Introduction to Philosophy

Classical and Contemporary Readings

FOURTH EDITION

Louis P. Pojman

United States Military Academy

James Fieser

The University of Tennessee at Martin

New York   Oxford
OXFORD UNIVERSITY PRESS
2008

Oxford University Press, Inc., publishes works that further Oxford University's objective of excellence in research, scholarship, and education.

Oxford   New York
Auckland   Cape Town   Dar es Salaam   Hong Kong   Karachi
Kuala Lumpur   Madrid   Melbourne   Mexico City Nairobi
New Delhi   Shanghai Taipei Tokyo Toronto

With offices in

Argentina Austria Brazil Chile Czech Republic France Greece
Guatemala Hungary Italy Japan Poland Portugal Singapore
South Korea Switzerland Thailand Turkey Ukraine Vietnam

Copyright © 2008 by Oxford University Press, Inc.

Published by Oxford University Press, Inc.
198 Madison Avenue, New York, New York 10016
http://www.oup.com

Library of Congress Cataloging-in-Publication Data

Introduction to philosophy : classical and contemporary readings / [edited by] Louis P.
Pojman. — 4th ed.
       p.   cm.
    Includes bibliographical references.
    ISBN 978-0-19-531161-7 (pbk.)
    1. Philosophy—Introductions. I. Pojman, Louis P.
BD21.I54 2008
100—dc22   2007038897

9 8 7 6 5 4 3 2 1

Printed in the United States of America
on acid-free paper

To Louis P. Pojman (1935–2005), who will always be remembered by his students, family, and friends.

Contents

PREFACE

The death of Louis Pojman in 2005 was a great loss to his many friends who had the joy of conversing, corresponding, and working with him over the years. Always generous with his time, he was particularly nurturing of students and young scholars who benefited from his help during critical moments of their academic and vocational advancement. His passing is also a major loss to the larger philosophical community, which has been the beneficiary of his steady outpouring of books and articles in so many of philosophy's subdisciplines, including epistemology, the philosophy of religion, ethics, and political philosophy, to name a few. Philosophy instructors throughout the English-speaking world know his works for their outstanding level of scholarship, timeliness, readability, and insights. This book, *Introduction to Philosophy: Classical and Contemporary Readings,* first appeared in 1991 and displayed these qualities in both its choice of readings and introductory essays. Successive editions preserved all the time-honored selections while moving forward with the most important selections from contemporary philosophers. It is in this spirit that the revised fourth edition is presented to the public with the following new selections:

Theory of Knowledge
    Sextus Empiricus, "Skepticism and Tranquility"
    Lorraine Code, "A Feminist Epistemology?"

Philosophy of Religion
    Samuel Clarke and David Hume, "The Argument from Contingency" (added critique
     by Hume)
    Voltaire, "The Best of All Possible Worlds?"

Philosophy of Mind
    René Descartes, "Interactive Dualism" (added section on the pineal gland)
    Anne Conway, "Mind and Body as a Continuum"

Freedom of the Will
    Epictetus, "Stoic Resignation to Fate"

Moral Philosophy
    David Hume, "Morality Not Derived from Reason"
    Alfred Jules Ayer, "Emotivism and Prescriptivism"

I express my gratitude to Trudy Pojman for her help with this transitional edition. I also thank Elmer Duncan, Gordon Pettit, David Pitt, and David Shier for their helpful suggestions.

James Fieser
April 26, 2007 (Hume's birthday)

PART I

What Is Philosophy?

> He that would seriously set upon the search of truth ought in the first
> place to prepare his mind with a love of it; . . . How a man may know
> whether he be [a lover of truth] in earnest, is worth inquiry; and I think
> there is one unerring mark of it, viz. The not entertaining any propo-
> sition with greater assurance than the proofs it is built upon will war-
> rant. Whoever goes beyond this measure of assent, it is plain receives
> not the truth in the love of it; loves not truth for truth's sake, but for
> some other bye-end.
>
> *John Locke,* An Essay Concerning Human Understanding

> The unexamined life is not worth living.
>
> *Socrates*

Philosophy is revolutionary and vitally important to the good life. It starts from an assumption, first announced by the founder of moral philosophy, Socrates (384–399 B.C.E.), that the unexamined life is not worth living and that while hard thinking about important issues disturbs, it also consoles. Philosophy, as Aristotle (384–322 B.C.E.) said over two thousand years ago, begins with wonder at the marvels and mysteries of the world. It begins in wonder in the pursuit of truth and wisdom and ends in a life lived in passionate moral and intellectual integrity. This is the classic philosophical ideal, begin-ning with the ancient Greeks down through Aquinas, Descartes, Kant, and Kierkegaard to the present. Of course, this thesis about the worth of philosophy is to be subject to ratio-nal scrutiny.

Philosophy is the love of wisdom (from the Greek *philos*, "love," and *sophia*, "wisdom"). It is the contemplation or study of the most important questions in existence, with the end of promoting illumination and understanding, a vision of the whole. It uses reason, sense perception, the imagination, and intuitions in its activities of *clarifying concepts* and *ana-lyzing and constructing arguments and theories* as possible answers to these perennial questions. It is revolutionary because its deliverances often disturb our common sense or our received tradition. Philosophy usually goes against the stream or the majority, since the majority opinion is often a composite of past intellectual struggles or "useful" biases. There is often deeper truth, better and new evidence that disturbs the status quo and that forces us to revise or reject some of our beliefs. This experience can be as painful as it is exciting.

The pain may lead us to give up philosophical inquiry, and a great deal of emotional health may be required in order to persevere in this pursuit. We may retreat into unreason and obey the commandment of Ignorance, "Think not, lest thou be confounded!" Truth (or what we seem justified in believing) may not always be edifying, but in the end the philosopher's faith is that Truth is good and worth pursuing for its own sake, and for its secondary benefits. The intelligent inquiry that philosophy promotes is liberating, freeing us from prejudice, self-deceptive notions, and half-truths. As Bertrand Russell (1872–1970) put it:

> The [person] who has no tincture of philosophy goes through life imprisoned in the prejudices derived from common sense, from the habitual beliefs of his age or his nation, and from convictions which have grown up in his mind without the co-operation or consent of his deliberate reason. . . . [W]hile diminishing our feeling of certainty as to what things are, [philosophy] greatly increases our knowledge as to what they may be; it removes the somewhat arrogant dogmatism of those who have never traveled into the region of liberating doubt, and it keeps alive the sense of wonder by showing familiar things in an unfamiliar light.[1]

Philosophy should result in a wider vision of life in which the impartial use of reason results in an appreciation of other viewpoints and other people's rights and needs. It typically engenders an attitude of philosophical modesty or *fallibilism* in the inquirer—an awareness that since in the past many of my firmest beliefs have been found to be false, the probability is that some of my present convictions are false. But different people react differently to philosophical inquiry. Some become radical skeptics, doubting what most accept as commonsense beliefs. Some become even more dogmatic, finding in philosophical method an instrument for certainty. Some nasty people seem to be able to do philosophy quite well without being transformed by it. But for the most part, those who have had the vision of a better life and have worked through arguments on substantive issues relating to human nature and destiny have been positively affected by the perennial pilgrimage. They march to a different drummer and show in their lives the fruits of their travail. This ability to live by reflective principle in spite of, and in the midst of, the noise of the masses is a hallmark of philosophy. This trait is illustrated by one of its heros, Socrates, whom we will encounter in our first reading, who stood alone against popular opinion of his day.

We mentioned that one of the tasks is clarifying concepts. Let me illustrate how this works with two examples. The American philosopher and psychologist William James (1842–1910), brother to the novelist Henry James, was vacationing with friends in New England one summer. Upon returning from a walk, he found his friends engaged in a fierce dispute. The problem was this: suppose a squirrel is clinging to the side of a tree and that you are trying to see the back of the squirrel. But as you walk around the tree, the clever squirrel moves edgewise around the tree on its other side so that you never get a look at the back of the squirrel. The question was: did you go around the squirrel? Half the group contended that you did go around, and half contended that you did not. What do you think the answer is?

Here is what William James said:

"Which party is right," I said, "depends on what you *practically mean* by 'going around' the squirrel. If you mean passing from north of him to the east, then to the south, then to the west, and then to the north of him again, obviously the man does go around him, for he occupies these successive positions. But if on the contrary you mean being first in front of him, then on the right of him, then behind him, then on his left, and finally in front again, it is quite obvious that the man fails to go round him, for by the compensating movements the squirrel makes, he keeps his belly turned towards the man all the time, and his back is burned away. Make the distinction, and there is no occasion for any further dispute.[2]

Here was a dispute over the concept of "going round something." The philosopher is trained to look at the frame of reference of the phrase, notes its inherent ambiguity, and, unraveling it, makes things clearer. In this case, once James had pointed out the equivocation in the idea of "going round," all dispute ceased. The first task in philosophy is to make your ideas (concepts, notions) as clear as possible.

A second illustration has to do with the difficult matter of whether abortion is morally permissible. It is often alleged that abortion is morally wrong because it is the killing of innocent human beings. Putting this in syllogistic form, we get the following:

1. It is morally wrong to kill innocent human beings.
2. Abortion is an act of killing an innocent human being.
Therefore 3. Abortion is morally wrong.

On the face of it, this looks like a good argument, and it is often used in opposition to abortion. There may be good arguments opposed to abortion, but this one, as it stands, is not one of them.

Early on in the debate over abortion, philosophers like Michael Tooley and Mary Anne Warren pointed out that the argument contained an equivocation over the term "human being."[3] We use "human being" ambiguously, sometimes meaning a biologic concept, the species *Homo sapiens*, and other times meaning a psychological-moral concept, *someone who has the characteristics that make humans of special moral worth*, such as rationality or rational self-consciousness. We sometimes refer to this second concept by the term *person*. It is being human beings as *persons*, as having requisite psychological qualities, and not merely our membership in a biological group, that gives us a serious moral right to life. But other beings may also have the required psychological qualities. Perhaps apes, dolphins, and Galacticans are also rationally self-conscious beings. Then they would be persons. And there are no doubt some *Homo sapiens* who do not possess minimally rational self-consciousness. They would not be persons. Applying this insight to our argument, we need to change the premises to read as follows:

1. It is morally wrong to kill innocent persons.
2. Abortion is an act of killing an innocent member of the species *Homo sapiens*.
Therefore 3. Abortion is morally wrong.

If the attempt at clarification has succeeded, this argument is not sound, for the original term "human beings" was being used differently in the premises.

The hallmark of the philosophical method is *argument*. Philosophers clarify concepts, analyze and test propositions and beliefs, but the major task is to analyze and construct arguments. Bertrand Russell said that one aim of philosophy is to begin with assumptions that no one would ever think of doubting and proceed through a careful process of valid reasoning to conclusions so preposterous to common sense that no one could help doubting. Indeed, in philosophy there is no "political correctness." No hypothesis, however outrageous to common sense or conventional thinking, is ruled out of court, *provided* only that you endeavor to support your claim with arguments, with reasons. Otherwise, anything goes.

Philosophical reasoning is closely allied to scientific reasoning in that both look for evidence and build hypotheses that are tested with the hope of coming closer to the truth. However, scientific experiments take place in laboratories and have testing procedures through which to record objective or empirically verifiable results. The laboratory of the philosopher is his or her mind, where imaginative thought experiments take place; the study, where ideas are written down and examined; and wherever conversation about the perennial questions takes place, where thesis and counterexample and counterthesis are considered. We will look more closely at this aspect in the next chapter.

Because philosophical questions are generally more complicated and metaphysical than scientific questions, most of philosophy's important theses cannot be proved or disproved. Yet some of what theoretical scientists do could be called "philosophical cosmology" or "philosophy of science." Only recently have the sciences made their way out of the family fold of philosophy as they systematized their decision-making procedures. In the words of philosopher Jeffrey Olen,

> First there were the great patriarch and matriarch, the searchers for knowledge and wisdom, who bore a large number of children. Mathematics, physics, ethics, psychology, logic, political thought, metaphysics, . . . and epistemology . . . —all belonged to the same family. Philosophers were not *just* philosophers, but mathematicians and physicists and psychologists as well. Indeed, in the beginning of the family's history, no distinction was made between philosophy and these other disciplines. . . .
>
> In the beginning, then, all systematic search for knowledge was philosophy. This fact is still reflected in the modern university, where the highest degree granted in all of the sciences and humanities is the Ph.D.—the doctor of philosophy.
>
> But the children gradually began to leave home. First to leave were physics and astronomy, as they began to develop experimental techniques of their own. This exodus, led by Galileo (1564–1642), Isaac Newton (1642–1727), and Johannes Kepler (1571–1630), created the first of many great family crises . . . . Eventually, psychology left home.[4]

The major areas of philosophy are as follows:

Metaphysics (concerned with such issues as the nature of ultimate reality). It deals with such questions as:

- What is ultimate reality?
- Is there one ultimate substance (e.g., matter) or more (e.g., mind and/or spirit)?
- Is there a God (or gods) who created us, to whom we owe our allegiance?
- What is mind?
- How is the mind related to the body?
- Is there life after death, or is this life all there is?
- Am I free, or is every act determined by antecedent conditions?
- What is a self or person, and under what conditions can I be said to be the same self or person through change over time?

Epistemology (regarding the nature of knowledge):

- What is knowledge?
- What can I know? Anything at all? Or must I remain skeptical about reality? Could I be mistaken about most of my beliefs?
- How reliable is sense perception? Does it give me the truth about the world?
- What is truth?
- How can I justify my beliefs?
- What, if any, are the limits of reason?
- Are there other ways to attain the truth besides rational inquiry—for example, through faith?

Value theory (study of values, including aesthetics, ethics, and political philosophy):

- What is value?
- Are values intrinsic in things or states of affairs, or are they simply a product of sentient desire?
- What is beauty?
- Is art intrinsically good or bad, or is aesthetic beauty simply in the eye of the beholder?
- What makes an action right or wrong? Good or bad?
- Are moral principles objectively valid, or are they relative to culture?
- Does morality depend on religion?
- Which is the correct moral theory?
- What is the correct political theory? How should society be organized?
- What justifies government? That is, why isn't anarchy justified? Or is it?
- Is civil disobedience ever justified, and under what circumstances?
- Are there natural rights, rights we have in virtue of our humanity?
- Are all human beings equal, or is human equality a myth?

Logic (having to do with the laws of thought and forms of argument):

- What is a valid and sound argument?
- How can our belief in induction be justified?
- How does logic contribute to our knowledge and belief justification?
- What is a logical fallacy, and what are some of the ways we go wrong in our thinking?

In addition to these central topics, there are secondary areas of philosophy that work on conceptual and/or theoretical problems arising within first-order nonphilosophical disciplines. Examples are philosophy of science, philosophy of psychology, philosophy of mathematics, philosophy of language, and philosophy of law. Wherever conceptual analysis or justification of a theoretical schema is needed, philosophical expertise is appropriate. More recently, as technology creates new possibilities and problems, applied ethics (e.g., biomedical ethics, business ethics, environmental ethics, and legal ethics) has arisen. History plays a dialectical role with regard to philosophy, for not only do philosophers practice philosophy while teaching the history of philosophy, but they also involve themselves in the critical examination of the principles that underlie historical investigation itself, creating a philosophy of history.

We will touch on many of these areas in this work: a little logic and history of philosophy; philosophy of religion; epistemology; metaphysics, including the mind-body problem, personal identity, immortality, and free will and determinism; and ethics. We shall also spend a little time with the question of whether there is meaning to life. These are more than enough for an *introduction* to philosophy.

Philosophical study is dialectic, proceeding as an intellectual conversation in which thesis and counterthesis, hypothesis and counterexample continue in a way that shows up the weaknesses of proposed solutions to the puzzles of existence and leaves some answers as more or less plausible. In this conversation, all sides of an issue should receive a fair hearing, and the reader is left to make up his or her own mind on each issue. Hence, in this work at least two opposing views are set forth on the issues discussed.

Philosophy, we noted, is centered in argument: it is a rational activity. You may have questions about just what this means. Sometimes students, especially in introductory classes, get annoyed, even angry, that their views are subjected to sharp critical scrutiny or that the views of philosophers of the past, who cannot defend themselves, get torn to pieces by their teacher. So they ask, "So what if [so and so's] argument is unsound. Why do we always have to follow the best reasons? Why don't philosophers respect leaps of faith or our nonrational beliefs?"

The initial response to this query is to ask whether the questioner wants a *rational* answer or a nonrational one. "Do you want a reason for justifying philosophical practice or just my own emotional prejudice?" Presumably, the former is wanted. Indeed, the question "Why?" implies that a reason is called for, so that even a question about the appropriateness of reason must be addressed by reason. If reason has limits, it is reason that discovers it and explains this fact.

The teacher may further point out that reason does recognize limits. Immanuel Kant (1724–1804) tried to show these limits in order to make room for religious faith. More problematically, Søren Kierkegaard (1813–1855) used rational argument to show that sometimes it is rational even to go against reason. What does this mean?

Here we have to distinguish two kinds of reason: practical reason and theoretical reason. Practical reason has to do with *acting* in order to realize a goal. For example, you desire to be healthy and so carry out a regimen of exercise, good nutrition, and general moderation. You have a goal (something you desire), you ask what are the necessary or best means of reaching that goal, and then, if you are rational in the practical sense, you act on your judgment.

Theoretical reason, on the other hand, has to do with *beliefs*. It asks what evidence there is for such and such a proposition or belief. What is it rational to believe about the best way to stay healthy or the existence of God or the existence of ghosts or life after death? Thus there are two types of rationality, the practical (having to do with actions) and the theoretical (having to do with beliefs).

But sometimes these types of reasoning may conflict. For instance, I may have evidence that my friend (or parent) has committed a crime. My evidence is substantial but perhaps not decisive. For practical reasons, I may ignore or dismiss the evidence, reasoning that to believe my friend is guilty would be an act of disloyalty or greatly damage our relationship (for I cannot hide my feelings very well). On another occasion, I may use theoretical reason to conclude that I should not use reason to analyze the best way to make baskets while I am playing basketball, for the act of shooting is more likely to succeed if

I don't think too much about what I am doing, but just do it. Or when I am reading literature, I may want to turn off my critical faculties in order to more fully enjoy the story.

If all this is accurate, it is sometimes rational not to be rational. Paradoxical? Yes, but explainable, and not contradictory. We are *practically* rational in not always using *theoretical* rationality when engaged in some activities. On one level, theoretical reason judges that we are justified in not using theoretical reason while engaging in practical activities but that we are practically rational in acting spontaneously, following our feelings, making leaps of faith.

But there are cases where theoretical reason is simply not an issue, where practical reasons are justified by theoretical reasoning. The more difficult question is: Is it ever right to allow ourselves to believe propositions where there is insufficient reason? Should practical reason sometimes *override* theoretical rationality? The British philosopher W. K. Clifford (1845–1879) said, "No, it is wrong always, everywhere, and for anyone to believe anything upon insufficient evidence." One problem with Clifford's absolute prohibition is that there seems to be insufficient evidence to support it, and if so, it is self-referentially incoherent (or self-refuting).

Other philosophers, such as Blaise Pascal (1623–1662), Kierkegaard, and William James argue the reverse: sometimes we are (practically) justified in getting ourselves to believe against the conclusions of (theoretical) reason, against the preponderance of evidence. We will examine some of these philosophers and arguments in Part II. For now we need only point out that this is a live philosophical issue.

Although a clearer understanding of the nature of philosophy will only emerge as you work through the arguments on the various issues you are going to study, I want to end this introduction with a set of guidelines for philosophical inquiry: the "Ten Commandments of Philosophy." I hope they will aid you in your own pilgrimage, as you build your own philosophy of life. Test them, refine them, and possibly reject some of them or add better ones, as you proceed on your own pursuit of wisdom.

Ten Commandments of Philosophy

1. *Allow the spirit of wonder to flourish in your breast*. Philosophy begins with deep wonder about the universe, about who we are, where we came from, and where we are going. What is this life all about? Speculate and explore different points of view and worldviews. Do not stifle childlike curiosity.

2. *Doubt everything unsupported by evidence until the evidence convinces you of its truth*. Be reasonably cautious, a moderate skeptic, suspicious of those who claim to have the truth. Doubt is the soul's purgative. Do not fear intellectual inquiry. As Goethe said, "The masses fear the intellectual, but it is stupidity that they should fear, if they only realized how dangerous it really is."

3. *Love the truth*. "Philosophy is the eternal search for truth, a search which inevitably fails and yet is never defeated; which continually eludes us, but which always guides us. This free, intellectual life of the mind is the noblest inheritance of the Western World; it is also the hope of our future." (W. T. Jones)

4. *Divide and conquer*. Divide each problem and theory into its smallest essential components in order to analyze each unit carefully. This is the analytic method.

5. *Collect and construct*. Build a coherent argument or theory from component parts. One should move from simple, secure foundations to the complex and

comprehensive, in the manner of Bertrand Russell that we mentioned earlier. The important thing is to have a coherent, well-founded, tightly reasoned set of beliefs that can withstand the opposition.

6. *Conjecture and refute.* Make a complete survey of possible objections to your position, looking for counterexamples and subtle mistakes. Following a suggestion of Karl Popper, philosophy is a system of conjecture and refutation. Seek bold hypotheses and seek disconfirmations of your favorite positions. In this way, by a process of elimination, you will negatively, indirectly, and gradually approach the Truth.

In this regard, seek to understand your opponent's position for, as John Stuart Mill wrote, "He who knows only his own side of the case knows little of that. If he is equally unable to refute the reasons on the opposite side, if he does not so much as know what they are, he has no ground for preferring either opinion." Mill further urges us to face squarely the best arguments our opponent can muster. The truth seeker "must know [the opponent's arguments] in their most plausible and persuasive form; he must feel the whole force of the difficulty which the true view of the subject has to encounter and dispose of, else he will never really possess himself of the portion of the truth which meets and removes that difficulty."[5]

7. *Revise and rebuild.* Be willing to revise, reject, and modify your beliefs and the degree to which you hold any belief. Acknowledge that you probably have many false beliefs and be grateful to those who correct you. This is the principle of fallibilism, the thesis that we are very likely incorrect in many of our beliefs and have a tendency toward self-deception in considering objections to our position.

8. *Seek simplicity.* This is the principle of parsimony, sometimes known as "Occam's razor." Prefer the simpler explanation to the more complex, all things being equal. Of course, all things are not always equal. Sometimes the truth is complex, but where two explanations are of relatively equal merit, prefer the simpler.

9. *Live the truth*! Appropriate your ideas in a personal way, so that even as the Objective Truth is a correspondence of the thought to the world, this Lived Truth will be a correspondence of the life to the thought. As Kierkegaard said, "Here is a definition of [subjective] truth: holding fast to an objective uncertainty in an appropriation process of the most passionate inwardness is the truth, the highest truth available for an existing individual."

10. *Live the good*! Let the practical conclusions of a philosophical reflection on the moral life inspire and motivate you to action. Let moral truth transform your life so that you shine like a jewel in its own light amid the darkness of ignorance.

Nondogmatically, pursuing truth and wisdom, harkening to the voice of wisdom, aim at letting the fruits of philosophy transform your life. This is what Socrates meant when he said, "The unexamined life is not worth living." My hope is that philosophy will add a vital dimension to your life.

To summarize, philosophy consists of the rational examination of worldviews, metaphysical theories, ethical systems, and even the limits of reason. It is the practice of giving reasons in support of one's beliefs and actions. Its ultimate goal is to arrive at a rationally justified position regarding one's beliefs about important issues, including what is the best way to live one's life and to organize society. More deeply, it aims at truth and wisdom, hopefully resulting in a life filled with meaning and moral goodness. Virtually all of the sciences arose from philosophy, which continues to ask questions wherever an empirical process is inadequate for a definitive answer.

FOR FURTHER REFLECTION

1. Consider the quotation by John Locke at the beginning of this introduction to Part I. Many people believe that philosophy, as reflected in this quotation, overemphasizes reason. "The heart has its reasons that the mind knows nothing of," said Pascal, and Kierkegaard echoes his refrain. They both contend that reason has limits. Do you agree? Discuss the matter, asking yourself, "Am I using *reason* even in inquiring about the limits of reason?" Is the contention that "reason is limited" a thesis that reason must adjudicate?

2. A man in one of the French writer Molière's plays discovered one day that he had been speaking prose all of his life without knowing it. Likewise, all of us have been doing amateur philosophy all of our lives. In a sense, philosophy is just hard thinking about the important issues of life. Mark Woodhouse illustrates how virtually every human activity has philosophical implications:

   a. A neurophysiologist, while establishing correlations between certain brain functions and the feeling of pain, begins to wonder whether the "mind" is distinct from the brain.

   b. A nuclear physicist, having determined that matter is mostly empty space containing colorless energy transformations, begins to wonder to what extent the solid, extended, colored world we perceive corresponds to what actually exists, and which world is the more "real." . . .

   c. A behavioral psychologist, having increasing success in predicting human behavior, questions whether any human actions can be called "free."

   d. Supreme court justices, when framing a law to distinguish obscene and nonobscene art forms, are drawn into questions about the nature and function of art.

   e. A theologian, in a losing battle with science over literal descriptions of the universe (or "reality"), is forced to redefine the whole purpose and scope of traditional theology.

   f. An anthropologist, noting that all societies have some conception of a moral code, begins to wonder just what distinguishes a moral from a nonmoral point of view.

   g. A linguist, in examining the various ways language shapes our view of the world, declares that there is no one "true reality" because all views of reality are conditioned and qualified by the language in which they are expressed.

   h. A perennial skeptic, accustomed to demanding and not receiving absolute proof for every view encountered, declares that it is impossible to know anything.

   i. A county commissioner, while developing new zoning ordinances, begins to wonder whether the *effect* or the *intent* (or both) of zoning laws makes them discriminatory.

    j. An IRS director, in determining which (religious) organizations should be exempted from tax, is forced to define what counts as a "religion" or "religious group."

    k. A concerned mother, having decided to convert her communist son, is forced to read the *Communist Manifesto* and to do some thinking about Marxist and capitalist ideologies.[6]

We could continue this list of examples indefinitely, but you can already see that, given a particularly relevant problem, even the nonphilosopher is lured into a modest amount of philosophical thinking. If the nonphilosopher fails to see any purpose in the discipline, try raising a philosophical problem of special relevance to his or her interests. In examining possible responses, that person will probably discover a commitment to certain philosophical theses.

    Find some examples in your life or in a newspaper or other media that illustrate philosophical inquiry and discuss them.

3. As you read and work your way through this book, it will help if you can think of some puzzling philosophical problems that you would like to make progress in solving for yourself. Pick out a few and try to think about them every day. Ask your friends for their ideas on the problems, and keep a journal on your own insights.

    We begin our readings with a selection from Plato's ancient classic, the *Apology*, which relates Socrates' defense of his career as a philosopher before the Athenian court. Next we read John Locke's description of philosophy as the love of truth. Finally, we read Bertrand Russell's modern interpretation of philosophy as an intrinsically worthwhile activity that enlarges our conception of what is possible, enriches our imagination, and diminishes our dogmatic assurance.

NOTES

1. Bertrand Russell, *The Problems of Philosophy* (Oxford: Oxford University Press, 1912), 156 f.
2. William James, *The Writings of William James* (New York: Random House, 1967), 367 f.
3. Michael Tooley, "Abortion and Infanticide," *Philosophy and Public Affairs* 2, 1 (1972); Mary Anne Warren, "On the Moral and Legal Status of Abortion," *The Monist* 57, 1 (1973). In my discussion I do not mean to imply that the equation of "rational self-consciousness" with being a person with a serious right to life is the correct answer to the personhood problem. This is controversial and needs a defense. I use it simply as a more plausible alternative to the biological equation of specieshood with personhood.
4. Jeffrey Olen, *Persons and Their World* (New York: Random House, 1983), 3 f.
5. John Stuart Mill, *On Liberty* (Indianapolis, IN: Hackett, 1978), 35.
6. Mark Woodhouse, *A Preface to Philosophy* (Belmont, CA: Wadsworth, 1984).

PLATO
〜

SOCRATIC WISDOM

Plato (427–347 B.C.E.) is one of the greatest philosophers who ever lived and the first philosopher to write systematically on philosophical subjects. He lived in Athens, the great Greek democratic city-state, on the eve of its glory under the great Athenian leader Pericles. During much of Plato's life, Athens was at war with Sparta, the Greek city-state to the south of Athens. He was Socrates' disciple, the founder of the first school of philosophy: the Academy in Athens, Aristotle's teacher, and an advisor to emperors. Among his important works are the *Republic*, the *Apology*, *Phaedo*, and *Timaeus*. British philosopher and mathematician Alfred North Whitehead called the whole history of Western philosophy "a series of footnotes to Plato."

Socrates (470–399 B.C.E.) is considered the father of moral philosophy. Socrates wrote nothing, and most of our knowledge about him comes to us from Plato's writings. Living in Athens, under the great leader Pericles, he enjoyed the freedoms of Greek democracy, where all free males had an equal voice in government. He spent much of his life in the marketplace of Athens, questioning and arguing with his contemporaries on philosophical issues (such as: What are justice, friendship, self-control, piety, virtue? How do we teach virtue? Does anyone do evil voluntarily? and so forth). He saw himself as the gafly of the Greek city-state, serving his fellow citizens without pay. But many of its leading citizens saw him as a big pain in the neck, and eventually they brought him to trial.

Our reading concerns this trial. Three Athenians—Meletus, Anytus, and Lycon—have brought charges against Socrates: they say he has corrupted the youth and doesn't believe in the Greek gods. The real cause of the trial is probably that Socrates has made a number of enemies in high places. He has defied the authorities when they ordered him to arrest a political opponent named Leon, against what Socrates considers the law. He has embarrassed many of the leading citizens, politicians, artisans, poets, and orators—often before their sons—by exposing their pretenses to knowledge. The anger has erupted in one of the most famous trials of all time. The following is Plato's account of the trial in *The Apology*.

I will begin at the beginning, and ask what is the accusation which has given rise to the slander of me, and in fact has encouraged Meletus to prefer this charge against me. Well, what do the slanderers say? They shall be my prosecutors, and I will sum up their words in an affidavit: "Socrates is an evil-doer, and a

From Plato, "The Apology," in *Dialogues of Plato*, trans. Benjamin Jowett (Oxford: Oxford University Press, 1896).

curious person, who searches into things under the earth and in heaven, and he makes the worse appear the better cause; and he teaches the aforesaid doctrines to others." Such is the nature of the accusation: it is just what you have yourselves seen in the comedy of Aristophanes, who has introduced a man whom he calls Socrates, going about and saying that he walks in air, and talking a deal of nonsense concerning matters of which I do not pretend to know either much or little—not that I mean to speak disparagingly of any one who is a student of natural philosophy. I should be very sorry if Meletus could bring so grave a charge against me. But the simple truth is, O Athenians, that I have nothing to do with physical speculations. Very many of those here present are witnesses to the truth of this, and to them I appeal. Speak then, you who have heard me, and tell your neighbours whether any of you have ever known me hold forth in few words or in many upon such matters. . . . You hear their answer. And from what they say of this part of the charge you will be able to judge of the truth of the rest.

As little foundation is there for the report that I am a teacher, and take money; this accusation has no more truth in it than the other. Although, if a man were really able to instruct mankind, to receive money for giving instruction would, in my opinion, be an honour to him. There is Gorgias of Leontium, and Prodicus of Ceos, and Hippias of Elis, who go the round of the cities, and are able to persuade the young men to leave their own citizens by whom they might be taught for nothing, and come to them whom they not only pay, but are thankful if they may be allowed to pay them. . . .

Here, O men of Athens, I must beg you not to interrupt me, even if I seem to say something extravagant. For the word which I will speak is not mine. I will refer you to a witness who is worthy of credit; that witness shall be the God of Delphi—he will tell you about my wisdom, if I have any, and of what sort it is. You must have known Chaerephon; he was early a friend of mine, and also a friend of yours, for he shared in the recent exile of the people, and returned with you. Well, Chaerephon, as you know, was very impetuous in all his doings, and he went to Delphi and boldly asked the oracle to tell him whether—as I was saying, I must beg you not to interrupt—he asked the oracle to tell him whether any one was wiser than I was, and the Pythian prophetess answered, that there was no man wiser. Chaerephon is dead himself; but his brother, who is in court, will confirm the truth of what I am saying.

Why do I mention this? Because I am going to explain to you why I have such an evil name. When I heard the answer, I said to myself, What can the god mean? and what is the interpretation of his riddle? for I know that I have no wisdom, small or great. What then can he mean when he says that I am the wisest of men? And yet he is a god, and cannot lie; that would be against his nature. After long consideration, I thought of a method of trying the question. I reflected that if I could only find a man wiser than myself, then I might go to the god with a refutation in my hand. I should say to him, "Here is a man who is wiser than I am; but you said that I was the wisest." Accordingly I went to one who had the reputation of wisdom, and observed him—his name I need not mention; he was a politician whom I selected for examination—and the result was as follows: When I began to talk with him, I could not help thinking that he was not really wise, although he was thought wise by many, and still wiser by himself; and thereupon I tried to explain to him that he thought himself wise, but was not really wise; and the consequence was that he hated me, and his enmity was shared by several who were present and heard me. So I left him, saying to myself, as I went away: Well, although I do not suppose that either of us knows anything really beautiful and good, I am better off than he is—for he knows nothing, and thinks that he knows; I neither know nor think that I know. In this latter particular, then, I seem to have slightly the advantage of him. Then I went to another who had still higher pretensions to wisdom, and my conclusion was exactly the same. Whereupon I made another enemy of him, and of many others besides him.

Then I went to one man after another, being not unconscious of the enmity which I provoked, and I lamented and feared this: But necessity was laid upon me,—the word of God, I thought, ought to be considered first. And I said to myself, Go I must to all who appear to know, and find out the meaning of the oracle. And I swear to you, Athenians, by the dog I swear!—for I must tell you the truth—the result of my mission was just this: I found that the men most in repute were all but the most foolish; and that others less esteemed were really wiser and better. I will tell you the tale of my wanderings and of the "Herculean" labours, as I may call them; which I endured only to find at last the oracle irrefutable. After the politicians, I went to the poets; tragic, dithyrambic, and all sorts. And there, I said to myself, you will be instantly detected; now you will find out that you are more ignorant than they are. Accordingly, I took them some of the most elaborate passages in their own writings, and asked what was the meaning of them—thinking that they would teach me something. Will you believe me? I am almost ashamed to confess the truth, but I must say that there is hardly a person present who would not have talked better about their poetry than they did themselves. Then I knew that not by wisdom do poets write poetry, but by a sort of genius and inspiration; they are like diviners or soothsayers who also say many fine things, but do not understand the meaning of them. The poets appeared to me to be much in the same case; and I further observed that upon the strength of their poetry they believed themselves to be the wisest of men in other things in which they were not wise. So I departed, conceiving myself to be superior to them for the same reason that I was superior to the politicians.

At last I went to the artisans, for I was conscious that I knew nothing at all, as I may say, and I was sure that they knew many fine things; and here I was not mistaken, for they did know many things of which I was ignorant, and in this they certainly were wiser than I was. But I observed that even the good artisans fell into the same error as the poets;—because they were good workmen they thought that they also knew all sorts of high matters, and this defect in them overshadowed their wisdom; and therefore I asked myself on behalf of the oracle, whether I would like to be as I was, neither having their knowledge nor their ignorance, or like them in both; and I made answer to myself and to the oracle that I was better off as I was.

This inquisition has led to my having many enemies of the worst and most dangerous kind, and has given occasion also to many calumnies. And I am called wise, for my hearers always imagine that I

myself possess the wisdom which I find wanting in others: but the truth is, O men of Athens, that God only is wise; and by his answer he intends to show that the wisdom of men is worth little or nothing; he is not speaking of Socrates, he is only using my name by way of illustration, as if he said, He, O men, is the wisest, who, like Socrates, knows that his wisdom is in truth worth nothing. And so I go about the world, obedient to the god, and search and make enquiry into the wisdom of any one, whether citizen or stranger, who appears to be wise; and if he is not wise, then in vindication of the oracle I show him that he is not wise; and my occupation quite absorbs me, and I have no time to give either to any public matter of interest or to any concern of my own, but I am in utter poverty by reason of my devotion to the god.

There is another thing:—young men of the richer classes, who have not much to do, come about me of their own accord; they like to hear the pretenders examined, and they often imitate me, and proceed to examine others; there are plenty of persons, as they quickly discover, who think that they know something, but really know little or nothing; and then those who are examined by them instead of being angry with themselves are angry with me: This confounded Socrates, they say; this villainous misleader of youth!— and then if somebody asks them, Why, what evil does he practise or teach? they do not know, and cannot tell; but in order that they may not appear to be at a loss, they repeat the ready-made charges which are used against all philosophers about teaching things up in the clouds and under the earth, and having no gods, and making the worse appear the better cause; for they do not like to confess that their pretence of knowledge has been detected—which is the truth; and as they are numerous and ambitious and energetic, and are drawn up in battle array and have persuasive tongues, they have filled your ears with their loud and inveterate calumnies. And this is the reason why my three accusers, Meletus and Anytus and Lycon, have set upon me; Meletus, who has a quarrel with me on behalf of the poets; Anytus, on behalf of the craftsmen and politicians; Lycon, on behalf of the rhetoricians: and as I said at the beginning, I cannot expect to get rid of such a mass of calumny all in a moment. And this, O men of Athens, is the truth and the whole truth;

I have concealed nothing, I have dissembled nothing. And yet, I know that my plainness of speech makes them hate me, and what is their hatred but a proof that I am speaking the truth?—Hence has arisen the prejudice against me; and this is the reason of it, as you will find out either in this or in any future enquiry.

I have said enough in my defence against the first class of my accusers; I turn to the second class. They are headed by Meletus, that good man and true lover of his country, as he calls himself. . . . He says that I am a doer of evil, and corrupt the youth; but I say, O men of Athens, that Meletus is a doer of evil, in that he pretends to be in earnest when he is only in jest, and is so eager to bring men to trial from a pretended zeal and interest about matters in which he really never had the smallest interest. And the truth of this I will endeavour to prove to you.

Come hither, Meletus, and let me ask a question of you. You think a great deal about the improvement of youth?

Yes, I do.

Tell the judges, then, who is their improver; for you must know, as you have taken the pains to discover their corrupter, and are citing and accusing me before them. Speak, then, and tell the judges who their improver is.—Observe, Meletus, that you are silent, and have nothing to say. But is not this rather disgraceful, and a very considerable proof of what I was saying, that you have no interest in the matter? Speak up, friend, and tell us who their improver is.

The laws.

But that, my good sir, is not my meaning. I want to know who the person is, who, in the first place, knows the laws.

The judges, Socrates, who are present in court.

What, do you mean to say, Meletus, that they are able to instruct and improve youth?

Certainly they are.

What, all of them, or some only and not others?

All of them.

By the goddess Herè, that is good news! There are plenty of improvers, then. And what do you say of the audience,—do they improve them?

Yes, they do.

And the senators?

Yes, the senators improve them.

But perhaps the members of the assembly corrupt them?—or do they too improve them?

They improve them.

Then every Athenian improves and elevates them; all with the exception of myself; and I alone am their corrupter? Is that what you affirm?

That is what I stoutly affirm.

I am very unfortunate if you are right. But suppose I ask you a question: How about horses? Does one man do them harm and all the world good? Is not the exact opposite the truth? One man is able to do them good, or at least not many;—the trainer of horses, that is to say, does them good, and others who have to do with them rather injure them? Is not that true, Meletus, of horses, or of any other animals? Most assuredly it is; whether you and Anytus say yes or no. Happy indeed would be the condition of youth if they had one corrupter only, and all the rest of the world were their improvers. But you, Meletus, have sufficiently shown that you never had a thought about the young: your carelessness is seen in your not caring about the very things which you bring against me.

And now, Meletus, I will ask you another question—by Zeus I will: Which is better, to live among bad citizens, or among good ones? Answer, friend, I say; the question is one which may be easily answered. Do not the good do their neighbours good, and the bad do them evil?

Certainly.

And is there any one who would rather be injured than benefited by those who live with him? Answer, my good friend, the law requires you to answer—does any one like to be injured?

Certainly not.

And when you accuse me of corrupting and deteriorating the youth, do you allege that I corrupt them intentionally or unintentionally?

Intentionally, I say.

But you have just admitted that the good do their neighbours good, and evil do them evil. Now, is that a truth which your superior wisdom has recognized thus early in life, and am I, at my age, in such darkness and ignorance as not to know that if a man with whom I have to live is corrupted by me, I am very likely to be harmed by him; and yet I corrupt him, and intentionally, too—so you say, although neither I nor any other human being is ever likely to be convinced by you. But either I do not corrupt them, or I corrupt them unintentionally; and on either view of the case you lie. If my offence is unintentional, the law has no cognizance of unintentional offences: you ought to have taken me privately, and warned and admonished me; for if I had been better advised, I should have left off doing what I only did unintentionally—no doubt I should; but you would have nothing to say to me and refused to teach me. And now you bring me up in this court, which is a place not of instruction, but of punishment.

It will be very clear to you, Athenians, as I was saying, that Meletus has no care at all, great or small, about the matter. But still I should like to know, Meletus, in what I am affirmed to corrupt the young. I suppose you mean, as I infer from your indictment, that I teach them not to acknowledge the gods which the state acknowledges, but some other new divinities or spiritual agencies in their stead. These are the lessons by which I corrupt the youth, as you say.

Yes, that I say emphatically.

Then, by the gods, Meletus, of whom we are speaking, tell me and the court, in somewhat plainer terms, what you mean! for I do not as yet understand whether you affirm that I teach other men to acknowledge some gods, and therefore that I do believe in gods, and am not an entire atheist—this you do not lay to my charge,—but only you say that they are not the same gods which the city recognizes—the charge is that they are different gods. Or, do you mean that I am an atheist simply, and a teacher of atheism?

I mean the latter—that you are a complete atheist.

What an extraordinary statement! Why do you think so, Meletus? Do you mean that I do not believe in the godhead of the sun or moon, like other men?

I assure you, judges, that he does not: for he says that the sun is stone, and the moon earth.

Friend Meletus, you think that you are accusing Anaxagoras: and you have but a bad opinion of the judges, if you fancy them illiterate to such a degree as not to know that these doctrines are found in the books of Anaxagoras the Clazomenian, which are full of them. And so, forsooth, the youth are said to be taught them by Socrates, when there are not unfrequently exhibitions of them at the theatre (price of admission one drachma at the most); and they might pay their money, and laugh at Socrates if he pretends to father these extraordinary views. And so, Meletus, you really think that I do not believe in any god?

I swear by Zeus that you believe absolutely in none at all.

Nobody will believe you, Meletus, and I am pretty sure that you do not believe yourself. I cannot help thinking, men of Athens, that Meletus is reckless and impudent, and that he has written this indictment in a spirit of mere wantonness and youthful bravado. Has he not compounded a riddle, thinking to try me? He said to himself:—I shall see whether the wise Socrates will discover my facetious contradiction, or whether I shall be able to deceive him and the rest of them. For he certainly does appear to me to contradict himself in the indictment as much as if he said that Socrates is guilty of not believing in the gods, and yet of believing in them—but this is not like a person who is in earnest.

I should like you, O men of Athens, to join me in examining what I conceive to be his inconsistency; and do you, Meletus, answer. And I must remind the audience of my request that they would not make a disturbance if I speak in my accustomed manner:

Did ever man, Meletus, believe in the existence of human things, and not of human beings? . . . I wish, men of Athens, that he would answer, and not be always trying to get up an interruption. Did ever any man believe in horsemanship, and not in horses? or in flute-playing, and not in flute-players? No, my friend; I will answer to you and to the court, as you refuse to answer for yourself. There is no man who ever did. But now please to answer the next question: Can a man believe in spiritual and divine agencies, and not in spirits or demigods?

He cannot.

How lucky I am to have extracted that answer, by the assistance of the court! But then you swear in the indictment that I teach and believe in divine or spiritual agencies (new or old, no matter for that); at any rate, I believe in spiritual agencies,—so you say and swear in the affidavit; and yet if I believe in divine beings, how can I help believing in spirits or demigods;—must I not? To be sure I must; and therefore I may assume that your silence gives consent.

Now what are spirits or demigods? are they not either gods or the sons of gods?

Certainly they are.

But this is what I call the facetious riddle invented by you: the demigods or spirits are gods, and you say first that I do not believe in gods, and then again that I do believe in gods; that is, if I believe in demigods. For if the demigods are the illegitimate sons of gods, whether by the nymphs or by any other mothers, of whom they are said to be the sons—what human being will ever believe that there are no gods if they are the sons of gods? You might as well affirm the existence of mules, and deny that of horses and asses. Such nonsense, Meletus, could only have been intended by you to make trial of me. You have put this into the indictment because you had nothing real of which to accuse me. But no one who has a particle of understanding will ever be convinced by you that the same men can believe in divine and superhuman things, and yet not believe that there are gods and demigods and heroes.

I have said enough in answer to the charge of Meletus: any elaborate defence is unnecessary; but I know only too well how many are the enmities which I have incurred, and this is what will be my destruction if I am destroyed;—not Meletus, nor yet Anytus, but the envy and detraction of the world, which has been the death of many good men, and will probably be the death of many more; there is no danger of my being the last of them.

Some one will say: And are you not ashamed, Socrates, of a course of life which is likely to bring you to an untimely end? To him I may fairly answer: There you are mistaken: a man who is good for anything ought not to calculate the chance of living or dying; he ought only to consider whether in doing anything he is doing right or wrong—acting the part of a good man or of a bad. . . .

Strange, indeed, would be my conduct, O men of Athens, if I who, when I was ordered by the generals whom you chose to command me at Potidaea and Amphipolis and Delium, remained where they placed me, like any other man, facing death—if now, when, as I conceive and imagine, God orders me to fulfil the philosopher's mission of searching into myself and other men, I were to desert my post through fear of death, or any other fear; that would indeed be strange, and I might justly be arraigned in court for denying the existence of the gods, if I disobeyed the oracle because I was afraid of death, fancying that I was wise when I was not wise. For the fear of death is indeed the pretence of wisdom, and not real wisdom, being a pretence of knowing the unknown; and no one knows whether death, which men in their fear apprehend to be the greatest evil, may not be the greatest good. Is not this ignorance of a disgraceful sort, the ignorance which is the conceit that man knows what he does not know? And in this respect only I believe myself to differ from men in general, and may perhaps claim to be wiser than they are:—that whereas I know but little of the world below, I do not suppose that I know: but I do know that injustice and disobedience to a better, whether God or man, is evil and dishonourable, and I will never fear or avoid a possible good rather than a certain evil. And therefore if you let me go now, and are not convinced by Anytus, who said that since I had been prosecuted I must be put to death . . . —if you say to me, Socrates, this time we will not mind Anytus, and you shall be let off, but upon one condition, that you are not to enquire and speculate in this way any more, and that if you are caught doing so again you shall die;—if this was the condition on which you let me go, I should reply: Men of Athens, I honour and love you; but I shall obey God rather than you, and while I have life and strength I shall never cease from the practice and teaching of philosophy, exhorting any one whom I meet and saying to him after my manner: You, my friend,—a citizen of the great and mighty and wise city of Athens,—are you not ashamed of heaping up the greatest amount of money and honour and reputation, and caring so little about wisdom and truth and the greatest improvement of the soul, which you never regard or heed at all? And if the person with whom I am arguing, says: Yes, but I do care; then I do not leave him or let him go at once; but I proceed to interrogate and examine and cross-examine him, and if I think that he has no virtue in him, but only says that he has, I reproach him with undervaluing the greater, and overvaluing the less. And I shall repeat the same words to every one whom I meet, young and old, citizen and alien, but especially to the citizens, inasmuch as they are my brethren. For know that this is the command of God; and I believe that no greater good has ever happened in the state than my service to the God. For I do nothing but go about persuading you all, old and young alike, not to take thought for your persons or your properties, but first and chiefly to care about the greatest improvement of the soul. I tell you that virtue is not given by money, but that from virtue comes money and every other good of man, public as well as private. This is my teaching, and if this is the doctrine which corrupts the youth, I am a mischievous person. But if any one says that this is not my teaching, he is speaking an untruth. Wherefore, O men of Athens, I say to you, do as Anytus bids or not as Anytus bids, and either acquit me or not; but whichever you do, understand that I shall never alter my ways, not even if I have to die many times. . . .

And now, Athenians, I am not going to argue for my own sake, as you may think, but for yours, that you may not sin against the God by condemning me, who am his gift to you. For if you kill me you will not easily find a successor to me, who, if I may use such a ludicrous figure of speech, am a sort of gadfly, given to the state by God; and the state is a great and noble steed who is tardy in his motions owing to his very size, and requires to be stirred into life. I am that gadfly which God has attached to the state, and all day long and in all places am always fastening upon you, arousing and persuading and reproaching you. You will not easily find another like me, and therefore I would advise you to spare me. . . .

[The vote is taken and he is found guilty by 281 votes to 220.]

There are many reasons why I am not grieved, O men of Athens, at the vote of condemnation. I expected it, and am only surprised that the votes are so nearly equal; for I had thought that the majority against me would have been far larger; but now, had thirty votes gone over to the other side, I should have been acquitted. And I may say, I think, that I have escaped Meletus. I may say more; for without the assistance of Anytus and Lycon, any one may see that he would not have had a fifth part of the votes, as the law requires, in which case he would have incurred a fine of a thousand drachmae.

And so he proposes death as the penalty. And what shall I propose on my part, O men of Athens? Clearly that which is my due. And what is my due? What return shall be made to the man who has never had the wit to be idle during his whole life; but has been careless of what the many care for—wealth, and family interests, and military offices, and speaking in the assembly, and magistracies, and plots, and parties. Reflecting that I was really too honest a man to be a politician and live, I did not go where I could do no good to you or to myself; but where I could do the greatest good privately to every one of you, thither I went, and sought to persuade every man among you that he must look to himself, and seek virtue and wisdom before he looks to his private interests, and look to the state before he looks to the interests of the state; and that this should be the order which he observes in all his actions. What shall be done to such an one? Doubtless some good thing, O men of Athens, if he has his reward; and the good should be of a kind suitable to him. What would be a reward suitable to a poor man who is your benefactor, and who desires leisure that he may instruct you? There can be no reward so fitting as maintenance in the Prytaneum, O men of Athens, a reward which he deserves far more than the citizen who has won the prize at Olympia in the horse or chariot race, whether the chariots were drawn by two horses or by many. For I am in want, and he has enough; and he only gives you the appearance of happiness, and I give you the reality. And if I am to estimate the penalty fairly, I should say that maintenance in the Prytaneum is the just return.

Perhaps you think that I am braving you in what I am saying now, as in what I said before about the tears and prayers. But this is not so. I speak rather because I am convinced that I never intentionally wronged any one, although I cannot convince you— the time has been too short; if there were a law at Athens, as there is in other cities, that a capital cause should not be decided in one day, then I believe that I should have convinced you. But I cannot in a moment refute great slanders; and, as I am convinced that I never wronged another, I will assuredly not wrong myself. I will not say of myself that I deserve any evil, or propose any penalty. Why should I? Because I am afraid of the penalty of death which

Meletus proposes? When I do not know whether death is a good or an evil, why should I propose a penalty which would certainly be an evil? Shall I say imprisonment? And why should I live in prison, and be the slave of the magistrates of the year—of the Eleven? Or shall the penalty be a fine, and imprisonment until the fine is paid? There is the same objection. I should have to lie in prison, for money I have none, and cannot pay. And if I say exile (and this may possibly be the penalty which you will affix), I must indeed be blinded by the love of life, if I am so irrational as to expect that when you, who are my own citizens, cannot endure my discourses and words, and have found them so grievous and odious that you will have no more of them, others are likely to endure me. No indeed, men of Athens, that is not very likely. And what a life should I lead, at my age, wandering from city to city, ever changing my place of exile, and always being driven out! For I am quite sure that wherever I go, there, as here, the young men will flock to me; and if I drive them away, their elders will drive me out at their request; and if I let them come, their fathers and friends will drive me out for their sakes.

Some one will say: Yes, Socrates, but cannot you hold your tongue, and then you may go into a foreign city, and no one will interfere with you? Now I have great difficulty in making you understand my answer to this. For if I tell you that to do as you say would be a disobedience to the God, and therefore that I cannot hold my tongue, you will not believe that I am serious; and if I say again that daily to discourse about virtue, and of those other things about which you hear me examining myself and others, is the greatest good of man, and that the unexamined life is not worth living, you are still less likely to believe me. Yet I say what is true, although a thing of which it is hard for me to persuade you. Also, I have never been accustomed to think that I deserve to suffer any harm. Had I money I might have estimated the offence at what I was able to pay, and not have been much the worse. But I have none, and therefore I must ask you to proportion the fine to my means. Well, perhaps I could afford a mina, and therefore I propose that penalty: Plato, Crito, Critobulus, and Apollodorus, my friends here, bid me say thirty minae, and they will be the sureties. Let thirty minae be the penalty; for which sum they will be ample security to you.

[2nd vote: The jury decides for the death penalty by a vote of 360 to 141.]

Not much time will be gained, O Athenians, in return for the evil name which you will get from the detractors of the city, who will say that you killed Socrates, a wise man; for they will call me wise, even although I am not wise, when they want to reproach you. If you had waited a little while, your desire would have been fulfilled in the course of nature. For I am far advanced in years, as you may perceive, and not far from death. . . . The difficulty, my friends, is not to avoid death, but to avoid unrighteousness; for that runs faster than death. I am old and move slowly, and the slower runner has overtaken me, and my accusers are keen and quick, and the faster runner, who is unrighteousness, has overtaken them. And now I depart hence condemned by you to suffer the penalty of death,—they too go their ways condemned by the truth to suffer the penalty of villainy and wrong; and I must abide by my award—let them abide by theirs. I suppose that these things may be regarded as fated,—and I think that they are well. . . .

Friends, who would have acquitted me, I would like also to talk with you about the thing which has come to pass, while the magistrates are busy, and before I go to the place at which I must die. Stay then a little, for we may as well talk with one another while there is time. You are my friends, and I should like to show you the meaning of this event which has happened to me. O my judges—for you I may truly call judges—I should like to tell you of a wonderful circumstance. Hitherto the divine faculty of which the internal oracle is the source has constantly been in the habit of opposing me even about trifles, if I was going to make a slip or error in any matter; and now as you see there has come upon me that which may be thought, and is generally believed to be, the last and worst evil. But the oracle made no sign of opposition, either when I was leaving my house in the morning, or when I was on my way to the court, or while I was speaking, at anything which I was going to say; and yet I have often been stopped in the middle of a speech, but now in nothing I either said or did touching the matter in hand has the oracle opposed me.

What do I take to be the explanation of this silence? I will tell you. It is an intimation that what has happened to me is a good, and that those of us who think that death is an evil are in error. For the customary sign would surely have opposed me had I been going to evil and not to good.

Let us reflect in another way, and we shall see that there is great reason to hope that death is a good; for one of two things—either death is a state of nothingness and utter unconsciousness, or, as men say, there is a change and migration of the soul from this world to another. Now if you suppose that there is no consciousness, but a sleep like the sleep of him who is undisturbed even by dreams, death will be an unspeakable gain. For if a person were to select the night in which his sleep was undisturbed even by dreams, and were to compare with this the other days and nights of his life, and then were to tell us how many days and nights he had passed in the course of his life better and more pleasantly than this one, I think that any man, I will not say a private man, but even the great king will not find many such days or nights, when compared with the others. Now if death be of such a nature, I say that to die is gain; for eternity is then only a single night. But if death is the journey to another place, and there, as men say, all the dead abide, what good, O my friends and judges, can be greater than this? If indeed when the pilgrim arrives in the world below, he is delivered from the professors of justice in this world, and finds the true judges who are said to give judgment there, Minos and Rhadamanthus and Aeacus and Triptolemus, and other sons of God who were righteous in their own life, that pilgrimage will be worth making. What would not a man give if he might converse with Orpheus and Musaeus and Hesiod and Homer? Nay, if this be true, let me die again and again. I myself, too, shall have a wonderful interest in there meeting and conversing with Palamedes, and Ajax the son of Telamon, and any other ancient hero who has suffered death through an unjust judgment; and there will be no small pleasure, as I think, in comparing my own sufferings with theirs. Above all, I shall then be able to continue my search into true and false knowledge; as in this world, so also in the next; and I shall find out who is wise, and who pretends to be wise, and is not. What would

not a man give, O judges, to be able to examine the leader of the great Trojan expedition; or Odysseus or Sisyphus, or numberless others, men and women too! What infinite delight would there be in conversing with them and asking them questions! In another world they do not put a man to death for asking questions: assuredly not. For besides being happier than we are, they will be immortal, if what is said is true.

Wherefore, O judges, be of good cheer about death, and know of a certainty, that no evil can happen to a good man, either in life or after death. He and his are not neglected by the gods; nor has my own approaching end happened by mere chance. But I see clearly that the time had arrived when it was better for me to die and be released from trouble; wherefore the oracle gave no sign. For which reason, also, I am not angry with my condemners, or with my accusers; they have done me no harm, although they did not mean to do me any good; and for this I may gently blame them.

Still I have a favour to ask of them. When my sons are grown up, I would ask you, O my friends, to punish them; and I would have you trouble them, as I have troubled you, if they seem to care about riches, or anything, more than about virtue; or if they pretend to be something when they are really nothing,—then reprove them, as I have reproved you, for not caring about that for which they ought to care, and thinking that they are something when they are really nothing. And if you do this, both I and my sons will have received justice at your hands.

The hour of departure has arrived, and we go our ways—I to die, and you to live. Which is better God only knows.

FOR FURTHER REFLECTION

1. Describe Socrates. What kind of man was he? What were his deepest beliefs?
2. Some have found a note of arrogance and insensitivity in Socrates and argue that he deserved what he got. Does this reading lend any support to that opinion?
3. Does Socrates think that we do evil voluntarily? Why do we do evil?

4. Can the good be harmed by the bad? How do we harm ourselves?

5. What does Socrates mean when he says that "the unexamined life is not worth living"?

JOHN LOCKE

PHILOSOPHY AS THE LOVE OF TRUTH VERSUS ENTHUSIASM

The English philosopher John Locke (1632–1704) was born in Bristol, England and raised as a Puritan. He was educated at Christ Church, Oxford University, where he became a tutor in Greek rhetoric and philosophy. Later he was a practicing physician and assistant to Lord Ashley, the Earl of Shaftesbury. In 1663, because of their Puritan sympathies, both were forced into exile in the Netherlands, where Locke wrote his two masterpieces, An Essay Concerning Human Understanding (published in 1689), from which this selection is taken, and Two Treatises on Government (published in 1690).

Locke held that since God was a God of Truth, He would never require that we believe anything against the natural light of reason—though some mysteries (for example, immortality) are beyond our understanding. Religious people, who have ample grounds for believing in God, must beware lest they allow their imagination and passion to run away with them. Reason and faith are compatible, so that every claim to faith must be supported with evidence. That is, we must be lovers of Truth, believing propositions according to their supporting evidence. Locke wrote in a letter to Anthony Collins, "To love the truth for truth's sake is the principal part of human perfection in this world, and the seed-plot of all other virtues" (October 29, 1703). Lady Masham wrote of Locke, "He was always, in the greatest and in the smallest affairs of human life, as well as in speculative opinions, disposed to follow reason, whosoever suggested it; he being ever a faithful servant, I had almost said a slave, to truth; never abandoning her for anything else, and following her for her own sake purely."[1]

Locke's use of the word *enthusiasm* contains the negative connotations that word held for many of the philosophers and theologians of his day, including Bishop Butler, Jonathan Swift, Henry More, and Bishop Warburton. Leibniz wrote, "Enthusiasm was originally a good term. Just as *sophism* properly indicates an exercise of wisdom, so enthusiasm signifies that there is a divinity in us. But these men having consecrated their passions, fancies, dreams, and even their anger, as something divine, *enthusiasm* began to signify a mental disturbance attributed to the influence of some divinity. . . . Since then, we attribute it to those who believe without foundation that their impulses come from God."[2]

---

[1]Quoted in A. S. Pringle-Pattison's edition of *An Essay Concerning Human Understanding* by John Locke (Oxford: Oxford University Press, 1924), p. 359.
[2]Ibid., p. 360.

1. He that would seriously set upon the search of truth, ought in the first place to prepare his mind with a love of it. For he that loves it not, will not take much pains to get it, nor be much concerned when he misses it. There is nobody in the commonwealth of learning, who does not profess himself a lover of truth; and there is not a rational creature that would not take it amiss to be thought otherwise of. And yet for all this, one may truly say, that there are very few lovers of truth for truth's sake, even amongst those who persuade themselves that they are so. How a man may know whether he be so in earnest, is worth inquiry: And I think there is one unerring mark of it, viz. the not entertaining any proposition with greater assurance than the proofs it is built upon will warrant. Whoever goes beyond this measure of assent, it is plain receives not the truth in the love of it; loves not truth for truth's sake, but for some other bye end. For the evidence that any proposition is true (except such as are self-evident) lying only in the proofs a man has of it, whatsoever degrees of assent he affords it beyond the degrees of that evidence, it is plain that all the surplusage of assurance is owing to some other affection, and not to the love of truth: It being as impossible, that the love of truth should carry my assent above the evidence there is to me that it is true, as that the love of truth should make me assent to any proposition for the sake of that evidence, which it has not, that it is true; which is in effect to love it as a truth, because it is possible or probable that it may not be true. In any truth that gets not possession of our minds by the irresistible light of self-evidence, or by the force of demonstration, the arguments that gain it assent are the vouchers and gage of its probability to us; and we can receive it for no other, than such as they deliver it to our understandings. Whatsoever credit or authority we give to any proposition, more than it receives from the principles and proofs it supports itself upon, is owing to our inclinations that way, and is so far a derogation from the love of truth as such: Which, as it can receive no evidence from our passions or interests, so it should receive no tincture from them.

2. The assuming an authority of dictating to others, and a forwardness to prescribe to their opinions, is a constant concomitant of this bias and corruption of our judgments. For how almost can it be otherwise, but that he should be ready to impose on another's belief, who has already imposed on his own? Who can reasonably expect arguments and conviction from him, in dealing with others, whose understanding is not accustomed to them in his dealing with himself? Who does violence to his own faculties, tyrannizes over his own mind, and usurps the prerogative that belongs to truth alone, which is to command assent by only its own authority, i.e., by and in proportion to that evidence which it carries with it.

3. Upon this occasion I shall take the liberty to consider a third ground of assent [the first two are reason and revelation, ed.], which with some men has the same authority, and is as confidently relied on as either faith or reason; I mean enthusiasm: Which laying by reason, would set up revelation without it. Whereby in effect it takes away both reason and revelation, and substitutes in the room of it the ungrounded fancies of a man's own brain, and assumes them for a foundation both of opinion and conduct.

4. Reason is natural revelation, whereby the eternal father of light, and fountain of all knowledge, communicates to mankind that portion of truth which he has laid within the reach of their natural faculties: Revelation is natural reason enlarged by a new set of discoveries communicated by God immediately, which reason vouches the truth of, by the testimony and proofs it gives, that they come from God. So that he that takes away reason, to make way for revelation, puts out the light of both, and does much—what the same, as if he would persuade a man to put out his eyes, the better to receive the remote light of an invisible star by a telescope.

5. Immediate revelation being a much easier way for men to establish their opinions and regulate their conduct, than the tedious and not always successful labor of strict reasoning, it is no wonder that some have been very apt to pretend to revelation, and to

From John Locke, *An Essay Concerning Human Understanding* (1689), Book IV.19.

persuade themselves that they are under the peculiar guidance of heaven in their actions and opinions, especially in those of them which they cannot account for by the ordinary methods of knowledge and principles of reason. Hence we see that in all ages, men, in whom melancholy has mixed with devotion, or whose conceit of themselves has raised them into an opinion of a greater familiarity with God, and a nearer admittance to his favor than is afforded to others, have often flattered themselves with a persuasion of an immediate intercourse with the Deity, and frequent communications from the Divine Spirit. God, I own, cannot be denied to be able to enlighten the understanding, by a ray darted into the mind immediately from the fountain of light; this they understand he has promised to do, and who then has so good a title to expect it as those who are his peculiar people, chosen by him, and depending on him?

6. Their minds being thus prepared, whatever groundless opinion comes to settle itself strongly upon their fancies, is an illumination from the spirit of God, and presently of divine authority: And whatsoever odd action they find in themselves a strong inclination to do, that impulse is concluded to be a call or direction from heaven, and must be obeyed; it is a commission from above, and they cannot err in executing it.

7. This I take to be properly enthusiasm, which, though founded neither on reason nor divine revelation, but rising from the conceits of a warmed or overweening brain, works yet, where it once gets footing, more powerfully on the persuasions and actions of men, than either of those two, or both together: Men being most forwardly obedient to the impulses they receive from themselves; and the whole man is sure to act more vigorously, where the whole man is carried by a natural motion. For strong conceit, like a new principle, carries all easily with it, when got above common sense, and freed from all restraint of reason, and check of reflection, it is heightened into a divine authority, in concurrence with our own temper and inclination.

8. Though the odd opinions and extravagant actions enthusiasm has run men into, were enough to warn them against this wrong principle, so apt to misguide them both in their belief and conduct; yet the love of something extraordinary, the ease and glory it is to be inspired, and be above the common and natural ways of knowledge, so flatters many men's laziness, ignorance, and vanity, that when once they are got into this way of immediate revelation, of illumination without search, and of certainty without proof, and without examination, it is a hard matter to get them out of it. Reason is lost upon them, they are above it: They see the light infused into their understandings, and cannot be mistaken; it is clear and visible there, like the light of bright sunshine; shows itself, and needs no other proof but its own evidence: They feel the hand of God moving them within, and the impulses of the spirit, and cannot be mistaken in what they feel. . . .

9. This is the way of talking of these men: They are sure, because they are sure: And their persuasions are right, because they are strong in them. For, when what they say is stripped of the metaphor of seeing and feeling, this is all it amounts to: And yet these similes so impose on them, that they serve them for certainty in themselves, and demonstration to others.

10. But to examine a little soberly this internal light, and this feeling on which they build so much. These men have, they say, clear light, and they see; they have awakened sense, and they feel; this cannot, they are sure, be disputed them. For when a man says he sees or feels, nobody can deny it him, that he does so. But here let me ask: This seeing, is it the perception of the truth of the proposition, or of this, that it is a revelation from God? This feeling, is it a perception of an inclination or fancy to do something, or of the spirit of God moving that inclination? These are two very different perceptions, and must be carefully distinguished, if we would not impose upon ourselves. I may perceive the truth of a proposition, and yet not perceive that it is an immediate revelation from God. I may perceive the truth of a proposition in Euclid, without its being or my perceiving it to be a revelation: Nay, I may perceive I came not by this knowledge in a natural way, and so may conclude it revealed, without perceiving that it is a revelation from God; because there be spirits, which, without being divinely commissioned, may excite those ideas in me, and lay them in such order before my mind, that I may perceive their connection. So that the knowledge of any proposition coming into my mind,

I know not how, is not a perception that it is from God. Much less is a strong persuasion, that it is true, a perception that it is from God, or so much as true. But however it be called light and seeing, I suppose it is at most but belief and assurance: And the proposition taken for a revelation, is not such as they know to be true, but take to be true. For where a proposition is known to be true, revelation is needless: And it is hard to conceive how there can be a revelation to any one of what he knows already. If therefore it be a proposition which they are persuaded, but do not know, to be true, whatever they may call it, it is not seeing, but believing. For these are two ways, whereby truth comes into the mind, wholly distinct, so that one is not the other. What I see I know to be so by the evidence of the thing itself: What I believe I take to be so upon the testimony of another: But this testimony I must know to be given, or else what ground have I of believing? I must see that it is God that reveals this to me, or else I see nothing. The question then here is, how do I know that God is the revealer of this to me; that this impression is made upon my mind by his Holy Spirit, and that therefore I ought to obey it? If I know not this, how great soever the assurance is that I am possessed with, it is groundless; whatever light I pretend to, it is but enthusiasm. For whether the proposition supposed to be revealed, be in itself evidently true, or visibly probable, or by the natural ways of knowledge uncertain, the proposition that must be well grounded, and manifested to be true, is this, that God is the revealer of it, and that what I take to be a revelation is certainly put into my mind by him, and is not an illusion dropped in by some other spirit, or raised by my own fancy. For if I mistake not, these men receive it for true, because they presume God revealed it. Does it not then stand upon them, to examine upon what grounds they presume it to be a revelation from God? or else all their confidence is mere presumption: And this light, they are so dazzled with, is nothing but an ignis fatuus that leads them constantly round in this circle; it is a revelation, because they firmly believe it, and they believe it, because it is a revelation.

11. In all that is of divine revelation, there is need of no other proof but that it is an inspiration from God: For he can neither deceive nor be deceived. But how shall it be known that any proposition in our minds is a truth infused by God; a truth that is revealed to us by him, which he declares to us, and therefore we ought to believe? Here it is that enthusiasm fails of the evidence it pretends to. For men thus possessed boast of a light whereby they say they are enlightened, and brought into the knowledge of this or that truth. But if they know it to be a truth, they must know it to be so, either by its own self-evidence to natural reason, or by the rational proofs that make it out to be so. If they see and know it to be a truth, either of these two ways, they in vain suppose it to be a revelation. For they know it to be true the same way, that any other man naturally may know that it is so without the help of revelation. For thus all the truths, of what kind soever, that men uninspired are enlightened with, came into their minds, and are established there. If they say they know it to be true because it is a revelation from God, the reason is good: But then it will be demanded how they know it to be a revelation from God. If they say, by the light it brings with it, which shines bright in their minds, and they cannot resist: I beseech them to consider whether this be any more than what we have taken notice of already, viz. that it is a revelation, because they strongly believe it to be true. For all the light they speak of is but a strong, though ungrounded, persuasion of their own minds, that it is a truth. For rational grounds from proofs that it is a truth, they must acknowledge to have none; for then it is not received as a revelation, but upon the ordinary grounds that other truths are received: And if they believe it to be true because it is a revelation, and have no other reason for its being a revelation, but because they are fully persuaded without any other reason that it is true; they believe it to be a revelation, only because they strongly believe it to be a revelation; which is a very unsafe ground to proceed on, either in our tenets or actions. And what readier way can there be to run ourselves into the most extravagant errors and miscarriages, than thus to set up fancy for our supreme and sole guide, and to believe any proposition to be true, any action to be right, only because we believe it to be so? The strength of our persuasions is no evidence at all of their own rectitude: Crooked things may be as stiff and inflexible as straight: And men may be as positive and peremptory in error as in

truth. How come else the untractable zealots in different and opposite parties? For if the light, which every one thinks he has in his mind, which in this case is nothing but the strength of his own persuasion, be an evidence that it is from God, contrary opinions have the same title to be inspirations; and God will be not only the father of lights, but of opposite and contradictory lights, leading men contrary ways; and contradictory propositions will be divine truths, if an ungrounded strength of assurance be an evidence, that any proposition is a divine revelation.

12. This cannot be otherwise, whilst firmness of persuasion is made the cause of believing, and confidence of being in the right is made an argument of truth. St. Paul himself believed he did well, and that he had a call to it when he persecuted the Christians, whom he confidently thought in the wrong: But yet it was he, and not they, who were mistaken. Good men are men still, liable to mistakes; and are sometimes warmly engaged in errors, which they take for divine truths, shining in their minds with the clearest light.

13. Light, true light, in the mind is, or can be nothing else but the evidence of the truth of any proposition; and if it be not a self-evident proposition, all the light it has, or can have, is from the cleanness and validity of those proofs, upon which it is received. To talk of any other light in the understanding is to put ourselves in the dark, or in the power of the Prince of darkness, and by our own consent to give ourselves up to delusion to believe a lie. For if strength of persuasion be the light, which must guide us; I ask how shall any one distinguish between the delusions of Satan, and the inspirations of the Holy Ghost? He can transform himself into an angel of light. And they who are led by this son of the morning, are as fully satisfied of the illumination, i.e., are as strongly persuaded, that they are enlightened by the spirit of God, as any one who is so: They acquiesce and rejoice in it, are acted by it: And nobody can be more sure, nor more in the right (if their own strong belief may be judge) than they.

14. He therefore that will not give himself up to all the extravagancies of delusion and error, must bring this guide of his light within to the trial. God, when he makes the prophet, does not unmake the man. He leaves all his faculties in the natural state, to enable him to judge of his inspirations, whether they be of divine origin or no. When he illuminates the mind with supernatural light, he does not extinguish that which is natural. If he would have us assent to the truth of any proposition, he either evidences that truth by the usual methods of natural reason, or else makes it known to be a truth which he would have us assent to, by his authority; and convinces us that it is from him, by some marks which reason cannot be mistaken in. Reason must be our last judge and guide in everything. I do not mean that we must consult reason, and examine whether a proposition revealed from God can be made out by natural principles, and if it cannot, that then we may reject it: But consult it we must, and by it examine, whether it be a revelation from God or no. And if reason finds it to be revealed from God, reason then declares for it, as much as for any other truth, and makes it one of her dictates. Every conceit that thoroughly warms our fancies must pass for an inspiration, if there be nothing but the strength of our persuasions, whereby to judge of our persuasions: If reason must not examine their truth by something extrinsic to the persuasions themselves, inspirations and delusions, truth and falsehood, will have the same measure, and will not be possible to be distinguished.

15. Thus we see the holy men of old, who had revelations from God, had something else besides that internal light of assurance in their own minds, to testify to them that it was from God. They were not left to their own persuasions alone, that those persuasions were from God; but had outward signs to convince them of the author of those revelations. And when they were to convince others, they had a power given them to justify the truth of their commission from heaven, and by visible signs to assert the divine authority of a message they were sent with. Moses saw the bush burn without being consumed, and heard a voice out of it. This was something besides finding an impulse upon his mind to go to Pharaoh, that he might bring his brethren out of Egypt: And yet he thought not this enough to authorize him to go with that message, till God, by another miracle of his rod that turned into a serpent, had assured him of a power to testify his mission, by the same miracle repeated before them, whom he was sent to. Gideon was sent by an angel to deliver Israel from the Midianites, and

yet he desired a sign to convince him that this commission was from God. These, and several the like instances to be found among the prophets of old, are enough to show that they thought not an inward seeing or persuasion of their own minds, without any other proof, a sufficient evidence that it was from God; though the scripture does not every where mention their demanding or having such proofs.

16. In what I have said I am far from denying that God can, or doth sometimes enlighten men's minds in the apprehending of certain truths, or excite them to good actions by the immediate inflence and assistance of the Holy Spirit, without any extraordinary signs accompanying it. But in such cases too we have reason and scripture, unerring rules to know whether it be from God or no. Where the truth embraced is consonant to the revelation in the written word of God, or the action conformable to the dictates of right reason or holy writ, we may be assured that we run no risk in entertaining it as such; because though perhaps it be not an immediate revelation from God, extraordinarily operating on our minds, yet we are sure it is warranted by that revelation which he has given us of truth. . . .

FOR FURTHER REFLECTION

1. Describe Locke's concept of the love of truth. What does he mean by this?
2. Do you agree with the high status Locke gives to truth? Some people think Locke overvalues truth. They say that happiness, peace of mind and freedom are also important and that sometimes we ought to sacrifice some truth to these values. What do you think? Write a paragraph on the value and meaning of loving the truth.
3. What does Locke mean by the term *enthusiasm?* Why does he condemn it?
4. Does Locke think that religious *revelations* must always be false? What does he say about distinguishing valid from invalid claims to revelation?

BERTRAND RUSSELL

THE VALUE OF PHILOSOPHY

Bertrand Russell (1872–1970) is one of the most important philosophers of the twentieth century. His works cover almost every area of philosophy, from logic and philosophy of mathematics (*Principia Mathematica*, published in 1910, written with Alfred North Whitehead) to philosophy of religion ("Mysticism" and "Why I Am Not a Christian") and ethics ("Science and Ethics"). Russell's concern to live out his philosophy in his life led him to found a special school on his philosophy of education, become a leader in Britain's "Ban the [atom] Bomb" movement, and speak out on moral and political issues, sometimes at personal risk.

In this reading, from the end of his brilliant essay *The Problems of Philosophy* (1912), Russell argues that the value of philosophy lies not in any ability to produce material goods ("Philosophy bakes no bread") or to make definitive conclusions about the nature of reality, but in its effect on the lives of those who take it seriously. In its contemplation of the perennial questions of life, it enlarges our understanding and results in spiritual liberation.

Having now come to the end of our brief and very incomplete review of the problems of philosophy, it will be well to consider, in conclusion, what is the value of philosophy and why it ought to be studied. It is the more necessary to consider this question, in view of the fact that many men, under the influence of science or of practical affairs, are inclined to doubt whether philosophy is anything better than innocent but useless trifling, hair-splitting distinctions, and controversies on matters concerning which knowledge is impossible.

This view of philosophy appears to result, partly from a wrong conception of the ends of life, partly from a wrong conception of the kind of goods which philosophy strives to achieve. Physical science, through the medium of inventions, is useful to innumerable people who are wholly ignorant of it; thus the study of physical science is to be recommended, not only, or primarily, because of the effect on the student, but rather because of the effect on mankind in general. Thus utility does not belong to philosophy. If the study of philosophy has any value at all for others than students of philosophy, it must be only indirectly, through its effects upon the lives of those who study it. It is in these effects, therefore, if anywhere, that the value of philosophy must be primarily sought.

But further, if we are not to fail in our endeavour to determine the value of philosophy, we must first free our minds from the prejudices of what are wrongly called "practical" men. The "practical" man, as this word is often used, is one who recognizes only material needs, who realizes that men must have food for the body, but is oblivious of the necessity of providing food for the mind. If all men were well off, if poverty and disease had been reduced to their lowest possible point, there would still remain much to be done to produce a valuable society; and even in the existing world the goods of the mind are at least as important as the goods of the body. It is exclusively among the goods of the mind that the value of philosophy is to be found; and only those who are not indifferent to these goods can be persuaded that the study of philosophy is not a waste of time.

Philosophy, like all other studies, aims primarily at knowledge. The knowledge it aims at is the kind of knowledge which gives unity and system to the body of the sciences, and the kind which results from a critical examination of the grounds of our convictions, prejudices, and beliefs. But it cannot be maintained that philosophy has had any very great measure of success in its attempts to provide definite answers to its questions. If you ask a mathematician, a mineralogist, a historian, or any other man of learning, what definite body of truths has been ascertained by his science, his answer will last as long as you are willing to listen. But if you put the same question to a philosopher, he will, if he is candid, have to confess that his study has not achieved positive results such as have been achieved by other sciences. It is true that this is partly accounted for by the fact that, as soon as definite knowledge concerning any subject becomes possible, this subject ceases to be called philosophy, and becomes a separate science. The whole study of the heavens, which now belongs to astronomy, was once included in philosophy; Newton's great work was called "the mathematical principles of natural philosophy." Similarly, the study of the human mind, which was a part of philosophy, has now been separated from philosophy and has become the science of psychology. Thus, to a great extent, the uncertainty of philosophy is more apparent than real: those questions which are already capable of definite answers are placed in the sciences, while those only to which, at present, no definite answer can be given, remain to form the residue which is called philosophy.

This is, however, only a part of the truth concerning the uncertainty of philosophy. There are many questions—and among them those that are of the profoundest interest to our spiritual life—which, so far as we can see, must remain insoluble to the human intellect unless its powers become of quite a different order from what they are now. Has the universe any unity of plan or purpose, or is it a fortuitous concourse of atoms? Is consciousness a permanent part of the universe, giving hope of indefinite growth in wisdom, or is it a transitory accident on a small planet

From Bertrand Russell, *The Problems of Philosophy* (Oxford: Oxford University Press, 1912).

on which life must ultimately become impossible? Are good and evil of importance to the universe or only to man? Such questions are asked by philosophy, and variously answered by various philosophers. But it would seem that, whether answers be otherwise discoverable or not, the answers suggested by philosophy are none of them demonstrably true. Yet, however slight may be the hope of discovering an answer, it is part of the business of philosophy to continue the consideration of such questions, to make us aware of their importance, to examine all the approaches to them, and to keep alive that speculative interest in the universe which is apt to be killed by confining ourselves to definitely ascertainable knowledge.

Many philosophers, it is true, have held that philosophy could establish the truth of certain answers to such fundamental questions. They have supposed that what is of most importance in religious beliefs could be proved by strict demonstration to be true. In order to judge of such attempts, it is necessary to take a survey of human knowledge, and to form an opinion as to its methods and its limitations. On such a subject it would be unwise to pronounce dogmatically; but if the investigations of our previous chapters have not led us astray, we shall be compelled to renounce the hope of finding philosophical proofs of religious beliefs. We cannot, therefore, include as part of the value of philosophy any definite set of answers to such questions. Hence, once more, the value of philosophy must not depend upon any supposed body of definitely ascertainable knowledge to be acquired by those who study it.

The value of philosophy is, in fact, to be sought largely in its very uncertainty. The man who has no tincture of philosophy goes through life imprisoned in the prejudices derived from common sense, from the habitual beliefs of his age or his nation, and from convictions which have grown up in his mind without the cooperation or consent of his deliberate reason. To such a man the world tends to become definite, finite, obvious; common objects rouse no questions, and unfamiliar possibilities are contemptuously rejected. As soon as we begin to philosophize, on the contrary, we find, as we saw in our opening chapters, that even the most everyday things lead to problems to which only very incomplete answers can be given. Philoso-

phy, though unable to tell us with certainty what is the true answer to the doubts which it raises, is able to suggest many possibilities which enlarge our thoughts and free them from the tyranny of custom. Thus, while diminishing our feeling of certainty as to what things are, it greatly increases our knowledge as to what they may be; it removes the somewhat arrogant dogmatism of those who have never travelled into the region of liberating doubt, and it keeps alive our sense of wonder by showing familiar things in an unfamiliar aspect.

Apart from its utility in showing unsuspected possibilities, philosophy has a value—perhaps its chief value—through the greatness of the objects which it contemplates, and the freedom from narrow and personal aims resulting from this contemplation. The life of the instinctive man is shut up within the circle of his private interests: family and friends may be included, but the outer world is not regarded except as it may help or hinder what comes within the circle of instinctive wishes. In such a life there is something feverish and confined, in comparison with which the philosophic life is calm and free. The private world of instinctive interests is a small one, set in the midst of a great and powerful world which must, sooner or later, lay our private world in ruins. Unless we can so enlarge our interests as to include the whole outer world, we remain like a garrison in a beleaguered fortress, knowing that the enemy prevents escape and that ultimate surrender is inevitable. In such a life there is no peace, but a constant strife between the insistence of desire and the powerlessness of will. In one way or another, if our life is to be great and free, we must escape this prison and this strife.

One way of escape is by philosophic contemplation. Philosophic contemplation does not, in its widest survey, divide the universe into two hostile camps—friends and foes, helpful and hostile, good and bad—it views the whole impartially. Philosophic contemplation, when it is unalloyed, does not aim at proving that the rest of the universe is akin to man. All acquisition of knowledge is an enlargement of the Self, but this enlargement is best attained when it is not directly sought. It is obtained when the desire for knowledge is alone operative, by a study which does not wish in advance that its objects should have this or that character, but adapts the Self to the characters which it finds in its objects. This enlargement of the Self is not obtained when, taking the Self as it is, we try to show that the world is so similar to this Self that knowledge of it is possible without any admission of what seems alien. The desire to prove this is a form of self-assertion and, like all self-assertion, it is an obstacle to the growth of Self which it desires, and of which the Self knows that it is capable. Self-assertion, in philosophic speculation as elsewhere, views the world as a means to its own ends; thus it makes the world of less account than Self, and the Self sets bounds to the greatness of its goods. In contemplation, on the contrary, we start from the not-Self, and through its greatness the boundaries of Self are enlarged; through the infinity of the universe the mind which contemplates it achieves some share in infinity.

For this reason greatness of soul is not fostered by those philosophies which assimilate the universe to Man. Knowledge is a form of union of Self and not-Self; like all union, it is impaired by dominion, and therefore by any attempt to force the universe into conformity with what we find in ourselves. There is a widespread philosophical tendency towards the view which tells us that Man is the measure of all things, that truth is manmade, that space and time and the world of universals are properties of the mind, and that, if there be anything not created by the mind, it is unknowable and of no account for us. This view, if our previous discussions were correct, is untrue; but in addition to being untrue, it has the effect of robbing philosophic contemplation of all that gives it value, since it fetters contemplation to Self. What it calls knowledge is not a union with the not-Self, but a set of prejudices, habits, and desires, making an impenetrable veil between us and the world beyond. The man who finds pleasure in such a theory of knowledge is like the man who never leaves the domestic circle for fear his word might not be law.

The true philosophic contemplation, on the contrary, finds its satisfaction in every enlargement of the not-Self, in everything that magnifies the objects contemplated, and thereby the subject contemplating. Everything, in contemplation, that is personal or private, everything that depends upon habit, self-interest, or desire, distorts the object, and hence impairs the

union which the intellect seeks. By thus making a barrier between subject and object, such personal and private things become a prison to the intellect. The free intellect will see as God might see, without a *here* and *now,* without hopes and fears, without the trammels of customary beliefs and traditional prejudices, calmly, dispassionately, in the sole and exclusive desire of knowledge—knowledge as impersonal, as purely contemplative, as it is possible for man to attain. Hence also the free intellect will value more the abstract and universal knowledge into which the accidents of private history do not enter, than the knowledge brought by the senses, and dependent, as such knowledge must be, upon an exclusive and personal point of view and a body whose sense-organs distort as much as they reveal.

The mind which has become accustomed to the freedom and impartiality of philosophic contemplation will preserve something of the same freedom and impartiality in the world of action and emotion. It will view its purposes and desires as parts of the whole, with the absence of insistence that results from seeing them as infinitesimal fragments in a world of which all the rest is unaffected by any one man's deeds. The impartiality which, in contemplation, is the unalloyed desire for truth, is the very same quality of mind which, in action, is justice, and in emotion is that universal love which can be given to all, and not only to those who are judged useful or admirable. Thus contemplation enlarges not only the objects of our thoughts, but also the objects of our actions and our affections: it makes us citizens of the universe, not only of one walled city at war with all the rest. In this citizenship of the universe consists man's true freedom, and his liberation from the thraldom of narrow hopes and fears.

Thus, to sum up our discussion of the value of philosophy: Philosophy is to be studied, not for the sake of any definite answers to its questions, since no definite answers can, as a rule, be known to be true, but rather for the sake of the questions themselves; because these questions enlarge our conception of what is possible, enrich our intellectual imagination and diminish the dogmatic assurance which closes the mind against speculation; but above all because, through the greatness of the universe which philosophy contemplates, the mind also is rendered great, and becomes capable of that union with the universe which constitutes its highest good.

FOR FURTHER REFLECTION

1. What are the aims of philosophy? Has it been successful in attaining them? Explain.
2. Compare Russell's essay with Socrates' thought.
3. Evaluate Russell's contention that "the man who has no tincture of philosophy goes through life imprisoned in the prejudices derived from common sense, from the habitual beliefs of his age or his nation, and from convictions which have grown up in his mind without the cooperation or consent of his deliberate reason. . . . Through the greatness of the universe which philosophy contemplates, the mind also is rendered great, and becomes capable of that union with the universe which constitutes its highest good."
4. A particularly poignant vignette revealing Russell's search for a philosophy to make sense out of life is recorded in *The Autobiography of Bertrand Russell* (London: Unwin and Hyman, 1953, vol. 1, p. 146), where he relates the experience of seeing Mrs. Whitehead in severe pain. The year is 1901.

> When we came home, we found Mrs. W. undergoing an unusually severe bout of pain. She seemed cut off from everyone and everything by walls of agony, and the sense of the solitude of each human soul suddenly overwhelmed me. Ever since my marriage, my emotional life had been calm and superficial. I had forgotten all the deeper issues, and had been content with flippant cleverness. Suddenly the ground seemed to give way beneath me, and I found myself in quite another region. Within five minutes I went thru some such reflections as the following: the loneliness of the human soul is unendurable; nothing can penetrate it except the highest intensity of the sort of love that religious teachers have preached; whatever does not spring from this motive is harmful, or at best useless; it follows that war is wrong, that a public school education is abominable, that the use of force is to be deprecated, and that in human relations one should penetrate to the core of loneliness in each person and speak to that. [Russell then describes his sudden awareness of Mrs. W's three-year-old son, with whom he then and there found an affinity.] . . . At the end of those five minutes, I had become a completely different person. For a time, a sort of mystic illumination possessed me. I felt that I knew the inmost thoughts of everybody that I met in the street, and though this was, no doubt, a delusion, I did in actual fact find myself in *far closer* touch than previously with all my friends, and many of my acquaintances. Having been an Imperialist, I became during those five minutes . . . a Pacificist. Having for years cared only for exactness and analysis, I found myself filled with semi-mystical feelings about beauty, and with an intense interest in children and with a desire almost as profound as that of the Buddha to find some philosophy which should make human life endurable. A strange excitement possessed me, containing intense pain but also some element of triumph through the fact that I could dominate pain, and make it, as I thought, a gateway to wisdom. The mystic insight which I then imagined myself to possess has largely faded, and the habit of analysis has reasserted itself. But something of what I thought I saw in that moment has remained always with me, *causing* my attitude during the first war, my interest in my children, my indifference to minor misfortunes and a certain emotional tone in all my human relations.

What view of philosophy do you see in this experience? Is it identical with what you read in Russell's essay, or does it add a new dimension? If you think it does bring in something new, what is that?

PART II

❦

Theory of Knowledge

What can we really know? How can we be certain that we have the truth? How can we be certain that we know anything at all? What is knowledge, and how is it different from belief? If we know something, must we know that we know it?

The theory of knowledge—*epistemology* (from the Greek, "the science of knowing")— inquires into the nature of knowledge and justification of belief. Many philosophers believe that this inquiry is central to philosophy: if philosophy is the quest for truth and wisdom, then we need to know how to find the truth and justify our beliefs. We need to know how to distinguish truth from falsity and justified from unwarranted beliefs.

The field of epistemology concerns several classical issues:

1. What is knowledge? That is, what are the essential characteristics of this concept?
2. Can we know anything at all? Or are we doomed to ignorance about the most important subjects in life?
3. How do we obtain knowledge—by using our senses, or our intellect, or both?

Let us examine each of these questions.

What is knowledge? The claim you know something is the claim that you possess a truth. If you claim to know that "10 × 10 = 100," you implicitly claim that the statement "10 × 10 = 100" is true. It would be misusing language to make statements like " I know that 10 × 10 = 13, but it is false," because knowledge claims are claims about grasping the truth. Of course, we may be wrong about our knowledge claims. The drunk claims to "know" that there are pink elephants in the room, the child claims to "know" that Santa Claus exists, and two witnesses may claim contradictory "knowledge" in describing an accident. We often believe falsely that we know. Sometimes the evidence on which we base a knowledge claim is inadequate or misleading, or we misremember or misperceive. Sometimes knowledge claims are contradicted by others, as when two people of different religious faiths each claims the only true religion, or when one person claims with

31

certainty that abortion is morally wrong and the other person claims with equal certainty that it is morally permissible.

Knowledge involves possessing the truth, but includes more than having a true belief. Imagine that I am holding up four cards so that I can see their faces but you can see only their backs. I ask you to guess what types of cards I am holding. You feel a hunch (that is, have a weak belief) that I am holding up four aces and correctly announce, "You are holding four aces in your hands." Although we both possess the truth, I have something you don't—an adequate justification for my belief that there are four aces in my hand. So knowledge differs from mere true belief in that the knower has an adequate justification for claiming truth.

Some further questions are as follows: How much justification is enough to transform a mere true belief into a state of knowledge? Must we be certain about a belief before it counts as knowledge? Is some knowledge self-evident, so that we do not need further evidence for our claim to know (such as the claim to know that we have free will)?

This path leads us to our second major question: Can we know anything at all? Or are we doomed to ignorance about the most important subjects in life? What do we really know? Could it be that we really know nothing at all? The theory that we do not have any knowledge is called *skepticism*. We cannot be completely certain that any of our beliefs are true. Radical skepticism goes even further, claiming that we cannot even be certain of *the belief that we cannot be completely certain that any of our beliefs are true*. In other words, we are even unable to know that we cannot have knowledge.

Skepticism does not deny that we should act from the best evidence available, but it insists that we can never be sure that our truth claims are correct. For all we know, the universe and everything in it could have been created ten minutes ago, and all our apparent memories created with it. Or the universe and everything in it may have doubled in size last night while we were sleeping. How could we check this? Would it help to use a ruler to measure our height, to see if we had doubled in size?

Further, do you know that you are not the only person who exists? Maybe everyone else is a robot programmed to speak and smile and write exams. Can you prove that other people have consciousness? Have you ever *felt* their consciousness, their pain, or their sense of the color green? In fact, how do you know that you're not dreaming right now? All that you are experiencing is part of a dream. Soon you will wake up and be surprised to discover that what you thought were dreams were really minidreams within your maxidream. How can you prove that you're not dreaming? Or, perhaps you are a brain suspended in a tub full of a chemical solution in a scientist's laboratory and wired to a computer that is feeding you simulated experiences. If you are under the control of an ingenious scientist, you would never discover it, for he or she has arranged that you will only be able to compare your beliefs to the simulated experiences. Your tub is your destiny!

Now we turn to our third question: How do we obtain knowledge? Through using our senses, or our intellect, or both? The two classic theories on how we acquire knowledge are called *rationalism* and *empiricism*. Both theories use reason in acquiring knowledge, but rationalists believe that reason is sufficient to discover truth, whereas empiricists hold that all knowledge originates through sense perception (seeing, hearing, touching, tasting, and smelling).

A. CLASSICAL THEORIES ON CERTAINTY AND THE SOURCES OF KNOWLEDGE

The earliest surviving texts in ancient Greek philosophy show a preoccupation and almost obsession with discovering the sources of human knowledge and the extent to which we can be certain about anything. Protagoras, the ancient Greek sophist, made the dramatic claim that "Man is the measure of all things: of existing things, that they exist; of nonexisting things, that they do not exist." His point is that we human beings create our own standards by which we judge the truth of everything. The source of knowledge, for Protagoras, is human convention, and the certainty that it gives is rather flimsy since our conventions are evershifting.

In the first selection, Plato rejects relativist conceptions of knowledge like Protagoras' and argues that we have genuine knowledge of absolute truths that are in no way dependent on changing human convention. Plato distinguishes between two approaches to knowledge: sense perception and reason. Sense perception cannot be adequate for grasping the truth because its objects change and decay. All we get in this way are beliefs about particular objects. Knowledge, however, goes beyond the particular and grasps universal truths or "forms," as Plato calls them. Plato argues that all knowledge involves knowing *objects*, and thus these forms (the objects of our knowledge) must exist in their own nonphysical real world. Philosophers, he maintains, are people who work their way through the world of becoming, the empirical world, to this higher reality. In Plato's dialogue *Meno*, the lead character Socrates teaches geometry to an uneducated slave and thereby claims to demonstrate that all learning comes about through recollecting the forms. The slave learns to double the size of a square simply by consulting his own inherent understanding. Plato believed in reincarnation and held that in a previous existence, we saw all essential truths but have since lost awareness of them through birth. Education should therefore be a stimulation of the soul, so that we recall what we really possess but have forgotten.

Plato's optimistic conception of knowledge became an important source of inspiration for many philosophers in the centuries that followed. Others, though, were quite suspicious about any claim to attain certainty, an important example of which is the ancient Greek skeptic Sextus Empiricus. According to Sextus in the second reading, every argument that we can offer in support of some knowledge claim can be countered by an argument in its opposition; the wise thing to do is be skeptical by neither believing nor disbelieving in knowledge claims and thereby achieve mental tranquility.

During the sixteenth and seventeenth centuries, Sextus's view of skepticism was revived, and this triggered a dramatic response by the French philosopher René Descartes, as can be seen in the third reading. Descartes agrees with skeptics that much of what we took for knowledge has turned out to be false or unsupported by clear evidence, and he wonders whether all his beliefs are unjustified. So he tries to suspend belief about all his claims to knowledge, in order to build a firm foundation and thereon a stronger house of knowledge. Descartes' approach is commonly called *rationalism* because of two distinct features. First, Descartes maintains that we are born with knowledge of an important set of truths—innate ideas as he calls them—which are the rational foundation of everything else that we know. Second, he argues that we further our knowledge through the reasoning process of deduction: from our innate ideas, we deduce other truths in much the way that we deduce theorems in geometry.

The fourth author in this section, John Locke, attacked both these features of rationalism. According to Locke, there are no innate ideas, and claims to knowledge must be founded on sense experience. Furthermore, while we often reason deductively, the manner in which we extend our knowledge is largely through sense experience, not through deduction. Thus, in contrast to the rationalistic approach, Locke's methodology is commonly called *empiricism* (from the Latin word *empeiria*, meaning "experience"). Locke dramatically illustrates his emphasis on experience here: "Let us then suppose the mind to be, as we say, white paper, void of all characters, without any ideas; how comes it by that vast store, which the busy and boundless fancy of man has painted on it with an almost endless variety? Whence has it all the materials of reason and knowledge? To this I answer, in one word, from experience: in that all our knowledge is founded." Locke sets forth a representational theory of knowledge, claiming that the core qualities of what we know are caused by the world itself, although some qualities are the products of the way our perceptual mechanisms are affected by the world. The former qualities, called *primary qualities*, such as motion, size, shape, and number, are the true building blocks of knowledge, whereas the latter, the *secondary qualities*, such as color, taste, and sensations of warmth and cold, are ways to apprehend the primary qualities.

The fifth reading is by Irish philosopher George Berkeley, who later in life became an Anglican bishop. Inspired by Locke, Berkeley held that knowledge comes to us from experience. However, he disagreed with Locke about the ultimate source behind our experiences; specifically, he rejected Locke's contention that material objects are the causes of our perceptions. There is no material world, says Berkeley, only ideas in minds. More precisely, God interjects perceptions of objects directly into our spirit-minds. Berkeley's position is called *idealism* (as in "idea-ism"), since perceptions of things are really just ideas in the spirit-minds of God and people. Berkeley makes his case in his work *Three Dialogues Between Hylas and Philonous* (1713). Part of his argument involves a rejection of Locke's distinction between primary and secondary qualities; for Berkeley, all qualities are essentially secondary and exist in the mind alone. Thus, Berkeley famously maintains that *to be is to be perceived*: all external objects are just mental phenomena that would cease to exist if they were not perceived. A careful reading of the *Dialogues* will give you Berkeley's answer as to why the world does not cease to exist when we go to sleep or cease to perceive parts of it.

In the sixth reading, Scottish philosopher David Hume carries on the empiricist tradition, but draws quite skeptical conclusions about our ability to have certainty about anything. Our knowledge of the world is confined to our experience of it and underlying mental habits that force us to think in certain ways. Concepts of so-called external objects and external causal forces are really just the result of mental habits that assimilate our sensory experiences; there is no way for us to know whether our concepts have anything at all to do with what goes on in the real world itself.

The German philosopher Immanuel Kant, author of the seventh reading, sought to reconcile empiricism with rationalism. First, he was compelled to accept the empiricist doctrine that all the content of knowledge comes to us by way of the senses. Yet he thought the rationalists were correct in pointing out that the knowing process has an innate element. The matter may be put this way: Every proposition is (1) either a priori or empirical—that is either known intuitively or through experience—and (2) either analytic or synthetic—that is, either true by definition or not true by definition. If we combine all the classifications, we get the following candidates for types of knowledge:

1. Analytic a priori propositions (true by definition and known intuitively, for example, "All mothers are women")
2. Analytic empirical propositions (true by definition and known through experience)
3. Synthetic a priori propositions (not true by definition and known intuitively)
4. Synthetic empirical propositions (not true by definition and known through experience, for example, "Mary is Joan's mother")

Kant agrees with empiricists, such as Hume, who accepted Types 1 and 4 and rejected Type 2 as incoherent. That is, for Kant and the empiricists, there are no analytic empirical truths; the notion seems contradictory. However, Kant parts company with the empiricists by accepting Type 3. The mind intuitively structures our knowledge so that everything that we know is organized in specific ways. Thus, there are synthetic a priori truths, consisting of knowledge that is part of the rigidly structured nature of sense perception and thinking itself. Examples of synthetic a priori knowledge are the concepts of time, space, and causality. These are all part of the structure of our minds, and without them, we cannot perceive or think about reality. Our minds impose these structures onto all experience in the way that a cookie cutter molds cookie dough into specific shapes. Regardless of whether these concepts have real existence in the world itself, we nevertheless are forced to rely on them when we think about the world.

PLATO

〜

THE THEORY OF THE FORMS AND
DOCTRINE OF RECOLLECTION

Plato (427–347 B.C.E.) distinguishes two approaches to belief and knowledge: sense perception and reason. Sense perception has as its object the fleeting world of particular objects, which appear differently at different times. Hence it is an unstable relationship, yielding only fallible opinion or belief, but not knowledge, the ultimate truth. Reason, however, grasps that which is absolute, unchanging, and universal, the *Forms* as they are called. Sense perception causes us to see specific horses, chairs, and people, but reason gives us understanding of the universal horse, chair, and person.

Sense perception may be the starting point for knowledge, but it can never by itself bring us to the realm of reality, the world of being. By itself, it leaves us in the realm of appearances, in the world of becoming. "As for the man who believes in beautiful things, but does not believe in beauty itself nor is able to follow if one lead him to the understanding of it—do you think his life is real or a dream? Is it not a dream? For whether a man be asleep or awake is it not dream-like to mistake the image for the real thing?" The role of the philosopher is to use the world of sense perception in order to lead the soul out of the dreamlike state of becoming and into the real world of being.

Plato's "Theory of Recollection" (from the *Meno*) is the classic expression of the doctrine that we are born with innate ideas or a priori knowledge, an implicit knowledge, prior to experience, which recollection makes explicit. This type of knowledge is the bridge between the two worlds of being and becoming.

In this selection, Meno wants to know whether virtue can be taught or whether it is learned by practice or some other way. He begins this section by noting Socrates' renowned ability to expose pretensions and reveal just how ignorant we all are.

Meno raises a35 puzzle about learning: how do you know when you have found the answer to your question? Either (1) you don't know the answer and so won't know when you've found it; or (2) you already know the answer, in which case why make an inquiry? Socrates set about to solve this riddle about the impossibility of learning anything new. Try to follow his reasoning with Meno's slave boy.

Men.: O Socrates, I used to be told, before I knew you, that you were always doubting yourself and making others doubt; and now you are casting your spells over me, and I am simply getting bewitched and enchanted, and am at my wits' end. And if I may venture to make a jest upon you, you seem to me both in your appearance and in your power over others to be very like the flat torpedo fish, who torpifies those who come near him and touch him, as you have now torpified me, I think. For my soul and my tongue are really torpid, and I do not know how to answer you; and though I have been delivered of an infinite variety of speeches about virtue before now, and to many persons—and very good ones they were, as I thought—at this moment I cannot even say what virtue is. And I think that you are very wise in not voyaging and going away from home, for if you did in other places as you do in Athens, you would be cast into prison as a magician.

Soc.: You are a rogue, Meno, and had all but caught me. . . .

. . . As to my being a torpedo, if the torpedo is torpid as well as the cause of torpidity in others, then indeed I am a torpedo, but not otherwise; for I perplex others, not because I am clear, but because I am utterly perplexed myself. And now I know not what virtue is, and you seem to be in the same case, although you did once perhaps know before you touched me. However, I have no objection to join with you in the enquiry.

Men.: And how will you enquire, Socrates, into that which you do not know? What will you put forth as the subject of enquiry? And if you find what you want, how will you ever know that this is the thing which you did not know?

Soc.: I know, Meno, what you mean; but just see what a tiresome dispute you are introducing. You argue that a man cannot enquire either about that which he knows, or about that which he does not know; for if he knows, he has no need to enquire; and if not, he cannot; for he does not know the very subject about which he is to enquire.

Men.: Well, Socrates, and is not the argument sound?

Soc.: I think not.

Men.: Why not?

Soc.: I will tell you why: I have heard from certain wise men and women who spoke of things divine that—

Men.: What did they say?

Soc.: They spoke of a glorious truth, as I conceive.

Men.: What was it? and who were they?

Soc.: Some of them were priests and priestesses, who had studied how they might be able to give a reason of their profession: there have been poets also, who spoke of these things by inspiration, like Pindar, and many others who were inspired. And they say—mark, now, and see whether their words are true—they say that the soul of man is immortal, and at one time has an end, which is termed dying, and at another time is born again, but is never destroyed. And the moral is, that a man ought to live always in perfect holiness. '*For in the ninth year Persephone sends the souls of those from whom she has received the penalty of ancient crime back again from beneath into the light of the sun above, and these are they who become noble kings and mighty men and great in wisdom and are called saintly heroes in after ages.*' The soul, then, as being immortal, and having been born again many times, and having seen all things that exist, whether in this world or in the world below, has knowledge of them all; and it is no wonder that she should be able to call to remembrance all that she ever knew about virtue, and about everything; for as all nature is akin, and the soul has learned all things, there is no difficulty in her eliciting or as men say learning, out of a single recollection all the rest, if a man is strenuous and does not faint; for all enquiry and all learning is but recollection. And therefore we ought not to listen to this sophistical argument about the impossibility of enquiry: for it will make us idle, and is sweet only to the sluggard; but the other saying will make us active and inquisitive. In that confiding, I will gladly enquire with you into the nature of virtue.

Men.: Yes, Socrates; but what do you mean by saying that we do not learn, and that what we call learning is only a process of recollection? Can you teach me how this is?

Soc.: I told you, Meno, just now that you were a rogue, and now you ask whether I can teach you, when I am saying that there is no teaching, but only recollection; and thus you imagine that you will involve me in a contradiction.

Men.: Indeed, Socrates, I protest that I had no such intention. I only asked the question from habit; but if you can prove to me that what you say is true, I wish that you would.

Soc.: It will be no easy matter, but I will try to please you to the utmost of my power. Suppose that you call one of your numerous attendants, that I may demonstrate on him.

From Plato, "Meno," in *Dialogues of Plato*, trans. Benjamin Jowett (Oxford: Oxford University Press, 1896).

Men.: Certainly. Come hither, boy.

Soc.: He is Greek, and speaks Greek, does he not?

Men.: Yes, indeed; he was born in the house.

Soc.: Attend now to the questions which I ask him, and observe whether he learns of me or only remembers.

Men.: I will.

Soc.: Tell me, boy, do you know that a figure like this is a square?

Boy: I do.

Soc.: And you know that a square figure has these four lines equal?

Boy: Certainly.

Soc.: And these lines which I have drawn through the middle of the square are also equal?

Boy: Yes.

Soc.: A square may be of any size?

Boy: Certainly.

Soc.: And if one side of the figure be of two feet, and the other side be of two feet, how much will the whole be? Let me explain: if in one direction the space was of two feet, and in the other direction of one foot, the whole would be of two feet taken once?

Boy: Yes.

Soc.: But since this side is also of two feet, there are twice two feet?

Boy: There are.

Soc.: Then the square is of twice two feet?

Boy: Yes.

Soc.: And how many are twice two feet? count and tell me.

Boy: Four, Socrates.

Soc.: And might there not be another square twice as large as this, and having like this the lines equal?

Boy: Yes.

Soc.: And of how many feet will that be?

Boy: Of eight feet.

Soc.: And now try and tell me the length of the line which forms the side of that double square: this is two feet—what will that be?

Boy: Clearly, Socrates, it will be double.

Soc.: Do you observe, Meno, that I am not teaching the boy anything, but only asking him questions; and now he fancies that he knows how long a line is necessary in order to produce a figure of eight square feet; does he not?

Men.: Yes.

Soc.: And does he really know?

Men.: Certainly not.

Soc.: He only guesses that because the square is double, the line is double.

Men.: True.

Soc.: Observe him while he recalls the steps in regular order. (*To the Boy.*) Tell me, boy, do you assert that a double space comes from a double line? Remember that I am not speaking of an oblong, but of a figure equal every way, and twice the size of this—that is to say of eight feet; and I want to know whether you still say that a double square comes from a double line?

Boy: Yes.

Soc.: But does not this line become doubled if we add another such line here?

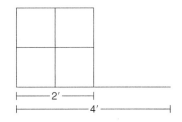

Boy: Certainly.

Soc.: And four such lines will make a space containing eight feet?

Boy: Yes.

Soc.: Let us describe such a figure: Would you not say that this is the figure of eight feet?

Boy: Yes.

Soc.: And are there not these four divisions in the figure, each of which is equal to the figure of four feet?

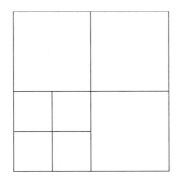

Boy: True.

Soc.: And is not that four times four?

Boy: Certainly.

Soc.: And four times is not double?

Boy: No, indeed.

Soc.: But how much?

Boy: Four times as much.

Soc.: Therefore the double line, boy, has given a space, not twice, but four times as much.

Boy: True.

Soc.: Four times four are sixteen—are they not?

Boy: Yes.

Soc.: What line would give you a space of eight feet, as this gives one of sixteen feet;—do you see?

Boy: Yes.

Soc.: And the space of four feet is made from this half line?

Boy: Yes.

Soc.: Good; and is not a space of eight feet twice the size of this, and half the size of the other?

Boy: Certainly.

Soc.: Such a space, then, will be made out of a line greater than this one, and less than that one?

Boy: Yes; I think so.

Soc.: Very good; I like to hear you say what you think. And now tell me, is not this a line of two feet and that of four?

Boy: Yes.

Soc.: Then the line which forms the side of eight feet ought to be more than this line of two feet, and less than the other of four feet?

Boy: It ought.

Soc.: Try and see if you can tell me how much it will be.

Boy: Three feet.

Soc.: Then if we add a half to this line of two, that will be the line of three. Here are two and there is one; and on the other side, here are two also and there is one: and that makes the figure of which you speak?

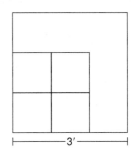

Boy: Yes.

Soc.: But if there are three feet this way and three feet that way, the whole space will be three times three feet?

Boy: That is evident.

Soc.: And how much are three times three feet?

Boy: Nine.

Soc.: And how much is the double of four?

Boy: Eight.

Soc.: Then the figure of eight is not made out of a line of three?

Boy: No.

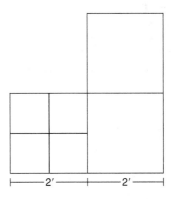

Soc.: But from what line?—tell me exactly; and if you would rather not reckon, try and show me the line.

Boy: Indeed, Socrates, I do not know.

Soc.: Do you see, Meno, what advances he has made in his power of recollection? He did not know at first, and he does not know now, what is the side of a figure of eight feet: but then he thought that he knew, and answered confidently as if he knew, and had no difficulty; now he has a difficulty, and neither knows nor fancies that he knows.

Men.: True.

Soc.: Is he not better off in knowing his ignorance?

Men.: I think that he is.

Soc.: If we have made him doubt, and given him the 'torpedo's shock,' have we done him any harm?

Men.: I think not.

Soc.: We have certainly, as would seem, assisted him in some degree to the discovery of the truth; and now he will wish to remedy his ignorance, but then he would have been ready to tell all the world again and again that the double space should have a double side.

Men.: True.

Soc.: But do you suppose that he would ever have enquired into or learned what he fancied that he knew, though he was really ignorant of it, until he had fallen into perplexity under the idea that he did not know, and had desired to know?

Men.: I think not, Socrates.

Soc.: Then he was the better for the torpedo's touch?

Men: I think so.

[Although the slave boy has never been educated, he possesses innate knowledge of geometry. Socrates claims that all he is doing is helping the slave bring to consciousness that which he already knows. That is, education is recollection of innate ideas.]

Soc.: Mark now the farther development. I shall only ask him, and not teach him, and he shall share the enquiry with me: and do you watch and see if you find me telling or explaining anything to him, instead of eliciting his opinion. Tell me, boy, is not this a square of four feet which I have drawn?

Boy: Yes.

Soc.: And now I add another square equal to the former one?

Boy: Yes.

Soc.: And a third, which is equal to either of them?

Boy: Yes.

Soc.: Suppose that we fill up the vacant corner?

Boy: Very good.

Soc.: Here, then, there are four equal spaces?

Boy: Yes.

Soc.: And how many times larger is this space than this other?

Boy: Four times.

Soc.: But it ought to have been twice only, as you will remember.

Boy: True.

Soc.: And does not this line, reaching from corner to corner, bisect each of these spaces? [BDEF]

Boy: Yes.

Soc.: And are there not here four equal lines which contain this space? [BD, DE, EF, and FB]

Boy: There are.

Soc.: Look and see how much this space is.

Boy: I do not understand.

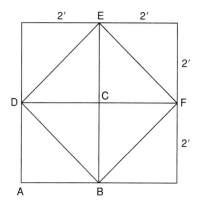

Soc.: Has not each interior line cut off half of the four spaces? [BD, DE, EF, and FB]

Boy: Yes.

Soc.: And how many spaces are there in this section? [BDEF]

Boy: Four.

Soc.: And how many in this? [ABCD]

Boy: Two.

Soc.: And four is how many times two?

Boy: Twice.

Soc.: And this space is of how many feet? [BDEF]

Boy: Of eight feet.

Soc.: And from what line do you get this figure?

Boy: From this. [EF]

Soc.: That is, from the line which extends from corner to corner of the figure of four feet?

Boy: Yes.

Soc.: And that is the line which the learned call the diagonal. And if this is the proper name, then you, Meno's slave, are prepared to affirm that the double space is the square of the diagonal?

Boy: Certainly, Socrates.

Soc.: What do you say of him, Meno? Were not all these answers given out of his own head?

Men.: Yes, they were all his own.

Soc.: And yet, as we were just now saying, he did not know?

Men.: True.

Soc.: But still he had in him those notions of his— had he not?

Men.: Yes.

Soc.: Then he who does not know may still have true notions of that which he does not know?

Men.: He has.

Soc.: And at present these notions have just been stirred up in him, as in a dream; but if he were frequently asked the same questions, in different forms, he would know as well as any one at last?

Men.: I dare say.

Soc.: Without any one teaching him he will recover his knowledge for himself, if he is only asked questions?

Men.: Yes.

Soc.: And this spontaneous recovery of knowledge in him is recollection?

Men.: True.

Soc.: And this knowledge which he now has must he not either have acquired or always possessed?

Men.: Yes.

Soc.: But if he always possessed this knowledge he would always have known; or if he has acquired the knowledge he could not have acquired it in this life, unless he has been taught geometry; for he may be made to do the same with all geometry and every other branch of knowledge. Now, has any one ever taught him all this? You must know about him, if, as you say, he was born and bred in your house.

Men.: And I am certain that no one ever did teach him.

Soc.: And yet he has the knowledge?

Men.: The fact, Socrates, is undeniable.

Soc.: But if he did not acquire the knowledge in this life, then he must have had and learned it at some other time?

Men.: Clearly he must.

Soc.: Which must have been the time when he was not a man?

Men.: Yes.

Soc.: And if there have been always true thoughts in him, both at the time when he was and was not a man, which only need to be awakened into knowledge by putting questions to him, his soul must have always possessed this knowledge, for he always either was or was not a man?

Men.: Obviously.

Soc.: And if the truth of all things always existed in the soul, then the soul is immortal. Wherefore be of good cheer, and try to recollect what you do not know, or rather what you do not remember.

Men.: I feel, somehow, that I like what you are saying.

Soc.: And I, Meno, like what I am saying. Some things I have said of which I am not altogether confident. But that we shall be better and braver and less helpless if we think that we ought to enquire, than we should have been if we indulged in the idle fancy that there was no knowing and no use in seeking to know what we do not know;—that is a theme upon which I am ready to fight, in word and deed, to the utmost of my power.

FOR FURTHER REFLECTION

1. What is the puzzle about learning that Meno points out? Why does it seem impossible to learn anything? What is Socrates' response to the puzzle? How do we learn, and why is learning possible?

2. Describe the process by which the boy reaches the correct answer. Does he truly have innate knowledge of geometry? Has Socrates proved his point? Is there another way to explain this phenomenon?

3. In this dialogue, Socrates maintains that we are born with knowledge of unchanging truths. Is this doctrine plausible?

SEXTUS EMPIRICUS

SKEPTICISM AND TRANQUILITY

While Plato's optimistic theory of knowledge and the forms had a dramatic impact on philosophy in the ancient world, it was counterbalanced by a more skeptical trend that questioned our ability to know anything with certainty. One of the founders of this tradition was an eccentric philosopher named Pyrrho (c. 365–c. 275 BCE) whose name quickly became synonymous with skepticism. Although none of his writings survives, the philosophical views of the skeptical tradition that he founded are preserved in the works of Sextus Empiricus (fl. 200 CE), particularly his book *Outlines of Pyrrhonism*.

In the selections presented here, Sextus describes skepticism as the suspension of judgment on any issue whatever—neither advocating nor opposing any view—and thereby achieving a mental state of tranquility. How, though, are we able to suspend our judgments with apparently obvious truths, such as "there is a red ball in front of me"? According to Sextus, there are ten methods of skeptical argumentation that help cast doubt on virtually any truth that we can think of. His discussion of the first method appears here, the underlying strategy of it forms the basis for the remaining nine. According to this first method, we begin by noting that an object, such as a red ball, will appear differently to different animals. To a dog, it may appear one shape or color; to a cow, another; to a housefly, another. However, we will never be in a position to say that the perceptions of one animal are more accurate than those of another. Thus, we must suspend our judgment about the true shape or color of the ball.

BOOK 1

1. *The Principal Differences Between Philosophers.* It is probable that those who seek after anything whatever, will either find it as they continue the search, will deny that it can be found and confess it to be out of reach, or will go on seeking it. Accordingly, some have said regarding the things sought in philosophy that they have found the truth, while others have declared it impossible to find, and still others continue to seek it. Those who think that they have found it are those who are especially called Dogmatists, as for example, the Schools of Aristotle and Epicurus, the Stoics and some others. Those who have declared it impossible to find are Clitomachus, Carneades, with their respective followers, and other Academicians. Those who still seek it are the Skeptics. Therefore, it appears reasonable to conclude that the three principal kinds of philosophy are the Dogmatic, the Academic, and the Skeptic. Other writers may suitably examine the first two Schools, but I will here give an outline of the Skeptical School. I must comment in advance, though, that I will not declare absolutely with

From Sextus Empiricus, *Outlines of Pyrrhonism* (c. 200 CE), Book 1.

anything I say that it is exactly as I describe it. Rather, I will state things empirically as they appear to me now.

2. *Ways of Examining Skepticism.* One way of examining the Skeptical philosophy is called general, and the other particular. The general method is that by which we set forth the character of Skepticism, declaring what its idea is, what its principles are, its method of reasoning, its criterion, and its aim. It also presents the method of doubt, and the way in which we should understand the Skeptical formula, and the distinction between Skepticism and the related Schools of philosophy. The particular method, on the contrary, is that by which we speak against each part of so-called philosophy. Let us then treat Skepticism at first in the general way, beginning our delineation with the terminology of the Skeptical School.

3. *The Definition of the Skeptical School.* The Skeptical School is also called the "Seeking School," from its spirit of research and examination; the "Suspending School," from the condition of mind in which one is left after the search, in regard to the things that one has examined; and the "Doubting School," either because, as some say, the Skeptics doubt and are seeking in regard to everything, or because they never know whether to deny or affirm. It is also called the Pyrrhonean School, because Pyrrho appears to us the best representative of Skepticism, and is more prominent than all who before him occupied themselves with it.

4. *What Is Skepticism?* Skepticism is *an ability to place appearances in opposition to judgments in any way whatever. By balancing reasons that are opposed to each other, we first reach the state of suspension of judgment, and afterwards that of tranquility.* To clarify, I do not use the word "ability" in any unusual sense, but simply mean that we are able to do something. By "appearances" I mean the things that we sense, as opposed to our judgments about them. The phrase "in any way whatever" may refer either to the word "ability" in its simple sense as I have said, or it may refer to the "placing of appearances in opposition to judgments." For we place appearances in opposition to each other in a variety of ways: appearances to appearances, and judgments to judgments, or appearances to judgments. Also, the phrase "in any way whatever" may refer to "appearances and judgments," so that we need not ask how appearances appear, or how thoughts are judged; rather, we should understand these things in a simple sense. By "reasons opposed to each other," I do not in any way mean that they deny or affirm anything, but simply that they offset each other. By "balancing" I mean equally likely and equally unlikely, so that the opposing reasons do not surpass each other in likelihood. "Suspension of judgment" means holding back opinion so that we neither deny nor affirm anything. "Tranquility" is repose and calmness of mind. I will later explain how tranquility accompanies suspension of judgment when I speak about the aim of skepticism.

5. *The Skeptic.* The notion of a "Pyrrhonean philosopher" follows from the above definition of the Skeptical School. He is the one who possesses the ability that I have described.

6. *The Primary Principle of Skepticism.* Skepticism arose in the beginning from the hope of attaining tranquility. People of the greatest intelligence were perplexed by the contradiction of various things, and being at a loss what to believe, they began to question what things are true, and what false. They then hoped to attain tranquility through some solution. The primary principle of the Skepticism, then, is to oppose every argument by one of equal weight, and in this way we finally reach the position where we have no dogmas.

7. *Does the Skeptic Dogmatize?* I say that the Skeptic does not dogmatize. I do not say this with regard to the popular meaning of the word "dogma," namely, that it is a dogma to assert to anything rather than another. For even the Skeptic assents to feelings that are a necessary result of sensation; for example, when he is warm or cold, he cannot say that he thinks he is not warm or cold. Rather, when I say that the Skeptic does

not dogmatize, I take the word "dogma" to mean the acceptance of any opinion in regard to the undetectable things investigated by science. For the Pyrrhonean assents to nothing that is undetectable.

Furthermore, the Skeptic does not dogmatize even when he utters the skeptical formula in regard to things that are undetectable, such as "Nothing is truer than another thing," or "I decide nothing," or any of the others which I will speak about later. For the dogmatist maintains that the things about which he dogmatizes actually exist in themselves. The Skeptic, however, does not regard these Skeptical formulas in any absolute sense, for he assumes that the saying "All is false" includes its own falsehood. Similarly, the saying "Nothing is true" and "Nothing is truer than another thing" implies that they are no truer than other things, and thus they cancel themselves out. We say the same also in regard to the other Skeptical expressions. In short, if he who dogmatizes assumes the truth about that which he dogmatizes, the Skeptic, on the contrary, expresses his sayings in a way that applies to the utterances themselves. Thus, we cannot say that the Skeptic dogmatizes in saying these things. The principal thing in uttering these formulas is that he says what appears to him, and communicates his own feelings in an unprejudiced way, without asserting anything in regard to external objects.

8. *Is Skepticism a System?* I respond in a similar way if I am asked whether Skepticism is a sect or not. If the word "system" is defined as meaning a body of persons who hold dogmas which are in conformity with each other, and also with appearances, and dogma means an assent to anything that is undetectable, then I reply that we have no sect. If, however, one means by sect, a school which follows a certain line of reasoning based on appearances, and that reasoning shows how it is possible to apparently live rightly (not understanding "rightly" as referring to virtue only, but in a broader sense); if, also, it leads one to be able to suspend judgment,

then I reply that we have a system. For we follow a certain kind of reasoning which is based upon appearances, and which shows us how to live according to the habits, laws, and teachings of our country, and our own feelings.

9. *Does the Skeptic Study Natural Science?* I reply similarly to the question whether the Skeptic should study natural science. For we do not study natural science in order to express ourselves with confidence regarding any of the dogmas that it teaches, but we take it up in order to be able to meet every argument by one of equal weight, and also for the sake of tranquility. In the same way we study the logical and ethical part of so-called philosophy.

10. *Do the Skeptics Deny Appearances?* Those who say that the Skeptics deny appearances are ignorant of our teachings. For as I said before, we do not deny the sensations which we think we have, and which lead us to assent involuntarily to them; we accept that we have appearances. When we are ask whether the object is such as it appears to be, we concede that it appears so and so; however, while we do not question the phenomenon, we do question what is asserted about the phenomenon, and that is different from doubting the phenomenon itself. For example, it appears to us that honey is sweet. This we concede, for we experience sweetness through sensation. We doubt, however, whether it is sweet by reason of its essence, which is not a question of the phenomenon, but of that which is asserted of the phenomenon. Should we, however, argue directly against appearances, it is not with the intention of denying their existence, but only to show the rashness of the Dogmatists. For if reasoning is such a deceiver that it snatches away genuine appearances from before our eyes, we should distrust it all the more in regard to things that are undetectable, and thus avoid rashly following it.

11. *The Criterion of Skepticism.* From what I say about the criterion of the Skeptical School it is evident that we pay careful attention to appearances. The word criterion is used in two

ways. First, it is understood as a proof of existence or non-existence, in regard to which I will
criticize later. Second, when it refers to action,
it means the criterion that we follow in life by
doing some things and refraining from doing
others. It is about this that I will now speak. I
say that the criterion of the Skeptical School is
appearance, and in calling it so, I mean the
image of what appears. This cannot be doubted,
since it arises from receptive to an involuntary
feeling. Hence virtually no one doubts that an
object appears to be such and such; but we do
question whether it is as it appears.

So, we cannot be entirely inactive with the
observances of daily life since we live by following appearances, and in an unprejudiced
way. Observance of daily life is of four different kinds. Sometimes it is directed by the guidance of nature, sometimes by the necessity of
feelings, sometimes by the tradition of laws and
of customs, and sometimes by the teaching of
skills. It is directed by the guidance of nature,
for by nature we are capable of sensation and
thought. It is directed by the necessity of feelings, since hunger leads us to food, and thirst to
drink. It is directed by the traditions of laws
and customs, since according to them we consider piety a good in daily life, and impiety an
evil. It is directed by the teaching of skills, for
we are not inactive in the skills we undertake. I
say all these things, however, without expressing a decided opinion.

12. *What Is the Aim of Skepticism?* It is natural to examine next the aim of the Skeptical
School. An aim is the end for which we do anything or think anything. It depends on nothing,
or in other words, it is the ultimate objective of
things to be desired. We say, then, that the aim
of the Skeptic is tranquility in those things
which pertain to the opinion, and moderation in
the things that life requires of us. In order to
attain tranquility, the Skeptic begins to philosophize about the ideas and to understand which
are true and which are false. He then faces contradictions of equal weight, and, being unable to
judge, he withholds his opinion. As if by fate,

while his judgment is in suspension he attains
tranquility in regard to matters of opinion. For
a person will always be troubled if he holds the
opinion that anything is either good or bad by
nature. For when he does not possess those
things that seem good to him, he feels tortured
by the things which are by nature bad, and pur-
sues those that he thinks to be good. But once
he acquires them, he becomes even unhappier
through his irrational and excessive excitement,
which makes him fear losing them and inclines
him to do everything in his power to retain the
things that seem good to him. On the other
hand, if a person is undecided about things that
are good and bad by nature, he will neither seek
nor avoid anything eagerly, and is therefore in
a state of tranquility.

A story is told about Apelles the painter that
applies to the Skeptic. It is said that Apelles
was once painting a horse and wished to depict
foam in the horse's mouth. When he failed to do
so, he gave up and threw a sponge at the picture
with which he had wiped the colors from the
painting. However, as soon as the sponge
touched the picture, it produced an excellent
representation of foam. Similarly, Skeptics initially hope to gain tranquility by making judgments about the irregularity between appearances
and their thoughts about them. When they are
unable to do this, they suspend their judgment.
As if by fate, while their judgment is in suspension, tranquility follows, just as a shadow
follows a body.

Nevertheless, I do not maintain that the
Skeptic is completely undisturbed, since he is
disturbed by some things that are inevitable. I
confess that sometimes he is cold and thirsty,
and that he suffers in these ways. However, in
similar circumstances, the ignorant are suffer in
two ways: first from the feelings themselves,
and, second, from the fact that they think these
conditions are bad by nature. The Skeptic, by
contrast, escapes more easily since he rejects
the opinion that anything is in itself bad by
nature. Therefore we say that the aim of the
Skeptic is tranquility in matters of opinion, and

moderation of feeling in those things that are inevitable. Some notable Skeptics have added also suspension of judgment in investigation.

13. *The General Methods of Suspending Judgment.* Since, as I have said, tranquility follows the suspension of judgment in regard to everything, it is important for me to explain how this suspension of judgment takes place. Generally speaking, it occurs by placing things in opposition to each other. We either place appearances in opposition to appearances, or thoughts in opposition to thoughts, or some combination of these. For example, we place appearances in opposition to appearances when we say that this tower appears round from a distance but square when near by. Thoughts are in opposition to thoughts when, for example, we take the view that providence exists because of the order in the heavens and oppose it to the fact that there is no providence since good people often suffer while evil people prosper. Thought is placed in opposition to appearances, when, for example, Anaxagoras opposed the fact that snow is white, by saying that snow is frozen water, and, as water is black, snow must also be black.

Likewise we sometimes place the present in opposition to the present, with reasoning similar to the above-mentioned cases. We sometimes also place the present in opposition to the past or the future. For example, when someone proposes an argument to us that we cannot refute, we say to him, "Before the founder of the School to which you belong was born, the argument which you propose had not appeared as a valid argument, but was dormant in nature; so in the same way it is possible that its refutation also exists in nature, but has not yet appeared to us, so that it is not at all necessary for us to agree with an argument that currently seems to be strong." In order to make it clearer to us what we mean by these oppositions, I will proceed to give the Methods through which suspension of judgment is produced. I will not say anything about their validity or their number, because they may be unsound and there may be more than I will enumerate.

14. *The Ten Methods.* Certain Methods were commonly handed down by the older Skeptics, by means of which suspension of judgment seems to take place. They are ten in number, and are synonymously called "arguments" and "points." They are these: the first is based upon the differences in animals; the second upon the differences in men; the third upon the difference in the constitution of the organs of sense; the fourth upon circumstances; the fifth upon position, distance, and place; the sixth upon mixtures; the seventh upon the quantity and constitution of objects; the eighth upon relation; the ninth upon frequency or rarity of occurrences; the tenth upon systems, customs, laws, mythical beliefs, and dogmatic opinions. I have made this order myself.

These Methods come under three general heads: the standpoint of the judge, the standpoint of the thing judged, and the standpoint of both together. Under the standpoint of the judge come the first four, for the judge is either an animal, or a man, or a sense, and exists under certain circumstances. Under the standpoint of that which is judged, come the seventh and the tenth. Under the one composed of both together, come the fifth and the sixth, the eighth and the ninth. Again, these three divisions are included under the Method of Relation, because that is the most general one. It includes the three special divisions, and these in turn include the ten. We say these things in regard to their probable number, and we proceed in the following chapter to speak of their meaning.

The first Method, I said, is the one based upon the differences in animals, and according to this Method, different animals do not get the same ideas of the same objects through the senses. This we conclude from the different origin of the animals, and also from the difference in the constitutions of their bodies.

In regard to the difference in origin, some animals originate without mixture of the sexes, while others originate through sexual intercourse. Of those which originate without intercourse of the sexes, some come from fire, as the little animals which appear in chimneys, others from stagnant water, as misquotes, others from fermented wine, as the stinging ants, others from the earth, others from the mud, like frogs, others from slime, as worms, others from donkeys, as beetles, others from cabbage, as caterpillars, others from fruit, as the gall insect from the wild figs, others from putrefied animals, as bees from bulls, and wasps from horses. Again, of those originating from intercourse of the sexes, some come from animals of the same kind, as in most cases, and others from those of different kinds, as mules. Again, of animals in general, some are born alive, as humans, others from eggs, as birds, and others are born a lump of flesh, as bears. It is probable therefore, that the inequalities and differences in origin cause great opposition in the animals, and the result is incompatibility, discord, and conflict between the sensations of the different animals.

Again, the differences in the principal parts of the body, especially in those fixed by nature to judge and to perceive, may cause the greatest differences in their ideas of objects, according to the differences in the animals themselves. For example, those who are jaundice call that yellow which appears to us white, and those who have bloodshot eyes call it blood-red. Accordingly, as some animals have yellow eyes, and others bloodshot ones, and still others whitish ones, and others eyes of other colors, it is probable that they have a different perception of colors. Furthermore, when we look steadily at the sun for a long time, and then look down at a book, the letters seem to us gold colored, and dance around. Now, some animals have by nature a luster in their eyes, and these emit a fine and sparkling light so that they see at night, and we may reasonably suppose that external things do not appear the same to them as to us.

Jugglers by lightly rubbing the wick of the lamp with metal rust, or with the dark yellow fluid of the sepia, make those who are present appear now copper-colored and now black, according to the amount of the mixture used. If this is so, it is reasonable to suppose that because of the mixture of different fluids in the eyes of animals, their ideas of objects would be different. Furthermore, when we press the eye on the side, the figures, forms and sizes of things seen appear elongated and narrow. It is therefore probable that animals which have the pupil oblique and long, as goats, cats, and similar animals, have ideas different

from those of the animals which have a round pupil. Mirrors, according to their different construction, sometimes show the external object smaller than reality, as concave ones, and sometimes long and narrow, as the convex ones do; others show the head of the one looking into it down, and the feet up. As some of the vessels around the eye fall entirely outside the eye, on account of their protuberance, while others are more sunken, and still others are placed in an even surface, it is probable that for this reason also the ideas vary, and dogs, fishes, lions, men, and grasshoppers do not see the same things, either of the same size, or of similar form, but according to the impression on the organ of sight of each animal respectively.

The same thing is true in regard to the other senses. For how can it be said that shellfish, birds of prey, animals covered with spines, those with feathers and those with scales would be affected in the same way by the sense of touch? And how can the sense of hearing perceive alike in animals which have the narrowest auditory passages, and in those that are furnished with the widest, or in those with hairy ears and those with smooth ones? For even humans hear differently when we partially stop up the ears, from what we do when we use them naturally. The sense of smell also varies according to differences in animals, since even our sense of smell is affected when we catch a cold and the phlegm is too abundant, and also when parts around our head are flooded with too much blood, for we then avoid odors that seem agreeable to others, and feel as if we were injured by them. Since also some of the animals are moist by nature and full of secretions, and others are very full of blood, and still others have either yellow or black bile prevalent and abundant, it is reasonable to think that odorous things appear different to each one of them.

It is the same with regard to things of taste, since some animals have the tongue rough and dry and others very moist. We too, when we have a dry tongue in fever, think that whatever we take is gritty, bad tasting, or bitter; and this we experience because of the varying degrees of the humors that are said to be in us. Since, then, different animals have different organs for taste, and a greater or less amount of the various humors, it may well be that they form different ideas of the same objects as regards their taste.

It is natural to suppose that external objects are regarded differently according to the different constitution of the animals which perceive them. This is similar to how the same food on being absorbed becomes in some places veins, in other places arteries, and in other places bones, nerves, or other tissues, showing different power according to the difference of the parts receiving it. This is just as the same water absorbed by the trees becomes in some places bark, in other places branches, and in other places fruit, perhaps a fig or a pomegranate, or something else. This is also just as the breath of the musician when blown into the flute becomes sometimes a high tone and sometimes a low one, or the same pressure of the hand upon the lyre sometimes causes a deep tone and sometimes a high tone.

We may see this more clearly in the things that are sought for and avoided by animals. For example, myrrh appears very agreeable to people and intolerable to beetles and bees. Oil also, which is useful to people, destroys wasps and bees if sprinkled on them; and sea-water, while it is unpleasant and poisonous to men if they drink it, is most agreeable and sweet to fish. Swine also prefer to wash in vile filth rather than in pure clean water. Furthermore, some animals eat grass and some eat herbs; some live in the woods, others eat seeds; some are carnivorous, and others lactivorous; some enjoy putrefied food, and others fresh food; some raw food, and others that which is prepared by cooking; and in general that which is agreeable to some is disagreeable and fatal to others, and should be avoided by them. Thus hemlock makes the quail fat, and henbane the hogs, and these, as it is known, enjoy eating lizards; deer also eat poisonous animals, and swallows the cantharid. Moreover, ants and flying ants, when swallowed by men, cause discomfort and colic, but the bear, on the contrary, whatever sickness he may have, becomes stronger by devouring them. The viper is benumbed if one twig of the oak touches it, as is also the bat by a leaf of the plane-tree. The elephant flees before the ram, and the lion before the cock, and seals from the rattling of beans that are being pounded, and the tiger from the sound of the drum. Many other examples could be given, but that we may not seem to dwell longer than is necessary on this subject, we conclude by saying

that since the same things are pleasant to some and unpleasant to others, and the pleasure and displeasure depend on the ideas, it must be that different animals have different ideas of objects.

Since the same things appear differently according to the difference in the animals, it will be possible for us to say how the external object appears to us, but as to how it is in reality we shall suspend our judgment. For we cannot ourselves judge between our own ideas and those of other animals, being ourselves involved in the difference, and therefore much more in need of being judged than being ourselves able to judge. Furthermore, we cannot give preference to our own mental representations over those of other animals, either without evidence or with evidence, for besides the fact that perhaps there is no evidence, as I will show, the evidence so called will be either manifest to us or not. If it is not manifest to us, then we cannot accept it with conviction. If it is manifest to us (since the question is in regard to what is manifest to animals, and we use as evidence that which is manifest to us who are animals), then it is to be questioned if it is true as it is manifest to us. It is absurd, however, to try to base the questionable on the questionable, because the same thing is to be believed and not to be believed, which is certainly impossible. The evidence is to be believed insofar as it will furnish a proof, and disbelieved insofar as it is itself to be proved. We therefore have no evidence according to which we can give preference to our own ideas over those of so-called irrational animals. Since ideas differ according to the difference in animals, and it is impossible to judge them, it is necessary to suspend the judgment in regard to external objects.

FOR FURTHER REFLECTION

1. Sextus maintains that skeptical doubt will lead to mental tranquility. How might it do so?
2. In Section 7 of this reading, Sextus argues that skepticism is not dogmatic, since it holds its own principles in doubt. Is this possible without self-contradiction?
3. Even if animals have different perceptions of the same object, might we still arrive at some

uniform and consistent knowledge about that object as it really is? If so, how?

4. Only the first method of skepticism is presented here, that regarding the different perceptions of the same thing by different animals. The second method is similar and involves different perceptions of the same object by different human beings. Think of an example of this method.

RENÉ DESCARTES

MEDITATIONS ON FIRST PHILOSOPHY

René Descartes (1596–1650) was born in France and educated by the Jesuits at the College of La Fleche. After a three-year career as a professional soldier, he traveled through Europe, trying to complete his education by reading the "great books of the world." Finally he settled in Holland and began to write philosophical treatises. These were radically innovative because, instead of starting with the accumulated authority of the medieval tradition, Descartes begins with his own experience and philosophizes from there. The self, instead of the tradition, becomes the center of authority. Descartes's two major Philosophy works are *Discourse on Method* (1637) and *Meditations on First Philosophy* (1641). The six "Meditations" of the letter work are presented here complate.

Descartes writes philosophy in the first person singular. He wants to know the truth, and he realizes that this quest will be difficult, because he has discovered (by painful experience) that much of what he has been taught and taken for granted is false. He must destroy his shaky house of "knowledge" and discover a new foundation on which to build an indestructible system. His method consists in doubting everything that can be doubted; on the pure remainder of certain truth, one can begin to construct a system of undoubtable knowledge. The result is a type of *rationalism* in which the only certainties are discovered by the mind, through self-evident insight and reasoning.

MEDITATION I

Of the Things Which May Be Brought within the Sphere of the Doubtful

It is now some years since I detected how many were the false beliefs that I had from my earliest youth admitted as true, and how doubtful was everything I had since constructed on this basis; and from that time I was convinced that I must once for all seriously undertake to rid myself of all the opinions which I had formerly accepted, and commence to build anew from the foundation, if I wanted to establish any firm and permanent structure in the sciences. But as this enterprise appeared

From René Descartes, *Meditations,* in *The Philosophical Works of Descartes,* trans. Elizabeth Haldane and G. Ross, (Cambridge University Press, 1931), vol. 1, pp. 144–199.

to be a very great one, I waited until I had attained an age so mature that I could not hope that at any later date I should be better fitted to execute my design. This reason caused me to delay so long that I should feel that I was doing wrong were I to occupy in deliberation the time that yet remains to me for action. Today, then, since very opportunely for the plan I have in view I have delivered my mind from every care [and am happily agitated by no passions] and since I have procured for myself an assured leisure in a peaceable retirement, I shall at last seriously and freely address myself to the general upheaval of all my former opinions.

Now for this object it is not necessary that I should show that all of these are false—I shall perhaps never arrive at this end. But inasmuch as reason already persuades me that I ought no less carefully to withhold my assent from matters which are not entirely certain and indubitable than from those which appear to me manifestly to be false, if I am able to find in each one some reason to doubt, this will suffice to justify my rejecting the whole. And for that end it will not be requisite that I should examine each in particular, which would be an endless undertaking; for owing to the fact that the destruction of the foundations of necessity brings with it the downfall of the rest of the edifice, I shall only in the first place attack those principles upon which all my former opinions rested.

All that up to the present time I have accepted as most true and certain I have learned either from the senses or through the senses; but it is sometimes proved to me that these senses are deceptive, and it is wiser not to trust entirely to any thing by which we have once been deceived.

But it may be that although the senses sometimes deceive us concerning things which are hardly perceptible, or very far away, there are yet many others to be met with as to which we cannot reasonably have any doubt, although we recognise them by their means. For example, there is the fact that I am here, seated by the fire, attired in a dressing gown, having this paper in my hands and other similar matters. And how could I deny that these hands and this body are mine, were it not perhaps that I compare myself to certain persons, devoid of sense, whose cerebella are so troubled and clouded by the violent vapours of black bile, that they constantly assure us that they think they

are kings when they are really quite poor, or that they are clothed in purple when they are really without covering, or who imagine that they have an earthenware head or are nothing but pumpkins or are made of glass. But they are mad, and I should not be any the less insane were I to follow examples so extravagant.

At the same time I must remember that I am a man, and that consequently I am in the habit of sleeping, and in my dreams representing to myself the same things or sometimes even less probable things, than do those who are insane in their waking moments. How often has it happened to me that in the night I dreamt that I found myself in this particular place, that I was dressed and seated near the fire, whilst in reality I was lying undressed in bed! At this moment it does indeed seem to me that it is with eyes awake that I am looking at this paper; that this head which I move is not asleep, that it is deliberately and of set purpose that I extend my hand and perceive it; what happens in sleep does not appear so clear nor so distinct as does all this. But in thinking over this I remind myself that on many occasions I have in sleep been deceived by similar illusions, and in dwelling carefully on this reflection I see so manifestly that there are no certain indications by which we may clearly distinguish wakefulness from sleep that I am lost in astonishment. And my astonishment is such that it is almost capable of persuading me that I now dream.

Now let us assume that we are asleep and that all these particulars, e.g., that we open our eyes, shake our head, extend our hands, and so on, are but false delusions; and let us reflect that possibly neither our hands nor our whole body are such as they appear to us to be. At the same time we must at least confess that the things which are represented to us in sleep are like painted representations which can only have been formed as the counterparts of something real and true, and that in this way those general things at least, i.e., eyes, a head, hands, and a whole body, are not imaginary things, but things really existent. For, as a matter of fact, painters, even when they study with the greatest skill to represent sirens and satyrs by forms the most strange and extraordinary, cannot give them natures which are entirely new, but merely make a certain medley of the members of different animals; or if their imagination is extravagant enough to invent something so novel that nothing similar has ever before been seen, and that then their work represents a thing purely fictitious and absolutely false, it is certain all the same that the colours of which this is composed are necessarily real. And for the same reason, although these general things, to wit, [a body], eyes, a head, hands, and such like, may be imaginary, we are bound at the same time to confess that there are at least some other objects yet more simple and more universal, which are real and true; and of these just in the same way as with certain real colours, all these images of things which dwell in our thoughts, whether true and real or false and fantastic, are formed.

To such a class of things pertains corporeal nature in general, and its extension, the figure of extended things, their quantity or magnitude and number, as also the place in which they are, the time which measures their duration, and so on.

That is possibly why our reasoning is not unjust when we conclude from this that Physics, Astronomy, Medicine and all other sciences which have as their end the consideration of composite things, are very dubious and uncertain; but that Arithmetic, Geometry and other sciences of that kind which only treat of things that are very simple and very general, without taking great trouble to ascertain whether they are actually existent or not, contain some measure of certainty and an element of the indubitable. For whether I am awake or asleep, two and three together always form five, and the square can never have more than four sides, and it does not seem possible that truths so clear and apparent can be suspected of any falsity [or uncertainty].

Nevertheless I have long had fixed in my mind the belief that an all-powerful God existed by whom I have been created such as I am. But how do I know that He has not brought it to pass that there is no earth, no heaven, no extended body, no magnitude, no place, and that nevertheless [I possess the perceptions of all these things and that] they seem to me to exist just exactly as I now see them? And, besides, as I sometimes imagine that others deceive themselves in the things which they think they know best, how do I know that I am not deceived every time that I add two and three, or count the sides of a square, or judge of things yet simpler, if anything simpler can be imagined? But possibly God has not desired that I should

be thus deceived, for He is said to be supremely good. If, however, it is contrary to His goodness to have made me such that I constantly deceive myself, it would also appear to be contrary to His goodness to permit me to be sometimes deceived, and nevertheless I cannot doubt that He does permit this.

There may indeed be those who would prefer to deny the existence of a God so powerful, rather than believe that all other things are uncertain. But let us not oppose them for the present, and grant that all that is here said of a God is a fable; nevertheless in whatever way they suppose that I have arrived at the state of being that I have reached—whether they attribute it to fate or to accident, or make out that it is by a continual succession of antecedents, or by some other method—since to err and deceive oneself is a defect, it is clear that the greater will be the probability of my being so imperfect as to deceive myself ever, as is the Author to whom they assign my origin the less powerful. To these reasons I have certainly nothing to reply, but at the end I feel constrained to confess that there is nothing in all that I formerly believed to be true, of which I cannot in some measure doubt, and that not merely through want of thought or through levity, but for reasons which are very powerful and maturely considered; so that henceforth I ought not the less carefully to refrain from giving credence to these opinions than to that which is manifestly false, if I desire to arrive at any certainty [in the sciences].

But it is not sufficient to have made these remarks, we must also be careful to keep them in mind. For these ancient and commonly held opinions still revert frequently to my mind, long and familiar custom having given them the right to occupy my mind against my inclination and rendered them almost masters of my belief; nor will I ever lose the habit of deferring to them or of placing my confidence in them, so long as I consider them as they really are, i.e., opinions in some measure doubtful, as I have just shown, and at the same time highly probable, so that there is much more reason to believe in than to deny them. That is why I consider that I shall not be acting amiss, if, taking of set purpose a contrary belief, I allow myself to be deceived, and for a certain time pretend that all these opinions are entirely false and imaginary, until at last, having thus balanced my former prejudices with my latter [so that they cannot divert my opinions more to one side than to the other], my judgment will no longer be dominated by bad usage or turned away from the right knowledge of the truth. For I am assured that there can be neither peril nor error in this course, and that I cannot at present yield too much to distrust, since I am not considering the question of action, but only of knowledge.

I shall then suppose, not that God who is supremely good and the fountain of truth, but some evil genius not less powerful than deceitful, has employed his whole energies in deceiving me; I shall consider that the heavens, the earth, colours, figures, sound, and all other external things are nought but the illusions and dreams of which this genius has availed himself in order to lay traps for my credulity; I shall consider myself as having no hands, no eyes, no flesh, no blood, nor any senses, yet falsely believing myself to possess all these things; I shall remain obstinately attached to this idea, and if by this means it is not in my power to arrive at the knowledge of any truth, I may at least do what is in my power [i.e. suspend my judgment], and with firm purpose avoid giving credence to any false thing, or being imposed upon by this arch deceiver, however powerful and deceptive he may be. But this task is a laborious one, and insensibly a certain lassitude leads me into the course of my ordinary life. And just as a captive who in sleep enjoys an imaginary liberty, when he begins to suspect that his liberty is but a dream, fears to awaken, and conspires with these agreeable illusions that the deception may be prolonged, so insensibly of my own accord I fall back into my former opinions, and I dread awakening from this slumber, lest the laborious wakefulness which would follow the tranquillity of this repose should have to be spent not in daylight, but in the excessive darkness of the difficulties which have just been discussed.

MEDITATION II

Of the Nature of the Human Mind; and That It Is More Easily Known Than the Body

The Meditation of yesterday filled my mind with so many doubts that it is no longer in my power to forget

them. And yet I do not see in what manner I can resolve them; and, just as if I had all of a sudden fallen into very deep water, I am so disconcerted that I can neither make certain of setting my feet on the bottom, nor can I swim and so support myself on the surface. I shall nevertheless make an effort and follow anew the same path as that on which I yesterday entered, i.e., I shall proceed by setting aside all that in which the least doubt could be supposed to exist, just as if I had discovered that it was absolutely false; and I shall ever follow in this road until I have met with something which is certain, or at least, if I can do nothing else, until I have learned for certain that there is nothing in the world that is certain. Archimedes, in order that he might draw the terrestrial globe out of its place, and transport it elsewhere, demanded only that one point should be fixed and immoveable; in the same way I shall have the right to conceive high hopes if I am happy enough to discover one thing only which is certain and indubitable.

I suppose, then, that all the things that I see are false; I persuade myself that nothing has ever existed of all that my fallacious memory represents to me. I consider that I possess no senses; I imagine that body, figure, extension, movement and place are but the fictions of my mind. What, then, can be esteemed as true? Perhaps nothing at all, unless that there is nothing in the world that is certain.

But how can I know there is not something different from those things that I have just considered, of which one cannot have the slightest doubt? Is there not some God, or some other being by whatever name we call it, who puts these reflections into my mind? That is not necessary, for is it not possible that I am capable of producing them myself? I myself, am I not at least something? But I have already denied that I had senses and body. Yet I hesitate, for what follows from that? Am I so dependent on body and senses that I cannot exist without these? But I was persuaded that there was nothing in all the world, that there was no heaven, no earth, that there were no minds, nor any bodies: was I not then likewise persuaded that I did not exist? Not at all; of a surety I myself did exist since I persuaded myself of something [or merely because I thought of something]. But there is some deceiver or other, very powerful and very cunning, who ever employs his ingenuity in deceiving me. Then without doubt I exist also if he deceives me, and let him deceive me as much as he will, he can never cause me to be nothing so long as I think that I am something. So that after having reflected well and carefully examined all things, we must come to the definite conclusion that this proposition: I am, I exist, is necessarily true each time that I pronounce it, or that I mentally conceive it.

But I do not yet know clearly enough what I am, I who am certain that I am; and hence I must be careful to see that I do not imprudently take some other object in place of myself, and thus that I do not go astray in respect of this knowledge that I hold to be the most certain and most evident of all that I have formerly learned. That is why I shall now consider anew what I believed myself to be before I embarked upon these last reflections; and of my former opinions I shall withdraw all that might even in a small degree be invalidated by the reasons which I have just brought forward, in order that there may be nothing at all left beyond what is absolutely certain and indubitable.

What then did I formerly believe myself to be? Undoubtedly I believed myself to be a man. But what is a man? Shall I say a reasonable animal? Certainly not; for then I should have to inquire what an animal is, and what is reasonable; and thus from a single question I should insensibly fall into an infinitude of others more difficult; and I should not wish to waste the little time and leisure remaining to me in trying to unravel subtleties like these. But I shall rather stop here to consider the thoughts which of themselves spring up in my mind, and which were not inspired by anything beyond my own nature alone when I applied myself to the consideration of my being. In the first place, then, I considered myself as having a face, hands, arms, and all that system of members composed of bones and flesh as seen in a corpse which I designated by the name of body. In addition to this I considered that I was nourished, that I walked, that I felt, and that I thought, and I referred all these actions to the soul: but I did not stop to consider what the soul was, or if I did stop, I imagined that it was something extremely rare and subtle like a wind, a flame, or an ether, which was spread throughout my grosser parts. As to body I had no manner of doubt about its nature, but thought I had a very clear knowledge of it; and if I had desired to explain it according to the notions that I had then formed of it, I should have described it thus: By the body I understand all that which can be defined by a certain figure: something which can be confined in a certain place, and which can fill a given space in such a way that every other body will be excluded from it; which can be perceived either by touch, or by sight, or by hearing, or by taste, or by smell: which can be moved in many ways not, in truth, by itself, but by something which is foreign to it, by which it is touched [and from which it receives impressions]: for to have the power of self-movement, as also of feeling or of thinking, I did not consider to appertain to the nature of body: on the contrary, I was rather astonished to find that faculties similar to them existed in some bodies.

But what am I, now that I suppose that there is a certain genius which is extremely powerful, and, if I may say so, malicious, who employs all his powers in deceiving me? Can I affirm that I possess the least of all those things which I have just said pertain to the nature of body? I pause to consider, I revolve all these things in my mind, and I find none of which I can say that it pertains to me. It would be tedious to stop to enumerate them. Let us pass to the attributes of soul and see if there is any one which is in me? What of nutrition or walking [the first mentioned]? But if it is so that I have no body it is also true that I can neither walk nor take nourishment. Another attribute is sensation. But one cannot feel without body, and besides I have thought I perceived many things during sleep that I recognised in my waking moments as not having been experienced at all. What of thinking? I find here that thought is an attribute that belongs to me; it alone cannot be separated from me. I am, I exist, that is certain. But how often? Just when I think; for it might possibly be the case if I ceased entirely to think, that I should likewise cease altogether to exist. I do not now admit anything which is not necessarily true: to speak accurately I am not more than a thing which thinks, that is to say a mind or a soul, or an understanding, or a reason, which are terms whose significance was formerly unknown to me. I am, however, a real thing and really exist; but what thing? I have answered: a thing which thinks.

And what more? I shall exercise my imagination [in order to see if I am not something more]. I am not a collection of members which we call the human body: I am not a subtle air distributed through these members, I am not a wind, a fire, a vapour, a breath, nor anything at all which I can imagine or conceive; because I have assumed that all these were nothing. Without changing that supposition I find that I only leave myself certain of the fact that I am somewhat. But perhaps it is true that these same things which I supposed were non-existent because they are unknown to me, are really not different from the self which I know. I am not sure about this, I shall not dispute about it now; I can only give judgment on things that are known to me. I know that I exist, and I inquire what I am, I whom I know to exist. But it is very certain that the knowledge of my existence taken in its precise significance does not depend on things whose existence is not yet known to me; consequently it does not depend on those which I can feign in imagination. And indeed the very term *feign* in imagination proves to me my error, for I really do this if I image myself a something, since to imagine is nothing else than to contemplate the figure or image of a corporeal thing. But I already know for certain that I am, and that it may be that all these images, and, speaking generally, all things that relate to the nature of body are nothing but dreams [and chimeras]. For this reason I see clearly that I have as little reason to say, "I shall stimulate my imagination in order to know more distinctly what I am," than if I were to say, "I am now awake, and I perceive somewhat that is real and true: but because I do not yet perceive it distinctly enough, I shall go to sleep of express purpose, so that my dreams may represent the perception with greatest truth and evidence." And, thus, I know for certain that nothing of all that I can understand by means of my imagination belongs to this knowledge which I have of myself, and that it is necessary to recall the mind from this mode of thought with the utmost diligence in order that it may be able to know its own nature with perfect distinctness.

But what then am I? A thing which thinks. What is a thing which thinks? It is a thing which doubts, understands, [conceives], affirms, denies, wills, refuses, which also imagines and feels.

Certainly it is no small matter if all these things pertain to my nature. But why should they not so pertain? Am I not that being who now doubts nearly everything, who nevertheless understands certain things, who affirms that one only is true, who denies all the others, who desires to know more, is averse from being deceived, who imagines many things, sometimes indeed despite his will, and who perceives many likewise, as by the intervention of the bodily organs? Is there nothing in all this which is as true as it is certain that I exist, even though I should always sleep and though he who has given me being employed all his ingenuity in deceiving me? Is there likewise any one of these attributes which can be distinguished from my thought, or which might be said to be separated from myself? For it is so evident of itself that it is I who doubts, who understands, and who desires, that there is no reason here to add anything to explain it. And I have certainly the power of imagining likewise; for although it may happen (as I formerly supposed) that none of the things which I imagine are true, nevertheless this power of imagining does not cease to be really in use, and it forms part of my thought. Finally, I am the same who feels, that is to say, who perceives certain things, as by the organs of sense, since in truth I see light, I hear noise, I feel heat. But it will be said that these phenomena are false and that I am dreaming. Let it be so; still it is at least quite certain that it seems to me that I see light, that I hear noise and that I feel heat. That cannot be false; properly speaking it is what is in me called feeling; and used in this precise sense that is no other thing than thinking.

From this time I begin to know what I am with a little more clearness and distinction than before; but nevertheless it still seems to me, and I cannot prevent myself from thinking, that corporeal things, whose images are framed by thought, which are tested by the senses, are much more distinctly known than that obscure part of me which does not come under the imagination. Although really it is very strange to say that I know and understand more distinctly these things whose existence seems to me dubious, which are unknown to me, and which do not belong to me, than others of the truth of which I am convinced, which are known to me and which pertain to my real nature, in a word, than myself. But I see clearly how the case stands: my mind loves to wander, and cannot yet suffer itself to be retained within the just limits of truth. Very good, let us once more give it the freest rein, so that, when afterwards we seize the proper occasion for pulling up, it may the more easily be regulated and controlled.

Let us begin by considering the commonest matters, those which we believe to be the most distinctly comprehended, to wit, the bodies which we touch and see; not indeed bodies in general, for these general ideas are usually a little more confused, but let us consider one body in particular. Let us take, for example, this piece of wax: it has been taken quite freshly from the hive, and it has not yet lost the sweetness of the honey which it contains; it still retains somewhat of the odour of the flowers from which it has been culled; its colour, its figure, its size are apparent; it is hard, cold, easily handled, and if you strike it with the finger, it will emit a sound. Finally all the things which are requisite to cause us distinctly to recognise a body, are met with in it. But notice that while I speak and approach the fire what remained of the taste is exhaled, the smell evaporates, the colour alters, the figure is destroyed, the size increases, it becomes liquid, it heats, scarcely can one handle it, and when one strikes it, no sound is emitted. Does the same wax remain after this change? We must confess that it remains; none would judge otherwise. What then did I know so distinctly in this piece of wax? It could certainly be nothing of all that the senses brought to my notice, since all these things which fall under taste, smell, sight, touch, and hearing, are found to be changed, and yet the same wax remains.

Perhaps it was what I now think, viz., that this wax was not that sweetness of honey, nor that agreeable scent of flowers, nor that particular whiteness, nor that figure, nor that sound, but simply a body which a little while before appeared to me as perceptible under these forms, and which is now perceptible under others. But what, precisely, is it that I imagine when I form such conceptions? Let us attentively consider this, and, abstracting from all that does not belong to the wax, let us see what remains. Certainly nothing remains excepting a certain extended thing which is flexible and movable. But what is the mean-

ing of flexible and movable? Is it not that I imagine that this piece of wax being round is capable of becoming square and of passing from a square to a triangular figure? No, certainly it is not that, since I imagine it admits of an infinitude of similar changes, and I nevertheless do not know how to compass the infinitude by my imagination, and consequently this conception which I have of the wax is not brought about by the faculty of imagination. What now is this extension? Is it not also unknown? For it becomes greater when the wax is melted, greater when it is boiled, and greater still when the heat increases; and I should not conceive [clearly] according to truth what wax is, if I did not think that even this piece that we are considering is capable of receiving more variations in extension than I have ever imagined. We must then grant that I could not even understand through the imagination what this piece of wax is, and that it is my mind alone which perceives it. I say this piece of wax in particular, for as to wax in general it is yet clearer. But what is this piece of wax which cannot be understood excepting by the [understanding or] mind? It is certainly the same that I see, touch, imagine, and finally it is the same which I have always believed it to be from the beginning. But what must particularly be observed is that its perception is neither an act of vision, nor of touch, nor of imagination, and has never been such although it may have appeared formerly to be so, but only an intuition of the mind, which may be imperfect and confused as it was formerly, or clear and distinct as it is at present, according as my attention is more or less directed to the elements which are found in it, and of which it is composed.

Yet in the meantime I am greatly astonished when I consider [the great feebleness of mind] and its proneness to fall [insensibly] into error; for although without giving expression to my thoughts I consider all this in my own mind, words often impede me and I am almost deceived by the terms of ordinary language. For we say that we see the same wax, if it is present, and not that we simply judge that it is the same from its having the same colour and figure. From this I should conclude that I knew the wax by means of vision and not simply by the intuition of the mind; unless by chance I remember that, when looking from a window and saying I see men who pass in the street,

I really do not see them, but infer that what I see is men, just as I say that I see wax. And yet what do I see from the window but hats and coats which may cover automatic machines? Yet I judge these to be men. And similarly solely by the faculty of judgment which rests in my mind, I comprehend that which I believed I saw with my eyes.

A man who makes it his aim to raise his knowledge above the common should be ashamed to derive the occasion for doubting from the forms of speech invented by the vulgar; I prefer to pass on and consider whether I had a more evident and perfect conception of what the wax was when I first perceived it, and when I believed I knew it by means of the external senses or at least by the common sense as it is called, that is to say by the imaginative faculty, or whether my present conception is clearer now that I have most carefully examined what it is, and in what way it can be known. It would certainly be absurd to doubt as to this. For what was there in this first perception which was distinct? What was there which might not as well have been perceived by any of the animals? But when I distinguish the wax from its external forms, and when, just as if I had taken from it its vestments, I consider it quite naked, it is certain that although some error may still be found in my judgment, I can nevertheless not perceive it thus without a human mind.

But finally what shall I say of this mind, that is, of myself, for up to this point I do not admit in myself anything but mind? What then, I who seem to perceive this piece of wax so distinctly, do I not know myself, not only with much more truth and certainty, but also with much more distinctness and clearness? For if I judge that the wax is or exists from the fact that I see it, it certainly follows much more clearly that I am or that I exist myself from the fact that I see it. For it may be that what I see is not really wax, it may also be that I do not possess eyes with which to see anything; but it cannot be that when I see, or (for I no longer take account of the distinction) when I think I see, that I myself who think am nought. So if I judge that the wax exists from the fact that I touch it, the same thing will follow, to wit, that I am; and if I judge that my imagination, or some other cause, whatever it is, persuades me that the wax exists, I shall still conclude the same. And what I have here remarked of wax may be applied to all other things which are external to me [and which are met with outside of me]. And further, if the [notion or] perception of wax has seemed to me clearer and more distinct, not only after the sight or the touch, but also after many other causes have rendered it quite manifest to me, with how much more [evidence] and distinctness must it be said that I now know myself, since all the reasons which contribute to the knowledge of wax, or any other body whatever, are yet better proofs of the nature of my mind! And there are so many other things in the mind itself which may contribute to the elucidation of its nature, that those which depend on body such as these just mentioned, hardly merit being taken into account.

But finally here I am, having insensibly reverted to the point I desired, for, since it is now manifest to me that even bodies are not properly speaking known by the senses or by the faculty of imagination, but by the understanding only, and since they are not known from the fact that they are seen or touched, but only because they are understood, I see clearly that there is nothing which is easier for me to know than my mind. But because it is difficult to rid oneself so promptly of an opinion to which one was accustomed for so long, it will be well that I should halt a little at this point, so that by the length of my meditation I may more deeply imprint on my memory this new knowledge.

MEDITATION III

Of God: That He Exists

I shall now close my eyes, I shall stop my ears, I shall call away all my senses, I shall efface even from my thoughts all the images of corporeal things, or at least (for that is hardly possible) I shall esteem them as vain and false; and thus holding converse only with myself and considering my own nature, I shall try little by little to reach a better knowledge of and a more familiar acquaintanceship with myself. I am a thing that thinks, that is to say, that doubts, affirms, denies, that knows a few things, that is ignorant of many [that loves, that hates], that wills, that desires, that also imagines and perceives; for as I remarked before, although the things which I perceive and imagine are perhaps nothing at all apart from me and in themselves, I am nevertheless assured that these modes of thought that I call perceptions and imaginations, inasmuch only as they are modes of thought, certainly reside [and are met with] in me.

And in the little that I have just said, I think I have summed up all that I really know, or at least all that hitherto I was aware that I knew. In order to try to extend my knowledge further, I shall now look around more carefully and see whether I cannot still discover in myself some other things which I have not hitherto perceived. I am certain that I am a thing which thinks; but do I not then likewise know what is requisite to render me certain of a truth? Certainly in this first knowledge there is nothing that assures me of its truth, excepting the clear and distinct perception of that which I state, which would not indeed suffice to assure me that what I say is true, if it could ever happen that a thing which I conceived so clearly and distinctly could be false; and accordingly it seems to me that already I can establish as a general rule that all things which I perceive very clearly and very distinctly are true.

At the same time I have before received and admitted many things to be very certain and manifest, which yet I afterwards recognised as being dubious. What then were these things? They were the earth, sky, stars and all other objects which I apprehended by means of the senses. But what did I clearly [and distinctly] perceive in them? Nothing more than that the ideas or thoughts of these things were presented to my mind. And not even now do I deny that these ideas are met with in me. But there was yet another thing which I affirmed, and which, owing to the habit which I had formed of believing it, I thought I perceived very clearly, although in truth I did not perceive it at all, to wit, that there were objects outside of me from which these ideas proceeded, and to which they were entirely similar. And it was in this that I erred, or, if perchance my judgment was correct, this was not due to any knowledge arising from my perception.

But when I took anything very simple and easy in the sphere of arithmetic or geometry into considera-tion, e.g. that two and three together made five, and other things of the sort, were not these present to my mind so clearly as to enable me to affirm that they were true? Certainly if I judged that since such matters could be doubted, this would not have been so for any other reason than that it came into my mind that perhaps a God might have endowed me with such a nature that I may have been deceived even concerning things which seemed to me most manifest. But every time that this preconceived opinion of the sovereign power of a God presents itself to my thought, I am constrained to confess that it is easy to Him, if He wishes it, to cause me to err, even in matters in which I believe myself to have the best evidence. And, on the other hand, always when I direct my attention to things which I believe myself to perceive very clearly, I am so persuaded of their truth that I let myself break out into words such as these: Let who will deceive me, He can never cause me to be nothing while I think that I am, or some day cause it to be true to say that I have never been, it being true now to say that I am, or that two and three make more or less than five, or any such thing in which I see a manifest contradiction. And, certainly, since I have no reason to believe that there is a God who is a deceiver, and as I have not yet satisfied myself that there is a God at all, the reason for doubt which depends on this opinion alone is very slight, and so to speak meta-physical. But in order to be able altogether to remove it, I must inquire whether there is a God as soon as the occasion presents itself; and if I find that there is a God, I must also inquire whether He may be a deceiver; for without a knowledge of these two truths I do not see that I can ever be certain of anything.

And in order that I may have an opportunity of inquiring into this in an orderly way [without interrupting the order of meditation which I have proposed to myself, and which is little by little to pass from the notions which I find first of all in my mind to those which I shall later on discover in it] it is requisite that I should here divide my thoughts into certain kinds, and that I should consider in which of these kinds there is, properly speaking, truth or error to be found. Of my thoughts some are, so to speak, images of the things, and to these alone is the title 'idea' properly applied; examples are my thought of a man or of a chimera, of heaven, of an angel, or [even] of God. But other thoughts possess other forms as well. For example in willing, fearing, approving, denying, though I always perceive something as the subject of the action of my mind, yet by this action I always add something else to the idea which I have of that thing; and of the thoughts of this kind some are called volitions or affections, and others judgments.

Now as to what concerns ideas, if we consider them only in themselves and do not relate them to anything else beyond themselves, they cannot properly speaking be false; for whether I imagine a goat or a chimera, it is not less true that I imagine the one than the other. We must not fear likewise that falsity can enter into will and into affections, for although I may desire evil things, or even things that never existed, it is not the less true that I desire them. Thus there remains no more than the judgments which we make, in which I must take the greatest care not to deceive myself. But the principal error and the commonest which we may meet with in them, consists in my judging that the ideas which are in me are similar or conformable to the things which are outside me; for without doubt if I considered the ideas only as certain modes of my thoughts, without trying to relate them to anything beyond, they could scarcely give me material for error.

But among these ideas, some appear to me to be innate, some adventitious, and others to be formed [or invented] by myself; for, as I have the power of understanding what is called a thing, or a truth, or a thought, it appears to me that I hold this power from no other source than my own nature. But if I now hear some sound, if I see the sun, or feel heat, I have hitherto judged that these sensations proceeded from certain things that exist outside of me; and finally it appears to me that sirens, hippogryphs, and the like, are formed out of my own mind. But again I may possibly persuade myself that all these ideas are of the nature of those which I term adventitious, or else that they are all innate, or all fictitious: for I have not yet clearly discovered their true origin.

And my principal task in this place is to consider, in respect to those ideas which appear to me to proceed from certain objects that are outside me, what are the reasons which cause me to think them similar to these objects. It seems indeed in the first place that I am taught this lesson by nature; and, secondly, I experience in myself that these ideas do not depend on my will nor therefore on myself—for they often present themselves to my mind in spite of my will. Just now, for instance, whether I will or whether I do not will, I feel heat, and thus I persuade myself that this feeling, or at least this idea of heat, is produced in me by something which is different from me, i.e., by the heat of the fire near which I sit. And nothing seems to me more obvious than to judge that this object imprints its likeness rather than anything else upon me.

Now I must discover whether these proofs are sufficiently strong and convincing. When I say that I am so instructed by nature, I merely mean a certain spontaneous inclination which impels me to believe in this connection, and not a natural light which makes me recognise that it is true. But these two things are very different; for I cannot doubt that which the natural light causes me to believe to be true, as, for example, it has shown me that I am from the fact that I doubt, or other facts of the same kind. And I possess no other faculty whereby to distinguish truth from falsehood, which can teach me that what this light shows me to be true is not really true, and no other faculty that is equally trustworthy. But as far as [apparently] natural impulses are concerned, I have frequently remarked, when I had to make active choice between virtue and vice, that they often enough led me to the part that was worse; and this is why I do not see any reason for following them in what regards truth and error.

And as to the other reason, which is that these ideas must proceed from objects outside me, since they do not depend on my will, I do not find it any the more convincing. For just as these impulses of which I have spoken are found in me, notwithstanding that they do not always concur with my will, so perhaps there is in me some faculty fitted to produce these ideas without the assistance of any external things, even though it is not yet known by me; just as, apparently, they have hitherto always been found in me during sleep without the aid of any external objects.

And finally, though they did proceed from objects different from myself, it is not a necessary consequence that they should resemble these. On the contrary, I have noticed that in many cases there was a great difference between the object and its idea. I find, for example, two completely diverse ideas of the sun in my mind; the one derives its origin from the senses, and should be placed in the category of adventitious ideas; according to this idea the sun seems to be extremely small; but the other is derived from astronomical reasonings, i.e., is elicited from certain notions that are innate in me, or else it is formed by me in some other manner; in accordance with it the sun appears to be several times greater than the earth. These two ideas cannot, indeed, both resemble the same sun, and reason makes me believe that the one which seems to have originated directly from the sun itself, is the one which is most dissimilar to it.

All this causes me to believe that until the present time it has not been by a judgment that was certain [or premeditated], but only by a sort of blind impulse that I believed that things existed outside of, and different from me, which, by the organs of my senses, or by some other method whatever it might be, conveyed these ideas or images to me [and imprinted on me their similitudes].

But there is yet another method of inquiring whether any of the objects of which I have ideas within me exist outside of me. If ideas are only taken as certain modes of thought, I recognise amongst them no difference or inequality, and all appear to proceed from me in the same manner; but when we consider them as images, one representing one thing and the other another, it is clear that they are very different one from the other. There is no doubt that those which represent to me substances are something more, and contain so to speak more objective reality within them [that is to say, by representation participate in a higher degree of being or perfection] than those that simply represent modes or accidents; and that idea again by which I understand a supreme God, eternal, infinite, [immutable], omniscient, omnipotent, and Creator of all things which are outside of Himself, has certainly more objective reality in itself than those ideas by which finite substances are represented.

Now it is manifest by the natural light that there must at least be as much reality in the efficient and total cause as in its effect. For, pray, whence can the effect derive its reality, if not from its cause? And in what way can this cause communicate this reality to it, unless it possessed it in itself? And from this it follows, not only that something cannot proceed from nothing, but likewise that what is more perfect—that is to say, which has more reality within itself—cannot proceed from the less perfect. And this is not only evidently true of those effects which possess actual or formal reality, but also of the ideas in which we consider merely what is termed objective reality. To take an example, the stone which has not yet existed not only cannot now commence to be unless it has been produced by something which possesses within itself, either formally or eminently, all that enters into the composition of the stone [i.e., it must possess the same things or other more excellent things than those which exist in the stone] and heat can only be produced in a subject in which it did not previously exist by a cause that is of an order [degree or kind] at least as perfect as heat, and so in all other cases. But further, the idea of heat, or of a stone, cannot exist in me unless it has been placed within me by some cause which possesses within it at least as much reality as that which I conceive to exist in the heat or the stone. For although this cause does not transmit anything of its actual or formal reality to my idea, we must not for that reason imagine that it is necessarily a less real cause; we must remember that [since every idea is a work of the mind] its nature is such that it demands of itself no other formal reality than that which it borrows from my thought, of which it is only a mode [i.e. a manner or way of thinking]. But in order that an idea should contain some one certain objective reality rather than another, it must without doubt derive it from some cause in which there is at least as much formal reality as this idea contains of objective reality. For if we imagine that something is found in an idea which is not found in the cause, it must then have been derived from nought; but however imperfect may be this mode of being by which a thing is objectively [or by representation] in the understanding by its idea, we cannot certainly say that this mode of being is nothing, nor, consequently, that the idea derives its origin from nothing.

Nor must I imagine that, since the reality that I consider in these ideas is only objective, it is not essential that this reality should be formally in the causes of my ideas, but that it is sufficient that it should be found objectively. For just as this mode of objective existence pertains to ideas by their proper nature, so does the mode of formal existence pertain to the causes of those ideas (this is at least true of the first and principal) by the nature peculiar to them. And although it may be the case that one idea gives birth to another idea, that cannot continue to be so indefinitely; for in the end we must reach an idea whose cause shall be so to speak an archetype, in which the whole reality [or perfection] which is so to speak objectively [or by representation] in these ideas is contained formally [and really]. Thus the light of nature causes me to know clearly that the ideas in me are like [pictures or] images which can, in truth, easily fall short of the perfection of the objects from which they have been derived, but which can never contain anything greater or more perfect.

And the longer and the more carefully that I investigate these matters, the more clearly and distinctly do I recognise their truth. But what am I to conclude from it all in the end? It is this, that if the objective reality of any one of my ideas is of such a nature as clearly to make me recognise that it is not in me either formally or eminently, and that consequently I cannot myself be the cause of it, it follows of necessity that I am not alone in the world, but that there is another being which exists, or which is the cause of this idea. On the other hand, had no such an idea existed in me, I should have had no sufficient argument to convince me of the existence of any being beyond myself; for I have made very careful investigation everywhere and up to the present time have been able to find no other ground.

But of my ideas, beyond that which represents me to myself, as to which there can here be no difficulty, there is another which represents a God, and there are others representing corporeal and inanimate things, others angels, others animals, and others again which represent to me men similar to myself.

As regards the ideas which represent to me other men or animals, or angels, I can however easily conceive that they might be formed by an admixture of the other ideas which I have of myself, of corporeal things, and of God, even although there were apart

from me neither men nor animals, nor angels, in all the world.

And in regard to the ideas of corporeal objects, I do not recognise in them anything so great or so excellent that they might not have possibly proceeded from myself; for if I consider them more closely, and examine them individually, as I yesterday examined the idea of wax, I find that there is very little in them which I perceive clearly and distinctly. Magnitude or extension in length, breadth, or depth, I do so perceive; also figure which results from a termination of this extension, the situation which bodies of different figure preserve in relation to one another, and movement or change of situation; to which we may also add substance, duration and number. As to other things such as light, colours, sounds, scents, tastes, heat, cold and the other tactile qualities, they are thought by me with so much obscurity and confusion that I do not even know if they are true or false, i.e., whether the ideas which I form of these qualities are actually the ideas of real objects or not [or whether they only represent chimeras which cannot exist in fact]. For although I have before remarked that it is only in judgments that falsity, properly speaking, or formal falsity, can be met with, a certain material falsity may nevertheless be found in ideas, i.e., when these ideas represent what is nothing as though it were something. For example, the ideas which I have of cold and heat are so far from clear and distinct that by their means I cannot tell whether cold is merely a privation of heat, or heat a privation of cold, or whether both are real qualities, or are not such. And inasmuch as [since ideas resemble images] there cannot be any ideas which do not appear to represent some things, if it is correct to say that cold is merely a privation of heat, the idea which represents it to me as something real and positive will not be improperly termed false, and the same holds good of other similar ideas.

To these it is certainly not necessary that I should attribute any author other than myself. For if they are false, i.e., if they represent things which do not exist, the light of nature shows me that they issue from nought, that is to say, that they are only in me in so far as something is lacking to the perfection of my nature. But if they are true, nevertheless because they exhibit so little reality to me that I cannot even clearly distinguish the thing represented from non-being, I do not see any reason why they should not be produced by myself.

As to the clear and distinct idea which I have of corporeal things, some of them seem as though I might have derived them from the idea which I possess of myself, as those which I have of substance, duration, number, and such like. For [even] when I think that a stone is a substance, or at least a thing capable of existing of itself, and that I am a substance also, although I conceive that I am a thing that thinks and not one that is extended, and that the stone on the other hand is an extended thing which does not think, and that thus there is a notable difference between the two conceptions—they seem, nevertheless, to agree in this, that both represent substances. In the same way, when I perceive that I now exist and further recollect that I have in former times existed, and when I remember that I have various thoughts of which I can recognise the number, I acquire ideas of duration and number which I can afterwards transfer to any object that I please. But as to all the other qualities of which the ideas of corporeal things are composed, to wit, extension, figure, situation and motion, it is true that they are not formally in me, since I am only a thing that thinks; but because they are merely certain modes of substance [and so to speak the vestments under which corporeal substance appears to us] and because I myself am also a substance, it would seem that they might be contained in me eminently.

Hence there remains only the idea of God, concerning which we must consider whether it is something which cannot have proceeded from me myself. By the name God I understand a substance that is infinite [eternal, immutable], independent, all-knowing, all-powerful, and by which I myself and everything else, if anything else does exist, have been created. Now all these characteristics are such that the more diligently I attend to them, the less do they appear capable of proceeding from me alone; hence, from what has been already said, we must conclude that God necessarily exists.

For although the idea of substance is within me owing to the fact that I am substance, nevertheless I should not have the idea of an infinite substance—since I am finite—if it had not proceeded from some substance which was veritably infinite.

Nor should I imagine that I do not perceive the infinite by a true idea, but only by the negation of the finite, just as I perceive repose and darkness by the negation of movement and of light; for, on the contrary, I see that there is manifestly more reality in infinite substance than in finite, and therefore that in some way I have in me the notion of the infinite earlier than the finite—to wit, the notion of God before that of myself. For how would it be possible that I should know that I doubt and desire, that is to say, that something is lacking to me, and that I am not quite perfect, unless I had within me some idea of a Being more perfect than myself, in comparison with which I should recognise the deficiencies of my nature?

And we cannot say that this idea of God is perhaps materially false and that consequently I can derive it from nought [i.e., that possibly it exists in me because I am imperfect], as I have just said is the case with ideas of heat, cold and other such things; for, on the contrary, as this idea is very clear and distinct and contains within it more objective reality than any other, there can be none which is of itself more true, nor any in which there can be less suspicion of falsehood. The idea, I say, of this Being who is absolutely perfect and infinite, is entirely true; for although, perhaps, we can imagine that such a Being does not exist, we cannot nevertheless imagine that His idea represents nothing real to me, as I have said of the idea of cold. This idea is also very clear and distinct; since all that I conceive clearly and distinctly of the real and the true, and of what conveys some perfection, is in its entirety contained in this idea. And this does not cease to be true although I do not comprehend the infinite, or though in God there is an infinitude of things which I cannot comprehend, nor possibly even reach in any way by thought; for it is of the nature of the infinite that my nature, which is finite and limited, should not comprehend it; and it is sufficient that I should understand this, and that I should judge that all things which I clearly perceive and in which I know that there is some perfection, and possibly likewise an infinitude of properties of which I am ignorant, are in God formally or eminently, so that the idea which I have of Him may become the most true, most clear, and most distinct of all the ideas that are in my mind.

But possibly I am something more than I suppose myself to be, and perhaps all those perfections which I attribute to God are in some way potentially in me, although they do not yet disclose themselves, or issue in action. As a matter of fact I am already sensible that my knowledge increases [and perfects itself] little by little, and I see nothing which can prevent it from increasing more and more into infinitude; nor do I see, after it has thus been increased [or perfected], anything to prevent my being able to acquire by its means all the other perfections of the Divine nature; nor finally why the power I have of acquiring these perfections, if it really exists in me, shall not suffice to produce the ideas of them.

At the same time I recognise that this cannot be. For, in the first place, although it were true that every day my knowledge acquired new degrees of perfection, and that there were in my nature many things potentially which are not yet there actually, nevertheless these excellences do not pertain to [or make the smallest approach to] the idea which I have of God in whom there is nothing merely potential [but in whom all is present really and actually]; for it is an infallible token of imperfection in my knowledge that it increases little by little. And further, although my knowledge grows more and more, nevertheless I do not for that reason believe that it can ever be actually infinite, since it can never reach a point so high that it will be unable to attain to any greater increase. But I understand God to be actually infinite, so that He can add nothing to His supreme perfection. And finally I perceive that the objective being of an idea cannot be produced by a being that exists potentially only, which properly speaking is nothing, but only by a being which is formal or actual.

To speak the truth, I see nothing in all that I have just said which by the light of nature is not manifest to anyone who desires to think attentively on the subject; but when I slightly relax my attention, my mind, finding its vision somewhat obscured and so to speak blinded by the images of sensible objects, I do not easily recollect the reason why the idea that I possess of a being more perfect than I, must necessarily have been placed in me by a being which is really more perfect; and this is why I wish here to go on to inquire whether I, who have this idea, can exist if no such being exists.

And I ask, from whom do I then derive my existence? Perhaps from myself or from my parents, or from some other source less perfect than God; for we can imagine nothing more perfect than God, or even as perfect as He is.

But [were I independent of every other and] were I myself the author of my being, I should doubt nothing and I should desire nothing, and finally no perfection would be lacking to me; for I should have bestowed on myself every perfection of which I possessed any idea and should thus be God. And it must not be imagined that those things that are lacking to me are perhaps more difficult of attainment than those which I already possess; for, on the contrary, it is quite evident that it was a matter of much greater difficulty to bring to pass that I, that is to say, a thing or a substance that thinks, should emerge out of nothing, than it would be to attain to the knowledge of many things of which I am ignorant, and which are only the accidents of this thinking substance. But it is clear that if I had of myself possessed this greater perfection of which I have just spoken [that is to say, if I had been the author of my own existence], I should not at least have denied myself the things which are the more easy to acquire [to wit, many branches of knowledge of which my nature is destitute]; nor should I have deprived myself of any of the things contained in the idea which I form of God, because there are none of them which seem to me specially difficult to acquire: and if there were any that were more difficult to acquire, they would certainly appear to me to be such (supposing I myself were the origin of the other things which I possess) since I should discover in them that my powers were limited.

But though I assume that perhaps I have always existed just as I am at present, neither can I escape the force of this reasoning, and imagine that the conclusion to be drawn from this is, that I need not seek for any author of my existence. For all the course of my life may be divided into an infinite number of parts, none of which is in any way dependent on the other; and thus from the fact that I was in existence a short time ago it does not follow that I must be in existence now, unless some cause at this instant, so to speak, produces me anew, that is to say, conserves me. It is as a matter of fact perfectly clear and evident to all those who consider with attention the nature of time, that, in order to be conserved in each moment in which it endures, a substance has need of the same power and action as would be necessary to produce and create it anew, supposing it did not yet exist, so that the light of nature shows us clearly that the distinction between creation and conservation is solely a distinction of the reason.

All that I thus require here is that I should interrogate myself, if I wish to know whether I possess a power which is capable of bringing it to pass that I who now am shall still be in the future; for since I am nothing but a thinking thing, or at least since thus far it is only this portion of myself which is precisely in question at present, if such a power did reside in me, I should certainly be conscious of it. But I am conscious of nothing of the kind, and by this I know clearly that I depend on some being different from myself.

Possibly, however, this being on which I depend is not that which I call God, and I am created either by my parents or by some other cause less perfect than God. This cannot be, because, as I have just said, it is perfectly evident that there must be at least as much reality in the cause as in the effect; and thus since I am a thinking thing, and possess an idea of God within me, whatever in the end be the cause assigned to my existence, it must be allowed that it is likewise a thinking thing and that it possesses in itself the idea of all the perfections which I attribute to God. We may again inquire whether this cause derives its origin from itself or from some other thing. For if from itself, it follows by the reasons before brought forward, that this cause must itself be God; for since it possesses the virtue of self-existence, it must also without doubt have the power of actually possessing all the perfections of which it has the idea, that is, all those which I conceive as existing in God. But if it derives its existence from some other cause than itself, we shall again ask, for the same reason, whether this second cause exists by itself or through another, until from one step to another, we finally arrive at an ultimate cause, which will be God.

And it is perfectly manifest that in this there can be no regression into infinity, since what is in question is not so much the cause which formerly created me, as that which conserves me at the present time.

Nor can we suppose that several causes may have concurred in my production, and that from one I have received the idea of one of the perfections which I attribute to God, and from another the idea of some other, so that all these perfections indeed exist somewhere in the universe, but not as complete in one unity which is God. On the contrary, the unity, the simplicity or the inseparability of all things which are in God is one of the principal perfections which I conceive to be in Him. And certainly the idea of this unity of all Divine perfections cannot have been placed in me by any cause from which I have not likewise received the ideas of all the other perfections; for this cause could not make me able to comprehend them as joined together in an inseparable unity without having at the same time caused me in some measure to know what they are [and in some way to recognise each one of them].

Finally, so far as my parents [from whom it appears I have sprung] are concerned, although all that I have ever been able to believe of them were true, that does not make it follow that it is they who conserve me, nor are they even the authors of my being in any sense, in so far as I am a thinking being; since what they did was merely to implant certain dispositions in that matter in which the self—i.e. the mind, which alone I at present identify with myself—is by me deemed to exist. And thus there can be no difficulty in their regard, but we must of necessity conclude from the fact alone that I exist, or that the idea of a Being supremely perfect—that is of God—is in me, that the proof of God's existence is grounded on the highest evidence.

It only remains to me to examine into the manner in which I have acquired this idea from God; for I have not received it through the senses, and it is never presented to me unexpectedly, as is usual with the ideas of sensible things when these things present themselves, or seem to present themselves, to the external organs of my senses; nor is it likewise a fiction of my mind, for it is not in my power to take from or to add anything to it; and consequently the only alternative is that it is innate in me, just as the idea of myself is innate in me.

And one certainly ought not to find it strange that God, in creating me, placed this idea within me to be like the mark of the workman imprinted on his work; and it is likewise not essential that the mark shall be something different from the work itself. For from the sole fact that God created me it is most probable that in some way he has placed his image and similitude upon me, and that I perceive this similitude (in which the idea of God is contained) by means of the same faculty by which I perceive myself—that is to say, when I reflect on myself I not only know that I am something [imperfect], incomplete and dependent on another, which incessantly aspires after something which is better and greater than myself, but I also know that He on whom I depend possesses in Himself all the great things towards which I aspire [and the ideas of which I find within myself], and that not indefinitely or potentially alone, but really, actually and infinitely; and that thus He is God. And the whole strength of the argument which I have here made use of to prove the existence of God consists in this, that I recognise that it is not possible that my nature should be what it is, and indeed that I should have in myself the idea of a God, if God did not veritably exist—a God, I say, whose idea is in me, i.e., who possesses all those supreme perfections of which our mind may indeed have some idea but without understanding them all, who is liable to no errors or defect [and who has none of all those marks which denote imperfection]. From this it is manifest that He cannot be a deceiver, since the light of nature teaches us that fraud and deception necessarily proceed from some defect.

But before I examine this matter with more care, and pass on to the consideration of other truths which may be derived from it, it seems to me right to pause for a while in order to contemplate God Himself, to ponder at leisure His marvellous attributes, to consider, and admire, and adore, the beauty of this light so resplendent, at least as far as the strength of my mind, which is in some measure dazzled by the sight, will allow me to do so. For just as faith teaches us that the supreme felicity of the other life consists only in this contemplation of the Divine Majesty, so we continue to learn by experience that a similar meditation, though incomparably less perfect, causes us to enjoy the greatest satisfaction of which we are capable in this life.

MEDITATION IV
Of the True and the False

I have been well accustomed these past days to detach my mind from my senses, and I have accurately observed that there are very few things that one knows with certainty respecting corporeal objects, that there are many more which are known to us respecting the human mind, and yet more still regarding God Himself; so that I shall now without any difficulty abstract my thoughts from the consideration of [sensible or] imaginable objects, and carry them to those which, being withdrawn from all contact with matter, are purely intelligible. And certainly the idea which I possess of the human mind inasmuch as it is a thinking thing, and not extended in length, width and depth, nor participating in anything pertaining to body, is incomparably more distinct than is the idea of any corporeal thing. And when I consider that I doubt, that is to say, that I am an incomplete and dependent being, the idea of a being that is complete and independent, that is of God, presents itself to my mind with so much distinctness and clearness—and from the fact alone that this idea is found in me, or that I who possess this idea exist, I conclude so certainly that God exists, and that my existence depends entirely on Him in every moment of my life—that I do not think that the human mind is capable of knowing anything with more evidence and certitude. And it seems to me that I now have before me a road which will lead us from the contemplation of the true God (in whom all the treasures of science and wisdom are contained) to the knowledge of the other objects of the universe.

For, first of all, I recognise it to be impossible that He should ever deceive me; for in all fraud and deception some imperfection is to be found, and although it may appear that the power of deception is a mark of subtilty or power, yet the desire to deceive without doubt testifies to malice or feebleness, and accordingly cannot be found in God.

In the next place I experienced in myself a certain capacity for judging which I have doubtless received from God, like all the other things that I possess; and as He could not desire to deceive me, it is clear that

He has not given me a faculty that will lead me to err if I use it aright.

And no doubt respecting this matter could remain, if it were not that the consequence would seem to follow that I can thus never be deceived; for if I hold all that I possess from God, and if He has not placed in me the capacity for error, it seems as though I could never fall into error. And it is true that when I think only of God [and direct my mind wholly to Him], I discover [in myself] no cause of error, or falsity; yet directly afterwards, when recurring to myself, experience shows me that I am nevertheless subject to an infinitude of errors, as to which, when we come to investigate them more closely, I notice that not only is there a real and positive idea of God or of a Being of supreme perfection present to my mind, but also, so to speak, a certain negative idea of nothing, that is, of that which is infinitely removed from any kind of perfection; and that I am in a sense something intermediate between God and nought, i.e., placed in such a manner between the supreme Being and non-being, that there is in truth nothing in me that can lead to error in so far as a sovereign Being has formed me; but that, as I in some degree participate likewise in nought or in non-being, i.e., in so far as I am not myself the supreme Being, and as I find myself subject to an infinitude of imperfections, I ought not to be astonished if I should fall into error. Thus do I recognise that error, in so far as it is such, is not a real thing depending on God, but simply a defect; and therefore, in order to fall into it, that I have no need to possess a special faculty given me by God for this very purpose, but that I fall into error from the fact that the power given me by God for the purpose of distinguishing truth from error is not infinite.

Nevertheless this does not quite satisfy me; for error is not a pure negation [i.e., is not the simple defect or want of some perfection which ought not to be mine], but it is a lack of some knowledge which it seems that I ought to possess. And on considering the nature of God it does not appear to me possible that He should have given me a faculty which is not perfect of its kind, that is, which is wanting in some perfection due to it. For if it is true that the more skilful the artizan, the more perfect is the work of his hands, what can have been produced by this supreme Creator of all things that is not in all its parts perfect? And certainly there is no doubt that God could have created me so that I could never have been subject to error; it is also certain that He ever wills what is best; is it then better that I should be subject to err than that I should not?

In considering this more attentively, it occurs to me in the first place that I should not be astonished if my intelligence is not capable of comprehending why God acts as He does; and that there is thus no reason to doubt of His existence from the fact that I may perhaps find many other things besides this as to which I am able to understand neither for what reason nor how God has produced them. For, in the first place, knowing that my nature is extremely feeble and limited, and that the nature of God is on the contrary immense, incomprehensible, and infinite, I have no further difficulty in recognising that there is an infinitude of matters in His power, the causes of which transcend my knowledge; and this reason suffices to convince me that the species of cause termed final, finds no useful employment in physical [or natural] things; for it does not appear to me that I can without temerity seek to investigate the [inscrutable] ends of God.

It further occurs to me that we should not consider one single creature separately, when we inquire as to whether the works of God are perfect, but should regard all his creations together. For the same thing which might possibly seem very imperfect with some semblance of reason if regarded by itself, is found to be very perfect if regarded as part of the whole universe; and although, since I resolved to doubt all things, I as yet have only known certainly my own existence and that of God, nevertheless since I have recognised the infinite power of God, I cannot deny that He may have produced many other things, or at least that He has the power of producing them, so that I may obtain a place as a part of a great universe.

Whereupon, regarding myself more closely, and considering what are my errors (for they alone testify to there being any imperfection in me), I answer that they depend on a combination of two causes, to wit, on the faculty of knowledge that rests in me, and on the power of choice or of free will—that is to say, of the understanding and at the same time of the will. For by the understanding alone I [neither assert nor deny anything, but] apprehend the ideas of things as to which I can form a judgment. But no error is properly speaking found in it, provided the word error is taken in its proper signification; and though there is possibly an infinitude of things in the world of which I have no idea in my understanding, we cannot for all that say that it is deprived of these ideas [as we might say of something which is required by its nature], but simply it does not possess these; because in truth there is no reason to prove that God should have given me a greater faculty of knowledge than He has given me; and however skilful a workman I represent Him to be, I should not for all that consider that He was bound to have placed in each of His works all the perfections which He may have been able to place in some. I likewise cannot complain that God has not given me a free choice or a will which is sufficient, ample and perfect, since as a matter of fact I am conscious of a will so extended as to be subject to no limits. And what seems to me very remarkable in this regard is that of all the qualities which I possess there is no one so perfect and so comprehensive that I do not very clearly recognise that it might be yet greater and more perfect. For, to take an example, if I consider the faculty of comprehension which I possess, I find that it is of very small extent and extremely limited, and at the same time I find the idea of another faculty much more ample and even infinite, and seeing that I can form the idea of it, I recognise from this very fact that it pertains to the nature of God. If in the same way I examine the memory, the imagination, or some other faculty, I do not find any which is not small and circumscribed, while in God it is immense [or infinite]. It is free-will alone or liberty of choice which I find to be so great in me that I can conceive no other idea to be more great; it is indeed the case that it is for the most part this will that causes me to know that in some manner I bear the image and similitude of God. For although the power of will is incomparably greater in God than in me, both by reason of the knowledge and the power which, conjoined with it, render it stronger and more efficacious, and by reason of its object, inasmuch as in God it extends to a great

many things; it nevertheless does not seem to me greater if I consider it formally and precisely in itself: for the faculty of will consists alone in our having the power of choosing to do a thing or choosing not to do it (that is, to affirm or deny, to pursue or to shun it), or rather it consists alone in the fact that in order to affirm or deny, pursue or shun those things placed before us by the understanding, we act so that we are unconscious that any outside force constrains us in doing so. For in order that I should be free it is not necessary that I should be indifferent as to the choice of one or the other of two contraries; but contrariwise the more I lean to the one—whether I recognise clearly that the reasons of the good and true are to be found in it, or whether God so disposes my inward thought—the more freely do I choose and embrace it. And undoubtedly both divine grace and natural knowledge, far from diminishing my liberty, rather increase it and strengthen it. Hence this indifference which I feel, when I am not swayed to one side rather than to the other by lack of reason, is the lowest grade of liberty, and rather evinces a lack or negation in knowledge than a perfection of will: for if I always recognised clearly what was true and good, I should never have trouble in deliberating as to what judgment or choice I should make, and then I should be entirely free without ever being indifferent.

From all this I recognise that the power of will which I have received from God is not of itself the source of my errors—for it is very ample and very perfect of its kind—any more than is the power of understanding; for since I understand nothing but by the power which God has given me for understanding, there is no doubt that all that I understand, I understand as I ought, and it is not possible that I err in this. Whence then come my errors? They come from the sole fact that since the will is much wider in its range and compass than the understanding, I do not restrain it within the same bounds, but extend it also to things which I do not understand: and as the will is of itself indifferent to these, it easily falls into error and sin, and chooses the evil for the good, or the false for the true.

For example, when I lately examined whether anything existed in the world, and found that from the very fact that I considered this question it followed very clearly that I myself existed, I could not prevent myself from believing that a thing I so clearly conceived was true: not that I found myself compelled to do so by some external cause, but simply because from great clearness in my mind there followed a great inclination of my will; and I believed this with so much the greater freedom or spontaneity as I possessed the less indifference towards it. Now, on the contrary, I not only know that I exist, inasmuch as I am a thinking thing, but a certain representation of corporeal nature is also presented to my mind; and it comes to pass that I doubt whether this thinking nature which is in me, or rather by which I am what I am, differs from this corporeal nature, or whether both are not simply the same thing; and I here suppose that I do not yet know any reason to persuade me to adopt the one belief rather than the other. From this it follows that I am entirely indifferent as to which of the two I affirm or deny, or even whether I abstain from forming any judgment in the matter.

And this indifference does not only extend to matters as to which the understanding has no knowledge, but also in general to all those which are not apprehended with perfect clearness at the moment when the will is deliberating upon them: for, however probable are the conjectures which render me disposed to form a judgment respecting anything, the simple knowledge that I have that those are conjectures alone and not certain and indubitable reasons, suffices to occasion me to judge the contrary. Of this I have had great experience of late when I set aside as false all that I had formerly held to be absolutely true, for the sole reason that I remarked that it might in some measure be doubted.

But if I abstain from giving my judgment on any thing when I do not perceive it with sufficient clearness and distinctness, it is plain that I act rightly and am not deceived. But if I determine to deny or affirm, I no longer make use as I should of my free will, and if I affirm what is not true, it is evident that I deceive myself; even though I judge according to truth, this comes about only by chance, and I do not escape the blame of misusing my freedom; for the light of nature teaches us that the knowledge of the understanding should always precede the determination of the will. And it is in the misuse of the free will that the privation which constitutes the characteristic nature of error

is met with. Privation, I say, is found in the act, in so far as it proceeds from me, but it is not found in the faculty which I have received from God, nor even in the act in so far as it depends on Him.

For I have certainly no cause to complain that God has not given me an intelligence which is more powerful, or a natural light which is stronger than that which I have received from Him, since it is proper to the finite understanding not to comprehend a multitude of things, and it is proper to a created understanding to be finite; on the contrary, I have every reason to render thanks to God who owes me nothing and who has given me all the perfections I possess, and I should be far from charging Him with injustice and with having deprived me of, or wrongfully withheld from me, these perfections which He has not bestowed upon me.

I have further no reason to complain that He has given me a will more ample than my understanding, for since the will consists only of one single element, and is so to speak indivisible, it appears that its nature is such that nothing can be abstracted from it [without destroying it]; and certainly the more comprehensive it is found to be, the more reason I have to render gratitude to the giver.

And, finally, I must also not complain that God concurs with me in forming the acts of the will, that is the judgment in which I go astray, because these acts are entirely true and good, inasmuch as they depend on God; and in a certain sense more perfection accrues to my nature from the fact that I can form them, than if I could not do so. As to the privation in which alone the formal reason of error or sin consists, it has no need of any concurrence from God, since it is not a thing [or an existence], and since it is not related to God as to a cause, but should be termed merely a negation [according to the significance given to these words in the Schools]. For in fact it is not an imperfection in God that He has given me the liberty to give or withhold my assent from certain things as to which He has not placed a clear and distinct knowledge in my understanding; but it is without doubt an imperfection in me not to make a good use of my freedom, and to give my judgment readily on matters which I only understand obscurely. I nevertheless perceive that God could easily have created me so that I never should err, although I still remained free, and endowed with a limited knowledge, viz., by giving to my understanding a clear and distinct intelligence of all things as to which I should ever have to deliberate; or simply by His engraving deeply in my memory the resolution never to form a judgment on anything without having a clear and distinct understanding of it, so that I could never forget it. And it is easy for me to understand that, in so far as I consider myself alone, and if there were only myself in the world, I should have been much more perfect than I am, if God had created me so that I could never err. Nevertheless I cannot deny that in some sense it is a greater perfection in the whole universe that certain parts should not be exempt from error as others are than that all parts should be exactly similar. And I have no right to complain if God, having placed me in the world, has not called upon me to play a part that excels all others in distinction and perfection.

And further I have reason to be glad on the ground that if He has not given me the power of never going astray by the first means pointed out above, which depends on a clear and evident knowledge of all the things regarding which I can deliberate, He has at least left within my power the other means, which is firmly to adhere to the resolution never to give judgment on matters whose truth is not clearly known to me; for although I notice a certain weakness in my nature in that I cannot continually concentrate my mind on one single thought, I can yet, by attentive and frequently repeated meditation, impress it so forcibly on my memory that I shall never fail to recollect it whenever I have need of it, and thus acquire the habit of never going astray.

And inasmuch as it is in this that the greatest and principal perfection of man consists, it seems to me that I have not gained little by this day's Meditation, since I have discovered the source of falsity and error. And certainly there can be no other source than that which I have explained; for as often as I so restrain my will within the limits of my knowledge that it forms no judgment except on matters which are clearly and distinctly represented to it by the understanding, I can never be deceived; for every clear and distinct conception is without doubt something, and hence cannot

derive its origin from what is nought, but must of necessity have God as its author—God, I say, who being supremely perfect, cannot be the cause of any error; and consequently we must conclude that such a conception [or such a judgment] is true. Nor have I only learned to-day what I should avoid in order that I may not err, but also how I should act in order to arrive at a knowledge of the truth; for without doubt I shall arrive at this end if I devote my attention sufficiently to those things which I perfectly understand; and if I separate from these that which I only understand confusedly and with obscurity. To these I shall henceforth diligently give heed.

MEDITATION V

Of the Essence of Material Things, and, Again, of God, That He Exists

Many other matters respecting the attributes of God and my own nature or mind remain for consideration; but I shall possibly on another occasion resume the investigation of these. Now (after first noting what must be done or avoided, in order to arrive at a knowledge of the truth) my principal task is to endeavour to emerge from the state of doubt into which I have these last days fallen, and to see whether nothing certain can be known regarding material things.

But before examining whether any such objects as I conceive exist outside of me, I must consider the ideas of them in so far as they are in my thought, and see which of them are distinct and which confused.

In the first place, I am able distinctly to imagine that quantity which philosophers commonly call continuous, or the extension in length, breadth, or depth, that is in this quantity, or rather in the object to which it is attributed. Further, I can number in it many different parts, and attribute to each of its parts many sorts of size, figure, situation and local movement, and, finally, I can assign to each of these movements all degrees of duration.

And not only do I know these things with distinctness when I consider them in general, but, likewise [however little I apply my attention to the matter], I discover an infinitude of particulars respecting numbers, figures, movements, and other such things, whose truth is so manifest, and so well accords with my nature, that when I begin to discover them, it seems to me that I learn nothing new, or recollect what I formerly knew—that is to say, that I for the first time perceive things which were already present to my mind, although I had not as yet applied my mind to them.

And what I here find to be most important is that I discover in myself an infinitude of ideas of certain things which cannot be esteemed as pure negations, although they may possibly have no existence outside of my thought, and which are not framed by me, although it is within my power either to think or not to think them, but which possess natures which are true and immutable. For example, when I imagine a triangle, although there may nowhere in the world be such a figure outside my thought, or ever have been, there is nevertheless in this figure a certain determinate nature, form, or essence, which is immutable and eternal, which I have not invented, and which in no wise depends on my mind, as appears from the fact that diverse properties of that triangle can be demonstrated, viz., that its three angles are equal to two right angles, that the greatest side is subtended by the greatest angle, and the like, which now, whether I wish it or do not wish it, I recognize very clearly as pertaining to it, although I never thought of the matter at all when I imagined a triangle for the first time, and which therefore cannot be said to have been invented by me.

Nor does the objection hold good that possibly this idea of a triangle has reached my mind through the medium of my senses, since I have sometimes seen bodies triangular in shape; because I can form in my mind an infinitude of other figures regarding which we cannot have the least conception of their ever having been objects of sense, and I can nevertheless demonstrate various properties pertaining to their nature as well as to that of the triangle, and these must certainly all be true since I conceive them clearly. Hence they are something, and not pure negation; for it is perfectly clear that all that is true is something, and I have already fully demonstrated that all that I know clearly is true. And even although I had not demonstrated this, the nature of my mind is such that

I could not prevent myself from holding them to be true so long as I conceive them clearly; and I recollect that even when I was still strongly attached to the objects of sense, I counted as the most certain those truths which I conceived clearly as regards figures, numbers, and the other matters which pertain to arithmetic and geometry, and, in general, to pure and abstract mathematics.

But now, if just because I can draw the idea of something from my thought, it follows that all which I know clearly and distinctly as pertaining to this object does really belong to it, may I not derive from this an argument demonstrating the existence of God? It is certain that I no less find the idea of God, that is to say, the idea of a supremely perfect Being, in me, than that of any figure or number whatever it is; and I do not know any less clearly and distinctly that an [actual and] eternal existence pertains to this nature than I know that all that which I am able to demonstrate of some figure or number truly pertains to the nature of this figure or number, and therefore, although all that I concluded in the preceding Meditations were found to be false, the existence of God would pass with me as at least as certain as I have ever held the truths of mathematics (which concern only numbers and figures) to be.

This indeed is not at first manifest, since it would seem to present some appearance of being a sophism. For being accustomed in all other things to make a distinction between existence and essence, I easily persuade myself that the existence can be separated from the essence of God, and that we can thus conceive God as not actually existing. But, nevertheless, when I think of it with more attention, I clearly see that existence can no more be separated from the essence of God than can its having its three angles equal to two right angles be separated from the essence of a [rectilinear] triangle, or the idea of a mountain from the idea of a valley; and so there is not any less repugnance to our conceiving a God (that is, a Being supremely perfect) to whom existence is lacking (that is to say, to whom a certain perfection is lacking), than to conceive of a mountain which has no valley.

But although I cannot really conceive of a God without existence any more than a mountain without a valley, still from the fact that I conceive of a mountain with a valley, it does not follow that there is such a mountain in the world; similarly although I conceive of God as possessing existence, it would seem that it does not follow that there is a God which exists; for my thought does not impose any necessity upon things, and just as I may imagine a winged horse, although no horse with wings exists, so I could perhaps attribute existence to God, although no God existed.

But a sophism is concealed in this objection; for from the fact that I cannot conceive a mountain without a valley, it does not follow that there is any mountain or any valley in existence, but only that the mountain and the valley, whether they exist or do not exist, cannot in any way be separated one from the other. While from the fact that I cannot conceive God without existence, it follows that existence is inseparable from Him, and hence that He really exists; not that my thought can bring this to pass, or impose any necessity on things, but, on the contrary, because the necessity which lies in the thing itself, i.e., the necessity of the existence of God determines me to think in this way. For it is not within my power to think of God without existence (that is of a supremely perfect Being devoid of a supreme perfection) though it is in my power to imagine a horse either with wings or without wings.

And we must not here object that it is in truth necessary for me to assert that God exists after having presupposed that He possesses every sort of perfection, since existence is one of these, but that as a matter of fact my original supposition was not necessary, just as it is not necessary to consider that all quadrilateral figures can be inscribed in the circle; for supposing I thought this, I should be constrained to admit that the rhombus might be inscribed in the circle since it is a quadrilateral figure, which, however, is manifestly false. [We must not, I say, make any such allegations because] although it is not necessary that I should at any time entertain the notion of God, nevertheless whenever it happens that I think of a first and a sovereign Being, and, so to speak, derive the idea of Him from the storehouse of my mind, it is necessary that I should attribute to Him every sort of perfection, although I do not get so far as to enumer-

ate them all, or to apply my mind to each one in particular. And this necessity suffices to make me conclude (after having recognised that existence is a perfection) that this first and sovereign Being really exists; just as though it is not necessary for me ever to imagine any triangle, yet, whenever I wish to consider a rectilinear figure composed only of three angles, it is absolutely essential that I should attribute to it all those properties which serve to bring about the conclusion that its three angles are not greater than two right angles, even although I may not then be considering this point in particular. But when I consider which figures are capable of being inscribed in the circle, it is in no wise necessary that I should think that all quadrilateral figures are of this number; on the contrary, I cannot even pretend that this is the case, so long as I do not desire to accept anything which I cannot conceive clearly and distinctly. And in consequence there is a great difference between the false suppositions such as this, and the true ideas born within me, the first and principal of which is that of God. For really I discern in many ways that this idea is not something factitious, and depending solely on my thought, but that it is the image of a true and immutable nature; first of all, because I cannot conceive anything but God himself to whose essence existence [necessarily] pertains; in the second place because it is not possible for me to conceive two or more Gods in this same position; and, granted that there is one such God who now exists, I see clearly that it is necessary that He should have existed from all eternity, and that He must exist eternally; and finally, because I know an infinitude of other properties in God, none of which I can either diminish or change.

For the rest, whatever proof or argument I avail myself of, we must always return to the point that it is only those things which we conceive clearly and distinctly that have the power of persuading me entirely. And although amongst the matters which I conceive of in this way, some indeed are manifestly obvious to all, while others only manifest themselves to those who consider them closely and examine them attentively; still, after they have once been discovered, the latter are not esteemed as any less certain than the former. For example, in the case of every right-angled triangle, although it does not so manifestly appear that the square of the base is equal to the squares of the two other sides as that this base is opposite to the greatest angle; still, when this has once been apprehended, we are just as certain of its truth as of the truth of the other. And as regards God, if my mind were not pre-occupied with prejudices, and if my thought did not find itself on all hands diverted by the continual pressure of sensible things, there would be nothing which I could know more immediately and more easily than Him. For is there anything more manifest than that there is a God, that is to say, a Supreme Being, to whose essence alone existence pertains?

And although for a firm grasp of this truth I have need of a strenuous application of mind, at present I not only feel myself to be as assured of it as of all that I hold as most certain, but I also remark that the certainty of all other things depends on it so absolutely, that without this knowledge it is impossible ever to know anything perfectly.

For although I am of such a nature that as long as I understand anything very clearly and distinctly, I am naturally impelled to believe it to be true, yet because I am also of such a nature that I cannot have my mind constantly fixed on the same object in order to perceive it clearly, and as I often recollect having formed a past judgment without at the same time properly recollecting the reasons that led me to make it, it may happen meanwhile that other reasons present themselves to me, which would easily cause me to change my opinion, if I were ignorant of the facts of the existence of God, and thus I should have no true and certain knowledge, but only vague and vacillating opinions. Thus, for example, when I consider the nature of a [rectilinear] triangle, I who have some little knowledge of the principles of geometry recognise quite clearly that the three angles are equal to two right angles, and it is not possible for me not to believe this so long as I apply my mind to its demonstration; but so soon as I abstain from attending to the proof, although I still recollect having clearly comprehended it, it may easily occur that I come to doubt its truth, if I am ignorant of there being a God. For I can persuade myself of having been so constituted by nature that I can easily deceive myself even in those matters which I believe myself to apprehend with the greatest evidence and certainty, especially when I recollect that I have frequently judged matters to be true and certain which other reasons have afterwards impelled me to judge to be altogether false.

But after I have recognised that there is a God—because at the same time I have also recognised that all things depend upon Him, and that He is not a deceiver, and from that have inferred that what I perceive clearly and distinctly cannot fail to be true—although I no longer pay attention to the reasons for which I have judged this to be true, provided that I recollect having clearly and distinctly perceived it no contrary reason can be brought forward which could ever cause me to doubt of its truth; and thus I have a true and certain knowledge of it. And this same knowledge extends likewise to all other things which I recollect having formerly demonstrated, such as the truths of geometry and the like; for what can be alleged against them to cause me to place them in doubt? Will it be said that my nature is such as to cause me to be frequently deceived? But I already know that I cannot be deceived in the judgment whose grounds I know clearly. Will it be said that I formerly held many things to be true and certain which I have afterwards recognised to be false? But I had not had any clear and distinct knowledge of these things, and not as yet knowing the rule whereby I assure myself of the truth, I had been impelled to give my assent from reasons which I have since recognised to be less strong than I had at the time imagined them to be. What further objection can then be raised? That possibly I am dreaming (an objection I myself made a little while ago), or that all the thoughts which I now have are no more true than the phantasies of my dreams? But even though I slept the case would be the same, for all that is clearly present to my mind is absolutely true.

And so I very clearly recognise that the certainty and truth of all knowledge depends alone on the knowledge of the true God, in so much that, before I knew Him, I could not have a perfect knowledge of any other thing. And now that I know Him I have the means of acquiring a perfect knowledge of an infinitude of things, not only of those which relate to God Himself and other intellectual matters, but also of those which pertain to corporeal nature in so far as it is the object of pure mathematics [which have no concern with whether it exists or not].

MEDITATION VI

Of the Existence of Material Things, and of the Real Distinction between the Soul and Body of Man

Nothing further now remains but to inquire whether material things exist. And certainly I at least know that these may exist in so far as they are considered as the objects of pure mathematics, since in this aspect I perceive them clearly and distinctly. For there is no doubt that God possesses the power to produce everything that I am capable of perceiving with distinctness, and I have never deemed that anything was impossible for Him, unless I found a contradiction in attempting to conceive it clearly. Further, the faculty of imagination which I possess, and of which, experience tells me, I make use when I apply myself to the consideration of material things, is capable of persuading me of their existence; for when I attentively consider what imagination is, I find that it is nothing but a certain application of the faculty of knowledge to the body which is immediately present to it, and which therefore exists.

And to render this quite clear, I remark in the first place the difference that exists between the imagination and pure intellection [or conception]. For example, when I imagine a triangle, I do not conceive it only as a figure comprehended by three lines, but I also apprehend these three lines as present by the power and inward vision of my mind, and this is what I call imagining. But if I desire to think of a chiliagon, I certainly conceive truly that it is a figure composed of a thousand sides, just as easily as I conceive of a triangle that it is a figure of three sides only; but I cannot in any way imagine the thousand sides of a chiliagon [as I do the three sides of a triangle], nor do I, so to speak, regard them as present [with the eyes of my mind]. And although in accordance with the habit I have formed of always employing the aid of my imagination when I think of corporeal things, it may happen that in imagining a chiliagon I confusedly represent to myself some

figure, yet it is very evident that this figure is not a chiliagon, since it in no way differs from that which I represent to myself when I think of a myriagon or any other many-sided figure; nor does it serve my purpose in discovering the properties which go to form the distinction between a chiliagon and other polygons. But if the question turns upon a pentagon, it is quite true that I can conceive its figure as well as that of a chiliagon without the help of my imagination; but I can also imagine it by applying the attention of my mind to each of its five sides, and at the same time to the space which they enclose. And thus I clearly recognise that I have need of a particular effort of mind in order to effect the act of imagination, such as I do not require in order to understand, and this particular effort of mind clearly manifests the difference which exists between imagination and pure intellection.

I remark besides that this power of imagination which is in one, inasmuch as it differs from the power of understanding, is in no wise a necessary element in my nature, or in [my essence, that is to say] the essence of my mind; for although I did not possess it I should doubtless ever remain the same as I now am, from which it appears that we might conclude that it depends on something which differs from me. And I easily conceive that if some body exists with which my mind is conjoined and united in such a way that it can apply itself to consider it when it pleases, it may be that by this means it can imagine corporeal objects; so that this mode of thinking differs from pure intellection only inasmuch as mind in its intellectual activity in some manner turns on itself, and considers some of the ideas which it possesses in itself; while in imagining it turns towards the body, and there beholds in it something conformable to the idea which it has either conceived of itself or perceived by the senses. I easily understand, I say, that the imagination could be thus constituted if it is true that body exists; and because I can discover no other convenient mode of explaining it, I conjecture with probability that body does exist; but this is only with probability, and although I examine all things with care, I nevertheless do not find that from this distinct idea of corporeal nature, which I have in my imagination, I can derive any argument from which there will necessarily be deduced the existence of body.

But I am in the habit of imagining many other things besides this corporeal nature which is the object of pure mathematics, to wit, the colours, sounds, scents, pain, and other such things, although less distinctly. And inasmuch as I perceive these things much better through the senses, by the medium of which, and by the memory, they seem to have reached my imagination, I believe that, in order to examine them more conveniently, it is right that I should at the same time investigate the nature of sense perception, and that I should see if from the ideas which I apprehend by this mode of thought, which I call feeling, I cannot derive some certain proof of the existence of corporeal objects.

And first of all I shall recall to my memory those matters which I hitherto held to be true, as having perceived them through the senses, and the foundations on which my belief has rested; in the next place I shall examine the reasons which have since obliged me to place them in doubt; in the last place I shall consider which of them I must now believe.

First of all, then, I perceived that I had a head, hands, feet, and all other members of which this body—which I considered as a part, or possibly even as the whole, of myself—is composed. Further I was sensible that this body was placed amidst many others, from which it was capable of being affected in many different ways, beneficial and hurtful, and I remarked that a certain feeling of pleasure accompanied those that were beneficial, and pain those which were harmful. And in addition to this pleasure and pain, I also experienced hunger, thirst, and other similar appetites, as also certain corporeal inclinations towards joy, sadness, anger, and other similar passions. And outside myself, in addition to extension, figure, and motions of bodies, I remarked in them hardness, heat, and all other tactile qualities, and, further, light and colour, and scents and sounds, the variety of which gave me the means of distinguishing the sky, the earth, the sea, and generally all the other bodies, one from the other. And certainly, considering the ideas of all these qualities which presented themselves to my mind, and which alone I perceived properly or immediately, it was not without reason that I believed myself to perceive objects quite different from my thought, to wit, bodies from which those

ideas proceeded; for I found by experience that these ideas presented themselves to me without my consent being requisite, so that I could not perceive any object, however desirous I might be, unless it were present to the organs of sense; and it was not in my power not to perceive it, when it was present. And because the ideas which I received through the senses were much more lively, more clear, and even, in their own way, more distinct than any of those which I could of myself frame in meditation, or than those I found impressed on my memory, it appeared as though they could not have proceeded from my mind, so that they must necessarily have been produced in me by some other things. And having no knowledge of those objects excepting the knowledge which the ideas themselves gave me, nothing was more likely to occur to my mind than that the objects were similar to the ideas which were caused. And because I likewise remembered that I had formerly made use of my senses rather than my reason, and recognised that the ideas which I formed of myself were not so distinct as those which I perceived through the senses, and that they were most frequently even composed of portions of these last, I persuaded myself easily that I had no idea in my mind which had not formerly come to me through the senses. Nor was it without some reason that I believed that this body (which by a certain special right I call my own) belonged to me more properly and more strictly than any other; for in fact I could never be separated from it as from other bodies; I experienced in it and on account of it all my appetites and affections, and finally I was touched by the feeling of pain and the titillation of pleasure in its parts, and not in the parts of other bodies which were separated from it. But when I inquired, why, from some, I know not what, painful sensation, there follows sadness of mind, and from the pleasurable sensation there arises joy, or why this mysterious pinching of the stomach which I call hunger causes me to desire to eat, and dryness of throat causes a desire to drink, and so on, I could give no reason excepting that nature taught me so; for there is certainly no affinity (that I at least can understand) between the craving of the stomach and the desire to eat, any more than between the perception of whatever causes pain and the thought of sadness which arises from this perception.

And in the same way it appeared to me that I had learned from nature all the other judgments which I formed regarding the objects of my senses, since I remarked that these judgments were formed in me before I had the leisure to weigh and consider any reasons which might oblige me to make them.

But afterwards many experiences little by little destroyed all the faith which I had rested in my senses; for I from time to time observed that those towers which from afar appeared to me to be round, more closely observed seemed square, and that colossal statues raised on the summit of these towers, appeared as quite tiny statues when viewed from the bottom; and so in an infinitude of other cases I found error in judgments founded on the external senses. And not only in those founded on the external senses, but even in those founded on the internal as well; for is there anything more intimate or more internal than pain? And yet I have learned from some persons whose arms or legs have been cut off, that they sometimes seemed to feel pain in the part which had been amputated, which made me think that I could not be quite certain that it was a certain member which pained me, even although I felt pain in it. And to those grounds of doubt I have lately added two others, which are very general; the first is that I never have believed myself to feel anything in waking moments which I cannot also sometimes believe myself to feel when I sleep, and as I do not think that these things which I seem to feel in sleep, proceed from objects outside of me, I do not see any reason why I should have this belief regarding objects which I seem to perceive while awake. The other was that being still ignorant, or rather supposing myself to be ignorant, of the author of my being, I saw nothing to prevent me from having been so constituted by nature that I might be deceived even in matters which seemed to me to be most certain. And as to the grounds on which I was formerly persuaded of the truth of sensible objects, I had not much trouble in replying to them. For since nature seemed to cause me to lean towards many things from which reason repelled me, I did not believe that I should trust much to the teachings of nature. And although the ideas which I receive by the senses do not depend on my will, I did not think that one should for that reason conclude that they proceeded from things different from myself, since possibly some faculty might be discovered in me—though hitherto unknown to me—which produced them.

But now that I begin to know myself better, and to discover more clearly the author of my being, I do not in truth think that I should rashly admit all the matters which the senses seem to teach us, but, on the other hand, I do not think that I should doubt them all universally.

And first of all, because I know that all things which I apprehend clearly and distinctly can be created by God as I apprehend them, it suffices that I am able to apprehend one thing apart from another clearly and distinctly in order to be certain that the one is different from the other, since they may be made to exist in separation at least by the omnipotence of God; and it does not signify by what power this separation is made in order to compel me to judge them to be different: and, therefore, just because I know certainly that I exist, and that meanwhile I do not remark that any other thing necessarily pertains to my nature or essence, excepting that I am a thinking thing, I rightly conclude that my essence consists solely in the fact that I am a thinking thing [or a substance whose whole essence or nature is to think]. And although possible (or rather certainly, as I shall say in a moment) I possess a body with which I am very intimately conjoined, yet because, on the one side, I have a clear and distinct idea of myself inasmuch as I am only a thinking and unextended thing, and as, on the other, I possess a distinct idea of body, inasmuch as it is only an extended and unthinking thing, it is certain that this I [that is to say, my soul by which I am what I am], is entirely and absolutely distinct from my body, and can exist without it.

I further find in myself faculties employing modes of thinking peculiar to themselves, to wit, the faculties of imagination and feeling, without which I can easily conceive myself clearly and distinctly as a complete being; while, on the other hand, they cannot be so conceived apart from me, that is without an intelligent substance in which they reside, for [in the notion we have of these faculties, or, to use the language of the Schools] in their formal concept, some kind of intellection is comprised, from which I infer that they are distinct from me as its modes are from a thing. I observe also in me some other faculties such as that of change of position, the assumption of different figures and such like, which cannot be conceived, any more than can the preceding, apart from some substance to which they are attached, and consequently cannot exist without it; but it is very clear that these faculties, if it be true that they exist, must be attached to some corporeal or extended substance, and not to an intelligent substance, since in the clear and distinct conception of these there is some sort of extension found to be present, but no intellection at all. There is certainly further in me a certain passive faculty of perception, that is, of receiving and recognising the ideas of sensible things, but this would be useless to me [and I could in no way avail myself of it], if there were not either in me or in some other thing another active faculty capable of forming and producing these ideas. But this active faculty cannot exist in me [inasmuch as I am a thing that thinks] seeing that it does not presuppose thought, and also that those ideas are often produced in me without my contributing in any way to the same, and often even against my will; it is thus necessarily the case that the faculty resides in some substance different from me in which all the reality which is objectively in the ideas that are produced by this faculty is formally or eminently contained, as I remarked before. And this substance is either a body, that is, a corporeal nature in which there is contained formally [and really] all that which is objectively [and by representation] in those ideas, or it is God Himself, or some other creature more noble than body in which that same is contained eminently. But, since God is no deceiver, it is very manifest that He does not communicate to me these ideas immediately and by Himself, nor yet by the intervention of some creature in which their reality is not formally, but only eminently, contained. For since He has given me no faculty to recognise that this is the case, but, on the other hand, a very great inclination to believe [that they are sent to me or] that they are conveyed to me by corporeal objects, I do not see how He could be defended from the accusation of deceit if these ideas were produced by causes other than corporeal objects. Hence we must allow that corporeal things exist. However, they are perhaps not exactly what we perceive by the senses, since this

comprehension by the senses is in many instances very obscure and confused; but we must at least admit that all things which I conceive in them clearly and distinctly, that is to say, all things which, speaking generally, are comprehended in the object of pure mathematics, are truly to be recognised as external objects.

As to other things, however, which are either particular only, as, for example, that the sun is of such and such a figure, etc., or which are less clearly and distinctly conceived, such as light, sound, pain and the like, it is certain that although they are very dubious and uncertain, yet on the sole ground that God is not a deceiver, and that consequently He has not permitted any falsity to exist in my opinion which He has not likewise given me the faculty of correcting, I may assuredly hope to conclude that I have within me the means of arriving at the truth even here. And first of all there is no doubt that in all things which nature teaches me there is some truth contained; for by nature, considered in general, I now understand no other thing than either God Himself or else the order and disposition which God has established in created things; and by my nature in particular I understand no other thing than the complexus of all the things which God has given me.

But there is nothing which this nature teaches me more expressly [nor more sensibly] than that I have a body which is adversely affected when I feel pain, which has need of food or drink when I experience the feelings of hunger and thirst, and so on; nor can I doubt there being some truth in all this.

Nature also teaches me by these sensations of pain, hunger, thirst, etc., that I am not only lodged in my body as a pilot in a vessel, but that I am very closely united to it, and so to speak so intermingled with it that I seem to compose with it one whole. For if that were not the case, when my body is hurt, I, who am merely a thinking thing, should not feel pain, for I should perceive this wound by the understanding only, just as the sailor perceives by sight when something is damaged in his vessel; and when my body has need of drink or food, I should clearly understand the fact without being warned of it by confused feelings of hunger and thirst. For all these sensations of hunger, thirst, pain, etc. are in truth none other than certain confused modes of thought which are produced by the union and apparent intermingling of mind and body.

But there are many other things which nature seems to have taught me, but which at the same time I have never really received from her, but which have been brought about in my mind by a certain habit which I have of forming inconsiderate judgments on things; and thus it may easily happen that these judgments contain some error. Take, for example, the opinion which I hold that all space in which there is nothing that affects [or makes an impression on] my senses is void; that in a body which is warm there is something entirely similar to the idea of heat which is in me; that in a white or green body there is the same whiteness or greenness that I perceive; that in a bitter or sweet body there is the same taste, and so on in other instances; that the stars, the towers, and all other distant bodies are of the same figure and size as they appear from far off to our eyes, etc. But in order that in this there should be nothing which I do not conceive distinctly, I should define exactly what I really understand when I say that I am taught somewhat by nature. For here I take nature in a more limited signification than when I term it the sum of all the things given me by God, since in this sum many things are comprehended which only pertain to mind (and to these I do not refer in speaking of nature) such as the notion which I have of the fact that what has once been done cannot ever be undone and an infinitude of such things which I know by the light of nature [without the help of the body]; and seeing that it comprehends many other matters besides which only pertain to body, and are no longer here contained under the name of nature, such as the quality of weight which it possesses and the like, with which I also do not deal; for in talking of nature I only treat of those things given by God to me as a being composed of mind and body. But the nature here described truly teaches me to flee from things which cause the sensation of pain, and seek after the things which communicate to me the sentiment of pleasure and so forth; but I do not see that beyond this it teaches me that from those diverse sense-perceptions we should ever form any conclusion regarding things outside of us, without having [carefully and maturely] mentally examined them beforehand. For it seems to

me that it is mind alone, and not mind and body in conjunction, that is requisite to a knowledge of the truth in regard to such things. Thus, although a star makes no larger an impression on my eye than the flame of a little candle there is yet in me no real or positive propensity impelling me to believe that it is not greater than that flame; but I have judged it to be so from my earliest years, without any rational foundation. And although in approaching fire I feel heat, and in approaching it a little too near I even feel pain, there is at the same time no reason in this which could persuade me that there is in the fire something resembling this heat any more than there is in it something resembling the pain; all that I have any reason to believe from this is, that there is something in it, whatever it may be, which excites in me these sensations of heat or of pain. So also, although there are spaces in which I find nothing which excites my senses, I must not from that conclude that these spaces contain no body; for I see in this, as in other similar things, that I have been in the habit of perverting the order of nature, because these perceptions of sense having been placed within me by nature merely for the purpose of signifying to my mind what things are beneficial or hurtful to the composite whole of which it forms a part, and being up to that point sufficiently clear and distinct, I yet avail myself of them as though they were absolute rules by which I might immediately determine the essence of the bodies which are outside me, as to which, in fact, they can teach me nothing but what is most obscure and confused.

But I have already sufficiently considered how, notwithstanding the supreme goodness of God, falsity enters into the judgments I make. Only here a new difficulty is presented—one respecting those things the pursuit or avoidance of which is taught me by nature, and also respecting the internal sensations which I possess, and in which I seem to have sometimes detected error [and thus to be directly deceived by my own nature]. To take an example, the agreeable taste of some food in which poison has been intermingled may induce me to partake of the poison, and thus deceive me. It is true, at the same time that in this case nature may be excused, for it only induces me to desire food in which I find a pleasant taste, and not to desire the poison which is unknown to it; and thus I can infer nothing from this fact, except that my nature is not omniscient, at which there is certainly no reason to be astonished, since man, being finite in nature, can only have knowledge the perfectness of which is limited.

But we not unfrequently deceive ourselves even in those things to which we are directly impelled by nature, as happens with those who when they are sick desire to drink or eat things hurtful to them. It will perhaps be said here that the cause of their deceptiveness is that their nature is corrupt, but that does not remove the difficulty, because a sick man is none the less truly God's creature than he who is in health; and it is therefore as repugnant to God's goodness for the one to have a deceitful nature as it is for the other. And as a clock composed of wheels and counter-weights no less exactly observes the laws of nature when it is badly made, and does not show the time properly, than when it entirely satisfies the wishes of its maker, and as, if I consider the body of a man as being a sort of machine so built up and composed of nerves, muscles, veins, blood and skin, that though there were no mind in it at all, it would not cease to have the same motions as at present, exception being made of those movements which are due to the direction of the will, and in consequence depend upon the mind [as opposed to those which operate by the disposition of its organs], I easily recognise that it would be as natural to this body, supposing it to be, for example, dropsical, to suffer the parchedness of the throat which usually signifies to the mind the feeling of thirst, and to be disposed by this parched feeling to move the nerves and other parts in the way requisite for drinking, and thus to augment its malady and do harm to itself, as it is natural to it, when it has no indisposition, to be impelled to drink for its good by a similar cause. And although, considering the use to which the clock has been destined by its maker, I may say that it deflects from the order of its nature when it does not indicate the hours correctly; and as, in the same way, considering the machine of the human body as having been formed by God in order to have in itself all the movements usually manifested there, I have reason for thinking that it does not follow the order of nature when, if the throat is dry, drinking does harm to the conservation of health, nevertheless I recognise at the same time

that this last mode of explaining nature is very different from the other. For this is but a purely verbal characterisation depending entirely on my thought, which compares a sick man and a badly constructed clock with the idea which I have of a healthy man and a well made clock, and it is hence extrinsic to the things to which it is applied; but according to the other interpretation of the term nature I understand something which is truly found in things and which is therefore not without some truth.

But certainly although in regard to the dropsical body it is only so to speak to apply an extrinsic term when we say that its nature is corrupted, inasmuch as apart from the need to drink, the throat is parched; yet in regard to the composite whole, that is to say, to the mind or soul united to this body, it is not a purely verbal predicate, but a real error of nature, for it to have thirst when drinking would be hurtful to it. And thus it still remains to inquire how the goodness of God does not prevent the nature of man so regarded from being fallacious.

In order to begin this examination, then, I here say, in the first place, that there is a great difference between mind and body, inasmuch as body is by nature always divisible, and the mind is entirely indivisible. For, as a matter of fact, when I consider the mind, that is to say, myself inasmuch as I am only a thinking thing, I cannot distinguish in myself any parts, but apprehend myself to be clearly one and entire; and although the whole mind seems to be united to the whole body, yet if a foot, or an arm, or some other part, is separated from my body, I am aware that nothing has been taken away from my mind. And the faculties of willing, feeling, conceiving, etc. cannot be properly speaking said to be its parts, for it is one and the same mind which employs itself in willing and in feeling and understanding. But it is quite otherwise with corporeal or extended objects, for there is not one of these imaginable by me which my mind cannot easily divide into parts, and which consequently I do not recognise as being divisible; this would be sufficient to teach me that the mind or soul of man is entirely different from the body, if I had not already learned it from other sources.

I further notice that the mind does not receive the impressions from all parts of the body immediately, but only from the brain, or perhaps even from one of its smallest parts, to wit, from that in which the common sense is said to reside, which, whenever it is disposed in the same particular way, conveys the same thing to the mind, although meanwhile the other portions of the body may be differently disposed, as is testified by innumerable experiments which it is unnecessary here to recount.

I notice, also, that the nature of body is such that none of its parts can be moved by another part a little way off which cannot also be moved in the same way by each one of the parts which are between the two, although this more remote part does not act at all. As, for example, in the cord *ABCD* [which is in tension] if we pull the last part *D,* the first part *A* will not be moved in any way differently from what would be the case if one of the intervening parts *B* or *C* were pulled, and the last part *D* were to remain unmoved. And in the same way, when I feel pain in my foot, my knowledge of physics teaches me that this sensation is communicated by means of nerves dispersed through the foot, which, being extended like cords from there to the brain, when they are contracted in the foot, at the same time contract the inmost portions of the brain which is their extremity and place of origin, and then excite a certain movement which nature has established in order to cause the mind to be affected by a sensation of pain represented as existing in the foot. But because these nerves must pass through the tibia, the thigh, the loins, the back and the neck, in order to reach from the leg to the brain, it may happen that although their extremities which are in the foot are not affected, but only certain ones of their intervening parts [which pass by the loins or the neck], this action will excite the same movement in the brain that might have been excited there by a hurt received in the foot, in consequence of which the mind will necessarily feel in the foot the same pain as if it had received a hurt. And the same holds good of all the other perceptions of our senses.

I notice finally that since each of the movements which are in the portion of the brain by which the mind is immediately affected brings about one particular sensation only, we cannot under the circumstances imagine anything more likely than that this movement,

amongst all the sensations which it is capable of impressing on it, causes mind to be affected by that one which is best fitted and most generally useful for the conservation of the human body when it is in health. But experience makes us aware that all the feelings with which nature inspires us are such as I have just spoken of; and there is therefore nothing in them which does not give testimony to the power and goodness of the God [who has produced them]. Thus, for example, when the nerves which are in the feet are violently or more than usually moved, their movement, passing through the medulla of the spine to the inmost parts of the brain, gives a sign to the mind which makes it feel somewhat, to wit, pain, as though in the foot, by which the mind is excited to do its utmost to remove the cause of the evil as dangerous and hurtful to the foot. It is true that God could have constituted the nature of man in such a way that this same movement in the brain would have conveyed something quite different to the mind; for example, it might have produced consciousness of itself either in so far as it is in the brain, or as it is in the foot, or as it is in some other place between the foot and the brain, or it might finally have produced consciousness of anything else whatsoever; but none of all this would have contributed so well to the conservation of the body. Similarly, when we desire to drink, a certain dryness of the throat is produced which moves its nerves, and by their means the internal portions of the brain; and this movement causes in the mind the sensation of thirst, because in this case there is nothing more useful to us than to become aware that we have need to drink for the conservation of our health; and the same holds good in other instances.

From this it is quite clear that, notwithstanding the supreme goodness of God, the nature of man, inasmuch as it is composed of mind and body, cannot be otherwise than sometimes a source of deception. For if there is any cause which excites, not in the foot but in some part of the nerves which are extended between the foot and the brain, or even in the brain itself, the same movement which usually is produced when the foot is detrimentally affected, pain will be experienced as though it were in the foot, and the sense will thus naturally be deceived; for since the same movement in the brain is capable of causing but one sensation in the mind, and this sensation is much more frequently excited by a cause which hurts the foot than by another existing in some other quarter, it is reasonable that it should convey to the mind pain in the foot rather than in any other part of the body. And although the parchedness of the throat does not always proceed, as it usually does, from the fact that drinking is necessary for the health of the body, but sometimes comes from quite a different cause, as is the case with dropsical patients, it is yet much better that it should mislead on this occasion than if, on the other hand, it were always to deceive us when the body is in good health; and so on in similar cases.

And certainly this consideration is of great service to me, not only in enabling me to recognise all the errors to which my nature is subject, but also in enabling me to avoid them or to correct them more easily. For knowing that all my senses more frequently indicate to me truth than falsehood respecting the things which concern that which is beneficial to the body, and being able almost always to avail myself of many of them in order to examine one particular thing, and, besides that, being able to make use of my memory in order to connect the present with the past, and of my understanding which already has discovered all the causes of my errors, I ought no longer to fear that falsity may be found in matters every day presented to me by my senses. And I ought to set aside all the doubts of these past days as hyperbolical and ridiculous, particularly that very common uncertainty respecting sleep, which I could not distinguish from the waking state; for at present I find a very notable difference between the two, inasmuch as our memory can never connect our dreams one with the other, or with the whole course of our lives, as it unites events which happen to us while we are awake. And, as a matter of fact, if someone, while I was awake, quite suddenly appeared to me and disappeared as fast as do the images which I see in sleep, so that I could not know from whence the form came nor whither it went, it would not be without reason that I should deem it a spectre or a phantom formed by my brain [and similar to those which I form in sleep], rather than a real man. But

when I perceive things as to which I know distinctly both the place from which they proceed, and that in which they are, and the time at which they appeared to me; and when, without any interruption, I can connect the perceptions which I have of them with the whole course of my life, I am perfectly assured that these perceptions occur while I am waking and not during sleep. And I ought in no wise to doubt the truth of such matters, if, after having called up all my senses, my memory, and my understanding, to examine them, nothing is brought to evidence by any one of them which is repugnant to what is set forth by the others. For because God is in no wise a deceiver, it follows that I am not deceived in this. But because the exigencies of action often oblige us to make up our minds before having leisure to examine matters carefully, we must confess that the life of man is very frequently subject to error in respect to individual objects, and we must in the end acknowledge the infirmity of our nature.

FOR FURTHER REFLECTION

1. Are you convinced by Descartes's argument? Is the self the most certain of objects? Explain your answer.
2. Is Descartes's argument against trusting the senses a valid argument? Why should we always distrust the senses? Discuss this issue, and when you get to the next reading, compare it with what Locke says. Descartes is a *rationalist,* believing that unaided reason can discover all truth, whereas Locke and Hume are *empiricists,* believing that sense perception is the only way to knowledge. Keep this difference in mind as you continue reading in this section of the book.
3. What is Descartes's criterion of knowledge?
4. Does Descartes convince you that the mind is more certain than matter? Why or why not?
5. Reconstruct Descartes's arguments for the existence of God. Do you find these arguments valid? Explain.
6. How does Descartes prove that there is a material world?

JOHN LOCKE

KNOWLEDGE THROUGH EXPERIENCE

The English philosopher John Locke (1632–1704) was educated at Oxford University, where he became a tutor in Greek rhetoric and philosophy. Later he practiced medicine and served as assistant to the Earl of Shaftesbury. His work on representative government and human rights greatly influenced the founders of the United States. His principal works are *Two Treatises on Government* (1689); *An Essay Concerning Human Understanding* (1690), from which the following reading is taken; and *The Reasonableness of Christianity* (1695).

Locke's work on the theory of knowledge is the first systematic assault on Cartesian rationalism, on the view that reason alone guarantees knowledge. Locke argues that to make any sense, our claims to knowledge must be derived from the world. He rejects the rationalist notion that we have *innate ideas* (actual prior knowledge of metaphysical truths, such as mathematical truths, universals, and the laws of nature). Locke argues that (1) no good deductive argument establishes the existence of such entities; (2) children and idiots do not seem to have them; and (3) an empirical way of knowing, which seems far more reasonable, has no place for such entities. Locke does believe that we have intuitive knowledge of our own existence and that the existence of God can be demonstrated by reason. Locke believes this assertion is not inconsistent: We know, on immediate reflection, that we exist because of the nature of consciousness, not because of any prior knowledge hidden within us. Nor do we have innate knowledge of God; but we can reason from empirical truths about the world to the existence of God (using such arguments as the cosmological and teleological arguments discussed in Part III of this book).

According to Locke, at birth your mind is a tabula rasa, a "blank slate." Your mind is like white paper, devoid of characteristics until it receives sense perceptions. All knowledge begins with sensory experience, on which the mind works, developing complex ideas, abstractions, and the like. Instead of the absolute certainty sought by the rationalists, Locke says that—apart from self-knowledge —most of what we "know," we infer in *degrees* of certainty from experience. For example, we see the sun rise every morning, and we infer that very probably it will rise again tomorrow (but we can't be absolutely sure).

INTRODUCTION

1. *An inquiry into the understanding pleasant and useful.* Since it is the *understanding* that sets man above the rest of sensible beings, and gives him all the advantage and dominion which he has over them; it is certainly a subject, even for its nobleness, worth our labour to inquire into. The understanding, like the eye, whilst it makes us see and perceive all other things, takes no notice of itself; and it requires art and

From John Locke, *An Essay Concerning Human Understanding* (1689), Books 1.1, 2.1, and 8, 4.11 and 15.

pains to set it at a distance and make it its own object. But whatever be the difficulties that lie in the way of this inquiry; whatever it be that keeps us so much in the dark to ourselves; sure I am that all the light we can let in upon our minds, all the acquaintance we can make with our own understandings, will not only be very pleasant, but bring us great advantage, in directing our thoughts in the search of other things.

2. *Design.* This, therefore, being my purpose—to inquire into the original, certainty, and extent of *human knowledge,* together with the grounds and degrees of *belief, opinion,* and *assent*—I shall not at present meddle with the physical consideration of the mind; or trouble myself to examine wherein its essence consists; or by what motions of our spirits or alterations of our bodies we come to have any *sensation* by our organs, or any *ideas* in our understandings; and whether those ideas do in their formation, any or all of them, depend on matter or not. These are speculations which, however curious and entertaining, I shall decline, as lying out of my way in the design I am now upon. It shall suffice to my present purpose, to consider the discerning faculties of a man, as they are employed about the objects which they have to do with. And I shall imagine I have not wholly misemployed myself in the thoughts I shall have on this occasion, if, in this historical, plain method, I can give any account of the ways whereby our understandings come to attain those notions of things we have; and can set down any measures of the certainty of our knowledge; or the grounds of those persuasions which are to be found amongst men, so various, different, and wholly contradictory; and yet asserted somewhere or other with such assurance and confidence, that he that shall take a view of the opinions of mankind, observe their opposition, and at the same time consider the fondness and devotion wherewith they are embraced, the resolution and eagerness wherewith they are maintained, may perhaps have reason to suspect, that either there is no such thing as truth at all, or that mankind hath no sufficient means to attain a certain knowledge of it.

3. *Method.* It is therefore worth while to search out the bounds between opinion and knowledge; and examine by what measures, in things whereof we have no certain knowledge, we ought to regulate our assent and moderate our persuasion. In order whereunto I shall pursue this following method:

First, I shall inquire into the original of those *ideas,* notions, or whatever else you please to call them, which a man observes, and is conscious to himself he has in his mind; and the ways whereby the understanding comes to be furnished with them.

Secondly, I shall endeavour to show what *knowledge* the understanding hath by those ideas; and the certainty, evidence, and extent of it.

Thirdly, I shall make some inquiry into the nature and grounds of *faith* or *opinion:* whereby I mean that assent which we give to any proposition as true, of whose truth yet we have no certain knowledge. And here we shall have occasion to examine the reasons and degrees of *assent.*

BOOK I

Chapter I

1. It is an established opinion amongst some men, that there are in the understanding certain *innate principles;* some primary notions, κοιναὶ ἔννοιαι, characters, as it were stamped upon the mind of man; which the soul receives in its very first being, and brings into the world with it. It would be sufficient to convince unprejudiced readers of the falseness of this supposition, if I should only show (as I hope I shall in the following parts of this Discourse) how men, barely by the use of their natural faculties, may attain to all the knowledge they have, without the help of any innate impressions; and may arrive at certainty, without any such original notions or principles. For I imagine any one will easily grant that it would be impertinent to suppose the ideas of colours innate in a creature to whom god hath given sight, and a power to receive them by the eyes from external objects: and no less unreasonable would it be to attribute several truths to the impressions of nature, and innate characters, when we may observe in ourselves faculties fit to attain as easy and certain knowledge of them as if they were originally imprinted on the mind.

But because a man is not permitted without censure to follow his own thoughts in the search of truth, when they lead him ever so little out of the common road, I shall set down the reasons that made me doubt of the truth of that opinion, as an excuse for my mistake, if I be in one; which I leave to be considered by those who, with me, dispose themselves to embrace truth wherever they find it.

2. There is nothing more commonly taken for granted than that there are certain *principles,* both *speculative* and *practical* (for they speak of both), universally agreed upon by all mankind: which therefore, they argue, must needs be the constant impressions which the souls of men receive in their first beings, and which they bring into the world with them, as necessarily and really as they do any of their inherent faculties.

3. This argument, drawn from universal consent, has this misfortune in it, that if it were true in matter of fact, that there were certain truths wherein all mankind agreed, it would not prove them innate, if there can be any other way shown how men may come to that universal agreement, in the things they do consent in, which I presume may be done.

4. But, which is worse, this argument of universal consent, which is made use of to prove innate principles, seems to me a demonstration that there are none such because there are none to which all mankind give an universal assent. I shall begin with the speculative, and instance in those magnified principles of demonstration, "Whatsoever is, is," and "It is impossible for the same thing to be and not to be"; which, of all others, I think have the most allowed title to innate. These have so settled a reputation of maxims universally received, that it will no doubt be thought strange if any one should seem to question it. But yet I take liberty to say, that these propositions are so far from having an universal assent, that there are a great part of mankind to whom they are not so much as known.

5. For, first, it is evident, that all children and idiots have not the least apprehension or thought of them. And the want of that is enough to destroy that universal assent which must needs be the necessary concomitant of all innate truths: it seeming to me near a contradiction to say, that there are truths imprinted on the soul, which it perceives or understands not: imprinting, if it signify anything, being nothing else but the making certain truths to be perceived. For to imprint anything on the mind without

the mind's perceiving it, seems to me hardly intelligible. If therefore children and idiots have souls, have minds, with those impressions upon them, *they* must unavoidably perceive them, and necessarily know and assent to these truths; which since they do not, it is evident that there are no such impressions. For if they are not notions naturally imprinted, how can they be innate? and if they are notions imprinted, how can they be unknown? To say a notion is imprinted on the mind, and yet at the same time to say that the mind is ignorant of it, and never yet took notice of it, is to make this impression nothing. No proposition can be said to be in the mind which it never yet knew, which it was never yet conscious of. For if any one may, then, by the same reason, all propositions that are true, and the mind is capable ever of assenting to, may be said to be in the mind, and to be imprinted: since, if any one can be said to be in the mind, which it never yet knew, it must be only because it is capable of knowing it; and so the mind is of all truths it ever shall know. Nay, thus truths may be imprinted on the mind which it never did, nor ever shall know; for a man may live long, and die at last in ignorance of many truths which his mind was capable of knowing, and that with certainty. So that if the capacity of knowing be the natural impression contended for, all the truths a man ever comes to know will, by this account, be every one of them innate; and this great point will amount to no more, but only to a very improper way of speaking; which, whilst it pretends to assert the contrary, says nothing different from those who deny innate principles. For nobody, I think, ever denied that the mind was capable of knowing several truths. The capacity, they say, is innate; the knowledge acquired. But then to what end such contest for certain innate maxims? If truths can be imprinted on the understanding without being perceived, I can see no difference there can be between any truths the mind is *capable* of knowing in respect of their original: they must all be innate or all adventitious: in vain shall a man go about to distinguish them. He therefore that talks of innate notions in the understanding, cannot (if he intend thereby any distinct sort of truths) mean such truths to be in the understanding as it never perceived, and is yet wholly ignorant of. For if these words "to be in the understanding" have any propriety, they signify to be understood. So that to be in the understanding, and not to be understood; to be in the mind and never to be perceived, is all one as to say anything is and is not in the mind or understanding. If therefore these two propositions, "Whatsoever is, is," and "It is impossible for the same thing to be and not to be," are by nature imprinted, children cannot be ignorant of them: infants, and all that have souls, must necessarily have them in their understandings, know the truth of them, and assent to it. . . .

BOOK II

Chapter I

1. Every man being conscious to himself that he thinks and that which his mind is applied about whilst thinking being the *ideas* that are there, it is past doubt that men have in their minds several ideas,—such as are those expressed by the words *whiteness, hardness, sweetness, thinking, motion, man, elephant, army, drunkenness,* and others: it is in the first place then to be inquired, *How he comes by them?*

I know it is a received doctrine, that men have native ideas, and original characters, stamped upon their minds in their very first being. This opinion I have at large examined already; and, I suppose what I have said in the foregoing Book will be much more easily admitted, when I have shown whence the understanding may get all the ideas it has; and by what ways and degrees they may come into the mind;—for which I shall appeal to every one's own observation and experience.

2. Let us then suppose the mind to be, as we say, white paper, void of all characters, without any ideas:—How comes it to be furnished? Whence comes it by that vast store which the busy and boundless fancy of man has painted on it with an almost endless variety? Whence has it all the *materials* of reason and knowledge? To this I answer, in one word, from EXPERIENCE. In that all our knowledge is founded; and from that it ultimately derives itself. Our observation employed either, about external sensible objects, or about the internal operations of our minds perceived and reflected

on by ourselves, is that which supplies our understandings with all the *materials* of thinking. These two are the fountains of knowledge, from whence all the ideas we have, or can naturally have, do spring.

3. First, our Senses, conversant about particular sensible objects, do convey into the mind several distinct perceptions of things, according to those various ways wherein those objects do affect them. And thus we come by those *ideas* we have of *yellow, white, heat, cold, soft, hard, bitter, sweet,* and all those which we call sensible qualities; which when I say the senses convey into the mind, I mean, they from external objects convey into the mind what produces there those perceptions. This great source of most of the ideas we have, depending wholly upon our senses, and derived by them to the understanding, I call SENSATION.

4. Secondly, the other fountain from which experience furnisheth the understanding with ideas is,—the perception of the operations of our own mind within us, as it is employed about the ideas it has got;—which operations, when the soul comes to reflect on and consider, do furnish the understanding with another set of ideas, which could not be had from things without. And such are *perception, thinking, doubting, believing, reasoning, knowing, willing,* and all the different actings of our own minds;—which we being conscious of, and observing in ourselves, do from these receive into our understandings as distinct ideas as we do from bodies affecting our senses. This source of ideas every man has wholly in himself, and though it be not sense, as having nothing to do with external objects, yet it is very like it, and might properly enough be called *internal sense.* But as I call the other Sensation, so I call this REFLECTION, the ideas it affords being such only as the mind gets by reflecting on its own operations within itself. By reflection then, in the following part of this discourse, I would be understood to mean, that notice which the mind takes of its own operations, and the manner of them, by reason whereof there come to be ideas of these operations in the understanding. These two, I say, viz. external material things, as the objects of SENSATION, and the operations of our own minds within, as the objects of REFLECTION, are to me the only originals from whence all our ideas take their beginnings. The term *operations* here I use in a large sense, as com-

prehending not barely the actions of the mind about its ideas, but some sort of passions arising sometimes from them, such as is the satisfaction or uneasiness arising from any thought.

5. The understanding seems to me not to have the least glimmering of any ideas which it doth not receive from one of these two. *External objects* furnish the mind with the ideas of sensible qualities, which are all those different perceptions they produce in us; and *the mind* furnishes the understanding with ideas of its own operations.

These, when we have taken a full survey of them, and their several modes, combinations, and relations, we shall find to contain all our whole stock of ideas; and that we have nothing in our minds which did not come in one of these two ways. Let any one examine his own thoughts, and thoroughly search into his understanding; and then let him tell me, whether all the original ideas he has there, are any other than of the objects of his senses, or of the operations of his mind, considered as objects of his reflection. And how great a mass of knowledge soever he imagines to be lodged there, he will, upon taking a strict view, see that he has not any idea in his mind but what one of these two have imprinted;—though perhaps, with infinite variety compounded and enlarged by the understanding, as we shall see hereafter.

6. He that attentively considers the state of a child, at his first coming into the world, will have little reason to think him stored with plenty of ideas, that are to be the matter of his future knowledge. It is *by degrees* he comes to be furnished with them. And though the ideas of obvious and familiar qualities imprint themselves before the memory begins to keep a register of time or order, yet it is often so late before some unusual qualities come in the way, that there are few men that cannot recollect the beginning of their acquaintance with them. And if it were worth while, no doubt a child might be so ordered as to have but a very few, even of the ordinary ideas, till he were grown up to a man. But all that are born into the world, being surrounded with bodies that perpetually and diversely affect them, variety of ideas, whether care be taken of it or not, are imprinted on the minds of children. Light and colours are busy at hand everywhere, when the eye is but open; sounds and some tan-

gible qualities fail not to solicit their proper senses, and force an entrance to the mind;—but yet, I think, it will be granted easily, that if a child were kept in a place where he never saw any other but black and white till he were a man, he would have no more ideas of scarlet or green, than he that from his childhood never tasted an oyster, or a pine-apple, has of those particular relishes. . . .

Chapter VIII

. . . 8. Whatsoever the mind perceives *in itself,* or is the immediate object of perception, thought, or understanding, that I call *idea;* and the power to produce any idea in our mind, I call *quality* of the subject wherein that power is. Thus a snowball having the power to produce in us the ideas of white, cold, and round,—the power to produce those ideas in us, as they are in the snowball, I call qualities; and as they are sensations or perceptions in our understandings, I call them ideas; which *ideas,* if I speak of sometimes as in the things themselves, I would be understood to mean those qualities in the objects which produce them in us.

9. Qualities thus considered in bodies are, *First,* such as are utterly inseparable from the body, in what state soever it be; and such as in all the alterations and changes it suffers, all the force can be used upon it, it constantly keeps; and such as sense constantly finds in every particle of matter which has bulk enough to be perceived; and the mind finds inseparable from every particle of matter, though less than to make itself single be perceived by our senses: v.g. Take a grain of wheat, divide it into two parts; each part has still solidity, extension, figure, and mobility: divide it again, and it retains still the same qualities; and so divide it on, till the parts become insensible; they must retain still each of them all those qualities. For division (which is all that a mill, or pestle, or any other body, does upon another, in reducing it to insensible parts) can never take away either solidity, extension, figure, or mobility from any body, but only makes two or more distinct separate masses of matter, of that which was but one before; all which distinct masses, reckoned as so many distinct bodies, after division, make a certain number. These I call *original* or *primary qualities* of body, which I think we may observe to produce simple ideas

in us, viz. solidity, extension, figure, motion or rest, and number.

10. *Secondly,* such qualities which in truth are nothing in the objects themselves but powers to produce various sensations in us by their primary qualities, i.e. by the bulk, figure, texture, and motion of their insensible parts, as colours, sounds, tastes, etc. These I call *secondary qualities.* To these might be added a *third* sort, which are allowed to be barely powers; though they are as much real qualities in the subject as those which I, to comply with the common way of speaking, call qualities, but for distinction, secondary qualities. For the power in fire to produce a new colour, or consistency, in *wax* or *clay,*—by its primary qualities, is as much a quality in fire, as the power it has to produce in *me* a new idea or sensation of warmth or burning, which I felt not before,—by the same primary qualities, viz. the bulk, texture, and motion of its insensible parts. . . .

13. . . . let us suppose at present that the different motions and figures, bulk and number, of such particles, affecting the several organs of our senses, produce in us those different sensations which we have from the colours and smells of bodies; v.g. that a violet, by the impulse of such insensible particles of matter, of peculiar figures and bulks, and in different degrees and modifications of their motions, causes the ideas of the blue colour, and sweet scent of that flower to be produced in our minds. It being no more impossible to conceive that God should annex such ideas to such motions, with which they have no similitude, than that he should annex the idea of pain to the motion of a piece of steel dividing our flesh, with which that idea hath no resemblance.

14. What I have said concerning colours and smells may be understood also of tastes and sounds, and the other like sensible qualities; which, whatever reality we by mistake attribute to them, are in truth nothing in the objects themselves, but powers to produce various sensations in us; and depend on those primary qualities, viz. bulk, figure, texture, and motion of parts as I have said.

15. From whence I think it easy to draw this observation,—that the ideas of primary qualities of bodies are resemblances of them, and their patterns do really exist in the bodies themselves, but the ideas produced in us by these secondary qualities have no resemblance of them at all. There is nothing like our ideas, existing in the bodies themselves. They are, in the bodies we denominate from them, only a power to produce those sensations in us: and what is sweet, blue, or warm in idea, is but the certain bulk, figure, and motion of the insensible parts, in the bodies themselves, which we call so.

16. Flame is denominated hot and light; snow, white and cold; and manna, white and sweet, from the ideas they produce in us. Which qualities are commonly thought to be the same in those bodies that those ideas are in us, the one the perfect resemblance of the other, as they are in a mirror, and it would by most men be judged very extravagant if one should say otherwise. And yet he that will consider that the same fire that, at one distance produces in us the sensation of warmth, does, at a nearer approach, produce in us the far different sensation of pain, ought to bethink himself what reason he has to say—that this idea of warmth, which was produced in him by the fire, is *actually in the fire;* and his idea of pain, which the same fire produced in him the same way, is *not* in the fire. Why are whiteness and coldness in snow, and pain not, when it produces the one and the other idea in us; and can do neither, but by the bulk, figure, number, and motion of its solid parts? . . .

21. Ideas being thus distinguished and understood, we may be able to give an account how the same water, at the same time, may produce the idea of cold by one hand and of heat by the other: whereas it is impossible that the same water, if those ideas were really in it, should at the same time be both hot and cold. For, if we imagine *warmth,* as it is in our hands, to be nothing but a certain sort and degree of motion in the minute particles of our nerves or animal spirits, we may understand how it is possible that the same water may, at the same time, produce the sensations of heat in one hand and cold in the other; which yet *figure* never does, that never producing the idea of a square by one hand which has produced the idea of a globe by another. But if the sensation of heat and cold be nothing but the increase or diminution of the motion of the minute parts of our bodies, caused by the corpuscles of any other body, it is easy to be under-

stood, that if that motion be greater in one hand than in the other; if a body be applied to the two hands, which has in its minute particles a greater motion than in those of one of the hands, and a less than in those of the other, it will increase the motion of the one hand and lessen it in the other; and so cause the different sensations of heat and cold that depend thereon. . . .

8. When children have, by repeated sensations, got ideas fixed in their memories, they begin by degrees to learn the use of signs. And when they have got the skill to apply the organs of speech to the framing of articulate sounds, they begin to make use of words, to signify their ideas to others. These verbal signs they sometimes borrow from others, and sometimes make themselves, as one may observe among the new and unusual names children often give to things in the first use of language.

9. The use of words then being to stand as outward marks of our internal ideas, and those ideas being taken from particular things, if every particular idea that we take in should have a distinct name, names must be endless. To prevent this, the mind makes the particular ideas received from particular objects to become general; which is done by considering them as they are in the mind such appearances,—separate from all other existences, and the circumstances of real existence, as time, place, or any other concomitant ideas. This is called ABSTRACTION, whereby ideas taken from particular beings become general representatives of all of the same kind; and their names general names, applicable to whatever exists conformable to such abstract ideas. Such precise, naked appearances in the mind, without considering how, whence, or with what others they came there, the understanding lays up (with names commonly annexed to them) as the standards to rank real existences into sorts, as they agree with these patterns, and to denominate them accordingly. Thus the same colour being observed to-day in chalk or snow, which the mind yesterday received from milk, it considers that appearance alone, makes it a representative of all of that kind; and having given it the name *whiteness,* it by that sound signifies the same quality wheresoever to be imagined or met with; and thus universals, whether ideas or terms, are made. . . .

BOOK IV

Chapter XI   *Of Our Knowledge of the Existence of Other Things*

1. The knowledge of our own being we have by intuition. The existence of a God, reason clearly makes known to us, as has been shown.

The knowledge of the existence of *any other thing* we can have only by *sensation:* for there being no necessary connexion of real existence with any *idea* a man hath in his memory; nor of any other existence but that of God with the existence of any particular man: no particular man can know the existence of any other being, but only when, by actual operating upon him, it makes itself perceived by him. For, the having the idea of anything in our mind, no more proves the existence of that thing, than the picture of a man evidences his being in the world, or the visions of a dream make thereby a true history.

2. It is therefore the *actual receiving* of ideas from without that gives us notice of the existence of other things, and makes us know, that something doth exist at that time without us, which causes that idea in us; though perhaps we neither know nor consider how it does it. For it takes not from the certainty of our senses, and the ideas we receive by them, that we know not the manner wherein they are produced: v.g. whilst I write this, I have, by the paper affecting my eyes, that idea produced in my mind, which, whatever object causes, I call *white;* by which I know that that quality or accident (i.e. whose appearance before my eyes always causes that idea) doth really exist, and hath a being without me. And of this, the greatest assurance I can possibly have, and to which my faculties can attain, is the testimony of my eyes, which are the proper and sole judges of this thing; whose testimony I have reason to rely on as so certain, that I can no more doubt, whilst I write this, that I see white and black, and that something really exists that causes that sensation in me, than that I write or move my hand; which is a certainty as great as human nature is capable of, concerning the existence of anything, but a man's self alone, and of God.

3. The notice we have by our senses of the existing of things without us, though it be not altogether so cer-

tain as our intuitive knowledge, or the deductions of our reason employed about the clear abstract ideas of our own minds; yet it is an assurance that deserves the name of *knowledge*. If we persuade ourselves that our faculties act and inform us right concerning the existence of those objects that affect them, it cannot pass for an ill-grounded confidence: for I think nobody can, in earnest, be so sceptical as to be uncertain of the existence of those things which he sees and feels. At least, he that can doubt so far (whatever he may have with his own thoughts), will never have any controversy with me; since he can never be sure I say anything contrary to his own opinion. As to myself, I think God has given me assurance enough of the existence of things without me: since, by their different application, I can produce in myself both pleasure and pain, which is one great concernment of my present state. This is certain: the confidence that our faculties do not herein deceive us, is the greatest assurance we are capable of concerning the existence of material beings. For we cannot act anything but by our faculties; nor talk of knowledge itself, but by the help of those faculties which are fitted to apprehend even what knowledge is.

But besides the assurance we have from our senses themselves, that they do not err in the information they give us of the existence of things without us, when they are affected by them, we are further confirmed in this assurance by other concurrent reasons:—

4. I. It is plain those perceptions are produced in us by exterior causes affecting our senses: because those that want the *organs* of any sense, never can have the ideas belonging to that sense produced in their minds. This is too evident to be doubted: and therefore we cannot but be assured that they come in by the organs of that sense, and no other way. The organs themselves, it is plain, do not produce them: for then the eyes of a man in the dark would produce colours, and his nose smell roses in the winter: but we see nobody gets the relish of a pineapple, till he goes to the Indies, where it is, and tastes it.

5. II. Because sometimes I find that *I cannot avoid the having those ideas produced in my mind.* For though, when my eyes are shut, or windows fast, I can at pleasure recall to my mind the ideas of light, or the sun, which former sensations had lodged in my memory; so I can at pleasure lay by *that* idea, and

take into my view that of the smell of a rose, or taste of sugar. But, if I turn my eyes at noon towards the sun, I cannot avoid the ideas which the light or sun then produces in me. So that there is a manifest difference between the ideas laid up in my memory (over which, if they were there only, I should have constantly the same power to dispose of them, and lay them by at pleasure), and those which force themselves upon me, and I cannot avoid having. And therefore it must needs be some exterior cause, and the brisk acting of some objects without me, whose efficacy I cannot resist, that produces those ideas in my mind, whether I will or no. Besides, there is nobody who doth not perceive the difference in himself between contemplating the sun, as he hath the idea of it in his memory, and actually looking upon it: of which two, his perception is so distinct, that few of his ideas are more distinguishable one from another. And therefore he hath certain knowledge that they are not *both* memory, or the actions of his mind, and fancies only within him; but that actual seeing hath a cause without. . . .

Chapter XV   Of Probability

1. As *demonstration* is the showing the agreement or disagreement of two ideas, by the intervention of one or more proofs, which have a constant, immutable, and visible connexion one with another; so *probability* is nothing but the appearance of such an agreement or disagreement, by the intervention of proofs, whose connexion is not constant and immutable, or at least is not perceived to be so, but is, or appears for the most part to be so, and is enough to induce the mind to judge the proposition to be true or false, rather than the contrary. For example: in the demonstration of it a man perceives the certain, immutable connexion there is of equality between the three angles of a triangle, and those intermediate ones which are made use of to show their equality to two right ones; and so, by an intuitive knowledge of the agreement or disagreement of the intermediate ideas in each step of the progress, the whole series is continued with an evidence, which clearly shows the agreement or disagreement of those three angles in equality to two right ones: and thus he has certain

knowledge that it is so. But another man, who never took the pains to observe the demonstration, hearing a mathematician, a man of credit, affirm the three angles of a triangle to be equal to two right ones, assents to it, i.e. receives it for true: in which case the foundation of his assent is the probability of the thing; the proof being such as for the most part carries truth with it: the man on whose testimony he receives it, not being wont to affirm anything contrary to or besides his knowledge, especially in matters of this kind: so that that which causes his assent to this proposition, that the three angles of a triangle are equal to two right ones, that which makes him take these ideas to agree, without knowing them to do so, is the wonted veracity of the speaker in other cases, or his supposed veracity in this.

2. Our knowledge, as has been shown, being very narrow, and we not happy enough to find certain truth in everything which we have occasion to consider; most of the propositions we think, reason, discourse— nay, act upon, are such as we cannot have undoubted knowledge of their truth: yet some of them border so near upon certainty, that we make no doubt at all about them; but assent to them as firmly, and act, according to that assent, as resolutely as if they were infallibly demonstrated, and that our knowledge of them was perfect and certain. But there being degrees herein, from the very neighbourhood of certainty and demonstration, quite down to improbability and unlikeness, even to the confines of impossibility; and also degrees of assent from full assurance and confidence, quite down to conjecture, doubt, and distrust: I shall come now (having, as I think, found out *the bounds of*

human knowledge and certainty), in the next place, to consider *the several degrees and grounds of probability, and assent or faith. . . .*

5. Probability wanting that intuitive evidence which infallibly determines the understanding and produces certain knowledge, the mind, if it *will proceed rationally,* ought to examine all the grounds of probability, and see how they make more or less for or against any proposition, before it assents to or dissents from it; and, upon a due balancing the whole, reject or receive it, with a more or less firm assent, proportionably to the preponderancy of the greater grounds of probability on one side or the other.

FOR FURTHER REFLECTION

1. Has Locke successfully refuted the theory of innate ideas? How does he account for our intuitive certainty of the laws of logic and for the reality of the self—two items that the rationalists consider innate knowledge?
2. Is Lockean empiricism plausible? Are our minds like empty paper until experience writes its message on them? Explain. (Note that Locke is not denying that the mind has capabilities and that some humans can learn more than others.)
3. How does Locke deal with the problems of skepticism regarding sensory experience, which concerns Descartes so much? Is he successful? Why or why not? (Hume disagrees with him, as you will see in a later reading.)

GEORGE BERKELEY

AN IDEALIST THEORY OF KNOWLEDGE

George Berkeley (1685–1753), an Irish philosopher and Anglican bishop, was educated at Trinity College, Dublin, where he subsequently taught. A deeply committed Christian, he sought to reconcile science with his faith, arguing that although matter does not exist, the laws of physics, being God's laws, govern a universe made up of ideas. To exist is to be perceived, and God is that being who, perceiving all things, causes them to exist as ideas in his mind. This position is called *philosophical idealism*. Berkeley's main works are *A Treatise on the Principles of Knowledge* (1710) and *Three Dialogues between Hylas and Philonous* (1713), from which the present selection is taken.

In the following dialogue, Berkeley defends his idealism—that is, the notion that only minds and ideas exist. "To be is to be perceived," is to be an idea in a mind; and hence matter, as existing apart from the mind, does not exist. In this dialogue Hylas (from the Greek word for "matter") debates with Philonous (from the Greek "love of mind"). Unlike traditional idealism (such as Plato's), Berkeley's idealism is not rationalistic. It doesn't assume independently existing ideas; rather, it assumes an empirical foundation. Berkeley agrees with Locke that all ideas originate in sense experience: all we ever experience is ideas, our sensations, or sense perceptions. The only reality to be known is perceivers and perceptions. To hold all this ideal reality together, a divine mind perceives us and hence creates us as ideas in his mind.

THE FIRST DIALOGUE

Philonous: Good morrow, Hylas. I did not expect to find you abroad so early.

Hylas: It is indeed something unusual; but my thoughts were so taken up with a subject I was discoursing of last night, that finding I could not sleep, I resolved to rise and take a turn in the garden.

Phil.: It happened well, to let you see what innocent and agreeable pleasures you lose every morning. Can there be a pleasanter time of the day or a more delightful season of the year? That purple sky, these wild but sweet notes of birds, the fragrant bloom upon the trees and flowers, the gentle influence of the rising sun—these and a thousand nameless beauties of nature inspire the soul with secret transports; its faculties, too, being at this time fresh and lively, are fit for those meditations which the solitude of a garden and tranquility of the morning naturally dispose us to. But I am afraid I interrupt your thoughts, for you seemed very intent on something.

Hyl.: It is true, I was, and shall be obliged to you if you will permit me to go on in the same vein; not that I would by any means deprive myself of your company, for my thoughts always flow more easily in conversation with a friend than when I am alone; but

From George Berkeley, *Three Dialogues between Hylas and Philonous* (1713).

my request is that you would suffer me to impart my reflections to you.

Phil.: With all my heart, it is what I should have requested myself if you had not prevented me.

Hyl.: I was considering the odd fate of those men who have in all ages, through an affectation of being distinguished from the vulgar, or some unaccountable turn of thought, pretended either to believe nothing at all or to believe the most extravagant things in the world. This, however, might be borne if their paradoxes and skepticism did not draw after them some consequences of general disadvantage to mankind. But the mischief lies here: that when men of less leisure see them who are supposed to have spent their whole time in the pursuits of knowledge professing an entire ignorance of all things or advancing such notions as are repugnant to plain and commonly received principles, they will be tempted to entertain suspicions concerning the most important truths, which they had hitherto held sacred and unquestionable.

Phil.: I entirely agree with you as to the ill tendency of the affected doubts of some philosophers and fantastical conceits of others. I am even so far gone of late in this way of thinking that I have quitted several of the sublime notions I had got in their schools for vulgar opinions. And I give it you on my word, since this revolt from metaphysical notions to the plain dictates of nature and common sense, I find my understanding strangely enlightened, so that I can now easily comprehend a great many things which before were all mystery and riddle.

Hyl.: I am glad to find there was nothing in the accounts I heard of you.

Phil.: Pray, what were those?

Hyl.: You were represented in last night's conversation as one who maintained the most extravagant opinion that ever entered into the mind of man, to wit, that there is no such thing as "material substance" in the world.

Phil.: That there is no such thing as what philosophers call "material substance," I am seriously persuaded; but if I were made to see anything absurd or skeptical in this, I should then have the same reason to renounce this that I imagine I have now to reject the contrary opinion.

Hyl.: What! Can anything be more fantastical, more repugnant to common sense or a more manifest piece of skepticism than to believe there is no such thing as matter?

Phil.: Softly, good Hylas. What if it should prove that you, who hold there is, are, by virtue of that opinion, a greater skeptic and maintain more paradoxes and repugnances to common sense than I who believe no such thing?

Hyl.: You may as soon persuade me the part is greater than the whole, as that, in order to avoid absurdity and skepticism, I should ever be obliged to give up my opinion in this point.

Phil.: Well then, are you content to admit that opinion for true which, upon examination, shall appear most agreeable to common sense and remote from skepticism?

Hyl.: With all my heart. Since you are for raising disputes about the plainest things in nature, I am content for once to hear what you have to say.

Phil.: Pray, Hylas, what do you mean by a "skeptic"?

Hyl.: I mean what all men mean, one that doubts of everything.

Phil.: He then who entertains no doubt concerning some particular point, with regard to that point cannot be thought a skeptic.

Hyl.: I agree with you.

Phil.: Whether does doubting consist in embracing the affirmative or negative side of a question?

Hyl.: In neither; for whoever understands English cannot but know that *doubting* signifies a suspense between both.

Phil.: He then that denies any point can no more be said to doubt of it than he who affirms it with the same degree of assurance.

Hyl.: True.

Phil.: And, consequently, for such his denial is no more to be esteemed a skeptic than the other.

Hyl.: I acknowledge it.

Phil.: How comes it to pass then, Hylas, that you pronounce me a skeptic because I deny what you affirm, to wit, the existence of matter? Since, for aught you can tell, I am as peremptory in my denial as you in your affirmation.

Hyl.: Hold, Philonous, I have been a little out in my definition; but every false step a man makes in discourse is not to be insisted on. I said indeed that a "skeptic" was one who doubted of everything, but I should have added: or who denies the reality and truth of things.

Phil.: What things? Do you mean the principles and theorems of sciences? But these you know are universal intellectual notions, and consequently independent of matter; the denial therefore of this does not imply the denying them.

Hyl.: I grant it. But are there no other things? What think you of distrusting the senses, of denying the real existence of sensible things, or pretending to know nothing of them. Is not this sufficient to denominate a man a skeptic?

Phil.: Shall we therefore examine which of us it is that denies the reality of sensible things or professes the greatest ignorance of them, since, if I take you rightly, he is to be esteemed the greatest skeptic?

Hyl.: That is what I desire.

Phil.: What mean you by "sensible things"?

Hyl.: Those things which are perceived by the senses. Can you imagine that I mean anything else?

Phil.: Pardon me, Hylas, if I am desirous clearly to apprehend your notions, since this may much shorten our inquiry. Suffer me then to ask you this further question. Are those things only perceived by the senses which are perceived immediately? Or may those things properly be said to be "sensible" which are perceived mediately, or not without the intervention of others?

Hyl.: I do not sufficiently understand you.

Phil.: In reading a book, what I immediately perceive are the letters, but mediately, or by means of these, are suggested to my mind the notions of God, virtue, truth, etc. Now, that the letters are truly sensible things, or perceived by sense, there is no doubt; but I would know whether you take the things suggested by them to be so too.

Hyl.: No, certainly; it were absurd to think God or virtue sensible things, though they may be signified and suggested to the mind by sensible marks with which they have an arbitrary connection.

Phil.: It seems, then, that by "sensible things" you mean those only which can be perceived immediately by sense.

Hyl.: Right.

Phil.: Does it not follow from this that, though I see one part of the sky red, and another blue, and that my reason does thence evidently conclude there must be some cause of that diversity of colors, yet that cause cannot be said to be a sensible thing or perceived by the sense of seeing?

Hyl.: It does.

Phil.: In like manner, though I hear variety of sounds, yet I cannot be said to hear the causes of those sounds.

Hyl.: You cannot.

Phil.: And when by my touch I perceive a thing to be hot and heavy, I cannot say, with any truth or propriety, that I feel the cause of its heat or weight.

Hyl.: To prevent any more questions of this kind, I tell you once for all that by "sensible things" I mean those only which are perceived by sense, and that in truth the senses perceive nothing which they do not perceive immediately, for they make no inferences. The deducing therefore of causes or occasions from effects and appearances, which alone are perceived by sense, entirely relates to reason.

Phil.: This point then is agreed between us—that *sensible things are those only which are immediately perceived by sense.* You will further inform me whether we immediately perceive by sight anything besides light and colors and figures; or by hearing, anything but sounds; by the palate, anything besides tastes; by the smell, besides odors; or by the touch, more than tangible qualities.

Hyl.: We do not.

Phil.: It seems, therefore, that if you take away all sensible qualities, there remains nothing sensible?

Hyl.: I grant it.

Phil.: Sensible things therefore are nothing else but so many sensible qualities or combinations of sensible qualities?

Hyl.: Nothing else.

Phil.: Heat is then a sensible thing?

Hyl.: Certainly.

Phil.: Does the reality of sensible things consist in being perceived, or is it something distinct from their being perceived, and that bears no relation to the mind?

Hyl.: To *exist* is one thing, and to be *perceived* is another.

Phil.: I speak with regard to sensible things only; and of these I ask, whether by their real existence you mean a subsistence exterior to the mind and distinct from their being perceived?

Hyl.: I mean a real absolute being, distinct from and without any relation to their being perceived.

Phil.: Heat therefore, if it be allowed a real being, must exist without the mind?

Hyl.: It must.

Phil.: Tell me, Hylas, is this real existence equally compatible to all degrees of heat, which we perceive, or is there any reason why we should attribute it to some and deny it to others? And if there be, pray, let me know that reason.

Hyl.: Whatever degree of heat we perceive by sense, we may be sure the same exists in the object that occasions it.

Phil.: What! the greatest as well as the least?

Hyl.: I tell you, the reason is plainly the same in respect of both: they are both perceived by sense; nay, the greater degree of heat is more sensibly perceived; and consequently, if there is any difference, we are more certain of its real existence than we can be of the reality of a lesser degree.

Phil.: But is not the most vehement and intense degree of heat a very great pain?

Hyl.: No one can deny it.

Phil.: And is any unperceiving thing capable of pain or pleasure?

Hyl.: No, certainly.

Phil.: Is your material substance a senseless being or a being endowed with sense and perception?

Hyl.: It is senseless, without doubt.

Phil.: It cannot, therefore, be the subject of pain?

Hyl.: By no means.

Phil.: Nor, consequently, of the greatest heat perceived by sense, since you acknowledge this to be no small pain?

Hyl.: I grant it.

Phil.: What shall we say then of your external object: is it a material substance, or no?

Hyl.: It is a material substance with the sensible qualities inhering in it.

Phil.: How then can a great heat exist in it, since you own it cannot in a material substance? I desire you would clear this point.

Hyl.: Hold, Philonous, I fear I was out in yielding intense heat to be a pain. It should seem rather that pain is something distinct from heat, and the consequence or effect of it.

Phil.: Upon putting your hand near the fire, do you perceive one simple uniform sensation or two distinct sensations?

Hyl.: But one simple sensation.

Phil.: Is not the heat immediately perceived?

Hyl.: It is.

Phil.: And the pain?

Hyl.: True.

Phil.: Seeing therefore they are both immediately perceived at the same time, and the fire affects you only with one simple or uncompounded idea, it follows that this same simple idea is both the intense heat immediately perceived and the pain; and, consequently, that the intense heat immediately perceived is nothing distinct from a particular sort of pain.

Hyl.: It seems so.

Phil.: Again, try in your thoughts, Hylas, if you can conceive a vehement sensation to be without pain or pleasure.

Hyl.: I cannot.

Phil.: Or can you frame to yourself an idea of sensible pain or pleasure, in general, abstracted from every particular idea of heat, cold, tastes, smells, etc.?

Hyl.: I do not find that I can.

Phil.: Does it not therefore follow that sensible pain is nothing distinct from those sensations or ideas—in an intense degree?

Hyl.: It is undeniable; and, to speak the truth, I begin to suspect a very great heat cannot exist but in a mind perceiving it.

Phil.: What! are you then in that *skeptical* state of suspense, between affirming and denying?

Hyl.: I think I may be positive in the point. A very violent and painful heat cannot exist without the mind.

Phil.: It has not therefore, according to you, any real being?

Hyl.: I own it.

Phil.: Is it therefore certain that there is no body in nature really hot?

Hyl.: I have not denied there is any real heat in bodies, I only say there is no such thing as an intense real heat.

Phil.: But did you not say before that all degrees of heat were equally real, or, if there was any difference, that the greater were more undoubtedly real than the lesser?

Hyl.: True; but it was because I did not then consider the ground there is for distinguishing between them, which I now plainly see. And it is this: because intense heat is nothing else but a particular kind of painful sensation, and pain cannot exist but in a perceiving being, it follows that no intense heat can really exist in an unperceiving corporeal substance. But this is no reason why we should deny heat in an inferior degree to exist in such a substance.

Phil.: But how shall we be able to discern those degrees of heat which exist only in the mind from those which exist without it?

Hyl.: That is no difficult matter. You know the least pain cannot exist unperceived; whatever, therefore, degree of heat is a pain exists only in the mind. But as for all other degrees of heat nothing obliges us to think the same of them.

Phil.: I think you granted before that no unperceiving being was capable of pleasure any more than of pain.

Hyl.: I did.

Phil.: And is not warmth, or a more gentle degree of heat than what causes uneasiness, a pleasure?

Hyl.: What then?

Phil.: Consequently, it cannot exist without the mind in an unperceiving substance, or body.

Hyl.: So it seems.

Phil.: Since, therefore, as well those degrees of heat that are not painful, as those that are, can exist only in a thinking substance, may we not conclude that external bodies are absolutely incapable of any degree of heat whatsoever?

Hyl.: On second thoughts, I do not think it is so evident that warmth is a pleasure as that a great degree of heat is pain.

Phil.: I do not pretend that warmth is as great a pleasure as heat is a pain. But if you grant it to be even a small pleasure, it serves to make good my conclusion.

Hyl.: I could rather call it an "indolence." It seems to be nothing more than a privation of both pain and pleasure. And that such a quality or state as this may

agree to an unthinking substance, I hope you will not deny.

Phil.: If you are resolved to maintain that warmth, or a gentle degree of heat, is no pleasure, I know not how to convince you otherwise than by appealing to your own sense. But what think you of cold?

Hyl.: The same that I do of heat. An intense degree of cold is a pain; for to feel a very great cold is to perceive a great uneasiness; it cannot therefore exist without the mind; but a lesser degree of cold may, as well as a lesser degree of heat.

Phil.: Those bodies, therefore, upon whose application to our own we perceive a moderate degree of heat must be concluded to have a moderate degree of heat or warmth in them; and those upon whose application we feel a like degree of cold must be thought to have cold in them.

Hyl.: They must.

Phil.: Can any doctrine be true that necessarily leads a man into an absurdity?

Hyl.: Without doubt it cannot.

Phil.: Is it not an absurdity to think that the same thing should be at the same time both cold and warm?

Hyl.: It is.

Phil.: Suppose now one of your hands is hot, and the other cold, and that they are both at once put into the same vessel of water, in an intermediate state, will not the water seem cold to one hand, and warm to the other?

Hyl.: It will.

Phil.: Ought we not therefore, by your principles, to conclude it is really both cold and warm at the same time, that is, according to your own concession, to believe an absurdity?

Hyl.: I confess it seems so.

Phil.: Consequently, the principles themselves are false, since you have granted that no true principle leads to an absurdity.

Hyl.: But, after all, can anything be more absurd than to say, *there is no heat in the fire?*

Phil.: To make the point still clearer; tell me whether, in two cases exactly alike, we ought not to make the same judgment?

Hyl.: We ought.

Phil.: When a pin pricks your finger, does it not rend and divide the fibres of your flesh?

Hyl.: It does.

Phil.: And when a coal burns your finger, does it any more?

Hyl.: It does not.

Phil.: Since, therefore, you neither judge the sensation itself occasioned by the pin, nor anything like it to be in the pin, you should not, conformably to what you have now granted, judge the sensation occasioned by the fire, or anything like it, to be in the fire.

Hyl.: Well, since it must be so, I am content to yield this point and acknowledge that heat and cold are only sensations existing in our minds. But there still remain qualities enough to secure the reality of external things.

Phil.: But what will you say, Hylas, if it shall appear that the case is the same with regard to all other sensible qualities, and that they can no more be supposed to exist without the mind than heat and cold?

Hyl.: Then, indeed, you will have done something to the purpose; but that is what I despair of seeing proved.

Phil.: Let us examine them in order. What think you of tastes—do they exist without the mind, or no?

Hyl.: Can any man in his senses doubt whether sugar is sweet or wormwood bitter?

Phil.: Inform me, Hylas. Is a sweet taste a particular kind of pleasure or pleasant sensation, or is it not?

Hyl.: It is.

Phil.: And is not bitterness some kind of uneasiness or pain?

Hyl.: I grant it.

Phil.: If therefore, sugar and wormwood are unthinking corporeal substances existing without the mind, how can sweetness and bitterness, that is, pleasure and pain, agree to them?

Hyl.: Hold, Philonous. I now see what it was [that] deluded me all this time. You asked whether heat and cold, sweetness and bitterness, were not particular sorts of pleasure and pain; to which I answered simply that they were. Whereas I should have thus distinguished: those qualities as perceived by us are pleasures or pains, but not as existing in the external objects. We must not therefore conclude absolutely that there is no heat in the fire or sweetness in the

sugar, but only that heat or sweetness, as perceived by us, are not in the fire or sugar. What say you to this?

Phil.: I say it is nothing to the purpose. Our discourse proceeded altogether concerning sensible things, which you defined to be "the things we immediately perceive by our senses." Whatever other qualities, therefore, you speak of, as distinct from these, I know nothing of them, neither do they at all belong to the point in dispute. You may, indeed, pretend to have discovered certain qualities which you do not perceive and assert those insensible qualities exist in fire and sugar. But what use can be made of this to your present purpose, I am at a loss to conceive. Tell me then once more, do you acknowledge that heat and cold, sweetness and bitterness (meaning those qualities which are perceived by the senses), do not exist without the mind?

Hyl.: I see it is to no purpose to hold out, so I give up the cause as to those mentioned qualities, though I profess it sounds oddly to say that sugar is not sweet.

Phil.: But, for your further satisfaction, take this along with you: that which at other times seems sweet shall, to a distempered palate, appear bitter, and nothing can be plainer than that divers persons perceive different tastes in the same food, since that which one man delights in, another abhors. And how could this be if the taste was something really inherent in the food?

Hyl.: I acknowledge I know not how.

Phil.: In the next place, odors are to be considered. And with regard to these I would fain know whether what has been said of tastes does not exactly agree to them? Are they not so many pleasing or displeasing sensations?

Hyl.: They are.

Phil.: Can you then conceive it possible that they should exist in an unperceiving thing?

Hyl.: I cannot.

Phil.: Or can you imagine that filth and ordure affect those brute animals that feed on them out of choice with the same smells which we perceive in them?

Hyl.: By no means.

Phil.: May we not therefore conclude of smells, as of the other forementioned qualities, that they cannot exist in any but a perceiving substance or mind?

Hyl.: I think so.

Phil.: Then as to sounds, what must we think of them, are they accidents really inherent in external bodies or not?

Hyl.: That they inhere not in the sonorous bodies is plain from hence; because a bell struck in the exhausted receiver of an air-pump sends forth no sound. The air, therefore, must be thought the subject of sound.

Phil.: What reason is there for that, Hylas?

Hyl.: Because, when any motion is raised in the air, we perceive a sound greater or less, in proportion to the air's motion; but without some motion in the air we never hear any sound at all.

Phil.: And granting that we never hear a sound but when some motion is produced in the air, yet I do not see how you can infer from thence that the sound itself is in the air.

Hyl.: It is this very motion in the external air that produces in the mind the sensation of sound. For, striking on the drum of the ear, it causes a vibration which by the auditory nerves being communicated to the brain, the soul is thereupon affected with the sensation called "sound."

Phil.: What! is sound then a sensation?

Hyl.: I tell you, as perceived by us it is a particular sensation in the mind.

Phil.: And can any sensation exist without the mind?

Hyl.: No, certainly.

Phil.: How then can sound, being a sensation, exist in the air if by the "air" you mean a senseless substance existing without the mind?

Hyl.: You must distinguish, Philonous, between sound as it is perceived by us, and as it is in itself; or (which is the same thing) between the sound we immediately perceive and that which exists without us. The former, indeed, is a particular kind of sensation, but the latter is merely a vibrative or undulatory motion in the air.

Phil.: I thought I had already obviated that distinction by the answer I gave when you were applying it in a like case before. But, to say no more of that, are you sure then that sound is really nothing but motion?

Hyl.: I am.

Phil.: Whatever, therefore, agrees to real sound may with truth be attributed to motion?

Hyl.: It may.

Phil.: It is then good sense to speak of "motion" as of a thing that is *loud, sweet, acute,* or *grave.*

Hyl.: I see you are resolved not to understand me. Is it not evident those accidents or modes belong only to sensible sound, or sound in the common acceptation of the word, but not to sound in the real and philosophic sense, which, as I just now told you, is nothing but a certain motion of the air?

Phil.: It seems then there are two sorts of sound— the one vulgar, or that which is heard, the other philosophical and real?

Hyl.: Even so.

Phil.: And the latter consists in motion?

Hyl.: I told you so before.

Phil.: Tell me, Hylas, to which of the senses, think you, the idea of motion belongs? To the hearing?

Hyl.: No, certainly; but to the sight and touch.

Phil.: It should follow then that, according to you, real sounds may possibly be *seen* or *felt,* but never *heard.*

Hyl.: Look you, Philonous, you may, if you please, make a jest of my opinion, but that will not alter the truth of things. I own, indeed, the inferences you draw me into sound something oddly, but common language, you know, is framed by, and for the use of, the vulgar. We must not therefore wonder if expressions adapted to exact philosophic notions seem uncouth and out of the way.

Phil.: Is it come to that? I assure you I imagine myself to have gained no small point since you make so light of departing from common phrases and opinions, it being a main part of our inquiry to examine whose notions are widest of the common road and most repugnant to the general sense of the world. But can you think it no more than a philosophical paradox to say that "real sounds are never heard," and that the idea of them is obtained by some other sense? And is there nothing in this contrary to nature and the truth of things?

Hyl.: To deal ingenuously, I do not like it. And, after the concessions already made, I had as well grant that sounds, too, have no real being without the mind.

Phil.: And I hope you will make no difficulty to acknowledge the same of colors.

Hyl.: Pardon me; the case of colors is very different. Can anything be plainer than that we see them on the objects?

Phil.: The objects you speak of are, I suppose, corporeal substances existing without the mind?

Hyl.: They are.

Phil.: And have true and real colors inhering in them?

Hyl.: Each visible object has that color which we see in it.

Phil.: How! is there anything visible but what we perceive by sight?

Hyl.: There is not.

Phil.: And do we perceive anything by sense which we do not perceive immediately?

Hyl.: How often must I be obliged to repeat the same thing? I tell you, we do not.

Phil.: Have patience, good Hylas, and tell me once more whether there is anything immediately perceived by the senses except sensible qualities. I know you asserted there was not; but I would now be informed whether you still persist in the same opinion.

Hyl.: I do.

Phil.: Pray, is your corporeal substance either a sensible quality or made up of sensible qualities?

Hyl.: What a question that is! Who ever thought it was?

Phil.: My reason for asking was, because in saying "each visible object has that color which we see in it," you make visible objects to be corporeal substances, which implies either that corporeal substances are sensible qualities or else that there is something besides sensible qualities perceived by sight; but as this point was formerly agreed between us, and is still maintained by you, it is a clear consequence that your corporeal substance is nothing distinct from sensible qualities.

Hyl.: You may draw as many absurd consequences as you please and endeavor to perplex the plainest things, but you shall never persuade me out of my senses. I clearly understand my own meaning.

Phil.: I wish you would make me understand it, too. But, since you are unwilling to have your notion of corporeal substance examined, I shall urge that

point no further. Only be pleased to let me know whether the same colors which we see exist in external bodies or some other.

Hyl.: The very same.

Phil.: What! are then the beautiful red and purple we see on yonder clouds really in them? Or do you imagine they have in themselves any other form than that of a dark mist of vapor?

Hyl.: I must own, Philonous, those colors are not really in the clouds as they seem to be at this distance. They are only apparent colors.

Phil.: "Apparent" call you them? How shall we distinguish these apparent colors from real?

Hyl.: Very easily. Those are to be thought apparent which, appearing only at a distance, vanish upon a nearer approach.

Phil.: And those, I suppose, are to be thought real which are discovered by the most near and exact survey.

Hyl.: Right.

Phil.: Is the nearest and exactest survey made by the help of a microscope or by the naked eye?

Hyl.: By a microscope, doubtless.

Phil.: But a microscope often discovers colors in an object different from those perceived by the unassisted sight. And, in case we had microscopes magnifying to any assigned degree, it is certain that no object whatsoever, viewed through them, would appear in the same color which it exhibits to the naked eye.

Hyl.: And what will you conclude from all this? You cannot argue that there are really and naturally no colors on objects because by artificial managements they may be altered or made to vanish.

Phil.: I think it may evidently be concluded from your own concessions that all the colors we see with our naked eyes are only apparent as those on the clouds, since they vanish on a more close and accurate inspection which is afforded us by a microscope. Then, as to what you say by way of prevention: I ask you whether the real and natural state of an object is better discovered by a very sharp and piercing sight or by one which is less sharp?

Hyl.: By the former without doubt.

Phil.: Is it not plain from dioptrics that microscopes make the sight more penetrating and represent objects as they would appear to the eye in case it were naturally endowed with a most exquisite sharpness?

Hyl.: It is.

Phil.: Consequently, the microscopical representation is to be thought that which best sets forth the real nature of the thing, or what it is in itself. The colors, therefore, by it perceived are more genuine and real than those perceived otherwise.

Hyl.: I confess there is something in what you say.

Phil.: Besides, it is not only possible but manifest that there actually are animals whose eyes are by nature framed to perceive those things which by reason of their minuteness escape our sight. What think you of those inconceivably small animals perceived by glasses? Must we suppose they are all stark blind? Or, in case they see, can it be imagined their sight has not the same use in preserving their bodies from injuries which appears in that of all other animals? And if it has, is it not evident they must see particles less than their own bodies, which will present them with a far different view in each object from that which strikes our senses? Even our own eyes do not always represent objects to us after the same manner. In the jaundice everyone knows that all things seem yellow. Is it not therefore highly probable those animals in whose eyes we discern a very different texture from that of ours, and whose bodies abound with different humors, do not see the same colors in every object that we do? From all which should it not seem to follow that all colors are equally apparent, and that none of those which we perceive are really inherent in any outward object?

Hyl.: It should.

Phil.: The point will be past all doubt if you consider that, in case colors were real properties or affections inherent in external bodies, they could admit of no alteration without some change wrought in the very bodies themselves; but is it not evident from what has been said that, upon the use of microscopes, upon a change happening in the humors of the eye, or a variation of distance, without any manner of real alteration in the thing itself, the colors of any object are either changed or totally disappear? Nay, all other circumstances remaining the same, change but the situation of some objects and they shall present different colors to the eye. The same thing happens upon viewing an object in various degrees of light. And what is more known than that the same bodies appear differently colored by candlelight from what they do in the open day? Add to these the experiment of a prism which, separating the heterogeneous rays of light alters the color of any object and will cause the whitest to appear of a deep blue or red to the naked eye. And now tell me whether you are still of opinion that every body has its true real color inhering in it; and if you think it has, I would fain know further from you what certain distance and position of the object, what peculiar texture and formation of the eye, what degree or kind of light is necessary for ascertaining that true color and distinguishing it from apparent ones.

Hyl.: I own myself entirely satisfied that they are all equally apparent and that there is no such thing as color really inhering in external bodies, but that it is altogether in the light. And what confirms me in this opinion is that in proportion to the light colors are still more or less vivid; and if there be no light, then are there no colors perceived. Besides, allowing there are colors on external objects, yet, how is it possible for us to perceive them? For no external body affects the mind unless it acts first on our organs of sense. But the only action of bodies is motion, and motion cannot be communicated otherwise than by impulse. A distant object, therefore, cannot act on the eye, nor consequently make itself or its properties perceivable to the soul. Whence it plainly follows that it is immediately some contiguous substance which, operating on the eye, occasions a perception of colors; and such is light.

Phil.: How! is light then a substance?

Hyl.: I tell you, Philonous, external light is nothing but a thin fluid substance whose minute particles, being agitated with a brisk motion and in various manners reflected from the different surfaces of outward objects to the eyes, communicate different motions to the optic nerves; which, being propagated to the brain, cause therein various impressions, and these are attended with the sensations of red, blue, yellow, etc.

Phil.: It seems, then, the light does no more than shake the optic nerves.

Hyl.: Nothing else.

Phil.: And, consequent to each particular motion of the nerves, the mind is affected with a sensation which is some particular color.

Hyl.: Right.

Phil.: And these sensations have no existence without the mind.

Hyl.: They have not.

Phil.: How then do you affirm that colors are in the light, since by "light" you understand a corporeal substance external to the mind?

Hyl.: Light and colors, as immediately perceived by us, I grant cannot exist without the mind. But in themselves they are only the motions and configurations of certain insensible particles of matter.

Phil.: Colors, then, in the vulgar sense, or taken for the immediate objects of sight, cannot agree to any but a perceiving substance.

Hyl.: That is what I say.

Phil.: Well then, since you give up the point as to those sensible qualities which are alone thought colors by all mankind besides, you may hold what you please with regard to those invisible ones of the philosophers. It is not my business to dispute them; only I would advise you to bethink yourself whether, considering the inquiry we are upon, it be prudent for you to affirm—*the red and blue which we see are not real colors, but certain unknown motions and figures which no man ever did or can see are truly so.* Are not these shocking notions, and are not they subject to as many ridiculous inferences as those you were obliged to renounce before in the case of sounds?

Hyl.: I frankly own, Philonous, that it is in vain to stand out any longer. Colors, sounds, tastes, in a word, all those termed "secondary qualities," have certainly no existence without the mind. But by this acknowledgment I must not be supposed to derogate anything from the reality of matter or external objects; seeing it is no more than several philosophers maintain, who nevertheless are the farthest imaginable from denying matter. For the clearer understanding of this you must know sensible qualities are by philosophers divided into "primary" and "secondary." The former are extension, figure, solidity, gravity, motion, and rest. And these they hold exist really in bodies. The latter are those above enumerated, or, briefly, all sensible qualities besides the primary, which they assert are

only so many sensations or ideas existing nowhere but in the mind. But all this, I doubt not, you are already apprised of. For my part I have been a long time sensible there was such an opinion current among philosophers, but was never thoroughly convinced of its truth till now.

Phil.: You are still then of opinion that *extension* and *figures* are inherent in external unthinking substances?

Hyl.: I am.

Phil.: But what if the same arguments which are brought against secondary qualities will hold good against these also?

Hyl.: Why then I shall be obliged to think they too exist only in the mind.

Phil.: Is it your opinion the very figure and extension which you perceive by sense exist in the outward object or material substance?

Hyl.: It is.

Phil.: Have all other animals as good grounds to think the same of the figure and extension which they see and feel?

Hyl.: Without doubt, if they have any thought at all.

Phil.: Answer me, Hylas. Think you the senses were bestowed upon all animals for their preservation and well-being in life? Or were they given to men alone for this end?

Hyl.: I make no question but they have the same use in all other animals.

Phil.: If so, is it not necessary they should be enabled by them to perceive their own limbs and those bodies which are capable of harming them?

Hyl.: Certainly.

Phil.: A mite therefore must be supposed to see his own foot, and things equal or even less than it, as bodies of some considerable dimension, though at the same time they appear to you scarce discernible or at best at so many visible points?

Hyl.: I cannot deny it.

Phil.: And to creatures less than the mite they will seem yet larger?

Hyl.: They will.

Phil.: Insomuch that what you can hardly discern will to another extremely minute animal appear as some huge mountain?

Hyl.: All this I grant.

Phil.: Can one and the same thing be at the same time in itself of different dimensions?

Hyl.: That were absurd to imagine.

Phil.: But from what you have laid down it follows that both the extension by you perceived and that perceived by the mite itself, as likewise all those perceived by lesser animals, are each of them the true extension of the mite's foot; that is to say, by your own principles you are led into an absurdity.

Hyl.: There seems to be some difficulty in the point.

Phil.: Again, have you not acknowledged that no real inherent property of any object can be changed without some change in the thing itself?

Hyl.: I have.

Phil.: But, as we approach to or recede from an object, the visible extension varies, being at one distance ten or a hundred times greater than at another. Does it not therefore follow from hence likewise that it is not really inherent in the object?

Hyl.: I own I am at a loss what to think.

Phil.: Your judgment will soon be determined if you will venture to think as freely concerning this quality as you have done concerning the rest. Was it not admitted as a good argument that neither heat nor cold was in the water because it seemed warm to one hand and cold to the other?

Hyl.: It was.

Phil.: It is not the very same reasoning to conclude there is no extension or figure in an object because to one eye it shall seem little, smooth, and round, when at the same time it appears to the other great, uneven, and angular?

Hyl.: The very same. But does this latter fact ever happen?

Phil.: You may at any time make the experiment by looking with one eye bare and with the other through a microscope.

Hyl.: I know not how to maintain it, and yet I am loath to give up *extension;* I see so many odd consequences following upon such a concession.

Phil.: Odd, say you? After the concessions already made, I hope you will stick at nothing for its oddness. But, on the other hand, should it not seem very odd if the general reasoning which includes all other sensible qualities did not also include extension? If it be allowed that no idea nor anything like an idea can exist in an unperceiving substance, then surely it follows that no figure or mode of extension, which we can either perceive or imagine, or have any idea of, can be really inherent in matter, not to mention the peculiar difficulty there must be in conceiving a material substance, prior to and distinct from extension, to be the *substratum* of extension. Be the sensible quality what it will—figure or sound or color—it seems alike impossible it should subsist in that which does not perceive it.

Hyl.: I give up the point for the present, reserving still a right to retract my opinion in case I shall hereafter discover any false step in my progress to it.

Phil.: That is a right you cannot be denied. Figures and extension being dispatched, we proceed next to *motion.* Can a real motion in any external body be at the same time both very swift and very slow?

Hyl.: It cannot.

Phil.: Is not the motion of a body swift in a reciprocal proportion to the time it takes up in describing any given space? Thus a body that describes a mile in an hour moves three times faster than it would in case it described only a mile in three hours.

Hyl.: I agree with you.

Phil.: And is not time measured by the succession of ideas in our minds?

Hyl.: It is.

Phil.: And is it not possible ideas should succeed one another twice as fast in your mind as they do in mine, or in that of some spirit of another kind?

Hyl.: I own it.

Phil.: Consequently, the same body may to another seem to perform its motion over any space in half the time that it does to you. And the same reasoning will hold as to any other proportion; that is to say, according to your principles (since the motions perceived are both really in the object) it is possible one and the same body shall be really moved the same way at once, both very swift and very slow. How is this consistent with common sense or with what you just now granted?

Hyl.: I have nothing to say to it.

Phil.: Then as for *solidity;* either you do not mean any sensible quality by that word, and so it is beside our inquiry; or if you do, it must be either hardness or resistance. But both the one and the other are plainly relative to our senses: it being evident that what seems hard to one animal may appear soft to another who has greater force and firmness of limbs. Nor is it less plain that the resistance I feel is not in the body.

Hyl.: I own the very sensation of resistance, which is all you immediately perceive, is not in the *body,* but the cause of that sensation is.

Phil.: But the causes of our sensations are not things immediately perceived, and therefore not sensible. This point I thought had been already determined.

Hyl.: I own it was; but you will pardon me if I seem a little embarrassed; I know not how to quit my old notions.

Phil.: To help you out, do but consider that if *extension* be once acknowledged to have no existence without the mind, the same must necessarily be granted of motion, solidity, and gravity, since they all evidently suppose extension. It is therefore superfluous to inquire particularly concerning each of them. In denying extension, you have denied them all to have any real existence.

Hyl.: I wonder, Philonous, if what you say be true, why those philosophers who deny the secondary qualities any real existence should yet attribute it to the primary. If there is no difference between them, how can this be accounted for?

Phil.: It is not my business to account for every opinion of the philosophers. But, among other reasons which may be assigned for this, it seems probable that pleasure and pain being rather annexed to the former than the latter may be one. Heat and cold, tastes and smells have something more vividly pleasing or disagreeable than the ideas of extension, figure, and motion affect us with. And, it being too visibly absurd to hold that pain or pleasure can be in an unperceiving substance, men are more easily weaned from believing the external existence of the secondary than the primary qualities. You will be satisfied there is something in this if you recollect the difference you made between an intense and more moderate degree of heat, allowing the one a real existence while you denied it to the other. But, after all, there is no rational ground for that distinction, for surely an indif-

ferent sensation is as truly a *sensation* as one more pleasing or painful, and consequently should not any more than they be supposed to exist in an unthinking subject.

Hyl.: It is just come into my head, Philonous, that I have somewhere heard of a distinction between *absolute* and *sensible* extension. Now though it be acknowledged that *great* and *small,* consisting merely in the relation which other extended beings have to the parts of our own bodies, do not really inhere in the substances themselves, yet nothing obliges us to hold the same with regard to *absolute* extension, which is something abstracted from *great* and *small,* from this or that particular magnitude or figure. So likewise as to motion: *swift* and *slow* are altogether relative to the succession of ideas in our own minds. But it does not follow, because those modifications of motion exist not without the mind, that therefore absolute motion abstracted from them does not.

Phil.: Pray what is it that distinguishes one motion, or one part of extension, from another? Is it not something sensible, as some degree of swiftness or slowness, some certain magnitude or figure peculiar to each?

Hyl.: I think so.

Phil.: These qualities, therefore, stripped of all sensible properties, are without all specific and numerical differences, as the schools call them.

Hyl.: They are.

Phil.: That is to say, they are extension in general, and motion in general.

Hyl.: Let it be so.

Phil.: But it is a universally received maxim that *everything which exists is particular.* How then can motion in general, or extension in general, exist in any corporeal substance?

Hyl.: I will take time to solve your difficulty.

Phil.: But I think the point may be speedily decided. Without doubt you can tell whether you are able to frame this or that idea. Now I am content to put our dispute on this issue. If you can frame in your thoughts a distinct abstract idea of motion or extension divested of all those sensible modes as swift and slow, great and small, round and square, and the like, which are acknowledged to exist only in the mind, I will then yield the point you contend for. But if you *cannot,* it will be unreasonable on your side to insist any longer upon what you have no notion of.

Hyl.: To confess ingenuously, I cannot.

Phil.: Can you even separate the ideas of extension and motion from the ideas of all those qualities which they who make the distinction term "secondary"?

Hyl.: What! is it not an easy matter to consider extension and motion by themselves, abstracted from all other sensible qualities? Pray how do the mathematicians treat of them?

Phil.: I acknowledge, Hylas, it is not difficult to form general propositions and reasonings about those qualities without mentioning any other, and, in this sense, to consider or treat of them abstractedly. But how does it follow that, because I can pronounce the word "motion" by itself, I can form the idea of it in my mind exclusive of body? Or because theorems may be made of extension and figures, without any mention of *great* or *small,* or any other sensible mode or quality, that therefore it is possible such an abstract idea of extension, without any particular size or figure or sensible quality, should be distinctly formed and apprehended by the mind? Mathematicians treat of quantity without regarding what other sensible qualities it is attended with, as being altogether indifferent to their demonstrations. But when, laying aside the words, they contemplate the bare ideas, I believe you will find they are not the pure abstracted ideas of extension.

Hyl.: But what say you to *pure intellect?* May not abstracted ideas be framed by that faculty?

Phil.: Since I cannot frame abstract ideas at all, it is plain I cannot frame them by the help of pure intellect, whatsoever faculty you understand by those words. Besides, not to inquire into the nature of pure intellect and its spiritual objects, as *virtue, reason, God,* or the like, thus much seems manifest that sensible things are only to be perceived by sense or represented by the imagination. Figures, therefore, and extension, being originally perceived by sense, do not belong to pure intellect; but, for your further satisfaction, try if you can frame the idea of any figure abstracted from all particularities of size or even from other sensible qualities.

Hyl.: Let me think a little—I do not find that I can.

Phil.: And can you think it possible that [an idea] should really exist in nature which implies a repugnancy in its conception?

Hyl.: By no means.

Phil.: Since therefore it is impossible even for the mind to disunite the ideas of extension and motion from all other sensible qualities, does it not follow that where the one exist there necessarily the other exist likewise?

Hyl.: It should seem so.

Phil.: Consequently, the very same arguments which you admitted as conclusive against the secondary qualities are, without any further application of force, against the primary, too. Besides, if you will trust your senses, is it not plain all sensible qualities coexist, or to them appear as being in the same place? Do they ever represent a motion or figure as being divested of all other visible and tangible qualities?

Hyl.: You need say no more on this head. I am free to own, if there be no secret error or oversight in our proceedings hitherto, that all sensible qualities are alike to be denied existence without the mind. But my fear is that I have been too liberal in my former concessions, or overlooked some fallacy or other. In short, I did not take time to think.

Phil.: For that matter, Hylas, you may take what time you please in reviewing the progress of our inquiry. You are at liberty to recover any slips you might have made, or offer whatever you have omitted which makes for your first opinion.

Hyl.: One great oversight I take to be this—that I did not sufficiently distinguish the *object* from the *sensation.* Now, though this latter may not exist without the mind, yet it will not thence follow that the former cannot.

Phil.: What object do you mean? The object of the senses?

Hyl.: The same.

Phil.: It is then immediately perceived?

Hyl.: Right.

Phil.: Make me to understand the difference between what is immediately perceived and a sensation.

Hyl.: The sensation I take to be an act of the mind perceiving; besides which there is something perceived, and this I call the "object." For example, there is red and yellow on that tulip. But then the act of perceiving those colors is in me only, and not in the tulip.

Phil.: What tulip do you speak of? Is it that which you see?

Hyl.: The same.

Phil.: And what do you see besides color, figure, and extension?

Hyl.: Nothing.

Phil.: What you would say then is that the red and yellow are coexistent with the extension; is it not?

Hyl.: That is not all; I would say they have a real existence without the mind, in some unthinking substance.

Phil.: That the colors are really in the tulip which I see is manifest. Neither can it be denied that this tulip may exist independent of your mind or mine; but that any immediate object of the senses—that is, any idea, or combination of ideas—should exist in an unthinking substance, or exterior to all minds, is in itself an evident contradiction. Nor can I imagine how this follows from what you said just now, to wit, that the red and yellow were on the tulip *you saw,* since you do not pretend to *see* that unthinking substance.

Hyl.: You have an artful way, Philonous, of diverting our inquiry from the subject.

Phil.: I see you have no mind to be pressed that way. To return then to your distinction between *sensation* and *object;* if I take you right, you distinguish in every perception two things, the one an action of the mind, the other not.

Hyl.: True.

Phil.: And this action cannot exist in, or belong to, any unthinking thing, but whatever besides is implied in a perception may?

Hyl.: That is my meaning.

Phil.: So that if there was a perception without any act of the mind, it were possible such a perception should exist in an unthinking substance?

Hyl.: I grant it. But it is impossible there should be such a perception.

Phil.: When is the mind said to be active?

Hyl.: When it produces, puts an end to, or changes anything.

Phil.: Can the mind produce, discontinue, or change anything but by an act of the will?

Hyl.: It cannot.

Phil.: The mind therefore is to be accounted *active* in its perceptions so far forth as *volition* is included in them?

Hyl.: It is.

Phil.: In plucking this flower I am active, because I do it by the motion of my hand, which was consequently upon my volition; so likewise in applying it to my nose. But is either of these smelling?

Hyl.: No.

Phil.: I act, too, in drawing the air through my nose, because my breathing so rather than otherwise is the effect of my volition. But neither can this be called "smelling," for if it were I should smell every time I breathed in that manner?

Phil.: Smelling then is somewhat consequent to all this?

Hyl.: It is.

Phil.: But I do not find my will concerned any further. Whatever more there is—as that I perceive such a particular smell, or any smell at all—this is independent of my will, and therein I am altogether passive. Do you find it otherwise with you, Hylas?

Hyl.: No, the very same.

Phil.: Then, as to seeing, is it not in your power to open your eyes or keep them shut, to turn them this or that way?

Hyl.: Without doubt.

Phil.: But does it in like manner depend on your will that in looking on this flower you perceive *white* rather than any other color? Or, directing your open eyes toward yonder part of the heaven, can you avoid seeing the sun? Or is light or darkness the effect of your volition?

Hyl.: No, certainly.

Phil.: You are then in these respects altogether passive?

Hyl.: I am.

Phil.: Tell me now whether *seeing* consists in perceiving light and colors or in opening and turning the eyes?

Hyl.: Without doubt, in the former.

Phil.: Since, therefore, you are in the very perception of light and colors altogether passive, what is become of that action you were speaking of as an ingredient in every sensation? And does it not follow from your own concessions that the perception of light and colors, including no action in it, may exist in an unperceiving substance? And is not this a plain contradiction?

Hyl.: I know not what to think of it.

Phil.: Besides, since you distinguish the *active* and *passive* in every perception, you must do it in that of pain. But how is it possible that pain, be it as little active as you please, should exist in an unperceiving substance? In short, do but consider the point and then confess ingenuously whether light and colors, tastes, sounds, etc., are not all equally passions or sensations in the soul. You may indeed call them "external objects" and give them in words what subsistence you please. But examine your own thoughts and then tell me whether it be not as I say?

Hyl.: I acknowledge, Philonous, that, upon a fair observation of what passes in my mind, I can discover nothing else but that I am a thinking being affected with variety of sensations; neither is it possible to conceive how a sensation should exist in an unperceiving substance. But then, on the other hand, when I look on sensible things in a different view, considering them as so many modes and qualities, I find it necessary to suppose a material *substratum,* without which they cannot be conceived to exist.

Phil.: "Material substratum" call you it? Pray, by which of your senses came you acquainted with that being?

Hyl.: It is not itself sensible; its modes and qualities only being perceived by the senses.

Phil.: I presume then it was by reflection and reason you obtained the idea of it?

Hyl.: I do not pretend to any proper positive idea of it. However, I conclude it exists because qualities cannot be conceived to exist without a support.

Phil.: It seems then you have only a relative notion of it, or that you conceive it not otherwise than by conceiving the relation it bears to sensible qualities?

Hyl.: Right.

Phil.: Be pleased, therefore, to let me know wherein that relation consists.

Hyl.: Is it not sufficiently expressed in the term "substratum" or "substance"?

Phil.: If so, the word "substratum" should import that it is spread under the sensible qualities or accidents?

Hyl.: True.

Phil.: And consequently under extension?

Hyl.: I own it.

Phil.: It is therefore somewhat in its own nature distinct from extension?

Hyl.: I tell you extension is only a mode, and matter is something that supports modes. And is it not evident the thing supported is different from the thing supporting?

Phil.: So that something distinct from, and exclusive of, extension is supposed to be the *substratum* of extension?

Hyl.: Just so.

Phil.: Answer me, Hylas, can a thing be spread without extension, or is not the idea of extension necessarily included in *spreading?*

Hyl.: It is.

Phil.: Whatsoever therefore you suppose spread under anything must have in itself an extension distinct from the extension of that thing under which it is spread?

Hyl.: It must.

Phil.: Consequently, every corporeal substance being the *substratum* of extension must have in itself another extension by which it is qualified to be a *substratum,* and so on to infinity? And I ask whether this be not absurd in itself and repugnant to what you granted just now, to wit, that the *substratum* was something distinct from and exclusive of extension?

Hyl.: Aye, but, Philonous, you take me wrong. I do not mean that matter is *spread* in a gross literal sense under extension. The word "substratum" is used only to express in general the same thing with "substance."

Phil.: Well then, let us examine the relation implied in the term "substance." Is it not that it stands under accidents?

Hyl.: The very same.

Phil.: But that one thing may stand under or support another, must it not be extended?

Hyl.: It must.

Phil.: Is not therefore this supposition liable to the same absurdity with the former?

Hyl.: You still take things in a strict literal sense; that is not fair, Philonous.

Phil.: I am not for imposing any sense on your words; you are at liberty to explain them as you please. Only, I beseech you, make me understand something by them. You tell me matter supports or stands under accidents. How! is it as your legs support your body?

Hyl.: No; that is the literal sense.

Phil.: Pray let me know any sense, literal or not literal, that you understand it in.—How long must I wait for an answer, Hylas?

Hyl.: I declare I know not what to say. I once thought I understood well enough what was meant by matter's supporting accidents. But now, the more I think on it, the less can I comprehend it; in short, I find that I know nothing of it.

Phil.: It seems then you have no idea at all, neither relative nor positive, of matter? you know neither what it is in itself nor what relation it bears to accidents?

Hyl.: I acknowledge it.

Phil.: And yet you asserted that you could not conceive how qualities or accidents should really exist without conceiving at the same time a material support of them?

Hyl.: I did.

Phil.: That is to say, when you conceive the real existence of qualities, you do withal conceive something which you cannot conceive?

Hyl.: It was wrong I own. But still I fear there is some fallacy or other. Pray, what think you of this? It is just come into my head that the ground of all our mistake lies in your treating of each quality by itself. Now I grant that each quality cannot singly subsist without the mind. Color cannot without extension, neither can figure without some other sensible quality. But, as the several qualities united or blended together form entire sensible things, nothing hinders why such things may not be supposed to exist without the mind.

Phil.: Either, Hylas, you are jesting or have a very bad memory. Though, indeed, we went through all the qualities by name one after another, yet my arguments, or rather your concessions, nowhere tended to prove that the secondary qualities did not subsist each alone by itself, but that they were not *at all* without the mind. Indeed, in treating of figure and motion we concluded they could not exist without the mind, because it was impossible even in thought to separate them

from all secondary qualities, so as to conceive them existing by themselves. But then this was not the only argument made use of upon that occasion. But (to pass by all that has been hitherto said and reckon it for nothing, if you will have it so) I am content to put the whole upon this issue. If you can conceive it possible for any mixture or combination of qualities, or any sensible object whatever, to exist without the mind, then I will grant it actually to be so.

Hyl.: If it comes to that the point will soon be decided. What more easy than to conceive a tree or house existing by itself, independent of, and unperceived by, any mind whatsoever? I do at this present time conceive them existing after that manner.

Phil.: How say you, Hylas, can you see a thing which is at the same time unseen?

Hyl.: No, that were a contradiction.

Phil.: Is it not as great a contradiction to talk of *conceiving* a thing which is *unconceived?*

Hyl.: It is.

Phil.: The tree or house, therefore, which you think of is conceived by you?

Hyl.: How should it be otherwise?

Phil.: And what is conceived is surely in the mind?

Hyl.: Without question, that which is conceived is in the mind.

Phil.: How then came you to say you conceived a house or tree existing independent and out of all minds whatsoever?

Hyl.: That was I own an oversight, but stay, let me consider what let me into it.—It is a pleasant mistake enough. As I was thinking of a tree in a solitary place where no one was present to see it, methought that was to conceive a tree as existing unperceived or unthought of, not considering that I myself conceived it all the while. But now I plainly see that all I can do is to frame ideas in my own mind. I may indeed conceive in my own thoughts the idea of a tree, or a house, or a mountain, but that is all. And this is far from proving that I can conceive them *existing out of the minds of all spirits.*

Phil.: You acknowledge then that you cannot possibly conceive how any one corporeal sensible thing should exist otherwise than in a mind?

Hyl.: I do.

Phil.: And yet you will earnestly contend for the truth of that which you cannot so much as conceive?

Hyl.: I profess I know not what to think; but still there are some scruples remain with me. Is it not certain I see things at a distance? Do we not perceive the stars and moon, for example, to be a great way off? Is not this, I say, manifest to the senses?

Phil.: Do you not in a dream, too, perceive those or the like objects?

Hyl.: I do.

Phil.: And have they not then the same appearance of being distant?

Hyl.: They have.

Phil.: But you do not thence conclude the apparitions in a dream to be without the mind?

Hyl.: By no means.

Phil.: You ought not therefore to conclude that sensible objects are without the mind, from their appearance or manner wherein they are perceived.

Hyl.: I acknowledge it. But does not my sense deceive me in those cases?

Phil.: By no means. The idea or thing which you immediately perceive, neither sense nor reason informs you that it actually exists without the mind. By sense you only know that you are affected with such certain sensations of light and colors, etc. And these you will not say are without the mind.

Hyl.: True, but, besides all that, do you not think the sight suggests something of *outness* or *distance?*

Phil.: Upon approaching a distant object, do the visible size and figure change perpetually or do they appear the same at all distances?

Hyl.: They are in a continual change.

Phil.: Sight, therefore, does not suggest or any way inform you that the visible object you immediately perceive exists at a distance, or will be perceived when you advance farther onward, there being a continued series of visible objects succeeding each other during the whole time of your approach.

Hyl.: It does not; but still I know, upon seeing an object, what object I shall perceive after having passed over a certain distance? no matter whether it be exactly the same or no, there is still something of distance suggested in the case.

Phil.: Good Hylas, do but reflect a little on the point, and then tell me whether there be any more in it than this. From the ideas you actually perceive by sight, you have by experience learned to collect what other ideas you will (according to the standing order of nature) be affected with, after such a certain succession of time and motion.

Hyl.: Upon the whole, I take it to be nothing else.

Phil.: Now is it not plain that if we suppose a man born blind was on a sudden made to see, he could at first have no experience of what may be suggested by sight?

Hyl.: It is.

Phil.: He would not then, according to you, have any notion of distance annexed to the things he saw, but would take them for a new set of sensations existing only in his mind?

Hyl.: It is undeniable.

Phil.: But to make it more plain: is not *distance* a line turned endwise to the eye?

Hyl.: It is.

Phil.: And can a line so situated be perceived by sight?

Hyl.: It cannot.

Phil.: Does it not therefore follow that distance is not properly and immediately perceived by sight?

Hyl.: It should seem so.

Phil.: Again, is it your opinion that colors are at a distance?

Hyl.: It must be acknowledged they are only in the mind.

Phil.: But do not colors appear to the eye as coexisting in the same place with extension and figures?

Hyl.: They do.

Phil.: How can you then conclude from sight that figures exist without, when you acknowledge colors do not; the sensible appearances being the very same with regard to both?

Hyl.: I know not what to answer.

Phil.: But allowing that distance was truly and immediately perceived by the mind, yet it would not thence follow it existed out of the mind. For whatever is immediately perceived is an idea; and can any *idea* exist out of the mind?

Hyl.: To suppose that were absurd; but, inform me, Philonous, can we perceive or know nothing besides our ideas?

Phil.: As for the rational deducing of causes from effects, that is beside our inquiry. And by the senses you can best tell whether you perceive anything which is not immediately perceived. And I ask you whether the things immediately perceived are other than your own sensations or ideas? You have indeed more than once, in the course of this conversation, declared yourself on those points, but you seem, by this last question, to have departed from what you then thought.

Hyl.: To speak the truth, Philonous, I think there are two kinds of objects: the one perceived immediately, which are likewise called "ideas"; the other are real things or external objects, perceived by the mediation of ideas which are their images and representations. Now I own ideas do not exist without the mind, but the latter sort of objects do. I am sorry I did not think of this distinction sooner; it would probably have cut short your discourse.

Phil.: Are those external objects perceived by sense or by some other faculty?

Hyl.: They are perceived by sense.

Phil.: How! is there anything perceived by sense which is not immediately perceived?

Hyl.: Yes, Philonous, in some sort there is. For example, when I look on a picture or statue of Julius Caesar, I may be said, after a manner, to perceive him (though not immediately) by my senses.

Phil.: It seems then you will have our ideas, which alone are immediately perceived, to be pictures of external things: and that these also are perceived by sense inasmuch as they have a conformity or resemblance to our ideas?

Hyl.: That is my meaning.

Phil.: And in the same way that Julius Caesar, in himself invisible, is nevertheless perceived by sight, real things, in themselves imperceptible, are perceived by sense.

Hyl.: In the very same.

Phil.: Tell me, Hylas, when you behold the picture of Julius Caesar, do you see with your eyes any more than some colors and figures, with a certain symmetry and composition of the whole?

Hyl.: Nothing else.

Phil.: And would not a man who had never known anything of Julius Caesar see as much?

Hyl.: He would.

Phil.: Consequently, he has his sight and the use of it in as perfect a degree as you?

Hyl.: I agree with you.

Phil.: Whence comes it then that your thoughts are directed to the Roman emperor, and his are not? This cannot proceed from the sensations or ideas of sense by you then perceived, since you acknowledge you have no advantage over him in that respect. It should seem therefore to proceed from reason and memory, should it not?

Hyl.: It should.

Phil.: Consequently, it will not follow from that instance that anything is perceived by sense which is not immediately perceived. Though I grant we may, in one acceptation, be said to perceive sensible things mediately by sense—that is, when, from a frequently perceived connection, the immediate perception of ideas by one sense suggest to the mind others, perhaps belonging to another sense, which are wont to be connected with them. For instance, when I hear a coach drive along the streets, immediately I perceive only the sound; but from the experience I have had that such a sound is connected with a coach, I am said to hear the coach. It is nevertheless evident that, in truth and strictness, nothing can be *heard* but *sound;* and the coach is not then properly perceived by sense, but suggested from experience. So likewise when we are said to see a red-hot bar of iron; the solidity and heat of the iron are not the objects of sight, but suggested to the imagination by the color and figure which are properly perceived by that sense. In short, those things alone are actually and strictly perceived by any sense which would have been perceived in case that same sense had then been first conferred on us. As for other things, it is plain they are only suggested to the mind by experience grounded on former perceptions. But, to return to your comparison of Caesar's picture, it is plain, if you keep to that, you must hold the real things or archetypes of our ideas are not perceived by sense, but by some internal faculty of the soul, as reason or memory. I would, therefore, fain know what arguments you can draw from reason for the existence of what you call "real things" or "material objects," or whether you remember to have seen them formerly as they are in themselves, or if you have heard or read of anyone that did.

Hyl.: Philonous, you are disposed to railery; but that will never convince me.

Phil.: My aim is only to learn from you the way to come at the knowledge of "material beings." Whatever we perceive is perceived either immedi-ately or mediately—by sense, or by reason and reflection. But, as you have excluded sense, pray show me what reason you have to believe their existence, or what *medium* you can possibly make use of to prove it, either to mine or your own understanding.

Hyl.: To deal ingenuously, Philonous, now [that] I consider the point, I do not find I can give you any good reason for it. But this much seems pretty plain, that it is at least possible such things may really exist. And as long as there is no absurdity in supposing them, I am resolved to believe as I did, till you bring good reasons to the contrary.

Phil.: What! is it come to this, that you only believe the existence of material objects, and that your belief is founded barely on the possibility of its being true? Then you will have me bring reasons against it, though another would think it reasonable the proof should lie on him who holds the affirmative. And, after all, this very point which you are now resolved to maintain, without any reason, is in effect what you have more than once during this discourse seen good reason to give up. But to pass over all this—if I understand you rightly, you say our ideas do not exist without the mind, but that they are copies, images, or representations of certain originals that do?

Hyl.: You take me right.

Phil.: They are then like external things?

Hyl.: They are.

Phil.: Have those things a stable and permanent nature, independent of our senses, or are they in a perpetual change, upon our producing any motions in our bodies, suspending, exerting, or altering our faculties or organs of sense?

Hyl.: Real things, it is plain, have a fixed and real nature, which remains the same notwithstanding any change in our senses or in the posture and motion of our bodies; which indeed may affect the ideas in our minds, but it were absurd to think they had the same effect on things existing without the mind.

Phil.: How then is it possible that things perpetually fleeting and variable as our ideas should be copies or images of anything fixed and constant? Or, in other words, since all sensible qualities, as size, figure, color, etc., that is, our ideas, are continually changing upon every alteration in the distance, medium, or instruments of sensation—how can any determinate material objects be properly represented or painted forth by several distinct things each of which is so different from and unlike the rest? Or, if you say it resembles some one only of our ideas, how shall we be able to distinguish the true copy from all the false ones?

Hyl.: I profess, Philonous, I am at a loss. I know not what to say to this.

Phil.: But neither is this all. Which are material objects in themselves—perceptible or imperceptible?

Hyl.: Properly and immediately nothing can be perceived but ideas. All material things, therefore, are in themselves insensible and to be perceived only by their ideas.

Phil.: Ideas then are sensible, and their archetypes or originals insensible?

Hyl.: Right.

Phil.: But how can that which is sensible be like that which is insensible? Can a real thing, in itself *invisible,* be like a *color,* or a real thing which is not *audible* be like a *sound?* In a word, can anything be like a sensation or idea, but another sensation or idea?

Hyl.: I must own, I think not.

Phil.: Is it possible there should be any doubt on the point? Do you not perfectly know your own ideas?

Hyl.: I know them perfectly, since what I do not perceive or know can be no part of my idea.

Phil.: Consider, therefore, and examine them, and then tell me if there be anything in them which can exist without the mind, or if you can conceive anything like them existing without the mind?

Hyl.: Upon inquiry I find it impossible for me to conceive or understand how anything but an idea can be like an idea. And it is most evident that *no idea can exist without the mind.*

Phil.: You are, therefore, by your principles forced to deny the reality of sensible things, since you made it to consist in an absolute existence exterior to the mind. That is to say, you are a downright skeptic. So I have gained my point, which was to show your principles led to skepticism.

Hyl.: For the present I am, if not entirely convinced, at least silenced.

Phil.: I would fain know what more you would require in order to obtain a perfect conviction. Have you not had the liberty of explaining yourself all manner of ways? Were any little slips in discourse laid hold and insisted on? Or were you not allowed to retract or reinforce anything you had offered, as best served your purpose? Has not everything you could say been heard and examined with all the fairness imaginable? In a word, have you not in every point been convinced out of your own mouth? And, if you can at present discover any flaw in any of your former concessions, or think of any remaining subterfuge, any new distinction, color, or comment whatsoever, why do you not produce it?

Hyl.: A little patience, Philonous. I am at present so amazed to see myself ensnared, and as it were imprisoned in the labyrinths you have drawn me into, that on the sudden it cannot be expected I should find my way out. You must give me time to look about me and recollect myself.

Phil.: Hark; is not this the college bell?

Hyl.: It rings for prayers.

Phil.: We will go in then, if you please, and meet here again tomorrow morning. In the meantime, you may employ your thoughts on this morning's discourse and try if you can find any fallacy in it, or invent any new means to extricate yourself.

Hyl.: Agreed.

THE SECOND DIALOGUE

Hylas: I beg your pardon, Philonous, for not meeting you sooner. All this morning my head was so filled with our late conversation that I had not leisure to think of the time of the day, or indeed of anything else.

Philonous: I am glad you were so intent upon it, in hopes if there were any mistakes in your concessions, or fallacies in my reasonings from them, you will now discover them to me.

Hyl.: I assure you I have done nothing ever since I saw you but search after mistakes and fallacies, and, with that [in] view, have minutely examined the whole series of yesterday's discourse; but all in vain, for the

notions it led me into, upon review, appear still more clear and evident; and the more I consider them, the more irresistibly do they force my assent.

Phil.: And is not this, think you, a sign that they are genuine, that they proceed from nature and are conformable to right reason? Truth and beauty are in this alike, that the strictest survey sets them both off to advantage, while the false luster of error and disguise cannot endure being reviewed or too nearly inspected.

Hyl.: I own there is a great deal in what you say. Nor can anyone be more entirely satisfied of the truth of those odd consequences so long as I have in view the reasonings that lead to them. But when these are out of my thoughts, there seems, on the other hand, something so satisfactory, so natural and intelligible in the modern way of explaining things that I profess I know not how to reject it.

Phil.: I know not what you mean.

Hyl.: I mean the way of accounting for our sensations or ideas.

Phil.: How is that?

Hyl.: It is supposed the soul makes her residence in some part of the brain, from which the nerves take their rise, and are thence extended to all parts of the body; and that outward objects, by the different impressions they make on the organs of sense, communicate certain vibrative motions to the nerves, and these, being filled with spirits, propagate them to the brain or seat of the soul, which, according to the various impressions or traces thereby made in the brain, is variously affected with ideas.

Phil.: And call you this an explication of the manner whereby we are affected with ideas?

Hyl.: Why not, Philonous; have you anything to object against it?

Phil.: I would first know whether I rightly understand your hypothesis. You make certain traces in the brain to be the causes or occasions of our ideas. Pray tell me whether by the "brain" you mean any sensible thing.

Hyl.: What else think you I could mean?

Phil.: Sensible things are all immediately perceivable; and those things which are immediately perceivable are ideas, and these exist only in the mind. This much you have, if I mistake not, long since agreed to.

Hyl.: I do not deny it.

Phil.: The brain therefore you speak of, being a sensible thing, exists only in the mind. Now I would fain know whether you think it reasonable to suppose that one idea or thing existing in the mind occasions all other ideas. And if you think so, pray how do you account for the origin of that primary idea or brain itself?

Hyl.: I do not explain the origin of our ideas by that brain which is perceivable to sense, this being itself only a combination of sensible ideas, but by another which I imagine.

Phil.: But are not things imagined as truly *in the mind* as things perceived?

Hyl.: I must confess they are.

Phil.: It comes, therefore, to the same thing; and you have been all this while accounting for ideas by certain motions or impressions of the brain, that is, by some alteration in an idea, whether sensible or imaginable it matters not.

Hyl.: I begin to suspect my hypothesis.

Phil.: Besides spirits, all that we know or conceive are our own ideas. When, therefore, you say all ideas are occasioned by impressions in the brain, do you conceive this brain or no? If you do, then you talk of ideas imprinted in an idea causing that same idea, which is absurd. If you do not conceive it, you talk unintelligibly, instead of forming a reasonable hypothesis.

Hyl.: I now clearly see it was a mere dream. There is nothing in it.

Phil.: You need not be much concerned at it, for, after all, this way of explaining things, as you called it, could never have satisfied any reasonable man. What connection is there between a motion in the nerves and the sensations of sound or color in the mind? Or how is it possible these should be the effect of that?

Hyl.: But I could never think it had so little in it as now it seems to have.

Phil.: Well then, are you at length satisfied that no sensible things have a real existence, and that you are in truth an arrant *skeptic?*

Hyl.: It is too plain to be denied.

Phil.: Look! are not the fields covered with a delightful verdure? Is there not something in the woods and groves, in the rivers and clear springs, that soothes, that delights, that transports the soul? At the prospect of the wide and deep ocean, or some huge mountain whose top is lost in the clouds, or of an old gloomy forest, are not our minds filled with a pleasing horror? Even in rocks and deserts is there not an agreeable wildness? How sincere a pleasure is it to behold the natural beauties of the earth! To preserve and renew our relish for them, is not the veil of night alternately drawn over her face, and does she not change her dress with the seasons? How aptly are the elements disposed! What variety and use in the meanest productions of nature! What delicacy, what beauty, what contrivance in animal and vegetable bodies! How exquisitely are all things suited, as well to their particular ends as to constitute apposite parts of the whole! And while they mutually aid and support, do they not also set off and illustrate each other? Raise now your thoughts from this ball of earth to all those glorious luminaries that adorn the high arch of heaven. The motion and situation of the planets, are they not admirable for use and order? Were those (miscalled "erratic") globes ever known to stray in their repeated journeys through the pathless void? Do they not measure areas round the sun ever proportioned to the times? So fixed, so immutable are the laws by which the unseen Author of nature actuates the universe. How vivid and radiant is the luster of the fixed stars! How magnificent and rich that negligent profusion with which they appear to be scattered throughout the whole azure vault! Yet, if you take the telescope, it brings into your sight a new host of stars that escape the naked eye. Here they seem contiguous and minute, but to a nearer view, immense orbs of light at various distances, far sunk in the abyss of space. Now you must call imagination to your aid. The feeble narrow sense cannot descry innumerable worlds revolving round the central fires, and in those worlds the energy of an all-perfect Mind displayed in endless forms. But neither sense nor imagination are big enough to comprehend the boundless extent with all its glittering furniture. Though the laboring mind exert and strain each power to its utmost reach, there still stands out ungrasped a surplusage immeasurable. Yet all the vast bodies that compose this mighty frame, how distant and remote soever, are by some secret mechanism, some divine art and force, linked in a mutual dependence and intercourse with each other, even with this earth, which was almost slipt from my thoughts and lost in the crowd of worlds. Is not the whole system immense, beautiful, glorious beyond expression and beyond thought! What treatment, then, do those philosophers deserve who would deprive these noble and delightful scenes of all reality? How should those principles be entertained that lead us to think all the visible beauty of the creation a false imaginary glare? To be plain, can you expect this skepticism of yours will not be thought extravagantly absurd by all men of sense?

Hyl.: Other men may think as they please, but for your part you have nothing to reproach me with. My comfort is you are as much a skeptic as I am.

Phil.: There, Hylas, I must beg leave to differ from you.

Hyl.: What! have you all along agreed to the premises, and do you now deny the conclusion and leave me to maintain those paradoxes by myself which you led me into? This surely is not fair.

Phil.: I deny that I agreed with you in those notions that led to skepticism. You indeed said the *reality* of sensible things consisted in an *absolute existence* out of the minds of spirits, or distinct from their being perceived. And, pursuant to this notion of reality, you are obliged to deny sensible things any real existence; that is, according to your own definition, you profess yourself a skeptic. But I neither said nor thought the reality of sensible things was to be defined after that manner. To me it is evident, for the reasons you allow of, that sensible things cannot exist otherwise than in a mind or spirit. Whence I conclude, not that they have no real existence, but that, seeing they depend not on my thought and have an existence distinct from being perceived by me, *there must be some other mind wherein they exist.* As sure, therefore, as the sensible world really exists, so sure is there an infinite omnipresent Spirit, who contains and supports it.

Hyl.: What! this is no more than I and all Christians hold; nay, and all others, too, who believe there is a God and that He knows and comprehends all things.

Phil.: Aye, but here lies the difference. Men commonly believe that all things are known or perceived by God, because they believe the being of a God; whereas I, on the other side, immediately and necessarily conclude the being of a God, because all sensible things must be perceived by him.

Hyl.: But so long as we all believe the same thing, what matter is it how we come by that belief?

Phil.: But neither do we agree in the same opinion. For philosophers, though they acknowledge all corporeal beings to be perceived by God, yet they attribute to them an absolute subsistence distinct from their being perceived by any mind whatever, which I do not. Besides, is there no difference between saying, *there is a God, therefore He perceives all things,* and saying, *sensible things do really exist; and if they really exist, they are necessarily perceived by an infinite mind: therefore there is an infinite mind, or God?* This furnishes you with a direct and immediate demonstration, from a most evident principle, of the *being of a God.* Divines and philosophers had proved beyond all controversy, from the beauty and usefulness of the several parts of the creation, that it was the workmanship of God. But that—setting aside all help of astronomy and natural philosophy, all contemplation of the contrivance, order and adjustment of things—an infinite mind should be necessarily inferred from the bare *existence* of the sensible world is an advantage peculiar to them only who have made this easy reflection, that the sensible world is that which we perceive by our several senses; and that nothing is perceived by the senses besides ideas; and that no idea or archetype of an idea can exist otherwise than in a mind. . . .

I do not pretend to be a setter-up of new notions. My endeavors tend only to unite and place in a clearer light that truth which was before shared between the vulgar and the philosophers, the former being of opinion that *those things they immediately perceive are the real things,* and the latter, that *the things immediately perceived are ideas which exist only in the mind.* Which two notions put together do, in effect, constitute the substance of what I advance.

Hyl.: I have been a long time distrusting my senses; methought I saw things by a dim light and through false glasses. Now the glasses are removed and a new light breaks in upon my understanding. I am clearly convinced that I see things in their native forms and am no longer in pain about their *unknown natures* or *absolute existence*. This is the state I find myself in at present, though, indeed, the course that brought me to it I do not yet thoroughly comprehend. You set out upon the same principles that Academics, Cartesians, and the like sects usually do, and for a long time it looked as if you were advancing their philosophical skepticism; but, in the end, your conclusions are directly opposite to theirs.

Phil.: You see, Hylas, the water of yonder fountain, how it is forced upwards in a round column, to a certain height, at which it breaks and falls back into the basin from whence it rose, its ascent as well as descent proceeding from the same uniform law or principle of gravitation. Just so, the same principles which, at first view, lead to skepticism, pursued to a certain point, bring men back to common sense.

FOR FURTHER REFLECTION

1. What is the most "extravagant opinion that ever entered into the mind of man"? How does Philonous respond to Hylas' surprise at his views? How does he seek to rebut the charge of skepticism?
2. How does Philonous convince Hylas that heat and pain are ideas in the mind? Go through the argument, step by step.
3. What does Hylas mean by saying, "To exist is one thing and to be perceived is another?"
4. Why does Philonous reject the notion of a material substratum—that is, matter that exists independently of our perceptions?
5. Do you agree with Berkeley that only ideas in the mind exist? Does it seem obvious that matter really does exist? If you disagree with Berkeley, show where he has made an error in his argument.
6. According to Berkeley, there is no sound independently of our hearing it and no reality but our experiencing it. Does this mean that when we leave our rooms, they disappear? There is an old Oxford limerick on this point:

> There was a young man who said, "God
> Must think it exceedingly odd
> If he finds that this tree
> Continues to be,
> When there's no one about in the quad."

> Dear Sir, your astonishment's odd
> I'm always about in the quad,
> And that's why the tree
> Continues to be,
> Since observed by,

> > Yours faithfully,
> > God

The question is, in whose mind does God exist? Does the notion of God fit into Berkeley's system? If so, how?

DAVID HUME

EXPERIENCE AND THE LIMITS OF HUMAN REASONING

The Scottish empiricist and skeptic David Hume (1711–1776) is one of the most brilliant philosophers who ever lived. His major philosophical work is the *Treatise of Human Nature* (1739), written when he was twenty-seven years old. His *Enquiry Concerning Human Understanding* (1748), from which the following selection is taken, is a briefer and more accessible version of material in the *Treatise.*

In this selection from the *Enquiry,* Hume first establishes his stance as an empiricist in the tradition of John Locke. All ideas in our minds, he argues, come from impressions, particularly sense experiences and internal feelings. We can even use this as a way of discovering whether our ideas have any true meaning or are just nonsense: to see if "a philosophical term is employed without any meaning . . . we need but inquire, from what impression is that supposed idea derived?" Hume next explores the limits of the human reasoning process. Human reasoning, he argues, is of two sorts. The first is about *relations of ideas*—truths of mathematics or logic that are true by definition, such as 1 + 1 = 2. The second is about *matters of fact*—facts about the world around us that require experience for us to know. Hume's key concern is to discover our reasoning process about matters of fact. Such reasoning, he maintains, is based on seeing causal relations in things, such as rain causing the grass to grow. Our ability to form causal relations is, in turn, based on generalizations that we make about our experiences, such as seeing the grass grow after each rainfall. Generalizations from experience, in turn, are grounded in the mental ability to form habits, for example, I habitually expect the grass to grow after it rains. This, according to Hume, is a rather skeptical explanation of human reasoning about matters of fact. What appears to be a fixed fact in the external world in the end hinges on a mere mental ability to form habits from experience.

SECTION II: OF THE ORIGIN OF IDEAS

Every one will allow that there is a considerable difference between the perception of the mind, when a man feels the pain of excessive heat, or the pleasure of moderate warmth, and when he afterwards recalls to his memory this sensation, or anticipates it by his imagination. These faculties may mimic or copy the perceptions of the senses; but they never can entirely reach the force and vivacity of the original sentiment. The utmost we say of them, even when they operate with greatest vigor, is, that they represent their object in so lively a manner, that we could almost say we feel or see it: But, except the mind be disordered by disease or madness, they never can arrive at such a pitch

From David Hume, *An Enquiry Concerning Human Understanding* (1748).

of vivacity, as to render these perceptions altogether undistinguishable. All the colours of poetry, however splendid, can never paint natural objects in such a manner as to make the description be taken for a real landscape. The most lively thought is still inferior to the dullest sensation.

We may observe a like distinction to run through all the other perceptions of the mind. A man in a fit of anger, is actuated in a very different manner from one who only thinks of that emotion. If you tell me, that any person is in love, I easily understand your meaning, and form a just conception of his situation; but never can mistake that conception for the real disorders and agitations of the passion. When we reflect on our past sentiments and affections, our thought is a faithful mirror, and copies its objects truly; but the colours which it employs are faint and dull, in comparison of those in which our original perceptions were clothed. It requires no nice discernment or metaphysical head to mark the distinction between them.

Here therefore we may divide all the perceptions of the mind into two classes or species, which are distinguished by their different degrees of force and vivacity. The less forcible and lively are commonly denominated Thoughts or Ideas. The other species want a name in our language, and in most others; I suppose, because it was not requisite for any, but philosophical purposes, to rank them under a general term or appellation. Let us, therefore, use a little freedom, and call them Impressions; employing that word in a sense somewhat different from the usual. By the term impression, then, I mean all our more lively perceptions, when we hear, or see, or feel, or love, or hate, or desire, or will. And impressions are distinguished from ideas, which are the less lively perceptions, of which we are conscious, when we reflect on any of those sensations or movements above mentioned.

Nothing, at first view, may seem more unbounded than the thought of man, which not only escapes all human power and authority, but is not even restrained within the limits of nature and reality. To form monsters, and join incongruous shapes and appearances, costs the imagination no more trouble than to conceive the most natural and familiar objects. And while

the body is confined to one planet, along which it creeps with pain and difficulty; the thought can in an instant transport us into the most distant regions of the universe; or even beyond the universe, into the unbounded chaos, where nature is supposed to lie in total confusion. What never was seen, or heard of, may yet be conceived; nor is any thing beyond the power of thought, except what implies an absolute contradiction.

But though our thought seems to possess this unbounded liberty, we shall find, upon a nearer examination, that it is really confined within very narrow limits, and that all this creative power of the mind amounts to no more than the faculty of compounding, transposing, augmenting, or diminishing the materials afforded us by the senses and experience. When we think of a golden mountain, we only join two consistent ideas, gold, and mountain, with which we were formerly acquainted. A virtuous horse we can conceive; because, from our own feeling, we can conceive virtue; and this we may unite to the figure and shape of a horse, which is an animal familiar to us. In short, all the materials of thinking are derived either from our outward or inward sentiment: The mixture and composition of these belongs alone to the mind and will. Or, to express myself in philosophical language, all our ideas or more feeble perceptions are copies of our impressions or more lively ones.

To prove this, the two following arguments will, I hope, be sufficient. First, when we analyze our thoughts or ideas, however compounded or sublime, we always find, that they resolve themselves into such simple ideas as were copied from a precedent feeling or sentiment. Even those ideas, which, at first view, seem the most wide of this origin, are found, upon a nearer scrutiny, to be derived from it. The idea of God, as meaning an infinitely intelligent, wise, and good Being, arises from reflecting on the operations of our own mind, and augmenting, without limit, those qualities of goodness and wisdom. We may prosecute this enquiry to what length we please; where we shall always find, that every idea which we examine is copied from a similar impression. Those who would assert that this position is not universally true nor without exception, have only one, and that an easy method of refuting it; by producing that idea, which, in their opinion, is not derived from this source. It will then be incumbent on us, if we would maintain our doctrine, to produce the impression, or lively perception, which corresponds to it.

Secondly, If it happen, from a defect of the organ, that a man is not susceptible of any species of sensation, we always find that he is as little susceptible of the correspondent ideas. A blind man can form no notion of colors; a deaf man of sounds. Restore either of them that sense, in which he is deficient; by opening this new inlet for his sensations, you also open an inlet for the ideas; and he finds no difficulty in conceiving these objects. The case is the same, if the object, proper for exciting any sensation, has never been applied to the organ. A Laplander or Negro, has no notion of the relish of wine. And though there are few or no instances of a like deficiency in the mind, where a person has never felt or is wholly incapable of a sentiment or passion that belongs to his species; yet we find the same observation to take place in a less degree. A man of mild manners can form no idea of inveterate revenge or cruelty; nor can a selfish heart easily conceive the heights of friendship and generosity. It is readily allowed, that other beings may possess many senses of which we can have no conception; because the ideas of them have never been introduced to us, in the only manner, by which an idea can have access to the mind, to wit, by the actual feeling and sensation.

There is, however, one contradictory phenomenon, which may prove, that it is not absolutely impossible for ideas to arise, independent of their correspondent impressions. I believe it will readily be allowed, that the several distinct ideas of colour, which enter by the eye, or those of sound, which are conveyed by the ear, are really different from each other; though, at the same time, resembling. Now if this be true of different colours, it must be no less so of the different shades of the same colour; and each shade produces a distinct idea, independent of the rest. For if this should be denied, it is possible, by the continual gradation of shades, to run a colour insensibly into what is most remote from it; and if you will not allow any of the means to be different, you cannot, without absurdity, deny the extremes to be the same. Suppose, therefore, a person to have enjoyed his sight

for thirty years, and to have become perfectly acquainted with colours of all kinds, except one particular shade of blue, for instance, which it never has been his fortune to meet with. Let all the different shades of that colour, except that single one, be placed before him, descending gradually from the deepest to the lightest; it is plain, that he will perceive a blank, where that shade is wanting, and will be sensible, that there is a greater distance in that place between the contiguous colours than in any other. Now I ask, whether it be possible for him, from his own imagination, to supply this deficiency, and raise up to himself the idea of that particular shade, though it had never been conveyed to him by his senses? I believe there are few but will be of opinion that he can: And this may serve as a proof, that the simple ideas are not always, in every instance, derived from the correspondent impressions; though this instance is so singular, that it is scarcely worth our observing, and does not merit, that for it alone we should alter our general maxim.

Here, therefore, is a proposition, which not only seems, in itself, simple and intelligible; but, if a proper use were made of it, might render every dispute equally intelligible, and banish all that jargon, which has so long taken possession of metaphysical reasonings, and drawn disgrace upon them. All ideas, especially abstract ones, are naturally faint and obscure: the mind has but a slender hold of them: they are apt to be confounded with other resembling ideas; and when we have often employed any term, though without a distinct meaning, we are apt to imagine it has a determinate idea annexed to it. On the contrary, all impressions, that is, all sensations, either outward or inward, are strong and vivid: The limits between them are more exactly determined: Nor is it easy to fall into any error or mistake with regard to them. When we entertain, therefore, any suspicion, that a philosophical term is employed without any meaning or idea (as is but too frequent), we need but enquire, from what impression is that supposed idea derived? And if it be impossible to assign any, this will serve to confirm our suspicion. By bringing ideas into so clear a light, we may reasonably hope to remove all dispute, which may arise, concerning their nature and reality.

SECTION IV: SCEPTICAL DOUBTS CONCERNING THE OPERATIONS OF THE UNDERSTANDING

Part I

All the objects of human reason or enquiry may naturally be divided into two kinds, to wit, Relations of Ideas, and Matters of Fact. Of the first kind are the sciences of Geometry, Algebra, and Arithmetic; and in short, every affirmation, which is either intuitively or demonstratively certain. That the square of the hypotenuse is equal to the squares of the two sides, is a proposition, which expresses a relation between these figures. That three times five is equal to the half of thirty, expresses a relation between these numbers. Propositions of this kind are discoverable by the mere operation of thought, without dependence on what is any where existent in the universe. Though there never were a circle or triangle in nature, the truths, demonstrated by Euclid, would for ever retain their certainty and evidence.

Matters of fact, which are the second objects of human reason, are not ascertained in the same manner; nor is our evidence of their truth, however great, of a like nature with the foregoing. The contrary of every matter of fact is still possible; because it can never imply a contradiction, and is conceived by the mind with the same facility and distinctness, as if ever so conformable to reality. That the sun will not rise tomorrow is no less intelligible a proposition, and implies no more contradiction, than the affirmation, that it will rise. We should in vain, therefore, attempt to demonstrate its falsehood. Were it demonstratively false, it would imply a contradiction, and could never be distinctly conceived by the mind.

It may, therefore, be a subject worthy of curiosity, to enquire what is the nature of that evidence, which assures us of any real existence and matter of fact, beyond the present testimony of our senses, or the records of our memory. This part of philosophy, it is observable, has been little cultivated, either by the ancients or moderns; and therefore our doubts and errors, in the prosecution of so important an enquiry, may be the more excusable; while we march through such difficult paths, without any guide or direction. They may even prove useful, by exciting curiosity, and destroying that implicit faith and security, which is the bane of all reasoning and free enquiry. The discovery of defects in the common philosophy, if any such there be, will not, I presume, be a discouragement, but rather an incitement, as is usual, to attempt something more full and satisfactory, than has yet been proposed to the public.

All reasonings concerning matter of fact seem to be founded on the relation of Cause and Effect. By means of that relation alone we can go beyond the evidence of our memory and senses. If you were to ask a man, why he believes any matter of fact, which is absent; for instance, that his friend is in the country, or in France; he would give you a reason; and this reason would be some other fact; as a letter received from him, or the knowledge of his former resolutions and promises. A man, finding a watch or any other machine in a desert island, would conclude, that there had once been men in that island. All our reasonings concerning fact are of the same nature. And here it is constantly supposed, that there is a connexion between the present fact and that which is inferred from it. Were there nothing to bind them together, the inference would be entirely precarious. The hearing of an articulate voice and rational discourse in the dark assures us of the presence of some person: Why? because these are the effects of the human make and fabric, and closely connected with it. If we anatomize all the other reasonings of this nature, we shall find, that they are founded on the relation of cause and effect, and that this relation is either near or remote, direct or collateral. Heat and light are collateral effects of fire, and the one effect may justly be inferred from the other.

If we would satisfy ourselves, therefore, concerning the nature of that evidence, which assures us of matters of fact, we must enquire how we arrive at the knowledge of cause and effect.

I shall venture to affirm, as a general proposition, which admits of no exception, that the knowledge of this relation is not, in any instance, attained by reasonings a priori; but arises entirely from experience, when we find, that any particular objects are constantly conjoined with each other. Let an object be presented to a man of ever so strong natural reason and abilities; if that object be entirely new to him, he will not be able, by the most accurate examination of its sensible qualities, to discover any of its causes or effects. Adam, though his rational faculties be supposed, at the very first, entirely perfect, could not have inferred from the fluidity, and transparency of water, that it would suffocate him, or from the light and warmth of fire, that it would consume him. No object ever discovers, by the qualities which appear to the senses, either the causes which produced it, or the effects which will arise from it; nor can our reason, unassisted by experience, ever draw any inference concerning real existence and matter of fact.

This proposition, that causes and effects are discoverable, not by reason but by experience, will readily be admitted with regard to such objects, as we remember to have once been altogether unknown to us; since we must be conscious of the utter inability, which we then lay under, of foretelling, what would arise from them. Present two smooth pieces of marble to a man, who has no tincture of natural philosophy; he will never discover, that they will adhere together, in such a manner as to require great force to separate them in a direct line, while they make so small a resistance to a lateral pressure. Such events, as bear little analogy to the common course of nature, are also readily confessed to be known only by experience; nor does any man imagine that the explosion of gunpowder, or the attraction of a loadstone, could ever be discovered by arguments a priori. In like manner, when an effect is supposed to depend upon an intricate machinery or secret structure of parts, we make no difficulty in attributing all our knowledge of it to experience. Who will assert that he can give the ultimate reason, why milk or bread is proper nourishment for a man, not for a lion or a tiger?

But the same truth may not appear, at first sight, to have the same evidence with regard to events, which have become familiar to us from our first appearance in the world, which bear a close analogy to the whole course of nature, and which are supposed to depend on the simple qualities of objects, without any secret structure of parts. We are apt to imagine, that we could discover these effects by the mere operation of our reason, without experience. We fancy, that were we brought, on a sudden, into this world, we could at first have inferred, that one Billiard-ball would communicate motion to another upon impulse; and that we needed not to have waited for the event, in order to pronounce with certainty concerning it. Such is the influence of custom, that, where it is strongest, it not only covers our natural ignorance, but even conceals itself, and seems not to take place, merely because it is found in the highest degree.

But to convince us, that all the laws of nature, and all the operations of bodies without exception, are known only by experience, the following reflections may, perhaps, suffice. Were any object presented to us, and were we required to pronounce concerning the effect, which will result from it, without consulting past observation; after what manner, I beseech you, must the mind proceed in this operation? It must invent or imagine some event, which it ascribes to the object as its effect; and it is plain that this invention must be entirely arbitrary. The mind can never possibly find the effect in the supposed cause, by the most accurate scrutiny and examination. For the effect is totally different from the cause, and consequently can never be discovered in it. Motion in the second Billiard-ball is a quite distinct event from motion in the first; nor is there any thing in the one to suggest the smallest hint of the other. A stone or piece of metal raised into the air, and left without any support, immediately falls: But to consider the matter a priori, is there any thing we discover in this situation, which can beget the idea of a downward, rather than an upward, or any other motion, in the stone or metal?

And as the first imagination or invention of a particular effect, in all natural operations, is arbitrary, where we consult not experience; so must we also esteem the supposed tie or connexion between the cause and effect, which binds them together, and renders it impossible, that any other effect could result from the operation of that cause. When I see, for instance, a Billiard-ball moving in a straight line towards another; even suppose motion in the second ball should by accident be suggested to me, as the result of their contact or impulse; may I not conceive, that a hundred different events might as well follow from that cause? May not both these balls remain at absolute rest? May not the first ball return in a straight line, or leap off from the second in any line or direction? All these suppositions are consistent and conceivable. Why then should we give the preference to one, which is no more consistent or conceivable than the rest? All our reasonings a priori will never be able to shew us any foundation for this preference.

In a word, then, every effect is a distinct event from its cause. It could not, therefore, be discovered in the cause, and the first invention or conception of it, a priori, must be entirely arbitrary. And even after it is suggested, the conjunction of it with the cause must appear equally arbitrary; since there are always many other effects, which, to reason, must seem fully as consistent and natural. In vain, therefore, should we pretend to determine any single event, or infer any cause or effect, without the assistance of observation and experience.

Hence we may discover the reason, why no philosopher, who is rational and modest, has ever pretended to assign the ultimate cause of any natural operation, or to show distinctly the action of that power, which produces any single effect in the universe. It is confessed, that the utmost effort of human reason is to reduce the principles, productive of natural phenomena, to a greater simplicity, and to resolve the many particular effects into a few general causes, by means of reasonings from analogy, experience, and observation. But as to the causes of these general causes, we should in vain attempt their discovery; nor shall we ever be able to satisfy ourselves, by any particular explication of them. These ultimate springs and principles are totally shut up from human curiosity and enquiry. Elasticity, gravity, cohesion of parts, communication of motion by impulse; these are probably the ultimate causes and principles which we shall ever discover in nature; and we may esteem ourselves sufficiently happy, if, by accurate enquiry and reasoning, we can trace up the particular phenomena to, or near to, these general principles. The most perfect philosophy of the natural kind only staves off our ignorance a little longer: As perhaps the most perfect philosophy of the moral or metaphysical kind serves only to discover larger portions of it. Thus the observation of human blindness and weakness is the result

of all philosophy, and meets us, at every turn, in spite of our endeavors to elude or avoid it.

Nor is geometry, when taken into the assistance of natural philosophy, ever able to remedy this defect, or lead us into the knowledge of ultimate causes, by all that accuracy of reasoning, for which it is so justly celebrated. Every part of mixed mathematics proceeds upon the supposition, that certain laws are established by nature in her operations; and abstract reasonings are employed, either to assist experience in the discovery of these laws, or to determine their influence in particular instances, where it depends upon any precise degree of distance and quantity. Thus, it is a law of motion, discovered by experience, that the moment or force of any body in motion is in the compound ratio or proportion of its solid contents and its velocity; and consequently, that a small force may remove the greatest obstacle or raise the greatest weight, if, by any contrivance or machinery, we can increase the velocity of that force, so as to make it an overmatch for its antagonist. Geometry assists us in the application of this law, by giving us the just dimensions of all the parts and figures, which can enter into any species of machine; but still the discovery of the law itself is owing merely to experience, and all the abstract reasonings in the world could never lead us one step towards the knowledge of it. When we reason a priori, and consider merely any object or cause, as it appears to the mind, independent of all observation, it never could suggest to us the notion of any distinct object, such as its effect; much less, shew us the inseparable and inviolable connexion between them. A man must be very sagacious, who could discover by reasoning that crystal is the effect of heat, and ice of cold, without being previously acquainted with the operation of these qualities.

Part II

But we have not, yet, attained any tolerable satisfaction with regard to the question first proposed. Each solution still gives rise to a new question as difficult as the foregoing, and leads us on to farther enquiries. When it is asked, What is the nature of all our reasonings concerning matter of fact? the proper answer seems to be, that they are founded on the relation of cause and effect. When again it is asked, What is the foundation of all our reasonings and conclusions concerning that relation? it may be replied in one word, Experience. But if we still carry on our sifting humor, and ask, What is the foundation of all conclusions from experience? this implies a new question, which may be of more difficult solution and explication. Philosophers, that give themselves airs of superior wisdom and sufficiency, have a hard task, when they encounter persons of inquisitive dispositions, who push them from every corner, to which they retreat, and who are sure at last to bring them to some dangerous dilemma. The best expedient to prevent this confusion, is to be modest in our pretensions; and even to discover the difficulty ourselves before it is objected to us. By this means, we may make a kind of merit of our very ignorance.

I shall content myself, in this section, with an easy task, and shall pretend only to give a negative answer to the question here proposed. I say then, that, even after we have experience of the operations of cause and effect, our conclusions from that experience are not founded on reasoning, or any process of the understanding. This answer we must endeavor, both to explain and to defend.

It must certainly be allowed, that nature has kept us at a great distance from all her secrets, and has afforded us only the knowledge of a few superficial qualities of objects; while she conceals from us those powers and principles, on which the influence of these objects entirely depends. Our senses inform us of the colour, weight, and consistence of bread; but neither sense nor reason can ever inform us of those qualities, which fit it for the nourishment and support of a human body. Sight or feeling conveys an idea of the actual motion of bodies; but as to that wonderful force or power, which would carry on a moving body for ever in a continued change of place, and which bodies never lose but by communicating it to others; of this we cannot form the most distant conception. But notwithstanding this ignorance of natural powers and principles, we always presume, when we see like sensible qualities, that they have like secret powers, and expect, that effects, similar to those which we have experienced, will follow from them. If a body of like colour and con-

sistence with that bread, which we have formerly eaten, be presented to us, we make no scruple of repeating the experiment, and foresee, with certainty, like nourishment and support. Now this is a process of the mind or thought, of which I would willingly know the foundation. It is allowed on all hands, that there is no known connexion between the sensible qualities and the secret powers; and consequently, that the mind is not led to form such a conclusion concerning their constant and regular conjunction, by any thing which it knows of their nature. As to past Experience, it can be allowed to give direct and certain information of those precise objects only, and that precise period of time, which fell under its cognizance: But why this experience should be extended to future times, and to other objects, which for aught we know, may be only in appearance similar; this is the main question on which I would insist. The bread, which I formerly eat, nourished me; that is, a body of such sensible qualities, was, at that time, endued with such secret powers: But does it follow, that other bread must also nourish me at another time, and that like sensible qualities must always be attended with like secret powers? The consequence seems nowise necessary. At least, it must be acknowledged, that there is here a consequence drawn by the mind; that there is a certain step taken; a process of thought, and an inference, which wants to be explained. These two propositions are far from being the same, I have found that such an object has always been attended with such an effect, and I foresee, that other objects, which are, in appearance, similar, will be attended with similar effects. I shall allow, if you please, that the one proposition may justly be inferred from the other: I know in fact, that it always is inferred. But if you insist, that the inference is made by a chain of reasoning, I desire you to produce that reasoning. The connexion between these propositions is not intuitive. There is required a medium, which may enable the mind to draw such an inference, if indeed it be drawn by reasoning and argument. What that medium is, I must confess, passes my comprehension; and it is incumbent on those to produce it, who assert, that it really exists, and is the origin of all our conclusions concerning matter of fact.

This negative argument must certainly, in process of time, become altogether convincing, if many penetrating and able philosophers shall turn their enquiries this way; and no one be ever able to discover any connecting proposition or intermediate step, which supports the understanding in this conclusion. But as the question is yet new, every reader may not trust so far to his own penetration, as to conclude, because an argument escapes his enquiry, that therefore it does not really exist. For this reason it may be requisite to venture upon a more difficult task; and enumerating all the branches of human knowledge, endeavor to shew, that none of them can afford such an argument.

All reasonings may be divided into two kinds, namely demonstrative reasoning, or that concerning relations of ideas, and moral reasoning, or that concerning matter of fact and existence. That there are no demonstrative arguments in the case, seems evident; since it implies no contradiction, that the course of nature may change, and that an object, seemingly like those which we have experienced, may be attended with different or contrary effects. May I not clearly and distinctly conceive, that a body, falling from the clouds, and which, in all other respects, resembles snow, has yet the taste of salt or feeling of fire? Is there any more intelligible proposition than to affirm, that all the trees will flourish in December and January, and decay in May and June? Now whatever is intelligible, and can be distinctly conceived, implies no contradiction, and can never be proved false by any demonstrative argument or abstract reasoning a priori.

If we be, therefore, engaged by arguments to put trust in past experience, and make it the standard of our future judgment, these arguments must be probable only, or such as regard matter of fact and real existence, according to the division above mentioned. But that there is no argument of this kind, must appear, if our explication of that species of reasoning be admitted as solid and satisfactory. We have said, that all arguments concerning existence are founded on the relation of cause and effect; that our knowledge of that relation is derived entirely from experience; and that all our experimental conclusions proceed upon the supposition, that the future will be conformable to the past. To endeavor, therefore, the

proof of this last supposition by probable arguments, or arguments regarding existence, must be evidently going in a circle, and taking that for granted, which is the very point in question.

In reality, all arguments from experience are founded on the similarity which we discover among natural objects, and by which we are induced to expect effects similar to those which we have found to follow from such objects. And though none but a fool or madman will ever pretend to dispute the authority of experience, or to reject that great guide of human life; it may surely be allowed a philosopher to have so much curiosity at least as to examine the principle of human nature, which gives this mighty authority to experience, and makes us draw advantage from that similarity, which nature has placed among different objects. From causes, which appear similar, we expect similar effects. This is the sum of all our experimental conclusions. Now it seems evident that, if this conclusion were formed by reason, it would be as perfect at first, and upon one instance, as after ever so long a course of experience. But the case is far otherwise. Nothing so like as eggs; yet no one, on account of this appearing similarity, expects the same taste and relish in all of them. It is only after a long course of uniform experiments in any kind, that we attain a firm reliance and security with regard to a particular event. Now where is that process of reasoning, which, from one instance, draws a conclusion, so different from that which it infers from a hundred instances, that are nowise different from that single one? This question I propose as much for the sake of information, as with an intention of raising difficulties. I cannot find, I cannot imagine any such reasoning. But I keep my mind still open to instruction, if any one will vouchsafe to bestow it on me.

Should it be said, that, from a number of uniform experiments, we infer a connexion between the sensible qualities and the secret powers; this, I must confess, seems the same difficulty, couched in different terms. The question still recurs, on what process of argument this inference is founded? Where is the medium, the interposing ideas, which join propositions so very wide of each other? It is confessed, that the colour, consistence, and other sensible qualities of bread appear not, of themselves, to have any connexion with the secret powers of nourishment and support. For otherwise we could infer these secret powers from the first appearance of these sensible qualities, without the aid of experience; contrary to the sentiment of all philosophers, and contrary to plain matter of fact. Here then is our natural state of ignorance with regard to the powers and influence of all objects. How is this remedied by experience? It only shows us a number of uniform effects, resulting from certain objects, and teaches us that those particular objects, at that particular time, were endowed with such powers and forces. When a new object, endowed with similar sensible qualities, is produced, we expect similar powers and forces, and look for a like effect. From a body of like colour and consistence with bread, we expect like nourishment and support. But this surely is a step or progress of the mind, which wants to be explained. When a man says, I have found, in all past instances, such sensible qualities conjoined with such secret powers: And when he says, Similar sensible qualities will always be conjoined with similar secret powers; he is not guilty of a tautology, nor are these propositions in any respect the same. You say that the one proposition is an inference from the other. But you must confess that the inference is not intuitive; neither is it demonstrative: Of what nature is it then? To say it is experimental, is begging the question. For all inferences from experience suppose, as their foundation, that the future will resemble the past, and that similar powers will be conjoined with similar sensible qualities. If there be any suspicion, that the course of nature may change, and that the past may be no rule for the future, all experience becomes useless, and can give rise to no inference or conclusion. It is impossible, therefore, that any arguments from experience can prove this resemblance of the past to the future; since all these arguments are founded on the supposition of that resemblance. Let the course of things be allowed hitherto ever so regular; that alone, without some new argument or inference, proves not, that, for the future, it will continue so. In vain do you pretend to have learned the nature of bodies from your past experience. Their secret nature, and consequently, all their effects and influence, may change, without any change in their sensible qualities. This happens sometimes, and with regard to some objects: Why may it not happen always, and with regard to all objects? What logic, what process of argument secures you against this supposition? My practice, you say, refutes my doubts. But you mistake the purport of my question. As an agent, I am quite satisfied in the point; but as a philosopher, who has some share of curiosity, I will not say scepticism, I want to learn the foundation of this inference. No reading, no enquiry has yet been able to remove my difficulty, or give me satisfaction in a matter of such importance. Can I do better than propose the difficulty to the public, even though, perhaps, I have small hopes of obtaining a solution? We shall, at least, by this means, be sensible of our ignorance, if we do not augment our knowledge.

I must confess, that a man is guilty of unpardonable arrogance, who concludes, because an argument has escaped his own investigation, that therefore it does not really exist. I must also confess, that, though all the learned, for several ages, should have employed themselves in fruitless search upon any subject, it may still, perhaps, be rash to conclude positively, that the subject must, therefore, pass all human comprehension. Even though we examine all the sources of our knowledge, and conclude them unfit for such a subject, there may still remain a suspicion, that the enumeration is not complete, or the examination not accurate. But with regard to the present subject, there are some considerations, which seem to remove all this accusation of arrogance or suspicion of mistake.

It is certain, that the most ignorant and stupid peasants, nay infants, nay even brute beasts, improve by experience, and learn the qualities of natural objects, by observing the effects which result from them. When a child has felt the sensation of pain from touching the flame of a candle, he will be careful not to put his hand near any candle; but will expect a similar effect from a cause, which is similar in its sensible qualities and appearance. If you assert, therefore, that the understanding of the child is led into this conclusion by any process of argument or ratiocination, I may justly require you to produce that argument; nor have you any pretense to refuse so equitable a demand. You cannot say, that the argument is abstruse, and may possibly escape your enquiry; since you confess, that it is obvious to the capacity of a mere infant. If you hesitate, therefore, a moment, or if, after reflection, you produce any intricate or profound argument, you, in a manner, give up the question, and confess, that it is not reasoning which engages us to suppose the past resembling the future, and to expect similar effects from causes, which are, to appearance, similar. This is the proposition which I intended to enforce in the present section. If I be right, I pretend not to have made any mighty discovery. And if I be wrong, I must acknowledge myself to be indeed a very backward scholar; since I cannot now discover an argument, which, it seems, was perfectly familiar to me, long before I was out of my cradle.

SECTION V: SCEPTICAL SOLUTION OF THESE DOUBTS

Part I

The passion for philosophy, like that for religion, seems liable to this inconvenience, that, though it aims at the correction of our manners, and extirpation of our vices, it may only serve, by imprudent management, to foster a predominant inclination, and push the mind, with more determined resolution, towards the side, which already draws too much, by the bias and propensity of the natural temper. It is certain, that, while we aspire to the magnanimous firmness of the philosophic sage, and endeavor to confine our pleasures altogether within our own minds, we may, at last, render our philosophy like that of Epictetus, and other Stoics, only a more refined system of selfishness, and reason ourselves out of all virtue, as well as social enjoyment. While we study with attention the vanity of human life, and turn all our thoughts towards the empty and transitory nature of riches and honors, we are, perhaps, all the while, flattering our natural indolence, which, hating the bustle of the world, and drudgery of business, seeks a presence of reason to give itself a full and uncontrolled indulgence. There is, however, one species of philosophy, which seems little liable to this inconvenience, and that because it

strikes in with no disorderly passion of the human mind, nor can mingle itself with any natural affection or propensity; and that is the Academic or Sceptical philosophy. The academics always talk of doubt and suspense of judgment, of danger in hasty determinations, of confining to very narrow bounds the enquiries of the understanding, and of renouncing all speculations which lie not within the limits of common life and practice. Nothing, therefore, can be more contrary than such a philosophy to the supine indolence of the mind, its rash arrogance, its lofty pretensions, and its superstitious credulity. Every passion is mortified by it, except the love of truth; and that passion never is, nor can be, carried to too high a degree. It is surprising, therefore, that this philosophy, which, in almost every instance, must be harmless and innocent, should be the subject of so much groundless reproach and obloquy. But, perhaps, the very circumstance, which renders it so innocent, is what chiefly exposes it to the public hatred and resentment. By flattering no irregular passion, it gains few partisans: By opposing so many vices and follies, it raises to itself abundance of enemies, who stigmatize it as libertine, profane, and irreligious.

Nor need we fear, that this philosophy, while it endeavors to limit our enquiries to common life, should ever undermine the reasonings of common life, and carry its doubts so far as to destroy all action, as well as speculation. Nature will always maintain her rights, and prevail in the end over any abstract reasoning whatsoever. Though we should conclude, for instance, as in the foregoing section, that, in all reasonings from experience, there is a step taken by the mind, which is not supported by any argument or process of the understanding, there is no danger, that these reasonings, on which almost all knowledge depends, will ever be affected by such a discovery. If the mind be not engaged by argument to make this step, it must be induced by some other principle of equal weight and authority; and that principle will preserve its influence as long as human nature remains the same. What that principle is, may well be worth the pains of enquiry.

Suppose a person, though endowed with the strongest faculties of reason and reflection, to be brought on a sudden into this world; he would, indeed, immediately observe a continual succession of objects, and one event following another; but he would not be able to discover any thing farther. He would not, at first, by any reasoning, be able to reach the idea of cause and effect; since the particular powers, by which all natural operations are performed, never appear to the senses; nor is it reasonable to conclude, merely because one event, in one instance, precedes another, that therefore the one is the cause, the other the effect. Their conjunction may be arbitrary and casual. There may be no reason to infer the existence of one from the appearance of the other. And in a word, such a person, without more experience, could never employ his conjecture or reasoning concerning any matter of fact, or be assured of any thing beyond what was immediately present to his memory and senses.

Suppose again, that he has acquired more experience, and has lived so long in the world as to have observed similar objects or events to be constantly conjoined together; what is the consequence of this experience? He immediately infers the existence of one object from the appearance of the other. Yet he has not, by all his experience, acquired any idea or knowledge of the secret power, by which the one object produces the other; nor is it, by any process of reasoning, he is engaged to draw this inference. But still he finds himself determined to draw it: And though he should be convinced that his understanding has no part in the operation, he would nevertheless continue in the same course of thinking. There is some other principle, which determines him to form such a conclusion.

This principle is Custom or Habit. For wherever the repetition of any particular act or operation produces a propensity to renew the same act or operation, without being impelled by any reasoning or process of the understanding; we always say, that this propensity is the effect of Custom. By employing that word, we pretend not to have given the ultimate reason of such a propensity. We only point out a principle of human nature, which is universally acknowledged, and which is well known by its effects. Perhaps, we can push our enquiries no farther, or pretend to give the cause of this cause; but must rest contented with it as the ultimate principle, which we can assign, of all our conclusions from

experience. It is sufficient satisfaction, that we can go so far; without repining at the narrowness of our faculties, because they will carry us no farther. And it is certain we here advance a very intelligible proposition at least, if not a true one, when we assert, that, after the constant conjunction of two objects, heat and flame, for instance, weight and solidity, we are determined by custom alone to expect the one from the appearance of the other. This hypothesis seems even the only one, which explains the difficulty, why we draw, from a thousand instances, an inference, which we are not able to draw from one instance, that is, in no respect, different from them. Reason is incapable of any such variation. The conclusions which it draws from considering one circle, are the same which it would form upon surveying all the circles in the universe. But no man, having seen only one body move after being impelled by another, could infer, that every other body will move after a like impulse. All inferences from experience, therefore, are effects of custom, not of reasoning.

Custom, then, is the great guide of human life. It is that principle alone, which renders our experience useful to us, and makes us expect, for the future, a similar train of events with those which have appeared in the past. Without the influence of custom, we should be entirely ignorant of every matter of fact, beyond what is immediately present to the memory and senses. We should never know how to adjust means to ends, or to employ our natural powers in the production of any effect. There would be an end at once of all action, as well as of the chief part of speculation.

But here it may be proper to remark that though our conclusions from experience carry us beyond our memory and senses, and assure us of matters of fact, which happened in the most distant places and most remote ages, yet some fact must always be present to the senses or memory, from which we may first proceed in drawing these conclusions. A man, who should find in a desert country the remains of pompous buildings, would conclude, that the country had, in ancient times, been cultivated by civilized inhabitants; but did nothing of this nature occur to him, he could never form such an inference. We learn the events of former ages from history; but then we must peruse the volumes, in which this instruction is contained, and thence carry up our inferences from one testimony to another, till we arrive at the eye-witnesses and spectators of these distant events. In a word, if we proceed not upon some fact, present to the memory or senses, our reasonings would be merely hypothetical; and however the particular links might be connected with each other, the whole chain of inferences would have nothing to support it, nor could we ever, by its means, arrive at the knowledge of any real existence. If I ask why you believe any particular matter of fact, which you relate, you must tell me some reason; and this reason will be some other fact, connected with it. But as you cannot proceed after this manner, in infinitum, you must at last terminate in some fact, which is present to your memory or senses; or must allow that your belief is entirely without foundation.

What then is the conclusion of the whole matter? A simple one; though, it must be confessed, pretty remote from the common theories of philosophy. All belief of matter of fact or real existence is derived merely from some object, present to the memory or senses, and a customary conjunction between that and some other object. Or in other words; having found, in many instances, that any two kinds of objects, flame and heat, snow and cold, have always been conjoined together; if flame or snow be presented anew to the senses, the mind is carried by custom to expect heat or cold, and to believe, that such a quality does exist, and will discover itself upon a nearer approach. This belief is the necessary result of placing the mind in such circumstances. It is an operation of the soul, when we are so situated, as unavoidable as to feel the passion of love, when we receive benefits: or hatred, when we meet with injuries. All these operations are a species of natural instincts, which no reasoning or process of the thought and understanding is able, either to produce, or to prevent.

At this point, it would be very allowable for us to stop our philosophical researches. In most questions, we can never make a single step farther; and in all questions, we must terminate here at last, after our most restless and curious enquiries. But still our curiosity will be pardonable, perhaps commendable, if it carry us on to still farther researches, and make us examine more accurately the nature of this belief, and of the customary conjunction, whence it is derived. By this means we may meet with some explications and

analogies, that will give satisfaction; at least to such as love the abstract sciences, and can be entertained with speculations, which, however accurate, may still retain a degree of doubt and uncertainty. As to readers of a different taste; the remaining part of this section is not calculated for them, and the following enquiries may well be understood, though it be neglected.

Part II

Nothing is more free than the imagination of man; and though it cannot exceed that original stock of ideas, furnished by the internal and external senses, it has unlimited power of mixing, compounding, separating, and dividing these ideas, in all the varieties of fiction and vision. It can feign a train of events, with all the appearance of reality, ascribe to them a peculiar time and place, conceive them as existent, and paint them out to itself with every circumstance, that belongs to any historical fact, which it believes with the greatest certainty. Wherein, therefore, consists the difference between such a fiction and belief? It lies not merely in any peculiar idea, which is annexed to such a conception as commands our assent, and which is wanting to every known fiction. For as the mind has authority over all its ideas, it could voluntarily annex this particular idea to any fiction, and consequently be able to believe whatever it pleases; contrary to what we find by daily experience. We can, in our conception, join the head of a man to the body of a horse; but it is not in our power to believe, that such an animal has ever really existed.

It follows, therefore, that the difference between fiction and belief lies in some sentiment or feeling, which is annexed to the latter, not to the former, and which depends not on the will, nor can be commanded at pleasure. It must be excited by nature, like all other sentiments; and must arise from the particular situation, in which the mind is placed at any particular juncture. Whenever any object is presented to the memory or the senses, it immediately, by the force of custom, carries the imagination to conceive that object, which is usually conjoined to it; and this conception is attended with a feeling or sentiment, different from the loose reveries of the fancy. In this consists the whole nature of belief. For as there is no matter of fact which we believe so firmly, that we cannot conceive the contrary, there would be no difference between the conception assented to, and that which is rejected, were it not for some sentiment, which distinguishes the one from the other. If I see a Billiard-ball moving towards another, on a smooth table, I can easily conceive it to stop upon contact. This conception implies no contradiction; but still it feels very differently from that conception, by which I represent to myself the impulse, and the communication of motion from one ball to another.

Were we to attempt a definition of this sentiment, we should, perhaps, find it a very difficult, if not an impossible task; in the same manner as if we should endeavor to define the feeling of cold or passion of anger, to a creature who never had any experience of these sentiments. Belief is the true and proper name of this feeling; and no one is ever at a loss to know the meaning of that term; because every man is every moment conscious of the sentiment represented by it. It may not, however, be improper to attempt a description of this sentiment; in hopes we may, by that means, arrive at some analogies, which may afford a more perfect explication of it. I say then, that belief is nothing but a more vivid, lively, forcible, firm, steady conception of an object, than what the imagination alone is ever able to attain. This variety of terms, which may seem so unphilosophical, is intended only to express that act of the mind, which renders realities, or what is taken for such, more present to us than fictions, causes them to weigh more in the thought, and gives them a superior influence on the passions and imagination. Provided we agree about the thing, it is needless to dispute about the terms. The imagination has the command over all its ideas, and can join and mix and vary them, in all the ways possible. It may conceive fictitious objects with all the circumstances of place and time. It may set them, in a manner, before our eyes, in their true colours, just as they might have existed. But as it is impossible, that this faculty of imagination can ever, of itself, reach belief, it is evident, that belief consists not in the peculiar nature or order of ideas, but in the manner of their conception, and in their feeling to the mind. I confess, that it is impossible perfectly to explain this feeling or manner of conception. We may make use of words, which

express something near it. But its true and proper name, as we observed before, is belief; which is a term, that every one sufficiently understands in common life. And in philosophy, we can go no farther than assert, that belief is something felt by the mind, which distinguishes the ideas of the judgment from the fictions of the imagination. It gives them more weight and influence; makes them appear of greater importance; enforces them in the mind; and renders them the governing principle of our actions. I hear at present, for instance, a person's voice, with whom I am acquainted; and the sound comes as from the next room. This impression of my senses immediately conveys my thought to the person, together with all the surrounding objects. I paint them out to myself as existing at present, with the same qualities and relations, of which I formerly knew them possessed. These ideas take faster hold of my mind, than ideas of an enchanted castle. They are very different to the feeling, and have a much greater influence of every kind, either to give pleasure or pain, joy or sorrow.

Let us, then, take in the whole compass of this doctrine, and allow, that the sentiment of belief is nothing but a conception more intense and steady than what attends the mere fictions of the imagination, and that this manner of conception arises from a customary conjunction of the object with something present to the memory or senses: I believe that it will not be difficult, upon these suppositions, to find other operations of the mind analogous to it, and to trace up these phenomena to principles still more general.

We have already observed, that nature has established connexions among particular ideas, and that no sooner one idea occurs to our thoughts than it introduces its correlative, and carries our attention towards it, by a gentle and insensible movement. These principles of connexion or association we have reduced to three, namely, Resemblance, Contiguity, and Causation: which are the only bonds, that unite our thoughts together, and beget that regular train of reflection or discourse, which, in a greater or less degree, takes place among all mankind. Now here arises a question, on which the solution of the present difficulty will depend. Does it happen, in all these relations, that, when one of the objects is presented to the senses or memory, the mind is not only carried to the conception of the correlative, but reaches a steadier and stronger conception of it than what otherwise it would have been able to attain? This seems to be the case with that belief, which arises from the relation of cause and effect. And if the case be the same with the other relations or principles of association, this may be established as a general law, which takes place in all the operations of the mind.

We may, therefore, observe, as the first experiment to our present purpose, that, upon the appearance of the picture of an absent friend, our idea of him is evidently enlivened by the resemblance, and that every passion, which that idea occasions, whether of joy or sorrow, acquires new force and vigor. In producing this effect, there concur both a relation and a present impression. Where the picture bears him no resemblance, at least was not intended for him, it never so much as conveys our thought to him: And where it is absent, as well as the person; though the mind may pass from the thought of the one to that of the other; it feels its idea to be rather weakened than enlivened by that transition. We take a pleasure in viewing the picture of a friend, when it is set before us; but when it is removed, rather choose to consider him directly, than by reflection in an image, which is equally distant and obscure.

The ceremonies of the Roman Catholic religion may be considered as instances of the same nature. The devotees of that superstition usually plead in excuse for the mummeries, with which they are upbraided, that they feel the good effect of those external motions, and postures, and actions, in enlivening their devotion and quickening their fervor, which otherwise would decay, if directed entirely to distant and immaterial objects. We shadow out the objects of our faith, say they, in sensible types and images, and render them more present to us by the immediate presence of these types, than it is possible for us to do, merely by an intellectual view and contemplation. Sensible objects have always a greater influence on the fancy than any other; and this influence they readily convey to those ideas, to which they are related, and which they resemble. I shall only infer from these practices, and this reasoning, that the effect of resemblance in enlivening the ideas is very common; and as in every case a resemblance and a

present impression must concur, we are abundantly supplied with experiments to prove the reality of the foregoing principle.

We may add force to these experiments by others of a different kind, in considering the effects of contiguity as well as of resemblance. It is certain, that distance diminishes the force of every idea, and that, upon our approach to any object; though it does not discover itself to our senses; it operates upon the mind with an influence, which imitates an immediate impression. The thinking on any object readily transports the mind to what is contiguous; but it is only the actual presence of an object, that transports it with a superior vivacity. When I am a few miles from home, whatever relates to it touches me more nearly than when I am two hundred leagues distant; though even at that distance the reflecting on any thing in the neighborhood of my friends or family naturally produces an idea of them. But as in this latter case, both the objects of the mind are ideas; notwithstanding there is an easy transition between them; that transition alone is not able to give a superior vivacity to any of the ideas, for want of some immediate impression.

No one can doubt but causation has the same influence as the other two relations of resemblance and contiguity. Superstitious people are fond of the relics of saints and holy men, for the same reason, that they seek after types or images, in order to enliven their devotion, and give them a more intimate and strong conception of those exemplary lives, which they desire to imitate. Now it is evident, that one of the best relics, which a devotee could procure, would be the handiwork of a saint; and if his cloths and furniture are ever to be considered in this light, it is because they were once at his disposal, and were moved and affected by him; in which respect they are to be considered as imperfect effects, and as connected with him by a shorter chain of consequences than any of those, by which we learn the reality of his existence.

Suppose, that the son of a friend, who had been long dead or absent, were presented to us; it is evident, that this object would instantly revive its correlative idea, and recall to our thoughts all past intimacies and familiarities, in more lively colours than they would otherwise have appeared to us. This is another phenomenon, which seems to prove the principle above-mentioned.

We may observe, that, in these phenomena, the belief of the correlative object is always presupposed; without which the relation could have no effect. The influence of the picture supposes, that we believe our friend to have once existed. Contiguity to home can never excite our ideas of home, unless we believe that it really exists. Now I assert, that this belief, where it reaches beyond the memory or senses, is of a similar nature, and arises from similar causes, with the transition of thought and vivacity of conception here explained. When I throw a piece of dry wood into a fire, my mind is immediately carried to conceive, that it augments, not extinguishes the flame. This transition of thought from the cause to the effect proceeds not from reason. It derives its origin altogether from custom and experience. And as it first begins from an object, present to the senses, it renders the idea or conception of flame more strong and lively than any loose, floating reverie of the imagination. That idea arises immediately. The thought moves instantly towards it, and conveys to it all that force of conception, which is derived from the impression present to the senses. When a sword is levelled at my breast, does not the idea of wound and pain strike me more strongly, than when a glass of wine is presented to me, even though by accident this idea should occur after the appearance of the latter object? But what is there in this whole matter to cause such a strong conception, except only a present object and a customary transition to the idea of another object, which we have been accustomed to conjoin with the former? This is the whole operation of the mind, in all our conclusions concerning matter of fact and existence; and it is a satisfaction to find some analogies, by which it may be explained. The transition from a present object does in all cases give strength and solidity to the related idea.

Here, then, is a kind of pre-established harmony between the course of nature and the succession of our ideas; and though the powers and forces, by which the former is governed, be wholly unknown to us; yet our thoughts and conceptions have still, we find, gone on in the same train with the other works of nature. Custom is that principle, by which this correspondence has been effected; so necessary to the subsistence of our species, and the regulation of our conduct, in every circumstance and occurrence of human life. Had not the presence of an object instantly excited the idea of those objects, commonly conjoined with it, all our knowledge must have been limited to the narrow sphere of our memory and senses; and we should never have been able to adjust means to ends, or employ our natural powers, either to the producing of good, or avoiding of evil. Those, who delight in the discovery and contemplation of final causes, have here ample subject to employ their wonder and admiration.

I shall add, for a further confirmation of the foregoing theory, that, as this operation of the mind, by which we infer like effects from like causes, and vice versa, is so essential to the subsistence of all human creatures, it is probable, that it could be trusted to the fallacious deductions of our reason, which is slow in its operations; appears not, in any degree, during the first years of infancy; and at best is, in every age and period of human life, extremely liable to error and mistake. It is more conformable to the ordinary wisdom of nature to secure so necessary an act of the mind, by some instinct or mechanical tendency, which may be infallible in its operations, may discover itself at the first appearance of life and thought, and may be independent of all the labored deductions of the understanding. As nature has taught us the use of our limbs, without giving us the knowledge of the muscles and nerves, by which they are actuated; so has she implanted in us an instinct, which carries forward the thought in a correspondent course to that which she has established among external objects; though we are ignorant of those powers and forces, on which this regular course and succession of objects totally depends.

FOR FURTHER REFLECTION

1. According to Hume, what is the origin of our ideas? How does Hume distinguish ideas from impressions? What two proofs does he offer for his thesis about ideas and impressions?

2. Hume's empiricism is more radical than Locke's because it leads to skepticism over metaphysical issues that Locke thought safe (such as the nature of the self, causality, and the

existence of God). Hume closes the *Enquiry* thus: "By way of conclusion to these reflections on diverse questions: When we run over libraries, persuaded of the principles here expounded, what havoc must we make? If we take in hand any volume, of divinity or metaphysics, for instance, let us ask: Does it contain any reasoning concerning quantity or number? No. Does it contain any experimental (probable) reasoning concerning matter of fact? No. Commit it then to the flames: for it can contain nothing but sophistry and illusion." Are you convinced by Hume's reasoning? If not, how would you argue against him?

3. How does Hume argue against justifying the belief that the future will resemble the past? Note that (1) the foundation of reasoning regarding matters of fact is the idea of causation; (2) the foundation of reasoning concerning causation is *experience;* and (3) the foundation of all conclusions regarding trust in experience is the principle of the uniformity of nature (for example, bread will continue to nourish us in the future because it has in the past, and the sun will rise tomorrow because it always has in the past). But why should we accept the uniformity of nature? There is no contradiction in supposing its opposite (let us say, that bread will no longer nourish us, or that the sun won't rise tomorrow). We cannot reason that something will continue to act in some way because it has always done so in the past, for that is begging the question. It seems that the foundation of the principle of the uniformity of nature is our trust in causation, of which the principle of the uniformity of nature is supposed to be the foundation. Do you see the circularity? Can you find anything wrong in Hume's reasoning?

Immanuel Kant

THE COPERNICAN REVOLUTION IN KNOWLEDGE

Immanuel Kant (1724–1804), who was born into a deeply pietistic Lutheran family in Königsberg, Germany, lived in that town his entire life and taught at the University of Königsberg. He lived a duty-bound, methodical life, so regular that citizens were said to have set their clocks by his walks. Kant is one of the premier philosophers in the Western tradition. In his monumental work *The Critique of Pure Reason* (1781), from which this selection is taken, he inaugurated a revolution in the theory of knowledge.

Who is right—the rationalists from Plato to Descartes, who argue that reason alone is the ultimate source of knowledge, or the empiricists, Locke and Hume, who argue that experience is the only source of knowledge? Are there innate ideas, as the rationalists contend, or are our minds completely blank at birth and need experience to write on them?

Kant began as a rationalist but on reading Hume was struck with the cogency of his argument. Hume "woke me from my dogmatic slumbers," Kant wrote, and henceforth accepted the idea that all our knowledge begins with experience. But Kant thought that Hume had made an invalid inference in concluding that all our knowledge arises from experience. Kant sought to demonstrate that the rationalists had an invaluable insight that had been lost in their flamboyant speculation—the insight that something determinate in the mind enables us to know what we know.

Kant argued that the mind is so structured and empowered that it imposes interpretive categories on our experience, so that we do not simply experience the world, as the empiricists claimed, but interpret it through the categorizing mechanisms of the mind. This theory is sometimes called Kant's Copernican revolution, for just as Copernicus showed that it was not the sun that revolved around the earth, but vice versa, that the earth revolved around the sun, likewise Kant showed that it was not the world that caused us to experience things the way we do but the categories of the mind that caused us to experience the world and everything else the way we do.

Here we need to say something about a priori and a posteriori knowledge. A priori knowledge is what we know before experience. It is opposed to a posteriori knowledge, which follows and is based on our experience. You may recall that Hume believes all knowledge claims regarding matters of fact are a posteriori, and only analytic statements (such as mathematical truths or statements such as "All mothers are women") are known a priori. But Kant believes it is possible to have a priori knowledge about matters of fact. Indeed, he thinks that mathematical truth is not analytic but synthetic (the predicate adds something to the subject) and that there are also other examples of synthetic a priori knowledge, such as knowledge of time, space, causality, and moral law.

PREFACE TO THE SECOND EDITION

. . . Until now we have assumed that all our knowledge must conform to objects. But every attempt to extend our knowledge of objects by establishing something in regard to them a priori, by means of concepts, have, on this assumption, ended in failure. Therefore, we must see whether we may have better success in our metaphysical task if we begin with the assumption that objects must conform to our knowledge. In this way we would have knowledge of objects a priori. We should then be proceeding in the same way as Copernicus in his revolutionary hypothesis. After he failed to make progress in explaining the movements of the heavenly bodies on the supposition that they all revolved around the observer, he decided to reverse the relationship and made the observer revolve around the heavenly body, the sun, which was at rest. A similar experiment can be done in meta-

physics with regard to the intuition of objects. If our intuition must conform to the constitution of the object, I do not see how we could know anything of the object a priori, but if the object of sense must conform to the constitution of our faculty of intuition, then a priori knowledge is possible. . . .

INTRODUCTION

I.—Of the Difference Between Pure and Empirical Knowledge

That all our knowledge begins with experience there can be no doubt. For how is it possible that the faculty of cognition should be awakened into exercise otherwise than by means of objects which affect our senses, and partly of themselves produce representations, partly rouse our powers of understanding into activity, to compare, to connect, or to separate these,

Preface from Immanuel Kant, *The Critique of Pure Reason* (1781), trans. Louis P. Pojman. Remainder of selection, trans. J. M. D. Meiklejohn (New York: Wiley, 1855); originally published 1781.

and so to convert the raw material of our sensuous impressions into a knowledge of objects, which is called experience? In respect of time, therefore, no knowledge of ours is antecedent to experience, but begins with it.

But, though all our knowledge begins with experience, it by no means follows that all arises out of experience. For, on the contrary, it is quite possible that our empirical knowledge is a compound of that which we receive through impressions, and that which the faculty of cognition supplies from itself (sensuous impressions giving merely the *occasion*), an addition which we cannot distinguish from the original element given by sense, till long practice has made us attentive to, and skilful in separating it. It is, therefore, a question which requires close investigation, and is not to be answered at first sight—whether there exists a knowledge altogether independent of experience, and even of all sensuous impressions? Knowledge of this kind is called a priori, in contradistinction to empirical knowledge, which has its sources a posteriori, that is, in experience.

But the expression, "a priori," is not as yet definite enough adequately to indicate the whole meaning of the question above stated. For, in speaking of knowledge which has its sources in experience, we are wont to say, that this or that may be known a priori, because we do not derive this knowledge immediately from experience, but from a general rule, which, however, we have itself borrowed from experience. Thus, if a man undermined his house, we say, "he might know a priori that it would have fallen"; that is, he needed not to have waited for the experience that it did actually fall. But still, a priori, he could not know even this much. For, that bodies are heavy, and, consequently, that they fall when their supports are taken away, must have been known to him previously, by means of experience.

By the term "knowledge a priori," therefore, we shall in the sequel understand, not such as is independent of this or that kind of experience, but such as is absolutely so of *all* experience. Opposed to this is empirical knowledge, or that which is possible only a posteriori, that is, through experience. Knowledge a priori is either pure or impure. Pure knowledge a priori is that with which no empirical element is mixed up. For example, the proposition, "Every change has a cause," is a proposition a priori, but impure, because change is a conception which can only be derived from experience.

II.—The Human Intellect, Even in an Unphilosophical State, Is in Possession of Certain Cognitions, A Priori

The question now is as to a *criterion*, by which we may securely distinguish a pure from an empirical cognition. Experience no doubt teaches us that this or that object is constituted in such and such a manner, but not that it could not possibly exist otherwise. Now, in the first place, if we have a proposition which contains the idea of necessity in its very conception, it is a judgment a priori; if, moreover, it is not derived from any other proposition, unless from one equally involving the idea of necessity, it is absolutely a priori. Secondly, an empirical judgment never exhibits strict and absolute, but only assumed and comparative universality (by induction); therefore, the most we can say is—so far as we have hitherto observed, there is no exception to this or that rule. If, on the other hand, a judgment carries with it strict and absolute universality, that is, admits of no possible exception, it is not derived from experience, but is valid absolutely a priori.

Empirical universality is, therefore, only an arbitrary extension of validity, from that which may be predicated of a proposition valid in most cases, to that which is asserted of a proposition which holds good in all; as, for example, in the affirmation, "all bodies are heavy." When, on the contrary, strict universality characterizes a judgment, it necessarily indicates another peculiar source of knowledge, namely, a faculty of cognition a priori. Necessity and strict universality, therefore, are infallible tests for distinguishing pure from empirical knowledge, and are inseparably connected with each other. But as in the use of these criteria the empirical limitation is sometimes more easily detected than the contingency of the judgment, or the unlimited universality which we attach to a judgment is often a more convincing proof than its necessity, it may be advisable to use the criteria separately, each being by itself infallible.

Now, that in the sphere of human cognition, we have judgments which are necessary, and in the strictest sense universal, consequently pure a priori, it will be an easy matter to show. If we desire an example from the sciences, we need only take any proposition in mathematics. If we cast our eyes upon the commonest operations of the understanding, the proposition, "every change must have a cause," will amply serve our purpose. In the latter case, indeed, the conception of a cause so plainly involves the conception of a necessity of connection with an effect, and of a strict universality of the law, that the very notion of a cause would entirely disappear, were we to derive it, like Hume, from a frequent association of what happens with that which precedes, and the habit thence originating of connecting representations—the necessity inherent in the judgment being therefore merely subjective. Besides, without seeking for such examples of principles existing a priori in cognition, we might easily show that such principles are the indispensable basis of the possibility of experience itself, and consequently prove their existence a priori. For whence could our experience itself acquire certainty, if all the rules on which it depends were themselves empirical, and consequently fortuitous? No one, therefore, can admit the validity of the use of such rules as first principles. But, for the present, we may content ourselves with having established the fact, that we do possess and exercise a faculty of pure a priori cognition; and, secondly, with having pointed out the proper tests of such cognition, namely, universality and necessity.

Not only in judgments, however, but even in conceptions, is an a priori origin manifest. For example, if we take away by degrees from our conceptions of a body all that can be referred to mere sensuous experience—color, hardness or softness, weight, even impenetrability—the body will then vanish; but the space which it occupied still remains, and this it is utterly impossible to annihilate in thought. Again, if we take away, in like manner, from our empirical conception of any object, corporeal or incorporeal, all properties which mere experience has taught us to connect with it, still we cannot think away those through which we cogitate it as substance, or adhering to substance, although our conception of substance is more determined than that of an object. Compelled,

therefore, by that necessity with which the conception of substance forces itself upon us, we must confess that it has its seat in our faculty of cognition a priori. . . .

IV.—Of the Difference Between Analytical and Synthetical Judgments

In all judgments wherein the relation of a subject to the predicate is thought (I mention affirmative judgments only here; the application to negative will be very easy), this relation is possible in two different ways. Either the predicate B belongs to the subject A, as somewhat which is contained (though covertly) in the conception A; or the predicate B lies completely out of the conception A, although it stands in connection with it. In the first instance, I term the judgment analytical, in the second, synthetical. Analytical judgments (affirmative) are therefore those in which the connection of the predicate with the subject is cogitated through identity; those in which this connection is cogitated without identity, are called synthetical judgments. The former may be called *explicative*, the latter *augmentative*[1] judgments; because the former add in the predicate nothing to the conception of the subject, but only analyze it into its constituent conceptions, which were thought already in the subject, although in a confused manner; the latter add to our conceptions of the subject a predicate which was not contained in it, and which no analysis could ever have discovered therein. For example, when I say, "all bodies are extended," this is an analytical judgment. For I need not go beyond the conception of *body* in order to find extension connected with it, but merely analyze the conception, that is, become conscious of the manifold properties which I think in that conception, in order to discover this predicate in it: it is therefore an analytical judgment. On the other hand, when I say, "all bodies are heavy," the predicate is something totally different from that which I think in the mere conception of a body. But the addition of such a predicate therefore, it becomes a synthetical judgment.

Judgments of experience, as such, are always synthetical. For it would be absurd to think of grounding an analytical judgment on experience, because in forming such a judgment, I need not go out of the sphere of my conceptions, and therefore recourse to the testimony of experience is quite unnecessary. That "bodies are extended" is not an empirical judgment, but a proposition which stands firm a priori. For before addressing myself to experience, I already have in my conception all the requisite conditions for the judgment, and I have only to extract the predicate from the conception, according to the principle of contradiction, and thereby at the same time become conscious of the necessity of the judgment, a necessity which I could never learn from experience. On the other hand, though at first I do not at all include the predicate of weight in my conception of body in general, that conception still indicates an object of experience, a part of the totality of experience, to which I can still add other parts; and this I do when I recognize by observation that bodies are heavy. I can cognize beforehand by analysis the conception of body through the characteristics of extension, impenetrability, shape, etc., all which are cogitated in this conception. But now I extend my knowledge, and looking back on experience from which I had derived this conception of body, I find weight at all times connected with the above characteristics, and therefore I synthetically add to my conceptions this as a predicate, and say, "all bodies are heavy." Thus it is experience upon which rests the possibility of the synthesis of the predicate of weight with the conception of body, because both conceptions, although the one is not contained in the other, still belong to one another (only contingently, however), as parts of a whole, namely, of experience, which is itself a synthesis of intuitions.

But to synthetical judgments a priori, such aid is entirely wanting. If I go out of and beyond the conception A, in order to recognize another B as connected with it, what foundation have I to rest on, whereby to render the synthesis possible? I have here no longer the advantage of looking out in the sphere of experience for what I want. Let us take, for example, the proposition, "everything that happens has a cause." In the conception of *something that happens,* I indeed think an existence which a certain time antecedes, and from this I can derive analytical judgments. But the conception of a cause lies quite out of the above conception, and indicates something entirely different from "that which happens,"

and is consequently not contained in that conception. How then am I able to assert concerning the general conception—"that which happens"—something entirely different from that conception, and to recognize the conception of cause although not contained in it, yet as belonging to it, and even necessarily? What is here the unknown = X, upon which the understanding rests when it believes it has found, out of the conception A a foreign predicate B, which it nevertheless considers to be connected with it? It cannot be experience, because the principle adduced annexes the two representations, cause and effect, to the representation existence, not only with universality, which experience cannot give, but also with the expression of necessity, therefore completely a priori and from pure conceptions. Upon such synthetical, that is augmentative propositions, depends the whole aim of our speculative knowledge a priori; for although analytical judgments are indeed highly important and necessary, they are so, only to arrive at that clearness of conceptions which is requisite for a sure and extended synthesis, and this alone is a real acquisition.

V.—In All Theoretical Sciences of Reason, Synthetical Judgments A Priori Are Contained as Principles

1. Mathematical judgments are always synthetical. Hitherto this fact, though incontestably true and very important in its consequences, seems to have escaped the analysts of the human mind, nay, to be in complete opposition to all their conjectures. For as it was found that mathematical conclusions all proceed according to the principle of contradiction (which the nature of every apodictic certainty requires), people became persuaded that the fundamental principles of the science also were recognized and admitted in the same way. But the notion is fallacious; for although a synthetical proposition can certainly be discerned by means of the principle of contradiction, this is possible only when another synthetical proposition precedes, from which the latter is deduced, but never of itself.

Before all, be it observed, that proper mathematical propositions are always judgments a priori, and not empirical, because they carry along with them the conception of necessity, which cannot be given by experience. If this be demurred to, it matters not; I will then limit my assertion to *pure* mathematics, the very conception of which implies, that it consists of knowledge altogether non-empirical and a priori.

We might, indeed, at first suppose that the proposition 7 + 5 = 12, is a merely analytical proposition, following (according to the principle of contradiction), from the conception of the sum of seven and five. But if we regard it more narrowly, we find that our conception of the sum of seven and five contains nothing more than the uniting of both sums into one, whereby it cannot at all be cogitated what this single number is which embraces both. The conception of twelve is by no means obtained by merely cogitating the union of seven and five; and we may analyze our conception of such a possible sum as long as we will, still we shall never discover in it the notion of twelve. We must go beyond these conceptions, and have recourse to an intuition which corresponds to one of the two—our five fingers, for example, or like Segner in his "Arithmetic," five points, and so by degrees, add the units contained in the five given in the intuition, to the conception of seven. For I first take the number 7, and, for the conception of five calling in the aid of the fingers of my hand as objects of intuition, I add the units, which I before took together to make up the number 5, gradually now by means of the material image my hand, to the number 7, and by this process, I at length see the number 12 arise. That 7 should be added to 5, I have certainly cogitated in my conception of a sum = 7 + 5, but not that this sum was equal to 12. Arithmetical propositions are therefore always synthetical, of which we may become more clearly convinced by trying large numbers. For it will thus become quite evident, that, turn and twist our conceptions as we may, it is impossible, without having recourse to intuition, to arrive at the sum total or product by means of the mere analysis of our conceptions. Just as little is any principle of pure geometry analytical. "A straight line between two points is the shortest," is a synthetical proposition. For my conception of *straight,* contains no notion of *quantity,* but is merely *qualitative.* The conception of the *shortest* is therefore wholly an addition, and by no analy-

sis can it be extracted from our conception of a straight line. Intuition must therefore here lend its aid, by means of which and thus only, our synthesis is possible.

Some few principles preposited by geometricians are, indeed, really analytical, and depend on the principle of contradiction. They serve, however, like identical propositions, as links in the chain of method, not as principles—for example, *a* = *a,* the whole is equal to itself, or (*a* + *b*) > *a,* the whole is greater than its part. And yet even these principles themselves, though they derive their validity from pure conceptions, are only admitted in mathematics because they can be presented in intuition. What causes us here commonly to believe that the predicate of such apodictic judgments is already contained in our conception, and that the judgment is therefore analytical, is merely the equivocal nature of the expression. We must join in thought a certain predicate to a given conception, and this necessity cleaves already to the conception. But the question is, not what we must join in thought to the given conception, but what we really think therein, though only obscurely, and then it becomes manifest, that the predicate pertains to these conceptions, necessarily indeed, yet not as thought in the conception itself, but by virtue of an intuition, which must be added to the conception.

2. The science of Natural Philosophy (Physics) contains in itself synthetical judgments a priori, as principles. I shall adduce two propositions. For instance, the proposition, "in all changes of the material world, the quantity of matter remains unchanged"; or, that, "in all communication of motion, action and reaction must always be equal." In both of these, not only is the necessity, and therefore their origin, a priori clear, but also that they are synthetical propositions. For in the conception of matter, I do not cogitate its permanency, but merely its presence in space, which it fills. I therefore really go out of and beyond the conception of matter, in order to think on to it something a priori, which I did not think in it. The proposition is therefore not analytical, but synthetical, and nevertheless conceived a priori; and so it is with regard to the other propositions of the pure part of natural philosophy.

3. As to Metaphysics, even if we look upon it merely as an attempted science, yet, from the nature of human reason, an indispensable one, we find that it must contain synthetical propositions a priori. It is not merely the duty of metaphysics to dissect, and thereby analytically to illustrate the conceptions which we form a priori of things; but we seek to widen the range of our a priori knowledge. For this purpose, we must avail ourselves of such principles as add something to the original conception—something not identical with, nor contained in it, and by means of synthetical judgments a priori, leave far behind us the limits of experience; for example, in the proposition, "the world must have a beginning," and such like. Thus metaphysics, according to the proper aim of the science, consists merely of synthetical a priori propositions.

NOTE

1. That is, judgments which really add to, and do not merely analyze or explain the conceptions which make up the sum of our knowledge.

FOR FURTHER REFLECTION

1. Explain Kant's Copernican revolution in knowledge.
2. What does Kant mean by saying that "though all our knowledge begins with experience, it by no means follows that all arises out of experience"?
3. Define a priori and a posteriori knowledge, according to Kant. What examples does he offer of a priori knowledge (or cognition)?
4. How does Kant distinguish between analytic and synthetic judgments?
5. Do you think this revolutionary system of combining empiricist with rationalist aspects is a successful compromise or synthesis? Or is something lost? For example, Kant affirms that we can never know reality in itself—the *Ding an Sich*—but can only know the appearances of reality filtered through the categories of the mind. But if causality is a category of the mind and doesn't exist in reality, how do we know the appearances have anything to do with reality?

B. CONTEMPORARY THEORIES ON THE LIMITS OF KNOWLEDGE

Classical philosophers focused on a range of epistemological issues, but foremost among their concerns were the issues of certainty and skepticism. On the one hand, there were optimists like Plato and Descartes, who believed that we could achieve complete certainty in our quest for truth, as long as we conducted our quest in the proper manner. On the other hand, there were pessimists like Sextus Empiricus and Hume, who raised serious questions about our ability to know anything at all. The nagging issues of certainty and skepticism set much of the agenda for contemporary epistemology.

The first reading, "Science and Myth" by John Maynard Smith, discusses the relationship of science to values. Both are important for the flourishing of human civilization, and both are created by people. Nevertheless, Smith argues, they are very different enterprises, and the key difference involves the notion of falsification: scientific theories are at least potentially capable of being disproved by new facts or experiments. Take, for example, the time-honored scientific contention that aspirin helps relieve pain. In spite of the wealth of scientific studies supporting this assertion, the possibility is still open that new and better-conducted studies will show that aspirin actually has no real effect on pain relief. All scientific theories carry this vulnerability, and that is a good thing, rather than a bad one, since it makes science directly dependent on evidence—both old and new evidence. Many values that we hold, though, are not like that, such as the view that Elvis Presley is the greatest singer of all time. If I'm committed to this view, no argument to the contrary will affect me; my view is unfalsifiable. Smith argues that many values masquerade as science, but, while science should be committed to some values, values have no role within the scientific theories themselves.

Norman Malcolm, in the second reading, draws a critical distinction between two types of knowledge: strong and weak. Strong knowledge takes place when nothing at all would count as evidence for the falsehood of a belief from the perspective of a person who holds that belief. For example, my belief that $2 + 2 = 4$ is strong, since nothing could convince me that I'm wrong about it. Weak knowledge, by contrast, allows for the possibility that a belief may be mistaken. For instance my belief that $92 \times 16 = 1472$ is weak, since I recognize that I could have miscalculated this equation.

In the third reading, Karl Popper argues that there is a realm of objective knowledge, is independent of particular knowers. He calls this the "third world" of knowledge, in contrast to the "first world" of knowledge, which is about physical things, and the "second world," which is about states of mental consciousness. The third world is the realm of propositions, scientific truths, and even ethical truths. An example that he gives is this: "From the entry 'Knowledge' in *the Oxford English Dictionary: knowledge* is a 'branch of learning; a science; an art.'" According to Popper, this third world is a creation of humans, but nevertheless has its own independent objective existence.

In stark contrast to Popper, in the fourth reading Richard Rorty attacks the notion of objective truth and argues that all our notions of reality depend on some underlying social convention that he calls "social solidarity." He resists classifying his view as "relativist" and instead sees it as pragmatic. To the extent that there are many different disciplines that devise their own conventions, the notion of truth "applies equally to the judgments of lawyers, anthropologists, physicists, philologists and literary critics." Their mutually shared approach, he believes, helps blur the distinction between these disciplines: they "denote communities whose boundaries were as fluid as the interests of their members."

In the fifth reading, Daniel Dennett attacks the trend in contemporary epistemology to see that truth is a mere relative concept. The recent intellectual movement called "postmodernism" champions such relativism. In epistemology, the basic theme of postmodernism is that old-fashioned conceptions of truth, objectivity, and rationality held by modern philosophers, such as Descartes, Locke, and Kant, are horribly misguided. All so-called facts are only beliefs that arise within some social convention, and interpretations of so-called reality may differ from social group to social group. This is largely the perspective taken by Rorty in the previous selection, and this is what Dennett opposes here. Dennett argues that in the evolutionary development of life on this planet, there are great survival benefits for organisms to differentiate correctly between appearance and reality and "get it right." Modern science, he believes, is on the right path to describing reality accurately; while there are imperfections in scientific methods, the methods are nonetheless "indefinitely perfectible."

In the sixth reading, Lorraine Code offers a middle ground position between relativists and objectivists. We should indeed recognize that the social perspective of the inquirer has a real impact on scientific inquiry; at the same time, though, we should recognize that there are realities in the world that restrict the range of claims that we can make. The downfall of traditional epistemology was its overemphasis on objectivity and impartiality—an approach, she charges, that owes to male ways of thinking. According to Code, a female approach to epistemology would reject rigid notions of objectivity and follow the middle-ground view that she outlines.

JOHN MAYNARD SMITH

SCIENCE AND MYTH

John Maynard Smith (b. 1920) is an evolutionary biologist who teaches at the University of Sussex in England. In this essay, he compares science with myth. By *myth*, he means the stories that embody nonscientific value. Sometimes he simply means *value*, such as moral principles, the value of truth, and the ideal of equal opportunity. Both myth and science are necessary for human survival and flourishing, but they have different structures. Scientific theories can be falsified, whereas myths cannot. For example, if I set forth a theory of the planets' orbits, I should be able to predict the location of Mars on a given night. If you, using adequate telescopes, don't observe Mars at that location, my theory is falsified; it fails the crucial test. Similarly, Lamarckian evolutionary theory was falsified when it was observed that animal offspring failed to inherit the learned traits of their parents. Myths are not testable in the same way. For a good discussion of the method of falsifiability, see "A Debate on the Rationality of Religious Belief" among Anthony Flew, R. M. Hare, and Basil Mitchell in Part IIIC.

Recently, after giving a radio talk on Charles Darwin, I received through the post a pamphlet by Don Smith entitled "Why Are There Gays at All? Why Hasn't Evolution Eliminated Gayness Millions of Years Ago?" The pamphlet points to a genuine concern: the prevalence of homosexual behavior in our species is not understood and is certainly not something that would be predicted from Darwinian theory. Smith wrote the pamphlet because he believes the persecution of gays has been strengthened and justified by the existence of a theory of evolution that asserts gays are unfit because they do not reproduce. He also believes that gays can be protected from future persecution only if it can be shown that they have played an essential and creative role in evolution.

His argument is that, in evolution, novelty arises when individuals adopt mating habits different from those typical of their species: it is summed up on a button that reads "Sexual deviation is the mainspring of evolution."

I do not find this argument particularly persuasive, but that is not the point I want to make. I think Smith would have been better advised to have written, "If people despise gays because gayness does not contribute to biological fitness, they are wrong to do so. It would be as sensible to persecute mathematicians because an ability to solve differential equations does not contribute to fitness. A scientific theory—Darwinism or any other—has nothing to say about the value of a human being."

The point I am making is that Smith is demanding of evolutionary biology that it be a myth; that is, a story with a moral message. He is not alone in this. Elaine Morgan's book *The Descent of Woman* is an account of the origin of *Homo sapiens* that is intended to give mythical support to the women's movement by emphasizing the role of the female sex and, in particular, the mother-child bond. She claims, with reason, that many other accounts of human evolution have, perhaps unconsciously, placed undue emphasis on the role of males. Earlier, George Bernard Shaw wrote *Back to Methuselah* (1922) avowedly as an evolutionary myth, because he found in Darwinism a justification of selfishness and brutality and because he wished instead to support the Lamarckian theory of the inheritance of acquired characters, which he saw as justifying free will and individual endeavor.

We should not be surprised by Don Smith, Elaine Morgan, and Bernard Shaw. In all societies, people have constructed myths about the origins of the universe and of humans. The function of these myths is to define our place in nature and thus to give us a sense of purpose and value. Since Darwinism is, among other things, an account of human origins, is it any wonder that it is expected to carry a moral message?

The people and the objects that figure in a myth stand not only for themselves but also as symbols of other things. To some extent, myths and their symbolic components develop simply because human beings find it difficult to accept any input as meaningless. Shown an inkblot, we see witches, bats, and dragons. This refusal to accept input as mere noise lies at the root of divination by tarot cards, tea leaves, the livers or shoulders of animals, or the sticks of the *I Ching*. It may also account for the strangely late development of a mathematical theory of probability or of any scientific theory with a chance element. As anthropologist Dan Sperber has written, "Symbolic thought is capable, precisely, of transforming noise into information."

Another—and in the present context, more important—function of myths is to give moral and evaluative guidance. Some mythmaking is quite conscious. In *Back to Methuselah,* for example, Shaw deliberately invented a story that would have the moral effect he desired. More usually, however, I suspect that a mythmaker conceives a story that moves him or her in a particular way—at its lowest, it reinforces prejudices, and at its highest, to borrow Aristotle's words, it evokes feelings of pity and fear. People repeat myths because they hope to persuade others to behave in certain ways.

This raises the question of why we use myths rather than simple statements of instruction. Why do we talk of King Alfred and the cakes, for example, instead of saying that people in important positions should be modest? Perhaps a story whose meaning has to be puzzled out or guessed at carries more conviction than a mere instruction. What we imagine is more important than what we are told.

Sometimes, I find it hard to discover how few people distinguish stories intended to give moral guidance from those meant simply to supply technical help. Confusion seems particularly likely to crop up when rituals are involved. For example, if, before going into battle, a man sharpens his spear and undergoes ritual purification (or, for that matter, cleans his rifle and goes to mass), he may regard the two procedures as equally efficacious. Indeed, they may well be so, one in preparing the spear and the other himself. If we regard the former as more practical, we do so only because we understand metallurgy better than psychology.

Despite the difficulty, most people do try to distinguish procedures and technical instructions that alter the external world from procedures and stories intended to alter our own state of consciousness or persuade us that certain things are right. Indeed, we take some trouble when educating our children to give hints about which category of information is being transmitted. For example, a surprisingly large proportion of the stories read aloud to children, particularly those with a moral message, are about talking animals or even talking steam engines. It is as if we wanted to be sure that the stories are not taken literally.

While such efforts may be successful in many spheres of human endeavor, the examples of Don Smith and Bernard Shaw show how hard it is for many people to separate science, and especially evolution, from myth. One reaction to this difficulty is to assert that there is no difference, that evolution theory has no more claim to objective truth than Genesis. Many scientists would be enraged by such an assertion, but rage is no substitute for argument. In the last century, it was widely held that the scientific method, conceived of as establishing theories by induction from observation, led to certain knowledge. Darwin and Einstein have robbed us of that certainty—or have liberated us from that prison. If, as Darwin showed, there is not a fixed and finite number of things in the universe, each with a knowable essence, then induction is logically impossible. Einstein, in turn, showed that what scientists had been most confident of—classical mechanics—was at worst false and at best a special case of a more general theory. After that twin blow, certain knowledge is something we can expect only at our funerals.

But it is one thing to admit that scientific knowledge cannot be certain and another to claim that there is no difference between science and myth. Karl Popper, perhaps the most influential contemporary philosopher of science, has told us that it was the impact of Einstein, and in particular the wish to distinguish Einstein's theory from those of Freud, Adler, and Marx, that led him to propose falsifiability as the criterion for separating science from pseudoscience. If a theory is scientific, he suggested, observations can be conceived of which, if they were accepted, would show the theory to be false. In contrast, he suggests that no conceivable pattern of human behavior could falsify Freudian theory.

Popper's views have been attacked, primarily on the grounds that there are no such things as theory-free observations. Every observation is subject to interpretation, conscious and unconscious. Consequently, there can never be certain grounds for rejecting a scientific theory, and hence the distinction between science and pseudoscience disappears.

This criticism seems to me largely to miss the point. If Popper were claiming that scientific knowledge were certain, then the impossibility of certain falsification would indeed be damaging. But he makes no such claim. He insists on two things. First, a scientific theory must assert that certain kinds of events cannot

happen, so that the theory is falsified if these events are subsequently observed, and second, there is inevitably a logical asymmetry in any attempt to test a theory, so that a theory can be falsified but cannot be proved true by the acceptance of observation.

There is, however, a tide of ideas that would deny the distinction. The emotional force behind this tide derives, in part, from an entirely proper disgust at some of the consequences of technology in the modern world and, in part, from an equally proper wish to treat the ideas of other peoples as of equal value to our own. What is common to these two reactions is the conviction, which I share, that scientific theories are not the only kind of idea that we need. A frequently drawn corollary of this conviction, which I do not share, is that scientific ideas are not distinguishable from other ideas.

. . . A crucial distinction must be made between the psychological sources of a theory and the testing of it. If Darwin's ideas, or Newton's, were accepted because they were socially appealing, then indeed science and myth would be indistinguishable. But I do not think that they were. They were accepted because of their explanatory power and ability to withstand experimental test. Of course, new ideas in science sometimes come from analogies with society, just as, in one scientific discipline, such as biology, they arise by analogy with others, such as physics and engineering. But what matters for the progress of science is not where the ideas come from but how they are treated.

Society influences the development of science through both the problems that seem worth solving and the resources available for their solution. I have little doubt that society also influences scientists, both as individuals and groups, by making some ideas seem worth pursuing and others implausible or unpromising. For example, my own caution about applying to humans ideas drawn from a study of animal societies—a caution that contrasts with the enthusiasm of such scientists as E. O. Wilson and Richard Alexander—probably arose because I grew up under the shadow of Hitler and the Nazi theories of racial superiority and biological determinism and not because of anything internal to biology or sociology.

There is, however, a caricature inherent in the externalist view of science that I reject emphatically. This is the idea that we can evaluate a scientific theory by reference to the society in which it was born, or to the moral and political conclusions that might be drawn from it. Once accept that view and science is dead, as genetics died in Russia in 1948, when Stalin supported Lysenko's Lamarckian views against the Mendelians. Stalin took his position partly in the hope of quick returns in agricultural productivity and partly because Lysenko's belief in the inheritance of acquired characters seemed to accord better with Marxism than did the orthodox—and, as it happens, more nearly correct—Mendelian doctrine that hereditary characteristics are transmitted from parent to offspring by genes and that the genetic message is independent from changes induced in the body of the parent during its lifetime.

I would not have spent so much time discussing the difference between scientific theories and myths if the difference between them were obvious. Indeed, they have much in common. Both are constructs of the human mind, and both are intended to have a significance wider than the direct assertions they contain. Popper suggested falsifiability as the criterion distinguishing them, and I think he was right. However, we can often also distinguish them by their function: the function of a scientific theory is to account for experience—often, it is true, the rather esoteric experience emerging from deliberate experiment; the function of a myth is to provide a source and justification for values. What, then, should be the relation between them?

Three views are tenable. The first, sometimes expressed as a demand for "normative science," is that the same mental constructs should serve both as myths and as scientific theories. If I am right, this widely held view underlies the criticism of Darwinism from gays, from the women's movement, from socialists, and so on. It explains the preference expressed by some churchmen for "big bang" as opposed to "steady state" theories of cosmology. Although well intentioned, it seems to me pernicious in its effects. Applied to evolution theory, it means either that we must embrace Darwinism and draw from it the conclusion that gays are unnatural and social services wicked or that we must embrace Lamarckism whether or not the genetic

evidence supports it. Normative science will be bad morality or bad science, and most probably both.

The second view is that we should do without myths and confine ourselves to science. This is the view I held at the age of twenty, but it really won't do. If, as I now believe, scientific theories say nothing about what is right but only about what is possible, we need some other source of values, and that source has to be myth, in the broadest sense of the term.

The third view, and I think the only sensible one, is that we need both myths and scientific theories, but that we must be as clear as we can about which is which. In essence, this was the view urged by the French molecular biologist Jaques Monod in *Chance and Necessity* (1972). Oddly, Monod was almost universally derided by his critics for arguing that one can derive values from science, when in fact he argued the precise opposite. His case was that there is no place in science for teleological, or value-laden, hypotheses. Yet, to do science, one must first be committed to some values—not least, to the value of seeking the truth. Since this value cannot be derived from science, it must be seen as a prior moral commitment, needed before science is possible. So far from values being derived from science, Monod saw science as depending on values.

Although I disagree with some aspects of his book, I agree with Monod on two basic points. First, values do not derive from science but are necessary for the practice of science. Second, we should distinguish as clearly as we can between science and myth. We should make this distinction, not because we could then discard the myths and retain only science, but because the roles they play are different. Scientific theories tell us what is possible; myths tell us what is desirable. Both are needed to guide proper action.

FOR FURTHER REFLECTION

1. According to John Maynard Smith, what are the respective roles of science and myth in human affairs? Are they really the same? If not, how do they differ?
2. Smith writes that Darwin and Einstein robbed us of the certainty that we once had about our beliefs and theories. What does he mean by this?

3. Smith says that a crucial distinction must be made between the psychological sources of a theory and testing that theory. What does this mean? Can you give an illustration?

4. Do you agree with Smith that science and values are both human inventions? Could they instead be discoveries?

NORMAN MALCOLM

TWO TYPES OF KNOWLEDGE

Norman Malcolm (b. 1911) was educated at Cambridge University, where he studied under Ludwig Wittgenstein, perhaps the most influential philosopher of this century, and taught philosophy for many years at Cornell University. He is the author of several works, including *Ludwig Wittgenstein: A Memoir* (1958), *Dreaming* (1959), and *Knowledge and Certainty* (1963). Malcolm begins this essay with a quotation from the British philosopher H. A. Prichard to the effect that we can discover in ourselves whether we *know* some proposition or whether we merely *believe* it. Does knowledge light up a different mental state than belief does? This thesis has a history that goes back to Plato and Descartes. Malcolm analyzes the thesis and rejects it on one level but then argues that it does convey a truth about the difference between strong and weak knowledge claims.

'We must recognize that when we know something we either do, or by reflecting, can know that our condition is one of knowing that thing, while when we believe something, we either do or can know that our condition is one of believing and not of knowing: so that we cannot mistake belief for knowledge or vice versa.' [1]

This remark is worthy of investigation. Can I discover *in myself* whether I know something or merely believe it?

Let us begin by studying the ordinary usage of "know" and "believe." Suppose, for example, that several of us intend to go for a walk and that you pro- pose that we walk in Cascadilla Gorge. I protest that I should like to walk beside a flowing stream and that at this season the gorge is probably dry. Consider the following cases:

(1) You say "I believe that it won't be dry although I have no particular reason for thinking so." If we went to the gorge and found a flowing stream we should not say that you *knew* that there would be water but that you thought so and were right.

(2) You say "I believe that it won't be dry because it rained only three days ago and usually water flows in the gorge for at least that long after a rain." If we found water we should be inclined to say that you

From Norman Malcolm, "Knowledge and Belief," originally published in *Mind* 51 (1952), 178–89. Reprinted in its revised form from *Knowledge and Certainty: Essays and Lectures by Norman Malcolm* (Englewood Cliffs, N.J.: Prentice-Hall, 1963), by permission of the author.

knew that there would be water. It would be quite natural for you to say "I knew that it wouldn't be dry"; and we should tolerate your remark. This case differs from the previous one in that here you had a *reason.*

(3) You say "I know that it won't be dry" and give the same reason as in (2). If we found water we should have very little hesitation in saying that you knew. Not only had you a reason, but you *said* "I know" instead of "I believe." It may seem to us that the latter should not make a difference—but it does.

(4) You say "I know that it won't be dry" and give a stronger reason, e.g., "I saw a lot of water flowing in the gorge when I passed it this morning." If we went and found water, there would be no hesitation at all in saying that you knew. If, for example, we later met someone who said "Weren't you surprised to see water in the gorge this afternoon?" you would reply "No, I *knew* that there would be water; I had been there earlier in the day." We should have no objection to this statement.

(5) Everything happens as in (4), except that upon going to the gorge we find it to be dry. We should not say that you knew, but that you *believed* that there would be water. And this is true even though you declared that you knew, and even though your evidence was the same as it was in case (4) in which you did know.

I wish to make some comments on the usage of "know," "knew," "believe," and "believed," as illustrated in the preceding cases:

(*a*) Whether we should say that you knew, depends in part on whether you had grounds for your assertion and on the strength of those grounds. There would certainly be less hesitation to say that you knew in case (4) than in case (3), and this can be due only to the difference in the strength of the grounds.

(*b*) Whether we should say that you knew, depends in part on how *confident* you were. In case (2), if you had said "It rained only three days ago and usually water flows in the gorge for at least that long after a rain; but, of course, I don't feel absolutely sure that there will be water," then we should *not* have said that you knew that there would be water. If you lack confidence that *p* is true then others do not say that you know that *p* is true, even though *they* know that *p* is

true. Being confident is a necessary condition for knowing.

(*c*) Prichard says that if we reflect we cannot mistake belief for knowledge. In case (4) you knew that there would be water, and in case (5) you merely believed it. Was there any way that you could have discovered by reflection, in case (5), that you did not know? It would have been useless to have reconsidered your grounds for saying that there would be water, because in case (4), where you *did* know, your grounds were identical. They could be at fault in (5) only if they were at fault in (4), and they were not at fault in (4). Cases (4) and (5) differ in only one respect—namely, that in one case you did subsequently find water and in the other you did not. Prichard says that we can determine by reflection whether we know something or merely believe it. But where, in these cases, is the material that reflection would strike upon? There is none.

There is only one way that Prichard could defend his position. He would have to say that in case (4) you did *not* know that there would be water. And it is obvious that he would have said this. But this is false. It is an enormously common usage of language to say, in commenting upon just such an incident as (4), "He knew that the gorge would be not dry because he had seen water flowing there that morning." It is a usage that all of us are familiar with. We so employ "know" and "knew" every day of our lives. We do not think of our usage as being loose or incorrect—and it is not. As philosophers we may be surprised to observe that it *can* be that the knowledge that *p* is true should differ from the belief that *p* is true *only* in the respect that in one case *p* is true and in the other false. But that is the fact.

There is an argument that one is inclined to use as a proof that you did not know that there would be water. The argument is the following: It could have turned out that you found no water; if it had so turned out you would have been mistaken in saying that you would find water; therefore you could have been mistaken; but if you could have been mistaken then you did not know.

Now it certainly *could* have turned out that the gorge was quite dry when you went there, even though you saw lots of water flowing through it only a few hours before. This does not show, however, that you did not know that there would be water. What it shows is that *although you knew you could have been mistaken.*[2] This would seem to be a contradictory result; but it is not. It seems so because our minds are fixed upon another usage of "know" and "knew"; one in which "It could have turned out that I was mistaken," implies "I did not know."

When is "know" used in this sense? I believe that Prichard uses it in this sense when he says that when we go through the proof of the proposition that the angles of a triangle are equal to two right angles we *know* that the proposition is true (p. 89). He says that if we put to ourselves the question: Is our condition one of knowing this, or is it only one of being convinced of it? then "We can only answer 'Whatever may be our state on other occasions, here we are knowing this.' And this statement is an expression of our *knowing* that we are knowing; for we do not *believe* that we are knowing this, we know that we are" (p. 89). He goes on to say that if someone were to object that we might be making a mistake "because for all we know we can later on discover some fact which is incompatible with a triangle's having angles that are equal to two right angles, we can answer that we *know* that there can be no such fact, for in knowing that a triangle must have such angles we also know that nothing can exist which is incompatible with this fact" (p. 90).

It is easy to imagine a non-philosophical context in which it would have been natural for Prichard to have said "I know that the angles of a triangle are equal to two right angles." Suppose that a young man just beginning the study of geometry was in doubt as to whether that proposition is true, and had even constructed an ingenious argument that appeared to prove it false. Suppose that Prichard was unable to find any error in the argument. He might have said to the young man: "There must be an error in it. I know that the angles of a triangle are equal to two right angles."

When Prichard says that "nothing can exist which is incompatible with" the truth of that proposition, is he prophesying that no one will ever have the ingenuity to construct a flawless-looking argument against it? I believe not. When Prichard says that "we" *know* (and implies that *he* knows) that the proposition is true

and *know* that nothing can exist that is incompatible with its being true, he is not making any *prediction* as to what the future will bring in the way of arguments or measurements. On the contrary, he is asserting that *nothing* that the future might bring could ever count as evidence against the proposition. He is implying that he would not *call* anything "evidence" against it. He is using "know" in what I shall call its "strong" sense. "Know" is used in this sense when a person's statement "I know that *p* is true" implies that the person who makes the statement would look upon nothing whatever as evidence that *p* is false.

It must not be assumed that whenever "know" is used in connexion with mathematical propositions it is used in the strong sense. A great many people have *heard* of various theorems of geometry, e.g., the Pythagorean. These theorems are a part of "common knowledge." If a schoolboy doing his geometry assignment felt a doubt about the Pythagorean theorem, and said to an adult "Are you *sure* that it is true?" the latter might reply "Yes, I know that it is." He might make this reply even though he could not give proof of it and even though he had never gone through a proof of it. If subsequently he was presented with a "demonstration" that the theorem is false, or if various persons reputed to have a knowledge of geometry soberly assured him that it is false, he might be filled with doubt or even be convinced that he was mistaken. When he said "Yes, I know that it is true," he did not pledge himself to hold to the theorem through thick and thin. He did not absolutely exclude the possibility that something could prove it to be false. I shall say that he used "know" in the "weak" sense.

Consider another example from mathematics of the difference between the strong and weak senses of "know." I have just now rapidly calculated that 92 times 16 is 1472. If I had done this in the commerce of daily life where a practical problem was at stake, and if someone had asked "Are you sure that $92 \times 16 = 1472$?" I might have answered "I *know* that it is; I have just now calculated it." But also I might have answered "I know that it is; but I will calculate it again to *make sure*." And here my language points to a distinction. I say that I *know* that $92 \times 16 = 1472$. Yet I am willing to *confirm* it—that is, there is something that I should *call* "making sure;" and, likewise, there is something that I should *call* "finding out that it is false." If I were to do this calculation again and obtain the result that 92 × 16 = 1372, and if I were to carefully check this latter calculation without finding any error, I should be disposed to say that I was previously mistaken when I declared that 92 × 16 = 1472. Thus when I say that I know that 92 × 16 = 1472, I allow for the possibility of a *refutation,* and so I am using "know" in its weak sense.

Now consider propositions like 2 + 2 = 4 and 7 + 5 = 12. It is hard to think of circumstances in which it would be natural for me to say that I know that 2 + 2 = 4, because no one ever questions it. Let us try to suppose, however, that someone whose intelligence I respect argues that certain developments in arithmetic have shown that 2 + 2 does not equal 4. He writes out a proof of this in which I can find no flaw. Suppose that his demeanour showed me that he was in earnest. Suppose that several persons of normal intelligence became persuaded that his proof was correct and that 2 + 2 does not equal 4. What would be my reaction? I should say "I can't see what is wrong with your proof; but it *is* wrong, because I *know* that 2 + 2 = 4." Here I should be using "know" in its strong sense. I should not admit that any argument or any future development in mathematics could show that it is false that 2 + 2 = 4.

The propositions 2 + 2 = 4 and 92 × 16 = 1472 do not have the same status. There *can* be a demonstration that 2 + 2 = 4. But a demonstration would be for me (and for any average person) only a curious exercise, a sort of *game.* We have no serious interest in proving that proposition. It does not *need* a proof. It stands without one, and would not fall if a proof went against it. The case is different with the proposition that 92 × 16 = 1472. We take an interest in the demonstration (calculation) because that proposition *depends* upon its demonstration. A calculation may lead me to reject it as false. But 2 + 2 = 4 does *not* depend on its demonstration. It does not depend on anything! And in the calculation that proves that 92 × 16 = 1472, there are steps that do not depend on any calculation (e.g., 2 × 6 = 12; 5 + 2 = 7; 5 + 9 = 14).

There is a correspondence between this dualism in the logical status of mathematical propositions and the two senses of "know." When I use "know" in the weak sense I am prepared to let an investigation

(demonstration, calculation) determine whether the something that I claim to know is true or false. When I use "know" in the strong sense I am not prepared to look upon anything as an *investigation;* I do not concede that anything whatsoever could prove me mistaken; I do not regard the matter as open to any *question;* I do not admit that my proposition could turn out to be false, that any future investigation *could* refute it or cast doubt on it.

We have been considering the strong sense of "know" in its application to mathematical propositions. Does it have application anywhere in the realm of *empirical* propositions—for example, to propositions that assert or imply that certain physical things exist? Descartes said that we have a "moral assurance" of the truth of some of the latter propositions but that we lack a "metaphysical certainty." Locke said that the perception of the existence of physical things is not "so certain as our intuitive knowledge, or the deductions of our reason" although "it is an assurance that deserves the name of knowledge." Some philosophers have held that when we make judgements of perception such as that there are peonies in the garden, cows in the field, or dishes in the cupboard, we are "taking for granted" that the peonies, cows, and dishes exist, but not knowing it in the "strict" sense. Others have held that all empirical propositions, including judgements of perception, are merely hypotheses. The thought behind this exaggerated mode of expression is that any empirical proposition whatever *could* be refuted by future experience—that is, it *could* turn out to be false. Are these philosophers right?

Consider the following propositions:

(i)   The sun is about ninety million miles from the earth.
(ii)   There is a heart in my body.
(iii) Here is an ink-bottle.

In various circumstances I should be willing to assert of each of these propositions that I know it to be true. Yet they differ strikingly. This I see when, with each, I try to imagine the possibility that it is false.

(i) If in ordinary conversation someone said to me 'The sun is about twenty million miles from the earth, isn't it?' I should reply "No, it is about ninety million miles from us." If he said "I think that you are confusing the sun with Polaris," I should reply, "I *know* that ninety million miles is roughly the sun's distance from the earth." I might invite him to verify the figure in an encyclopedia. A third person who overheard our conversation could quite correctly report that I knew the distance to the sun, whereas the other man did not. But this knowledge of mine is little better than hearsay. I have seen that figure mentioned in a few books. I know nothing about the observations and calculations that led astronomers to accept it. If tomorrow a group of eminent astronomers announced that a great error had been made and that the correct figure is twenty million miles, I should not insist that they were wrong. It would surprise me that such an enormous mistake could have been made. But I should no longer be willing to say that I *know* that ninety million is the correct figure. Although I should *now* claim that I know the distance to be about ninety million miles, it is easy for me to envisage the possibility that some future investigation will prove this to be false.

(ii) Suppose that after a routine medical examination the excited doctor reports to me that the X-ray photographs show that I have no heart. I should tell him to get a new machine. I should be inclined to say that the fact that I have a heart is one of the few things that I can count on as absolutely certain. I can feel it beat. I know it's there. Furthermore, how could my blood circulate if I didn't have one? Suppose that later on I suffer a chest injury and undergo a surgical operation. Afterwards the astonished surgeons solemnly declare that they searched my chest cavity and found no heart, and that they made incisions and looked about in other likely places but found it not. They are convinced that I am without a heart. They are unable to understand how circulation can occur or what accounts for the thumping in my chest. But they are in agreement and obviously sincere, and they have clear photographs of my interior spaces. What would be my attitude? Would it be to insist that they were all mistaken? I think not. I believe that I should eventually accept their testimony and the evidence of the photographs. I should consider to be false what I now regard as an absolute certainty.

(iii) Suppose that as I write this paper someone in the next room were to call out to me "I can't find an ink-bottle; is there one in the house?" I should reply "Here is an ink-bottle." If he said in a doubtful tone

"Are you sure? I looked there before," I should reply "Yes, I know there is; come and get it."

Now could it turn out to be false that there is an ink-bottle directly in front of me on this desk? Many philosophers have thought so. They would say that many things could happen of such a nature that if they did happen it would be proved that I am deceived. I agree that many extraordinary things could happen, in the sense that there is no logical absurdity in the supposition. It could happen that when I next reach for this ink-bottle my hand should seem to pass *through* it and I should not feel the contact of any object. It could happen that in the next moment the ink-bottle will suddenly vanish from sight; or that I should find myself under a tree in the garden with no ink-bottle about; or that one or more persons should enter this room and declare with apparent sincerity that they see no ink-bottle on this desk; or that a photograph taken now of the top of the desk should clearly show all of the objects on it except the ink-bottle. Having admitted that these things *could happen,* am I compelled to admit that if they did happen then it would be proved that there is no ink-bottle here *now?* Not at all! I could say that when my hand seemed to pass through the ink-bottle I should *then* be suffering from hallucination; that if the ink-bottle suddenly vanished it would have miraculously ceased to exist; that the other persons were conspiring to drive me mad, or were themselves victims of remarkable concurrent hallucinations; that the camera possessed some strange flaw or that there was trickery in developing the negative. I admit that in the next moment I could find myself under a tree or in the bathtub. But this is not to admit that it could be revealed in the next moment that I am now dreaming. For what I admit is that I might be instantaneously transported to the garden, but not that in the next moment I might *wake up* in the garden. There is nothing that could happen to me in the next moment that I should call "waking up;" and therefore nothing that could happen to me in the next moment would be accepted by me now as proof that I now dream.

Not only do I not *have* to admit that those extraordinary occurrences would be evidence that there is no ink-bottle here; the fact is that I *do not* admit it. There is nothing whatever that could happen in the next moment or the next year that would by me be called *evidence* that there is not an ink-bottle here now. No future experience or investigation could prove to me that I am mistaken. Therefore, if I were to say "I know that there is an ink-bottle here," I should be using "know" in the strong sense.

It will appear to some that I have adopted an *unreasonable* attitude towards that statement. There is, however, nothing unreasonable about it. It seems so because one thinks that the statement that here is an ink-bottle *must* have the same status as the statements that the sun is ninety million miles away and that I have a heart and that there will be water in the gorge this afternoon. But this is a *prejudice.*

In saying that I should regard nothing as evidence that there is no ink-bottle here now, I am not *predicting* what I should do if various astonishing things happened. If other members of my family entered this room and, while looking at the top of this desk, declared with apparent sincerity that they see no ink-bottle, I might fall into a swoon or become mad. I *might* even come to believe that there is not and has not been an ink-bottle here. I cannot foretell with certainty how I should react. But if it is *not* a prediction, what is the meaning of my assertion that I should regard nothing as evidence that there is no ink-bottle here?

That assertion describes my *present* attitude towards the statement that here is an ink-bottle. It does not prophesy what my attitude *would* be if various things happened. My present attitude towards that statement is radically different from my present attitude towards those other statements (e.g., that I have a heart). I do *now* admit that certain future occurrences would disprove the latter. Whereas no imaginable future occurrence would be considered by me *now* as proving that there is not an ink-bottle here.

These remarks are not meant to be autobiographical. They are meant to throw light on the common concepts of evidence, proof, and disproof. Every one of us upon innumerable occasions of daily life takes this same attitude towards various statements about physical things, e.g., that here is a torn page, that this dish is broken, that the thermometer reads 70, that no rug is on the floor. Furthermore, the concepts of proof, disproof, doubt, and conjecture *require* us to take this attitude. In order for it to be possible that any statements about physical things should *turn out to be false* it is necessary that some statements about physical things *cannot* turn out to be false.

This will be made clear if we ask ourselves the question, When do we *say* that something turned out to be false? When do we use those words? Someone asks you for a dollar. You say "There is one in this drawer." You open the drawer and look, but it is perfectly empty. Your statement turned out to be false. This can be said because you *discovered* an empty drawer. It could not be said if it were only probable that the drawer is empty or were still open to question. Would it make sense to say "I had better make sure that it is empty; perhaps there is a dollar in it after all?" Sometimes; but not always. Not if the drawer lies open before your eyes. That remark is the prelude to a search. What search can there be when the emptiness of the drawer confronts you? In certain circumstances there is nothing that you would call "making sure" that the drawer is empty; and likewise nothing that you would call "its turning out to be false" that the drawer is empty. You *made* sure that the drawer is empty. One statement about physical things *turned out to be false* only because you *made sure* of another statement about physical things. The two concepts cannot exist apart. Therefore it is impossible that *every* statement about physical things *could* turn out to be false.

In a certain important respect some a priori statements and some empirical statements possess the same logical character. The statements that $5 \times 5 = 25$ and that here is an ink-bottle, both lie beyond the reach of doubt. On both, my judgement and reasoning *rests*. If you could somehow undermine my confidence in either, you would not teach me *caution.* You would fill my mind with chaos! I could not even make *conjectures* if you took away those fixed points of certainty; just as a man cannot *try* to climb whose body has no support. A conjecture implies an understanding of what certainty would be. If it is not a certainty that $5 \times 5 = 25$ and that here is an ink-bottle, then I do not understand what it is. You cannot make me doubt either of these statements or treat them as hypotheses. You cannot persuade me that future experience could refute them. With both of them it is perfectly unintelligible to me to speak of a "possibility" that they are false. This is to say that I know both of them to be true, in the strong sense of "know." And I am inclined to think that the strong sense of "know" is what various philosophers have had in mind when they have spoken of "perfect," "metaphysical," or "strict certainty."

It will be thought that I have confused a statement about my "sensations," or my "sense-data," or about the way something *looks* or *appears* to me, with a statement about physical things. It will be thought that the things that I have said about the statement "Here is an ink-bottle" could be true only if that statement is interpreted to mean something like "There appears to me to be an ink-bottle here," i.e., interpreted so as not to assert or imply that any physical thing exists. I wish to make it clear that my statement "Here is an ink-bottle" is *not* to be interpreted in that way. It would be utterly fantastic for me in my present circumstances to say "There appears to me to be an ink-bottle here."

If someone were to call me on the telephone and say that he urgently needed an ink-bottle I should invite him to come here and get this one. If he said that it was extremely urgent that he should obtain one immediately and that he could not afford to waste time going to a place where there might not be one, I should tell him that it is an absolute certainty that there is one here, that nothing could be more certain, that it is something I absolutely guarantee. But if my statement "There is an ink-bottle here" were a statement about my "sensations" or "sense-data," or if it meant that there *appears* to me to be an ink-bottle here or that something here *looks* to me like an ink-bottle, and if that is all that I meant by it—then I should react quite differently to his urgent request. I should say that there is probably an ink-bottle here but that I could not *guarantee* it, and that if he needs one very desperately and at once then he had better look elsewhere. In short, I wish to make it clear that my statement "Here is an ink-bottle" is strictly about physical things and not about "sensations," "sense-data," or "appearances."

Let us go back to Prichard's remark that we can determine by reflection whether we know something or merely believe it. Prichard would think that "knowledge in the weak sense" is mere belief and not knowledge. This is wrong. But if we let ourselves speak this way, we can then see some justification for Prichard's remark. For then he would be asserting, among other things, that we can determine by reflection whether we

know something in the strong sense or in the weak sense. This is not literally true; however, there is this truth in it—that reflection can make us realize that we are *using* "I know it" in the strong (or weak) sense in a particular case. Prichard says that reflection can show us that "our condition is one of knowing" a certain thing, or instead that "our condition is one of believing and not of knowing" that thing. I do not understand what could be meant here by "our condition." The way I should put it is that reflection on *what we should think* if certain things were to happen may make us realize that we should (or should not) call those things "proof" or "evidence" that what we claim to know is not so. I have tried to show that the distinction between strong and weak knowledge does not run parallel to the distinction between a priori and empirical knowledge but cuts across it, i.e., these two kinds of knowledge may be distinguished *within* a priori knowledge and *within* empirical knowledge.

Reflection can make me realize that I am using "know" in the strong sense; but can reflection show me that I *know* something in the strong sense (or in the weak)? It is not easy to state the logical facts here. On the one hand, if I make an assertion of the form "I know that *p*" it does not follow that *p,* whether or not I am using "know" in the strong sense. If I have said to someone outside my room "Of course, I know that Freddie is in here," and I am speaking in the strong sense, it does not *follow* that Freddie is where I claim he is. This logical fact would not be altered even if I *realized* that I was using "know" in the strong sense. My reflection on what I should say if . . . , cannot show me that I *know* something. From the fact that I should not call anything "evidence" that Freddie is not here, it does not follow that he *is* here; therefore, it does not follow that I *know* he is here.

On the other hand, in an actual case of my using "know" in the strong sense, I cannot envisage a possibility that what I say to be true should turn out to be not true. If I were speaking of *another person's* assertion about something, I *could* think both that he is using "know" in the strong sense and that nonetheless what he claims he knows to be so might turn out to be not so. But *in my own case* I cannot have this conjunction of thoughts, and this is a logical and not a psychological fact. When *I* say that I know something to be so, using "know" in the strong sense, it is unintelligible *to me* (although perhaps not to others) to suppose that anything could prove that it is not so and, therefore, that I do not know it.

NOTES

1. H. A. Prichard, *Knowledge and Perception* (Oxford: Clarendon Press, 1950), p. 88.
2. Some readers seem to have thought that I was denying here that "I knew that *p*" entails "that *p*." That was not my intention, and my words do not have that implication. If I had said *"although you knew you were mistaken,"* I should have denied the above entailment and, also, I should have misused "knew." The difference between the strong and weak senses of "know" (and "knew") is not that this entailment holds for the strong but not for

the weak sense. It holds for both. If it is false that *p*, then one does not (and did not) know that *p*.

FOR FURTHER REFLECTION

1. Are you convinced by Malcolm's argument that one cannot discover the difference between belief and knowledge merely by looking within oneself? Why or why not?
2. Is Malcolm correct in insisting that *certainty* is a necessary condition for knowledge? Could you *know* the answer to a question without being certain of it? Explain your answers.
3. Outline the difference between strong and weak knowledge. Can you find counterexamples to Malcolm's thesis?

KARL POPPER
∽

EPISTEMOLOGY WITHOUT A KNOWING SUBJECT

Karl Popper (1902–1994), an Austrian-born philosopher, spent most of his career at the London School of Economics. He is the author of several works in philosophy of science, epistemology, and political philosophy.

In "Epistemology Without a Knowing Subject," Popper argues that there really are three different worlds existing in the same universe: the physical world of matter, the mental world of consciousness and mental events, and the Platonic world of propositions, theories, arguments, and problems. This third world, an idea anticipated by Gottlob Frege, is objective and autonomous. Although it has been created by humans, it doesn't depend on humans for its continued existence. As long as a record (e.g., a library) survived the extinction of humanity, a new race might discover these ideas and bring them back to the public domain. Unlike Jacques Derrida and the deconstructivists, this world of ideas does not depend on human interpretation. The *text* remains objective and autonomous, even though individuals may interpret it differently (or misinterpret it).

From Karl Popper, *Objective Knowledge: An Evolutionary Approach* (revised ed., 1979), by permission of Oxford University Press.

Allow me to start with a confession. Although I am a very happy philosopher I have, after a lifetime of lecturing, no illusions about what I can convey in a lecture. For this reason I shall make no attempt in this lecture to convince you. Instead I shall make an attempt to challenge you, and, if possible, to provoke you.

I. THREE THESES ON EPISTEMOLOGY AND THE THIRD WORLD

I might have challenged those who have heard of my adverse attitude towards Plato and Hegel by calling my lecture *"A theory of the Platonic world,"* or *"A theory of the objective spirit."*

The main topic of this lecture will be what I often call, for want of a better name, *"the third world."* To explain this expression I will point out that, without taking the words "world" or "universe" too seriously, we may distinguish the following three worlds or universes: first, the world of physical objects or of physical states; secondly, the world of states of consciousness, or of mental states, or perhaps of behavioural dispositions to act; and thirdly, the world of *objective contents of thought*, especially of scientific and poetic thoughts and of works of art.

Thus what I call "the third world" has admittedly much in common with Plato's theory of Forms or Ideas, and therefore also with Hegel's objective spirit, though my theory differs radically, in some decisive respects, from Plato's and Hegel's. It has more in common still with Bolzano's theory of a universe of propositions in themselves and of truths in themselves, though it differs from Bolzano's also. My third world resembles most closely the universe of Frege's objective contents of thought.

It is not part of my view or of my argument that we might not enumerate our worlds in different ways, or not enumerate them at all. We might, especially, distinguish more than three worlds. My term "the third world" is merely a matter of convenience.

In upholding an objective third world I hope to provoke those whom I call *"belief philosophers"*: those who, like Descartes, Locke, Berkeley, Hume, Kant, or Russell, are interested in our subjective beliefs, and their basis or origin. Against these belief philosophers I urge that our problem is to find better and bolder theories; and that *critical preference* counts, but *not belief*.

I wish to confess, however, at the very beginning, that I am a realist: I suggest, somewhat like a naive realist, that there are physical worlds and a world of states of consciousness, and that these two interact. And I believe that there is a third world, in a sense which I shall explain more fully.

Among the inmates of the "third world" are, more especially, *theoretical systems*; but inmates just as important are *problems* and *problem situations*. And I will argue that the most important inmates of this world are *critical arguments*, and what may be called—in analogy to a physical state or to a state of consciousness—*the state of discussion* or the *state of a critical argument*; and, of course, the contents of journals, books, and libraries.

Most opponents of the thesis of an objective third world will of course admit that there are problems, conjectures, theories, arguments, journals, and books. But they usually say that all these entities are, essentially, symbolic or linguistic *expressions* of subjective mental states, or perhaps of behavioural dispositions to act; further, that these entities are means of *communication*—that is to say, symbolic or linguistic means to evoke in others similar mental states or behavioural dispositions to act.

Against this, I have often argued that one cannot relegate all these entities and their content to the second world.

Let me repeat one of my standard arguments[1] for the (more or less) *independent existence of the third world*.

I consider two thought experiments:

Experiment (1). All our machines and tools are destroyed, and all our subjective learning, including our subjective knowledge of machines and tools, and how to use them. But *libraries and our capacity to learn from them* survive. Clearly, after much suffering, our world may get going again.

Experiment (2). As before, machines and tools are destroyed, and our subjective learning, including our subjective knowledge of machines and tools, and how to use them. But this time, *all libraries are destroyed also*, so that our capacity to learn from books becomes useless.

If you think about these two experiments, the reality, significance, and degree of autonomy of the third world (as well as its effects on the second and first worlds) may perhaps become a little clearer to you. For in the second case there will be no reemergence of our civilization for many millennia.

I wish to defend in this lecture three main theses, all of which concern epistemology. Epistemology I take to be the theory of *scientific knowledge*.

My first thesis is this. Traditional epistemology has studied knowledge or thought in a subjective sense—in the sense of the ordinary usage of the words "I know" or "I am thinking." This, I assert, has led students of epistemology into irrelevances: while intending to study scientific knowledge, they studied in fact something which is of no relevance to scientific knowledge. For *scientific knowledge* simply is not knowledge in the sense of the ordinary usage of the words "I know." While knowledge in the sense of "I know" belongs to what I call the "second world," the world of *subjects*, scientific knowledge belongs to the third world, to the world of objective theories, objective problems, and objective arguments.

Thus my first thesis is that the traditional epistemology, of Locke, Berkeley, Hume, and even of Russell, is irrelevant, in a pretty strict sense of the word. It is a corollary of this thesis that a large part of contemporary epistemology is irrelevant also. This includes modern epistemic logic, if we assume that it aims at a theory of *scientific knowledge*. However, any epistemic logician can easily make himself completely immune from my criticism, simply by making clear that he does not aim at contributing to the *theory of scientific knowledge*.

My first thesis involves the existence of two different senses of knowledge or of thought: (1) *knowledge or thought in the subjective sense*, consisting of a state of mind or of consciousness or a disposition to behave or to react, and (2) *knowledge or thought in an objective sense*, consisting of problems, theories, and arguments as such. Knowledge in this objective sense is totally independent of anybody's claim to know; it is also independent of anybody's belief, or disposition to assent; or to assert, or to act. Knowledge in the objective sense is *knowledge without a knower*: it is *knowledge without a knowing subject*.

Of though in the objective sense Frege wrote: "I understand by a *thought* not the subjective act of thinking but its *objective content*. . . ."

The two senses of thought and their interesting interrelations can be illustrated by the following highly convincing quotation from Heyting (1962, p. 195), who says about Brouwer's act of inventing his theory of the continuum: "If recursive functions had been invented before, he [Brouwer] would perhaps not have formed the notion of a choice sequence which, I think, would have been unlucky."

This quotation refers on the one hand to some *subjective thought processes* of Brouwer's and says that they might not have occurred (which would have been unfortunate) had the *objective problem situation* been different. Thus Heyting mentions certain possible *influences* upon Brouwer's subjective thought processes, and he also expresses his opinion regarding the value of these subjective thought processes. Now it is interesting that influences, qua influences, must be subjective: only Brouwer's subjective acquaintance with recursive functions could have had that unfortunate effect of preventing him from inventing free choice sequences.

On the other hand, the quotation from Heyting points to a certain objective relationship between the *objective contents* of two thoughts or theories: Heyting does not refer to the subjective conditions or the electrochemistry of Brouwer's brain processes, but to an *objective problem situation in mathematics* and its possible influences on Brouwer's subjective acts of thought which were bent on solving these objective problems. I would describe this by saying that Heyting's remark is about the objective or third-world *situational logic* of Brouwer's invention, and that Heyting's remark implies that the third-world situation may affect the second world. Similarly, Heyting's suggestion that it would have been unfortunate if Brouwer had not invented choice sequences is a way of saying that the *objective content* of Brouwer's thought was valuable and interesting; valuable and interesting, that is, in the way it changed the objective problem situation in the third world.

To put the matter simply, if I say "Brouwer's thought was influenced by Kant" or even "Brouwer rejected Kant's theory of space" then I speak at least partly about acts of thought in the subjective sense: the word "influence" indicates a context of thought processes or acts of thinking. If I say, however, "Brouwer's thought differs vastly from Kant's," then it is pretty clear that I speak mainly about contents. And, ultimately, if I say 'Brouwer's thoughts are incompatible with Russell's,' then, by using a *logical term* such as *"incompatible,"* I make it unambiguously clear that I am using the word "thought" only in Frege's objective sense, and that I am speaking only about the objective content, or the logical content, of theories.

Just as ordinary language unfortunately has no separate terms for "thought" in the sense of the second world and in the sense of the third world, so it has no separate terms for the corresponding two senses of "I know" and of "knowledge."

In order to show that both senses exist, I will first mention three subjective or second-world examples:

(1) "I *know* you are trying to provoke me, but I will not be provoked."
(2) "I *know* that Fermat's last theorem has not been proved, but I believe it will be proved one day."
(3) From the entry "Knowledge" in *The Oxford English Dictionary*: *knowledge* is a "state of being aware or informed."

Next I will mention three objective or third-world examples:

(1) From the entry "Knowledge" in *The Oxford English Dictionary*: *knowledge* is a "branch of learning; a science; an art."
(2) "Taking account of the present state of *metamathematical knowledge*, it seems possible that Fermat's last theorem may be undecidable."
(3) "I certify that this thesis is an original and significant *contribution to knowledge*."

These very trite examples have only the function of helping to clarify what I mean when I speak of "knowledge in the objective sense." My quoting *The Oxford English Dictionary* should not be interpreted as either a concession to language analysis or as an attempt to appease its adherents. It is not quoted in an attempt to prove that "ordinary usage" covers "knowledge" in the objective sense of my third world. In fact, I was surprised to find in *The Oxford English Dictionary* examples of objective usages of "knowledge." (I was even more surprised to find some at least *partly* objective usages of "know": "to distinguish . . . to be acquainted with (a thing, a place, a person); . . . to understand." That these usages may be partly objective will emerge from the sequel.) At any rate, my examples are not intended as arguments. They are intended solely as illustrations.

My *first thesis*, so far not argued but only illustrated, was that traditional epistemology with its concentration on the second world, or on knowledge in the subjective sense, is irrelevant to the study of scientific knowledge.

My *second thesis* is that what is relevant for epistemology is the study of scientific problems and problem situations, of scientific conjectures (which I take as merely another word for scientific hypotheses or theories), of scientific discussions, of critical arguments, and of the role played by evidence in arguments; and therefore of scientific journals and books, and of experiments and their evaluation in scientific arguments; or, in brief, that the study of a *largely autonomous* third world of objective knowledge is of decisive importance for epistemology.

An epistemological study as described in my second thesis shows that scientists very often do not claim that their conjectures are true, or that they "know" them in the subjective sense of "know," or that they believe in them. Although in general they do not claim to know, in developing their research programmes they act on the basis of guesses about what is and what is not fruitful, and what line of research promises further results in the third world of objective knowledge. In other words, scientists act on the basis of a guess or, of you like, of a *subjective belief* (for we may so call the subjective basis of an action) concerning what is promising of impending *growth in the third world of objective knowledge.*

This, I suggest, furnishes an argument in favour of both my *first thesis* (of the irrelevance of a subjectivist epistemology) and of my *second thesis* (of the relevance of an objectivist epistemology).

But I have a *third thesis*. It is this. An objectivist epistemology which studies the third world can help to throw an immense amount of light upon the second world of subjective consciousness, especially upon the subjective thought processes of scientists; but *the converse is not true*.

These are my three main theses.

In addition to my three main theses, I offer three supporting theses.

The first of these is that the third world is a natural product of the human animal, comparable to a spider's web.

The second supporting thesis (and an almost crucial thesis, I think) is that the third world is largely *autonomous*, even though we constantly act upon it and are acted upon by it: it is autonomous in spite of the fact that it is our product and that it has a strong feed-back effect upon us; that is to say, upon us qua inmates of the second and even of the first world.

The third supporting thesis is that it is through this interaction between ourselves and the third world that objective knowledge grows, and that there is a close analogy between the growth of knowledge and biological growth; that is, the evolution of plants and animals.

2. A BIOLOGICAL APPROACH TO THE THIRD WORLD

In the present section of my talk I shall try to defend the existence of an autonomous world by a kind of biological or evolutionary argument.

A biologist may be interested in the behaviour of animals; but he may also be interested in some of the *non-living structures* which animals produce, such as spiders' webs, or nests built by wasps or ants, the burrows of badgers, dams constructed by beavers, or paths made by animals in forests.

I will distinguish between two main categories of problems arising from the study of these structures. The first category consists of problems concerned with *the methods used* by the animals, or *the ways the animals behave* when constructing these structures. This first category thus consists *of problems concerned with the acts of production*; with the behavioural dispositions of the animal; and with the relationships between the animal and the product. The second category of problems is concerned with the *structures themselves*. It is concerned with the chemistry of the materials used in the structure; with their geometrical and physical properties; with their evolutionary changes, depending upon special environmental conditions; and with their dependence upon or their adjustments to these environmental conditions. *Very* important also is the *feedback relation* from the properties of the structure to the behaviour of the animals. In dealing with this second category of problems—that is, with the structures themselves—we shall also have to look upon the structures from the point of view of their biological *functions*. Thus some problems of the first category will admittedly arise when we discuss problems of the second category; for example "How was this nest built?" and "What aspects of its structure are typical (and thus presumably traditional or inherited) and what aspects are variants adjusted to special conditions?"

As my last example of a problem shows, problems of the first category—that is, problems concerned with the production of the structure—will sometimes be suggested by problems of the second category. This must be so, since both categories of problems are dependent upon *the fact that such objective structures exist*, a fact which itself belongs to the second category. Thus the existence of the *structures themselves* may be said to create both categories of problems. We may say that the second category of problems—problems connected with the structures themselves—is more fundamental: all that it presupposes from the first category is the bare fact that the structures are somehow *produced by* some animals.

Now these simple considerations may of course also be applied to products of *human* activities, such as houses, or tools, and also to works of art. Especially important for us, they apply to what we call "language," and to what we call "science."

The connection between these biological considerations and the topic of my present lecture can be made clear by reformulating my three main theses. My first thesis can be put by saying that in the present problem situation in philosophy, few things are as important as the awareness of the distinction between the two categories of problems—production problems on the one hand and problems connected with the produced structures themselves on the other. My second thesis is that we should realize that the second category of problems, those concerned with the products in themselves, is in almost every respect more important than the first category, the problems of production. My third thesis is that the problems of the second category are basic for understanding the production problems: contrary to first impressions, we can learn more about production behaviour by studying the products themselves than we can learn about the products by studying production behaviour. This third thesis may be described as an anti-behaviouristic and anti-psychologistic thesis.

In their application to what may be called "knowledge" my three theses may be formulated as follows.

(1) We should constantly be aware of the distinction between problems connected with our personal contributions to the production of scientific knowledge on the one hand, and problems connected with the structure of the various products, such as scientific theories or scientific arguments, on the other.
(2) We should realize that the study of the products is vastly more important than the study of the production, even for an understanding of the production and its methods.
(3) We can learn more about the heuristics and the methodology and even about the psychology of research by studying theories, and the arguments offered for or against them, than by any direct behaviouristic or psychological or sociological approach. In general, we may learn a great deal about behaviour and psychology from the study of the products.

In what follows I will call the approach from the side of the products—the theories and the arguments—the "objective" approach or the "third-world" approach. And I will call the behaviourist, the psy-

chological, and the sociological approach to scientific knowledge the "subjective" approach or the "second-world" approach.

The appeal of the subjective approach is largely due to the fact that it is *causal*. For I admit that the objective structures for which I claim priority are caused by human behaviour. Being causal, the subjective approach may seem to be more scientific than the objective approach which, as it were, starts from effects rather than causes.

Though I admit that the objective structures are products of behaviour, I hold that the argument is mistaken. In all sciences, the ordinary approach is from the effects to the causes. The effect raises the problem—the problem to be explained, the explicandum—and the scientist tries to solve it by constructing an explanatory hypothesis.

My three main theses with their emphasis on the objective product are therefore neither teleological nor unscientific.

3. THE OBJECTIVITY AND THE AUTONOMY OF THE THIRD WORLD

One of the main reasons for the mistaken subjective approach to knowledge is the feeling that a book is nothing without a reader: only if it is understood does it really become a book; otherwise it is just paper with black spots on it.

This view is mistaken in many ways. A wasp's nest is a wasp's nest even after it has been deserted; even though it is never again used by wasps as a nest. A bird's nest is a bird's nest even if it was never lived in. Similarly a book remains a book—a certain type of product—even if it is never read (as may easily happen nowadays).

Moreover, a book, or even a library, need not even have been written by anybody: a series of books of logarithms, for example, may be produced and printed by a computer. It may be the best series of books on logarithms—it may contain logarithms up to, say, fifty decimal places. It may be sent out to libraries, but it may be found too cumbersome for use; at any rate, years may elapse before anybody uses it; and many figures in it (which represent mathematical theorems) may never be looked at as long as men live on earth. Yet each of these figures contains what I call "objective knowledge"; and the question of whether or not I am entitled to call it by this name is of no interest.

The example of these books of logarithms may seem farfetched. But it is not. I should say that almost every book is like this: it contains objective knowledge, true or false, useful or useless; and whether anybody ever reads it and really grasps its contents is almost accidental. A man who reads a book with understanding is a rare creature. But even if he were more common, there would always be plenty of misunderstandings and misinterpretations; and it is not the actual and somewhat accidental avoidance of such misunderstandings which turns black spots on white paper into a book, or an instance of knowledge in the objective sense. It is its possibility or potentiality of being understood, its dispositional character of being understood or interpreted, or misunderstood or misinterpreted, which makes a thing a book. And this potentiality or disposition may exist without every being actualized or realized.

To see this more clearly, we may imagine that after the human race has perished, some books or libraries may be found by some civilized successors of ours (no matter whether these are terrestrial animals which have become civilized, or some visitors from outer space). These books may be deciphered. They may be those logarithm tables never read before, for argument's sake. This makes it quite clear that neither its composition by thinking animals nor the fact that it has not actually been read or understood is essential for making a think a book, and that it is sufficient that it might be deciphered.

Thus I do admit that in order to belong to the third world of objective knowledge, a book should—in principle, or virtually—be capable of being grasped (or deciphered, or understood, or 'known') by somebody. But I do not admit more.

We can thus say that there is a kind of Platonic (or Bolzanoesque) third world of books in themselves, theories in themselves, problems in themselves, problem situations in themselves, arguments in themselves, and so on. And I assert that even though this third world is a human product, there are many theories in themselves and arguments in themselves and problem situations in themselves which have never been produced or understood and may never be produced or understood by men.

The thesis of the existence of such a third world of problem situations will strike many as extremely metaphysical and dubious. But it can be defended by pointing out its biological analogue. For example, it has its full analogue in the realm of birds' nests. Some years ago I got a present for my garden—a nesting-box for birds. It was a human product, of course, not a bird's product—just as our logarithm table was a computer's product rather than a human product. But in the context of the bird's world, it was part of an objective problem situation, and an objective opportunity. For some years the birds did not even seem to notice the nesting-box. But after some years, it was carefully inspected by some blue tits who even started building in it, but gave up very soon. Obviously, here was a graspable opportunity, though not, it appears, a particularly valuable one. At any rate, here was a problem situation. And the problem may be solved in another year by other birds. If it is not, another box may prove more adequate. On the other hand, a most adequate box may be removed before it is ever used. The question of the adequacy of the box is clearly an objective one; and whether the box is ever used is partly accidental. So it is with all ecological niches. They are potentialities and may be studied as such in an objective way, up to a point independently of the question of whether these potentialities will ever be actualized by any living organisms. A bacteriologist knows how to prepare such an ecological niche for the culture of certain bacteria or moulds. It may be perfectly adequate for its purpose. Whether it will ever be used and inhabited is another question.

A large part of the objective third world of actual and potential theories and books and arguments arises as an unintended by-product of the actually produced books and arguments. We may also say that it is a by-product of human language. Language itself, like a bird's nest, is an unintended by-product of actions which were directed at other aims.

How does an animal path in the jungle arise? Some animals may break through the undergrowth in order to get to a drinking-place. Other animals find it easiest to use the same track. Thus it may be widened and improved by use. It is not planned—it is an unintended consequence of the need for easy or swift movement. This is how a path is originally made—perhaps even by men—and how language and any other institutions which are useful may arise, and how they may owe their existence and development to their usefulness. They are not planned or intended, and there was perhaps no need for them before they came into existence. But they may create a new need, or a new set of aims: the aim-structure of animals or men is not "given", but it develops, with the help of some kind of feedback mechanism, out of earlier aims, and out of results which were or were not aimed at.

In this way, a whole new universe of possibilities or potentialities may arise: a world which is to a large extent *autonomous*.

A very obvious example is a garden. Even though it may have been planned with great care, it will as a rule turn out partly in unexpected ways. But even if it turns out as planned, some unexpected interrelationships between the planned objects may give rise to a whole universe of possibilities, of possible new aims, and of new *problems*.

The world of language, of conjectures, theories, and arguments—in brief, the universe of objective knowledge—is one of the most important of these man-created, yet at the same time largely autonomous, universes. . . .

NOTE

1. The argument is adapted from Popper, 1962, vol. ii; cp. p. 108.

FOR FURTHER REFLECTION

1. What according to Popper are the three worlds of knowledge? What is the content of Popper's third world?
2. Who are the traditional "belief philosophers," and how does Popper's theory differ from their epistemology? How does he differ from the deconstructivists like Derrida and Rorty (selection 10)?
3. How can there be knowledge without a knowing subject? How would the traditional epistemologists respond to Popper's theory? 4. What is Popper's evolutionary argument for his theory?

RICHARD RORTY

DISMANTLING TRUTH
Solidarity versus Objectivity

Richard Rorty is professor of comparative literature at Stanford University and the author of several works, including *Philosophy and the Mirror of Nature* (1979).

In this selection, Rorty attacks the distinction between objectivity and subjectivity as well as the correspondence theory of truth. He sides with Thomas Kuhn in arguing that we can have no theory-independent notion of reality and proposes to erase the essential difference between science and the humanities and arts. Embracing the title of "the new fuzzies," Rorty proposes that a notion of social solidarity replace the enlightenment notion of objective truth.

In our culture, the notions of "science," "rationality," "objectivity" and "truth" are bound up with one another. Science is thought of as offering "hard," "objective" truth—truth as correspondence to reality, the only sort of truth worthy of the name. Humanists—philosophers, theologians, historians, literary critics—have to worry about whether they are being "scientific"—whether they are entitled to think of their conclusions, no matter how carefully argued, as worthy of the term "true." We tend to identify seeking "objective truth" with "using reason," and so we think of the natural sciences as paradigms of rationality. We also think of rationality as a matter of following procedures laid down in advance, of being "methodical." So we tend to use "methodical," "rational," "scientific" and "objective" as synonyms.

Worries about "cognitive status" and "objectivity" are characteristic of a secularized culture in which the scientist replaces the priest. The scientist is now seen as the person who keeps humanity in touch with something beyond itself. As the universe was depersonalized, beauty (and, in time, even moral goodness) came to be thought of as "subjective." So truth is now thought of as the only point at which human beings are responsible to something non-human. A commitment to "rationality" and to "method" is thought to be a recognition of this responsibility. The scientist becomes a moral exemplar, one who selflessly exposes himself again and again to the hardness of facts.

One result of this way of thinking is that any academic discipline which wants a place at the trough, but is unable to offer the predictions and the technology provided by the natural sciences, must either pretend to imitate science or find some way of obtaining "cognitive status" without the necessity of discovering facts. Practitioners of these disciplines must either affiliate themselves with this quasi-priestly order by using terms like "behavioral sciences" or else find something other than "fact" to be concerned with. People in the humanities typically choose the latter

From Richard Rorty, "Science and Solidarity," in John S. Nelson, Allan Megill, and Donald N. McCloskey, *The Rhetoric of the Human Sciences* (1987), by permission of the University of Wisconsin Press.

strategy. They describe themselves either as concerned with "values" as opposed to facts, or as developing and inculcating habits of "critical reflection."

Neither sort of rhetoric is very satisfactory. No matter how much humanists talk about "objective values," the phrase always sounds vaguely confused. It gives with one hand what it takes back with the other. The distinction between the objective and the subjective was designed to parallel that between fact and value, so an objective value sounds vaguely mythological as a winged horse. Talk about the humanists' special skill at critical reflection fares no better. Nobody really believes that philosophers or literary critics are better at critical thinking, or at taking big broad views of things, than theoretical physicists or microbiologists. So society tends to ignore both these kinds of rhetoric. It treats humanities as on a par with the arts, and thinks of both as providing pleasure rather than truth. Both are, to be sure, thought of as providing "high" rather than "low" pleasure. But an elevated and spiritual sort of pleasure is still a long way from the grasp of a truth.

These distinctions between hard facts and soft values, truth and pleasure, and objectivity and subjectivity are awkward and clumsy instruments. They are not suited to divide up culture; they create more difficulties than they resolve. It would be best to find another vocabulary, to start afresh. But in order to do so we first have to find a new way of describing the natural sciences. It is not a question of debunking or downgrading the natural sciences, but simply of ceasing to see him on the model of the priest. We need to stop thinking of science as the place where the human mind confronts the world. We need a way of explaining why scientists are, and deserve to be, moral exemplars which does not depend on a distinction between objective fact and something softer, squishier and more dubious.

To get to such a way of thinking we can start by distinguishing two senses of the term "rationality." In one sense, the one I have already discussed, to be rational is to be methodical: that is, to have criteria for success laid down in advance. We think of poets and painters as using some other faculty than "reason" in their work because, by their own confession, they are not sure of what they want to do before they have

done it. They make up new standards of achievement as they go along. By contrast, we think of judges as knowing in advance what criteria a brief will have to satisfy in order to invoke a favorable decision, and of businessmen as setting well-defined goals and being judged by their success in achieving them. Law and business are good examples of rationality, but the scientist, knowing in advance what would count as disconfirming his hypothesis and prepared to abandon that hypothesis as a result of the unfavorable outcome of a single experiment, seems a truly heroic example. Further, we seem to have a clear criterion of the success of a scientific theory—namely, its ability to predict, and thereby to enable us to control some portion of the world. If to be rational means to be able to lay down criteria in advance, then it is plausible to take natural science as the paradigm of rationality.

The trouble is that in this sense of "rational" the humanities are never going to qualify as rational activities. If the humanities are concerned with ends rather than means, then there is no way to evaluate their success in terms of antecedently specified criteria. If we already knew what criteria we wanted to satisfy, we would not worry about whether we were pursuing the right ends. If we thought we knew the goals of culture and society in advance, we would have no use for the humanities—as totalitarian societies in fact do not. It is characteristic of democracies and pluralistic societies to redefine their goals continually. But if to be rational means to satisfy criteria, then this process of redefinition will be bound to be non-rational. So if the humanities are to be viewed as rational activities, rationality will have to be thought of as something other than the satisfaction of criteria which are statable in advance.

[The second] meaning of "rational" is, in fact, available. In this sense, the word means something like "sane" or "reasonable" rather than "methodical." It names a set of moral virtues: tolerance, respect for the opinion of those around one, willingness to listen, reliance on persuasion rather than force. These are the virtues which members of a civilized society must possess if the society is to endure. In this sense of "rational," the word means something more like "civilized" than like "methodical." When so construed, the distinction between the rational and the irrational has nothing in particular to do with the difference between the arts and the sciences. On this construction, to be rational is simply to discuss any topic— religious, literary, or scientific—in a way which eschews dogmatism, defensiveness, and righteous indignation.

There is no problem about whether, in this latter, weaker sense the humanities are "rational disciplines." Usually humanists display the moral virtues in question. Sometimes they do not, but then sometimes scientists don't either. Yet these moral virtues are felt to be not enough. Both humanists and the public hanker after rationality in the first, stronger sense of the term: a sense which is associated with objective truth, correspondence to reality, method and criteria.

We should not try to satisfy this hankering, but rather try to eradicate it. No matter what one's opinion of the secularization of culture, it was a mistake to try to make the natural scientist into a new sort of priest, a link between the human and the non-human. So was the idea that some sorts of truths are "objective" whereas others are merely "subjective" or "relative"—the attempt to divide up the set of true sentences into "genuine knowledge" and "mere opinion," or into the "factual" and the "judgmental." So was the idea that the scientist has a special method which, if only the humanists would apply it to ultimate values, would give us the same kind of self-confidence about moral ends as we now have about technological means. I think that we should content ourselves with the second, "weaker" conception of rationality and avoid the first, "stronger" conception. We should avoid the idea that there is some special virtue in knowing in advance what criteria you are going to satisfy, in having standards by which to measure progress.

[IS SCIENCE RATIONAL?]

One can make these issues somewhat more concrete by taking up the current controversy among philosophers about the "rationality of science." For some twenty years, ever since the publication of Thomas Kuhn's book, *The Structure of Scientific Revolutions* philosophers have been debating the question of

"whether science is rational." Attacks on Kuhn for being "irrational" are now as frequent and urgent as, in the 1930s and 1940s, were attacks on the logical positivists for saying that moral judgments were "meaningless." We are constantly being warned of the danger of "relativism" which will beset us if we give up our attachment to objectivity and to the idea of rationality as obedience to criteria.

Whereas Kuhn's enemies routinely accuse him of reducing science to "mob psychology," and pride themselves on having (by a new theory of meaning or reference or verisimilitude) vindicated the "rationality of science," his pragmatic friends (such as myself) routinely congratulate him on having softened the distinction between science and non-science. . . . [H]e has said that "there is no theory-independent way to reconstruct phrases like "really there." He has asked whether it really helps "to imagine that there is some one full, objective, true account of nature and that the proper measure of scientific achievement is the extent to which it brings us closer to the ultimate goal." We pragmatists quote these passages incessantly in the course of our effort to enlist Kuhn in our campaign to drop the objective-subjective distinction altogether.

What I am calling "pragmatism" might also be called "left-wing Kuhnianism." It has also been rather endearingly called (by one of its critics, Clark Glymour) "the new fuzziness," because it is an attempt to blur just those distinctions between the objective and the subjective and between fact and value which the criterial conception of rationality has developed. We fuzzies would like to substitute the idea of "unforced agreement" for that of "objectivity." We should like to put all culture on an epistemological level (or get rid of the idea of "epistemological level"). . . . On our view, "truth" is a univocal term. It applies equally to the judgments of lawyers, anthropologists, physicists, philologists and literary critics. There is point in assigning degrees of "objectivity" or "hardness" to such disciplines. For the presence of unforced agreement in all of them gives us everything in the way of "objective truth" which one could possibly want: namely, intersubjective agreement.

As soon as one says that all there is to objectivity is intersubjectivity, one is likely to be accused of being a relativist. That is the epithet traditionally applied to pragmatists. But this epithet is ambiguous. It can name any of three different views:

1. The silly and self-refuting view that every belief is as good as every other.
2. The wrong-headed view that "true" is an equivocal term, having as many meanings as there are contexts of justification.
3. The ethnocentric view that there is nothing to be said about either truth or rationality apart from descriptions of the familiar procedures of justification which a given society—*ours*—uses in one or another area of inquiry.

The pragmatist does hold this third, ethnocentric view. But he does not hold the first or the second view of relativism.

But "relativism" is not an appropriate term to describe this sort of ethnocentrism. For we pragmatists are not holding a positive theory which says that something is relative to something else. Instead, we are making the purely *negative* point that we would be better off without the traditional distinctions between knowledge and opinion, construed as the distinction between truth as correspondence to reality and truth as a commendatory term for well-justified beliefs. Our opponents call this negative claim "relativistic" because they cannot imagine that anybody would seriously deny that truth has an intrinsic nature. So when we say that there is nothing to be said about truth save that each of us will commend as true those beliefs which he or she finds good to believe, the realist is inclined to interpret this as one more positive theory about the nature of truth: a theory according to which truth is simply the contemporary opinion of a chosen individual or group. Such a theory would, of course, be self-refuting. But we pragmatists do not have a theory of truth, much less a relativistic one. As partisans of solidarity, our account of the value of cooperative human enquiry has only an ethical base, not an epistemological or metaphysical one.

To say that we must be ethnocentric may sound suspicious, but this will only happen if we identify ethnocentrism with pigheaded refusal to talk to representatives of other communities. In my sense of ethnocentrism, to be ethnocentric is simply to work by our own lights. The defense of ethnocentrism is simply that there are no other lights to work by. Beliefs suggested by another individual or another culture must be tested by trying to weave them together with beliefs which we already have. . . .

This way of thinking runs counter to the attempts, familiar since the eighteenth century, to think of political liberalism as based on a conception of the nature of man. To most thinkers of the Enlightenment, it seemed clear that the access to Nature which physical science had provided should now be followed by the establishment of social, political and economic institutions which were "in accordance with Nature." Ever since, liberal social thought has centered around social reform as made possible by objective knowledge of what human beings are like—not knowledge of what Greeks or Frenchmen or Chinese are like, but of humanity as such. This tradition dreams of a universal human community which will exhibit a nonparochial solidarity because it is the expression of an ahistorical human nature.

Philosophers who belong to this tradition, who wish to ground solidarity in objectivity, have to construe truth as correspondence to reality. So they must construct an epistemology which has room for a kind of justification which is not merely social but natural, springing from human nature itself, and made possible by a link between that part of nature and the rest of nature. By contrast we pragmatists, who wish to reduce objectivity to solidarity, do not require either a metaphysics or an epistemology. . . . We see the gap between truth and justification not as something to be bridged by isolating a natural and transcultural sort of rationality which can be used to criticize certain cultures and praise others, but simply as the gap between the actual good and the possible better. From a pragmatist point of view, to say that what is rational for us now to believe may not be *true*, is simply to say that somebody may come up with a better idea. . . .

Another reason for describing us as "relativistic" is that we pragmatists drop the idea that enquiry is destined to converge to a single point—that Truth is "out there" waiting for human beings to arrive at it. This idea seems to us an unfortunate attempt to carry a religious conception over into a secular culture. All that is worth preserving of the claim that rational inquiry will converge to a single point is the claim that we must be able to explain why past false views were held in the past, and thus explain how we go about re-educating our benighted ancestors. To say that we think we're heading in the right direction is just to say, with Kuhn, that we can, by hindsight, tell the story of the past as a story of progress.

But the fact that we can trace such a direction and tell such a story does not mean that we have come closer to a goal which is out there waiting for us. We cannot, I think, imagine a moment at which the human race could settle back and say, "Well, now that we've finally arrived at the Truth we can relax." Paul Feyerabend is right in suggesting that we should discard the metaphor of inquiry, and human activity generally, as converging rather than proliferating, becoming more unified rather than more diverse. On the contrary, we should *relish* that thought that the sciences as well as the arts will *always* provide a spectacle of fierce competition between alternative theories, movements and schools. The end of human activity is not rest, but rather richer and better human activity. We should think of human progress as making it possible for human beings to do more interesting things and be more interesting people, not as heading toward a place which has somehow been prepared for us in advance. To drop the criterial conception of rationality in favor of the pragmatist conception would be to give up the idea of Truth as something to which we were responsible. Instead we should think of "true" as a word which applies to those beliefs upon which we are able to agree, as roughly synonymous with "justified." . . .

. . . Pragmatists would like to replace the desire for objectivity—the desire to be in touch with a reality which is more than some community with which we identify ourselves—with the desire for solidarity with that community. They think that the habits of relying on persuasion rather than force, of respect for opinions of colleagues, of curiosity and eagerness for new data and ideas, are the *only* virtues which scientists have. They do not think that there is an intellectual virtue called "rationality" over and above these moral virtues. . . .

Pragmatists interpret the goal of inquiry (in any sphere of culture) as the attainment of an appropriate mixture of unforced agreement with tolerant dis-agreement (where what counts as appropriate is determined, within that sphere, by trial and error). Such a reinterpretation of our sense of responsibility would, if carried through, gradually make unintelligible the subject-object model of enquiry, the child-parent model of moral obligation, and the correspondence theory of truth. A world in which those models, and that theory, no longer had any intuitive appeal would be a pragmatist's paradise.

When Dewey urged that we try to create such a paradise he was said to be irresponsible. For, it was said, he left us bereft of weapons to use against our enemies; he gave us nothing with which to "answer the Nazis." When we new fuzzies try to revive Dewey's repudiation of criteriology we are said to be "relativistic." We must, people say, believe that every coherent view is as good as every other, since we have no "outside" touchstone for choice among such views. We are said to leave the general public defenseless against the witch doctor, the defender of creationism, or anyone else who is clever and patient enough to deduce a consistent and wide-ranging set of theorems from his "alternative first principles."

Nobody is convinced when we fuzzies say that we can be just as morally indignant as the next philosopher. We are suspected of being contritely fallibilist when righteous fury is called for. Even when we actually display appropriate emotions we get nowhere, for we are told that we have no *right* to these emotions. When we suggest that one of the few things we know (or need to know) about truth is that it is what wins in a free and open encounter, we are told that we have defined "true" as "satisfies the standards of our community." But we pragmatists do not hold this relativist view. We do not infer from "There is no way to step outside communities to a neutral standpoint" to "There is no rational way to justify liberal communities over totalitarian communities." For that inference involves just the notion of "rationality" as a set of ahistorical principles which pragmatists abjure. What we in fact infer is that there is no way to beat totalitarians in argument by appealing to shared common premises, and no point in pretending that a common human nature makes the totalitarians unconsciously hold such premises.

The claim that we fuzzies have no right to be furious at moral evil, no right to commend our views as true unless we simultaneously refute ourselves by claiming that there are objects out there which *make* those views true, begs all the theoretical questions. But it gets to the practical and moral heart of the matter. This is the question of whether notions like "unforced agreement" and "free and open encounter"—descriptions of social situations—can take the place in our moral lives of notions like "the world," "the will of God," "the moral law," "what our beliefs are trying to represent accurately" and "what makes our beliefs true." All the philosophical presuppositions which make Hume's fork seem inevitable are ways of suggesting that human communities must justify their existence by striving to attain a non-human goal. To suggest that we can forget about Hume's fork [the radical separation of facts from values], forget about being responsible to what is "out there," is to suggest that human communities can justify their existence only by comparisons with other actual and possible human communities. . . .

Imagine . . . that a few years from now you open your copy of the *New York Times* and read that the philosophers, in convention assembled, have unanimously agreed that values are objective, science rational, truth a matter of correspondence to reality, etc. Recent breakthroughs in semantics and meta-ethics, the report goes on, have caused the last remaining non-cognitivists in ethics to recant. Similarly breakthroughs in the philosophy of science have led Kuhn formally to abjure his claim that there is no theory-independent way to reconstruct statements about what is "really there." All the new fuzzies have repudiated all their former views. By way of making amends for the intellectual confusion which the philosophical profession has recently caused, the philosophers have adopted a short, crisp set of standards of rationality and morality. Next year the convention is expected to adopt the report of the committee charged with formulating a standard of aesthetic taste.

Surely the public reaction to this would not be "Saved!" but rather "Who on earth do these philosophers think they *are?*" It is one of the best things about the form of intellectual life we Western liberals lead that this *would* be our reaction. No matter how

much we moan about the disorder and confusion of the current philosophical scene, about the treason of the clerks, we do not really want things any other way. What prevents us from relaxing and enjoying the new fuzziness is perhaps no more than cultural lag, the fact that the rhetoric of the Enlightenment praised the emerging natural sciences in a vocabulary which was left over from a less liberal and tolerant era. This rhetoric enshrined all the old philosophical opposition between mind and world, appearance and reality, subject and object, truth and pleasure. Dewey thought that it was the continued prevalence of such opposition which prevented us from seeing that modern science was a new and promising invention, a way of life which had not existed before and which ought to be encouraged and imitated, something which required a new rhetoric rather than justification by an old one.

Suppose that Dewey were right about this, and that eventually we learn to find the fuzziness which results from breaking down such opposition spiritually comforting rather than morally offensive. What would the rhetoric of the culture, and in particular of the humanities, sound like? Presumably it would be more Kuhnian, in the sense that it would mention particular concrete achievements—paradigms—more, and "method" less. There would be less talk about rigor and more about originality. The image of the great scientist would not be of somebody who got it right but of somebody who made it new. The new rhetoric would draw more on the vocabulary of Romantic poetry and socialist politics, and less on that of Greek metaphysics, religious morality or Enlightenment scientism. A scientist would rely on a sense of solidarity with the rest of her profession, rather than a picture of herself as battling through the veils of illusion, guided by the light of reason.

If all this happened, the term "science," and thus the opposition between the humanities, the arts and the sciences might gradually fade away. Once "science" was deprived of an honorific sense, we might not need it for taxonomy. . . . The people now called "scientists" would no longer think of themselves as members of a quasi-priestly order, nor would the public think of themselves as in the care of such an order.

In this situation, the "humanities" would no longer think of themselves as such, nor would they share a common rhetoric. Each of the disciplines which now fall under that rubric would worry as little about its method, cognitive status or "philosophical foundations" as do mathematics, civil engineering or sculpture. For terms which denoted disciplines would not be thought to divide "subject matter," chunks of the world which had "interfaces" with each other. Rather, they would be thought to denote communities whose boundaries were as fluid as the interests of their members. In this heyday of the fuzzies, there would be as little reason to be self-conscious about the nature and status of one's discipline as, in the ideal democratic community, about the nature and status of one's race or sex. For one's ultimate loyalty would be to the larger community which permitted and encouraged this kind of freedom and insouciance. This community would serve no higher end than its own preservation and self-improvement, the preservation and enhancement of civilization. It would identify rationality with that effort, rather than with the desire for objectivity. So it would feel no need for a foundation more solid than reciprocal loyalty.

FOR FURTHER REFLECTION

1. What are the major motivations of Rorty in rejecting the correspondence theory of truth and the object-subject distinction? Why does he think that the notion of intersubjective agreement (or unforced agreement) is a better idea? What are the strengths and weaknesses of Rorty's proposal?

2. Rorty distinguishes three types of relativism. What are they, and which does he choose? Do you agree with his argument here? Explain your answer.

3. What does Rorty mean that pragmatic truth has only an ethical base, not an epistemological or metaphysical one? What is his argument for this? Is it sound?

4. Has Rorty successfully eliminated metaphysical and epistemological notions? Has he argued successfully against the distinction between the ideas of objectivity and subjectivity and against the correspondence theory of truth? Critique his argument.

5. Do you detect any hidden assumptions in this article? Who is the community with which Rorty identifies? What are its values? Does it include religious people? conservatives? socialists? Explain your answer.

6. Elsewhere in *Philosophy and the Mirror of Nature* (p. 176), Rorty describes "truth" as "what you can defend against all comers, . . . what our peers will *ceteris paribus* let us get away with saying." Analyze this characterization of truth.

DANIEL DENNETT

POSTMODERNISM AND TRUTH

Daniel Dennett is Distinguished Arts and Science Professor at Tufts University and the author of several works in philosophy of mind and science, including *Consciousness Explained* (1991) and *Darwin's Dangerous Idea* (1995). He has been the president of the American Philosophical Association. In this essay Dennett contends that postmodernism fails to come to grips with the concept of truth. The postmodernists either reject for an irrational cognitive relativism or undervalue, as having minor significance, a *vegetarian* concept of truth.

Here is a story you probably haven't heard, about how a team of American researchers inadvertently introduced a virus into a third world country they were studying.[1] They were experts in their field, and they had the best intentions; they thought they were helping the people they were studying, but in fact they had never really seriously considered whether what they were doing might have ill effects. It had not occurred to them at all that a side-effect of their research might be damaging to the fragile ecology of the country they were studying. The virus they introduced had some dire effects indeed: it raised infant mortality rates, led to a general decline in the health and wellbeing of women and children, and, perhaps worst of all, indirectly undermined the only effective political force for democracy in the country, strengthening the hand of the traditional despot who ruled the nation. These American researchers had something to answer for, surely, but when confronted with the devastation they had wrought, their response was frustrating, to say the least: they still thought that what they were doing was, all things considered, in the interests of the people, and declared that the standards by which this so-called devastation was being measured were simply not appropriate. Their critics, they contended, were trying to impose "Western" standards in a cultural environment that had no use for such standards. In this strange defense they were warmly supported by the country's leaders—not surprisingly—and little was heard—not surprisingly—from those who *might* have been said, by Western standards, to have suffered as a result of their activities.

These researchers were not biologists intent on introducing new strains of rice, nor were they agribusiness chemists testing new pesticides, or doctors trying out vaccines that couldn't legally be tested in the U.S.A They were postmodernist science critics and other multiculturalists who were arguing, in the course of their professional researches on the culture and traditional "science" of this country, that Western science was just one among many equally valid narratives, not to be "privileged" in its competition with native traditions which other researchers—biologists, chemists, and others—were eager to supplant. The virus they introduced was not a macromolecule but a meme (a replicating idea): the idea that science was a "colonial" imposition, not a worthy substitute for the practices and beliefs that had carried the third-world country to its current condition. And the reason you have not heard of this particular incident is that I made

Reprinted by permission of Daniel Dennett.

it up, to dramatize the issue and to try to unsettle what seems to be the current orthodoxy among the *literati* about such matters. But it is inspired by real incidents—that is to say, true reports. Events of just this sort have occurred in India and elsewhere, reported, movingly, by a number of writers, among them:

Meera Nanda, "The Epistemic Charity of the Social Constructivist Critics of Science and Why the Third World Should Refuse the Offer," in N. Koertge, ed., *A House Built on Sand: Exposing Postmodernist Myths about Science*, Oxford University Press, 1998, pp. 286–311.

Reza Afshari, "An Essay on Islamic Cultural Relativism in the Discourse of Human Rights," in *Human Rights Quarterly*, 16, 1994, pp. 235–76.

Susan Okin, "Is Multiculturalism Bad for Woman?" *Boston Review*, October/November, 1997, pp. 25–28.

Pervez Hoodbhoy, *Islam and Science: Religious Orthodoxy and the Battle for Rationality*, London and New Jersey, Zed Books Ltd., 1991.

My little fable is also inspired by a wonderful remark of E. O. Wilson, in *Atlantic Monthly* a few months ago: "Scientists, being held responsible for what they say, have not found postmodernism useful." Actually, of course, we are all held responsible for what we say. The laws of libel and slander, for instance, exempt none of us, but most of us—including scientists in many or even most fields—do not typically make assertions that, independently of libel and slander considerations, might bring harm to others, even indirectly. A handy measure of this fact is the evident ridiculousness we discover in the idea of malpractice insurance for . . . literary critics, philosophers, mathemeticians, historians, cosmologists. What on earth could a mathematician or literary critic do, in the course of executing her professional duties, that might need the security blanket of malpractice insurance? She might inadvertently trip a student in the corridor, or drop a book on somebody's head, but aside from such *outré* side-effects, our activities are paradigmatically innocuous. One would think. But in those fields where the stakes are higher—and more direct—there is a longstanding tradition of being especially cautious, and of taking particular responsibility for ensuring that no harm results (as explicitly honored in the Hippocratic Oath). Engineers, knowing that thousands of people's safety may depend on the bridge they design, engage in focussed exercises with specified constraints designed to determine that, according to all current knowledge, their designs are safe and sound. Even economists—often derided for the risks they take with *other* people's livelihoods—when the find themselves in positions to endorse specific economic measures considered by government bodies or by their private clients, are known to attempt to put a salutory strain on their underlying assumptions, just to be safe. They are used to asking themselves, and to being expected to ask themselves: "What if I'm wrong?" We others seldom ask ourselves this question, since we have spent our student and professional lives working on topics that are, according both to tradition and common sense, incapable of affecting any lives in ways worth worrying about. If my topic is whether or not Vlastos had the best interpretation of Plato's *Parmenides* or how the wool trade affected imagery in Tudor poetry, or what the best version of string theory says about time, or how to recast proofs in topology in some new formalism, if I am wrong, dead wrong, in what I say, the only damage I am likely to do is to my own scholarly reputation. But when we aspire to have a greater impact on the "real" (as opposed to "academic") world—and many philosophers do aspire to this today—we need to adopt the attitudes and habits of these more applied disciplines. We need to hold ourselves responsible for what we say, recognizing that our words, if believed, can have profound effects for good or ill.

When I was a young untenured professor of philosophy, I once received a visit from a colleague from the Comparative Literature Department, an eminent and fashionable literary theorist, who wanted some help from me. I was flattered to be asked, and did my best to oblige, but the drift of his questions about various philosophical topics was strangely perplexing to me. For quite a while we were getting nowhere, until finally he managed to make clear to me what he had come for. He wanted "an epistemology," he said. *An* epistemology. Every self-respecting literary theorist had to sport an epistemology that season, it seems, and without one he felt naked, so he had come to me for an epistemology to wear—it was the very next fashion, he was sure, and he wanted the *dernier cri* in epistemologies. It didn't matter to him that it be sound, or defensible, or (as one might as well say) *true*; it just had to be new and different and stylish. Accessorize, my good fellow, or be overlooked at the party.

At that moment I perceived a gulf between us that I had only dimly seen before. It struck me at first as simply the gulf between being serious and being frivolous. But that initial surge of self-righteousness on my part was, in fact, a naive reaction. My sense of outrage, my sense that my time had been wasted by this man's bizarre project, was in its own way as unsophisticated as the reaction of the first-time theatergoer who leaps on the stage to protect the heroine from the villain. "Don't you understand?" we ask incredulously. "It's *make believe*. Its *art*. It isn't *supposed* to be taken literally!" Put in that context, perhaps this man's quest was not so disreputable after all. I would not have been offended, would I, if a colleague in the Drama Department had come by and asked if he could borrow a few yards of my books to put on the shelves of the set for his production of Tom Stoppard's play, *Jumpers*. What if anything would be wrong in outfitting this fellow with a snazzy set of outrageous epistemological doctrines with which he could titillate or confound his colleagues?

What would be wrong would be that since this man didn't acknowledge the gulf, didn't even recognize that it existed, my acquiescence in his shopping spree would have contributed to the debasement of a precious commodity, the erosion of a valuable distinction. Many people, including both onlookers and participants, don't see this gulf, or actively deny its existence, and therein lies the problem. The sad fact is that in some intellectual circles, inhabited by some of our more advanced thinkers in the arts and humanities, this attitude passes as a sophisticated appreciation of the futility of proof and the relativity of all knowledge claims. In fact this opinion, far from being sophisticated, is the height of sheltered naiveté, made possible only by flatfooted ignorance of the proven methods of scientific truth-seeking and their power. Like many other naif, these thinkers, reflecting on the manifest inability of *their* methods of truth-seeking to achieve stable and valuable results, innocently generalize from their own cases and conclude that nobody *else* knows how to discover the truth either.

Among those who contribute to this problem, I am sorry to say, is, my good friend Dick Rorty. Richard Rorty and I have been constructively disagreeing with each other for over a quarter of a century now. Each of us has taught the other a great deal, I believe, in the reciprocal process of chipping away at our residual points of disagreement. I can't name a living philosopher from whom I have learned more. Rorty has opened up the horizons of contemporary philosophy, shrewdly showing us philosophers many things about how our own projects have grown out of the philosophical projects of the distant and recent past, while boldly describing and prescribing future paths for us to take. But there is one point over which he and I do not agree at all—not yet—and that concerns his attempt over the years to show that philosophers' debates about Truth and Reality really do erase the gulf, really do license a slide into some form of relativism. In the end, Rorty tells us, it is all just "conversations," and there are only political or historical or aesthetic grounds for taking one role or another in an ongoing conversation.

Rorty has often tried to enlist me in his campaign, declaring that he could find in my own work one explosive insight or another that would help him with his project of destroying the illusory edifice of objectivity. One of his favorite passages is the one with which I ended my book *Consciousness Explained* (1991):

> It's just a war of metaphors, you say—but metaphors are not "just" metaphors; metaphors are the tools of thought. No one can think about consciousness without them, so it is important to equip yourself with the best set of tools available. Look what we have built with our tools. Could you have imagined it without them? [p. 455]

"I wish," Rorty says, "he had taken one step further, and had added that such tools are all that inquiry can ever provide, because inquiry is never 'pure' in the sense of [Bernard] Williams' 'project of pure inquiry.' It is always a matter of getting us something we want." ("Holism, Intrinsicality, Transcendence," in Dahlbom, ed., *Dennett and his Critics*, 1993.) But I would never take that step, for although metaphors are indeed irreplaceable tools of thought, they are not the only such tools. Microscopes and mathematics and MRI scanners are among the others. Yes, any inquiry is a matter of getting us something we want: the truth about something that matters to us, if all goes as it should.

When philosophers argue about truth, they are arguing about how not to inflate the truth about truth into the Truth about Truth, some absolutistic doctrine that makes indefensible demands on our systems of thought. It is in this regard similar to debates about, say, the reality of time, or the reality of the past. There are some deep, sophisticated, worthy philosophical investigations into whether, properly speaking, the past is real. Opinion is divided, but you entirely misunderstand the point of these disagreements if you suppose that they undercut claims such as the following:

Life first emerged on this planet more than three thousand million years ago.
The Holocaust happened during World War II.
Jack Ruby shot and killed Lee Harvey Oswald at 11:21 am, Dallas time, November 24, 1963.

These are truths about events that really happened. Their denials are falsehoods. No sane philosopher has ever thought otherwise, though in the heat of battle, they have sometimes made claims that could be so interpreted.

Richard Rorty deserves his large and enthralled readership in the arts and humanities, and in the "humanistic" social sciences, but when his readers enthusiastically interpret him as encouraging their postmodernist skepticism about truth, they trundle down paths he himself has refrained from traveling. When I press him on these points, he concedes that there is indeed a useful concept of truth that survives intact after all the corrosive philosophical objections have been duly entered. This serviceable, modest concept of truth, Rorty acknowledges, has its uses: when we want to compare two maps of the countryside for reliability, for instance, or when the issue is whether the accused did or did not commit the crime as charged.

Even Richard Rorty, then, acknowledges the gap, and the importance of the gap, between appearance and reality, between those theatrical exercises that

may entertain us without pretense of truth-telling, and those that aim for, and often hit, the truth. He calls it a "vegetarian" concept of truth. Very well, then, let's all be vegetarians about the truth. Scientists never wanted to go the whole hog anyway.

So now, let's ask about the sources or foundations of this mild, uncontroversial, vegetarian concept of truth.

Right now, as I speak, billions of organisms on this planet are engaged in a game of hide and seek. It is not just a game for them. It is a matter of life and death. *Getting it right*, not making mistakes, has been of paramount importance to every living thing on this planet for more than three billion years, and so these organisms have evolved thousands of different ways of finding out about the world they live in, discriminating friends from foes, meals from mates, and ignoring the rest for the most part. It matters to them that they not be misinformed about these matters—indeed nothing matters more—but they don't, as a rule, appreciate this. They are the beneficiaries of equipment exquisitely designed to get what matters right but when their equipment malfunctions and gets matters wrong, they have no resources, as a rule, for noticing this, let alone deploring it. They soldier on, unwittingly. The difference between how things seem and how things really are is just as fatal a gap for them as it can be for us, but they are largely oblivious to it. The *recognition* of the difference between appearance and reality is a human discovery. A few other species—some primates, some cetaceans, maybe even some birds—show signs of appreciating the phenomenon of "false belief"—*getting it wrong*. They exhibit sensitivity to the errors of others, and perhaps even some sensitivity to their own errors as errors, but they lack the capacity for the reflection required to *dwell* on this possibility, and so they cannot use this sensitivity in the deliberate design of repairs or improvements of their own seeking gear or hiding gear. That sort of bridging of the gap between appearance and reality is a wrinkle that we human beings alone have mastered.

We are the species that discovered doubt. Is there enough food laid by for winter? Have I miscalculated? Is my mate cheating on me? Should we have moved south? Is it safe to enter this cave? Other creatures are often visibly agitated by their own uncertainties about just such questions, but because they cannot actually *ask themselves these questions*, they cannot articulate their predicaments for themselves or take steps to improve their grip on the truth. They are stuck in a world of appearances, making the best they can of how things seem and seldom if ever worrying about whether how things seem is how they truly are.

We alone can be wracked with doubt, and we alone have been provoked by that epistemic itch to seek a remedy: better truth-seeking methods. Wanting to keep track of our food supplies, our territories, our families, our enemies, we discovered the benefits of talking it over with others, asking questions, passing on lore. We invented culture. Then we invented measuring, and arithmetic, and maps, and writing. These communicative and recording innovations come with a built-in ideal: truth. The point of asking questions is to find *true* answers; the point of measuring is to measure *accurately*; the point of making maps is to *find your way* to your destination. There may be an Island of the Colour-blind (allowing Oliver Sacks his usual large dose of poetic license), but no Island of the People Who Do Not Recognize Their Own Children. The Land of the Liars could exist only in philosophers' puzzles; there are no traditions of False Calendar Systems for mis-recording the passage of time. In short, the goal of truth goes without saying, in every human culture.

We human beings use our communicative skills not just for truth-telling, but also for promise-making, threatening, bargaining, story-telling, entertaining, mystifying, inducing hypnotic trances, and just plain kidding around, but prince of these activities is truth-telling, and for this activity we have invented ever better tools. Alongside our tools for agriculture, building, warfare, and transportation, we have created a technology of truth: science. Try to draw a straight line, or a circle, "freehand." Unless you have considerable artistic talent, the result will not be impressive. With a straight edge and a compass, on the other hand, you can practically eliminate the sources of human variability and get a nice, clean, objective result, the same every time.

Is the line really straight? How straight is it? In response to these questions, we develop ever finer tests, and then tests of the accuracy of those tests, and so forth, bootstrapping our way to ever greater accu-

racy and objectivity. Scientists are just as vulnerable to wishful thinking, just as likely to be tempted by base motives, just as venal and gullible and forgetful as the rest of humankind. Scientists don't consider themselves to be saints; they don't even pretend to be priests (who according to tradition are supposed to do a better job than the rest of us at fighting off human temptation and frailty). Scientists take themselves to be just as weak and fallible as anybody else, but recognizing those very sources of error in themselves and in the groups to which they belong, they have devised elaborate systems to tie their own hands, forcibly preventing their frailties and prejudices from infecting their results.

It is not just the implements, the physical tools of the trade, that are designed to be resistant to human error. The organization of methods is also under severe selection pressure for improved reliability and objectivity. The classic example is the double blind experiment, in which, for instance, neither the human subjects nor the experimenters themselves are permitted to know which subjects get the test drug and which the placebo, so that nobody's subliminal hankerings and hunches can influence the perception of the results. The statistical design of both individual experiments and suites of experiments, is then embedded in the larger practice of routine attempts at replication by independent investigators, which is further embedded in a tradition—flawed, but recognized—of publication of both positive and negative results.

What inspires faith in arithmetic is the fact that hundreds of scribblers, working independently on the same problem, will all arrive at the same answer (except for those negligible few whose errors can be found and identified to the mutual satisfaction of all). This unrivalled objectivity is also found in geometry and the other branches of mathematics, which since antiquity have been the very model of certain knowledge set against the world of flux and controversy. In Plato's early dialogue, the *Meno*, Socrates and the slave boy work out together a special case of the Pythagorean theorem. Plato's example expresses the frank recognition of a standard of truth to be aspired to by all truth-seekers, a standard that has not only never been seriously challenged, but that has been tacitly accepted—indeed heavily relied upon, even in matters of life and death—by the most vigorous opponents of science. (Or do you know a church that keeps track of its flock, and their donations, without benefit of arithmetic?)

Yes, but science almost never looks as uncontroversial, as cut-and-dried, as arithmetic. Indeed rival scientific factions often engage in propaganda battles as ferocious as anything to be found in politics, or even in religious conflict. The fury with which the defenders of scientific orthodoxy often defend their doctrines against the heretics is probably unmatched in other arenas of human rhetorical combat. These competitions for alliance—and, of course, funding—are designed to capture attention, and being well-designed, they typically succeed. This has the side effect that the warfare on the cutting edge of any science draws attention away from the huge uncontested background, the dull metal heft of the axe that gives the cutting edge its power. What goes without saying, during these heated disagreements, is an organized, encyclopedic collection of agreed-upon, humdrum scientific fact.

Robert Proctor usefully draws our attention to a distinction between neutrality and objectivity. Geologists, he notes, know a lot more about oil-bearing shales than about other rocks—for the obvious economic and political reasons—but they do *know* objectively about oil bearing shales. And much of what they learn about oil-bearing shales can be generalized to other, less favored rocks. We want science to be objective; we should not want science to be neutral. Biologists know a lot more about the fruit-fly, *Drosophila*, than they do about other insects—not because you can get rich off fruit flies, but because you can get knowledge out of fruit flies easier than you can get it out of most other species. Biologists also know a lot more about mosquitoes than about other insects, and here it is because mosquitoes are more harmful to people than other species that might be much easier to study. Many are the reasons for concentrating attention in science, and they all conspire to make the paths of investigation far from neutral; they do not, in general, make those paths any less objective. Sometimes, to be sure, one bias or another leads to a violation of the canons of scientific method. Studying the pattern of a disease in men, for instance, while neglecting to gather the data on the same disease in women, is not just not neutral; it is bad science, as indefensible in scientific terms as it is in political terms.

It is true that past scientific orthodoxies have themselves inspired policies that hindsight reveals to be seriously flawed. One can sympathize, for instance, with Ashis Nandy, editor of the passionately anti-scientific anthology, *Science, Hegemony and Violence: A Requiem for Modernity*, Delhi: Oxford Univ. Press, 1988. Having lived through Atoms for Peace, and the Green Revolution, to name two of the most ballyhooed scientific juggernauts that have seriously disrupted third world societies, he sees how "the adaptation in India of decades-old western technologies are advertised and purchased as great leaps forward in science, even when such adaptations turn entire disciplines or areas of knowledge into mere intellectual machines for the adaptation, replication and testing of shop-worn western models which have often been given up in the west itself as too dangerous or as ecologically nonviable." (p. 8) But we should recognize this as a political misuse of science, not as a fundamental flaw in science itself.

The methods of science aren't foolproof, but they are indefinitely perfectible. Just as important: there is a tradition of criticism that enforces improvement whenever and wherever flaws are discovered. The methods of science, like everything else under the sun, are themselves objects of scientific scrutiny, as *method* becomes *methodology*, the analysis of methods. Methodology in turn falls under the gaze of *epistemology*, the investigation of investigation itself—nothing is off limits to scientific questioning. The irony is that these fruits of scientific reflection, showing us the ineliminable smudges of imperfection, are sometimes used by those who are suspicious of science as their grounds for denying it a privileged status in the truth-seeking department—as if the institutions and practices they see competing with it were no worse off in these regards. But where are the examples of religious orthodoxy being simply abandoned in the face of irresistible evidence? Again and again in science, yesterday's heresies have become today's new orthodoxies. No religion exhibits that pattern in its history.

NOTE

1. Portions of this paper are derived from "Faith in the Truth," my Amnesty Lecture, Oxford, February 17, 1997.

FOR FURTHER REFLECTION

1. Examine Dennett's parable of the American researchers introducing a virus into a third world country. What is the message of this story?

2. Evaluate Dennett's rejection of cognitive relativism, the idea that there is no objective truth, but that truth is relative to each person or culture. How does Dennett argue against this thesis?

3. What is the role of science in the pursuit of objective truth? What does Dennett mean when he says science is not neutral with regard to truth?

4. Compare Dennett's essay with the previous one by Richard Rorty. Discuss their comparative merits and demerits.

5. Is there something self-referentially incoherent in the postmodernist claim that *there is no objective truth*? Are they claiming that that statement is objectively true?

6. What is the "*vegetarian concept of truth*"? What does Dennett say about it? How important is it for our lives?or

LORRAINE CODE

A FEMINIST EPISTEMOLOGY?

Lorraine Code is a philosophy professor at York University in Canada and a prominent author in feminist philosophy; her writings include *What Can She Know?* (1991) and *Ecological Thinking: The Politics of Epistemic Location* (2006). In the selection presented here from the former of these works, Code argues that traditional epistemology is androcentric—that is, maleoriented—because of its devotion to objectivity, impartiality, and universality. Contrary to this tradition, Code maintains that facts are often created by people and social institutions and are not objectively or impartially discovered. Feminism is antithetical to this androcentric perspective, and, thus, there can be no feminist epistemology in the traditional empiricist manner that epistemology has been done. However, Code argues, feminists should engage in epistemological discussions to critique epistemology's traditional assumptions. To this end, feminist epistemological analysis requires *positionality*, that is, "an open middle ground where an inquirer can take up a position, a standpoint, within a forest of absolutes." This will offer a diversity of methods for epistemological and scientific inquiry that will recognize the special perspective of the inquirer. Code reassures her reader that positionality will not open the door to rampant absolute relativism in which any view is as valid as another. For example,

From Lorraine Code, *What Can She Know? Feminist Theory and the Construction of Knowledge* (Ithaca, N.Y.: Cornell University Press, 1991), chap. 8. Reprinted with permission of the publisher.

a view that endorses violence against women would be opposed by the experiences of count-less women. Rejecting absolute relativism, feminists should instead accept a mitigated skep-ticism that, on the one hand, recognizes that something in the world itself constrains the possibilities of knowledge, while, on the other hand, recognizes the perspective of the knower. From this middle-ground position, feminists can "perceive interconnections among various traditionally separate 'branches' of philosophy, and of philosophy with other disci-plines and projects."

The product of my investigations in this book cannot unequivocally be called "a feminist episte-mology." Indeed, my principal conclusion is that the question whether a feminist epistemology is possi-ble or desirable must be left unanswered. So seem-ingly outrageous a claim, at this stage, demands an explanation.

As long as "epistemology" bears the stamp of the postpositivist, empiricist project of determining nec-essary and sufficient conditions for knowledge and devising strategies to refute skepticism, there can be no feminist epistemology. I have shown that the con-ceptions of knowledge and subjective agency that inform this project are inimical to feminist concerns on many levels: ontological, epistemological, moral, political. Ideals central to the project—ideals of objectivity, impartiality, and universality—are andro-centrically derived. Their articulation maps onto typ-ical middle-class white male experiences to suppress the very possibility that the sex of the knower could be epistemologically significant. But my project has been to take that possibility very seriously and to argue that once its implications are examined, "the epistemological project" will demand reconstruction. It would not be possible to develop a feminist epis-temology that retained allegiance to the pivotal ideas around which epistemology—for all its variations—has defined itself. Hence there can be no femi¬nist epistemology in any of the traditional senses of the term.

Feminists can be epistemologists, however, and epistemologists can be feminists. Feminists have to understand "the epistemological project" to be in a position to see its androcentrism and to comprehend the political consequences of its hegemony. They need to engage in dialogues with the tradition to analyze its strengths and limitations; they need to develop polit-ically informed critiques and to create space for pro-ductive relocations of knowledge in human lives. My contention that feminists have to engage in episte-mological analysis without articulating their project as the creation of "a feminist epistemology" is not merely a semantic quibble. Epistemological analyses that are compatible with feminist political commit-ments—however varied—sit uneasily with amalga-mating the labels while attempting to decenter androcentricity so that it can include women. Femi-nists cannot participate in the construction of a mono-lithic, comprehensive epistemological *theory* removed from the practical-political issues a theory of knowl-edge has to address. My discussions of women and madness, of the nurses in the Grange Inquiry, and of the creation of the Poverty Game have shown why theories that transcend the specificities of gendered and otherwise situated subjectivities are impotent to come to terms with the politics of knowledge. So there can be no feminist epistemology in the received sense—yet epistemological questions are fundamen-tal to feminist inquiry.

Even if androcentricity could be decentered to make space for gynocentric concerns, it is not obvious that "a feminist epistemology" would be the most desirable result. A feminist epistemology would seem to require a basis in assumptions about the essence of women and of knowledge. Hence it would risk replicating the exclusionary, hegemonic structures of the masculinist epistemology, in its various manifestations, that has claimed absolute sovereignty over the epistemic ter-rain. A politically adequate "successor epistemology" would have to give pride of place to questions such as, Whose knowledge are we talking about? Is it the knowledge that interchangeable observers have of cups, pens, and books on tables, or is it knowledge that committed Marxists have about capitalism? that committed supporters of apartheid have about blacks? Is it the knowledge of privileged intellectuals with the leisure to analyze the nature of freedom and oppression, or is it the knowledge that women who desperately need work must have so that they can weigh the dangers of radiation in a factory job against the humiliation of unemployment and welfare? The diversity of situations and circumstances in which people need to be in a position to know makes it difficult to see how a theory of knowledge, *an* epistemology, could respond to their questions.

Some of these reservations bear on the difficulty of seeing in feminist empiricism the best alternative to androcentric epistemology.[1] Feminist empiricism advocates a new empiricist project informed by the privileged vision of feminist consciousness and hence peculiarly equipped to eradicate sexism and androcentrism, represented as social biases. In its feminist dimension, it disrupts the smooth impartiality of the standard empiricist credo by introducing a specificity—a declaration of specific interests—to contest the very possibility of a disinterested epistemology. Hence it can claim subversive potential. But its scope is constricted by the fact that it makes these claims from within a structure that is itself indelibly tainted.

In arguing that social biases permeate "the context of discovery" in any inquiry so thoroughly that it would be naive to hope for their eradication in the "context of justification," feminist empiricism demonstrates its radical potential. In requiring—especially in the social sciences—that researchers locate themselves on the same critical plane as their "objects of study," feminist empiricism takes issue with the very idea that there could be valid, detached observation. And in urging more rigor in scientific and other inquiry, to detect the influence of gender bias in shaping research, feminist empiricism refuses to accept any claims for value-free inquiry.[2] Paradoxically, by acknowledging its engaged, interested position and taking the socio-political identity of inquirers into account *epistemologically*, feminist empiricism promises enhanced objectivity and diminished bias.

Yet that very emphasis on screening for bias restricts the promise of feminist empiricism. The idea that a "truer" account of reality, a more rigorously empirical and hence objective account, can be achieved through self-conscious stripping away of bias threatens to reproduce the old liberal split between "the individual" and the discourses and power structures constitutive of her or his place on the epistemic terrain. It evinces a belief in a detached position from which biases will indeed be visible and can be washed away. The thought that the—possibly unconscious—androcentrism of mainstream epistemology is imposed and maintained from outside on an otherwise neutral subject matter fails to take into account the constitutive role of ideologies, stereotypes, and structures of epistemic privilege in creating the only institutionally legitimate possibilities for the construction and growth of knowledge. It does not grant sufficient credence to the claim that facts are often made, not found. Feminist empiricism—like the master discourse from which it takes its name—opts for a position outside the material and historical conditions that most urgently require analysis. Hence, despite its subversive potential, it cannot, alone, provide the theoretical position that feminist epistemologists require.[3]

How, then, can the terrain be remapped so that the space required for feminist epistemological analyses can be created? A productive imagery is that of creating a clearing, an open middle ground where an inquirer can take up a position, a standpoint, within a forest of absolutes: the exigencies of objectivism, the fervor of ideology, the quietism of extreme relativism, and the hegemony of universal Truth—to mention only a few. This idea of "taking up a position" resumes the positionality analyses of previous chapters. Positionality, I think, is a sophisticated elaboration of earlier feminist standpoint theories that argued for the possibility of developing a unified, authoritative construction of reality anchored in the experiences and socioeconomic positions of women, deriving their inspiration from Marxist analyses of the standpoint of the proletariat.[4] Recent feminist concentration on differences and specificities makes the possibility of a feminist standpoint both remote and suspect, for it would presuppose an artificial unity in diversity. Intricated as it is with a complex configuration of specificities, *positionality* responds more adequately to the historical/political exigencies of the 1990s.

On this middle ground, responsible critical inquiry could take place, and effective forms of cognitive agency could thrive. Yet middle grounds have a bad name in professional philosophy. Too often, occupying such a position is condemned as a refusal to take a stand, a plea for undecidability and indifferent tolerance, a desire to have things both—or all—ways, hence a feeble form of fence sitting. Moreover, as I have shown in Chapter 2, the dichotomous thinking of most mainstream philosophy obliterates the very possibility of "middle grounds." My claim, however, is that a well-mapped middle ground offers a place to take up positions of strength and maximum productivity from which exclusionary theories can be tapped critically and creatively for criticism and reconstruction. Occupancy of these positions is compatible with a strong commitment to engagement in practices designed to eradicate women's oppression and to the creation of environments ecologically committed to the promotion of social/political well-being. It draws on the theoretical and practical resources that surround it to incorporate what is best in them and to reject what is damaging and oppressive. From these positions it is clear that analyses of damage, constraint, well-being, and empowerment are all themselves situated and revisable, based on the best, understanding available at the time, open to renegotiation. The provisionality—the revisability—of the resources no more leaves them "undecided," unstable sites for theory building and activism than a "fallibilist" standpoint in scientific inquiry would make it impossible to proceed with research. Like scientific research, politically informed activism and theory building have to go on, from where they are, for the gaps in their knowledge will not become visible except in practice, in further research that shows where revision is demanded. "Second wave" feminists made remarkable progress working from the hypothesis that women could be analyzed as a class; that same progress destabilized the hypothesis, yet while it was in place it made quantities of high-quality, emancipatory research and action possible.

Feminists committed to breaking with the monolithic, hegemonic tradition, to working as philosophers and feminists at once, have revealed gaps in the malestream totalizing discourse which leave them no choice but to refuse obedience to it. These refusals are anarchic in breaking away from the rules of established methodologies, challenging the most taken-for-granted philosophical assumptions, theories and goals.[5] Challenges and refusals are marks not of truculence and aimless rebellion, but of strategies for uncovering the structures of an order that is imposed to check an imagined threat of "chaos," the exaggeration of whose dangers conceals its emancipatory potential. This is a "chaos" of plurality, ambiguity, and differences: plurality of methods and methodologies; ambiguity in theoretical conclusions; differences that refuse the reductivism of universality and univocity. Only by thinkers wedded to a rigid conception of order and orthodoxy could this multiplicity be interpreted as chaotic in a derogatory sense. Yet such thinkers prevail, and such interpretations are the stuff of which their theories are made. For Stenstad, an anarchist persists in "questioning, working and playing with ambiguities, being alert for the presence of the strange within the familiar, and allowing for concealment or unclarity in the midst of disclosure."[6] The questioning takes place *from somewhere* and is committed to finding answers that make action possible.

One of the traditionally problematic features of a middle ground is that a refusal to occupy a position of pure objectivism is equated with an assertion of value in relativism. I have made such a claim at many places in this book. I have done so cognizant of the fact that there are cogent and persuasive arguments against relativism available in the philosophical tradition: that relativism can take an "anything goes" form that would make criticism and responsible epistemic choice into meaningless ephemera—hence that absolute relativism forces perfect tolerance, which would have to include tolerance of sexism, racism, homophobia, and other oppressive practices. But the middle ground has no place for absolutes, relativist or otherwise. Participants in standard objectivist/relativist debates work with a false dichotomy according to which any move toward relativism amounts to a flat rejection of realism. My claim is that epistemological relativism does not entail antirealism.

Politically, feminists could not opt for an absolute relativism that recognized no facts of the matter—no objective, external reality—but only my, your, or our negotiated reality. Consider feminist concern with what "science has proved" about women's natural inferiority to men, about the safety of drugs to safeguard or prevent pregnancy, about the harmlessness of pesticides and nuclear power. That concern will not be put to rest by an assurance that there are many ways of looking at these things, all equally valid. No politically informed woman will be convinced by an argument that it is all relative—that for some people these things are wrong or harmful and for others they are valid and harmless. Nor could feminists agree that "the realities" of sexism, the wage gap, violence against women, inadequate day care, class and racial injustices are all in their minds. It would fly in the face of the well-documented experiences of countless women to deny that these are realities, if perhaps not in the idealized physical science sense. If there are no objective social realities—in a sense that allows for perspectival differences—there are no tools for the realization of feminist political projects.

However various their political allegiances, feminists are united in their commitments to ending women's oppression in patriarchal societies. Their ideological differences may produce different causal analyses of oppression and prompt diverse solutions. Yet differences in knowledge about oppression do not preclude possibilities of transformative dialogue. Were the oppression not demonstrably there *at all*, no debate would be possible; were it known identically by everyone, no debate would be necessary. Hence the impact of feminism on epistemology recommends a mitigated relativism. Mitigated relativism takes different perspectives into account. The claim that it must be mitigated affirms that there is something there, in the world, to know and act on—hence to constrain possibilities of knowledge and analysis. Were this not so, the findings of feminist research could simply be dismissed as one set of opinions, no better than any others. Indeed, they could be read as manifestations of ideological paranoia, and a relativist would have no way of countering the charge. Feminists need to demonstrate the reality of social injustices and practices and to work as hard for

change in larger social structures and institutions as for change in the "personal" areas of women's lives. Because of the dominance of received "objectivist" knowledge in producing the social institutions in which they live, women cannot opt for a *radical* relativism that is unable to name those institutions and productions. They can, and I think must, opt for the mitigated, critical relativism implicit in asking, *Whose* knowledge are we talking about? Such a relativism would recognize the perspectival, locatedness of knowledge *and* its associations with subjective purposes. Yet it would develop strategies for evaluating perspectives and purposes.

This claim for evaluative possibilities might appear to recommend a mitigated *objectivism* instead of a mitigated relativism, and the suggestion would be plausible.[7] On a continuum between extreme objectivism and radical relativism, the mitigated versions of each would approach one another quite closely. I prefer to characterize the position I advocate as a *mitigated* relativism, however, for the freedom it offers from the homogenizing effects of traditional objectivism, in which differences, discrepancies, and deviations are smoothed out for the sake of achieving a unified theory. With its commitment to difference, critical relativism is able to resist reductivism and to accommodate divergent perspectives. Mitigated in its constraints by "the facts" of material objects and social/political artifacts, yet ready to account for the mechanisms of power (in a Foucauldian sense) and prejudice (in a Gadamerian sense) that produce knowledge of these facts, and committed to the self-critical stance that its mitigation requires, such relativism is a resourceful epistemological position.

Wariness of relativism may be prompted by a suspicion that only knowers of supreme privilege, able to step outside the harsher constraints of inadequate material and epistemic resources, could claim the possibility—and right—to construct "their world" from their own vantage point. The suspicion is not unfounded. But it cannot, I think, justifiably be countered with a move to objectivism with its history of laying claim to "a view from nowhere." That view will never be available to everyone; only God and his would-be successors can pretend to a God's-eye view. Those who are not sufficiently privileged to occupy such a position will always find that their position is constructed relative to it, and the old illusions and oppressions will remain firmly in place.

No single, monolithic scheme has been able to claim adequate explanatory power; and projects to devise such a scheme have been impressive for their failure to acknowledge their gaps, exclusions, and suppressions. Yet the fact that the scheme that has claimed absolute authority has proved wanting does not count as a reason to conclude that no scheme is better than any other. Perspectival explanations are constrained by reality: relativism is stopped in its feared slide into nihilism, solipsism, or subjectivism by the "brute facts" of the world and by the discursive limits of speaking positions. Sexism, racism, and environmental harm are as demonstrably part of the world as tables and chairs, though they are open to more varying interpretations. So an endorsement of relativism in no way amounts to a denial of realism.

The adversarial method gains strong endorsement from the antirelativism of objectivist theories. On the adversarial paradigm, any philosopher worthy of the name—hence any philosopher worth engaging with in adversarial combat—will have located himself in an entrenched position to which his allegiance is complete and perfect. One could not be a bit of a utilitarian, with Kantian and existentialist sympathies, and claim respect as a disputant under the adversarial paradigm. So a philosopher who finds truth in Kantian ethics but believes that it would offer better guidance to real people if it were tempered with consequentialist, situational, and care-oriented considerations will have difficulty claiming the credentials of a bona fide moral philosopher. To occupy a utilitarian position for some situations, a Kantian one in others, is to occupy a middle ground where the malestream assumes that no debate can take place and that only inferior philosophy, therefore, can be done. Analogous charges are advanced against self-proclaimed epistemologists who argue the advantages of reliabilism, coherentism, foundationalism, and perspectivism, or claim that knowledge is both objective and subjective.

The occupancy of a middle ground is a political act that refuses confinement within the narrow, cramped space that the adversarial paradigm allows for philo-

sophical conversation. This refusal is not simply a negative act. It amounts to an explicit requirement for openness to debate; it resists closure and is committed to developing a politics of difference. Nor is it merely a reactive gesture. It is true that it creates clearings in the middle of the absolutes out of a radical disillusionment with the pretensions and political implications of unified theory building. So it would be preposterous for the refusal to amount simply to constructing an alternative theory of just the same kind, with "masculine" modes simply displaced by "feminine" ones. But only within the adversarial paradigm is the lack of a whole, universal theory equated with impotence. The middle ground is located within experiences, histories, social structures, material circumstances. Its occupants are committed to examining the resources and contradictions these experiences and circumstances yield. Its openness is a source of power in which the productiveness of an ambiguity that refuses closure can be realized. De Beauvoir argues that "the notion of ambiguity must not be confused with that of absurdity." Nor, in this context, must it be confused with anti-realism or irrationalism. She continues: "To say that [existence] is ambiguous is to assert that its meaning is never fixed, that it must constantly be won . . . it is because man's [sic] condition is ambiguous that he seeks, through failure and outrageousness, to save his existence."[8]

An ecological analysis of how, from a middle-ground position, feminists could engage in viable epistemological critique and reconstruction would emphasize the power of feminist philosophy as a collective, not an adversarial, project. Its nature is apparent in the practice of citing and drawing on one another's work as sources for theoretical-practical growth, bases for constructive critique, contributions to ongoing conversations committed to understanding the environments and structural locations where people are positioned and position themselves. Feminist philosophy in general, and epistemological inquiry in particular, engages with traditional philosophical discourse and takes a stand in relation to it. From its middle-ground position it can perceive interconnections among various traditionally separate "branches" of philosophy, and of philosophy with other disciplines and projects. It is committed to developing "an *explanatory diagnostic analysis* of women's [epistemic] oppression across history, culture and societies, and [to] articulating an *anticipatory-utopian critique*" of current epistemological norms and values—to developing new modes of cooperative existence and "of relating to ourselves and to nature in the future."[9] Ecologically mapped, the epistemic terrain can accommodate many locations on a middle ground, whose influence spreads to promote other transfomations and emancipatory strategies, which go on to inspire still others, and so on.

In Chapter 4 I note that, despite its problems of autonomy and austerity, Kantian philosophy affords a resource for the process of taking subjectivity into account while resisting the slide into subjectivism. Kant's revolutionary contribution to the history of philosophy is in his demonstration that knowledge is a construct—not a *construct* ex nihilo, or out of whole cloth, but one in which cognitive agents have considerable freedom. Feminist unmaskings of the political implications of constructive processes demonstrate that it matters how responsibly the project is undertaken. Feminist demonstrations of the interweaving of epistemological issues with moral political and ontological questions reveal the intricacy and ubiquity of accountability requirements.

Committed at once to emancipatory and ecologically sensitive goals, feminists have to devise strategies for remapping the epistemic terrain which acknowledge the demands of social-political-moral accountability while addressing specific, located, structurally produced needs. The point is not that scientific inquiry, or knowledge production more generally, should eschew its commitment to objectivity and accurate prediction. But such commitments have to be balanced against ecological and emancipatory projects—balanced responsibly so that investigators *consciously* control for sexism, for insensitivity to other specificities, and for human and environmental exploitation. Hence there must be an explicit acknowledgment that methods and methodologies always raise ethical-political questions, and inquirers must ensure that they can address these questions. In science, ecological commitments demand the development of cooperative, noninvasive ways of understanding nature and using its resources. Scientists cannot continue to present themselves as free, autonomous, asocial agents who can follow lithe lure of the technically sweet"[10] without regard for its social-political impact. Feminist involvement in the ecology and peace movements requires a reconstruction of all projects of inquiry, from the microcosmic to the macrocosmic, toward a productive, critical elaboration of strategies for promoting and fostering cooperation—among people and with the environment.

Writing of her vision for women, in the concluding paragraphs of *The Second Sex*, de Beauvoir remarks: "It remains only for women to continue their ascent, and the successes they are obtaining are an encouragement for them to do so. It seems almost certain that sooner or later they will arrive at complete economic and social equality, which will bring about an inner metamorphosis."[11] That ascent has been slower and more arduous than de Beauvoir anticipated, yet the transformations in women's lives have been more wide-ranging and radical than she envisaged. Each success has revealed another step to be taken. Women have far to go to end economic, political, and social oppression, and they will not achieve it until they succeed in obliterating epistemic oppression. But the impact of the women's movement has been nothing short of astonishing. The metamorphosis de Beauvoir envisages is not confined to "inner," private transformations; it is visible in transformations in social structures; in women's refusals to remain Other.

Posing the question Whose knowledge are we talking about? is a revolutionary step in this refusal. The next steps cannot merely be the addition of some notes about women's subjugated knowledge to the existing corpus of received knowledge, or the integration of women on equal terms into received epistemological theories. They must transform the terms of the discourse, challenge the structures of the epistemological project. Such transformations will reveal that the discourses feminists are developing are themselves empowering, informing innovative practices, and producing a resistance against domination that signals profound inner metamorphoses.

NOTES

1. In examining feminist empiricism and a version of feminist standpoint theory as possible "successor epistemologies," I am drawing on Harding's classifications in *The Science Question in Feminism*. In her "Conclusion: Epistemological Questions" in *Feminism and Methodology*, Harding characterizes them aptly as *transitional epistemologies* (p. 186). It will be apparent that the "standpoint" I sketch here is somewhat different from Harding's.

2. In her book *Toward a Feminist Epistemology* (Savage, Md.: Rowman & Littlefield, 1990), which I read after this book had gone to press, Jane Duran develops a version of empiricism that draws on "naturalized epistemologies." Her analysis aims to make it possible for empiricists to take human specificities more plausibly into account while retaining their central empiricist commitments.

3. Wylie notes that "feminist empiricists are caught in the awkward position of exploiting the epistemic advantages of their standpoint as women while endorsing the ideal that scientific inquiry is objective in that an inquirer's social, political standpoint is irrelevant." Wylie, *"The Philosophy of Ambivalence: Sandra Harding on The Science Question in Feminism,"* in Hanen and Nielson, eds., *Science, Morality, and Feminist Theory*, p. 64.

4. A landmark feminist standpoint position is elaborated in Nancy Hartsock, "The Feminist Standpoint: Developing the Ground for a Specifically Feminist Historical Materialism," in Harding and Hintikka, eds., *Discovering Reality*.

5. I borrow the "anarchic" characterization from Stenstad, "Anarchic Thinking."

6. Ibid., p. 89.

7. Marilyn Friedman made this suggestion to me.

8. De Beauvoir, *Ethics of Ambiguity*, p. 129.

9. The phrases are from Benhabib, "Generalized and Concrete Other," pp. 80–81.

10. The phrase is attributed to Robert Oppenheimer, by James Eayrs, in *Science and Conscience* (Toronto: C.B.C. Publications, 1968), the transcript of a Canadian Broadcasting Corporation television symposium (p. 5).

11. De Beauvoir, *The Second Sex*, p. 811.

FOR FURTHER REFLECTION

1. Do you agree with Code that the epistemological notions of objectivity, impartiality, and universality are maleoriented? Explain why or why not.

2. Is there anything especially female about the notion that some facts are created by people and social institutions? Explain why or why not.

3. Code recommends the concept of "positionality," which is "an open middle ground where an inquirer can take up a position, a standpoint, within a forest of absolutes." Would this be a good or bad thing for scientific inquiry?

4. Code believes that the middle ground of positionality will not give way to the disastrous effects of absolute relativism. Is she correct?

5. Is there any practical distinction between mitigated relativism and mitigated objectivism as Code claims?

Part III

Philosophy of Religion

If God exists, then the grounding reality is not ultimately groundless, the supporting reality is not ultimately unsupported, and evolving reality is not ultimately without aim. . . . affirmation of God implies an ultimately justified fundamental trust in reality. If someone affirms God, he knows why he can trust reality.

Hans Kung, Does God Exist?

The basis of irreligious criticism is this: man makes religion; religion does not make man. Religion is indeed man's self-consciousness and self-awareness so long as he has not found himself or has lost himself again. But man is not an abstract being, squatting outside the world. Man is the human world, the state, society. This state, this society, produces religion, which is an inverted world consciousness, because they are in an inverted world. Religion is the general theory of this world, its encyclopedic compendium, its logic in popular form, its spiritual point d'honneur, its enthusiasm, its moral sanction, its solemn complement, its general basis of consolation and justification. It is the fantastic realization of the human being inasmuch as the human being possesses no true reality. . . . Religious suffering is at the same time an expression of real suffering and a protest against real suffering. Religion is the sigh of the oppressed creature, the sentiment of a heartless world, and the soul of soulless conditions. It is the opium of the people.

Karl Marx, Critique of Hegel

Does God exist? Is there a supremely powerful, completely benevolent being who created the universe and all that is in it and who is presently and providentially active in caring for us? The question is perhaps the most profound that human beings ask. It is the ultimate metaphysical issue, for if there is such a being, then it is of paramount importance that we come to know that fact and as much as possible about God and his or her plan.

Implications follow that affect our understanding of the world and ourselves. If God exists, the world is not accidental, a product of mere chance and necessity, but a home that has been designed for rational and sentient beings, a place of personal purposefulness. If there is a God, we ought to do everything possible to discover this fact, including using reason to make the discovery itself or to test its validity.

On the other hand, perhaps a supreme, benevolent being does not exist. Karl Marx may be right: religion may be just a human invention, the "opium of the people." But if there is no God, we want to know this, too. Whether or not we believe in God makes a difference in the way we view the universe and in the way we live.

These are two extremes: (1) a supreme being who is all-powerful (omnipotent), all-knowing (omniscient), and all-good (omnibenevolent); or (2) no deity at all. The belief in an omnipotent, omniscient, omnibenevolent deity, who is providentially active in the world, is called *theism* (from the Greek word for God, *theos*) or *monotheism*, the belief in one god. The belief that there is no god is called *atheism*. There are positions in between these: *deism*, the belief that an ingenious being designed and created the world but then left it; *polytheism*, the belief in many gods; *pantheism*, the belief that everything is God; and *limited theism*, the view that God is very powerful but not omnipotent and omniscient. While all of these positions are interesting, the Western tradition, influenced by Judaism, Christianity, and Islam as well as Greek philosophical monotheism, has been theist. The central debate has been between theism and atheism or *agnosticism*, the view that we cannot know whether there is a God. The readings in this part reflect this central debate.

Philosophy of religion is the study of the concepts and arguments surrounding the idea of a supreme being or beings, a God or gods. Even if God does not exist, the arguments centering on this quest are interesting for their ingenuity and subtlety. It may be argued that the Judeo-Christian tradition is so important in the world, especially in Western civilization, that every person who wants to be well-informed must come to grips with the arguments and counterarguments surrounding its claims. Hence, even if you reject the assertions of religion, it is important to understand what you are rejecting and why.

In the first two sections (A and B) of this part, we examine arguments for and against the existence of God: the cosmological argument, the teleological argument, the ontological argument, the argument from religious experience, and the argument from evil. In section C, we examine the relation of faith to reason, asking whether it is rational to hold religious beliefs and to live a life governed by those beliefs.

A. TRADITIONAL ARGUMENTS FOR THE EXISTENCE OF GOD

Can the existence of God be demonstrated or made probable by argument? The debate between those who believe that reason can demonstrate that God exists and those who do not has an ancient lineage, going back to Protagoras and Plato. One of the earliest references to arguments for the existence of God is found in Plato's Laws, where the following dialogue takes place:

Clinias: Why, surely, sir, it looks easy enough to speak the truth in saying that gods exist.

Athenian: And on what grounds?

Clinias: Why, to begin with, think of the earth, and sun, and planets, and everything! And the wonderful and beautiful order of the seasons with its distinctions of years and months! Besides, there is the fact that all mankind, Greek and non-Greek alike, believe in the existence of gods.[1]

Two arguments can be identified here: the teleological (purposefulness) argument, which states that the design manifested in the world shows the hand of a grand designer; and the *consensus gentium*, the argument from the consensus of humanity, which states that virtually all cultures exhibit belief in gods.

Even before Plato, the psalmist of the Hebrew scriptures has offered us the argument from design: "The heavens declare the glory of god; and the firmament sheweth his handiwork. Day unto day uttereth speech, and night unto night sheweth knowledge. There is no speech nor language where their voice is not heard." (Psalm 19) In the New Testament Paul writes, "For the invisible things of God from the creation of the world are clearly understood by the things that are made, even His eternal power and God-head; so that [those who fail to act on this knowledge] are without excuse." (Romans 1:20)

Arguments for the existence of God divide into two main groups: a priori and a posteriori. An a posteriori argument is based on premises that can be known only by means of experience of the world (for example, that there is a world, events have causes, and so forth). An a priori argument, in contrast, rests on premises that can be known to be true independently of experience of the world: one need only clearly conceive of such a proposition in order to see that it is true. In this book, all but one of the arguments are a posteriori arguments for the existence of God; only the ontological argument is an a priori argument.

The questions before us in this part of our work are: "What do the arguments for the existence of God establish? Do any of them demonstrate beyond reasonable doubt the existence of a supreme being or deity? Do any of them make it probable, given the evidence at hand, that such a being exists?"

The first two readings, by Saint Thomas Aquinas and Samuel Clarke, plus the debate between Father F. C. Copleston and Bertrand Russell, contain various forms of the cosmological argument. All versions of this argument begin with the a posteriori assumptions that (1) the universe exists, and that (2) something outside the universe is required to explain the existence of the universe. That is, the universe is *contingent*, depending on something outside of itself for its existence. That "something else" is logically prior to the universe. It constitutes the reason for the existence of the universe. God is such a being.

One version of the cosmological argument is called the "first-cause argument." The first two arguments given by Saint Thomas Aquinas serve as examples of it. The general outline goes something like this:

1. Everything in the universe has a cause.
2. An infinite regression is impossible. The series of causes and effects cannot go on indefinitely but must have a beginning.

3. So there must be a first cause (outside the universe) capable of producing everything besides itself (which is not produced, but a necessary being).
4. Such a being must be an infinite, necessary being; that is, God.

This sort of argument can be challenged at every point, and you will find some of these
challenges in Bertrand Russell's comments, in his dialogue with Father Copleston.

The next two readings concern the teleological argument, or the argument from design.
The teleological argument for God's existence begins with the premise that the world
shows intelligent purpose or order, and concludes that there must be, or probably is, a
divine intelligence, a supreme designer to account for the observed or perceived intelligent purpose or order. Although this argument has been cited in Plato, in Paul's letter to
the Romans, and in Saint Thomas's "fifth way," the clearest sustained treatment is found
in William Paley's *Natural Theology* (1802), our fourth selection, in which Paley offers
his famous "watch" argument.

Just as we infer an intelligent designer to account for the purpose-revealing watch, says
Paley, we must analogously infer an intelligent grand designer to account for the purpose-
revealing world. "Every indication of contrivance, every manifestation of design, which
existed in the watch, exists in the works of nature; with the difference, on the side of
nature, of being greater and more, and that in a degree which exceeds all computation."

Ironically, Paley's argument was attacked even before he had written it down, for
David Hume had already written his famous *Dialogues Concerning Natural Religion*
(published posthumously in 1779), the classic critique of the teleological argument.
Paley seems to have been unaware of Hume's work. A selection from the *Dialogues* is
our fifth reading. In it, the natural theologian Cleanthes debates the orthodox believer
Demea and the skeptic or critic Philo, who does most of the serious arguing.

Through Philo, Hume attacks the argument from design from several angles. First of
all, he argues that the universe is not enough like the products of human design to support the argument. As Philo puts it:

> But can you think, Cleanthes, that your usual phlegm and philosophy have been preserved
> in so wide a step as you have taken, when you compared to the universe, houses, ships, fur-
> niture, machines; and from their similarity in some circumstances inferred a similarity in
> their causes? . . . but can a conclusion, with any propriety, be transferred from the parts to
> the whole? Does not the great disproportion bar all comparison and inferences? From
> observing the growth of a hair, can we learn anything concerning the generation of a man?

Hume is saying that we cannot argue from the parts of something to the whole. For
example, just because we see part of a forest filled with pine trees, we cannot infer that
the entire forest is made up of pine trees. Try testing this judgment with possible counterexamples of your own.

Philo's second objection is that the analogy from artifact to divine designer fails
because we have no other universe with which to compare this one—and we need to compare, in order to decide if it is the kind of universe designed or simply the kind that developed on its own. But, as C. S. Peirce put it, "Universes are not as plentiful as blackberries." Since
there is only one universe, we have no standard of comparison by which to judge it.
Paley's answer would be that one clear instance of purposefulness in nature (for example, the eye) would let us conclude that there is probably an intelligent designer.

A third objection is that to use the analogy from artifact to designer, we would have to infer a grand, anthropomorphic designer, a human writ large, who has all the features we have. "Why not become a perfect anthropomorphite? Why not assert the Deity or Deities to be corporeal, and to have eyes, a nose, mouth, ears, etc.?"

Hume makes several other points against the design argument. The universe resembles an animal in some ways and a plant in other ways; so the argument fails, because it depends upon our seeing the world as a grand machine. The world might well be the result of mere chance. And, finally, the argument is weak because the world exhibits not only order, but much disorder.

A modern objection to the argument, anticipated by Hume, is based on Darwinian evolution, which casts doubt on the notion of teleological explanations altogether. In his *Origin of Species* (1859), Charles Darwin maintained that the process from simpler organisms to more complex ones took place gradually over many centuries and millennia, through an apparently nonpurposive process of trial and error, of natural selection and survival of the fittest. As Julian Huxley (*Evolution as Process*, p. 4) put it, the evolutionary process "results immediately and automatically from the basic property of living matter—that of self-copying, but with occasional errors. Self-copying leads to multiplication and competition; the errors in self-copying are what we call mutations, that will inevitably confer different degrees of biological advantage or disadvantage on their possessors. The consequence will be differential reproduction down the generations—in other words, natural selection."

As important as Darwin's contribution is in offering us an alternative model for biological development, it doesn't altogether destroy the argument from design: the theist can still argue that natural selection is the *way* an ultimate designer is working out his or her purpose for the world. You can decide for yourself whether this argument is sound and whether you can meet Hume's objections.

The third argument for the existence of God given in this section is the ontological argument, one of the most intriguing and remarkable arguments in philosophy. First set forth by Anselm, archbishop of Canterbury in the eleventh century, the argument has continued to puzzle and fascinate philosophers ever since. The argument is important not only because it claims to be an a priori proof for the existence of God, but also because it raises such philosophical problems as (1) whether existence is a property and (2) whether the notion of necessary existence is intelligible. Furthermore, it has special religious significance because it is the only traditional argument that clearly defines the necessary properties of God; that is, omnipotence, omniscience, omnibenevolence, and other great-making properties. There are many versions of the ontological argument (and many interpretations of some of these versions); the essential form of Anselm's version is given in the second chapter of his *Proslogium*. Anselm believes that God's existence is absolutely certain, so that only a fool would doubt or deny it, yet he desires understanding to fulfill his faith. "And so, Lord, do thou, who dost give understanding to faith, give me, so far as thou knowest it to be profitable, to understand that thou art as we believe; and that thou art that which we believe. And indeed, we believe that thou art a being than which nothing greater can be conceived. Or is there no such nature, since the fool hath said in his heart, there is no God?"

The argument that follows may be treated as a reductio ad absurdum argument. That is, it begins with a supposition (S) that is contradictory to what one desires to prove and then goes about showing that (S) together with other certain or self-evident assumptions (A-1 and A-2) yields a contradiction, which in turn demonstrates that the contradictory of (S) must be true.

Anselm's argument goes like this:

1. Suppose that the greatest conceivable being (GCB) exists in the mind alone (and not in reality). (S)
2. Existence in reality is greater than existence in the mind alone. (A-1)
3. We can conceive of a GCB that exists in reality as well as in the mind. (A-2)
4. Therefore, there is a being that is greater than the GCB. (from 1, 2, and 3)
5. But this is impossible, for it is a contradiction.
6. Therefore, it is false that a GCB exists in the mind alone and not in reality (from 1 and 5). So a GCB must exist in reality as well as in the mind. This being is, *per definition*, God.

Anselm's contemporary, Gaunilo, sets forth the first objection to Anselm's argument. Accusing Anselm of pulling rabbits out of hats, he tells the story of a delectable lost island, one that is more excellent than all lands. Since it is better that such a perfect island exist in reality than simply in the mind alone, this Island of the Blest must necessarily exist. Anselm replies that the analogy fails, for—unlike the greatest possible being—the greatest possible island can be conceived of as not existing. Alvin Plantinga has clarified Anselm's point: There simply are some properties that do have intrinsic maximums and some properties that do not have them. No matter how wonderful you make the Island of the Blest, we can conceive of a more wonderful island. The greatness of islands is like the greatness of numbers in this respect. There is no greatest natural number, for no matter how large the number you choose is, we can always conceive of a number twice as large. However, the properties of God have intrinsic maximums. For example, we can define perfect knowledge this way: for any proposition, an omniscient being knows whether it is true or false.

Our fourth argument for the existence of God is the argument from religious experience, which appeals to mystical experiences and claims of extraordinary revelations as evidence for God's existence. The problem with religious experiences is that they are private. You may have the sense of God forgiving you or an angel speaking to you, but I, who am in the same room with you, neither hear nor feel anything unusual. You are praying and suddenly feel transported by grace and sense the unity of all reality while I, who am sitting next to you, wonder at the strange expression on your face and ask if something is wrong. Perhaps you are having an epileptic seizure?

Yet religious experiences of various varieties have been reported by numerous people over the centuries, from dairymaids like Joan of Arc to mystics like Teresa of Avila and Saint John of the Cross. They cannot be simply dismissed without serious analysis.

There are two levels of problem here. First, to what degree, if any, is the subject of a religious experience justified in inferring from the psychological experience (the subjective aspect) to the existential or ontological reality of the object of the experience (the objective aspect)? And second, to what degree, if any, does the cumulative witness of people who have religious experiences justify the claim that there is a God or transcendent reality?

Traditionally, the argument from religious experience has not been one of the "proofs" for God's existence. At best, is has confirmed or branded on the soul what the proofs conveyed with icy logic. Many people, such as William James, believe that even without valid proofs, religious experiences are self-authenticating for the subject. Others, such as Bertrand Russell (see seventh reading), argue that a subjective experience itself is never adequate for making an existential claim (of an object existing outside oneself). It is a mistake to argue that the psychological experience of X proves the reality of X. In our readings, F. C. Copleston and C. D. Broad dispute this claim and go even further, arguing that a sort of *consensus mysticum*, an enormous agreement among mystics about what they have experienced, is itself evidence for the reality of a divine being. Russell denies that there is such agreement but, even if there were, would give a psychological or naturalistic explanation for it.

Many psychological explanations of religious experience cast doubt on its validity. One of the most famous is the Freudian interpretation. Sigmund Freud says that religious experience is the result of projecting one's father image out onto reality. The progression goes like this. When you were a child, you looked upon your father as a powerful hero who could do everything, meet all your needs, and overcome the normal obstacles that hindered your way at every step. When you grew older, you sadly realized that your father was fallible and very finite indeed, but you still had the need of the benevolent, all-powerful Father. So, subconsciously you projected your need for that long-lost father onto the empty heavens and invented a god for yourself. This is a common phenomenon, and all of us who have successfully projected Daddy into the Big Sky go to church or synagogue or the mosque or temple and worship the illusion on our favorite holy days. But it is a myth. The sky is empty, and the sooner we realize it the better for everyone.

This is one explanation of religious experience and of religion in general. It is not a disproof of God's existence, simply a hypothesis. Even if it is true psychologically that we tend to think of God as a powerful and loving parent, perhaps the parental relationship is God's way of teaching us about himself—by analogy.

Another explanatory theory is naturalism, which states that all reality can be explained by reference to physical processes, so that there is no need to bring in mysterious spiritual entities. There is no soul, nor spiritual reality, although there are values and consciousness, which are explained by reference to physical states. Consciousness or mind is a function of brain states, nothing more or less. The brain processes spatiotemporal experiences communicated through the senses; all learning is produced in this way. The mechanisms of the brain modify and coordinate the experiences, but there is no good reason to believe that the brain has access to extra-physical reality. Naturalism has problems of its own, but it is a coherent explanatory theory, and a rival to theism.

In our final reading in this section, C. D. Broad considers to what extent we can infer God's existence from human religious experience. Broad likens the religious sense to an ear for music. A few people on the negative end are spiritually tone deaf and a few on the positive end are the founders of religion, the Bachs and Beethovens of religion. In between are the ordinary followers who are like the average musical listener, and above them are the saints, who are like people who have the very finest ear for music.

The chief difference is that religion, unlike music, says something about the nature of reality. Is what it says true? Does religious experience support the truth claims of religion? Is religious experience "veridical," and are the claims about "the nature of reality which are an integral part of the experience, true or probable"? Broad considers the argument from mystical agreement:

1. There is an enormous unanimity among the mystics concerning the spiritual nature of reality.
2. When there is such unanimity among observers as to what they take themselves to be experiencing, it is reasonable to conclude that their experiences are veridical (unless we have good reason to believe that they are deluded).
3. There are no positive reasons for thinking that mystical experiences are delusory.
4. Therefore it is reasonable to believe that mystical experiences are veridical.

The weak premise is number 3, because there is evidence that mystics are neuropathic or sexually repressed. Broad considers these charges and admits some plausibility, but suggests that they are not conclusive. Regarding the charge of neuropathology, he urges that "one might need to be slightly 'cracked' in order to have some peep-holes into the super-sensible world." And, regarding sexual abnormality, perhaps no one who was "incapable of strong sexual desires and emotions could have anything worth calling religious experience."

His own guarded judgment is that, given what we know about the origins of religious belief and emotions, there is no reason to think that religious experience is "specially likely to be delusive or misdirected." Yet the evidence suggests that the concepts and beliefs of even the best religions are "extremely inadequate to the facts which they express; that they are highly confused and are mixed up with a great deal of positive error and sheer nonsense; and that, if the human race goes on and continues to have religious experiences and to reflect on them, they will be altered and improved almost out of recognition."

NOTE

1. Plato, *Laws*, Book X 886, trans. A. E. Taylor (London: Everyman, 1934). Originally written c. fourth century B.C.E.

St. Thomas Aquinas

THE FIVE WAYS

Many people consider the Dominican monk Thomas Aquinas (1225–1274) to be the greatest theologian in Western religion. The five arguments given here are versions of the cosmological argument, already described in the introduction to this part of the book. Put simply, their strategies are as follows. The first argument begins with the fact that there is change and argues that there must be an unmoved mover who originates all change (or motion) but itself is not moved. The second argument is from causation: there must be a first cause to explain the existence of cause. The third argument is from contingency: there are dependent beings (such as humans), so there must be an independent or necessary being on whom the dependent beings rely for their subsistence. The fourth argument is from excellence: there are degrees of excellence, so there must be a perfect being from whence cometh all excellences. The final argument is from the harmony of things: the harmony of nature calls for an explanation, and the only sufficient explanation is that a divine designer planned such harmony.

THE FIRST WAY: THE ARGUMENT FROM CHANGE

The existence of God can be shown in five ways. The first and clearest is taken from the idea of motion. (1) Now it is certain, and our senses corroborate it, that some things in this world are in motion. (2) But everything which is in motion is moved by something else. (3) For nothing is in motion except in so far as it is in potentiality in relation to that towards which it is in motion. (4) Now a thing causes movement in so far as it is in actuality. For to cause movement is nothing else than to bring something from potentiality to actuality; but a thing cannot be brought from potentiality to actuality except by something which exists in actuality, as, for example, that which is hot in actuality, like fire, makes wood, which is only hot in potentiality, to be hot in actuality, and thereby causes movement in it and alters it. (5) But it is not possible that the same thing should be at the same time in actuality and potentiality in relation to the same thing, but only in relation to different things; for what is hot in actuality cannot at the same time be hot in potentiality, though it is at the same time cold in potentiality. (6) It is impossible, therefore, that in relation to the same thing and in the same way anything should both cause movement and be caused, or that it should cause itself to move. (7) Everything therefore that is in motion must be moved by something else. If therefore the thing which causes it to move be in motion, this too must be moved by something else, and so on. (8) But we cannot proceed to infinity in this way, because in that case there would be no first mover, and in consequence, neither would there be any other mover; for secondary movers do not cause movement except they be moved by a first mover, as, for example, a stick cannot cause movement unless it is moved by the hand. Therefore it is necessary to stop at some first

From Thomas Aquinas, *Summa Theologica,* trans. Laurence Shapcote (London: O. P. Benziger Brothers, 1911).

mover which is moved by nothing else. And this is what we all understand God to be.

THE SECOND WAY: THE ARGUMENT FROM CAUSATION

The Second Way is taken from the idea of the Efficient Cause. (1) For we find that there is among material things a regular order of efficient causes. (2) But we do not find, nor indeed is it possible, that anything is the efficient cause of itself, for in that case it would be prior to itself, which is impossible. (3) Now it is not possible to proceed to infinity in efficient causes. (4) For if we arrange in order all efficient causes, the first is the cause of the intermediate, and the intermediate the cause of the last, whether the intermediate be many or only one. (5) But if we remove a cause the effect is removed; therefore, if there is no *first* among efficient causes, neither will there be a last or an intermediate. (6) But if we proceed to infinity in efficient causes there will be no first efficient cause, and thus there will be no ultimate effect, nor any intermediate efficient causes, which is clearly false. Therefore it is necessary to suppose the existence of some first efficient cause, and this men call God.

THE THIRD WAY: THE ARGUMENT FROM CONTINGENCY

The Third Way rests on the idea of the "contingent" and the "necessary" and is as follows: (1) Now we find that there are certain things in the Universe which are capable of existing and of not existing, for we find that some things are brought into existence and then destroyed, and consequently are capable of being or not being. (2) But it is impossible for all things which exist to be of this kind, because anything which is capable of not existing, at some time or other does not exist. (3) If therefore *all* things are capable of not existing, there was a time when nothing existed in the Universe. (4) But if this is true there would also be nothing in existence now; because anything that does

not exist cannot begin to exist except by the agency of something which has existence. If therefore there was once nothing which existed, it would have been impossible for anything to begin to exist, and so nothing would exist now. (5) This is clearly false. Therefore all things are not contingent, and there must be something which is necessary in the Universe. (6) But everything which is necessary either has or has not the cause of its necessity from an outside source. Now it is not possible to proceed to infinity in necessary things which have a cause of their necessity, as has been proved in the case of efficient causes. Therefore it is necessary to suppose the existence of something which is necessary in itself, not having the cause of its necessity from any outside source, but which is the cause of necessity in others. And this "something" we call God.

THE FOURTH WAY: THE ARGUMENT FROM DEGREES OF EXCELLENCE

The Fourth Way is taken from the degrees which are found in things. (1) For among different things we find that one is more or less good or true or noble; and likewise in the case of other things of this kind. (2) But the words "more" or "less" are used of different things in proportion as they approximate in their different ways to something which has the particular quality in the highest degree—e.g., we call a thing hotter when it approximates more nearly to that which is hot in the highest degree. There is therefore something which is true in the highest degree, good in the highest degree and noble in the highest degree; (3) and consequently there must be also something which has being in the highest degree. For things which are true in the highest degree also have being in the highest degree (see Aristotle, *Metaphysics,* 2). (4) But anything which has a certain quality of any kind in the highest degree is also the cause of all the things of that kind, as, for example, fire which is hot in the highest degree is the cause of all hot things (as is said in the same book). (5) Therefore there exists something which is the cause of being, and goodness, and of every perfection in all existing things; and this we call God.

THE FIFTH WAY:
THE ARGUMENT FROM
HARMONY

The Fifth Way is taken from the way in which nature is governed. (1) For we observe that certain things which lack knowledge, such as natural bodies, work for an End. This is obvious, because they always, or at any rate very frequently, operate in the same way so as to attain the best possible result. (2) Hence it is clear that they do not arrive at their goal by chance, but by purpose. (3) But those things which have no knowledge do not move towards a goal unless they are guided by someone or something which does possess knowledge and intelligence—e.g., an arrow by an archer. Therefore, there does exist something which possesses intelligence by which all natural things are directed to their goal; and this we call God.

FOR FURTHER REFLECTION

1. Outline Aquinas's arguments, and analyze them.
2. Which of these arguments are the clearest? (Don't be intimidated by the terms *potential* and *actual* as used in the first argument. These Aristotelian terms are not widely used in the same way today. If you ignore them, you should still be able to get to the heart of the argument.)
3. Has Aquinas proved the existence of God? Why or why not? What do you think the value of these arguments is?

SAMUEL CLARKE AND
DAVID HUME

THE CAUSAL ARGUMENT FOR GOD

Born iNowrich, England Samuel Clarke (1675–1729) was one of the most prominent philo-sophical theologians of his time. Clarke's presentation of the causal argument for God's existence was the most systematic and compelling version of that proof during the eighteenth Century, and even today it remains among the most important versions. His basic argument is this:

1.   The world contains an infinite series of dependent objects.
2.   The explanation of the series is either within the series itself or a necessary being outside that series.
3.   The explanation of the series cannot reside in the series iteself, since the very fact of the series' existence would still need an explantion.
4.   Therefore, the explanation of the series consists of a necessary.being out side the series

From Samuel Clarke, *A Demonstration of the Being and Attributes of God* (1705), Part 2; David Hume, *Dialogues Concerning Natural Religion* (1779), Part 9. Section headings have been added, and spelling and punctuation have been modernized by the editor.

Clarke's argument came under attack by Scottish skeptical philosopher David Hume (1711–1776) in his book *Dialogues Concerning Natural Religion* (1779). In this work, the character Demea presents a summary version of Clarke's famous argument; it is then criticized by the character Cleanthes. Hume's main criticism, as expressed by the character Cleanthes, is that the existence of the entire series of dependent beings is fully explained by the existence of each thing in the series. Clarke's original argument and Hume's analysis are both presented next.

CLARKE'S ARGUMENT

There has existed from eternity some one unchangeable and independent being. For since something must needs have been from eternity (as has been already proved, and is granted on all hands): either [on the one hand] there has always existed one unchangeable and *independent* Being, from which all other beings that are or ever were in the universe, have received their original, or else [on the other hand] there has been an infinite succession of changeable and *dependent* beings, produced one from another in an endless progression, without any original cause at all. Which latter supposition is so very absurd, that though all atheism must in its account of most things (as shall be shown hereafter) terminate in it, yet I think very few atheists ever were so weak as openly and directly to defend it. For it is plainly impossible and contradictory to itself.

I shall not argue against it from the supposed impossibility of infinite succession, barely and absolutely considered in itself, for a reason which shall be mentioned hereafter. But, if we consider such an infinite progression, as one entire endless series of dependent beings; it is plain this whole series of beings can have no cause from without, of its existence: because in it are supposed to be included all things that are or ever were in the universe. And it is plain it can have no reason within itself of its existence, because no one being in this infinite succession is supposed to be self-existent or necessary (which is the only ground or reason of existence of any thing, that can be imagined within the thing itself, as will presently more fully appear). But every one [must be] dependent on the foregoing. And where no part is necessary, it is manifest the whole cannot be neces-

sary, [since] absolute necessity of existence, not being an outward, relative, and accidental determination, but an inward and essential property of the nature of the thing which so exists. An infinite succession therefore of merely dependent beings, without any original independent cause, is a series of beings, that has neither necessity nor cause, nor any reason at all of its existence, neither within itself nor from without. That is, it is an express contradiction and impossibility. It is a supposing something to be caused, (because it is granted in every one of its stages of succession, not to be necessary and from itself), and yet that in the whole it is caused absolutely by nothing, which every man knows is a contradiction to be done in time. And because duration in this case makes no difference, it is equally a contradiction to suppose it done from eternity. And consequently there must on the contrary, of necessity have existed from eternity, some one immutable and independent Being. . . .

HUME'S CRITICISM

The Argument from Necessity Presented

[Demea:] The argument, replied Demea, which I would insist on, is the common one. Whatever exists must have a cause or reason of its existence; it being absolutely impossible for any thing to produce itself, or be the cause of its own existence. In mounting up, therefore, from effects to causes, we must either go on in tracing an infinite succession, without any ultimate cause at all; or must at last have recourse to some ultimate cause, that is necessarily existent: Now, that the first supposition is absurd, may be thus proved. In the infinite chain or succession of causes and effects, each single effect is determined to exist by the power and efficacy of that cause which immediately preceded; but the whole eternal chain or succession, taken together, is not determined or caused by any thing; and yet it is evident that it requires a cause or reason, as much as any particular object which begins to exist in time. The question is still reasonable, why this particular succession of causes existed from eternity, and not any other succession, or no succession at all. If there be no necessarily existent being, any supposition which can be formed is equally possible; nor is there any more absurdity in Nothing's having existed from eternity, than there is in that succession of causes which constitutes the universe. What was it, then, which determined Something to exist rather than Nothing, and bestowed being on a particular possibility, exclusive of the rest? External causes, there are supposed to be none. Chance is a word without a meaning. Was it Nothing? But that can never produce any thing. We must, therefore, have recourse to a necessarily existent Being, who carries the reason of his existence in himself, and who cannot be supposed not to exist, without an express contradiction. There is, consequently, such a Being; that is, there is a Deity.

The Failure of A Priori Arguments

[Cleanthes:] I shall begin with observing, that there is an evident absurdity in pretending to demonstrate a matter of fact, or to prove it by any arguments a priori. Nothing is demonstrable, unless the contrary implies a contradiction. Nothing, that is distinctly conceivable, implies a contradiction. Whatever we conceive as existent, we can also conceive as non-existent. There is no being, therefore, whose non-existence implies a contradiction. Consequently there is no being, whose existence is demonstrable. I propose this argument as entirely decisive, and am willing to rest the whole controversy upon it.

It is pretended that the Deity is a necessarily existent being; and this necessity of his existence is attempted to be explained by asserting, that if we knew his whole essence or nature, we should perceive it to be as impossible for him not to exist, as for twice two not to be four. But it is evident that this can

never happen, while our faculties remain the same as at present. It will still be possible for us, at any time, to conceive the non-existence of what we formerly conceived to exist; nor can the mind ever lie under a necessity of supposing any object to remain always in being; in the same manner as we lie under a necessity of always conceiving twice two to be four. The words, therefore, *necessary existence*, have no meaning; or, which is the same thing, none that is consistent.

But further, why may not the material universe be the necessarily existent Being, according to this pretended explication of necessity? We dare not affirm that we know all the qualities of matter; and for aught we can determine, it may contain some qualities, which, were they known, would make its non-existence appear as great a contradiction as that twice two is five. I find only one argument employed to prove, that the material world is not the necessarily existent Being: and this argument is derived from the contingency both of the matter and the form of the world. "Any particle of matter," it is said, "may be *conceived* to be annihilated; and any form may be *conceived* to be altered. Such an annihilation or alteration, therefore, is not impossible." But it seems a great partiality not to perceive, that the same argument extends equally to the Deity, so far as we have any conception of him; and that the mind can at least imagine him to be non-existent, or his attributes to be altered. It must be some unknown, inconceivable qualities, which can make his non-existence appear impossible, or his attributes unalterable: And no reason can be assigned, why these qualities may not belong to matter. As they are altogether unknown and inconceivable, they can never be proved incompatible with it.

Add to this, that in tracing an eternal succession of objects, it seems absurd to inquire for a general cause or first author. How can any thing, that exists from eternity, have a cause, since that relation implies *a priority* in time, and a beginning of existence?

In such a chain, too, or succession of objects, each part is caused by that which preceded it, and causes that which succeeds it. Where then is the difficulty? But the *whole*, you say, wants a cause. I answer, that the uniting of these parts into a whole, like the uniting of several distinct countries into one kingdom, or several distinct members into one body, is performed merely by an arbitrary act of the mind, and has no influence on the nature of things. Did I show you the particular causes of each individual in a collection of twenty particles of matter, I should think it very unreasonable, should you afterwards ask me, what was the cause of the whole twenty. This is sufficiently explained in explaining the cause of the parts.

FOR FURTHER REFLECTION

1. According to Clarke, the explanation of the series of dependent beings cannot reside within the series itself, since the very fact of the series' existence would still need an explanation. Explain his point.

2. What is Hume's general objection to a priori arguments, as expressed by the character Cleanthes?

3. What precisely about Clarke's proof makes it an a priori argument?

4. According to Hume, the existence of the entire series of dependent beings is fully explained by the existence of each thing in the series. Explain his point and say whether you agree.

F. C. Copleston and Bertrand Russell

∽

A DEBATE ON THE ARGUMENT FROM CONTINGENCY

Father F. C. Copleston (1907–1994) was a professor of philosophy at Heythrop College and London University in England and at the Gregorian University in Rome. He is famous for his multivolume *A History of Philosophy*. Bertrand Russell (1872–1970), one of the most important philosophers of this century, was an agnostic who argued against Christian belief. His works cover almost every area of philosophy, from logic and philosophy of mathematics (*Principia Mathematica*, published 1910, written with Alfred North Whitehead) to philosophy of religion ("Mysticism" and *Why I Am Not a Christian*) and ethics ("Science and Ethics"). Russell's concern to live out his philosophy in his life led him to found a special school on his philosophy of education, become a leader in Britain's "Ban the [atom] Bomb" movement, and speak out on moral and political issues, sometimes at personal risk. He spent time in prison during World War I for his pacifist opposition to the war.

In this famous BBC radio debate of 1948, Copleston defends the argument from contingency while Russell attacks it.

From Bertrand Russell, *Why I Am Not a Christian* (London: Allen & Unwin, 1957). Copyright © 1957, 1985 by Allen & Unwin Ltd. Reprinted by permission of Taylor & Francis Books UK and The Bertrand Russell Peace Foundation.

Copleston: As we are going to discuss the existence of God, it might perhaps be as well to come to some provisional agreement as to what we understand by the term "God." I presume that we mean a supreme personal being—distinct from the world and creator of the world. Would you agree—provisionally at least—to accept this statement as the meaning of the term "God"?

Russell: Yes, I accept this definition.

Copleston: Well, my position is the affirmative position that such a being actually exists, and that His existence can be proved philosophically. Perhaps you would tell me if your position is that of agnosticism or of atheism. I mean, would you say that the non-existence of God can be proved?

Russell: No, I should not say that: my position is agnostic.

Copleston: Would you agree with me that the problem of God is a problem of great importance? For example, would you agree that if God does not exist, human beings and human history can have no other purpose than the purpose they choose to give themselves, which—in practice—is likely to mean the purpose which those impose who have the power to impose it?

Russell: Roughly speaking, yes, though I should have to place some limitation on your last clause.

Copleston: Would you agree that if there is no God—no absolute Being—there can be no absolute values? I mean, would you agree that if there is no absolute good that the relativity of values results?

Russell: No, I think these questions are logically distinct. Take, for instance, G. E. Moore's *Principia Ethica,* where he maintains that there is a distinction of good and evil, that both of these are definite concepts. But he does not bring the idea of God to support that contention.

Copleston: Well, suppose we leave the question of good till later, till we come to the moral argument, and I give first a metaphysical argument. I'd like to put the main weight on the metaphysical argument based on Leibniz's argument from "Contingency" and then later we might discuss the moral argument. Suppose I give a brief statement on the metaphysical argument and that then we go on to discuss it?

Russell: That seems to me to be a very good plan.

Copleston: Well, for clarity's sake, I'll divide the argument into distinct stages. First of all, I should say, we know that there are at least some beings in the world which do not contain in themselves the reason for their existence. For example, I depend on my parents, and now on the air, and on food, and so on. Now, secondly, the world is simply the real or imagined totality or aggregate of individual objects, none of which contain in themselves alone the reason for their existence. There isn't any world distinct from the objects which form it, any more than the human race is something apart from the members. Therefore, I should say, since objects or events exist, and since no object of experience contains within itself the reason of its existence, this reason, the totality of objects, must have a reason external to itself. That reason must be an existent being. Well, this being is either itself the reason for its own existence, or it is not. If it is, well and good. If it is not, then we must proceed farther. But if we proceed to infinity in that sense, then there's no explanation of existence at all. So, I should say, in order to explain existence, we must come to a being which contains within itself the reason for its own existence, that is to say, which cannot not exist.

Russell: This raises a great many points and it is not altogether easy to know where to begin, but I think that, perhaps, in answering your argument, the best point at which to begin is the question of necessary being. The word "necessary," I should maintain, can only be applied significantly to propositions. And, in fact, only to such as are analytic—that is to say—such as it is self-contradictory to deny. I could only admit a necessary being if there were a being whose existence it is self-contradictory to deny. I should like to know whether you would accept Leibniz's division of propositions into truths of reason and truths of fact. The former—the truths of reason—being necessary.

Copleston: Well, I certainly should not subscribe to what seems to be Leibniz's idea of truths of reason and truths of fact, since it would appear that, for him, there are in the long run only analytic propositions. It would seem that for Leibniz truths of fact are ultimately reducible to truths of reason. That is to say, to analytic propositions, at least for an omniscient mind. Well, I couldn't agree with that. For one thing it would fail to meet the requirements of the experience of freedom. I don't want to uphold the whole philosophy of Leibniz. I have made use of his argument from contingent to necessary being, basing the argument on the principle of sufficient reason, simply because it seems to me a brief and clear formulation of what is, in my opinion, the fundamental metaphysical argument for God's existence.

Russell: But, to my mind, "a necessary proposition" has got to be analytic. I don't see what else it can mean. And analytic propositions are always complex and logically somewhat late. "Irrational animals are animals" is an analytic proposition; but a proposition such as "This is an animal" can never be analytic. In fact, all the propositions that can be analytic are somewhat late in the build-up of propositions.

Copleston: Take the proposition "If there is a contingent being then there is a necessary being." I consider that that proposition hypothetically expressed is a necessary proposition. If you are going to call every necessary proposition an analytic proposition, then—in order to avoid a dispute in terminology—I would agree to call it analytic, though I don't consider it a tautological proposition. But the proposition is a necessary proposition only on the supposition that there is a contingent being. That there is a contingent being actually existing has to be discovered by experience, and the proposition that there is a contingent being is certainly not an analytic proposition, though once you know, I should maintain, that there is a contingent being, it follows of necessity that there is a necessary being.

Russell: The difficulty of this argument is that I don't admit the idea of a necessary being and I don't admit that there is any particular meaning in calling other beings "contingent." These phrases don't for me have any significance except within a logic that I reject.

Copleston: Do you mean that you reject these terms because they won't fit in with what is called "modern logic"?

Russell: Well, I can't find anything that they could mean. The word "necessary," it seems to me, is a useless word, except as applied to analytic propositions, not to things.

Copleston: In the first place, what do you mean by "modern logic"? As far as I know, there are somewhat differing systems. In the second place, not all modern logicians surely would admit the meaninglessness of metaphysics. We both know, at any rate, one very eminent modern thinker whose knowledge of modern logic was profound, but who certainly did not think that metaphysics are meaningless or, in particular, that the problem of God is meaningless. Again, even if all modern logicians held that metaphysical terms are meaningless, it would not follow that they were right. The proposition that metaphysical terms are meaningless seems to me to be a proposition based on an assumed philosophy. The dogmatic position behind it seems to be this: What will not go into my machine is non-existent, or it is meaningless; it is the expression of emotion. I am simply trying to point out that anybody who says that a particular system of modern logic is the sole criterion of meaning is saying something that is over-dogmatic; he is dogmatically insisting that a part of philosophy is the whole of philosophy. After all, a "contingent" being is a being which has not in itself the complete reason for its existence, that's what I mean by a contingent being. You know, as well as I do, that the existence of neither of us can be explained without reference to something or somebody outside us, our parents, for example. A "necessary" being, on the other hand, means a being that must and cannot not exist. You may say that there is no such being, but you will find it hard to convince me that you do not understand the terms I am using. If you do not understand them, then how can you be entitled to say that such a being does not exist, if that is what you do say?

Russell: Well, there are points here that I don't propose to go into at length. I don't maintain the meaninglessness of metaphysics in general at all. I maintain the meaninglessness of certain particular terms—not on any general ground, but simply because I've not been able to see an interpretation of those particular terms. It's not a general dogma—it's a particular thing. But those points I will leave out for a moment. And I will say that what you have been saying brings us back, it seems to me, to the ontological argument that there is a being whose essence involves existence, so that his existence is analytic. That seems to me to be impossible, and it raises, of course, the question what one means by existence, and as to this, I think a subject named can never be significantly said to exist but only a subject described. And that existence, in fact, quite definitely is not a predicate.

Copleston: Well, you say, I believe, that it is bad grammar, or rather bad syntax to say for example "T. S. Eliot exists"; one ought to say, for example, "He, the author of *Murder in the Cathedral,* exists." Are you going to say that the proposition, "The cause of the world exists," is without meaning? You may say that the world has no cause; but I fail to see how you can say that the proposition that the "cause of the world exists" is meaningless. Put it in the form of a question: "Has the world a cause?" or "Does a cause of the world exist?" Most people surely would understand the question, even if they don't agree about the answer.

Russell: Well, certainly the question "Does the cause of the world exist?" is a question that has meaning. But if you say, "Yes, God is the cause of the world" you're using God as a proper name; then "God exists" will not be a statement that has meaning; that is the position that I'm maintaining. Because, therefore, it will follow that it cannot be an analytic proposition ever to say that this or that exists. For example, suppose you take as your subject "the existent round-square," it would look like an analytic proposition that "the existent round-square exists," but it doesn't exist.

Copleston: No, it doesn't, then surely you can't say it doesn't exist unless you have a conception of what existence is. As to the phrase "existent round-square," I should say that it has no meaning at all.

Russell: I quite agree. Then I should say the same thing in another context in reference to a "necessary being."

Copleston: Well, we seem to have arrived at an impasse. To say that a necessary being is a being that must exist and cannot not exist has for me a definite meaning. For you it has no meaning.

Russell: Well, we can press the point a little, I think. A being that must exist and cannot not exist, would surely, according to you, be a being whose essence involves existence.

Copleston: Yes, a being the essence of which is to exist. But I should not be willing to argue the existence of God simply from the idea of His essence because I don't think we have any clear intuition of God's essence as yet. I think we have to argue from the world of experience to God.

Russell: Yes, I quite see the distinction. But, at the same time, for a being with sufficient knowledge, it would be true to say "Here is this being whose essence involves existence!"

Copleston: Yes, certainly, if anybody saw God, he would see that God must exist.

Russell: So that I mean there is a being whose essence involves existence although we don't know that essence. We only know there is such a being.

Copleston: Yes, I should add we don't know the essence *a priori.* It is only *a posteriori* through our experience of the world that we come to a knowledge of the existence of that being. And then one argues, the essence and existence must be identical. Because if God's essence and God's existence were not identical, then some sufficient reason for this existence would have to be found beyond God.

Russell: So it all turns on this question of sufficient reason, and I must say you haven't defined "sufficient reason" in a way that I can understand—what do you mean by sufficient reason? You don't mean cause?

Copleston: Not necessarily. Cause is a kind of sufficient reason. Only contingent being can have a cause. God is His own sufficient reason; and He is not cause of Himself. By sufficient reason in the full sense I mean an explanation adequate for the existence of some particular being.

Russell: But when is an explanation adequate? Suppose I am about to make a flame with a match. You may say that the adequate explanation of that is that I rub in on the box.

Copleston: Well, for practical purposes—but theoretically, that is only a partial explanation. An adequate explanation must ultimately be a total explana-tion, to which nothing further can be added.

Russell: Then I can only say that you're looking for something which can't be got, and which one ought not to expect to get.

Copleston: To say that one has not found it is one thing; to say that one should not look for it seems to me rather dogmatic.

Russell: Well, I don't know. I mean, the explana-tion of one thing is another thing which makes the other thing dependent on yet another, and you have to grasp this sorry scheme of things entire to do what you want, and that we can't do.

Copleston: But are you going to say that we can't, or we shouldn't even raise the question of the exis-tence of the whole of this sorry scheme of things — of the whole universe?

Russell: Yes, I don't think there's any meaning in it at all. I think the word "universe" is a handy word in some connections, but I don't think it stands for anything that has a meaning.

Copleston: If the word is meaningless, it can't be so very handy. In any case, I don't say that the uni-verse is something different from the objects which compose it (I indicated that in my brief summary of the proof); what I'm doing is to look for the reason, in this case the cause of the objects—the real or imag-ined totality of which constitute what we call the uni-verse. You say, I think, that the universe—or my existence if you prefer, or any other existence—is unintelligible?

Russell: First may I take up the point that if a word is meaningless it can't be handy. That sounds well but isn't in fact correct. Take, say, such a word as "the" or "than." You can't point to any object that those words mean, but they are very useful words; I should say the same of "universe." But leaving that point, you ask whether I consider that the universe is unintelligible. I shouldn't say unintelligible—I think it is without explanation. Intelligible, to my mind, is a different thing. Intelligible has to do with the thing itself intrinsically and not with its relations.

Copleston: Well, my point is that what we call the world is intrinsically unintelligible, apart from the existence of God. You see, I don't believe that the infinity of the series of events—I mean a horizontal

series, so to speak—if such an infinity could be proved, would be in the slightest degree relevant to the situation. If you add up chocolates you get choco-lates after all and not a sheep. If you add up chocolates to infinity, you presumably get an infinite number of chocolates. So if you add up contingent beings to infinity, you still get contingent beings, not a neces-sary being. An infinite series of contingent beings will be, to my way of thinking, as unable to cause itself as one contingent being. However, you say, I think, that it is illegitimate to raise the question of what will explain the existence of any particular object?

Russell: It's quite all right if you mean by explain-ing it, simply finding a cause for it.

Copleston: Well, why stop at one particular object? Why shouldn't one raise the question of the cause of the existence of all particular objects?

Russell: Because I see no reason to think there is any. The whole concept of cause is one we derive from our observation of particular things; I see no reason whatsoever to suppose that the total has any cause whatsoever.

Copleston: Well, to say that there isn't any cause is not the same thing as saying that we shouldn't look for a cause. The statement that there isn't any cause should come, if it comes at all, at the end of the inquiry, not the beginning. In any case, if the total has no cause, then to my way of thinking it must be its own cause, which seems to me impossible. Moreover, the statement that the world is simply there if in answer to a question, presupposes that the question has meaning.

Russell: No, it doesn't need to be its own cause, what I'm saying is that the concept of cause is not applicable to the total.

Copleston: Then you would agree with Sartre that the universe is what he calls "gratuitous"?

Russell: Well, the word "gratuitous" suggests that it might be something else; I should say that the uni-verse is just there, and that's all.

Copleston: Well, I can't see how you can rule out the legitimacy of asking the question how the total, or anything at all comes to be there. Why something rather than nothing, that is the question? The fact that we gain our knowledge of causality empirically, from particular causes, does not rule out the possibility of asking what the cause of the series is. If the word "cause" were meaningless or if it could be shown that Kant's view of the matter were correct, the question would be illegitimate I agree; but you don't seem to hold that the word "cause" is meaningless, and I do not suppose you are a Kantian.

Russell: I can illustrate what seems to me your fallacy. Every man who exists has a mother, and it seems to me your argument is that therefore the human race must have a mother, but obviously the human race hasn't a mother—that's a different logical sphere.

Copleston: Well, I can't really see any parity. If I were saying "every object has a phenomenal cause, therefore, the whole series has a phenomenal cause," there would be a parity; but I'm not saying that; I'm saying, every object has a phenomenal cause if you insist on the infinity of the series—but the series of phenomenal causes is an insufficient explanation of the series. Therefore, the series has not a phenomenal cause but a transcendent cause.

Russell: That's always assuming that not only every particular thing in the world, but the world as a whole must have a cause. For that assumption I see no ground whatever. If you'll give me a ground I'll listen to it.

Copleston: Well, the series of events is either caused or it's not caused. If it is caused, there must obviously be a cause outside the series. If it's not caused then it's sufficient to itself, and if it's sufficient to itself it is what I call necessary. But it can't be necessary since each member is contingent, and we've agreed that the total has no reality apart from its members, therefore, it can't be necessary. Therefore, it can't be (caused)—uncaused—therefore it must have a cause. And I should like to observe in passing that the statement "the world is simply there and is inexplicable" can't be got out of logical analysis.

Russell: I don't want to seem arrogant, but it does seem to me that I can conceive things that you say the human mind can't conceive. As for things not having a cause, the physicists assure us that individual quantum transitions in atoms have no cause.

Copleston: Well, I wonder now whether that isn't simply a temporary inference.

Russell: It may be, but it does show that physicists' minds can conceive it.

Copleston: Yes, I agree, some scientists—physicists—are willing to allow for indetermination within a restricted field. But very many scientists are not so willing. I think that Professor Dingle, of London University, maintains that the Heisenberg uncertainty principle tells us something about the success (or the lack of it) of the present atomic theory in correlating observations, but not about nature in itself, and many physicists would accept this view. In any case, I don't see how physicists can fail to accept the theory in practice, even if they don't do so in theory. I cannot see how science could be conducted on any other assumption than that of order and intelligibility in nature. The physicist presupposes, at least tacitly, that there is some sense in investigating nature and looking for the causes of events, just as the detective presupposes that there is some sense in looking for the cause of a murder. The metaphysician assumes that there is sense in looking for the reason or cause of phenomena, and, not being a Kantian, I consider that the metaphysician is as justified in his assumption as the physicist. When Sartre, for example, says that the world is gratuitous, I think that he has not sufficiently considered what is implied by "gratuitous."

Russell: I think—there seems to me a certain unwarrantable extension here; a physicist looks for causes; that does not necessarily imply that there are causes everywhere. A man may look for gold without assuming that there is gold everywhere; if he finds gold, well and good, if he doesn't he's had bad luck. The same is true when the physicists look for causes. As for Sartre, I don't profess to know what he means, and I shouldn't like to be thought to interpret him, but for my part, I do think the notion of the world having an explanation is a mistake. I don't see why one should expect it to have, and I think what you say about what the scientist assumes is an over-statement.

Copleston: Well, it seems to me that the scientist does make some such assumption. When he experiments to find out some particular truth, behind that experiment lies the assumption that the universe is not simply discontinuous. There is the possibility of finding out a truth by experiment. The experiment may be a bad one, it may lead to no result, or not to the result that he wants, but that at any rate there is the possibility, through experiment, of finding out the truth that he assumes. And that seems to me to assume an ordered and intelligible universe.

Russell: I think you're generalizing more than is necessary. Undoubtedly the scientist assumes that this sort of thing is likely to be found and will often be found. He does not assume that it will be found, and that's a very important matter in modern physics.

Copleston: Well I think he does assume or is bound to assume it tacitly in practice. It may be that, to quote Professor Haldane, "when I light the gas under the kettle, some of the water molecules will fly off as vapor, and there is no way of finding out which will do so," but it doesn't follow necessarily that the idea of chance must be introduced except in relation to our knowledge.

Russell: No it doesn't—at least if I may believe what he says. He's finding out quite a lot of things— the scientist is finding out quite a lot of things that are happening in the world, which are, at first, beginnings of causal chains—first causes which haven't in themselves got causes. He does not assume that everything has a cause.

Copleston: Surely that's a first cause within a certain selected field. It's a relatively first cause.

Russell: I don't think he'd say so. If there's a world in which most events, but not all, have causes, he will then be able to depict the probabilities and uncertainties by assuming that this particular event you're interested in probably has a cause. And since in any case you won't get more than probability that's good enough.

Copleston: It may be that the scientist doesn't hope to obtain more than probability, but in raising the question he assumes that the question of explanation has a meaning. But your general point then, Lord Russell, is that it's illegitimate even to ask the question of the cause of the world?

Russell: Yes, that's my position.

Copleston: If it's a question that for you has no meaning, it's of course very difficult to discuss it, isn't it?

Russell: Yes, it is very difficult. What do you say—shall we pass on to some other issue?

. . .

Copleston: Well, perhaps it's time I summed up my position. I've argued two things. First, that the existence of God can be philosophically proved by a metaphysical argument; secondly, that it is only the existence of God that will make sense of man's moral experience and of religious experience. Personally, I think that your way of accounting for man's moral judgments leads inevitably to a contradiction between what your theory demands and your own spontaneous judgments. Moreover, your theory explains moral obligation away, and explaining away is not explanation. As regards the metaphysical argument, we are apparently in agreement that what we call the world consists simply of contingent beings. That is, of beings no one of which can account for its own existence. You say that the series of events needs no explanation: I say that if there were no necessary being, no being which must exist and cannot not exist, nothing would exist. The infinity of the series of contingent beings, even if proved, would be irrelevant. Something does exist; therefore, there must be something which accounts for this fact, a being which is outside the series of contingent beings. If you had admitted this, we could then have discussed whether that being is personal, good, and so on. On the actual point discussed, whether there is or is not a necessary being, I find myself, I think, in agreement with the great majority of classical philosophers.

You maintain, I think, that existing beings are simply there, and that I have no justification for raising the question of the explanation of their existence. But I would like to point that this position cannot be substantiated by logical analysis; it expresses a philosophy which itself stands in need of proof. I think we have reached an impasse because our ideas of philosophy are radically different; it seems to me that what I call a part of philosophy, that you call the whole, in so far at least as philosophy is rational. It seems to me, if you will pardon my saying so, that besides your own logical system—which you call "modern" in opposition to antiquated logic (a tendentious adjective)—you maintain a philosophy which cannot be substantiated by logical analysis. After all, the problem of God's existence is an existential problem whereas logical analysis does not deal directly with problems of existence. So it seems to me, to declare that the terms involved in one set of problems are meaningless because they are not required in dealing with another set of problems, is to settle from the beginning the nature and extent of philosophy, and that is itself a philosophical act which stands in need of justification.

Russell: Weli, I should like to say just a few words by way of summary on my side. First, as to the metaphysical argument: I don't admit the connotations of such a term as "contingent" or the possibility of explanation in Father Copleston's sense. I think the word "contingent" inevitably suggests the possibility of something that wouldn't have this what you might call accidental character of just being there, and I don't think this is true except in the purely causal sense. You can sometimes give a causal explanation of one thing as being the effect of something else, but that is merely referring one thing to another thing and there's no—to my mind—explanation in Father Copleston's sense of anything at all, nor is there any meaning in calling things "contingent" because there isn't anything else they could be. That's what I should say about that, but I should like to say a few words about Father Copleston's accusation that I regard logic as all philosophy—that is by no means the case. I don't by any means regard logic as all philosophy. I think logic is an essential part of philosophy and logic has to be used in philosophy, and in that I think he and I are at one. When the logic that he uses was new—namely, in the time of Aristotle, there had to be a great deal of fuss made about it; Aristotle made a lot of fuss about that logic. Nowadays it's become old and respectable, and you don't have to make so much fuss about it. The logic that I believe in is comparatively new, and therefore I have to imitate Aristotle in making a fuss about it; but it's not that I think it's all philosophy by any means—I don't think so. I think it's an important part of philosophy, and when I say that, I don't find a meaning for this or that word, that is a position of detail based upon what I've found out about that particular word, from thinking about it. It's not a general position that all words that are used in metaphysics are nonsense, or anything like that which I don't really hold.

As regards the moral argument, I do find that when one studies anthropology or history, there are people who think it their duty to perform acts which I think abominable, and I certainly can't, therefore, attribute Divine origin to the matter of moral obligation, which Father Copleston doesn't ask me to; but I think even the form of moral obligation, when it takes the form of enjoining you to eat your father or what not, doesn't seem to me to be such a very beautiful and noble thing; and, therefore, I cannot attribute a Divine origin to this sense of moral obligation, which I think is quite easily accounted for in quite other ways.

FOR FURTHER REFLECTION

1. Outline the argument from contingency set forth by Copleston. Are all its premises clear to you? If not, what premises seem unclear, and why?
2. How do Copleston and Russell disagree over the concept of *necessity?* How could we make a rational decision in this disagreement?
3. Consider the question "Why is there something rather than nothing?" Is this a meaningful question? Does it open up a fruitful discussion about the possible existence of a supreme being? What do Russell and Copleston think about such questions? What do you think?
4. What lessons can we learn from this debate? Why can't Copleston and Russell come to an agreement here? Does the disagreement show the limits of reason, or is one of the debators just being irrational?

WILLIAM PALEY

THE WATCH AND THE WATCHMAKER

William Paley (1743–1805), archdeacon of Carlisle, was a leading evangelical apologist. His most important work is *Natural Theology, or Evidences of the Existence and Attributes of the Deity Collected from the Appearances of Nature* (1802), of which the first chapter follows. Paley argues that just as we infer an intelligent designer to account for the purpose-revealing watch, so likewise we must analogously infer an intelligent grand designer to account for the purpose-revealing world.

STATEMENT OF THE ARGUMENT

In crossing a heath, suppose I pitched my foot against a *stone,* and were asked how the stone came to be there, I might possibly answer, that, for anything I knew to the contrary, it had lain there for ever; nor would it, perhaps, be very easy to show the absurdity of this answer. But suppose I found a *watch* upon the ground, and it should be inquired how the watch happened to be in that place, I should hardly think of the answer which I had given—that, for anything I knew, the watch might have always been there. Yet why should not this answer serve for the watch as well as for the stone? why is it not as admissible in the second case as in the first? For this reason, and for no other; viz., that, when we come to inspect the watch, we perceive (what we could not discover in the stone) that its several parts are framed and put together for a purpose, e.g. that they are so formed and adjusted as to produce motion, and that motion so regulated as to point out the hour of the day; that, if the different parts had been differently shaped from what they are, if a different size from what they are, or placed after any other manner, or in any other order than that in which they are placed, either no motion at all would have been carried on in the machine, or none which would have answered the use that is now served by it. To reckon up a few of the plainest of these parts, and of their offices, all tending to one result:—We see a cylindrical box containing a coiled elastic spring, which, by its endeavor to relax itself, turns round the box. We next observe a flexible chain (artificially wrought for the sake of flexure) communicating the action of the spring from the box to the fusee. We then find a series of wheels, the teeth of which catch in, and apply to, each other, conducting the motion from the fusee to the balance, and from the balance to the pointer, and, at the same time, by the size and shape of those wheels, so regulating that motion as to terminate in causing an index, by an equable and measured progression, to pass over a given space in a given time. We take notice that the wheels are made of brass, in order to keep them from rust; the springs of steel, no other metal being so elastic; that over the face of the watch there is placed a glass, a material em-

From William Paley, *Natural Theology, or Evidences of the Existence and Attributes of the Deity Collected from the Appearances of Nature* (1802).

ployed in no other part of the work, but in the room of which, if there had been any other than a transparent substance, the hour could not be seen without opening the case. This mechanism being observed, (it requires indeed an examination of the instrument, and perhaps some previous knowledge of the subject, to perceive and understand it); but being once, as we have said, observed and understood, the inference, we think, is inevitable, that the watch must have had a maker; that there must have existed, at some time, and at some place or other, an artificer or artificers who formed it for the purpose which we find it actually to answer; who comprehended its construction, and designed its use.

I. Nor would it, I apprehend, weaken the conclusion, that we had never seen a watch made; that we had never known an artist capable of making one; that we were altogether incapable of executing such a piece of workmanship ourselves, or of understanding in what manner it was performed; all this being no more than what is true of some exquisite remains of ancient art, of some lost arts, and, to the generality of mankind, of the more curious productions of modern manufacture. Does one man in a million know how oval frames are turned? Ignorance of this kind exalts our opinion of the unseen and unknown artist's skill, if he be unseen and unknown, but raises no doubt in our minds of the existence and agency of such an artist, at some former time, and in some place or other. Nor can I perceive that it varies at all the inference, whether the question arise concerning a human agent, or concerning an agent of a different species, or an agent possessing, in some respect, a different nature.

II. Neither, secondly, would it invalidate our conclusion, that the watch sometimes went wrong, or that it seldom went exactly right. The purpose of the machinery, the design, and the designer, might be evident, and, in the case supposed, would be evident, in whatever way we accounted for the irregularity of the movement, or whether we could account for it or not. It is not necessary that a machine be perfect, in order to show with what design it was made; still less necessary, where the only question is, whether it were made with any design at all.

III. Nor, thirdly, would it bring any uncertainty into the argument, if there were a few parts of the watch, concerning which we could not discover, or had not yet discovered, in what manner they conduced to the general effect; or even some parts, concerning which we could not ascertain whether they conduced to that effect in any manner whatever. For, as to the first branch of the case, if by the loss, or disorder, or decay of the parts in question, the movement of the watch were found in fact to be stopped, or disturbed, or retarded, no doubt would remain in our minds as to the utility or intention of these parts, although we should be unable to investigate the manner according to which, or the connection by which, the ultimate effect depended upon their action or assistance; and the more complex is the machine, the more likely is this obscurity to arise. Then, as to the second thing supposed, namely, that there were parts which might be spared without prejudice to the movement of the watch, and that he had proved this by experiment, these superfluous parts, even if we were completely assured that they were such, would not vacate the reasoning which we had instituted concerning other parts. The indication of contrivance remained, with respect to them, nearly as it was before.

IV. Nor, fourthly, would any man in his senses think the existence of the watch, with its various machinery, accounted for, by being told that it was one out of possible combinations of material forms; that whatever he had found in the place where he found the watch, must have contained some internal configuration or other; and that this configuration might be the structure now exhibited, viz., of the works of a watch, as well as a different structure.

V. Nor, fifthly, would it yield his inquiry more satisfaction, to be answered, that there existed in things a principle of order, which had disposed the parts of the watch into their present form and situation. He never knew a watch made by the principle of order; nor can he even form to himself an idea of what is meant by a principle of order, distinct from the intelligence of the watchmaker.

VI. Sixthly, he would be surprised to hear that the mechanism of the watch was no proof of contrivance, only a motive to induce the mind to think so:

VII. And not less surprised to be informed, that the watch in his hand was nothing more than the result of the laws of *metallic* nature. It is a perversion of language to assign any law as the efficient, operative cause of anything. A law presupposes an agent; for it is only the mode according to which an agent proceeds; it implies a power; for it is the order according to which that power acts. Without this agent, without this power, which are both distinct from itself, the *law* does nothing, is nothing. The expression, "the law of metallic nature," may sound strange and harsh to a philosophic ear; but it seems quite as justifiable as some others which are more familiar to him such as "the law of vegetable nature," "the law of animal nature," or, indeed, as "the law of nature" in general, when assigned as the cause of phenomena in exclusion of agency and power, or when it is substituted into the place of these.

VIII. Neither, lastly, would our observer be driven out of his conclusion, or from his confidence in its truth, by being told that he knew nothing at all about the matter. He knows enough for his argument: he knows the utility of the end: he knows the subserviency and adaptation of the means to the end. These points being known, his ignorance of other points, his doubts concerning other points, affect not the certainty of his reasoning. The consciousness of knowing little need not beget a distrust of that which he does know. . . .

APPLICATION OF THE ARGUMENT

Every indication of contrivance, every manifestation of design, which existed in the watch, exists in the works of nature; with the difference, on the side of nature, of being greater and more, and that in a degree which exceeds all computation. I mean that the contrivances of nature surpass the contrivances of art, in the complexity, subtilty, and curiosity of the mechanism; and still more, if possible, do they go beyond them in number and variety; yet in a multitude of cases, are not less evidently mechanical, not less evidently contrivances, not less evidently accommodated to their end, or suited to their office, than are the most perfect productions of human ingenuity.

FOR FURTHER REFLECTION

1. What does Paley consider the inherent differences between a stone and a watch? What inferences does each permit about its origins?
2. What analogy can be made between the watch and the world? Does the analogy persuade you? Does the universe reveal design or order that points to a grand designer? Why or why not?

DAVID HUME

A CRITIQUE OF THE TELEOLOGICAL ARGUMENT

Scottish empiricist and skeptic David Hume (1711–1776), as noted earlier, is one of the most important philosophers who ever lived. His *Dialogues Concerning Natural Religion* (published posthumously in 1779) contains the classic critique of the argument from design. The following reading is from Parts II and V of this critique. Cleanthes, who opens our selection, is a natural theologian, the Paley of his time, who opposes both the orthodox believer Demea and the skeptic Philo. Philo puts forth the major criticisms against the argument from design.

Cleanthes: Look round the world: Contemplate the whole and every part of it: You will find it to be nothing but one great machine, subdivided into an infinite number of lesser machines, which again admit of subdivisions to a degree beyond what human senses and faculties can trace and explain. All these various machines, and even their most minute parts, are adjusted to each other with an accuracy which ravishes into admiration all men who have ever contemplated them. The curious adapting of means to ends, throughout all nature, resembles exactly, though it much exceeds, the productions of human contrivance; of human design, thought, wisdom, and intelligence. Since therefore the effects resemble each other, we are led to infer, by all the rules of analogy, that the causes also resemble, and that the Author of Nature is somewhat similar to the mind of man, though possessed of much larger faculties, proportioned to the grandeur of the work which he has executed. By this argument *a posteriori,* and by this argument alone, do we prove at once the existence of a Deity and his similarity to human mind and intelligence.

Demea: I shall be so free, *Cleanthes,* as to tell you that from the beginning I could not approve of your conclusion concerning the similarity of the Deity to men; still less can I approve of the mediums by which you endeavor to establish it. What! No demonstration of the Being of God! No abstract arguments! No proofs a priori! Are these which have hitherto been so much insisted on by philosophers all fallacy, all sophism? Can we reach no farther in this subject than experience and probability? I will say not that this is betraying the cause of a Deity; but surely, by this affected candor, you give advantages to atheists which they never could obtain by the mere dint of argument and reasoning.

Philo: What I chiefly scruple in this subject, is not so much that all religious arguments are by *Cleanthes* reduced to experience, as that they appear not be even the most certain and irrefragable of that inferior kind. That a stone will fall, that fire will burn, that the earth has solidity, we have observed a thousand and a thousand times; and when any new instance of this nature is presented, we draw without hesitation the accustomed inference. The exact similarity of the cases gives us a perfect assurance of a similar event, and a stronger evidence is never desired nor sought after. But wherever you depart, in the least, from the

From David Hume, *Dialogues Concerning Natural Religion* (1779).

similarity of the cases, you diminish proportionably the evidence; and may at last bring it to a very weak *analogy,* which is confessedly liable to error and uncertainty. After having experienced the circulation of the blood in human creatures, we make no doubt that it takes place in *Titius* and *Maevius;* but from its circulation in frogs and fishes it is only a presumption, though a strong one, from analogy that it takes place in men and other animals. The analogical reasoning is much weaker when we infer the circulation of the sap in vegetables from our experience that the blood circulates in animals; and those who hastily followed that imperfect analogy are found, by more accurate experiments to have been mistaken.

If we see a house, *Cleanthes,* we conclude, with the greatest certainty, that it had an architect or builder because this is precisely that species of effect which we have experienced to proceed from that species of cause. But surely you will not affirm that the universe bears such a resemblance to a house that we can with the same certainty infer a similar cause, or that the analogy is here entire and perfect. The dissimilitude is so striking that the utmost you can here pretend to is a guess, a conjecture, a presumption concerning a similar cause; and how that pretension will be received in the world, I leave you to consider.

Cleanthes: It would surely be very ill received, and I should be deservedly blamed and detested did I allow that the proofs of a Deity amounted to no more than a guess or conjecture. But is the whole adjustment of means to ends in a house and in the universe so slight a resemblance? The economy of final causes? The order, proportion, and arrangement of every part? Steps of a stair are plainly contrived that human legs may use them in mounting; and this inference is certain and infallible. Human legs are also contrived for walking and mounting; and this inference, I allow, is not altogether so certain because of the dissimilarity which you remark; but does it, therefore, deserve the name only of presumption or conjecture?

Demea: Good God! Where are we? Zealous defenders of religion allow that the proofs of a Deity fall short of perfect evidence! And you, *Philo,* on whose assistance I depended in proving the adorable mysteriousness of the Divine Nature, do you assent to all these extravagant opinions of *Cleanthes?* For what

other name can I give them? or, why spare my censure when such principles are advanced, supported by such an authority, before so young a man as *Pamphilus?*

Philo: You seem not to apprehend that I argue with *Cleanthes* in his own way, and, by showing him the dangerous consequences of his tenets, hope at last to reduce him to our opinion. But what sticks most with you, I observe, is the representation which *Cleanthes* has made of the argument a posteriori; and, finding that that argument is likely to escape your hold and vanish into air, you think it so disguised that you can scarcely believe it to be set in its true light. Now, however much I may dissent, in other respects, from the dangerous principle of *Cleanthes,* I must allow that he has fairly represented that argument, and I shall endeavor so to state the matter to you that you will entertain no further scruples with regard to it.

Were a man to abstract from everything which he knows or has seen, he would be altogether incapable, merely from his own ideas, to determine what kind of scene the universe must be, or to give the preference to one state or situation of things above another. For as nothing which he clearly conceives could be esteemed impossible or implying a contradiction, every chimera of his fancy would be upon an equal footing; nor could he assign any just reason why he adheres to one idea or system, and rejects the others which are equally possible.

Again, after he opens his eyes and contemplates the world as it really is, it would be impossible for him at first to assign the cause of any one event, much less of the whole of things, or of the universe. He might set his fancy a rambling, and she might bring him in an infinite variety of reports and representations. These would all be possible; but, being all equally possible, he would never of himself give a satisfactory account for his preferring one of them to the rest. Experience alone can point out to him the true cause of any phenomenon.

Now, according to this method of reasoning, *Demea,* it follows (and is, indeed, tacitly allowed by *Cleanthes* himself) that order, arrangement, or the adjustment of final causes, is not of itself any proof of design, but only so far as it has been experienced to proceed from that principle. For aught we can know *a priori,* matter may contain the source or spring of order originally within itself, as well as mind does; and there is no more difficulty in conceiving that the several elements, from an internal unknown cause, may fall into the most exquisite arrangement, than to conceive that their ideas, in the great universal mind, from a like internal unknown cause, fall into that arrangement. The equal possibility of both these suppositions is allowed. But, by experience, we find, according to *Cleanthes,* that there is a difference between them. Throw several pieces of steel together, without shape or form; they will never arrange themselves so as to compose a watch. Stone and mortar and wood, without an architect, never erect a house. But the ideas in a human mind, we see, by an unknown, inexplicable economy, arrange themselves so as to form the plan of a watch or house. Experience, therefore, proves that there is an original principle of order in mind, not in matter. From similar effects we infer similar causes. The adjustment of means to ends is alike in the universe, as in a machine of human contrivance. The causes, therefore, must be resembling.

I was from the beginning scandalized, I must own, with this resemblance which is asserted between the Deity and human creatures, and must conceive it to imply such a degradation of the Supreme Being as no sound theist could endure. With your assistance, therefore, *Demea,* I shall endeavor to defend what you justly call the adorable mysteriousness of the Divine Nature, and shall refute this reasoning of *Cleanthes,* provided he allows that I have made a fair representation of it.

When *Cleanthes* had assented, *Philo,* after a short pause, proceeded in the following manner.

That all inferences, *Cleanthes,* concerning fact are founded on experience, and that all experimental reasonings are founded on the supposition that similar causes prove similar effects, and similar effects similar causes, I shall not at present much dispute with you. But observe, I entreat you, with what extreme caution all just reasoners proceed in the transferring of experiments to similar cases. Unless the cases be exactly similar, they repose no perfect confidence in applying their past observation to any particular phenomenon. Every alteration of circumstances occasions a doubt concerning the event; and it requires new experiments to prove certainly that the new circumstances are of no

moment or importance. A change in bulk, situation, arrangement, age, disposition of the air, or surrounding bodies; any of these particulars may be attended with the most unexpected consequences. And unless the objects be quite familiar to us, it is the highest temerity to expect with assurance, after any of these changes, an event similar to that which before fell under our observation. The slow and deliberate steps of philosophers here, if anywhere, are distinguished from the precipitate march of the vulgar, who, hurried on by the smallest similitude, are incapable of all discernment or consideration.

But can you think, *Cleanthes,* that your usual phlegm and philosophy have been preserved in so wide a step as you have taken when you compared to the universe houses, ships, furniture, machines; and, from their similarity in some circumstances, inferred a similarity in their causes? Thought, design, intelligence, such as we discover in men and other animals, is no more than one of the springs and principles of the universe, as well as heat or cold, attraction or repulsion, and a hundred others which fall under daily observation. It is an active cause by which some particular parts of nature, we find, produce alterations on other parts. But can a conclusion, with any propriety, be transferred from parts to the whole? Does not the great disproportion bar all comparison and inference? From observing the growth of a hair, can we learn anything concerning the generation of a man? Would the manner of a leaf's blowing, even though perfectly known, afford us any instruction concerning the vegetation of a tree?

But allowing that we were to take the *operations* of one part of nature upon another for the foundation of our judgment concerning the *origin* of the whole (which never can be admitted), yet why select so minute, so weak, so bounded a principle as the reason and design of animals is found to be upon this planet? What peculiar privilege has this little agitation of the brain which we call "thought", that we must thus make it the model of the whole universe? Our partiality in our own favor does indeed present it on all occasions, but sound philosophy ought carefully to guard against so natural an illusion.

So far from admitting that the operations of a part can afford us any just conclusion concerning the origin of the whole, I will not allow any one part to form a rule for another part if the latter be very remote from the former. Is there any reasonable ground to conclude that the inhabitants of other planets possess thought, intelligence, reason, or anything similar to these faculties in men? When nature has so extremely diversified her manner of operation in this small globe, can we imagine that she incessantly copies herself throughout so immense a universe? And if thought, as we may well suppose, be confined merely to this narrow corner, and has even there so limited a sphere of action, with what propriety can we assign it for the original cause of all things? The narrow views of a peasant who makes his domestic economy the rule for the government of kingdoms is in comparison a pardonable sophism.

But were we ever so much assured that a thought and reason resembling the human were to be found throughout the whole universe, and were its activity elsewhere vastly greater and more commanding than it appears in this globe; yet I cannot see why the operations of a world constituted, arranged, adjusted, can with any propriety be extended to a world which is in its embryo state, and is advancing towards that constitution and arrangement. By observation we know somewhat of the economy, action, and nourishment of a finished animal; but we must transfer with great caution that observation to the growth of a foetus in the womb, and still more to the formation of an animalcule in the loins of its male parent. Nature, we find, even from our limited experience, possesses an infinite number of springs and principles which incessantly discover themselves on every change of her position and situation. And what new and unknown principles would actuate her in so new and unknown a situation as that of the formation of a universe, we cannot, without the utmost temerity, pretend to determine.

A very small part of this great system, during a very short time, is very imperfectly discovered to us; and do we thence pronounce decisively concerning the origin of the whole?

Admirable conclusion! Stone, wood, brick, iron, brass, have not, at this time, in this minute globe of earth, an order or arrangement without human art and contrivance; therefore, the universe could not origi-

nally attain its order and arrangement without something similar to human art. But is a part of nature a rule for another part very wide of the former? Is it a rule for the whole? Is a very small part a rule for the universe? Is nature in one situation a certain rule for nature in another situation vastly different from the former?

And can you blame me, *Cleanthes,* if I here imitate the prudent reserve of *Simonides,* who, according to the noted story, being asked by *Hiero, What God was?* desired a day to think of it, and then two days more; and after that manner continually prolonged the term, without ever bringing in his definition or description? Could you even blame me if I had answered, at first, *that I did not know,* and was sensible that this subject lay vastly beyond the reach of my faculties? You might cry out skeptic and rallier, as much as you pleased; but, having found in so many other subjects much more familiar the imperfections and even contradictions of human reason, I never should expect any success from its feeble conjectures in a subject so sublime and so remote from the sphere of our observation. When two *species* of objects have always been observed to be conjoined together, I can *infer,* by custom, the existence of one wherever I see the existence of the other; and this I call an argument from experience. But how this argument can have place where the objects, as in the present case, are single, individual, without parallel or specific resemblance, may be difficult to explain. And will any man tell me with a serious countenance that an orderly universe must arise from some thought and art like the human because we have experience of it? To ascertain this reasoning it were requisite that we had experience of the origin of worlds; and it is not sufficient, surely, that we have seen ships and cities arise from human art and contrivance. . . .

Philo: But to show you still more inconveniences in your anthropomorphism, please to take a new survey of your principles. *Like effects prove like causes.* This is the experimental argument; and this, you say too, is the sole theological argument. Now it is certain that the liker the effects are which are seen and the liker the causes which are inferred, the stronger is the argument. Every departure on either side diminishes the probability and renders the experiment less conclusive. You cannot doubt of the principle; neither ought you to reject its consequences.

All the new discoveries in astronomy which prove the immense grandeur and magnificence of the works of nature are so many additional arguments for a Deity, according to the true system of theism; but, according to your hypothesis of experimental theism, they become so many objections, by removing the effect still farther from all resemblance to the effects of human art and contrivance. For if *Lucretius,* even following the old system of the world, could exclaim:

> Who is strong enough to rule the sun, who to hold in hand and control the mighty bridle of the unfathomable deep? who to turn about all the heavens at one time, and warm the fruitful worlds with ethereal fires, or to be present in all places and at all times.[1]

If Tully[2] esteemed this reasoning so natural as to put it into the mouth of his Epicurean:

> What power of mental vision enabled your master Plato to descry the vast and elaborate architectural process which, as he makes out, the deity adopted in building the structure of the universe? What method of engineering was employed? What tools and levers and derricks? What agents carried out so vast an understanding? And how were air, fire, water, and earth enabled to obey and execute the will of the architect?

If this argument, I say, had any force in former ages, how much greater must it have at present when the bounds of nature are so infinitely enlarged and such a magnificent scene is opened to us? It is still more unreasonable to form our idea of so unlimited a cause from our experience of the narrow productions of human design and invention.

The discoveries by microscopes, as they open a new universe in miniature, are still objections, according to you; arguments, according to me. The farther we push our researches of this kind, we are still led to infer the universal cause of all to be vastly different from mankind, or from any object of human experience and observation.

And what say you to the discoveries in anatomy, chemistry, botany? . . .

Cleanthes: These surely are no objections; they only discover new instances of art and contrivance. It is still the image of mind reflected on us from innumerable objects.

Philo: Add a mind *like the human.*

Cleanthes: I know of no other.

Philo: And the liker, the better.

Cleanthes: To be sure.

Philo: Now, *Cleanthes,* mark the consequences. *First,* by this method of reasoning you renounce all claim to infinity in any of the attributes of the Deity. For, as the cause ought only to be proportioned to the effect, and the effect, so far as it falls under our cognizance, is not infinite: What pretensions have we, upon your suppositions, to ascribe that attribute to the Divine Being? You will still insist that, by removing him so much from all similarity to human creatures, we give in to the most arbitrary hypothesis, and at the same time weaken all proofs of his existence.

Secondly, you have no reason, on your theory, for ascribing perfection to the Deity, even in his finite capacity; or for supposing him free from every error, mistake, or incoherence, in his undertakings. There are many inexplicable difficulties in the works of Nature which, if we allow a perfect author to be proved *a priori,* are easily solved, and become only seeming difficulties from the narrow capacity of man, who cannot trace infinite relations. But according to your method of reasoning, these difficulties become all real; and, perhaps, will be insisted on as new instances of likeness to human art and contrivance. At least, you must acknowledge that it is impossible for us to tell, from our limited views, whether this system contains any great faults or deserves any considerable praise if compared to other possible and even real systems. Could a peasant, if the *Aeneid* were read to him, pronounce that poem to be absolutely faultless, or even assign to it its proper rank among the productions of human wit, he who had never seen any other production?

But were this world ever so perfect a production, it must still remain uncertain whether all the excellences of the work can justly be ascribed to the workman. If we survey a ship, what an exalted idea must we form of the ingenuity of the carpenter who framed so complicated, useful, and beautiful a machine? And what surprise must we feel when we find him a stupid mechanic who imitated others, and copied an art which, through a long succession of ages, after multiplied trials, mistakes, corrections, deliberations, and controversies, had been gradually improving? Many worlds might have been botched and bungled, throughout an eternity, ere this system was struck out; much labor lost; many fruitless trials made; and a slow but continued improvement carried on during infinite ages in the art of world-making. In such subjects, who can determine where the truth, nay, who can conjecture where the probability lies, amidst a great number of hypotheses which may be proposed, and a still greater which may be imagined?

And what shadow of an argument can you produce from your hypothesis to prove the unity of the Deity? A great number of men join in building a house or ship, in rearing a city, in framing a commonwealth; why may not several deities combine in contriving and framing a world? This is only so much greater similarity to human affairs. By sharing the work among several, we may so much further limit the attributes of each, and get rid of that extensive power and knowledge which must be supposed in one deity, and which, according to you, can only serve to weaken the proof of his existence. And if such foolish, such vicious creatures as man can yet often unite in framing and executing one plan, how much more those deities or demons, whom we may suppose several degrees more perfect?

To multiply causes without necessity is indeed contrary to true philosophy, but this principle applies not to the present case. Were one deity antecedently proved by your theory who were possessed of every attribute requisite to the production of the universe, it would be needless, I own (though not absurd), to suppose any other deity existent. But while it is still a question whether all these attributes are united in one subject or dispersed among several independent beings; by what phenomena in nature can we pretend to decide the controversy? Where we see a body raised in a scale, we are sure that there is in the opposite scale, however concealed from sight, some counterpoising weight equal to it; but it is still allowed to doubt whether that weight be an aggregate of several distinct bodies or one uniform united mass. And if the weight requisite very much exceeds anything which we have ever seen conjoined in any single

body, the former supposition becomes still more probable and natural. An intelligent being of such vast power and capacity as is necessary to produce a universe, or, to speak in the language of ancient philosophy, so prodigious an animal, exceeds all analogy and even comprehension.

But further, *Cleanthes,* men are mortal, and renew their species by generation; and this is common to all living creatures. The two great sexes of male and female, says *Milton,* animate the world. Why must this circumstance, so universal, so essential, be excluded from those numerous and limited deities? Behold, then, the theogeny of ancient times brought back upon us.

And why not become a perfect anthropomorphite? Why not assert the deity or deities to be corporeal, and to have eyes, a nose, mouth, ears, etc.? *Epicurus* maintained that no man had ever seen reason but in a human figure; therefore, the gods must have a human figure. And this argument, which is deservedly so much ridiculed by *Cicero,* becomes, according to you, solid and philosophical.

In a word, *Cleanthes,* a man who follows your hypothesis is able, perhaps, to assert or conjecture that the universe sometime arose from something like design: But beyond that position he cannot ascertain one single circumstance, and is left afterwards to fix every point of his theology by the utmost license of fancy and hypothesis. This world, for aught he knows, is very faulty and imperfect, compared to a superior standard; and was only the first rude essay of some infant deity who afterwards abandoned it, ashamed of his lame performance: It is the work only of some dependent, inferior deity, and is the object of derision to his superiors: It is the production of old age and dotage in some superannuated deity; and ever since his death has run on at adventures, from the first impulse and active force which it received from him. . . . You justly give signs of horror, *Demea,* at these strange suppositions; but these, and a thousand more of the same kind, are *Cleanthes'* suppositions, not mine. From the moment the attributes of the Deity are supposed finite, all these have place. And I cannot, for my part, think that so wild and unsettled a system of theology is, in any respect, preferable to none at all.

Cleanthes: These suppositions I absolutely disown: They strike me, however, with no horror, especially when proposed in that rambling way in which they drop from you. On the contrary, they give me pleasure when I see that, by the utmost indulgence of your imagination, you never get rid of the hypothesis of design in the universe, but are obliged at every turn to have recourse to it. To this concession I adhere steadily; and this I regard as a sufficient foundation for religion.

NOTES

1. *On the Nature of Things,* II, 1096–1099 (trans. by W. D. Rouse).
2. Tully was a common name for the Roman lawyer and philosopher, Marcus Tullius Cicero, 106–43 B.C.E. The excerpt is from *The Nature of the Gods,* I, viii, 19 (trans. by H. Rackham).

FOR FURTHER REFLECTION

1. Identify the positions of Demea, Cleanthes, and Philo. Outline Cleanthes' argument from design.
2. List six objections that Philo makes to the design argument and evaluate them. Can you think of ways of responding to Philo on any of these?
3. How effective are Hume's (Philo's) criticisms of the argument? Consider his contention that we can't argue from the part to a whole. Is that always true? Can we soetimes make valid inferences from a part to its whole? For example, if I discover that Pacific Ocean salt water taken from near a beach in southern California is undrinkable, can't I infer that the rest of the water in the Pacific Ocean is also probably undrinkable? This argument may be weak, but doesn't the part lend some probability to conclusions about the whole?

Anselm versus Gaunilo

THE ONTOLOGICAL ARGUMENT

Anselm (1003–1109), the great medieval philosopher, was born in the Italian province of Burgundy, joined a monastery in Normandy, and later in life became Archbishop of Canterbury in England. Anselm created one of the most intriguing arguments for God's existence ever devised, now known as the *ontological argument.* Although there are now many versions and interpretations of this argument, Anselm's proof, as it appears in his book *Proslogium* (1077), is the definitive version that philosophers continually turn to. The main elements of his argument are here:

1. God is that than which nothing greater can be conceived (i.e., the greatest possible being).
2. God exists at least in the understanding.
3. God might have existed in reality.
4. Existence in reality is greater than existence in the understanding alone.
5. Therefore, God exists in reality as well as in the understanding.

While Anselm was still alive, a monk named Gaunilo criticized that Anselm's type of argument would show the existence of the greatest possible anything. For example, if we begin with the imaginary concept of "an island than which none greater can be conceived," then, using Anselm's reasoning, we will conclude that this island actually exists. Anselm's reply to Gaunilo was that the ontological argument works only with the concept of the greatest possible being.

Things like islands are finite and composed of parts and, thus, the concept of "the greatest possible island" will never require its own existence.

ANSELM'S PRESENTATION

Chapter 2: Truly There Is a God

And so, Lord, you who gives understanding to faith, give me as much understanding as you know would be profitable, to know that you are as we believe and are that which we believe. And indeed, we believe that you are a being than which nothing greater can be conceived. Or is there no such thing, since the fool has said in his heart, there is no God? (Psalms 14:1). But in any case, this very fool, when he hears of this being of which I speak—a being than which nothing greater can be conceived—understands what he hears, and what he understands is in his thought, even though he does not understand it to exist.

For, it is one thing for an object to be in the understanding, and another to understand that the object exists. When a painter first conceives of what he will afterwards paint, he has it in his understanding, but he does not yet understand it to be, because he has not yet painted it. But after he has made the painting, he both has it in his understanding, and he understands that it exists, because he has made it.

Hence, even the fool is convinced that something exists in the understanding, at least, than which nothing greater can be conceived. For, when he hears of this, he understands it. And whatever is understood, exists in the understanding. And certainly that, than which nothing greater can be conceived, cannot exist in the understanding alone. For, suppose it exists in the understanding alone: then it can be conceived to exist in reality, which is greater.

Therefore, if that, than which nothing greater can be conceived, exists in the understanding alone, the very being than which nothing greater can be conceived, is one, than which a greater can be conceived. But obviously this is impossible. Therefore, there is no doubt that there exists a being than which nothing greater can be conceived, and it exists both in the understanding and in reality.

Chapter 3: God Cannot Be Conceived Not to Exist

And it certainly exists so truly, that it cannot be conceived not to exist. For, it is possible to conceive of a being which cannot be conceived not to exist; and this is greater than one which can be conceived not to exist. Hence, if that, than which nothing greater can be conceived, can be conceived not to exist, it is not that than which nothing greater can be conceived. But this is an irreconcilable contradiction. There is, then, so truly a being than which nothing greater can be conceived to exist, that it cannot even be conceived not to exist. And you, Lord God, are this being.

So certainly do you exist, Lord God, that you cannot be conceived not to exist. And rightly so since if a mind could conceive of a being better than you, the creature would rise above the Creator, which is absurd. And, indeed, whatever else there is aside from you alone can be conceived not to exist. You alone exist more truly than all other beings and in a higher degree than all others. For, whatever else exists does not exist so certainly, and hence in a less degree it belongs to it to exist. Why then did the fool said in his

From Anselm, *Prosolgium* (1077), Ch. 2–5; Gaunilo, *On Behalf of the Fool.*

heart "there is no God," since it is so evident to a rational mind that you do exist in the highest degree of all? Why, except that he is dense and foolish?

Chapter 4: How the Fool Has Said in His Heart What Cannot Be Conceived

But how has the fool said in his heart what he could not conceive? Or how is it that he could not conceive what he said in his heart, since it is the same to say in the heart, and to conceive?

But if he really he conceived it because he said it in his heart, and did not say in his heart, because he could not conceive, then there must be more than one way in which a thing is said in the heart or conceived. For, in one sense, an object is conceived when the word signifying it is conceived. In another sense it is conceived when the very entity, which the object is, is understood.

In this first sense, then, God can be conceived not to exist; but not at all in this second sense. For no one who understands what fire and water are can conceive fire to be water, according to the nature of the facts themselves, although this is possible according to the words. Thus, no one who understands what God is can conceive that God does not exist, although he says these words in his heart, either without any or with some foreign meaning. For, God is that than which a greater cannot be conceived. And he who thoroughly understands this, certainly understands that this being so truly exists, that not even in concept can it be non–existent. Therefore, he who understands that God so exists, cannot conceive that he does not exist.

I thank you, gracious Lord, I thank you, because what I formerly believed by your gift I now understand through your illumination, that if I were unwilling to believe that you do exist, I should not be able to not understand this to be true.

Chapter 5: God Is Whatever It Is Better to Be Than Not to Be

What are you, then, Lord God, than whom nothing greater can be conceived? But what are you, except that which, as the highest of all beings, alone exists through itself, and creates all other things from nothing? For, whatever is not this is less than a thing which can be conceived of. But this cannot be conceived of you. What good, therefore, does the supreme Good lack, through which every good is? Therefore, you are just, truthful, holy, and whatever it is better to be than not to be. For it is better to be just than not just; better to be holy than not holy.

GAUNILON'S CRITICISM

It is said that somewhere in the ocean is an island, which, because of the difficulty and even impossibility of discovering what does not exist, is called the lost island. And they say that this island has an immeasurable wealth of all types of riches and delicacies in greater abundance than is said about the Islands of the Blessed [that is, Hesperides in Greek mythology]. Having no owner or residents, it is more excellent in its stockpile of abundance than all other countries that are inhabited by humans.

Now if someone would tell me that there is such an island, I would easily understand his words; this presents no difficulty. But suppose that he went on to say, as if by a logical inference: "You can no longer doubt that this island which is more excellent than all lands exists somewhere, since you have no doubt that it is in your understanding. And since it is more excellent not to be in the understanding alone, but to exist both in the understanding and in reality, for this reason it must exist. For if it does not exist, any land which really exists will be more excellent than it; and so the island already understood by you to be more excellent will not be more excellent."

Suppose that a person tried to prove to me by this reasoning that this island actually exists, and that its existence should no longer be doubted. Either I would believe that he was joking, or I would not know which I ought to regard as the greater fool: perhaps myself for supposing that I should allow this proof, perhaps him for supposing that he had established with any certainty the existence of this island. For he ought to first show that the hypothetical excellence of this island exists as a real and positive fact, and in no way as an unreal object or one whose existence is uncertain in my understanding.

ANSELM'S REPLY

You say it is as if one should suppose an island in the ocean, which surpasses all lands in its fertility, and which, because of the difficulty and even impossibility of discovering what does not exist, is called a lost island. And one should say further that there can be no doubt that this island actually exists in reality since one who hears it described easily understands what he hears.

Now I confidently promise that if any person devises anything existing either in reality or in concept alone (except that than which a greater be conceived) to which he can adapt the sequence of my reasoning, I will discover that thing, and will give him his lost island, not to be lost again.

But it now appears that this being than which a greater is inconceivable cannot be conceived not to be, because it exists on so assured a ground of truth. For otherwise it would not exist at all.

Hence, if any one says that he conceives this being not to exist, I say that at the time when he conceives of this either he conceives of a being than which a greater is inconceivable, or he does not conceive at all. If he does not conceive, he does not conceive of the non–existence of that of which he does not conceive. But if he does conceive, he certainly conceives of a being which cannot be even conceived not to exist. For if it could be conceived not to exist, it could be conceived to have a beginning and an end. But this is impossible.

He, then, who conceives of this being conceives of a being which cannot be even conceived not to exist; but he who conceives of this being does not conceive that it does not exist; otherwise he conceives what is inconceivable. The non–existence, then, of that than which a greater cannot be conceived is inconceivable.

You say, moreover, that whereas I assert that this supreme being cannot be conceived not to exist, it might better be said that its non–existence, or even the possibility of its non–existence, cannot be understood.

But it would be more proper to say that it cannot be conceived. For if I had said that the object itself cannot be understood not to exist, possibly you yourself (who say that in accordance with the true meaning of the term what is unreal cannot be understood) would offer the objection that nothing which is can be understood not to be, for the non–existence of what exists is unreal. Hence God would not be the only being about which it could be said that it is impossible to understand its non–existence. For thus one of those beings which most certainly exist can be understood not to exist in the same way in which certain other real objects can be understood not to exist.

But this objection certainly cannot be urged against the term conception, if one considers the matter well. For although no objects which exist can be understood not to exist, yet all objects, except that which exists in the highest degree, can be conceived not to exist. For all those objects, and those alone, can be conceived not to exist, which have a beginning or end or composition of parts (also, as I have already said, whatever at any place or at any time does not exist as a whole).

That being alone, on the other hand, cannot be conceived not to exist, in which any conception discovers neither beginning nor end nor composition of parts, and which any conception finds always and everywhere as a whole.

Be assured, then, that you can conceive of your own non–existence, although you are most certain that you exist. I am surprised that you should have admitted that you are ignorant of this. For we conceive of the non–existence of many objects which we know to exist, and of the existence of many which we know not to exist. We do not do this by forming the opinion that they so exist, but by imagining that they exist as we conceive of them.

And indeed, we can conceive of the non–existence of an object, although we know it to exist, because at the same time we can conceive of the former and know the latter. And we cannot conceive of the nonexistence of an object, so long as we know it to exist, because we cannot conceive at the same time of existence and non–existence.

If, then, one will thus distinguish these two senses of this statement, he will understand that nothing, so long as it is known to exist, can be conceived not to exist. And whatever exists, except that being than which a greater cannot be conceived, can be conceived not to exist, even when it is known to exist.

So, then, it is of God alone that we can say that it is impossible to conceive of his non–existence, even though in one sense there are many objects which, so long as they exist, cannot be conceived not to exist. But in what sense God is to be conceived not to exist, I think has been shown clearly enough in my book.

FOR FURTHER REFLECTION

1. Anselm begins his argument with a prayer to God indicating that he already believes in God through faith, but seeks understanding. Is this significant for understanding his argument?

2. Explain Gaunilo's argument using your own example, such as "a rock star than which none greater can be conceived." Explain whether or not your example sufficiently parallels Anselm's argument regarding "a being than which nothing greater can be conceived."

3. Some philosophers have objected that Anselm misunderstands the concept of *being*. Being is not an ordinary concept like *red* or *horse*; rather, it is a primary concept that asserts that these other secondary concepts are present (e.g., a being that is red, a being that is a horse). Anselm seems to make being a secondary concept (e.g., a thing that is a being), which makes no sense. Is the critic correct? Why or why not?

4. Could an argument similar to Anselm's be used to prove that a perfectly powerful devil exists as the supreme being and creator of the universe?

F. C. COPLESTON AND BERTRAND RUSSELL

A DEBATE ON THE ARGUMENT FROM RELIGIOUS EXPERIENCE

This selection continues the debate begun in an earlier reading. Here Copleston turns to the argument from religious experience, "a loving, but unclear, awareness of some object which irresistibly seems to the experiencer as something transcending the self, something transcending all the normal objects of experience, something which cannot be pictured or conceptualized, but of the reality of which doubt is impossible—at least during the experience." Russell argues that such experience cannot be used to infer the existence of a supreme being and that it can have natural explanations.

From Bertrand Russell, *Why I Am Not a Christian* (London: Allen & Unwin, 1957). Copyright © 1957, 1985 by Allen & Unwin Ltd. Reprinted by permission of Taylor & Francis Books UK and The Bertrand Russell Peace Foundation.

Copleston: . . . Well, perhaps I might say a word about religious experience, and then we can go on to moral experience. I don't regard religious experience as a strict proof of the existence of God, so the character of the discussion changes somewhat, but I think it's true to say that the best explanation of it is the existence of God. By religious experience I don't mean simply feeling good. I mean a loving, but unclear, awareness of some object which irresistibly seems to the experiencer as something transcending the self, something transcending all the normal objects of experience, something which cannot be pictured or conceptualized, but of the reality of which doubt is impossible—at least during the experience. I should claim that cannot be explained adequately and without residue, simply subjectively. The actual basic experience at any rate is most easily explained on the hypothesis that there is actually some objective cause of that experience.

Russell: I should reply to that line of argument that the whole argument from our own mental states to something outside us, is a very tricky affair. Even where we all admit its validity, we only feel justified in doing so, I think, because of the consensus of mankind. If there's a crowd in a room and there's a clock in a room, they can all see the clock. The fact that they can all see it tends to make them think that it's not an hallucination: whereas the religious experiences do tend to be very private.

Copleston: Yes, they do. I'm speaking strictly of mystical experience proper, and I certainly don't include, by the way, what are called visions. I mean simply the experience, and I quite admit it's indefinable, of the transcendent object or of what seems to be a transcendent object. I remember Julian Huxley in some lecture saying that religious experience, or mystical experience, is as much a real experience as falling in love or appreciating poetry and art. Well, I believe that when we appreciate poetry and art we appreciate definite poems or a definite work of art. If we fall in love, well, we fall in love with somebody and not with nobody.

Russell: May I interrupt for a moment here. That is by no means always the case. Japanese novelists never consider that they have achieved a success

unless large numbers of real people commit suicide for love of the imaginary heroine.

Copleston: Well, I must take your word for these goings on in Japan. I haven't committed suicide, I'm glad to say, but I have been strongly influenced in the taking of two important steps in my life by two biographies. However, I must say I see little resemblance between the real influence of those books on me and the mystic experience proper, so far, that is, as an outsider can obtain an idea of that experience.

Russell: Well, I mean we wouldn't regard God as being on the same level as the characters in a work of fiction. You'll admit there's a distinction here?

Copleston: I certainly should. But what I'd say is that the best explanation seems to be the not purely subjectivist explanation. Of course, a subjectivist explanation is possible in the case of certain people in whom there is little relation between the experience and life, in the case of deluded people and hallucinated people, and so on. But when you get what one might call the pure type, say St. Francis of Assisi, when you get an experience that results in an overflow of dynamic and creative love, the best explanation of that it seems to me is the actual existence of an objective cause of the experience.

Russell: Well, I'm not contending in a dogmatic way that there is not a God. What I'm contending is that we don't know that there is. I can only take what is recorded as I should take other records and I do find that a very great many things are reported, and I am sure you would not accept things about demons and devils and what not—and they're reported in exactly the same tone of voice and with exactly the same conviction. And the mystic, if his vision is veridical, may be said to know that there are devils. But I don't know that there are.

Copleston: But surely in the case of the devils there have been people speaking mainly of visions, appearances, angels or demons and so on. I should rule out the visual appearances, because I think they can be explained apart from the existence of the object which is supposed to be seen.

Russell: But don't you think there are abundant recorded cases of people who believe that they've heard Satan speaking to them in their hearts, in just the same way as the mystics assert God—and I'm not talking now of an external vision, I'm talking of a purely mental experience. That seems to be an experience of the same sort as mystics' experience of God, and I don't see that from what mystics tell us you can get any argument for God which is not equally an argument for Satan.

Copleston: I quite agree, of course, that people have imagined or thought they have heard or seen Satan. And I have no wish in passing to deny the existence of Satan. But I do not think that people have claimed to have experienced Satan in the precise way in which mystics claim to have experienced God. Take the case of a non-Christian, Plotinus. He admits the experience is something inexpressible, the object is an object of love, and therefore, not an object that causes horror and disgust. And the effect of that experience is, I should say, borne out, or I mean the validity of the experience is borne out in the records of the life of Plotinus. At any rate it is more reasonable to suppose that he had that experience if we're willing to accept Porphyry's account of Plotinus's general kindness and benevolence.

Russell: The fact that a belief has a good moral effect upon a man is no evidence whatsoever in favor of its truth.

Copleston: No, but if it could actually be proved that the belief was actually responsible for a good effect on a man's life, I should consider it a presumption in favor of some truth, at any rate of the positive part of the belief if not of its entire validity. But in any case I am using the character of the life as evidence in favor of the mystic's veracity and sanity rather than as a proof of the truth of his beliefs.

Russell: But even that I don't think is any evidence. I've had experiences myself that have altered my character profoundly. And I thought at the time at any rate that it was altered for the good. Those experiences were important, but they did not involve the existence of something outside me, and I don't think that if I'd thought they did, the fact that they had a wholesome effect would have been any evidence that I was right.

Copleston: No, but I think that the good effect would attest your veracity in describing your experi-

ence. Please remember that I'm not saying that a mystic's mediation or interpretation of his experience should be immune from discussion or criticism.

Russell: Obviously the character of a young man may be—and often is—immensely affected for good by reading about some great man in history, and it may happen that the great man is a myth and doesn't exist, but the boy is just as much affected for good as if he did. There have been such people. Plutarch's *Lives* take Lycurgus as an example, who certainly did not exist, but you might be very much influenced by reading Lycurgus under the impression that he had previously existed. You would then be influenced by an object that you'd loved, but it wouldn't be an existing object.

Copleston: I agree with you on that, of course, that a man may be influenced by a character in fiction. Without going into the question of what it is precisely that influences him (I should say a real value) I think that the situation of that man and of the mystic are different. After all the man who is influenced by Lycurgus hasn't got the irresistible impression that he's experienced in some way the ultimate reality.

Russell: I don't think you've quite got my point about these historical characters—these unhistorical characters in history. I'm not assuming what you call an effect on the reason. I'm assuming that the young man reading about this person and believing him to be real loves him—which is quite easy to happen, and yet he's loving a phantom.

Copleston: In one sense he's loving a phantom, that's perfectly true, in the sense, I mean, that he's loving X or Y who doesn't exist. But at the same time, it is not, I think, the phantom as such that the young man loves; he perceives a real value, an idea which he recognizes as objectively valid, and that's what excites his love.

Russell: Well, in the same sense we had before about the characters in fiction.

Copleston: Yes, in one sense the man's loving a phantom—perfectly true. But in another sense he's loving what he perceives to be a value.

FOR FURTHER REFLECTION

1. Outline Copleston's argument that religious experience justifies belief in God's existence.

2. What are Russell's objections to Copleston's argument? Are they compelling considerations? Why or why not?

C. D. BROAD

THE ARGUMENT FROM RELIGIOUS EXPERIENCE

C. D. Broad (1887–1971) was a professor of philosophy at Cambridge University who wrote prolifically on philosophy of mind, philosophy of religion, and psychical research. In his article "The Argument from Religious Experience," he considers the extent to which we can infer from religious experience to the existence of God. Broad likens the religious sense to an ear for music. There are a few people on the negative end who are spiritually tone deaf and a few on the positive end who are the founders of religions, the Bachs and Beethovens. In between are the ordinary followers of religion, who are like the average musical listeners, and above them are the saints, who are likened to those with a very fine ear for music.

The chief difference is that religion, unlike music, says something about the nature of reality. Is what it says true? And does religious experience lend any support to the truth claims of religion? Is religious experience veridical? Are the claims about the "nature of reality," which are an integral part of the experience, true or probable? Broad carefully considers these questions.

I shall confine myself in this article to specifically religious experience and the argument for the existence of God which has been based on it.

This argument differs in the following important respect from the other two empirical types of argument. The Argument from Design and the arguments from ethical premises start from facts which are common to every one. But some people seem to be almost wholly devoid of any specifically religious experience; and among those who have it the differences of kind and degree are enormous. Founders of religions and saints, e.g., often claim to have been in direct contact with God, to have seen and spoken with Him, and so on. An ordinary religious man would certainly not make any such claim, though he might say that he had had experiences which assured him of the existence and presence of God. So the first thing that we have to notice is that capacity for religious experience is in certain respects like an ear for music. There are a few people who are unable to recognize

Reprinted from C. D. Broad, "Arguments for the Existence of God," in *The Journal of Theological Studies* 40 (1939), by permission of Oxford University Press.

and distinguish the simplest tune. But they are in a minority, like the people who have absolutely no kind of religious experience. Most people have some light appreciation of music. But the differences of degree in this respect are enormous, and those who have not much gift for music have to take the statements of accomplished musicians very largely on trust. Let us, then, compare tone-deaf persons to those who have no recognizable religious experience at all; the ordinary followers of a religion to men who have some taste for music but can neither appreciate the more difficult kinds nor compose; highly religious men and saints to persons with an exceptionally fine ear for music who may yet be unable to compose it; and the founders of religions to great musical composers, such as Bach and Beethoven.

This analogy is, of course, incomplete in certain important respects. Religious experience raises three problems, which are different though closely interconnected. (i) What is the *psychological analysis* of religious experience? Does it contain factors which are present also in certain experiences which are not religious? Does it contain any factor which never occurs in any other kind of experience? If it contains no such factor, but is a blend of elements each of which can occur separately or in non-religious experiences, its psychological peculiarity must consist in the characteristic way in which these elements are blended in it. Can this peculiar structural feature of religious experience be indicated and described? (ii) What are the *genetic and causal conditions* of the existence of religious experience? Can we trace the origin and development of the disposition to have religious experiences (*a*) in the human race, and (*b*) in each individual? Granted that the disposition is present in nearly all individuals at the present time, can we discover and state the variable conditions which call it into activity on certain occasions and leave it in abeyance on others? (iii) Part of the content of religious experience is alleged knowledge or well-founded belief about the nature of reality, e.g., that we are dependent on a being who loves us and whom we ought to worship, that values are somehow conserved in spite of the chances and changes of the material world at the mercy of which they seem *prima facie* to be, and so on. Therefore there is a third problem.

Granted that religious experience exists, that it has such-and-such a history and conditions, that it seems vitally important to those who have it, and that it produces all kinds of effects which would not otherwise happen, is it *veridical?* Are the claims to knowledge or well-founded belief about the nature of reality, which are an integral part of the experience, *true or probable?* Now, in the case of musical experience, there are analogies to the psychological problem and to the genetic or causal problem, but there is no analogy to the epistemological problem of validity. For, so far as I am aware, no part of the content of musical experience is alleged knowledge about the nature of reality; and therefore no question of its being veridical or delusive can arise.

Since both musical experience and religious experience certainly exist, any theory of the universe which was incompatible with their existence would be false, and any theory which failed to show the connexion between their existence and the other facts about reality would be inadequate. So far the two kinds of experience are in exactly the same position. But a theory which answers to the condition that it allows of the *existence* of religious experience and indicates the *connexion* between its existence and other facts about reality may leave the question as to its *validity* quite unanswered. Or, alternatively, it may throw grave doubt on its cognitive claims, or else it may tend to support them. Suppose, e.g., that it could be shown that religious experience contains no elements which are not factors in other kinds of experience. Suppose further it could be shown that this particular combination of factors tends to originate and to be activated only under certain conditions which are known to be very commonly productive of false beliefs held with strong conviction. Then a satisfactory answer to the questions of psychological analysis and causal antecedents would have tended to answer the epistemological question of validity in the negative. On the other hand, it might be that the only theory which would satisfactorily account for the origin of the religious disposition and for the occurrence of actual religious experiences under certain conditions was a theory which allowed some of the cognitive claims made by religious experience to be true or probable. Thus the three problems, though entirely distinct from each other, may be very closely connected; and it is the existence of the third problem in connexion with religious experience which puts it, for the present purpose, in a different category from musical experience.

In spite of this essential difference the analogy is not to be despised, for it brings out at least one important point. If a man who had no ear for music were to give himself airs on that account, and were to talk *de haut en bas* about those who can appreciate music and think it highly important, we should regard him, not as an advanced thinker, but as a self-satisfied Philistine. And, then if he did not do this but only propounded theories about the nature and causation of musical experience, we might think it reasonable to feel very doubtful whether his theories would be adequate or correct. In the same way, when persons without religious experience regard themselves as being *on that ground* superior to those who have it, their attitude must be treated as merely silly and offensive. Similarly, any theories about religious experience constructed by persons who have little or none of their own should be regarded with grave suspicion. (For that reason it would be unwise to attach very much weight to anything that the present writer may say on this subject.)

On the other hand, we must remember that the possession of a great capacity for religious experience, like the possession of a great capacity for musical appreciation and composition, is no guarantee of high general intelligence. A man may be a saint or a magnificent musician and yet have very little common sense, very little power of accurate introspection or of seeing causal connexions, and scarcely any capacity for logical criticism. He may also be almost as ignorant about other aspects of reality as the non-musical or non-religious man is about musical or religious experience. If such a man starts to theorize about music or religion, his theories may be quite as absurd, though in a different way, as those made by persons who are devoid of musical or religious experience. Fortunately it happens that some religious mystics of a high order have been extremely good at introspecting and describing their own experiences. And some highly religious persons have had very great critical and philosophical abilities. St.

Teresa is an example of the first, and St. Thomas Aquinas of the second.

Now I think it must be admitted that, if we compare and contrast the statements made by religious mystics of various times, races, and religions, we find a common nucleus combined with very great differences of detail. Of course the interpretations which they have put on their experiences are much more varied than the experiences themselves. It is obvious that the interpretations will depend in a large measure on the traditional religious beliefs in which various mystics have been brought up. I think that such traditions probably act in two different ways.

(i) The tradition no doubt affects the theoretical interpretation of experiences which would have taken place even if the mystic had been brought up in a different tradition. A feeling of unity with the rest of the universe will be interpreted very differently by a Christian who has been brought up to believe in a personal God and by a Hindu mystic who has been trained in a quite different metaphysical tradition.

(ii) The traditional beliefs, on the other hand, probably determine many of the details of the experience itself. A Roman Catholic mystic may have visions of the Virgin and the saints, whilst a Protestant mystic pretty certainly will not.

Thus the relations between the experiences and the traditional beliefs are highly complex. Presumably the outlines of the belief are determined by the experience. Then the details of the belief are fixed for a certain place and period by the special peculiarities of the experiences had by the founder of a certain religion. These beliefs then become traditional in that religion. Thenceforth they in part determine the details of the experiences had by subsequent mystics of that religion, and still more do they determine the interpretations which these mystics will put upon their experiences. Therefore, when a set of religious beliefs has once been established, it no doubt tends to produce experiences which can plausibly be taken as evidence for it. If it is a tradition in a certain religion that one can communicate with saints, mystics of that religion will seem to see and to talk with saints in their mystical visions; and this fact will be taken as further evidence for the belief that one can communicate with saints.

Much the same double process of causation takes place in sense-perception. On the one hand, the beliefs and expectations which we have at any moment largely determine what *interpretation* we shall put on a certain sensation which we should in any case have had then. On the other hand, our beliefs and expectations do to some extent determine and modify some of the sensible characteristics of the *sensa themselves.* When I am thinking only of diagrams a certain visual stimulus may produce a sensation of a sensibly flat sensum; but a precisely similar stimulus may produce a sensation of a sensibly solid sensum when I am thinking of solid objects.

Such explanations, however, plainly do not account for the first origin of religious beliefs, or for the features which are common to the religious experiences of persons of widely different times, races, and traditions.

Now, when we find that there are certain experiences which, though never very frequent in a high degree of intensity, have happened in a high degree among a few men at all times and places; and when we find that, in spite of differences in detail which we can explain, they involve certain fundamental conditions which are common and peculiar to them; two alternatives are open to us. (i) We may suppose that these men are in contact with an aspect of reality which is not revealed to ordinary persons in their everyday experience. And we may suppose that the characteristics which they agree in ascribing to reality on the basis of these experiences probably do belong to it. Or (ii) we may suppose that they are all subject to a delusion from which other men are free. In order to illustrate these alternatives it will be useful to consider three partly analogous cases, two of which are real and the third imaginary.

(*a*) Most of the detailed facts which biologists tells us about the minute structure and changes in cells can be perceived only by persons who have had a long training in the use of the microscope. In this case we believe that the agreement among trained microscopists really does correspond to facts which untrained persons cannot perceive. (*b*) Persons of all races who habitually drink alcohol to excess eventually have perceptual experiences in which they seem to themselves to see snakes or rats crawling about

their rooms or beds. In this case we believe that this agreement among drunkards is merely a uniform hallucination. (*c*) Let us now imagine a race of beings who can walk about and touch things but cannot see. Suppose that eventually a few of them developed the power of sight. All that they might tell their still blind friends about colour would be wholly unintelligible to and unverifiable by the latter. But they would also be able to tell their blind friends a great deal about what the latter would feel if they were to walk in certain directions. These statements would be verified. This would not, of course, *prove* to the blind ones that the unintelligible statements about colour correspond to certain aspects of the world which they cannot perceive. But it would show that the seeing persons had a source of additional information about matters which the blind ones could understand and test for themselves. It would not be unreasonable then for the blind ones to believe that probably the seeing ones are also able to perceive other aspects of reality which they are describing correctly when they make their unintelligible statements containing colour-names. The question then is whether it is reasonable to regard the agreement between the experiences of religious mystics as more like the agreement among trained microscopists about the minute structure of cells, or as more like the agreement among habitual drunkards about the infestation of their rooms by pink rats or snakes, or as more like the agreement about colours which the seeing men would express in their statements to the blind men.

Why do we commonly believe that habitual excess of alcohol is a cause of a uniform delusion and not a source of additional information? The main reason is as follows. The things which drunkards claim to perceive are not fundamentally different in kind from the things that other people perceive. We have all seen rats and snakes, though the rats have generally been grey or brown and not pink. Moreover the drunkard claims that the rats and snakes which he sees are literally present in his room and on his bed, in the same sense in which his bed is in his room and his quilt is on his bed. Now we may fairly argue as follows. Since these are the sort of things which we could see if they were there, the fact that we cannot see them makes it highly probable that they are not there. Again, we know what kinds of perceptible effect would generally follow from the presence in a room of such things as rats or snakes. We should expect fox-terriers or mongooses to show traces of excitement, cheese to be nibbled, corn to disappear from bins, and so on. We find that no such effects are observed in the bedrooms of persons suffering from *delirium tremens*. It therefore seems reasonable to conclude that the agreement among drunkards is a sign, not of a revelation, but of a delusion.

Now the assertions in which religious mystics agree are not such that they conflict with what we can perceive with our senses. They are about the structure and organization of the world as a whole and about the relations of men to the rest of it. And they have so little in common with the facts of daily life that there is not much chance of direct collision. I think that there is only one important point on which there is conflict. Nearly all mystics seem to be agreed that time and change and unchanging duration are unreal or extremely superficial, whilst these seem to plain men to be the most fundamental features of the world. But we must admit, on the one hand, that these temporal characteristics present very great philosophical difficulties and puzzles when we reflect upon them. On the other hand, we may well suppose that the mystic finds it impossible to state clearly in ordinary language what it is that he experiences about the facts which underlie the appearance of time and change and duration. Therefore it is not difficult to allow that what we experience as the temporal aspect of reality corresponds in some sense to certain facts, and yet that these facts appear to us in so distorted a form in our ordinary experience that a person who sees them more accurately and directly might refuse to apply temporal names to them.

Let us next consider why we feel fairly certain that the agreement among trained microscopists about the minute structure of cells expresses an objective fact, although we cannot get similar experiences. One reason is that we have learned enough, from simpler cases of visual perception, about the laws of optics to know that the arrangement of lenses in a microscope is such that it will reveal minute structure, which is otherwise invisible, and will not simply create optical delusions. Another reason is that we know of other cases in which trained persons can detect things which untrained people will overlook, and that in many cases the existence of these things can be verified by indirect methods. Probably most of us have experienced such results of training in our own lives.

Now religious experience is not in nearly such a strong position as this. We do not know much about the laws which govern its occurrence and determine its variations. No doubt there are certain standard methods of training and meditation which tend to produce mystical experiences. These have been elaborated to some extent by certain Western mystics and to a very much greater extent by Eastern Yogis. But I do not think that we can see here, as we can in the case of microscopes and the training which is required to make the best use of them, any conclusive reason why these methods should produce veridical rather than delusive experiences. Uniform methods of training and meditation would be likely to produce more or less similar experiences, whether these experiences were largely veridical or wholly delusive.

Is there any analogy between the facts about religious experience and the fable about the blind men some of whom gained the power of sight? It might be said that many ideals of conduct and ways of life, which we can all recognize now to be good and useful, have been introduced into human history by the founders of religions. These persons have made actual ethical discoveries which others can afterwards recognize to be true. It might be said that this is at least roughly analogous to the case of the seeing men telling the still blind men of facts which the latter could and did verify for themselves. And it might be said that this makes it reasonable for us to attach some weight to what founders of religions tell us about things which we cannot understand or verify for ourselves; just as it would have been reasonable for the blind men to attach some weight to the unintelligible statements which the seeing men made to them about colours.

I think that this argument deserves a certain amount of respect, though I should find it hard to estimate how much weight to attach to it. I should be inclined to sum up as follows. When there is a nucleus of agreement between the experiences of men in different places, times, and traditions, and when they all tend to put much the same kind of interpretation on the cognitive content of these experiences, it is reasonable to ascribe this agreement to their all being in contact with a certain objective aspect of reality *unless* there be some positive reason to think otherwise. The practical postulate which we go upon everywhere else is to treat cognitive claims as veridical unless there be some positive reason to think them delusive. This, after all, is our only guarantee for believing that ordinary sense-perception is veridical. We cannot *prove* that what people agree in perceiving really exists independently of them; but we do always assume that ordinary waking sense-perception is veridical unless we can produce some positive ground for thinking that it is delusive in any given case. I think it would be inconsistent to treat the experiences of religious mystics on different principles. So far as they agree they should be provisionally accepted as veridical unless there be some positive ground for thinking that they are not. So the next question is whether there is any positive ground for holding that they are delusive.

There are two circumstances which have been commonly held to cast doubt on the cognitive claims of religious and mystical experience. (i) It is alleged that founders of religions and saints have nearly always had certain neuropathic symptoms or certain bodily weaknesses, and that these would be likely to produce delusions. Even if we accept the premisses, I do not think that this is a very strong argument. (*a*) It is equally true that many founders of religions and saints have exhibited great endurance and great power of organization and business capacity which would have made them extremely successful and competent in secular affairs. There are very few offices in the cabinet or in the highest branches of the civil service which St. Thomas Aquinas could not have held with conspicuous success. I do not, of course, regard this as a positive reason *for* accepting the metaphysical doctrines which saints and founders of religions have based on their experiences; but it is relevant as a *rebuttal* of the argument which we are considering. (*b*) Probably very few people of extreme genius in science or art are perfectly normal mentally or physically, and some of them are very crazy and eccentric indeed. Therefore it would be rather surprising if persons of religious genius were completely normal,

whether their experiences be veridical or delusive. (*c*) Suppose, for the sake of argument, that there is an aspect of the world which remains altogether outside the ken of ordinary persons in their daily life. Then it seems very likely that some degree of mental and physical abnormality would be a necessary condition for getting sufficiently loosened from the objects of ordinary sense-perception to come into cognitive contact with this aspect of reality. Therefore the fact that those persons who claim to have this peculiar kind of cognition generally exhibit certain mental and physical abnormalities is rather what might be anticipated if their claims were true. One might need to be slightly 'cracked' in order to have some peep-holes into the super-sensible world. (*d*) If mystical experience were veridical, it seems quite likely that it would *produce* abnormalities of behaviour in those who had it strongly. Let us suppose, for the sake of argument, that those who have religious experience are in frequent contact with an aspect of reality of which most men get only rare and faint glimpses. Then such persons are, as it were, living in two worlds, while the ordinary man is living in only one of them. Or, again, they might be compared to a man who has to conduct his life with one ordinary eye and another of a telescopic kind. Their behaviour may be appropriate to the aspect of reality which they alone perceive and think all-important; but, for that very reason, it may be inappropriate to those other aspects of reality which are all that most men perceive or judge to be important and on which all our social institutions and conventions are built.

(ii) A second reason which is commonly alleged for doubt about the claims of religious experience is the following. It is said that such experience always originates from and remains mixed with certain other factors, e.g., sexual emotion, which are such that experiences and beliefs that arise from them are very likely to be delusive. I think that there are a good many confusions on this point, and it will be worth while to begin by indicating some of them.

When people say that B "originated from" A, they are liable to confuse at least three different kinds of connexion between A and B. (i) It might be that A is a necessary but insufficient condition of the existence of B. (ii) It might be that A is a necessary and sufficient condition of the existence of B. Or (iii) it might be that B simply *is* A in a more complex and disguised form. Now, when there is in fact evidence only for the first kind of connexion, people are very liable to jump to the conclusion that there is the third kind of connexion. It may well be the case, e.g., that no one who was incapable of strong sexual desires and emotions could have anything worth calling religious experience. But it is plain that the possession of a strong capacity for sexual experience is not a *sufficient* condition of having a religious experience; for we know that the former quite often exists in persons who show hardly any trace of the latter. But, even if it could be shown that a strong capacity for sexual desire and emotion is *both* necessary and sufficient to produce religious experience, it would not follow that the latter is just the former in disguise. In the first place, it is not at all easy to discover the exact meaning of this metaphorical phrase when it is applied to psychological topics. And, if we make use of physical analogies, we are not much helped. A mixture of oxygen and hydrogen in presence of a spark is necessary and sufficient to produce water accompanied by an explosion. But water accompanied by an explosion is not a mixture of oxygen and hydrogen and a spark "in a disguised form", whatever that may mean.

Now I think that the present rather vaguely formulated objection to the validity of the claims of religious experience might be stated somewhat as follows. "In the individual, religious experience originates from, and always remains mixed with, sexual desires and emotions. The other generative factor of it is the religious tradition of the society in which he lives, the teachings of his parents, nurses, schoolmasters, etc. In the race religious experience originated from a mixture of false beliefs about nature and man, irrational fears, sexual and other impulses, and so on. Thus the religious tradition arose from beliefs which we now recognize to have been false and from emotions which we now recognize to have been irrelevant and misleading. It is now drilled into children by those who are in authority over them at a time of life when they are intellectually and emotionally at much the same stage as the primitive savages among whom it originated. It is, therefore, readily accepted, and it determines beliefs and emotional dispositions which persist long after the child has grown up and acquired more adequate knowledge of nature and of himself."

Persons who use this argument might admit that it does not definitely *prove* that religious beliefs are false and groundless. False beliefs and irrational fears in our remote ancestors *might* conceivably be the origin of true beliefs and of an appropriate feeling of awe and reverence in ourselves. And, if sexual desires and emotions be an essential condition and constituent of religious experience, the experience *may* nevertheless be veridical in important respects. We might merely have to rewrite one of the beatitudes and say "Blessed are the *impure* in heart, for they shall see God." But, although it is logically possible that such causes should produce such effects, it would be said that they are most unlikely to do so. They seem much more likely to produce false beliefs and misplaced emotions.

It is plain that this argument has considerable plausibility. But it is worth while to remember that modern science has almost as humble an ancestry as contemporary religion. If the primitive witch-smeller is the spiritual progenitor of the Archbishop of Canterbury, the primitive rain-maker is equally the spiritual progenitor of the Cavendish Professor of Physics. There has obviously been a gradual refinement and purification of religious beliefs and concepts in the course of history, just as there has been in the beliefs and concepts of science. Certain persons of religious genius, such as some of the Hebrew prophets and the founders of Christianity and of Buddhism, do seem to have introduced new ethico-religious concepts and beliefs which have won wide acceptance, just as certain men of scientific genius, such as Galileo, Newton, and Einstein, have done in the sphere of science. It seems somewhat arbitrary to count this process as a continual approximation to true knowledge of the material aspect of the world in the case of science, and to refuse to regard it as at all similar in the case of religion. Lastly, we must remember that all of us have accepted the current common-sense and scientific view of the material world on the authority of our parents, nurses, masters, and companions at a time when we had neither the power nor the inclination to criticize it. And most of us accept, without even understanding, the more recondite doctrines of contemporary physics simply on the authority of those whom we have been taught to regard as experts.

On the whole, then, I do not think that what we know of the conditions under which religious beliefs and emotions have arisen in the life of the individual and the race makes it reasonable to think that they are *specially* likely to be delusive or misdirected. At any rate any argument which starts from that basis and claims to reach such a conclusion will need to be very carefully handled if its destructive effects are to be confined within the range contemplated by its users. It is reasonable to think that the concepts and beliefs of even the most perfect religions known to us are extremely inadequate to the facts which they express; that they are highly confused and are mixed up with a great deal of positive error and sheer nonsense; and that, if the human race goes on and continues to have religious experiences and to reflect on them, they will be altered and improved almost out of recognition. But all this could be said, *mutatis mutandis,* of scientific concepts and theories. The claim of any particu-

lar religion or sect to have complete or final truth on these subjects seems to me to be too ridiculous to be worth a moment's consideration. But the opposite extreme of holding that the whole religious experience of mankind is a gigantic system of pure delusion seems to me to be almost (though not quite) as far-fetched.

FOR FURTHER REFLECTION

1. Is Broad's analogy between religious experience and music valid? Why or why not?
2. Broad's principle of credulity can be summarized thus: that if there is no positive reason for thinking that certain experiences are delusive, then if there is considerable agreement among observers as to what they are experiencing, it is reasonable to conclude that the experiences are veridical. Do you agree? Explain.
3. Discuss the idea that religious experiences can be adequately explained by natural causes.

B. THE PROBLEM OF EVIL

> Is he willing to prevent evil, but not able? then he is impotent. Is he able, but not willing? then he is malevolent. Is he both able and willing? whence then is evil?
>
> *Epicurus, 341–270 B.C.E.*

We have been looking at arguments in favor of God's existence. The agnostic and atheist usually base their cases on the *absence* of evidence of God's existence. But they also have an argument *for* disbelief: the existence of evil. From it the "atheologian" (someone who argues against the existence of God) hopes either (1) to neutralize any positive evidence for God's existence based on whatever in the traditional arguments survives his or her criticism, or (2) to demonstrate that it is unreasonable to believe in God.

The problem of evil arises because it is paradoxical of an omnibenevolent, omnipotent deity to allow the existence of evil. The Judeo-Christian tradition has affirmed these three propositions:

1. *God is all-powerful (including omniscient).*
2. *God is perfectly good.*
3. *Evil exists.*

But if he is perfectly good, why does he allow evil to exist? Why didn't he create a better world, if not with no evil, at least with substantially less evil than in this world? Many have contended that this paradox, first schematized by Epicurus, is worse than a paradox—it is an implicit contradiction, because it contains premises that are inconsistent with one another. These people argue something like the following:

4. *If God (an all-powerful, omniscient, omnibenevolent being) existed, there would be no (or no unnecessary) evil in the world.*
5. *There is evil (or unnecessary evil) in the world.*
6. *Therefore, God does not exist.*

In order to see whether they are right, let us review each of the basic propositions that generate the paradox.

Proposition 1, the notion that "God is all-powerful," has been a cornerstone of Christian theology since the early centuries of the Church. Although it is debatable whether one can show that the biblical writers had such a strong concept (or whether the exact formulation is derived from a Platonic and Aristotelian metaphysics), most Judeo-Christian theologians have believed that any adequate view of deity entailed omnipotence. Some philosophers and theologians—for example, John Stuart Mill, William James, Alfred North Whitehead, Charles Hartshorne, and John Cobb—have relinquished the claim to God's omnipotence in order to get God off the hook with regard to evil. Many more believe that it either doesn't get God off the hook or that it tends to diminish God's essence. That is, even if God is not all-powerful, he (or she) certainly must be exceedingly powerful (and knowledgeable), and if so, he should have been able to prevent evil (or most of the evil) in the world. Yet if God is not so powerful, why do we call him "God" and not a demiurge and why don't we worship instead the ideal of moral goodness? Such theologians and philosophers (usually in a tradition called *process theology*) may have a case, but it may not be any better than some of the alternative solutions. Many will find it too radical altogether.

Finally, when theists speak of God being omnipotent, they usually mean that God can do anything that is *logically possible.* God cannot make a stone heavier than he can lift, cannot will that he never had existed, and cannot make "2 + 2 = 5." This limitation on God is important in defending theism against the atheologians.

Proposition 2, the idea that "God is all good," is necessary to the Judeo-Christian tradition. If you take the property of benevolence away from God, what is the difference between God and a supreme Devil? Somehow God has moral obligations and cannot do evil. One tradition (very Greek in origin) contends that God cannot change, so he cannot *do* anything (cannot have obligations). But this surely is unbiblical, for the God of the Bible is one who *creates* the heavens and the earth, as well as humanity, and *redeems* people from sin and despair. He is a God who acts, and who acts well.

Proposition 3, that "there is evil," may be denied by some Eastern religions, which view it as an illusion, but the Judeo-Christian tradition has always taken it as a fundamental datum to be overcome, if not explained. Suffering and pain, disease and death, cruelty and violence, rape and murder, poverty and natural havoc have all been viewed as the enemy of the good.

Generally, Western thought has distinguished between moral and natural evil. Moral evil includes all those bad things for which humans are morally responsible. Natural evil or *surd evil* stands for all those terrible events that nature itself does, such as hurricanes, tornados, earthquakes, volcanic eruptions, natural diseases, which bring suffering to humans and animals. However, some defenders of theism affirm that all evil is essentially moral evil: the devil causes natural evil.

The main defense of theism, given evil, is the free-will defense, going back as far as St. Augustine (354–430) and receiving modern treatment by John Hick, Alvin Plantinga, Stephen Davis and Richard Swinburne (see the last reading in this section: "A Theistic Response to the Problem of Evil"). The free-will defense adds another proposition to Epicurus' paradox in order to show that Propositions 1–3 are consistent and not contradictory:

7. *It is logically impossible for God to create free creatures and guarantee that they will never do evil.*

Since it is a good thing to create free creatures who are morally responsible agents, there is no assurance that they will not also do evil. Imagine that God considered an infinite set of possible worlds. In some of them he (or she) saw humans as not sinning, but in those they were not free; in some he saw humans as free and doing less evil than in this world. But he chose to create this world, with its enormous amount of good and evil. Perhaps he could have created other worlds with more good or less evil, but he would not create a world with a worse proportion of good to evil than this one has, and no world he could have created could have a better proportion of good over evil. This is the best an omnipotent, omnibenevolent God could do.

This defense assumes a libertarian view of freedom of the will. That is, humans are free to choose between good and evil acts. They are not caused (although they may be influenced) to do one deed rather than the other, but rather they are causally underdetermined. Given two identically similar situations, with identical causal antecedents, an agent could do Act A at one time and B at the other. This view is opposed to determinism as well as to compatibilism (a view that tries to reconcile freedom of action with determinism). If you are committed to compatibilism or determinism, the free-will defense will not be effective against the argument from evil. We examine this issue in Part V of this book.

To return to the issue at hand, the proponent of the free-will defense claims that all moral evil derives from creature freedom of the will. But what about natural evil? How does the theist account for it? There are two different ways. The first one, favored by Alvin Plantinga and Stephen Davis, is to attribute natural evil to the work of the devil and his or her angels. Disease and tornados are caused by the devil and his or her minions. The second way, favored by Swinburne, argues that natural evil is part and parcel of the nature of things: a result of the combination of deterministic physical laws that are necessary for consistent action and the responsibility given to humans to exercise their freedom.

Our four readings in this section take opposite views of the problem of evil. Voltaire raises the question why God permits evil, and he criticizes the view that evil is all for the best. Fyodor Dostoyevsky argues that the suffering of innocent animals and children seems to serve no greater good, and we especially expect God to prevent those things. Then Bruce Russell also asks why God allows so much suffering, much of which seems gratuitous. He contends that the burden of proof is on the theist to explain why God does not intervene to stop the suffering of the world. If by the mere pressing of a button I could have caused Hitler to have had a heart attack before starting World War II, I would have been obliged to do so. Why did God not intervene in 1939, and why does he not intervene in the sufferings of millions all over the world?

Richard Swinburne argues that there is no logical inconsistency between (1) the proposition that God is all-powerful and all good and (2) the proposition that there is evil in the world. He attempts to meet arguments like Russell's by appealing to the free-will defense: There are two kinds of evil: natural and moral. All moral evil is caused by free agents making the wrong choices; we humans are responsible for the social ills we experience.

Swinburne argues that natural evil is simply part of an orderly process of nature. The laws of nature are necessarily such that the good is interconnected with the bad. The same rain that causes one farmer's sown field to germinate may flood and ruin another farmer's field. Although there are, no doubt, limits to the amount of evil God will allow, he cannot constantly intervene without eroding human responsibility or the laws of nature. Where those limits of evil are, none of us finite humans can know. It would be presumptuous to think we knew.

VOLTAIRE
୬

THE BEST OF ALL POSSIBLE WORLDS?

Francois Marie Arout, better known by his chosen name Voltaire (1694–1778), was one of the most prominent writers of eighteenth-century France. He is noted for his defense of civil liberties, deistic religious views; and satirical literary works, such as his novel *Candide* (1759), which attacks Leibniz's view that this is the best of all possible worlds. His principal contribution to philosophy is his multivolume *Philosophical Dictionary*, published over a several year period (1764–69), from which the following selection is taken.

As in *Candide*, Voltaire's discussion in this selection similarly attacks Leibniz's optimistic view of God and human suffering. For Leibniz, in the grand scheme of things, the suffering that we experience helps make the world a much better place than it would have been otherwise, and, hence, God's ultimate goodness is consistent with the presence of suffering.

From Voltaire, "Optimism," *The Philosophical Dictionary* (1764), adapted from *The Works of Voltaire* (1901), Vol. 6.

Voltaire responds that this flies in the face of common sense: no clear good can result for us or God from the abundance of suffering. Rather, there is a genuine conflict between the existence of suffering and the idea of a God who is all-powerful and all-good. Voltaire notes a range of futile theological attempts to solve the problem, such as through the Christian view of original sin, and the non-Christian view of dual deities, one good the other evil. Several philosophers of Voltaire's time, though, resolved the issue by maintaining that the universe is divinely governed by unchanging laws, and suffering is simply part of that process. But this, Voltaire argues, "represents the author of nature as a powerful and malevolent monarch." Voltaire's solution is for us just to confess ignorance on the whole subject.

Please explain to me how everything is for the best, for I do not understand it. Does it mean that everything is arranged and ordered according to the laws of the impelling power? That I understand and acknowledge. Do you mean that everyone is well and possesses the means of living and that nobody suffers? You know that this is not the case. Are you of the opinion that the appalling tragedies that afflict the earth are good in reference to God, and that he takes pleasure in them? I do not give any credit to this horrible doctrine; neither do you.

Please have the goodness to explain how all is for the best. Plato, the dialectician, humbly allows to God the liberty of making five worlds; because, said Plato, there are five regular solids in geometry, the tetrahedron, the cube, the hexahedron, the dodecahedron, and the icosahedron. But why restrict divine power in this way? Why not permit the sphere, which is still more regular, and even the cone, the pyramid of many sides, the cylinder, etc.?

According to Plato, God necessarily chose the best of all possible worlds; and this system has been embraced by many Christian philosophers, although it appears opposed to the doctrine of original sin. After the disobedience of the first sin, our globe was no longer the best of all possible worlds. If it was ever so it might be so still, but many people believe it to be the worst of worlds instead of the best.

Leibniz takes the position of Plato. More readers than one complain of their inability to understand either of these writers, and for myself, having read both of them more than once, I confess my ignorance according to custom. Since the gospel has revealed nothing on the subject, we remain in darkness without remorse.

Leibniz, who writes on every subject, discusses original sin. Since every system-builder introduces into his plan something contradictory, Leibniz imagined that the disobedience towards God, with the frightful misfortunes which followed it, were integral parts of the best of worlds, and necessary ingredients of all possible happiness.

What! To be chased from a delightful place, where we might have lived forever only because of eating an apple? What! To produce unhappy children in misery who will suffer everything, and in return produce others to suffer after them? What! To experience all troubles, feel all pains, die in the midst of grief, and by way of compensation be burned to all eternity: is this fate the best possible? It certainly is not good for us, and in what manner can it be so for God? Leibniz felt that nothing could be said to these objections, but nevertheless he made great books in which he did not even understand himself.

[The Roman statesman] Lucullus, in good health, enjoying a good dinner with his friends and his mistress in the hall of Apollo, may jokingly deny the existence of evil. But let him put his head out of the window and he will see miserable people in abundance; let him be gripped with a fever, and he will be a miserable person himself.

I do not like to quote; it is typically a tricky matter. Nevertheless, what precedes and what follows the passage I just quoted is too frequently neglected; and thus a thousand objections may rise. I must, notwith-standing, quote Lactantius, one of the [early Christ-ian] fathers, who, in the thirteenth chapter on *The Anger of God*, makes Epicurus speak as follows: "God can either take away evil from the world and will not; or being willing to do so, cannot; or he nei-ther can nor will; or, lastly, he is both able and will-ing. If he is willing to remove evil and cannot, then he is not omnipotent. If he can, but will not remove it, then he is not benevolent; if he is neither able nor will-ing, then he is neither powerful nor benevolent; lastly, if he is both able and willing to eliminate evil, why does evil exist?"

The argument is weighty, and Lactantius replies to it very poorly by saying that God wills evil, but has given us wisdom to obtain the good. It must be con-fessed that this answer is very weak in comparison with the objection since it implies that God could bestow wisdom only by allowing evil—a pleasant wisdom truly! The origin of evil has always been an abyss, the depth of which no one has been able to measure. It was this difficulty that forced so many ancient philosophers and legislators to resort to two principles—the one good, the other evil. Typhon was the evil principle among the Egyptians, Arimanes among the Persians. The Manicheans, it is said, adopted this theory; but as these people have never spoken either of a good or of a bad principle, we have nothing to prove it.

Among the absurdities abounding in this world which may also be placed among the variety of our evils, here is a very considerable one. It presumes the existence of two all-powerful beings, fighting over which will succeed most in this world. They then make a treaty like the two physicians in Molière: "Allow me the vomit-inducer, and I will allow you the scalpel."

Along with the Platonists of the first century of the church, Basilides maintained that God assigned the task of making our world to his inferior angels, and these, being unskilled, have constructed it as we per-ceive. This theological fable is laid flat by the over-whelming objection that it is not in the nature of an all-powerful and all-wise deity to assign the con-struction of a world to incompetent architects.

Simon, who felt the force of this objection, side-steps it by saying that the angel who presided over the workers is damned for having done his business so carelessly. But the roasting of this angel gives no com-pensation. The adventure of Pandora among the Greeks scarcely meets the objection better. The box in which every evil is enclosed, and at the bottom of which remains Hope, is indeed a charming allegory; but Pandora was made by Vulcan only to avenge him-self on Prometheus, who had stolen fire to create a man of clay.

The Indians have succeeded no better. God having created man, gave him a drug which would insure him permanent bodily health. The man loaded his donkey with the drug; the donkey was thirsty, so the serpent directed him to a fountain, and while the donkey was drinking, the serpent stole the drug.

The Syrians said that man and woman were cre-ated in the fourth heaven; the couple decided to eat a cake instead of their natural food which was ambrosia; upon digestion, ambrosia was expelled through their pores. But after eating cake, they needed to relieve themselves in the usual manner. The man and the woman requested an angel to direct them to a toilet. The angel said "Observe that petty globe which is almost of no size at all; it is situated about 150 mil-lion miles from this place, and is the toilet of the uni-verse; go there as quickly as you can. The man and woman obeyed the angel and came here, where they have ever since remained. Since that time the world has been as we now find it. The Syrians will forever be asked why God allowed man to eat the cake and experience such a multitude of dreadful evils.

I pass with speed from the fourth heaven to Lord Bolingbroke. This writer, who doubtless was a great genius, gave to the celebrated [poet Alexander] Pope his plan of "all for the best," as it is found word for word in the posthumous works of Lord Bolingbroke, and recorded by Lord Shaftesbury in his book *Char-acteristics*. We read in Shaftesbury's chapter on "The Moralists" the following passage:

> Much may be replied to these complaints of the defects of nature—How came it so powerless and defective from the hands of a perfect Being?—But I deny that it is defective. Beauty is the result of con-

trast, and universal concord springs out of a perpetual conflict. . . . It is necessary that everything be sacrificed to other things—vegetables to animals, and animals to the earth. . . . The laws of the central power of gravitation, which give to the celestial bodies their weight and motion, are not to be deranged in consideration of a pitiful animal, who, protected as he is by the same laws, will soon be reduced to dust.

Bolingbroke, Shaftesbury, and Pope, their working artisan, resolve their general question no better than the rest. Their motto "all for the best" says no more than that all is governed by unchanging laws; and who did not know that? We learn nothing when we remark, after the manner of little children, that flies are created to be eaten by spiders, spiders by swallows, swallows by hawks, hawks by eagles, eagles by men, men killed by one another, to provide food for worms—except about one in a thousand—by devils.

There is a constant and regular order established among animals of all kinds, a universal order. When a stone is formed in my bladder, the mechanical process is admirable. Sandy particles pass by small degrees into my blood; they are filtered by the veins; and passing the urethra, deposit themselves in my bladder; where, uniting delightfully according to Newton's theory of attraction, a stone is formed. It gradually increases, and I suffer pains a thousand times worse than death, all by means of the most admirable mechanism in the world. A surgeon who is an expert in the art of Tubalcain [i.e., metalworking], thrusts a sharp instrument into me. Cutting into the perineum, grabs hold of the stone with his pincers, which breaks during the event by the necessary laws of mechanics. Owing to the same mechanism, I die in frightful torments. All this is "for the best," being the evident result of unchanging physical principles, agreeably to which I know as well as you that I die.

If we were incapable of feeling, there would be nothing to say against this system of physics; but that is not the point here. I ask whether there are physical evils, and from where do they originate? There is no absolute evil, says Pope in his "Essay on Man"; and

if there are particular evils, they are part of a general good. It is a singular general good that is composed of the kidney stone and the gout, of all sorts of crime and suffering, and of death and damnation.

The fall of man is our ointment for all these particular maladies of body and soul, which you call "the general health." But Shaftesbury and Bolingbroke have attacked original sin. Pope says nothing about it; but it is clear that their system undermines the foundations of the Christian religion, and explains nothing at all.

In the meantime, this system has been since accepted by many theologians, who willingly embrace contradictions. So be it. We ought to leave to everybody the privilege of reasoning in their own way upon the flood of suffering that overwhelm us. It would be as reasonable to prevent incurable patients from eating what they please. "God," says Pope, "beholds, with an equal eye, a hero perish or a sparrow fall; the destruction of an atom, or the ruin of a thousand planets; the bursting of a bubble, or the dissolution of a world."

This, I must confess, is a pleasant consolation! Who does not find a comfort in the declaration of Lord Shaftesbury who asserts "that God will not derange his general system for so miserable an animal as man?" It must be confessed at least that this pitiful creature has a right to cry out humbly, and, while moaning about himself, to try to understand why these eternal laws do not include the good of every individual.

This system of "all for the best" represents the author of nature as a powerful and malevolent monarch, who cares neither for the destruction of four or five hundred thousand men, nor for the many more who in consequence spend the rest of their days in poverty and tears, so long as he succeeds in his designs.

Thus, the view that "this is the best of all possible worlds" gives us no consolation, and is instead a hopeless doctrine to the philosophers who embrace it. The question of good and evil remains in permanent chaos for those who seek to understand it in reality. It is a mere mental sport to the disputants who are like prisoners that play with their chains. As to unreasoning people, they resemble the fish that are transported from a river to a reservoir, with no more suspicion that they are to be eaten during the approaching season of Lent, than we have ourselves of the facts which originate our destiny.

Let us place at the end of every chapter of metaphysics the two letters used by the Roman judges when they did not understand a pleading: N. L., *non liquet*, that is, "it is not clear." Let us, above all, silence the scoundrels who, overloaded like ourselves with the weight of human tragedy, add the injury of their slander. Let us refute their appalling dishonesty by turning instead to faith and providence.

Some reasoners hold the opinion that it is inconsistent with the nature of the Great Being of Beings for things to be otherwise than they are. It is a rough system, and I am too ignorant to attempt to examine it.

FOR FURTHER REFLECTION

1. Voltaire states that the fall of humanity does not make God any less responsible for the origin of suffering. What is Voltaire's reasoning, and do you agree with it?
2. Voltaire considers several non-Christian myths that attempt to explain the origin of evil. Why does he find these inadequate, and do you agree with his reasoning?
3. Voltaire quotes Shaftesbury's essay "The Moralist," which discusses God's role in evil. Do you agree with Voltaire's critique of Shaftesbury's view?
4. In the fourth to the last paragraph, Voltaire states that "This system of 'all for the best' represents the author of nature as a powerful and malevolent monarch." Why does Voltaire believe this, and is his reasoning sound?

FYODOR DOSTOYEVSKY

WHY IS THERE EVIL?

Fyodor Dostoyevsky (1822–1881), one of the greatest Russian novelists, was born in Moscow. His revolutionary sympathies and a penchant for gambling managed to keep him in constant danger. Among his famous writings are *Crime and Punishment* (1866), *The Idiot* (1868), and *The Brothers Karamazov* (1880), from which our reading is taken. In this scene from Dostoyevsky's most famous work, Ivan Karamazov is explaining to his pious brother, Alyosha, a Christian monk, why he cannot accept God.

"Well, tell me where to begin, give your orders. The existence of God, eh?"

"Begin where you like. You declared yesterday at father's that there was no God." Alyosha looked searchingly at his brother.

"I said that yesterday at dinner on purpose to tease you and I saw your eyes glow. But now I've no objection to discussing with you, and I say so very seriously. I want to be friends with you, Alyosha, for I have no friends and want to try it. Well, only fancy,

From Fyodor Dostoyevsky, *The Brothers Karamazov,* trans. Constance Garnett (London: Heinemann, 1912).

perhaps I too accept God," laughed Ivan, "that's a surprise for you, isn't it?"

"Yes of course, if you are not joking now."

"Joking? I was told at the elder's yesterday that I was joking. You know, dear boy, there was an old sinner in the eighteenth century who declared that, if there were no God, he would have to be invented. . . . And man has actually invented God. And what's strange, what would be marvelous, is not that God should really exist; the marvel is that such an idea, the idea of the necessity of God, could enter the head of such a savage, vicious beast as man. So holy it is, so touching, so wise and so great a credit it does to man. As for me, I've long resolved not to think whether man created God or God man. . . . For what are we aiming at now? I am trying to explain as quickly as possible my essential nature, that is what manner of man I am, what I believe in, and for what I hope, that's it, isn't it? And therefore I tell you that I accept God simply. But you must note this: if God exists and if He did create the world, then, as we all know, He created it according to the geometry of Euclid and the human mind with the conception of only three dimensions in space. Yet there have been and still are geometricians and philosophers, and even some of the most distinguished, who doubt whether the whole universe, or to speak more widely the whole of being, was only created in Euclid's geometry; they even dream that two parallel lines, which according to Euclid can never meet on earth, may meet somewhere in infinity. I have come to the conclusion that, since I can't understand even that, I can't expect to understand about God. I acknowledge humbly that I have no faculty for settling such questions. I have a Euclidian earthly mind, and how could I solve problems not of this world? And I advise you never to think about it either, my dear Alyosha, especially about God, whether He exists or not. All such questions are utterly inappropriate for a mind created with an idea of only three dimensions. And so I accept God and am glad to, and what's more I accept His wisdom, His purpose—which are utterly beyond our ken; I believe in the underlying order and the meaning of life; I believe in the eternal harmony in which they shall one day be blended. I believe in the Word to Which the uni-

verse is striving, and Which Itself was 'with God,' and Which Itself is God and so on, and so on, to infinity. There are all sorts of phrases for it. I seem to be on the right path, don't I? Yet would you believe it, in the final result I don't accept this world of God's, and, although I know it exists, I don't accept it at all. It's not that I don't accept God, you must understand, it's the world created by Him I don't and cannot accept. Let me make it plain. I believe like a child that suffering will be healed and made up for, that all the humiliating absurdity of human contradictions will vanish like a pitiful mirage, like the despicable fabrication of the impotent and infinitely small Euclidian mind of man, that in the world's finale, at the moment of eternal harmony, something so precious will come to pass that it will suffice for all hearts, for the comforting of all resentments, for the atonement of all the crimes of humanity, of all the blood they've shed; that it will make it not only possible to forgive but to justify all that has happened with men—but though all that may come to pass, I don't accept it. I won't accept it. Even if parallel lines do meet and I see it myself, I shall see it and say that they've met, but still I won't accept it. That's what's at the root of me, Alyosha; that's my creed.

" . . . Do you understand why this infamy must be and is permitted? Without it, I am told, man could not have known good and evil. Why should he know that diabolical good and evil when it costs so much? Why, the whole world of knowledge is not worth that child's prayer to 'dear, Kind God'! I say nothing of the sufferings of grown-up people, they have eaten the apple, damn them, and the devil take them all! But these little ones! I am making you suffer, Alyosha, you are not yourself. I'll leave off if you like."

"Never mind. I want to suffer too," muttered Alyosha.

"One picture, only one more, because it's so curious, so characteristic, and I have only just read it in some collection of Russian antiquities. I've forgotten the name. I must look it up. It was in the darkest days of serfdom at the beginning of the century, and long live the Liberator of the People! There was in those days a general of aristocratic connections, the owner of great estates, one of these men—somewhat exceptional, I believe, even then—who, retiring from the service into a life of leisure, are convinced that they've earned absolute power over the lives of their subjects. There were such men then. So our general, settled on his property of two thousand souls, lives in pomp and domineers over his poor neighbors as though they were dependents and buffoons. He has kennels of hundreds of hounds and nearly a hundred dog-boys—all mounted, and in uniform. One day a serf boy, a little child of eight, threw a stone in play and hurt the paw of the general's favorite hound. 'Why is my favorite dog lame?' He is told that the boy threw a stone that hurt the dog's paw. 'So you did it.' The general looked the child up and down. 'Take him.' He was taken—taken from his mother and kept shut up all night. Early that morning the general comes out on horseback, with the hounds, his dependents, dog-boys, and huntsmen, all mounted around him in full hunting parade. The servants summoned for their edification, and in front of them all stands the mother of the child. The child is brought from the lockup. It's a gloomy, cold, foggy autumn day, a capital day for hunting. The general orders the child to be undressed; the child is stripped naked. He shivers, numb with terror not daring to cry. . . . 'Make him run,' commands the general. 'Run! run!' shout the dog-boys. The boy runs. . . . 'At him!' yells the general, and he sets the whole pack of hounds on the child. The hounds catch him, and tear him to pieces before his mother's eyes! . . . I believe the general was afterwards declared incapable of administering his estates. Well—what did he deserve? To be shot? to be shot for the satisfaction of our moral feelings? Speak, Alyosha!"

"To be shot," murmured Alyosha, lifting his eyes to Ivan with a pale twisted smile.

"Bravo!" cried Ivan delighted. "If even you say so . . . You're a pretty monk! So there is a little devil sitting in your heart, Alyosha Karamazov!"

"What I said was absurd, but—"

"That's just the point that 'but'!" cried Ivan. "Let me tell you, novice, that the absurd is only too necessary on earth. The world stands on absurdities, and perhaps nothing would have come to pass in it without them. We know what we know!"

"What do you know?"

"I understand nothing," Ivan went on, as though in delirium. "I don't want to understand anything now. I want to stick to the fact. I made up my mind long ago not to understand. If I try to understand anything, I shall be false to the fact and I have determined to stick to the fact."

"Why are you trying me?" Alyosha cried, with sudden distress. "Will you say what you mean at last?"

"Of course, I will; that's what I've been leading up to. You are dear to me, I don't want to let you go, and I won't give you up to your Zossima."

Ivan for a minute was silent, his face became all at once very sad.

"Listen! I took the case of the children only to make my case clearer. Of the other tears of humanity with which the earth is soaked from its crust to its center, I will say nothing. I have narrowed my subject on purpose. I am a bug, and I recognize in all humility that I cannot understand why the world is arranged as it is. Men are themselves to blame, I suppose; they were given paradise, they wanted freedom, and stole fire from heaven, though they knew they would become unhappy, so there is no need to pity them. With my pitiful, earthly, Euclidian understanding, all I know is that there is suffering and that there are none guilty; that cause follows effect, simply and directly; that everything flows and finds its level—I must have justice, or I will destroy myself. I have believed in it. I want to see it, and if I am dead by then, let me rise again, for if it all happens without me, it will be too unfair. Surely I haven't suffered, simply that I, my crimes and my sufferings, may manure the soil of the future harmony for somebody else. I want to see with my own eyes the hind lie down with the lion and the victim rise up and embrace his murderer. I want to be there when everyone suddenly understands what it has all been for. All the religions of the world are built on this longing, and I am a believer. But then there are the children, and what am I to do about them? That's a question I can't answer. For the hundredth time I repeat, there are numbers of questions, but I've only taken the children, because in their case what I mean is so unanswerably clear. Listen! If all must suffer to pay for the eternal harmony, what have children to do with it, tell me, please? It's beyond all comprehension why they should suffer, and why they should pay for the harmony. Why should they, too, furnish material to enrich the soil for the harmony of the future? I understand solidarity in sin among men. I understand solidarity in retribution, too; but there can be no such solidarity with children. And if it is really true that they must share responsibility for all their fathers' crimes, such a truth is not of this world and is beyond my comprehension. Some jester will say, perhaps, that the child would have grown up and have sinned, but you see he didn't grow up, he was torn to pieces by the dogs, at eight years old. Oh, Alyosha, I am not blaspheming! I understand, of course, what an upheaval of the universe it will be, when everything in heaven and earth blends in one hymn of praise and everything that lives and has lived cries aloud: 'Thou art just, O Lord, for Thy ways are revealed,' when the mother embraces the fiend who threw her child to the dogs, and all three cry aloud with tears, 'Thou are just, O Lord!' then, of course, the crown of knowledge will be reached and all will be made clear. But what pulls me up here is that I can't accept that harmony. And while I am on earth, I make haste to take my own measures. You see, Alyosha, perhaps it really may happen that if I live to that moment, or rise again to see it, I, too, perhaps, may cry aloud with the rest, looking at the mother embracing the child's torturer, 'Thou art just, O Lord!' but I don't want to cry aloud then. While there is still time, I hasten to protect myself and so renounce the higher harmony altogether. It's not worth the tears of that one tortured child who beat itself on the breast with its little fist and prayed in its stinking outhouse, with its unexpiated tears to 'dear, kind God'! It's not worth it, because those tears are unatoned for. They must be atoned for, or there can be no harmony. But how? How are you going to atone for them? Is it possible? By their being avenged? But what do I care for avenging them? What do I care for a hell for oppressors? What good can hell do, since those children have already been tortured? And what becomes of harmony, if there is hell? I want to forgive. I want to embrace. I don't want more suffering. And if the sufferings of children go to swell the sum of sufferings which was necessary to pay for truth, then I protest that the truth is not worth such a price. I don't want the mother to embrace the oppressor who threw her son to the dogs! She dare not forgive him! Let her forgive him for herself, if she will, let her forgive the torturer for the immeasurable suffering of her mother's heart. But the sufferings of her tortured child she has no right to forgive; she dare not forgive the torturer, even if the child were to forgive him! And if that is so, if they dare not forgive, what becomes of harmony? Is there in the whole world a being who would have the right to forgive and could forgive? I don't want harmony. From love for humanity I don't want it. I would rather be left with the unavenged suffering. I would rather remain with my unavenged and unsatisfied indignation, *even if I were wrong.* Besides, too high a price is asked for harmony; it's beyond our means to pay so much to enter on it. And so I hasten to give back my entrance ticket, and if I am an honest man I am bound to give it back as soon as possible. And that I am doing. It's not God that I don't accept, Alyosha, only I most respectfully return Him the ticket."

"That's rebellion," murmured Alyosha, looking down.

"Rebellion? I am sorry you call it that," said Ivan earnestly. "One can hardly live in rebellion, and I want to live. Tell me yourself, I challenge you—answer. Imagine that you are creating a fabric of human destiny with the object of making men happy in the end, giving them peace and rest at last, but that it was essential and inevitable to torture to death only one tiny creature—that baby beating its breast with its fist, for instance—and to found that edifice on its unavenged tears, would you consent to be the architect on those conditions? Tell me, and tell the truth."

"No, I wouldn't consent," said Alyosha softly.

FOR FURTHER REFLECTION

1. There are three propositions involved in the traditional formulation of the problem of evil: (a) God is all-powerful (including omniscience); (b) God is perfectly good; and (c) evil exists. How would Ivan deal with them?

2. Do you think that the fact of evil counts against the proposition that God exists? Explain why or why not.

3. Some people believe that we are completely causally determined, a subject that will be discussed in Part V. What will they make of the free-will defense?

BRUCE RUSSELL

THE PROBLEM OF EVIL
Why Is There So Much Suffering?

Bruce Russell is professor and chair of philosophy at Wayne State University. His areas of specialization are ethics, epistemology, and the philosophy of religion. His main interest is the question of what makes an action or belief justified. This explains why he is interested in whether we are justified in believing in God and also explains his interest in the "why be moral?" question. He has a book forthcoming titled *Introduction to Philosophy through Film* in which he discusses a variety of philosophical problems raised in mostly recent films.

1. BACKGROUND

Any discussion of the problem of evil should start with examples of unspeakable cruelty or unbearable suffering. That is not because my version of the argument proceeds by claiming that God would not allow *any* such suffering but because the argument is that God would not allow so much terrible suffering *of that sort*.[1] The examples help us focus on the type of suffering at issue.

One such example involves two-year-old Ariana Swinson. On September 6, 2000, Edward Swinson and Linda Paling pleaded guilty to second-degree murder and first degree child abuse involving their daughter, two-year-old Ariana. Jack Kresnak, a writer for the *Detroit Free Press*, wrote the following on September 26, 2000:

> St. Clair County Assistant Prosecutor Jean Sturtridge asked for long prison terms based on Ariana's many bruises, broken right elbow, 4-inch skull fracture, brain hemorrhaging, ears that showed signs of tearing and sharp blows to the girl's mouth that tore the small piece of skin that holds the upper lip to the gum.

On January 31, 2000, the couple killed Ariana after throwing her to the floor for not eating properly and "then pouring water into the mouth of the unconscious child, causing her to drown." Ariana was malnourished, dehydrated, and had lost more than half her blood on the day of her death. The parents waited nearly an hour after Ariana's death to call police, using the time to coach their other two young children to take the fall for Ariana's death. Ariana had been raised for eighteen months by Paling's sister and brother-in-law, Valerie and Barney McDaniel, but was returned to her parents over their protests, and the protests of other members of Paling's family, following a dispute between the McDaniels and a foster care worker.

This is a case of pointless suffering in the sense that anyone who knew about what was happening to Ariana and could easily have prevented it should have. In other words, it is a case where it would be wrong for people who knew about the situation and easily could have changed things to fail to intervene. Surely, at the very least, anyone who could easily have stopped Swinson and Paling from *murdering* Ariana on January 31, 2000, should have prevented the murder.

The Swinson case is just one particularly brutal example of adults causing harm to children. We have all read of the Catholic priests who molested young boys in their charge. On a single day in July in 2002 the newspapers carried stories of the recent kidnapping, rape, and killing of 5-year-old Samantha Runnion in Orange County, CA; the 1998 kidnapping and slaying of 13-year-old Christina Williams of Seattle, WA; the rape, beating, and sodomizing of a 94-year-old woman in Palo Alto, CA; the death of Chandra Levy; and Dr. Harold Shipman, of Hyde, England, who is suspected of killing 215 of his patients over 23 years. Of course, this is only the tip of the iceberg. Many, many more acts of brutality that would make you cringe or cry if you knew the details occur everyday all over the world. And we should not forget Hitler, Pol Pot, the genocide in Rwanda, and all the terrible suffering that results from natural disasters and disease.

II. THE ARGUMENT

There are several versions of the argument from evil against the existence of God. One given by William Rowe goes like this:

1. An all-powerful, all-knowing, perfectly good being would prevent the occurrence of any intense suffering he could, unless he could not do so without thereby losing some greater good or permitting some evil equally bad or worse.
2. Not all such suffering has been prevented.
3. Therefore, there is no all-powerful, all-knowing, perfectly good being.[2]

Peter van Inwagen has criticized the moral premise, premise 1, on the grounds that a good being could cause, or allow, more evil than is necessary to bring about some good because there may be no minimum amount of evil that will bring about that good. For instance, there may be no minimum parking fine that will deter people from parking illegally or, even if there is, it may be permissible for a good person to impose a fine anywhere between, say, $50 and $55 to deter illegal parking. In another scenario van Inwagen asks us to imagine that Atlantis is sinking and that 1,000 people will drown if they are not rescued by ship. If the captain of the ship puts none on board he is certain to reach port safely; if he puts all 1,000 on board the ship will definitely sink and all will drown. For each person he puts on board, the likelihood of the ship's sinking is increased by 0.1%. Van Inwagen says that the captain must put at least a handful on board and not take aboard all but a handful. In between those extremes, everything is permitted. So it would be permissible for the captain to put, say, 100 on board, thereby leaving 900 to drown as Atlantis goes under, even though he *could* prevent more from dying by taking more aboard. According to van Inwagen, it is not wrong for him to take 100 aboard when he could have taken 125, even though taking 100 means at least 25 will needlessly drown on Atlantis. So it can be permissible for a good being to cause, or allow, needless suffering.[3]

However, van Inwagen recognizes that a good being would not allow *much more* evil than is needed to bring about some greater good or to prevent something equally bad or worse. For instance, a good captain would not put, say, only 10 aboard and allow 990 people to go down with Atlantis since he stands a good chance of getting to shore if, say, only 900 are allowed to drown and 100 put on board. And it would be wrong to assign a parking fine of $1,000 when one between $50 and $55 will achieve the sought after deterrent effect.

Against van Inwagen, someone might say that there must always be some least amount of evil that must be allowed to bring about a certain amount of good, or to prevent even more evil. There must be some lowest fine, say, $48.75, that will achieve the level of deterrence that is sought. We just do not know what it is, though God would if he existed. There must be some number of people such that if that number were left on Atlantis the ship would make it safely to port but if one more were taken aboard, it would sink. We just do not know what that number is, though God would if he existed.

Van Inwagen could reply that even if that is true *we* will not be able to judge that there is more terrible suffering than God would allow because *we* do not know what the least amount of suffering needed to bring about the relevant amount of good is. We are in no position to judge what the lowest fine is that would yield the desired deterrent effect, nor what the maximum number of people is that the ship can carry and safely reach shore. All we can say is that some fines are too small to achieve the desired deterrent effect, and some too large to be just. All we can say is that the captain must take at least a handful of people and must not take all but a handful. Except at the extremes, we are in no position to judge that the relevant action is required or wrong.

Does something similar hold with respect to the amount of evil in the world? I believe it does: we do not know what the least amount of evil is that would have to be allowed to bring about a certain amount of good, either because there is no such least amount or, even if there is, our capacities are not adequate for determining what it is. But contra van Inwagen, I believe that we are justified in believing that there is an *extreme* amount of suffering, *way more* than is needed to bring about any relevant good or to prevent some comparable evil. To allow all that horrible suffering is both unnecessary and *excessive*, just as a fine of $1,000 for illegal parking or letting 995 drown on Atlantis would be. And allowing excessive and unnecessary suffering is wrong, even if it is not always wrong to allow unnecessary suffering.

Now the issue becomes whether we are *justified in believing* that there is excessive suffering. There certainly appears to be. It seems that we could let people exercise their freedom and allow them to develop compassion, perseverance, and generosity with much, much less suffering.

Does the fact that we do not see a reason why God would allow so much suffering justify us in believing that there is no such reason? Some would argue that it does not since failure to see something (an elephant, a person, a reason) gives us reason to believe it is not

there *only if* we are justified in believing that if it were there we would see it. But we are not justified in believing that we would see God's reasons for allowing so much suffering even if those reasons existed. So not seeing any does not justify us in believing there are none.

Sometimes we argue in this way, and rightly so. For instance, the reason we are justified in believing there are no elephants in the room upon seeing none is that we have reason to believe that if there were any we would see them. The reason chess-grandmaster Kasparov is justified in believing that some novice player cannot get out of check, upon seeing no way for him to get out, is that Kasparov has reason to believe if there were a way he would see it. On the other hand, the reason we are *not justified* in believing that, say, a field mouse is not in a distant pasture, on the basis of failing to see any, is that we *do not* have reason to believe we would see such a mouse if one were there.

These examples seem to support the view that we are justified in believing that something is not there if *and only if* we have reason to believe that we would see that thing if it were there.

But I do not believe that this claim is true. *One way* for you to be justified in believing that something is not there is for you to fail to see it and to be justified in believing that if it were there you would see it. However, we are justified in believing that we are *not* in The Matrix (as in the film of that name) even though we *do not* have reason to believe that if we were in The Matrix we would see it, that is, would realize we were in it. Here, what justifies us in believing that we are in a world of real buildings, chairs, and people, and not in The Matrix, is that the hypothesis that we are in the real world better explains our sensations and experiences than the Matrix hypothesis that says we are being made to falsely believe we are in the real world through the activities of some supercomputers. Other things being equal, a simpler hypothesis is better than a more complex one that contains hidden causal mechanisms, or ones whose causal nature is obscure. And the simpler hypothesis to explain our perceptual sensations is that there are real buildings, people, and chairs that cause them, not some hidden supercomputers whose methods of causing them are obscure. So we can be justified in believing that something is not there, say, in believing that supercomputers *are not* causing our perceptual sensations, even though *it is false* that we have reason to believe we would "see" the supercomputers and their activities if they were there.

This opens up the possibility that we can be justified in believing that God "is not there," that is, does not exist, even though we *do not* have reason to believe that if he were there, that is, did exist, we would "see" the reason. More specifically, it opens up the possibility that we can be justified in believing there is no point to so much terrible suffering even though we *do not* have reason to believe that we would see the point if there were one. There are two possible explanations of the fact that we do not see why there is so much horrible suffering. The first is simply that there is no point; it is genuinely pointless suffering. The second is that there is a point that God sees, but we do not.

These explanations are similar to two explanations of our not seeing, say, a black leather sofa in our room. One explanation is that there is no such sofa in our room. Another is that we are in The Matrix and the supercomputers have not programmed an image of a black leather sofa into our experiences. Clearly, the simplest explanation of why we do not see a black leather sofa in the room is that there is none, not that the supercomputers have just failed to program such an experience in us. Barring evidence to the contrary, we should accept the simplest hypothesis, namely, the one that says there is no black leather sofa in the room. Similarly, barring evidence for the existence of God, we should accept the simplest hypothesis to explain why we see no sufficient moral reason to justify the existence of so much horrible suffering. The simplest hypothesis is that there is no such reason, not the hypothesis that God knows of such a reason but it is beyond our ken. Other things being equal, it is better to explain things by hypotheses that do not posit hidden entities whose plans and ways of making things happen are obscure (like The Matrix and God hypotheses) than hypotheses that do.

Suppose some people are not convinced. They still think that failing to see a reason why God would allow so much horrible suffering does not justify us

in thinking there is no such reason. After all, failing to make sense of what some eminent physicists say does not give us reason to believe that what they say is nonsense, for we have no reason to believe that it would make sense *to us* if it really did make sense.

What could *these* people say to someone who maintains that the earth was created 100 years ago by God, with all its signs of age, that is, with deep river valleys, fossil remains, old books and newspapers, etc., for reasons beyond our ken? They might say that God is no deceiver so we have reason to believe he would not create the earth 100 years ago with all its signs of age. But while it is *prima facie* wrong to deceive another, sometimes it is morally permitted, even required. A favorite example of philosophers is one where someone is trusted by the Nazis but also hiding Jews. If the Nazis ask this person if she is hiding Jews, she should lie and say "no," provided she has good reason to believe she will not be caught. So the defender of the 100 year-old earth can reply that, for all we know, God has reasons beyond our ken for deceiving us and creating the earth 100 years ago while making it look much older. Sometimes deception is not wrong. So the believer in God must hold that when it comes to a 100 year-old earth, we *do* have reason to believe that God would not deceive us into thinking that the earth is well over 100 years old. But then we must have reason to believe that there are no weighty reasons beyond our ken that God might have for deceiving us about the age of the earth. Because the cases are parallel, the believer should also hold that we are justified in believing that there are *no* reasons beyond our grasp weighty enough to justify God in allowing all the horrible suffering we observe.

My argument that God does not exist is that the best explanation of all the apparently pointless suffering we see is that it has no point, not that it has one beyond our ken. It is a better explanation because it does not introduce hidden entities to explain what we observe, and the other explanation leads to skepticism about whether God created the earth a short time ago. Because the best explanation of apparently pointless suffering is the existence of pointless suffering, we are justified in believing that God does not exist. Even if he could allow unnecessary suffering, he cannot allow excessive unnecessary suffering for that would be to allow morally indefensible suffering.

II. OBJECTIONS AND REPLIES

A. We are too ignorant to judge

Many critics of the argument from evil charge that we are in no position to judge that there is gratuitous evil since we are ignorant of too many things. William Alston argues that we are ignorant of whether there is an afterlife, of what sort of alternative worlds are metaphysically possible, of all the possibilities that are metaphysically possible, and of whether there are "modes of value beyond those of which we are aware."[4] And having justified beliefs about what the alternatives to preventing horrific evil are and what goods can only be realized, or what worse evils can only be prevented, by allowing those evils, would seem to be required for us to have justified beliefs about the existence of gratuitous evil.

Kirk Durston argues that to judge that some evil is gratuitous we must judge that the consequences of some alternative are better or that allowing the evil to occur involves unfairness because it involves uncompensated harm to some individual. He thinks that we are in no position to judge those consequences, or that any apparent unfairness really does involve *uncompensated* harm. Durston argues that "an event can lead to an exponentially increasing number of consequences, affecting an increasing number of causal chains."[5] If Lady Randolph Churchill had not slept with her husband on the night that she did, and had not slept in the very position she had, Winston Churchill would not have been conceived. If he had not been conceived, then World War II might have gone very differently. So little things can make big differences. Thus, for all we know, if God had intervened to prevent some horrific evil, things would have been much worse on balance, and, for all we know, innocent children and animals that suffer terribly will be justly compensated in an afterlife.

The problem with these arguments that claim we are too ignorant for our judgments about gratuitous evil to be justified is that they can be used to show that we are in no position to judge that the earth is more

than 100-years old. Perhaps God wants us to think that the world is older because he wants us to believe that natural disasters, wars, slavery and other horrible things have happened but also to have some idea of how they, or their consequences, can be overcome by examples of what we think are actual cases where they have been overcome. But it is better for us to have this information without, rather than with, the relevant suffering and injustice. So, for all we know, God deceives us about the age of the earth for our own good. So we are in no position to judge that the earth is over 100-years old. We should remain agnostic about whether it is.

Of course, this conclusion is absurd. But the arguments that conclude that we are too ignorant to be in a position to judge that there is gratuitous evil are the basis of this parallel argument with this absurd conclusion. Hence, we should reject objections to the argument from evil that rest on arguments that conclude we are too ignorant to judge whether there is gratuitous evil.

B. On the total evidence, it is not unreasonable to believe that God exists

Suppose you grant me that if there were no evidence for God's existence, the amount of terrible suffering experienced by innocents would require us to believe that God does not exist. Still, you might object, when all the evidence is considered we are not required to believe that God does not exist. Rather, we are either required to believe he does, or at least to suspend judgment on his existence.

The only traditional argument that concludes that a perfect, and so an all-knowing, all-powerful, wholly good being exists is the ontological argument, and it has been greatly criticized. The design and cosmological arguments at most argue to the existence of an intelligent cause of the universe or the order in it. And these arguments have also been severely criticized.

But I think most non-philosophers do not depend on any of these arguments anyway for their belief in God. I believe that more often than not they implicitly believe that the best explanation of events that they have observed in life involves the existence and activity of God. About a week after the newspapers carried stories of the kidnapping, rapes, and killings of girls and old women that I mentioned earlier, there was a story about how nine miners in Pennsylvania were saved in the summer of 2002. Without knowing where the trapped miners were in an area of about a square mile, rescuers drilled a 6-inch air pipe that broke through to the miners who were huddled in a 20 by 50 foot air pocket 24 stories below the surface of the earth. In addition, a drill broke, and drilling was stopped for 18 hours, when rescuers were drilling a 36-inch rescue shaft. During that time water rose in the 20 by 50 foot compartment. If the drill had not broken, rescuers may have pierced the compartment at a time when it was full of water, concluded that all the miners had drowned, and stopped the rescue effort.

Francis X. Clines of the *New York Times* wrote,

> This blue-collar, Bible-friendly town did not hesitate to use the word "miracle" in describing the intricate, roll-of-the-dice rescue operation that recovered the men.[6]

Is the best explanation of the rescue of the miners that God intervened to aid the effort? I do not think so. The rescuers did check mine maps to see what the points of highest elevation were before drilling the air-shaft. Furthermore, to make a rational judgment on this case you have to consider what has happened in similar cases. There are many cases where people died because rescuers were unable to reach them in time. You would expect by chance that some victims of disaster get saved and many others do not, and that is what we find. So it seems that luck is a better explanation of the rescue of the miners than God's intervention.

Because there is so much relevant evidence, it is hard to be certain that the best explanation of both so much horrible suffering and some remarkable and beneficial events is that there is no God, but that people are sometimes lucky. Such an explanation seems better than one that says that God intervenes and sometimes helps bring about good outcomes and other times allows bad outcomes for reasons beyond our ken. That theistic explanation has two strikes against it in that we cannot understand how an immaterial being can act on the material world, and it posits the existence of hidden reasons, those beyond our

ken. Whether it has three strikes against it depends on whether luck is an adequate explanation of events like the saving of the nine miners in Pennsylvania, the so-called Quecreek miracle. I think luck is an adequate explanation, but this is where I predict people will disagree, just as they sometimes disagree on whether a batter has checked his swing or gone around—especially if it involves a possible third strike in the late innings of a very important game.

NOTES

1. Earlier versions of the argument from evil have maintained the following: necessarily, if God exists, then he does not allow *any* suffering or evil. Against this claim people have rightly argued that it is possible for God to allow *necessary evils, or suffering*, that is, evils or suffering that God must allow in order to bring about a greater good or to prevent a greater evil. God might allow some suffering so that people can develop compassion, and he might allow some people to sometimes exercise their free wills in ways that harm others because it would be better for them to exercise their wills and to have the resultant harm than to have neither. My version of the argument allows that God *can allow some* suffering and evil. It just says that he cannot allow *a lot of horrible* suffering.

2. See Rowe, p. 2. I have switched premises 1 and 2 around, and I refer to an *all-powerful*, all-knowing, wholly good being whereas Rowe leaves out (I'm sure by oversight) reference to omnipotence in his formulation of the premise in his argument that corresponds to my 1.

3. Van Inwagen gives the Atlantis example in "Reflections on the Chapters by Draper, Russell, and Gale" in *The Evidential Argument from Evil*, p. 234. His point about their being no sharp cut off line between a penalty that is an effective deterrent and one that is not is made in his "The Magnitude, Duration, and Distribution of Evil: A Theodicy," *Philosophical Topics* 16 (1988), pp. 161–87, esp., pp. 167–68; and in "The Problems of Evil, Air, and Silence" in *The Evidential Argument from Evil*, pp. 172–73, note 11.

4. In "The Inductive Argument from Evil and the Human Cognitive Condition," in *The Evidential Argument from Evil*, p. 120.

5. Kirk Durston, "The consequential complexity of history and gratuitous evil," *Religious Studies* 36 (2000), pp. 65–80.

6. *The Press Democrat*, July 29, 2002, p. A11.

FOR FURTHER REFLECTION

1. Could Russell's argument against the existence of God be answered by bringing in free will or the idea that the world is a place of "soul making"?

2. Even if the problem of evil gives us some reason to believe that God does not exist, aren't there lots of good reasons to believe He does that Russell does not consider?

3. To be justified in believing that there are no goods that are good enough to justify allowing all the horrible suffering Russell refers to, wouldn't he have to be justified in believing that the goods we are aware of are a "representative sample" of all the goods there are? And how can he know that?

4. Even if Russell has shown that there is no all-powerful, all-knowing, wholly good being, he has not shown that there is no God of any sort. Why aren't we justified in believing in a "lesser" God?

5. Suppose someone objects to the way the problem of evil is set forth, arguing that the problem is unjustifiably anthropomorphic. As one person wrote me, "Who put human beings at the center of the definition of evil?" Should we take a more global view of evil, considering the harm done to animals and the environment? Is it a self-serving bias (sometimes called *speciesism*) that makes humanity the ultimate object of concern here?

RICHARD SWINBURNE

A THEISTIC RESPONSE TO THE PROBLEM OF EVIL

Richard Swinburne is Nolloth Professor of Philosophy of Religion at Oxford University. He is one of the leading philosophers of religion in the Western world, having written several important works in this area, including *The Existence of God* (1979), *Faith and Reason* (1981), and *Evolution of the Soul* (1986). In this essay, he distinguishes two major types of evil: active and passive. He uses the free-will defense to account for active evil (that caused by humans directly) and the notion of a lawlike universe to explain evil that either is caused by human acts, indirectly, or by nature itself.

God is, by definition, omniscient, omnipotent, and perfectly good. By "omniscient" I understand "one who knows all true propositions." By "omnipotent" I understand "able to do anything logically possible."

From *Reason and Religion,* edited by Stuart C. Brown. Copyright © 1977 by the Royal Institute of Philosophy. Used by permission of the publisher, Cornell University Press. Subheads added; footnotes deleted.

By "perfectly good" I understand "one who does no morally bad action," and I include among actions omissions to perform some action. The problem of evil is then often stated as the problem whether the existence of God is compatible with the existence of evil. Against the suggestion of compatibility, an atheist often suggests that the existence of evil entails the nonexistence of God. For, he argues, if God exists, then being omniscient, he knows under what circumstances evil will occur, if he does not act; and being omnipotent, he is able to prevent its occurrence. Hence, being perfectly good, he will prevent its occurrence and so evil will not exist. Hence the existence of God entails the nonexistence of evil. Theists have usually attacked this argument by denying the claim that necessarily a perfectly good being, foreseeing the occurrence of evil and able to prevent it, will prevent it. And indeed, if evil is understood in the very wide way in which it normally is understood in this context, to include physical pain of however slight a degree, the cited claim is somewhat implausible. For it implies that if through my neglecting frequent warnings to go to the dentist, I find myself one morning with a slight toothache, then necessarily, there does not exist a perfectly good being who foresaw the evil and was able to have prevented it. Yet it seems fairly obvious that such a being might well choose to allow me to suffer some mild consequences of my folly—as a lesson for the future which would do me real harm.

The threat to theism seems to come, not from the existence of evil as such, but rather from the existence of evil of certain kinds and degrees—severe undeserved physical pain or mental anguish, for example. I shall therefore list briefly the kinds of evil which are evident in our world, and ask whether their existence in the degrees in which we find them is compatible with the existence of God. I shall call the man who argues for compatibility the theodicist, and his opponent the antitheodicist. The theodicist will claim that it is not morally wrong for God to create or permit the various evils, normally on the grounds that doing so is providing the logically necessary conditions of greater goods. The antitheodicist denies these claims by putting forward moral principles which have as consequences that a good God would not under any circumstances create or permit the evils in question. I shall argue that these moral principles are not, when carefully examined, at all obvious, and indeed that there is a lot to be said for their negations. Hence I shall conclude that it is plausible to suppose that the existence of these evils is compatible with the existence of God.

Since I am discussing only the compatibility of various evils with the existence of God, I am perfectly entitled to make occasionally some (non-self-contradictory) assumption, and argue that if it was true, the compatibility would hold. For if p is compatible with q, given r (where r is not self-contradictory), then p is compatible with q simpliciter. It is irrelevant to the issue of compatibility whether these assumptions are true. If, however, the assumptions which I make are clearly false, and if also it looks as if the existence of God is compatible with the existence of evil *only* given those assumptions, the formal proof of compatibility will lose much of interest. To avoid this danger, I shall make only such assumptions as are not clearly false—and also in fact the ones which I shall make will be ones to which many theists are already committed for entirely different reasons.

THE PROBLEM OF EVIL: TYPES

What then is wrong with the world? First, there are painful sensations, felt both by men, and, to a lesser extent, by animals. Second, there are painful emotions, which do not involve pain in the literal sense of this word—for example, feelings of loss and failure and frustration. Such suffering exists mainly among men, but also, I suppose, to some small extent among animals too. Third, there are evil and undesirable states of affairs, mainly states of men's minds, which do not involve suffering. For example, there are the states of mind of hatred and envy; and such states of the world as rubbish tipped over a beauty spot. And fourth, there are the evil actions of men, mainly actions having as foreseeable consequences evils of the first three types, but perhaps other actions as well—such as lying and promise breaking with no such foreseeable consequences. As before, I include among actions, omissions to perform some actions. If there are rational agents other than men and God (if he exists), such as angels or devils or strange beings on distant planets, who suffer and perform evil actions, then their evil feelings, states, and actions must be added to the list of evils.

I propose to call evil of the first type physical evil, evil of the second type mental evil, evil of the third type state evil, and evil of the fourth type moral evil. Since there is a clear contrast between evils of the first three types, which are evils that happen to men or animals or the world, and evils of the fourth type, which are evils that men do, there is an advantage in having one name for evils of any of the first three types—I shall call these passive evils. I distinguish evil from mere absence of good. Pain is not simply the absence of pleasure. A headache is a pain, whereas not having the sensation of drinking whiskey is, for many people, mere absence of pleasure. Likewise, the feeling of loss in bereavement is an evil involving suffering, to be contrasted with the mere absence of the pleasure of companionship. Some thinkers have, of course, claimed that a good God would create a "best of all (logically) possible worlds" (i.e., a world than which no better is logically possible), and for them the mere absence of good creates a problem since it looks as if a world would be a better world if it had that good. For most of us, however, the mere absence of good seems less of a threat to theism than the presence of evil, partly because it is not at all clear whether any sense can be given to the concept of a best of all possible worlds (and if it cannot then of logical necessity there will be a better world than any creatable world) and partly because even if sense can be given to this concept it is not at all obvious that God has an obligation to create such a world—to whom would he be doing an injustice if he did not? My concern is with the threat to theism posed by the existence of evil.

OBJECTION 1: GOD OUGHT NOT TO CREATE EVILDOERS

Now much of the evil in the world consists of the evil actions of men and the passive evils brought about by those actions. (These include the evils brought about intentionally by men, and also the evils which result from long years of slackness by many generations of men. Many of the evils of 1975 are in the latter category, and among them many state evils. The hatred and jealousy which many men and groups feel today result from an upbringing consequent on generations of neglected opportunities for reconciliations.) The antitheodicist suggests as a moral principle (P1) that a creator able to do so ought to create only creatures such that necessarily they do not do evil actions. From this it follows that God would not have made men who do evil actions. Against this suggestion the theodicist naturally deploys the free-will defense, elegantly expounded in recent years by Alvin Plantinga. This runs roughly as follows: it is not logically possible for an agent to make another agent such that necessarily he freely does only good actions. Hence if a being G creates a free agent, he gives to the agent power of choice between alternative actions, and how he will exercise that power is something which G cannot control while the agent remains free. It is a good thing that there exist free agents, but a logically necessary consequence of their existence is that their power to choose to do evil actions may sometimes be realized. The price is worth paying, however, for the existence of agents performing free actions remains a good thing even if they sometimes do evil. Hence it is not logically possible that a creator create free creatures "such that necessarily they do not do evil actions." But it is not a morally bad thing that he create free creatures, even with the possibility of their doing evil. Hence the cited moral principle is implausible.

The free-will defense as stated needs a little filling out. For surely there could be free agents who did not have the power of moral choice, agents whose only opportunities for choice were between morally indifferent alternatives—between jam and marmalade for breakfast, between watching the news on BBC 1 or the news on ITV. They might lack this power either because they lacked the power of making moral judgments (i.e., lacked moral discrimination); or because all their actions which were morally assessable were caused by factors outside their control; or because they saw with complete clarity what was right and wrong and had no temptation to do anything except the right. The free-will defense must claim, however, that it is a good thing that there exist free agents with the power and opportunity of choosing between morally good and morally evil actions, agents with sufficient moral discrimination to have some idea of the difference and some (though not overwhelming) temptation to do other than the morally good. Let us call such agents humanly free agents. The defense must then go on to claim that it is not logically possible to create humanly free agents such that necessarily they do not do morally evil actions. Unfortunately, this latter claim is highly debatable, and I have no space to debate it. I propose therefore to circumvent this issue as follows. I shall add to the definition of humanly free agents, that they are agents whose choices do not have fully deterministic precedent causes. Clearly then it will not be logically possible to create humanly free agents whose choices go one way rather than another, and so not logically possible to create humanly free agents such that necessarily they do not do evil actions. Then the free-will defense claims that $(P1)$ is not universally true; it is not morally wrong to create humanly free agents—despite the real possibility that they will do evil. Like many others who have discussed this issue, I find this a highly plausible suggestion. Surely as parents we regard it as a good thing that our children have power to do free actions of moral significance—even if the consequence is that they sometimes do evil actions. This conviction is likely to be stronger, not weaker, if we hold that the free actions with which we are concerned are ones which do not have fully deterministic precedent causes. In this way we show the existence of God to be compatible with the existence of moral evil—but only subject to a very big assumption—that men are humanly free agents. If they are not, the compatibility shown by the free-will defense is of little interest. For the agreed exception to $(P1)$ would not then justify a creator making men who did evil actions; we should need a different exception to avoid incompatibility. The assumption seems to me not clearly false, and is also one which most theists affirm for quite other reasons. Needless to say, there is no space to discuss the assumption here.

OBJECTION 2: AGAINST PASSIVE EVIL

All that the free-will defense has shown so far, however (and all that Plantinga seems to show), is grounds for supposing that the existence of moral evil is compatible with the existence of God. It has not given grounds for supposing that the existence of evil consequences of moral evils is compatible with the existence of God. In an attempt to show an incompatibility, the antitheodicist may suggest instead of $(P1)$, $(P2)$—that a creator able to do so ought always to ensure that any creature whom he creates does not cause passive evils, or at any rate passive evils which hurt creatures other than himself. For could not God have made a world where there are humanly free creatures, men with the power to do evil actions, but where those actions do not have evil consequences, or at any rate evil consequences which affect others— e.g., a world where men cannot cause pain and distress to other men? Men might well do actions which are evil either because they were actions which they believed would have evil consequences or because they were evil for some other reason (e.g., actions which involved promise breaking) without them in fact having any passive evils as consequences. Agents in such a world would be like men in a simulator training to be pilots. They can make mistakes, but no one suffers through those mistakes. Or men might do evil actions which did have the evil consequences which were foreseen but which damaged only themselves. . . .

I do not find $(P2)$ a very plausible moral principle. A world in which no one except the agent was affected by his evil actions might be a world in which men had freedom but it would not be a world in which men had responsibility. The theodicist claims that it would not be wrong for God to create interdependent humanly free agents, a society of such agents responsible for each other's well-being, able to make or mar each other.

Fair enough, the antitheodicist may again say. It is not wrong to create a world where creatures have responsibilities for each other. But might not those responsibilities simply be that creatures had the opportunity to benefit or to withhold benefit from each other, not a world in which they had also the opportunity to cause each other pain? One answer to this is that if creatures have only the power to benefit and not the power to hurt each other, they obviously lack any very strong responsibility for each other. To bring out the point by a caricature—a world in which I could choose whether or not to give you sweets, but not whether or not to break your leg or make you unpopular, is not a world in which I have a very strong influence on your destiny, and so not a world in which I have a very full responsibility for you. Further, however, there is a point which will depend on an argument which I will give further on. In the actual world very often a man's withholding benefits from another is correlated with the latter's suffering some passive evil, either physical or mental. Thus if I withhold from you certain vitamins, you will suffer disease. Or if I deprive you of your wife by persuading her to live with me instead, you will suffer grief at the loss. Now it seems to me that a world in which such correlations did not hold would not necessarily be a better world than the world in which they do. The appropriateness of pain to bodily disease or deprivation, and of mental evils to various losses or lacks of a more spiritual kind, is something for which I shall argue in detail a little later.

So then the theodicist objects to (P2) on the grounds that the price of possible passive evils for other creatures is a price worth paying for agents to have great responsibilities for each other. It is a price which (logically) must be paid if they are to have those responsibilities. Here again a reasonable antitheodicist may see the point. In bringing up our own children, in order to give them responsibility, we try not to interfere too quickly in their quarrels— even at the price, sometimes, of younger children getting hurt physically. We try not to interfere, first, in order to train our children for responsibility in later life and second, because responsibility here and now is a good thing in itself. True, with respect to the first reason, whatever the effects on character produced by training, God could produce without training. But if he did so by imposing a full character on a humanly free creature, this would be giving him a character which he had not in any way chosen or adopted for himself. Yet it would seem a good

thing that a creator should allow humanly free creatures to influence by their own choices the sort of creatures they are to be, the kind of character they are to have. That means that the creator must create them immature, and allow them gradually to make decisions which affect the sort of beings they will be. And one of the greatest privileges which a creator can give to a creature is to allow him to help in the process of education, in putting alternatives before his fellows.

OBJECTION 3: THE QUANTITY OF EVIL

Yet though the antitheodicist may see the point, in theory, he may well react to it rather like this. "Certainly some independence is a good thing. But surely a father ought to interfere if his younger son is really getting badly hurt. The ideal of making men free and responsible is a good one, but there are limits to the amount of responsibility which it is good that men should have, and in our world men have too much responsibility. A good God would certainly have intervened long ago to stop some of the things which happen in our world." Here, I believe, lies the crux— it is simply a matter of quantity. The theodicist says that a good God could allow men to do to each other the hurt they do, in order to allow them to be free and responsible. But against him the antitheodicist puts forward as a moral principle (P3) that a creator able to do so ought to ensure that any creature whom he creates does not cause passive evils as many and as evil as those in our world. He says that in our world freedom and responsibility have gone too far—produced too much physical and mental hurt. God might well tolerate a boy hitting his younger brothers, but not Belsen.

The theodicist is in no way committed to saying that a good God will not stop things getting too bad. Indeed, if God made our world, he has clearly done so. There are limits to the amount and degree of evil which are possible in our world. Thus there are limits to the amount of pain which a person can suffer—persons live in our world only so many years and the amount which they can suffer at any given time (if mental goings-on are in any way correlated with bodily ones) is limited by their physiology. Further, theists often claim that from time to time God intervenes in the natural order which he has made to prevent evil which would otherwise occur. So the theodicist can certainly claim that a good God stops too much sufferings—it is just that he and his opponent draw the line in different places. The issue as regards the passive evils caused by men turns ultimately to the quantity of evil. To this crucial matter I shall return toward the end of the paper.

THE INTERCONNECTEDNESS OF GOOD AND EVIL

We shall have to turn next to the issue of passive evils not apparently caused by men. But, first, I must consider a further argument by the theodicist in support of the free-will defense and also an argument of the antitheodicist against it. The first is the argument that various evils are logically necessary conditions for the occurrence of actions of certain especially good kinds. Thus for a man to bear his suffering cheerfully there has to be suffering for him to bear. There have to be acts which irritate for another to show tolerance of them. Likewise, it is often said, acts of forgiveness, courage, self-sacrifice, compassion, overcoming temptation, etc., can be performed only if there are evils of various kinds. Here, however, we must be careful. One might reasonably claim that all that is necessary for some of these good acts (or acts as good as these) to be performed is belief in the existence of certain evils, not their actual existence. You can show compassion toward someone who appears to be suffering, but is not really; you can forgive someone who only appeared to insult you, but did not really. But if the world is to be populated with imaginary evils of the kind needed to enable creatures to perform acts of the above specially good kinds, it would have to be a world in which creatures are generally and systematically deceived about the feelings of their fellows— in which the behavior of creatures generally and unavoidably belies their feelings and intentions. I suggest, in the tradition of Descartes (*Meditations* 4, 5 and 6), that it would be a morally wrong act of a cre-

ator to create such a deceptive world. In that case, given a creator, then, without an immoral act on his part, for acts of courage, compassion, etc., to be acts open to men to perform, there have to be various evils. Evils give men the opportunity to perform those acts which show men at their best. A world without evils would be a world in which men could show no forgiveness, no compassion, no self-sacrifice. And men without that opportunity are deprived of the opportunity to show themselves at their noblest. For this reason God might well allow some of his creatures to perform evil acts with passive evils as consequences, since these provide the opportunity for especially noble acts.

Against the suggestion of the developed free-will defense that it would be justifiable for God to permit a creature to hurt another for the good of his or the other's soul, there is one natural objection which will surely be made. This is that it is generally supposed to be the duty of men to stop other men hurting each other badly. So why is it not God's duty to stop men hurting each other badly? Now the theodicist does not have to maintain that it is never God's duty to stop men hurting each other; but he does have to maintain that it is not God's duty in circumstances where it clearly is our duty to stop such hurt if we can—e.g., when men are torturing each other in mind or body in some of the ways in which they do this in our world and when, if God exists, he does not step in.

Now different views might be taken about the extent of our duty to interfere in the quarrels of others. But the most which could reasonably be claimed is surely this—that we have a duty to interfere in three kinds of circumstances—(1) if an oppressed person asks us to interfere and it is probable that he will suffer considerably if we do not, (2) if the participants are children or not of sane mind and it is probable that one or other will suffer considerably if we do not interfere, or (3) if it is probable that considerable harm will be done to others if we do not interfere. It is not very plausible to suppose that we have any duty to interfere in the quarrels of grown sane men who do not wish us to do so, unless it is probable that the harm will spread. Now note that in the characterization of each of the circumstances in which we would have a duty to interfere there occurs the word "probable," and it is being used in the "epistemic" sense—as "made probable by the total available evidence." But then the "probability" of an occurrence varies crucially with which community or individual is assessing it, and the amount of evidence which they have at the time in question. What is probable relative to your knowledge at t_1 may not be at all probable relative to my knowledge at t_2. Hence a person's duty to interfere in quarrels will depend on their probable consequences relative to that person's knowledge. Hence it follows that one who knows much more about the probable consequences of a quarrel may have no duty to interfere where another with less knowledge does have such a duty—and conversely. Hence a God who sees far more clearly than we do the consequences of quarrels may have duties very different from ours with respect to particular such quarrels. He may know that the suffering that A will cause B is not nearly as great as B's screams might suggest to us and will provide (unknown to us) an opportunity to C to help B recover and will thus give C a deep responsibility which he would not otherwise have. God may very well have reason for allowing particular evils which it is our bounden duty to attempt to stop at all costs simply because he knows so much more about them than we do. And this is no ad hoc hypothesis—it follows directly from the characterization of the kind of circumstances in which persons have a duty to interfere in quarrels.

We may have a duty to interfere in quarrels when God does not for a very different kind of reason. God, being our creator, the source of our beginning and continuation of existence, has rights over us which we do not have over our fellow-men. To allow a man to suffer for the good of his or someone else's soul one has to stand in some kind of parental relationship toward him. I don't have the right to let some stranger Joe Bloggs suffer for the good of his soul or of the soul of Bill Snoggs, but I do have *some* right of this kind in respect of my own children. I may let the younger son suffer *somewhat* for the good of his and his brother's soul. I have this right because in small part I am responsible for his existence, its beginning and continuance. If this is correct, then a fortiori, God who is, ex hypothesi, so much more the author of our

being than are our parents, has so many more rights in this respect. God has rights to allow others to suffer, while I do not have those rights and hence have a duty to interfere instead. In these two ways the theodicist can rebut the objection that if we have a duty to stop certain particular evils which men do to others, God must have this duty too.

OBJECTION 4: PASSIVE EVIL NOT DUE TO HUMAN ACTION

In the free-will defense, as elaborated above, the theist seems to me to have an adequate answer to the suggestion that necessarily a good God would prevent the occurrence of the evil which men cause—if we ignore the question of the quantity of evil, to which I will return at the end of my paper. But what of the passive evil apparently not due to human action? What of the pain caused to men by disease or earthquake or cyclone, and what too of animal pain which existed before there were men? There are two additional assumptions, each of which has been put forward to allow the free-will defense to show the compatibility of the existence of God and the existence of such evil. The first is that, despite appearances, men are ultimately responsible for disease, earthquake, cyclone, and much animal pain. There seem to be traces of this view in Genesis 3 : 16–20. One might claim that God ties the goodness of man to the well-being of the world and that a failure of one leads to a failure of the other. Lack of prayer, concern, and simple goodness lead to the evils in nature. This assumption, though it may do some service for the free-will defense, would seem unable to account for the animal pain which existed before there were men. The other assumption is that there exist humanly free creatures other than men, which we may call fallen angels, who have chosen to do evil, and have brought about the passive evils not brought about by men. These were given the care of much of the material world and have abused that care. For reasons already given, however, it is not God's moral duty to interfere to prevent the passive evils caused by such creatures. This defense has recently been used by, among others, Plantinga. This assumption, it seems to me, will do the job, and is not *clearly* false. It is also an assumption which was part of the Christian tradition long before the free-will defense was put forward in any logically rigorous form. I believe that this assumption may indeed be indispensable if the theist is to reconcile with the existence of God the existence of passive evils of certain kinds, e.g., certain animal pain. But I do not think that the theodicist need deploy it to deal with the central cases of passive evils not caused by men—mental evils and the human pain that is a sign of bodily malfunctioning. Note, however, that if he does not attribute such passive evils to the free choice of some other agent, the theodicist must attribute them to the direct action of God himself, or rather, what he must say is that God created a universe in which passive evils must necessarily occur in certain circumstances, the occurrence of which is necessary or at any rate not within the power of a humanly free agent to prevent. The antitheodicist then naturally claims, that although a creator might be justified in allowing free creatures to produce various evils, nevertheless (*P4*) a creator is never justified in creating a world in which evil results except by the action of a humanly free agent. Against this the theodicist tries to sketch reasons which a good creator might have for creating a world in which there is evil not brought about by humanly free agents. One reason which he produces is one which we have already considered earlier in the development of the free-will defense. This is the reason that various evils are logically necessary conditions for the occurrence of actions of certain especially noble kinds. This was adduced earlier as a reason why a creator might allow creatures to perform evil acts with passive evils as consequences. It can also be adduced as a reason why he might himself bring about passive evils—to give further opportunities for courage, patience, and tolerance. I shall consider here one further reason that, the theodicist may suggest, a good creator might have for creating a world in which various passive evils were implanted, which is another reason for rejecting (*P4*). It is, I think, a reason which is closely connected with some of the other reasons which we have been considering why a good creator might permit the existence of evil.

A creator who is going to create humanly free agents and place them in a universe has a choice of the kind of universe to create. First, he can create a finished universe in which nothing needs improving. Humanly free agents know what is right, and pursue it; and they achieve their purposes without hindrance. Second, he can create a basically evil universe, in which everything needs improving, and nothing can be improved. Or, third, he can create a basically good but half-finished universe—one in which many things need improving, humanly free agents do not altogether know what is right, and their purposes are often frustrated; but one in which agents can come to know what is right and can overcome the obstacles to the achievement of their purposes. In such a universe the bodies of creatures may work imperfectly and last only a short time; and creatures may be morally ill-educated, and set their affections on things and persons which are taken from them. The universe might be such that it requires long generations of cooperative effort between creatures to make perfect. While not wishing to deny the goodness of a universe of the first kind, I suggest that to create a universe of the third kind would be no bad thing, for it gives to creatures the privilege of making their own universe. Genesis 1 in telling of a God who tells men to "subdue" the earth pictures the creator as creating a universe of this third kind; and fairly evidently—given that men are humanly free agents—our universe is of this kind.

Now a creator who creates a half-finished universe of this third kind has a further choice as to how he molds the humanly free agents which it contains. Clearly he will have to give them a nature of some kind, that is, certain narrow purposes which they have a natural inclination to pursue until they choose or are forced to pursue others—e.g., the immediate attainment of food, sleep, and sex. There could hardly be humanly free agents without some such initial purposes. But what is he to do about their knowledge of their duty to improve the world—e.g., to repair their bodies when they go wrong, so that they can realize long-term purposes, to help others who cannot get food to do so, etc.? He could just give them a formal hazy knowledge that they had such reasons for action without giving them any strong inclination to pursue them. Such a policy might well seem an excessively laissez-faire one. We tend to think that parents who give their children no help toward taking the right path are less than perfect parents. So a good creator might well help agents toward taking steps to improve the universe. We shall see that he can do this in one of two ways.

An action is something done for a reason. A good creator, we supposed, will give to agents some reasons for doing right actions—e.g., that they are right, that they will improve the universe. These reasons are ones of which men can be aware and then either act on or not act on. The creator could help agents toward doing right actions by making these reasons more effective causally; that is, he could make agents so that by nature they were inclined (though not perhaps compelled) to pursue what is good. But this would be to impose a moral character on agents, to give them wide general purposes which they naturally pursue, to make them naturally altruistic, tenacious of purpose, or strong-willed. But to impose a character on creatures might well seem to take away from creatures the privilege of developing their own characters and those of their fellows. We tend to think that parents who try too forcibly to impose a character, however good a character, on their children, are less than perfect parents.

The alternative way in which a creator could help creatures to perform right actions is by sometimes providing additional reasons for creatures to do what is right, reasons which by their very nature have a strong causal influence. Reasons such as improving the universe or doing one's duty do not necessarily have a strong causal influence, for as we have seen creatures may be little influenced by them. Giving a creature reasons which by their nature were strongly causally influential on a particular occasion on any creature whatever his character, would not impose a particular character on a creature. It would, however, incline him to do what is right on that occasion and maybe subsequently too. Now if a reason is by its nature to be strongly causally influential it must be something of which the agent is aware which causally inclines him (whatever his character) to perform some action, to bring about some kind of change. What kind of reason could this be except the existence of an unpleasant feeling, either a sensation such as pain or an emotion such as a feeling of loss or deprivation? Such feelings are things of which agents are conscious, which cause them to do whatever action will

get rid of those feelings, and which provide reason for performing such action. An itch causally inclines a man to do whatever will cause the itch to cease, e.g., scratch, and provides a reason for doing that action. Its causal influence is quite independent of the agent—saint or sinner, strong-willed or weak-willed, will all be strongly inclined to get rid of their pains (though some may learn to resist the inclination). Hence a creator who wished to give agents some inclination to improve the world without giving them a character, a wide set of general purposes which they naturally pursue, would tie some of the imperfections of the world to physical or mental evils.

To tie desirable states of affairs to pleasant feelings would not have the same effect. Only an existing feeling can be causally efficacious. An agent could be moved to action by a pleasant feeling only when he had it, and the only action to which he could be moved would be to keep the world as it is, not to improve it. For men to have reasons which move men of any character to actions of perfecting the world, a creator needs to tie its imperfections to unpleasant feelings, that is, physical and mental evils.

There is to some considerable extent such tie-up in our universe. Pain normally occurs when something goes wrong with the working of our body which is going to lead to further limitation on the purposes which we can achieve; and the pain ends when the body is repaired. The existence of the pain spurs the sufferer, and others through the sympathetic suffering which arises when they learn of the sufferer's pain, to do something about the bodily malfunctioning. Yet giving men such feelings which they are inclined to end involves the imposition of no character. A man who is inclined to end his toothache by a visit to the dentist may be saint or sinner, strong-willed or weak-willed, rational or irrational. Any other way of which I can conceive of giving men an inclination to correct what goes wrong, and generally to improve the universe, would seem to involve imposing a character. A creator could, for example, have operated exclusively by threats and promises, whispering in men's ears, "unless you go to the dentist, you are going to suffer terribly," or "if you go to the dentist, you are going to feel wonderful." And if the order of nature is God's creation, he does indeed often provide us with such threats and promises—not by whispering in our ears but by providing inductive evidence. There is plenty of inductive evidence that unattended cuts and sores will lead to pain; that eating and drinking will lead to pleasure. Still, men do not always respond to threats and promises or take the trouble to notice inductive evidence (e.g., statistics showing the correlation between smoking and cancer). A creator could have made men so that they naturally took more account of inductive evidence. But to do so would be to impose character. It would be to make men, apart from any choice of theirs, rational and strong-willed.

Many mental evils too are caused by things going wrong in a man's life or in the life of his fellows and often serve as a spur to a man to put things right, either to put right the cause of the particular mental evil or to put similar things right. A man's feeling of frustration at the failure of his plans spurs him either to fulfill those plans despite their initial failure or to curtail his ambitions. A man's sadness at the failure of the plans of his child will incline him to help the child more in the future. A man's grief at the absence of a loved one inclines him to do whatever will get the loved one back. As with physical pain, the spur inclines a man to do what is right but does so without imposing a character—without, say, making a man responsive to duty, or strong-willed.

Physical and mental evils may serve as spurs to long-term cooperative research leading to improvement of the universe. A feeling of sympathy for the actual and prospective suffering of many from tuberculosis or cancer leads to acquisition of knowledge and provision of cure for future sufferers. Cooperative and long-term research and cure is a very good thing, the kind of thing toward which men need a spur. A man's suffering is never in vain if it leads through sympathy to the work of others which eventually provides a long-term cure. True, there could be sympathy without a sufferer for whom the sympathy is felt. Yet in a world made by a creator, there cannot be sympathy on the large scale without a sufferer, for whom the sympathy is felt, unless the creator planned for creatures generally to be deceived about the feelings of their fellows; and that, we have claimed, would be morally wrong.

So generally many evils have a biological and psychological utility in producing spurs to right action without imposition of character, a goal which it is hard to conceive of being realized in any other way. This point provides a reason for the rejection of (P4). There are other kinds of reason which have been adduced reasons for rejecting (P4)—e.g., that a creator could be justified in bringing about evil as a punishment—but I have no space to discuss these now. I will, however, in passing, mention briefly one reason why a creator might make a world in which certain mental evils were tied to things going wrong. Mental suffering and anguish are a man's proper tribute to losses and failures, and a world in which men were immunized from such reactions to things going wrong would be a worse world than ours. By showing proper feelings a man shows his respect for himself and others. Thus a man who feels no grief at the death of his child or the seduction of his wife is rightly branded by us as insensitive, for he has failed to pay the proper tribute of feeling to others, to show in his feeling how much he values them, and thereby failed to value them properly—for valuing them properly involves having proper reactions of feeling to their loss. Again, only a world in which men feel sympathy for losses experienced by their friends, is a world in which love has full meaning.

So, I have argued, there seem to be kinds of justification for the evils which exist in the world, available to the theodicist. Although a good creator might have very different kinds of justification for producing, or allowing others to produce, various different evils, there is a central thread running through the kind of theodicy which I have made my theodicist put forward. This is that it is a good thing that a creator should make a half-finished universe and create immature creatures, who are humanly free agents, to inhabit it; and that he should allow them to exercise some choice over what kind of creatures they are to become and what sort of universe is to be (while at the same time giving them a slight push in the direction of doing what is right); and that the creatures should have power to affect not only the development of the inanimate universe but the well-being and moral character of their fellows, and that there should be opportunities for creatures to develop noble characters and do especially noble actions. My theodicist has argued that if a creator is to make a universe of this kind, then evils of various kinds may inevitably—at any rate temporarily—belong to such a universe; and that it is not a morally bad thing to create such a universe despite the evils.

THE QUANTITY OF EVIL

Now a morally sensitive antitheodicist might well in principle accept some of the above arguments. He may agree that in principle it is not wrong to create humanly free agents, despite the possible evils which might result, or to create pains as biological warnings. But where the crunch comes, it seems to me, is in the amount of evil which exists in our world. The antitheodicist says, all right, it would not be wrong to create men able to harm each other, but it would be wrong to create men able to put each other in Belsen. It would not be wrong to create backaches and headaches, even severe ones, as biological warnings, but not the long severe incurable pain of some diseases. In reply the theodicist must argue that a creator who allowed men to do little evil would be a creator who gave them little responsibility; and a creator who gave them only coughs and colds, and not cancer and cholera would be a creator who treated men as children instead of giving them real encouragement to subdue the world. The argument must go on with regard to particular cases. The antitheodicist must sketch in detail and show his adversary the horrors of particular wars and diseases. The theodicist in reply must sketch in detail and show his adversary the good which such disasters make possible. He must show to his opponent men working together for good, men helping each other to overcome disease and famine; the heroism of men who choose the good in spite of temptation, who help others not merely by giving them food but who teach them right and wrong, give them something to live for and something to die for. A world in which this is possible can only be a world in which there is much evil as well as great good. Interfere to stop the evil and you cut off the good.

Like all moral arguments this one can be settled only by each party pointing to the consequences of his opponent's moral position and trying to show that his opponent is committed to implausible consequences. They must try, too, to show that each other's moral principles do or do not fit well with other moral principles which each accepts. The exhibition of consequences is a long process, and it takes time to convince an opponent even if he is prepared to be rational, more time than is available in this paper. All that I claim to have *shown* here is that there is no *easy proof* of incompatibility between the existence of evils of the kinds we find around us and the existence of God. Yet my sympathies for the outcome of any more detailed argument are probably apparent, and indeed I may have said enough to convince some readers as to what that outcome would be.

My sympathies lie, of course, with the theodicist. The theodicist's God is a god who thinks the higher goods so worthwhile that he is prepared to ask a lot of man in the way of enduring evil. Creatures determining in cooperation their own character and future, and that of the universe in which they live, coming in the process to show charity, forgiveness, faith, and self-sacrifice is such a worthwhile thing that a creator would not be unjustified in making or permitting a certain amount of evil in order that they should be realized. No doubt a good creator would put a limit on the amount of evil in the world and perhaps an end to the struggle with it after a number of years. But if he allowed creatures to struggle with evil, he would allow them a real struggle with a real enemy, not a parlor game. The antitheodicist's mistake lies in extrapolating too quickly from *our* duties when faced with evil to the duties of a creator, while ignoring the enormous differences in the circumstances of each. Each of us at one time can make the existing universe better or worse only in a few particulars. A creator can choose the kind of universe and the kind of creatures there are to be. It seldom becomes us in our ignorance and weakness to do anything more than remove the evident evils—war, disease, and famine. We seldom have the power or the knowledge or the right to use such evils to forward deeper and longer-term goods. To make an analogy, the duty of the weak and ignorant is to eliminate cowpox and not to spread it, while the doctor has a duty to spread it (under carefully controlled conditions). But a creator who made or permitted his creatures to suffer much evil and asked them to suffer more is a very demanding creator, one with high ideals who expects a lot. For myself I can say that I would not be too happy to worship a creator who expected too little of his creatures. Nevertheless such a God does ask a lot of creatures. A theodicist is in a better position to defend a theodicy such as I have outlined if he is prepared also to make the further additional claim—that God knowing the worthwhileness of the conquest of evil and the perfecting of the universe by men, shared with them this task by subjecting himself as man to the evil in the world. A creator is more justified in creating or permitting evils to be overcome by his creatures if he is prepared to share with them the burden of the suffering and effort.

FOR FURTHER REFLECTION

1. Has Swinburne successfully met the challenges thrown to him by Russell? Given the free-will defense, can you agree with Swinburne that an all-powerful and all-good God could allow the evil that exists? Why or why not?

2. Evaluate Swinburne's arguments for the existence of passive evil. How cogent are they? What would someone like Russell say in reply?

3. The free-will defense only works if human beings are truly free. The question is, "Are we free, or are we determined by antecedent causes and the laws of nature?" Many philosophers believe that we are totally determined. Keep this issue in mind when you turn to the subject of free will and determinism in Part V.

C. Faith and Reason

> Our passional nature not only lawfully may, but must, decide an option between propositions, whenever it is a genuine option that cannot by its nature be decided on intellectual grounds; for to say under such circumstances, "Do not decide, but leave the question open," is itself a passional decision, —just like deciding yes or no,—and is attended with the same risk of losing truth.
>
> *William James,* The Will to Believe

> It is wrong always, everywhere, and for anyone, to believe anything upon insufficient evidence.
>
> *W. K. Clifford,* The Ethics of Belief

One of the most important focuses of philosophy of religion is on the relationship between faith and reason. Is religious belief rational? Or is faith essentially irrational or, at least, *a*rational? If we can't prove the claims of religious belief, is it nevertheless reasonable to believe these claims? For example, even if we *don't* have a deductive proof for the existence of God, is it *nevertheless* reasonable to believe that God exists? This debate has been dominated by two opposing positions. The first position asserts that faith and reason are commensurable (that is, it is rational to believe in God). The second position denies this assertion. People who hold the first position disagree about how compatible faith and reason are; most, like Aquinas, relegate the compatibility to the "preambles of faith" (the existence of God, and God's nature) and don't include the "articles of faith" (such as the doctrine of the incarnation). Few have gone as far as Immanuel Kant, who maintained that there was complete harmony between reason and faith; that is, that religious belief could be held by reason alone.

The second position has two subpositions. One asserts that faith is opposed to reason (making unlikely bedfellows of such men as David Hume and Søren Kierkegaard) and considers faith irrational. The second subposition asserts that faith is higher than reason, transcends reason. John Calvin and Karl Barth assert that a natural theology is inappropriate because it seeks to meet unbelief on its own ground (on the ground of ordinary, finite reason). Revelation, however, is "self-authenticating," "carrying with it its own evidence." We can call this position the "transrational" view of faith. Faith is not so much *against* reason as *above* it and *beyond* its proper domain. Kierkegaard holds that the two subpositions are compatible, because he holds that faith is both above reason (superior to it) and against reason (because human reason has been affected by sin). These irrationalist and transrationalist positions are sometimes hard to distinguish. Faith seems to be so highly valued that reason ends up looking not just inadequate but even culpable: using reason where faith claims the victory is not only inappropriate but irreverent—and faithless.

This section of Part III begins with a brief debate that took place in 1948 among three Oxford University philosophers. First, Antony Flew challenges theists to state the conditions under which they would give up their faith. He argues that unless one can state what would "falsify" one's belief, one does not have a meaningful (testable, definable) belief. If nothing *could* count against the belief, it doesn't make a definite assertion. Serious truth claims must be testable.

Second, R. M. Hare argues that Flew's way of describing faith is wrong, because religious faith consists of a set of profound, unfalsifiable assumptions (which he calls *bliks*) that govern all of a person's other beliefs. There are both rational and irrational bliks. Examples of rational bliks are the beliefs that "Every event has a cause" and that "It is wrong to cause unnecessary harm." Most of us hold these beliefs very deeply but cannot prove them. An example of an irrational blik is the paranoid's belief that everyone hates him (or her) and is conspiring to harm him. Hare argues that we cannot live without some bliks. Not all our beliefs can be proved. Theistic religion is a rational blik for many of us. Although it is not subject to rational scrutiny, it is not insane or irrational.

Third, Basil Mitchell suggests a compromise. Rational considerations do enter the debate on religious faith, but no one can say exactly when a gradual accumulation of evidence begins to count enough against a belief so that the believer feels obliged to stop believing it. Rational considerations count against religious belief, but the believer struggles to keep them from counting decisively against the belief.

Can faith be rationally justified? Is it rationally acceptable to believe in God? This is the rationalist challenge to religion. Can it and should it be met?

The next readings in this section of Part III deal with a *pragmatic* or *practical* justification for religious belief. That is, even if we cannot find good evidence for religious belief, would it perhaps be in our interest to get ourselves to believe in these propositions anyway? And would such believing be morally permissible? In the first essay, "Faith Is a Rational Wager," Blaise Pascal argues that a cost-benefit analysis of the matter shows it is very reasonable to believe that God exists, regardless of whether we have good evidence for that belief. The argument goes something like this: regarding the proposition

"God exists," reason is neutral. It can neither prove nor disprove it. But we must choose, because not choosing *for* God is in effect choosing *against* him, and thus losing the possible benefits of belief. Since these benefits promise to be infinite and the loss equally infinite, we might set forth the possibilities thus:

	God exists	**God does not exist**
I believe	A. Infinite gain with minimal finite loss	B. Overal finite loss in terms of sacrifice of earthly goods
I do not believe	C. Infinite loss with finite gain	D. Overall finite gain

Some sacrifice of earthly pleasures is involved with belief in God, but by multiplying the various combinations we find that there is an incommensurability between A and C on one hand and B and D on the other. No matter how enormous the *finite* gain, the mere possibility of *infinite* gain will always make the latter infinitely preferable to the former. So the only relevant considerations are A and C. Since A (believing in God) promises infinite happiness and C (not believing in God) infinite unhappiness, a rational cost-benefit analysis leaves no doubt about what we should do. We have a clear self-interested reason for believing in God.

Go over this argument closely. Are there any weaknesses in it? Does it show that we all should do whatever is necessary to come to believe that God exists? Is such a belief necessary and sufficient for eternal happiness?

In the next essay, "The Ethics of Belief," the British philosopher W. K. Clifford sets up reason's roadblock to such pragmatic justifications for religious belief. Clifford argues that there is an ethics to believing: all belief without sufficient evidence is immoral. Pragmatic justifications are not justifications at all but counterfeits of genuine justifications, which must always be based on evidence.

Clifford illustrates his thesis with the example of a shipowner who sends to sea a ship full of emigrants. He knows the ship is old and badly built, but he doesn't have the ship inspected. Dismissing from his mind all doubts and suspicions of the ship's unseaworthiness, he trusts in Providence. Thus he feels sincere and comfortable, and after the ship sinks, killing all the passengers, he collects his insurance money without a trace of guilt.

Clifford comments that although the shipowner sincerely believed all was well with the ship, his sincerity doesn't excuse him, because "he had no right to believe on such evidence as was before him." One has an obligation to believe propositions only on sufficient evidence. Furthermore, it is not valid to object that the shipowner had an obligation to *act* in a certain way (inspect the ship), not to *believe* in a certain way. Although he has an obligation to inspect the ship, the objection overlooks the function of belief as guiding action. "No man holding a strong belief on one side of a question, or even wishing to hold a belief on one side, can investigate it with such fairness and completeness as if he were really in doubt and unbiassed; so that the existence of a belief not founded on fair inquiry unfits a man for the performance of this necessary duty." The general conclusion is that it is wrong *always and for anyone* to believe anything on insufficient evidence.

The classic response to Clifford's ethics of belief is U.S. philosopher William James's "The Will to Believe" (1896), the next essay in this section. James argues that life would become much poorer if we believed only such a stingy, Scroogelike epistemology as Clifford proposes. In everyday life, where the evidence for important propositions is often unclear, we must either live by faith or stop acting at all. Although we may not make leaps of faith to just anywhere, sometimes practical need forces us to decide on propositions that don't have their truth value written all over their faces, like prices on windshields at used car lots.

In "The Sentiment of Rationality" (1879), James defines "faith" as "a belief in something concerning which doubt is still theoretically possible; and as the test of belief is willingness to act, one may say that faith is the readiness to act in a cause the prosperous issue of which is not certified to us in advance." In "The Will to Believe," James speaks of "belief" as a live, important hypothesis, on which we can't avoid deciding, because not choosing is, in effect, choosing against the hypothesis. For example, in "The Sentiment of Rationality," a mountain climber finds himself in a position from which he can only escape by making an enormous leap. If he tries to add up the evidence that he can make the leap successfully, and won't believe on insufficient evidence, he will become paralyzed by emotions of fear and mistrust, and hence be lost. This climber would be better off getting himself to believe that he can and will make the leap. "In this case . . . the part of wisdom clearly is to believe what one desires; for the belief is one of the indispensable preliminary conditions of the realization of its object. *There are then cases where faith creates its own verification*" (italics in original).

James claims that religion may be such a genuine option for many people, and where it is an option the individual has the right to believe the better story rather than the worse. To do so, one must use willpower to believe, to bridge the gap left by inadequate evidence.

Keep in mind two questions while you read these articles: one is descriptive and the other is normative. The first is whether it is possible to believe propositions at will. How can we get ourselves to believe propositions that the evidence doesn't force on us? Surely we can't believe that the world is flat or that "2 + 2 = 5" simply by willing to do so, but which propositions (if any) *are* subject to willpower? Is it psychologically possible to make the kinds of moves that Pascal and James advise? Do such moves involve self-deception? If we know that the only cause for believing in a religious proposition is our desire to believe, can we, if we are rational, continue to believe? Are willed beliefs self-defeating?

The second question deals with the ethics of belief, stressed by Clifford. Supposing that we can get ourselves to believe or disbelieve propositions, is this self-manipulation morally permissible? What are the arguments for and against integrity of belief?

In the final reading, Alvin Plantinga argues that the believer, who does not have arguments to support his or her belief in God, does not violate the ethics of belief. Nor is he or she being irrational, because such a belief is "properly basic."

ANTONY FLEW, R. M. HARE, AND BASIL MITCHELL

A DEBATE ON THE RATIONALITY OF RELIGIOUS BELIEF

Antony Flew is professor of philosophy emeritus at the University of Reading in England. R. M. Hare (recently deceased) and Basil Mitchell were, until their retirement, professors of philosophy at Oxford University. All three were educated at Oxford, where they all began their teaching careers. In this 1948 Oxford symposium, Flew challenges theists to state the conditions under which they would give up their faith, because, he contends, unless one can state what would falsify one's belief, the belief isn't meaningful. If nothing could count against the belief, it doesn't make a genuine assertion, because serious truth claims must be subject to possible falsification.

R. M. Hare responds that, on the contrary, religious faith consists of a set of profoundly unfalsifiable assumptions (which he calls *bliks*), which govern all of a person's other beliefs. There are insane and sane bliks, and everyone has some blik or other. Even the scientist makes these fundamental assumptions. So religion should not be subject to the kind of rational scrutiny Flew urges.

Basil Mitchell seeks a compromise. Rational considerations enter the debate on faith, but no one can say exactly when a gradual accumulation of evidence is enough to overthrow religious belief. Although rational considerations do count against faith, the believer will not let them count *decisively* against it.

ANTONY FLEW

Let us begin with a parable. It is a parable developed from a tale told by John Wisdom in his haunting and revelatory article "Gods." Once upon a time two explorers came upon a clearing in the jungle. In the clearing were growing many flowers and many weeds. One explorer says, "Some gardener must tend this plot." The other disagrees, "There is no gardener." So they pitch their tents and set a watch. No gardener is ever seen. "But perhaps he is an invisible gardener." So they set up a barbed-wire fence. They electrify it. They patrol with bloodhounds. (For they remember how H. G. Wells's *The Invisible Man* could be both smelt and touched though he could not be seen.) But no shrieks ever suggest that some intruder has received a shock. No movements of the wire ever betray an invisible climber. The bloodhounds never

From *New Essays in Philosophical Theology*, edited by Antony Flew and Alasdair McIntyre (London: SCM Press, 1955), pp. 96–108. Copyright © 1955 by Antony Flew and Alasdair McIntyre. Footnotes edited.

give cry. Yet still the Believer is not convinced. "But there is a gardener, invisible, intangible, insensible to electric shocks, a gardener who has no scent and makes no sound, a gardener who comes secretly to look after the garden which he loves." At last the Sceptic despairs. "But what remains of your original assertion? Just how does what you call an invisible, intangible, eternally elusive gardener differ from an imaginary gardener or even from no gardener at all?"

In this parable we can see how what starts as an assertion, that something exists or that there is some analogy between certain complexes of phenomena, may be reduced step by step to an altogether different status, to an expression perhaps of a "picture preference." The Sceptic says there is no gardener. The Believer says there is a gardener (but invisible, etc.). One man talks about sexual behaviour. Another man prefers to talk of Aphrodite (but knows that there is not really a superhuman person additional to, and somehow responsible for, all sexual phenomena). The process of qualification may be checked at any point before the original assertion is completely withdrawn and something of that first assertion will remain (Tautology). Mr. Wells's invisible man could not, admittedly, be seen, but in all other respects he was a man like the rest of us. But though the process of qualification may be, and of course usually is, checked in time, it is not always judiciously so halted. Someone may dissipate his assertion completely without noticing that he has done so. A fine brash hypothesis may thus be killed by inches, the death by a thousand qualifications.

And in this, it seems to me, lies the peculiar danger, the endemic evil, of theological utterance. Take such utterances as "God has a plan," "God created the world," "God loves us as a father loves his children." They look at first sight very much like assertions, vast cosmological assertions. Of course, this is no sure sign that they either are, or are intended to be, assertions. But let us confine ourselves to the cases where those who utter such sentences intend them to express assertions. (Merely remarking parenthetically that those who intend or interpret such utterances as crypto-commands, expressions of wishes, disguised ejaculations, concealed ethics, or as anything else but assertions, are unlikely to succeed in making them either properly orthodox or practically effective.)

Now to assert that such and such is the case is necessarily equivalent to denying that such and such is not the case. Suppose then that we are in doubt as to what someone who gives vent to an utterance is asserting, or suppose that, more radically, we are sceptical as to whether he is really asserting anything at all, one way of trying to understand (or perhaps it will be to expose) his utterance is to attempt to find what he would regard as counting against, or as being incompatible with, its truth. For if the utterance is indeed an assertion, it will necessarily be equivalent to a denial of the negation of that assertion. And anything which would count against the assertion, or which would induce the speaker to withdraw it and to admit that it had been mistaken, must be part of (or the whole of) the meaning of the negation of that assertion. And to know the meaning of the negation of an assertion, is as near as makes no matter, to know the meaning of that assertion. And if there is nothing which a putative assertion denies then there is nothing which it asserts either: and so it is not really an assertion. When the Sceptic in the parable asked the Believer, "Just how does what you call an invisible, intangible, eternally elusive gardener differ from an imaginary gardener or even from no gardener at all?" he was suggesting that the Believer's earlier statement had been so eroded by qualification that it was no longer an assertion at all.

Now it often seems to people who are not religious as if there was no conceivable event or series of events the occurrence of which would be admitted by sophisticated religious people to be a sufficient reason for conceding "There wasn't a God after all" or "God does not really love us then." Someone tells us that God loves us as a father loves his children. We are reassured. But then we see a child dying of inoperable cancer of the throat. His earthly father is driven frantic in his efforts to help, but this Heavenly Father reveals no obvious sign of concern. Some qualification is made—God's love is "not a merely human love" or it is "an inscrutable love," perhaps—and we realize that such sufferings are quite compatible with the truth of the assertion that "God loves us as a father (but, of course, . . .)." We are reassured again. But then perhaps we ask: what is this assurance of God's (appropriately qualified) love worth, what is this apparent guarantee really a guarantee against? Just what would have to happen not merely (morally and wrongly) to tempt but also (logically and rightly) to entitle us to say "God does not love us" or even "God does not exist?" I therefore put to the succeeding symposiasts the simple central questions, "What would have to occur or to have occurred to constitute for you a disproof of the love of, or of the existence of, God?"

R. M. HARE

I wish to make it clear that I shall not try to defend Christianity in particular, but religion in general—not because I do not believe in Christianity, but because you cannot understand what Christianity is, until you have understood what religion is.

I must begin by confessing that, on the ground marked out by Flew, he seems to me to be completely victorious. I therefore shift my ground by relating another parable. A certain lunatic is convinced that all dons want to murder him. His friends introduce him to all the mildest and most respectable dons that they can find, and after each of them has retired, they say, "You see, he doesn't really want to murder you; he spoke to you in a most cordial manner; surely you are convinced now?" But the lunatic replies, "Yes, but that was only his diabolical cunning; he's really plotting against me the whole time, like the rest of them; I know it I tell you." However many kindly dons are produced, the reaction is still the same.

Now we say that such a person is deluded. But what is he deluded about? About the truth or falsity of an assertion? Let us apply Flew's test to him. There is no behaviour of dons that can be enacted which he will accept as counting against his theory; and therefore his theory, on this test, asserts nothing. But it does not follow that there is no difference between what he thinks about dons and what most of us think about them—otherwise we should not call him a lunatic and ourselves sane, and dons would have no reason to feel uneasy about his presence in Oxford.

Let us call that in which we differ from this lunatic, our respective *bliks*. He has an insane *blik* about dons; we have a sane one. It is important to realize that we

have a sane one, not no *blik* at all; for there must be two sides to any argument—if he has a wrong *blik,* then those who are right about dons must have a right one. Flew has shown that a *blik* does not consist in an assertion or system of them; but nevertheless it is very important to have the right *blik*.

Let us try to imagine what it would be like to have different *bliks* about other things than dons. When I am driving my car, it sometimes occurs to me to wonder whether my movements of the steering-wheel will always continue to be followed by corresponding alterations in the direction of the car. I have never had a steering failure, though I have had skids, which must be similar. Moreover, I know enough about how the steering of my car is made, to know the sort of thing that would have to go wrong for the steering to fail—steel joints would have to part, or steel rods break, or something—but how do I know that this won't happen? The truth is, I don't know; I just have a *blik* about steel and its properties, so that normally I trust the steering of my car; but I find it not at all difficult to imagine what it would be like to lose this *blik* and acquire the opposite one. People would say I was silly about steel; but there would be no mistaking the reality of the difference between our respective *bliks*—for example, I should never go in a motor-car. Yet I should hesitate to say that the difference between us was the difference between contradictory assertions. No amount of safe arrivals or bench-tests will remove my *blik* and restore the normal one: for my *blik* is compatible with any finite number of such tests.

It was Hume who taught us that our whole commerce with the world depends upon our *blik* about the world; and that differences between *bliks* about the world cannot be settled by observation of what happens in the world. That was why, having performed the interesting experiment of doubting the ordinary man's *blik* about the world, and showing that no proof could be given to make us adopt one *blik* rather than another, he turned to backgammon to take his mind off the problem. It seems, indeed, to be impossible even to formulate as an assertion the normal *blik* about the world which makes me put my confidence in the future reliability of steel joints, in the continued ability of the road to support my car, and not gape beneath it revealing nothing below; in the general nonhomicidal tendencies of dons; in my own continued well-being (in some sense of that word that I may not now fully understand) if I continued to do what is right according to my lights; in the general likelihood of people like Hitler coming to a bad end. But perhaps a formulation less inadequate than most is to be found in the Psalms: "The earth is weak and all the inhabiters thereof: I bear up the pillars of it."

The mistake of the position which Flew selects for attack is to regard this kind of talk as some sort of *explanation,* as scientists are accustomed to use the word. As such, it would obviously be ludicrous. We no longer believe in God as an Atlas—*nous n'avons pas besoin de cette hypothèse.* But it is nevertheless true to say that, as Hume saw, without a *blik* there can be no explanation; for it is by our *bliks* that we decide what is and what is not an explanation. Suppose we believed that everything that happened, happened by pure chance. This would not of course be an assertion; for it is compatible with anything happening or not happening, and so, incidentally, is its contradictory. But if we had this belief, we should not be able to explain or predict or plan anything. Thus, although we should not be *asserting* anything different from those of a more normal belief, there would be a great difference between us; and this is the sort of difference that there is between those who really believe in God and those who really disbelieve in him.

The word "really" is important, and may excite suspicion. I put it in, because when people have had a good Christian upbringing, as have most of those who now profess not to believe in any sort of religion, it is very hard to discover what they really believe. The reason why they find it so easy to think that they are not religious, is that they have never got into the frame of mind of one who suffers from the doubts to which religion is the answer. Not for them the terrors of the primitive jungle. Having abandoned some of the more picturesque fringes of religion, they think that they have abandoned the whole thing—whereas in fact they still have got, and could not live without, a religion of a comfortably substantial, albeit highly sophisticated, kind, which differs from that of many "religious people" in little more than this, that "religious people" like to sing Psalms about theirs—a very natural and proper thing to do. But nevertheless there

may be a big difference lying behind—the difference between two people who, though side by side, are walking in different directions. I do not know in what direction Flew is walking; perhaps he does not know either. But we have had some examples recently of various ways in which one can walk away from Christianity, and there are any number of possibilities. After all, man has not changed biologically since primitive times; it is his religion that has changed, and it can easily change again. And if you do not think that such changes make a difference, get acquainted with some Sikhs and some Mussulmans of the same Punjabi stock; you will find them quite different sorts of people.

There is an important difference between Flew's parable and my own which we have not yet noticed. The explorers do not *mind* about their garden; they discuss it with interest, but not with concern. But my lunatic, poor fellow, minds about dons; and I mind about the steering of my car; it often has people in it that I care for. It is because I mind very much about what goes on in the garden in which I find myself, that I am unable to share the explorers' detachment.

BASIL MITCHELL

Flew's article is searching and perceptive, but there is, I think, something odd about his conduct of the theologian's case. The theologian surely would not deny that the fact of pain counts against the assertion that God loves men. This very incompatibility generates the most intractable of theological problems—the problem of evil. So the theologian *does* recognize the fact of pain as counting against Christian doctrine. But it is true that he will not allow it—or anything—to count decisively against it; for he is committed by his faith to trust in God. His attitude is not that of the detached observer, but of the believer.

Perhaps this can be brought out by yet another parable. In time of war in an occupied country, a member of the resistance meets one night a stranger who deeply impresses him. They spend that night together in conversation. The Stranger tells the partisan that he himself is on the side of the resistance—

indeed that he is in command of it, and urges the partisan to have faith in him no matter what happens. The partisan is utterly convinced at that meeting of the Stranger's sincerity and constancy and undertakes to trust him.

They never meet in conditions of intimacy again. But sometimes the Stranger is seen helping members of the resistance, and the partisan is grateful and says to his friends, "He is on our side."

Sometimes he is seen in the uniform of the police handing over patriots to the occupying power. On these occasions his friends murmur against him: but the partisan still says, "He is on our side." He still believes that, in spite of appearances, the Stranger did not deceive him. Sometimes he asks the Stranger for help and receives it. He is then thankful. Sometimes he asks and does not receive it. Then he says, "The Stranger knows best." Sometimes his friends, in exasperation, say "Well, what *would* he have to do for you to admit that you were wrong and that he is not on our side?" But the partisan refuses to answer. He will not consent to put the Stranger to the test. And sometimes his friends complain, "Well, if *that's* what you mean by his being on our side, the sooner he goes over to the other side the better."

The partisan of the parable does not allow anything to count decisively against the proposition "The Stranger is on our side." This is because he has committed himself to trust the Stranger. But he of course recognizes that the Stranger's ambiguous behavior *does* count against what he believes about him. It is precisely this situation which constitutes the trial of his faith.

When the partisan asks for help and doesn't get it, what can he do? He can (*a*) conclude that the stranger is not on our side or: (*b*) maintain that he is on our side, but that he has reasons for withholding help.

The first he will refuse to do. How long can he uphold the second position without its becoming just silly?

I don't think one can say in advance. It will depend on the nature of the impression created by the Stranger in the first place. It will depend, too, on the manner in which he takes the Stranger's behaviour. If he blandly dismisses it as of no consequence, as having no bearing upon his belief, it will be assumed that he is thoughtless or insane. And it quite obviously won't do for him to say easily, "Oh, when used of the Stranger the phrase 'is on our side' *means* ambiguous behavior of this sort." In that case he would like the religious man who says blandly of a terrible disaster "It is God's will." No, he will only be regarded as sane and reasonable in his belief, if he experiences in himself the full force of the conflict.

It is here that my parable differs from Hare's. The partisan admits that many things may and do count against belief: whereas Hare's lunatic who has a *blik* about dons doesn't admit that anything counts against his *blik*. Nothing *can* count against *bliks*. Also the partisan has a reason for having in the first instance committed himself, viz. the character of the Stranger; whereas the lunatic has no reason for his *blik* about dons—because, of course, you can't have reasons for *bliks*.

This means that I agree with Flew that theological utterances must be assertions. The partisan is making an assertion when he says, "The Stranger is on our side."

Do I want to say that the partisan's belief about the Stranger is, in any sense, an explanation? I think I do. It explains and makes sense of the Stranger's behaviour: it helps to explain also the resistance movement in the context of which he appears. In each case it differs from the interpretation which the others put upon the same facts.

"God loves men" resembles "the Stranger is on our side" (and many other significant statements, e.g. historical ones) in not being conclusively falsifiable. They can both be treated in at least three different ways: (1) As provisional hypotheses to be discarded if experience tells against them; (2) As significant articles of faith; (3) As vacuous formulae (expressing, perhaps, a desire for reassurance) to which experience makes no difference and which make no difference to life.

The Christian, once he has committed himself, is precluded by his faith from taking up the first attitude: "Thou shalt not tempt the Lord thy God." He is in constant danger, as Flew has observed, of slipping into the third. But he need not; and, if he does, it is a failure in faith as well as in logic.

FOR FURTHER REFLECTION

1. What does the "garden" parable mean? How does Flew interpret it? Do you agree with him? Why or why not?

2. What does Flew mean by saying that a brash hypothesis can be "killed by inches, the death by a thousand qualifications"?

3. Analyze the different strategies in our three philosophers' statements. Who has made the best case? Explain your choice.

4. Should the believer follow Flew's advice and state what would count against his or her faith? Should one's faith be open to revision or rejection on the basis of arguments? Discuss your answers.

5. Must the believer be able to cite evidence before he or she can affirm that it is rational to believe in God? Why or why not?

BLAISE PASCAL

FAITH IS A RATIONAL WAGER

Blaise Pascal (1623–1662) was a French scientist, philosopher, and mathematician. He founded probability theory and made important contributions to science through his studies of barometric pressure. On converting to a radical form of Catholicism in 1653, he turned all his attention to religious matters. In this famous section from his *Pensées* (or *Thoughts*), Pascal argues that a cost-benefit analysis shows it is eminently reasonable to get ourselves to believe that God exists, regardless of whether we have good evidence for that belief. The argument goes something like this: Reason can neither prove nor disprove the proposition "God exists." But we must make a choice, because not to choose for God is in effect to choose against him and thus to lose the possible benefits of belief. Since these benefits promise to be infinite— and the loss equally infinite—gamble on faith.

Infinite—nothing.—Our soul is cast into a body, where it finds number, time, dimension. Thereupon it reasons, and calls this nature, necessity, and can believe nothing else.

Unity joined to infinity adds nothing to it, no more than one foot to an infinite measure. The finite is annihilated in the presence of the infinite, and becomes a pure nothing. So our spirit before God, so our justice before divine justice. There is not so great disproportion between our justice and that of God, as between unity and infinity.

The justice of God must be vast like His compassion. Now, justice to the outcast is less vast, and ought less to offend our feelings than mercy towards the elect.

We know that there is an infinite, and are ignorant of its nature. As we know it to be false that numbers

From Blaise Pascal, *Thoughts,* trans. W. F. Trotter (New York: Collier & Son, 1910).

are finite, it is therefore true that there is an infinity in number. But we do not know what it is. It is false that it is even, it is false that it is odd; for the addition of a unit can make no change in its nature. Yet it is a number, and every number is odd or even (this is certainly true of every finite number). So we may well know that there is a God without knowing what He is. Is there not one substantial truth, seeing there are so many things which are not the truth itself?

We know then the existence and nature of the finite, because we also are finite and have extension. We know the existence of the infinite, and are ignorant of its nature, because it has extension like us, but not limits like us. But we know neither the existence nor the nature of God, because He has neither extension nor limits.

But by faith we know His existence; in glory we shall know His nature. Now, I have already shown that we may well know the existence of a thing, without knowing its nature.

Let us now speak according to natural lights.

If there is a God, He is infinitely incomprehensible, since, having neither parts nor limits, He has no affinity to us. We are then incapable of knowing either what He is or if He is. This being so, who will dare to undertake the decision of the question? Not we, who have no affinity to Him.

Who then will blame Christians for not being able to give a reason for their belief, since they profess a religion for which they cannot give a reason? They declare, in expounding it to the world, that it is a foolishness, *stultitiam;* and then you complain that they do not prove it! If they proved it, they would not keep their words; it is in lacking proofs, that they are not lacking in sense. "Yes, but although this excuses those who offer it as such, and takes away from them the blame of putting it forward without reason, it does not excuse those who receive it." Let us then examine this point, and say, "God is, or He is not." But to which side shall we incline? Reason can decide nothing here. There is an infinite chaos which separates us. A game is being played at the extremity of this infinite distance where heads or tails will turn up. What will you wager? According to reason, you can do neither the one thing nor the other; according to reason, you can defend neither of the propositions.

Do not then reprove for error those who have made a choice; for you know nothing about it. "No, but I blame them for having made, not this choice, but a choice; for again both he who chooses heads and he who chooses tails are equally at fault, they are both in the wrong. The true course is not to wager at all."

—Yes; but you must wager. It is not optional. You are embarked. Which will you choose then; Let us see. Since you must choose, let us see which interests you least. You have two things to lose, the true and the good; and two things to stake, your reason and your will, your knowledge and your happiness; and your nature has two things to shun, error and misery. Your reason is no more shocked in choosing one rather than the other, since you must of necessity choose. This is one point settled. But your happiness? Let us weigh the gain and the loss in wagering that God is. Let us estimate these two chances. If you gain, you gain all; if you lose, you lose nothing. Wager them without hesitation that He is.—"That is very fine. Yes, I must wager; but I may perhaps wager too much."—Let us see. Since there is an equal risk of gain and of loss, if you had only to gain two lives, instead of one, you might still wager. But if there were three lives to gain, you would have to play (since you are under the necessity of playing), and you would be imprudent, when you are forced to play, not to chance your life to gain three at a game where there is an equal risk of loss and gain. But there is an eternity of life and happiness. And this being so, if there were an infinity of chances, of which one only would be for you, you would still be right in wagering one to win two, and you would act stupidly, being obliged to play, by refusing to stake one life against three at a game in which there was out of an infinity an infinitely happy life to gain. But there is here an infinity of an infinitely happy life to gain, a chance of gain against a finite number of chances of loss, and what you stake is finite. It is all divided; wherever the infinite is and there is not an infinity of chances of loss against that of gain, there is no time to hesitate, you must give all. And thus, when one is forced to play, he must renounce reason to preserve his life, rather than risk it for infinite gain, as likely to happen as the loss of nothingness.

For it is no use to say it is uncertain if we will gain, and it is certain that we risk, and that the infinite distance between the *certainty* of what is staked and the *uncertainty* of what will be gained, equals the finite good which is certainly staked against the uncertain infinite. It is not so, as every player stakes a certainty to gain an uncertainty, and yet he stakes a finite certainty to gain a finite uncertainty, without transgressing against reason. There is not an infinite distance between the certainty staked and the uncertainty of the gain; that is untrue. In truth, there is an infinity between the certainty of gain and the certainty of loss. But the uncertainty of the gain is proportioned to the certainty of the stake according to the proportion of the chances of gain and loss. Hence it comes that, if there are as many risks on one side as on the other, the course is to play even; and then the certainty of the stake is equal to the uncertainty of the gain, so far is it from the fact that there is an infinite distance between them. And so our proposition is of infinite force, when there is the finite to stake in a game where there are equal risks of gain and of loss, and the infinite to gain. This is demonstrable; and if men are capable of any truths, this is one.

"I confess it, I admit it. But still is there no means of seeing the faces of the cards?"—Yes, Scripture and the rest, &c.—"Yes, but I have my hands tied and my mouth closed; I am forced to wager, and am not free. I am not released, and am so made that I cannot believe. What then would you have me do?"

True. But at least learn your inability to believe, since reason brings you to this, and yet you cannot believe. Endeavour then to convince yourself, not by increase of proofs of God, but by the abatement of your passions. You would like to attain faith, and do not know the way; you would like to cure yourself of unbelief, and ask the remedy for it. Learn of those who have been bound like you, and who now stake all their possessions. These are people who know the way which you would follow, and who are cured of an ill of which you would be cured. Follow the way by which they began; by acting as if they believe, taking the holy water, having masses said, &c. Even this will naturally make you believe, and deaden your acute-

ness.—"But this is what I am afraid of."—And why? What have you to lose?

But to show you that this leads you there, it is this which will lessen the passions, which are your stumbling-blocks.

The end of this discourse.—Now what harm will befall you in taking this side? You will be faithful, honest, humble, grateful, generous, a sincere friend, truthful. Certainly you will not have those poisonous pleasures, glory and luxury; but will you not have others? I will tell you that you will thereby gain in this life, and that, at each step you take on this road, you will see so great certainty of gain, so much nothingness in what you risk, that you will at last recognize that you have wagered for something certain and infinite, for which you have given nothing.

"Ah! This discourse transports me, charms me," &c.

If this discourse pleases you and seems impressive, know that it is made by a man who has knelt, both before and after it, in prayer to that Being, infinite and without parts, before whom he lays all he has, for you also to lay before Him all you have for your own good and for His glory, so that strength may be given to lowliness.

FOR FURTHER REFLECTION

1. What is the wager that Pascal advocates, and how does he calculate the cost-benefit ratio?
2. Do you agree with Pascal that a cost-benefit analysis shows it is good common sense to wager on God? Why or why not?
3. Could other religions make similar or even more striking claims and use Pascal's argument to urge us to give up our religion and join theirs? Explain your answer.
4. Might God—if there be one—disdain making faith in God an outcome of a wager, rather than an honest estimation of the evidence? Why or why not?

W. K. CLIFFORD

THE ETHICS OF BELIEF

In this essay the British philosopher W. K. Clifford (1845–1879) argues against Pascalian pragmatic (or "wager") justification for religious belief. Clifford argues that an ethics of belief makes all believing that lacks sufficient evidence immoral. Pragmatic justifications are not justifications at all, but are counterfeits; genuine justifications must always be based on evidence.

Clifford illustrates his thesis with the example of a shipowner who sends to sea a ship full of emigrants. He knows that the ship is old and poorly built, but he doesn't have the ship inspected. Dismissing his doubts and suspicions of the vessel's unseaworthiness, he trusts in Providence. He feels sincere and comfortable, and after the ships sinks and all the passengers are drowned, he collects his insurance money without a trace of guilt. Clifford argues that sincerity in no way excuses the shipowner, because "he had no right to believe on such evidence as was before him." One is obligated to believe propositions only on sufficient evidence. Clifford concludes that it is wrong *always and for anyone* to believe anything on insufficient evidence.

A shipowner was about to send to sea an emigrant ship. He knew that she was old, and not over-well built at the first; that she had seen many seas and climes, and often had needed repairs. Doubts had been suggested to him that possibly she was not seaworthy. These doubts preyed upon his mind and made him unhappy; he thought that perhaps he ought to have her thoroughly overhauled and refitted, even though this should put him to great expense. Before the ship sailed, however, he succeeded in overcoming these melancholy reflections. He said to himself that she had gone safely through so many voyages and weathered so many storms that it was idle to suppose she would not come safely home from this trip also. He would put his trust in Providence, which could hardly fail to protect all these unhappy families that were leaving their fatherland to seek for better times elsewhere. He would dismiss from his mind all ungener- ous suspicions about the honesty of builders and contractors. In such ways he acquired a sincere and comfortable conviction that his vessel was thoroughly safe and seaworthy; he watched her departure with a light heart, and benevolent wishes for the success of the exiles in their strange new home that was to be; and he got his insurance money when she went down in midocean and told no tales.

What shall we say of him? Surely this, that he was verily guilty of the death of those men. It is admitted that he did sincerely believe in the soundness of his ship; but the sincerity of his conviction can in no wise help him, because *he had no right to believe on such evidence as was before him.* He had acquired his belief not by honestly earning it in patient investigation, but by stifling his doubts. And although in the end he may have felt so sure about it that he could not think otherwise, yet inasmuch as he had knowingly

From W. K. Clifford, *Lectures and Essays* (London: Macmillan, 1879).

and willingly worked himself into that frame of mind, he must be held responsible for it.

Let us alter the case a little, and suppose that the ship was not unsound after all; that she made her voyage safely, and many others after it. Will that diminish the guilt of her owner? Not one jot. When an action is once done, it is right or wrong forever; no accidental failure of its good or evil fruits can possibly alter that. The man would not have been innocent, he would only have been not found out. The question of right or wrong has to do with the origin of his belief, not the matter of it; not what it was, but how he got it; not whether it turned out to be true or false, but whether he had a right to believe on such evidence as was before him.

There was once an island in which some of the inhabitants professed a religion teaching neither the doctrine of original sin nor that of eternal punishment. A suspicion got abroad that the professors of this religion had made use of unfair means to get their doctrines taught to children. They were accused of wresting the laws of their country in such a way as to remove children from the care of their natural and legal guardians; and even of stealing them away and keeping them concealed from their friends and relations. A certain number of men formed themselves into a society for the purpose of agitating the public about this matter. They published grave accusations against individual citizens of the highest position and character, and did all in their power to injure those citizens in the exercise of their professions. So great was the noise they made, that a Commission was appointed to investigate the facts; but after the Commission had carefully inquired into all the evidence that could be got, it appeared that the accused were innocent. Not only had they been accused on insufficient evidence, but the evidence of their innocence was such as the agitators might easily have obtained, if they had attempted a fair inquiry. After these disclosures the inhabitants of that country looked upon the members of the agitating society, not only as persons whose judgment was to be distrusted, but also as no longer to be counted honorable men. For although they had sincerely and conscientiously believed in the charges they had made, *yet they had no right to believe on such evidence as was before them.* Their sin-

cere convictions, instead of being honestly earned by patient inquiring, were stolen by listening to the voice of prejudice and passion.

Let us vary this case also, and suppose, other things remaining as before, that a still more accurate investigation proved the accused to have been really guilty. Would this make any difference in the guilt of the accusers? Clearly not; the question is not whether their belief was true or false, but whether they entertained it on wrong grounds. They would no doubt say, "Now you see that we were right after all; next time perhaps you will believe us." And they might be believed, but they would not thereby become honorable men. They would not be innocent, they would only be not found out. Every one of them, if he chose to examine himself *in foro conscientiae,* would know that he had acquired and nourished a belief, when he had no right to believe on such evidence as was before him; and therein he would know that he had done a wrong thing.

It may be said, however, that in both of these supposed cases it is not the belief which is judged to be wrong, but the action following upon it. The shipowner might say, "I am perfectly certain that my ship is sound, but still I feel it my duty to have her examined, before trusting the lives of so many people to her." And it might be said to the agitator, "However convinced you were of the justice of your cause and the truth of your convictions, you ought not to have made public attack upon any man's character until you had examined the evidence on both sides with the utmost patience and care."

In the first place, let us admit that, so far as it goes, this view of the case is right and necessary; right, because even when a man's belief is so fixed that he cannot think otherwise, he still has a choice in regard to the action suggested by it, and so cannot escape the duty of investigating on the ground of the strength of his convictions; and necessary, because those who are not yet capable of controlling their feelings and thoughts must have a plain rule dealing with overt acts.

But this being premised as necessary, it becomes clear that it is not sufficient, and that our previous judgment is required to supplement it. For it is not possible so to sever the belief from the action it suggests as to condemn the one without condemning the other. No man holding a strong belief on one side of a question, or even wishing to hold a belief on one side, can investigate it with such fairness and completeness as if he were really in doubt and unbiased; so that the existence of a belief not founded on fair inquiry unfits a man for the performance of this necessary duty.

Nor is that truly a belief at all which has not some influence upon the actions of him who holds it. He who truly believes that which prompts him to an action has looked upon the action to lust after it, he has committed it already in his heart. If a belief is not realized immediately in open deeds, it is stored up for the guidance of the future. It goes to make a part of that aggregate of beliefs which is the link between sensation and action at every moment of all our lives, and which is so organized and compacted together that no part of it can be isolated from the rest, but every new addition modifies the structure of the whole. No real belief, however trifling and fragmentary it may seem, is ever truly insignificant; it prepares us to receive more of its like, confirms those which resembled it before, and weakens others; and so gradually it lays a stealthy train in our inmost thoughts, which may some day explode into overt action, and leave its stamp upon our character forever.

And no one man's belief is in any case a private matter which concerns himself alone. Our lives are guided by that general conception of the course of things which has been created by society for social purposes. Our words, our phrases, our forms and processes and modes of thought are common property, fashioned and perfected from age to age; an heirloom which every succeeding generation inherits as a precious deposit and a sacred trust to be handed on to the next one, not unchanged but enlarged and purified, with some clear marks of its proper handiwork. Into this, for good or ill, is woven every belief of every man who has speech of his fellows. An awful privilege, and an awful responsibility, that we should help to create the world in which posterity will live.

In the two supposed cases which have been considered, it has been judged wrong to believe on insufficient evidence, or to nourish belief by suppressing doubts and avoiding investigation. The reason of this judgment is not far to seek; it is that in both these cases the belief held by one man was of great importance to other men. But for as much as no belief held by one man, however seemingly trivial the belief, and however obscure the believer, is ever actually insignificant or without its effect on the fate of mankind, we have no choice but to extend our judgment to all cases of belief whatever. Belief, that sacred faculty which prompts the decisions of our will, and knits into harmonious working all the compacted energies of our being, is ours not for ourselves but for humanity. It is rightly used on truths which have been established by long experience and waiting toil, and which have stood in the fierce light of free and fearless questioning. Then it helps to bind men together, and to strengthen and direct their common action. It is desecrated when given to unproved and unquestioned statements, for the solace and private pleasure of the believer; to add a tinsel splendor to the plain straight road of our life and display a bright mirage beyond it; or even to drown the common sorrows of our kind by a self-deception which allows them not only to cast down, but also to degrade us. Whoso would deserve well of his fellows in this matter will guard the purity of his belief with a very fanaticism of jealous care, lest at any time it should rest on an unworthy object, and catch a stain which can never be wiped away.

It is not only the leader of men, statesman, philosopher, or poet, that owes this bounden duty to mankind. Every rustic who delivers in the village alehouse his slow, infrequent sentences, may help to kill or keep alive the fatal superstitions which clog his race. Every hard-worked wife of an artisan may transmit to her children beliefs which shall knit society together, or rend it in pieces. No simplicity of mind, no obscurity of station, can escape the universal duty of questioning all that we believe.

It is true that this duty is a hard one, and the doubt which comes out of it is often a very bitter thing. It leaves us bare and powerless where we thought that we were safe and strong. To know all about anything is to know how to deal with it under all circumstances. We feel much happier and more secure when we think we know precisely what to do, no matter what happens, than when we have lost our way and do not know where to turn. And if we have supposed ourselves to know all about anything, and to be capable of doing what is fit in regard to it, we naturally do not like to find that we are really ignorant and powerless, that we have to begin again at the beginning, and try to learn what the thing is and how it is to be dealt with—if indeed anything can be learned about it. It is the sense of power attached to a sense of knowledge that makes men desirous of believing, and afraid of doubting.

This sense of power is the highest and best of pleasures when the belief on which it is founded is true belief, and has been fairly earned by investigation. For then we may justly feel that it is common property, and holds good for others as well as for ourselves. Then we may be glad, not that *I* have learned secrets by which I am safer and stronger, but that *we men* have got mastery over more of the world; and we shall be strong, not for ourselves, but in the name of Man and in his strength. But if the belief has been accepted on insufficient evidence, the pleasure is a stolen one. Not only does it deceive ourselves by giving us a sense of power which we do not really possess, but it is sinful, because it is stolen in defiance of our duty to mankind. That duty is to guard ourselves from such beliefs as from a pestilence, which may shortly master our own body and then spread to the rest of the town. What would be thought of one who, for the sake of a sweet fruit, should deliberately run the risk of bringing a plague upon his family and his neighbors?

And, as in other such cases, it is not the risk only which has to be considered; for a bad action is always bad at the time when it is done, no matter what happens afterwards. Every time we let ourselves believe for unworthy reasons, we weaken our powers of self-control, of doubting, of judicially and fairly weighing evidence. We all suffer severely enough from the maintenance and support of false beliefs and the fatally wrong actions which they lead to, and the evil born when one such belief is entertained is great and wide. But a greater and wider evil arises when the credulous character is maintained and supported, when a habit of believing for unworthy reasons is fostered and made permanent. If I steal money from any person, there may be no harm done by the mere transfer of possession; he may not feel the loss, or it may

prevent him from using the money badly. But I cannot help doing this great wrong towards Man, that I make myself dishonest. What hurts society is not that it should lose its property, but that it should become a den of thieves; for then it must cease to be society. This is why we ought not to do evil that good may come; for at any rate this great evil has come, that we have done evil and are made wicked thereby. In like manner, if I let myself believe anything on insufficient evidence, there may be no great harm done by the mere belief; it may be true after all, or I may never have occasion to exhibit it in outward acts. But I cannot help doing this great wrong toward Man, that I make myself credulous. The danger to society is not merely that it should believe wrong things, though that is great enough; but that it should become credulous, and lose the habit of testing things and inquiring into them; for then it must sink back into savagery.

The harm which is done by credulity in a man is not confined to the fostering of a credulous character in others, and consequent support of false beliefs. Habitual want of care about what I believe leads to habitual want of care in others about the truth of what is told to me. Men speak the truth to one another when each reveres the truth in his own mind and in the other's mind; but how shall my friend revere the truth in my mind when I myself am careless about it, when I believe things because I want to believe them, and because they are comforting and pleasant? Will he not learn to cry, "Peace," to me, when there is no peace? By such a course I shall surround myself with a thick atmosphere of falsehood and fraud, and in that I must live. It may matter little to me, in my cloud-castle of sweet illusions and darling lies; but it matters much to Man that I have made my neighbors ready to deceive. The credulous man is father to the liar and the cheat; he lives in the bosom of this his family, and it is no marvel if he should become even as they are. So closely are our duties knit together, that whoso shall keep the whole law, and yet offend in one point, he is guilty of all.

To sum up; it is wrong always, everywhere, and for anyone, to believe anything upon insufficient evidence.

If a man, holding a belief which he was taught in childhood or persuaded of afterwards, keeps down and pushes away any doubts which arise about it in his mind, purposely avoids the reading of books and the company of men that call in question or discuss it, and regards as impious those questions which cannot easily be asked without disturbing it—the life of that man is one long sin against mankind.

If this judgment seems harsh when applied to those simple souls who have never known better, who have been brought up from the cradle with a horror of doubt, and taught that their eternal welfare depends on what they believe, then it leads to the very serious question. Who hath made Israel to sin? . . .

Inquiry into the evidence of a doctrine is not to be made once for all, and then taken as finally settled. It is never lawful to stifle a doubt; for either it can be honestly answered by means of the inquiry already made, or else it proves that the inquiry was not complete.

"But," says one, "I am a busy man; I have no time for the long course of study which would be necessary to make me in any degree a competent judge of certain questions, or even able to understand the nature of the arguments." Then he would have no time to believe. . . .

FOR FURTHER REFLECTION

1. Describe Clifford's ethics of belief. Does Clifford exaggerate our duty to believe exactly according to the evidence? Does he falsely suppose that we can measure the evidence? Explain your position.

2. Is Clifford's shipowner example relevant to religious belief, or are there significant dissimilarities? If so, describe them.

3. Is it sometimes permissible to believe some proposition without strong evidence? Consider the following situation: There is evidence that your best friend has committed a crime, but something deep inside of you tells you that he is innocent and you find yourself believing against the evidence? If it turned out that you were right, would this justify you in your confidence in your friend? Would this serve as a counterexample to Clifford's rationalism? Or can Clifford give a plausible account of this sort of situation? Explain.

WILLIAM JAMES

THE WILL TO BELIEVE

William James (1842–1910), a U.S. philosopher and psychologist, was born in New York City and educated at Harvard. He was the brother of Henry James, the novelist. James struggled much of his life with ill health. He was assailed by doubts over freedom of the will and the existence of God, and he developed the philosophy of pragmatism partly in response to these difficulties. His principal works are *The Principles of Psychology* (1890), *The Varieties of Religious Experience* (1902), and *The Will to Believe* (1897), from which this selection is taken.

This essay has been regarded as the classic response to Clifford's ethics of belief (see previous reading). James argues that life would be greatly impoverished if we confined our beliefs to such a Scroogelike epistemology as Clifford proposes. In everyday life, where the evidence for important propositions is often unclear, we must live by faith or cease to act at all. Although we may not make leaps of faith just anywhere, sometimes practical necessity forces us to make decisions on propositions whose truth value is not clear. "Belief" is defined as a live, momentous optional hypothesis on which we cannot avoid a decision, because not to choose is, in effect, to choose against the hypothesis. James claims that where religion is such an optional hypothesis, people have the right to believe the better story rather than the worse. To do so, one must will to believe what the evidence alone is inadequate to support.

. . . I have long defended to my own students the lawfulness of voluntarily adopted faith; but as soon as they have got well imbued with the logical spirit, they have as a rule refused to admit my contention to be lawful philosophically, even though in point of fact they were personally all the time chock-full of some faith or other themselves. I am all the while, however, so profoundly convinced that my own position is correct, that your invitation has seemed to me a good occasion to make my statements more clear. Perhaps your minds will be more open than those with which I have hitherto had to deal. I will be as little technical as I can, though I must begin by setting up some technical distinctions that will help us in the end.

Let us give the name of *hypothesis* to anything that may be proposed to our belief; and just as the electricians speak of live and dead wires, let us speak of any hypothesis as either *live* or *dead*. A live hypothesis is one which appeals as a real possibility to him to whom it is proposed. If I ask you to believe in the Mahdi, the notion makes no electric connection with your nature—it refuses to scintillate with any credibility at all. As an hypothesis it is completely dead. To an Arab, however (even if he be not one of the Mahdi's followers), the hypothesis is among the mind's possibilities: it is alive. This shows that deadness and liveness in an hypothesis are not intrinsic properties, but relations to the individual

From William James, *The Will to Believe* (1897).

thinker. They are measured by his willingness to act. The maximum of liveness in an hypothesis means willingness to act irrevocably. Practically, that means belief; but there is some believing tendency wherever there is willingness to act at all.

Next, let us call the decision between two hypotheses an *option*. Options may be of several kinds. They may be—1, *living* or *dead;* 2, *forced* or *avoidable;* 3, *momentous* or *trivial;* and for our purposes we may call an option a *genuine* option when it is of the forced, living, and momentous kind.

1. A living option is one in which both hypotheses are live ones. If I say to you: "Be a theosophist or be a Mohammedan," it is probably a dead option, because for you neither hypothesis is likely to be alive. But if I say: "Be an agnostic or be a Christian," it is otherwise: trained as you are, each hypothesis makes some appeal, however small, to your belief.

2. Next, if I say to you: "Choose between going out with your umbrella or without it," I do not offer you a genuine opinion, for it is not forced. You can easily avoid it by not going out at all. Similarly, if I say, "Either love me or hate me," "Either call my theory true or call it false," your option is avoidable. You may remain indifferent to me, neither loving nor hating, and you may decline to offer any judgment as to my theory. But if I say, "Either accept this truth or go without it," I put on you a forced opinion, for there is no standing place outside of the alternative. Every dilemma based on a complete logical disjunction, with no possibility of not choosing, is an option of this forced kind.

3. Finally, if I were Dr. Nansen and proposed to you to join my North Pole expedition, your option would be momentous; for this would probably be your only similar opportunity, and your choice now would either exclude you from the North Pole sort of immortality altogether or put at least the chance of it into your hands. He who refuses to embrace a unique opportunity loses the prize as surely as if he tried and failed. *Per contra,* the option is trivial when the opportunity is not unique, when the stake is insignificant, or when the decision is reversible if it later prove unwise. Such trivial options abound in the scientific life. A chemist finds an hypothesis live enough to spend a year in its verification: he believes in it to

that extent. But if his experiments prove inconclusive either way, he is quit for his loss of time, no vital harm being done.

It will facilitate our discussion if we keep all these distinctions well in mind. . . .

The thesis I defend is, briefly stated, this: *Our passional nature not only lawfully may, but must, decide an option between propositions, whenever it is a genuine option that cannot by its nature be decided on intellectual grounds; for to say, under such circumstances, "Do not decide, but leave the question open," is itself a passional decision, just like deciding yes or no, and is attended with the same risk of losing the truth. . . .*

Wherever the option between losing truth and gaining it is not momentous, we can throw the chance of *gaining truth* away, and at any rate save ourselves from any chance of *believing falsehood,* by not making up our minds at all till objective evidence has come. In scientific questions, this is almost always the case; and even in human affairs in general, the need of acting is seldom so urgent that a false belief to act on is better than no belief at all. Law courts, indeed, have to decide on the best evidence attainable for the moment, because a judge's duty is to make law as well as to ascertain it, and (as a learned judge once said to me) few cases are worth spending much time over: the great thing is to have them decided on *any* acceptable principle, and got out of the way. But in our dealings with objective nature we obviously are recorders, not makers, of the truth; and decisions for the mere sake of deciding promptly and getting on to the next business would be wholly out of place. Throughout the breadth of physical nature facts are what they are quite independently of us, and seldom is there any such hurry about them that the risks of being duped by believing a premature theory need be faced. The questions here are always trivial options, the hypotheses are hardly living (at any rate not living for us spectators), the choice between believing truth or falsehood is seldom forced. The attitude of sceptical balance is therefore the absolutely wise one if we would escape mistakes. What difference, indeed, does it make to most of us whether we have or have not a theory of the Röntgen rays, whether we believe or not in mind-stuff, or have a conviction about the causality of conscious states? It makes no difference. Such options are not forced on us. On every account it is better not to make them, but still keep weighing reasons *pro et contra* with an indifferent hand.

I speak, of course, here of the purely judging mind. For purposes of discovery such indifference is to be less highly recommended, and science would be far less advanced than she is if the passionate desires of individuals to get their own faiths confirmed had been kept out of the game. . . . On the other hand, if you want an absolute duffer in an investigation, you must, after all, take the man who has no interest whatever in its results; he is the warranted incapable, the positive fool. The most useful investigator, because the most sensitive observer, is always he whose eager interest in one side of the question is balanced by an equally keen nervousness lest he become deceived. Science has organized this nervousness into a regular *technique,* her so-called method of verification; and she has fallen so deeply in love with the method that one may even say she has ceased to care for truth by itself at all. It is only truth as technically verified that interests her. The truth of truths might come in merely affirmative form, and she would decline to touch it. Such truth as that, she might repeat with Clifford, would be stolen in defiance of her duty to mankind. Human passions, however, are stronger than technical rules. "Le coeur a ses raisons," as Pascal says, "que la raison ne connaît pas" [The heart has its reasons that reason does not know.—Ed.]; and however indifferent to all but the bare rules of the game the umpire, the abstract intellect, may be, the concrete players who furnish him the materials to judge of are usually, each one of them, in love with some pet 'live hypothesis' of his own. Let us agree, however, that wherever there is no forced option, the dispassionately judicial intellect with no pet hypothesis, saving us, as it does, from dupery at any rate, ought to be our ideal.

The question next arises: Are there not somewhere forced options in our speculative questions, and can we (as men who may be interested at least as much in positively gaining truth as in merely escaping dupery) always wait with impunity till the coercive evidence shall have arrived? It seems *a priori* improbable that the truth should be so nicely adjusted to our needs and powers as that. In the great boarding-house of nature, the cakes and the butter and the syrup seldom come out so even and leave the plates so clean. Indeed, we should view them with scientific suspicion if they did.

Moral questions immediately present themselves as questions whose solution cannot wait for sensible proof. A moral question is a question not of what sensibly exists, but of what is good, or would be good if it did exist. Science can tell us what exists; but to compare the *worths,* both of what exists and of what does not exist, we must consult not science, but what Pascal calls our heart. Science herself consults her heart when she lays it down that the infinite ascertainment of fact and correction of false belief are the supreme goods for man. Challenge the statement, and science can only repeat it oracularly, or else prove it by showing that such ascertainment and correction bring man all sorts of other goods which man's heart in turn declares. The question of having moral beliefs at all or not having them is decided by our will. Are our moral preferences true or false, or are they only odd biological phenomena, making things good or bad for *us,* but in themselves indifferent? How can your pure intellect decide? If your heart does not *want* a world of moral reality, your head will assuredly never make you believe in one. Mephistophelian scepticism, indeed, will satisfy the head's play-instincts much better than any rigorous idealism can. Some men (even at the student age) are so naturally cool-hearted that the moralistic hypothesis never has for them any pungent life, and in their supercilious presence the hot young moralist always feels strangely ill at ease. The appearance of knowingness is on their side, of *naiveté* and gullibility on his. Yet, in the inarticulate heart of him, he clings to it that he is not a dupe, and that there is a realm in which (as Emerson says) all their wit and intellectual superiority is no better than the cunning of a fox. Moral scepticism can no more be refuted or proved by logic than intellectual scepticism. When we stick to it that there *is* truth (be it of either kind), we do so with our whole nature, and resolve to stand or fall by the results. The sceptic with his whole nature adopts the doubting attitude; but which of us is the wiser, Omniscience only knows.

Turn now from these wide questions of good to a certain class of questions of fact, questions concerning personal relations, states of mind between one man and another. *Do you like me or not?*—for example. Whether you do or not depends, in countless instances, on whether I meet you half-way, am willing to assume that you must like me, and show you trust and expectation. The previous faith on my part in your liking's existence is in such cases what makes your liking come. But if I stand aloof, and refuse to budge an inch until I have objective evidence, until you shall have done something apt, as the absolutists say, *ad extorquendum assensum meum,* ten to one your liking never comes. How many women's hearts are vanquished by the mere sanguine insistence of some man that they *must* love him! he will not consent to the hypothesis that they cannot. The desire for a certain kind of truth here brings about that special truth's existence; and so it is in innumerable cases of other sorts. Who gains promotions, boons, appointments, but the man in whose life they are seen to play the part of live hypotheses, who discounts them, sacrifices other things for their sake before they have come, and takes risks for them in advance? His faith acts on the powers above him as a claim, and creates its own verification.

A social organism of any sort whatever, large or small, is what it is because each member proceeds to his own duty with a trust that the other members will simultaneously do theirs. Wherever a desired result is achieved by the co-operation of many independent persons, its existence as a fact is a pure consequence of the precursive faith in one another of those immediately concerned. A government, an army, a commercial system, a ship, a college, an athletic team, all exist in this condition, without which not only is nothing achieved, but nothing is even attempted. A whole train of passengers (individually brave enough) will be looted by a few highwaymen, simply because the latter can count on one another, while each passenger fears that if he makes a movement of resistance, he will be shot before any one else backs him up. If we believed that the whole car-full would rise at once with us, we should each severally rise, and train-robbing would never even be attempted. There are, then, cases where a fact cannot come at all unless a preliminary faith exists in its coming. *And where faith in a fact can help create the fact,* that would be an insane

logic which should say that faith running ahead of scientific evidence is the 'lowest kind of immorality' into which a thinking being can fall. Yet such is the logic by which our scientific absolutists pretend to regulate our lives!

In truths dependent on our personal action, then, faith based on desire is certainly a lawful and possibly an indispensable thing.

But now, it will be said, these are all childish human cases, and have nothing to do with great cosmical matters, like the question of religious faith. Let us then pass on to that. Religions differ so much in their accidents that in discussing the religious question we must make it very generic and broad. What then do we now mean by the religious hypothesis? Science says things are; morality says some things are better than other things; and religion says essentially two things.

First, she says that the best things are the more eternal things, the overlapping things, the things in the universe that throw the last stone, so to speak, and say the final word. "Perfection is eternal,"—this phrase of Charles Secrétan seems a good way of putting his first affirmation of religion, an affirmation which obviously cannot yet be verified scientifically at all.

The second affirmation of religion is that we are better off even now if we believe her first affirmation to be true.

Now, let us consider what the logical elements of this situation are *in case the religious hypothesis in both its branches be really true.* (Of course, we must admit that possibility at the outset. If we are to discuss the question at all, it must involve a living option. If for any of you religion be a hypothesis that cannot, by any living possibility be true, then you need go no farther. I speak to the 'saving remnant' alone.) So proceeding, we see, first, that religion offers itself as a *momentous* option. We are supposed to gain, even now, by our belief, and to lose by our nonbelief, a certain vital good. Secondly, religion is a *forced* option, so far as that good goes. We cannot escape the issue by remaining sceptical and waiting for more light, because, although we do avoid error in that way *if religion be untrue,* we lose the good, *if it be true,* just as certainly as if we positively chose to disbelieve. It is as if a man should hesitate indefinitely to ask a certain woman to marry him because he was not perfectly sure that she would prove an angel after he brought her home. Would he not cut himself off from that particular angel-possibility as decisively as if he went and married some one else? Scepticism, then, is not avoidance of option; it is option of a certain particular kind of risk. *Better risk loss of truth than chance of error,*—that is your faith-vetoer's exact position. He is actively playing his stake as much as the believer is; he is backing the field against the religious hypothesis, just as the believer is backing the religious hypothesis against the field. To preach scepticism to us as a duty until 'sufficient evidence' for religion be found, is tantamount therefore to telling us, when in presence of the religious hypothesis, that to yield to our fear of its being error is wiser and better than to yield to our hope that it may be true. It is not intellect against all passions, then; it is only intellect with one passion laying down its law. And by what, forsooth, is the supreme wisdom of this passion warranted? Dupery for dupery, what proof is there that dupery through hope is so much worse than dupery through fear? I, for one, can see no proof; and I simply refuse obedience to the scientist's command to imitate his kind of option, in a case where my own stake is important enough to give me the right to choose my own form of risk. If religion be true and the evidence for it be still insufficient, I do not wish, by putting your extinguisher upon my nature (which feels to me as if it had after all some business in this matter), to forfeit my sole chance in life of getting upon the winning side,—that chance depending, of course, on my willingness to run the risk of acting as if my passional need of taking the world religiously might be prophetic and right.

All this is on the supposition that it really may be prophetic and right, and that, even to us who are discussing the matter, religion is a live hypothesis which may be true. Now, to most of us religion comes in a still further way that makes a veto on our active faith even more illogical. The more perfect and more eternal aspect of the universe is represented in our religions as having personal form. The universe is no longer a mere *It* to us, but a *Thou,* if we are religious; and any relation that may be possible from person to person might be possible here. For instance, although

in one sense we are passive portions of the universe, in another we show a curious autonomy, as if we were small active centres on our own account. We feel, too, as if the appeal of religion to us were made to our own active good-will, as if evidence might be forever withheld from us unless we met the hypothesis half-way. To take a trivial illustration: just as a man who in a company of gentlemen made no advances, asked a warrant for every concession, and believed no one's word without proof, would cut himself off by such churlishness from all the social rewards that a more trusting spirit would earn,—so here, one who should shut himself up in snarling logicality and try to make the gods extort his recognition willy-nilly, or not get it at all, might cut himself off forever from his only opportunity of making the gods' acquaintance. This feeling, forced on us we know not whence, that by obstinately believing that there are gods (although not to do so would be so easy both for our logic and our life) we are doing the universe the deepest service we can, seems part of the living essence of the religious hypothesis. If the hypothesis *were* true in all its parts, including this one, then pure intellectualism, with its veto on our making willing advances, would be an absurdity; and some participation of our sympathetic nature would be logically required. I, therefore, for one, cannot see my way to accepting the agnostic rules for truth-seeking, or wilfully agree to keep my willing nature out of the game. I cannot do so for this plain reason, that *a rule of thinking which would absolutely prevent me from acknowledging certain kinds of truth if those kinds of truth were really there, would be an irrational rule.* That for me is the long and short of the formal logic of the situation, no matter what the kinds of truth might materially be.

I confess I do not see how this logic can be escaped. But sad experience makes me fear that some of you may still shrink from radically saying with me, *in abstracto,* that we have the right to believe at our own risk any hypothesis that is live enough to tempt our will. I suspect, however, that if this is so, it is because you have got away from the abstract logical point of view altogether, and are thinking (perhaps without realizing it) of some particular religious hypothesis which for you is dead. The freedom to 'believe what we will' you apply to the case of some patent superstition; and the faith you think of is the faith defined by the schoolboy when he said, "Faith is when you believe something that you know ain't true." I can only repeat that this is misapprehension. *In concreto,* the freedom to believe can only cover living options which the intellect of the individual cannot by itself resolve; and living options never seem absurdities to him who has them to consider. When I look at the religious question as it really puts itself to concrete men, and when I think of all the possibilities which both practically and theoretically it involves, then this command that we shall put a stopper on our heart, instincts, and courage, and *wait*—acting of course meanwhile more or less as if religion were *not* true—till doomsday, or till such time as our intellect and senses working together may have raked in evidence enough,—this command, I say, seems to me the queerest idol ever manufactured in the philosophic cave. Were we scholastic absolutists, there might be more excuse. If we had an infallible intellect with its objective certitudes, we might feel ourselves disloyal to such a perfect organ of knowledge in not trusting to it exclusively, in not waiting for its releasing word. But if we are empiricists, if we believe that no bell in us tolls to let us know for certain when truth is in our grasp, then it seems a piece of idle fantasticality to preach so solemnly our duty of waiting for the bell. Indeed we *may* wait if we will,—I hope you do not think that I am denying that—but if we do so, we do so at our peril as much as if we believed. In either case we *act,* taking our life in our hands. No one of us ought to issue vetoes to the other, nor should we bandy words of abuse. We ought, on the contrary, delicately and profoundly to respect one another's mental freedom: then only shall we bring about the intellectual republic: then only shall we have that spirit of inner tolerance without which all our outer tolerance is soulless, and which is empiricism's glory; then only shall we live and let live, in speculative as well as in practical things. . . .

FOR FURTHER REFLECTION

1. Explain what James means by a "genuine" option. Is he correct in calling religious belief a genuine option? Why or why not?
2. Has James successfully met Clifford's objections to religious belief, or has he confused self-creating beliefs with wishful thinking? That is, by getting myself into the state where I believe I am capable of winning a race (although there's not enough evidence to decide the likelihood of the matter), I may actually increase my chances of winning the race; but my *believing* that God exists doesn't increase the probability that God does exist, because God either exists, or does not exist, independently of my beliefs. How would James or one of his followers respond to this objection?
3. Can we obtain beliefs simply by *willing* to have them, or is this an exercise in futility? Explain your answer.

ALVIN PLANTINGA

RELIGIOUS BELIEF WITHOUT EVIDENCE

Alvin Plantinga (b. 1932) is a professor of philosophy at the University of Notre Dame. He has written widely in metaphysics and philosophy of religion, including *The Nature of Necessity* (1974) and *God, Freedom and Evil* (1974). In the following essay, he argues that it is rational to believe in God despite the lack of evidence for such belief. Those (like W. K. Clifford) who insist that we must have evidence for all our beliefs simply fail to make their case, because the evidentialists have not set forth clear criteria that would account for all the clear cases of justified beliefs and that would exclude the belief in God. Plantinga outlines the position of the foundationalist-evidentialist as claiming that all justified beliefs must either (1) be "properly basic" by fulfilling certain criteria, or (2) be based on other beliefs that eventually result in a treelike construction with properly basic beliefs at the bottom, or foundation. Plantinga shows that many beliefs we seem to be justified in holding do not fit into the foundationalist framework; such beliefs as memory beliefs (for example, that I ate breakfast this morning), belief in an external world, and belief in other minds. These beliefs do not depend on other beliefs, yet neither are they self-evident, incorrigible (impossible not to believe), or evident to the senses.

Having shown the looseness of what we can accept as "properly basic," Plantinga next shows that the Protestant reformers saw belief in God as "properly basic." He asks us to consider this belief as a legitimate option, and examines possible objections to it.

I. THE EVIDENTIALIST OBJECTION TO THEISTIC BELIEF

Many philosophers—Clifford, Blanshard, Russell, Scriven, and Flew, to name a few—have argued that belief in God is irrational, or unreasonable, or not rationally acceptable, or intellectually irresponsible, or somehow noetically below par because, as they say, there is *insufficient evidence* for it.[1] Bertrand Russell was once asked what he would say if, after dying, he were brought into the presence of God and asked why he hadn't been a believer. Russell's reply: "I'd say, 'Not enough evidence, God! Not enough evidence!'"[2] I don't know just how such a response would be received; but Russell, like many others, held that theistic belief is unreasonable because there is insufficient evidence for it. We all remember W. K. Clifford, that delicious *enfant terrible*, as William James called him, and his insistence that it is immoral, wicked, and monstrous, and maybe even impolite to accept a belief for which you don't have sufficient evidence:

From *Religious Experience and Religious Belief,* ed. Joseph Runzo and Craig Ihara (New York: University Press of America, 1986). Reprinted with permission.

Whoso would deserve well of his fellows in this matter will guard the purity of his belief with a very fanaticism of jealous care, lest at any time it should rest on an unworthy object, and catch a stain which can never be wiped away.

He adds that if a

belief has been accepted on insufficient evidence, the pleasure is a stolen one. Not only does it deceive ourselves by giving us a sense of power which we do not really possess, but it is sinful, because it is stolen in defiance of our duty to mankind. That duty is to guard ourselves from such beliefs as from a pestilence which may shortly master our body and spread to the rest of the town.

and finally:

To sum up: it is wrong always, everywhere, and for anyone to believe anything upon insufficient evidence.

(It is not hard to detect, in these quotations, the "tone of robustious pathos" with which James credits him.) Clifford, of course, held that one who accepts belief in God *does* accept that belief on insufficient evidence, and has indeed defied his duty to mankind. More recently, Bertrand Russell has endorsed the evidentialist injunction "Give to any hypothesis which is worth your while to consider, just that degree or credence which the evidence warrants."

More recently, Antony Flew[3] has commended what he calls Clifford's "luminous and compulsive essay" (perhaps "compulsive" here is a misprint for "compelling"); and Flew goes on to claim that there is, in his words a "presumption of atheism." What is a presumption of atheism, and why should we think there is one? Flew puts it as follows:

The debate about the existence of God should properly begin from the presumption of atheism . . . the onus of proof must lie upon the theist. The word "atheism," however, has in this contention to be construed unusually. Whereas nowadays the usual meaning of "atheist" in English is "someone who asserts there is no such being as God," I want the word to be understood not positively but negatively. I want the original Greek prefix "a" to be read in the same way in "atheist" as it is customarily read in such other Greco-English words as "amoral," "atypical," and

"asymmetrical." In this interpretation an atheist becomes: not someone who positively asserts the non-existence of God; but someone who is simply not a theist.

What the protagonist of my presumption of atheism wants to show is that the debate about the existence of God ought to be conducted in a particular way, and that the issue should be seen in a certain perspective. His thesis about the onus of proof involves that it is up to the theist: first to introduce and to defend his proposed concept of God; and second, to provide sufficient reason for believing that this concept of his does in fact have an application.

How shall we understand this? What does it mean, for example, to say that the debate "should properly begin from the presumption of atheism"? What sorts of things do debates begin from, and what is it for one to begin from such a thing? Perhaps Flew means something like this: to speak of where a debate should begin is to speak of the sorts of premises to which the affirmative and negative sides can properly appeal in arguing their cases. Suppose you and I are debating the question whether, say, the United States has a right to seize Mideast oil fields if the OPEC countries refuse to sell us oil at what we think is a fair price. I take the affirmative, and produce for my conclusion an argument one premise of which is the proposition that the United States has indeed a right to seize these oil fields under those conditions. Doubtless that maneuver would earn me very few points. Similarly, a debate about the existence of God cannot sensibly start from the assumption that God does indeed exist. That is to say, the affirmative can't properly appeal, in its arguments, to such premises as that there is such a person as God; if it could, it'd have much too easy a time of it. So in this sense of "start," Flew is quite right: the debate can't start from the assumption that God exists.

Of course, it is also true that the debate can't start from the assumption that God does *not* exist; using "atheism" in its ordinary sense, there is equally a presumption of aatheism (which, by a familiar principle of logic, reduces to theism). So it looks as if there is in Flew's sense a presumption of atheism, all right, but in that same sense an equal presumption of aatheism. If this is what Flew means, then what he says is entirely correct, if something of a truism.

In another passage, however, Flew seems to understand the presumption of atheism in quite another different fashion:

> It is by reference to this inescapable demand for grounds that the presumption of atheism is justified. If it is to be established that there is a God, then we have to have good grounds for believing that this is indeed so. Until or unless some such grounds are produced we have literally no reason at all for believing; and in that situation the only reasonable posture must be that of either the negative atheist or the agnostic.

Here we have the much more substantial suggestion that it is unreasonable or irrational to accept theistic belief in the absence of sufficient grounds or reasons. And of course Flew, along with Russell, Clifford, and many others, holds that in fact there aren't sufficient grounds or evidence for belief in God. The evidentialist objection, therefore, appeals to the following two premises:

(A) It is irrational or unreasonable to accept theistic belief in the absence of sufficient evidence or reasons.

and

(B) There is no evidence, or at any rate not sufficient evidence, for the proposition that God exists.

(B), I think, is at best dubious. At present, however, I'm interested in the objector's other premise—the claim that it is irrational or unreasonable to accept theistic belief in the absence of evidence or reasons. Why suppose *that's* true? Why suppose a theist must have evidence or reason to think there *is* evidence for this belief, if he is not to be irrational? This isn't just *obvious,* after all.

Now many Reformed thinkers and theologians[4] have rejected *natural theology* (thought of as the attempt to provide proofs or arguments for the existence of God). They have held not merely that the proffered arguments are unsuccessful, but that the whole enterprise is in some way radically misguided. I have argued (1980) that the Reformed rejection of natural theology is best construed as an inchoate and unfocused rejection of (A). What these Reformed thinkers really mean to hold, I think, is that belief in God is properly basic: it need not be based on argument or evidence from other propositions at all. They mean to hold that the believer is entirely within his intellectual right in believing as he does, even if he doesn't know of any good theistic argument (deductive or inductive), even if he doesn't believe that there is any such argument, and even if in fact no such argument exists. They hold that it is perfectly rational to accept belief in God without accepting it on the basis of any other beliefs or propositions at all. Why suppose that the believer must have evidence if he is not to be irrational? Why should anyone accept (A)? What is to be said in its favor?

Suppose we begin by asking what the objector means by describing a belief as *irrational.* What is the force of his claim that the theistic belief is irrational and how is it to be understood? The first thing to see is that this claim is rooted in a *normative* contention. It lays down conditions that must be met by anyone whose system of beliefs is *rational;* and here "rational" is to be taken as a normative or evaluative term. According to the objector, there is a right way and a wrong way with respect to belief. People have responsibilities, duties and obligations with respect to their believings just as they do with respect to their actions—or if we think believings are a kind of action, their *other* actions. Professor Brand Blanshard puts this clearly:

> everywhere and always belief has an ethical aspect. There is such a thing as a general ethics of the intellect. The main principle of that ethic I hold to be the same inside and outside religion. This principle is simple and sweeping: Equate your assent to the evidence. (*Reason and Belief,* p. 401)

and according to Michael Scriven:

> Now even belief in something for which there is no evidence, i.e., a belief which goes beyond the evidence, although a lesser sin than a belief in something which is contrary to well-established laws, is plainly irrational in that it simply amounts to attaching belief where it is not justified. So the proper alternative, when there is no evidence, is not mere suspension of belief, e.g., about Santa Claus, it is disbelief. It most certainly is not faith. (*Primary Philosophy,* p. 103)

Perhaps this sort of obligation is really a special case of a more general moral obligation; or perhaps, on the other hand, it is *sui generis*. In any event, says the objector, there are such obligations: to conform to them is to be rational and to go against them is to be irrational.

Now here the objector seems right; there are duties and obligations with respect to beliefs. One's own welfare and that of others sometimes depends on what one believes. If we're descending the Grand Teton and I'm setting the anchor for the 120-foot rappel into the Upper Saddle, I have an obligation to form such beliefs as *this anchor point is solid* only on the basis of careful scrutiny and testing. One commissioned to gather intelligence—the spies Joshua sent into Canaan, for example—has an obligation to get it right. I have an obligation with respect to the belief that Justin Martyr was a Latin apologist—an obligation arising from the fact that I teach medieval philosophy, must make a declaration on this issue, and am obliged not to mislead my students here. The precise *form* of these obligations may be hard to specify: am I obliged to believe that J. M. was a Latin apologist if and only if J. M. *was* a Latin apologist? Or to form a belief on this topic only after the appropriate amount of checking and investigating? Or maybe just to tell the students the truth about it, whatever I myself believe in the privacy of my own study? Or to tell them what's generally thought by those who should know? In the rappel case: Do I have a duty to believe that the anchor point is solid if and only if it is? Or just to check carefully before forming the belief? Or perhaps there's no obligation to believe at all, but only to *act on* a certain belief only after appropriate investigation. In any event, it seems plausible to hold that there are obligations and norms with respect to belief, and I do not intend to contest this assumption.

The objector begins, therefore, from the plausible contention that there are duties or obligations with respect to belief: call them *intellectual duties.* These duties can be understood in several ways. First, we could construe them teleologically; we could adopt an intellectual utilitarianism. Here the rough idea is that our intellectual obligations arise out of a connection between our beliefs and what is intrinsically good and intrinsically bad; and our intellectual obligations are just a special case of the general obligation so to act to maximize good and minimize evil. Perhaps this is how W. K. Clifford thinks of the matter. If people accepted such propositions as *this DC-10 is airworthy* when the evidence is insufficient, the consequences could be disastrous: so perhaps some of us, at any rate, have an obligation to believe that proposition only in the presence of adequate evidence. The intellectual utilitarian could be an ideal utilitarian; he could hold that certain epistemic states are intrinsically valuable—knowledge, perhaps, or believing the truth, or a skeptical and judicial temper that is not blown about by every wind of doctrine. Among our duties, then, is a duty to try to bring about these valuable states of affairs. Perhaps this is how Professor Roderick Chisholm is to be understood when he says

> Let us consider the concept of what might be called an "intellectual requirement." We may assume that every person is subject to a purely intellectual requirement: that of trying his best to bring it about that, for every proposition that he considers, he accepts it if and only if it is true. (*Theory of Knowledge,* 2nd ed., p. 9)

Secondly, we could construe intellectual obligations *aretetically;* we could adopt what Professor Frankena calls a "mixed ethics of virtue" with respect to the intellect. There are valuable noetic or intellectual states (whether intrinsically or extrinsically valuable); there are also the corresponding intellectual virtues, the habits of acting so as to produce or promote or enhance those valuable states. One's intellectual obligations, then, are to try to produce and enhance these intellectual virtues in oneself and others.

Thirdly, we could construe intellectual obligations *deontologically;* we could adopt a *pure* ethics of obligation with respect to the intellect. Perhaps there are intellectual obligations that do not arise from any connection with good or evil, but attach to us just by virtue of our having the sorts of noetic powers human beings do in fact display. The quotation from Chisholm could also be understood along these lines.

Intellectual obligations, therefore, can be understood teleologically or aretetically or deontologically. And perhaps there are purely intellectual obligations of the following sorts. Perhaps I have a duty not to take as basic a proposition whose denial seems self-evident. Perhaps I have a duty to take as basic the proposition *I seem to see a tree* under certain conditions. With respect to certain kinds of propositions, perhaps I have a duty to believe them only if I have evidence for them, and a duty to proportion the strength of my belief to the strength of my evidence.

Of course, these would be prima facie obligations. One presumably has an obligation not to take bread from the grocery store without permission and another to tell the truth. Both can be overridden, in specific circumstances, by other obligations—in the first case, perhaps, an obligation to feed my starving children and in the second, an obligation to protect a human life. So we must distinguish prima facie duties or obligations from *all-things-considered* or *on-balance (ultima facie?)* obligations. I have a *prima facie* obligation to tell the truth; in a given situation, however, that obligation may be overridden by others, so that my duty, all things considered, is to tell a lie. This is the grain of truth contained in situation ethics and the ill-named "new morality."

And prima facie intellectual obligations can conflict, just as obligations of other sorts. Perhaps I have a prima facie obligation to believe what seems to me self-evident, and what seems to me to follow self-evidently from what seems to me self-evident. But what if, as in the Russell paradoxes, something that seems self-evidently false apparently follows, self-evidently, from what seems self-evidently true? Here prima facie intellectual obligations conflict, and no matter what I do I will violate a prima facie obligation. Another example: in reporting the Grand Teton rappel, I neglected to mention the violent electrical storm coming in from the southwest; to escape it we must get off in a hurry, so that I have a prima facie obligation to inspect the anchor point carefully, but anchor to set up the rappel rapidly, which means I can't spend a lot of time inspecting the anchor point.

Thus lightly armed, suppose we return to the evidential objector. Does he mean to hold that the theist without evidence is violating some intellectual obligation? If so, which one? Does he claim, for example, that the theist is violating his *ultima facie* intellectual obligation in thus believing? Perhaps he thinks anyone who believes in God without evidence is vio-

lating his all-things-considered intellectual duty. This, however, seems unduly harsh. What about the fourteen-year-old theist brought up to believe in God in a community where everyone believes? This fourteen-year-old theist, we may suppose, doesn't believe on the basis of evidence. He doesn't argue thus: everyone around here says God loves us and cares for us; most of what everyone around here says is true; so probably *that's* true. Instead, he simply believes what he's taught. Is he violating an all-things-considered intellectual duty? Surely not. And what about the mature theist—Thomas Aquinas, let's say—who thinks he *does* have adequate evidence? Let's suppose he's wrong; let's suppose all of his arguments are failures. Nevertheless, he has reflected long, hard, and conscientiously on the matter and thinks he *does* have adequate evidence. Shall we suppose he's violating an all-things-considered intellectual duty here? I should think not. So construed, the objector's contention is totally implausible.

Perhaps, then, he is to be understood as claiming that there is a prima facie intellectual duty not to believe in God without evidence. This duty can be overridden by circumstances, of course; but there is a prima facie obligation to believe propositions of this sort only on the basis of evidence. But here too there are problems. The suggestion is that I now have the prima facie obligation to believe propositions of this sort only on the basis of evidence. I have a prima facie duty to comply with the following command: either have evidence or don't believe. But this may be a command I can't comply with. The objector thinks there *isn't* adequate evidence for this belief, so presumably I can't *have* adequate evidence for it, unless we suppose I could create some. And it is also not within my power to refrain from believing this proposition. My beliefs aren't for the most part directly within my control. If you order me now, for example, to cease believing that the earth is very old, there's no way I can comply with your order. But in the same way it isn't within my power to cease believing in God now. So this alleged prima facie duty is one it isn't within my power to comply with. But how can I have a prima facie duty to do what isn't within my power to do?

Presumably, then, the objector means to be understood in still another fashion. Although it is not within my power now to cease believing now, there may be a series of actions now, such that I can now take the first, and after taking the first, will be able to take the second, and so on; and after taking the whole series of actions, I will no longer believe in God. Perhaps the objector thinks it is my prima facie duty to undertake whatever sort of regimen will at some time in the future result in my not believing without evidence. Perhaps I should attend a Universalist Unitarian Church, for example, and consort with members of the Rationalist Society of America. Perhaps I should read a lot of Voltaire and Bertrand Russell. Even if I can't now stop believing without evidence, perhaps there are other actions I can now take, such that if I do take them, then at some time in the future I won't be in this deplorable condition.

There is still another option available to the objector. He need not hold that the theist without evidence is violating some duty, prima facie, *ultima facie* or otherwise. Consider someone who believes that Venus is smaller than Mercury, not because he has evidence, but because he finds it amusing to believe what everyone disbelieves—or consider someone who holds this belief on the basis of an outrageously bad argument. Perhaps there is no obligation he has failed to meet; nevertheless his intellectual condition is defective in some way; or perhaps alternatively there is a commonly achieved excellence he fails to display. Perhaps he is like someone who is easily gulled, or walks with a limp, or has a serious astigmatism, or is unduly clumsy. And perhaps the evidentialist objection is to be understood, not as the claim that the theist without evidence has failed to meet some obligation, but that he suffers from a certain sort of intellectual deficiency. If this is the objector's view, then his proper attitude towards the theist would be one of sympathy rather than censure.

These are some of the ways, then, in which the evidentialist objection could be developed; and of course there are still other possibilities. For ease of exposition, let us take the claim deontologically; what I shall say will apply *mutatis mutandis* if we take it one of the other ways. The evidentialist objector, then, holds that it is irrational to believe in God without evidence. He doesn't typically hold, however, that the same goes for *every* proposition; for

given certain plausible conditions on the evidence relation it would follow that if we believe anything, then we are under obligation to believe infinitely many propositions. Let's say that proposition *p* is *basic* for a person *S* if *S* believes *p* but does not have evidence for *p;* and let's say that *p* is *properly basic* for *S* if *S* is within his epistemic rights in taking *p* as basic. The evidentialist objection, therefore, presupposes some view about what sorts of propositions are correctly or rightly or justifiably taken as basic; it presupposes a view about what is properly basic. And the minimally relevant claim for the evidentialist objector is that belief in God is *not* properly basic. Typically this objection has been rooted in some form of *classical foundationalism,* an enormously popular picture or total way of looking at faith, knowledge, justified belief, rationality and allied topics. This picture had been widely accepted ever since the days of Plato and Aristotle; its near relatives, perhaps, remain the dominant ways of thinking about these topics. According to the classical foundationalist, some propositions are *properly* or *rightly* basic for a person and some are not; those that are not rationally accepted only on the basis of *evidence* where the evidence must trace back, ultimately, to what is properly basic. Now there are two varieties of classical foundationalism. According to the ancient and medieval variety, a proposition is properly basic for a person *S* if and only if it is either self-evident to *S* or "evident to the senses," to use Aquinas' term for *S;* according to the modern variety, a proposition is properly basic for *S* if and only if it is either self-evident to *S* or incorrigible for him. For ease of exposition, let's say that classical foundationalism is the disjunction of ancient and medieval with modern foundationalism; according to the classical foundationalist, then, a proposition is properly basic for a person *S* if and only if it is either self-evident to *S* or incorrigible for *S* or evident to the senses for *S*.

Now I said that the evidentialist objection to theistic belief is typically rooted in classical foundationalism. Insofar as it is so rooted, it is *poorly* rooted. For classical foundationalism is self-referentially incoherent. Consider the main tenet of classical foundationalism:

(C) p is properly basic for S if and only if p is self-evident, incorrigible, or evident to the senses for S.

Now of course the classical foundationalist accepts (C) and proposes that we do so as well. And either he takes (C) as basic or he doesn't. If he doesn't, then if he is rational in accepting it, he must by his own claims have an argument for it from propositions that are properly basic, by argument forms whose corresponding conditionals are properly basic. Classical foundationalists do not, so far as I know, offer such arguments for (C). I suspect the reason is that they don't know of any arguments of that sort for (C). It is certainly hard to see what such an argument would be. Accordingly, classical foundationalists probably take (C) as basic. But then according to (C) itself, if (C) is properly taken as basic, it must be either self-evident, incorrigible, or evident to the senses for the foundationalist, and clearly it isn't any of those. If the foundationalist takes (C) as basic, therefore, he is self-referentially inconsistent. We must conclude, I think, that the classical foundationalist is in self-referential hot water—his own acceptance of the central tenet of his view is irrational by his own standards.

II. OBJECTIONS TO TAKING BELIEF IN GOD AS BASIC

Insofar as the evidentialist objection is rooted in classical foundationalism, it is poorly rooted indeed; and so far as I know, no one has developed and articulated any other reason for supporting that belief in God is not properly basic. Of course it doesn't follow that it *is* properly basic; perhaps the class of properly basic propositions is broader than classical foundationalists think, but still not broad enough to admit belief in God. But why think so? What might be the objections to the Reformed view that belief in God is properly basic?

I've heard it argued that if I have no evidence for the existence of God, then if I accept that proposition, my belief will be *groundless,* or *gratuitous,* or *arbitrary.* I think this is an error; let me explain.

Suppose we consider perceptual beliefs, memory beliefs, and beliefs ascribing mental states to other persons: such beliefs as

(1) I see a tree.
(2) I had breakfast this morning.
(3) That person is angry.

Although beliefs of this sort are typically and properly taken as basic, it would be a mistake to describe them as *groundless.* Upon having experience of a certain sort, I believe that I am perceiving a tree. In the typical case I do not hold this belief on the basis of other beliefs; it is nonetheless not groundless. My having that characteristic sort of experience—to use Professor Chisholm's language, my being appeared treely to—plays a crucial role in the formation and justification of that belief. We might say this experience, together, perhaps, with other circumstances, is what *justifies* me in holding it; this is the *ground* of my justification, and, by extension, the ground of the belief itself.

If I see someone displaying typical pain behavior, I take it that he or she is in pain. Again, I don't take the displayed behavior as *evidence* for that belief; I don't infer that belief from others I hold; I don't accept it on the basis of other beliefs. Still, my perceiving the pain behavior plays a unique role in the formation and justification of that belief; as in the previous case, it forms the ground of my justification for the belief in question. The same holds for memory beliefs. I seem to remember having breakfast this morning; that is, I have an inclination to believe the proposition that I had breakfast, along with a certain past-tinged experience that is familiar to all but hard to describe. Perhaps we should say that I am appeared to pastly; but perhaps that insufficiently distinguishes the experience in question from that accompanying beliefs about the past not grounded in my own memory. The phenomenology of memory is a rich and unexplored realm; here I have no time to explore it. In this case as in the others, however, there is a justifying circumstance present, a condition that forms the ground of my justification for accepting the memory belief in question.

In each of these cases, a belief is taken as basic, and in each case properly taken as basic. In each case there is some circumstance or condition that confers justification; there is a circumstance that serves as the *ground* of justification. So in each case there will be some true proposition of the sort:

(4) In condition *C, S* is justified in taking *p* as basic. Of course *C* will vary with *p*.

For a perceptual judgment such as

(5) I see a rose-colored wall before me,

C will include my being appeared to in a certain fashion. No doubt *C* will include more. If I'm appeared to in the familiar fashion but know that I am wearing rose-colored glasses, or that I am suffering from a disease that causes me to be thus appeared to, no matter what the color of the nearby objects, then I am not justified in taking (5) as basic. Similarly for memory. Suppose I know that my memory is unreliable; it often plays me tricks. In particular, when I seem to remember having breakfast, then, more often than not, I *haven't* had breakfast. Under these conditions I am not justified in taking it as basic that I had breakfast, even though I seem to remember that I did.

So being appropriately appeared to, in the perceptual case, is not sufficient for justification; some further condition—a condition hard to state in detail—is clearly necessary. The central point, here, however, is that a belief is properly basic only in certain conditions; these conditions are, we might say, the ground of its justification and, by extension, the ground of the belief itself. In this sense, basic beliefs are not, or are not necessarily, *groundless* beliefs.

Now similar things may be said about belief in God. When the Reformers claim that this belief is properly basic, they do not mean to say, of course, that there are no justifying circumstances for it, or that it is in that sense groundless or gratuitous. Quite the contrary. Calvin holds that God "reveals and daily discloses himself in the whole workmanship of the universe," and the divine art "reveals itself in the innumerable and yet distinct and well-ordered variety of the heavenly host." God has so created us that we have a tendency or disposition to see his hand in the world about us. More precisely, there is in us a disposition to believe propositions of the sort *this flower was created by God* or *this vast and intricate uni-*verse *was created by God* when we contemplate the flower or behold the starry heavens or think about the vast reaches of the universe.

Calvin recognizes, at least implicitly, that other sorts of conditions may trigger this disposition. Upon reading the Bible, one may be impressed with a deep sense that God is speaking to one. Upon having done what I know is cheap, or wrong, or wicked, I may feel guilty in God's sight and form the belief *God disapproves of what I've done.* Upon confession and repentance, I may feel forgiven, forming the belief *God forgives me for what I've done.* A person in grave danger may turn to God, asking for His protection and help; and of course he or she then forms the belief that God is indeed able to hear and help if He sees fit. When life is sweet and satisfying, a spontaneous sense of gratitude may well up within the soul; someone in this condition may thank and praise the Lord for His goodness, and will of course form the accompanying belief that indeed the Lord is to be thanked and praised.

There are therefore many conditions and circumstances that call forth belief in God: guilt, gratitude, danger, a sense of God's presence, a sense that He speaks, perception of various parts of the universe. A complete job would explore the phenomenology of all these conditions and of more besides. This is a large and important topic; but here I can only point to the existence of these conditions.

Of course, none of the beliefs I mentioned a moment ago is the simple belief that God exists. What we have instead are such beliefs as

(6) God is speaking to me.
(7) God has created all this.
(8) God disapproves of what I have done.
(9) God forgives me.
(10) God is to be thanked and praised.

These propositions are properly basic in the right circumstances. But it is quite consistent with this to suppose that the proposition *there is such a person as God* is neither properly basic nor taken as basic by those who believe in God. Perhaps what they take as basic are such propositions as (6)–(10), believing in the existence of God on the basis of such propositions. From this point of view, it isn't exactly right to say that belief in God is properly basic; more exactly, what are properly basic are such propositions (6)–(10), each of which self-evidently entails that God exists. It isn't the relatively high level and general proposition *God exists* that is properly basic, but instead propositions detailing some of His attributes or actions.

Suppose we return to the analogy between belief in God and belief in the existence of perceptual objects, other persons, and the past. Here too it is relatively specific and concrete propositions rather than their more general and abstract colleagues that are properly basic. Perhaps such items as

(11) There are trees.
(12) There are other persons.
(13) The world has existed for more than 5 minutes

are not properly basic; it is instead such propositions as

(14) I see a tree.
(15) That person is pleased.
(16) I had breakfast more than an hour ago

that deserve the accolade. Of course, propositions of the latter sort immediately and self-evidently entail propositions of the former sort; and perhaps there is thus no harm in speaking of the former as properly basic, even though so to speak is to speak a bit loosely.

The same must be said about belief in God. We may say, speaking loosely, that belief in God is properly basic; strictly speaking, however, it is probably not that proposition but such propositions as (6)–(10) that enjoy that status. But the main point, here, is this: belief in God or (6)–(10) are properly basic; to say so, however, is not to deny that there are justifying conditions for these beliefs, or conditions that confer justification on one who accepts them as basic. They are therefore not groundless or gratuitous.

A second objection I've often heard: If belief in God is properly basic, why can't *just any* belief be properly basic? What about voodoo or astrology? What about the belief that the Great Pumpkin returns every Halloween? Could I properly take *that* as basic? And if I can't, why can I properly take belief in God as basic? Suppose I believe that if I flap my arms with sufficient vigor, I can take off and fly about the room; could I defend myself against the charge of irrationality by claiming this belief is basic? If we say that

belief in God is properly basic, won't we be committed to holding that just anything, or nearly anything, can properly be taken as basic, thus throwing wide the gates to irrationalism and superstition?

Certainly not. What might lead one to think the Reformed epistemologist is in this kind of trouble? The fact that he rejects the criteria for proper basicality purveyed by classical foundationalism? But why should *that* be thought to commit him to such tolerance or irrationality? Consider an analogy. In the balmy days of positivism, the positivists went about confidently wielding their verifiability criterion and declaring meaningless much that was obviously meaningful. Now suppose someone rejected a formulation of that criterion—the one to be found in the second edition of A. J. Ayer's *Language, Truth and Logic,* for example. Would that mean she was committed to holding that

(17) 'Twas brillig; and the slithy toves did gyre and gimble in the wabe

contrary to appearances, makes good sense? Of course not. But then the same goes for the Reformed epistemologist; the fact that he rejects the Classical Foundationalist's criterion of proper basicality does not mean that he is committed to supposing just anything is properly basic.

But what then is the problem? Is it that the Reformed epistemologist not only rejects those criteria for proper basicality, but seems in no hurry to produce what he takes to be a better substitute? If he has no such criterion, how can he fairly reject belief in the Great Pumpkin as properly basic?

This objection betrays an important misconception. How do we rightly arrive at or develop criteria for meaningfulness, or justified belief, or proper basicality? Where do they come from? Must one have such a criterion before one can sensibly make any judgments—positive or negative—about proper basicality? Surely not. Suppose I don't know of a satisfactory substitute for the criteria proposed by Classical Foundationalism; I am nevertheless entirely within my rights in holding that certain propositions are not properly basic in certain conditions. Some propositions seem self-evident when in fact they are not; that is the lesson of some of the Russell paradoxes. Nevertheless it would be irrational to take as basic the denial of a proposition that seems self-evident to you. Similarly, suppose it seems to you that you see a tree; you would then be irrational in taking as basic the proposition that you don't see a tree, or that there aren't any trees. In the same way, even if I don't know of some illuminating criterion of meaning, I can quite properly declare (17) meaningless.

And this raises an important question—one Roderick Chisholm has taught us to ask. What is the status of the criteria for knowledge, or proper basicality, or justified belief? Typically, these are universal statements. The modern foundationalist's criterion for proper basicality, for example, is doubly universal:

(18) For any proposition *A* and person *S, A* is properly basic for *S* if and only if *A* is incorrigible for *S* or self-evident to *S*.

But how could one know a thing like that? What are its credentials? Clearly enough, (18) isn't self-evident or just obviously true. But if it isn't, how does one arrive at it? What sorts of arguments would be appropriate? Of course, a foundationalist might find (18) so appealing, he simply takes it to be true, neither offering argument for it, nor accepting it on the basis of other things he believes. If he does so, however, his noetic structure will be self-referentially incoherent. (18) itself is neither self-evident nor incorrigible; hence in accepting (18) as basic, the modern foundationalist violates the condition of proper basicality he himself lays down in accepting it. On the other hand, perhaps the foundationalist will try to produce some argument for it from premises that are self-evident or incorrigible: it is exceedingly hard to see, however, what such an argument might be like. And until he has produced such arguments, what shall the rest of us do—we who do not find (18) at all obvious or compelling? How could he use (18) to show us that belief in God, for example, is not properly basic? Why should we believe (18), or pay it any attention?

The fact is, I think, that neither (18) nor any other revealing necessary and sufficient condition for proper basicality follows from clearly self-evident premises by clearly acceptable arguments. And hence the proper way to arrive at such a criterion is, broadly speaking, *inductive*. We must assemble examples of beliefs and conditions such that the former are obviously properly basic in the latter, and examples of beliefs and conditions such that the former are obviously *not* properly basic in the latter. We must then frame hypotheses on the necessary and sufficient conditions of proper basicality and test these hypotheses by reference to those examples. Under the right conditions, for example, it is clearly rational to believe that you see a human person before you: a being who has thoughts and feelings, who knows and believes things, who makes decisions and acts. It is clear, furthermore, that you are under no obligation to reason to this belief from others you hold; under those conditions that belief is properly basic for you. But then (18) must be mistaken; the belief in question, under those circumstances, is properly basic, though neither self-evident nor incorrigible for you. Similarly, you may seem to remember that you had breakfast this morning, and perhaps you know of no reason to suppose your memory is playing you tricks. If so, you are entirely justified in taking that belief as basic. Of course it isn't properly basic on the criteria offered by classical foundationalists; but that fact counts not against you but against those criteria.

Accordingly, criteria for proper basicality must be reached from below rather than above; they should not be presented as *obiter dicta,* but argued to and tested by a relevant set of examples. But there is no reason to assume, in advance, that everyone will agree on the examples. The Christian will of course suppose that belief in God is entirely proper and rational; if he doesn't accept this belief on the basis of other propositions, he will conclude that it is basic for him and quite properly so. Followers of Bertrand Russell and Madelyn Murray O'Hare may disagree, but how is that relevant? Must my criteria, or those of the Christian community, conform to their examples? Surely not. The Christian community is responsible to *its* set of examples, not to theirs.

Accordingly, the Reformed epistemologist can properly hold that belief in the Great Pumpkin is not properly basic, even though he holds that belief in God *is* properly basic and even if he has no full-fledged criterion of proper basicality. Of course he is committed to supposing that there is a relevant *difference* between belief in God and belief in the Great

Pumpkin, if he holds that the former, but not the latter, is properly basic. But this should prove no great embarrassment; there are plenty of candidates. These candidates are to be found in the neighborhood of the conditions I mentioned in the last section that justify and ground belief in God. Thus, for example, the Reformed epistemologist may concur with Calvin in holding that God has implanted in us a natural tendency to see his hand in the world around us; the same cannot be said for the Great Pumpkin, there being no Great Pumpkin and no natural tendency to accept beliefs about the Great Pumpkin.

By way of conclusion, then: being self-evident, or incorrigible, or evident to the senses is not a necessary condition of proper basicality. Furthermore, one who holds that belief in God *is* properly basic is not thereby committed to the idea that belief in God is groundless or gratuitous or without justifying circumstances. And even if he lacks a general criterion of proper basicality, he is not obliged to suppose that just any, or nearly any, belief—belief in the Great Pumpkin, for example—is properly basic. Like everyone should, he begins with examples; and he may take belief in the Great Pumpkin, in certain circumstances, as a paradigm of irrational basic belief.

NOTES

1. See, for example, Blanshard, *Reason and Belief,* pp. 400ff; Clifford, "The Ethics of Belief," pp. 345ff; Flew, *The Presumption of Atheism,* p. 22; Russell, "Why I Am Not a Christian," pp. 3ff; and Scriven, *Primary Philosophy,* pp. 87ff. In Plantinga, "Is Belief in God Rational?" I consider and reject the evidentialist objection to theistic belief.
2. W. Salmon, "Religion and Science: A New Look at Hume's Dialogues," *Philosophical Studies* 33 (1978), p. 176.
3. A. G. N. Flew, *The Presumption of Atheism* (London: Pemberton Publishing Co., 1976).
4. A Reformed thinker or theologian is one whose intellectual sympathies lie with the Protestant tradition going back to John Calvin (not someone who was formerly a theologian and has since seen the light).

FOR FURTHER REFLECTION

1. Has Plantinga successfully defended the view that one has no rational obligation to support one's belief in God with evidence? Explain. Compare Plantinga's view with the argument that anyone who claims that something exists must be able to give good reasons for its existence.
2. Is there a relevant difference between believing in the Great Pumpkin and believing in God? Could a worshiper of a devil use Plantinga's argument to claim that there is a natural human tendency to believe in a Creator Devil?

PART IV

❧

Philosophy of Mind

Do we have souls inside our bodies? Is the mind of a different substance, separate from the body or brain? How does the mind relate to the body? What is consciousness? What is the nature of the self? Are you the same person over time, or do you change your identity? Are you really the same person you were when you were one month old or four years old, and are you the same person you will be at ninety, should "you" live that long? Will you survive your death? Is the self immortal?

These are the kinds of questions considered by students of the philosophy of mind. We want to understand the nature of the mind, and the nature of our own minds. We want to understand who we are and whether we will live again after we are dead.

The idea of a separate soul or mind in humans has a long history. The ancient Hebrews used the word "breath" (*ruach*, which also means "spirit") to refer to the soul, believing that it was a gift from God that animated us. The ancient Greeks, particularly Pythagoras and Plato, thought that the soul (*psyche*, from which we get our word "psychology," the study of the soul) was lodged in the body like a captain of a ship. The soul was the rational and animating principle within us. It was immortal, having neither beginning nor end. When a person died, the soul left the body and was reincarnated in another body. Hinduism holds a similar belief, with the addition that the soul at last will be absorbed into a greater soul in Nirvana. Most Christians throughout the ages have believed that the soul is created by God, animates the body, and will live forever in another realm after death. Other Christians, basing their belief on Paul's words in I Corinthians 15, believe that it is not a separate soul but a resurrected body (a whole, embodied person) that will survive death.

Today these ideas are under attack. Neuroscience studies brain states, which many scientists believe are sufficient to explain mental life. They argue that there is no place nor need for a separate soul or mind. If they are correct, our religious heritage needs to be modified or abandoned. But many philosophers argue that there are good reasons for holding to traditional beliefs about the soul or mind and about its survival after death. Both sides of the dispute are included in the readings that follow.

The sections in this part examine three important subjects in philosophy of mind: (A) the mind-body problem, (B) the problem of personal identity, and (C) survival after death.

Each section depends on the previous section, so formulate your ideas on the body-mind problem before taking up the questions of personal identity and survival after death.

A. The Mind-Body Problem

> The curiosity of Man and the cunning of his Reason have revealed much of what nature held hidden. The structure of spacetime, the constitution of matter, the many forms of energy, the nature of life itself; all of these mysteries have become open books to us. To be sure, deep questions remain unanswered and revolutions await us still, but it is difficult to exaggerate the explosion in scientific understanding we humans have fashioned over the past 500 years. Despite this general advance, a central mystery remains largely a mystery: the nature of *conscious intelligence*.
>
> *Paul Churchland,* Matter and Consciousness

Intuitively, we seem to distinguish two different types of reality: material and mental, bodies and minds. *Bodies* are solid, material entities, extended in three-dimensional space, publicly observable, measurable, capable of causing things to happen in accordance with invariant laws of mechanics.

Minds have none of these properties. Consciousness is not solid or material, is not extended in three-dimensional space, does not occupy space at all, is directly observable only by the person who owns it, cannot be measured, and seems incapable of causing things to happen in accordance with the invariant laws of mechanics. Individuals can only think their own thoughts, feel their own emotions, and suffer their own pain. Although neurosurgeons can open skulls and observe brains, they cannot observe minds, or their beliefs, sensations, emotions, or desires.

Unlike physical bodies, mental entities have no shape, weight, length, width, height, color, mass, velocity, or temperature. It would sound odd, indeed, to speak of a belief weighing 16 ounces like a box of cereal, or to describe a feeling of love measuring 4 inches × 4 inches × 10 feet, like a piece of lumber, a pain as heavy as a cement bag, or a desire as green and having a temperature of 103°F.

Yet common sense tells us that these two entities somehow interact. If you step on a nail, it pierces your skin, sending a message through your nervous system that results in something altogether different from the shape or size of the nail or skin, something that doesn't have size or shape and that can't be seen, smelled, tasted, or heard—a feeling of distress or pain. Whereas the nail is public, the pain is private. Still, your mind tells you it would be good to throughly clean and bandage the wound, so your mind causes you to move your body. Your legs carry you to sink and medicine cabinet, where you stop and use your arms and hands to go through the various motions needed to attend to the wound. You then call on your memory to tell you when you had your last tetanus shot.

In situations like these, the body affects the mind and the mind in turn affects the body. So common sense shows that there is a close interactive relationship between these two radically different entities. This position is called *dualist interactionism*. We can represent it as follows. Let "BS" represent "brain state" and "MS," "mental state," and let "→" represent causal relationships. The dualist interactive process looks like this:

$$
\begin{array}{ccccc}
\text{MS 1} & & \text{MS 2} & \rightarrow & \text{MS 3} \\
\uparrow & \searrow & \nearrow & & \searrow \\
\text{BS 1} & \text{BS 2} & & & \text{BS 3}
\end{array}
$$

For example, stepping on the nail causes brain state BS 1, which in turn causes mental state MS 1, the feeling of pain, which in turn causes you, via a brain state, to decide to move your foot (BS 2), which in turn brings relief from the pain (MS 2) as well as the intention to care for the wound (MS 3), which leads to the brain state BS 3, which causes you to move toward the sink and medicine cabinet.

But the question arises, how exactly does this transaction between the mind and brain occur, and where does it occur? Could it be, as *materialists* contend, that the mind is really simply a function of the body, not a separate substance at all? Or could the *idealist monists* be correct: the body is really an illusion, and there is only one substance, the mind alone? The following schema may guide you through the readings in this part of the work (Berkeley's idealism was already considered in Part II):

Theory	Nature of Substance	Theorist
Dualist interactionism	Mental and physical	Plato and Moreland
		Descartes and Locke
		John Eccles and Karl Popper
Ideal monism	Mental	Berkeley
		Hinduism and Christian Science
Material monism	Physical	Hobbes and Russell
		Churchland

There are several types of dualism besides *interactionism*. The most notable is *epiphenomenalism*, which posits a one-way causal relationship: the body affects the mind, causing mental events, but the mind does not affect the body. Mental events are like the babbling of brooks, the exhaust from a car's engine, or the smoke from trains' chimneys; they are effects of physical processes, but do not themselves cause motion in the water, the car, or the train. Epiphenomenalism is represented in the following schema:

$$
\begin{array}{ccccc}
\text{MS 1} & & \text{MS 2} & & \text{MS 3} \\
\downarrow & & \uparrow & & \uparrow \\
\text{BS 1} & \rightarrow & \text{BS 2} & \rightarrow & \text{BS 3}
\end{array}
$$

There is also a view known as *parallelism*, which holds that there are two parallel realities, one mental and one physical, connected with human action:

$$
\begin{array}{ccccc}
\text{MS 1} & \rightarrow & \text{MS 2} & \rightarrow & \text{MS 3} \\
\uparrow & & & & \\
\text{BS 1} & \rightarrow & \text{BS 2} & \rightarrow & \text{BS 3}
\end{array}
$$

Finally, there is a view called *panpsychism*, which holds that everything in nature has mind or a soul. Panpsychism is a correlate of *pantheism*, which holds that everything is God or contains God. According to panpsychism, there is soul or mind in the ultimate particles of physics, and that is why we can experience consciousness.

There are also several versions of materialism. The simplest is *metaphysical behaviorism*, which either denies mental events or denies their importance in understanding behavior. Actually, behaviorism is not so much a theory about the mind-body problem as it is a theory about how to understand the language we use in describing events. All talk about beliefs, desires, and sensations should be analyzed into language describing dispositions to behave in certain ways. For example, the statement, "Sam fears snakes" should be analyzed as, "If Sam saw a rattlesnake he would flee, or if Sam saw a green garter snake, he would flee," and so forth. The sentence, "Mary dislikes pain" should be analyzed as, "If Mary's C-fibers are firing, she will look for a pain reliever in the medicine cabinet." Though metaphysical behaviorism arose within a materialist context, one who accepts this account of language use could be a dualist behaviorist. In any case, metaphysical behaviorism has largely been abandoned by philosophers, for two reasons: (1) its ignoring of inner states was a colossal blunder, for inner mental states really exist and must be recognized as such. For example, to dismiss pain as simply a disposition to wince or withdraw is to ignore the obvious fact that pain hurts. It feels bad. These raw feelings or sensations (including smells, sounds, and color sensations) are called *qualia*. Behaviorism lacks an adequate account of qualia. (2) Behaviorism's dispositional account of mental locutions turns out to be infinitely long, too long to be useful. For example, think of the possible behaviors that might describe pain behavior: wincing, screaming, taking a pain reliever, taking more medicine, calling a doctor, pulling a needle (or knife) out of one's arm, using acupuncture, engaging in self-hypnosis, stoically grinning and bearing it, masochistically embracing it.

A reaction to behaviorism by materialists U. T. Place and J. J. C. Smart sought to recognize mental states within a materialist framework, *producing reductive materialism in the form of the identity thesis*. Mental states, they argued, are *identical* with *brain states*. For example, the inner state of pain is really the excitation of C-fibers or, possibly, delta-fibers.

However, it was quickly pointed out by Hilary Putnam and Jerry Fodor that the identity theory was guilty of an unwarranted assumption in supposing that mental states could be reduced to specific types of brain states. Why couldn't it be the case that there are different configurations of brain activity? Perhaps C-fibers firing cause pain in most people, but some may have a combination of delta-fibers firing that give rise to similar conscious states. Or suppose that inhabitants of Galactica have nervous systems with a silicon base rather than a carbon base like ours. To accept on present evidence that all mental states are like ours is a version of neural chauvinism. Perhaps neuroscientists will design complicated artificial persons who have mental states but whose physical hardware is very different from ours. What is important is not the specific material involved in causing mental phenomena or qualia, but the causal role that an operation plays in the process. This theory of multiple realizability is called *functionalism*. Just as there are many ways to catch mice (e.g., mousetraps, poison, etc.) and many ways to get from San Francisco to New York City (fly, bicycle, drive straight through via route 80, drive a southern route through Arizona, hike, etc.), so likewise there could be several ways for the nervous system to produce a given mental state. *Functionalism* can be viewed as the chastened and corrected successor to *behaviorism*, and like *behaviorism*, which is usually held by materialists, it could be accepted by dualists. Paul Churchland gives a more critical account of *functionalism* in his second essay in this part of our book.

Finally, there is *eliminative materialism*, which contends that the ordinary conceptual framework in which we talk about mental events is mistaken. Our commonsense conceptual scheme is labeled *folk psychology*, and includes our concepts of belief, desire, emotions, perceptions, and sensations. As we learn more about our brains and the way they work, we will be able to replace this subjectivist speech with a more scientific discourse. For example, instead of talking about a headache, you might talk about certain C-fibers firing in your brain.

In my experience most philosophers and students find the debate between interactive dualism and forms of materialism the most interesting and important. We will spend most of our time in this section examining these theories. A discussion of functionalism, which may be equally important, is also included.

First we turn to Descartes's classic rendition of interactive dualism. According to Descartes, three kinds of objects or substances exist in the universe: (1) the eternal substance, God; (2) his creation in terms of mind; and (3) his creation in terms of matter. Humans are made up of the latter two types of substance. Descartes says, "We may thus easily have two clear and distinct notions or ideas, the one of created substance which thinks, and the other of corporeal substances, provided we carefully separate all the attributes of thought from those of extension."

We are thinking substances or embodied minds, says Descartes, "for I am not only lodged in my body as a pilot in a ship, but I am very closely united to it, and so to speak so intermingle with it that I seem to compose with it one whole. For if that were not the case, when my body is hurt, I, who am merely a thinking thing, should perceive this wound by the understanding only, just as the sailor perceives by sight when something is damaged in his vessel."

The two kinds of substances that make us each a person intermingle in such a way that they causally act on each other. Although it might be that a mind interacts with each part of its body separately, Descartes believes that mind interacts only with the brain. The material event that causally stimulates one of your five senses (light hitting the retina of your eye) results in a chain of physical causation that leads to a certain brain process from which a certain sensation results. Then, in turn, being affected by your brain, your mind, through mental events, acts on your brain, which in turn affects your body.

Descartes thought he could pinpoint the place in the brain where the interaction between mind and brain took place: "The part of the body in which the soul exercises its function immediately is in nowise the heart, nor the whole of the brain, but merely the most inward of all its parts, to wit, a certain very small gland which is situated in the middle of its substance." This gland, the seat of the mind, is the pineal gland. It functions as the intermediary that transmits the effects of the mind to the brain and the effects of the brain to the mind. We shall disregard his mistake about the pineal gland (there is no evidence that it is the seat of consciousness), but accept the essential structure of Descartes's theory as the classic expression of dualist interactionism.

The second reading, by Anne Conway, takes the view that mind and body are not radically distinct things as Descartes believed. Instead, there is a graded progression from heavy body to light body to heavy spirit to light spirit, where each level impacts those next to it. Thus, light spirit communicates with heavy body through this continuum.

Next, we look at a contemporary overview on the problem of dualism and materialism by Jerome Shaffer. In our fourth reading, Paul Churchland critiques this position. Then, in our fifth reading, Churchland critiques functionalism and defends materialism, especially *eliminative materialism*, which attempts to eliminate all talk of mental states and claims that the language of mental events is an outmoded legacy of folk mythology, called *folk psychology*, which includes our concepts of belief, pain, desire, emotion and intention. As we learn more about our brains and how they work, Churchland argues, we will be able to replace this subjectivist language with more scientific discourse.

Our sixth reading, Thomas Nagel's "What Is It Like to Be a Bat?" is a critique of this kind of objectivism, the view that we can give a complete and accurate description of the world by omitting the subjective point of view. Nagel argues that subjectivity, conscious awareness, is an integral part of both our experience and the world itself. In our sixth reading David Chalmers argues in favor of naturalistic dualism and against reductive materialism.

Finally, we turn to the question of whether computers can think. The British genius A. N. Turing proposed a test, now called the *Turing test,* in which a sophisticated questioner could not tell the difference between the answers of a computer and a human being. In our final selection, "Minds, Brains, and Computers," John Searle uses a thought experiment called the "Chinese room" to argue that while it may be possible for a computer to fool a sophisticated questioner, the computer will lack something a human possesses— namely, *understanding* of the meanings of the symbols that are being manipulated. Since what we mean by thinking involves interpretation of symbols and understanding, the computer, unlike us, cannot think.

RENÉ DESCARTES

INTERACTIVE DUALISM

French philosopher René Descartes (1596–1650) is perhaps the leading defender of the position known as *interactive dualism*. In this view, my body is composed of physical stuff, while my mind is a nonphysical spiritual entity. While metaphysically distinct entities, my spirit-mind and physical body nonetheless interact with each other. My body sends sensory information to my mind, and my mind issues commands to my body that make it move. Descartes lays out his position in two works, selections from which are presented here. First, in his *Discourse on the Method* (1637), he describes his mental self as a thinking thing that is distinct from—and can even exist apart from—his physical body. He then describes the functioning of the body as a machine that is guided by the mind. In the process of describing the relationships between mind and body, he argues that animals are mere machines. Second, in *The Passions of the Soul* (1649), Descartes argues that the interactive gateway between these realms of the spirit-mind and physical body is the pineal gland in the brain.

THE MIND DISTINCT FROM THE BODY

The Mind Is a Thinking Thing Distinct from the Body

I had long before remarked that from practical considerations it is sometimes necessary to adopt almost beyond doubt opinions that we observe to be highly uncertain. But as I then desired to give my attention solely to the search after truth, I thought that a procedure exactly the opposite was needed. I ought to reject as absolutely false all opinions in regard to which I could suppose the least ground for doubt, in order to ascertain whether after that there remained [anything] in my belief that was wholly indubitable. Accordingly, seeing that our senses sometimes deceive us, I was willing to suppose that there existed nothing really such as they presented to us. And because some people err in reasoning, . . . even on the simplest matters of geometry, I, convinced that I was as open to error as any other, rejected as false all the reasonings that I had before taken for demonstrations. Finally, when I considered that the very same thoughts that we experience when awake may also be experienced when we are asleep, while there is at that time not one of them true, I supposed that all the objects that had ever entered into my mind when awake, had in them no more truth than the illusions of my dreams. But immediately I observed that, while I thus wished to think that everything was false, it was absolutely necessary that I, who thus thought, should to some extent exist. I observed that this truth,

I think, therefore I am, was so certain and of such evidence, that no ground of doubt, however extravagant, could be maintained by the skeptics capable of shaking it. I concluded that I might, without scruple, accept it as the first principle of the philosophy of which I was in search.

In the next place, I attentively examined what I was. I observed that I could suppose that I had no body, and that there was no world, nor any place in which I might be. But I could not therefore suppose that I was not. On the contrary, from the very circumstance that I thought to doubt the truth of other things, it most clearly and certainly followed that I was. On the other hand, if I had only ceased to think, although all the other objects which I had ever imagined had been in reality existent, I would have had no reason to believe that I existed. I concluded from this that I was a substance whose whole essence or nature consists only in thinking, and which, that it may exist, has need of no place, nor is dependent on any material thing. Thus the "I" (that is to say, the mind by which I am what I am) is wholly distinct from the body. It is even more easily known than the [body], and is such that even if the [body] did not exist, [my mind] would still continue to be all that it is.

The Mechanical Nature of the Body

I had expounded all these matters with sufficient detail in the treatise which I formerly thought of publishing. And after these, I had shown what must be the fabric of the nerves and muscles of the human body to give

From René Descartes, *Discourse on the Method* (1637), Part 4, and *The Passions of the Soul* (1649), Part 1. Section titles have been added by the editor.

the animal spirits contained in it the power to move the limbs. We see this, for example, when heads shortly after they have been cut off still move and bite the earth, although no longer animated. [We also see this] in the changes that must take place in the brain to produce waking, sleep, and dreams. [We also see this] with how light, sounds, odors, tastes, heat, and all the other qualities of external objects impress it with different ideas by means of the senses, and similarly with how hunger, thirst, and the other internal passions can likewise impress upon it divers ideas. [We also see this] in what must be understood by the "common sense" in which these ideas are received by the memory which retains them, by the imagination which can change them in various ways and out of them compose new ideas, and which, by the same means, distributing the animal spirits through the muscles, can cause the members of such a body to move in as many different ways, and in a manner as suited, whether to the objects that are presented to its senses or to its internal passions, as can take place in our own case apart from the guidance of the will.

Nor will this appear at all strange to those who are acquainted with the variety of movements performed by the different automata, or moving machines created by human engineering, and that with help of but few pieces compared with the great multitude of bones, muscles, nerves, arteries, veins, and other parts that are found in the body of each animal. Such persons will look upon this body as a machine made by the hands of God, which is incomparably better arranged, and adequate to movements more admirable than is any machine of human invention. And here I especially stopped to show that, were there such machines exactly resembling in organs and outward form an ape or any other irrational animal, we could have no means of knowing that they were in any respect of a different nature from these animals.

On the other hand, if there were machines resembling our bodies, and capable of imitating our actions as far as it is morally possible, there would still remain two most certain tests whereby to know that they were not really human. Of these the first is that they could never use words or other signs arranged in such a manner as is competent to us in order to declare our thoughts to others. For, we may easily conceive a machine to be so constructed that it utters words, and even that it utters some in response to the action upon it of external objects which cause a change in its organs. For example, if touched in a particular place it may ask what we wish to say to it. If touched in another it may cry out that it is hurt, and such like. But it would not arrange them variously so as to reply appropriately to what is said in its presence, as people of the lowest level of intellect can do. The second test is that, although such machines might execute many things with equal or perhaps greater perfection than any of us, they would, without doubt, fail in certain others from which it could be discovered that they did not act from knowledge, but solely from the construction of their organs. For, while reason is a universal instrument that is available for every contingency, these organs, on the contrary, need a particular arrangement for each particular action. Accordingly, it must be morally impossible that there should exist in any machine a diversity of organs sufficient to enable it to act in all the occurrences of life, in the way in which our reason enables us to act.

Animals Have Bodies with No Minds or Reason

Again, by means of these two tests we may likewise know the difference between humans and animals. For it is highly noteworthy that there are no people so dull and stupid, not even idiots, as to be incapable of joining together different words, and thereby constructing a declaration by which to make their thoughts understood; and that on the other hand, there is no other animal, however perfect or happily circumstanced, which can do the like. Nor does this inability arise from the lack of organs: for we observe that magpies and parrots can utter words like ourselves, and are yet unable to speak as we do, that is, so as to show that they understand what they say. Yet there are people who are born deaf and dumb (and thus not less, but rather more than the brutes) and thus destitute of the organs which others use in speaking. Yet, they are in the habit of spontaneously inventing certain signs by which they express their thoughts to those who, being usually in their company, have time to learn their language. And this proves not only that animals have less reason than humans, but that they have none at all. For we see that very little is required to enable a person to speak. And since a certain inequality of capacity is observable among animals of the same species, as well as among people, and since some are more capable of being instructed than others, it is incredible that the most perfect ape or parrot of its species, should not in this be equal to the most stupid infant of its kind, or at least to one that was partly insane, unless the soul of animals were of a nature wholly different from ours.

We should also not confuse speech with the natural movements that display the passions, and can be imitated by machines as well as manifested by animals. Nor must it be thought, as some ancient writers did, that animals speak although we do not understand their language. For if such were the case, since they are endowed with many organs analogous to ours, they could as easily communicate their thoughts to us as to their fellows. It is also very worthy of remark that, though there are many animals that display more skill than we do in certain of their actions, the same animals are yet observed to show none at all in many other actions. Thus, just because they do better than we do, this does not prove that they are possessed with minds. For it would then follow that they possessed greater reason than any of us, and could surpass us in all things. On the contrary: it rather proves that they are destitute of reason, and that it is nature which acts in them according to the disposition of their organs. Thus it is seen that a clock composed only of wheels and weights can number the hours and measure time more exactly than we with all our skill.

After this I described the rational soul, and showed that it could by no means be deduced from the power of matter, as the other things of which I had spoken. Instead, it must be expressly created. Further, it is not sufficient for it to be lodged in the human body exactly like a pilot in a ship, unless perhaps to move its members; rather, it is necessary for it to be joined and united more closely to the body, in order to have sensations and appetites similar to ours, and thus constitute a real person.

In conclusion, I have elaborated on the subject of the soul since it is a topic of considerable importance. For after the error of those who deny the existence of God (an error which I think I have already sufficiently refuted), there is none that is more powerful in leading feeble minds astray from the straight path of virtue than the supposition that the soul of the brutes is of the same nature as our own (and, consequently, that after this life we have nothing to hope for or fear any more than flies and ants). Instead, when we know how far animals differ from us, we much better understand the reasons which establish that the soul is of a nature entirely independent of the body, and that consequently it is not liable to die with the latter. Finally, because we observe no other causes that are capable of destroying the soul, we are naturally led to judge that it is immortal.

MIND AND BODY CONNECTED IN THE BRAIN

31. *That there is a small gland in the brain in which the soul exercises its function more particularly than in the other parts.* It is likewise necessary to know that although the soul is joined to the whole body, there is yet in that a certain part in which it exercises its functions more particularly than in all the others. And it is usually believed that this part is the brain, or possibly the heart. It is believed to be the brain because it is with it that the organs of sense are connected. And it is believed to be the heart because it is apparently in it that we experience the passions. But, in examining the matter with care, it seems as though I had clearly ascertained that the part of the body in which the soul exercises its functions immediately is in nowise the heart, nor the whole of the brain. Instead, it is merely the most inward of all its parts, namely, a certain very small gland which is situated in the middle of its substance and so suspended above the duct whereby the animal spirits in its anterior cavities have communication with those in the posterior. It is such that the slightest movements which take place in it may alter very greatly the course of these spirits. And, reciprocally, the smallest changes which occur in the course of the spirits may do much to change the movements of this gland.

32. *How we know that this gland is the main seat of the soul.* The reason which persuades me that the soul cannot have any other seat in all the body than this

gland wherein to exercise its functions immediately, is that I reflect that the other parts of our brain are all of them double, just as we have two eyes two hands, two ears, and finally all the organs of our outside senses are double. And inasmuch as we have but one solitary and simple thought of one particular thing at one and the same moment, it must necessarily be the case that there must somewhere be a place where the two images which come to us by the two eyes, where the two other impressions which proceed from a single object by means of the double organs of the other senses, can unite before arriving at the soul, in order that they may not represent to it two objects instead of one. And it is easy to see how these images or other impressions might unite in this gland by the intermission of the spirits which fill the cavities of the brain. But there is no other place in the body where they can be thus united unless they are so in this gland.

34. *How the soul and the body act on one another.* Let us then conceive here that the soul has its principal seat in the little gland which exists in the middle of the brain. For, from this spot it radiates forth through all the remainder of the body by means of the animal spirits, nerves, and even the blood, which, participating in the impressions of the spirits, can carry them by the arteries into all the members. Recall what has been said above about the machine of our body, that is, that the little filaments of our nerves are so distributed in all its parts, that on the occasion of the diverse movements which are there excited by sensible objects, they open in different ways the pores of the brain. This, in turn, causes the animal spirit contained in these cavities to enter in different ways into the muscles, by which means they can move the members in all the different ways in which they are capable of being moved. And also, recall all the other causes which are capable of moving the spirits in different ways and which suffice to conduct them into different muscles. Let us here add that the small gland which is the main seat of the soul is so suspended between the cavities which contain the spirits that it

can be moved by them in as many different ways as there are sensible differences in the object. Further, it may also be moved in different ways by the soul, whose nature is such that it receives in itself as many different impressions, that is to say, that it possesses as many different perceptions as there are different movements in this gland. Reciprocally, likewise, the machine of the body is so formed that from the simple fact that this gland is differently moved by the soul (or by such other cause, whatever it is) it thrusts the spirits which surround it towards the pores of the brain, which conduct them by the nerves into the muscles, by which means it causes them to move the limbs.

FOR FURTHER REFLECTION

1. Descartes argues that our minds are nonphysical spirits, since I can imagine existing without a body, but I cannot imagine that I do not think. Leibniz criticized Descartes as follows: "Someone who thinks that the soul is corporeal . . . will admit that you can doubt (as long as you are ignorant of the nature of the soul) whether anything corporeal exists or does not exist. And as you nevertheless see clearly that your soul exists, he will admit that this one thing follows: that you can still doubt whether the soul is corporeal. But no amount of torture can extort anything more from this argument." What is Leibniz's point, and is he correct?

2. What is Descartes' argument for why even sophisticated machines will never have the capacity to reason? Do you agree?

3. What is Descartes' argument for why animals are incapable of reasoning and have no soul? Do you agree?

4. Explain why Descartes says the pineal gland in the center of the brain is the gateway between our physical bodies and mental spirits. Is there a problem with his theory?

ANNE CONWAY

MIND AND BODY AS A CONTINUUM

During an era in which philosophy was overwhelmingly dominated by male writers, Anne Conway (1631–1678) composed her sole work *The Principles of the Most Ancient and Modern Philosophy*, which appeared after her death, first in Latin (1690), then in English (1692). She was born in London into an aristocratic family and later became acquainted with Henry More, the Cambridge Platonist philosopher.

A key feature of her book is its rejection of Descartes' radical distinction between physical body and metal spirit; instead she advocates the view that body and spirit are more or less the same thing, differing only in degree, not in kind. Bodies and spirits are on a continuum, she argues, starting with heavy bodies, then light bodies, then heavy spirits, then light spirits. Each level intermingles with the next, and thus the entire continuum of body and spirit are connected. In this manner, my mental spirit interacts with my physical body by exchanging signals back and forth through my body-spirit continuum.

BODY AND SOUL DIFFER ONLY IN DEGREE, NOT IN KIND

To prove that spirit and body differ not essentially, but gradually, I shall deduce my fourth argument from the intimate band or union, which intercedes between bodies and spirits. [It is] by means whereof the spirits have dominion over the bodies with which they are united, that they move them from one place to another, and use them as instruments in their various operations. For if spirit and body are so contrary one to another (so that a spirit is only life, or a living and sensible substance, but a body a certain mass merely dead; a spirit penetrable and indiscerpible [i.e., indivisible into parts], which are all contrary attributes) what (I pray you) is that which does so join or unite them together? Or, what are those links or chains, whereby they have so firm a connection, and that for so long a space of time? Moreover also, when the spirit or soul is separated from the body, so that it has no longer dominion or power over it to move it as it had before, what is the cause of this separation?

If it be said, that the vital agreement ([which] the soul has to the body) is the cause of the said union, and that the body being corrupted that vital agreement ceases, I answer, we must first inquire in what this vital agreement does consist. For if they cannot tell us wherein it does consist, they only trifle with empty words, which give a sound, but want a signification. For certainly in the sense which they take body and spirit in, there is no agreement at all between them. For a body is always a dead thing, void of life and sense, no less when the spirit is in it, than when it is gone out of it. Hence there is no agreement at all between them. And if there is any agreement, that certainly will remain the same, both, when the body is sound and when it is corrupted.

From Anne Conway, *The Principles of the Most Ancient and Modern Philosophy* (1692), Chapters 8 and 9. Section headings have been added, and spelling and punctuation have been modernized by the editor.

If they deny this, because a spirit requires an organized body (by means whereof it performs its vital acts of the external senses—moves and transports the body from place to place, which organical action ceases when the body is corrupted) certainly by this the difficulty is never the better solved. For why does the spirit require such an organized body? ex. gr. Why does it require a corporeal eye so wonderfully formed and organized that I can see by it? Why does it need a corporeal light to see corporeal objects? Or, why is it requisite that the image of the object should be sent to it, through the eye, that I may see it? If the same were entirely nothing but a spirit, and no way corporeal, why does it need so many several corporeal organs, so far different from the nature of it?

Furthermore, how can a spirit move its body, or any of its members, if a spirit (as they affirm) is of such a nature that no part of its body can in the least resist it, even as one body is wont to resist another, when it is moved by it, by reason of its impenetrability? For if a spirit could also easily penetrate all bodies, wherefore does it not leave the body behind it when it is moved from place to place, seeing it can so easily pass out without the least resistance? For certainly this is the cause of all motions which we see in the world, where one thing moves another, viz. because both are impenetrable in the sense aforesaid. For, were it not for this impenetrability, one creature could not move another because this would not oppose that nor at all resist it. An example whereof we have in the sails of a ship, by which the wind drives the ship, and that so much the more vehemently, by how much the fewer holes, vents, and passages, the same finds in the sails against which it drives. When on the contrary, if, instead of sails, nets were expanded, through which the wind would have a freer passage, certainly by these the ship would be but little moved, although it blew with great violence. Hence we see how this impenetrability causes resistance, and this makes motion. But if there were no impenetrability, as in the case of body and spirit, then there would be no resistance, and by consequence the spirit could make no motion in the body. . . .

For we may easily understand how one body is united with another, by that true agreement that one has with another in its own nature. And so the most subtle and spiritual body may be united with a body that is very gross and thick, sc, by means of certain bodies partaking of subtlety and grossness, according to diverse degrees consisting between two extremes. And these middle bodies are indeed the links and chains by which the soul, which is so subtle and spiritual, is conjoined with a body so gross—which middle spirits (if they cease, or are absent) the union is broken or dissolved. So from the same foundation we may easily understand how the soul moves the body, viz. as one subtle body can move another gross and thick body. And seeing the body itself is a sensible life, or an intellectual substance, it is no less clearly conspicuous how one body can wound, or grieve, or gratify, or please another. [It is] because things of one or alike nature can easily affect each other. . . .

I shall draw a fifth argument from what we observe in all visible bodies, as in earth, water, stones, wood, etc. What abundance of spirits is in all these things? For earth and water continually produce animals, as they have done from the beginning, so that a pool filled with water may produce fishes though none were ever put there to increase or breed. And seeing that all other things do more originally proceed from earth and water, it necessarily follows that the spirits of all animals were in the water. And therefore it is said in *Genesis*, that the spirit of God moved upon the face of the waters, viz. that from hence he might produce whatsoever was afterwards created.

But if it be said, this argument does not prove that all spirits are bodies, but that all bodies have in them the spirits of all animals (so that every body has a spirit in it, and likewise a spirit and body, and although they are thus united, yet they still remain different in nature one from another, and so cannot be changed one into another) to this I answer. If every body, even the least, has in it the spirits of all animals, and other things, even as matter is said to have in it all forms, now I demand, whether a body has actually all those spirits in it, or potentially only? If actually, how is it possible that so many spirits essentially distinct from body can actually exist in their distinct essences in so small a body (even in the least that can be conceived) unless it be by intrinsic presence, which is not communicable to any creature, as already proved. For if all kinds of spirits are in any, even the least body, how comes it to pass that such an animal is produced of this body and not another? Yea, how comes it to pass that all kinds of animals are not immediately produced out of one and the same body, which experience denies. For we see that nature keeps her order in all operations, whence one animal is formed of another, and one species proceeds from another, as well when it ascends to a farther perfection, as when it descends to a viler state and condition.

But if they say, all spirits are contained in any body, not actually in their distinct essences, but only potentially as they term it, then it must be granted, that the body and all those spirits are one and the same thing. That is, that a body may be turned into them, as when we say wood is potentially fire (that is, can be turned into fire), water is potentially air (that is, may be changed into air). . . .

AGAINST DESCARTES, HOBBES, AND SPINOZA

From what has been lately said, and from diverse reasons alleged, that spirit and body are originally in their first substance but one and the same thing, it evidently appears that the philosophers (so called) which have taught otherwise, whether ancient or modern, have generally erred. . . .

And none can object that all this philosophy is no other than that of Descartes or Hobbes under a new mask. For, first, as touching the Cartesian philosophy, this says that every body is a mere dead mass, not only void of all kind of life and sense, but utterly incapable thereof to all eternity. This grand error also is to be imputed to all those who affirm body and spirit to be contrary things, and inconvertible one into another, so as to deny a body all life and sense, but utterly incapable thereof to all eternity. This grand error also is to be imputed to all those who affirm body and spirit to be contrary things, and inconvertible one into another, so as to deny a body all life and sense, which is quite contrary to the grounds of this our philosophy. Wherefore it is so far from being a *Cartesian* principle, under a new mask, that it may be

truly said it is *anti-Cartesian*, in regard of their fundamental principles—although, it cannot be denied that Descartes taught many excellent and ingenious things concerning the mechanical part of natural operations, and how all natural motions proceed according to rules and laws mechanical, even as indeed nature herself, i.e., the creature, as an excellent mechanical skill and wisdom in itself (given it from God, who is the fountain of all wisdom) by which it operates. But yet in nature, and her operations, they are far more than merely mechanical, and the same is not a mere organical body, like a clock, wherein there is not a vital principle of motion, but a living body, having life and sense, which body is far more sublime than a mere mechanism, or mechanical motion.

But, secondly, as to what pertains to Hobbes's opinion, this is more contrary to this our philosophy than that of Descartes. For Descartes acknowledged God to be plainly immaterial and an incorporeal spirit. Hobbes affirms God himself to be material and corporeal—yea, nothing else but matter and body—and so confounds God and the creatures in their essences, and denies that there is any essential distinction between them. These and many more the worst of consequences are the dictates of Hobbes's philosophy, to which may be added that of Spinoza, for this Spinoza also confounds God and the creatures together and makes but one being of both, all which are diametrically opposite to the philosophy here delivered by us.

FOR FURTHER REFLECTION

1. Conway criticizes Cartesian interactive dualism with an analogy of a ship that uses nets as sails. Explain the analogy and say whether it is an effective criticism.

2. Conway gives examples of how physical things interact with spiritual things; for example, she says that "earth and water continually produce animals." Is this a good example of physical things interacting with spiritual things? Explain why or why not.

3. Conway does not give exact details about what part of you is a heavy spirit and what part of you

is a light body and how those two parts of you might interact. Speculate about what part of you might occupy these two roles.

4. What, according to Conway, is wrong with Hobbes's view that God is material, and do you agree with her?

JEROME SHAFFER

CONSCIOUSNESS AND THE MIND-BODY PROBLEM

Jerome Shaffer (b. 1929) is a philosophy professor at the University of Connecticut and has made significant contributions in philosophy of mind. This excerpt is taken from *Philosophy of Mind* (1968).

In this selection Shaffer examines the traditional mind-body problem, focusing on interactive dualism and reductive materialism (the identity theory) and showing the strengths and weaknesses associated with each position. Shaffer provides the best overview of the problem available in the literature.

It would seem to be an undeniable fact that consciousness does exist and that any account of the world will have to give some place to it. But what place? What is the relation of consciousness to whatever else does exist? In particular, what is the relation of consciousness to the organic and inorganic matter that makes up so great a part of the world? And more particularly, what is the relation of consciousness to those organic systems we know as human bodies? . . . We can begin our inquiry by asking what is the subject of consciousness, in other words, *what* is conscious when consciousness exists? Well, what sorts of things have consciousness? One pretty indisputable case is that of . . . human beings. But what is a . . . human being? Is he just a particular kind of matter formed in a particular way? Or is there more to the story, and if so what more? If a man is *more* than a particularly

formed kind of matter, then is it some part of that *more* which is the subject of consciousness?

To make the discussion manageable, let us confine ourselves to that form of consciousness which consists in having what I shall call mental events: those particular occasions which consist in the having of some thought, the feeling of some sensation, the imaging of some mental picture, the entertaining of some wish, etc. Our problem, then, will be to determine *what* it is that has the thought, feels the sensation, images the mental picture, entertains the wish, etc.

[Shaffer now contrasts *dualist theories,* which state that the mind is nonmaterial and fundamentally different from the body, with materialist theories, which state that mental events are reducible to physical events.]

From Jerome Schaffer, *Philosophy of Mind* (1968), pp. 35–55, by permission of the author and Pearson Education, Upper Saddle River, N.J.

DUALISM

The most systematic dualistic theory is that which was presented by the French philosopher Descartes. He held that the subject of consciousness is the *mind* and that the mind is a thing or entity separate and distinct from the body. The body is a thing or entity whose essence (defining characteristic) is occupying space, i.e., having shape, size, and location in space; and it is in no sense conscious. The mind, on the other hand, is completely different in its nature. It is utterly nonspatial, having neither shape, size, nor location. Its essence (defining characteristic) is simply having consciousness, that is, thoughts, feelings, memories, perceptions, desires, emotions, etc.

Descartes held that since the mind and the body are separate entities, each can exist without the other. It is obvious and undeniable that Descartes is at least correct in holding that *some* bodies—e.g., stones and lakes—do indeed exist without minds. Descartes himself believed that animals (other than man) were also examples of bodies without minds. Some people might disagree with him there, and there would be even more disagreement with his thesis that minds could exist without bodies. Descartes believed that minds were immortal, that they continue to exist as disembodied minds after the body has perished in death.

There is an important gap in Descartes' account, a gap which can be noted in the summary just given. From the fact that the essence of the mind is one thing, having consciousness, and the essence of the body is another, occupying space, it does not follow that the mind and the body are *two separate entities.* What is to rule out the possibility that one and the same thing can have *both* these properties, be *both* a thinking thing and at the very same time an extended thing? The essence, that is, the defining characteristic, of being a husband is being a married man and the essence of being a parent is having offspring, but one and the same person can be both a husband *and* a parent (and, obviously, can be one without being the other). This gap in Descartes' reasoning was first pointed out by Spinoza, who had been a follower of Descartes. Spinoza realized that "although two attributes may be conceived as really distinct," and here he has in mind thinking and extension, "we cannot nevertheless thence conclude that they constitute two

beings or two different substances."[1] Then, breaking decisively with Descartes, Spinoza went on to maintain that in the case of human beings (and, as a matter of fact, for Spinoza, in everything else as well), both thinking *and* space-occupancy were characteristics of one and the same thing. This view shall be discussed later under the heading of double aspect theory.

Nevertheless, Descartes held that one and the same thing could not be both a space-occupier and a thinking thing. He seems to have thought that these characteristics were simply so different in their natures that one and the same thing *could* not have both. Thus he cites the fact that extended things are divisible, whereas thinking things are not divisible (see his sixth *Meditation*). But this is a very weak line of argument. Since thinking and occupying space are different characteristics, there will naturally be differences between them. Extended things will necessarily be divisible (I take it Descartes is here thinking of *spatially* dividing something), and things which are nonextended, say disembodied minds, will not be so divisible. But this is just to say that we have different characteristics here. A thing which thinks would be divisible if it were at the same time an extended thing. So pointing out differences between extension and thinking does not show us that things which have the one characteristic cannot have the other. Perhaps Descartes had in mind the point that extension and thinking are *so very* different, so basically different. Of course one object could be both red and round, he might say, but could one object be both red and thinking? Here again, however, the line of argument is weak. Being red and being valuable and being holy are *very* different sorts of properties, yet one and the same object, say a particular jewel, might be all three. So we still do not have a very good reason for thinking that thinking things could not be extended and vice versa.

Even if the dualist fails to give us a reason for holding that thinking things and extended things are *different* entities, still such a view might be correct. And we have not yet seen any reason for thinking it is *not* correct. So let us, for the moment, grant the dualist his claim that they are different entities. If we do so, the question arises how these two different entities are related to each other, if at all. Here we find ourselves faced with what is traditionally known in philosophy as the mind-body problem.

THE TRADITIONAL MIND-BODY PROBLEM

. . . In order to get a better grasp of dualism we will here take a brief look at the various theories [of the mind-body problem] that have been proposed. Descartes himself believed that sometimes the mind could causally affect the body and sometimes the body could causally affect the mind; this view is called interactionism. An example of the former would be a case in which, after deliberation, I decide (a mental event) to press the button and then my hand reaches out to press it (a bodily event); an example of the latter would be a case in which the moving hand (a bodily event) comes in contact with the button, causing in me a feeling of fear (a mental event) at what will happen if I do press the button.

Interactionism is not the only dualistic theory of the relation between mind and body. Some philosophers have held that there is only *one-way* causality, from body to mind; this view is known as epiphenomenalism. The epiphenomenalist accepts one half of the interactionist contention, that part which holds that bodily events can cause mental events. But he denies the other half; he denies that mental events can ever cause bodily events. Whatever happens in the mind is merely a by-product of bodily activity (most plausibly, brain activity). No important philosopher has ever held what we might call reverse epiphenomenalism, namely that bodily events are *always* merely effects of mental activity. The religion of Christian Science comes somewhat close to this view, holding that bodily events, particularly those concerning health and disease, are results of mental activity. Many Christian Scientists would go so far as to maintain that *all* bodily events, for example the activity in our sense organs during perception, are caused solely by mental activity. This is the view of the eighteenth-century Irish philosopher George Berkeley, that anything that ever happens at all happens only in the mind. Berkeley's view is no longer dualism; he holds that only minds exist and that matter and in particular bodies do not exist at all, except in the mind.

Finally, there is the dualist theory known as parallelism. The parallelist admits the close connection of events in the mind and events in the body, but does not wish to say that the connection is a causal one, for he holds that the mind and the body are too utterly different to be able to interact causally with each other. So the parallelist holds that the mind and the body are like two clocks, each with its own mechanism and with no causal connection between them, yet always in phase keeping the same time.

OBJECTIONS TO DUALISM

Dualist theories are not very much in favor these days. There are two main sources of discontent with them. (1) Many philosophers have grave doubts that the notion of the mind as a thing or entity can be rendered intelligible. (2) Even if it could be made intelligible, the view of the world which results seems to many unnecessarily complex. We will discuss these two sources of discontent in order.

(1) Dualists tell us that in addition to the familiar objects of everyday life, tables, rocks, hair, trees, clouds, air, in short material things, there also exist things of a quite different kind—minds. These minds are real things, real objects, real entities, but they are fundamentally different sorts of things from material things. Well then, what is a mind? Is it a peculiar kind of stuff, immaterial matter, insubstantial substance, bodiless body? It is supposed to have no extension, that is, no shape, size, or capacity to occupy space; it is not visible to the eye, tangible to the touch, nor is it visible under any microscope however powerful, [or] tangible to the most delicate of probing instruments. Perhaps the mind is like a gravitational, magnetic, or electrical field? But it cannot be, for on the dualist's hypothesis the mind is in no way physical; if it were like them, or like physical energy of some sort, then it would be a *physical* phenomenon and we would no longer be dualists. Yet if it is in no way like such things, in what sense is the mind a thing at all? What meaning can we give to the notion of the mind as an existent thing?

The problem comes out in two particular ways, in the problem of identification and the problem of individuation. The former problem concerns how we can tell when we are in the presence of some other mind A rather than B or even in the presence of any other mind at all. Since, on the dualist account, another mind is not detectible by any observations we could make, it is impossible that we should have any reason to think we could ever identify another mind as mind A or B. So we could never justifiably believe we were, for example, talking to someone. And a concept of a mind which made it impossible justifiably to apply that concept to any other thing would be utterly useless, even if intelligible.

The problem of individuation concerns what makes two minds distinct, assuming there could be two distinct minds. One answer might be that they have different mental histories, each having had different mental events at certain times. But it seems perfectly intelligible to suppose that at some time we might have two distinct minds with exactly the same history of mental events (each might have grown up in exactly the same way). And, if this supposition of two exactly similar minds is intelligible, then what would make them two distinct minds rather than one and the same mind? The dualist does not seem to have an answer. He must say they are distinct, and yet he cannot say how or in what respect they differ. Does that make any sense?

(2) Even if we were able to give some *meaning* to the claim that minds exist, many contemporary philosophers would reject the claim that in fact minds do exist. They would make the remark attributed to the French astronomer Laplace in reply to Napoleon's question about the role of God in the system: said Laplace, "Sire, I have no need of that hypothesis." Thus many philosophers would argue that everything that happens in the world can be explained without using the notion of minds, strictly on the basis of physical phenomena and physical laws.

The view that minds do not exist at all and that only the physical exists is called materialism. We shall now turn to this view.

MATERIALISM

Materialism is one of the very oldest theories. It was a familiar doctrine to the ancient Greeks of the fourth and fifth centuries B.C. The spokesman for this view, Democritus, held that nothing exists but material atoms and the void and that everything in the world is nothing but the interactions of these atoms as they move through the void. Even the most complex behavior of human beings can be resolved into interactions between the atoms. A modern materialist would allow a more complicated picture than "atoms and the void." He would bring in subatomic particles and antiparticles, electromagnetic waves, a relativized view of "the void," various kinds of forces and energies, and the rest of the conceptual apparatus of contemporary physics. But he would still hold that nothing exists but such physical phenomena; if such terms as "thought," "feeling," "wish," etc., have any meaning at all, they must refer in the last analysis to physical phenomena. So-called mental events are really nothing but physical events occurring to physical objects.

We should, at the outset, distinguish materialism as characterized here from another doctrine which has already been mentioned, epiphenomenalism. . . . The latter is a dualistic theory which allows that the mind is separate and distinct from the body but also insists that the mind is utterly dependent causally upon the body, that everything which happens in the mind is a result of events in the body, and that the mind is utterly powerless to affect the body in any way. Such a view is often called materialistic, since it places the highest *importance* on the material side of things. It is in this sense that Karl Marx was materialistic, for he held that "conceiving, thinking, the mental intercourse of men, appear at [the earliest] stage as the direct efflux of their material behavior."[2] Notice that Marx is not saying men's conceiving, thinking, and mental intercourse *are nothing but* their material behavior. That would be materialism as here characterized. He is saying that they are the "efflux," i.e., a *separate, nonmaterial* outflow which originates and derives from material behavior. Such a view is not materialistic in our sense.

The materialist holds that nothing but the physical exists—matter, energy, and the void. But then what *are* thoughts, feelings, wishes, and the other so-called mental phenomena? Here four different answers have been seriously proposed. The most radical view, supported by very few, is that such terms have *no real meaning at all* and should be dropped from the language. They represent an accretion to our language which was conceived in ignorance and superstition, nurtured by the vested interests of religion and the black arts, and condoned by human lethargy. On this view, mentalistic terms should be allowed to suffer the fate of the language of witchcraft and demonic possession. Let us call this the unintelligibility thesis.

The unintelligibility thesis has not gained much support among contemporary philosophers. In the first place, it is clear why notions of witchcraft and demonic possession died out—it has been shown pretty conclusively by science that no such phenomena in fact exist. There might have been witches, and, in that case, there could have been a science which studied them and the ways in which they achieved their effects; but the evidence indicates that there are no such things. But this is hardly the case with mentalistic terms. What kind of discoveries could show that in fact there are no thoughts, feelings, wishes, and the like? On the contrary, is it not as plain as anything can be that there are such things? And, secondly, we could not dispense with mentalistic terms, even if our theories told us it was most desirable to do so, nor does it seem likely we will be able to do for the foreseeable future. This is because we often want to tell our thoughts, describe our feelings, express our wishes, and there is no other way available of doing so than saying I just had the thought . . . , I feel . . . , I wish. . . . To abandon such expressions would be to impoverish our language to the point of bankruptcy.

Another materialistic reply to the question "What are thoughts, feelings, wishes, and the like?" is called the avowal theory. This theory allows that sentences like "I feel bored" have meaning all right, but are not used to make *statements,* are not used to describe or report or assert anything. They are simply bits of behavior, the effects of certain inner (physical) conditions. If I yawn, twiddle my thumbs, or say "Ho hum," I am not describing, reporting, or asserting anything; I am not making a statement which is either true or false. The avowal theory takes "I feel bored" to be a (learned) bit of behavior, like "Ho hum," which results from certain inner (physical) conditions, and not a statement, description, report, or assertion at all. And the same

would go for utterances of the form "I just had the thought that . . . ," "I wish that . . . ," and the like.

It cannot be denied that there is some truth in the avowal theory. Certainly such utterances are sometimes used in this way, as expressions of inner states—"I feel bored" is sometimes uttered in the way that "God, I'm bored!" or even "Oh God, what boredom!" is uttered, and it is clear at least in the latter case that no statement, description, report, or assertion is being made. Yet the avowal theory falls down in two important respects. First, it is utterly implausible when applied to third-person statements, e.g., "He is bored." In no way can such a remark be taken as the expression of an inner state. Second, even in their first-person use, such utterances are often used merely to report or describe. If someone asks me why I keep looking at my watch, I may say "Because I am bored," making a report which explains my behavior. Furthermore, I can use such utterances to make *false* statements, as when I am lying. "Ho hum" cannot be used to explain anything or to lie about anything. So the avowal theory will not do.

Another materialistic account is to allow that expressions referring to thoughts, feelings, wishes, and the like have meaning, but to insist that their meanings can be expressed in purely physicalistic terms. What physicalistic terms? The most plausible candidate is the set of terms which refer to physical *behavior.* This account [is] known as behaviorism. . . .

This behavioristic version of materialism has had a strong appeal for philosophers over the years. In contrast with the unintelligibility thesis, it allows sentences containing mentalistic terms to have meaning, and, in contrast with the avowal theory, it allows them to be either true or false in the situations in which they are used. And by using the concept of *disposition to behave,* it allows such sentences to be true even where the person is not at that moment behaving in any particular fashion. Yet by tying the meaning to *behavior* the theory allows sentences with mentalistic terms to be testable by observation in an open and public way. To determine whether someone has a headache we only have to see if, under suitable conditions, he behaves in the appropriate ways.

This view, however, is open to a fundamental objection. . . . No matter what sort of behavior or behavioral dispositions we imagine as allegedly constituting a particular mental event, we can always imagine just that behavior or those dispositions *without* that mental event. We can imagine that behavior as coming from some *other* cause, or even as inexplicably *spontaneous*. Therefore behavior and behavioral dispositions do not furnish an exhaustive analysis of these mentalistic terms. There is something left out by such accounts.

The last version of materialism we shall consider, and currently the most seriously discussed, is known as the identity theory. It is the theory that thoughts, feelings, wishes, and the rest of so-called mental phenomena are identical with, one and the same thing as, states and processes of the *body* (and, perhaps, more specifically, states and processes of the nervous system, or even of the brain alone). Thus the having of a thought is identical with having such and such bodily cells in such and such states, other cells in other states.

In one respect the identity theory and behaviorism are very much alike. This comes out when we ask ourselves what the "dispositions" of the behaviorist are. If an object has a "disposition," then *it is in a particular state* such that when certain things happen to it, other things will happen to it. Thus if an object is brittle, it is in a particular state such that when subject to a sudden force it will shatter. And similarly dispositions of a body to behave in particular ways are *states of that body*. So it is fair to say that both identity theorists and behaviorists identify the mental with *bodily states*. But one important way in which they differ concerns how those states are to be defined or characterized. As we have seen, behaviorists wish to define those states in terms of what changes they result in when certain specifiable conditions obtain. Identity theorists wish to define them in terms of identifiable structures of the body, ongoing processes and states of the bodily organs, and, in the last analysis, the very cells which go to make up those organs.

There is another important respect in which the identity theory differs from behaviorism. The behaviorist offered his notion of dispositions to behave in certain ways as an analysis of the very meaning of mentalistic terms. But the identity theorist grants that it is wildly implausible to claim that what I *mean* when I say, for example, that I just had a particular

thought is that certain events were going on in my nervous system. For I have no idea what those events are, nor does even the most advanced neurophysiologist at the present time, and yet I know what I mean when I say I just had a particular thought. So, since I know what I mean by those words, I cannot mean by them something I know nothing about (viz., unknown events in my nervous system). Hence the identity theory is not intended to be an analysis of the *meanings* of mentalistic terms as behaviorism purports to be. What, then, is the theory that mental phenomena are "identical" with the body intended to be?

The sense of "identity" relevant here is that in which we say, for example, that the morning star is "identical" with the evening star. It is not that the expression "morning star" means the same as the expression "evening star"; on the contrary, these expressions mean something different. But the object referred to by the two expressions is one and the same; there is just one heavenly body, namely, Venus, which when seen in the morning is called the morning star and when seen in the evening is called the evening star. The morning star is identical with the evening star; they are one and the same object.

Of course, the identity of the mental with the physical is not exactly of this sort, since it is held to be simultaneous identity rather than the identity of a thing at one time with the same thing at a later time. To take a closer example, one can say that lightning is a particularly massive electrical discharge from one cloud to another or to the earth. Not that the word "lightning" *means* "a particularly massive electrical discharge . . . "; when Benjamin Franklin discovered that lightning was electrical, he did not make a discovery about the meaning of words. Nor when it was discovered that water was H_2O was a discovery made about the meanings of words; yet water is identical with H_2O.

In a similar fashion, the identity theorists can hold that thoughts, feelings, wishes, and the like are identical with physical states. Not "identical" in the sense that mentalistic terms are synonymous in meaning with physicalistic terms but "identical" in the sense that the actual events picked out by mentalistic terms are one and the same events as those picked out by physicalistic terms.

It is important to note that the identity theory does not have a chance of being true unless a particular sort of correspondence obtains between mental events and physical events, namely, that whenever a mental event occurs, a physical event of a particular sort (or at least one of a number of particular sorts) occurs, and vice versa. If it turned out to be the case that when a particular mental event occurred it seemed a matter of chance what physical events occurred or even whether any physical event at all occurred, or vice versa, then the identity theory would not be true. So far as our state of knowledge at the present time is concerned, it is still too early to say what the empirical facts are, although it must be said that many scientists do believe that there exists the kind of correspondences needed by identity theorists. But even if these correspondences turn out to exist, that does not mean that the identity theory will be true. For identity theorists do not hold merely that mental and physical events are correlated in a particular way but that they are one and the same events, i.e., not like lightning and thunder (which are correlated in lawful ways but not identical) but like lightning and electrical discharges (which always go together because they are one and the same).

What are the advantages of the identity theory? As a form of materialism, it does not have to cope with a world which has in it both mental phenomena and physical phenomena, and it does not have to ponder how they might be related. There exist only the physical phenomena, although there do exist two different ways of talking about such phenomena: physicalistic terminology and, in at least some situations, mentalistic terminology. We have here a dualism of language, but not a dualism of entities, events, or properties.

SOME DIFFICULTIES IN THE IDENTITY THEORY

But do we have merely a dualism of languages and no other sort of dualism? In the case of Venus, we do indeed have only one object, but the expression "morning star" picks out one phase of that object's history, where it is in the mornings, and the expression "evening star" picks out another phase of that object's history, where it is in the evenings. If that object did not have these two distinct aspects, it would not have been a *discovery* that the morning star and the evening star were indeed one and the same body, and, further, there would be no point to the different ways of referring to it.

Now it would be admitted by identity theorists that physicalistic and mentalistic terms do not refer to different phases in the history of one and the same object. What sort of identity is intended? Let us turn to an allegedly closer analogy, that of the identity of lightning and a particular sort of electrical phenomenon. Yet here again we have two distinguishable aspects, the appearance to the naked eye on the one hand and the physical composition on the other. And this is also not the kind of identity which is plausible for mental and physical events. The appearance *to the naked eye* of a neurological event is utterly different from the experience of having a thought or a pain.

It is sometimes suggested that the physical aspect results from looking at a particular event "from the outside," whereas the mental results from looking at the same event "from the inside." When the brain surgeon observes my brain he is looking at it from the outside, whereas when I experience a mental event I am "looking" at my brain "from the inside."

Such an account gives us only a misleading analogy, rather than an accurate characterization of the relationship between the mental and the physical. The analogy suggests the difference between a man who knows his own house from the inside, in that he is free to move about within, seeing objects from different perspectives, touching them, etc., but can never get outside to see how it looks from there, and a man who cannot get inside and therefore knows only the outside appearance of the house, and perhaps what he can glimpse through the windows. But what does this have to do with the brain? Am I free to roam about inside my brain, observing what the brain surgeon may never see? Is not the "inner" aspect of my brain far more accessible to the brain surgeon than to me? He has the X rays, probes, electrodes, scalpels, and scissors for getting at the inside of my brain. If it is replied that this is only an analogy, not to be taken literally, then the question still remains how the mental and the physical are related.

Usually identity theorists at this point flee to even vaguer accounts of the relationship. They talk of different "levels of analysis," or of different "perspectives," or of different "conceptual schemes," or of different "language games." The point of such suggestions is that the difference between the mental and the physical is not a basic, fundamental, or intrinsic one, but rather a difference which is merely relative to different human purposes or standpoints. The difference is supposed to exist not in the thing itself but in the eye of the beholder.

But these are only hints. They do not tell us in precise and literal terms how the mental and the physical differ and are related. They only try to assure us that the difference does not matter to the real nature of things. But until we are given a theory to consider, we cannot accept the identity theorists' assurance that some theory will do only he does not know what it is.

One of the leading identity theorists, J. J. C. Smart, holds tht mentalistic discourse is simply a vaguer, more indefinite way of talking about what could be talked about more precisely by using physiological terms. If I report a red afterimage, I mean (roughly) that something is going on which is like what goes on when I really see a red patch. I do not actually *mean* that a particular sort of brain process is occurring, but when I say something is going on I refer (very vaguely, to be sure) to just that brain process. Thus the thing referred to in my report of an afterimage is a brain process. Hence there is no need to bring in any nonphysical features. Thus even the taint of dualism is avoided.

Does this ingenious attempt to evade dualistic implications stand up under philosophical scrutiny? I am inclined to think it will not. Let us return to the man reporting the red afterimage. He was aware of the occurrence of something or other, of some feature or other. Now it seems to me obvious that he was not necessarily aware of the state of his brain at that time (I doubt that most of us are ever aware of the state of our brain) nor, in general, necessarily aware of any physical features of his body at that time. He might, of course, have been incidentally aware of some physical feature but not insofar as he was aware of the red afterimage as such. Yet he was definitely aware of

something, or else how could he have made that report? So he must have been aware of some nonphysical feature. That is the only way of explaining how he was aware of anything at all.

Of course, the thing that our reporter of the afterimage was aware of might well have had further features which he was *not* aware of, particularly, in this connection, physical features. I may be aware of certain features of an object without being aware of others. So it is not ruled out that the event our reporter is aware of might be an event with predominantly physical features—he just does not notice those. But he must be aware of some of its features, or else it would not be proper to say he was aware of *that* event. And if he is not aware of any physical features, he must be aware of something else. And that shows that we cannot get rid of those nonphysical features in the way that Smart suggests.

One would not wish to be dogmatic in saying that identity theorists will never work out this part of their theory. Much work is being done on this problem at the present time, for it arises in other areas of philosophy as well as in the philosophy of mind. In particular philosophers of science are concerned with the problem. We saw that the identity theory used such analogies as the identity of lightning with electrical phenomena and the identity of water with molecules consisting of hydrogen and oxygen. But the question to be raised is what kind of identity we are dealing with in such cases. Do we have mere duality of terms in these cases, duality of features, properties, or aspects, or even duality of substances? Very similar issues arise. So it is quite possible that further work on this problem of identity will be useful in clarifying the identity theory of the mental and the physical. But at the present the matter is by no means as clear as it should be.

Even if the identity theorist could clarify the sense of "identity" to be used in his theory, he would still face two other problems. These concern coexistence in time and space. Coexistence in time and space are conditions that must be met if there is to be identity. That is to say, for two apparently different things to turn out to be one and the same, they must exist at the same time and in the same location. If we could show that Mr. A existed at a time when Mr. B did not, or that Mr. A existed in a place where Mr. B did not, then this would show that Mr. A and Mr. B were different men. It is by virtue of these facts about identity that an alibi can exonerate a suspect: if Mr. A was not in Chicago at the time, then he could not be one and the same with the man who stole the diamonds in Chicago.

So if mental events are to be identical with physical events, then they must fulfill the conditions of coexistence in time and space. The question is, Do they?

So far as coexistence in time is concerned, very little is known. The most relevant work consists in direct stimulation of an exposed part of the brain during surgery. Since only a local anesthetic is necessary in many such cases the patient may well be fully conscious. Then, as the surgeon stimulates different parts of his brain, the patient may report the occurrence of mental events—memories, thoughts, sensations. Do the physical events in the brain and the mental events occur at precisely the same time? It is impossible to say. All that would be required is a very small time gap to prove that the physical events were not identical with the mental events. But it is very difficult to see how the existence of so small a time gap could be established. And even if it were, what would it prove? Only that the mental event was not identical with just that physical event; it would not prove it was nonidentical with any physical event. So it could well be that coexistence in time is present or is not. I do not think that we shall get much decisive information from empirical work of the sort here described. The identity theorist, then, does not have to fear refutation from this quarter, at least not for a long time.

How about coexistence in space? Do mental events occur in the same place the corresponding physical events occur? This is also a very difficult question to answer, for two reasons. First our present ignorance of neurophysiology, especially concerning the brain and how it functions, allows us to say very little about the location of the relevant physical events. This much does seem likely: they are located in the brain. Much more than that we do not at present know, although as the time passes, we should learn much more. The second reason for our difficulty in telling if there is coexistence in space has to do with the location of

mental events. Where do thoughts, feelings, and wishes occur? Do they occur in the brain? Suppose you suddenly have the thought that it is almost suppertime; where does that occur? The most sensible answer would be that it occurs wherever you are when you have that thought. If you are in the library when you have that thought, then the thought occurs in the library. But it would be utterly unnatural to ask where inside your body the thought occurred; in your foot, or your liver, or your heart, or your head? It is not that any one of these places is more likely than another. They are all wrong. Not because thoughts occur somewhere *else* within your body than your foot, liver, heart, or head—but because it *makes no sense at all* to locate the occurrence of a thought at some place within your body. We would not understand someone who pointed to a place in his body and claimed that it was *there* that his entertaining of a thought was located. Certainly, if one *looked* at that place, one would not *see* anything resembling a thought. If it were replied to this that pains can be located in the body without being seen there, then it should be pointed out that one *feels* the pain there but one hardly feels a thought in the body.

The fact that it makes no sense at all to speak of mental events as occurring at some point within the body has the result that the identity theory cannot be true. This is because the corresponding physical events do occur at some point within the body, and if those physical events are identical with mental events, then those mental events must occur at the same point within the body. But those mental events do not occur at any point within the body, because any statement to the effect that they occurred here, or there, would be senseless. Hence the mental events cannot meet the condition of coexistence in space, and therefore cannot be identical with physical events.

Our inability to give the location within the body of mental events is different from our inability to give the location of the corresponding physical events within the body. In the latter case, it is that we do not know enough about the body, particularly the brain. Some day, presumably, we will know enough to pin down pretty exactly the location of the relevant physical events. But in the case of mental events it is not simply that at present we are ignorant but that some-day we may well know. What would it be like to discover the location of a thought in the brain? What kind of information would we need to be able to say that the thought occurred exactly *here?* If by X rays or some other means we were able to see every event which occurred in the brain, we would never get a glimpse of a thought. If, to resort to fantasy, we could so enlarge a brain or so shrink ourselves that we could wander freely through the brain, we would still never observe a thought. All we could ever observe in the brain would be the *physical* events which occur in it. If mental events had location in the brain, there should be some means of detecting them there. But of course there is none. The very idea of it is senseless.

Some identity theorists believe this objection can be met. One approach is to reply that this objection begs the question: if the identity theory is true, and mental events are identical with brain events, then, paradoxical as it may sound, mental events do indeed have location, and are located precisely where the physical events are located. Another approach is to reply that the relevant physical events should be construed as events which happen to the body as a whole, and therefore occur where the body as a whole is located; then it is not so paradoxical to give location to the mental events, for they would be located where the body is located but would not be located in any particular part of the body.

We have carried our discussion of the identity theory to the very frontier of present philosophical thinking. We can only leave it to the reader to decide how well it can meet the objections which are raised to it. . . .

A RECONSIDERATION OF DUALISM

In view of the grave difficulties in materialism and the person theory, it might be useful to review the objections to dualism and see if they can be met in some way. After all, dualism does have the advantage over materialism of accounting for the inability to reduce mental phenomena to material phenomena and the advantage over the person theory of allowing for the

treatment of the human body as a material body in principle no different from other material bodies. It would be desirable to preserve these advantages, if we could overcome the disadvantages which seem to rule dualism out.

We noted that one source of discontent with dualism was that it seemed to commit us to the existence of a very peculiar kind of entity, a something which persists in time, has states, undergoes changes, and engages in processes, and yet is invisible, intangible, without size or shape or mass. What a curious something it is; it does not even seem *intelligible* that there should be such a thing. Nothing can be said about it except that it is a subject of consciousness! And that hardly makes clear what it is.

I do not think that this difficulty can be met directly. If the dualist is correct, then the notion of a nonmaterial subject of consciousness is perplexing and obscure, and nothing can be done about that. But we can weaken the force of the difficulty. It depends upon an implicit comparison of the immaterial subject of consciousness with the material subject of material states, material events, and material processes. It is suggested by this implicit comparison that the notion of the latter is clear and intelligible whereas the notion of the former is not. But it is not true that the notion of a material thing is clear and intelligible. We can raise parallel objections to it. We may ask of a material thing which has states, undergoes changes, and engages in processes: *What is it* which has these states, undergoes changes, and engages in processes? What *is* a material thing? On reflection we will see that the only thing which can be said is that it is a something which is the subject of certain sorts of states, events, and processes, namely material ones. Nothing more can be said than that. But precisely that sort of thing, no more and no less, can be said of an immaterial thing, namely that it is a something which is the subject of certain sorts of states, events, and processes, namely ones involving consciousness. So in this respect, immaterial things are no worse off than material things.

However, we are still left with two particular problems here, which we referred to earlier as the problem of identification and the problem of individuation. . . .

So far as identification is concerned, it does seem to be the case that we can only tell we are in the presence of another consciousness and can only tell whose consciousness it is by observing *physical* phenomena. We have no way of getting at the other mind directly. Of course, the problem of identification would be easier if mental telepathy were a common phenomenon. Then one could communicate with another mind without resort to ordinary sense observation and one might tell, by the content of the communication, whom one was communicating with. Thus if it communicated information which only your uncle could know, that would be good reason to think it was your uncle you were in communication with. There is some question even here how much such inferences are based upon what we know about the world through sense observation; for example, you would think it was something only your uncle could know because you know, perhaps, that only he was in the room at the time (as established by observing, through the window, his body and the otherwise empty room). So if in the end sense observation must be depended upon, telepathy will not help. But even if it did help it is not available to us for determining the identity of other consciousnesses. So we must depend upon sense observations of material bodies, especially human bodies. And that leaves mental things in a weaker position, at least epistemologically, than material things.

So far as individuation is concerned, too, mental entities seem to have a weaker status than material entities. For it does seem to be possible for there to be two different persons who have exactly the same mental history, exactly the same set of mental states and events throughout their life. The only thing that could distinguish the two would be the existence of different bodies in different places (although having exactly similar mental histories would necessitate their having exactly similar bodies and environments). This indicates that mental entities depend in part on material entities for their individuation.

We must conclude that any theory of the nature of the subject of consciousness must include some reference to the material bodies, although it may not be necessary to *identify* the subject of consciousness with the material body. Indeed, we have seen that there are grave difficulties in attempts to defend such an identification. Yet a dualism which includes the concept of an immaterial subject of consciousness utterly independent of material bodies is unable to deal with the problems of identification and individuation. . . .

NOTES

1. *Ethics,* Part I, Prop. x, note.
2. Karl Marx and Friedrich Engels, *The German Ideology* (New York: International Publishers, 1947), p. 14.

FOR FURTHER REFLECTION

1. Go over Shaffer's arguments for and against dualism and materialism. In light of his analysis, what do you think is the best position? Do you think there is a solution to the mind-body problem? Explain.

PAUL CHURCHLAND

A CRITIQUE OF DUALISM

Paul Churchland (b. 1942) is a philosophy professor at the University of California at San Diego. He has written a number of books and articles in philosophy of mind, including *Scientific Realism and the Plasticity of Mind* (1979) and *Matter and Consciousness* (1984), from which latter book the next two selections are taken. His work has won him a reputation for clarity and insight.

In this selection, Churchland examines various forms of dualism and discusses their merits and demerits, concluding that the evidence is against all forms of dualism and in favor of some form of materialism.

What is the real nature of mental states and processes? In what medium do they take place, and how are they related to the physical world? Will my consciousness survive the disintegration of my physical body? Or will it disappear forever as my brain ceases to function? Is it possible that a purely physical system such as a computer could be constructed so as to enjoy real conscious intelligence? Where do minds come from? What are they?

These are some of the questions we shall confront in this chapter. Which answers we should give to them depends on which theory of mind proves to be the most reasonable theory on the evidence, to have the greatest explanatory power, predictive power, coherence, and simplicity. Let us examine the available theories, and the considerations that weigh for and against each.

1. DUALISM

The dualistic approach to mind encompasses several quite different theories, but they are all agreed that the essential nature of conscious intelligence resides in something *nonphysical,* in something forever beyond the scope of sciences like physics, neurophysiology, and computer science. Dualism is not the most widely held view in the current philosophical and scientific community, but it is the most common theory of mind in the public at large, it is deeply entrenched in most of the world's popular religions, and it has been the dominant theory of mind for most of Western history. It is thus an appropriate place to begin our discussion.

Substance Dualism

The distinguishing claim of this view is that each mind is a distinct nonphysical thing, an individual "package" of nonphysical substance, a thing whose identity is independent of any physical body to which it may be temporarily "attached." Mental states and activities derive their special character, on this view, from their being states and activities of this unique, nonphysical substance.

From Paul Churchland, *Matter and Consciousness* (Cambridge, MA: MIT Press, 1984), by permission of the author and publisher.

This leaves us wanting to ask for more in the way of a *positive* characterization of the proposed mind-stuff. It is a frequent complaint with the substance dualist's approach that his characterization of it is so far almost entirely negative. This need not be a fatal flaw, however, since we no doubt have much to learn about the underlying nature of mind, and perhaps the deficit here can eventually be made good. On this score, the philosopher René Descartes (1596–1650) has done as much as anyone to provide a positive account of the nature of the proposed mind-stuff, and his views are worthy of examination.

Descartes theorized that reality divides into two basic kinds of substance. The first is ordinary matter, and the essential feature of this kind of substance is that it is extended in space: any instance of it has length, breadth, height, and occupies a determinate position in space. Descartes did not attempt to play down the importance of this type of matter. On the contrary, he was one of the most imaginative physicists of his time, and he was an enthusiastic advocate of what was then called "the mechanical philosophy." But there was one isolated corner of reality he thought could not be accounted for in terms of the mechanics of matter: the conscious reason of Man. This was his motive for proposing a second and radically different kind of substance, a substance that has no spatial extension or spatial position whatever, a substance whose essential feature is the activity of *thinking*. This view is known as *Cartesian dualism.*

As Descartes saw it, the real *you* is not your material body, but rather a nonspatial thinking substance, an individual unit of mind-stuff quite distinct from your material body. This nonphysical mind is in systematic causal interaction with your body. The physical state of your body's sense organs, for example, causes visual/auditory/tactile experiences in your mind. And the desires and decisions of your nonphysical mind cause your body to behave in purposeful ways. Its causal connections to your mind are what make your body yours, and not someone else's.

The main reasons offered in support of this view were straightforward enough. First, Descartes thought that he could determine, by direct introspection alone, that he was essentially a thinking substance and nothing else. And second, he could not imagine how a purely physical system could ever use *language* in a relevant way, or engage in mathematical *reasoning,* as any normal human can. Whether these are good reasons, we shall discuss presently. Let us first notice a difficulty that even Descartes regarded as a problem.

If "mind-stuff" is so utterly different from "matter-stuff" in its nature—different to the point that it has no mass whatever, no shape whatever, and no position anywhere in space—then how is it possible for my mind to have any causal influence on my body at all? As Descartes himself was aware (he was one of the first to formulate the law of the conservation of momentum), ordinary matter in space behaves according to rigid laws, and one cannot get bodily movement (= momentum) from nothing. How is this utterly insubstantial "thinking substance" to have any influence on ponderous matter? How can two such different things be in any sort of causal contact? Descartes proposed a very subtle material substance—"animal spirits"—to convey the mind's influence to the body in general. But this does not provide us with a solution, since it leaves us with the same problem with which we started: how something ponderous and spatial (even "animal spirits") can interact with something entirely nonspatial.

In any case, the basic principle of division used by Descartes is no longer as plausible as it was in his day. It is now neither useful nor accurate to characterize ordinary matter as that-which-has-extension-in-space. Electrons, for example, are bits of matter, but our best current theories describe the electron as a point-particle with no extension whatever (it even lacks a determinate spatial position). And according to Einstein's theory of gravity, an entire star can achieve this same status, if it undergoes a complete gravitational collapse. If there truly is a division between mind and body, it appears that Descartes did not put his finger on the dividing line.

Such difficulties with Cartesian dualism provide a motive for considering a less radical form of substance dualism, and that is what we find in a view I shall call *popular dualism.* This is the theory that a person is literally a "ghost in a machine," where the machine is the human body, and the ghost is a spiritual substance, quite unlike physical matter in its internal constitution, but fully possessed of spatial properties even so. In particular, minds are commonly held to be *inside* the bodies they control: inside the head, on most views, in intimate contact with the brain.

This view need not have the difficulties of Descartes'. The mind is right there in contact with the brain, and their interaction can perhaps be understood in terms of their exchanging energy of a form that our science has not yet recognized or understood. Ordinary matter, you may recall, is just a form or manifestation of energy. (You may think of a grain of sand as a great deal of energy condensed or frozen into a small package, according to Einstein's relation, $E = mc^2$.) Perhaps mind-stuff is a well-behaved form or manifestation of energy also, but a different form of it. It is thus *possible* that a dualism of this alternative sort be consistent with familiar laws concerning the conservation of momentum and energy. This is fortunate for dualism, since those particular laws are very well established indeed.

This view will appeal to many for the further reason that it at least holds out the possibility (though it certainly does not guarantee) that the mind might survive the death of the body. It does not guarantee the mind's survival because it remains possible that the peculiar form of energy here supposed to constitute a mind can be produced and sustained only in conjunction with the highly intricate form of matter we call the brain, and must disintegrate when the brain disintegrates. So the prospects for surviving death are quite unclear even on the assumption that popular dualism is true. But even if survival were a clear consequence of the theory, there is a pitfall to be avoided here. Its promise of survival might be a reason for *wishing* dualism to be true, but it does not constitute a reason for *believing* that it *is* true. For that, we would need independent empirical evidence that minds do indeed survive the permanent death of the body. Regrettably, and despite the exploitative blatherings of the supermarket tabloids (TOP DOCS PROVE LIFE AFTER DEATH!!!), we possess no such evidence.

As we shall see later in this section, when we turn to evaluation, positive evidence for the existence of this novel, nonmaterial, thinking *substance* is in general on the slim side. This has moved many dualists to articulate still less extreme forms of dualism, in hopes of narrowing further the gap between theory and available evidence.

Property Dualism

The basic idea of the theories under this heading is that while there is no *substance* to be dealt with here beyond the physical brain, the brain has a special set of *properties* possessed by no other kind of physical object. It is these special properties that are nonphysical: hence the term *property dualism.* The properties in question are the ones you would expect: the property of having a pain, of having a sensation of red, of thinking that *P,* of desiring that *Q,* and so forth. These are the properties that are characteristic of conscious intelligence. They are held to be nonphysical in the sense that they cannot ever be reduced to or explained solely in terms of the concepts of the familiar physical sciences. They will require a wholly new and autonomous science—the 'science of mental phenomena'—if they are ever to be adequately understood.

From here, important differences among the positions emerge. Let us begin with what is perhaps the oldest version of property dualism: *epiphenomenalism.* This term is rather a mouthful, but its meaning is simple. The Greek prefix "epi-" means "above", and the position at issue holds that mental phenomena are not a part of the physical phenomena in the brain that ultimately determine our actions and behavior, but rather ride "above the fray." Mental phenomena are thus *epi*phenomena. They are held to just appear or emerge when the growing brain passes a certain level of complexity.

But there is more. The epiphenomenalist holds that while mental phenomena are caused to occur by the various activities of the brain, *they do not have any causal effects in turn.* They are entirely impotent with respect to causal effects on the physical world. They are *mere* epiphenomena. (To fix our ideas, a vague metaphor may be helpful here. Think of our conscious mental states as little sparkles of shimmering light that occur on the wrinkled surface of the brain, sparkles which are caused to occur by physical activity in the brain, but which have no causal effects on the brain in return.) This means that the universal conviction that one's actions are determined by one's desires, decisions, and volitions is false! One's actions are exhaustively determined by physical events in the brain, which events *also* cause the epiphenomena we call desires, decisions, and volitions. There is therefore a constant conjunction between volitions and actions. But according to the epiphenomenalist, it is mere illusion that the former cause the latter.

What could motivate such a strange view? In fact, it is not too difficult to understand why someone might take it seriously. Put yourself in the shoes of a neuroscientist who is concerned to trace the origins of behavior back up the motor nerves to the active cells in the motor cortex of the cerebrum, and to trace in turn their activity into inputs from other parts of the brain, and from the various sensory nerves. She finds a thoroughly physical system of awesome structure and delicacy, and much intricate activity, all of it unambiguously chemical or electrical in nature, and she finds no hint at all of any nonphysical inputs of the kind that substance dualism proposes. What is she to think? From the standpoint of her researches, human behavior is exhaustively a function of the activity of the physical brain. And this opinion is further supported by her confidence that the brain has the behavior-controlling features it does exactly because those features have been ruthlessly selected for during the brain's long evolutionary history. In sum, the seat of human behavior appears entirely physical in its constitution, in its origins, and in its internal activities.

On the other hand, our neuroscientist has the testimony of her own introspection to account for as well. She can hardly deny that she has experiences, beliefs, and desires, nor that they are connected in some way with her behavior. One bargain that can be struck here is to admit the *reality* of mental properties, as nonphysical properties, but demote them to the status of impotent epiphenomena that have nothing to do with the scientific explanation of human and animal behavior. This is the position the epiphenomenalist takes, and the reader can now perceive the rationale behind it. It is a bargain struck between the desire to respect a rigorously scientific approach to the explanation of behavior, and the desire to respect the testimony of introspection.

The epiphenomenalist's "demotion" of mental properties—to causally impotent byproducts of brain activity—has seemed too extreme for most property dualists, and a theory closer to the convictions of common sense has enjoyed somewhat greater popularity. This view, which we may call *interactionist property dualism,* differs from the previous view in only one essential respect: the interactionist asserts that mental properties do indeed have causal effects on the brain, and thereby, on behavior. The mental properties of the brain are an integrated part of the general causal fray, in systematic interaction with the brain's physical properties. One's actions, therefore, are held to be caused by one's desires and volitions after all.

As before, mental properties are here said to be *emergent* properties, properties that do not appear at all until ordinary physical matter has managed to organize itself, through the evolutionary process, into a system of sufficient complexity. Examples of properties that are emergent in this sense would be the property of being *solid,* the property of being *colored,* and the property of being *alive.* All of these require matter to be suitably organized before they can be displayed. With this much, any materialist will agree. But any property dualist makes the further claim that mental states and properties are *irreducible,* in the sense that they are not just organizational features of physical matter, as are the examples cited. They are said to be novel properties beyond prediction or explanation by physical science.

This last condition—the irreducibility of mental properties—is an important one, since this is what makes the position a dualist position. But it sits poorly with the joint claim that mental properties emerge from nothing more than the organizational achievements of physical matter. If that is how mental properties are produced, then one would expect a physical account of them to be possible. The simultaneous claim of evolutionary emergence *and* physical irreducibility is prima facie puzzling.

A property dualist is not absolutely bound to insist on both claims. He could let go the thesis of evolutionary emergence, and claim that mental properties are *fundamental* properties of reality, properties that have been here from the universe's inception, properties on a par with length, mass, electric charge, and other fundamental properties. There is even an historical precedent for a position of this kind. At the turn of this century it was still widely believed that electromagnetic phenomena (such as electric charge and magnetic attraction) were just an unusually subtle manifestation of purely *mechanical* phenomena. Some scientists thought that a reduction of electromagnetics to mechanics was more or less in the bag. They thought that radio waves, for example, would turn out to be just travelling oscillations in a very subtle but jellylike aether that fills space everywhere. But the aether turned out not to exist. So electromagnetic properties turned out to be fundamental properties in their own right, and we were forced to add electric charge to the existing list of fundamental properties (mass, length, and duration).

Perhaps mental properties enjoy a status like that of electromagnetic properties: irreducible, but not emergent. Such a view may be called *elemental-property dualism,* and it has the advantage of clarity over the previous view. Unfortunately, the parallel with electromagnetic phenomena has one very obvious failure. Unlike electromagnetic properties, which are displayed at all levels of reality from the subatomic level on up, mental properties are displayed only in large physical systems that have evolved a very complex internal organization. The case for the evolutionary emergence of mental properties through the organization of matter is extremely strong. They do not appear to be basic or elemental at all. This returns us, therefore, to the issue of their irreducibility. Why should we accept this most basic of the dualist's claims? Why be a dualist?

ARGUMENTS FOR DUALISM

Here we shall examine some of the main considerations commonly offered in support of dualism. Criticism will be postponed for a moment so that we may appreciate the collective force of these supporting considerations.

A major source of dualistic convictions is the religious belief many of us bring to these issues. Each of the major religions is in its way a theory about the cause or purpose of the universe, and Man's place within it, and many of them are committed to the notion of an immortal soul—that is, to some form of substance dualism. Supposing that one is consistent, to consider disbelieving dualism is to consider disbelieving one's religious heritage, and some of us find that difficult to do. Call this the *argument from religion.*

A more universal consideration is the *argument from introspection.* The fact is, when you center your attention on the contents of your consciousness, you do not clearly apprehend a neural network pulsing with electrochemical activity: you apprehend a flux of thoughts, sensations, desires, and emotions. It seems that mental states and properties, as revealed in introspection, could hardly be more different from physical states and properties if they tried. The verdict of introspection, therefore, seems strongly on the side of some form of dualism—on the side of property dualism, at a minimum.

A cluster of important considerations can be collected under the *argument from irreducibility.* Here one points to a variety of mental phenomena where it seems clear that no purely physical explanation could possibly account for what is going on. Descartes has already cited our ability to use language in a way that is relevant to our changing circumstances, and he was impressed also with our faculty of Reason, particularly as it is displayed in our capacity for mathematical reasoning. These abilities, he thought, must surely be beyond the capacity of any physical system. More recently, the introspectible qualities of our sensations (sensory "qualia"), and the meaningful content of our thoughts and beliefs, have also been cited as phenomena that will forever resist reduction to the physical. Consider, for example, seeing the color or smelling the fragrance of a rose. A physicist or chemist might know everything about the molecular structure of the rose, and of the human brain, argues the dualist, but that knowledge would not enable him to predict or anticipate the quality of these inexpressible experiences.

Finally, parapsychological phenomena are occasionally cited in favor of dualism. Telepathy (mind reading), precognition (seeing the future), telekinesis (thought control of material objects), and clairvoyance (knowledge of distant objects) are all awkward to explain within the normal confines of psychology and physics. If these phenomena are real, they might well be reflecting the superphysical nature that the dualist ascribes to the mind. Trivially they are *mental* phenomena, and if they are also forever beyond physical explanation, then at least some mental phenomena must be irreducibly nonphysical.

Collectively, these considerations may seem compelling. But there are serious criticisms of each, and we must examine them as well. Consider first the argument from religion. There is certainly nothing wrong in principle with appealing to a more general theory that bears on the case at issue, which is what the appeal to religion amounts to. But the appeal can only be as good as the scientific credentials of the religion(s) being appealed to, and here the appeals tend to fall down rather badly. In general, attempts to decide scientific questions by appeal to religious orthodoxy have a very sorry history. That the stars are other suns, that the earth is not the center of the universe, that diseases are caused by microorganisms, that the earth is billions of years old, that life is a physicochemical phenomenon; all of these crucial insights were strongly and sometimes viciously resisted, because the dominant religion of the time happened to think otherwise. Giordano Bruno was burned at the stake for urging the first view; Galileo was forced by threat of torture in the Vatican's basement to recant the second view; the firm belief that disease was a punishment visited by the Devil allowed public health practices that brought chronic plagues to most of the cities of Europe; and the age of the earth and the evolution of life were forced to fight an uphill battle against religious prejudice even in an age of supposed enlightenment.

History aside, the almost universal opinion that one's own religious convictions are the reasoned outcome of a dispassionate evaluation of all of the major alternatives is almost demonstrably false for humanity in general. If that really were the genesis of most people's convictions, then one would expect the major faiths to be distributed more or less randomly or evenly over the globe. But in fact they show a very strong tendency to cluster: Christianity is centered in Europe and the Americas, Islam in Africa and the Middle East, Hinduism in India, and Buddhism in the Orient. Which illustrates what we all suspected anyway: that *social forces* are the primary determinants of religious belief for people in general. To decide scientific questions by appeal to religious orthodoxy would therefore be to put social forces in place of empirical evidence. For all of these reasons, professional scientists and philosophers concerned with the nature of mind generally do their best to keep religious appeals out of the discussion entirely.

The argument from introspection is a much more interesting argument, since it tries to appeal to the direct experience of everyman. But the argument is deeply suspect, in that it assumes that our faculty of inner observation or introspection reveals things as they really are in their innermost nature. This assumption is suspect because we already know that our other forms of observation—sight, hearing, touch, and so on—do no such thing. The red surface of an apple does not *look* like a matrix of molecules reflecting photons at certain critical wavelengths, but that is what it is. The sound of a flute does not *sound* like a sinusoidal compression wave train in the atmosphere, but that is what it is. The warmth of the summer air does not *feel* like the mean kinetic energy of millions of tiny molecules, but that is what it is. If one's pains and hopes and beliefs do not *introspectively* seem like electrochemical states in a neural network, that may be only because our faculty of introspection, like our other senses, is not sufficiently penetrating to reveal such hidden details. Which is just what one would expect anyway. The argument from introspection is therefore entirely without force, unless we can somehow argue that the faculty of introspection is quite different from all other forms of observation.

The argument from irreducibility presents a more serious challenge, but here also its force is less than first impression suggests. Consider first our capacity for mathematical reasoning which so impressed Descartes. The last ten years have made available, to anyone with fifty dollars to spend, electronic calculators whose capacity for mathematical reasoning—the calculational part, at least—far surpasses that of any normal human. The fact is, in the centuries since Descartes' writings, philosophers, logicians, mathematicians, and computer scientists have managed to isolate the general principles of mathematical reasoning, and electronics engineers have created machines that compute in accord with those principles. The result is a hand-held object that would have astonished Descartes. This outcome is impressive not just because machines have proved capable of some of the capacities boasted by human reason, but because some of those achievements invade areas of human reason that past dualistic philosophers have held up as forever closed to mere physical devices.

Although debate on the matter remains open, Descartes' argument from language use is equally dubious. The notion of a *computer language* is by now a commonplace: consider BASIC, Pascal, FORTRAN, APL, LISP, and so on. Granted, these artificial "languages" are much simpler in structure and content than human natural language, but the differences may be differences only of degree, and not of kind. As well, the theoretical work of Noam Chomsky and the generative grammar approach to linguistics have done a great deal to explain the human capacity for language use in terms that invite simulation by computers. I do not mean to suggest that truly conversational computers are just around the corner. We have a great deal yet to learn, and fundamental problems yet to solve (mostly having to do with our capacity for inductive or theoretical reasoning). But recent progress here does nothing to support the claim that language use must be forever impossible for a purely physical system. On the contrary, such a claim now appears rather arbitrary and dogmatic. . . .

The next issue is also a live problem: How can we possibly hope to explain or to predict the intrinsic qualities of our sensations, or the meaningful content of our beliefs and desires, in purely physical terms? This is a major challenge to the materialist. But as we shall see in later sections, active research programs are already under way on both problems, and positive suggestions are being explored. It is in fact not impossible to imagine how such explanations might go, though the materialist cannot yet pretend to have solved either problem. Until he does, the dualist will retain a bargaining chip here, but that is about all. What the dualists need in order to establish their case is the conclusion that a physical reduction is outright

impossible, and that is a conclusion they have failed to establish. Rhetorical questions, like the one that opens this paragraph, do not constitute arguments. And it is equally difficult, note, to imagine how the relevant phenomena could be explained or predicted solely in terms of the substance dualist's nonphysical mind-stuff. The explanatory problem here is a major challenge to everybody, not just to the materialist. On this issue then, we have a rough standoff.

The final argument in support of dualism urged the existence of parapsychological phenomena such as telepathy and telekinesis, the point being that such mental phenomena are (a) real, and (b) beyond purely physical explanation. This argument is really another instance of the argument from irreducibility discussed above, and as before, it is not entirely clear that such phenomena, even if real, must forever escape a purely physical explanation. The materialist can already suggest a possible mechanism for telepathy, for example. On his view, thinking is an electrical activity within the brain. But according to electromagnetic theory, such changing motions of electric charges must produce electromagnetic waves radiating at the speed of light in all directions, waves that will contain information about the electrical activity that produced them. Such waves can subsequently have effects on the electrical activity of other brains, that is, on their thinking. Call this the "radio transmitter/receiver" theory of telepathy.

I do not for a moment suggest that this theory is true: the electromagnetic waves emitted by the brain are fantastically weak (billions of times weaker than the ever present background electromagnetic flux produced by commercial radio stations), and they are almost certain to be hopelessly jumbled together as well. This is one reason why, in the absence of systematic, compelling, and repeatable evidence for the existence of telepathy, one must doubt its possibility. But it is significant that the materialist has the theoretical resources to suggest a detailed possible explanation of telepathy, if it were real, which is more than any dualist has so far done. It is not at all clear, then, that the materialist *must* be at an explanatory disadvantage in these matters. Quite the reverse.

Put the preceding aside, if you wish, for the main difficulty with the argument from parapsychological phenomena is much, much simpler. Despite the endless pronouncements and anecdotes in the popular press, and despite a steady trickle of serious research on such things, there is no significant or trustworthy evidence that such phenomena even exist. The wide gap between popular conviction on this matter, and the actual evidence, is something that itself calls for research. For there is not a single parapsychological effect that can be repeatedly or reliably produced in any laboratory suitably equipped to perform and control the experiment. Not one. Honest researchers have been repeatedly hoodwinked by "psychic" charlatans with skills derived from the magician's trade, and the history of the subject is largely a history of gullibility, selection of evidence, poor experimental controls, and outright fraud by the occasional researcher as well. If someone really does discover a repeatable parapsychological effect, then we shall have to reevaluate the situation, but as things stand, there is nothing here to support a dualist theory of mind.

Upon critical examination, the arguments in support of dualism lose much of their force. But we are not yet done: there are arguments against dualism, and these also require examination.

Arguments Against Dualism

The first argument against dualism urged by the materialists appeals to the greater *simplicity* of their view. It is a principle of rational methodology that, if all else is equal, the simpler of two competing hypotheses should be preferred. This principle is sometimes called "Ockham's Razor"—after William of Ockham, the medieval philosopher who first enunciated it—and it can also be expressed as follows: "Do not multiply entities beyond what is strictly necessary to explain the phenomena." The materialist postulates only one kind of substance (physical matter), and one class of properties (physical properties), whereas the dualist postulates two kinds of matter and/or two classes of properties. And to no explanatory advantage, charges the materialist.

This is not yet a decisive point against dualism, since neither dualism nor materialism can yet explain all of the phenomena to be explained. But the objection does have some force, especially since there is no

doubt at all that physical matter exists, while spiritual matter remains a tenuous hypothesis.

If this latter hypothesis brought us some definite explanatory advantage obtainable in no other way, then we would happily violate the demand for simplicity, and we would be right to do so. But it does not, claims the materialist. In fact, the advantage is just the other way around, he argues, and this brings us to the second objection to dualism: the relative *explanatory impotence* of dualism as compared to materialism.

Consider, very briefly, the explanatory resources already available to the neurosciences. We know that the brain exists and what it is made of. We know much of its microstructure: how the neurons are organized into systems and how distinct systems are connected to one another, to the motor nerves going out to the muscles, and to the sensory nerves coming in from the sense organs. We know much of their microchemistry: how the nerve cells fire tiny electrochemical pulses along their various fibers, and how they make other cells fire also, or cease firing. We know some of how such activity processes sensory information, selecting salient or subtle bits to be sent on to higher systems. And we know some of how such activity initiates and coordinates bodily behavior. Thanks mainly to neurology (the branch of medicine concerned with brain pathology), we know a great deal about the correlations between damage to various parts of the human brain, and various behavioral and cognitive deficits from which the victims suffer. There are a great many isolated deficits—some gross, some subtle—that are familiar to neurologists (inability to speak, or to read, or to understand speech, or to recognize faces, or to add/subtract, or to move a certain limb, or to put information into long-term memory, and so on), and their appearance is closely tied to the occurrence of damage to very specific parts of the brain.

Nor are we limited to cataloguing traumas. The growth and development of the brain's microstructure is also something that neuroscience has explored, and such development appears to be the basis of various kinds of learning by the organism. Learning, that is, involves lasting chemical and physical changes in the brain. In sum, the neuroscientist can tell us a great deal about the brain, about its constitution and the physical laws that govern it; he can already explain much of our behavior in terms of the physical, chemical, and electrical properties of the brain; and he has the theoretical resources available to explain a good deal more as our explorations continue. . . .

Compare now what the neuroscientist can tell us about the brain, and what he can do with that knowledge, with what the dualist can tell us about spiritual substance, and what he can do with those assumptions. Can the dualist tell us anything about the internal constitution of mind-stuff? Of the nonmaterial elements that make it up? Of the laws that govern their behavior? Of the mind's structural connections with the body? Of the manner of its operations? Can he explain human capacities and pathologies in terms of its structures and its defects? The fact is, the dualist can do none of these things, because no detailed theory of mind-stuff has ever been formulated. Compared to the rich resources and explanatory successes of current materialism, dualism is less a theory of mind than it is an empty space waiting for a genuine theory of mind to be put in it.

Thus argues the materialist. But again, this is not a completely decisive point against dualism. The dualist can admit that the brain plays a major role in the administration of both perception and behavior—on his view the brain is the *mediator* between the mind and the body—but he may attempt to argue that the materialist's current successes and future explanatory prospects concern only the mediative functions of the brain, not the *central* capacities of the nonphysical mind, capacities such as reason, emotion, and consciousness itself. On these latter topics, he may argue, both dualism *and* materialism currently draw a blank.

But this reply is not a very good one. So far as the capacity for reasoning is concerned, machines already exist that execute in minutes sophisticated deductive and mathematical calculations that would take a human a lifetime to execute. And so far as the other two mental capacities are concerned, studies of such things as depression, motivation, attention, and sleep have revealed many interesting and puzzling facts about the neurochemical and neurodynamical basis of both emotion and consciousness. The *central* capacities, no less than the peripheral, have been addressed with profit by various materialist research programs.

In any case, the (substance) dualist's attempt to draw a sharp distinction between the unique 'mental' capacities proper to the nonmaterial mind, and the merely mediative capacities of the brain, prompts an argument that comes close to being an outright refutation of (substance) dualism. If there really is a distinct entity in which reasoning, emotion, and consciousness take place, and if that entity is dependent on the brain for nothing more than sensory experiences as input and volitional executions as output, *then one would expect reason, emotion, and consciousness to be relatively invulnerable to direct control or pathology by manipulation or damage to the brain.* But in fact the exact opposite is true. Alcohol, narcotics, or senile degeneration of nerve tissue will impair, cripple, or even destroy one's capacity for rational thought. Psychiatry knows of hundreds of emotion-controlling chemicals (lithium, chlorpromazine, amphetamine, cocaine, and so on) that do their work when vectored into the brain. And the vulnerability of consciousness to the anesthetics, to caffeine, and to something as simple as a sharp blow to the head, shows its very close dependence on neural activity in the brain. All of this makes perfect sense if reason, emotion, and consciousness are activities of the brain itself. But it makes very little sense if they are activities of something else entirely.

We may call this the argument from the *neural dependence* of all known mental phenomena. Property dualism, note, is not threatened by this argument, since, like materialism, property dualism reckons the brain as the seat of all mental activity. We shall conclude this section, however, with an argument that cuts against both varieties of dualism: the argument from *evolutionary history.*

What is the origin of a complex and sophisticated species such as ours? What, for that matter, is the origin of the dolphin, the mouse, or the housefly? Thanks to the fossil record, comparative anatomy, and the biochemistry of proteins and nucleic acids, there is no longer any significant doubt on this matter. Each existing species is a surviving type from a number of variations on an earlier type of organism; each earlier type is in turn a surviving type from a number of variations on a still earlier type of organism; and so on down the branches of the evolutionary tree until, some three billion years ago, we find a trunk of just one or a handful of very simple organisms. These organisms, like their more complex offspring, are just self-repairing, self-replicating, energy-driven molecular structures. (That evolutionary trunk has its own roots in an earlier era of purely chemical evolution, in which the molecular elements of life were themselves pieced together.) The mechanism of development that has structured this tree has two main elements: (1) the occasional blind variation in types of reproducing creatures, and (2) the selective survival of some of these types due to the relative reproductive advantage enjoyed by individuals of those types. Over periods of geological time, such a process can produce an enormous variety of organisms, some of them very complex indeed.

For purposes of our discussion, the important point about the standard evolutionary story is that the human species and all of its features are the wholly physical outcome of a purely physical process. Like all but the simplest of organisms, we have a nervous system. And for the same reason: a nervous system permits the discriminative guidance of behavior. But a nervous system is just an active matrix of cells, and a cell is just an active matrix of molecules. We are

notable only in that our nervous system is more complex and powerful than those of our fellow creatures. Our inner nature differs from that of simpler creatures in degree, but not in kind.

If this is the correct account of our origins, then there seems neither need, nor room, to fit any nonphysical substances or properties into our theoretical account of ourselves. We are creatures of matter. And we should learn to live with that fact.

Arguments like these have moved most (but not all) of the professional community to embrace some form of materialism. This has not produced much unanimity, however, since the differences between the several materialist positions are even wider than the differences that divide dualism. . . .

FOR FURTHER REFLECTION

1. Go over Churchland's arguments for and against dualism. Do you think that he has dealt fairly with the arguments? Could the dualist respond to any of his attacks? Explain your answers.

PAUL CHURCHLAND

ON FUNCTIONALISM AND MATERIALISM

We continue with Churchland's work on the mind-body problem. In this selection Church-land examines functionalism and the two prominent versions of materialism in philosophy of mind. Reductivism claims that there is an identity of mental states with brain states. Functionalism rejects any one-to-one correlation between mental types and physical types, and concentrates on the relationship between inputs and outputs. For example, the mental event of pain could be similar in two beings who have altogether different types of bodies and brains. Most functionalists are materialists, but someone could be a functionalist *and* be a non-materialist. Eliminative materialism is more radical than either of these other theories and seeks to eliminate "folk psychology"—talk of beliefs, feelings, and perceptions—in favor of more scientific descriptions of what is going on in the brain. Churchland concludes that the truth may be a combination of the two theories, although the evidence points more in the direction of eliminativism.

I. REDUCTIVE MATERIALISM (THE IDENTITY THEORY)

Reductive materialism, more commonly known as *the identity theory,* is the most straightforward of the several materialist theories of mind. Its central claim is simplicity itself: Mental states *are* physical states of the brain. That is, each type of mental state or process is *numerically identical with* (is one and the very same thing as) some type of physical state or process within the brain or central nervous system. At present we do not know enough about the intricate functionings of the brain actually to state the relevant identities, but the identity theory is committed to the idea that brain research will eventually reveal them. . . .

Historical Parallels

As the identity theorist sees it, the result here predicted has familiar parallels elsewhere in our scientific history. Consider sound. We now know that sound is just a train of compression waves traveling through the air, and that the property of being high pitched is identical with the property of having a high oscillatory frequency. We have learned that light is just electromagnetic waves, and our best current theory says that the color of an object is identical with a triplet of reflectance efficiencies the object has, rather like a musical chord that it strikes, though the "notes" are struck in electromagnetic waves instead of in sound waves. We now appreciate that the warmth or coolness of a body is just the energy of motion of the molecules that make it up: warmth is identical with high average molecular kinetic energy, and coolness is identical with low average molecular kinetic energy. We know that lightning is identical with a sudden large-scale discharge of electrons between clouds, or between the atmosphere and the ground. What we now think of as 'mental states,'

From Paul Churchland, *Matter and Consciousness* (Cambridge, MA: MIT Press, 1984) by permission of the author and publisher.

argues the identity theorist, are identical with brain states in exactly the same way.

Intertheoretic Reduction

These illustrative parallels are all cases of successful *intertheoretic reduction.* That is, they are all cases where a new and very powerful theory turns out to entail a set of propositions and principles that mirror perfectly (or almost perfectly) the propositions and principles of some older theory or conceptual framework. The relevant principles entailed by the new theory have the same structure as the corresponding principles of the old framework, and they apply in exactly the same cases. The only difference is that where the old principles contained (for example) the notions of "heat," "is hot," and "is cold," the new principles contain instead the notions of "total molecular kinetic energy," "has a high mean molecular kinetic energy," and "has a low mean molecular kinetic energy."

If the new framework is far better than the old at explaining and predicting phenomena, then we have excellent reason for believing that the theoretical terms of the *new* framework are the terms that describe reality correctly. But if the old framework worked adequately, so far as it went, and if it parallels a portion of the new theory in the systematic way described, then we may properly conclude that the old terms and the new terms refer to the very same things, or express the very same properties. We conclude that we have apprehended the very same reality that is incompletely described by the old framework, but with a new and more penetrating conceptual framework. And we announce what philosophers of science call "intertheoretic identities": light *is* electromagnetic waves, temperature *is* mean molecular kinetic energy, and so forth.

The examples of the preceding two paragraphs share one more important feature in common. They are all cases where the things or properties on the receiving end of the reduction are *observable* things and properties within our *common-sense* conceptual framework. They show that intertheoretic reduction occurs not only between conceptual frameworks in the theoretical stratosphere: common-sense observ-ables can also be reduced. There would therefore be nothing particularly surprising about a reduction of our familiar introspectible mental states to physical states of the brain. All that would be required would be that an explanatorily successful neuroscience develop to the point where it entails a suitable "mirror image" of the assumptions and principles that constitute our common-sense conceptual framework for mental states, an image where brain-state terms occupy the positions held by mental-state terms in the assumptions and principles of common sense. If this (rather demanding) condition were indeed met, then, as in the historical cases cited, we would be justified in announcing a reduction, and in asserting the identity of mental states with brain states.

Arguments for the Identity Theory

What reasons does the identity theorist have for believing that neuroscience will eventually achieve the strong conditions necessary for the reduction of our "folk" psychology? There are at least four reasons, all directed at the conclusion that the correct account of human-behavior-and-its-causes must reside in the physical neurosciences.

We can point first to the purely physical origins and ostensibly physical constitution of each individual human. One begins as a genetically programmed monocellular organization of molecules (a fertilized ovum), and one develops from there by the accretion of further molecules whose structure and integration is controlled by the information coded in the DNA molecules of the cell nucleus. The result of such a process would be a purely physical system whose behavior arises from its internal operations and its interactions with the rest of the physical world. And those behavior-controlling internal operations are precisely what the neurosciences are about.

This argument coheres with a second argument. The origins of each *type* of animal also appear exhaustively physical in nature. The argument from evolutionary history discussed earlier . . . lends further support to the identity theorist's claim, since evolutionary theory provides the only serious explanation we have for the behavior-controlling capacities of the brain and central nervous system. Those systems were selected for because of the many advantages (ultimately, the reproductive advantage) held by creatures whose behavior was thus controlled. Again our behavior appears to have its basic causes in neural activity.

The identity theorist finds further support in the argument, discussed earlier, from the neural dependence of all known mental phenomena. . . . This is precisely what one should expect, if the identity theory is true. Of course, systematic neural dependence is also a consequence of property dualism, but here the identity theorist will appeal to considerations of simplicity. Why admit two radically different classes of properties and operations if the explanatory job can be done by one?

A final argument derives from the growing success of the neurosciences in unraveling the nervous systems of many creatures and in explaining their behavioral capacities and deficits in terms of the structures discovered. The preceding arguments all suggest that neuroscience should be successful in this endeavor, and the fact is that the continuing history of neuroscience bears them out. Especially in the case of very simple creatures (as one would expect), progress has been rapid. And progress has also been made with humans, though for obvious moral reasons exploration must be more cautious and circumspect. In sum, the neurosciences have a long way to go, but progress to date provides substantial encouragement to the identity theorist.

Even so, these arguments are far from decisive in favor of the identity theory. No doubt they do provide an overwhelming case for the idea that the causes of human and animal behavior are essentially physical in nature, but the identity theory claims more than just this. It claims that neuroscience will discover a taxonomy of neural states that stand in a one-to-one correspondence with the mental states of our common-sense taxonomy. Claims for intertheoretic identity will be justified only if such a match-up can be found. But nothing in the preceding arguments guarantees that the old and new frameworks will match up in this way, even if the new framework is a roaring success at explaining and predicting our behavior. Furthermore, there are arguments from other positions within the materialist camp to the effect that such convenient match-ups are rather unlikely. Before exploring

those, however, let us look at some more traditional objections to the identity theory.

Arguments Against the Identity Theory

We may begin with the argument from introspection discussed earlier. Introspection reveals a domain of thoughts, sensations, and emotions, not a domain of electrochemical impulses in a neural network. Mental states and properties, as revealed in introspection, appear radically different from any neurophysiological states and properties. How could they possibly be the very same things?

The answer, as we have already seen, is, "Easily." In discriminating red from blue, sweet from sour, and hot from cold, our external senses are actually discriminating between subtle differences in intricate electromagnetic, stereochemical, and micromechanical properties of physical objects. But our senses are not sufficiently penetrating to reveal on their own the detailed nature of those intricate properties. That requires theoretical research and experimental exploration with specially designed instruments. The same is presumably true of our "inner" sense: introspection. It may discriminate efficiently between a great variety of neural states, without being able to reveal on its own the detailed nature of the states being discriminated. Indeed, it would be faintly miraculous if it did reveal them, just as miraculous as if unaided sight were to reveal the existence of interacting electric and magnetic fields whizzing by with an oscillatory frequency of a million billion hertz and a wavelength of less than a millionth of a meter. For despite "appearances," that is what light is. The argument from introspection, therefore, is quite without force.

The next objection argues that the identification of mental states with brain states would commit us to statements that are literally unintelligible, to what philosophers have called "category errors," and that the identification is therefore a case of sheer conceptual confusion. We may begin the discussion by noting a most important law concerning numerical identity. Leibniz' Law states that two items are numerically identical just in case any property had by either one of them is also had by the other: in logical notation,

$$(x)(y)[(x = y) \equiv (F)(Fx \equiv Fy)].$$

This law suggests a way of refuting the identity theory: find some property that is true of brain states, but not of mental states (or vice versa), and the theory would be exploded.

Spatial properties were often cited to this end. Brain states and processes must of course have some specific spatial location: in the brain as a whole, or in some part of it. And if mental states are identical with brain states, then they must have the very same spatial location. But it is literally meaningless, runs the argument, to say that my feeling-of-pain is located in my ventral thalamus, or that my belief-that-the-sun-is-a-star is located in the temporal lobe of my left cerebral hemisphere. Such claims are as meaningless as the claim that the number 5 is green, or that love weighs twenty grams.

Trying the same move from the other direction, some have argued that it is senseless to ascribe the various *semantic* properties to brain states. Our thoughts and beliefs, for example, have a meaning, a specific propositional content; they are either true or false; and they can enjoy relations such as consistency and entailment. If thoughts and beliefs were brain states, then all these semantic properties would have to be true of brain states. But it is senseless, runs the argument, to say that some resonance in my association cortex is true, or logically entails some other resonance close by, or has the meaning that *P.*

Neither of these moves has the same bite it did twenty years ago, since familiarity with the identity theory and growing awareness of the brain's role have tended to reduce the feelings of semantic oddity produced by the claims at issue. But even if they still struck all of us as semantically confused, this would carry little weight. The claim that sound has a wavelength, or that light has a frequency, must have seemed equally unintelligible in advance of the conviction that both sound and light are wave phenomena. (See, for example, Bishop Berkeley's eighteenth-century dismissal of the idea that sound is a vibratory motion of the air, in Dialogue I of his *Three Dialogues.* The objections are voiced by Philonous.) The claim that warmth is measured in kilogram · meters^2/seconds^2 would have seemed semantically perverse before

we understood that temperature is mean molecular kinetic energy. And Copernicus' sixteenth-century claim that the earth *moves* also struck people as absurd to the point of perversity. It is not difficult to appreciate why. Consider the following argument.

> Copernicus' claim that the earth moves is sheer conceptual confusion. For consider what it *means* to say that something moves: "*x* moves" means "*x* changes position relative to the earth." Thus, to say that the earth moves is to say that the earth changes position relative to itself! Which is absurd. Copernicus' position is therefore an abuse of language.

The *meaning analysis* here invoked might well have been correct, but all that would have meant is that the speaker should have set about changing his meanings. The fact is, any language involves a rich network of assumptions about the structure of the world, and if a sentence S provokes intuitions of semantic oddness, that is usually because S violates one or more of those background assumptions. But one cannot always reject S for that reason alone, since the overthrow of those background assumptions may be precisely what the facts require. The "abuse" of accepted modes of speech is often an essential feature of real scientific progress! Perhaps we shall just have to get used to the idea that mental states have anatomical locations and brain states have semantic properties.

While the charge of sheer senselessness can be put aside, the identity theorist does owe us some account of exactly how physical brain states can have semantic properties. The account currently being explored can be outlined as follows. Let us begin by asking how it is that a particular *sentence* (= utterance type) has the specific propositional content it has: the sentence "La pomme est rouge," for example. Note first that a sentence is always an integrated part of an entire system of sentences: a language. Any given sentence enjoys many relations with countless other sentences: it entails many sentences, is entailed by many others, is consistent with some, is inconsistent with others, provides confirming evidence for yet others, and so forth. And speakers who use that sentence within that language draw inferences in accordance with those relations. Evidently, each sentence (or each set of equivalent sentences) enjoys a unique pattern of such entailment relations: it plays a distinct inferential role in a complex linguistic economy. Accordingly, we say that the sentence "La pomme est rouge" has the propositional content, *the apple is red,* because the sentence "La pomme est rouge" plays *the same role* in French that the sentence "The apple is red" plays in English. To have the relevant propositional content is just to play the relevant inferential role in a cognitive economy.

Returning now to types of brain states, there is no problem in principle in assuming that one's brain is the seat of a complex inferential economy in which types of brain states are the role-playing elements. According to the theory of meaning just sketched, such states would then have propositional content, since having content is not a matter of whether the contentful item is a pattern of sound, a pattern of letters on paper, a set of raised Braille bumps, or a pattern of neural activity. What matters is the inferential role the item plays. Propositional content, therefore, seems within the reach of brain states after all.

We began this subsection with an argument against materialism that appealed to the qualitative *nature* of our mental states, as revealed in introspection. The next argument appeals to the simple fact that they are introspectible at all.

1. My mental states are introspectively known by me as states of my conscious self.
2. My brain states are *not* introspectively known by me as states of my conscious self.

Therefore, by Leibniz' Law (that numerically identical things must have exactly the same properties),

3. My mental states are not identical with my brain states.

This, in my experience, is the most beguiling form of the argument from introspection, seductive of freshmen and faculty alike. But it is a straightforward instance of a well-known fallacy, which is clearly illustrated in the following parallel arguments:

1. Muhammad Ali is widely known as a heavyweight champion.
2. Cassius Clay is *not* widely known as a heavyweight champion.

Therefore, by Leibniz' Law,

3. Muhammad Ali is not identical with Cassius Clay.

or,

1. Aspirin is recognized by John to be a pain reliever.
2. Acetylsalicylic acid is *not* recognized by John to be a pain reliever.

Therefore, by Leibniz' Law,

3. Aspirin is not identical with acetylsalicylic acid.

Despite the truth of the relevant premises, both conclusions are false: the identities are wholly genuine. Which means that both arguments are invalid. The problem is that the "property" ascribed in premise (1), and withheld in premise (2), consists only in the subject item's being *recognized, perceived,* or *known* as something-or-other. But such apprehension is not a genuine property of the item itself, fit for divining identities, since one and the same subject may be successfully recognized under one name or description, and yet fail to be recognized under another (accurate, coreferential) description. Bluntly, Leibniz' Law is not valid for these bogus "properties." The attempt to use them as above commits what logicians call an *intensional* fallacy. The premises may reflect, not the failure of certain objective identities, but only our continuing failure to appreciate them.

A different version of the preceding argument must also be considered, since it may be urged that one's brain states are more than merely not (yet) known by introspection: they are not know*able* by introspection under any circumstances. Thus,

1. My mental states are knowable by introspection.
2. My brain states are *not* knowable by introspection.

Therefore, by Leibniz' Law,

3. My mental states are not identical with my brain states.

Here the critic will insist that being know*able* by introspection *is* a genuine property of a thing, and that this modified version of the argument is free of the "intensional fallacy" discussed above.

And so it is. But now the materialist is in a position to insist that the argument contains a false premise—premise (2). For if mental states are indeed brain states, then it is really brain states we have been introspecting all along, though without fully appreciating what they are. And if we can learn to think of and recognize those states under mentalistic descriptions, as we all have, then we can certainly learn to think of and recognize them under their more penetrating neurophysiological descriptions. At the very least, premise (2) simply begs the question against the identity theorist. The mistake is amply illustrated in the following parallel argument:

1. Temperature is knowable by feeling.
2. Mean molecular kinetic energy is *not* knowable by feeling.

Therefore, by Leibniz' Law,

3. Temperature is not identical with mean molecular kinetic energy.

This identity, at least, is long established, and this argument is certainly unsound: premise (2) is false. Just as one can learn to feel that the summer air is about 70°F, or 21°C, so one can learn to feel that the mean KE of its molecules is about 6.2×10^{-21} joules, for whether we realize it or not, that is what our discriminatory mechanisms are keyed to. Perhaps our brain states are similarly accessible. . . .

Consider now a final argument, again based on the introspectible qualities of our sensations. Imagine a future neuroscientist who comes to know everything there is to know about the physical structure and activity of the brain and its visual system, of its actual and possible states. If for some reason she has never actually *had* a sensation-of-red (because of color blindness, say, or an unusual environment), then there will remain something she does *not* know about certain sensations: *what it is like to have a sensation-of-red.* Therefore, complete knowledge of the physical facts of visual perception and its related brain activity still leaves something out. Accordingly, materialism

cannot give an adequate account of all mental phenomena, and the identity theory must be false.

The identity theorist can reply that this argument exploits an unwitting equivocation on the term "know." Concerning our neuroscientist's utopian knowledge of the brain, "knows" means something like "has mastered the relevant set of neuroscientific propositions." Concerning her (missing) knowledge of what it is like to have a sensation-of-red, "knows" means something like "has a prelinguistic representation of redness in her mechanisms for noninferential discrimination." It is true that one might have the former without the latter, but the materialist is not committed to the idea that having knowledge in the former sense automatically constitutes having knowledge in the second sense. The identity theorist can admit a duality, or even a plurality, of different *types of knowledge* without thereby committing himself to a duality in *types of things known*. The difference between a person who knows all about the visual cortex but has never enjoyed the sensation-of-red, and a person who knows no neuroscience but knows well the sensation-of-red, may reside not in *what* is respectively known by each (brain states by the former, nonphysical *qualia* by the latter), but rather in the different *type,* or *medium,* or *level* of representation each has of exactly the same thing: brain states.

In sum, there are pretty clearly more ways of "having knowledge" than just having mastered a set of sentences, and the materialist can freely admit that one has "knowledge" of one's sensations in a way that is independent of the neuroscience one may have learned. Animals, including humans, presumably have a prelinguistic mode of sensory representation. This does not mean that sensations are beyond the reach of physical science. *It just means that the brain uses more modes and media of representation than the mere storage of sentences.* All the identity theorist needs to claim is that those other modes of representation will also yield to neuroscientific explanation.

The identity theory has proved to be very resilient in the face of these predominantly antimaterialist objections. But further objections, rooted in competing forms of materialism, constitute a much more serious threat, as the following sections will show.

II. FUNCTIONALISM

According to *functionalism,* the essential or defining feature of any type of mental state is the set of causal relations it bears to (1) environmental effects on the body, (2) other types of mental states, and (3) bodily behavior. Pain, for example, characteristically results from some bodily damage or trauma; it causes distress, annoyance, and practical reasoning aimed at relief; and it causes wincing, blanching, and nursing of the traumatized area. Any state that plays exactly that functional role is a pain, according to functionalism. Similarly, other types of mental states (sensations, fears, beliefs, and so on) are also defined by their unique causal roles in a complex economy of internal states mediating sensory inputs and behavioral outputs.

This view may remind the reader of behaviorism, and indeed it is the heir to behaviorism, but there is one fundamental difference between the two theories. Where the behaviorist hoped to define each type of mental state solely in terms of environmental input and behavioral output, the functionalist denies that this is possible. As he sees it, the adequate characterization of almost any mental state involves an ineliminable reference to a variety of other mental states with which it is causally connected, and so a reductive definition solely in terms of publicly observable inputs and outputs is quite impossible. Functionalism is therefore immune to one of the main objections against behaviorism.

Thus the difference between functionalism and behaviorism. The difference between functionalism and the identity theory will emerge from the following argument raised against the identity theory.

Imagine a being from another planet, says the functionalist, a being with an alien physiological constitution, a constitution based on the chemical element silicon, for example, instead of on the element carbon, as ours is. The chemistry and even the physical structure of the alien's brain would have to be systematically different from ours. But even so, that alien brain could well sustain a functional economy of internal states whose mutual *relations* parallel perfectly the mutual relations that define our own mental

states. The alien may have an internal state that meets all the conditions for being a pain state, as outlined earlier. That state, considered from a purely physical point of view, would have a very different makeup from a human pain state, but it could nevertheless be identical to a human pain state from a purely functional point of view. And so for all of his functional states.

If the alien's functional economy of internal states were indeed *functionally isomorphic* with our own internal economy—if those states were causally connected to inputs, to one another, and to behavior in ways that parallel our own internal connections—then the alien would have pains, and desires, and hopes, and fears just as fully as we, despite the differences in the physical system that sustains or realizes those functional states. What is important for mentality is not the matter of which the creature is made, but the structure of the internal activities which that matter sustains.

If we can think of one alien constitution, we can think of many, and the point just made can also be made with an artificial system. Were we to create an electronic system—a computer of some kind—whose internal economy were functionally isomorphic with our own in all the relevant ways, then it too would be the subject of mental states.

What this illustrates is that there are almost certainly many more ways than one for nature, and perhaps even for man, to put together a thinking, feeling, perceiving creature. And this raises a problem for the identity theory, for it seems that there is no single type of physical state to which a given type of mental state must always correspond. Ironically, there are *too many* different kinds of physical systems that can realize the functional economy characteristic of conscious intelligence. If we consider the universe at large, therefore, and the future as well as the present, it seems quite unlikely that the identity theorist is going to find the one-to-one match-ups between the concepts of our common-sense mental taxonomy and the concepts of an overarching theory that encompasses all of the relevant physical systems. But that is what intertheoretic reduction is standardly said to require. The prospects for universal identities, between types of mental states and types of brain states, are therefore slim.

If the functionalists reject the traditional "mental-type = physical type" identity theory, virtually all of them remain committed to a weaker "mental token = physical token" identity theory, for they still maintain that each *instance* of a given type of mental state is numerically identical with some specific physical state in some physical system or other. It is only universal (type/type) identities that are rejected. Even so, this rejection is typically taken to support the claim that the science of psychology is or should be *methodologically autonomous* from the various physical sciences such as physics, biology, and even neurophysiology. Psychology, it is claimed, has its own irreducible laws and its own abstract subject matter.

As this book is written, functionalism is probably the most widely held theory of mind among philosophers, cognitive psychologists, and artificial intelligence researchers. Some of the reasons are apparent from the preceding discussion, and there are further reasons as well. In characterizing mental states as essentially functional states, functionalism places the concerns of psychology at a level that abstracts from the teeming detail of a brain's neurophysiological (or crystallographic, or microelectronic) structure. The science of psychology, it is occasionally said, is methodologically autonomous from those other sciences (biology, neuroscience, circuit theory) whose concerns are with what amount to engineering details. This provides a rationale for a great deal of work in cognitive psychology and artificial intelligence, where researchers postulate a system of abstract functional states and then test the postulated system, often by way of its computer simulation, against human behavior in similar circumstances. The aim of such work is to discover in detail the functional organization that makes us what we are.

Arguments Against Functionalism

Current popularity aside, functionalism also faces difficulties. The most commonly posed objection cites an old friend: sensory qualia. Functionalism may escape one of behaviorism's fatal flaws, it is said, but it still falls prey to the other. By attempting to make its *rela-tional* properties the definitive feature of any mental state, functionalism ignores the "inner" or qualitative nature of our mental states. But their qualitative nature is the essential feature of a great many types of mental state (pain, sensations of color, of temperature, of pitch, and so on), runs the objection, and functionalism is therefore false.

The standard illustration of this apparent failing is called "the inverted spectrum thought-experiment." It is entirely conceivable, runs the story, that the range of color sensations that I enjoy upon viewing standard objects is simply inverted relative to the color sensations that you enjoy. When viewing a tomato, I may have what is really a sensation-of-green where you have the normal sensation-of-red; when viewing a banana, I may have what is really sensation-of-blue where you have the normal sensation-of-yellow; and so forth. But since we have no way of comparing our inner qualia, and since I shall make all the same observational discriminations among objects that you will, there is no way to tell whether my spectrum is inverted relative to yours.

The problem for functionalism arises as follows. Even if my spectrum is inverted relative to yours, we remain functionally isomorphic with one another. My visual sensation upon viewing a tomato is *functionally* identical with your visual sensation upon viewing a tomato. According to functionalism, therefore, they are the very same type of state, and it does not even make sense to suppose that my sensation is "really" a sensation-of-green. If it meets the functional conditions for being a sensation-of-red, then by definition it is a sensation-of-red. According to functionalism, apparently, a spectrum inversion of the kind described is ruled out by definition. But such inversions are entirely conceivable, concludes the objection, and if functionalism entails that they are not conceivable, then functionalism is false.

Another qualia-related worry for functionalism is the so-called "absent qualia problem." The functional organization characteristic of conscious intelligence can be instantiated (= realized or instanced) in a considerable variety of physical systems, some of them radically different from a normal human. For example, a giant electronic computer might instantiate it, and there are more radical possibilities still. One writer asks us to imagine the people of China—all 10^9 of them—organized into an intricate game of mutual interactions so that collectively they constitute a giant brain which exchanges inputs and outputs with a single robot body. That system of the robot-plus-10^9-unit-brain could presumably instantiate the relevant functional organization (though no doubt it would be much slower in its activities than a human or a computer), and would therefore be the subject of mental states, according to functionalism. But surely, it is urged, the complex states that there play the functional roles of pain, pleasure, and sensations-of-color would not have intrinsic qualia as ours do, and would therefore fail to be genuine mental states. Again, functionalism seems at best an incomplete account of the nature of mental states.

It has recently been argued that both the inverted-qualia and the absent-qualia objections can be met, without violence to functionalism and without significant violence to our common-sense intuitions about qualia. Consider the inversion problem first. I think the functionalist is right to insist that the type-identity of our visual sensations be reckoned according to their functional role. But the objector is also right in insisting that a relative inversion of two people's qualia, without functional inversion, is entirely conceivable. The apparent inconsistency between these positions can be dissolved by insisting that (1) our functional states (or rather, their physical realizations) do indeed have an intrinsic nature on which our introspective identification of those states depends; while also insisting that (2) such intrinsic natures are nevertheless not essential to the type-identity of a given mental state, and may indeed *vary* from instance to instance of the same type of mental state.

What this means is that the qualitative character of your sensation-of-red might be different from the qualitative character of my sensation-of-red, slightly or substantially, and a third person's sensation-of-red might be different again. But so long as all three states are standardly caused by red objects and standardly cause all three of us to believe that something is red, then all three states are sensations-of-red, whatever their intrinsic qualitative character. Such intrinsic qualia merely serve as salient features that permit the quick introspective identification of sensations, as black-on-orange stripes serve as a salient feature for the quick visual identification of tigers. But specific qualia are not essential to the type-identity of mental states, any more than black-on-orange stripes are essential to the type-identity of tigers.

Plainly, this solution requires the functionalist to admit the *reality* of qualia, and we may wonder how there can be room for qualia in his materialist world-picture. Perhaps they can be fit in as follows: *identify* them with physical properties of whatever physical states instantiate the mental (functional) states that display them. For example, identify the qualitative nature of your sensations-of-red with that physical feature (of the brain state that instantiates it) to which your mechanisms of introspective discrimination are in fact responding when you judge that you have a sensation-of-red. If materialism is true, then there must *be* some internal physical feature or other to which your discrimination of sensations-of-red is keyed: *that* is the quale of your sensations-of-red. If the pitch of a sound can turn out to be the frequency of an oscillation in air pressure, there is no reason why the quale of a sensation cannot turn out to be, say, a spiking frequency in a certain neural pathway. ("Spikes" are the tiny electrochemical pulses by which our brain cells communicate.)

This entails that creatures with a constitution different from ours may have qualia different from ours, despite being psychologically isomorphic with us. It does not entail that they *must* have different qualia, however. If the qualitative character of my sensation-of-red is really a spiking frequency of 90 hertz in a certain neural pathway, it is possible that an electro-mechanical robot might enjoy the very same qualitative character if, in reporting sensations-of-red, the robot were responding to a spiking frequency of 90 hertz in a corresponding *copper* pathway. It might be the spiking frequency that matters to our respective mechanisms of discrimination, not the nature of the medium that carries it.

This proposal also suggests a solution to the absent qualia problem. So long as the physical system at issue is functionally isomorphic with us, to the last detail, then it will be equally capable of subtle introspective discriminations among its sensations. Those discriminations must be made on some systematic physical basis, that is, on some characteristic physical features of the states being discriminated. Those features at the objective focus of the system's discriminatory mechanisms, *those* are its sensory qualia—though the alien system is no more likely to appreciate their true physical nature than we appreciate the true physical nature of our own qualia. Sensory qualia are therefore an inevitable concomitant of any system with the kind of functional organization at issue. It may be difficult or impossible to "see" the qualia in an alien system, but it is equally difficult to "see" them even when looking into a human brain.

I leave it to the reader to judge the adequacy of these responses. If they are adequate, then, given its other virtues, functionalism must be conceded a very strong position among the competing contemporary theories of mind. It is interesting, however, that the defense offered in the last paragraph found it necessary to take a leaf from the identity theorist's book (types of qualia are reduced to or identified with types of physical states), since the final objection we shall consider also tends to blur the distinction between functionalism and reductive materialism.

Consider the property of *temperature,* runs the objection. Here we have a paradigm of a physical property, one that has also been cited as the paradigm of a successfully *reduced* property, as expressed in the intertheoretic identity

> "temperature = mean kinetic energy of constituent molecules."

Strictly speaking, however, this identity is true only for the temperature of a gas, where simple particles are free to move in ballistic fashion. In a *solid,* temperature is realized differently, since the interconnected molecules are confined to a variety of vibrational motions. In a *plasma,* temperature is something else again, since a plasma has no constituent molecules; they, and their constituent atoms, have been ripped to pieces. And even a *vacuum* has a so-called "blackbody" temperature—in the distribution of electromagnetic waves coursing through it. Here temperature has nothing to do with the kinetic energy of particles.

It is plain that the physical property of temperature enjoys 'multiple instantiations' no less than do psy-

chological properties. Does this mean that thermodynamics (the theory of heat and temperature) is an "autonomous science," separable from the rest of physics, with its own irreducible laws and its own abstract nonphysical subject matter?

Presumably not. What it means, concludes the objection, is that *reductions are domain-specific:*

> temperature-in-a-gas = the mean kinetic energy of the gas's molecules,

whereas

> temperature-in-a-vacuum = the blackbody distribution of the vacuum's transient radiation.

> Similarly, perhaps

> joy-in-a-human = resonances in the lateral hypothalamus,

whereas

> joy-in-a-Martian = something else entirely.

This means that we may expect some type/type reductions of mental states to physical states after all, though they will be much narrower than was first suggested. Furthermore, it means that functionalist claims concerning the radical autonomy of psychology cannot be sustained. And last, it suggests that functionalism is not so profoundly different from the identity theory as was first made out.

As with the defense of functionalism outlined earlier, I leave the evaluation of this criticism to the reader. We shall have occasion for further discussion of functionalism in later chapters. At this point, let us turn to the final materialist theory of mind, for functionalism is not the only major reaction against the identity theory.

III. ELIMINATIVE MATERIALISM

The identity theory was called into doubt not because the prospects for a materialist account of our mental capacities were thought to be poor, but because it seemed unlikely that the arrival of an adequate materialist theory would bring with it the nice one-to-one match-ups, between the concepts of folk psychology and the concepts of theoretical neuroscience, that intertheoretic reduction requires. The reason for that doubt was the great variety of quite different physical systems that could instantiate the required functional organization. *Eliminative materialism* also doubts that the correct neuroscientific account of human capacities will produce a neat reduction of our common-sense framework, but here the doubts arise from a quite different source.

As the eliminative materialists see it, the one-to-one match-ups will not be found, and our common-sense psychological framework will not enjoy an intertheoretic reduction, *because our common-sense psychological framework is a false and radically misleading conception of the causes of human behavior and the nature of cognitive activity.* On this view, folk psychology is not just an incomplete representation of our inner natures; it is an outright *mis*representation of our internal states and activities. Consequently, we cannot expect a truly adequate neuroscientific account of our inner lives to provide theoretical categories that match up nicely with the categories of our common-sense framework. Accordingly, we must expect that the older framework will simply be eliminated, rather than be reduced, by a matured neuroscience.

Historical Parallels

As the identity theorist can point to historical cases of successful intertheoretic reduction, so the eliminative materialist can point to historical cases of the outright elimination of the ontology of an older theory in favor of the ontology of a new and superior theory. For most of the eighteenth and nineteenth centuries, learned people believed that heat was a subtle fluid held in bodies, much in the way water is held in a sponge. A fair body of moderately successful theory described the way this fluid substance—called "caloric"—flowed within a body, or from one body to another, and how it produced thermal expansion, melting, boiling, and so forth. But by the end of the last century it had become abundantly clear that heat was not a substance at all, but just the energy of

motion of the trillions of jostling molecules that make up the heated body itself. The new theory—the "corpuscular/kinetic theory of matter and heat"—was much more successful than the old in explaining and predicting the thermal behavior of bodies. And since we were unable to *identify* caloric fluid with kinetic energy (according to the old theory, caloric is a material *substance;* according to the new theory, kinetic energy is a form of *motion*), it was finally agreed that there is *no such thing* as caloric. Caloric was simply eliminated from our accepted ontology.

A second example. It used to be thought that when a piece of wood burns, or a piece of metal rusts, a spiritlike substance called "phlogiston" was being released: briskly, in the former case, slowly in the latter. Once gone, that "noble" substance left only a base pile of ash or rust. It later came to be appreciated that both processes involve, not the loss of something, but the *gaining* of a substance taken from the atmosphere: oxygen. Phlogiston emerged, not as an incomplete description of what was going on, but as a radical misdescription. Phlogiston was therefore not suitable for reduction to or identification with some notion from within the new oxygen chemistry, and it was simply eliminated from science.

Admittedly, both of these examples concern the elimination of something nonobservable, but our history also includes the elimination of certain widely accepted "observables." Before Copernicus' views became available, almost any human who ventured out at night could look up at *the starry sphere of the heavens,* and if he stayed for more than a few minutes he could also see that it *turned,* around an axis through Polaris. What the sphere was made of (crystal?) and what made it turn (the gods?) were theoretical questions that exercised us for over two millennia. But hardly anyone doubted the existence of what everyone could observe with their own eyes. In the end, however, we learned to reinterpret our visual experience of the night sky within a very different conceptual framework, and the turning sphere evaporated.

Witches provide another example. Psychosis is a fairly common affliction among humans, and in earlier centuries its victims were standardly seen as cases of demonic possession, as instances of Satan's spirit itself, glaring malevolently out at us from behind the victims' eyes. That witches exist was not a matter of any controversy. One would occasionally see them, in any city or hamlet, engaged in incoherent, paranoid, or even murderous behavior. But observable or not, we eventually decided that witches simply do not exist. We concluded that the concept of a witch is an element in a conceptual framework that misrepresents so badly the phenomena to which it was standardly applied that literal application of the notion should be permanently withdrawn. Modern theories of mental dysfunction led to the elimination of witches from our serious ontology.

The concepts of folk psychology—belief, desire, fear, sensation, pain, joy, and so on—await a similar fate, according to the view at issue. And when neuroscience has matured to the point where the poverty of our current conceptions is apparent to everyone, and the superiority of the new framework is established, we shall then be able to set about *re*conceiving our internal states and activities, within a truly adequate conceptual framework at last. Our explanations of one another's behavior will appeal to such things as our neuropharmacological states, the neural activity in specialized anatomical areas, and whatever other states are deemed relevant by the new theory. Our private introspection will also be transformed, and may be profoundly enhanced by reason of the more accurate and penetrating framework it will have to work with— just as the astronomer's perception of the night sky is much enhanced by the detailed knowledge of modern astronomical theory that he or she possesses.

The magnitude of the conceptual revolution here suggested should not be minimized: it would be enormous. And the benefits to humanity might be equally great. If each of us possessed an accurate neuroscientific understanding of (what we now conceive dimly as) the varieties and causes of mental illness, the factors involved in learning, the neural basis of emotions, intelligence, and socialization, then the sum total of human misery might be much reduced. The simple increase in mutual understanding that the new framework made possible could contribute substantially toward a more peaceful and humane society. Of course, there would be dangers as well: increased knowledge means increased power, and power can always be misused.

Arguments for Eliminative Materialism

The arguments for eliminative materialism are diffuse and less than decisive, but they are stronger than is widely supposed. The distinguishing feature of this position is its denial that a smooth intertheoretic reduction is to be expected—even a species-specific reduction—of the framework of folk psychology to the framework of a matured neuroscience. The reason for this denial is the eliminative materialist's conviction that folk psychology is a hopelessly primitive and deeply confused conception of our internal activities. But why this low opinion of our common-sense conceptions?

There are at least three reasons. First, the eliminative materialist will point to the widespread explanatory, predictive, and manipulative failures of folk psychology. So much of what is central and familiar to us remains a complete mystery from within folk psychology. We do not know what *sleep* is, or why we have to have it, despite spending a full third of our lives in that condition. (The answer, "For rest," is mistaken. Even if people are allowed to rest continuously, their need for sleep is undiminished. Apparently, sleep serves some deeper functions, but we do not yet know what they are.) We do not understand how *learning* transforms each of us from a gaping infant to a cunning adult, or how differences in *intelligence* are grounded. We have not the slightest idea how *memory* works, or how we manage to retrieve relevant bits of information instantly from the awesome mass we have stored. We do not know what *mental illness* is, nor how to cure it.

In sum, the most central things about us remain almost entirely mysterious from within folk psychology. And the defects noted cannot be blamed on inadequate time allowed for their correction, for folk psychology has enjoyed no significant changes or advances in well over 2,000 years, despite its manifest failures. Truly successful theories may be expected to reduce, but significantly unsuccessful theories merit no such expectation.

This argument from explanatory poverty has a further aspect. So long as one sticks to normal brains, the poverty of folk psychology is perhaps not strikingly evident. But as soon as one examines the many perplexing behavioral and cognitive deficits suffered by people with *damaged* brains, one's descriptive and explanatory resources start to claw the air. . . . As with other humble theories asked to operate successfully in unexplored extensions of their old domain (for example, Newtonian mechanics in the domain of velocities close to the velocity of light, and the classical gas law in the domain of high pressures or temperatures), the descriptive and explanatory inadequacies of folk psychology become starkly evident.

The second argument tries to draw an inductive lesson from our conceptual history. Our early folk theories of motion were profoundly confused, and were eventually displaced entirely by more sophisticated theories. Our early folk theories of the structure and activity of the heavens were wildly off the mark, and survive only as historical lessons in how wrong we can be. Our folk theories of the nature of fire, and the nature of life, were similarly cockeyed. And one could go on, since the vast majority of our past folk conceptions have been similarly exploded. All except folk psychology, which survives to this day and has only recently begun to feel pressure. But the phenomenon of conscious intelligence is surely a more complex and difficult phenomenon than any of those just listed. So far as accurate understanding is concerned, it would be a *miracle* if we had got *that* one right the very first time, when we fell down so badly on all the others. Folk psychology has survived for so very long, presumably, not because it is basically correct in its representations, but because the phenomena addressed are so surpassingly difficult that any useful handle on them, no matter how feeble, is unlikely to be displaced in a hurry.

A third argument attempts to find an a priori advantage for eliminative materialism over the identity theory and functionalism. It attempts to counter the common intuition that eliminative materialism is distantly possible, perhaps, but is much less probable than either the identity theory or functionalism. The focus again is on whether the concepts of folk psychology will find vindicating match-ups in a matured neuroscience. The eliminativist bets no; the other two bet yes. (Even the functionalist bets yes, but expects the match-ups to be only species-specific, or only person-specific. Functionalism, recall, denies the existence only of *universal* type/type identities.)

The eliminativist will point out that the requirements on a reduction are rather demanding. The new theory must entail a set of principles and embedded concepts that mirrors very closely the specific conceptual structure to be reduced. And the fact is, there are vastly many more ways of being an explanatorily successful neuroscience while *not* mirroring the structure of folk psychology, than there are ways of being an explanatorily successful neuroscience while also *mirroring* the very specific structure of folk psychology. Accordingly, the a priori probability of eliminative materialism is not lower, but substantially *higher* than that of either of its competitors. One's initial intuitions here are simply mistaken.

Granted, this initial a priori advantage could be reduced if there were a very strong presumption in favor of the truth of folk psychology—true theories are better bets to win reduction. But according to the first two arguments, the presumptions on this point should run in precisely the opposite direction.

Arguments Against Eliminative Materialism

The initial plausibility of this rather radical view is low for almost everyone, since it denies deeply entrenched assumptions. That is at best a question-begging complaint, of course, since those assumptions are precisely what is at issue. But the following line of thought does attempt to mount a real argument.

Eliminative materialism is false, runs the argument, because one's introspection reveals directly the existence of pains, beliefs, desires, fears, and so forth. Their existence is as obvious as anything could be.

The eliminative materialist will reply that this argument makes the same mistake that an ancient or medieval person would be making if he insisted that he could just see with his own eyes that the heavens form a turning sphere, or that witches exist. The fact is, all observation occurs within some system of concepts, and our observation judgments are only as good as the conceptual framework in which they are expressed. In all three cases—the starry sphere, witches, and the familiar mental states—precisely what is challenged is the integrity of the background conceptual frameworks in which the observation judgments are expressed. To insist on the validity of one's experiences, *traditionally interpreted,* is therefore to beg the very question at issue. For in all three cases, the question is whether we should *re*conceive the nature of some familiar observational domain.

A second criticism attempts to find an incoherence in the eliminative materialist's position. The bald statement of eliminative materialism is that the familiar mental states do not really exist. But that statement is meaningful, runs the argument, only if it is the expression of a certain *belief,* and an *intention* to communicate, and a *knowledge* of the language, and so forth. But if the statement is true, then no such mental states exist, and the statement is therefore a meaningless string of marks or noises, and cannot be true. Evidently, the assumption that eliminative materialism is true entails that it cannot be true.

The hole in this argument is the premise concerning the conditions necessary for a statement to be meaningful. It begs the question. If eliminative materialism is true, then meaningfulness must have some different source. To insist on the "old" source is to insist on the validity of the very framework at issue. Again, an historical parallel may be helpful here. Consider the medieval theory that being biologically *alive* is a matter of being ensouled by an immaterial *vital spirit.* And consider the following response to someone who has expressed disbelief in that theory.

> My learned friend has stated that there is no such thing as vital spirit. But this statement is incoherent. For if it is true, then my friend does not have vital spirit, and must therefore be *dead.* But if he is dead, then his statement is just a string of noises, devoid of meaning or truth. Evidently, the assumption that antivitalism is true entails that it cannot be true! Q.E.D.

This second argument is now a joke, but the first argument begs the question in exactly the same way.

A final criticism draws a much weaker conclusion, but makes a rather stronger case. Eliminative materialism, it has been said, is making mountains out of molehills. It exaggerates the defects in folk psychology, and underplays its real successes. Perhaps the arrival of a matured neuroscience will require the elimination of the occasional folk-psychological concept, continues the criticism, and a minor adjustment in certain folk-psychological principles may have to be endured. But the large-scale elimination forecast by the eliminative materialist is just an alarmist worry or a romantic enthusiasm.

Perhaps this complaint is correct. And perhaps it is merely complacent. Whichever, it does bring out the important point that we do not confront two simple and mutually exclusive possibilities here: pure reduction versus pure elimination. Rather, these are the end points of a smooth spectrum of possible outcomes, between which there are mixed cases of partial elimination and partial reduction. Only empirical research . . . can tell us where on that spectrum our own case will fall. Perhaps we should speak here, more liberally, of "revisionary materialism," instead of concentrating on the more radical possibility of an across-the-board elimination. Perhaps we should. But it has been my aim in this section to make it at least intelligible to you that our collective conceptual destiny lies substantially toward the revolutionary end of the spectrum.

FOR FURTHER REFLECTION

1. Evaluate the arguments for and against reductive and eliminative materialism. Do you agree with Churchland's assessment? Explain.
2. Try to imagine how we would describe our beliefs, perceptions, feelings, and desires within an eliminative framework. Describe two people talking to each other who have just fallen in love. Eliminative materialism does sound revolutionary, but the question is, is it true?
3. Compare Churchland's account of the mind-body problem with Shaffer's. How do they differ?

THOMAS NAGEL

WHAT IS IT LIKE TO BE A BAT?

Thomas Nagel is professor of philosophy at New York University and the author of several works in ethics and philosophy of mind, including *The View from Nowhere* (1986). Much of Nagel's work involves showing the incongruities between objective and subjective perspectives, especially between the scientific explanation of humanness and our subjective experience of it. Something vital is lost in the reduction of mental states to brain states.

In this article Nagel argues against the view that the objective perspective is the correct one. He contends that the peculiarity of the subjective character experience is that increased objectivity actually takes us further from its real nature.

Consciousness is what makes the mind-body problem really intractable. Perhaps that is why current discussions of the problem give it little attention or get to it obviously wrong. The recent wave of reductionist euphoria has produced several analyses of mental phenomena and mental concepts designed to explain the possibility of some variety of materialism, psychophysical identification, or reduction. But the problems dealt with are those common to this type of reduction and other types, and what makes the mind-body problem unique, and unlike the water–H_2O problem or the Turing machine–IBM machine problem or the lightning-electrical discharge problem or the gene-DNA problem or the oak tree– hydrocarbon problem, is ignored. Every reductionist has his favorite analogy from modern science. It is most unlikely that any of these unrelated examples of successful reduction will shed light on the relation of mind to brain. But philosophers share the general human weakness for explanations of what is incomprehensible in terms suited for what is familiar and well understood, though entirely different. This has led to the acceptance of implausible accounts of the mental largely because they would permit familiar kinds of reduction. I shall try to explain why the usual examples do not help us to understand the relation between mind and body—why, indeed, we have at present no conception of what an explanation of the physical nature of a mental phenomenon would be. Without consciousness the mind-body problem would be much less interesting. With consciousness it seems hopeless. The most important and characteristic feature of conscious mental phenomena is very poorly understood. Most reductionist theories do not even try to explain it. And careful examination will show that no currently available concept of reduction is applicable to it. Perhaps a new theoretical form can be devised for the purpose, but such a solution, if it exists, lies in the distinct intellectual future.

Conscious experience is a widespread phenomenon. It occurs at many levels of animal life, though we cannot be sure of its presence in the simpler organisms, and it is very difficult to say in general what provides evidence of it. (Some extremists have been

From Thomas Nagel, "What Is It Like to Be a Bat?" in *Philosophical Review* (October 1974). Footnotes edited.

prepared to deny it even of mammals other than man.) No doubt it occurs in countless forms totally unimaginable to us, on other planets in other solar systems throughout the universe. But no matter how the form may vary, the fact that an organism has conscious experience *at all* means, basically, that there is something it is like to *be* that organism. There may be further implications about the form of the experience; there may even (though I doubt it) be implications about the behavior of the organism. But fundamentally an organism has conscious mental states if and only if there is something that it is like to *be* that organism—something it is like *for* the organism.

We may call this the subjective character of experience. It is not captured by any of the familiar, recently devised reductive analyses of the mental, for all of them are logically compatible with its absence. It is not analyzable in terms of any explanatory system of functional states, or intentional states, since these could be ascribed to robots or automata that behaved like people though they experienced nothing. It is not analyzable in terms of the causal role of experiences in relation to typical human behavior—for similar reasons. I do not deny that conscious mental states and events cause behavior, nor that they may be given functional characterizations. I deny only that this kind of thing exhausts their analysis. Any reductionist program has to be based on an analysis of what is to be reduced. If the analysis leaves something out, the problem will be falsely posed. It is useless to base the defense of materialism on any analysis of mental phenomena that fails to deal explicitly with their subjective character. For there is no reason to suppose that a reduction which seems plausible when no attempt is made to account for consciousness can be extended to include consciousness. Without some idea, therefore, of what the subjective character of experience is, we cannot know what is required of a physicalist theory.

While an account of the physical basis of mind must explain many things, this appears to be the most difficult. It is impossible to exclude the phenomenological features of experience from a reduction in the same way that one excludes the phenomenal features of an ordinary substance from a physical or chemical reduction of it—namely, by explaining them as effects on the minds of human observers. If physicalism is to be defended, the phenomenological features must themselves be given a physical account. But when we examine their subjective character it seems that such a result is impossible. The reason is that every subjective phenomenon is essentially connected with a single point of view, and it seems inevitable that an objective, physical theory will abandon that point of view.

Let me first try to state the issue somewhat more fully than by referring to the relation between the subjective and the objective, or between the *pour-soi* and the *en-soi*. This is far from easy. Facts about what it is like to be an *X* are very peculiar, so peculiar that some may be inclined to doubt their reality, or the significance of claims about them. To illustrate the connection between subjectivity and a point of view, and to make evident the importance of subjective features, it will help to explore the matter in relation to an example that brings out clearly the divergence between the two types of conception, subjective and objective.

I assume we all believe that bats have experience. After all, they are mammals, and there is no more doubt that they have experience than that mice or pigeons or whales have experience. I have chosen bats instead of wasps or flounders because if one travels too far down the phylogenetic tree, people gradually shed their faith that there is experience there at all. Bats, although more closely related to us than those other species, nevertheless present a range of activity and a sensory apparatus so different from ours that the problem I want to pose is exceptionally vivid (though it certainly could be raised with other species). Even without the benefit of philosophical reflection, anyone who has spent some time in an enclosed space with an excited bat knows what it is to encounter a fundamentally *alien* form of life.

I have said that the essence of the belief that bats have experience is that there is something that it is like to be a bat. Now we know that most bats (the microchiroptera, to be precise) perceive the external world primarily by sonar, or echolocation, detecting the reflections, from objects within range, of their own rapid, subtly modulated, high-frequency shrieks. Their brains are designed to correlate the outgoing impulses with the subsequent echoes, and the information thus acquired enables bats to make precise discrimination of distance, size, shape, motion, and texture comparable to those we make by vision. But bat sonar, though clearly a form of perception, is not similar in its operation to any sense that we possess, and there is no reason to suppose that it is subjectively like anything we can experience or imagine. This appears to create difficulties for the notion of what it is like to be a bat. We must consider whether any method will permit us to extrapolate to the inner life of the bat from our own case,[1] and if not, what alternative methods there may be for understanding the notion.

Our own experience provides the basic material for our imagination, whose range is therefore limited. It will not help to try to imagine that one has webbing on one's arms, which enables one to fly around at dusk and dawn catching insects in one's mouth; that one has very poor vision, and perceives the surrounding world by a system of reflected high-frequency sound signals; and that one spends the day hanging upside down by one's feet in an attic. Insofar as I can imagine this (which is not very far), it tells me only what it would be like for *me* to behave as a bat behaves. But that is not the question. I want to know what it is like for a *bat* to be a bat. Yet if I try to imagine this, I am restricted to the resources of my own mind, and those resources are inadequate to the task. I cannot perform it either by imagining additions to my present experience, or by imagining segments gradually subtracted from it, or by imagining some combination of additions, subtractions, and modifications.

To the extent that I could look and behave like a wasp or a bat without changing my fundamental structure, my experiences would not be anything like the experiences of those animals. On the other hand, it is doubtful that any meaning can be attached to the supposition that I should possess the internal neurophysiological constitution of a bat. Even if I could by gradual degrees be transformed into a bat, nothing in my present constitution enables me to imagine what the experiences of such a future stage of myself thus metamorphosed would be like. The best evidence would come from the experiences of bats, if we only knew what they were like.

So if extrapolation from our own case is involved in the idea of what it is like to be a bat, the extrapolation must be incompletable. We cannot form more than a schematic conception of what it *is* like. For example, we may ascribe general *types* of experience on the basis of the animal's structure and behavior. Thus we describe bat sonar as a form of three-dimensional forward perception; we believe that bats feel some versions of pain, fear, hunger, and lust, and that they have other, more familiar types of perception besides sonar. But we believe that these experiences also have in each case a specific subjective character, which it is beyond our ability to conceive. And if there is conscious life elsewhere in the universe, it is likely that some of it will not be describable even in the most general experiential terms available to us.[2] (The problem is not confined to exotic cases, however, for it exists between one person and another. The subjective character of the experience of a person deaf and blind from birth is not accessible to me, for example, nor presumably is mine to him. This does not prevent us each from believing that the other's experience has such a subjective character.)

If anyone is inclined to deny that we can believe in the existence of facts like this whose exact nature we cannot possibly conceive, he should reflect that in contemplating the bats we are in much the same position that intelligent bats or Martians[3] would occupy if they tried to form a conception of what it was like to be us. The structure of their own minds might make it impossible for them to succeed, but we know they would be wrong to conclude that there is not anything precise that it is like to be us: that only certain general types of mental state could be ascribed to us (perhaps perception and appetite would be concepts common to us both; perhaps not). We know they would be wrong to draw such a skeptical conclusion because we know what it is like to be us. And we know that while it includes an enormous amount of variation and complexity, and while we do not possess the vocabulary to describe it adequately, its subjective character is highly specific, and in some respects describable in terms that can be understood only by creatures like us. The fact that we cannot expect ever to accommodate in our language a detailed description of Martian or bat phenomenology should not lead us to dismiss as meaningless the claim that bats and Martians have experiences fully comparable in richness of detail to our own. It would be fine if someone were to develop concepts and a theory that enabled us to think about those things, but such an understanding may be permanently denied to us by the limits of our nature. And to deny the reality or logical significance of what we can never describe or understand is the crudest form of cognitive dissonance.

This brings us to the edge of a topic that requires much more discussion than I can give it here: namely, the relation between facts on the one hand and conceptual schemes or systems of representation on the other. My realism about the subjective domain in all its forms implies a belief in the existence of facts beyond the reach of human concepts. Certainly it is possible for a human being to believe that there are facts which humans never *will* possess the requisite concepts to represent or comprehend. Indeed, it would be foolish to doubt this, given the finiteness of humanity's expectations. After all, there would have been transfinite numbers even if everyone had been wiped out by the Black Death before Cantor discovered them. But one might also believe that there are facts which *could* not ever be represented or comprehended by human beings, even if the species lasted for ever—simply because our structure does not permit us to operate with concepts of the requisite type. This impossibility might even be observed by other beings, but it is not clear that the existence of such beings, or the possibility of their existence, is a precondition of the significance of the hypothesis that there are humanly inaccessible facts. (After all, the nature of beings with access to humanly inaccessible facts is presumably itself a humanly inaccessible fact.) Reflection on what it is like to be a bat seems to lead us, therefore, to the conclusion that there are facts that do not consist in the truth of propositions expressible in a human language. We can be compelled to recognize the existence of such facts without being able to state or comprehend them.

I shall not pursue this subject, however. Its bearing on the topic before us (namely, the mind-body problem) is that it enables us to make a general observation about the subjective character of experience. Whatever may be the status of facts about what it is like to be a human being, or a bat, or a Martian, these appear to be facts that embody a particular point of view.

I am not adverting here to the alleged privacy of experience to its possessor. The point of view in question is not one accessible only to a single individual. Rather it is a *type*. It is often possible to take up a point of view other than one's own, so the comprehension of such facts is not limited to one's own case. There is a sense in which phenomenological facts are perfectly objective: One person can know or say of another what the quality of the other's experience is. They are subjective, however, in the sense that even this objective ascription of experience is possible only for someone sufficiently similar to the object of ascription to be able to adopt his point of view—to understand the ascription in the first person as well as in the third, so to speak. The more different from oneself the other experiencer is, the less success one can expect with this enterprise. In our own case we occupy the relevant point of view, but we will have as much difficulty understanding our own experience properly if we approach it from another point of view as we would if we tried to understand the experience of another species without taking up *its* point of view.

This bears directly on the mind-body problem. For if the facts of experience—facts about what it is like *for* the experiencing organism—are accessible only from one point of view, then it is a mystery how the true character of experiences could be revealed in the physical operation of that organism. The latter is a domain of objective facts *par excellence*—the kind that can be observed and understood from many points of view and by individuals with differing perceptual systems. There are no comparable imaginative obstacles to the acquisition of knowledge about bat neurophysiology by human scientists, and intelligent bats or Martians might learn more about the human brain than we ever will.

This is not by itself an argument against reduction. A Martian scientist with no understanding of visual perception could understand the rainbow, or lightning, or clouds as physical phenomena, though he would never be able to understand the human concepts of rainbow, lightning, or cloud, or the place these things occupy in our phenomenal world. The objective nature of the things picked out by these concepts could be apprehended by him because, although the concepts themselves are connected with a particular point of view and a particular visual phenomenology, the things apprehended from that point of view are not: They are observable from the point of view but external to it; hence they can be comprehended from other points of view also, either by the same organisms or by others. Lightning has an objective character that is not exhausted by its visual appearance, and this can be investigated by a Martian without vision. To be precise, it has a *more* objective character than is revealed in its visual appearance. In speaking of the move from subjective characterization, I wish to remain noncommittal about the existence of an end point, the completely objective intrinsic nature of the thing, which one might or might not be able to reach. It may be more accurate to think of objectivity as a direction in which the understanding can travel. And in understanding a phenomenon like lightning, it is legitimate to go as far away as one can from a strictly human viewpoint.

In the case of experience, on the other hand, the connexion with a particular point of view seems much closer. It is difficult to understand what could be meant by the *objective* character of an experience, apart from the particular point of view from which its subject apprehends it. After all, what would be left of what it was like to be a bat if one removed the viewpoint of the bat? But if experience does not have, in addition to its subjective character, an objective nature that can be apprehended from many different points of view, then how can it be supposed that a Martian investigating my brain might be observing physical processes which were my mental processes (as he might observe physical processes which were bolts of lightning), only from a different point of view? How, for that matter, could a human physiologist observe them from another point of view?[4]

We appear to be faced with a general difficulty about psychophysical reduction. In other areas the process of reduction is a move in the direction of greater objectivity, toward a more accurate view of the real nature of things. This is accomplished by reducing our dependence on individual or species-specific points of view toward the object of investigation. We describe it not in terms of the impressions it makes on our senses, but in terms of its more general effects and of properties detectable by means other than the human senses. The less it depends on a specifically human viewpoint, the more objective is our description. It is possible to follow this path because although the concepts and ideas we employ in thinking about the external world are initially applied from a point of view that involves our perceptual apparatus, they are used by us to refer to things beyond themselves—toward which we *have* the phenomenal point of view. Therefore we can abandon it in favor of another, and still be thinking about the same things.

Experience itself, however, does not seem to fit the pattern. The idea of moving from appearance to reality seems to make no sense here. What is the analogue in this case to pursuing a more objective understanding of the same phenomena by abandoning the initial subjective viewpoint toward them in favour of another that is more objective but concerns the same thing? Certainly it *appears* unlikely that we will get closer to the real nature of human experience by leaving behind the particularity of our human point of view and striving for a description in terms accessible to beings that could not imagine what it was like to be us. If the subjective character of experience is fully comprehensible only from one point of view, then any shift to greater objectivity—that is, less attachment to a specific viewpoint—does not take us nearer to the real nature of the phenomenon: It takes us farther away from it.

In a sense, the seeds of this objection to the reducibility of experience are already detectable in successful cases of reduction; for in discovering sound to be, in reality, a wave phenomenon in air or other media, we leave behind one viewpoint to take up another, and the auditory, human or animal viewpoint that we leave behind remains unreduced. Members of radically different species may both understand the same physical events in objective terms, and this does not require that they understand the phenomenal forms in which those events appear to the senses of members of the other species. Thus it is a condition of their referring to a common reality that their more particular viewpoints are not part of the common reality that they both apprehend. The reduction can succeed only if the species-specific viewpoint is omitted from what is to be reduced.

But while we are right to leave this point of view aside in seeking a fuller understanding of the external world, we cannot ignore it permanently, since it is the essence of the internal world, and not merely a point of view on it. Most of the neobehaviorism of recent philosophical psychology results from the effort to substitute an objective concept of mind for the real thing, in order to have nothing left over which cannot be reduced. If we acknowledge that a physical theory of mind must account for the subjective character of experience, we must admit that no presently available conception gives us a clue how this could be done. The problem is unique. If mental processes are indeed physical processes, then there is something it is like, intrinsically, to undergo certain physical processes. What it is for such a thing to be the case remains a mystery.

What moral should be drawn from these reflections, and what should be done next? It would be a mistake to conclude that physicalism must be false. Nothing is proved by the inadequacy of physicalist hypotheses that assume a faulty objective analysis of mind. It would be truer to say that physicalism is a position we cannot understand because we do not at present have any conception of how it might be true. Perhaps it will be thought unreasonable to require such a conception as a condition of understanding. After all, it might be said, the meaning of physicalism is clear enough: Mental states are states of the body; mental events are physical events. We do not know *which* physical states and events they are, but that should not prevent us from understanding the hypothesis. What could be clearer than the words "is" and "are"?

But I believe it is precisely this apparent clarity of the word "is" that is deceptive. Usually, when we are told that X is Y we know how it is supposed to be true, but that depends on a conceptual or theoretical background and is not conveyed by the "is" alone. We know how both "X" and "Y" refer, and the kinds of things to which they refer, and we have a rough idea how the two referential paths might converge on a single thing, be it an object, a person, a process, an event or whatever. But when the two terms of the

identification are very disparate it may not be so clear how it could be true. We may not have even a rough idea of how the two referential paths could converge, or what kind of things they might converge on, and a theoretical framework may have to be supplied to enable us to understand this. Without the framework, an air of mysticism surrounds the identification.

This explains the magical flavor of popular presentations of fundamental scientific discoveries, given out as propositions to which one must subscribe without really understanding them. For example, people are now told at an early age that all matter is really energy. But despite the fact that they know what "is" means, most of them never form a conception of what makes this claim true, because they lack the theoretical background.

At the present time the status of physicalism is similar to that which the hypothesis that matter is energy would have had if uttered by a pre-Socratic philosopher. We do not have the beginnings of a conception of how it might be true. In order to understand the hypothesis that a mental event is a physical event, we require more than an understanding of the word "is." The idea of how a mental and a physical term might refer to the same thing is lacking, and the usual analogies with theoretical identification in other fields fail to supply it. They fail because if we construe the reference of mental terms to physical events on the usual model, we either get a reappearance of separate subjective events as the effects through which mental reference to physical events is secured, or else we get a false account of how mental terms refer (for example, a causal behaviorist one).

Strangely enough, we may have evidence for the truth of something we cannot really understand. Suppose a caterpillar is locked in a sterile safe by someone unfamiliar with insect metamorphosis, and weeks later the safe is reopened, revealing a butterfly. If the person knows that the safe has been shut the whole time, he has reason to believe that the butterfly is or was once the caterpillar, without having any idea in what sense this might be so. (One possibility is that the caterpillar contained a tiny winged parasite that devoured it and grew into the butterfly.) It is conceivable that we are in such a position with regard to physicalism. Donald Davidson has argued that if mental events have physical causes and effects, they must have physical descriptions. He holds that we have reason to believe this even though we do not—and in fact *could* not—have a general psychophysical theory. His argument applies to intentional mental events, but I think we also have some reason to believe that sensations are physical processes, without being in a position to understand how. Davidson's position is that certain physical events have irreducibly mental properties, and perhaps some view describable in this way is correct. But nothing of which we can now form a conception corresponds to it; nor have we any idea what a theory would be like that enabled us to conceive of it. Very little work has been done on the basic question (from which mention of the brain can be entirely omitted) whether any sense can be made of experiences' having an objective character at all. Does it make sense, in other words, to ask what my experiences are *really* like, as opposed to how they appear to me? We cannot genuinely understand the hypothesis that their nature is captured in a physical description unless we understand the more fundamental idea that they *have* an objective nature (or that objective processes can have a subjective nature).

I should like to close with a speculative proposal. It may be possible to approach the gap between subjective and objective from another direction. Setting aside temporarily the relation between the mind and the brain, we can pursue a more objective understanding of the mental in its own right. At present we are completely unequipped to think about the subjective character of experience without relying on the imagination—without taking up the point of view of the experiential subject. This should be regarded as a challenge to form new concepts and devise a new method—an objective phenomenology not dependent on empathy or the imagination. Though presumably it would not capture everything, its goal would be to describe, at least in part, the subjective character of experiences.

We would have to develop such a phenomenology to describe the sonar experiences of bats; but it would also be possible to begin with humans. One might try, for example, to develop concepts that could be used to explain to a person blind from birth what it was like to see. One would reach a blank wall eventually, but

it should be possible to devise a method of expressing in objective terms much more than we can at present, and with much greater precision. The loose intermodal analogies—for example, 'Red is like the sound of a trumpet'—which crop up in discussions of this subject are of little use. That should be clear to anyone who has both heard a trumpet and seen red. But structural features of perception might be more accessible to objective description, even though something would be left out. And concepts alternative to those we learn in the first person may enable us to arrive at a kind of understanding even of our own experience which is denied us by the very ease of description and lack of distance that subjective concepts afford.

Apart from its own interest, a phenomenology that is in this sense objective may permit questions about the physical basis of experience to assume a more intelligible form. Aspects of subjective experience that admitted this kind of objective description might be better candidates for objective explanations of a more familiar sort. But whether or not this guess is correct, it seems unlikely that any physical theory of mind can be contemplated until more thought has been given to the general problem of subjective and objective. Otherwise we cannot even pose the mind-body problem without sidestepping it.

NOTES

1. By "our own case," I do not mean just "my own case," but rather the mentalistic ideas that we apply unproblematically to ourselves and other human beings.
2. Therefore the analogical form of the English expression "what it is *like*" is misleading. It does not mean "what (in our experience) it *resembles*," but rather "how it is for the subject himself."
3. Any intelligent extraterrestrial beings totally different from us.
4. The problem is not just that when I look at the *Mona Lisa,* my visual experience has a certain quality, no trace of which is to be found by someone looking into my brain. For even if he did observe there a tiny image of the *Mona Lisa,* he would have no reason to identify it with the experience.

FOR FURTHER REFLECTION

1. Explain Nagel's case against reductionism. How strong is it? What would Churchland be likely to say in response to Nagel's arguments?

2. In another place Nagel states his thesis this way:

> There are things about the world and life and ourselves that cannot be adequately understood from a maximally objective standpoint, however much it may extend our understanding beyond the point from which we started. A great deal is essentially connected to a particular point of view, and the attempt to give a complete account of the world in objective terms detached from these perspectives inevitably leads to false reductions or to outright denials that certain patently real phenomena exist at all. To the extent that such no-nonsense theories have an effect, they merely threaten to impoverish the intellectual landscape for a while by inhibiting the serious expression of certain questions. In the name of liberation, these movements have offered us intellectual repression (*A View from Nowhere* [Oxford: Oxford University Press, 1986], pp. 7, 11).

Do you agree with Nagel? Or is the objective perspective really the true perspective? Or is the objective compatible with the subjective? Explain your answer.

DAVID CHALMERS

AGAINST MATERIALISM
Can Consciousness Be Reductively Explained?

David Chalmers is professor of philosophy at the University of California at Santa Cruz and the author of several works in the philosophy of mind, including *The Conscious Mind* (Oxford University Press, 1996), from which this selection is taken. Chalmers holds that consciousness is a mystery that has eluded materialist explanation. More specifically, he argues that reductive materialism fails to provide a convincing argument for the connection between the brain and consciousness. He argues, in the zombie argument, against the supervenience relationship. One set of properties A logically supervenes on another set B when there are no two logically possible situations in which B properties are the same but A properties differ. Chalmers then goes on to answer objections to his arguments and elaborate on the implications.

From David, J. Chalmers, *The Conscious Mind* (Oxford University Press, 1996), by permission. Endnotes deleted.

1. IS CONSCIOUSNESS LOGICALLY SUPERVENIENT ON THE PHYSICAL?

Almost everything in the world can be explained in physical terms; it is natural to hope that consciousness might be explained this way, too. In this chapter, however, I will argue that consciousness escapes the net of reductive explanation. No explanation given wholly in physical terms can ever account for the emergence of conscious experience. This may seem to be a negative conclusion, but it leads to some strong positive consequences that I will bring out in later chapters.

To make the case against reductive explanation, we need to show that consciousness is not logically supervenient on the physical. In principle, we need to show that it does not supervene *globally*—that is, that all the microphysical facts in the world do not entail the facts about consciousness. In practice, it is easier to run the argument *locally*, arguing that in an individual, microphysical facts do not entail the facts about consciousness. When it comes to consciousness, local and global supervenience plausibly stand and fall together, so it does not matter which way we run the argument: if consciousness supervenes at all, it almost certainly supervenes locally. If this is disputed, however, all the arguments can be run at the global level with straightforward alterations.

How can we argue that consciousness is not logically supervenient on the physical? There are various ways. We can think about what is conceivable, in order to argue directly for the logical possibility of a situation in which the physical facts are the same but the facts about experience are different. We can appeal to epistemology, arguing that the right sort of link between knowledge of physical facts and knowledge of consciousness is absent. And we can appeal directly to the concept of consciousness, arguing that there is no analysis of the concept that could ground an entailment from the physical to the phenomenal. In what follows I will give arguments using all three of these strategies. The first two are essentially arguments from conceivability, the second two are arguments from epistemology, and the fifth is an argument from analysis. There is some element of redundancy among the five arguments, but together they make a strong case.

One can also do things more directly, making the case against reductive explanation without explicitly appealing to logical supervenience. I have taken that route elsewhere, but here I will give the more detailed analysis to allow a fuller case. All the same, the case against reductive explanation and the critique of existing reductive accounts (in section 2 onward) should make sense even without this analysis. Some readers might like to proceed there directly, at least on a first reading.

(A technical note: The burden of this chapter is to argue, in effect, that there is no a priori entailment from physical facts to phenomenal facts. The sort of necessity that defines the relevant supervenience relation is the a priori version of logical necessity, where primary intensions are central. . . . [T]his is the relation that is relevant to issues about explanation; matters of a posteriori necessity can be set to one side. In the next chapter, issues of ontology rather than explanation are central, and I argue separately that there is no a posteriori necessary connection between physical facts and phenomenal facts.)

Argument 1: The Logical Possibility of Zombies

The most obvious way (although not the only way) to investigate the logical supervenience of consciousness is to consider the logical possibility of a *zombie*: someone or something physically identical to me (or to any other conscious being), but lacking conscious experiences altogether. At the global level, we can consider the logical possibility of a *zombie world*: a world physically identical to ours, but in which there are no conscious experiences at all. In such a world, everybody is a zombie.

So let us consider my zombie twin. This creature is molecule for molecule identical to me, and identical in all the low-level properties postulated by a completed physics, but he lacks conscious experience entirely. (Some might prefer to call a zombie "it," but I use the personal pronoun; I have grown quite fond of my zombie twin.) To fix ideas, we can imagine that right now I am gazing out the window, experiencing some nice green sensations from seeing the trees outside, having pleasant taste experience through munching on a chocolate bar, and feeling a dull aching sensation in my right shoulder.

What is going on in my zombie twin? He is physically identical to me, and we may as well suppose that he is embedded in an identical environment. He will certainly be identical to me *functionally*: he will be processing the same sort of information, reacting in a similar way to inputs, with his internal configurations being modified appropriately and with indistinguishable behavior resulting. He will be *psychologically* identical to me. . . . He will be perceiving the trees outside, in the functional sense, and tasting the chocolate, in the psychological sense. All of this follows logically from the fact that he is physically identical to me, by virtue of the functional analyses of psychological notions. He will even be "conscious" in the functional senses described earlier—he will be awake, able to report the contents of his internal states, able to focus attention in various places, and so on. It is just that none of this functioning will be accompanied by any real conscious experience. There will be no phenomenal feel. There is nothing it is like to be a zombie.

This sort of zombie is quite unlike the zombies found in Hollywood movies, which tend to have significant functional impairments. The sort of consciousness that Hollywood zombies most obviously lack is a psychological version: typically, they have little capacity for introspection and lack a refined ability to voluntarily control behavior. They may or may not lack phenomenal consciousness; as Block (1995) points out, it is reasonable to suppose that there is something it tastes like when they eat their victims. We can call these *psychological zombies*; I am concerned with the *phenomenal zombies*, which are physically and functionally identical, but which lack experience. (Perhaps it is not surprising that phenomenal zombies have not been popular in Hollywood, as there would be obvious problems with their depiction.)

The idea of zombies as I have described them is a strange one. For a start, it is unlikely that zombies are naturally possible. In the real world, it is likely that any replica of me would be conscious. For this reason, it is most natural to imagine unconscious creatures as physically different from conscious ones—exhibiting

impaired behavior, for example. But the question is not whether it is plausible that zombies could exist in our world, or even whether the idea of a zombie replica is a natural one; the question is whether the notion of a zombie is conceptually coherent. The mere intelligibility of the notion is enough to establish the conclusion.

Arguing for a logical possibility is not entirely straightforward. How, for example, would one argue that a mile-high unicycle is logically possible? It just seems obvious. Although no such thing exists in the real world, the description certainly appears to be coherent. If someone objects that it is not logically possible—it merely seems that way—there is little we can say, except to repeat the description and assert its obvious coherence. It seems quite clear that there is no hidden contradiction lurking in the description.

I confess that the logical possibility of zombies seems equally obvious to me. A zombie is just something physically identical to me, but which has no conscious experience—all is dark inside. While this is probably empirically impossible, it certainly seems that a coherent situation is described; I can discern no contradiction in the description. In some ways an assertion of this logical possibility comes down to a brute intuition, but no more so than with the unicycle. Almost everybody, it seems to me, is capable of conceiving of this possibility. Some may be led to deny the possibility in order to make some theory come out right, but the justification of such theories should ride on the question of possibility, rather than the other way around.

In general, a certain burden of proof lies on those who claim that a given description is logically *impossible*. If someone truly believes that a mile-high unicycle is logically impossible, she must give us some idea of where a contradiction lies, whether explicit or implicit. If she cannot point out something about the intensions of the concepts "mile-high" and "unicycle" that might lead to a contradiction, then her case will not be convincing. On the other hand, it is no more convincing to give an obviously false analysis of the notions in question—to assert, for example, that for something to qualify as a unicycle it must be shorter than the Statue of Liberty. If no reasonable analysis of the terms in question points toward a contradiction, or even makes the existence of a contradiction plausible, then there is a natural assumption in favor of logical possibility.

That being said, there are some positive things that proponents of logical possibility can do to bolster their case. They can exhibit various indirect arguments, appealing to what we know about the phenomena in question and the way we think about hypothetical cases involving these phenomena, in order to establish that the obvious logical possibility really is a logical possibility, and really is obvious. One might spin a fantasy about an ordinary person riding a unicycle, when suddenly the whole system expands a thousandfold. Or one might describe a series of unicycles, each bigger than the last. In a sense, these are all appeals to intuition, and an opponent who wishes to deny the possibility can in each case assert that our intuitions have misled us, but the very obviousness of what we are describing works in our favor, and helps shift the burden of proof further onto the other side.

For example, we can indirectly support the claim that zombies are logically possible by considering *nonstandard realizations* of my functional organization. My functional organization—that is, the pattern of causal organization embodied in the mechanisms responsible for the production of my behavior—can in principle be realized in all sorts of strange ways. To use a common example (Block 1978), the people of a large nation such as China might organize themselves so that they realize a causal organization isomorphic to that of my brain, with every person simulating the behavior of a single neuron, and with radio links corresponding to synapses. The population might control an empty shell of a robot body, equipped with sensory transducers and motor effectors.

Many people find it implausible that a set-up like this would give rise to conscious experience—that somehow a "group mind" would emerge from the overall system. I am not concerned here with whether or not conscious experience would *in fact* arise; I suspect that in fact it would. . . . All that matters here is that the idea that such a system lacks conscious experience is *coherent*. A meaningful possibility is being expressed, and it is an open question whether consciousness arises or not. We can make a similar point

by considering my silicon isomorph, who is organized like me but who has silicon chips where I have neurons. Whether such an isomorph would *in fact* be conscious is controversial, but it seems to most people that those who deny this are expressing a coherent possibility. From these cases it follows that the existence of my conscious experience is not logically entailed by the facts about my functional organization.

But given that it is conceptually coherent that the group-mind set-up or my silicon isomorph could lack conscious experience, it follows that my zombie twin is an equally coherent possibility. For it is clear that there is no more of a *conceptual* entailment from biochemistry to consciousness than there is from silicon or from a group of homunculi. If the silicon isomorph without conscious experience is conceivable, we need only substitute neurons for silicon in the conception while leaving functional organization constant, and we have my zombie twin. Nothing in this substitution could force experience into the conception; these implementational differences are simply not the sort of thing that could be conceptually relevant to experience. So consciousness fails to logically supervene on the physical.

The argument for zombies can be made without an appeal to these non-standard realizations, but these have a heuristic value in eliminating a source of conceptual confusion. To some people, intuitions about the logical possibility of an unconscious physical replica seem less than clear at first, perhaps because the familiar co-occurrence of biochemistry and consciousness can lead one to suppose a conceptual connection. Considerations of the less familiar cases remove these empirical correlations from the picture, and therefore make judgments of logical possibility more straightforward. But once it is accepted that these nonconscious functional replicas are logically possible, the corresponding conclusion concerning a physical replica cannot be avoided.

Some may think that conceivability arguments are unreliable. For example, sometimes it is objected that we cannot really imagine in detail the many billions of neurons in the human brain. Of course this is true; but we do not need to imagine each of the neurons to make the case. Mere complexity among neurons could not conceptually entail consciousness; if all that neural structure is to be relevant to consciousness, it must be relevant *in virtue* of some higher-level properties that it enables. So it is enough to imagine the system at a coarse level, and to make sure that we conceive it with appropriately sophisticated mechanisms of perception, categorization, high-band-with access to information contents, reportability, and the like. No matter how sophisticated we imagine these mechanisms to be, the zombie scenario remains as coherent as ever. Perhaps an opponent might claim that all the unimagined neural detail is conceptually relevant in some way independent of its contribution to sophisticated functioning; but then she owes us an account of what that way might be, and none is available. Those implementational details simply lie at the wrong level to be conceptually relevant to consciousness.

It is also sometimes said that conceivability is an imperfect guide to possibility. The may way that conceivability and possibility can come apart is tied to the phenomenon of a posteriori necessity: for example, the hypothesis that water is not H_2O seems conceptually coherent, but water is arguably H_2O in all possible worlds. But a posteriori necessity is irrelevant to the concerns of this chapter. As we saw in the last chapter, explanatory connections are grounded in a priori entailments from physical facts to high-level facts. The relevant kind of possibility is to be evaluated using the primary intensions of the terms involved, instead of the secondary intensions that are relevant to a posteriori necessity. So even if a zombie world is conceivable only in the sense in which it is conceivable that water is not H_2O, that is enough to establish that consciousness cannot be reductively explained.

Those considerations aside, the main way in which conceivability arguments can go wrong is by subtle conceptual confusion: if we are insufficiently reflective we can overlook an incoherence in a purported possibility, by taking a conceived-of situation and *misdescribing* it. For example, one might think that one can conceive of a situation in which Fermat's last theorem is false, by imagining a situation in which leading mathematicians declare that they have found a counterexample. But given that the theorem is actually true, this situation is being misdescribed: it is really a scenario in which Fermat's last theorem is true, and in which some mathematicians make a mistake. Importantly, though, this kind of mistake always lies in the a priori domain, as it arises from the incorrect application of the primary intensions of our concepts to a conceived situation. Sufficient reflection will reveal that the concepts are being incorrectly applied, and that the claim of logical possibility is not justified.

So the only route available to an opponent here is to claim that in describing the zombie world as a zombie world, we are misapplying the concepts, and that in fact there is a conceptual contradiction lurking in the description. Perhaps if we thought about it clearly enough we would realize that by imagining a physically identical world we are thereby *automatically* imagining a world in which there is conscious experience. But then the burden is on the opponent to give us some idea of where the contradiction might lie in the apparently quite coherent description. If no internal incoherence can be revealed, then there is a very strong case that the zombie world is logically possible.

As before, I can detect no internal incoherence; I have a clear picture of what I am conceiving when I conceive of a zombie. Still, some people find conceivability arguments difficult to adjudicate, particularly where strange ideas such as this one are concerned. It is therefore fortunate that every point made using zombies can also be made in other ways, for example by considering epistemology and analysis. To many, arguments of the latter sort (such as arguments 3–5 below) are more straightforward and therefore make a stronger foundation in the argument against logical supervenience. But zombies at least provide a vivid illustration of important issues in the vicinity. . . .

Argument 3: From Epistemic Asymmetry

As we saw earlier, consciousness is a surprising feature of the universe. Our grounds for belief in consciousness derive solely from our own experience of it. Even if we knew every last detail about the physics of the universe—the configuration, causation, and evolution among all the fields and particles in the spatiotemporal manifold—*that* information would not lead us to postulate the existence of conscious experience. My knowledge of consciousness, in the first instance, comes from my own case, not from any external observation. It is my first-person experience of consciousness that forces the problem on me.

From all the low-level facts about physical configurations and causation, we can in principle derive all sorts of high-level facts about macroscopic systems, their organization, and the causation among. One could determine all the facts about biological function, and about human behavior and the brain mechanisms by which it is caused. But nothing in this vast causal story would lead one who had not experienced it directly to believe that there should be any *consciousness*. The very idea would be unreasonable; almost mystical, perhaps.

It is true that the physical facts about the world might provide some indirect evidence for the existence of consciousness. For example, from these facts one could ascertain that there were a lot of organisms that *claimed* to be conscious, and said they had mysterious subjective experiences. Still, this evidence would be quite inconclusive, and it might be most natural to draw an eliminativist conclusion—that there was in fact no *experience* present in these creatures, just a lot of talk.

Eliminativism about conscious experience is an unreasonable position *only* because of our own acquaintance with it. If it were not for this direct knowledge, consciousness could go the way of the vital spirit. To put it another way, there is an *epistemic asymmetry* in our knowledge of consciousness that is not present in our knowledge of other phenomena. Our knowledge that conscious experience exists derives primarily from our own case, with external evidence playing at best a secondary role.

The point can also be made pointing to the existence of a problem of other minds. Even when we know everything physical about the other creatures we do not *know* for certain that they are conscious, or what their experiences are (although we may gave good reason to believe that they are). It is striking that there is no problem of "other lives," or of "other economies," or of "other heights." There is no epistemic asymmetry in those cases, precisely because those phenomena are logically supervenient on the physical.

The epistemic asymmetry in knowledge of consciousness makes it clear that consciousness cannot logically supervene. If it were logically supervenient, there would be no such epistemic asymmetry; a logically supervenient property can be detected straightforwardly on the basis of external evidence, and there is no special role for the first-person case. To be sure, there are some supervenient properties—memory, perhaps—that are more easily detected in the first-person case. But this is just a matter of how hard one has to work. The presence of memory is just as accessible from the third person, in principle, as from the first person. The epistemic asymmetry associated with consciousness is much more fundamental, and it tells us that no collection of facts about complex causation in physical systems adds up to a fact about consciousness. . . .

Argument 5: From the Absence of Analysis

If proponents of reductive explanation are to have any hope of defeating the arguments above, they will have to give us some idea of how the existence of consciousness *might* be entailed by physical facts. While it is not fair to expect all the details, one at least needs an account of how such an entailment might *possibly* go. But any attempt to demonstrate such an entailment is doomed to failure. For consciousness to be entailed by a set of physical facts, one would need some kind of analysis of the notion of consciousness—the kind of analysis whose satisfaction physical facts could imply—and there is no such analysis to be had.

The only analysis of consciousness that seems even remotely tenable for these purposes is a functional analysis. Upon such an analysis, it would be seen that all there is to the notion of something's being conscious is that it should play a certain functional role. For example, one might say that all there is to a state's being conscious is that it be verbally reportable, or that it be the result of certain kinds of perceptual discrimination, or that it make information available to later processes in a certain way, or whatever. But on the face of it, these fail miserably as analyses. They simply miss what it means to be a conscious experience. Although conscious states may play various causal roles, they are not *defined* by the causal roles. Rather, what makes them conscious is that they have a certain phenomenal feel, and this feel is not something that can be functionally defined away.

To see how unsatisfactory these analyses are, note how they trivialize the problem of explaining consciousness. Suddenly, all we have to do to explain consciousness is explain our ability to make certain verbal reports, or to perform certain sorts of discrimination, or to manifest some other capacity. But on the face of it, it is entirely conceivable that one could explain all these things without explaining a thing about consciousness itself; that is, without explaining the *experience* that accompanies the report or the discrimination. To analyze consciousness in terms of some functional notion is either to change the subject or to define away the problem. One might as well define "world peace" as "a ham sandwich." Achieving world peace becomes much easier, but it is a hollow achievement.

Functional analyses of consciousness can also be argued against on more specific grounds. For example, any functionally analyzed concept will have a degree of semantic indeterminacy. Does a mouse have beliefs? Do bacteria learn? Is a computer virus alive? The best answer to these questions is usually in a sense yes, in a sense no. It all depends on how we draw the boundaries in the concepts, and in any high-level functional concepts the boundaries will be vague. But compare: Does a mouse have conscious experience? Does a virus? These are not matters for stipulation. Either there is something that it is like to be a mouse or there is not, and it is not up to us to define the mouse's experiences into or out of existence. To be sure, there is probably a continuum of conscious experience from the very faint to the very rich; but if something has conscious experience, however faint, we cannot stipulate it away. This determinacy could not be derived from any functional analysis of the concepts in the vicinity of consciousness, as the functional concepts in the vicinity are all somewhat vague. If so, it follows that the notion of consciousness cannot be functionally analyzed.

Another objection is that the functional analysis collapses the important distinction . . . between the notions of awareness and consciousness. Presumably if consciousness is to be functionally analyzed, it will be analyzed roughly as we analyzed awareness then: in terms of a certain accessibility of information in later processing and in the control of behavior. Awareness is a perfectly good concept, but it is quite distinct from the concept of conscious experience. The functionalist treatment collapses the two notions of consciousness and awareness into one, and therefore does not do justice to our conceptual system.

The alternatives to functional analysis look even worse. It is most unclear that there could be any other kind of analysis appropriate for reductive explanation. The only alternative might be a structural analysis—perhaps consciousness could be analyzed as some sort of biochemical structure—but that analysis would be even more clearly inadequate. Whether or not consciousness *is* a biochemical structure, that is not what "consciousness" *means*. To analyze consciousness that way again trivializes the explanatory problem by changing the subject. It seems that the concept of consciousness is irreducible, being characterizable only in terms of concepts that themselves involve consciousness.

Note that this is quite unlike the sort of irreducibility that is sometimes supposed to hold for high-level concepts in general. We have seen that many high-level notions have no crisp definitions, and no manageable analyses in terms of necessary and sufficient conditions. Nevertheless, as we saw in the last chapter, these concepts at least have rough-and-ready analyses that get us into the ballpark, although they will inevitably fail to do justice to the details. Most importantly, it is easy to see that properties such as life, learning, and so on can be analyzed as functional properties, even if spelling out the details of just *which* functional property is a difficult matter. Even though these properties lack crisp functional definitions, they are nevertheless quite compatible with entailment by the physical facts.

The problems with consciousness are in a different league. Here, the purported analyses do not even get into the ballpark. In a much starker way, they completely fail to characterize what needs to be explained. There is no temptation to even *try* to add epicycles to a purported functional analysis of consciousness in order to make it satisfactory, as there is with similar analyses of life and of learning. Consciousness is simply not to be characterized as a functional property in the first place. The same goes for analyses of consciousness as a structural property, or in other reductive terms. There is therefore no way for an entailment from physical facts to consciousness to get off the ground.

2. THE FAILURE OF REDUCTIVE EXPLANATION

The failure of consciousness to logically supervene on the physical tells us that no reductive explanation of consciousness can succeed. Given any account of the physical processes purported to underlie consciousness, there will always be a further question: Why are these processes accompanied by conscious experience? For most other phenomena, such a question is easily answered: the physical facts about those processes *entail* the existence of the phenomena. For a phenomenon such as life, for example, the physical facts imply that certain functions will be performed, and the performance of those functions is all we need to explain in order to explain life. But no such answer will suffice for consciousness.

Physical explanation is well suited to the explanation of *structure* and of *function*. Structural properties and functional properties can be straightforwardly entailed by a low-level physical story, and so are clearly apt for reductive explanation. And almost all the high-level phenomena that we need to explain ultimately come down to structure or function: think of the explanation of waterfalls, planets, digestion, reproduction, language. But the explanation of consciousness is not just a matter of explaining structure and function. Once we have explained all the physical structure in the vicinity of the brain, and we have explained how all the various brain functions are performed, there is a further sort of explanandum: consciousness itself. Why should all this structure and function give rise to experience? The story about the physical processes does not say.

We can put this in terms of the thought experiments given earlier. Any story about physical processes applies equally to me and to my zombie twin. It follows that nothing in that story says why, in my case, consciousness arises. Similarly, any story about physical processes applies equally to my inverted twin, who sees blue where I see red: it follows that nothing in that story says why my experience is of one variety rather than another. The very fact that it is logically possible that the physical facts could be the same while the facts about consciousness are different shows us that as Levine (1983) has put it, there is an *explanatory gap* between the physical level and conscious experience.

If this is right, the fact that consciousness accompanies a given physical process is a *further fact*, not explainable simply by telling the story about the physical facts. In a sense, the accompaniment must be taken as brute. We might try to systematize and explain these brute facts in terms of some simple underlying pattern, but there will always remain an element here that is logically independent of the physical story. Perhaps we might get some kind of explanation by combining the underlying physical facts with certain further *bridging* principles that link the physical facts with consciousness, but this explanation will not be a reductive one. The very need for explicit bridging principles shows us that consciousness is not being explained reductively, but is being explained on its own terms.

Of course nothing I have said implies that physical facts are *irrelevant* to the explanation of consciousness. We can still expect physical accounts to play a significant role in a theory of consciousness, giving information about the physical *basis* of consciousness, for example, and perhaps yielding a detailed correspondence between various aspects of physical processing and aspects of conscious experience. Such accounts may be especially useful in helping to understand the *structure* of consciousness: the patterns of similarity and difference between experiences, the geometric structure of phenomenal fields, and so on. . . . But a physical account, alone, is not *enough*.

At this point, a number of objections naturally arise.

Objection 1: Are We Setting the Standards Too High?

Some might argue that explanation of *any* high-level phenomena will postulate "bridge laws" in addition to a low-level account, and that it is only with the aid of these bridges that the details of the high-level phenomena are derived. However, as the discussion in the last chapter suggests (and as is carefully argued by Horgan [1978]), in such cases the bridge laws are not further facts about the world. Rather, the connecting principles themselves are logically supervenient on the low-level facts. The extreme case of such a bridging principle is a supervenience conditional, which we have seen is usually a conceptual truth. Other more "localized" bridging principles, such as the link between molecular motion and heat, can at least be derived from the physical facts. For consciousness, by contrast, such bridging principles must be taken as primitive.

It is interesting to see how a typical high-level property—such as life, say—evades the arguments put forward in the case of consciousness. First, it is straightforwardly inconceivable that there could be a physical replica of a living creature that was not itself alive. Perhaps a problem might arise due to context-dependent properties (would a replica that forms randomly in a swamp be alive, or be human?), but fixing environmental facts eliminates even that possibility. Second, there is no "inverted life" possibility analogous to the inverted spectrum. Third, when one knows all the physical facts about an organism (and possibly about its environment), one has enough material to know all the biological facts. Fourth, there is no epistemic asymmetry with life; facts about life in others are as accessible, in principle, as facts about life in ourselves. Fifth, the concept of life is plausibly analyzable in functional terms: to be alive is roughly to possess certain capacities to adapt, reproduce, and metabolize. As a general point, most high-level phenomena come down to matters of physical structure and function, and we have good reason to believe that structural and functional properties are logically supervenient on the physical.

Objection 2: Couldn't a Vitalist Have Said the Same Thing about Life?

All this notwithstanding, a common reaction to the sort of argument I have given is to reply that a vitalist about life might have said the same things. For example, a vitalist might have claimed that it is logically possible that a physical replica of me might not be *alive*, in order to establish that life cannot be reductively explained. And a vitalist might have argued that life is a further fact, not explained by any account of the physical facts. But the vitalist would have been *wrong*. By analogy, might not the opponent of reductive explanation for consciousness also be wrong?

I think this reaction misplaces the source of vitalist objections. Vitalism was mostly driven by doubt about whether physical mechanisms could perform all the complex *functions* associated with life: adaptive behavior, reproduction, and the like. At the time, very little was known about the enormous sophistication of biochemical mechanisms, so this sort of doubt was quite natural. But implicit in these very doubts is the conceptual point that when it comes to explaining life, it is the performance of various functions that needs to be explained. Indeed, it is notable that as physical explanation of the relevant functions gradually appeared, vitalist doubts mostly melted away. With consciousness, by contrast, the problem persists even when the various functions are explained.

Presented with a full physical account showing how physical processes perform the relevant functions, a reasonable vitalist would concede that life has been explained. There is not even *conceptual* room for the performance of these functions without life. Perhaps some ultrastrong vitalist would deny even this, claiming that something is left out by a functional account of life—the vital spirit, perhaps. But the obvious rejoinder is that unlike experience, the vital spirit is not something we have independent reason to believe in. Insofar as there was ever any reason to believe in it, it was as an explanatory construct—"We *must* have such a thing in order to be able to do such amazing stuff." But as an explanatory construct, the vital spirit can be eliminated when we find a better explanation of how the functions are performed. Conscious experience, by contrast, forces itself on one as an explanandum and cannot be eliminated so easily.

One reason a vitalist might think something is left out of a functional explanation of life is precisely that nothing in a physical account explains why there is something it is like to be alive. Perhaps some element of belief in a "vital spirit" was tied to the phenomena of one's inner life. Many have perceived a link between the concepts of life and experience, and even today it seems reasonable to say that one of the things that needs to be explained about life is the fact that many living creatures are conscious. But the existence of *this* sort of vitalist doubt is of no comfort to the proponent of reductive explanation of consciousness, as it is a doubt that has never been overturned.

Objection 3: Is Conceivability a Guide to Possibility?

Philosophers are often suspicious of arguments that give a key role to conceivability, frequently responding that conceivability does not suffice for possibility. This is a subtle issue that I have discussed earlier and will discuss again: but here, the subtleties are not especially relevant. When it comes to matters of *explanation*, it is clear that conceivability is central. If on reflection we find it conceivable that all these physical processes could take place in the absence of consciousness, then no reductive explanation of consciousness will be satisfactory: the further question of why *we* exist and not zombies will always arise. Even if conceivability is tied to the limits of human capacity, explanation is tied to the limits of human capacity in a similar way.

Another way to put the point is to note that reductive explanation of a phenomenon in terms of the physical requires an *a priori* implication from the physical facts to the relevant high-level facts (logical supervenience according to primary intension, as I put it earlier). If such a connection does not hold, then we will always be able to raise the further question of why the physical processes give rise to consciousness. We have seen that in almost all domains, the right sort of connection holds, making reductive

explanation possible; but it does not seem to hold for conscious experience. One can question whether *ontological* views such as materialism turn on these *a priori* links—I discuss that matter in the next chapter—but when it comes to reductive explanation, such links are crucial.

Objection 4: Isn't This a Collection of Circular Intuitions?

It might be further objected that the arguments I have given consist, at bottom, in a collection of intuitions. There is certainly a sense in which all these arguments are based on intuition, but I have tried to make clear just how natural and plain these intuitions are, and how forced it is to deny them. The main intuition at work is that *there is something to be explained*—some phenomenon associated with first-person experience that presents a problem not presented by observation of cognition form the third-person point of view. Given the premise that some explanandum is forced on us by first-person experience that is not forced on us by third-person observation, most of the arguments above fall out. It follows immediately, for example, that what needs to be explained cannot be analyzed as the playing of some functional role, for the latter phenomenon is revealed to us by third-person observation and is much more straightforward.

The "intuition" at work here is the very raison d'être of the problem of consciousness. The only consistent way to get around the intuitions is to deny the problem and the phenomenon altogether. One can always, at least when speaking "philosophically," deny the intuitions altogether, and deny that there is anything (apart from the performance of various functions) that needs explaining. But if one takes consciousness seriously, the conclusions for which I am arguing must follow.

Objection 5: Doesn't All Explanation Have to Stop Somewhere?

A final objection is that no explanation gives one something for nothing: all explanation has to stop somewhere. In explaining the motion of the planets, for example, one takes the laws of gravity and the existence of mass for granted. Perhaps we should simply take something for granted in this case, too? I am sympathetic with this point; I think we do have to take something for granted in explaining consciousness. But in doing so we inevitably move beyond a *reductive* explanation. Indeed, this sort of analogy lends support to the nonreductive position I am advocating. We take the laws of physics for granted because they are *fundamental* laws. If we take a link between physical processes and conscious experience for granted, this suggests that the link should be taken as fundamental in the same way. . . .

5. THE APPEAL TO NEW PHYSICS

Sometimes it is held that the key to the explanation of consciousness may lie in a new sort of physical theory. Perhaps, in arguing that consciousness is not entailed by the physics of our world, we have been tacitly assuming that the physics of our world is something like physics as we understand it today, consisting in an arrangement of particles and fields in the spatiotemporal manifold, undergoing complex processes of causation and evolution. An opponent might agree that nothing in *this* sort of physics entails the existence of consciousness, but argue that there might be a new kind of physical theory from which consciousness falls out as a consequence.

It is not easy to evaluate this claim in the absence of any detailed proposal. One would at least like to see an example of how such a new physics might *possibly* go. Such an example need not be plausible in the light of current theories, but there would have to be a sense in which it would recognizably be physics. The crucial question is: How could a theory that is recognizably a physical theory entail the existence of consciousness? If such a theory consists in a description of the structure and dynamics of fields, waves, particles, and the like, then all the usual problems will apply. And it is unclear that *any* sort of physical theory could be different enough from this to avoid the problems.

The trouble is that the basic elements of physical theories seem always to come down to two things: the structure and dynamics and physical processes. Different theories invoke different sorts of structure. Newtonian physics invokes a Euclidean space-time; relativity theory invokes a non-Euclidean differential manifold; quantum theory invokes a Hilbert space for wave functions. And different theories invoke different kinds of dynamics within those structures: Newton's laws, the principles of relativity, the wave equations of quantum mechanics. But from structure and dynamics, we can only get more structure and dynamics. This allows the possibility of satisfying explanations of all sorts of high-level structural and functional properties, but conscious experience will remain untouched. No set of facts about physical structure and dynamics can add up to a fact about phenomenology.

Of course, there is a sense in which the physics of the universe *must* entail the existence of consciousness, if one *defines* physics as the fundamental science from whose facts and laws everything else follows. This construal of physics, however, trivializes the question involved. If one allows physics to include theories developed specifically to deal with the phenomenon of consciousness, unmotivated by more basic considerations, then we may get an "explanation" of consciousness, but it will certainly not be a reductive one. For our purposes, it is best to take physics to be the fundamental science developed to explain observations of the external world. If this kind of physics entailed the facts about consciousness, without invoking consciousness itself in a crucial role, then consciousness would truly be reductively explained. For the reasons I have given, however, there is good reason to believe that no such reductive explanation is possible.

Almost all existing proposals concerning the use of physics to explain consciousness focus on the most puzzling part of physics, namely quantum mechanics. This is understandable: for physics to explain consciousness would take something extraordinary, and quantum mechanics is by far the most extraordinary part of contemporary physics. But in the end it does not seem to be extraordinary enough.

For example, Penrose (1994) suggests that the key to understanding consciousness may lie in a theory that reconciles quantum theory with the theory of general relativity. He suggests that gravitational effects not yet understood may be responsible for the collapse of the quantum wave function, leading to a nonalgorithmic element in the laws of nature. Drawing on the ideas of Hameroff (1994), he suggests that human cognition may depend on quantum collapse in microtubules, which are protein structures found in the skeleton of a neuron. Indeed, Penrose and Hameroff suggest that quantum collapse in microtubules may be the physical basis of conscious experience.

These ideas are extremely speculative, but they could at least *conceivably* help to explain certain elements of human cognitive functioning. Penrose suggests that the nonalgorithmic element in collapse could explain certain aspects of our mathematical insight, which he believes goes beyond the capacity of any algorithmic system. Hameroff suggests that the collapse of a superposed wave function might help explain certain aspects of human decision making. But nothing here seems to help with the explanation of conscious experience. Why should quantum processes in microtubules give rise to consciousness? The question here is just as hard as the corresponding question about classical processes in a classical brain. When it comes to the problem of experience, nonalgorithmic and algorithmic processes are in the same boat.

Some have suggested that the *nonlocality* of quantum mechanics, as suggested by recent experiments bearing on the Einstein-Podolsky-Rosen paradox and Bell's theorem, might be the key to a theory of consciousness. But even if physics is nonlocal, it is hard to see how this should help in the explanation of consciousness. Even given a nonlocal physical process, it remains logically possible that the process could take place in the absence of consciousness. The explanatory gap is as wide as ever.

The most frequently noted connection between consciousness and quantum mechanics lies in the fact that on some interpretations of the latter, measurement by a conscious observer is required to bring about the collapse of the wave function. On this sort of interpretation, consciousness plays a central role in the dynamics of the physical theory. These interpretations are highly controversial, but in any case it is notable that they do nothing to provide an *explanation* of consciousness. Rather, they simply *assume* the existence of consciousness, and use it to help explain certain physical phenomena. Theories of consciousness that exploit this relationship are occasionally put forward (e.g., Hodgson 1988; Stapp 1993), but they are certainly not reductive theories.

One cannot rule out the possibility that fundamental physical theories such as quantum mechanics will play a key role in a theory of consciousness. For example, perhaps consciousness will turn out to be associated with certain fundamental physical properties, or with certain configurations of those properties, or perhaps there will be a more subtle link. But all the same, there is little hope that this sort of theory will provide a wholly physical *explanation* of consciousness. When it comes to reductive explanation, physics-based theories are no better off than neurobiological and cognitive theories.

6. EVOLUTIONARY EXPLANATION

Even those who take consciousness seriously are often drawn to the idea of an evolutionary explanation of consciousness. After all, consciousness is such a ubiquitous and central feature that it seems that it must have arisen during the evolutionary process for a *reason*. In particular, it is natural to suppose that it arose because there is some function that it serves that could not be achieved without it. If we could get a clear enough idea of the relevant function, then we would have some idea of why consciousness exists.

Unfortunately, this idea overestimates what an evolutionary explanation can provide us. The process of natural selection cannot distinguish between me and my zombie twin. Evolution selects properties according to their functional role, and my zombie twin performs all the functions that I perform just as well as I do; in particular he leaves around just as many copies of his genes. It follows that evolution alone cannot explain why conscious creatures rather than zombies evolved.

Some may be tempted to respond, "But a zombie *couldn't* do all the things that I can." But my zombie twin is by definition physically identical to me over its history, so it certainly produces indistinguishable behavior. Anyone wishing to question zombie capacity must therefore find something wrong with the arguments at the start of this chapter, rather than raising the question here.

To see the point in a different way, note that the real problem with consciousness is to explain the principles in virtue of which consciousness arises from physical systems. Presumably these principles—whether they are conceptual truths, metaphysical necessities, or natural laws—are constant over space-time: if a physical replica of me had popped into existence a million years ago, it would have been just as conscious as I am. The connecting principles themselves are therefore independent of the evolutionary process. While evolution can be very useful in explaining why particular physical systems have evolved, it is irrelevant to the explanation of the bridging principles in virtue of which some of the systems are conscious.

7. WHITHER REDUCTIVE EXPLANATION?

It is not uncommon for people to agree with critiques of specific reductive accounts, but to qualify this agreement: "Of course *that* doesn't explain consciousness, but if we just wait a while, an explanation will come along." I hope the discussion here has made it clear that the problems with this kind of explanation of consciousness are more fundamental than that. The problems with the models and theories presented here do not lie in the *details*; at least, we have not needed to consider the details in order to see what is wrong with them. The problem lies in the overall explanatory strategy. These models and theories are simply not the *sort* of thing that could explain consciousness.

It is inevitable that increasingly sophisticated reductive "explanations" of consciousness will be put forward, but these will only produce increasingly sophisticated explanations of cognitive functions.

Even such "revolutionary" developments as the invocation of connectionist networks, nonlinear dynamics, artificial life, and quantum mechanics will provide only more powerful functional explanations. This may make for some very interesting cognitive science, but the mystery of consciousness will not be removed.

Any account given in purely physical terms will suffer from the same problem. It will ultimately be given in terms of the structural and dynamical properties of physical processes, and no matter how sophisticated such an account is, it will yield only more structure and dynamics. While this is enough to handle most natural phenomena, the problem of consciousness goes beyond any problem about the explanation of structure and function, so a new sort of explanation is needed.

It might be supposed that there could eventually be a reductive explanatory technique that explained something other than structure and function, but it is very hard to see how this could be possible, given that the laws of physics are ultimately cast in terms of structure and dynamics. The existence of consciousness will always be a further fact relative to structural and dynamic facts, and so will always be unexplained by a physical account.

For an explanation of consciousness, then, we must look elsewhere. We certainly need not give up on explanation; we need only give up on *reductive* explanation. The possibility of explaining consciousness nonreductively remains open. This would be a very different sort of explanation, requiring some radical changes in the way we think about the structure of the world.   But if we make these changes, the beginnings of a theory of consciousness may become visible in the distance.

REFERENCES

Block, N. 1978. "Troubles with functionalism" in N. Block, ed. *Readings in the Philosophy of Psychology*. Cambridge, MA: Harvard University Press.

Block, N., 1995. "On a confusion about a function of consciousness." *Behavioral & Brain Sciences* 18: 227–47.

Hameroff, S. R., 1994. "Quantum coherence in microtubules." *Journal of Consciousness Studies* 1: 91–118.

Hodgson, D. 1988. *The Mind Matters: Consciousness & Choices in a Quantum World*. Oxford: Oxford University Press.

Horgan, T. 1978. "Supervenient Bridge Laws." *Philosophy of Science* 45: 227–49.

Levine, J. 1983. "Materialism and Qualia: The Explanatory Gap." *Pacific Philosophical Quarterly* 64: 354–61.

Penrose, R. 1994. *Shadows of the Mind*. Oxford: Oxford University Press.

FOR FURTHER REFLECTION

1. Discuss Chalmers's three arguments against reductive materialism. Does he defeat the thesis of a supervenience relationship between mental and physical states?
2. Explain Chalmers's view on functional analysis of consciousness.

JOHN SEARLE

MINDS, BRANS, AND COMPUTERS

John Searle is professor of philosophy at the University of California, Berkeley, and the author of several works in the philosophy of language and the philosophy of mind, including *Intentionality* (1983) and *The Rediscovery of the Mind* (1992). In this essay, Searle argues that although weak AI (artificial intelligence), which states that the mind functions somewhat like a computer, might be correct, strong AI, which states that the appropriately programmed computer *is* mind and has intentions, is false.

What psychological and philosophical significance should we attach to recent efforts at computer simulations of human cognitive capacities? In answering this question, I find it useful to distinguish what I will call "strong" AI from "weak" or "cautious" AI (artificial intelligence). According to weak AI, the principal value of the computer in the study of the mind is that it gives us a very powerful tool. For example, it enables us to formulate and test hypotheses in a more rigorous and precise fashion. But according to strong AI, the computer is not merely a tool in the study of the mind; rather, the appropriately programmed computer really *is* a mind, in the sense that computers given the right programs can be literally said to *understand* and have other cognitive states. In strong AI, because the programmed computer has cognitive states, the programs are not mere tools that enable us to test psychological explanations; rather, the programs are themselves the explanations.

I have no objection to the claims of weak AI, at least as far as this article is concerned. My discussion here will be directed at the claims I have defined as those of strong AI, specifically the claim that the appropriately programmed computer literally has cognitive states and that the programs thereby explain human cognition. When I hereafter refer to AI, I have in mind the strong version, as expressed by these two claims.

I will consider the work of Roger Schank and his colleagues at Yale (Schank and Abelson 1977), because I am more familiar with it than I am with any other similar claims, and because it provides a very clear example of the sort of work I wish to examine. But nothing that follows depends upon the details of Schank's programs. The same arguments would apply to Winograd's SHRDLU (Winograd 1973), Weizenbaum's ELIZA (Weizenbaum 1965), and indeed any Turing machine simulation of human mental phenomena. . . .

Very briefly, and leaving out the various details, one can describe Schank's program as follows: The aim of the program is to simulate the human ability to understand stories. It is characteristic of human beings' story-understanding capacity that they can answer questions about the story even though the information that they give was never explicitly stated in the story. Thus, for example, suppose you are given the following story: "A man went into a restaurant and ordered a hamburger. When the hamburger arrived it was burned to a crisp, and the man stormed out of the restaurant angrily, without paying for the hamburger or leaving a tip." Now, if you are asked "Did the man eat the hamburger?" you will presumably answer, "No, he did not." Similarly, if you are given the following story: "A man went into a restaurant and ordered a hamburger; when the hamburger came he was very pleased with it; and as he left the restaurant he gave the waitress a large tip before paying his bill," and you are asked the question, "Did the man eat the hamburger?" you will presumably answer, "Yes, he ate the hamburger." Now Schank's machines can similarly answer questions about restaurants in this fashion. To do this, they have a "representation" of the sort of information that human beings have about restaurants, which enables them to answer such questions as those above, given these sorts of stories. When the machine is given the story and then asked the question, the machine will print out answers of the sort that we would expect human beings to give if told similar stories. Partisans of strong AI claim that in this question and answer sequence the machine is not only simulating a human ability but also (1) that the machine can literally be said to *understand* the story and provide the answers to questions, and (2) that what the machine and its programs do *explains* the human ability to understand the story and answer questions about it.

Both claims seem to me to be totally unsupported by Schank's work, as I will attempt to show in what follows. I am not, of course, saying that Schank himself is committed to these claims. One way to test any theory of the mind is to ask oneself what it would be like if my mind actually worked on the principles that the theory says all minds work on. Let us apply this test to the Schank program with the following thought experiment. Suppose that I'm locked in a room and given a large batch of Chinese writing. Suppose furthermore (as is indeed the case) that I know no Chinese, either written or spoken, and that I'm not even confident that I could recognize Chinese writing as Chinese writing distinct from, say, Japanese writing or meaningless squiggles. To me, Chinese writing is just so many meaningless squiggles. Now suppose further that after this first batch of Chinese writing I am given a second batch of Chinese script together with a set of rules for correlating the second batch with the first batch. The rules are in English, and I understand these rules as well as any other native speaker of English. They enable me to correlate one set of formal symbols with another set of formal symbols, and all that "formal" means here is that I can identify the symbols entirely by their shapes. Now suppose also that I am given a third batch of Chinese symbols together with some instructions, again in English, that enable me to correlate elements of this third batch with the first two batches, and these rules instruct me how to give back certain Chinese symbols with certain sorts of shapes in response to certain sorts of shapes given me in the third batch. Unknown to me, the people who are giving me all of these symbols call the first batch a "script," they call the second batch a "story," and they call the third batch "questions." Furthermore, they call the symbols I give them back in response to the third batch "answers to the questions," and the set of rules in English that they gave me, they call the "program." Now just to complicate the story a little, imagine that these people also give me stories in English, which I understand, and they then ask me questions in English about these stories, and I give them back answers in English. Suppose also that after a while, I get so good at following the instructions for manipulating the Chinese symbols and the programmers get so good at writing the programs that from the external point of view—that is, from the point of view of somebody outside the room in which I am locked—my answers to the questions are absolutely indistinguishable from those of native Chinese speakers. Nobody just looking at my answers can tell that I don't speak a word of Chinese. Let us also suppose that my answers to the English questions are, as they no doubt would be, indistinguishable from those of other native English speakers, for the simple reason that I am a native English speaker. From the external point of view—from the point of view of someone reading my "answers"—the answers to the Chinese questions and English questions are equally good. But in the Chinese case, unlike the English case, I produce the answers by manipulating uninterpreted formal symbols. As far as the Chinese is concerned, I simply behave like a computer; I perform computational operations on formally specified elements. For the purposes of the Chinese, I am simply an instantiation of the computer program.

Now the claims made by strong AI are that the programmed computer understands the stories and that the program in some sense explains human understanding. But we are now in a position to examine these claims in light of our thought experiment.

1. As regards the first claim, it seems to me quite obvious in the example that I do not understand a word of the Chinese stories. I have in-puts and outputs that are indistinguishable from those of the native Chinese speaker, and I can have any formal program you like, but I still understand nothing. For the same reasons, Schank's computer understands nothing of any stories, whether in Chinese, English, or whatever, since in the Chinese case the computer is me, and in cases where the computer is not me, the computer has nothing more than I have in the case where I understand nothing.

2. As regards the second claim, that the program explains human understanding, we can see that the computer and its program do not provide sufficient conditions of understanding since the computer and the program are functioning, and there is no understanding. But does it even provide a necessary condition or a significant contribution to understanding? One of the claims made by the supporters of strong AI is that when I understand a story in English, what I am doing is exactly the same—or perhaps more of the same—as what I was doing in manipulating the Chinese symbols. It is simply more formal symbol manipulation that distinguishes the case in English, where I do understand, from the case in Chinese, where I don't. I have not demonstrated that this claim is false, but it would certainly appear an incredible claim in the example. Such plausibility as the claim has derives from the supposition that we can construct a program that will have the same inputs and outputs as native speakers, and in addition we assume that speakers have some level of description where they are also instantiations of a program. On the basis of these two assumptions we assume that even if Schank's program isn't the whole story about understanding, it may be part of the story. Well, I suppose that is an empirical possibility, but not the slightest reason has so far been given to believe that it is true, since what is suggested—though certainly not demonstrated—by the example is that the computer program is simply irrelevant to my understanding of the story. In the Chinese case I have everything that artificial intelligence can put into me by way of a program, and I understand nothing; in the English case I understand everything, and there is so far no reason at all to suppose that my understanding has anything to do with computer programs, that is, with computational operations on purely formally specified elements. As long as the program is defined in terms of computational operations on purely formally defined elements, what the example suggests is that these by themselves have no interesting connection with understanding. They are certainly not sufficient conditions, and not the slightest reason has been given to suppose that they are necessary conditions or even that they make a significant contribution to understanding. Notice that the force of the argument is not simply that different machines can have the same input and output while operating on different formal principles—that is not the point at all. Rather, whatever purely formal principles you put into the computer, they will not be suf-

ficient for understanding, since a human will be able to follow the formal principles without understanding anything. No reason whatever has been offered to suppose that such principles are necessary or even contributory, since no reason has been given to suppose that when I understand English I am operating with any formal program at all.

Well, then, what is it that I have in the case of the English sentences that I do not have in the case of the Chinese sentences? The obvious answer is that I know what the former mean, while I haven't the faintest idea what the latter mean. But in what does this consist and why couldn't we give it to a machine, whatever it is? . . .

I have had the occasions to present this example to several workers in artificial intelligence, and, interestingly, they do not seem to agree on what the proper reply to it is. . . .

. . . I want to block some common misunderstandings about "understanding": In many of these discussions one finds a lot of fancy footwork about the word "understanding." My critics point out that there are many different degrees of understanding; that "understanding" is not a simple two-place predicate; that there are even different kinds and levels of understanding, and often the law of excluded middle doesn't even apply in a straightforward way to statements of the form "*x* understands *y*"; that in many cases it is a matter for decision and not a simple matter of fact whether *x* understands *y,* and so on. To all of these points I want to say: of course, of course. But they have nothing to do with the points at issue. There are clear cases in which "understanding" literally applies and clear cases in which it does not apply; and these two sorts of cases are all I need for this argument. I understand stories in English; to a lesser degree I can understand stories in French; to a still lesser degree, stories in German; and in Chinese, not at all. My car and my adding machine, on the other hand, understand nothing: they are not in that line of business.[1] We often attribute "understanding" and other cognitive predicates by metaphor and analogy to cars, adding machines, and other artifacts, but nothing is proved by such attributions. We say, "The door *knows* when to open because of its photoelectric cell," "The adding machine *knows how* (*understands how,* is

able) to do addition and subtraction but not division," and "The thermostat *perceives* changes in the temperature." The reason we make these attributions is quite interesting, and it has to do with the fact that in artifacts we extend our own intentionality;[2] our tools are extensions of our purposes, and so we find it natural to make metaphorical attributions of intentionality to them; but I take it no philosophical ice is cut by such examples. The sense in which an automatic door "understands instructions" from its photoelectric cell is not at all the sense in which I understand English. If the sense in which Schank's programmed computers understand stories is supposed to be the metaphorical sense in which the door understands, and not the sense in which I understand English, the issue would not be worth discussing. But Newell and Simon (1963) write that the kind of cognition they claim for computers is exactly the same as for human beings. I like the straightforwardness of this claim, and it is the sort of claim I will be considering. I will argue that in the literal sense the programmed computer understands what the car and the adding machine understand, namely, exactly nothing. The computer's understanding is not just (like my understanding of German) partial or incomplete; it is zero. . . .

By way of concluding I want to try to state some of the general philosophical points implicit in the argument. For clarity I will try to do it in a question-and-answer fashion, and begin with that old chestnut of a question:

"Could a machine think?"

The answer is, obviously, yes. We are precisely such machines.

"Yes, but could an artificial, a man-made machine, think?"

Assuming it is possible to produce artificially a machine with a nervous system, neurons, with axons and dendrites, and all the rest of it, sufficiently like ours, again the answer to the question seems to be obviously, yes. If you can exactly duplicate the causes, you could duplicate the effects. And indeed it might be possible to produce consciousness, intentionality, and all the rest of it using some other sorts of chemical principles than those that human beings use. It is, as I said, an empirical question.

"OK, but could a digital computer think?"

If by "digital computer" we mean anything at all that has a level of description where it can correctly be described as the instantiation of a computer program, then again the answer is, of course, yes, since we are the instantiations of any number of computer programs, and we can think.

"But could something think, understand, and so on *solely* by virtue of being a computer with the right sort of program? Could instantiating a program, the right program of course, by itself be a sufficient condition of understanding?" This I think is the right question to ask, though it is usually confused with one or more of the earlier questions, and the answer to it is no.

"Why not?"

Because the formal symbol manipulations by themselves don't have any intentionality; they are quite meaningless; they aren't even *symbol* manipulations, since the symbols don't symbolize anything. In the linguistic jargon, they have only a syntax but no semantics. Such intentionality as computers appear to have is solely in the minds of those who program them and those who use them, those who send in the input and those who interpret the output.

The aim of the Chinese room example was to try to show this by showing that as soon as we put something into the system that really does have intentionality (a man), and we program him with the formal program, you can see that the formal program carries no additional intentionality. It adds nothing, for example, to a man's ability to understand Chinese.

Precisely that feature of AI that seemed so appealing—the distinction between the program and the realization—proves fatal to the claim that simulation could be duplication. The distinction between the program and its realization in the hardware seems to be parallel to the distinction between the level of mental operations and the level of brain operations. And if we could describe the level of mental operations as a formal program, then it seems we could describe what was essential about the mind without doing either introspective psychology or neurophysiology of the brain. But the equation "mind is to brain as program is to hardware" breaks down at several points, among them the following three:

First, the distinction between program and realization has the consequence that the same program could have all sorts of crazy realizations that had no form of intentionality. Weizenbaum (1976, Ch. 2), for example, shows in detail how to construct a computer using a roll of toilet paper and a pile of small stones. Similarly, the Chinese story understanding-program can be programmed into a sequence of water pipes, a set of wind machines, or a monolingual English speaker, none of which thereby acquires an understanding of Chinese. Stones, toilet paper, wind, and water pipes are the wrong kind of stuff to have intentionality in the first place—only something that has the same causal powers as brains can have intentionality—and though the English speaker has the right kind of stuff for intentionality you can easily see that he doesn't get any extra intentionality by memorizing the program, since memorizing it won't teach him Chinese.

Second, the program is purely formal, but the intentional states are not in that way formal. They are defined in terms of their content, not their form. The belief that it is raining, for example, is not defined as a certain formal shape, but as a certain mental content with conditions of satisfaction, a direction of fit (see Searle 1979), and the like. Indeed the belief as such hasn't even got a formal shape in this syntactic sense, since one and the same belief can be given an indefinite number of different syntactic expressions in different linguistic systems.

Third, as I mentioned before, mental states and events are literally a product of the operation of the brain, but the program is not in that way a product of the computer.

"Well if programs are in no way constitutive of mental processes, why have so many people believed the converse? That at least needs some explanation."

I don't really know the answer to that one. The idea that computer simulations could be the real thing ought to have seemed suspicious in the first place because the computer isn't confined to simulating mental operations, by any means. No one supposes that computer simulations of a five-alarm fire will burn the neighborhood down or that a computer simulation of a rainstorm will leave us all drenched. Why on earth would anyone suppose that a computer simulation of understanding actually understood anything? It is sometimes said that it would be frightfully hard to get computers to feel pain or fall in love, but love and pain are neither harder nor easier than cognition or anything else. For simulation, all you need is the right input and output and a program in the middle that transforms the former into the latter. That is all the computer has for anything it does. To confuse simulation with duplication is the same mistake, whether it is pain, love, cognition, fires, or rainstorms.

Still, there are several reasons why AI must have seemed—and to many people perhaps still does seem—in some way to reproduce and thereby explain mental phenomena, and I believe we will not succeed in removing these illusions until we have fully exposed the reasons that give rise to them.

First, and perhaps most important, is a confusion about the notion of "information processing": Many people in cognitive science believe that the human brain, with its mind, does something called "information processing," and analogously the computer with its program does information processing; but fires and rainstorms, on the other hand, don't do information processing at all. Thus, though the computer can simulate the formal features of any process whatever, it stands in a special relation to the mind and brain because when the computer is properly programmed, ideally with the same program as the brain, the information processing is identical in the two cases, and this information processing is really the essence of the mental. But the trouble with this argument is that it rests on an ambiguity in the notion of "information." In the sense in which people "process information" when they reflect, say, on problems in arithmetic or when they read and answer questions about stories, the programmed computer does not do "information processing." Rather, what it does is manipulate formal symbols. The fact that the programmer and the interpreter of the computer output use the symbols to stand for objects in the world is totally beyond the scope of the computer. The computer, to repeat, has a syntax but no semantics. Thus, if you type into the computer "2 plus 2 equals?" it will type out "4." But it has no idea that "4" means 4 or that it means anything at all. And the point is not that it lacks some second-order information about the interpretation of its first-order symbols, but rather that its first-order symbols don't have any interpretations

as far as the computer is concerned. All the computer has is more symbols. The introduction of the notion of "information processing" therefore produces a dilemma: Either we construe the notion of "information processing" in such a way that it implies intentionality as part of the process or we don't. If the former, then the programmed computer does not do information processing: it only manipulates formal symbols. If the latter, then, though the computer does information processing, it is only doing so in the sense in which adding machines, typewriters, stomachs, thermostats, rainstorms, and hurricanes do information processing; namely, they have a level of description at which we can describe them as taking information in at one end, transforming it, and producing information as output. But in this case it is up to outside observers to interpret the input and output as information in the ordinary sense. And no similarity is established between the computer and the brain in terms of any similarity of information processing.

Second, in much of AI there is a residual behaviorism or operationalism. Since appropriately programmed computers can have input-output patterns similar to those of human beings, we are tempted to postulate mental states in the computer similar to human mental states. But once we see that it is both conceptually and empirically possible for a system to have human capacities in some realm without having any intentionality at all, we should be able to overcome this impulse. My desk adding machine has calculating capacities, but no intentionality, and in this paper I have tried to show that a system could have input and output capabilities that duplicated those of a native Chinese speaker and still not understand Chinese, regardless of how it was programmed. The Turing test is typical of the tradition in being unashamedly behavioristic and operationalistic, and I believe that if AI workers totally repudiated behaviorism and operationalism, much of the confusion between simulation and duplication would be eliminated.

Third, this residual operationalism is joined to a residual form of dualism; indeed strong AI only makes sense given the dualistic assumption that, where the mind is concerned, the brain doesn't matter. In strong AI (and in functionalism, as well) what matters are programs, and programs are independent of their realization in machines; indeed, as far as AI is concerned, the same program could be realized by an electronic machine, a Cartesian mental substance, or a Hegelian world spirit. The single most surprising discovery that I have made in discussing these issues is that many AI workers are quite shocked by my idea that actual human mental phenomena might be dependent on actual physical-chemical properties of actual human brains. But if you think about it a minute you can see that I should not have been surprised; for unless you accept some form of dualism, the strong AI project hasn't got a chance. The project is to reproduce and explain the mental by designing programs, but unless the mind is not only conceptually but empirically independent of the brain you couldn't carry out the project, for the program is completely independent of any realization. Unless you believe that the mind is separable from the brain both conceptually and empirically—dualism in a strong form—you cannot hope to reproduce the mental by writing and running programs since programs must be independent of brains or any other particular forms of instantiation. If mental operations consist in computational operations on formal symbols, then it follows that they have no interesting connection with the brain; the only connection would be that the brain just happens to be one of the indefinitely many types of machines capable of instantiating the program. This form of dualism is not the traditional Cartesian variety that claims there are two sorts of *substances,* but it is Cartesian in the sense that it insists that what is specifically mental about the mind has no intrinsic connection with the actual properties of the brain. This underlying dualism is masked from us by the fact that AI literature contains frequent fulminations against "dualism"; what the authors seem to be unaware of is that their position presupposes a strong version of dualism.

"Could a machine think?" My own view is that *only* a machine could think, and indeed only very special kinds of machines, namely brains and machines that had the same causal powers as brains. And that is the main reason strong AI has had little to tell us about thinking, since it has nothing to tell us about machines. By its own definition, it is about programs, and programs are not machines. Whatever else intentionality is, it is a biological phenomenon, and it is as likely to be as causally dependent on the specific biochemistry of its origins as lactation, photosynthesis, or any other biological phenomena. No one would suppose that we could produce milk and sugar by running a computer simulation of the formal sequences in lactation and photosynthesis, but where the mind is concerned many people are willing to believe in such a miracle because of a deep and abiding dualism: The mind they suppose is a matter of formal processes and is independent of quite specific material causes in the way that milk and sugar are not.

In defense of this dualism the hope is often expressed that the brain is a digital computer (early computers, by the way, were often called "electronic brains"). But that is no help. Of course the brain is a digital computer. Since everything is a digital computer, brains are too. The point is that the brain's causal capacity to produce intentionality cannot consist in its instantiating a computer program, since for any program you like it is possible for something to instantiate that program and still not have any mental states. Whatever it is that the brain does to produce intentionality, it cannot consist in instantiating a program since no program, by itself, is sufficient for intentionality.

REFERENCES

Newell, A. & Simon, H. A. (1963). GPS, a program that simulates human thought. In *Computers and thought*, ed. A. Feigenbaum & V. Feldman, pp. 279–93. New York: McGraw Hill.

Schank, R. C. & Abelson, R. P. (1977). *Scripts, plans, goals, and understanding.* Hillsdale, N.J.: Lawrence Erlbaum Press.

Searle, J. R. (1979). Intentionality and the use of language. In *Meaning and use*, ed. A. Margalit. Dordrecht: Reidel.

Weizenbaum, J. (1965). Eliza—A computer program for the study of natural language communication between man and machine. *Communication of the Association for Computing machinery* 9:36–45.

———(1976). *Computer power and human reason.* San Francisco: W. H. Freeman.

Winograd, T. (1973) A procedural model of language understanding. In *Computer models of thought and language*, ed. R. Schank & K. Colby. San Francisco: W. H. Freeman.

NOTES

1. Also, "understanding" implies both the possession of mental (intentional) states and the truth (validity, success) of these states. For the purposes of this discussion we are concerned only with the possession of the states.
2. Intentionality is by definition that feature of certain mental states by which they are directed at or about objects and states of affairs in the world. Thus, beliefs, desires, and intentions are intentional states; undirected forms of anxiety and depression are not.

FOR FURTHER REFLECTION

1. Evaluate Searle's argument against strong AI. Can you see any weaknesses in it? How might a proponent of strong AI defend his or her position?
2. Suppose we could devise a robot with a television camera inside enabling it to see and a voice machine to utter meaningful sentences in response to its environmental input. Would this be an advance on the Schank program that would meet Searle's objections?
3. Here is one reply of an AI proponent discussed in Searle's original essay:

> Your whole argument presupposes that AI is only about analog and digital computers. But that just happens to be the present state of technology. Whatever these causal processes are that you say are essential for intentionality, eventually we will be able to build devices that have these causal processes, and that will be artificial intelligence. So your arguments are in no way directed at the ability of artificial intelligence to produce and explain cognition (*The Many Mansions Reply* [Berkeley]).

Evaluate this response. Does it show that artificial intelligence could eventually become conscious, have intentional states, and understand language?

B. The Problem of Personal Identity

Suppose you wake up tomorrow in a strange room. There are pictures of unfamiliar people on the light blue walls. The furniture in the room is very odd. You wonder how you got here. You remember being in the hospital, where you were dying of cancer. Your body was wasting away, and your death was thought to be a few days away. Dr. Jekyll had kindly given you an extra dose of morphine to kill the pain. That's all you can remember. You notice a calendar on the wall in front of you. The date is January 1, 2000. "This can't be," you think, "for yesterday was December 2, 1999." "Where have I been all this time?" Suddenly, you see a mirror. You reel back, for it's not your body that you spy in the glass, but a slim, pale, freckled woman's body. You have blue eyes and look years older. You feel tired and confused and frightened, and you start to cry. Soon a strange man comes into your room. "I was wondering when you'd wake up, Maria. The doctor said that I should let you sleep as long as possible, but I didn't think that you would sleep for two whole days! Anyway, the operation was a success! We were afraid the accident had ended your life. The children will be so happy to see you awake. How do you feel?"

"Can this be a bad joke?" you wonder. "Who is this strange man, and who am I?" Unbeknownst to "you," your physician, Dr. Jekyll, needed a living brain to implant in the head of Maria Ganz, mother of four children. She had been in a car accident and arrived at the hospital on a ventilator but brain dead. Your brain was in excellent shape but lacked a healthy body. Ganz's body was intact but needed a brain. Being an enterprising brain surgeon, Dr. Jekyll saw the chance of performing the first successful brain transplant. Later that day Jekyll congratulates "you" on being the first human to survive a brain transplant. "You" would have been dead had the operation not been performed. Frightened and confused, "you" wonder if this fate is not worse than death. The fact that the operation was a success is of little comfort to you, for you're not sure you're still you!

The problem of personal identity is one of the most fascinating in the history of philosophy. It is especially complicated because it involves not one but three, and possibly four, philosophical questions: (1) What is it to be a person? (2) What is identity? (3) What is personal identity? and (4) How is survival possible, given the problems of personal identity? Let's look briefly at each of these questions with reference to the readings in this part of the book.

1. *What is it to be a person?* In our first reading, John Locke says that a person is defined as "a thinking intelligent being, that has reason and reflection, and can consider itself as itself, the same thinking thing, in different times and places; which it does only by that consciousness which is inseparable from thinking, and, as it seems to me, essential to it." That is, our ability to reason, introspect, and survey our memories and intentions sets us apart from the animals as being of greater value. The view may be challenged by the materialist who says that it is really your brain (or your brain and body) that defines your personhood. Your more developed brain sets you apart from other animals. Of course, we are conscious beings. Although we do not understand how consciousness works, the physicalist believes that consciousness is a function of the brain. In the second reading, David Hume argues that the notion of a self or soul is very likely a fiction. "You" are merely a bundle of perceptions. You have consciousness of a continuing succession of experiences, but not of a continuing experiencer. This view is compatible with the physicalist view of personhood.

2. *What is identity?* This question sounds absurdly simple. Identity is the fact that each thing is itself and not another. In logic, the law of identity "A = A" formally states the definition. But we are interested not in a formal definition of mere identity but of identity *over time,* or reidentification (sometimes this is referred to as "numerical identity"). What is it to be the *same* thing over time? Suppose you go to an automobile dealership to buy a new car. You see several blue Fords parked side by side. They resemble each other so much that you cannot tell them apart. They are the same type of car and are exactly similar to each other. Suppose you pick one out at random and buy it. But your car is different from the other blue Fords even though you couldn't tell the difference between them. A year passes, and your blue Ford now has 20,000 miles on it and a few scratches. Is it the same car that you originally bought? Most of us would probably agree that it is. The changes have altered it but not destroyed its identity as the blue car that you bought and have driven for 20,000 miles.

What causes your blue Ford to be the same car over the period of one year? A common history, continuity over time. The car is linked together by a succession of spatiotemporal events from its origins in Detroit to its present place in your parking lot. This continuity distinguishes it from all the other Fords that were ever built, no matter how similar they appear. So we might conclude that *continuity over time* is the criterion of identity.

But immediately we find problems with this criterion. The Rio Grande River dries up in places in New Mexico every summer, only to reappear as a running river in early spring.

Is the Rio Grande the same river this year as it was the last? There isn't any continuity over time of water flowing over its bed. Perhaps we can escape the problem by saying that by "river" we really mean the riverbed, which must hold running water sometimes but need not always convey it. Does this solve the problem?

Consider another counterexample: The Chicago White Sox are playing the New York Yankees in Yankee Stadium in late April. The game is called in the fifth inning, with the Yankees leading 3 to 2. Shortly afterward there is a baseball strike, and all the players take to the picket lines while a new set of players come up from the minor leagues to fill their positions. The "game" is continued in Chicago in August with a whole new set of players on both sides. The White Sox win, and the game decides who wins the division. Suppose a Yankee player who has had some philosophy argues that this latter game was not part of the original game played in April. There was no *continuity* between them. He demands that a new game be played from the start since it is impossible to play the same game as was played four months ago or even four days ago. Would he have a point? Should the commissioner of baseball call for a makeup game?

The most perplexing problem with regard to the notion of "sameness" or identity over time is illustrated by the ancient tale of Theseus' ship. Suppose you have a small ship in need of some repairs. You begin (at Time t_1) to replace the old planks and material with new planks and material, until after one year (Time t_2) the ship is completely made up of different material. Do you have the same ship at t_2 as you had at t_1? If so, at what point did it (call it *Theseus 2*) become a different ship?

People disagree as to whether Theseus' ship has changed its identity. Suppose that you argue that it has not changed its identity, for it had a continuous history over time and therefore is the same ship. But now suppose that your friend takes the material discarded from the original *Theseus* and reconstructs *that* ship (call it *Theseus 3*). Which ship is now Theseus' ship? There is temporal continuity between *Theseus 1* and *Theseus 2* but material continuity between *Theseus 1* and *Theseus 3*. If it worries you that there was a time when the material of *Theseus 1* was not functioning as a ship, we could alter the example and suppose that as the planks were taken from *Theseus 1* they were transferred to another ship *Argos,* where they replaced the *Argos'* planks, ending up with a ship that contained every board and nail from the original *Theseus* (call this transformed *Argos, Theseus 4*). Which is now the original *Theseus?*

Is there something peculiar about the notion of identity?

3. *What is personal identity?* What is it to be the same person over time? Are you the same person that you were when you were one year old or even sixteen years old? We recall Locke's idea that the mental characteristics (ability to reflect or introspect) constitute personhood. Personal identity is indicated by the successive memories that the person has, the continuity over time of a set of experiences that are remembered. We may call this the *psychological states criterion of personal identity.* The main competitor of this view is the *brain criterion of personal identity,* although some philosophers hold to a *body criterion.* Let us examine each of these briefly.

The psychological states criterion holds that your memories constitute your identity over time. You are the same person you were at ten years of age because you have a continuous set of memories that contains all those you had at age ten, plus others that continued after that year. There are several problems with this view. In the first place, your memories are not continuous in our consciousness. When you sleep, you cease to have memories at all. In partial amnesia, do you cease to be who you were? Thomas Reid suggests a problem of transitivity in memories. Suppose you are a gallant officer, age twenty-five, who is a hero in a battle; and you remember getting a flogging in your childhood. Later, at sixty-five, you recall the heroic deed done at twenty-five but cannot recall the flogging. Since you cannot remember the earlier deed, are you at sixty-five the same person you were when you did remember it? Can Locke answer Reid?

What about the phenomenon of split personalities and multiple personalities, the most famous of which is Sybil, who allegedly expressed sixteen different personalities with sixteen different sets of memories? In giving a psychological-states account, would we have to say that Sybil's one body contained sixteen persons? Are there different people inside each of us, expressed by different "sides" of our personality?

Sometimes a person expresses apparent memories of events that occurred in distant times and to different "persons." Is the body of the contemporary being "possessed" by another person? If your friend suddenly starts reminiscing about the Battle of Waterloo and the beautiful Empress Josephine, has Napoleon suddenly come alive in your friend's body? This would truly be a case of reincarnation. But what if two of your friends came to you with the same "foreign" memories? And what is to prohibit complete soul flow, a different person inside you each day? How do you know that the soul that is remembering today is the same soul that remembered yesterday? You might object that this couldn't be the case, because you have the same body; but that objection won't work, because the body has nothing to do with the psychological states criterion. If you think the body is important, this might indicate that the memory criterion is inadequate on its own and depends on a physical body for continuity.

The body criterion has difficulties, one of which is the fact that the body can undergo radical changes and we would still want to call the person the same person. Almost all the cells of the human body change every seven years. But does each person become a *new* person every seven years? Or think of the story at the beginning of this section in which Dr. Jekyll transplants your brain into Maria Ganz's body. Wouldn't you still be you?

This suggests the third criterion, the brain criterion of personal identity. Our memories are contained within our brain, so we might want to say that having the same brain constitutes the same person. But this thesis has difficulties, as are brought out in the third reading, by Derek Parfit and Godfrey Vesey. It is well known that if the corpus callosum, the great band of fibers that unites the two hemispheres of the brain, is cut, two different centers of consciousness can be created. When either side of the cerebral cortex brain is destroyed, the person can live on as a conscious being. It is also possible in principle to transplant brains. Suppose that your body is destroyed and neurologists transplant each half of your brain into a different body. Dr. Jekyll transplants one-half of your brain into Maria Ganz and the other half into the head of a seven-foot-tall basketball player. "You" wake up with two personalities. Do "you" survive the operation? There seem to be just three possible answers: (1) you do not survive; (2) you survive as one of the two; and (3) you survive as two people.

All these options seem unsatisfactory. It seems absurd to say (Answer 1) that you don't survive, for there is continuity of consciousness (in the Lockean sense) as though you had gone to sleep and awakened. If you had experienced the destruction of one-half of your brain, we would still say you survived with half a brain, so why not say so now when each half is autonomous? The logic of this thesis would seem to say that double life equals death.

But Answer 2 seems arbitrary. Why say that you only survive as one of the two, and which one is it? And Answer 3, that you survive as both, is not satisfactory either, because it gives up the notion of identity. You cannot be numerically one, with two centers of consciousness and two spatiotemporal bodies. Otherwise we might say when you wreck your new Ford that the other one left in the automobile dealer's parking lot (the blue Ford that was exactly like yours) was indeed yours.

If this analysis of the personal identity problem is accurate, what sense can we make of the concept? Not much, according to Parfit. We should speak of survival of the person, not the identity of the person. Persons, as psychological states, survive and gradually merge (like Theseus' rebuilt ship) into descendant persons. Your memories and personality gradually emerged from the sixteen-year-old who gradually developed from the ten-year-old who bore your name. These were your ancestor selves. But you too will merge with future or descendant selves as you have different experiences, take on new memories, and forget old ones. Suppose every year neurologists could transplant half of your brain into another body, in which a new half would duplicate the present state of the transferred half. In this way a treelike operation would continue to spread successors of yourself as though by psychological parthenogenesis. You would survive in a sense but it would make no sense to speak of personal identity, a concept that Parfit wants to get rid of. We could also imagine a neurological game of musical hemispheres as half of your brain was merged with half of someone else's brain in a third person's head. You could continue the hemisphere-moving game every six months so that you might even get reemerged with your own other half at some future time—kind of like meeting your spouse again after other adventures. You'd have a lot to talk about through the medium of the corpus callosum!

Of course, Parfit's point is that we are going through significant changes all the time, so that as we have new experiences we take on new selfhood. Something in us survives, but with a difference. If Parfit is right about the relativity of identity in survival, then we might be less interested in our distant future than in our immediate future. After all, that person ten years down the line is less like us than is the person we'll be tomorrow. This fact might encourage a sort of general utilitarianism, for since our distant interests really are not as pressing, we could be free to work for the total greater good. On the other hand, it could have the opposite effect of making us indifferent to the future of society. This notion of proximate identity also raises the question of whether we should be concerned about our distant death fifty years down the line, which one of our successor selves will have to face. This view might also cause us to prohibit long-term prison sentences for criminal actions, for why punish a descendant for what one of his or her ancestors did? Finally, it could be used to argue against exorbitant awards in malpractice litigation. Often a jury is asked to award a sum of money (as high as $12 million) to a severely retarded child whose damage has been incurred through medical malpractice. The justification for the large sum is the expectation that the child would have become a professional (physician or lawyer) and made an enormous sum of money in his or her lifetime. But if we were to take the notion of proximate identity seriously, we could only sue the physician for the damages done to the immediate person, not to his or her descendant selves.

What is the truth about personal identity? Are you the same person that you were at age sixteen? And will you be still the same person at age sixty-five?

JOHN LOCKE

THE SELF AS PSYCHOLOGICAL PROPERTIES

In this selection, Locke sets forth his psychological-states theory of personal identity, locating the criterion of personal identity in terms of consciousness, especially memory. The soul or essence of the person, defined as a reflective being, could take on different bodily forms and still preserve the same identity. (See Part II for a biographical sketch of Locke.)

. . . If the identity of *soul alone* makes the same *man,* and there be nothing in the nature of matter why the same individual spirit may not be united to different bodies, it will be possible that those men, living in distant ages, and of different tempers, may have been the same man: which way of speaking must be from a very strange use of the word man, applied to an idea out of which body and shape are excluded. . . .

An animal is a living organized body; and consequently the same animal, as we have observed, is the same continued *life* communicated to different particles of matter, as they happen successively to be united to that organized living body. And whatever is talked of other definitions, ingenious observation puts it past doubt, that the idea in our minds, of which the sound "man" in our mouths is the sign, is nothing else but of an animal of such a certain form. . . .

I presume it is not the idea of a thinking or rational being alone that makes the *idea of a man* in most people's sense: but of a body, so and so shaped, joined to it; and if that be the idea of a man, the same successive body not shifted all at once, must, as well as the same immaterial spirit, go to the making of the same man.

This being premised, to find wherein personal identity consists, we must consider what *person* stands for;—which, I think, is a thinking intelligent being, that has reason and reflection, and can consider itself as itself, the same thinking thing, in different times and places; which it does only by that consciousness which is inseparable from thinking, and, as it seems to me, essential to it: it being impossible for any one to perceive without *perceiving* that he does perceive. When we see, hear, smell, taste, feel, meditate, or will anything, we know that we do so. Thus it is always as to our present sensations and perceptions: and by this every one is to himself that which he calls self:—it not being considered, in this case, whether the same self be continued in the same or divers substances. For, since consciousness always accompanies thinking, and it is that which makes every one to be what he calls self, and thereby distinguishes himself from all other thinking things, in this alone consists personal identity, i.e., the sameness of a rational being: and as far as this consciousness can be extended backwards to any past action or thought, so far reaches the identity of that person; it is the same self now it was then; and it is by the same self with this present one that now reflects on it, that that action was done.

But it is further inquired, whether it be the same identical substance. This few would think they had

From John Locke, "Of Ideas of Identity and Diversity (1690)," in *An Essay Concerning Understanding,* Book II, Chapter 27.

reason to doubt of, if these perceptions, with their consciousness, always remained present in the mind, whereby the same thinking thing would be always consciously present, and, as would be thought, evidently the same to itself. But that which seems to make the difficulty is this, that this consciousness being interrupted always by forgetfulness, there being no moment of our lives wherein we have the whole train of all our past actions before our eyes in one view, but even the best memories losing the sight of one part whilst they are viewing another; and we sometimes, and that the greatest part of our lives, not reflecting on our past selves, being intent on our present thoughts, and in sound sleep having no thoughts at all, or at least none with that consciousness which remarks our waking thoughts,—I say, in all these cases, our consciousness being interrupted, and we losing the sight of our past selves, doubts are raised whether we are the same thinking thing, i.e. the same *substance* or no. Which, however reasonable or unreasonable, concerns not *personal* identity at all. The question being what makes the same person; and not whether it be the same identical substance, which always thinks in the same person, which, in this case, matters not at all: different substances, by the same consciousness (where they do partake in it) being united into one person, as well as different bodies by the same life are united into one animal, whose identity is perceived in that change of substances by the unity of one continued life. For, it being the same consciousness that makes a man be himself to himself, personal identity depends on that only, whether it be annexed solely to one individual substance, or can be continued in a succession of several substances. For as far as any intelligent being *can* repeat the idea of any past action with the same consciousness it had of it at first, and with the same consciousness it has of any present action; so far it is the same personal self. For it is by the consciousness it has of its present thoughts and actions, that it is *self to itself* now, and so will be the same self, as far as the same consciousness can extend to actions past or to come; and would be by distance of time, or change of substance, no more two persons, than a man be two men by wearing other clothes today than he did yesterday, with a long or a short sleep between: the same

consciousness uniting those distant actions in the same person, whatever substances contributed to their production.

That this is so, we have some kind of evidence in our very bodies, all whose particles, whilst vitally united to this same thinking conscious self, so that *we feel* when they are touched, and are affected by, and conscious of good or harm that happens to them, are a part of ourselves; i.e., of our thinking conscious self. Thus, the limbs of his body are to every one a part of himself; he sympathizes and is concerned for them. Cut off a hand, and thereby separate it from that consciousness he had of its heat, cold, and other affections, and it is then no longer a part of that which is himself, any more than the remotest part of matter. Thus, we see the *substance* whereof personal self consisted at one time may be varied at another, without the change of personal identity; there being no question about the same person, though the limbs which but now were a part of it, be cut off. . . .

And thus may we be able, without any difficulty, to conceive the same person at the resurrection, though in a body not exactly in make or parts the same which he had here,—the same consciousness going along with the soul that inhabits it. But yet the soul alone, in the change of bodies, would scarce to any one but to him that makes the soul the man, be enough to make the same man. For should the soul of a prince, carrying with it the consciousness of the prince's past life, enter and inform the body of a cobbler, as soon as deserted by his own soul, every one sees he would be the same *person* with the prince, accountable only for the prince's actions: but who would say it was the same *man?* The body too goes to the making the man, and would, I guess, to everybody determine the man in this case, wherein the soul, with all its princely thoughts about it, would not make another man: but he would be the same cobbler to every one besides himself. I know that, in the ordinary way of speaking, the same person, and the same man, stand for one and the same thing. And indeed every one will always have a liberty to speak as he pleases, and to apply what articulate sounds to what ideas he thinks fit, and change them as often as he pleases. But yet, when we will inquire what makes the same *spirit, man,* or *person,* we must fix the ideas of spirit, man, or person in our minds; and having resolved with ourselves what we mean by them, it will not be hard to determine in either of them, or the like, when it is the same, and when not.

But though the immaterial substance or soul does not alone, wherever it be, and in whatsoever state, make the same *man;* yet it is plain, consciousness, as far as ever it can be extended—should it be to ages past—unites existences and actions very remote in time into the same *person,* as well as it does the existences and actions of the immediately preceding moment: so that whatever has the consciousness of present and past actions, is the same person to whom they both belong. Had I the same consciousness that I saw the ark and Noah's flood, as that I saw an overflowing of the Thames last winter, or as that I write now, I could no more doubt that I who write this now, that saw the Thames overflowed last winter, and that viewed the flood at the general deluge, was the same *self,*—place that self in what *substance* you please—than that I who write this am the same *myself* now whilst I write (whether I consist of all the same substance, material or immaterial, or no) that I was yesterday. For as to this point of being the same self, it matters not whether this present self be made up of the same or other substances —I being as much concerned, and as justly accountable for any action that was done a thousand years since, appropriated to me now by this self-consciousness, as I am for what I did the last moment. . . .

But yet possibly it will still be objected,—Suppose I wholly lose the memory of some parts of my life, beyond a possibility of retrieving them, so that perhaps I shall never be conscious of them again; yet am I not the same person that did those actions, had those thoughts that I once was conscious of, though I have now forgot them? To which I answer, that we must here take notice what the word *I* is applied to; which, in this case, is the *man* only. And the same man being presumed to be the same person, I is easily here supposed to stand also for the same person. But if it be possible for the same man to have distinct incommunicable consciousness at different times, it is past doubt the same man would at different times make different persons; which, we see, is the sense of mankind in the solemnest declaration of their opin-

ions, human laws not punishing the mad man for the sober man's actions, nor the sober man for what the mad man did,—thereby making them two persons: which is somewhat explained by our way of speaking in English when we say such an one is "not himself," or is "beside himself"; in which phrases it is insinuated, as if those who now, or at least first used them, though that self was changed; the selfsame person was no longer in that man.

But yet it is hard to conceive that Socrates, the same individual man, should be two persons. To help us a little in this, we must consider what is meant by Socrates, or the same individual *man.*

First, it must be either the same individual, immaterial, thinking substance; in short, the same numerical soul, and nothing else.

Secondly, or the same animal, without any regard to the immaterial soul.

Thirdly, or the same immaterial spirit united to the same animal.

Now, take which of these suppositions you please, it is impossible to make personal identity to consist in anything but consciousness; or reach any further than that does.

FOR FURTHER REFLECTION

1. How would Locke respond to the objection that memories are not continuous in our consciousness? When we sleep, we cease to have memories at all. In partial amnesia, do we cease to be who we were? Recall Thomas Reid's suggestion of the problem of transitivity in memories. Suppose there is a gallant officer who at age twenty-five is a hero in a battle and who remembers getting a flogging in his childhood. Later, at age sixty-five, he recalls the heroic deed done at twenty-five but cannot recall the flogging. Since he cannot remember the earlier deed, is he the same person he was when he did remember it? Can Locke answer Reid?

2. What about the phenomenon of split personalities and multiple personalities, also discussed in the introduction to this section, the most famous of which is Sybil, who allegedly

expressed sixteen different personalities with sixteen different sets of memories? On a psychological-states account, would we have to say that one body contains sixteen persons? Are there different persons inside each of us, expressed by different "sides" of our personalities?

DAVID HUME

THE SELF AS A BUNDLE OF PERCEPTIONS

Hume denies that we have any basis in experience for believing in the existence of a permanent, "substantial" self. For Hume, you may recall from Part II, all learning comes from sensory impressions. Since there does not seem to be a separate impression of the self that we experience, there is no reason to believe that we have a self. The most we can identify ourselves with is our consciousness, and that constantly changes. There is no separate, permanent self that endures over time. Hence, personal identity is a fiction. (See the biographical sketch of Hume in Part II.)

There are some philosophers, who imagine we are every moment intimately conscious of what we call our Self; that we feel its existence and its continuance in existence; and are certain, beyond the evidence of a demonstration, both of its perfect identity and simplicity. . . .

Unluckily all these positive assertions are contrary to that very experience, which is pleaded for them, nor have we any idea of *self,* after the manner it is here explained. For from what impression could this idea be derived? This question 'tis impossible to answer without a manifest contradiction and absurdity; and yet 'tis a question, which must necessarily be answered, if we would have the idea of self pass for clear and intelligible. It must be some one impression, that gives rise to every real idea. But self or person is not any one impression, but that to which our several impressions and ideas are supposed to have a reference. If any impression gives rise to the idea of self, that impression must continue invariably the same, through the whole course of our lives; since self is supposed to exist after that manner. But there is no impression constant and invariable. Pain and pleasure, grief and joy, passions and sensations succeed each other, and never all exist at the same time. It cannot, therefore, be from any of these impressions, or from any other, that the idea of self is derived; and consequently there is no such idea.

But farther, what must become of all our particular perceptions upon this hypothesis? All these are different, and distinguishable, and separable from each other, and may be separately considered, and may exist separately, and have no need of any thing to support their existence. After what manner, there-

From David Hume, *A Treatise of Human Nature* (1739).

fore, do they belong to self; and how are they connected with it? For my part, when I enter most intimately into what I call *myself,* I always stumble on some particular perception or other, of heat or cold, light or shade, love or hatred, pain or pleasure. I never can catch *myself* at any time without a perception, and never can observe any thing but the perception. When my perceptions are removed for any time, as by sound sleep; so long am I insensible of *myself,* and may truly be said not to exist. And were all my perceptions removed by death, and could I neither think, nor feel, nor see, nor love, nor hate after the dissolution of my body, I should be entirely annihilated, nor do I conceive what is farther requisite to make me a perfect nonentity. If any one upon serious and unprejudiced reflection, thinks he has a different notion of *himself,* I must confess I can reason no longer with him. All I can allow him is, that he may be in the right as well as I, and that we are essentially different in this particular. He may, perhaps, perceive something simple and continued, which he calls *himself;* though I am certain there is no such principle in me.

But setting aside some metaphysicians of this kind, I may venture to affirm of the rest of mankind, that they are nothing but a bundle or collection of different perceptions, which succeed each other with an inconceivable rapidity, and are in a perpetual flux and movement. Our eyes cannot turn in their sockets without varying our perceptions. Our thought is still more variable than our sight; and all our other senses and faculties contribute to this change; nor is there any single power of the soul, which remains unalterably the same, perhaps for one moment. The mind is a kind of theatre, where several perceptions successively make their appearance; pass, re-pass, glide away, and mingle in an infinite variety of postures and situations. There is properly no *simplicity* in it at one time, nor *identity* in different; whatever natural propension we may have to imagine that simplicity and identity. The comparison of the theatre must not mislead us. They are the successive perceptions only, that constitute the mind; nor have we the most distant notion of the place, where these scenes are represented, or of the materials, of which it is composed.

What then gives us so great a propension to ascribe an identity to these successive perceptions, and to

suppose ourselves possessed of an invariable and uninterrupted existence through the whole course of our lives? . . .

We have a distinct idea of an object, that remains invariable and uninterrupted through a supposed variation of time; and this idea we call that of *identity* or *sameness.* We have also a distinct idea of several different objects existing in succession, and connected together by a close relation; and this to an accurate view affords as perfect a notion of *diversity,* as if there was no manner of relation among the objects. But though these two ideas of identity, and a succession of related objects be in themselves perfectly distinct, and even contrary, yet 'tis certain, that in our common way of thinking they are generally confounded with each other. That action of the imagination, by which we consider the uninterrupted and invariable object, and that by which we reflect on the succession of related objects, are almost the same to the feeling, nor is there much more effort of thought required in the latter case than in the former. The relation facilitates the transition of the mind from one object to another, and renders its passage as smooth as if it contemplated one continued object. This resemblance is the cause of the confusion and mistake, and makes us substitute the notion of identity, instead of that of related objects. . . .

Thus we feign the continued existence of the perceptions of our senses, to remove the interruption; and run into the notion of a *soul,* and *self,* and *substance,* to disguise the variation. But we may farther observe, that where we do not give rise to such a fiction, our propension to confound identity with relation is so great, that we are apt to imagine something unknown and mysterious, connecting the parts, beside their relation; and this I take to be the case with regard to the identity we ascribe to plants and vegetables. And even when this does not take place, we still feel a propensity to confound these ideas, though we are not able fully to satisfy ourselves in that particular, nor find any thing invariable and uninterrupted to justify our notion of identity.

Thus the controversy concerning identity is not merely a dispute of words. For when we attribute identity, in an improper sense, to variable or interrupted objects, our mistake is not confined to the expression, but is commonly attended with a fiction, either of something invariable and uninterrupted, or of something mysterious and inexplicable, or at least with a propensity to such fictions. What will suffice to prove this hypothesis to the satisfaction of every fair enquirer, is to show from daily experience and observation, that the objects, which are variable or interrupted, and yet are supposed to continue the same, are such only as consist of a succession of parts, connected together by resemblance, contiguity, or causation. . . .

A ship, of which a considerable part has been changed by frequent reparations, is still considered as the same; nor does the difference of the materials hinder us from ascribing an identity to it. The common end, in which the parts conspire, is the same under all their variations, and affords an easy transition of the imagination from one situation of the body to another. . . .

Though every one must allow, that in a very few years both vegetables and animals endure a *total* change, yet we still attribute identity to them, while their form, size, and substance are entirely altered. An oak, that grows from a small plant to a large tree, is still the same oak; though there be not one particle of matter, or figure of its parts the same. An infant becomes a man, and is sometimes fat, sometimes lean, without any change in his identity. . . . A man, who hears a noise, that is frequently interrupted and renewed, says, it is still the same noise; though 'tis evident the sounds have only a specific identity or resemblance, and there is nothing numerically the same, but the cause, which produced them. In like manner it may be said without breach of the propriety of language, that such a church, which was formerly of brick, fell to ruin, and that the parish rebuilt the same church of freestone, and according to modern architecture. Here neither the form nor materials are the same, nor is there any thing common to

the two objects, but their relation to the inhabitants of the parish; and yet this alone is sufficient to make us denominate them the same. . . .

From thence it evidently follows, that identity is nothing really belonging to these different perceptions, and uniting them together; but is merely a quality, which we attribute to them, because of the union of their ideas in the imagination, when we reflect upon them. . . .

The only question, therefore, which remains, is, by what relations this uninterrupted progress of our thought is produced, when we consider the successive existence of a mind or thinking person. And here 'tis evident we must confine ourselves to resemblance and causation. . . . Also, as memory alone acquaints us with the continuance and extent of this succession of perceptions, 'tis to be considered, upon that account chiefly, as the source of personal identity. Had we no memory, we never should have any notion of causation, nor consequently of that chain of causes and effects, which constitute our self or person.

FOR FURTHER REFLECTION

1. What does Hume mean by saying that the self is not any one impression, and what significance does this have for him?
2. Kant criticized Hume for reducing the mind to a stream of consciousness. The fact to be explained, says Kant, is not the succession of awarenesses, but an awareness of succession. If that which is aware passed with the awareness, there would be no awareness of succession, but it doesn't pass with the awareness. This continuity suggests that there is a transcendent self beyond the stream of consciousness of which Hume speaks. What do you make of this objection to Hume?

DEREK PARFIT AND GODFREY VESEY

BRAIN TRANSPLANTS AND PERSONAL IDENTITY
A Dialogue

Derek Parfit is an English philosopher who was educated and now teaches at Oxford University. He has made outstanding contributions to the subjects of ethical theory and the problem of personal identity. His major work is *Reasons and Persons* (1984). Godfrey Vesey was educated at Cambridge University and is a professor of philosophy at Open University. His principal works are *Perception* (1971) and *Personal Identity* (1974).

In this dialogue, Vesey introduces the problem of split-brain transplants. That is, a brain is divided into two, and half is put into each of two other people's brainless heads. Does the original person survive? Parfit then responds by developing his ideas of personal identity as psychological identity.

BRAIN TRANSPLANTS

In 1973 in the *Sunday Times* there was a report of how a team from the Metropolitan Hospital in Cleveland under Dr. R. J. White had successfully transplanted a monkey's head on to another monkey's body.[1] Dr. White was reported as having said, "Technically a human head transplant is possible," and as hoping that "it may be possible eventually to transplant *parts* of the brain or other organs inside the head."

The possibility of brain transplants gives rise to a fascinating philosophical problem. Imagine the following situation:

Two men, a Mr. Brown and a Mr. Robinson, had been operated on for brain tumours and brain extractions had been performed on both of them. At the end of the operations, however, the assistant inadvertently put Brown's brain in Robinson's head, and

Robinson's brain in Brown's head. One of these men immediately dies, but the other, the one with Robinson's body and Brown's brain, eventually regains consciousness. Let us call the latter "Brownson." Upon regaining consciousness Brownson exhibits great shock and surprise at the appearance of his body. Then, upon seeing Brown's body, he exclaims incredulously "That's me lying there!" Pointing to himself he says "This isn't my body; the one over there is!" When asked his name he automatically replies "Brown." He recognizes Brown's wife and family (whom Robinson had never met), and is able to describe in detail events in Brown's life, always describing them as events in his own life. Of Robinson's past life he evinces no knowledge at all. Over a period of time he is observed to display all of the personality traits, mannerisms, interests, likes and dislikes, and so on, that had previously characterized Brown, and to act and talk in ways completely alien to the old Robinson.[2]

From "Brain Transplants and Personal Identity," in *Philosophy in the Open*, ed. Godfrey Vesey, 1974. Reprinted by permission of Open University Press.

The next step is to suppose that Brown's brain is not simply transplanted whole into someone else's brainless head, but is divided in two and half put into each of *two* other people's brainless heads. The same memory having been coded in many parts of the cortex, they *both* then say they are Brown, are able to describe events in Brown's life as if they are events in their own lives, etc. What should we say now?

The implications of this case for what we should say about personal identity are considered by Derek Parfit in a paper entitled "Personal Identity." Parfit's own view is expressed in terms of a relationship he calls "psychological continuity." He analyses this relationship partly in terms of what he calls "*q*-memory" ("*q*" stands for "quasi"). He sketches a definition of "*q*-memory" as follows:

> I am *q*-remembering an experience if (1) I have a belief about a past experience which seems in itself like a memory belief, (2) someone did have such an experience, and (3) my belief is dependent upon this experience in the same way (whatever that is) in which a memory of an experience is dependent upon it.[3]

The significance of this definition of *q*-memory is that *two* people can, in theory, *q*-remember doing what only one person did. So two people can, in theory, be psychologically continuous with one person.

Parfit's thesis is that there is nothing more to personal identity than this "psychological continuity." This is *not* to say that whenever there is a sufficient degree of psychological continuity there is personal identity, for psychological continuity could be a one-two, or "branching," relationship, and we are able to speak of "identity" only when there is a one-one relationship. It *is* to say that a common belief—in the special nature of personal identity—is mistaken.

In the discussion that follows I began by asking Parfit what he thinks of this common belief.

PERSONAL IDENTITY

Vesey: Derek, can we begin with the belief that you claim most of us have about personal identity? It's this: whatever happens between now and some future time either I shall still exist or I shan't. And any future experience will either be my experience or it won't. In other words, personal identity is an all or nothing matter: either I survive or I don't. Now what do you want to say about that?

Parfit It seems to me just false. I think the true view is that we can easily describe and imagine large numbers of cases in which the question, "Will that future person be me—or someone else?" is both a question which doesn't have any answer at all, and there's no puzzle that there's no answer.

Vesey: Will you describe one such case.

Parfit One of them is the case discussed in the correspondence material, the case of division in which we suppose that each half of my brain is to be transplanted into a new body and the two resulting people will both seem to remember the whole of my life, have my character and be psychologically continuous with me in every way. Now in this case of division there were only three possible answers to the question, "What's going to happen to *me?*" And all three of them seem to me open to very serious objections. So the conclusion to be drawn from the case is that the question of what's going to happen to me, just doesn't have an answer. I think the case also shows that that's not mysterious at all.

Vesey: Right, let's deal with these three possibilities in turn.

Parfit Well, the first is that I'm going to be both of the resulting people. What's wrong with that answer is that it leads very quickly to a contradiction.

Vesey: How?

Parfit The two resulting people are going to be different people from each other. They're going to live completely different lives. They're going to be as different as any two people are. But if they're different people from each other it can't be the case that I'm going to be both of them. Because if I'm both of them, then one of the resulting people is going to be the same person as the other.

Vesey: Yes. They can't be different people and be the same person, namely me.

Parfit Exactly. So the first answer leads to a contradiction.

Vesey: Yes. And the second?

Parfit Well, the second possible answer is that I'm not going to be both of them but just one of them. This doesn't lead to a contradiction, it's just wildly implausible. It's implausible because my relation to each of the resulting people is exactly similar.

Vesey: Yes, so there's no reason to say that I'm one rather than the other?

Parfit It just seems absurd to suppose that, when you've got exactly the same relation, one of them is identity and the other is nothing at all.

Vesey: It does seem absurd, but there are philosophers who would say that sort of thing. Let's go on to the third.

Parfit Well, the only remaining answer, if I'm not going to be both of them or only one of them, is that I'm going to be neither of them. What's wrong with this answer is that it's grossly misleading.

Vesey: Why?

Parfit If I'm going to be neither of them, then there's not going to be anyone in the world after the operation who's going to be me. And that implies, given the way we now think, that the operation is as bad as death. Because if there's going to be no one who's going to be me, then I cease to exist. But it's obvious on reflection that the operation isn't as bad as death. It isn't bad in any way at all. That this is obvious can be shown by supposing that when they do the operation only one of the transplants succeeds and only one of the resulting people ever comes to consciousness again.

Vesey: Then I think we would say that this person is me. I mean we'd have no reason to say that he wasn't.

Parfit On reflection I'm sure we would all think that I would survive as that one person.

Vesey: Yes.

Parfit Yes. Well, if we now go back to the case where both operations succeed . . .

Vesey: Where there's a double success . . .

Parfit It's clearly absurd to suppose that a double success is a failure.

Vesey: Yes.

Parfit So the conclusion that I would draw from this case is firstly, that to the question, "What's going to happen to me?," there's no true answer.

Vesey: Yes.

Parfit Secondly, that if we decide to say one of the three possible answers, what we say is going to obscure the true nature of the case.

Vesey: Yes.

Parfit And, thirdly, the case isn't in any way puzzling. And the reason for that is this. My relation to each of the resulting people is the relation of full psychological continuity. When I'm psychologically continuous with only one person, we call it identity. But if I'm psychologically continuous with two future people, we can't call it identity. It's not puzzling because we know exactly what's going to happen.

Vesey: Yes, could I see if I've got this straight? Where there is psychological continuity in a one-one case, this is the sort of case which we'd ordinarily talk of in terms of a person having survived the operation, or something like that.

Parfit Yes.

Vesey: Now what about when there is what you call psychological continuity—that's to say, where the people seem to remember having been me and so on—in a one-two case? Is this survival or not?

Parfit Well, I think it's just as good as survival, but the block we have to get over is that we can't say that anyone in the world after the operation is going to be me.

Vesey: No.

Parfit Well, we can say it but it's very implausible. And we're inclined to think that if there's not going to be anyone who is me tomorrow, then I don't survive. What we need to realize is that my relation to each of those two people is just as good as survival. Nothing is missing at all in my relation to both of them, as compared with my relation to myself tomorrow.

Vesey: Yes.

Parfit So here we've got survival without identity. And that only seems puzzling if we think that identity is a further fact over and above psychological continuity.

Vesey: It is very hard not to think of identity being a further fact, isn't it?

Parfit Yes, I think it is. I think that the only way to get rid of our temptation to believe this is to consider many more cases than this one case of division. Perhaps I should give you another one. Suppose that the following is going to happen to me. When I die in a normal way, scientists are going to map the states of all the cells in my brain and body and after a few months they will have constructed a perfect duplicate of me out of organic matter. And this duplicate will wake up fully psychologically continuous with me, seeming to remember my life with my character, etc.

Vesey: Yes.

Parfit Now in this case, which is a secular version of the Resurrection, we're very inclined to think that the following question arises and is very real and very important. The question is, "Will that person who wakes up in three months be me or will he be some quite other person who's merely artificially made to be exactly like me?"

Vesey: It does seem to be a real question. I mean in the one case, if it is going to be me, then I have expectations and so on, and in the other case, where it isn't me, I don't.

Parfit I agree, it seems as if there couldn't be a bigger difference between it being me and it being someone else.

Vesey: But you want to say that the two possibilities are in fact the same?

Parfit I want to say that those two descriptions, "It's going to be me" and "It's going to be someone who is merely exactly like me," don't describe different outcomes, different courses of events, only one of which can happen. They are two ways of describing one and the same course of events. What I mean by that perhaps could be shown if we take an exactly comparable case involving not a person but something about which I think we're not inclined to have a false view.

Vesey: Yes.

Parfit Something like a club. Suppose there's some club in the nineteenth century . . .

Vesey: The Sherlock Holmes Club or something like that?

Parfit Yes, perhaps. And after several years of meeting it ceases to meet. The club dies.

Vesey: Right.

Parfit And then two of its members, let's say, have emigrated to America, and after about fifteen years they get together and they start up a club. It has exactly the same rules, completely new membership except for the first two people, and they give it the same name. Now suppose someone came along and said: "There's a real mystery here, because the fol-

lowing question is one that must have an answer. But how can we answer it?" The question is, "Have they started up the very same club—is it the same club as the one they belonged to in England—or is it a completely new club that's just exactly similar?"

Vesey: Yes.

Parfit Well, in that case we all think that this man's remark is absurd; there's no difference at all. Now that's my model for the true view about the case where they make a duplicate of me. It seems that there's all the difference in the world between its being me and its being this other person who's exactly like me. But if we think there's no difference at all in the case of the clubs, why do we think there's a difference in the case of personal identity, and how can we defend the view that there's a difference?

Vesey: I can see how some people would defend it. I mean, a dualist would defend it in terms of a soul being a simple thing, but . . .

Parfit Let me try another case which I think helps to ease us out of this belief we're very strongly inclined to hold.

Vesey: Go on.

Parfit Well, this isn't a single case, this is a whole range of cases. A whole smooth spectrum of different cases which are all very similar to the next one in the range. At the start of this range of cases you suppose that the scientists are going to replace one per cent of the cells in your brain and body with exact duplicates.

Vesey: Yes.

Parfit Now if that were to be done, no one has any doubt that you'd survive. I think that's obvious because after all you can *lose* one per cent of the cells and survive. As we get further along the range they replace a larger and larger percentage of cells with exact duplicates, and of course at the far end of this range, where they replace a hundred per cent, then we've got my case where they just make a duplicate out of wholly fresh matter.

Vesey: Yes.

Parfit Now on the view that there's all the difference in the world between its being me and its being this other person who is exactly like me, we ought in consistency to think that in some case in the middle of that range, where, say, they're going to replace fifty per cent, the same question arises: it is going to be me or this completely different character? I think that even the most convinced dualist who believes in the soul is going to find this range of cases very embarrassing, because he seems committed to the view that there's some crucial percentage up to which it's going to be him and after which it suddenly ceases to be him. But I find that wholly unbelievable.

Vesey: Yes. He's going to have to invent some sort of theory about the relation of mind and body to get round this one. I'm not quite sure how he would do it. Derek, could we go on to a related question? Suppose that I accepted what you said, that is, that there isn't anything more to identity than what you call psychological continuity in a one-one case. Suppose I accept that, then I would want to go on and ask you, well, what's the philosophical importance of this?

Parfit The philosophical importance is, I think, that psychological continuity is obviously, when we think about it, a matter of degree. So long as we think that identity is a further fact, one of the things we're inclined to think is that it's all or nothing, as you said earlier. Well, if we give up that belief and if we realize that what matters in my continued existence is a matter of degree, then this does make a difference in actual cases. All the cases that I've considered so far are of course bizarre science fiction cases. But I think that in actual life it's obvious on reflection that, to give an example, the relations between me now and me next year are much closer in every way than the relations between me now and me in twenty years. And the sorts of relations that I'm thinking of are relations of memory, character, ambition, intention—all of those. Next year I shall remember much more of this year than I will in twenty years. I shall have a much more similar character. I shall be carrying out more of the same plans, ambitions and, if that is so, I think there are various plausible implications for our moral beliefs and various possible effects on our emotions.

Vesey: For our moral beliefs? What have you in mind?

Parfit Let's take one very simple example. On the view which I'm sketching it seems to me much more plausible to claim that people deserve much less punishment, or even perhaps no punishment, for what they did many years ago as compared with what they did very recently. Plausible because the relations between them now and them many years ago when they committed the crime are so much weaker.

Vesey: But they are still the people who are responsible for the crime.

Parfit I think you say that because even if they've changed in many ways, after all it was just as much they who committed the crime. I think that's true, but on the view for which I'm arguing, we would come to think that it's a completely trivial truth. It's like the following truth: it's like the truth that all of my relatives are just as much my relatives. Suppose I in my will left more money to my close relatives and less to my distant relatives; a mere pittance to my second cousin twenty-nine times removed. If you said, "But that's clearly unreasonable because all of your relatives are just as much your relatives," there's a sense in which that's true but it's obviously too trivial to make my will an unreasonable will. And that's because what's involved in kinship is a matter of degree.

Vesey: Yes.

Parfit Now, if we think that what's involved in its being the same person now as the person who committed the crime is a matter of degree, then the truth that it was just as much him who committed the crime, will seem to us trivial in the way in which the truth that all my relatives are equally my relatives is trivial.

Vesey: Yes. So you think that I should regard myself in twenty years' time as like a fairly distant relative of myself?

Parfit Well, I don't want to exaggerate; I think the connections are much closer.

Vesey: Suppose I said that this point about psychological continuity being a matter of degree—suppose I said that this isn't anything that anybody denies?

Parfit I don't think anybody does on reflection deny that psychological continuity is a matter of degree. But I think what they may deny, and I think what may make a difference to their view, if they come over to the view for which I'm arguing—what they may deny is that psychological continuity is all there is to identity. Because what I'm arguing against is this further belief which I think we're all inclined to hold even if we don't realize it. The belief that however much we change, there's a profound sense in which the changed us is going to be just as much us. That even if some magic wand turned me into a completely different sort of person—a prince with totally different character, mental powers—it would be just as much me. That's what I'm denying.

Vesey: Yes. This is the belief which I began by stating, and I think that if we did lose that belief that would be a change indeed.

NOTES

1. *Sunday Times,* 9 December, 1973, p. 13.
2. Shoemaker (1963), pp. 23–24.
3. Parfit (1971), p. 15.

FOR FURTHER REFLECTION

1. Is Parfit's analysis of the problem of the split-brain case plausible? Do you think that he correctly construes the issue, or does he already presuppose controversial premises? Explain.
2. What are the three possible answers to the question "What's going to happen to me?" in the split-brain case, and how does Parfit treat them? What is Parfit's solution to the problem? Could you suggest another solution to the problem of personal identity?

C. Personal Identity and Survival: Will I Survive My Death?

Suppose the ingenious neurologist Dr. Jekyll were to design a brain just like yours in his laboratory, and suppose he were to design a body like yours but virtually indestructible (well, a nuclear bomb could destroy it, but failing that it would be impervious to alteration). The brain is now dormant, but at your death Dr. Jekyll will activate it and bring it to life within the prosthetic body. Now Jekyll tells you that he needs to kill you in order to allow your alter ego to exist. You complain, but Jekyll assures you that one exactly similar to you will live again with all your memories (or copies of them, but Alter Ego won't know the difference). Would you be comforted by that news? Would you take comfort in the fact that you will live again?

Where does all this leave us with regard to survival after death? If there is no continuity of consciousness, is it the same person who would be resurrected or reconstituted by God at some future time? Or would the reconstituted person be like Jekyll's replica? A different token of the same generic type? Could God make several tokens of your type—say five of you—which could be reconstituted and go on to live a new and eternal life? Quintuple resurrection!

Are the disembodied memories of a person enough to satisfy you for survival? The question is perplexing. It seems that your identity is somehow tied to your psychological states (such as memories and personality traits), which don't seem to depend on a body. But if this is so, would you survive if a computer stored much of the information about your personalities and memory states?

We seem to need both a body and a brain to instantiate our consciousness and personalities. It is hard to imagine any learning or experiencing or communication with others without a recognizable body. And the brain seems to be the locus of conscious experience. But bodies and brains die and are disintegrated. What happens to your consciousness and your personal identity? Is the gap between the present conscious life and the next simply like a long sleep during which God prepares a new and glorified body for your personality? Or does the fact that there will have to be a new creation rule out the possibility of personal survival altogether? Or can it be that there is an intrinsically spiritual character to your self that both survives the death of the body and persists in a life beyond this one?

The issue is as difficult as it is important to us. In this section, the first reading, from Plato's *Phaedo,* sets forth a view of the soul that is separate and of infinitely higher value than the body. The soul is good and the body evil. The body is really an encumbrance of the soul, which longs to be liberated from it. Death releases the soul from the body so that it can attain a wholly spiritual existence devoid of evil. In the second reading, Bertrand Russell challenges the notion of survival after death and argues that it is essentially incoherent. In the third reading, John Hick responds to those who say that personal immortality is impossible. He sets forth conditions for justifying our belief in survival and shows that those conditions could be met. According to Hick, there is nothing incoherent about the notion of immortality.

PLATO

~~

ARGUMENTS FOR THE IMMORTALITY OF THE SOUL

Plato (427–347 B.C.E.) believed that human beings were composed of two substances, a body and a soul. Of these, the true self is the soul, which lives on after the death of the body. The following selection is from the *Phaedo,* which describes Socrates' final days in prison before his death. In this dialogue between Socrates and his disciples, Cebes and Simmias, Socrates argues that it is certain that our souls survive our death.

(See the biographical sketch of Plato in Part I.)

Socrates: What again shall we say of the actual acquirement of knowledge?—is the body, if invited to share in the inquiry, a hinderer or a helper? I mean to say, have sight and hearing any truth in them? Are they not, as the poets are always telling us, inaccurate witnesses? and yet, if even they are inaccurate and indistinct, what is to be said of the other senses?—for you will allow that they are the best of them?

From Plato, *Phaedo,* trans. Benjamin Jowett, 1896.

Simmias: Certainly.

Soc.: Then when does the soul attain truth?—for in attempting to consider anything in company with the body she is obviously deceived.

Sim.: Yes, that is true.

Soc.: Then must not existence be revealed to her in thought, if at all?

Sim.: Yes.

Soc.: And thought is best when the mind is gathered into herself and none of these things trouble her—neither sounds nor sights nor pain nor any pleasure,—when she has as little as possible to do with the body, and has no bodily sense of feeling, but is aspiring after being?

Sim.: That is true.

Soc.: And in this the philosopher dishonors the body; his soul runs away from the body and desires to be alone and by herself?

Sim.: That is true.

Soc.: Well, but there is another thing, Simmias: Is there or is there not an absolute justice?

Sim.: Assuredly there is.

Soc.: And an absolute beauty and absolute good?

Sim.: Of course.

Soc.: But did you ever behold any of them with your eyes?

Sim.: Certainly not.

Soc.: Or did you ever reach them with any other bodily sense? (and I speak not of these alone, but of absolute greatness, and health, and strength, and of the essence of true nature of everything). Has the reality of them ever been perceived by you through the bodily organs? or rather, is not the nearest approach to the knowledge of their several natures made by him who so orders his intellectual vision as to have the most exact conception of the essence of that which he considers?

Sim.: Certainly.

Soc.: And he attains to the knowledge of them in their highest purity who goes to each of them with the mind alone, not allowing when in the act of thought the intrusion or introduction of sight or any other sense in the company of reason, but with the very light of the mind in her clearness penetrates into the very light of truth in each; he has got rid, as far as he can, of eyes and ears and of the whole body, which he conceives of only as a disturbing element, hindering the soul from the acquisition of knowledge when in company with her—is not this the sort of man who, if ever man did, is likely to attain the knowledge of existence?

Sim.: There is admirable truth in that, Socrates.

Soc.: And when they consider all this, must not true philosophers make a reflection, of which they will speak to one another in such words as these: We have found, they will say, a path of speculation which seems to bring us and the argument to the conclusion, that while we are in the body, and while the soul is mingled with this mass of evil, our desire will not be satisfied, and our desire is of the truth. For the body is a source of endless trouble to us by reason of the mere requirement of food; and also is liable to diseases which overtake and impede us in the search after truth: and by filling us so full of loves, and lusts, and fears, and fancies, and idols, and every sort of folly, prevents our ever having, as people say, so much as a thought. From whence come wars, and fightings, and factions? whence but from the body and the lusts of the body? For wars are occasioned by the love of money, and money has to be acquired for the sake and in the service of the body; and in consequence of all these things the time which ought to be given to philosophy is lost. Moreover, if there is time and an inclination toward philosophy, yet the body introduces a turmoil and confusion and fear into the course of speculation, and hinders us from seeing the truth, and all experience shows that if we would have pure knowledge of anything we must be quit of the body, and the soul in herself must behold all things in themselves: then I suppose that we shall attain that which we desire, and of which we say that we are lovers, and that is wisdom; not while we live, but after death, as the argument shows; for if while in company with the body, the soul cannot have pure knowledge, one of two things seems to follow—either knowledge is not to be attained at all, or, if at all, after death. For then, and not till then, the soul will be in herself alone and without the body. In this present life, I reckon that we make the nearest approach to knowledge when we have the least possible concern or interest in the body, and are not saturated with the bodily nature, but remain pure until the hour when God himself is pleased to release us. And then the foolishness of the body will be cleared away and we shall be pure and hold converse with other pure souls, and know of ourselves the clear light everywhere; and this is surely the light of truth. For no impure thing is allowed to approach the pure. These are the sort of words, Simmias, which the true lovers of wisdom cannot help saying to one another, and thinking. You will agree with me in that?

Sim.: Certainly, Socrates.

Soc.: But if this is true, O my friend, then there is great hope that, going whither I go, I shall there be satisfied with that which has been the chief concern of you and me in our past lives. And now that the hour of departure is appointed to me, this is the hope with which I depart, and not I only, but every man who believes that he has his mind purified.

Sim.: Certainly.

Soc.: And what is purification but the separation of the soul from the body, as I was saying before; the habit of the soul gathering and collecting herself into herself, out of all the courses of the body; the dwelling in her own place alone, as in another life, so also in this, as far as she can; the release of the soul from the chains of the body?

Sim.: Very true.

Soc.: And what is that which is termed death, but this very separation and release of the soul from the body?

Sim.: To be sure.

Soc.: And the true philosophers, and they only, study and are eager to release the soul. Is not the separation and release of the soul from the body their especial study?

Sim.: That is true.

Soc.: And as I was saying at first, there would be a ridiculous contradiction in men studying to live as nearly as they can in a state of death, and yet repining when death comes.

Sim.: Certainly.

Soc.: Then Simmias, as the true philosophers are ever studying death, to them, of all men, death is the least terrible. Look at the matter in this way: how inconsistent of them to have been always enemies of the body, and wanting to have the soul alone, and when this is granted to them, to be trembling and

repining; instead of rejoicing at their departing to that place where, when they arrive, they hope to gain that which in life they loved (and this was wisdom), and at the same time to be rid of the company of their enemy. Many a man has been willing to go to the world below in the hope of seeing there an earthly love, or wife, or son, and conversing with them. And will he who is a true lover of wisdom, and is persuaded in like manner that only in the world below he can worthily enjoy her, still repine at death? Will he not depart with joy? Surely, he will, my friend, if he be a true philosopher. For he will have a firm conviction that there only, and nowhere else, he can find wisdom in her purity. And if this be true, he would be very absurd, as I was saying, if he were to fear death. . . .

And were we not saying long ago that the soul when using the body as an instrument of perception, that is to say, when using the sense of sight or hearing or some other sense (for the meaning of perceiving through the body is perceiving through the senses),— were we not saying that the soul too is then dragged by the body into the region of the changeable, and wanders and is confused; the world spins round her, and she is like a drunkard when under their influence?

Cebes: Very true.

Soc.: But when returning into herself she reflects; then she passes into the realm of purity, and eternity, and immortality, and unchangeableness, which are her kindred, and with them she ever lives, when she is by herself and is not let or hindered; then she ceases from her erring ways, and being in communion with the unchanging is unchanging. And this state of the soul is called wisdom?

Cebes: That is well and truly said, Socrates.

Soc.: And to which class is the soul more nearly alike and akin, as far as may be inferred from this argument, as well as from the preceding one?

Cebes: I think, Socrates, that, in the opinion of every one who follows the argument, the soul will be infinitely more like the unchangeable,—even the most stupid person will not deny that.

Soc.: And the body is more like the changing?

Cebes: Yes.

Soc.: Yet once more consider the matter in this light: When the soul and the body are united, then nature orders the soul to rule and govern, and the body to obey and serve. Now which of these two functions is akin to the divine? and which to the mortal? Does not the divine appear to you to be that which naturally orders and rules, and the mortal that which is subject and servant?

Cebes: True.

Soc.: And which does the soul resemble?

Cebes: The soul resembles the divine, and the body the mortal—there can be no doubt of that, Socrates.

Soc.: Then reflect, Cebes: is not the conclusion of the whole matter this,—that the soul is in the very likeness of the divine, and immortal, and intelligible, and uniform, and indissoluble, and unchangeable; and the body is in the very likeness of the human, and mortal, and unintelligible, and multiform, and dissoluble, and changeable. Can this, my dear Cebes, be denied?

Cebes: No indeed.

Soc.: But if this is true, then is not the body liable to speedy dissolution? and is not the soul almost or altogether indissoluble?

Cebes: Certainly.

Soc.: And do you further observe, that after a man is dead, the body, which is the visible part of man, and has a visible framework, which is called a corpse, and which would naturally be dissolved and decomposed and dissipated, is not dissolved or decomposed at once, but may remain for a good while, if the constitution be sound at the time of death, and the season of the year favorable? For the body when shrunk and embalmed, as is the custom in Egypt, may remain almost entire through infinite ages; and even in decay, still there are some portions, such as the bones and ligaments, which are practically indestructible. You allow that?

Cebes: Yes.

Soc.: And are we to suppose that the soul, which is invisible, in passing to the true Hades, which like her is invisible, and pure, and noble, and on her way to the good and wise God, whither, if God will, my soul is also soon to go,—that the soul, I repeat, if this be her nature and origin, is blown away and perishes immediately on quitting the body, as the many say? That can never be, my dear Simmias and Cebes. The truth rather is, that the soul which is pure at departing draws after her no bodily taint, having never voluntarily had connection with the body, which she is ever avoiding, herself gathered into herself (for such abstraction has been the study of her life). And what does this mean but that she has been a true disciple of philosophy, and has practiced how to die easily? And is not philosophy the practice of death?

Cebes: Certainly.

Soc.: That soul, I say, herself invisible, departs to the invisible world,—to the divine and immortal and rational: thither arriving, she lives in bliss and is released from the error and folly of men, their fears and wild passions and all other human ills, and forever dwells, as they say of the initiated, in company with the gods? Is not this true, Cebes?

Cebes: Yes, beyond a doubt.

FOR FURTHER REFLECTION

1. Are Plato's arguments in this dialogue persuasive? Do the arguments depend overly much on his theory of the Forms, which gives ideas separate existence? Explain.
2. Is Plato correct in thinking that the body always hinders pure thought? How might a contemporary materialist respond to Plato?

BERTRAND RUSSELL

THE ILLUSION OF IMMORTALITY

In this brief essay, the eminent British philosopher Bertrand Russell (1872–1970) outlines some of the major objections to the idea of life after death. Russell argues that it is not reasonable to believe that our personality and memories will survive the destruction of our bodies. He claims that the inclination to believe in immortality comes from emotional factors, notably the fear of death.

(See the biographical sketch of Russell in Part I.)

Before we can profitably discuss whether we shall continue to exist after death, it is well to be clear as to the sense in which a man is the same person as he was yesterday. Philosophers used to think that there were definite substances, the soul and the body, that each lasted on from day to day, that a soul, once created, continued to exist throughout all future time, whereas a body ceased temporarily from death till the resurrection of the body.

The part of this doctrine which concerns the present life is pretty certainly false. The matter of the body is continually changing by processes of nutriment and wastage. Even if it were not, atoms in physics are no longer supposed to have continuous existence; there is no sense in saying: this is the same atom as the one that existed a few minutes ago. The continuity of a human body is a matter of appearance and behavior, not of substance.

The same thing applies to the mind. We think and feel and act, but there is not, in addition to thoughts and feelings and actions, a bare entity, the mind or the soul, which does or suffers these occurrences. The mental continuity of a person is a continuity of habit and memory: there was yesterday one person whose feelings I can remember, and that person I regard as myself of yesterday; but, in fact, myself of yesterday was only certain mental occurrences which are now remembered and are regarded as part of the person who now recollects them. All that constitutes a person is a series of experiences connected by memory and by certain similarities of the sort we call habit.

If, therefore, we are to believe that a person survives death, we must believe that the memories and habits which constitute the person will continue to be exhibited in a new set of occurrences.

No one can prove that this will not happen. But it is easy to see that it is very unlikely. Our memories and habits are bound up with the structure of the brain, in much the same way in which a river is connected with the riverbed. The water in the river is always changing, but it keeps to the same course because previous rains have worn a channel. In like manner, previous events have worn a channel in the brain, and our thoughts flow along this channel. This is the cause of memory and mental habits. But the brain, as a structure, is dissolved at death, and memory therefore may be expected to be also dissolved. There is no more reason to think otherwise than to expect a river

From Bertrand Russell, *Why I Am Not a Christian* (London: George Allen & Unwin, 1957), pp. 88–93. Copyright © 1957 by Allen & Unwin. Reprinted by permission of Taylor & Francis Books UK and The Bertrand Russell Peace Foundation.

to persist in its old course after an earthquake has raised a mountain where a valley used to be.

All memory, and therefore (one may say) all minds, depend upon a property which is very noticeable in certain kinds of material structures but exists little if at all in other kinds. This is the property of forming habits as a result of frequent similar occurrences. For example: a bright light makes the pupils of the eyes contract; and if you repeatedly flash a light in a man's eyes and beat a gong at the same time, the gong alone will, in the end, cause his pupils to contract. This is a fact about the brain and nervous system—that is to say, about a certain material structure. It will be found that exactly similar facts explain our response to language and our use of it, our memories and the emotions they arouse, our moral or immoral habits of behavior, and indeed everything that constitutes our mental personality, except the part determined by heredity. The part determined by heredity is handed on to our posterity but cannot, in the individual, survive the disintegration of the body. Thus both the hereditary and the acquired parts of a personality are, so far as our experience goes, bound up with the characteristics of certain bodily structures. We all know that memory may be obliterated by an injury to the brain, that a virtuous person may be rendered vicious by encephalitis lethargica, and, that a clever child can be turned into an idiot by lack of iodine. In view of such familiar facts, it seems scarcely probable that the mind survives the total destruction of brain structure which occurs at death.

It is not rational arguments but emotions that cause belief in a future life.

The most important of these emotions is fear of death, which is instinctive and biologically useful. If we genuinely and wholeheartedly believed in the future life, we should cease completely to fear death. The effects would be curious, and probably such as most of us would deplore. But our human and subhuman ancestors have fought and exterminated their enemies throughout many geological ages and have profited by courage; it is therefore an advantage to the victors in the struggle for life to be able, on occasion, to overcome the natural fear of death. Among ani-

mals and savages, instinctive pugnacity suffices for this purpose; but at a certain stage of development, as the Mohammedans first proved, belief in Paradise has considerable military value as reinforcing natural pugnacity. We should therefore admit that militarists are wise in encouraging the belief in immortality, always supposing that this belief does not become so profound as to produce indifference to the affairs of the world.

Another emotion which encourages the belief in survival is admiration of the excellence of man. As the Bishop of Birmingham says, "His mind is a far finer instrument than anything that had appeared earlier—he knows right and wrong. He can build Westminster Abbey. He can make an airplane. He can calculate the distance of the sun. . . . Shall, then, man at death perish utterly? Does that incomparable instrument, his mind, vanish when life ceases?"

The Bishop proceeds to argue that "the universe has been shaped and is governed by an intelligent purpose," and that it would have been unintelligent, having made man, to let him perish.

To this argument there are many answers. In the first place, it has been found, in the scientific investigation of nature, that the intrusion of moral or aesthetic values has always been an obstacle to discovery. It used to be thought that the heavenly bodies must move in circles because the circle is the most perfect curve, that species must be immutable because God would only create what was perfect and what therefore stood in no need of improvement, that it was useless to combat epidemics except by repentance because they were sent as a punishment for sin, and so on. It has been found, however, that, so far as we can discover, nature is indifferent to our values and can only be understood by ignoring our notions of good and bad. The Universe may have a purpose, but nothing that we know suggests that, if so, this purpose has any similarity to ours.

Nor is there in this anything surprising. Dr. Barnes tells us that man "knows right and wrong." But, in fact, as anthropology shows, men's views of right and wrong have varied to such an extent that no single item has been permanent. We cannot say, therefore, that man knows right and wrong, but only that some men do. Which men? Nietzsche argued in favor of an ethic profoundly different from Christ's, and some powerful governments have accepted his teaching. If knowledge of right and wrong is to be an argument for immortality, we must first settle whether to believe Christ or Nietzsche, and then argue that Christians are immortal, but Hitler and Mussolini are not, or vice versa. The decision will obviously be made on the battlefield, not in the study. Those who have the best poison gas will have the ethic of the future and will therefore be the immortal ones.

Our feelings and beliefs on the subject of good and evil are, like everything else about us, natural facts, developed in the struggle for existence and not having any divine or supernatural origin. In one of Aesop's fables, a lion is shown pictures of huntsmen catching lions and remarks that, if he had painted them, they would have shown lions catching huntsmen. Man, says Dr. Barnes, is a fine fellow because he can make airplanes. A little while ago there was a popular song about the cleverness of flies in walking upside down on the ceiling, with the chorus: "Could Lloyd George do it? Could Mr. Baldwin do it? Could Ramsay Mac do it? Why, NO." On this basis a very telling argument could be constructed by a theologically-minded fly, which no doubt the other flies would find most convincing.

Moreover, it is only when we think abstractly that we have such a high opinion of man. Of men in the concrete, most of us think the vast majority very bad. Civilized states spend more than half their revenue on killing each other's citizens. Consider the long history of the activities inspired by moral fervor: human sacrifices, persecutions of heretics, witch-hunts, pogroms leading up to wholesale extermination by poison gases, which one at least of Dr. Barnes's episcopal colleagues must be supposed to favor, since he holds pacifism to be un-Christian. Are these abominations, and the ethical doctrines by which they are prompted, really evidence of an intelligent Creator? And can we really wish that the men who practice them should live forever? The world in which we live can be understood as a result of muddle and accident; but if it is the outcome of deliberate purpose, the purpose must have

been that of a fiend. For my part, I find accident a less painful and more plausible hypothesis.

FOR FURTHER REFLECTION

1. How strong is Russell's argument against survival? Does his notion of personal identity lead to his conclusion, and is that the place to look more carefully? Explain.

2. In his famous study of near-death or "out-of-body" experiences, *Life After Life* (New York: Bantam, 1976, p. 21), Raymond Moody documents several cases of clinically dead people who were revived and who reported remarkably similar out-of-body experiences. Moody sets down a composite outline of their reports in the following passage:

> A man is dying and, as he reaches the point of greatest physical distress, he hears himself pronounced dead by his doctor. He begins to hear an uncomfortable noise, a loud ringing or buzzing, and at the same time feels himself moving very rapidly through a long dark tunnel. After this, he suddenly finds himself outside of his own physical body, but still in the immediate physical environment, and he sees his own body from a distance, as though he is a spectator. He watches the resuscitation attempt from this unusual vantage point and is in a state of emotional upheaval.
>
> After a while, he collects himself and becomes more accustomed to his odd condition. He notices that he still has a "body," but one of a very different nature and with very different powers from the physical body he has left behind. Soon other things begin to happen. Others come to meet and to help him. He glimpses the spirits of relatives and friends who have already died, and a loving, warm spirit of a kind he has never encountered before—a being of light—appears before him. This being asks him a question, nonverbally, to make him evaluate his life and helps him along by showing him a panoramic, instantaneous playback of the major events of his life. At some point he finds himself approaching some sort of barrier or border, apparently rep-

resenting the limit between earthly life and the next life. Yet, he finds that he must go back to the earth, that the time for his death has not yet come. At this point he resists, for by now he is taken up with his experiences in the afterlife and does not want to return. He is over-

whelmed by intense feelings of joy, love, and peace. Despite his attitude, though, he somehow reunites with his physical body and lives.

How would Russell respond to this sort of near-death experience?

JOHN HICK

IN DEFENSE OF LIFE AFTER DEATH

John Hick, a retired British philosopher and theologian, examines the Platonic notion of the immortality of the soul and argues that it is filled with problems. In its place he argues for the New Testament view of the re-creation of the psychophysical person, a holistic person who is body-soul in one. He then offers a thought experiment of "John Smith" reappearances to persuade us that the idea of re-creation of the same person is conceivable and worthy of rational belief. In the last part of his essay, Hick considers whether parapsychology can provide evidence for our survival after death.

THE IMMORTALITY OF THE SOUL

Some kind of distinction between physical body and immaterial or semimaterial soul seems to be as old as human culture; the existence of such a distinction has been indicated by the manner of burial of the earliest human skeletons yet discovered. Anthropologists offer various conjectures about the origin of the distinction: perhaps it was first suggested by memories of dead persons; by dreams of them; by the sight of reflections of oneself in water and on other bright surfaces; or by meditation upon the significance of religious rites which grew up spontaneously in face of the fact of death.

It was Plato (427–347 B.C.E.), the philosopher who has most deeply and lastingly influenced Western culture, who systematically developed the body-mind dichotomy and first attempted to prove the immortality of the soul.[1]

Plato argues that although the body belongs to the sensible world,[2] and shares its changing and impermanent nature, the intellect is related to the unchanging realities of which we are aware when we think not of particular good things but of Goodness itself, not of specific just acts but of Justice itself, and of the other "universals" or eternal Ideas in virtue of which physical things and events have their own specific characteristics. Being related to this higher and abiding realm, rather than to the evanescent world of

From John Hick, *Philosophy of Religion* (1983), 3rd ed., pp. 122–32, by permission of Pearson Education, Inc., Upper Saddle River, NJ.

sense, reason or the soul is immortal. Hence, one who devotes his life to the contemplation of eternal realities rather than to the gratification of the fleeting desires of the body will find at death that whereas his body turns to dust, his soul gravitates to the realm of the unchanging, there to live forever. Plato painted an awe-inspiring picture, of haunting beauty and persuasiveness, which has moved and elevated the minds of men in many different centuries and lands. Nevertheless, it is not today (as it was during the first centuries of the Christian era) the common philosophy of the West; and a demonstration of immortality which presupposes Plato's metaphysical system cannot claim to constitute a proof for the twentieth-century disbeliever.

Plato used the further argument that the only things that can suffer destruction are those that are composite, since to destroy something means to disintegrate it into its constituent parts. All material bodies are composite; the soul, however, is simple and therefore imperishable. This argument was adopted by Aquinas and has become standard in Roman Catholic theology, as in the following passage from the modern Catholic philosopher, Jacques Maritain:

> A spiritual soul cannot be corrupted, since it possesses no matter; it cannot be disintegrated, since it has no substantial parts; it cannot lose its individual unity, since it is self-subsisting, nor its internal energy, since it contains within itself all the sources of its energies. The human soul cannot die. Once it exists, it cannot disappear; it will necessarily exist for ever, endure without end. Thus, philosophic reason, put to work by a great metaphysician like Thomas Aquinas, is able to prove the immortality of the human soul in a demonstrative manner.[3]

This type of reasoning has been criticized on several grounds. Kant pointed out that although it is true that a simple substance cannot disintegrate, consciousness may nevertheless cease to exist through the diminution of its intensity to zero.[4] Modern psychology has also questioned the basic premise that the mind is a simple entity. It seems instead to be a structure of only relative unity, normally fairly stable and tightly integrated but capable under stress of various degrees of division and dissolution. This comment

from psychology makes it clear that the assumption that the soul is a simple substance is not an empirical observation but a metaphysical theory. As such, it cannot provide the basis for a general proof of immortality.

The body-soul distinction, first formulated as a philosophical doctrine in ancient Greece, was baptized into Christianity, ran through the medieval period, and entered the modern world with the public status of a self-evident truth when it was redefined in the seventeenth century by Descartes. Since World War II, however, the Cartesian mind-matter dualism, having been taken for granted for many centuries, has been strongly criticized by philosophers of the contemporary analytical school.[5] It is argued that the words that describe mental characteristics and operations—such as "intelligent," "thoughtful," "carefree," "happy," "calculating" and the like—apply in practice to types of human behavior and to behavioral dispositions. They refer to the empirical individual, the observable human being who is born and grows and acts and feels and dies, and not to the shadowy proceedings of a mysterious "ghost in the machine." Man is thus very much what he appears to be—a creature of flesh and blood, who behaves and is capable of behaving in a characteristic range of ways—rather than a nonphysical soul incomprehensibly interacting with a physical body.

As a result of this development much mid-twentieth-century philosophy has come to see man in the way he is seen in the biblical writings, not as an eternal soul temporarily attached to a mortal body, but as a form of finite, mortal, psychophysical life. Thus, the Old Testament scholar, J. Pedersen, says of the Hebrews that for them ". . . the body is the soul in its outward form."[6] This way of thinking has led to quite a different conception of death from that found in Plato and the neo-Platonic strand of European thought.

THE RE-CREATION OF THE PSYCHOPHYSICAL PERSON

Only toward the end of the Old Testament period did after-life beliefs come to have any real importance in

Judaism. Previously, Hebrew religious insight had focused so fully upon God's covenant with the nation, as an organism that continued through the centuries while successive generations lived and died, that the thought of a divine purpose for the individual, a purpose that transcended this present life, developed only when the breakdown of the nation as a political entity threw into prominence the individual and the problem of his personal destiny.

When a positive conviction arose of God's purpose holding the individual in being beyond the crisis of death, this conviction took the non-Platonic form of belief in the resurrection of the body. By the turn of the eras, this had become an article of faith for one Jewish sect, the Pharisees, although it was still rejected as an innovation by the more conservative Sadducees.

The religious difference between the Platonic belief in the immortality of the soul, and the Judaic-Christian belief in the resurrection of the body is that the latter postulates a special divine act of re-creation. This produces a sense of utter dependence upon God in the hour of death, a feeling that is in accordance with the biblical understanding of man as having been formed out of "the dust of the earth,"[7] a product (as we say today) of the slow evolution of life from its lowly beginnings in the primeval slime. Hence, in the Jewish and Christian conception, death is something real and fearful. It is not thought to be like walking from one room to another, or taking off an old coat and putting on a new one. It means sheer unqualified extinction—passing out from the lighted circle of life into "death's dateless night." Only through the sovereign creative love of God can there be a new existence beyond the grave.

What does "the resurrection of the dead" mean? Saint Paul's discussion provides the basic Christian answer to this question.[8] His conception of the general resurrection (distinguished from the unique resurrection of Jesus) has nothing to do with the resuscitation of corpses in a cemetery. It concerns God's re-creation or reconstitution of the human psychophysical individual, not as the organism that has died but as a *soma pneumatikon,* a "spiritual body," inhabiting a spiritual world as the physical body inhabits our present physical world.

A major problem confronting any such doctrine is that of providing criteria of personal identity to link the earthly life and the resurrection life. Paul does not specifically consider this question, but one may, perhaps, develop his thought along lines such as the following.[9]

Suppose, first, that someone—John Smith—living in the USA were suddenly and inexplicably to disappear from before the eyes of his friends, and that at the same moment an exact replica of him were inexplicably to appear in India. The person who appears in India is exactly similar in both physical and mental characteristics to the person who disappeared in America. There is continuity of memory, complete similarity of bodily features including fingerprints, hair and eye coloration, and stomach contents, and also of beliefs, habits, emotions, and mental dispositions. Further, the "John Smith" replica thinks of himself as being the John Smith who disappeared in the USA. After all possible tests have been made and have proved positive, the factors leading his friends to accept "John Smith" as John Smith would surely prevail and would cause them to overlook even his mysterious transference from one continent to another, rather than treat "John Smith," with all John Smith's memories and other characteristics, as someone other than John Smith.

Suppose, second, that our John Smith, instead of inexplicably disappearing, dies, but that at the moment of his death a "John Smith" replica, again complete with memories and all other characteristics, appears in India. Even with the corpse on our hands we would, I think, still have to accept this "John Smith" as the John Smith who died. We would have to say that he had been miraculously re-created in another place.

Now suppose, third, that on John Smith's death the "John Smith" replica appears, not in India, but as a resurrection replica in a different world altogether, a resurrection world inhabited only by resurrected persons. This world occupies its own space distinct from that with which we are now familiar. That is to say, an object in the resurrection world is not situated at any distance or in any direction from the objects in our present world, although each object in either world is spatially related to every other object in the same world.

This supposition provides a model by which one may conceive of the divine re-creation of the embodied human personality. In this model, the element of the strange and the mysterious has been reduced to a minimum by following the view of some of the early Church Fathers that the resurrection body has the same shape as the physical body,[10] and ignoring Paul's own hint that it may be as unlike the physical body as a full grain of wheat differs from the wheat seed.[11]

What is the basis for this Judaic-Christian belief in the divine re-creation or reconstitution of the human personality after death? There is, of course, an argument from authority, in that life after death is taught throughout the New Testament (although very rarely in the Old Testament). But, more basically, belief in the resurrection arises as a corollary of faith in the sovereign purpose of God, which is not restricted by death and which holds man in being beyond his natural mortality. In the words of Martin Luther, "Anyone with whom God speaks, whether in wrath or in mercy, the same is certainly immortal. The Person of God who speaks, and the Word, show that we are creatures with whom God wills to speak, right into eternity, and in an immortal manner."[12] In a similar vein it is argued that if it be God's plan to create finite persons to exist in fellowship with himself, then it contradicts both his own intention and his love for the creatures made in his image if he allows men to pass out of existence when his purpose for them remains largely unfulfilled.

It is this promised fulfillment of God's purpose for man, in which the full possibilities of human nature will be realized, that constitutes the "heaven" symbolized in the New Testament as a joyous banquet in which all and sundry rejoice together. As we saw when discussing the problem of evil, no theodicy can succeed without drawing into itself this eschatological[13] faith in an eternal, and therefore infinite, good which thus outweighs all the pains and sorrows that have been endured on the way to it.

Balancing the idea of heaven in Christian tradition is the idea of *hell*. This, too, is relevant to the problem of theodicy. For just as the reconciling of God's goodness and power with the fact of evil requires that out of the travail of history there shall come in the end

an eternal good for man, so likewise it would seem to preclude man's eternal misery. The only kind of evil that is finally incompatible with God's unlimited power and love would be utterly pointless and wasted suffering, pain which is never redeemed and worked into the fulfilling of God's good purpose. Unending torment would constitute precisely such suffering; for being eternal, it could never lead to a good end beyond itself. Thus, hell as conceived by its enthusiasts, such as Augustine or Calvin, is a major part of the problem of evil! If hell is construed as eternal torment, the theological motive behind the idea is directly at variance with the urge to seek a theodicy. However, it is by no means clear that the doctrine of eternal punishment can claim a secure New Testament basis.[14] If, on the other hand, "hell" means a continuation of the purgatorial suffering often experienced in this life, and leading eventually to the high good of heaven, it no longer stands in conflict with the needs of theodicy. Again, the idea of hell may be deliteralized and valued as a *mythos,* as a powerful and pregnant symbol of the grave responsibility inherent in man's freedom in relation to his Maker.

DOES PARAPSYCHOLOGY HELP?

The spiritualist movement claims that life after death has been proved by well-attested cases of communication between the living and the "dead." During the closing quarter of the nineteenth century and the decades of the present century this claim has been made the subject of careful and prolonged study by a number of responsible and competent persons.[15] This work, which may be approximately dated from the founding in London of the Society for Psychical Research in 1882, is known either by the name adopted by that society or in the United States by the name parapsychology.

Approaching the subject from the standpoint of our interest in this chapter, we may initially divide the phenomena studied by the parapsychologist into two groups. There are those phenomena that involve no reference to the idea of a life after death, chief among these being psychokinesis and extrasensory perception (ESP) in its various forms (such as telepathy, clairvoyance, and precognition). And there are those phenomena that raise the question of personal survival after death, such as the apparitions and other sensory manifestations of dead persons and the "spirit messages" received through mediums. This division is, however, only of preliminary use, for ESP has emerged as a clue to the understanding of much that occurs in the second group. We shall begin with a brief outline of the reasons that have induced the majority of workers in this field to be willing to postulate so strange an occurrence as telepathy.

Telepathy is a name for the mysterious fact that sometimes a thought in the mind of one person apparently causes a similar thought to occur to someone else when there are no normal means of communication between them, and under circumstances such that mere coincidence seems to be excluded.

For example, one person may draw a series of pictures or diagrams on paper and somehow transmit an impression of these to someone else in another room who then draws recognizable reproductions of them. This might well be a coincidence in the case of a single successful reproduction; but can a series consist entirely of coincidences?

Experiments have been devised to measure the probability of chance coincidence in supposed cases of telepathy. In the simplest of these, cards printed in turn with five different symbols are used. A pack of fifty, consisting of ten bearing each symbol, is then thoroughly shuffled, and the sender concentrates on the cards one at a time while the receiver (who of course can see neither sender nor cards) tries to write down the correct order of symbols. This procedure is repeated, with constant reshuffling, hundreds or thousands of times. Since there are only five different symbols, a random guess would stand one chance in five of being correct. Consequently, on the assumption that only "chance" is operating, the receiver should be right in about 20 per cent of his tries, and wrong in about 80 per cent; and the longer the series, the closer should be the approach to this proportion. However, good telepathic subjects are right in a far larger number of cases than can be reconciled with random guessing. The deviation from chance expectation can be converted mathematically into "odds against

chance" (increasing as the proportion of hits is maintained over a longer and longer series of tries). In this way, odds of over a million to one have been recorded. J. B. Rhine (Duke University) has reported results showing "antichance" values ranging from seven (which equals odds against chance of 100,000 to one) to eighty-two (which converts the odds against chance to billions).[16] S. G. Soal (London University) has reported positive results for precognitive telepathy with odds against chance of $10^{35} \times 5$, or of billions to one.[17] Other researchers have also recorded confirming results. In the light of these reports, it is difficult to deny that some positive factor, and not merely "chance," is operating. "Telepathy" is simply a name for this unknown positive factor.

How does telepathy operate? Only negative conclusions seem to be justified to date. It can, for example, be said with reasonable certainty that telepathy does not consist in any kind of physical radiation, analogous to radio waves. For, first, telepathy is not delayed or weakened in proportion to distance, as are all known forms of radiation; and, second, there is no organ in the brain or elsewhere that can plausibly be regarded as its sending or receiving center. Telepathy appears to be a purely mental occurrence.

It is not, however, a matter of transferring or transporting a thought out of one mind into another—if, indeed, such an idea makes sense at all. The telepathized thought does not leave the sender's consciousness in order to enter that of the receiver. What happens would be better described by saying that the sender's thought gives rise to a mental "echo" in the mind of the receiver. This "echo" occurs at the unconscious level, and consequently the version of it that rises into the receiver's consciousness may be only fragmentary and may be distorted or symbolized in various ways, as in dreams.

According to one theory that has been tentatively suggested to explain telepathy, our minds are separate and mutually insulated only at the conscious (and preconscious) level. But at the deepest level of the unconscious, we are constantly influencing one another, and it is at this level that telepathy takes place.

How is a telepathized thought directed to one particular receiver among so many? Apparently the thoughts are directed by some link of emotion or common interest. For example, two friends are sometimes telepathically aware of any grave crisis or shock experienced by the other, even though they are at opposite ends of the earth.

We shall turn now to the other branch of parapsychology, which has more obvious bearing upon our subject. The *Proceedings of the Society for Psychical Research* contains a large number of carefully recorded and satisfactorily attested cases of the appearance of the figure of someone who has recently died to living people (in rare instances to more than one at a time) who were, in many cases, at a distance and unaware of the death. The S.P.R. reports also establish beyond reasonable doubt that the minds that operate in the mediumistic trance, purporting to be spirits of the departed, sometimes give personal information the medium could not have acquired by normal means and at times even give information, later verified, which had not been known to any living person.

On the other hand, physical happenings, such as the "materializations" of spirit forms in a visible and tangible form, are much more doubtful. But even if we discount the entire range of physical phenomena, it remains true that the best cases of trance utterance are impressive and puzzling, and taken at face value are indicative of survival and communication after death. If, through a medium, one talks with an intelligence that gives a coherent impression of being an intimately known friend who has died and establishes identity by a wealth of private information and indefinable personal characteristics—as has occasionally happened—then we cannot dismiss without careful trial the theory that what is taking place is the return of a consciousness from the spirit world.

However, the advance of knowledge in the other branch of parapsychology, centering upon the study of extrasensory perception, has thrown unexpected light upon this apparent commerce with the departed. For it suggests that unconscious telepathic contact between the medium and his or her client is an important and possibly a sufficient explanatory factor. This was vividly illustrated by the experience of two women who decided to test the spirits by taking into their minds, over a period of weeks, the personality and atmosphere of an entirely imaginary character in

an unpublished novel written by one of the women. After thus filling their minds with the characteristics of this fictitious person, they went to a reputable medium, who proceeded to describe accurately their imaginary friend as a visitant from beyond the grave and to deliver appropriate messages from him.

An even more striking case is that of the "direct voice" medium (i.e., a medium in whose seances the voice of the communicating "spirit" is heard apparently speaking out of the air) who produced the spirit of one "Gordon Davis" who spoke in his own recognizable voice, displayed considerable knowledge about Gordon Davis, and remembered his death. This was extremely impressive until it was discovered that Gordon Davis was still alive; he was, of all ghostly occupations, a real-estate agent, and had been trying to sell a house at the time when the séance took place!

Such cases suggest that genuine mediums are simply persons of exceptional telepathic sensitiveness who unconsciously derive the "spirits" from their clients' minds.

In connection with "ghosts," in the sense of apparitions of the dead, it has been established that there can be "meaningful hallucinations," the source of which is almost certainly telepathic. To quote a classic and somewhat dramatic example: a woman sitting by a lake sees the figure of a man running toward the lake and throwing himself in. A few days later a man commits suicide by throwing himself into this same lake. Presumably, the explanation of the vision is that the man's thought while he was contemplating suicide had been telepathically projected onto the scene via the woman's mind.

In many of the cases recorded there is delayed action. The telepathically projected thought lingers in the recipient's unconscious mind until a suitable state of inattention to the outside world enables it to appear to his conscious mind in a dramatized form—for example, by a hallucinatory voice or vision—by means of the same mechanism that operates in dreams.

If phantoms of the living can be created by previously experienced thoughts and emotions of the person whom they represent, the parallel possibility arises that phantoms of the dead are caused by thoughts and emotions that were experienced by the person represented when he was alive. In other words, ghosts may be "psychic footprints," a kind of mental trace left behind by the dead, but not involving the presence or even the continued existence of those whom they represent.

These considerations tend away from the hopeful view that parapsychology will open a window onto another world. However, it is too early for a final verdict; and in the meantime one should be careful not to confuse absence of knowledge with knowledge of absence.

NOTES

1. *Phaedo.*
2. The world known to us through our physical senses.
3. Jacques Maritain, *The Range of Reason* (London: Geoffrey Bles Ltd. and New York: Charles Scribner's Sons, 1953), p. 60.
4. Kant, *Critique of Pure Reason, Transcendental Dialectic,* "Refutation of Mendelessohn's Proof of the Permanence of the Soul."
5. Gilbert Ryle's *The Concept of Mind* (London: Hutchinson & Co., Ltd., 1949) is a classic statement of this critique.
6. *Israel* (London: Oxford University Press, 1926), I, 170.
7. Genesis 2:7; Psalm 103:14.
8. 1 Corinthians 15.
9. The following paragraphs are adapted, with permission, from a section of my article, "Theology and Verification," published in *Theology Today* (April, 1960) and reprinted in *The Existence of God* (New York: The Macmillan Company, 1964).
10. For example, Irenaeus, *Against Heresies,* Book II, Chap. 34, para. I.
11. 1 Corinthians 15:37.
12. Quoted by Emil Brunner, *Dogmatics,* II, 69.
13. From the Greek *eschaton,* end.
14. The Greek word *aionios,* which is used in the New Testament and which is usually translated as "eternal" or "everlasting," can bear either this meaning or the more limited meaning of "for the aeon, or age."
15. The list of past presidents of the Society for Psychical Research includes the philosophers Henri Bergson, William James, Hans Driesch, Henry Sidgwick, F. C. S. Schiller, C. D. Broad, and H. H. Price; the psychologists William McDougall, Gardner Murphy, Franklin Prince, and R. H. Thouless; the physicists Sir William Crookes, Sir Oliver Lodge, Sir William Barrett, and Lord Rayleigh; and the classicist Gilbert Murray.
16. J. B. Rhine, *Extrasensory Perception* (Boston: Society for Psychical Research, 1935), Table XLIII, p. 162. See also Rhine, *New Frontiers of the Mind* (New York: Farrar and Rinehart, Inc., 1937), pp. 69f.
17. S. G. Soal, *Proceedings of the Society for Psychical Research,* XLVI, 152–98 and XLVII, 21–150. See also S. G. Soal's *The Experimental Situation in Psychical Research* (London: The Society for Psychical Research, 1947).

FOR FURTHER REFLECTION

1. Has Hick successfully shown the plausibility of survival after death? Has he made the Judeo-Christian view intelligible in the light of modern psychology? Explain.
2. How would Hick respond to the charge that this sort of argument only establishes that someone "exactly similar" to you or me might be recreated, but does not show that you or I may survive?

PART V

Freedom of the Will,
Responsibility, and Punishment

> If I were capable of correct reasoning, and if, at the same time, I had
> a complete knowledge both of his disposition and of all the events by
> which he was surrounded, I should be able to foresee the line of con-
> duct which, in consequence of those events, he would adopt.
>
> *H. T. Buckle,* History of Civilization in England

> One of the strongest supports for the free choice thesis is the unmis-
> takable intuition of virtually every human being that he is free to
> make the choices he does and that the deliberations leading to those
> choices are also free flowing. The normal man feels too, after he has
> made a decision, that he could have decided differently. That is why
> regret or remorse for a past choice can be so disturbing. One can
> refrain from a certain action, and that non-action is likewise a choice.
>
> *Corliss Lamont,* Freedom of Choice Affirmed

Let us pose three questions:

1. Are we really free, or is free will an illusion? (Are we completely determined by
   antecedent causes?)
2. What does it mean to be morally responsible for our actions? (Does moral responsibility entail that the agent has free will?)
3. Is moral responsibility a necessary condition for justified punishment? (*or*, Is the
   concept "punishment" either a confused concept or entirely based on deterring
   crime?)

These three questions about freedom, responsibility, and punishment form the subject
matter of this part of the book. They focus on metaphysical problems connected with the

broad subject of freedom of the will and determinism. We want to know in what sense, if any, we have free will: in what sense, if any, we can be held morally responsible for our actions, and in what sense, if any, punishment is justified.

Free will, responsibility, and punishment are connected issues, and the view you take on any one of these will influence the view you hold on another. People have commonly thought that unless we have free will, we cannot be held morally responsible for any of our acts, and that unless we can be held morally responsible for an act, we cannot be praised or blamed for that act. But if you cannot be praised or blamed for your actions, then it makes no sense to speak of just desert in terms of reward and punishment. So, according to the common view, all depends on the acceptance of free will. At this point, stop and reflect on this reasoning. Do you see any problems with it? Do you believe that free will is necessary for being held responsible for your actions? In my experience, most people believe we have free will and that it is required for being held morally responsible for our actions. But is this common position correct?

In what follows, some essays support the common view; others reject it. In section A we consider whether we really have free will or whether we are wholly determined by antecedent causes or whether freedom and determinism are compatible. In section B we discuss the nature of moral responsibility and what kind of freedom is necessary for it. In section C we focus on the relationship between free will, responsibility, and punishment, attempting to discover the moral basis of punishment. Now let us turn to the topic of free will and determinism.

A. Free Will and Determinism

The antagonism between free will and determinism is one of the most intriguing and difficult problems in all philosophy. It constitutes a paradox. If you look at yourself, at your ability to deliberate and make choices, it seems obvious that you are free. Yet if you look at what you believe about causality (that is, that every event and thing must have a cause), then it appears that you do not have free will, but your acts are determined. So you seem to have inconsistent beliefs.

Let's look more closely at these theses, to see how they work and what support there is for each of them.

1. *Determinism* is the theory that everything in the universe (or at least the macroscopic universe) is entirely determined by causal laws, so that whatever happens at any given moment is the effect of some antecedent cause.

2. *Libertarianism* is the theory that claims that some actions are exempt from the causal laws. The individual is the sole (or decisive) cause of these acts, and the act originates ex nihilo (out of nothing), cut off from all other causes but the self's origination.

3. *Compatibilism, or soft determinism,* the third position, tries to reconcile causal determinism with free will. It holds that although determinism is true, we can still be said to act freely so long as our acts are done voluntarily.

DETERMINISM (SOMETIMES CALLED HARD DETERMINISM)

Baron Paul Henri Thiry, d'Holbach in our first selection states the determinist thesis in its classic form:

In whatever manner man is considered, he is connected to universal nature, and submitted to the necessary and immutable laws that she imposes on all the beings she contains, according to their peculiar essences or to the respective properties with which, without consulting them, she endows particular species. Man's life is a line that nature commands him to outline upon the surface of the earth, without his ever being able to swerve from it, even for an instant. He is born without his own consent; his organization does in nowise depend upon himself; his ideas come to him involuntarily; his habits are in the power of those who cause him to contract them; he is unceasingly modified by causes, whether visible or concealed, over which he has no control, which necessarily regulate his mode of existence, give the hue to his way of thinking, and determine his manner of acting. He is good or bad, happy or miserable, wise or foolish, reasonable or irrational, without his will counting for anything in these various states.[1]

Determinism, as d'Holbach's quotation indicates, is the theory that everything in the universe is governed by causal laws. That is, everything in the universe is entirely determined, so that whatever happens at any given moment is the effect of some antecedent cause. If you were omniscient, you could right now predict exactly everything that would happen for the rest of this hour, for the rest of time itself, simply because you would know how everything hitherto is causally related. This theory—which, it is claimed, is the basic presupposition of science—entails that there is no such thing as an uncaused event. (Sometimes this inference is modified to include only the macrocosmic world, leaving the microcosmic world in doubt.) Hence since all human actions are events, human actions are not undetermined, are not *free* in a radical sense, but are also the product of a causal process. So although you may self-importantly imagine that you are autonomous and have free will, in reality you are totally conditioned by heredity and environment.

The outline of the argument for determinism goes something like this:

1. Every event (state of affairs) must have a cause.
2. Human actions (as well as the agent who gives rise to those actions) are events (or states of affairs).
3. Therefore, every human action (including the agent him- or herself) is caused.

The principle of universal causality cannot be proven—we can't examine every event or state of affairs in the universe to determine its sufficient cause. But neither can it be disproven. This principle is unfalsifiable. Take any event or state of affairs that you consider uncaused. How do you know it is uncaused? Simply because you haven't found the cause does not mean that there isn't one. You just have not been able to locate it. Although the hypothesis of universal causality cannot be proven, it is something we usually assume—either because of considerable inductive evidence or as an a priori truth that seems to impose itself on our thinking about the world. Though an uncaused event is logically conceivable, we have difficulty imagining such an event in ordinary life. For example, imagine your reaction if, on visiting your doctor to seek relief for a severe headache, she were to conclude an elaborate examination with the remark, "I can certainly see that you are in great pain because of your headache, but I'm afraid that I can't help you, for there is no cause for this headache." Perhaps she calls her partner over to examine you. After his examination, he reports, "Sure enough, this is one of those interesting noncausal cases. Sorry, but we don't have any treatment for you. No medicine or other treatment can affect a noncausal headache. We really don't encounter many of these noncausal headaches anymore."

Why do we believe that every event and object in the world has a cause? Many philosophers have echoed John Stuart Mill's answer, that the doctrine of universal causality is a conclusion based on inductive reasoning. We have had an enormous range of experiences wherein we have found causal explanations for individual events, which in turn seem to participate in further causal chains. The problem with this reasoning, however, is that we have only experienced a very small part of the world, not enough of it to warrant a universal conclusion about every event and object having a cause.

David Hume (see Part II) pointed out that the idea of universal causality is not a necessary truth, such as the notion that a triangle has three sides. The hypothesis that every event has a cause arises from the observation of sequences of events in regular conjunctions: "When many uniform instances appear, and the same object is always followed by the same event, we then begin to entertain the notion of cause and connexion."[2] So after a number of successful tries at pouring water over a fire and observing the fire extinguish, we conclude that heat (or fire) causes water to disappear (or vaporize, turn into gas). But we cannot prove that water will always act in this way in the future, nor that it is responsible for every past instance of evaporation. We cannot prove universal causality. All we observe are two events in constant spatiotemporal order, and, from this, we infer a binding relation between them. We see one billiard ball (A) hit another (B), then we see B move away from A, and we judge that A's hitting B at a certain velocity is the cause of B's moving away as it did.

Immanuel Kant (see Part II) argued that the principle of universal causality is a synthetic a priori, that is, an assumption that we cannot prove by experience but is simply part of our noetic makeup. Our mental construction determines that we interpret all experience in the light of the principle of causality. We have no knowledge of what the world is in itself, or whether the principle is universally valid, but we cannot understand experience except by means of causal explanation. We are programmed to read our experience in the causal script.

Kant saw that there was a powerful incentive to believe in the principle of universal causation, and, thus, to believe in determinism, but he also thought that moral responsibility required that agents possess free will. Hence Kant's dilemma.

The man who used the idea of determinism more effectively for practical purposes than any one before him was the great U.S. criminal lawyer Clarence Darrow. In the 1920s, in a sensational crime, two teenage geniuses named Leopold and Loeb, who were both students at the University of Chicago, committed what they regarded as the perfect murder. They grotesquely dismembered a child and buried the parts of his body in a prairie. Caught, they faced an outraged public who demanded the death penalty. The defense attorney was Darrow, champion of lost causes. He conceded that the boys had committed the deed, but argued that they were, nevertheless, "innocent." His argument was based on the theory of determinism. It is worth reading part of the plea.

We are all helpless . . . this weary world goes on, begetting, with birth and with living and with death; and all of it is blind from the beginning to the end. I do not know what it was that made these two boys do this mad act, but I do know there is a reason for it. I know they did not beget themselves. I know that any of an infinite number of causes reaching back to the beginning might be working out in these boys' minds, whom you are asked to hang in malice and in hatred and injustice. . . .

Nature is strong and she is pitiless. She works in her own mysterious way, and we are her victims. We have not much to do with it ourselves. Nature takes this job in hand, and we play our part. In the words of old Omar Khayam, we are:

> But helpless in the game He plays
> Upon the chess board of nights and days;
> Hither and thither moves, and checks and slays,
> And one by one back in the closet lays.

What had this boy to do with it? He was not his own father, he was not his own mother; he was not his own grandparents. All of this was handed to him. He did not surround himself with governesses and wealth. He did not make himself. And yet he is to be compelled to pay.[3]

This plea convinced the judge to go against public opinion and recommend a life sentence instead of the death penalty. If Leopold and Loeb were determined by antecedent causes to do the deed they did, says Darrow, we cannot blame them for what they did any more than we can blame a cow for not being able to fly.

Determinism has received new attention and respect because of modern neurological studies suggesting that there is a one-to-one correlation between mental states and brain states. For example, electrodes set to stimulate certain parts of a patient's cerebral cortex evoke conscious states in the research subject. The hypothesis is that every conscious state can be traced back to a brain state.

Finally, we must distinguish determinism from fatalism. Fatalism is the doctrine that no matter what you—or what anyone else does—certain events will occur. For example, fatalists suppose that President John F. Kennedy was fated to be assassinated in Dallas, Texas, in November 1963. Nothing he or anyone else could have done would have made a difference. Or, the fatalist supposes that it is fixed by the stars or the gods that you will die in an airplane crash at noon on November 10, 2005, no matter what you do. Of course, you would also be destined to board an airplane—one way or another. Determinism, in contrast, acknowledges that human choices and actions can make a difference, but holds that these choices and actions are subject to causal laws. In this section, Baron d'Holbach and John Hospers present the case for hard determinism.

LIBERTARIANISM

Libertarianism is the theory that says we do have free wills. It contends that given the same antecedent conditions at time *t-1*, an agent *S* could do either act *A* or *A-2*. That is, it is up to *S* what the world will look like after *t-1*, and that his act is causally undetermined, the self making the unexplained difference. Libertarians do not contend that all our actions are free—only some of them are—nor do they offer an explanatory theory of free will. Their arguments are indirect. They offer four arguments for their position: from deliberation, from agent causation, from moral responsibility, and from quantum mechanics. I'll postpone discussion of moral responsibility to section B, and focus on the other three arguments here.

The Argument from Deliberation

The position is nicely summed up in the words of Corliss Lamont: "[There] is the unmistakable intuition of virtually every human being that he is free to make the choices he does and that the deliberations leading to those choices are also free flowing. The normal man feels too, after he has made a decision, that he could have decided differently. That is why regret or remorse for a past choice can be so disturbing."[4]

There is a difference between a knee jerk and purposely kicking a football. In the first case, the behavior is involuntary, a reflex reaction, while in the second case you deliberate, notice that you have an alternative (not kicking the ball), consciously choose to kick the ball, and, if successful, find your body moving in the requisite manner, so that the ball is kicked.

Deliberation may take a short or long time, be foolish or wise, but the process is a conscious one wherein you believe that you really can do either of the actions (or any of many possible actions). That is, in deliberating, you assume that we are free to choose among alternatives and that you are not determined to do simply one action. Otherwise why deliberate? This link should seem obvious to everyone who introspects on what it is to deliberate.

Furthermore, there seems to be something psychologically lethal about accepting determinism in human relations; it tends to curtail deliberation and paralyze actions. If people really believe that they and their actions are totally determined, the tendency is for them to excuse their behavior. Human effort seems pointless. As Arthur Eddington put it, "What significance is there to my mental struggle tonight whether I shall or shall not give up smoking, if the laws which govern the matter of the physical universe already preordain for the morrow a configuration of matter consisting of pipe, tobacco, and smoke connected to my lips?"[5] The determinist has an objection to this argument, which you will encounter in Hospers's essay, A4); the libertarian has a counterresponse in terms of agent causation, a version to which we now turn.

The Argument from Agent Causation

Some libertarians, such as Roderick Chisholm and Richard Taylor (in section A) and Lois Walker (section B), respond to the determinist view that motivation is caused by unconscious processes by putting forward an alternate picture of causation to account for actions. According to Chisholm, sometimes the *agent him- or herself* is the cause of his or her own acts. That is, the agent causes actions without him- or herself changing in any essential way. No account need be given of how this possible. Taylor puts it this way:

> The only conception of action that accords with our data is one according to which men . . . are sometimes, but of course not always, self-determining beings; that is, beings which are sometimes the causes of their own behavior. In the case of an action that is free, it must be such that it is caused by the agent who performs it, but such that no antecedent conditions were sufficient for his performing just that action. In the case of an action that is both free

and rational, it must be that the agent who performed it did so for some reason, but this reason cannot have been the cause of it.[6]

This notion of the self as agent differs from Hume's notion that the self is simply a bundle of perceptions, insisting instead that it is a substance and a self-moving being. Human beings are not simply assemblages of material processes but complex wholes, with a different metaphysical status than physical objects. Furthermore, this view sees the self as a substance and not an event. It is a being that initiates action without being caused to act by antecedent causes. If you raise your hand, it is not the events leading up to the raising of your hand that cause this act; rather, you yourself are the cause.

In a sense, the self becomes a "god," creating ex nihilo, in that reasons may influence but do not determine the acts. In the words of Chisholm, "If we are responsible, and if what I have been trying to say [about agent causality] is true, then we have a prerogative which some would attribute only to God: each of us, when we act, is a prime unmoved mover. In doing what we do, we cause certain events to happen and nothing—or no one—causes us to cause those events to happen."[7] Perhaps the libertarian draws some support for this thesis from Genesis 1:26, where God says, "Let us make man in our image." The image of God may be our ability to make free, causally underdetermined decisions. In a sense, every libertarian believes in at least one "god," and in creative miracles.

This theory, while attractive in that it preserves the notion of free agency, suffers from the fact that it leaves agent causation unexplained. The self is a mystery that is unaccounted for. Actions are seen as miracles that are unrelated to antecedent causal chains, detached from the laws of nature. Nevertheless, something like the argument from agency seems to be intuitively satisfying on introspection: we do feel that we are free agents.

Along these lines, the libertarian dismisses the determinist's hypothesis of a complete causal explanation based on a correlation of brain events with mental events. Although memories may be stored in the brain, the self is not. Whether as an emergent property or as a transcendent entity or simply as an unexplained mystery, the self must be regarded as primitive. In a Cartesian manner, it is to be accepted as more certain than anything else and the source of all other certainties.

Of course, determinists like Wood and Hospers have serious objections to this way of viewing human actions.

The Argument from Quantum Physics (A Peephole of Free Will)

At this point libertarians sometimes refer to an argument from quantum mechanics in order to defend themselves against determinists who insist that science agrees with them in espousing universal causality.[8] The argument from quantum mechanics is negative and supports the libertarian thesis indirectly. According to physicists and Nobel laureates Neils Bohr and Max Born, the behavior of subatomic particles does not follow causal processes but instead yields only statistically predictable behavior. That is, we cannot predict the motions of individual particles, but we can successfully predict the percentage that will act in certain ways. A certain randomness seems to operate on this subatomic level. Hence, there is a case for indeterminacy.

This thesis of quantum mechanics is controversial. Albert Einstein never accepted it. "God doesn't play dice!" he said. Quantum physics may only indicate the fact that we do not know the causes operative at subatomic levels; after all, we are only in the kinder-garten stage of the discipline. So, the indeterminist may be committing the fallacy of igno-rance by reading too much into the inability of quantum physicists to give causal explanations of subatomic behavior.

On the other hand, perhaps quantum physics should prompt impartial persons to reconsider what they mean by "causality," and whether it may be an unclear concept in the first place. The fact that our notion of "causality" is vague and unanalyzed was pointed out long ago by David Hume, and reiterated in the twentieth century by William James, who wrote,

> The principle of causality . . . what is it but a postulate, an empty name, covering simply a demand that the sequence of events shall some day manifest a deeper kind of belonging of one thing with another than the mere arbitrary juxtaposition which now phenomenally appears? It is as much an altar to an unknown god as the one that Saint Paul found at Athens. All our scientific and philosophic ideas are altars to unknown gods.[9]

Recent work by philosophers on the subject of causality has not substantially improved this state of affairs. The notion, while enjoying an intuitively privileged position in our noetic structure, is still an enigma.

Nevertheless, while the quantum theory and doubts about causality may cause us to loosen our grip on the notion of universal causality, it does not help the libertarians in any positive way for, at best, it only demonstrates that there is randomness in the world, not that there is purposeful, free agency. Uncaused behavior suggests erratic, impulsive, reflex motion without any rhyme or reason, the behavior of the maniac, lacking all pre-dictability and explanation, behavior out of rational control. But free action must be under your control if it is to be counted as your behavior. That is, the thesis of libertarianism is that agents are underdetermined when they make purposeful, rational decisions. All that quantum mechanics entails is that random events in the brain or wherever yield unpre-dictable behavior for which the agent is not responsible.

If this is so, indeterminism does not help the libertarian. The argument may be put this way:

1. If determinism is true, human actions are not free (since they are determined by antecedent causes).
2. If indeterminism is true, human actions are not free (since free actions must be pur-posive, rather than random).
3. So whether determinism or indeterminism is true, human actions are not free.

The challenge to the libertarian is to maneuver between the horns of this dilemma. The libertarian must reject determinism without accepting randomness as the explanation of our actions. But an alternative strategy is to deny that causal determinism entails hard determinism. To this strategy we now turn.

Compatibilism (Sometimes Called Soft Determinism)

However, there is another response to the problem of free will and determinism, similar to that of Kant but perhaps more subtle. It may be called "reconciling determinism," or "soft determinism" or "compatibilism." The position argues although we are determined, we still have moral responsibilities: the basis of the distinction is between *voluntary* and *involuntary* behavior.

The language of freedom and the language of determinism are only two different ways of talking about certain human or rational events, both necessary for humanity. One approach is necessary for science, and the other is necessary for morality and personal relationships. The compatibilist argues that the fact that we are determined does not affect our interpersonal relations. We still have feelings with which we must deal, using internalist insights. We still feel resentment when someone hurts us "on purpose." We still feel grateful for services rendered and hold people responsible for their actions. However, we acknowledge that from the external perspective, the determinist's account of all this is correct.

Along these lines, Walter T. Stace, in the third reading, argues that the problem of freedom and determinism is really only a semantic one, a dispute about the meaning of words. Freedom has to do with acts done voluntarily, and determinism has to do with the causal processes that underlie all behavior and events. These need not be incompatible. Mahatma Gandhi's fasting because he wanted to liberate India from British rule was a voluntary or free act, whereas a man starving in the desert is not doing so voluntarily or as a free act. A thief purposefully and voluntarily steals, whereas a kleptomaniac cannot help stealing. In both cases, each act or event has causal antecedents, but the former in each set are free while the latter are unfree. Stace notes, "Acts freely done are those whose immediate causes are psychological states in the agent. Acts not freely done are those whose immediate causes are states of affairs external to the agent."

The position that rejects the reconciliation of free will with determinism is called *incompatibilism*. In the following readings, compatibilism is attacked both by the determinist John Hospers and by libertarians Richard Taylor (section A), and Lois H. Walker (section B). They would agree with another incompatibilist, William James, who called compatibilism a "quagmire of evasion." Harry Frankfurt, in the last reading in this section, and Michael Levin in section B give further defenses of compatibilism.

NOTES

1. Paul Henri Thiry, Baron d'Holbach, *System of Nature*, trans. H. D. Robinson (London: Hogden, 1770), Chapter 11.
2. David Hume, *An Enquiry Concerning Human Understanding* (1748; reprint, New York: Oxford University Press, 1999), 78.
3. Clarence Darrow, *Attorney for the Damned* (New York: Simon & Schuster, 1957).
4. Corliss Lamont, *Freedom of Choice Affirmed* (New York: Horizon, 1967), 3.
5. Arthur Eddington, *The Nature of the Physical World* (New York: Macmillan, 1928).
6. Richard Taylor, *Metaphysics* (Englewood Cliffs, NJ: Prentice-Hall, 1974), 51.
7. Roderick Chisholm, *Human Freedom and the Self*, Lindley Lecture, University of Kansas, 1964.
8. See J. R. Lucas, *The Freedom of the Will* (Oxford: Oxford University Press, 1970).
9. William James, "The Dilemma of Determinism," in *The Will to Believe* (New York: Holt, 1912).

BARON PAUL HENRI D'HOLBACH

A DEFENSE OF DETERMINISM

Baron Paul Henri d'Holbach (1723–1789), born in Edesheim, Germany, and growing up in France, was one of the leading philosophers of the French Enlightenment. He was a materialist who believed that nature is one grand machine, and humans are particular machines within this grand machine—a machine that needs no machinist. He was a significant contributor to the *Encyclopedie* and a friend of Diderot, Hume, and Rousseau. His principal writings are *Christianity Unveiled* (1767), *The System of Nature* (1770), from which the present selection is taken, and *Common Sense, or Natural Ideas Opposed to Supernatural Ideas* (1772).

d'Holbach is one of the first philosophers to provide a sustained systematic critique of the doctrine of free will. According to him, if we accept science, which he equates with a system of material particles operating according to fixed laws of motion, then we will see that free will is an illusion. There is no such entity as a soul, but we are simply material objects in motion, having very complicated brains that lead the unreflective to believe that they are free.

Those who have affirmed that the *soul* is distinguished from the body, is immaterial, draws its ideas from its own peculiar source, acts by its own energies, without the aid of any exterior object, have, by a consequence of their own system, enfranchised [liberated] it from those physical laws according to which all beings of which we have a knowledge are obliged to act. They have believed that the soul is mistress of its own conduct, is able to regulate its own peculiar operations, has the faculty to determine its will by its own natural energy; in a word, they have pretended that man is a *free agent*.

It has been already sufficiently proved that the soul is nothing more than the body considered relatively to some of its functions more concealed than others: it has been shown that this soul, even when it shall be supposed immaterial, is continually modified conjointly with the body, is submitted to all its motion, and that without this it would remain inert and dead; that, consequently, it is subjected to the influence of those material and physical causes which give impulse to the body; of which the mode of existence, whether habitual or transitory, depends upon the material elements by which it is surrounded, that form its texture, constitute its temperament, enter into it by means of the aliments, and penetrate it by their subtility. The faculties which are called *intellectual*, and those qualities which are styled *moral*, have been explained in a manner purely physical and natural. In the last place it has been demonstrated that all the ideas, all the systems, all the affections, all the opinions, whether true or false, which man forms to himself, are to be attributed to his physical and material senses. Thus man is a being purely physical; in whatever manner he is considered, he is connected to universal nature, and submitted to the necessary and immutable laws that she imposes on all the beings she contains, according to their peculiar essences or to the

From Baron d'Holbach "Of the System of Man's Free Agency," in *The System of Nature* (1770).

respective properties with which, without consulting them, she endows each particular species. Man's life is a line that nature commands him to describe upon the surface of the earth, without his ever being able to swerve from it, even for an instant. He is born without his own consent; his organization does in nowise depend upon himself; his ideas come to him involuntarily; his habits are in the power of those who cause him to contract them; he is unceasingly modified by causes, whether visible or concealed, over which he has no control, which necessarily regulate his mode of existence, give the hue to his way of thinking, and determine his manner of acting. He is good or bad, happy or miserable, wise or foolish, reasonable or irrational, without his will being for any thing in these various states. Nevertheless, in despite of the shackles by which he is bound, it is pretended he is a free agent, or that independent of the causes by which he is moved, he determines his own will, and regulates his own condition.

However slender the foundation of this opinion, of which every thing ought to point out to him the error, it is current at this day and passes for an incontestable truth with a great number of people, otherwise extremely enlightened; it is the basis of religion, which, supposing relations between man and the unknown being she has placed above nature, has been incapable of imagining how man could either merit reward or deserve punishment from this being, if he was not a free agent. Society has been believed interested in this system; because an idea has gone abroad, that if all the actions of man were to be contemplated as necessary, the right of punishing those who injure their associates would no longer exist. At length human vanity accommodated itself to a hypothesis which, unquestionably, appears to distinguish man from all other physical beings, by assigning to him the special privilege of a total independence of all other causes, but of which a very little reflection would have shown him the impossibility. . . .

The will . . . is a modification of the brain, by which it is disposed to action, or prepared to give play to the organs. This will is necessarily determined by the qualities, good or bad, agreeable or painful, of the object or the motive that acts upon his senses, or of which the idea remains with him, and is resuscitated by his memory. In consequence, he acts necessarily, his action is the result of the impulse he receives either from the motive, from the object, or from the idea which has modified his brain, or disposed his will. When he does not act according to this impulse, it is because there comes some new cause, some new motive, some new idea, which modifies his brain in a different manner, gives him a new impulse, determines his will in another way, by which the action of the former impulse is suspended: thus, the sight of an agreeable object, or its idea, determines his will to set him in action to procure it; but if a new object or a new idea more powerfully attracts him, it gives a new direction to his will, annihilates the effect of the former, and prevents the action by which it was to be procured. This is the mode in which reflection, experience, reason, necessarily arrests or suspends the action of man's will: without this he would of necessity have followed the anterior impulse which carried him towards a then desirable object. In all this he always acts according to necessary laws, from which he has no means of emancipating himself.

If when tormented with violent thirst, he figures to himself in idea, or really perceives a fountain, whose limpid streams might cool his feverish want, is he sufficient master of himself to desire or not to desire the object competent to satisfy so lively a want? It will no doubt be conceded, that it is impossible he should not be desirous to satisfy it; but it will be said—if at this moment it is announced to him that the water he so ardently desires is poisoned, he will, notwithstanding his vehement thirst, abstain from drinking it: and it has, therefore, been falsely concluded that he is a free agent. The fact, however, is, that the motive in either case is exactly the same: his own conservation. The same necessity that determined him to drink before he knew the water was deleterious, upon this new discovery equally determines him not to drink; the desire of conserving himself either annihilates or suspends the former impulse; the second motive becomes stronger than the preceding, that is, the fear of death, or the desire of preserving himself, necessarily prevails over the painful sensation caused by his eagerness to drink; but, it will be said, if the thirst is very parching, an inconsiderate man without regarding the danger will risk swallowing the water. Nothing is gained by this remark: in this case the anterior impulse only regains the ascendency; he is persuaded that life may possibly be longer preserved, or that he shall derive a greater good by drinking the poisoned water than by enduring the torment, which, to his mind, threatens instant dissolution: thus the first becomes the strongest and necessarily urges him on to action. Nevertheless, in either case, whether he partakes of the water, or whether he does not, the two actions will be equally necessary; they will be the effect of that motive which finds itself most puissant; which consequently acts in the most coercive manner upon his will.

This example will serve to explain the whole phenomena of the human will. This will, or rather the brain, finds itself in the same situation as a ball, which, although it has received an impulse that drives it forward in a straight line, is deranged in its course whenever a force superior to the first obliges it to change its direction. The man who drinks the poisoned water appears a madman; but the actions of fools are as necessary as those of the most prudent individuals. The motives that determine the voluptuary and the debauchee to risk their health, are as powerful, and their actions are as necessary, as those which decide the wise man to manage his. But, it will be insisted, the debauchee may be prevailed on to change his conduct: this does not imply that he is a free agent; but that motives may be found sufficiently powerful to annihilate the effect of those that previously acted upon him; then these new motives determine his will to the new mode of conduct he may adopt as necessarily as the former did to the old mode.

Man is said to *deliberate*, when the action of the will is suspended; this happens when two opposite motives act alternately upon him. *To deliberate*, is to hate and to love in succession; it is to be alternately attracted and repelled; it is to be moved, sometimes by one motive, sometimes by another. Man only deliberates when he does not distinctly understand the quality of the objects from which he receives impulse, or when experience has not sufficiently apprised him of the effects, more or less remote, which his actions will produce. He would take the air, but the weather is uncertain; he deliberates in consequence; he weighs the various motives that urge his will to go out or to stay at home; he is at length determined by that motive which is most probable; this removes his indecision, which necessarily settles his will, either to remain within or to go abroad: his motive is always either the immediate or ultimate advantage he finds, or thinks he finds, in the action to which he is persuaded.

Man's will frequently fluctuates between two objects, of which either the presence or the ideas move him alternately: he waits until he has contemplated the objects, or the ideas they have left in his brain which solicit him to different actions; he then compares these objects or ideas; but even in the time of deliberation, during the comparison, pending these alternatives of love and hatred which succeed each other, sometimes with the utmost rapidity, he is not a free agent for a single instant; the good or the evil which he believes he finds successively in the objects, are the necessary motives of these momentary wills; of the rapid motion of desire or fear, that he experiences as long as his uncertainty continues. From this it will be obvious that deliberation is necessary; that uncertainty is necessary; that whatever part he takes, in consequence of this deliberation, it will always necessarily be that which he has judged, whether well or ill, is most probable to turn to his advantage.

When the soul is assailed by two motives that act alternately upon it, or modify it successively, it deliberates; the brain is in a sort of equilibrium, accompanied with perpetual oscillations, sometimes towards one object, sometimes towards the other, until the most forcible carries the point, and thereby extricates it from this state of suspense, in which consists the indecision of his will. But when the brain is simultaneously assailed by causes equally strong that move it in opposite directions, agreeable to the general law of all bodies when they are struck equally by contrary powers, it stops . . . it is neither capable to will nor to act; it waits until one of the two causes has obtained sufficient force to overpower the other; to determine its will; to attract it in such a manner that it may prevail over the efforts of the other cause.

This mechanism, so simple, so natural, suffices to demonstrate why uncertainty is painful, and why suspense is always a violent state for man. The brain, an organ so delicate and so mobile, experiences such rapid modifications that it is fatigued; or when it is urged in contrary directions, by causes equally powerful, it suffers a kind of compression, that prevents the activity which is suitable to the preservation of the whole, and which is necessary to procure what is advantageous to its existence. This mechanism will also explain the irregularity, the indecision, the inconstancy of man, and account for that conduct which frequently appears an inexplicable mystery, and which is, indeed, the effect of the received systems. In consulting experience, it will be found that the soul is submitted to precisely the same physical laws as the material body. If the will of each individual, during a given time, was only moved by a single cause or passion, nothing would be more easy than to foresee his actions; but his heart is frequently assailed by contrary powers, by adverse motives, which either act on him simultaneously or in succession; then his brain, attracted in opposite directions, is either fatigued, or else tormented by a state of compression, which deprives it of activity. Sometimes it is in a state of incommodious inaction; sometimes it is the sport of the alternate shocks it undergoes. Such, no doubt, is the state in which man finds himself when a lively passion solicits him to the commission of crime, whilst fear points out to him the danger by which it is attended; such, also, is the condition of him whom remorse, by the continued labour of his distracted soul, prevents from enjoying the objects he has criminally obtained.

Choice by no means proves the free agency of man: he only deliberates when he does not yet know which to choose of the many objects that move him; he is then in an embarrassment, which does not terminate until his will is decided by the greater advantage he believes he shall find in the object he chooses, or the action he undertakes. From whence it may be seen, that choice is necessary, because he would not determine for an object, or for an action, if he did not believe that he should find in it some direct advantage. That man should have free agency it were needful that he should be able to will or choose without motive, or that he could prevent motives coercing his will. Action always being the effect of his will once determined, and as his will cannot be determined but by a motive which is not in his own power, it follows that he is never the master of the determination of his own peculiar will; that consequently he never acts as a free agent. It has been believed that man was a free agent because he had a will with the power of choosing; but attention has not been paid to the fact that even his will is moved by causes independent of himself; is owing to that which is inherent in his own organization, or which belongs to the nature of the beings acting on him. Is he the master of willing not to withdraw his hand from the fire when he fears it will be burnt? Or has he the power to take away from fire the property which makes him fear it? Is he the master of not choosing a dish of meat, which he knows to be agreeable or analogous to his palate; of not preferring it to that which he knows to be disagreeable or dangerous? It is always according to his sensations, to his own peculiar experience, or to his suppositions, that he judges of things, either well or ill; but whatever may be his judgment, it depends necessarily on his mode of feeling, whether habitual or accidental, and the qualities he finds in the causes that move him, which exist in despite of himself. . . .

When it is said, that man is not a free agent, it is not pretended to compare him to a body moved by a simple impulsive cause: he contains within himself causes inherent to his existence; he is moved by an interior organ, which has its own peculiar laws, and is itself necessarily determined in consequence of ideas formed from perceptions resulting from sensations which it receives from exterior objects. As the mechanism of these sensations, of these perceptions, and the manner they engrave ideas on the brain of man, are not known to him; because he is unable to unravel all these motions; because he cannot perceive the chain of operations in his soul, or the motive principle that acts within him, he supposes himself a free agent; which, literally translated, signifies, that he moves himself by himself; that he determines himself without cause: when he rather ought to say, that he is ignorant how or for why he acts in the manner he does. It is true the soul enjoys an activity peculiar to itself; but it is equally certain that this activity would never be displayed, if some motive or some cause did not put it in a condition to exercise itself: at least it will not be pretended that the soul is able either to love or to hate without being moved, without knowing the objects, without having some idea of their qualities.

Gunpowder has unquestionably a particular activity, but this activity will never display itself, unless fire be applied to it; this, however, immediately sets it in motion.

It is the great complication of motion in man, it is the variety of his action, it is the multiplicity of causes that move him, whether simultaneously or in continual succession, that persuades him he is a free agent: if all his motions were simple, if the causes that move him did not confound themselves with each other, if they were distinct, if his machine were less complicated, he would perceive that all his actions were necessary, because he would be enabled to recur instantly to the cause that made him act. A man who should be always obliged to go towards the west, would always go on that side; but he would feel that, in so going, he was not a free agent: if he had another sense, as his actions or his motion, augmented by a sixth, would be still more varied and much more complicated, he would believe himself still more a free agent than he does with his five senses.

It is, then, for want of recurring to the causes that move him; for want of being able to analyze, from not being competent to decompose the complicated motion of his machine, that man believes himself a free agent; it is only upon his own ignorance that he founds the profound yet deceitful notion he has of his free agency; that he builds those opinions which he brings forward as a striking proof of his pretended freedom of action. If, for a short time, each man was willing to examine his own peculiar actions, search out their true motives to discover their concatenation, he would remain convinced that the sentiment he has of his natural free agency, is a chimera that must speedily be destroyed by experience.

Nevertheless it must be acknowledged that the multiplicity and diversity of the causes which continually act upon man, frequently without even his knowledge, render it impossible, or at least extremely difficult for him to recur to the true principles of his own peculiar actions, much less the actions of others: they frequently depend upon causes so fugitive, so remote from their effects, and which, superficially examined, appear to have so little analogy, so slender a relation with them, that it requires singular sagacity to bring them into light. This is what renders the study of the moral man a task of such difficulty; this is the reason why his heart is an abyss, of which it is frequently impossible for him to fathom the depth. He is then obliged to content himself with a knowledge of the general and necessary laws by which the human heart is regulated: for the individuals of his own species these laws are pretty nearly the same; they vary only in consequence of the organization that is peculiar to each, and of the modification it undergoes: This, however, cannot be rigorously the same in any two. It suffices to know, that by his essence, man tends to conserve himself, and to render his existence happy: this granted, whatever may be his actions, if he recur back to this first principle, to this general, this necessary tendency of his will, he never can be deceived with regard to his motives.

FOR FURTHER REFLECTION

1. Has d'Holbach proved that we do not have free will? Is his argument that science precludes such a notion convincing?

2. d'Holbach points out that without the doctrine of free will, the notion of just punishment crumbles: that religion could not justify God's sending people to hell for their sins, and the Law could not justify its system of punishments without the doctrine. Do you agree with d'Holbach?

3. Could we go even further and say that we would not have any place for moral praise or blame without a notion of free will? What would d'Holbach make of moral responsibility?

4. J. B. S. Haldane has written, "If my mental processes are determined wholly by the motion of atoms in my brain, I have no reason to suppose that my beliefs are true . . . and hence I have no reason for supposing my brain to be composed of atoms." Does this show that determinism is self-refuting?

RICHARD TAYLOR

LIBERTARIANISM
Defense of Free Will

Richard Taylor (b. 1919) taught philosophy for many years at the University of Rochester, Brown University, and Union College. He has written widely in moral and social philosophy as well as in philosophy of mind. He has a reputation for clarity and creativity.

In this essay Taylor argues for three theses: (1) soft determinism (or compatibilism) does not preserve moral responsibility,(2) indeterminism (the theory that some events lack causal determinants) must not be confused with freedom of the will and provides no support for it, and (3) the agency theory of free, will preserves our notions of deliberation and responsibility.

SOFT DETERMINISM

. . . All versions of this theory have in common three claims, by means of which, it is naively supposed, a reconciliation is achieved between determinism and freedom. Freedom being, furthermore, a condition of moral responsibility and the only condition that metaphysics seriously questions, it is supposed by the partisans of this view that determinism is perfectly compatible with such responsibility. This, no doubt, accounts for its great appeal and wide acceptance, even by some men of considerable learning.

The three claims of soft determinism are (1) that the thesis of determinism is true, and that accordingly all human behavior, voluntary or other, like the behavior of all other things, arises from antecedent conditions, given which no other behavior is possible—in short, that all human behavior is caused and determined; (2) that voluntary behavior is nonetheless free to the extent that it is not externally constrained or impeded; and (3) that, in the absence of such obstacles and constraints, the causes of voluntary behavior are certain states, events, or conditions within the agent himself; namely, his own acts of will or volitions, choices, decisions, desires, and so on.

Thus, on this view, I am free, and therefore sometimes responsible for what I do, provided nothing prevents me from acting according to my own choice, desire, or volition, or constrains me to act otherwise. There may, to be sure, be other conditions for my responsibility—such as, for example, an understanding of the probable consequences of my behavior, and that sort of thing—but absence of constraint or impediment is, at least, one such condition. And, it is claimed, it is a condition that is compatible with the supposition that my behavior is caused—for it is, by hypothesis, caused by my own inner choices, desires, and volitions.

THE REFUTATION OF THIS

The theory of soft determinism looks good at first—so good that it has for generations been solemnly taught from numberless philosophical chairs and

From Richard Taylor, Metaphysics (1974), 2nd ed., pp. 44–53, by permission of Pearson Education, Inc., Upper Saddle River, NJ.

implanted in the minds of students as sound philoso-phy—but no great acumen is needed to discover that far from solving any problem, it only camouflages it.

My free actions are those unimpeded and uncon-strained motions that arise from my own inner desires, choices, and volitions; let us grant this provisionally. But now, whence arise those inner states that deter-mine what my body shall do? Are they within my con-trol or not? Having made my choice or decision and acted upon it, could I have chosen otherwise or not?

Here the determinist, hoping to surrender nothing and yet to avoid the problem implied in that question, bids us not to ask it; the question itself, he announces, is without meaning. For to say that I could have done otherwise, he says, means only that I *would* have done otherwise *if* those inner states that determined my action had been different; if, that is, I had decided or chosen differently. To ask, accordingly, whether I could have chosen or decided differently is only to ask whether, had I decided to decide differently or chosen to choose differently, or willed to will differently, I would have decided or chosen or willed differently. And this, of course, *is* unintelligible nonsense.

But it is not nonsense to ask whether the causes of my actions—my own inner choices, decisions, and desires—are themselves caused. And of course they are, if determinism is true, for on that thesis every-thing is caused and determined. And if they are, then we cannot avoid concluding that, given the causal conditions of those inner states, I could not have decided, willed, chosen, or desired otherwise than I in fact did, for this is a logical consequence of the very definition of determinism. Of course we can still say that, *if* the causes of those inner states, whatever they were, had been different, then their effects, those inner states themselves, would have been different, and that in this hypothetical sense I could have decided, chosen, willed, or desired differently—but that only pushes our problem back still another step. For we will then want to know whether the causes of those inner states were within my control; and so on, *ad infinitum*. We are, at each step, permitted to say "could have been otherwise" only in a provisional sense—provided, that is, something else had been different—but must then retract it and replace it with "could not have been otherwise" as soon as we discover, as we

must at each step, that whatever would have to have been different could not have been different.

EXAMPLES

Such is the dialectic of the problem. The easiest way to see the shadowy quality of soft determinism, how-ever, is by means of examples.

Let us suppose that my body is moving in various ways, that these motions are not externally con-strained or impeded, and that they are all exactly in accordance with my own desires, choices, or acts of will and whatnot. When I will that my arm should move in a certain way, I find it moving in that way, unobstructed and unconstrained. When I will to speak, my lips and tongue move, unobstructed and uncon-strained, in a manner suitable to the formation of the words I choose to utter. Now given that this is a cor-rect description of my behavior, namely, that it con-sists of the unconstrained and unimpeded motions of my body in response to my own volitions, then it fol-lows that my behavior is free, on the soft determinist's definition of "free." It follows further that I am responsible for that behavior; or at least, that if I am not, it is not from any lack of freedom on my part.

But if the fulfillment of these conditions renders my behavior free—that is to say, if my behavior sat-isfies the conditions of free action set forth in the theory of soft determinism—then my behavior will be no less free if we assume further conditions that are perfectly consistent with those already satisfied.

We suppose further, accordingly, that while my behavior is entirely in accordance with my own voli-tions, and thus "free" in terms of the conception of freedom we are examining, my volitions themselves are caused. To make this graphic, we can suppose that an ingenious physiologist can induce in me any voli-tion he pleases, simply by pushing various buttons on an instrument to which, let us suppose, I am attached by numerous wires. All the volitions I have in that sit-uation are, accordingly, precisely the ones he gives me. By pushing one button, he evokes in me the voli-tion to raise my hand; and my hand, being unimpeded, rises in response to that volition. By pushing another, he induces the volition in me to kick, and my foot, being unimpeded, kicks in response to that volition. We can even suppose that the physiologist puts a rifle in my hands, aims it at some passerby, and then, by pushing the proper button, evokes in me the volition to squeeze my finger against the trigger, whereupon the passerby falls dead of a bullet wound.

This is the description of a man who is acting in accordance with his inner volitions, a man whose body is unimpeded and unconstrained in its motions, these motions being the effects of those inner states. It is hardly the description of a free and responsible agent. It is the perfect description of a puppet. To render a man your puppet, it is not necessary forcibly to constrain the motions of his limbs, after the fashion that real puppets are moved. A subtler but no less effective means of making a man your puppet would be to gain complete control of his inner states, and ensuring, as the theory of soft determinism does ensure, that his body will move in accordance with them.

The example is somewhat unusual, but it is no worse for that. It is perfectly intelligible, and it does appear to refute the soft determinist's conception of freedom. One might think that, in such a case, the agent should not have allowed himself to be so rigged in the first place, but this is irrelevant; we can suppose that he was not aware that he was, and was hence unaware of the source of the those inner states that prompted his bodily motions. The example can, moreover, be modified in perfectly realistic ways, so as to coincide with actual and familiar cases. One can, for instance, be given a compulsive desire for certain drugs, simply by having them administered to him over a course of time. Suppose, then, that I do, with neither my knowledge nor consent, thus become a victim of such a desire and act upon it. Do I act freely, merely by virtue of the fact that I am unimpeded in my quest for drugs? In a sense I do, surely, but I am hardly free with respect to whether or not I shall use drugs. I never chose to have the desire for them inflicted upon me.

Nor does it, of course, matter whether the inner states which allegedly prompt all my "free" activity are evoked in me by another agent or by perfectly impersonal forces. Whether a desire which causes my body to behave in a certain way is inflicted upon me by another person, for instance, or derived from hereditary factors, or indeed from anything at all, matters not the least. In any case, if it is in fact the cause of my bodily behavior, I cannot but act in accordance with it. Wherever it came from, whether from personal or impersonal origins, it was entirely caused or determined, and not within my control. Indeed, if determinism is true, as the theory of soft determinism holds it to be, all those inner states which cause my body to behave in whatever ways it behaves must arise from circumstances that existed before I was born; for the chain of causes and effects is infinite, and none could have been the least different, given those that preceded.

SIMPLE INDETERMINISM

We might at first now seem warranted in simply denying determinism, and saying that, insofar as they are free, my actions are not caused; or that, if they are caused by my own inner states—my own desires, impulses, choices, volitions, and whatnot—then these, in any case, are not caused. This is a perfectly clear sense in which a man's action, assuming that it was free, could have been otherwise. If it was uncaused, then, even given the conditions under which it occurred and all that preceded, some other act was nonetheless possible, and he did not have to do what he did. Or if his action was the inevitable consequence of his own inner states, and could not have been otherwise given these, we can nevertheless say that these inner states, being uncaused, could have been otherwise, and could thereby have produced different actions.

Only the slightest consideration will show, however, that this simple denial of determinism has not the slightest plausibility. For let us suppose it is true, and that some of my bodily motions—namely, those that I regard as my free acts—are not caused at all or, if caused by my own inner states, that these are not caused. We shall thereby avoid picturing a puppet, to be sure—but only by substituting something even less like a man; for the conception that now emerges is not that of a free man, but of an erratic and jerking phantom, without any rhyme or reason at all.

Suppose that my right arm is free, according to this conception; that is, that its motions are uncaused. It moves this way and that from time to time, but nothing causes these motions. Sometimes it moves forth vigorously, sometimes up, sometimes down, sometimes it just drifts vaguely about—these motions all being wholly free and uncaused. Manifestly I have nothing to do with them at all; they just happen, and neither I nor anyone can ever tell what this arm will be doing next. It might seize a club and lay it on the head of the nearest bystander, no less to my astonishment than his. There will never be any point in asking why these motions occur, or in seeking any explanation of them, for under the conditions assumed there is no explanation. They just happen, from no causes at all.

This is no description of free, voluntary, or responsible behavior. Indeed, so far as the motions of my body or its parts are entirely uncaused, such motions cannot even be ascribed to me as my behavior in the first place, since I have nothing to do with them. The behavior of my arm is just the random motion of a foreign object. Behavior that is mine must be behavior that is within my control, but motions that occur from no causes are without the control of anyone. I can have no more to do with, and no more control over, the uncaused motions of my limbs than a gambler has over the motions of an honest roulette wheel. I can only, like him, idly wait to see what happens.

Nor does it improve things to suppose that my bodily motions are caused by my own inner states, so long as we suppose these to be wholly uncaused. The result will be the same as before. My arm, for example, will move this way and that, sometimes up and sometimes down, sometimes vigorously and sometimes just drifting about, always in response to certain inner states, to be sure. But since these are supposed to be wholly uncaused, it follows that I have no control over them and hence none over their effects. If my hand lays a club forcefully on the nearest bystander, we can indeed say that this motion resulted from an inner club-wielding desire of mine; but we must add that I had nothing to do with that desire, and that it arose, to be followed by its inevitable effect, no less to my astonishment than to his. Things like this do, alas, sometimes happen. We are all sometimes seized by compulsive impulses that arise we know not whence

and we do sometimes act upon these. But because they are far from being examples of free, voluntary, and responsible behavior, we need only to learn that behavior was of this sort to conclude that it was not free, voluntary, or responsible. It was erratic, impulsive, and irresponsible.

DETERMINISM AND SIMPLE INDETERMINISM AS THEORIES

Both determinism and simple indeterminism are loaded with difficulties, and no one who has thought much on them can affirm either of them without some embarrassment. Simple indeterminism has nothing whatever to be said for it, except that it appears to remove the grossest difficulties of determinism, only, however, to imply perfect absurdities of its own. Determinism, on the other hand, is at least initially plausible. Men seem to have a natural inclination to believe in it; it is, indeed, almost required for the very exercise of practical intelligence. And beyond this, our experience appears always to confirm it, so long as we are dealing with everyday facts of common experience, as distinguished from the esoteric researches of theoretical physics. But determinism, as applied to human behavior, has implications which few men can casually accept, and they appear to be implications which no modification of the theory can efface.

Both theories, moreover, appear logically irreconcilable to the two items of data that we set forth at the outset; namely, (1) that my behavior is sometimes the outcome of my deliberation, and (2) that in these and other cases it is sometimes up to me what I do. Because these were our data, it is important to see, as must already be quite clear, that these theories cannot be reconciled to them.

I can deliberate only about my own future actions, and then only if I do not already know what I am going to do. If a certain nasal tickle warns me that I am about to sneeze, for instance, then I cannot deliberate whether to sneeze or not; I can only prepare for the impending convulsion. But if determinism is true, then there are always conditions existing antecedently to everything I do, sufficient for my doing just that, and such as to render it inevitable. If I can know what those conditions are and what behavior they are sufficient to produce, then I can in every such case know what I am going to do and cannot then deliberate about it.

By itself this only shows, of course, that I can deliberate only in ignorance of the causal conditions of my behavior; it does not show that such conditions cannot exist. It is odd, however, to suppose that deliberation should be a mere substitute for clear knowledge. Ignorance is a condition of speculation, inference, and guesswork, which have nothing whatever to do with deliberation. A prisoner awaiting execution may not know when he is going to die, and he may even entertain the hope of reprieve, but he cannot deliberate about this. He can only speculate, guess—and wait.

Worse yet, however, it now becomes clear that I cannot deliberate about what I am going to do, if it is even possible for me to find out in advance, whether I do in fact find out in advance or not. I can deliberate only with the view to deciding what to do, to making up my mind; and this is impossible if I believe that it could be inferred what I am going to do, from conditions already existing, even though I have not made that inference myself. If I believe that what I am going to do has been rendered inevitable by conditions already existing, and could be inferred by anyone having the requisite sagacity, then I cannot try to decide whether to do it or not, for there is simply nothing left to decide. I can at best only guess or try to figure it out myself or, all prognostics failing, I can wait and see; but I cannot deliberate. I deliberate in order to *decide* what *to* do, not to *discover* what it is that I am *going* to do. But if determinism is true, then there are always antecedent conditions sufficient for everything that I do, and this can always be inferred by anyone having the requisite sagacity; that is, by anyone having a knowledge of what those conditions are and what behavior they are sufficient to produce.

This suggests what in fact seems quite clear, that determinism cannot be reconciled with our second datum either, to the effect that it is sometimes up to me what I am going to do. For if it is ever really up to me whether to do this thing or that, then, as we have seen, each alternative course of action must be such that I can do it; not that I can do it in some abstruse

or hypothetical sense of "can"; not that I could do it if only something were true that is not true; but in the sense that it is then and there within my power to do it. But this is never so, if determinism is true, for on the very formulation of that theory whatever happens at any time is the only thing that can then happen, given all that precedes it. It is simply a logical consequence of this that whatever I do at any time is the only thing I can then do, given the conditions that precede my doing it. Nor does it help in the least to interpose, among the causal antecedents of my behavior, my own inner states, such as my desires, choices, acts of will, and so on. For even supposing these to be always involved in voluntary behavior—which is highly doubtful in itself—it is a consequence of determinism that these, whatever they are at any time, can never be other that what they then are. Every chain of causes and effects, if determinism is true, is infinite. This is why it is not now up to me whether I shall a moment hence be male or female. The conditions determining my sex have existed through my whole life, and even prior to my life. But if determinism is true, the same holds of anything that I ever am, ever become, or ever do. It matters not whether we are speaking of the most patent facts of my being, such as my sex; or the most subtle, such as my feelings, thoughts, desires, or choices. Nothing could be other than it is, given what was; and while we may indeed say, quite idly, that something—some inner state of mind, for instance—*could* have been different, had only something *else* been different, any consolation of this thought evaporates as soon as we add that whatever would have to have been different could not have been different.

It is even more obvious that our data cannot be reconciled to the theory of simple indeterminism. I can deliberate only about my own actions; this is obvious. But the random, uncaused motion of any body whatever, whether it be a part of my body or not, is no action of mine and nothing that is within my power. I might try to guess what these motions will be, just as I might try to guess how a roulette wheel will behave, but I cannot deliberate about them or try to decide what they shall be, simply because these things are not up to me. Whatever is not caused by anything is not caused by me, and nothing could be more plainly inconsistent with saying that it is nevertheless up to me what it shall be.

THE THEORY OF AGENCY

The only conception of action that accords with our data is one according to which men—and perhaps some other things too—are sometimes, but of course not always, self-determining beings; that is, beings which are sometimes the causes of their own behavior. In the case of an action that is free, it must be such that it is caused by the agent who performs it, but such that no antecedent conditions were sufficient for his performing just that action. In the case of an action that is both free and rational, it must be such that the agent who performed it did so for some reason, but this reason cannot have been the cause of it.

Now this conception fits what men take themselves to be; namely, beings who act, or who are agents, rather than things that are merely acted upon, and whose behavior is simply the causal consequence of conditions which they have not wrought. When I believe that I have done something, I do believe that it was I who caused it to be done, I who made something happen, and not merely something within me, such as one of my own subjective states, which is not identical with myself. If I believe that something not identical with myself was the cause of my behavior—some event wholly external to myself, for instance, or even one internal to myself, such as a nerve impulse, volition, or whatnot—then I cannot regard that behavior as being an act of mine, unless I further believe that I was the cause of that external or internal event. My pulse, for example, is caused and regulated by certain conditions existing within me, and not by myself. I do not, accordingly, regard this activity of my body as my action, and would be no more tempted to do so if I became suddenly conscious within myself of those conditions or impulses that produce it. This behavior with which I have nothing to do, behavior that is not within my immediate control, behavior that is not only not free activity, but not even the activity of an agent to begin with; it is nothing but a mechanical reflex. Had I never learned that my very life depends on this pulse beat, I would regard it with complete indiffer-

ence, as something foreign to me, like the oscillations of a clock pendulum that I idly contemplate.

Now this conception of activity, and of an agent who is the cause of it, involves two rather strange metaphysical notions that are never applied elsewhere in nature. The first is that of a *self* or *person*—for example, a man—who is not merely a collection of things or events, but a substance and a self-moving being. For on this view it is a man himself, and not merely some part of him or something within him, that is the cause of his own activity. Now we certainly do not know that a man is anything more than an assemblage of physical things and processes, which act in accordance with those laws that describe the behavior of all other physical things and processes. Even though a man is a living being, of enormous complexity, there is nothing, apart from the requirements of this theory, to suggest that his behavior is so radically different in its origin from that of other physical objects, or that an understanding of it must be sought in some metaphysical realm wholly different from that appropriate to the understanding of non-living things. Second, this conception of activity involves an extraordinary conception of causation, according to which an agent, which is a substance and not an event, can nevertheless be the cause of an event. Indeed, if he is a free agent then he can, on this conception, cause an event to occur—namely, some act of his own—without anything else causing him to do so. This means that an agent is sometimes a cause, without being an antecedent sufficient condition; for if I affirm that I am the cause of some act of mine, then I am plainly not saying that my very existence is sufficient for its occurrence, which would be absurd. If I say that my hand causes my pencil to move, then I am saying that the motion of my hand is, under the other conditions then prevailing, sufficient for the motion of the pencil. But if I then say that I cause my hand to move, I am not saying anything remotely like this, and surely not that the motion of my self is sufficient for the motion of my arm and hand, since these are the only things about me that are moving.

This conception of the causation of events by beings or substances that are not events is, in fact, so different from the usual philosophical conception of a cause that it should not even bear the same name, for "being a cause" ordinarily just means "being an antecedent sufficient condition or set of conditions." Instead, then, of speaking of agents as *causing* their own acts, it would perhaps be better to use another word entirely, and say, for instance, that they *originate* them, *initiate* them, or simply that they *perform* them.

Now this is on the face of it a dubious conception of what a man is. Yet it is consistent with our data, reflecting the presuppositions of deliberation, and appears to be the only conception that is consistent with them, as determinism and simple indeterminism are not. The theory of agency avoids the absurdities of simple indeterminism by conceding that human behavior is caused, while at the same time avoiding the difficulties of determinism by denying that every chain of causes and effects is infinite. Some such causal chains, on this view, have beginnings, and they begin with agents themselves. Moreover, if we are to suppose that it is sometimes up to me what I do, and understand this in a sense which is not consistent with determinism, we must suppose that I am an agent or a being who initiates his own actions, sometimes under conditions which do not determine what action he shall perform. Deliberation becomes, on this view, something that is not only possible but quite rational, for it does make sense to deliberate about activity that is truly my own and that depends in its outcome upon me as its author, and not merely upon something more or less esoteric that is supposed to be intimately associated with me, such as my thoughts, volitions, choices, or whatnot.

One can hardly affirm such a theory of agency with complete comfort, however, and wholly without embarrassment, for the conception of men and their powers which is involved in it is strange indeed, if not positively mysterious. In fact, one can hardly be blamed here for simply denying our data outright, rather than embracing this theory to which they do most certainly point. Our data—to the effect that men do sometimes deliberate before acting, and that when they do, they presuppose among other things that it is up to them what they are going to do—rest upon nothing more than fairly common consent. These data might simply be illusions. It might in fact be that no man ever deliberates, but only imagines that he does, that from pure conceit he supposes himself to be the master of his behavior and the author of his acts. Spinoza has suggested that if a stone, having been thrown into the air, were suddenly to become conscious, it would suppose itself to be the source of its own motion, being then conscious of what it was doing but not aware of the real cause of its behavior. Certainly men are *sometimes* mistaken in believing that they are behaving as a result of choice deliberately arrived at. A man might, for example, easily imagine that his embarking upon matrimony is the result of the most careful and rational deliberation, when in fact the causes, perfectly sufficient for that behavior, might be of an entirely physiological, unconscious origin. If it is sometimes false that we deliberate and then act as the result of a decision deliberately arrived at, even when we suppose it to be true, it might always be false. No one seems able, as we have noted, to describe deliberation without metaphors, and the conception of a thing's being "within one's power" or "up to him" seems to defy analysis or definition altogether, if taken in a sense which the theory of agency appears to require.

These are, then, dubitable conceptions, despite their being so well implanted in the common sense of mankind. Indeed, when we turn to the theory of fatalism, we shall find formidable metaphysical considerations which appear to rule them out altogether. Perhaps here, as elsewhere in metaphysics, we should be content with discovering difficulties, with seeing what is and what is not consistent with such convictions as we happen to have, and then drawing such satisfaction as we can from the realization that, no matter where we begin, the world is mysterious and the men who try to understand it are even more so. This realization can, with some justification, make one feel wise, even in the full realization of his ignorance.

FOR FURTHER REFLECTION

1. Compare Taylor's critique of soft determinism with Stace's defense of it. Who has the better argument? Can you find a way to preserve a sense of moral responsibility within a compatibilist theory?

2. Examine Taylor's notion of agent causation. What is the evidence for it? What are the problems with it?

W. T. STACE

COMPATIBILISM
Free Will Is Consistent with Determinism

W. T. Stace (1886–1967) was born in Britain and educated at Trinity College, Dublin. After serving in the British Civil Service in Ceylon (1910–1932), he came to the United States to teach at Princeton University. He is especially known for his attempt to reconcile empiricism with mysticism. Among his works are *The Concept of Morals* (1937), *Time and Eternity* (1952), and *Mysticism and Philosophy* (1960). His *A Critical History of Greek Philosophy* (1920) is one of the best introductions to Greek philosophy.

Stace attempts to reconcile free will with causal determinism. He takes the position James labeled "soft determinism" and what is sometimes called "compatibilism." It is necessary that we have free will in order to be held morally responsible, and yet it seems plausible that all our actions are caused. How can these two apparently inconsistent ideas be brought together? Stace argues that the problem is merely a verbal dispute, and that, rightly understood, there is no inconsistency in holding to both doctrines. Free actions are those we do voluntarily, whereas unfree actions are those that we do involuntarily.

[A] great problem which the rise of scientific naturalism has created for the modern mind concerns the foundations of morality. The old religious foundations have largely crumbled away, and it may well be thought that the edifice built upon them by generations of men is in danger of collapse. A total collapse of moral behavior is, as I pointed out before, very unlikely. For a society in which this occurred could not survive. Nevertheless the danger to moral standards inherent in the virtual disappearance of their old religious foundations is not illusory.

I shall first discuss the problem of free will, for it is certain that if there is no free will there can be no morality. Morality is concerned with what men ought and ought not to do. But if a man has no freedom to choose what he will do, if whatever he does is done under compulsion, then it does not make sense to tell him that he ought not to have done what he did and that he ought to do something different. All moral precepts would in such case be meaningless. Also if he acts always under compulsion, how can he be held morally responsible for his actions? How can he, for example, be punished for what he could not help doing?

It is to be observed that those learned professors of philosophy or psychology who deny the existence of free will do so only in their professional moments and in their studies and lecture rooms. For when it comes to doing anything practical, even of the most trivial kind, they invariably behave as if they and others were free. They inquire from you at dinner whether you will choose this dish or that dish. They

From Walter T. Stace, *Religion and the Modern Mind* (New York: Lippincott, 1952), by permission of HarperCollins Publishers. Inc.

will ask a child why he told a lie, and will punish him for not having chosen the way of truthfulness. All of which is inconsistent with a disbelief in free will. This should cause us to suspect that the problem is not a real one; and this, I believe, is the case. The dispute is merely verbal, and is due to nothing but a confusion about the meanings of words. It is what is now fashionably called a semantic problem.

How does a verbal dispute arise? Let us consider a case which, although it is absurd in the sense that no one would ever make the mistake which is involved in it, yet illustrates the principle which we shall have to use in the solution of the problem. Suppose that someone believed that the word "man" means a certain sort of five-legged animal; in short that "five-legged animal" is the correct *definition* of man. He might then look around the world, and rightly observing that there are no five-legged animals in it, he might proceed to deny the existence of men. This preposterous conclusion would have been reached because he was using an incorrect definition of "man." All you would have to do to show him his mistake would be to give him the correct definition; or at least to show him that his definition was wrong. Both the problem and its solution would, of course, be entirely verbal. The problem of free will, and its solution, I shall maintain, is verbal in exactly the same way. The problem has been created by the fact that learned men, especially philosophers, have assumed an incorrect definition of free will, and then finding that there is nothing in the world which answers to their definition, have denied its existence. As far as logic is concerned, their conclusion is just as absurd as that of the man who denies the existence of men. The only difference is that the mistake in the latter case is obvious and crude, while the mistake which the deniers of free will have made is rather subtle and difficult to detect.

Throughout the modern period, until quite recently, it was assumed, both by the philosophers who denied free will and by those who defended it, that *determinism is inconsistent with free will*. If a man's actions were wholly determined by chains of causes stretching back into the remote past, so that they could be predicted beforehand by a mind which knew all the causes, it was assumed that they could not in that case be free. This implies that a certain definition of

actions done from free will was assumed, namely that they are actions *not* wholly determined by causes or predictable beforehand. Let us shorten this by saying that free will was defined as meaning indeterminism. This is the incorrect definition which has led to the denial of free will. As soon as we see what the true definition is we shall find that the question whether the world is deterministic, as Newtonian science implied, or in a measure indeterministic, as current physics teaches, is wholly irrelevant to the problem.

Of course there is a sense in which one can define a word arbitrarily in any way one pleases. But a definition may nevertheless be called correct or incorrect. It is correct if it accords with a *common usage* of the word defined. It is incorrect if it does not. And if you give an incorrect definition, absurd and untrue results are likely to follow. For instance, there is nothing to prevent you from arbitrarily defining a man as a five-legged animal, but this is incorrect in the sense that it does not accord with the ordinary meaning of the word. Also it has the absurd result of leading to a denial of the existence of men. This shows that *common usage is the criterion for deciding whether a definition is correct or not.* And this is the principle which I shall apply to free will. I shall show that indeterminism is not what is meant by the phrase "free will" *as it is commonly used.* And I shall attempt to discover the correct definition by inquiring how the phrase is used in ordinary conversation.

Here are a few samples of how the phrase might be used in ordinary conversation. It will be noticed that they include cases in which the question whether a man acted with free will is asked in order to determine whether he was morally and legally responsible for his acts.

Jones: I once went without food for a week.
Smith: Did you do that of your own free will?
Jones: No. I did it because I was lost in a desert and could find no food.

But suppose that the man who had fasted was Mahatma Gandhi. The conversation might then have gone:

Gandhi: I once fasted for a week.
Smith: Did you do that of your own free will?

Gandhi: Yes. I did it because I wanted to compel the British Government to give India its independence.

Take another case. Suppose that I had stolen some bread, but that I was as truthful as George Washington. Then, if I were charged with the crime in court, some exchange of the following sort might take place:

Judge: Did you steal the bread of your own free will?

Stace: Yes. I stole it because I was hungry.

Or in different circumstances the conversation might run:

Judge: Did you steal of your own free will?

Stace: No. I stole because my employer threatened to beat me if I did not.

At a recent murder trial in Trenton some of the accused had signed confessions, but afterwards asserted that they had done so under police duress. The following exchange might have occurred:

Judge: Did you sign this confession of your own free will?

Prisoner: No. I signed it because the police beat me up.

Now suppose that a philosopher had been a member of the jury. We could imagine this conversation taking place in the jury room.

Foreman of the Jury: The prisoner says he signed the confession because he was beaten, and not of his own free will.

Philosopher: This is quite irrelevant to the case. There is no such thing as free will.

Foreman: Do you mean to say that it makes no difference whether he signed because his conscience made him want to tell the truth or because he was beaten?

Philosopher: None at all. Whether he was caused to sign by a beating or by some desire of his own—the desire to tell the truth, for example—in either case his signing was causally determined, and therefore in neither case did he act of his own free will. Since there is no such thing as free will, the question

whether he signed of his own free will ought not to be discussed by us.

The foreman and the rest of the jury would rightly conclude that the philosopher must be making some mistake. What sort of mistake could it be? There is only one possible answer. The philosopher must be using the phrase "free will" in some peculiar way of his own which is not the way in which men usually use it when they wish to determine a question of moral responsibility. That is, he must be using an incorrect definition of it as implying action not determined by causes.

Suppose a man left his office at noon, and were questioned about it. Then we might hear this:

Jones: Did you go out of your own free will?

Smith: Yes. I went out to get my lunch.

But we might hear:

Jones: Did you leave your office of your own free will?

Smith: No. I was forcibly removed by the police.

We have now collected a number of cases of actions which, in the ordinary usage of the English language, would be called cases in which people have acted of their own free will. We should also say in all these cases that they *chose* to act as they did. We should also say that they could have acted otherwise, if they had chosen. For instance, Mahatma Gandhi was not compelled to fast; he chose to do so. He could have eaten if he had wanted to. When Smith went out to get his lunch, he chose to do so. He could have stayed and done some more work, if he had wanted to. We have also collected a number of cases of the opposite kind. They are cases in which men were not able to exercise their free will. They had no choice. They were compelled to do as they did. The man in the desert did not fast of his own free will. He had no choice in the matter. He was compelled to fast because there was nothing for him to eat. And so with the other cases. It ought to be quite easy, by an inspection of these cases, to tell what we ordinarily mean when we say that a man did or did not exercise free will. We ought therefore to be able to extract from them the proper definition of the term. Let us put the cases in a table:

Free Acts	Unfree Acts
Gandhi fasting because he wanted to free India.	The man fasting in the desert because there was no food.
Stealing bread because one is hungry.	Stealing because one's employer threatened to beat one.
Signing a confession because one wanted to tell the truth.	Signing because the police beat one.
Leaving the office because one wanted one's lunch.	Leaving because forcibly removed.

It is obvious that to find the correct definition of free acts we must discover what characteristic is common to all the acts in the left-hand column, and is, at the same time, absent from all the acts in the right-hand column. This characteristic which all free acts have, and which no unfree acts have, will be the defining characteristic of free will.

Is being uncaused, or not being determined by causes, the characteristic of which we are in search? It cannot be, because although it is true that all the acts in the right-hand column have causes, such as the beating by the police or the absence of food in the desert, so also do the acts in the left-hand column. Mr. Gandhi's fasting was caused by his desire to free India, the man leaving his office by his hunger, and so on. Moreover there is no reason to doubt that these causes of the free acts were in turn caused by prior conditions, and that these were again the results of causes, and so on back indefinitely into the past. Any physiologist can tell us the causes of hunger. What caused Mr. Gandhi's tremendously powerful desire to free India is no doubt more difficult to discover. But it must have had causes. Some of them may have lain in peculiarities of his glands or brain, others in his past experiences, others in his heredity, others in his education. Defenders of free will have usually tended to deny such facts. But to do so is plainly a case of special pleading, which is unsupported by any scrap of evidence. The only reasonable view is that all human actions, both those which are freely done and those which are not, are either wholly determined by causes, or at least as much determined as other events in nature. It may be true, as the physicists tell us, that nature is not as deterministic as was once thought. But whatever degree of determinism prevails in the world, human actions appear to be as much determined as anything else. And if this is so, it cannot be the case that what distinguishes actions freely chosen from those which are not free is that the latter are determined by causes while the former are not. Therefore, being uncaused or being undetermined by causes, must be an incorrect definition of free will.

What, then, is the difference between acts which are freely done and those which are not? What is the characteristic which is present to all the acts in the left-hand column and absent from all those in the right-hand column? Is it not obvious that, although both sets of actions have causes, the causes of those in the left-hand column are *of a different kind* from the causes of those in the right-hand column? The free acts are all caused by desires, or motives, or by some sort of internal psychological states of the agent's mind. The unfree acts, on the other hand, are all caused by physical forces or physical conditions, outside the agent. Police arrest means physical force exerted from the outside; the absence of food in the desert is a physical condition of the outside world. We may therefore frame the following rough definitions. *Acts freely done are those whose immediate causes are psychological states in the agent. Acts not freely done are those whose immediate causes are states of affairs external to the agent.*

It is plain that if we define free will in this way, then free will certainly exists, and the philosopher's denial of its existence is seen to be what it is—nonsense. For it is obvious that all those actions of men which we should ordinarily attribute to the exercise of their free will, or of which we should say that they freely chose to do them, are in fact actions which have been caused by their own desires, wishes, thoughts, emotions, impulses, or other psychological states.

In applying our definition we shall find that it usually works well, but that there are some puzzling cases which it does not seem exactly to fit. These puzzles can always be solved by paying careful attention to the ways in which words are used, and remembering that they are not always used consistently. I have space for only one example. Suppose that a thug threatens to shoot you unless you give him your wallet, and suppose that you do so. Do you, in giving him your wallet, do so of your own free will or not? If we apply our definition, we find that you acted freely, since the immediate cause of the action was not an actual outside force but the fear of death, which is a psychological cause. Most people, however, would say that you did not act of your own free will but under compulsion. Does this show that our definition is wrong? I do not think so. Aristotle, who gave a solution of the problem of free will substantially the same as ours (though he did not use the term "free will") admitted that there are what he called "mixed" or borderline cases in which it is difficult to know whether we ought to call the acts free or compelled. In the case under discussion, though no actual force was used, the gun at your forehead so nearly approximated to actual force that we tend to say the case was one of compulsion. It is a borderline case.

Here is what may seem like another kind of puzzle. According to our view an action may be free though it could have been predicted beforehand with certainty. But suppose you told a lie, and it was certain beforehand that you would tell it. How could one then say, "You could have told the truth"? The answer is that it is perfectly true that you could have told the truth *if* you had wanted to. In fact you would have done so, for in that case the causes producing your action, namely your desires, would have been different, and would therefore have produced different effects. It is a delusion that predictability and free will are incompatible. This agrees with common sense. For if, knowing your character, I predict that you will act honorably, no one would say when you do act honorably, that this shows you did not do so of your own free will.

Since free will is a condition of moral responsibility, we must be sure that our theory of free will gives a sufficient basis for it. To be held morally responsible for one's actions means that one may be justly punished or rewarded, blamed or praised, for them.

But it is not just to punish a man for what he cannot help doing. How can it be just to punish him for an action which it was certain beforehand that he would do? We have not attempted to decide whether, as a matter of fact, all events, including human actions, are completely determined. For that question is irrelevant to the problem of free will. But if we assume for the purposes of argument that complete determinism is true, but that we are nevertheless free, it may then be asked whether such a deterministic free will is compatible with moral responsibility. For it may seem unjust to punish a man for an action which it could have been predicted with certainty beforehand that he would do.

But that determinism is incompatible with moral responsibility is as much a delusion as that it is incompatible with free will. You do not excuse a man for doing a wrong act because, knowing his character, you felt certain beforehand that he would do it. Nor do you deprive a man of a reward or prize because, knowing his goodness or his capabilities, you felt certain beforehand that he would win it.

Volumes have been written on the justification of punishment. But so far as it affects the question of free will, the essential principles involved are quite simple. The punishment of a man for doing a wrong act is justified, either on the ground that it will correct his own character, or that it will deter other people from doing similar acts. The instrument of punishment has been in the past, and no doubt still is, often unwisely used; so that it may often have done more harm than good. But that is not relevant to our present problem. Punishment, if and when it is justified, is justified only on one or both of the grounds just mentioned. The question then is how, if we assume determinism, punishment can correct character or deter people from evil actions.

Suppose that your child develops a habit of telling lies. You give him a mild beating. Why? Because you believe that his personality is such that the usual motives for telling the truth do not cause him to do so. You therefore supply the missing cause, or motive, in the shape of pain and the fear of future pain if he repeats his untruthful behavior. And you hope that a few treatments of this kind will condition him to the habit of truth-telling, so that he will come to tell the truth without the infliction of pain. You assume that his actions are determined by causes, but that the usual causes of truth-telling do not in him produce their usual effects. You therefore supply him with an artificially injected motive, pain and fear, which you think will in the future cause him to speak truthfully.

The principle is exactly the same where you hope, by punishing one man, to deter others from wrong actions. You believe that the fear of punishment will cause those who might otherwise do evil to do well.

We act on the same principle with non-human, and even with inanimate, things, if they do not behave in the way we think they ought to behave. The rose bushes in the garden produce only small and poor blooms, whereas we want large and rich ones. We supply a cause which will produce large blooms, namely fertilizer. Our automobile does not go properly. We supply a cause which will make it go better, namely oil in the works. The punishment for the man, the fertilizer for the plant, and the oil for the car, are all justified by the same principle and in the same way. The only difference is that different kinds of things require different kinds of causes to make them do what they should. Pain may be the appropriate remedy to apply, in certain cases, to human beings, and oil to the machine. It is, of course, of no use to inject motor oil into the boy or to beat the machine.

Thus we see that moral responsibility is not only consistent with determinism, but requires it. The assumption on which punishment is based is that human behavior is causally determined. If pain could not be a cause of truth-telling there would be no justification at all for punishing lies. If human actions and volitions were uncaused, it would be useless either to punish or reward, or indeed to do anything else to correct people's bad behavior. For nothing that you could do would in any way influence them. Thus moral responsibility would entirely disappear. If there were no determinism of human beings at all, their actions would be completely unpredictable and capricious, and therefore irresponsible. And this is in itself a strong argument against the common view of philosophers that free will means being undetermined by causes.

FOR FURTHER REFLECTION

1. What is Stace's strategy in consulting common language usage in order to show that free will is compatible with determinism? What semantic confusion gives rise to the problem of free will? Are determinists semantically confused? Explain your answer.

2. Has Stace successfully reconciled free will with determinism? Does his analysis of ordinary language settle the matter? Why or why not? The next reading examines John Hospers's evaluation of that claim. You may want to turn to that essay before you decide on the matter.

JOHN HOSPERS

DETERMINISM
Free Will and Psychoanalysis

John Hospers was professor of philosophy at the University of Southern California and the editor of *The Personalist*. He founded the Libertarian Party and was that party's candidate for the president of the United States in 1972. He is the author of several books, including *Libertarianism: A Political Philosophy for Tomorrow* (1971). Note that political libertarianism is a different theory from metaphysical libertarianism, against which Hospers here argues.

Hospers rejects both libertarianism and the compatibilist's attempt to reconcile free will and determinism, arguing that compatibilism is founded on a superficial view of being *compelled*. The compatibilist proceeds as though all compulsion were external, but in fact, argues Hospers, psychoanalysis shows that there is deep inward compulsion, and this factor counts against the distinction that the compatibilist makes. Hospers argues that psychoanalytic research destroys the compatibilist's case and leads us to accept hard determinism.

(Note: Hospers makes reference to a German-Austrian philosopher named Moritz Schlick [1882–1936]. Schlick's position and argument were the same as Stace's compatibilist position and argument.)

I

It is extremely common for nonprofessional philosophers and iconoclasts to deny that human freedom exists, but at the same time to have no clear idea of what it is that they are denying to exist. The first thing that needs to be said about the free-will issue is that any meaningful term must have a meaningful opposite: If it is meaningful to assert that people are not free, it must be equally meaningful to assert that people *are* free, whether this latter assertion is in fact true or not. Whether it is true, of course, will depend on the meaning that is given the weasel-word "free." For example, if freedom is made dependent on inde- terminism, it may well be that human freedom is nonexistent. But there seem to be no good grounds for asserting such a dependence, especially since lack of causation is the furthest thing from people's minds when they call an act free. Doubtless there are other senses that can be given to the word "free"—such as "able to do anything we want to do"—in which no human beings are free. But the first essential point about which the denier of freedom must be clear is *what* it is that he is denying. If one knows what it is like for people not to be free, one must know what it *would* be like for them to *be* free.

Philosophers have advanced numerous senses of "free" in which countless acts performed by human

From John Hospers, "Men and Free Will," *Philosophy and Phenomenological Research, 10,* no. 3 (March 1950), 307–27, by permission of the publisher.

beings can truly be called free acts. The most common conception of a free act is that according to which an act is free if and only if it is a *voluntary* act. But the word "voluntary" does not always carry the same meaning. Sometimes to call an act voluntary means that we can do the act *if* we choose to do it: In other words, that it is physically and psychologically possible for us to do it, so that the occurrence of the act follows upon the decision to do it. (One's decision to raise his arm is in fact followed by the actual raising of his arm, unless he is a paralytic; one's decision to pluck the moon from the sky is not followed by the actual event.) Sometimes a voluntary act is conceived . . . as an act which would not have occurred if, just beforehand, the agent had chosen not to perform it. But these senses are different from the sense in which a voluntary act is an act resulting from *deliberation,* or perhaps merely from *choice.* For example, there are many acts which we could have avoided, if we had chosen to do so, but which we nevertheless did not *choose* to perform, much less *deliberate* about them. The act of raising one's leg in the process of taking a step while out for a walk is one which a person could have avoided by choosing to, but which, after one has learned to walk, takes place automatically or semi-automatically through habit, and thus is not the result of choice. (One may have chosen to take the walk, but not to take this or that step while walking.) . . .

Now, no matter in which of the above ways we may come to define "voluntary," there are still acts which are voluntary *but which we would be very unlikely to think of as free.* Thus, when a person submits to the command of an armed bandit, he may do so voluntarily in every one of the above senses: He may do so as a result of choice, even of deliberation, and he could have avoided doing it by willing not to—he could, instead, have refused and been shot. The man who reveals a state secret under torture does the same: He could have refused and endured more torture. Yet such acts, and persons in respect of such acts, are not generally called free. We said that they were performed *under compulsion,* and if an act is performed under compulsion we do not call it free. We say, "He wasn't free because he was forced to do as he did," though of course his act was voluntary.

This much departure from the identification of free acts with voluntary acts almost everyone would admit. Sometimes, however, it would be added that this is all the departure that can be admitted. According to Schlick, for example,

> Freedom means the opposite of compulsion; a man is *free* if he does not act under *compulsion,* and he is compelled or unfree when he is hindered from without in the realization of his natural desires. Hence he is unfree when he is locked up, or chained, or when someone forces him at the point of a gun to do what otherwise he would not do. This is quite clear, and everyone will admit that the everyday or legal notion of the lack of freedom is thus correctly interpreted, and that a man will be considered quite free . . . if no such external compulsion is exerted upon him.[1]

Schlick adds that the entire vexed free-will controversy in philosophy is so much wasted ink and paper, because compulsion has been confused with causality and necessity with uniformity. If the question is asked whether every event is caused, the answer is doubtless yes; but if it is whether every event is compelled, the answer is clearly no. Free acts are uncompelled acts, not uncaused acts. Again, when it is said that some state of affairs (such as water flowing downhill) is necessary, if "necessary" means "compelled," the answer is no; if it means merely that it always happens that way, the answer is yes: Universality of application is confused with compulsion. And this, according to Schlick, is the end of the matter.

Schlick's analysis is indeed clarifying and helpful to those who have fallen victim to the confusions he exposes—and this probably includes most persons in their philosophical growing-pains. But *is* this the end of the matter? Is it true that all acts, though caused, are free as long as they are not compelled in the sense which he specifies? May it not be that, while the identification of "free" with "uncompelled" is acceptable, the area of compelled acts is vastly greater than he or most other philosophers have ever suspected? . . . We remember statements about human beings being pawns of their early environment, victims of conditions beyond their control, the result of causal influences stemming from their parents, and the like, and we ponder and ask, "Still, are we really free?" Is there not something in what generations of sages have said about man being fettered? Is there not perhaps something too facile, too sleight-of-hand, in Schlick's cutting of the Gordian knot? For example, when a metropolitan newspaper headlines an article with the words "Boy Killer Is Doomed Long Before He Is Born,"[2] and then goes on to describe how a twelve-year-old boy has been sentenced to prison for the murder of a girl, and how his parental background includes records of drunkenness, divorce, social maladjustment, and paresis, are we still to say that his act, though voluntary and assuredly *not* done at the point of a gun, is free? The boy has early displayed a tendency toward sadistic activity to hide an underlying masochism and "prove that he's a man"; being coddled by his mother only worsens this tendency until, spurned by a girl in his attempt on her, he kills her—not simply in a fit of anger, but calculatingly, deliberately. Is he free in respect of his criminal act, or for that matter in most of the acts of his life? Surely to ask this question is to answer it in the negative. Perhaps I have taken an extreme case; but it is only to show the superficiality of the Schlick analysis the more clearly. Though not everyone has criminotic tendencies, everyone has been molded by influences which in large measure at least determine his present behavior; he is literally the product of these influences, stemming from periods prior to his "years of discretion," giving him a host of character traits that he cannot change now even if he would. So obviously does what a man is depend upon how a man comes to be, that it is small wonder that philosophers and sages have considered man far indeed from being the master of his fate. It is not as if man's will were standing high and serene above the flux of events that have molded him; it is itself caught up in this flux, itself carried along on the current. An act is free when it is determined by the man's character, say moralists; but what if the most decisive aspects of his character were already irrevocably acquired before he could do anything to mold them? What if even the degree of will power available to him in shaping his habits and disciplining himself now to overcome the influence of his early environment is a factor over which he has no control? What are we to say of this kind of "freedom"? Is it not rather like the freedom of the machine to stamp labels on cans when it has been devised for just that purpose?

Some machines can do so more efficiently than others, but only because they have been better constructed.

II

It is not my purpose here to establish this thesis in general, but only in one specific respect which has received comparatively little attention, namely, the field referred to by psychiatrists as that of unconscious motivation. In what follows I shall restrict my attention to it because it illustrates as clearly as anything the points I wish to make.

Let me try to summarize very briefly the psychoanalytic doctrine on this point.[3] The conscious life of the human being, including the conscious decisions and volitions, is merely a mouthpiece for the unconscious—not directly for the enactment of unconscious drives, but of the compromise between unconscious drives and unconscious reproaches. There is a Big Three behind the scenes which the automaton called the conscious personality carries out: The id, an "eternal gimme," presents its wish and demands its immediate satisfaction; the super-ego says no to the wish immediately upon presentation; and the unconscious ego, the mediator between the two, tries to keep peace by means of compromise.[4]

To go into examples of the functioning of these three "bosses" would be endless; psychoanalytic case books supply hundreds of them. The important point for us to see in the present context is that *it is the unconscious that determines what the conscious impulse and the conscious action shall be.* . . .

We have always been conscious of the fact that we are not masters of our fate in every respect—that there are many things which we cannot do, that nature is more powerful than we are, that we cannot disobey laws without danger of reprisals, etc. We have become "officially" conscious, too, though in our private lives we must long have been aware of it, that we are not free with respect to the emotions that we feel—whom we love or hate, what types we admire, and the like. More lately still we have been reminded that there are unconscious motivations for our basic attractions and repulsions, our compulsive actions or inabilities to act. But what is not welcome news is that our very acts of volition, and the entire train of deliberations leading up to them, are but façades for the expression of unconscious wishes, or rather, unconscious compromises and defenses.

A man is faced by a choice: Shall he kill another person or not? Moralists would say, "Here is a free choice—the result of deliberation, an action consciously entered into." And yet, though the agent himself does not know it, and has no awareness of the forces that are at work within him, his choice is already determined for him: His conscious will is only an instrument, a slave, in the hands of a deep unconscious motivation which determines his action. If he has a great deal of what the analyst calls "free-floating guilt," he will not; but if the guilt is such as to demand immediate absorption in the form of self-damaging behavior, this accumulated guilt will have to be discharged in some criminal action. The man himself does not know what the inner clockwork is; he is like the hands on the clock, thinking they move freely over the face of the clock.

A woman has married and divorced several husbands. Now she is faced with a choice for the next marriage: shall she marry Mr. A, or Mr. B, or nobody at all? She may take considerable time to "decide" this question and her decision may appear as a final triumph of her free will. Let us assume that A is a normal, well-adjusted, kind and generous man while B is a leech, an impostor, one who will become entangled constantly in quarrels with her. If she belongs to a certain classifiable psychological type, she will inevitably choose B, and she will do so even if her previous husbands have resembled B, so that one would think that she "had learned from experience." Consciously, she will of course "give the matter due consideration," etc., etc. To the psychoanalyst all this is irrelevant chaff in the wind—only a camouflage for the inner workings about which she knows nothing consciously. If she is of a certain kind of masochistic strain, as exhibited in her previous set of symptoms, she *must* choose B: Her super-ego, always out to maximize the torment in the situation, seeing what dazzling possibilities for self-damaging behavior are promised by the choice of B, compels her to make the choice she does, and even to conceal the real basis of the choice behind an elaborate façade of rationalization. . . .

A man has wash-compulsion. He must be constantly washing his hands—he uses up perhaps 400 towels a day. Asked why he does this, he says, "I need to, my hands are dirty"; and if it is pointed out to him that they are not really dirty, he says, "They feel dirty anyway, I feel better when I wash them." So once again he washes them. He "freely decides" every time; he feels that he must wash them, he deliberates for a moment perhaps, but he always ends by washing them. What he does not see, of course, are the invisible wires inside him pulling him inevitably to do the thing he does: The infantile id-wish concerns preoccupation with dirt, the super-ego charges him with this, and the terrified ego must respond, "No, I don't like dirt, see how clean I like to be, look how I wash my hands!"

Let us see what further "free acts" the same patient engages in (this is an actual case history): He is taken to a concentration camp and given the worst of treatment by the Nazi guards. In the camp he no longer chooses to be clean, does not even try to be—on the contrary, his choice is now to wallow in filth as much as he can. All he is aware of now is a disinclination to be clean, and every time he must choose he chooses not to be. Behind the scenes, however, another drama is being enacted: The super-ego, perceiving that enough torment is being administered from the outside, can afford to cease pressing its charges in this quarter—the outside world is doing the torturing now, so the super-ego is relieved of the responsibility. Thus, the ego is relieved of the agony of constantly making terrified replies in the form of washing to prove that the super-ego is wrong. The defense no longer being needed, the person slides back into what is his natural predilection anyway, for filth. This becomes too much even for the Nazi guards: They take hold of him one day, saying "We'll teach you how to be clean!" drag him into the snow, and pour bucket after bucket of icy water over him until he freezes to death. Such is the end-result of an original id-wish, caught in the machinations of a destroying super-ego.

Let us take, finally, a less colorful, more everyday example. A student at a university, possessing wealth, charm, and all that is usually considered essential to popularity, begins to develop the following personality-pattern: Although well taught in the graces of social conversation, he always makes a *faux pas* somewhere, and always in the worst possible situation; to his friends he makes cutting remarks which hurt deeply—and always apparently aimed in such a way as to hurt the most: A remark that would not hurt A but would hurt B he invariably makes to B rather than to A, and so on. None of this is conscious. Ordinarily he is considerate of people, but he contrives always (unconsciously) to impose on just those friends who would resent it most, and at just the times when he should know that he should not impose: At 3 o'clock in the morning, without forewarning, he phones a friend in a nearby city demanding to stay at his apartment for the weekend; naturally the friend is offended, but the person himself is not aware that he has provoked the grievance ("common sense" suffers a temporary eclipse when the neurotic pattern sets in, and one's intelligence, far from being of help in such a situation, is used in the interest of the neurosis), and when the friend is cool to him the next time they meet, he wonders why and feels unjustly treated. Aggressive behavior on his part invites resentment and aggression in turn, but all that he consciously sees is others' behavior toward him—and he considers himself the innocent victim of an unjustified "persecution."

Each of these acts is, from the moralist's point of view, free: He chose to phone his friend at 3 A.M.; he chose to make the cutting remark that he did, etc. What he does not know is that an ineradicable masochistic pattern has set in. His unconscious is far more shrewd and clever than is his conscious intellect; it sees with uncanny accuracy just what kind of behavior will damage him most, and unerringly forces him into that behavior. Consciously, the student "doesn't know why he did it"—he gives different "reasons" at different times, but they are all, once again, rationalizations cloaking the unconscious mechanism which propels him willy-nilly into actions which his "common sense" eschews.

The more of this sort of thing one observes, the more he can see what the psychoanalyst means when he talks about *the illusion of freedom*. And the more of a psychiatrist one becomes, the more he is overcome with a sense of what an illusion this free-will can be. In some kinds of cases most of us can see it already: It takes no psychiatrist to look at the epilep-

tic and sigh with sadness at the thought that soon this person before you will be as one possessed, not the same thoughtful intelligent person you knew. But people are not aware of this in other contexts, for example when they express surprise at how a person whom they have been so good to could treat them so badly. Let us suppose that you help a person financially or morally or in some other way, so that he is in your debt; suppose further that he is one of the many neurotics who unconsciously identify kindness with weakness and aggression with strength. Then he will unconsciously take your kindness to him as weakness and use it as the occasion for enacting some aggression against you. He can't help it, he may regret it himself later; still, he will be driven to do it. If we gain a little knowledge of psychiatry, we can look at him with pity, that a person otherwise so worthy should be so unreliable—but we will exercise realism too, and be aware that there are some types of people that you cannot be good to in "free" acts of their conscious volition; they will use your own goodness against you. . . .

We talk about free-will, and we say, for example, the person is free to do so-and-so if he can do so *if* he wants to—and we forget that his wanting to is itself caught up in the stream of determinism, that unconscious forces drive him into the wanting or not wanting to do the thing in question. The analogy of the puppet whose motions are manipulated from behind by invisible wires, or better still, by springs inside, is a telling one at almost every point.

And the glaring fact is that it all started so early, before we knew what was happening. The personality-structure is inelastic after the age of five, and comparatively so in most cases after the age of three. Whether one acquires a neurosis or not is determined by that age—and just as involuntarily as if it had been a curse of God. If, for example, a masochistic pattern was set up, under pressure of hyper-narcissism combined with real or fancied infantile deprivation, then the masochistic snowball was on its course downhill long before we or anybody else knew what was happening, and long before anyone could do anything about it. To speak of human beings as "puppets" in such a context is no idle metaphor, but a stark rendering of a literal fact: Only the psychiatrist knows what puppets people really are; and it is no wonder that the protestations of philosophers that "the act which is the result of a volition, a deliberation, a conscious decision, is free" leave these persons, to speak mildly, somewhat cold.

But, one may object, all the states thus far described have been abnormal, neurotic ones. The well-adjusted (normal) person at least is free.

Leaving aside the question of how clearly and on what grounds one can distinguish the neurotic from the normal, let me use an illustration of a proclivity that everyone would call normal, namely, the decision of a man to support his wife and possibly a family, and consider briefly its genesis, according to psychoanalytic accounts.[5]

Every baby comes into the world with a full-fledged case of megalomania—interested only in himself, acting as if believing that he is the center of the universe and that others are present only to fulfill his wishes, and furious when his own wants are not satisfied immediately no matter for what reason. Gratitude, even for all the time and worry and care expended on him by the mother, is an emotion entirely foreign to the infant, and as he grows older it is inculcated in him only with the greatest difficulty; his natural tendency is to assume that everything that happens to him is due to himself, except for denials and frustrations, which are due to the "cruel, denying" outer world, in particular the mother; and that he owes nothing to anyone, is dependent on no one. This omnipotence-complex, or illusion of nondependence, has been called the "autarchic fiction." Such a conception of the world is actually fostered in the child by the conduct of adults, who automatically attempt to fulfill the infant's every wish concerning nourishment, sleep, and attention. The child misconceives causality and sees in these wish-fulfillments not the results of maternal kindness and love, but simply the result of his own omnipotence.

This fiction of omnipotence is gradually destroyed by experience, and its destruction is probably the deepest disappointment of the early years of life. First of all, the infant discovers that he is the victim of organic urges and necessities: hunger, defecation, urination. More important, he discovers that the maternal breast, which he has not previously distinguished

from his own body (he has not needed to, since it was available when he wanted it), is not a part of himself after all, but of another creature upon whom he is dependent. He is forced to recognize this, e.g., when he wants nourishment and it is at the moment not present; even a small delay is most damaging to the "autarchic fiction." Most painful of all is the experience of weaning, probably the greatest tragedy in every baby's life, when his dependence is most cruelly emphasized; it is a frustrating experience because what he wants is no longer there at all; and if he has been able to some extent to preserve the illusion of nondependence heretofore, he is not able to do so now—it is plain that the source of his nourishment is not dependent on him, but he on it. The shattering of the autarchic fiction is a great disillusionment to every child, a tremendous blow to his ego which he will, in one way or another, spend the rest of his life trying to repair. How does he do this?

First of all, his reaction to frustration is anger and fury; and he responds by kicking, biting, etc., the only way he knows. But he is motorically helpless, and these measures are ineffective, and only serve to emphasize his dependence the more. Moreover, against such responses of the child the parental reaction is one of prohibition, often involving deprivation of attention and affection. Generally the child soon learns that this form of rebellion is profitless, and brings him more harm than good. He wants to respond to frustration with violent aggression, and at the same time learns that he will be punished for such aggression, and that in any case the latter is ineffectual. What face-saving solution does he find? Since he must "face facts," since he must in any case "conform" if he is to have any peace at all, he tries to make it seem as if he himself is the source of the commands and prohibitions: The *external* prohibitive force is *internalized*—and here we have the origin of conscience. By making the prohibitive agency seem to come from within himself, the child can "save face"—as if saying, "The prohibition comes from within me, not from outside, so I'm not subservient to external rule, I'm only obeying rules I've set up myself," and thus to some extent saving the autarchic fiction, and at the same time avoiding unpleasant consequences directed against himself by complying with parental commands.

Moreover, the boy[6] has unconsciously never forgiven the mother for his dependence on her in early life, for nourishment and all other things. It has upset his illusion of nondependence. These feelings have been repressed and are not remembered; but they are acted out in later life in many ways—e.g., in the constant deprecation man has for woman's duties such as cooking and housework of all sorts ("All she does is stay home and get together a few meals, and she calls that work"), and especially in the man's identification with the mother is his sex experiences with women. By identifying with someone one cancels out in effect the person with whom he identifies—replacing that person, unconsciously denying his existence, and the man, identifying with his early mother, playing the active rôle in "giving" to his wife as his mother has "given" to him, is in effect the denial of his mother's existence, a fact which is narcissistically embarrassing to his ego because it is chiefly responsible for shattering his autarchic fiction. In supporting his wife, he can unconsciously deny that his mother gave to him, and that he was dependent on her giving. Why is it that the husband plays the provider, and wants his wife to be dependent on no one else, although twenty years before he was nothing but a parasitic baby? This is a face-saving device on his part: He can act out the reasoning. "See, I'm not the parasitic baby, on the contrary I'm the provider, the giver." His playing the provider is a constant face-saving device, to deny his early dependence which is so embarrassing to his ego. It is no wonder that men generally dislike to be reminded of their babyhood, when they were dependent on women.

Thus, we have here a perfectly normal adult reaction which is unconsciously motivated. The man "chooses" to support a family—and his choice is as unconsciously motivated as anything could be. (I have described here only the "normal" state of affairs, uncomplicated by the well-nigh infinite number of variations that occur in actual practice.)

III

Now, what of the notion of responsibility? What happens to it on our analysis?

Let us begin with an example, not a fictitious one. A woman and her two-year-old baby are riding on a train to Montreal in mid-winter. The child is ill. The woman wants badly to get to her destination. She is, unknown to herself, the victim of a neurotic conflict whose nature is irrelevant here except for the fact that it forces her to behave aggressively toward the child, partly to spite her husband whom she despises and who loves the child, but chiefly to ward off super-ego charges of masochistic attachment. Consciously she loves the child, and when she says this she says it sincerely, but she must behave aggressively toward it nevertheless, just as many children love their mothers but are nasty to them most of the time in neurotic pseudo-aggression. The child becomes more ill as the train approaches Montreal; the heating system of the train is not working, and the conductor pleads with the woman to get off the train at the next town and get the child to a hospital at once. The woman refuses. Soon after, the child's condition worsens, and the mother does all she can to keep it alive, without, however, leaving the train, for she declares that it is absolutely necessary that she reach her destination. But before she gets there the child is dead. After that, of course, the mother grieves, blames herself, weeps hysterically, and joins the church to gain surcease from the guilt that constantly overwhelms her when she thinks of how her aggressive behavior has killed her child.

Was she responsible for her deed? In ordinary life, after making a mistake, we say, "Chalk it up to experience." Here we should say, "Chalk it up to the neurosis." *She* could not help it if her neurosis forced her to act this way—she didn't even know what was going on behind the scenes; her conscious self merely acted out its assigned part. This is far more true than is generally realized: Criminal actions in general are not actions for which their agents are responsible; the agents are passive, not active—they are victims of a neurotic conflict. Their very hyper-activity is unconsciously determined.

To say this is, of course, not to say that we should not punish criminals. Clearly, for our own protection, we must remove them from our midst so that they can no longer molest and endanger organized society. And of course, if we use the word "responsible" in such a way that justly to hold someone responsible for a deed is by definition identical with being justified in punishing him, then we can and do hold people responsible. But this is like the sense of "free" in which free acts are voluntary ones. It does not go deep enough. In a deeper sense we cannot hold the person responsible: We can hold his neurosis responsible, but *he is not responsible for his neurosis,* particularly since the age at which its onset was inevitable was an age before he could even speak.

The neurosis is responsible—but isn't the neurosis a part of *him?* We have been speaking all the time as if the person and his unconscious were two separate beings; but isn't he one personality, including conscious and unconscious departments together?

I do not wish to deny this. But it hardly helps us here; for what people want when they talk about freedom, and what they hold to when they champion it, is the idea that the *conscious* will is the master of their destiny. "I am the master of my fate, I am the captain of my soul"—and they surely mean their conscious self, the self that they can recognize and search and introspect. Between an unconscious which willy-nilly determines your actions, and an external force which pushes you, there is little if anything to choose. The unconscious is just *as if* it were an outside force; and indeed, psychiatrists will assert that the inner Hitler (your super-ego) can torment you far more than any external Hitler can. Thus, the kind of freedom that people want, the only kind they will settle for, is precisely the kind that psychiatry says that they cannot have.

Heretofore it was pretty generally thought that, while we could not rightly blame a person for the color of his eyes or the morality of his parents, or even for what he did at the age of three, or to a large extent what impulses he had and whom he fell in love with, one *could* do so for other of his adult activities, particularly the acts he performed voluntarily and with premeditation. Later this attitude was shaken. Many voluntary acts came to be recognized at least in some circles, as compelled by the unconscious. . . . The usual examples, such as the kleptomaniac and the schizophrenic, apparently satisfy most philosophers, and with these exceptions removed, the rest of mankind is permitted to wander in the vast and alluring fields of freedom and responsibility. So far, the inroads upon freedom

left the vast majority of humanity untouched; they began to hit home when psychiatrists began to realize, though philosophers did not, that the domination of the conscious by the unconscious extended not merely to a few exceptional individuals, but to all human beings, that the "big three behind the scenes" are not respecters of persons, and dominate us all, even including that *sanctum sanctorum* of freedom, our conscious will. To be sure, the domination by the unconscious in the case of "normal" individuals is somewhat more benevolent than the tyranny and despotism exercised in neurotic cases, and therefore the former have evoked less comment; but the principle remains in all cases the same: The unconscious is the master of every fate and the captain of every soul.

We speak of a machine turning out good products most of the time but every once in a while turning out a "lemon." We do not, of course, hold the product responsible for this, but the machine, and via the machine, its maker. Is it silly to extend to inanimate objects the idea of responsibility? Of course, but is it any less so to employ the notion in speaking of human creatures? Are not the two kinds of cases analogous in countless important ways? Occasionally a child turns out badly too, even when his environment and training are the same as that of his brothers and sisters who turn out "all right." He is the "bad penny." His acts of rebellion against parental discipline in adult life (such as the case of the gambler, already cited) are traceable to early experiences of real or fancied denial of infantile wishes. Sometimes the denial has been real, though many denials are absolutely necessary if the child is to grow up to observe the common decencies of civilized life; sometimes, if the child has an unusual quantity of narcissism, every event that occurs is interpreted by him as a denial of his wishes, and nothing a parent could do, even granting every humanly possible wish, would help. In any event, the later neurosis can be attributed to this. Can the person himself be held responsible? Hardly. If he engaged in activities which are a menace to society, he must be put into prison, of course, but responsibility is another matter. The time when the events occurred which rendered his neurotic behavior inevitable was a time long before he was capable of thought and decision. As an adult, he is a victim of a world he never made—only this world is inside him.

What about the children who turn out "all right?" All we can say is that "it's just lucky for them" that what happened to their unfortunate brother didn't happen to them; *through no virtue of their own* they are not doomed to the life of unconscious guilt, expiation, conscious depression and terrified ego-gestures for the appeasement of a tyrannical super-ego that he is. The machine turned them out with a minimum of damage. But if the brother cannot be blamed for his evils, neither can they be praised for their good; unless, of course, we should blame people for what is not their fault, and praise them for lucky accidents.

We all agree that machines turn out "lemons," we all agree that nature turns out misfits in the realm of biology—the blind, the crippled, the diseased; but we hesitate to include the realm of the personality, for here, it seems, is the last retreat of our dignity as human beings. Our ego can endure anything but this; this island at least must remain above the encroaching flood. But may not precisely the same analysis be made here also? Nature turns out psychological "lemons" too, in far greater quantities than any other kind; and indeed all of us are "lemons" in some respect or other, the difference being one of degree. Some of us are lucky enough not to have a gambling-neurosis or criminotic tendencies or masochistic mother-attachment or overdimensional repetition-compulsion to make our lives miserable, but most of our actions, those usually considered the most important, are unconsciously dominated just the same. And, if a neurosis may be likened to a curse of God, let those of us, the elect, who are enabled to enjoy a measure of life's happiness without the hell-fire of neurotic guilt, take this not as our own achievement, but simply for what it is—a gift of God.

IV

Assuming the main conclusions of this paper to be true, is there any room left for freedom?

This, of course, all depends on what we mean by "freedom." In the senses suggested at the beginning of this paper, there are countless free acts, and unfree ones as well. When "free" means "uncompelled," and only external compulsion is admitted, again there are countless free acts. But now we have extended the notion of compulsion to include determination by unconscious forces. With this sense in mind, our question is, "With the concept of compulsion thus extended, and in the light of present psychoanalytic knowledge, is there any freedom left in human behavior?"

If practicing psychoanalysts were asked this question, there is little doubt that their answer would be along the following lines: They would say that they were not accustomed to using the term "free" at all, but that if they had to suggest a criterion for distinguishing the free from the unfree, they would say that a person's freedom is present *in inverse proportion to his neuroticism;* in other words, the more his acts are determined by a *malevolent* unconscious, the less free he is. Thus, they would speak of *degrees* of freedom. They would say that as a person is cured of his neurosis, he becomes more free—free to realize capabilities that were blocked by the neurotic affliction. The psychologically well-adjusted individual is in this sense comparatively the most free. Indeed, those who are cured of mental disorders are sometimes said to have *regained their freedom:* They are freed from the tyranny of a malevolent unconscious which formerly exerted as much of a domination over them as if they had been the abject slaves of a cruel dictator.

But suppose one says that a person is free only to the extent that his acts are *not unconsciously determined at all,* be they unconsciously benevolent *or* malevolent? If this is the criterion, psychoanalysts would say, most human behavior cannot be called free at all: Our impulses and volitions having to do with our basic attitudes toward life, whether we are optimists or pessimists, tough-minded or tender-minded, whether our tempers are quick or slow, whether we are "naturally self-seeking" or "naturally benevolent" (and *all the acts consequent upon these things*), what things annoy us, whether we take to blondes or brunettes, old or young, whether we become philosophers or artists or businessmen—all this has its basis in the unconscious. If people generally call most acts free, it is not because they believe that compelled acts should be called free; it is rather through not knowing how large a proportion of our acts actually are compelled. Only the comparatively "vanilla-flavored" aspects of our lives—such as our behavior toward people who don't really matter to us—are exempted from this rule.

These, I think, are the two principal criteria for distinguishing freedom from the lack of it which we might set up on the basis of psychoanalytic knowledge. Conceivably we might set up others. In every case, of course, it remains trivially true that "it all depends on how we choose to use the word." The facts are what they are, regardless of what words we choose for labeling them. But if we choose to label them in a way which is not in accord with what human beings, however vaguely, have long had in mind in applying these labels, as we would be doing if we labeled as "free" many acts which we know as much about as we now do through modern psychoanalytic methods, then we shall only be manipulating words to mislead our fellow creatures.

NOTES

1. *The Problems of Ethics,* Rynin translation, p. 150.
2. *New York Post,* Tuesday, May 18, 1948, p. 4.
3. I am aware that the theory presented below is not accepted by all practicing psychoanalysts. Many non-Freudians would disagree with the conclusions presented below. But I do not believe that this fact affects my argument, as long as the concept of unconscious motivation is accepted. I am aware, too, that much of the language employed in the following descriptions is animistic and metaphorical; but as long as I am presenting a view I would prefer to "go the whole hog" and present it in its most dramatic form. The theory can in any case be made clearest by the use of such language, just as atomic theory can often be made clearest to students with the use of models.
4. This view is very clearly developed in Edmund Bergler, *Divorce Won't Help,* especially Chapter 1.
5. E.g., Edmund Bergler, *The Battle of the Conscience,* Chapter 1.
6. The girl's development after this point is somewhat different. Society demands more aggressiveness of the adult male, and hence there are more super-ego strictures on tendencies toward passivity in the male; accordingly his defenses must be stronger.

FOR FURTHER REFLECTION

1. Hospers bases his argument on the doctrine of psychoanalysis. What is the evidence that psychoanalysis is true or completely true? What debatable premises, if any, can you detect in the content mentioned by Hospers?
2. Compare Hospers's argument with Stace's argument. Do you think that Hospers has successfully refuted compatibilism? Has he been as successful in refuting libertarianism? Explain your answers.

HARRY FRANKFURT

FREEDOM OF THE WILL AND THE CONCEPT OF A PERSON

Harry Frankfurt (b. 1929) is a professor of philosophy emeritus at Princeton University who has made important contributions to the study of free will and to Descartes scholarship. Frankfurt, like Stace, is a compatibilist. But whereas Stace and most compatibilists defend their position by a controversial hypothetical interpretation of the formula "S is free just in case S *could have done otherwise*," Frankfurt offers a theory of the will in order to account for our notion of freedom. What distinguishes humans from other animals is our ability to deliberate and choose courses of actions. The strategy goes like this: Both animals and humans have straightforward or *first-order* desires—for example, desires to eat, to be comfortable, to sleep—but whereas animals act directly on their wants, humans can weigh them and accept or reject them. For example, Joan may have the first-order desire to smoke a cigarette, but she may also want to be healthy. She compares the two desires and forms a *second-order* desire, say, to refrain from smoking based on her desire to remain healthy. But since it is possible that she may have the second-order desire to refrain from smoking without wanting to act on it, there is one more step in the process. She must make her desire her will, her *volition*, and be committed to act on the desire not to smoke. The person must *identify* himself or herself with the second-order desire and thereby make it a second-order volition. As Frankfurt writes in another article, "To the extent that a person identifies himself with the springs of his actions, he takes a responsibility for those actions and acquires moral responsibility for them" ("Three Concepts of Free Action," in *Moral Responsibility*, ed. John Martin Fischer, Ithaca, NY: Cornell University Press, 1986, p. 120).

What philosophers have lately come to accept as analysis of the concept of a person is not actually analysis of *that* concept at all. Strawson, whose usage represents the current standard, identifies the concept of a person as "the concept of a type of entity such that *both* predicates ascribing states of consciousness *and* predicates ascribing corporeal characteristics . . . are equally applicable to a single individual of that single type."[1] But there are many entities besides persons that have both mental and physical properties. As it happens—though it seems extraordinary that this should be so—there is no common English word for the type of entity Strawson has in mind, a type that includes not only human beings but animals of various lesser species as well. Still, this hardly justifies the misappropriation of a valuable philosophical term.

Whether the members of some animal species are persons is surely not to be settled merely by deter-

From Harry Frankfurt, *Journal of Philosophy*, vol. lxviii, No. 1 (Jan. 1971), pp. 5–20, by permission of the author and the *Journal of Philosophy*. Some notes deleted, others renumbered.

mining whether it is correct to apply to them, in addition to predicates ascribing corporeal characteristics, predicates that ascribe states of consciousness. It does violence to our language to endorse the application of the term "person" to those numerous creatures which do have both psychological and material properties but which are manifestly not persons in any normal sense of the word. This misuse of language is doubtless innocent of any theoretical error. But although the offence is "merely verbal," it does significant harm. For it gratuitously diminishes our philosophical vocabulary, and it increases the likelihood that we will overlook the important area of inquiry with which the term "person" is most naturally associated. It might have been expected that no problem would be of more central and persistent concern to philosophers than that of understanding what we ourselves essentially are. Yet this problem is so generally neglected that it has been possible to make off with its very name almost without being noticed and, evidently, without evoking any widespread feeling of loss.

There is a sense in which the word "person" is merely the singular form of "people" and in which both terms connote no more than membership in a certain biological species. In those senses of the word which are of greater philosophical interest, however, the criteria for being a person do not serve primarily to distinguish the members of our own species from the members of other species. Rather, they are designed to capture those attributes which are the subject of our most humane concern with ourselves and the source of what we regard as most important and most problematical in our lives. Now these attributes would be of equal significance to us even if they were not in fact peculiar and common to the members of our own species. What interests us most in the human condition would not interest us less if it were also a feature of the condition of other creatures as well.

Our concept of ourselves as persons is not to be understood, therefore, as a concept of attributes that are necessarily species-specific. It is conceptually possible that members of novel or even of familiar non-human species should be persons; and it is also conceptually possible that some members of the human species are not persons. We do in fact assume, on the other hand, that no member of another species

is a person. Accordingly, there is a presumption that what is essential to persons is a set of characteristics that we generally suppose—whether rightly or wrongly—to be uniquely human.

It is my view that one essential difference between persons and other creatures is to be found in the structure of a person's will. Human beings are not alone in having desires and motives, or in making choices. They share these things with the members of certain other species, some of whom even appear to engage in deliberation and to make decisions based upon prior thought. It seems to be peculiarly characteristic of humans, however, that they are able to form what I shall call "second-order desires" or "desires of the second order."

Besides wanting and choosing and being moved *to do* this or that, men may also want to have (or not to have) certain desires and motives. They are capable of wanting to be different, in their preferences and purposes, from what they are. Many animals appear to have the capacity for what I shall call "first-order desires" or "desires of the first order," which are simply desires to do or not to do one thing or another. No animal other than man, however, appears to have the capacity for reflective self-evaluation that is manifested in the formation of second-order desires.

I

The concept designated by the verb "to want" is extraordinarily elusive. A statement of the form "*A* want to *X*"—taken by itself, apart from a context that serves to amplify or to specify its meaning—conveys remarkably little information. Such a statement may be consistent, for example, with each of the following statements: (a) the prospect of doing *X* elicits no sensation or introspectible emotional response in *A;* (b) *A* is unaware that he wants to *X;* (c) *A* believes that he does not want to *X;* (d) *A* wants to refrain from *X*-ing; (e) *A* wants to *Y* and believes that it is impossible for him both to *Y* and to *X;* (f) *A* does not "really" want to *X;* (g) *A would rather die than X;* and so on. It is therefore hardly sufficient to formulate the distinction between first-order and second-order desires, as I have done, by suggesting merely that someone has a first-order desire when he wants to do or not to do such-and-such, and that he has a second-order desire when he wants to have or not to have a certain desire of the first order.

As I shall understand them, statements of the form "*A* wants to *X*" cover a rather broad range of possibilities. They may be true even when statements like (a) through (g) are true: when *A* is unaware of any feelings concerning *X*-ing, when he is unaware that he wants to *X,* when he deceives himself about what he wants and believes falsely that he does not want to *X,* when he also has other desires that conflict with his desire to *X,* or when he is ambivalent. The desires in question may be conscious or unconscious, they need not be univocal, and *A* may be mistaken about them. There is a further source of uncertainty with regard to statements that identify someone's desires, however, and here it is important for my purposes to be less permissive.

Consider first those statements of the form "*A* wants to *X*" which identify first-order desires—that is, statements in which the term "to *X*" refers to an action. A statement of this kind does not, by itself, indicate the relative strength of *A*'s desire to *X*. It does not make it clear whether this desire is at all likely to play a decisive role in what *A* actually does or tries to do. For it may correctly be said that *A* wants to *X* even when his desire to *X* is only one among his desires and when it is far from being paramount among them. Thus, it may be true that *A* wants to *X* when he strongly prefers to do something else instead; and it may be true that he wants to *X* despite the fact that, when he acts, it is not the desire to *X* that motivates him to do what he does. On the other hand, someone who states that *A* wants to *X* may mean to convey that it is this desire that is motivating or moving *A* to do what he is actually doing or that *A* will in fact be moved by this desire (unless he changes his mind) when he acts.

It is only when it is used in the second of these ways that, given the special usage of "will" that I propose to adopt, the statement identifies *A*'s will. To identify an agent's will is either to identify the desire (or desires) by which he is motivated in some action he performs or to identify the desire (or desires) by which he will or would be motivated when or if he

acts. An agent's will, then, is identical with one or more of his first-order desires. But the notion of the will, as I am employing it, is not coextensive with the notion of first-order desires. It is not the notion of something that merely inclines an agent in some degree to act in a certain way. Rather, it is the notion of an *effective* desire—one that moves (or will or would move) a person all the way to action. Thus the notion of the will is not coextensive with the notion of what an agent intends to do. For even though someone may have a settled intention to do *X,* he may none the less do something else instead of doing *X* because, despite his intention, his desire to do *X* proves to be weaker or less effective than some conflicting desire.

Now consider those statements of the form "*A* wants to *X*" which identify second-order desires— that is, statements in which the term "to *X*" refers to a desire of the first order. There are also two kinds of situation in which it may be true that *A* wants to want to *X*. In the first place, it might be true of *A* that he wants to have a desire to *X* despite the fact that he has a univocal desire, altogether free of conflict and ambivalence, to refrain from *X*-ing. Someone might want to have a certain desire, in other words, but univocally want that desire to be unsatisfied.

Suppose that a physician engaged in psychotherapy with narcotics addicts believes that his ability to help his patients would be enhanced if he understood better what it is like for them to desire the drug to which they are addicted. Suppose that he is led in this way to want to have a desire for the drug. If it is a genuine desire that he wants, then what he wants is not merely to feel the sensations that addicts characteristically feel when they are gripped by their desires for the drug. What the physician wants, in so far as he wants to have a desire, is to be inclined or moved to some extent to take the drug.

It is entirely possible, however, that, although he wants to be moved by a desire to take the drug, he does not want this desire to be effective. He may not want it to move him all the way to action. He need not be interested in finding out what it is like to take the drug. And in so far as he now wants only to *want* to take it, and not to *take* it, there is nothing in what he now wants that would be satisfied by the drug itself. He may now have, in fact, an altogether univocal desire *not* to take the drug; and he may prudently arrange to make it impossible for him to satisfy the desire he would have if his desire to want the drug should in time be satisfied.

It would thus be incorrect to infer, from the fact that the physician now wants to desire to take the drug, that he already does desire to take it. His second-order desire to be moved to take the drug does not entail that he has a first-order desire to take it. If the drug were now to be administered to him, this might satisfy no desire that is implicit in his desire to want to take it. While he wants to want to take the drug, he may have *no* desire to take it; it may be that *all* he wants is to taste the desire for it. That is, his desire to have a certain desire that he does not have may not be a desire that his will should be at all different than it is.

Someone who wants only in this truncated way to want to X stands at the margin of preciosity, and the fact that he wants to want to X is not pertinent to the identification of his will. There is, however, a second kind of situation that may be described by "A wants to X"; and when the statement is used to describe a situation of this second kind, then it does pertain to what A wants his will to be. In such cases the statement means that A wants the desire to X to be the desire that moves him effectively to act. It is not merely that he wants the desire to X to be among the desires by which, to one degree or another, he is moved or inclined to act. He wants this desire to be effective— that is, to provide the motive in what he actually does. Now when the statement that A wants to want to X is used in this way, it does entail that A already has a desire to X. It could not be true both that A wants the desire to X to move him into action and that he does not want to X. It is only if he does want to X that he can coherently want the desire to X not merely to be one of his desires but, more decisively, to be his will.

Suppose a man wants to be motivated in what he does by the desire to concentrate on his work. It is necessarily true, if this supposition is correct, that he already wants to concentrate on his work. This desire is now among his desires. But the question of whether or not his second-order desire is fulfilled does not turn merely on whether the desire he wants is one of his desires. It turns on whether this desire is, as he wants it to be, his effective desire or will. If, when the chips are down, it is his desire to concentrate on his work that moves him to do what he does, then what he wants at that time is indeed (in the relevant sense) what he wants to want. If it is some other desire that actually moves him when he acts, on the other hand, then what he wants at that time is not (in the relevant sense) what he wants to want. This will be so despite the fact that the desire to concentrate on his work continues to be among his desires.

II

Someone has a desire of the second order either when he wants simply to have a certain desire or when he wants a certain desire to be his will. In situations of the latter kind, I shall call his second-order desires "second-order volitions" or "volitions of the second order." Now it is having second-order volitions, and not having second-order desires generally, that I regard as essential to being a person. It is logically possible, however unlikely, that there should be an agent with second-order desires but with no volitions of the second order. Such a creature, in my view, would not be a person. I shall use the term "wanton" to refer to agents who have first-order desires but who are not persons because, whether or not they have desires of the second order, they have no second-order volitions.

The essential characteristic of a wanton is that he does not care about his will. His desires move him to do certain things, without its being true of him either that he wants to be moved by those desires or that he prefers to be moved by other desires. The class of wantons includes all non-human animals that have desires and all very young children. Perhaps it also includes some adult human beings as well. In any case, adult humans may be more or less wanton; they may act wantonly, in response to first-order desires concerning which they have no volitions of the second order, more or less frequently.

The fact that a wanton has no second-order volitions does not mean that each of his first-order desires is translated heedlessly and at once into action. He may have no opportunity to act in accordance with some of his desires. Moreover, the translation of his desires into action may be delayed or precluded either by conflicting desires of the first order or by the intervention of deliberation. For a wanton may possess and employ rational faculties of a high order. Nothing in the concept of a wanton implies that he cannot reason or that he cannot deliberate concerning how to do what he wants to do. What distinguishes the rational wanton from other rational agents is that he is not concerned with the desirability of his desires themselves. He ignores the question of what his will is to be. Not only does he pursue whatever course of action he is most strongly inclined to pursue, but he does not care which of his inclinations is the strongest.

Thus a rational creature, who reflects upon the suitability to his desires of one course of action or another, may none the less be a wanton. In maintaining that the essence of being a person lies not in reason but in will, I am far from suggesting that a creature without reason may be a person. For it is only in virtue of his rational capacities that a person is capable of becoming critically aware of his own will and of forming volitions of the second order. The structure of a person's will presupposes, accordingly, that he is a rational being.

The distinction between a person and a wanton may be illustrated by the difference between two narcotics addicts. Let us suppose that the physiological condition accounting for the addiction is the same in both men, and that both succumb inevitably to their periodic desires for the drug to which they are addicted. One of the addicts hates his addiction and always struggles desperately, although to no avail, against its thrust. He tries everything that he thinks might enable him to overcome his desires for the drug. But these desires are too powerful for him to withstand, and invariably, in the end, they conquer him. He is an unwilling addict, helplessly violated by his own desires.

The unwilling addict has conflicting first-order desires: he wants to take the drug, and he also wants to refrain from taking it. In addition to these first-order desires, however, he has a volition of the second order. He is not a neutral with regard to the conflict between his desire to take the drug and his desire to refrain from taking it. It is the latter desire, and not the former, that he wants to constitute his will; it is the latter desire,

rather than the former, that he wants to be effective and to provide the purpose that he will seek to realize in what he actually does.

The other addict is a wanton. His actions reflect the economy of his first-order desires, without his being concerned whether the desires that move him to act are desires by which he wants to be moved to act. If he encounters problems in obtaining the drug or in administering it to himself, his responses to his urges to take it may involve deliberation. But it never occurs to him to consider whether he wants the relation among his desires to result in his having the will he has. The wanton addict may be an animal, and thus incapable of being concerned about his will. In any event he is, in respect of his wanton lack of concern, no different from an animal.

The second of these addicts may suffer a first-order conflict similar to the first-order conflict suffered by the first. Whether he is human or not, the wanton may (perhaps due to conditioning) both want to take the drug and want to refrain from taking it. Unlike the unwilling addict, however, he does not prefer that one of his conflicting desires should be paramount over the other; he does not prefer that one first-order desire rather than the other should constitute his will. It would be misleading to say that he is neutral as to the conflict between his desires, since this would suggest that he regards them as equally acceptable. Since he has no identity apart from his first-order desires, it is true neither that he prefers one to the other nor that he prefers not to take sides.

It makes a difference to the unwilling addict, who is a person, which of his conflicting first-order desires wins out. Both desires are his, to be sure; and whether he finally takes the drug or finally succeeds in refraining from taking it, he acts to satisfy what is in a literal sense his own desire. In either case he does something he himself wants to do, and he does it not because of some external influence whose aim happens to coincide with his own but because of his desire to do it. The unwilling addict identifies himself, however, through the formation of a second-order volition, with one rather than with the other of his conflicting first-order desires. He makes one of them more truly his own and, in so doing, he withdraws himself from the other. It is in virtue of this identification and withdrawal, accomplished through the formation of a second-order volition, that the unwilling addict may meaningfully make the analytically puzzling statements that the force moving him to take the drug is a force other than his own, and that it is not of his own free will but rather against his will that this force moves him to take it.

The wanton addict cannot or does not care which of his conflicting first-order desires wins out. His lack of concern is not due to his inability to find a convincing basis for preference. It is due either to his lack of capacity for reflection or to his mindless indifference to the enterprise of evaluating his own desires and motives. There is only one issue in the struggle to which his first-order conflict may lead: whether the one or the other of his conflicting desires is stronger. Since he is moved by both desires, he will not be altogether satisfied by what he does no matter which of them is effective. But it makes no difference *to him* whether his craving or his aversion gets the upper hand. He has no stake in the conflict between them and so, unlike the unwilling addict, he can neither win nor lose the struggle in which he is engaged. When a *person* acts, the desire by which he is moved is either the will he wants or a will he wants to be without. When a *wanton* acts, it is neither.

III

There is a very close relationship between the capacity for forming second-order volitions and another capacity that is essential to persons—one that has often been considered a distinguishing mark of the human condition. It is only because a person has volitions of the second order that he is capable both of enjoying and of lacking freedom of the will. The concept of a person is not only, then, the concept of a type of entity that has both first-order desires and volitions of the second order. It can also be construed as the concept of a type of entity for whom the freedom of its will may be a problem. This concept excludes all wantons, both infrahuman and human, since they fail to satisfy an essential condition for the enjoyment of freedom of the will. And it excludes those suprahuman beings, if any, whose wills are necessarily free.

Just what kind of freedom is the freedom of the will? This question calls for an identification of the special area of human experience to which the concept of freedom of the will, as distinct from the concepts of other sorts of freedom, is particularly germane. In dealing with it, my aim will be primarily to locate the problem with which a person is most immediately concerned when he is concerned with the freedom of his will.

According to one familiar philosophical tradition, being free is fundamentally a matter of doing what one wants to do. Now the notion of an agent who does what he wants to do is by no means an altogether clear one: both the doing and the wanting, and the appropriate relation between them as well, require elucidation. But although its focus needs to be sharpened and its formulation refined, I believe that this notion does capture at least part of what is implicit in the idea of an agent who *acts* freely. It misses entirely, however, the peculiar content of the quite different idea of an agent whose *will* is free.

We do not suppose that animals enjoy freedom of the will, although we recognize that an animal may be free to run in whatever direction it wants. Thus, having the freedom to do what one wants to do is not a sufficient condition of having a free will. It is not a necessary condition either. For to deprive someone of his freedom of action is not necessarily to undermine the freedom of his will. When an agent is aware that there are certain things he is not free to do, this doubtless affects his desires and limits the range of choices he can make. But suppose that someone, without being aware of it, has in fact lost or been deprived of his freedom of action. Even though he is no longer free to do what he wants to do, his will may remain as free as it was before. Despite the fact that he is not free to translate his desires into actions or to act according to the determinations of his will, he may still form those desires and make those determinations as freely as if his freedom of action had not been impaired.

When we ask whether a person's will is free we are not asking whether he is in a position to translate his first-order desires into actions. That is the question of whether he is free to do as he pleases. The question of the freedom of his will does not concern the relation between what he does and what he wants to do. Rather, it concerns his desires themselves. But what question about them is it?

It seems to me both natural and useful to construe the question of whether a person's will is free in close analogy to the question of whether an agent enjoys freedom of action. Now freedom of action is (roughly, at least) the freedom to do what one wants to do. Analogously, then, the statement that a person enjoys freedom of the will means (also roughly) that he is free to want what he wants to want. More precisely, it means that he is free to will what he wants to will, or to have the will he wants. Just as the question about the freedom of an agent's action has to do with whether it is the action he wants to perform, so the question about the freedom of his will has to do with whether it is the will he wants to have.

It is in securing the conformity of his will to his second-order volitions, then, that a person exercises freedom of the will. And it is in the discrepancy between his will and his second-order volitions, or in his awareness that their coincidence is not his own doing but only a happy chance, that a person who does not have this freedom feels its lack. The unwilling addict's will is not free. This is shown by the fact that it is not the will he wants. It is also true, though in a different way, that the will of the wanton addict is not free. The wanton addict neither has the will he wants nor has a will that differs from the will he wants. Since he has no volitions of the second order, the freedom of his will cannot be a problem for him. He lacks it, so to speak, by default.

People are generally far more complicated than my sketchy account of the structure of a person's will may suggest. There is as much opportunity for ambivalence, conflict, and self-deception with regard to desires of the second order, for example, as there is with regard to first-order desires. If there is an unresolved conflict among someone's second-order desires, then he is in danger of having no second-order volition; for unless this conflict is resolved, he has no preference concerning which of his first-order desires is to be his will. This condition, if it is so severe that it prevents him from identifying himself in a sufficiently decisive way with *any* of his conflicting

first-order desires, destroys him as a person. For it either tends to paralyse his will and to keep him from acting at all, or it tends to remove him from his will so that his will operates without his participation. In both cases he becomes, like the unwilling addict though in a different way, a helpless bystander to the forces that move him.

Another complexity is that a person may have, especially if his second-order desires are in conflict, desires and volitions of a higher order than the second. There is no theoretical limit to the length of the series of desires of higher and higher orders; nothing except common sense and, perhaps, a saving fatigue prevents an individual from obsessively refusing to identify himself with any of his desires until he forms a desire of the next higher order. The tendency to generate such a series of acts of forming desires, which would be a case of humanization run wild, also leads toward the destruction of a person.

It is possible, however, to terminate such a series of acts without cutting it off arbitrarily. When a person identifies himself *decisively* with one of his first-order desires, this commitment "resounds" throughout the potentially endless array of higher orders. Consider a person who, without reservation or conflict, wants to be motivated by the desire to concentrate on his work. The fact that his second-order volition to be moved by this desire is a decisive one means that there is no room for questions concerning the pertinence of desires or volitions of higher orders. Suppose the person is asked whether he wants to want to concentrate on his work. He can properly insist that this question concerning a third-order desire does not arise. It would be a mistake to claim that, because he has not considered whether he wants the second-order volition he has formed, he is indifferent to the question of whether it is with this volition or with some other that he wants his will to accord. The decisiveness of the commitment he has made means that he has decided that no further question about his second-order volition, at any higher order, remains to be asked. It is relatively unimportant whether we explain this by saying that this commitment implicitly generates an endless series of confirming desires of higher orders, or by saying that the commitment is tantamount to a dissolution of the pointedness of all questions concerning higher orders of desire.

Examples such as the one concerning the unwilling addict may suggest that volitions of the second order, or of higher orders, must be formed deliberately and that a person characteristically struggles to ensure that they are satisfied. But the conformity of a person's will to his higher-order volitions may be far more thoughtless and spontaneous than this. Some people are naturally moved by kindness when they want to be kind, and by nastiness when they want to be nasty, without any explicit forethought and without any need for energetic self-control. Others are moved by nastiness when they want to be kind and by kindness when they intend to be nasty, equally without forethought and without active resistance to these violations of their higher-order desires. The enjoyment of freedom comes easily to some. Others must struggle to achieve it.

IV

My theory concerning the freedom of the will accounts easily for our disinclination to allow that this freedom is enjoyed by the members of any species inferior to our own. It also satisfies another condition that must be met by any such theory, by making it apparent why the freedom of the will should be regarded as desirable. The enjoyment of a free will means the satisfaction of certain desires—desires of the second or of higher orders—whereas its absence means their frustration. The satisfactions at stake are those which accrue to a person of whom it may be said that his will is his own. The corresponding frustrations are those suffered by a person of whom it may be said that he is estranged from himself, or that he finds himself a helpless or a passive bystander to the forces that move him.

A person who is free to do what he wants to do may yet not be in a position to have the will he wants. Suppose, however, that he enjoys both freedom of action and freedom of the will. Then he is not only free to do what he wants to do; he is also free to want what he wants to want. It seems to me that he has, in

that case, all the freedom it is possible to desire or to conceive. There are other good things in life, and he may not possess some of them. But there is nothing in the way of freedom that he lacks.

It is far from clear that certain other theories of the freedom of the will meet these elementary but essential conditions: that it be understandable why we desire this freedom and why we refuse to ascribe it to animals. Consider, for example, Roderick Chisholm's quaint version of the doctrine that human freedom entails an absence of causal determination.[2] Whenever a person performs a free action, according to Chisholm, it's a miracle. The motion of a person's hand, when the person moves it, is the outcome of a series of physical causes; but some event in this series, "and presumably one of those that took place within the brain, was caused by the agent and not by any other events" (18). A free agent has, therefore, "a prerogative which some would attribute only to God: each of us, when we act, is a prime mover unmoved" (23).

This account fails to provide any basis for doubting that animals of subhuman species enjoy the freedom it defines. Chisholm says nothing that makes it seem less likely that a rabbit performs a miracle when it moves its leg than that a man does so when he moves his hand. But why, in any case, should anyone *care* whether he can interrupt the natural order of causes in the way Chisholm describes? Chisholm offers no reason for believing that there is a discernible difference between the experience of a man who miraculously initiates a series of causes when he moves his hand and a man who moves his hand without any such breach of the normal causal sequence. There appears to be no concrete basis for preferring to be involved in the one state of affairs rather than in the other.

It is generally supposed that, in addition to satisfying the two conditions I have mentioned, a satisfactory theory of the freedom of the will necessarily provides an analysis of one of the conditions of moral responsibility. The most common recent approach to the problem of understanding the freedom of the will has been, indeed, to inquire what is entailed by the assumption that someone is morally responsible for what he has done. In my view, however, the relation between moral responsibility and the freedom of the will has been very widely misunderstood. It is not true that a person is morally responsible for what he has done only if his will was free when he did it. He may be morally responsible for having done it even though his will was not free at all.

A person's will is free only if he is free to have the will he wants. This means that, with regard to any of his first-order desires, he is free either to make that desire his will or to make some other first-order desire his will instead. Whatever his will, then, the will of the person whose will is free could have been otherwise; he could have done otherwise than to constitute his will as he did. It is a vexed question just how 'he could have done otherwise' is to be understood in contexts such as this one. But although this question is important to the theory of freedom, it has no bearing on the theory of moral responsibility. For the assumption that a person is morally responsible for what he has done does not entail that the person was in a position to have whatever will he wanted.

This assumption *does* entail that the person did what he did freely, or that he did it of his own free will. It is a mistake, however, to believe that someone acts freely only when he is free to do whatever he wants or that he acts of his own free will only if his will is free. Suppose that a person has done what he wanted to do, that he did it because he wanted to do it, and that the will by which he was moved when he did it was his will because it was the will he wanted. Then he did it freely and of his own free will. Even supposing that he could have done otherwise, he would not have done otherwise; and even supposing that he could have had a different will, he would not have wanted his will to differ from what it was. Moreover, since the will that moved him when he acted was his will because he wanted it to be, he cannot claim that his will was forced upon him or that he was a passive bystander to its constitution. Under these conditions, it is quite irrelevant to the evaluation of his moral responsibility to inquire whether the alternatives that he opted against were actually available to him.

In illustration, consider a third kind of addict. Suppose that his addiction has the same physiological basis and the same irresistible thrust as the addictions of the unwilling and wanton addicts, but that he is altogether delighted with his condition. He is a willing addict, who would not have things any other way. If the grip of his addiction should somehow weaken, he would do whatever he could to reinstate it; if his desire for the drug should begin to fade, he would take steps to renew its intensity.

The willing addict's will is not free, for his desire to take the drug will be effective regardless of whether or not he wants this desire to constitute his will. But when he takes the drug, he takes it freely and of his own free will. I am inclined to understand his situation as involving the overdetermination of his first-order desire to take the drug. This desire is his effective desire because he is physiologically addicted. But it is his effective desire also because he wants it to be. His will is outside his control, but, by his second-order desire that his desire for the drug should be effective, he has made this will his own. Given that it is therefore not only because of his addiction that his desire for the drug is effective, he may be morally responsible for taking the drug.

My conception of the freedom of the will appears to be neutral with regard to the problem of determinism. It seems conceivable that it should be causally determined that a person is free to want what he wants to want. If this is conceivable, then it might be causally determined that a person enjoys a free will. There is no more than an innocuous appearance of paradox in the proposition that it is determined, ineluctably and by forces beyond their control, that certain people have free wills and that others do not. There is no incoherence in the proposition that some agency other than a person's own is responsible (even *morally* responsible) for the fact that he enjoys or fails to enjoy freedom of the will. It is possible that a person should be morally responsible for what he does of his own free will and that some other person should also be morally responsible for his having done it.

On the other hand, it seems conceivable that it should come about by chance that a person is free to have the will he wants. If this is conceivable, then it might be a matter of chance that certain people enjoy freedom of the will and that certain others do not. Perhaps it is also conceivable, as a number of philosophers believe, for states of affairs to come about in a way other than by chance or as the outcome of a sequence of natural causes. If it is indeed conceivable for the relevant states of affairs to come about in some third way, then it is also possible that a person should in that third way come to enjoy the freedom of the will.

NOTES

1. P. F. Strawson, *Individuals* (London: Methuen, 1959), 101–2. Ayer's usage of "person" is similar: "it is characteristic of persons in this sense that besides having various physical properties . . . they are also credited with various forms of consciousness" [A. J. Ayer, *The Concept of a Person* (New York: St. Martin's, 1963), 82]. What concerns Strawson and Ayer is the problem of understanding the relation between mind and body, rather than the quite different problem of understanding what it is to be a creature that not only has a mind and a body but is also a person.
2. "Freedom and Action," in *Freedom and Determinism,* ed. Keith Lehrer (New York: Random House, 1966), 11–44.

FOR FURTHER REFLECTION

1. Compare Frankfurt's version of compatibilism with Stace's version. Is Frankfurt's analysis superior? Does it make compatibilism plausible? Can we be both free and determined? Explain your answers.
2. Philosopher Gary Watson (University of California at Irvine) criticized Frankfurt's theory as being too desire oriented. We not only weigh our conflicting desires in deciding what to do, but we make *evaluations* as to the appropriateness or moral status of our desires. These evaluations are not just other desires, but have a life of their own, so that although I may want to cheat very badly, I reject that desire on moral grounds. Is Watson correct in his analysis? Why or why not?
3. Is Frankfurt's equation of identification with freedom satisfactory? Consider this counterexample: John, who is tempted to cheat on his English test, deliberates on the matter and identifies with the second-order desire to cheat. However, unbeknownst to John, he has been hypnotized (to have a desire to cheat) by a clever psychologist, so that he cannot help willing as he does. Would you say that John acts freely? How would Frankfurt respond to such counterexamples?
4. Now that you have read through several essays on free will, determinism, and compatibilism, which arguments are the best and which position has the most evidence in its favor? Explain.

B. Moral Responsibility

Imagine that it is a cold January day and you are walking along the boardwalk over-looking the sea, eagerly making your way toward some exciting destination. Suddenly someone pushes you off the boardwalk and into the shallow water three feet below. Getting up from the cold water, you realize that your clothes are soaking wet and you won't be able to get to your date. You glare angrily at the man who pushed you, blaming him, holding him morally accountable for the mess you are in. Whatever possessed him to do it? Let's look at six possible ways to describe the man's act.

1. The man was angry at the world and just wanted to strike back. You were the unlucky victim. His wife had run off with another man, and he had just been fired from his job. You somehow reminded him of one of the people in his sad saga, and he just lashed blindly out at you.
2. The man was mentally ill. In fact, he had just been discharged from an institution (prematurely, it turns out). He cannot control episodes of sudden, violent behavior. Examinations have revealed a defect in his brain that most likely accounts for his condition. He is now very sorry, and helps you up out of the water.
3. The man has been hypnotized and ordered by the hypnotist to push someone into the water. He is not sure why he did it, but believes that he pushed you of his own free will.
4. The man has a nervous condition that sometimes causes violent muscle reflexes. He had an attack, and his arm shot out, knocking you into the water.
5. The man was actually trying to save your life. He had just seen your enemy behind you, ready to pull the trigger of a gun that was aimed at your head. By pushing you into the water, the man saved you from injury and possible death.
6. The man deliberated about whether to push someone into the water and, realizing it would mess up your plans, decided that the pleasure he would get in seeing your plans disrupted would outweigh whatever qualms of conscience he might have later.

In all of these situations, the basic fact is the same: The man knocked you into the water. In that sense he is at least partially *causally* responsible for your being wet and not on your way to your date. But in which cases is he *morally* responsible?

We would tend to *excuse* the man's behavior in cases 2, 3, and 4, for he was not in control of his behavior. We would still hold him accountable in 1, but acknowledge mitigating circumstances and characterize him as having *diminished* responsibility. Only cases 5 and 6 look like clear examples of fully responsible behavior. Case 5 is a case of praiseworthy behavior (let's assume for the sake of illustration that the act was fully in accord with the man's character and moral commitments), and case 6 is a case of blameworthy behavior. In case 1, the man was partly free, while in cases 5 and 6 he was fully free.

But suppose a determinist such as John Hospers or Clarence Darrow objects, saying that all of the acts in these cases were caused by antecedent causes, so that the man was not free in doing any of them. The only difference between the mentally ill man and the man who acts deliberately is that the latter man has reflected desires conforming to his act—but he is no more free than the hypnotized man, who also wants to push you into the water. The hypnotized man's act is caused by the hypnotist, but the reflective man made his decision because of antecedent causes and the laws of nature. He might have felt free in deciding to do what he did, but his intuitions do not touch the subconscious causes that shaped his intuition as well as his decision.

Both the hard determinist and the libertarian (incompatibilist) agree that if determinism is true, we do not have moral responsibility. Compatibilists, however, argue that moral responsibility is consistent with causal determinism, because *responsibility* refers to the way the decision is made or the act done—whether it is deliberate or voluntary, or results from some involuntary process such as ignorance or compulsion.

Aristotle, author of the first reading in this section, is often cited as the first philosopher to offer a compatibilist theory of human action. According to Aristotle, voluntary acts were the only ones for which a person could be praised or blamed. He defines a voluntary act as "that of which the moving principle is in the agent himself, he being aware of the particular circumstances of the action," and an involuntary act one that "takes place under compulsion or owing to ignorance." Moral responsibility simply designates the set of voluntary actions for which a person can be praised or blamed. He believes that impulsive acts, occasioned by desire or anger, are voluntary. His main argument is that such behavior comes from a person's character, and each person is to some extent responsible for his or her moral character.

Aristotle simply ignores any discussion of determinism, leading many philosophers to conclude that we need not dispute about whether behavior is governed entirely by causal laws. We should confine ourselves to asking the kinds of questions that Aristotle asked: was the action voluntary or involuntary, or was it a borderline case? Then we should withhold or apply moral praise and censure accordingly.

In the second reading, stoic philosopher Epictetus acknowledges that everything in the cosmos is determind by fate. However, for our human vantage, our attitudes and actions appear to be within our control, while everything else is beyond our control. We should thus adjust our attitudes to accept what fate has in store for us.

Galen Strawson challenges the notion of moral responsibility, arguing that the idea rests on an incoherent premise—that an agent can bring himself (his motivational patterns) into existence (*causa sui*).

Michael Levin is a compatibilist of the other variety, a soft determinist. He accepts the thesis that all human actions are governed by causal laws, but nevertheless holds that this determinism is not at odds with moral responsibility.

Lois Hope Walker, a libertarian, challenges the compatibilist approach, arguing that if our behavior is completely explainable in terms of antecedent events and the laws of nature, then these things, not the agent, are responsible for his or her behavior. Unless libertarianism is true, no one is morally responsible for any act whatsoever.

ARISTOTLE

VOLUNTARY ACTION AND RESPONSIBILITY

Aristotle (384–322 B.C.E.), Greek physician, Plato's prize pupil, tutor to Alexander the Great, and one of the most important philosophers who ever lived, wrote important contributions on every major field in philosophy: metaphysics, philosophy of science, philosophical psychology, esthetics, ethics, and politics. He is also the father of formal logic.

In this section from the *Nicomachean Ethics*, Aristotle discusses the nature of moral responsibility as those actions that are voluntarily done. A person is praised and blamed only for his or her voluntary acts. Involuntary acts, committed in ignorance or under compulsion, are excusable. To say an act is morally virtuous implies that the act has followed a choice that is the result of deliberation. Aristotle's discussion is especially significant, not only because it is the first philosophical discussion of voluntary action, but also because it omits all reference to nonagent causality or determinism. This omission has been praised and used as a paradigm by compatibilists, who accordingly argue that we can separate the truth of responsibility from any discussion of determinism or libertarianism.

CHAPTER 1

As virtue is concerned with emotion and action, and emotions and actions that are voluntary are objects for praise or blame, while those that are involuntary are objects for pardon and sometimes for pity, we must, I think, in a study of virtue distinguish the voluntary from the involuntary. It will also be useful for lawmakers for its bearing on the award of honors and punishments.

Acts done under compulsion or from ignorance are generally considered involuntary. An act is compulsory if its origin is external to the doer or sufferer, that is, if it is one to which the doer or sufferer contributes nothing, as if, for example, the wind, or people who have us in their power, were to carry us in a certain direction. But if an act is performed for fear of some greater evil or for some noble end, as, for example, if a tyrant, who had our parents and children in his power, were to order us to do some shameful act on condition that, if we did it, their lives would be spared, and, if not, they would be put to death, it is questionable whether such an act is voluntary or involuntary. The act of throwing goods overboard during a storm at sea is of the same sort; for nobody would voluntarily make such a sacrifice in the abstract, yet every sensible person will make it for his own safety and that of his companions. Acts like these are of a mixed character, yet more like voluntary than involuntary acts, for they are the results of choice at the time, and the end of the act is a result of the choice made at the moment of performing it. When we speak then of an action as voluntary or involuntary, we must regard the occasion when it was performed. The person[1] whose acts we are here considering acts voluntarily; for in acts like his the power which sets the machin-

From Aristotle, *Nicomachean Ethics*, trans. James E. C. Weldon (New York: Macmillan, 1897).

ery of his limbs in motion is in himself, and when the origin of anything is in the person himself, it lies with him either to do it or not to do it. Such actions then are voluntary, although in the abstract they may be called involuntary; because nobody would choose any such act in itself.

Such acts are at times objects of praise, when men submit to something shameful or painful for the sake of gaining something great and noble; in a contrary case they are objects of blame, for only a bad man would submit to something utterly shameful, if his object were ignoble or only trivial. Some acts are pardonable, though not praiseworthy, as when a person is induced to do wrong by pressure too strong for human nature, that no one could resist. Yet there are acts, perhaps, we cannot be compelled to do; we should rather suffer the most dreadful form of death than do them. So the reasons which forced Alcmaeon in Euripides[2] to murder his mother are clearly ridiculous.

It is sometimes difficult to determine what ought to be chosen or endured in order to obtain or avoid a certain result. But it is still more difficult to abide by our decisions; for it generally happens that the consequence we expect is painful and the act we are forced to do is shameful; therefore we receive blame or praise according as we yield or do not yield to the constraint.

What class of acts then may rightly be called compulsory? Acts may be called absolutely compulsory whenever the cause is external to the doer and he contributes nothing. But when an act, though involuntary in itself, is chosen at a particular time and for a particular end, and when its cause is in the doer himself, then, though the act is involuntary in itself, it is voluntary at that time and for that end. Such an act is more like a voluntary than an involuntary act; for actions come under the class of particular things, and in the supposed case the particular act is voluntary. And what kind of acts should be chosen for what ends it is not easy to state, as particular cases admit of many differences.

Someone might argue that whatever is pleasant or noble is compulsory on us, because pleasure and nobleness are forces external to ourselves; but if that were so, every act would be compulsory, as these are the motives of all our acts. Also, if a person acts under compulsion and against his will, his act is painful to him; but if he is influenced to act by pleasure and nobleness, it is pleasant. It is absurd to lay the blame of our wrongdoings on external causes, rather than on the facility with which we are caught by such influences, and take the credit of our noble actions ourselves, while laying the blame of our shameful acts on pleasure. An act then is compulsory if its origin is outside the doer, or if the person who is compelled contributes nothing to the act.

CHAPTER 2

An act committed in ignorance is never voluntary; but it is not involuntary, unless it is followed by pain and regret. For a person who does something, whatever it may be, from ignorance and yet feels no distress at his act, has not, it is true, acted voluntarily, since he did not know what he was doing, but on the other hand he has not acted involuntarily, so long as he feels no regret. If a person who has acted from ignorance regrets what he has done, he may be called an involuntary agent; but a person who does not regret it is in a different case, and he may be called a non-voluntary agent, for, since he differs from the other, it is better he should have a special name.

There is a difference too, it would seem, between acting from ignorance and acting in ignorance. Thus, if a person is intoxicated or enraged, he is not regarded as acting from ignorance, but as acting from intoxication or rage; yet he does not act consciously but in ignorance.

Every wicked person, we know, is ignorant of what he ought to do and what he ought not to do, and ignorance is the error which makes people unjust and generally bad. But when we speak of an action as involuntary, we do not mean merely that a person is ignorant of his true interest. The ignorance which causes involuntary action, as distinguished from that which causes wickedness, is not that which affects the moral purpose, nor again is it ignorance of the universal,[3] for that is blameworthy. It is rather ignorance of particulars, that is, of the particular circumstances and occasion of the act. Where this ignorance exists, there is room for pity and forgiveness, since one who is ignorant of such particulars is an involuntary actor.

It will be well then to define the nature and number of these particulars. They are

1. who is acting
2. what is the act
3. the occasion or circumstances of the act

Sometimes also

4. the instrument; for instance, the tool
5. the aim; for instance, safety
6. the manner of doing the act; for instance, gently or violently.

Nobody but a madman could be ignorant of all these particulars. Clearly too no one could be ignorant of the actor; for how could a person be ignorant of himself? But he might not know what he was doing, as when people say a word slipped from them unawares or they did not know something was secret, like Aeschylus[4] when he revealed the mysteries; or he might only have meant to show the working of a weapon when he discharged it, like the man who discharged the catapult. Again, a person might take his son for an enemy, like Merope,[5] or a pointed foil for one with its button on, or a solid stone for a pumice stone; or he might kill somebody by a drink that was meant to save him; or he might strike a fatal blow while only intending, as in a sparring match, to show how to strike. Since there may be ignorance in regard to all these particular circumstances of an act, a person may be said to have acted involuntarily, if he was ignorant of any one of them, and especially of the most important circumstances of the act and its end. But if an action is to be called involuntary because of such ignorance, it should be painful to the agent and excite in him a feeling of regret.

CHAPTER 3

As an act is involuntary if done under compulsion or from ignorance, it would seem to follow that it is voluntary if the actor starts it in full knowledge of the particular circumstances of his act. It is probably wrong to call all acts of passion or desire involuntary. For on that principle, in the first place, none of the lower animals could be said to act voluntarily, nor could children; and, secondly, is it suggested that nothing we do

from desire or passion is voluntary? Or are our noble acts done voluntarily, and our shameful acts involuntarily? Surely the latter view is ridiculous, if one and the same feeling is the cause of both kinds of act. It would seem strange to say that the things we ought to desire we desire involuntarily; there are things about which we ought to be angry, and things, such as health and learning, which we ought to desire. Again, we think the involuntary is painful; but what we do from desire is pleasant. Again, what difference is there as to involuntariness between errors committed in cold reason and errors committed in anger? It is our duty to avoid both; but the irrational emotions seem to be as truly human as reason itself. So the acts that spring from passion and desire are no less the acts of the man than his rational acts; it is absurd therefore to regard them as involuntary.

CHAPTER 4

Having thus distinguished voluntary from involuntary action, we must go on to discuss moral purpose. For moral purpose is evidently most closely related to virtue, and is a better test of character than acts are.

Moral purpose is clearly something voluntary. Still moral purpose and the will are not identical; the will is the broader term. For children and the lower animals have a share in will; they do not share in moral purpose. Also, we speak of acts done on the spur of the moment as voluntary, but not as done with a moral purpose.

Those then who define moral purpose as desire, or passion, or wish, or opinion of some sort are mistaken. For moral purpose is not like desire and passion, common both to irrational creatures and to man. Again, an intemperate person acts from desire but not from moral purpose. On the other hand a temperate person acts from moral purpose but not from desire. Desire too is opposed to moral purpose, but desire is not opposed to desire. Desire too, though not moral purpose, is directed toward pleasures and pains. Still less can moral purpose be the same as passion; for no acts seem so little directed by moral purpose as those which spring from angry passion. Nor, again, is moral purpose the same as wishing, although it seems nearly allied to it. For moral purpose does not apply to impossibilities; anyone who said he had a purpose of achieving the impossible would be thought a fool. But there is such a thing as wishing for the impossible, as, for example, for immortality. Again, we may wish for things which could not possibly be won by our own efforts, as for the victory of a certain actor or athlete. But we cannot purpose such things; we only purpose what we think we can bring to pass by our own act. Again, a wish is directed rather to an end but a moral purpose to the means. Thus we wish to be healthy but we purpose or choose the means of keeping our health. Or, again, we wish to be happy and say so; but we cannot appropriately say that we purpose or choose to be happy. For in general our moral purpose seems limited to things that lie within our own power.

Nor, once more, can moral purpose be opinion; for the sphere of opinion is everywhere; we have opinions on things which are eternal or impossible as much as on things within our own power. Opinion too, unlike moral purpose, is distinguished as true or false, not as good or evil. Nobody, perhaps, maintains that moral purpose is identical with opinion generally; but neither is it identical with opinion of any particular kind. For according as we purpose or choose what is good or evil, and not according as we hold particular opinions, are we men of a certain character. Again, we choose to accept or avoid something and so on, but we have opinions as to what a thing is, or for whom or how it is beneficial. We have no opinion not to accept or avoid a thing. Again, moral purpose is praised more for being directed to a proper end than for being correct; opinion is praised for being true. Again, we purpose or choose what we best know to be good; but we form an opinion of things of which we have little knowledge. Again, it is not the people who make the best moral choice who form the best opinions. Some, who form a better opinion than others, are prevented by vice from making the right choice. Opinion may precede moral purpose or follow it, but that is not the point; the question we are considering is simply this, whether moral purpose is identical with opinions of some kind.

What then is the nature and character of moral purpose, since it is none of the things we have men-

tioned? It is clearly voluntary, but there are things which are voluntary and yet not purposed. Is it then the result of previous deliberation, for moral purpose implies reason and thought? The very name seems to indicate something chosen deliberately in preference to other things.

CHAPTER 5

The question is, do we deliberate about everything? Is everything a matter for deliberation, or are there some things that are not subjects for deliberation? Presumably we understand by "a matter for deliberation" not that about which a fool or a madman would deliberate, but about which a sensible person would.

Nobody deliberates about eternal things, that is, the unchangeable, such as the universe or the incommensurability of the diagonal and the side of a square; or about things in motion that always follow the same course, whether of necessity or by nature or for some other cause, as the solstices and the risings of the sun; or about things which are wholly irregular, like droughts and showers; or about chance happenings, such as the finding of a treasure. Nor, again, are all human affairs matters of deliberation; thus no Spartan will deliberate about the best constitution for the Scythians. The reason we do not deliberate about these things is that none of them can be affected by our action. The matters about which we deliberate are practical matters, lying within our power. There is in fact no other class of matters left; for the causes of things are evidently nature, necessity, chance, and besides these only intelligence and human agency in its various forms. Now different classes of people do deliberate about things that depend on their own efforts. The sciences which are exact and complete in themselves do not admit of deliberation, as, for example, writing; for we are in no doubt as to the proper way of writing. But a thing that depends on our own effort and is not invariable is a matter of deliberation, such as problems of medicine or finance. Navigation is more so than gymnastic, for it is less thoroughly systematized, and similarly all other arts. The arts are more matters of deliberation than the sciences, since we are in more doubt about them.

We deliberate over cases which fall under general rules, when it is uncertain what the issue will be, and when we can make no absolute decision. We invite the help of other people in our deliberations over questions of importance, when we distrust our own ability to decide them.

We deliberate not about ends but about means to ends. Thus a doctor does not deliberate whether he shall cure his patients, nor an orator whether he shall persuade his audience, nor a statesman whether he shall produce law and order; nor does anyone else deliberate about his end. They all set up a certain end and then consider how and by what means it can be attained; and if it apparently can be attained by several means, they consider what will be the easiest and best means of attaining it; and if there is but one means of attaining it, how to attain it by this means, and by what means the means can be attained, until they come to the first cause, which in the order of discovery is last. For deliberation, it seems, as we have described it, is a process of investigation and analysis. It is like the analysis of a geometrical figure.[6] Not all investigation, however, is deliberation; mathematical investigation is not; but deliberation is always investigation, and that which comes last in the order of analysis is first in the order of action.

If in a deliberation we come on an impossibility, we abandon our task, as, for instance, if we need money and cannot get it. But if the thing appears possible, we set about doing it. By possibilities I mean things that may be brought about by our own efforts; for what is done by our friends we may call done by ourselves, since the origin of it lies in ourselves. Sometimes the question is what tools are necessary and at other times how to use them. Similarly, in all cases it is sometimes the means of doing a thing and at other times the method or the agency that is the question. . . .

If the object of our moral purpose is that which, being in our power, is after deliberation the object of our desire, it follows that moral purpose is a deliberate desire for something in our power; for first we deliberate on a thing and, after reaching a decision on it, we desire it in accordance with our deliberation. Let us now leave this sketch of the moral purpose. We have shown what are the matters with which it deals and that it is directed to means rather than to ends.

NOTES

1. That is, the person who acts at the command of a tyrant or when he is at sea, under stress of stormy weather.

2. Euripides was the famous Athenian writer of psychological tragedies of the generation before Aristotle. Alcmaeon is said to have murdered his mother, Eriphyle, in revenge for the murder of his father, but as the play of Euripides is lost, it is impossible to say what "the reasons" alleged in it were.

3. That is, of the universal laws of right and moral conduct.

4. The usual story, although it hardly suits the present passage, is that the great dramatist Aeschylus was accused before the Areopagus of having revealed the Eleusinian mysteries and defended himself by declaring that he had never been initiated in them.

5. Merope, wife of Cresphontes, was on the point of murdering her son Aepytus by mistake, as Aristotle relates, *Poetics,* chap. 14.

6. The point of the comparison is that if we wish to learn how to construct a geometrical figure, the best way is often to assume the figure as already constructed and then to work backwards to the conditions necessary for constructing it.

FOR FURTHER REFLECTION

1. Aristotle's discussion of voluntary action has been criticized as being almost entirely negative: an act is voluntary to the extent that it is *not* done under conditions of ignorance or compulsion. John Locke offers a counterexample in which a man may be acting under compulsion and ignorance but nevertheless be free:

   > Suppose a man be carried whilst fast asleep into a room where there is a person he longs to see and speak with, and that he is there locked in, beyond his power to get out. He awakes and is glad to find himself in so desir-

able company. . . . He willingly stays in; that is, he prefers his stay to going away. I ask: is not this stay voluntary? I think nobody will doubt it, and yet being locked fast in, it is evident that he is not at liberty *not* to stay; he has not freedom to be gone (*An Essay Concerning Human Understanding,* vol. 1, ed. A. C. Fraser [Oxford: Oxford University Press, 1894], p. 317).

Has Locke successfully disconfirmed Aristotle's notion of voluntary action? If he has, what are the implications for the notion of moral responsibility?

EPICTETUS

STOIC RESIGNATION TO FATE

One of the great Stoic philosophers of Roman times was Epictetus (c. 55–c.135), a former slave who, upon gaining his freedom, founded an influential Stoic school. His surviving writings include *The Discourses* and *The Handbook.*

According to ancient Greek Stoic philosophy, everything is determined by fate, including events in the natural world outside of us and the thoughts and actions that come from within us. In that sense, our thoughts and actions are very much determined. However, from our perspective as humans, there is one component of control that we seem to have, namely, control over our moral choice, which involves the capacity to desire or not desire something. From our human perspective, then, we feel that we are responsible for what we desire and how we act upon our desires. In the selections presented here from his *Handbook,* Epictetus argues that our chief responsibility is to adjust our attitudes to the inevitable events that occur outside our control and just accept what happens. When we fail to do this, we will become overwhelmed with sorrow when a loved one dies or our lives otherwise fall to pieces. Epictetus' advice is brutal: we should turn away from pleasurable things to avoid depending on them and thereby shield ourselves from disappointment if we lose them. We should even constantly view our family members as though they are mortal, so if one dies, we will not be overcome with sorrow.

1. Some things are in our control and others not. Things in our control are opinion, pursuit, desire, aversion, and, in a word, whatever are our own actions. Things not in our control are body, property, reputation, career, and, in one word, whatever are not our own actions.

   The things in our control are by nature free, unrestrained, unhindered; but those not in our

From Epictetus, *The Handbook* (c. 135 C.E.).

control are weak, slavish, restrained, belonging to others. Remember, then, that if you suppose that things which are slavish by nature are also free, and that what belongs to others is your own, then you will be hindered. You will lament, you will be disturbed, and you will find fault both with gods and men. But if you suppose that only to be your own which *is* your own, and what belongs to others such as it really is, then no one will ever compel you or restrain you. Further, you will find fault with no one or accuse no one. You will do nothing against your will. No one will hurt you, you will have no enemies, and you will not be harmed.

Aiming therefore at such great things, remember that you must not allow yourself to be carried, even with a slight tendency, towards the attainment of lesser things. Instead, you must entirely quit some things and for the present postpone the rest. But if you would both have these great things, along with power and riches, then you will not gain even the latter, because you aim at the former too: but you will absolutely fail of the former, by which alone happiness and freedom are achieved.

Work, therefore to be able to say to every harsh appearance, "You are but an appearance, and not absolutely the thing you appear to be." And then examine it by those rules which you have, and first, and chiefly, by this: whether it concerns the things which are in our own control, or those which are not; and, if it concerns anything not in our control, be prepared to say that it is nothing to you.

2. Remember that following desire promises the attainment of that of which you are desirous; and aversion promises the avoiding that to which you are averse. However, he who fails to obtain the object of his desire is disappointed, and he who incurs the object of his aversion wretched. If, then, you confine your aversion to those objects only which are contrary to the natural use of your faculties, which you have in your own control, you will never incur anything to which you are averse. But if you are averse to sickness, or death, or poverty, you will be wretched. Remove aversion, then, from all things that are not in our control, and transfer it to things contrary to the nature of what is in our control. But, for the present, totally suppress desire: for, if you desire any of the things which are not in your own control, you must necessarily be disappointed; and of those which are, and which it would be laudable to desire, nothing is yet in your possession. Use only the appropriate actions of pursuit and avoidance; and even these lightly, and with gentleness and reservation.

3. With regard to whatever objects give you delight, are useful, or are deeply loved, remember to tell yourself of *what general nature they are*, beginning from the most insignificant things. If, for example, you are fond of a specific cup, remind yourself that it is merely a cup of which you are fond. Then, if it breaks, you will not be disturbed. If you kiss your child or your wife, say that you only kiss things that are mortal, and thus you will not be disturbed if either of them dies.

4. When you are going about any action, remind yourself what nature the action is. If you are going to bathe, picture to yourself the things which usually happen in the bath: some people splash the water, some push, some use abusive language, and others steal. Thus you will more safely go about this action if you say to yourself, "I will now go bathe, and keep my choice in a state conformable to nature." And in the same manner with regard to every other action. For thus, if any hindrance arises in bathing, you will have it ready to say, "It was not only to bathe that I desired, but to keep my choice in a state conformable to nature; and I will not keep it if I am bothered at things that happen.

5. Men are disturbed, not by things, but by the principles and notions which they form concerning things. Death, for instance, is not terrible, else it would have appeared so to Socrates. But the terror consists in our notion of death that it is terrible. When therefore we are hindered, or disturbed, or grieved, let us never attribute it to others, but to ourselves; that is, to

our own principles. An uninstructed person will lay the fault of his own bad condition upon others. Someone just starting instruction will lay the fault on himself. Some who is perfectly instructed will place blame neither on others nor on himself.

6. Don't be prideful with any excellence that is not your own. If a horse should be prideful and say, " I am handsome," it would be supportable. But when you are prideful, and say, " I have a handsome horse," know that you are proud of what is, in fact, only the good of the horse. What, then, is your own? Only your reaction to the appearances of things. Thus, when you behave conformably to nature in reaction to how things appear, you will be proud with reason; for you will take pride in some good of your own.

7. Consider when, on a voyage, your ship is anchored; if you go on shore to get water you may along the way amuse yourself with picking up a shellfish, or a truffle. However, your thoughts and continual attention ought to be bent towards the ship, waiting for the captain to call on board. You must then immediately leave all these things, otherwise you will be thrown into the ship, bound neck and feet like a sheep. So it is with life. If, instead of an onion or a shellfish, you are given a wife or child, that is fine. But if the captain calls, you must run to the ship, leaving them, and regarding none of them. But if you are old, never go far from the ship: lest, when you are called, you should be unable to come in time.

8. Don't demand that things happen as you wish, but wish that they happen as they *do* happen, and you will go on well.

9. Sickness is a hindrance to the body, but not to your ability to choose, unless that is your choice. Lameness is a hindrance to the leg, but not to your ability to choose. Say this to yourself with regard to everything that happens, then you will see such obstacles as hindrances to something else, but not to yourself.

10. With every accident, ask yourself what abilities you have for making a proper use of it. If you see an attractive person, you will find that self-restraint is the ability you have against your desire. If you are in pain, you will find fortitude. If you hear unpleasant language, you will find patience. And thus habituated, the appearances of things will not hurry you away along with them.

11. Never say of anything, "I have lost it"; but, "I have returned it." Is your child dead? It is returned. Is your wife dead? She is returned. Is your estate taken away? Well, and is not that likewise returned? "But he who took it away is a bad man." What difference is it to you who the giver assigns to take it back? While he gives it to you to possess, take care of it; but don't view it as your own, just as travelers view a hotel.

12. If you want to improve, reject such reasonings as these: "If I neglect my affairs, I'll have no income; if I don't correct my servant, he will be bad." For it is better to die with hunger, exempt from grief and fear, than to live in affluence with perturbation; and it is better your servant should be bad, than you unhappy.

Begin therefore from little things. Is a little oil spilt? A little wine stolen? Say to yourself, "This is the price paid for being without passion, for tranquility, and nothing is to be had for nothing." When you call your servant, it is possible that he may not come; or, if he does, he may not do what you want. But he is by no means of such importance that it should be in his power to give you any disturbance.

13. If you want to improve, be content to be thought foolish and stupid with regard to external things. Don't wish to be thought to know anything; and even if you appear to be somebody important to others, distrust yourself. For, it is difficult to both keep your faculty of choice in a state conformable to nature, and at the same time acquire external things. But while you are careful about the one, you must of necessity neglect the other.

14. If you wish your children, and your wife, and your friends to live forever, you are foolish; for you wish to be in control of things which you cannot, you wish for things that belong to others to be your own. So likewise, if you wish your servant to be without fault, you are a fool; for

you wish vice not to be vice," but something else. But, if you wish to have your desires undisappointed, this is in your own control. Exercise, therefore, what is in your control. He is the master of every other person who is able to confer or remove whatever that person wishes either to have or to avoid. Whoever, then, would be free, let him wish nothing, let him decline nothing, which depends on others else he must necessarily be a slave.

15. Remember that you must behave in life as at a dinner party. Is anything brought around to you? Put out your hand and take your share with moderation. Does it pass by you? Don't stop it. Is it not yet come? Don't stretch your desire towards it, but wait till it reaches you. Do this with regard to children, to a wife, to careers, to riches, and you will eventually be a worthy partner of the feasts of the gods. And if you don't even take the things which are set before you, but are able even to reject them, then you will not only be a partner at the feasts of the gods, but also of their empire. For, by doing this, Diogenes, Heraclitus and others like them, deservedly became, and were called, divine.

16. When you see anyone weeping in grief because his son has gone abroad, or is dead, or because he has suffered in his affairs, be careful that the appearance may not misdirect you. Instead, distinguish within your own mind, and be prepared to say, "It's not the accident that distresses this person, because it doesn't distress another person; it is the judgment which he makes about it." As far as words go, however, don't reduce yourself to his level, and certainly do not moan with him. Do not moan inwardly either.

17. Remember that you are an actor in a drama which depends upon the judgment of the author. If he wants it short, then it is short; if long, then it is long. If it is his pleasure, you should act a poor man, a cripple, a governor, or a private person, see that you act it naturally. For it is your job to act well the role that is assigned you; it is another's job to choose your role.

50. Whatever moral rules you have deliberately proposed to yourself, abide by them as they were laws, and as if you would be guilty of impiety by violating any of them. Don't regard what anyone says of you, for this, after all, is no concern of yours. How long, then, will you put off thinking yourself worthy of the highest improvements and follow the distinctions of reason? You have received the philosophical theorems, with which you ought to be familiar, and you have been familiar with them. What other master, then, do you wait for, to throw upon that the delay of reforming yourself? You are no longer a boy, but a grown man. If, therefore, you will be negligent and slothful, and always add procrastination to procrastination, purpose to purpose, and fix day after day in which you will attend to yourself, you will insensibly continue without proficiency, and, living and dying, persevere in being one of the vulgar. This instant, then, think yourself worthy of living as a man grown up, and a proficient. Let whatever appears to be the best be to you an inviolable law. And if any instance of pain or pleasure, or glory or disgrace, is set before you, remember that now is the combat, now the Olympiad comes on, nor can it be put off. By once being defeated and giving way, proficiency is lost, or by the contrary preserved. Thus Socrates became perfect, improving himself by everything, attending to nothing but reason. And though you are not yet a Socrates, you ought nevertheless to live with the desire of becoming a Socrates.

FOR FURTHER REFLECTION

1. Stoics argue that everything is determined by fate, including our thoughts and actions, but from our personal perspective as humans, we believe we have some choice, particularly over our own thoughts and actions. Is this notion of "choice" a mere illusion and, if so, why?

2. Epictetus argues that we have no control over our body, property, reputation, and career. Is this true?

3. Epictetus argues that we have control only over our own attitudes and actions—or, at least, it appears to us that way. Are some attitudes and actions outside our control, and, if so, what are they?

4. In Section 3 of this selection, Epictetus recommends that we continually remind ourselves that out loved ones are mortal, so that if one dies, we will not be disturbed. Is there anything wrong with this advice?

GALEN STRAWSON

THE IMPOSSIBILITY OF MORAL RESPONSIBILITY

Galen Strawson teaches philosophy at Reading University and is the author of several works in metaphysics, including *Freedom and Belief* (1986). In this article Strawson develops in several forms what he calls the "Basic Argument," which holds that in order for us to be ultimately morally responsible for our actions, we must, in some significant sense, be the cause of ourselves (the *causa sui*). But since no one can be the cause of himself or herself, no one is ultimately morally responsible for one's actions. Since desert claims, rewards, and punishments (for example, the kind of punishment and reward attached to hell and heaven) seem to require responsibility for actions, it would follow that no one deserves rewards and punishments. Strawson points out that the argument resists the compatibilist's claim that free will and determinism are compatible, since the compatibilist cannot avoid the crucial premise about self-causation (*causa sui*). Nor does the libertarian defense get around the problem, since all that the incompatibilist libertarian can show is that indeterminism may be true. But indeterminism only gives us randomness, not purposeful action, let alone self-causation. So it seems that the Basic Argument survives criticism. Moral responsibility is impossible, and no one deserves rewards and punishments.

Strawson admits that while this creates severe problems for ethics, it doesn't eliminate it. We need to rethink our moral categories to take into consideration the Basic Argument.

I

There is an argument, which I will call the Basic Argument, which appears to prove that we cannot be truly or ultimately morally responsible for our actions. According to the Basic Argument, it makes no difference whether determinism is true or false. We cannot be truly or ultimately morally responsible for our actions in either case.

The Basic Argument has various expressions in the literature of free will, and its central idea can be quickly conveyed. (1) Nothing can be *causa sui*—nothing can be the cause of itself. (2) In order to be truly morally responsible for one's actions one would have to be causa sui, at least in certain crucial mental respects. (3) Therefore nothing can be truly morally responsible.

In this paper I want to reconsider the Basic Argument, in the hope that anyone who thinks that we can be truly or ultimately morally responsible for our actions will be prepared to say exactly what is wrong with it. I think that the point that it has to make is obvious, and that it has been underrated in recent discussion of free will—perhaps because it admits of no answer. I suspect that it is obvious in such a way that insisting on it too much is likely to make it seem less obvious than it is, given the innate contrasuggestibility of human beings in general and philosophers in particular. But I am not worried about making it seem less obvious than it is so long as it gets adequate attention. As far as its validity is concerned, it can look after itself.

A more cumbersome statement of the Basic Argument goes as follows.

(1) Interested in free action, we are particularly interested in actions that are performed for a reason (as opposed to "reflex" actions or mindlessly habitual actions).

(2) When one acts for a reason, what one does is a function of how one is, mentally speaking. (It is also a function of one's height, one's strength, one's place and time, and so on. But the mental factors are crucial when moral responsibility is in question.)

(3) So if one is to be truly responsible for how one acts, one must be truly responsible for how one is, mentally speaking—at least in certain respects.

(4) But to be truly responsible for how one is, mentally speaking, in certain respects, one must have brought it about that one is the way one is, mentally speaking, in certain respects. And it is not merely that one must have caused oneself to be the way one is, mentally speaking. One must have consciously and explicitly chosen to be the way one is, mentally speaking, in certain respects, and one must have succeeded in bringing it about that one is that way.

(5) But one cannot really be said to choose, in a conscious, reasoned, fashion, to be the way one is mentally speaking, in any respect at all, unless one already exists, mentally speaking, already equipped with some principles of choice, "P1"—preferences, values, pro-attitudes, ideals—in the light of which one chooses how to be.

(6) But then to be truly responsible, on account of having chosen to be the way one is, mentally speaking, in certain respects, one must be truly responsible for one's having the principles of choice P1 in the light of which one chose how to be.

(7) But for this to be so one must have chosen P1, in a reasoned, conscious, intentional fashion.

(8) But for this, i.e. (7), to be so one must already have had some principles of choice P2, in the light of which one chose P1.

(9) And so on. Here we are setting out on a regress that we cannot stop. True self-determination is impossible because it requires the actual completion of an infinite series of choices of principles of choice.

(10) So true moral responsibility is impossible, because it requires true self-determination, as noted in (3).

This may seem contrived, but essentially the same argument can be given in a more natural form. (1) It is undeniable that one is the way one is, initially, as a result of heredity and early experience, and it is undeniable that these are things for which one cannot be held to be in any way responsible (morally or otherwise). (2) One cannot at any later stage of life hope to accede to true moral responsibility for the way one is by trying to change the way one already is as a result of heredity and previous experience. For (3) both the particular way in which one is moved to try to change oneself, and the degree of one's success in one's attempt at change, will be determined by how one

Reprinted From Galen Strawson in *Philosophical Studies,* 75 (1994), by permission.

already is as a result of heredity and previous experience. And (4) any further changes that one can bring about only after one has brought about certain initial changes will in turn be determined, via the initial changes, by heredity and previous experience. (5) This may not be the whole story, for it may be that some changes in the way one is are traceable not to heredity and experience but to the influence of indeterministic or random factors. But it is absurd to suppose that indeterministic or random factors, for which one is ex hypothesi in no way responsible, can in themselves contribute in any way to one's being truly morally responsible for how one is.

The claim, then, is not that people cannot change the way they are. They can, in certain respects (which tend to be exaggerated by North Americans and underestimated, perhaps, by Europeans). The claim is only that people cannot be supposed to change themselves in such a way as to be or become truly or ultimately morally responsible for the way they are, and hence for their actions.

II

I have encountered two main reactions to the Basic Argument. On the one hand it convinces almost all the students with whom I have discussed the topic of free will and moral responsibility.[1] On the other hand it often tends to be dismissed, in contemporary discussion of free will and moral responsibility, as wrong, or irrelevant, or fatuous, or too rapid, or an expression of metaphysical megalomania.

I think that the Basic Argument is certainly valid in showing that we cannot be morally responsible in the way that many suppose. And I think that it is the natural light, not fear, that has convinced the students I have taught that this is so. That is why it seems worthwhile to restate the argument in a slightly different—simpler and looser—version, and to ask again what is wrong with it.

Some may say that there is nothing wrong with it, but that it is not very interesting, and not very central to the free will debate. I doubt whether any non-philosopher or beginner in philosophy would agree with this view. If one wants to think about free will

and moral responsibility, consideration of some version of the Basic Argument is an overwhelmingly natural place to start. It certainly has to be considered at some point in a full discussion of free will and moral responsibility, even if the point it has to make is obvious. Belief in the kind of absolute moral responsibility that it shows to be impossible has for a long time been central to the Western religious, moral, and cultural tradition, even if it is now slightly on the wane (a disputable view). It is a matter of historical fact that concern about moral responsibility has been the main motor—indeed the *ratio essendi*—of discussion of the issue of free will. The only way in which one might hope to show (1) that the Basic Argument was not central to the free will debate would be to show (2) that the issue of moral responsibility was not central to the free will debate. There are, obviously, ways of taking the word "free" in which (2) can be maintained. But (2) is clearly false none the less.

In saying that the notion of moral responsibility criticized by the Basic Argument is central to the Western tradition, I am not suggesting that it is some artificial and local Judaeo-Christian-Kantian construct that is found nowhere else in the history of the peoples of the world, although even if it were that would hardly diminish its interest and importance for us. It is natural to suppose that Aristotle also subscribed to it,[2] and it is significant that anthropologists have suggested that most human societies can be classified either as "guilt cultures" or as "shame cultures." It is true that neither of these two fundamental moral emotions necessarily presupposes a conception of oneself as truly morally responsible for what one has done. But the fact that both are widespread does at least suggest that a conception of moral responsibility similar to our own is a natural part of the human moral-conceptual repertoire.

In fact the notion of moral responsibility connects more tightly with the notion of guilt than with the notion of shame. In many cultures shame can attach to one because of what some member of one's family—or government—has done, and not because of anything one has done oneself; and in such cases the feeling of shame need not (although it may) involve some obscure, irrational feeling that one is somehow responsible for the behaviour of one's family or government. The case of guilt is less clear. There is no doubt that people can feel guilty (or can believe that they feel guilty) about things for which they are not responsible, let alone morally responsible. But it is much less obvious that they can do this without any sense or belief that they are in fact responsible.

III

Such complications are typical of moral psychology, and they show that it is important to try to be precise about what sort of responsibility is under discussion. What sort of "true" moral responsibility is being said to be both impossible and widely believed in?

An old story is very helpful in clarifying this question. This is the story of heaven and hell. As I understand it, true moral responsibility is responsibility of such a kind that, if we have it, then it *makes sense,* at least, to suppose that it could be just to punish some of us with (eternal) torment in hell and reward others with (eternal) bliss in heaven. The stress on the words "makes sense" is important, for one certainly does not have to believe in any version of the story of heaven and hell in order to understand the notion of true moral responsibility that it is being used to illustrate. Nor does one have to believe in any version of the story of heaven and hell in order to believe in the existence of true moral responsibility. On the contrary: many atheists have believed in the existence of true moral responsibility. The story of heaven and hell is useful simply because it illustrates, in a peculiarly vivid way, the *kind* of absolute or ultimate accountability or responsibility that many have supposed themselves to have. It very clearly expresses its scope and force.

But one does not have to refer to religious faith in order to describe the sorts of everyday situations that are perhaps primarily influential in giving rise to our belief in true responsibility. Suppose you set off for a shop on the evening of a national holiday, intending to buy a cake with your last ten pound note. On the steps of the shop someone is shaking an Oxfam tin. You stop, and it seems completely clear to you that it is entirely up to you what you do next. That is, it seems to you that you are truly, radically free to

choose, in such a way that you will be ultimately morally responsible for whatever you do choose. Even if you believe that determinism is true, and that you will in five minutes time be able to look back and say that what you did was determined, this does not seem to undermine your sense of the absoluteness and inescapability of your freedom, and of your moral responsibility for your choice. The same seems to be true even if you accept the validity of the Basic Argument stated in section I, which concludes that one cannot be in any way ultimately responsible for the way one is and decides. In both cases, it remains true that as one stands there, one's freedom and true moral responsibility seem obvious and absolute to one.

Large and small, morally significant or morally neutral, such situations of choice occur regularly in human life. I think they lie at the heart of the experience of freedom and moral responsibility. They are the fundamental source of our inability to give up belief in true or ultimate moral responsibility. There are further questions to be asked about why human beings experience these situations of choice as they do. It is an interesting question whether any cognitively sophisticated, rational, self-conscious agent must experience situations of choice in this way. But they are the experiential rock on which the belief in true moral responsibility is founded.

IV

I will restate the Basic Argument. First, though, I will give some examples of people who have accepted that some sort of true or ultimate responsibility for the way one is is a necessary condition of true or ultimate moral responsibility for the way one acts, and who, certain that they are truly morally responsible for the way they act, have believed the condition to be fulfilled.

E. H. Carr held that "normal adult human beings are morally responsible for their own personality." Jean-Paul Sartre talked of "the choice that each man makes of his personality," and held that "man is responsible for what he is." In a later interview he judged that his earlier assertions about freedom were incautious; but he still held that "in the end one is always responsible for what is made of one" in some absolute sense. Kant described the position very clearly when he claimed that "man *himself* must make or have made himself into whatever, in a moral sense, whether good or evil, he is to become. Either condition must be an effect of his free choice; for otherwise he could not be held responsible for it and could therefore be *morally* neither good nor evil." Since he was committed to belief in radical moral responsibility, Kant held that such self-creation does indeed take place, and wrote accordingly of "man's character, which he himself creates" and of "knowledge of oneself as a person who . . . is his own originator." John Patten, the current British Minister for Education, a Catholic apparently preoccupied by the idea of sin, has claimed that "it is . . . self-evident that as we grow up each individual chooses whether to be good or bad." It seems clear enough that he sees such choice as sufficient to give us true moral responsibility of the heaven-and-hell variety.[3]

The rest of us are not usually so reflective, but it seems that we do tend, in some vague and unexamined fashion, to think of ourselves as responsible for—answerable for—how we are. The point is quite a delicate one, for we do not ordinarily suppose that we have gone through some sort of active process of self-determination at some particular past time. Nevertheless it seems accurate to say that we do unreflectively experience ourselves, in many respects, rather as we might experience ourselves if we did believe that we had engaged in some such activity of self-determination.

Sometimes a part of one's character—a desire or tendency—may strike one as foreign or alien. But it can do this only against a background of character traits that are not experienced as foreign, but are rather "identified" with (it is a necessary truth that it is only relative to such a background that a character trait can stand out as alien). Some feel tormented by impulses that they experience as alien, but in many a sense of general identification with their character predominates, and this identification seems to carry within itself an implicit sense that one is, generally, somehow in control of and answerable for how one is (even, perhaps, for aspects of one's character that one does not like). Here, then, I suggest that we find, semi-dormant in common thought, an implicit recognition of the idea

that true moral responsibility for what one does somehow involves responsibility for how one is. Ordinary thought is ready to move this way under pressure.

There is, however, another powerful tendency in ordinary thought to think that one can be truly morally responsible even if one's character is ultimately wholly non-self-determined—simply because one is fully self-consciously aware of oneself as an agent facing choices. I will return to this point later on.

V

Let me now restate the Basic argument in very loose—as it were conversational—terms. New forms of words allow for new forms of objection, but they may be helpful none the less.

(1) You do what you do, in any situation in which you find yourself, because of the way you are.

So

(2) To be truly morally responsible for what you do you must be truly responsible for the way you are—at least in certain crucial mental respects.

Or:

(1) What you intentionally do, given the circumstances in which you (believe you) find yourself, flows necessarily from how you are.

Hence

(2) You have to get to have some responsibility for how you are in order to get to have some responsibility for what you intentionally do, given the circumstances in which you (believe you) find yourself.

Comment. Once again the qualification about "certain mental respects" is one I will take for granted. Obviously one is not responsible for one's sex, one's basic body pattern, one's height, and so on. But if one were not responsible for anything about oneself, how one could be responsible for what one did, given the truth of (1)? This is the fundamental question, and it seems clear that if one is going to be responsible for any aspect of oneself, it had better be some aspect of one's mental nature.

I take it that (1) is incontrovertible, and that it is (2) that must be resisted. For if (1) and (2) are conceded the case seems lost, because the full argument runs as follows:

(1) You do what you do because of the way you are.

So

(2) To be truly morally responsible for what you do you must be truly responsible for the way you are—at least in certain crucial mental respects.

But

(3) You cannot be truly responsible for the way you are, so you cannot be truly responsible for what you do.

Why can't you be truly responsible for the way you are? Because

(4) To be truly responsible for the way you are, you must have intentionally brought it about that you are the way you are, and this is impossible.

Why is it impossible? Well, suppose it is not. Suppose that

(5) You have somehow intentionally brought it about that you are the way you now are, and that you have brought this about in such a way that you can now be said to be truly responsible for being the way you are now.

For this to be true

(6) You must already have had a certain nature N in the light of which you intentionally brought it about that you are as you now are.

But then

(7) For it to be true you and you alone are truly responsible for how you now are, you must be truly responsible for having had the nature N in the light of which you intentionally brought it about that you are the way you now are.

So

(8) You must have intentionally brought it about that you had that nature N, in which case you must have existed already with a prior nature in the light of which you intentionally brought it

about that you had the nature N in the light of which you intentionally brought it about that you are the way you now are . . .

Here one is setting off on the regress. Nothing can be *causa sui* in the required way. Even if such causal "aseity" is allowed to belong unintelligibly to God, it cannot plausibly be supposed to be possessed by ordinary finite human beings. "The *causa sui* is the best self-contradiction that has been conceived so far," as Nietzsche remarked in 1886:

> it is a sort of rape and perversion of logic. But the extravagant ride of man has managed to entangle itself profoundly and frightfully with just this non-sense. The desire for "freedom of the will" in the superlative metaphysical sense, which still holds sway, unfortunately, in the minds of the half-edu-cated; the desire to bear the entire and ultimate responsibility for one's actions oneself, and to absolve God, the world, ancestors, chance, and soci-ety involves nothing less than to be precisely this *causa sui* and, with more than Baron Münchhausen's audacity, to pull oneself up into existence by the hair, out of the swamps of nothingness . . .
>
> (*Beyond Good and Evil*, *§21*).

The rephrased argument is essentially exactly the same as before, although the first two steps are now more simply stated. It may seem pointless to repeat it, but the questions remain. Can the Basic Argument simply be dismissed? Is it really of no importance in the discussion of free will and moral responsibility? (No and No) Shouldn't any serious defense of free will and moral responsibility thoroughly acknowledge the respect in which the Basic Argument is valid before going on to try to give its own positive account of the nature of free will and moral responsibility? Doesn't the argument go to the heart of things if the heart of the free will debate is a concern about whether we can be truly morally responsible in the absolute way that we ordinarily suppose? (Yes and Yes)

We are what we are, and we cannot be thought to have made ourselves *in such a way* that we can be held to be free in our actions *in such a way* that we can be held to be morally responsible for our actions *in such a way* that any punishment or reward for our actions is ultimately just or fair. Punishments and rewards may seem deeply appropriate or intrinsically "fitting" to us in spite of this argument, and many of the various institutions of punishment and reward in human society appear to be practically indispensable in both their legal and non-legal forms. But if one takes the notion of justice that is central to our intellectual and cultural tradition seriously, then the evident consequence of the Basic Argument is that there is a fundamental sense in which no punishment or reward is ever ultimately just. It is exactly as just to punish or reward people for their actions as it is to punish or reward them for the (natural) colour of their hair or the (natural) shape of their faces. The point seems obvious, and yet it contradicts a fundamental part of our natural self-conception, and there are elements in human thought that move very deeply against it. When it comes to questions of responsibility, we tend to feel that we are somehow responsible for the way we are. Even more importantly, perhaps, we tend to feel that our explicit self-conscious awareness of ourselves as agents who are able to deliberate about what to do, in situations of choice, suffices to constitute us as morally responsible free agents in the strongest sense, whatever the conclusion of the Basic Argument.

VI

I have suggested that it is step (2) of the restated Basic Argument that must be rejected, and of course it can be rejected, because the phrases 'truly responsible' and 'truly morally responsible' can be defined in many ways. I will briefly consider three sorts of response to the Basic Argument, and I will concentrate on their more simple expressions, in the belief that truth in philosophy, especially in areas of philosophy like the present one, is almost never very complicated.

(I) The first is *compatibilist*. Compatibilists believe that one can be a free and morally responsible agent even if determinism is true. Roughly, they claim, with many variations of detail, that one may correctly be said to be truly responsible for what one does, when one acts, just so long as one is not caused to act by any of a certain set of constraints (kleptomaniac impulses, obsessional neuroses, desires that are experienced as alien, post-hypnotic commands, threats,

instances of *force majeure,* and so on). Clearly, this sort of compatibilist responsibility does not require that one should be truly responsible for how one is in any way at all, and so step (2) of the Basic Argument comes out as false. One can have compatibilist responsibility even if the way one is is totally determined by factors entirely outside one's control.

It is for this reason, however, that compatibilist responsibility famously fails to amount to any sort of true *moral* responsibility, given the natural, strong understanding of the notion of true moral responsibility (characterized above by reference to the story of heaven and hell). One does what one does entirely because of the way one is, and one is in no way ultimately responsible for the way one is. So how can one be justly punished for anything one does? Compatibilists have given increasingly refined accounts of the circumstances in which punishment may be said to be appropriate or intrinsically fitting. But they can do nothing against this basic objection.

Many compatibilists have never supposed otherwise. They are happy to admit the point. They observe that the notions of true moral responsibility and justice that are employed in the objection cannot possibly have application to anything real, and suggest that the objection is therefore not worth considering. In response, proponents of the Basic Argument agree that the notions of true moral responsibility and justice in question cannot have application to anything real; but they make no apologies for considering them. They consider them because they are central to ordinary thought about moral responsibility and justice. So far as most people are concerned, they are the subject, if the subject is moral responsibility and justice.

(II) The second response is *libertarian*. Incompatibilists believe that freedom and moral responsibility are incompatible with determinism, and some of them are libertarians, who believe that we are free and morally responsible agents, and that determinism is therefore false. In an ingenious statement of the incompatibilist-libertarian case, Robert Kane argues that agents in an undetermined world can have free will, for they can "have the power to make choices for which they have ultimate responsibility." [4] That is, they can "have the power to make choices which can only and finally be explained in terms of their own wills (i.e. character, motives, and efforts of will)." Roughly, Kane sees this power as grounded in the possible occurrence, in agents, of efforts of will that have two main features: first, they are partly indeterministic in their nature, and hence indeterminate in their outcome; second, they occur in cases in which agents are trying to make a difficult choice between the options that their characters dispose them to consider. (The paradigm cases will be cases in which they face a conflict between moral duty and non-moral desire.)

But the old objection to libertarianism recurs. How can this indeterminism help with *moral* responsibility? Granted that the truth of determinism rules out true moral responsibility, how can the falsity of determinism help? How can the occurrence of partly random or indeterministic events contribute in any way to one's being truly morally responsible either for one's actions or for one's character? If my efforts of will shape my character in an admirable way, and in so doing are partly indeterministic in nature, while also being shaped (as Kane grants) by my already existing character, why am I not merely lucky?

The general objection applies equally whether determinism is true or false, and can be restated as follows. We are born with a great many genetically determined predispositions for which we are not responsible. We are subject to many early influences for which we are not responsible. These decisively shape our characters, our motives, the general bent and strength of our capacity to make efforts of will. We may later engage in conscious and intentional shaping procedures—call them S-procedures—designed to affect and change our characters, motivational structure, and wills. Suppose we do. The question is then why we engage in the particular S-procedures that we do engage in, and why we engage in them in the particular way that we do. The general answer is that we engage in the particular S-procedures that we do engage in, given the circumstances in which we find ourselves, because of certain features of the way we already are. (Indeterministic factors may also play a part in what happens, but these will not help to make us responsible for what we do.) And these features of the way we already are—call them character features, or C-features—are either wholly the products of genetic or environmental influences, deterministic or

random, for which we are not responsible, or are at least partly the result of earlier S-procedures, which are in turn either wholly the product of C-features for which we are not responsible, or are at least partly the product of still earlier S-procedures, which are in turn either the products of C-features for which we are not responsible, or the product of such C-features together with still earlier S-procedures—and so on. In the end, we reach the first S-procedure, and this will have been engaged in, and engaged in the particular way in which it was engaged in, as a result of genetic or environmental factors, deterministic or random, for which we were not responsible.

Moving away from the possible role of indeterministic factors in character or personality formation, we can consider their possible role in particular instances of deliberation and decision. Here too it seems clear that indeterministic factors cannot, in influencing what happens, contribute to true moral responsibility in any way. In the end, whatever we do, we do it either as a result of random influences for which we are not responsible, or as a result of non-random influences for which we are not responsible, or as a result of influences for which we are proximally responsible but not ultimately responsible. The point seems obvious. Nothing can be ultimately *causa sui* in any respect at all. Even if God can be, we can't be.

Kane says little about moral responsibility in his paper, but his position seems to be that true moral responsibility is possible if indeterminism is true. It is possible because in cases of "moral, prudential and practical struggle we . . . are truly 'making ourselves' in such a way that we are ultimately responsible for the outcome." This "making of ourselves" means that "we can be ultimately responsible for our present motives and character by virtue of past choices which helped to form them and for which we were ultimately responsible" (op. cit., p. 252). It is for this reason that we can be ultimately responsible and morally responsible not only in cases of struggle in which we are "making ourselves," but also for choices and actions which do not involve struggle, flowing unopposed from our character and motives.

In claiming that we can be ultimately responsible for our present motives and character, Kane appears to *accept* step (2) of the Basic Argument. He appears to accept that we have to "make ourselves," and so be ultimately responsible for ourselves, in order to be morally responsible for what we do. The problem with this suggestion is the old one. In Kane's view, a person's "ultimate responsibility" for the outcome of an effort of will depends essentially on the partly indeterministic nature of the outcome. This is because it is only the element of indeterminism that prevents prior character and motives from fully explaining the outcome of the effort of will (op. cit., p. 236). But how can this indeterminism help with moral responsibility? How can the fact that my effort of will is indeterministic in such a way that its outcome is indeterminate make me truly responsible for it, or even help to make me truly responsible for it? How can it help in any way at all with moral responsibility? How can it make punishment—or reward—ultimately just?

There is a further, familiar problem with the view that moral responsibility depends on indeterminism. If one accepts the view, one will have to grant that it is impossible to know whether any human being is ever morally responsible. For moral responsibility now depends on the falsity of determinism, and determinism is unfalsifiable. There is no more reason to think that determinism is false than that it is true, in spite of the impression sometimes given by scientists and popularizers of science.

(III) The third option begins by accepting that one cannot be held to be ultimately responsible for one's character or personality or motivational structure. It accepts that this is so whether determinism is true or false. It then directly challenges step (2) of the Basic Argument. It appeals to a certain picture of the self in order to argue that one can be truly free and morally responsible in spite of the fact that one cannot be held to be ultimately responsible for one's character or personality or motivational structure. This picture has some support in the "phenomenology" of human choice—we sometimes experience our choices and decisions as if the picture were an accurate one. But it is easy to show that it cannot be accurate in such a way that we can be said to be truly or ultimately morally responsible for our choices or actions.

It can be set out as follows. One is free and truly morally responsible because one's self is, in a crucial

sense, independent of one's character or personality or motivational structure—one's CPM, for short. Suppose one is in a situation which one experiences as a difficult choice between A, doing one's duty, and B, following one's non-moral desires. Given one's CPM, one responds in a certain way. One's desires and beliefs develop and interact and constitute reasons for both A and B. One's CPM makes one tend towards A or B. So far the problem is the same as ever: whatever one does, one will do what one does because of the way one's CPM is, and since one neither is nor can be ultimately responsible for the way one's CPM is, one cannot be ultimately responsible for what one does.

Enter one's self, S. S is imagined to be in some way independent of one's CPM. S (i.e., one) considers the deliverances of one's CPM and decides in the light of them, but it—S—incorporates a power of decision that is independent of one's CPM in such a way that one can after all count as truly and ultimately morally responsible in one's decisions and actions, even though one is not ultimately responsible for one's CPM. Step (2) of the Basic Argument is false because of the existence of S.

The trouble with the picture is obvious. S (i.e., one) decides on the basis of the deliverances of one's CPM. But whatever S decides, it decides as it does because of the way it is (or else partly or wholly because of the occurrence in the decision process of indeterministic factors for which it—i.e., one—cannot be responsible, and which cannot plausibly be thought to contribute to one's true moral responsibility). And this returns us to where we started. To be a source of true or ultimate responsibility, S must be responsible for being the way it is. But this is impossible, for the reasons given in the Basic Argument.

The story of S and CPM adds another layer to the description of the human decision process, but it cannot change the fact that human beings cannot be ultimately self-determining in such a way as to be ultimately morally responsible for how they are, and thus for how they decide and act. The story is crudely presented, but it should suffice to make clear that no move of this sort can solve the problem.

"Character is destiny," as Novalis is often reported as saying. The remark is inaccurate, because external circumstances are part of destiny, but the point is well taken when it comes to the question of moral responsibility. Nothing can be *causa sui,* and in order to be truly morally responsible for one's actions one would have to be *causa sui,* at least in certain crucial mental respects. One cannot institute oneself in such a way that one can take over true or assume moral responsibility for how one is in such a way that one can indeed be truly morally responsible for what one does. This fact is not changed by the fact that we may be unable not to think of ourselves as truly morally responsible in ordinary circumstances. Nor is it changed by the fact that it may be a very good thing that we have this inability—so that we might wish to take steps to preserve it, if it looked to be in danger of fading. As already remarked, many human beings are unable to resist the idea that it is their capacity for fully explicit self-conscious deliberation, in a situation of choice, that suffices to constitute them as truly morally responsible agents in the strongest possible sense. The Basic Argument shows that this is a mistake. However self-consciously aware we are, as we deliberate and reason, every act and operation of our mind happens as it does as a result of features for which we are ultimately in no way responsible. But the conviction that self-conscious awareness of one's situation can be a sufficient foundation of strong free will is very powerful. It runs deeper than rational argument, and it survives untouched, in the everyday conduct of life, even after the validity of the Basic Argument has been admitted.

VII

There is nothing new in the somewhat incantatory argument of this paper. It restates certain points that may be in need of restatement. "Everything has been said before," said André Gide, echoing La Bruyère, "but since nobody listens we have to keep going back and beginning all over again." This is an exaggeration, but it may not be a gross exaggeration, so far as general observations about the human condition are concerned.

The present claim, in any case, is simply this: time would be saved, and a great deal of readily available clarity would be introduced into the discussion of the nature of moral responsibility, if the simple point that is established by the Basic Argument were more generally acknowledged and clearly stated. Nietzsche thought that thoroughgoing acknowledgment of the point was long overdue, and his belief that there might be moral advantages in such an acknowledgement may deserve further consideration.

NOTES

1. Two have rejected it in fifteen years. Both had religious commitments, and argued, on general and radical sceptical grounds, that we can know almost nothing, and cannot therefore know that true moral responsibility is not possible in some way that we do not understand.
2. Cf. *Nicomachean Ethics* III. 5.
3. Carr in *What Is History?,* p. 89; Sartre in *Being and Nothingness, Existentialism and Humanism,* p. 29, and in the *New Left Review* 1969 (quoted in Wiggins, 1975); Kant in *Religion within the Limits of Reason Alone,* p. 40, *The Critique of Practical Reason,* p. 101 (Ak. V. 98), and in *Opus Postumum,* p. 213; Patten in *The Spectator,* January 1992.

    These quotations raise many questions which I will not consider. It is often hard, for example, to be sure what Sartre is saying. But the occurrence of the quoted phrases is significant on any plausible interpretation of his views. As for Kant, it may be thought to be odd that he says what he does, in so far as he grounds the possibility of our freedom in our possession of an unknowable, non-temporal noumenal nature. It is, however, plausible to suppose that he thinks that radical or ultimate self-determination must take place even in the noumenal realm, in some unintelligibly non-temporal manner, if there is to be true moral responsibility.
4. Robert Kane, *The Significance of Free Will* (New York: Oxford University Press, 1996).

FOR FURTHER REFLECTION

1. Put the Basic Argument in your own words. Examine the major premises. Do you agree that it is valid and sound (i.e., that moral responsibility is impossible)?

2. What does *causa sui* mean? Why is it crucial to the Basic Argument?

3. Examine Strawson's responses to libertarians and compatibilists. Do libertarians and compatibilists have an adequate response to the Basic Argument? Explain your answer.

4. How would we have to revise our morality if the Basic Argument is sound? Could morality survive if people were not held responsible for their actions? How would we have to revise the law?

MICHAEL LEVIN

A COMPATIBILIST DEFENSE OF MORAL RESPONSIBILITY

Michael Levin teaches philosophy at City College of New York and the Graduate Center of the City University of New York. He has published extensively on topics in epistemology, philosophy of language, and the significance of human genetic differences. In this article he defends compatibilism, the view that free will and robust ascriptions of moral responsibility are consistent with the causal determination of human behavior by forces ultimately beyond human control. The key argument is that "freedom" just means "doing what you want," so that where our wants ultimately originate is irrelevant to whether we are free. Likewise, people are "responsible" for doing what they want because wants can be controlled by reward and punishment. Levin emphasizes that these translations are faithful to our commonsense view of ourselves as active, creative agents, and seeks to meet a variety of objections and counterexamples.

I. INTRODUCTION

Compatibilism (a.k.a. "soft determinism") is the view that free will and responsibility are consistent with causal determinism. Emphatically, compatibilists seek to preserve freedom in its full robust sense, which includes moral responsibility and the power to do other than we do (and are causally determined to do). These ideas belong to our ordinary conception of ourselves, leaving any account of freedom that rejects them of little interest.

There are arguments purporting to show that determinism rules out freedom, and other arguments purporting to show that indeterminism rules out freedom. Some philosophers, accepting arguments of both sorts, conclude that freedom is impossible.[1] Compatibilists usually agree that free will does require behavior at least to be determined, since you cannot freely do what is beyond your control, and what happens causelessly, randomly, is beyond anyone's control. But they deny that what is necessitated must also be beyond anyone's control, at least as "control" and cognate notions are normally understood. Indeed, compatibilism rests, essentially, on three explicative definitions:

The Freedom clause: "Freedom" means "doing what you want to."

The Responsibility clause: "Agent A is responsible for action X" means "X happened because A wanted X to happen."

The Power clause: "A could have done otherwise" means "A would have done otherwise, had he wanted to."

These definitions need polishing,[2] but they are a start.

The Freedom clause certainly seems to capture the everyday meaning of "free." A country is free to the extent its government lets its citizens do and say what they want. On a free afternoon you can, within understood limits, do as you please. Admission is free when you can pay what you please, including nothing. Competitors in freestyle swimming events may use any stroke they prefer. As a first approximation, then, "freedom" is another word for doing what you want, will, wish, choose, intend, or prefer. These pro-attitudes differ subtly, of course; one may want one thing but choose another he wants more, or choose something he doesn't want because the alternatives are worse. (Recall the captain who jettisons cargo to save his ship.) But it is clear on even this crude picture why there is no great puzzle whether we are free. We all act freely whenever we eat, work, marry or drive as fast as we want to. Note that this analysis also agrees with common sense that freedom comes in degrees; the more an individual can do what he wants, the freer he is. But everyone is free to some extent: it is the rare man bound in a dungeon, and even he can squirm.

As promised, the Freedom clause reconciles freedom with universal causal determinism. Under it, the causes of individual thoughts and actions may trace back to the Big Bang and certainly precede the birth of anyone now alive, yet still everyone acts freely every day. And this point of logic needs no explicit discussion of determinism generally, or genes, upbringing, environment, laws of nature, quantum mechanics, chaos dynamics or divine foreknowledge. How so, when for many people the main problem is that science threatens to reveal the hidden causes of

human behavior which we fondly tell ourselves do not exist? Easily: if freedom is doing what you want, these causes are irrelevancies: an agent's wants can be effects of factors beyond his control, indeed preceding his birth, *and* the action they lead to be free, so long as the action is an effect of the wants. The sources of his wants don't matter; freedom is consistent with any account of those sources, including fully deterministic ones. Thus, my daily jog may well be a product of my genes, upbringing and current environmental stimuli, none of which I had a say in, yet I jog of my own free will since I jog because I want to (whatever caused that want). Genes, upbringing and environment produced a desire to exercise, and that desire—not kidnappers, not a gust of wind—causes me to move along the running track. (My desire does not "make" me run, as if *it* wants me to run and *I* want me to stay home.) I acted freely when I jogged yesterday, says compatibilism, insofar as I did what I wanted, and there, pending refinements, the analysis ends. Perhaps I inherited a gene that coded for proteins that created nerve cells that disposed me to like the outdoors; nonetheless I go where I go of my own free will. Freedom abides even if all behavior falls under natural laws.

Note: compatibilism does not say that the past creates a range of desires one of which the agent freely chooses to act on, which would assume the very idea of freedom to be explained, and add a mysterious executive self lording it over supplicant appetites. No; the past causes desires, desires cause action, and (details aside) there isn't any more.

I stress again how thoroughly soft determinism captures the way we think when not struggling with the Free Will Riddle. Most advocates of the other standard positions—hard determinists, libertarian indeterminists, impossibilists—agree that for all practical purposes including assessment of moral and legal liability, "it happened because he wanted it to" suffices for "he did it freely." Virtually all discussants agree that other things equal people should be allowed to do what they wish, whether or not this leaves them free in some more arcane sense. "Hard" determinists in particular have lacked the chutzpah to propose repeal of constitutional protections of speech on grounds that no-one is free anyway—although B. F.

Skinner, in *Walden Two*, may be an exception, and Ted Honderich thinks sensible determinists will vote Labour.[3]

Incompatibilists typically reply that compatibilist freedom, though good enough for everyday life, is not "true" or "ultimate" freedom (Strawson's favored phrases). This answer is deeply suspect, given that "true" and "ultimate" are intensifiers without cognitive content. Nothing can be a tree, for instance, without being truly or really or ultimately a tree. We might on occasion call a mighty oak a "true tree," opposing it to a bonsai, because oaks are paradigms, the sort of tree best suited to teach children what "tree" means. Still, peripheral, pedagogically useless instances of a kind remain of that kind—bonsais are trees—and anyway people doing what they want are the paradigms by which children learn "free." In fairness Strawson does attempt to characterize "ultimate responsibility," as what an agent would bear were he to choose not only his actions but also his choice of actions, his choice of that choice . . . , and so back forever—in other words, were he responsible (as defined by the Responsibility clause) for his actions, and for the causes of whatever he is responsible for. To avoid the tendentious "ultimate," let us call this responsibility.* Now, the compatibilist, like Strawson, denies that anyone is ever responsible* for anything, since responsibility* calls for a self-creating self, something that would have to exist, absurdly enough, before it exists. The interesting question is whether in being irremediably irresponsible* we thereby disappoint our deepest hopes for ourselves. In effect, this whole paper is meant to show that the answer is no.[4]

Keeping concrete cases in mind is helpful. Driving from New York to Albany you suddenly announce that you may not be free to exit at Yonkers. "Why," your passenger asks: "Is the steering out? Have they blocked the off-ramps? Were you threatened? Did you recall a deathbed promise never to go there?" "No," you say; "The car is fine, the road is clear"—but your intention to bypass Yonkers may be the result of environmental factors stimulating your brain, a brain shaped by genes and upbringing determined in turn by your parents' genes and upbringing . . . *That* is why you may not be free. Far from disputing this rigmarole, a passenger uncorrupted by philosophy will impatiently deny its relevance. He will say that what matters is not why you want to bypass Yonkers, but whether the car goes where you want it to. You are free to turn because the motion of the car depends on you. You are in the driver's seat. The hardest determinist will agree with the giddiest indeterminist that if you run a red light the ensuing accident is your fault, and side with the court in dismissing a plea that your DNA and upbringing, having created a desire to save time, forced you to break the law.

It abuses language to say you are "not free" when the car goes where you aim it. Use fixes meaning, and "free" is used of actions flowing from preference. Such actions are therefore free by definition—the Freedom clause—whatever the origins of the preferences themselves.[5]

II. MARS ATTACKS!

Peter van Inwagen[6] has voiced a widespread objection to this defense of soft determinism, one arising from the broad point that agreement in usage does not guarantee correctness. We speak of sunrise, and readily teach children to tell sunrise from sunset, although the sun only seems to move because of the Earth's rotation. Yet this appearance has fooled enough people to lock "sunrise" into language. Or consider that children learn "cat" by associating it with certain household objects. It does not follow that there must be cats no matter what science discovers, for if these paradigms turned out to be robot Martian observation platforms, camouflaged in synthetic "fur" and outfitted with fake internal organs, our so-called cats would have proven not to be cats at all.

Specifically, van Inwagen asks us to imagine that all beliefs, desires and choices are produced by chips secretly placed by Martians in our brains at birth. Our behavior would still be caused by those choices, hence on the compatibilist analysis free—an absurdity, since our choices would then be the work of Martians. "Free," it appears, is no mere name for desire-driven behavior; its correct application also assumes no alien implants. This in itself is no great difficulty, since the implant story is fiction, but van Inwagen will want to know what distinguishes control by implant from control by genes and environment. Either way behavior is the product of factors the individual does not control, factors not up to him. Either way he is unfree. Imaginary implants simply vivify the conflict of free will with sheer *determination*. They invite us to conclude that correctly describing behavior as "free" or "up to us" assumes not merely no implants, but no determinative causes period. The quotidian distinction between "free" and "unfree" does not demonstrate free will. If behavior normally described as "free" is also caused, it is misdescribed.

Compatibilists reply[7] by noting the patent differences between standard causes and implants to which intuition responds. The most obvious is that implants put an individual's behavior under the sway of another *agent*; the individual decides what someone else *decides* he will decide. Usually, an individual is the sole decider among the proximate causes of his action. Assuming I chose to jog because a genetic proneness to exercise issued in an action via nerve cells, still genes and nerve cells are not agents who literally want or choose anything.

Covert implants destroy freedom by their idiosyncratic connection to meddlesome outsiders, not just by being causes. That is why the average person is not troubled by the idea that his decision to eat lunch is caused by physiologically triggered hunger pangs, yet is troubled indeed by the idea of his appetite being controlled by a mad scientist. It is also why we do not fear the coming day when people will be able to control themselves with implants. Aware of his temper, Homer (we may imagine) has surgeons place a serotonin releaser in his brain, set to be triggered by surges of emotion, to calm him when provoked. I expect we do—or in time will—regard him to be as free as a man who calms himself by counting to ten, since in both cases the decision to change the agent's decision-making process is the agent's own. Technologically assisted choice is halfway here with biofeedback, which has never been felt to threaten freedom. Ordinary "free" self-regulation thus differs from regulation by Martian.[8]

The defectiveness of choices chosen by others is one of the instructions for using freedom-words. Children learn quickly to distinguish Bart's doing something because he wanted to from his doing it because Nelson made him, a line I expect they would draw for themselves were it not pointed out. Children readily learn or surmise that Bart was made to shout in class and is not to blame when he shouts because Nelson twisted his arm or credibly threatened to do so, but was not made to shout and is to blame when he does it as a lark, or because Lisa talked him into it. Children observe that strong-arm tactics bypass the internal cognitive-affective processes that mediate persuasion, because of whose engagement Lisa cannot be said to decide what Bart will do, as bully Nelson does decide for his victim Bart.

First deciders take precedence among the causes of action for reasons having to do with the element of fault. (Now the Responsibility clause comes into play.) The fact is, children acquire the word "free" late in the language game, after they learn the more exigent game of blame-placing. The blame game concerns the conditions under which people are held responsible—that is, subject to reward and punishment. Having first mastered blameworthiness, children then learn to reserve "free," "could be helped" and their ilk for behavior subject to reinforcement, and "unfree," "beyond control" and *their* ilk for behavior not so subject.

It is natural to question the propriety and certainly the priority of the blame game—to argue that it must first be shown in general that people are free before they can be held responsible, and in any particular case that the accused could have done otherwise before the punitive boom is lowered. And such is the order in which these topics have traditionally been treated: freedom grounds responsibility, which in turn justifies punishment, hence is presupposed by blame and punishment both. Compatibilism inverts the order of explanation: the facts of punishment explain the practice of holding responsible, which rationalizes (because it is equivalent to) attribution of freedom. Blame with its repercussions comes first, and can be understood without reference to free will. Reward and punishment are the levers by which people get each other to change their ways, so much so that punishment is often *defined* as whatever—including indignation—weakens behavior, and reward as whatever—including praise—strengthens it. Exertion of effort is especially reinforceable, as it is relatively independent of environmental accidents. (You may be unable to open the door because it is locked, but you are almost certainly able to try to open it.) Sanctions are prices: by adjusting the cost of various traits society regulates their supply. Making a trait more expensive by punishing it more harshly ensures less of it—with the important exception of traits whose supply is inelastic. No normal incentive can induce Bart to ignore a twisted arm; no incentive whatever can induce him not to fall when tripped. Only actions resulting from choices (preeminently exertions of effort) can be influenced by prospective gain or loss, or vicarious appreciation of the fates of others. Linking reinforcement to unchosen behavior is pointless, which is why people are not held responsible for what they do not do by choice, why desert is felt to depend so heavily on effort, and why Bart is let off the hook if Nelson twisted his arm or tripped him. Nothing is gained by penalizing Bart and warning others about to be tripped, since however badly Bart wants not to fall— no matter how hard he tries not to—he will go down anyway, the fall being of Nelson's, not Bart's, devising. Hence, when taught how to assign liability we are told to look to the choice on which an action depended. Typically only one choice, the agent's, is even a candidate, no others being closely linked to his action. But where more than one choice leads up to action, as when Nelson chooses to make Bart choose to shout by threatening to break his arm, we learn to look to the choice most amenable to reinforcement. One learns to blame the disruption on Nelson, not Bart, for there is no practical way to get anyone to prefer silence and a broken arm to a shout and relief from pain, hence no practical way to get Bart to ignore Nelson. Nelson on the other hand is apt to be more easily deterred, unless someone is twisting *his* arm. For the same reason, a man is not blamed for decisions controlled by Martians: punishing him won't change his decisions, since punishing him won't faze the Martians. To faze Martians you must punish *them*. That is why everyday choices are distinguished from choices chosen by Martians.

Compatibilists as tough-minded as Hume have fretted about the implications for freedom of the existence of an "Author of all our volitions." On one hand, it seems unfair to hold men responsible for actions that result from choices designed down to the last detail by an omniscient, omnipotent God, a Martian writ large. On the other, it seems facile to excuse all of man's sins because of what happened eons ago. Why the ambivalence, the many unsatisfactory compromises? Because, I suggest, of an ambiguity in the rule "pin blame where the pinning does most good." The rule seems at first to direct attention away from man, whose choices were chosen for him, and toward God, whose choices were not, since the best way to change human minds is to change the mind of their maker. But the rule also counsels disregarding God, since He is impervious to conditioning. (Prayer implies belief that God can be influenced—but is prayer a reward?—and prayers for strength ask Him to influence our decisions. But many prayers are for concrete actions.) A further complication Hume notes is that from where we are now human choice certainly *looks* reinforceable. These divergent pulls leave us unsure whether to pin sin on God or man, whereas we know whom to blame—the presumably deterrable Martians—for the [mis]deeds of their human puppets. *Should* God be blamed? In my view this is undecidable, one of those cases for which prior usage (here, of "responsible") made no provision.

As this treatment of the theological puzzle suggests, I see compatibilism as primarily a descriptive thesis aimed at explaining, not justifying, intuitions. The Responsibility clause seeks to state the conditions under which responsibility *is* ascribed, *not* conditions which *warrant* its ascription. It asserts that individuals are in fact held responsible when what happens happens because they want it to. Compatibilism, mine anyway, does not say we are *entitled* to hold people responsible when they are susceptible to conditioning, but rather that this is when they *are* held responsible, and is, near enough, what "responsible" actually denotes. Not that being caused by an agent's careful decision is a bad reason to hold an act to his account. Who *else* is to blame (or, depending on the act, credit)? What more would it take to blame him? (Are hard determinists suggesting that World War II was nobody's fault, that it just happened?) Granted, blame*worthi*ness is normative, hence not equivalent to the purely descriptive idea of causation by decision, so perhaps compatibilism should be said to explicate our ordinary non-contingent criteria for responsibility. Be that subtlety as it may, asking whether people *should* be held responsible for behavior whose shape is a function of reward is like asking whether chickens should be called "chickens." Let me repeat: I am not saying, as some have, that a man is responsible when it is "fair" or "appropriate" to punish him. Such a move would surrender all the ground gained by tracing judgments of responsibility to judgments of sheer susceptibility to punishment. "Responsible" is the name for such behavior. Calling someone "responsible" carries practical consequences which calling something a "chicken" does not, to be sure, but only because of a prior decision to punish the undesired behavior and reward the desired behavior to which the word applies.

III. VIVA LAS VEGAS

Never mind Mars; what about Las Vegas, where degenerate gamblers do their gambling thing yet are still unfree, bound by their compulsion. No simple account in terms of preference can tell their whole story, since even though a compulsive gambler placing a bet is doing what he wants, plainly he differs from normals. A plausible suggestion[9] is that despite doing what he wants, he also wants, impotently, not to want what he wants; he wants not to want to gamble. Normals by contrast accept their desires. They eat when hungry and don't bemoan their getting hungry every few hours. A gambler does bemoan his urge to bet the rent and his yielding to it: he will hate himself tomorrow, and however much he wins he will be spurred to keep going until he loses. Yet despite these misgivings he bets, opening a gap between his preference and what he wants his preference to be. The tenacity of his preference thwarts his freedom, because he wants to banish or muffle it yet cannot do so.

To exclude compulsives, then, freedom should be defined more narrowly as acting from desires you do not deplore. Imagine a magic dial that can change your motivational make-up; not turning it leaves your motivational make-up as is. *If you wouldn't touch the dial,* anything you do as a result of your present desires is free. According to compatibilism, to be sure, minding or accepting one's desires is as much an effect of past causes as the desires themselves. Still, so long as nothing (including the agent himself) stops the agent from doing what he wants, he acts freely. Analysis of compulsion and weakness of will into a first-order desire plus a higher-order desire about that desire refines the core idea of freedom as doing what one wants. The compulsive has two desires: to gamble, and to cease desiring to gamble. He satisfies one, the gambling desire, but not the other, the desire to suppress the desire to gamble, since the desire he desires to suppress stays as strong as ever. He gambles freely but does not freely choose to gamble.

Odd though it sounds at first, the distinction between doing freely and choosing freely is most helpful. Consider this problem:[10] One day Homer hears that beer is healthier than wine, which causes him to want beer, which leads him to drink beer. But in Homer's brain is an implant (yes, the Martians are back) that would have made him want beer no matter what he heard. Had he started to want wine, the chip would have made him think of that great beer taste that doesn't fill you up. Most philosophers accept that (A) Homer did not drink beer freely even though he drank beer because he wanted to, and moreover that (B) he is responsible for his drinking beer. (A) challenges compatibilism directly, and (B) challenges the precept, which I said should be saved at all costs, that responsibility requires the ability to do otherwise. But these difficulties are illusory; Homer is free, and could have drunk wine. The implant does not stand ready to stop him from drinking wine if wine he wants; rather, it stands ready to stop him from wanting wine. Homer cannot choose wine, and will end up drinking beer, but it does not follow and is not true that he would end up drinking beer no matter what he wanted. So far as the story goes, he would have drunk wine had he wanted to, so by compatibilist lights *is* free to drink it and could have drunk it. He is not free to *want* or to *will* to drink wine, since, were he to want to want wine, he would (nevertheless) end up not wanting it.[11]

Perhaps inability to will or choose otherwise seems to entail inability to do otherwise because, as suggested earlier, failure to want what one wants to want is rarer than failure to act as one wants to act. One assumes therefore that doing is harder than wanting, hence that inability to do the easier thing, namely want, entails inability to do the harder, namely act. But in fact, wanting is sometimes harder than doing. I can listen to a Berlioz CD easily enough, but I cannot imagine what could make me want to listen to a Berlioz CD. Inability to want does not imply inability to do.

I suggest that the worry that we are unfree because our actions are caused by desires (caused by genes and environment) in effect treats all desires as compulsions, external forces pushing the self where it doesn't want to go. This idea is plainly incoherent, since the self cannot *want* to resist desires without having (further) desires of its own. Do the self's own desires, if caused, coerce it? But then the self must have a further desire to fight its own desires, . . . and a regress is under way. This regress is stopped by identifying the self, metaphorically, with the desires and thoughts it is customarily said to have, or, less metaphorically, with whatever entity—brain or soul—those desires and thoughts are states of. Wherever their origin, your desires can't push you around, since they pretty much *are* you. Compulsions are felt as alien because they work against the bulk of other desires, hence are necessarily exceptional.[12]

The doctrine that freedom is acting on choices you don't deplore also sharpens the old idea that freedom involves Reason. Compulsives make clear that being fully free requires more than merely acting on desire, but so on second thought do infants, animals, the retarded and the highly labile, all of whom do what they want yet are less free than reflective, stable adults. The mark of the actions of a sane adult is internal intellectual processing. He looks before leaping and stays put unless he likes the view. No rigid rules govern the length or object of his reflection, but the sane adult usually considers an action's likely effects, its conduciveness to his immediate goals, the coherence of these goals with his longer-term ones, the origin of his goals and the kind of person his actions and goals make him. We might deplore his final decision yet recognize his weighings as Reasonable.[13]

Infants, animals and lunatics fall short in the Reason department because they think too little, compulsives because their thinking, however thorough, is impotent.

Reason also smoothes a kink that has historically made compatibilists seem cynical. They often meet the recurrent question—what good is doing what you choose if your choices are caused?—with blunt denial of freedom of choice. "We can do as we please," quipped Bertrand Russell, "but not please as we please," a reply at once unsatisfying and gratuitous. Unsatisfying, because freedom is expected to reach to the faculties of desire and choice. Gratuitous, because this expectation can be met, for with Reason's help we often do please as we please. To return to the example of rage, a man seized by an impulse to smash his computer but aware of the folly of indulging it may count to ten to let it pass; after calm returns, he feels more benign toward his computer because he wanted to, hence by the Freedom clause he freely feels more benign. Or he may put his computer under a timelock, to frustrate destructive urges in advance. Any subsequent urges will be impotent because he wanted them to be; in other words he will have freely immobilized them. A familiar device for outflanking preferences is the promise, e.g., a promise to meet friends for a run insures that later laziness will be pitted against shame at not showing up.

The pinball game of internal processing whereby desires and beliefs bounce off each other, rack up points, and sometimes (witness Hamlet) send the system into tilt also buffers behavior from the world, response from stimulus. By transforming input, Reason makes the agent more than a transparent medium or (as one incompatibilist put it to me) "conduit" through which causes pass from and back into the environment. Conduits do not change their contents; humans do. A human listener's interpretation of sounds from a radio as the words "Highway congestion" prompts him to ponder whether to take a longer alternate route, whether he should change his plans, whether pondering whether to change his plans is an excuse not to go. Finally he sets out one way or the other—a conversion of noise into purpose nothing like the transduction of acoustic energy from the radio into mechanical energy in the wall opposite. What human beings emit may depend on what goes in, but thanks to Reason the output differs enough for human action to "originate" in a way incompatibilists customarily insist free actions must and deny that mere effects can. Incidentally, don't say that caused origination is a contradiction in terms because effects already exist "in" their causes. Containment is a bad metaphor for causation; as Yogi Berra might have said, effects don't happen until they happen.

Some critics deny that high-order reasoning actually informs most action.[14] Homer wanted a beer, so he took one from the fridge. He could have mulled over his desire for a beer, and had he done so he would have okayed it and gotten a beer anyway, but the fact is he didn't. So is his getting a beer less than free? My oblique reply is that complex human behavior is due to its antecedents in a variety of ways, rather like those in which the actions of governments are due to underlying social processes. Consider Hume's observation that all governments rest ultimately on opinion,[15] true on (but only on) a broad understanding of "rest" and "opinion." Typically, one minority faction actively supports the current regime, another faction is actively hostile, and everyone else takes the regime as a fact of life. Yet were the acquiescent majority to grow restive—ignoring government officials, for instance—the regime would collapse. So it endures because of its active supporters, despite its detractors, but also because of indifference, the passive failure of the remainder to oppose it. Governments do "rest on opinion"—in several ways, on opinions of several sorts. Likewise for individual actions. One small part of Homer, his beer desire (of course) and its allies (e.g., his thirst) think the beer desire is just great; another part, his sobriety desire and its friends (his need to keep his job), actively opposes it; the majority of Homer—his desires for nice weather, a bowling trophy—doesn't care. The yea-thinking beer alliance is running things, the nay-thinking sobriety party has been outmaneuvered, but he drinks most of all because most of him is inert, "because" in the counterfactual sense that he would not have drunk had most of him moved against the alliance. His walk to the fridge resulted from inward consent in the multi-dimensional way that public consent explains the persistence of governments.

IV. CALL ME IRRESPONSIBLE*

To admit, nay insist, that preferences about preferences are also caused may prompt a new spasm of the old qualm: Is the shift to wanting what you want to want progress if your wanting to want it is caused? An irked compatibilist will ask critics what progress would be, since they are unimpressed by the difference, which he has painstakingly marked out, between a frog snaring flies and a traveler self-consciously adopting an itinerary. Some critics explain themselves with one more variant of the mischievous Martians. Suppose a hypnotist makes Homer want to eat sugary donuts, endorse that preference (Homer now discounts health), and, if need be, endorse his second-order endorsement. Then although he acts from a taste he doesn't deplore, Homer's eating sugary donuts is still not intuitively free. Now, this intuition has already been traced to the utility, for limiting donut consumption, of punishing the hypnotist, but a further obscurity of this case concerns Homer's ability to find out where his taste for donuts came from. Will the hypnotist let him discover that it is a post-hypnotic suggestion? It is a fact that people care where their preferences came from. They find some modes of desire-formation tolerable, others not; whether one wishes to maintain a desire may depend on how he thinks he got it. Following Nozick,[16] a desire that would survive knowledge of its origin may be said to be in equilibrium; part of a desire's being "undeplored" is that it is in equilibrium. As people generally would want to shed desires produced by hypnosis, because like implanted desires they are the work of alien agents, we may suppose that Homer's taste for donuts is unstable, hence that his consuming them is not free. But what if Homer does know but *doesn't care* that his desire is a post-hypnotic suggestion, if he now thanks the hypnotist for letting him see the advantage of gustatory pleasure over health? In that case the compatibilist, confident that common sense will follow, declares Homer free. Homer likes donuts, he likes liking donuts, and appreciates having been hypnotized. Perhaps so profound a shake-up has replaced the old Homer with a new one. So be it; new-Homer at any rate munches donuts freely (and is responsible for his intake) while thanking the hypnotist for creating him. If the reader's intuition balks, that may be because we expect Homer to rebel—to repudiate his donut habit—on learning of the hypnotist, and therefore doubt the stability of his desire. But the implausibility of the example is no fault of compatibilism.

So: we are responsible for what we do, insofar as it is chosen for reasons we accept. We are also mostly responsible for our choices, most of which are allowed to stand if only in the passive, Humean sense that we would have blocked them had we wanted to. About the choices governing first-order choices matters grow murkier. I weigh my first-order choices on the scales of my character, endorsing (say) a decision to write a paper instead of watch TV because I am a philosopher. I probably could not extirpate my dedication to philosophy even if for some reason I deplored it, so I'm probably not responsible for it— no great concern to me precisely because this value is so entrenched in my character. And only a Woody Allen neurotic would even seek to identify the principles responsible for the values by which he judges his choices, let alone worry whether to change them. All this, I think, conforms to common sense. We are responsible for much but not everything, hence free of a responsibility* we never miss.

V. IFS AND CANS

Soft determinism, like all forms of determinism, permits just one state of the universe at any one time. As Homer picks up the remote and settles into his favorite chair, the laws of nature plus the state of the world, including his state of mind, imply that he will watch TV. This is why so many people assume determinism is incompatible with free will, since it seems obvious that for Homer to watch TV freely he must also be able to do something else, like read a book. He can't do anything freely unless he could have done otherwise, and Homer appears unable to do otherwise given determinism. Hard determinists conclude that Homer is unfree. Libertarians, convinced of Homer's freedom, conclude that the world is indeterministic. We compatibilists prefer to have our cake and eat it.

Soft determinists are determinists—that's our cake—yet, as I keep saying, we agree that freedom requires the ability to do otherwise. Who wouldn't? (Us, according to Mark Bernstein: "libertarian free will, unlike a compatibilist version of free will, demands the ability, in the very circumstances that the individual finds himself, to choose among various alternative courses of action."[17]) We hold that Homer could have read a book because of the Power clause: talk of what he could have done posits a different past, as a consequence of which Homer chooses some alternative. That's how we eat our cake. "Homer could have read a book" means "Homer would have read a book if he had wanted to." One imagines Homer's genes or rearing or just-prior experiences different enough to have caused him to want to read, in which case he would have. In every "can" an "if" lies buried.

For Kant this was "a wretched subterfuge," for James "a quagmire of evasion." Freedom is possible, they say, only if "Homer could have read" means that reading was in Homer's power given the same genes, upbringing and day's events—the very same world— as that in which he watches TV. According to Timothy O'Connor, when I ask what is in my power, "I am wondering what is open to me, given the way things are and have been."[18] John Martin Fischer expresses this as the principle that the possible must extend the actual.[19]

These critics are charging at an open door, since compatibilists agree that Homer could have done otherwise given exactly the way the world is—in fact, they agree to this *just by asserting* that Homer could have done otherwise. *Whatever* "Homer could have done otherwise" means, it is equivalent to "Homer could have done otherwise given the way things are." Here is why. It is a logical law that, if p is assumed to be true, any statement q is equivalent to the conjunction "p and q." Hence, when "given that" is understood as conjunction, and p is a complete description of the way things truly are, p is redundant in "Given p, q." For instance, if "Homer could have done otherwise" means "Homer would have done otherwise had things differed" then "Given how things actually are, Homer could have done otherwise" means "Given how things actually are, Homer would have done otherwise had things differed," i.e., that Homer would have done otherwise had things differed. To say that reading *War and Peace* is in Homer's power given actuality is just to say that reading *War and Peace* is in his power, regardless of the analysis of "power." The point is nearly as trivial when "given that" is read as conditional probability. By assuming p one sets the probability of p equal to 1; and for any q, the probability of q given p obviously then equals the probability of q by itself. Hence the probability of Homer doing otherwise given the history of the world = the probability of Homer doing otherwise, whatever Homer's doing otherwise consists in.

Some contemporary indeterminists invoke possible worlds, to their unwitting detriment. Let A be the actual world, where Homer watches TV. For Homer to be free, it is said, he must be able to read *in A*, not merely in some other possible but unactual world. Unfortunately for these contemporaries, the assertion that Homer could have read Tolstoy in a world W is taken by modal logicians to mean that there is another possible world V suitably related to W in which Homer does read Tolstoy. In other words, Homer could read in the actual world A just in case he does read in another possible world suitably related to this one, i.e., he would read were things a little different from how they are—what compatibilists have been saying all along. Indeterminists may reply that what could be true at A is not "Homer reads Tolstoy" but "Homer reads Tolstoy in A." However, the usual understanding of possible worlds make nonsense of claims of the form "p in W is true in W." Worlds are constituted by what happens in them, so if Homer does not read in W, "Homer reads in W" cannot be true and is probably undefined. Even more obscure is "Homer does not read in W, but he might have read in W." Instead of requesting the evaluation of possibility statements at worlds, which is legitimate, the indeterminist is now requesting the evaluation in worlds of statements *about worlds*, including possibility statements about worlds, which is not. Ironically, the world-indexed statements with which incompatibilists rebuke compatibilists, e.g., "Homer watched TV in A, but he might have read in A instead" are at best necessarily false.

Perhaps incompatibilists are trying to say that for Homer to be able to read Tolstoy in A at a time t there has to be a world exactly like A in all facts and laws up to t, in which Homer then reads Tolstoy at t. To introduce some notation, let W/t be world W up to t. Then, according to this version of incompatibilism, what people ordinarily mean when they say that given A still p is possible, where p is some falsehood, is that there is a world A′ such that A/t = A′/t and in which p. However, the intuition of common sense, namely A/t & possibly p, must be scrupulously distinguished from: possibly (A/t & p), which is what the existence of A′ amounts to. For one thing, there is a world with the same laws and past as ours yet a divergent future only if our world is indeterministic, which it may not be. More important, to suppose that A/t & possibly p requires a world matching ours up to t begs the question against the Power clause, according to which statements about what Homer could have but did not do assume a world whose past differs somewhat from the actual one. In the jargon, Homer's powers depend on what he does in worlds near A, and the abruptness of the divergence of A′ from A at t may mean that A′ and A are very distant.

Forgive and forget technicalities. The basic indeterminist protest that the possible must extend the actual rests on an equivocation. Of course estimates of power must spring from and comport with reality. But "reality" in this context does not mean the world down to the smallest detail, but rather its big facts, laws, and patterns. In *On the Waterfront*, Terry Malloy laments to his brother Charlie that he coulda been a contender. Charlie might concur: "You're right. You had great hands." Or he might demur: "No way. Kid KO punched harder." In making his assessment Charlie holds fixed Terry's reflexes, motivation, and the quality of opponents, not the force to the erg of every punch he ever threw. Holding each punch constant would leave Terry exactly what he is today, which is a bum.

The passage cited earlier from O'Connor runs in full:

> When I wonder what it is now in my power to do, I am wondering what is open to me, given the way things are and have been and the laws that constrain how things might be. And I am not, of course, merely wondering what general abilities I have.[20]

"Of course"? To the contrary, that is *precisely* what is at issue. Another sports story. When I was in high school, my handball team reached the New York City finals. I lost my game and with it the match and the city championship, and for years I brooded over whether I could have won. What was I wondering? The indeterminist will not accept: whether I would have won if I had played differently, since I am supposedly concerned with what could have happened had everything been exactly the same. But I can hardly have wondered whether I could have won if I had played exactly as I did and hence my opponent as he did, for had we played exactly as we did I would have lost a duplicate game by the identical score. No; I wondered what would have happened *if* the ref had been fairer, *if* I had practiced more, *if* I had tried harder—small deviations from history consonant with my athletic skills, the latter factor too large to vary while keeping things as they are. Homer can read as he contentedly watches TV because he is literate and there is printed matter in his home. All he need do is try.

Many indeterminists propose that Homer could have read Tolstoy just in case he would have read Tolstoy had he tried harder to resist TV *and* he could have tried harder to resist. This proposal is triply useless. First, it dilates the subject. The plain fact supposedly at odds with compatibilism is that Homer could have read Tolstoy, not that he could have done (that and) something else, such as try harder to be high-brow. No doubt he could have tried harder, but the two could-haves are distinct and one cannot do duty for the other. Second, construing "Homer could have read" as "Homer would have read had he . . . ," where the ellipsis is filled by "tried harder," capitulates to compatibilism. The compatibilist insists that can's always cloak if's; he is less particular on just what the if's are. Nor (the third difficulty) does he see why trying is as magical as indeterminists evidently take it to be. He interprets "Homer could have tried harder" as per the Power clause, viz. "Homer would have tried harder not to wallow in front of the TV had he felt guiltier about wallowing, or had he been raised more literately, or had he tried to try harder." In the last, ideal, case in which Homer would have tried harder to read if he had tried to try harder (for instance by sur-

rounding himself with books), his trying would have been free. Effort is one more variable whose value depends on those of prior causal factors.

Compatibilism is too ambitious a thesis to be established in one essay. Many troublesome issues remain. Nonetheless, I hope the reader has begun to accept that our view of ourselves as shaping our own fates can be reconciled with scientific determinism.

NOTES

1. See Galen Strawson, "The Impossibility of Moral Responsibility."
2. An obvious counterexample to the Responsibility clause: At an auction I tell you of my decision to bid; ever helpful, you push my arm up, a bid under house rules. My deciding caused my action, but in the wrong way. What way is right? To say "the way intention usually leads to action" is uninstructive. A reasonably counterexample-resistant account is that A does X when A's intending a sequence of events that culminates in X causes that sequence. At the auction, my bid did not eventuate as planned.

    "Lehrer cases" trouble the Power clause. In a crackdown on people who don't wish to sacrifice, the Department of Homeland Piety impounds Socrates' chicken, so he cannot sacrifice it. However, if Socrates wanted to sacrifice he would, because the DHP would return his chicken, so Socrates seems unable to do something that he would do if he wanted to. But in fact Socrates *can* sacrifice a chicken; he need only ask. He seems unable because the example presents his unwillingness to sacrifice as sufficient for his inability, which obscures the fact that his unwillingness is also *necessary*. And necessary it must be, for if Socrates might not sacrifice even if he wanted to, we cannot say that if he wanted to he would, and the Power clause would face no counterexample.
3. See his *How Free are You?*, 2nd ed. (New York: Oxford University Press, 2002).
4. As evidence of mankind holding itself responsible*, Strawson cites Nietzsche—whose imputation of this belief to others is no proof that others do hold it—two Britons who consider men responsible for their character, Kant and Sartre. But Kant based his view on denial of the reality of time, and

Sartre's metaphysics is indecipherable. Neither can be taken to speak for the human race at large.

5. I should mention the approach taken by my student Phyllis Liang, that an agent is free when his appetitive mechanisms are performing their evolutionarily adaptive functions. This natural extension of compatibilism handles the various problem cases considered below, and deserves development it cannot receive here.

6. *An Essay on Free Will* (New York: Oxford University Press, 1983), pp. 106–114.

7. J. Koons, "Is Hard Determinism a Form of Compatibilism?" *The Philosophical Forum* 33 (1), Spring 2002: 81–99 treats the Martians similarly.

8. Van Inwagen admits it is "of the highest importance" whether a person's behavior is "chosen for him by a non-human intelligence" (p. 111). Yet he finds it "hard to see . . . the relevance of [this] incontestably important fact." How can a fact be incontestably important but irrelevant?

9. Harry Frankfurt's, going back to Locke.

10. Also Frankfurt's.

11. Oddly, Frankfurt does not deploy his distinction between orders of desire to handle the puzzle in this simple manner.

12. Writes Strawson: "We are born with a great many genetically determined predispositions for which we are not responsible. We are subject to many early influences for which we are not responsible. These decisively shape our characters, our motives . . . our capacity to make efforts of will." Who is this "we" so much befalls? Was I not created by my genes? Aren't they my essence? If so, no coherent thought is expressed by "responsibility for one's genes," hence no coherent thought is expressed by its denial.

13. Compatibilists reject the curious tradition that only right action can be done freely.

14. See David Shatz, "Free Will and the Structure of Motivation," *Midwest Studies in Philosophy* 10 (1986): 451–482.

15. "Of the First Principles on Government," in *Hume's Moral and Political Philosophy*, ed. H. D. Aiken (Darien, CT: Hafner, 1970), p. 307.

16. *Philosophical Explanations* (Cambridge: Harvard University Press, 1981), 348–352. Desires out of equilibrium with respect to some possible history are "unfrozen." Nozick denies that acting from stable unfrozen desires suffices for freedom on the question-begging ground that the agent might have been caused to embrace the origin of his desires.

17. "Fatalism," in R. Kane, ed., *Oxford Handbook of Free Will* (New York: Oxford University Press, 2002), p. 74. Daniel Dennett denies that freedom entails ability to do otherwise on the ground that Martin Luther could "do no other" when he freely took his stand. Surely Luther exaggerated for rhetorical effect, and was declaring that he *would* do no other, or perhaps that he constitutionally could not want other. But had he not wanted to take his stand he surely would have sat down.

18. *Persons and Causes* (New York: Oxford University Press, 2000), p. 17.

19. *The Metaphysics of Free Will* (Malden, MA: Blackwell, 1995).

20. Op. cit.

FOR FURTHER REFLECTION

1. Is Levin's understanding of the use of "freedom" correct?

2. Go over the Martian objection: that we have been programmed by Martians or neurologists to feel free when we do what we have been programmed to do, and if so, we would not be free or responsible. Does Levin successfully meet this objection? Explain.

3. According to Levin, how does the compatibilist *invert* the order of explanation with regard to responsibility?

LOIS HOPE WALKER

A LIBERTARIAN DEFENSE OF MORAL RESPONSIBILITY

"Lois Walker" is a nom de plume for an author who wishes to remain anonymous. In this essay, she argues that the soft determinists like Michael Levin are misleading when they argue that determinism is compatible with free will. Soft determinist arguments for moral responsibility fail, so the only valid basis for attributing moral responsibility to people is by accepting the doctrine of libertarian free will. She also points out that the doctrine of free will is necessary to theism, for unless *humans* are freely responsible for evil acts, *God* must be—which makes God evil.

If one cannot be responsible for consequences of one's acts due to factors beyond one's control, or for antecedents of one's acts that are properties of temperament not subject to one's will, or for the circumstances that pose one's moral choices, then how can one be responsible even for the stripped-down acts of the will itself, if *they* are the product of antecedent circumstances outside of the will's control? The area of genuine agency, and therefore legitimate moral judgment, seems to shrink under this scrutiny to an extensionless point.

Thomas Nagel, Mortal Questions

In recent years there has been an exodus by philosophers from a libertarian position to soft determinism, sometimes called "compatibilism." Bewitched by the attraction of neurobiology, which promises to explain all human behavior via brain behavior, philosophers have been running over each other in their eagerness to endorse the latest hypotheses of the neurologist-philosophers. Witness the number of books and articles defending compatibilist positions.[1] In this moblike stampede, I find myself going against the traffic. Having embraced determinism as an undergraduate,

in my old age I have become disillusioned with this youthful friend. In this essay I want to defend the libertarian view of moral responsibility. In particular, I want to argue two theses: (1) soft determinist arguments for moral responsibility are invalid; (2) the libertarian position is rationally justified. In the process of defending Thesis 2, I point out that the soft determinist often misrepresents the libertarian position on this matter. Although the free will–determinism problem is one of the most difficult paradoxes in philosophy, and intelligent people can differ as to solution, the argument from moral responsibility seems to shift the weight of evidence in the libertarian's direction.

THE ARGUMENT FROM MORAL RESPONSIBILITY

Determinism seems to conflict with the thesis that we have moral responsibilities, for responsibility implies that we could have done otherwise than we did. We do not hold a dog morally responsible for chewing up our philosophy book or hold a one-month-old baby re-

This essay was written for this book and initially appeared in the first edition.

sponsible for crying, because they could not help it, but we do hold a twenty-year-old student responsible for his cheating because (we believe) he could have done otherwise. Blackbacked seagulls will tear apart a stray baby herring seagull without the slightest suspicion that their act may be immoral, but if humans lack this sense we judge them as pathological, as substandard.

Moral responsibility is something we take very seriously. We believe we do have duties, oughts, over which we feel rational guilt at failure to perform. But there can be no such things as duties, oughts, praise, blame, or rational guilt, if we are not actually free. The argument is the following.

1. Since "ought" implies "can," in order to have a duty to do Act A we must be able to do A *and* able to refrain from doing A.
2. Being morally responsible for doing A entails that I could have done otherwise if I had chosen to do so and that at some previous time I could have chosen to have done otherwise (or chosen some course of action that would have enabled me to do A).
3. But if determinism is true, and our actions are merely the product of the laws of nature and antecedent states of affairs, then it is not up to us to choose what we do.
4. But if it is not up to us to choose what we do, we cannot be said to be responsible for what we do.
5. So if determinism is true, we are not responsible for what we do.
6. But our belief in moral responsibility is self-evident, and more worthy of acceptance than belief in universal causality.
7. So if we believe that we have moral responsibilities, determinism cannot be accepted.
8. Therefore, since we justifiably believe in moral responsibility, we must reject the notion of determinism even if we cannot give a full explanatory account of how agents choose.

Is this argument sound? Interestingly enough, both hard determinists and libertarians accept the first five premises. Together they make up the group known as *incompatibilists,* for they claim that free will and moral responsibility are incompatible with determinism.

Here the determinist usually bites the bullet and admits that we do not have moral responsibilities, and that it is just an illusion that we do. But we are determined to have such an illusion, so there is nothing we can do about it. We cannot consciously live as determinists, but why should we think that we can? We are finite and fallible creatures, whose behavior is entirely governed by causal laws, but with self-consciousness that makes us aware of part (but only a part) of the process that governs our behavior.

Let us look more closely at the key premises in the argument. The notion that *ought* implies *can* was first pointed out by Immanuel Kant. It simply makes no sense to say that I have an obligation to do something that I do not have the power to do. Suppose that I have been hypnotized and have been ordered to go to shake hands with every person in my class. I do so, feeling that I am acting under my own free will, but I am not acting freely and I am not responsible for my behavior. Or suppose through some deep brain defect and poor early upbringing I am a kleptomaniac. I am not able to refrain from stealing, so that I am not responsible for my behavior—even though I may feel free while doing so. I am excused for my behavior and, one may hope, treated.

But suppose that I have acquired my habit of theft through giving in to the temptation to steal over a period of time, and now cannot refrain. Even though I now cannot refrain, I am responsible for the state I am now in. I am responsible for my character and morally responsible for my thievery. This conclusion is conveyed by Premise 2: "Being morally responsible for doing A entails that I could have done otherwise if I had chosen to do so and that at some previous time I could have chosen to have done otherwise (or chosen some course of action that would have enabled me to do A)."

The compatibilist usually responds at this point that the phrase "Could have done otherwise" should be translated hypothetically as "Would have done otherwise if I had chosen differently." When pressed and asked whether at the time in question I could have *chosen* otherwise, the compatibilist *qua* determinist must answer no. I could not have chosen differently. But if I could not have chosen differently, then what sense does it make to say that freedom amounts to being able to do differently if one chooses to do so? If I could never choose to do other than I do, I cannot be said to be able to do any other act but the one I actually do. The hypothetical interpretation is a red herring, amounting to little more than the truth that if things had been different, they would have been different. That is, if I had been *determined* to choose differently, I would have been *determined* to do otherwise than I did.

Premise 3 contends that if determinism is true, then we do not have the power to refrain from doing A (if A is what we indeed do). For any time *t* there is only one act open to us, that caused by the state of the world plus the laws of nature, together. But if antecedent states of affairs cause A to happen, then they are responsible for what we "do," and we ourselves are not responsible for those acts (Premise 4). We are puppets in the hands of nature.

So 5, "If determinism is true, we are not responsible for what we do." If nature is responsible for our actions, then nature should be praised or blamed for what we do, not us. The determinist may argue that in punishing or rewarding us we are really punishing or rewarding nature, but this, of course, is hyperbolic persiflage, for the notions of reward and punishment presuppose that the subject in question be conscious and have interests, neither of which apply to nature.

But if we are not responsible for our actions, then we are mere objects of nature, without selves worthy of respect in their own right. As Nagel says, "The area of genuine agency and therefore of legitimate moral judgment seems to shrink under this scrutiny to an extensionless point."

It is at this point that more sophisticated compatibilists such as Harry Frankfurt revise the meaning of free will in terms of identification with one's second-order desire. Humans, unlike other animals, have the ability to deliberate and choose courses of actions. Although both animals and humans have basic *first-order* desires (such as desires to eat, to be warm and to copulate), animals act directly on their wants,

whereas humans can weigh them and accept or reject them. For example, you may have the first-order desire to stay in bed rather than come to class today, but you may also have a first-order desire to learn more about the problem of free will and determinism. So you compare the two desires and form a *second-order* desire that one of the first-order desires be the one that motivates you—we hope it's the one enjoining you to come to class, based on your passionate desire to understand the free-will problem. So you choose to let your second-order desire affect your behavior. Frankfurt calls this your second-order *volition.* "To the extent that a person identifies himself with the springs of his actions, he takes a responsibility for those actions and acquires moral responsibility for them."[2]

Frankfurt may have described the phenomenology of free choice, but he hasn't shown that this saves the compatibilist account of free will. He has given only necessary but not sufficient conditions for free choice. For consider, suppose that you are deciding whether to get up from bed to go to class. You weigh the alternatives of staying in bed and experiencing the delicious taste of another hour of twilight dreams, against the intellectual pleasures of your philosophy class. You decide to get up, to make learning your second-order volition, to "identify yourself with the springs of this action," and so you rise.

But it turns out that a brilliant neurologist has been controlling your decisions through electronic waves that affect your neurons and brain patterns, *causing* you to choose to get up. Would you want to say that you *freely* got up? It sounds like you weren't free at all. You could not have avoided getting up, for your behavior was caused by the brilliant neurologist, and in spite of making "rising from the bed" your second-order volition, it can be said that you were not free at the moment to do otherwise.

The point is that the compatibilist's notion of second-order volitions turns out to be simply a subtler version of the "brilliant neurologist" story, because nature and antecedent causes cause you to form the second-order volition to get up and to get up. You could not have done anything else at that moment. The idea that you could was only an illusion.

We turn, then, to Premise 6: the idea that the belief that we are morally responsible is better justified than is our opinion of universal causality. If there is one thing we are sure of it is that we have selves, that we exist with moral obligations. There is nothing more certain than that I ought not kill innocent people, break promises simply for my own advantage, harm others without due cause, or cheat. I have a duty to help my aging parents, to protect my children, and to support my spouse and friends. But if determinism is true, all this obligation is a mere illusion.

And what are determinism's credentials for its horrendous freedom-denying claims? Simply, an atavistic faith in universal causality. Everything in the world must have a cause, so all my behavior and all my mental states are caused.

But this is unduly fideistic. Strange that philosophers should have turned up their noses at simple theists for lacking evidence for belief in a God, and yet should themselves have erected a shrine to the despot Omnicausality![3] As David Hume pointed out in his *Enquiry,* the notion of causality is not a necessary truth, nor one of which we have a clear idea. We just observe regularities in nature and sum up these constant conjunctions of behavior in lawlike statements. It is very difficult to define "causality" (to my mind, no one has given an adequate definition) or "natural law," and quantum physics tells us that on the most basic level of physical reality causal relationships do not operate. Until we can solve these problems in the philosophy of science, it behooves us to be modest about our claims that all behavior and states of affairs, including the self, are caused.

For my part, if I have to compare the propositions (1) "Every event and state of affairs in the world is caused" and (2) "I have moral responsibilities," I have not the slightest doubt about which I must choose.

At this point the determinist—both the soft kind and the hard variety—object that it is only through having determinate character that we can be said to be good or bad, that actions without determined character are capricious and arbitrary. To quote Sidney Hook,

The great difficulty with the indeterminist view in most forms is the suggestion it carries that choices

and actions, if not determined, are capricious. Caprice and responsibility are more difficult to reconcile than determinism and responsibility, for it seems easier to repudiate a choice or action which does not follow from one's character, or history, or nature, or self, than an act which does follow.[4]

But, as Hook himself recognizes, it is not necessary to equate free will with indeterminism. All that is necessary is to have a self that in deliberation can *weigh* desires and values. The self can exercise control, can veto desires or confirm them, can subscribe to reason or reject it in defiance, and this self itself transcends the ordinary laws of nature. C. A. Campbell and Robert Nozick think the self intervenes thus only on rare and momentous occasions, but I suspect that this claim is unduly modest. If it happens at all, why can't it happen every time the self deliberates?[5]

Of course, we may not be able to give a convincing explanation of the self or agency, because what will count for an explanation in the determinist's eyes is only a causal explanation, and that is exactly what is in question.

Many philosophers who work in this area of the debate tend to be religious agnostics, so that one explanation of the self-cum-free-will is cut off from them; that is, the idea of a Supreme Self, or God. If God is a free agent, self-determined, then if he (or she) creates humans in his image, why shouldn't we suppose that humans also are self-determining beings? Indeed, the Jewish-Christian tradition supposes that God did create us as free agents and that we have sinned against God; that is, we have misused our freedom for disobedience and wrongdoing. We are responsible for our actions and so can be held accountable for them. The alternative is to make God strongly responsible for the evil in the world (at least the moral evil), which is blasphemy to any theist. It may be in a weak or indirect sense, as omniscient creator, that God is responsible for *allowing* humans to sin and create evil, but he is not responsible in any direct sense. In this case, we must conclude that either God was not able to create a better world—one with a greater proportion of good over evil—than this one or else that God will bring good out of the evil in the world.

Since the theist will typically hold to the free-will defense to account for the evil in the world, he or she will typically embrace the doctrine of free will. The comprehensive theory, which stands or falls as a whole, carries the theist past the state of agnosticism on this matter. Of course, if it turns out that we are wholly determined by antecedent causes, then (supposing one understands this fact) one would have to give up the free-will defense, and perhaps theism itself. A lot is at stake in this dispute.

In conclusion, I have argued that the compatibilist strategy for saving moral responsibility is an illusion and that only libertarianism has a creditable notion of accountability. I have admitted that the problem of free will and determinism is fraught with paradox, but have argued that we have no good reason to distrust our intuitions about having a responsible self with moral obligations. I have also argued that if one is inclined to theism, one has additional reasons for preferring the libertarian position over its deterministic rivals.

NOTES

1. For example, Daniel Dennett, *Elbowroom* (Cambridge, MA: MIT Press, 1985); Michael Levin, *Philosophy of Mind* (Oxford: Oxford University Press, 1979); see most of the articles in John Martin Fischer, ed., *Moral Responsibility* (Ithaca, NY: Cornell University Press, 1986); and Gary Watson, ed., *Free Will* (Oxford: Oxford University Press, 1982); Wright Neely, "Freedom and Desire," *Philosophical Review 83,* 1974; and P. F. Strawson, "Freedom and Resentment," *Proceedings of the British Academy 48,* 1962.

2. "Three Concepts of Free Action," *Moral Responsibility,* ed. John Martin Fischer (Ithaca, NY: Cornell University Press, 1986), p. 120.

3. *Omnicausality* is the name for the doctrine that every event and state of affairs in the universe is caused by antecedent causes.

4. Sidney Hook, "Moral Responsibility in a Determined World," *Quest for Being* (New York: St. Martin's Press, 1961).

5. Robert Nozick, *Philosophical Explorations* (Cambridge, MA: Harvard University Press, 1981), Chapter 4.

FOR FURTHER REFLECTION

1. Walker alleges that without the free-will defense for the existence of God, theism probably collapses. Why does she come to this conclusion? Is this correct? Note that Augustine (354–430 C.E.) and most of the Protestant Reformers (such as Martin Luther and John Calvin) believed in the predestination of souls to heaven and hell, thus denying the idea that humans had free will (at least regarding salvation). How would they defend their position to Walker?

C. Punishment

To be responsible for a past act is to be liable to praise or blame. If the act was especially good we go further than praise, and reward it. If it was especially evil we go further than blame, and punish it. In this section, I want to apply the notion of responsibility to that of punishment. In particular, I want to discover under what conditions, if any, criminal punishment is justified. Three answers to this problem are presented: the retributivist, the utilitarian, and the rehabilitationist responses.

Even though few of us will ever become criminals or be indicted on criminal charges, most of us feel very strongly about the matter of criminal punishment. Something about crime touches the deepest nerves of our imaginations. Consider the following situations:

1. A drug addict knifes to death a vibrant, gifted twenty-two-year-old graduate student who is dedicated to helping others.
2. A sex pervert lures little children into his home, sexually abuses them, and then kills them. What if the "pervert" is himself a child of ten, as in a recently reported case?
3. The CEO, other leading officials, and accountants, employed by a major stockholding company, alter their account books and reports to reflect false earnings. As a result, many thousands of people lose not only their jobs but their pension funds as well.

How does hearing of these incidents make you feel?

What within us rises up in violent indignation at the thought of such atrocities? What should happen to the criminals in these cases? How can the victims (or their loved ones) ever be compensated for such crimes? We feel conflicting emotional judgments of both harsh vengeance and humane concern that we don't ourselves become violent and irrational in our quest for revenge.

THE DEFINITION OF PUNISHMENT

We may define "punishment" as a harm inflicted by a person in a position of authority on another person who is judged to have violated a rule. As such, the concept can be analyzed into five concepts:

1. *Punishment is an evil*, unpleasantness, suffering (not necessarily physical pain). Regarding this concept, the question is "Under what conditions is it right to cause harm or inflict suffering?"
2. *Punishment is done for an offense*. Must the offense be moral, or merely legal? Should we punish everyone who commits a moral offense? Need the offense already have been committed?
3. *Punishment is done to the offender*. At least, the recipient must be judged or believed to be guilty of a crime. Does this condition rule out the possibility of punishing innocent? What should we call the process of framing the innocent and "punishing" them?
4. *Punishment is carried out by a personal agency*. It is not the work of natural consequences. Nature cannot punish. Only humans or conscious beings can do so.
5. *Punishment is imposed by an authority*. It is conferred through the institutions that have to do with maintaining laws or the social code. This condition would seem to disqualify vigilante executions as punishment.

Now let us turn to the three main theories of punishment: retributivism, utilitarian deterrence, and rehabilitation.

THEORIES OF PUNISHMENT

Retributivist theories make infliction of punishment depend on what the agent deserves as one who has done wrong, rather than on any future social utility that might result from inflicting suffering on the criminal. Retribution is *backward looking*, assessing the nature of the misdeed. In the readings, Immanuel Kant and C. S. Lewis hold to this position, which has three theses:

1. Guilt is a necessary condition for justified punishment.
2. Guilt is a sufficient condition for justified punishment.
3. The proper amount of punishment to be inflicted on the morally (or legally) guilty offender is that amounts that fits (is appropriate to) the gravity of the offense.

Punishment restores the balance of the scales of justice, the social equilibrium of benefits and burdens; and hence it looks backward. We might put the argument this way:

1. In breaking the primary rule (*PR*) of society, A obtains an unfair advantage over others.
2. Unfair advantage ought to be redressed by society if possible.
3. A certain punishment (*P,1*) is a form of redressing the unfair advantage.

    Therefore, we ought to punish *A* with *P,1* for breaking *PR*. *P,1* restores the social equilibrium of burdens and benefits by taking from *A* what he (or she) unfairly got and now owes—that is, by exacting payment of his debt.

Utilitarian theories are theories of deterrence and prevention. The emphasis is not on the gravity of the evil done, but on deterring and preventing future evil. Their motto might be "Don't cry over spilt milk!" Unlike retributive theories, utilitarian theories look *forward* and are aimed at *social improvement*. Jeremy Bentham and John Stuart Mill are classic utilitarians. In our readings, Jonathan Glover and John Rawls represent this position, although Rawls's position also tries to incorporate the insight of the retributivist. Their position can be broken up into three theses:

1. Social utility (correction, prevention, and deterrence) is a necessary condition for justified punishment.
2. Social utility is a sufficient condition for justified punishment.
3. The proper amount of punishment to be inflicted on the offender is the amount that will do the most good (or the lest harm) to all those who will be affected by it. As Anthony Benn puts it, "The margin of increment of harm inflicted on the offender should be preferable to the harm avoided [by prospective criminals to other people] by fixing that penalty rather than one slightly lower."

Punishment is a technique of social control, justified so long as it prevents more evil than it produces. If a system of social control (for example, rehabilitation) will give a greater balance of good to evil, then the utilitarian will opt for that system. The utilitarian does not accept draconian punishments that would deter, because the punishment would be worse than the crime and cause greater suffering. The justification of punishment is based on only three criteria: (1) Will the punishment prevent a repetition? (2) Will the punishment or the threat of punishment deter potential offenders? And possibly, (3) Will the criminal be rehabilitated (this process need not be seen as punishment, but may involve it)?

To the utilitarian, the threat of punishment is everything! Every *act* of punishment is an admission that the *threat* of punishment has failed. If the threat is successful, there is no punishment to justify.

Rehabilitative theories consider that crime is a disease and that the criminal is a sick person who needs to be cured. Thus all punishment is cruel and unjustified treatment. "Criminals need therapy, not torture!" might well be the motto of this theory. Of course, we need to confine criminals for society's good, but criminals are not responsible for their deeds and should not be treated as free agents. Benjamin Karpman, a proponent of rehabilitation, puts it this way:

> Basically, criminality is but a symptom of insanity, using the term in its widest generic sense to express unacceptable social behavior based on unconscious motivation flowing from a disturbed instinctive and emotional life, whether this appears in frank psychoses, or in less obvious form in neuroses and unrecognized psychoses. . . . If criminals are products of early environmental influences in the same sense that psychotics and neurotics are, then it should be possible to reach them psychotherapeutically.[1]

In the readings, Karl Menninger holds this position.

The last essay in this section, John Rawls's "Two Concepts of Punishment," is especially interesting because it tries to do justice to both the retributive and the utilitarian theories of punishment. Rawls argues that there is a difference between justifying an *institution* and justifying a given *instance* where the institution is applied. Apply to punishment the questions, "Why do we have a system of punishment?" and "Why are we harming John for his misdeed?" Each requires a different sort of answer. When we seek to justify the institution of punishment, we resort to utilitarian considerations: (1) a society in which the wicked prosper is one that provides inadequate inducement of virtue; and (2) society will function better if some rules are made and enforced than if there are no rules or they are not enforced. But when we seek to justify an individual application of punishment, we resort to retributivist considerations; for example, the criminal committed a breach against the law, which merits a fitting harm in retribution.

NOTE

1. Benjamin Karpman, "Criminal Psychodynamics," *Journal of Criminal Law and Criminology* 47 (1956): 9.

IMMANUEL KANT

THE RIGHT TO PUNISH
Retributivism

In this essay, Kant (see the biography in Part II) gives the classic argument for retributivism (*jus talionis*). The moral law (what he calls the *categorical imperative*) states that a moral principle is such only if every rational person would will it to be universal law. Kant argues that while criminals do not actually will their own punishment, their rational selves will the system of laws that involves the punishment that they deserve. The punishment must be in exact proportion to the severity of the wrongdoing, and in being carried out punishment restores the balance of justice: "The penal law is a categorical imperative; and woe to him who creeps through the serpent-windings of utilitarianism to discover some advantage that may discharge him from the justice of punishment, or even from the due measure of it. . . . For if justice and righteousness perish, human life would no longer have any value in the world. . . . Whoever has committed murder must die" (Kant, *The Philosophy of Law*).

The right of administering punishment, is the right of the sovereign as the supreme power to inflict pain upon a subject on account of a crime committed by him. The head of the state cannot therefore be punished; but his supremacy may be withdrawn from him. Any transgression of the public law which makes him who commits it incapable of being a citizen, constitutes a crime, either simply as a private crime, or also as a *public* crime. Private crimes are dealt with by a civil court; public crimes by a criminal court.—Embezzlement or peculation of money or goods entrusted in trade, fraud in purchase or sale, if done before the eyes of the party who suffers, are private crimes. On the other hand, coining false money or forging bills of exchange, theft, robbery, etc., are public crimes, because the commonwealth, and not merely some particular individual, is endangered thereby. Such crimes may be divided into those of a *base* character and those of a *violent* character.

Judicial or juridical punishment is to be distinguished from natural punishment, in which crime as vice punishes itself, and does not as such come within the cognizance of the legislator. Juridical punishment can never be administered merely as a means for promoting another good, either with regard to the criminal himself or to civil society, but must in all cases be imposed only because the individual on whom it is inflicted *has committed a crime*. For one man ought never to be dealt with merely as a means subservient to the purpose of another, nor be mixed up with the subjects of real right. Against such treatment his inborn personality has a right to protect him, even although he may be condemned to lose his civil personality. He must first be found guilty and *punishable*, before there can be any thought of drawing from his punishment any benefit for himself or his fellow-citizens. The penal law is a categorical imperative; and woe to him who creeps through the serpent-windings of utilitari-

Immanuel Kant, *The Philosophy of Law*, Part II, trans. W. Hastie (Edinburgh: Clark, 1887), pp. 194–98. Latin words have been deleted where they were provided for comparison with translated words.

anism to discover some advantage that may discharge him from the justice of punishment, or even from the due measure of it, according to the pharisaic maxim: "It is better that *one* man should die than that the whole people should perish." For if justice and righteousness perish, human life would no longer have any value in the world.—What, then, is to be said of such a proposal as to keep a criminal alive who has been condemned to death, on his being given to understand that if he agreed to certain dangerous experiments being performed upon him, he would be allowed to survive if he came happily through them? It is argued that physicians might thus obtain new information that would be of value to the commonweal. But a court of justice would repudiate with scorn any proposal of this kind if made to it by the medical faculty; for justice would cease to be justice, if it were bartered away for any consideration whatever.

But what is the mode and measure of punishment which public justice takes as its principle and standard? It is just the principle of equality, by which the pointer of the scale of justice is made to incline no more to the one side than the other. It may be rendered by saying that the undeserved evil which any one commits on another, is to be regarded as perpetrated on himself. Hence it may be said: "If you slander another, you slander yourself; if you steal from another, you steal from yourself; if you strike another, you strike yourself; if you kill another, you kill yourself." This is the right of retaliation (*jus talionis*); and properly understood, it is the only principle which in regulating a public court, as distinguished from mere private judgment, can definitely assign both the quality and the quantity of a just penalty. All other standards are wavering and uncertain; and on account of other considerations involved in them, they contain no principle conformable to the sentence of pure and strict justice. It may appear, however, that difference of social status would not admit the application of the principle of retaliation, which is that of "like with like." But although the application may not in all cases be possible according to the letter, yet as regards the effect it may always be attained in practice, by due regard being given to the disposition and sentiment of the parties in the higher social sphere. Thus a pecuniary penalty on account of a verbal injury, may have

no direct proportion to the injustice of slander; for one who is wealthy may be able to indulge himself in this offence for his own gratification. Yet the attack committed on the honour of the party aggrieved may have its equivalent in the pain inflicted upon the pride of the aggressor, especially if he is condemned by the judgment of the court, not only to retract and apologize, but to submit to some meaner ordeal, as kissing the hand of the injured person. In like manner, if a man of the highest rank has violently assaulted an innocent citizen of the lower orders, he may be condemned not only to apologize but to undergo a solitary and painful imprisonment, whereby, in addition to the discomfort endured, the vanity of the offender would be painfully affected, and the very shame of his position would constitute an adequate retaliation after the principle of "like with like." But how then would we render the statement: "If you *steal* from another, you steal from yourself?" In this way, that whoever steals anything makes the property of all insecure; he therefore robs himself of all security in property, according to the right of retaliation. Such a one has nothing, and can acquire nothing, but he has the will to live; and this is only possible by others supporting him. But as the state should not do this gratuitously, he must for this purpose yield his powers to the state to be used in penal labour; and thus he falls for a time, or it may be for life, into a condition of slavery.—But whoever has committed murder, must *die*. There is, in this case, no juridical substitute or surrogate, that can be given or taken for the satisfaction of justice. There is no *likeness* or proportion between life, however painful, and death; and therefore there is no equality between the crime of murder and the retaliation of it but what is judicially accomplished by the execution of the criminal. His death, however, must be kept free from all maltreatment that would make the humanity suffering in his person loathsome or abominable. Even if a civil society resolved to dissolve itself with the consent of all its members—as might be supposed in the case of a people inhabiting an island resolving to separate and scatter themselves throughout the whole world—the last murderer lying in the prison ought to be executed before the resolution was carried out. This ought to be done in order that every one may realize the desert of his deeds, and that bloodguiltiness may not remain upon the people; for otherwise they might all be regarded as participators in the murder as a public violation of justice.

The equalization of punishment with crime, is therefore only possible by the cognition of the judge extending even to the penalty of death, according to the right of retaliation.

FOR FURTHER REFLECTION

1. Does Kant's version of retributivism seem too harsh? Does it lack a notion of mercy? Explain your answers.

2. Try to formulate Kant's argument that crime causes the scale of justice to be imbalanced and punishment restores the balance? What problems, if any, do you see with the argument?

3. How much weight does Kant place on the notion of free will and responsibility? Does he exaggerate our freedom? That is, are there not crimes partly due to deterministic factors over which we have no control or very little control? Explain.

4. Consider George Orwell's description of a hanging:

It is curious, but till that moment I had never realized what it means to destroy a healthy, conscious man. When I saw the prisoner step aside to avoid the puddle I saw the mystery, the unspeakable wrongness, of cutting a life short when it is in full tide. This man was not dying, he was alive just as we are alive. All the organs of his body were working—bowels digesting food, skin renewing itself, nails growing, tissue forming—all toiling away in solemn foolery. His nails would still be growing when he stood on the drop, when he was falling through the air with a tenth of a second to live. His eyes saw the yellow gravel and the grey walls, and his brain still remembered, foresaw, reasoned, even about puddles. He and we were a party of men walking together, seeing, hearing, feeling, understanding the same world; and in two minutes, with a sudden snap, one of us would be gone—one mind less, one world less. ("A Hanging," *Adelphi,* 1931, quoted in Jonathan Glover's *Causing Death and Saving Lives,* Harmondsworth, Eng.: Penguin, 1977, p. 228)

4. How would Kant or a retributivist respond to these sentiments? Does Orwell point to an unnecessary evil in capital punishment? Explain.

JONATHAN GLOVER

UTILITARIANISM AND PUNISHMENT

Jonathan Glover is professor of philosophy at the University of London. He has written widely on moral and social philosophy. Among his works are *Responsibility* (1970), *Causing Death and Saving Lives* (1977), and *What Kind of People Should There Be?* (1984).

In this essay, Glover provides a utilitarian view of punishment and specifically of capital punishment. He rejects both the absolutist abolitionist view that prohibits capital punishment in all instances and the retributivist view since it does not increase utility. Glover concludes his analysis by opposing capital punishment at this time because it has not been shown to be an effective deterrent.

The debate about capital punishment for murder is, emotionally at least, dominated by two absolutist views. On the retributive view, the murderer must be given the punishment he deserves, which is death. On the other view, analogous to pacifism about war, there is in principle no possibility of justifying capital punishment: in execution there is only "the unspeakable wrongness of cutting a life short when it is in full tide." Supporters of these two approaches agree only in rejecting the serpent-windings of utilitarianism.

Let us look first at the retributive view. According to retributivism in its purest form, the aim of punishment is quite independent of any beneficial social consequences it may have. To quote Kant again:

> Even if a Civil Society resolved to dissolve itself with the consent of all its members —as might be supposed in the case of a people inhabiting an island resolving to separate and scatter themselves throughout the whole world—the last Murderer lying in the prison ought to be executed before the resolution was carried out. This ought to be done in order that everyone may realize the desert of his deeds, and that

blood-guiltiness may not remain upon the people; for otherwise they might all be regarded as participators in the murder as a public violation of justice.

This view of punishment, according to which it has a value independent of its contribution to reducing the crime rate, is open to the objection that acting on it leads to what many consider to be pointless suffering. To impose suffering or deprivation on someone, or to take his life, is something that those of us who are not retributivists think needs very strong justification in terms of benefits, either to the person concerned or to other people. The retributivist has to say either that the claims of justice can make it right to harm someone where no one benefits, or else to cite the curiously metaphysical "benefits" of justice being done, such as Kant's concern that we should have "blood-guiltiness" removed. I have no way of refuting these positions, as they seem to involve no clear intellectual mistake. I do not expect to win the agreement of those who hold them, and I am simply presupposing the other view, that there is already enough misery in the world, and that adding to it requires a justification in terms of non-metaphysical benefits to people.

This is not to rule out retributive moral principles perhaps playing a limiting role in a general theory of punishment. There is a lot to be said for the retributive restrictions that *only* those who deserve punishment should receive it and that they should never get more punishment than they deserve. (The case for this, which at least partly rests on utilitarian considerations, has been powerfully argued by H. L. A. Hart.)[1] But the approach to be adopted here rules out using retributive considerations to justify any punishment not already justifiable in terms of social benefits. In particular it rules out the argument that capital punishment can be justified, whether or not it reduces the crime rate, because the criminal deserves it.

This approach also has the effect of casting doubt on another way of defending capital punishment, which was forthrightly expressed by Lord Denning: "The ultimate justification of any punishment is not that it is a deterrent, but that it is the emphatic denunciation by the community of a crime: and from this point of view, there are some murders which, in the present state of public opinion, demand the most emphatic denunciation of all, namely the death penalty.[2]" The question here is whether the point of the denunciation is to reduce the murder rate, in which case this turns out after all to be a utilitarian justification, or whether denunciation is an end in itself. If it is an end in itself, it starts to look like the retributive view in disguise, and should be rejected for the same reasons.

If we reject retribution for its own sake as a justification for capital punishment, we are left with two alternative general approaches to the question. One is an absolute rejection in principle of any possibility of capital punishment being justified. . . . The other is the rather more messy approach, broadly utilitarian in character, of weighing up likely social costs and benefits.

1. THE ABSOLUTIST REJECTION OF CAPITAL PUNISHMENT

To some people, it is impossible to justify the act of killing a fellow human being. They are absolute paci-fists about war and are likely to think of capital punishment as "judicial murder." They will sympathize with Beccaria's question: "Is it not absurd that the laws which detest and punish homicide, in order to prevent murder, publicly commit murder themselves.?"

The test of whether an opponent of capital punishment adopts this absolutist position is whether he would still oppose it if it could be shown to save many more lives than it cost: if, say, every execution deterred a dozen potential murderers. The absolutist, unlike the utilitarian opponent of the death penalty, would be unmoved by any such evidence. This question brings out the links between the absolutist position and the acts and omissions doctrine. For those of us who reject the acts and omissions doctrine, the deaths we fail to prevent have to be given weight, as well as the deaths we cause by execution. So those of us who do not accept the acts and omissions doctrine cannot be absolutist opponents of capital punishment.

There is a variant on the absolutist position which at first sight seems not to presuppose the acts and omissions doctrine. On this view, while saving a potential murder victim is in itself as important as not killing a murderer, there is something so cruel about the kind of death involved in capital punishment that this rules out the possibility of its being justified. Those of us who reject the acts and omissions doctrine have to allow that sometimes there can be side-effects associated with an act of killing, but not with failure to save a life, which can be sufficiently bad to make a substantial moral difference between the two. When this view is taken of the cruelty of the death penalty, it is not usually the actual method of execution which is objected to, though this can seem important, as in the case where international pressure on General Franco led him to substitute shooting for the garrotte. What seems peculiarly cruel and horrible about capital punishment is that the condemned man has the period of waiting, knowing how and when he is to be killed. Many of us would rather die suddenly than linger for weeks or months knowing we were fatally ill, and the condemned man's position is several degrees worse than that of the person given a few months to live by doctors. He has the additional horror of knowing exactly when he will die, and of knowing that his death will be in a ritualized killing by other people, symbolizing his ultimate rejection by the members of his community. The whole of his life may seem to have a different and horrible meaning when he sees it leading up to this end.

For reasons of this kind, capital punishment can plausibly be claimed to fall under the United States constitution's ban on "cruel and unusual punishments," so long as the word "unusual" is not interpreted too strictly. The same reasons make the death penalty a plausible candidate for falling under a rather similar ethical ban, which has been expressed by H. L. A. Hart: "There are many different ways in which we think it morally incumbent on us to *qualify* or *limit* the pursuit of the utilitarian goal by methods of punishment. Some punishments are ruled out as too barbarous to use *whatever their social utility*[3]" (final italics mine). Because of the extreme cruelty of capital punishment, many of us would, if forced to make a choice between two horrors, prefer to be suddenly murdered rather than be sentenced to death and executed. This is what makes it seem reasonable to say that the absolutist rejection of the death penalty need not rest on the acts and omissions doctrine.

But this appearance is illusory. The special awfulness of capital punishment may make an execution even more undesirable than a murder (though many would disagree on the grounds that this is outweighed by the desirability that the guilty rather than the innocent should die). Even if we accept that an execution is worse than an average murder, it does not follow from this that capital punishment is too barbarous to use *whatever its social utility*. For supposing a single execution deterred many murders? Or suppose that some of the murders deterred would themselves have been as cruel as an execution? When we think of the suffering imposed in a famous kidnapping case, where the mother received her son's ear through the post, we may feel uncertain even that capital punishment is more cruel than some "lesser" crimes than murder. The view that some kinds of suffering are too great to impose, whatever their social utility, rules out the possibility of justifying them, however much more suffering they would prevent. And this does presuppose the acts and omissions doctrine, and so excludes some of us even from this version of absolutism.

2. A UTILITARIAN APPROACH

It is often supposed that the utilitarian alternative to absolutism is simply one of adopting an unqualified maximizing policy. On such a view, the death penalty would be justified if, and only if, it was reasonable to think the number of lives saved exceeded the number of executions. (The question of what to do where the numbers exactly balance presupposes a fineness of measurement that is unattainable in these matters.) On any utilitarian view, numbers of lives saved must be a very important consideration. But there are various special features that justify the substantial qualification of a maximizing policy.

The special horror of the period of waiting for execution may not justify the absolutist rejection of the death penalty, but it is a powerful reason for thinking that an execution may normally cause more misery than a murder, and so for thinking that, if capital punishment is to be justified, it must do better than break even when lives saved through deterrence are compared with lives taken by the executioner.

This view is reinforced when we think of some of the other side-effects of the death penalty. It must be appalling to be told that your husband, wife or child has been murdered, but this is surely less bad than the experience of waiting a month or two for your husband, wife or child to be executed. And those who think that the suffering of the murderer himself matters less than that of an innocent victim will perhaps not be prepared to extend this view to the suffering of the murderer's parents, wife and children.

There is also the possibility of mistakenly executing an innocent man, something which it is very probable happened in the case of Timothy Evans. The German Federal Ministry of Justice is quoted in the Council of Europe's report on *The Death Penalty in European Countries* as saying that in the hundred years to 1953, there were twenty-seven death sentences "now established or presumed" to be miscarriages of justice. This point is often used as an argument against capital punishment, but what is often not noticed is that its force must depend on the special horrors of execution as compared with other forms of death, including being murdered. For the victim of murder is innocent too, and he also has no form of redress. It is only the (surely correct) assumption that an innocent man faces something much worse in execution than in murder that gives this argument its claim to prominence in this debate. For, otherwise, the rare cases of innocent men being executed would be completely overshadowed by the numbers of innocent men being murdered. (Unless, of course, the acts and omissions doctrine is again at work here, for execution is something that we, as a community, *do,* while a higher murder rate is something we at most *allow.*)

The death penalty also has harmful effects on people other than the condemned man and his family. For most normal people, to be professionally involved with executions, whether as judge, prison warder or chaplain, or executioner, must be highly disturbing. Arthur Koestler quotes the case of the executioner Ellis, who attempted suicide a few weeks after he executed a sick woman "whose insides fell out before she vanished through the trap.[4]" (Though the chances must be very small of the experience of Mr. Pierrepoint, who describes in his autobiography how he had to execute a friend with whom he often sang duets in a pub.[5]) And there are wider effects on society at large. When there is capital punishment, we are all involved in the horrible business of a long-premeditated killing, and most of us will to some degree share in the emotional response George Orwell had so strongly when he had to be present. It cannot be good for children at school to know that there is an execution at the prison down the road. And there is another bad effect, drily stated in the *Report of the Royal Commission on Capital Punishment:* "No doubt the ambition that prompts an average of five applications a week for the post of hangman, and the craving that draws a crowd to the prison where a notorious murderer is being executed, reveal psychological qualities that no state would wish to foster in its citizens."

Capital punishment is also likely to operate erratically. Some murderers are likely to go free because the death penalty makes juries less likely to convict. (Charles Dickens, in a newspaper article quoted in the 1868 Commons debate, gave the example of a forgery case, where a jury found a £10 note to be worth 39 shillings, in order to save the forger's life.) There are also great problems in operating a reprieve system without arbitrariness, say, in deciding whether being pregnant or having a young baby should qualify a woman for a reprieve.

Finally, there is the drawback that the retention or re-introduction of capital punishment contributes to a tradition of cruel and horrible punishment which we might hope would wither away. Nowadays we never think of disembowelling people or chopping off their hands as a punishment. Even if these punishments would be specially effective in deterring some very serious crimes, they are not regarded as a real possibility. To many of us, it seems that the utilitarian benefits from this situation outweigh the loss of any deterrent power they might have if re-introduced for some repulsive crime like kidnapping. And the longer we leave capital punishment in abeyance, the more its use will seem as out of the question as the no more cruel punishment of mutilation. (At this point, I come near to Hart's view that some punishments are too barbarous to use whatever their social utility. The difference is that I think that arguments for and against a punishment should be based on social utility, but that a widespread view that some things are unthinkable is itself of great social utility.)

For these reasons, a properly thought-out utilitarianism does not enjoin an unqualified policy of seeking the minimum loss of life, as the no trade-off view does. Capital punishment has its own special cruelties and horrors, which change the whole position. In order to be justified, it must be shown, with good evidence, that it has a deterrent effect not obtainable by less awful means, and one which is quite substantial rather than marginal.

3. DETERRENCE AND MURDER

The arguments over whether capital punishment deters murder more effectively than less drastic methods are of two kinds: statistical and intuitive. The statistical arguments are based on various kinds of comparisons of murder rates. Rates are compared before and after abolition in a country, and, where possible, further comparisons are made with rates after reintroduction of capital punishment. Rates are compared in neighbouring countries, or neighbouring states of the U.S.A., with and without the death penalty. I am not a statistician and have no special competence to discuss the issue, but will merely purvey the received opinion of those who have looked into the matter. Those who have studied the figures are agreed that there is no striking correlation between the absence of capital punishment and any alteration in the curve of the murder rate. Having agreed on this point, they then fall into two schools. On one view, we can conclude that capital punishment is not a greater deterrent to murder than the prison sentences that are substituted for it. On the other, more cautious, view, we can only conclude that we do not know that capital punishment is a deterrent. I shall not attempt to choose between these interpretations. For, given that capital punishment is justified only where there is good evidence that it is a substantial deterrent, either interpretation fails to support the case for it.

If the statistical evidence were conclusive that capital punishment did not deter more than milder punishments, this would leave no room for any further discussion. But, since the statistical evidence may be inconclusive, many people feel there is room left for intuitive arguments. Some of these deserve examination. The intuitive case was forcefully stated in 1864 by Sir James Fitzjames Stephen:[6]

> No other punishment deters men so effectually from committing crimes as the punishment of death. This is one of those propositions which it is difficult to prove, simply because they are in themselves more obvious than any proof can make them. It is possible to display ingenuity in arguing against it, but that is all. The whole experience of mankind is in the other direction. The threat of instant death is the one to which resort has always been made when there was an absolute necessity for producing some result. . . . No one goes to certain inevitable death except by compulsion. Put the matter the other way. Was there ever yet a criminal who, when sentenced to death and brought out to die, would refuse the offer of a commutation of his sentence for the severest secondary punishment? Surely not. Why is this? It can only be because 'All that a man has will he give for his life.' In any secondary punishment, however

terrible, there is hope; but death is death; its terrors cannot be described more forcibly.

These claims turn out when scrutinized to be much more speculative and doubtful than they at first sight appear.

The first doubt arises when Stephen talks of "certain inevitable death." The Royal Commission, in their *Report,* after quoting the passage from Stephen above, quote figures to show that, in the fifty years from 1900 to 1949, there was in England and Wales one execution for every twelve murders known to the police. In Scotland in the same period there was less than one execution for every twenty-five murders known to the police. Supporters of Stephen's view could supplement their case by advocating more death sentences and fewer reprieves, or by optimistic speculations about better police detection or greater willingness of juries to convict. But the reality of capital punishment as it was in these countries, unmodified by such recommendations and speculations, was not one where the potential murderer faced certain, inevitable death. This may incline us to modify Stephen's estimate of its deterrent effect, unless we buttress his view with the further speculation that a fair number of potential murderers falsely believed that what they would face was certain, inevitable death.

The second doubt concerns Stephen's talk of "the threat of instant death." The reality again does not quite fit this. By the time the police conclude their investigation, the case is brought to trial, and verdict and sentence are followed by appeal, petition for reprieve and then execution, many months have probably elapsed, and when this time factor is added to the low probability of the murderers being executed, the picture looks very different. For we often have a time bias, being less affected by threats of future catastrophes than by threats of instant ones. The certainty of immediate death is one thing; it is another thing merely to increase one's chances of death in the future. Unless this were so, no one would smoke or take on such high-risk jobs as diving in the North Sea.

There is another doubt when Stephen very plausibly says that virtually all criminals would prefer life imprisonment to execution. The difficulty is over whether this entitles us to conclude that it is therefore a more effective deterrent. For there is the possibility that, compared with the long term of imprisonment that is the alternative, capital punishment is what may appropriately be called an "overkill." It may be that, for those who will be deterred by threat of punishment, a long prison sentence is sufficient deterrent. I am not suggesting that this is so, but simply that it is an open question whether a worse alternative here generates any additional deterrent effect. The answer is *not* intuitively obvious.

Stephen's case rests on the speculative psychological assumptions that capital punishment is not an overkill compared with a prison sentence; and that its additional deterrent effect is not obliterated by time bias, nor by the low probability of execution, nor by a combination of these factors. Or else it must be assumed that, where the additional deterrent effect would be obliterated by the low probability of death, either on its own or in combination with time bias, the potential murderer thinks the probability is higher than it is. Some of these assumptions may be true, but, when they are brought out into the open, it is by no means obvious that the required combination of them can be relied upon.

Supporters of the death penalty also sometimes use what David A. Conway, in his valuable discussion of this issue, calls "the best-bet argument."[7] On this view, since there is no certainty whether or not capital punishment reduces the number of murders, either decision about it involves gambling with lives. It is suggested that it is better to gamble with the lives of murderers than with the lives of their innocent potential victims. This presupposes the attitude, rejected here, that a murder is a greater evil than the execution of a murderer. But, since this attitude probably has overwhelmingly widespread support, it is worth noting that, even if it is accepted, the best-bet argument is unconvincing. This is because, as Conway has pointed out, it overlooks the fact that we are not choosing between the chance of a murderer dying and the chance of a victim dying. In leaving the death penalty, we are opting for the certainty of the murderer dying which we hope will give us a chance of a potential victim being saved. This would look like a good bet only if we thought an execution substantially preferable to a murder and either the statistical

evidence or the intuitive arguments made the effectiveness of the death penalty as a deterrent look reasonably likely.

Since the statistical studies do not give any clear indication that capital punishment makes any difference to the number of murders committed, the only chance of its supporters discharging the heavy burden of justification would be if the intuitive arguments were extremely powerful. We might then feel justified in supposing that other factors distorted the murder rate, masking the substantial deterrent effect of capital punishment. The intuitive arguments, presented as the merest platitudes, turn out to be speculative and unobvious. I conclude that the case for capital punishment as a substantial deterrent fails.

NOTES

1. H. L. A. Hart, "Prolegomenon to the Principles of Punishment," *Proceedings of the Aristotelian Society,* 1959–1960.
2. Quoted in the *Report of the Royal Commission on Capital Punishment,* 1953.
3. H. L. A. Hart, "Murder and the Principles of Punishment," *Northwestern Law Review,* 1958.
4. Arthur Koestler, *Reflections on Hanging* (London, 1956).
5. Albert Pierrepoint, *Executioner: Pierrepoint* (London, 1974).
6. James Fitzjames Stephen, "Capital Punishments," *Fraser's Magazine,* 1864.
7. David A. Conway, "Capital Punishment and Deterrence," *Philosophy and Public Affairs,* 1974.

FOR FURTHER REFLECTION

1. Compare Glover's utilitarian view of punishment with Kant's retributivist view. Which do you favor as a theory of punishment? Why?
2. Does utilitarianism have any serious problems? Suppose there was a town hostilely divided between Ethnic Groups A and B. Further suppose a girl in Group B claimed that a man from Group A had raped her and this caused the citizens in B to begin a riot. The situation was getting out of hand and people were getting killed.

You, as the sheriff, could stop the riot by framing an innocent derelict from Group A and, after a setup trial, hang him in the town square. No one would know that the man was innocent (except you, and you won't tell). You are virtually certain that doing this will quell the riot and save many lives. It will do great utilitarian good and serve as a deterrent against future acts of this kind. What should you do?

KARL MENNINGER
⮌

THE CRIME OF PUNISHMENT
The Humanitarian Theory

Karl Menninger (1893–1990) is a cofounder of the Menninger Clinic in Kansas and the author of several books on psychoanalysis. In this essay, he argues that criminal behavior is not something criminals do of their own free will. Criminals are helpless victims who act in maladaptive and destructive ways. Crime is an illness that should be treated with "education, medication, counseling and training." Menninger urges us to change our present punitive attitude to a "therapeutic attitude" where we see crime as a "state of impaired functioning of such a nature that the public expects the sufferer to repair to the physician for help." The criminal should be treated as a patient in the care of a physician.

Few words in our language arrest our attention as do "crime," "violence," "revenge," and "injustice." We abhor crime; we adore justice; we boast that we live by the rule of law. Violence and vengefulness we repudiate as unworthy of our civilization, and we assume this sentiment to be unanimous among all human beings.

Yet crime continues to be a national disgrace and a world-wide problem. It is threatening, alarming, wasteful, expensive, abundant, and apparently increasing! In actuality it is decreasing in frequency of occurrence, but it is certainly increasing in visibility and the reactions of the public to it.

Our system for controlling crime is ineffective, unjust, expensive. Prisons seem to operate with revolving doors—the same people going in and out and in and out. *Who cares?*

Our city jails and inhuman reformatories and wretched prisons are jammed. They are known to be unhealthy, dangerous, immoral, indecent, crime-breeding dens of iniquity. Not everyone has smelled them, as some of us have. Not many have heard the groans and the curses. Not everyone has seen the hate and despair in a thousand blank, hollow faces. But, in a way, we all know how miserable prisons are. *We want them to be that way.* And they are. *Who cares?*

Professional and big-time criminals prosper as never before. Gambling syndicates flourish. White-collar crime may even exceed all others, but goes undetected in the majority of cases. We are all being robbed and we know who the robbers are. They live nearby. *Who cares?*

The public filches millions of dollars worth of food and clothing from stores, towels and sheets from hotels, jewelry and knick-knacks from shops. The public steals, and the same public pays it back in higher prices. *Who cares?*

Time and time again somebody shouts about this state of affairs, just as I am shouting now. The magazines shout. The newspapers shout. The television and radio commentators shout (or at least they "deplore"). Psychologists, sociologists, leading jurists, wardens, and intelligent police chiefs join the chorus. Governors and mayors and Congressmen are sometimes heard. They shout that the situation is bad, bad, bad, and getting worse. Some suggested that we immediately replace obsolete procedures with scientific methods. A few shout contrary sentiments. Do the clear indications derived from scientific discovery for appropriate changes continue to fall on deaf ears? Why is the public so long-suffering, so apathetic, and thereby so continuingly self-destructive? How many Presidents (and other citizens) do we have to lose before we do something?

The public behaves as a sick patient does when a dreaded treatment is proposed for his ailment. We all know how the aching tooth may suddenly quiet down in the dentist's office, or the abdominal pain disappear in the surgeon's examining room. Why should a sufferer seek relief and shun it? Is it merely the fear of the pain of the treatment? Is it the fear of unknown complications? Is it distrust of the doctor's ability? All of these, no doubt.

But, as Freud made so incontestably clear, the sufferer is always somewhat deterred by a kind of subversive, internal opposition to the work of cure. He suffers on the one hand from the pains of his affliction and yearns to get well. But he suffers at the same time from traitorous impulses that fight against the accomplishment of any change in himself, even recovery! Like Hamlet, he wonders whether it may be better after all to suffer the familiar pains and aches associated with the old method than to face the complications of a new and strange, even though possibly better, way of handling things.

The inescapable conclusion is that society *wants* crime, *needs* crime, and gains definite satisfactions from the present mishandling of it! We condemn crime; we punish offenders for it; but we need it. The crime and punishment ritual is a part of our lives. We need crimes to wonder at, to enjoy vicariously, to discuss and speculate about, and to publicly deplore. We need criminals to identify ourselves with, to envy secretly, and to punish stoutly. They do for us the forbidden, illegal things we *wish* to do, and, like scapegoats of old, they bear the burdens of our displaced guilt and punishment—"the iniquities of us all." . . .

Fifty years ago, Winston Churchill declared that the mood and temper of the public in regard to crime and criminals is one of the unfailing tests of the civilization of any country. Judged by this standard, how civilized are we?

The chairman of the President's National Crime Commission . . . declared recently that organized crime flourishes in America because enough of the public wants its services, and most citizens are apathetic about its impact. It will continue uncurbed as long as Americans accept it as inevitable and, in some instances, desirable.

Are there steps that we can take which will reduce the aggressive stabs and self-destructive lurches of our less well-managing fellow men? Are there ways to prevent and control the grosser violations, other than the clumsy traditional maneuvers which we have inherited? These depend basically upon intimidation and slow-motion torture. We call it punishment, and justify it with our "feeling." We know it doesn't work.

Yes, there *are* better ways. There are steps that could be taken; some *are* taken. But we move too slowly. Much better use, it seems to me, could be made of the members of my profession and other behavioral scientists than having them deliver courtroom pronunciamentos. The consistent use of a diagnostic clinic would enable trained workers to lay what they can learn about an offender before the judge who would know best how to implement the recommendation.

This would no doubt lead to a transformation of prisons, if not to their total disappearance in their present form and function. Temporary and permanent detention will perhaps always be necessary for a few, especially the professionals, but this could be more effectively and economically performed with new types of "facility" (that strange, awkward word for institution).

I assume it to be a matter of common and general agreement that our object in all this is to protect the community from a repetition of the offense by the most economical method consonant with our other purposes. Our "other purposes" include the desire to prevent these offenses from occurring, to reclaim offenders for social usefulness, if possible, and to detain them in protective custody, if reclamation is *not* possible. But how?

The treatment of human failure or dereliction by the infliction of pain is still used and believed in by many nonmedical people. "Spare the rod and spoil the child" is still considered wise counsel by many.

Whipping is still used by many secondary schoolmasters in England, I am informed, to stimulate study, attention, and the love of learning. Whipping was long a traditional treatment for the "crime" of disobedience on the part of children, pupils, servants, apprentices, employees. And slaves were treated for centuries by flogging for such offenses as weariness, confusion, stupidity, exhaustion, fear, grief, and even overcheerfulness. It was assumed and stoutly defended that these "treatments" cured conditions for which they were administered.

Meanwhile, scientific medicine was acquiring many new healing methods and devices. Doctors can now transplant organs and limbs; they can remove brain tumors and cure incipient cancers; they can halt pneumonia, meningitis, and other infections; they can correct deformities and repair breaks and tears and scars. But these wonderful achievements are accomplished on *willing* subjects, people who voluntarily ask for help by even heroic measures. And the reader will be wondering, no doubt, whether doctors can do anything with or for people who *do not want* to be treated at all, in any way! Can doctors cure willful aberrant behavior? Are we to believe that crime is a *disease* that can be reached by scientific measures? Isn't it merely "natural meanness" that makes all of us do wrong things at times even when we "know

better"? And are not self-control, moral stamina, and will power the things needed? Surely there is no medical treatment for the lack of those!

Let me answer this carefully, for much misunderstanding accumulates here. I would say that according to the prevalent understanding of the words, crime is *not* a disease. Neither is it an illness, although I think it *should* be! It *should* be treated, and it could be; but it mostly isn't.

These enigmatic statements are simply explained. Diseases are undesired states of being which have been described and defined by doctors, usually given Greek or Latin appellations, and treated by long-established physical and pharmacological formulae. Illness, on the other hand, is best defined as a state of impaired functioning of such a nature that the public expects the sufferer to repair to the physician for help. The illness may prove to be a disease; more often it is only vague and nameless misery, but something which doctors, not lawyers, teachers, or preachers, are supposed to be able and willing to help.

When the community begins to look upon the expression of aggressive violence as the symptom of an illness or as indicative of illness, it will be because it believes doctors can do something to correct such a condition. At present, some better-informed individuals do believe and expect this. However angry at or sorry for the offender, they want him "treated" in an effective way so that he will cease to be a danger to them. And they know that traditional punishment, "treatment-punishment," will not effect this.

What *will?* What effective treatment is there for such violence? It will surely have to begin with motivating or stimulating or arousing in a cornered individual the wish and hope and intention to change his methods of dealing with the realities of life. Can this be done by education, medication, counseling, training? I would answer *yes.* It can be done successfully in a majority of cases, if undertaken in time.

The present penal system and the existing legal philosophy do not stimulate or even expect such a change to take place in the criminal. Yet change is what medical science always aims for. The prisoner, like the doctor's other patients, should emerge from his treatment experience a different person, differently equipped, differently functioning, and headed in a different direction than when he began the treatment.

It is natural for the public to doubt that this can be accomplished with criminals. But remember that the public *used* to doubt that change could be effected in the mentally ill. No one a hundred years ago believed mental illness to be curable. Today *all* people know (or should know) that *mental illness is curable* in the great majority of instances and that the prospects and rapidity of cure are directly related to the availability and intensity of proper treatment.

The forms and techniques of psychiatric treatment used today number in the hundreds. No one patient requires or receives all forms, but each patient is studied with respect to his particular needs, his basic assets, his interests, and his special difficulties. A therapeutic team may embrace a dozen workers—as in a hospital setting—or it may narrow down to the doctor and the spouse. Clergymen, teachers, relatives, friends, and even fellow patients often participate informally but helpfully in the process of readaptation.

All of the participants in this effort to bring about a favorable change in the patient—i.e., in his vital balance and life program—are imbued with what we may call a *therapeutic attitude.* This is one in direct antithesis to attitudes of avoidance, ridicule, scorn, or punitiveness. Hostile feelings toward the subject, however justified by his unpleasant and even destructive behavior, are not in the curriculum of therapy or in the therapist. This does not mean that therapists approve of the offensive and obnoxious behavior of the patient; they distinctly disapprove of it. But they recognize it as symptomatic of continued imbalance and disorganization, which is what they are seeking to change. They distinguish between disapproval, penalty, price, and punishment.

Doctors charge fees; they impose certain "penalties" or prices, but they have long since put aside primitive attitudes of retaliation toward offensive patients. A patient may cough in the doctor's face or may vomit on the office rug; a patient may curse or scream or even struggle in the extremity of his pain. But these acts are not "punished." Doctors and nurses have no time or thought for inflicting unnecessary pain even upon patients who may be difficult, disagreeable, provocative, and even dangerous. It is their

duty to care for them, to try to make them well, and to prevent them from doing themselves or others harm. This requires love, not hate. This is the deepest meaning of the therapeutic attitude. Every doctor knows this; every worker in a hospital or clinic knows it (or should).

There is another element in the therapeutic attitude. It is the quality of hopefulness. If no one believes that the patient can get well, if no one—not even the doctor—has any hope, there probably won't be any recovery. Hope is just as important as love in the therapeutic attitude.

"But you were talking about the mentally ill," readers may interject, "those poor, confused, bereft, frightened individuals who yearn for help from you doctors and nurses. Do you mean to imply that willfully perverse individuals, our criminals, can be similarly reached and rehabilitated? Do you really believe that effective treatment of the sort you visualize can be applied to people *who do not want any help,* who are so willfully vicious, so well aware of the wrongs they are doing, so lacking in penitence or even common decency that punishment seems to be the only thing left?"

Do I believe there is effective treatment for offenders, and that they *can* be changed? *Most certainly and definitely I do.* Not all cases, to be sure; there are also some physical afflictions which we cannot cure at the moment. Some provision has to be made for incurables—pending new knowledge—and these will include some offenders. But I believe the majority of them would prove to be curable. The willfulness and the viciousness of offenders are part of the thing for which they have to be treated. These must not thwart the therapeutic attitude.

It is simply not true that most of them are "fully aware" of what they are doing, nor is it true that they want no help from anyone, although some of them say so. Prisoners are individuals: Some want treatment, some do not. Some don't know what treatment is. Many are utterly despairing and hopeless. Where treatment is made available in institutions, many prisoners seek it even with the full knowledge that doing so will not lessen their sentences. In some prisons, seeking treatment by prisoners is frowned upon by the officials.

Various forms of treatment are even now being tried in some progressive courts and prisons over the country—educational, social, industrial, religious, recreational, and psychological treatments. Socially acceptable behavior, new work-play opportunities, new identity and companion patterns all help toward community reacceptance. Some parole officers and some wardens have been extremely ingenious in developing these modalities of rehabilitation and reconstruction—more than I could list here even if I knew them all. But some are trying. The secret of success in all programs, however, is the replacement of the punitive attitude with a therapeutic attitude.

Offenders with propensities for impulsive and predatory aggression should not be permitted to live among us unrestrained by some kind of social control. *But the great majority of offenders, even "criminals," should never become prisoners if we want to "cure" them.*

There are now throughout the country many citizens' action groups and programs for the prevention and control of crime and delinquency. With such attitudes of inquiry and concern, the public could acquire information (and incentive) leading to a change of feeling about crime and criminals. It will discover how unjust is much so-called "justice," how baffled and frustrated many judges are by the ossified rigidity of old-fashioned, obsolete laws and state constitutions which effectively prevent the introduction of sensible procedures to replace useless, harmful ones.

I want to proclaim to the public that things are not what it wishes them to be, and will only become so if it will take an interest in the matter and assume some responsibility for its own self-protection.

Will the public listen?

If the public does become interested, it will realize that we must have more facts, more trial projects, more checked results. It will share the dismay of the President's Commission in finding that no one knows much about even the incidence of crime with any definiteness or statistical accuracy.

The average citizen finds it difficult to see how any research would in any way change his mind about a man who brutally murders his children. But just such inconceivably awful acts most dramati-cally point up the need for research. Why should—how can—a man become so dreadful as that in our culture? How is such a man made? Is it comprehensible that he can be born to become so depraved?

There are thousands of questions regarding crime and public protection which deserve scientific study. What makes some individuals maintain their interior equilibrium by one kind of disturbance of the social structure rather than by another kind, one that would have landed him in a hospital? Why do some individuals specialize in certain types of crime? Why do so many young people reared in areas of delinquency and poverty and bad example never become habitual delinquents? (Perhaps this is a more important question than why some of them do.)

The public has a fascination for violence, and clings tenaciously to its yen for vengeance, blind and deaf to the expense, futility, and dangerousness of the resulting penal system. But we are bound to hope that this will yield in time to the persistent, penetrating light of intelligence and accumulating scientific knowledge. The public will grow increasingly ashamed of its cry for retaliation, its persistent demand to punish. This is its crime, *our* crime against criminals—and, incidentally, our crime against ourselves. For before we can diminish our sufferings from the ill-controlled aggressive assaults of fellow citizens, we must renounce the philosophy of punishment, the obsolete, vengeful penal attitude. In its place we would seek a comprehensive constructive social attitude—therapeutic in some instances, restraining in some instances, but preventive in its total social impact.

In the last analysis this becomes a question of personal morals and values. No matter how glorified or how piously disguised, vengeance as a human motive must be personally repudiated by each and every one of us. This is the message of old religions and new psychiatries. Unless this message is heard, unless we, the people—the man on the street, the housewife in the home—can give up our delicious satisfactions in opportunities for vengeful retaliation on scapegoats, we cannot expect to preserve our peace, our public safety, or our mental health.

FOR FURTHER REFLECTION

1. What are the strengths and weaknesses of Menninger's views?
2. Does Menninger's theory undermine human freedom? Can the therapeutic approach be just as "oppressive" as retributivism? Is it really a disguised form of punishment? Explain your position.

C. S. LEWIS

AGAINST THE HUMANITARIAN THEORY OF REHABILITATION

Clive Staples Lewis (1898–1963) was a professor of medieval and Renaissance English at Cambridge University. He wrote children's literature and Christian philosophy. Among his works are *The Problem of Pain* (1944), *The Abolition of Man* (1947), and *Miracles* (1963).

In this essay, Lewis argues against views such as Menninger's, which he sarcastically calls "the Humanitarian theory of Punishment," for in spite of its therapeutic claims, it really controls and manipulates the "diseased" person as much as—if not more than—any usual punishment. Lewis argues that punishment must be linked to deserts and that people, including criminals, should be treated with respect as free agents. To treat them as sick and diseased rather than as responsible agents is to deny their freedom and dignity.

In England we have lately had a controversy about Capital Punishment. I do not know whether a murderer is more likely to repent and make a good end on the gallows a few weeks after his trial or in the prison infirmary thirty years later. I do not know whether the fear of death is an indispensable deterrent. I need not, for the purpose of this article, decide whether it is a morally permissible deterrent. Those are questions which I propose to leave untouched. My subject is not Capital Punishment in particular, but that theory of punishment in general which the controversy showed to be almost universal among my fellow-countrymen.

It may be called the Humanitarian Theory. Those who hold it think that it is mild and merciful. In this I believe that they are seriously mistaken. I believe that the "Humanity" which it claims is a dangerous illusion and disguises the possibility of cruelty and injustice without end. I urge a return to the traditional or Retributive theory not solely, nor even primarily, in the interests of society but in the interests of the criminal.

According to the Humanitarian theory, to punish a man because he deserves it, and as much as he deserves, is mere revenge, and, therefore, barbarous and immoral. It is maintained that the only legitimate motives for punishing are the desire to deter others by example or to mend the criminal. When this theory is combined, as frequently happens, with the belief that all crime is more or less pathological, the idea of mending tails off into that of healing or curing and punishment becomes therapeutic. Thus it appears at first sight that we have passed from the harsh and self-righteous notion of giving the wicked their deserts to the charitable and enlightened one of tending the psychologically sick. What could be more amiable? One little point which is taken for granted in this theory needs, however, to be made explicit. The things done to the criminal, even if they are called cures, will be just as compulsory as they were in the old days when we called them punishments. If a tendency to steal can be cured by psychotherapy, the thief will no doubt be forced to undergo the treatment. Otherwise, society cannot continue.

My contention is that this doctrine, merciful though it appears, really means that each one of us, from the moment he breaks the law, is deprived of the rights of a human being.

The reason is this. The Humanitarian theory removes from Punishment the concept of Desert. But the concept of Desert is the only connecting link between punishment and justice. It is only as deserved or undeserved that a sentence can be just or unjust. I do not here contend that the question "Is it deserved?" is the only one we can reasonably ask about a punishment. We may very properly ask whether it is likely to deter others and to reform the criminal. But neither of these two last questions is a question about justice. There is no sense in talking about a "just deterrent" or a "just cure." We demand of a deterrent not whether it is just but whether it will deter. We demand of a cure not whether it is just but whether it succeeds. Thus when we cease to consider what the criminal deserves and consider only what will cure him or deter others, we have tacitly removed him from the sphere of justice altogether; instead of a person, a subject of rights, we now have a mere object; a patient, a "case."

The distinction will become clearer if we ask who will be qualified to determine sentences when sentences are no longer held to derive their propriety from the criminal's deservings. On the old view the problem of fixing the right sentence was a moral problem. Accordingly, the judge who did it was a person trained in jurisprudence; trained, that is, in a science which deals with rights and duties, and which, in origin at least, was consciously accepting guidance from the Law of Nature, and from Scripture. We must admit that in the actual penal code of most countries at most times these high originals were so much modified by local custom, class interests, and utilitarian concessions, as to be very imperfectly recognizable. But the code was never in principle, and not always in fact, beyond the control of the conscience of the society. And when (say, in Eighteenth Century England) actual punishments conflicted too violently with the moral sense of the community, juries refused to convict and reform was finally brought about. This was possible because, so long as we are thinking in terms of Desert, the propriety of the penal code, being a moral question, is a question on which every man has the right to an opinion, not because he follows this or that profession, but because he is simply a man, a rational animal enjoying the Natural Light. But all this is changed when we drop the concept of Desert. The only two questions we may now ask about a punishment are whether it deters and whether it cures. But these are not questions on which anyone is entitled to have an opinion simply because he is a man. He is not entitled to an opinion even if, in addition to being a man, he should happen also to be a jurist, a Christian, and a moral theologian. For they are not questions about principle but about matter of fact; and for such *cuiquam in sua arte credendum* ("Experts must be believed."). Only the expert "penologist" (let barbarous things have barbarous names), in the light of previous experiment, can tell us what is likely to deter; only the psychotherapist can tell us what is likely to cure. It will be in vain for the rest of us, speaking simply as men, to say, "but this punishment is hideously unjust, hideously disproportionate to the criminal's deserts." The experts with perfect logic will reply, "but nobody was talking about deserts. No one was talking about *punishment* in your archaic vindictive sense of the word. Here are the statistics proving that this treatment cures. What is your trouble?"

The Humanitarian theory, then, removes sentences from the hands of jurists whom the public conscience is entitled to criticize and places them in the hands of technical experts whose special sciences do not even employ such categories as Rights or Justice. It might be argued that since this transference results from an abandonment of the old idea of punishment, and, therefore, of all vindictive motives, it will be safe to leave our criminals in such hands. I will not pause to comment on the simple minded view of fallen human nature which such a belief implies. Let us rather remember that the "cure" of criminals is to be compulsory; and let us then watch how the theory actually works in the mind of the Humanitarian. The immediate starting point of this article was a letter I read in one of our Leftist weeklies. The author was pleading that a certain sin, now treated by our Laws as a crime, should henceforward be treated as a disease. And he complained that under the present system the offender, after a term in gaol, was simply let out to return to his original environment where he would probably relapse. What he complained of was not the shutting up but the letting out. On his remedial view of punishment the offender should, of course, be detained until he was cured. And of course the official straighteners are the only people who can say when that is. The first result of the Humanitarian theory is, therefore, to substitute for a definite sentence (reflecting to some extent the community's moral judgment on the degree of ill-desert involved) an indefinite sentence terminable only by the word of those experts—and they are not experts in moral theology nor even in the Law of Nature—who inflict it. Which of us, if he stood in the dock, would not prefer to be tried by the old system?

It may be said that by the continued use of the word Punishment and the use of the verb "inflict" I am misrepresenting the Humanitarians. They are not punishing, not inflicting, only healing. But do not let us be deceived by a name. To be taken without consent from my home and friends; to lose my liberty; to undergo all those assaults on my personality which modern psychotherapy knows how to deliver; to be remade after some pattern of "normality" hatched in a Viennese laboratory to which I never professed allegiance; to know that this process will never end until either my captors have succeeded or I have grown wise enough to cheat them with apparent success—

who cares whether this is called Punishment or not? That it includes most of the elements for which any punishment is feared—shame, exile, bondage and years eaten by the locust—is obvious. Only enormous ill-desert could justify it; but ill-desert is the very conception which the Humanitarian theory has thrown overboard.

If we turn from the curative to the deterrent justification of punishment we shall find the new theory even more alarming. When you punish a man *in terrorem,* make of him an "example" to others, you are admittedly using him as a means to an end; someone else's end. This, in itself, would be a very wicked thing to do. On the classical theory of Punishment it was of course justified on the ground that the man deserved it. That was assumed to be established before any question of "making him an example" arose. You then, as the saying is, killed two birds with one stone; in the process of giving him what he deserved you set an example to others. But take away desert and the whole morality of the punishment disappears. Why, in Heaven's name, am I to be sacrificed to the good of society in this way?—unless, of course, I deserve it.

But that is not the worst. If the justification of exemplary punishment is not to be based on desert but solely on its efficacy as a deterrent, it is not absolutely necessary that the man we punish should even have committed the crime. The deterrent effect demands that the public should draw the moral, "If we do such an act we shall suffer like that man." The punishment of a man actually guilty whom the public think innocent will not have the desired effect; the punishment of a man actually innocent will, provided the public think him guilty. But every modern State has powers which make it easy to fake a trial. When a victim is urgently needed for exemplary purposes and a guilty victim cannot be found, all the purposes of deterrence will be equally served by the punishment (call it "cure" if you prefer) of an innocent victim, provided that the public can be cheated into thinking him guilty. It is no use to ask me why I assume that our rulers will be so wicked. The punishment of an innocent, that is, an undeserving, man is wicked only if we grant the traditional view that righteous punishment means deserved punishment. Once we have abandoned that criterion, all punishments have to be justified, if at all, on other grounds that have nothing to do with desert. Where the punishment of the innocent can be justified on those grounds (and it could in some cases be justified as a deterrent) it will be no less moral than any other punishment. Any distaste for it on the part of a Humanitarian will be merely a hang-over from the Retributive theory.

It is, indeed, important to notice that my argument so far supposes no evil intentions on the part of the Humanitarian and considers only what is involved in the logic of his position. My contention is that good men (not bad men) consistently acting upon that position would act as cruelly and unjustly as the greatest tyrants. They might in some respects act even worse. Of all tyrannies a tyranny sincerely exercised for the good of its victims may be the most oppressive. It may be better to live under robber barons than under omnipotent moral busybodies. The robber baron's cruelty may sometimes sleep, his cupidity may at some point be satiated; but those who torment us for our own good will torment us without end for they do so with the approval of their own conscience. They may be more likely to go to Heaven yet at the same time likelier to make a Hell of earth. Their very kindness stings with intolerable insult. To be "cured" against one's will and cured of states which we may not regard as disease is to be put on a level with those who have not yet reached the age of reason or those who never will; to be classed with infants, imbeciles, and domestic animals. But to be punished, however severely, because we have deserved it, because we "ought to have known better," is to be treated as a human person made in God's image.

In reality, however, we must face the possibility of bad rulers armed with a Humanitarian theory of punishment. A great many popular blue prints for a Christian society are merely what the Elizabethans called "eggs in moonshine" because they assume that the whole society is Christian or that the Christians are in control. This is not so in most contemporary States. Even if it were, our rulers would still be fallen men, and, therefore, neither very wise nor very good. As it is, they will usually be unbelievers. And since wisdom and virtue are not the only or the commonest qualifications for a place in the government, they will not

often be even the best unbelievers. The practical problem of Christian politics is not that of drawing up schemes for a Christian society, but that of living as innocently as we can with unbelieving fellow-subjects under unbelieving rulers who will never be perfectly wise and good and who will sometimes be very wicked and very foolish. And when they are wicked the Humanitarian theory of Punishment will put in their hands a finer instrument of tyranny than wickedness ever had before. For if crime and disease are to be regarded as the same thing, it follows that any state of mind which our masters choose to call "disease" can be treated as crime; and compulsorily cured. It will be vain to plead that states of mind which displease government need not always involve moral turpitude and do not therefore always deserve forfeiture of liberty. For our masters will not be using the concepts of Desert and Punishment but those of disease and cure. We know that one school of psychology already regards religion as a neurosis. When this particular neurosis becomes inconvenient to government what is to hinder government from proceeding to "cure" it? Such "cure" will, of course, be compulsory; but under the Humanitarian theory it will not be called by the shocking name of Persecution. No one will blame us for being Christians, no one will hate us, no one will revile us. The new Nero will approach us with the silky manners of a doctor, and though all will be in fact as compulsory as the *tunica molesta* or Smithfield or Tyburn, all will go on within the unemotional therapeutic sphere where words like "right" and "wrong" or "freedom" and "slavery" are never heard. And thus when the command is given every prominent Christian in the land may vanish overnight into Institutions for the Treatment of the Ideologically Unsound, and it will rest with the expert gaolers to say when (if ever) they are to re-emerge. But it will not be persecution. Even if the treatment is painful, even if it is life-long, even if it is fatal, that will be only a regrettable accident; the intention was purely therapeutic. Even in ordinary medicine there were painful operations and fatal operations; so in this. But because they are "treatment," not punishment, they can be criticized only by fellow-experts and on technical grounds, never by men as men and on grounds of justice.

This is why I think it essential to oppose the Humanitarian theory of Punishment, root and branch, wherever we encounter it. It carries on its front a semblance of Mercy which is wholly false. That is how it can deceive men of good will. The error began, perhaps, with Shelley's statement that the distinction between Mercy and Justice was invented in the courts of tyrants. It sounds noble, and was indeed the error of a noble mind. But the distinction is essential. The older view was that Mercy "tempered" Justice, or (on the highest level of all) that Mercy and Justice had met and kissed. The essential act of Mercy was to pardon; and pardon in its very essence involves the recognition of guilt and ill-desert in the recipient. If crime is only a disease which needs cure, not sin which deserves punishment, it cannot be pardoned. How can you pardon a man for having a gum-boil or a club foot? But the Humanitarian theory wants simply to abolish Justice and substitute Mercy for it. This means that you start being "kind" to people before you have considered their rights, and then force upon them supposed kindnesses which they in fact had a right to refuse, and finally kindnesses which no one but you will recognize as kindnesses and which the recipient will feel as abominable cruelties. You have overshot the mark. Mercy, detached from Justice, grows unmerciful. That is the important paradox. As there are plants which will flourish only in mountain soil, so it appears that Mercy will flower only when it grows in the crannies of the rock of Justice; transplanted to the marshlands of mere Humanitarianism, it becomes a man-eating weed, all the more dangerous because it is still called by the same name as the mountain variety. But we ought long ago to have learned our lesson. We should be too old now to be deceived by those humane pretensions which have served to usher in every cruelty of the revolutionary period in which we live. These are the "precious balms" which will "break our heads."

There is a fine sentence in Bunyan: "It came burning hot into my mind, whatever he said, and however he flattered, when he got me home to his house, he would sell me for a slave." There is a fine couplet, too, in John Ball:

> Be ware ere ye be wo.
> Know your friend from your foe.

One last word. You may ask why I send this to an Australian periodical. The reason is simple and perhaps worth recording; I can get no hearing for it in England.

FOR FURTHER REFLECTION

1. Do you agree with Lewis that the rehabilitation approach is "a dangerous illusion and disguises the possibility of cruelty and injustice without end"? Why or why not? What would proponents of the rehabilitation view say to counter Lewis's accusations?

2. C. S. Lewis was a devout Christian, and the New Testament instructs Christians to love their enemies and to do good to those who despitefully use them. Is there something paradoxical about Lewis's espousal of retributivism in the light of his Christian faith? Explain. How might Lewis or other Christians holding his view reconcile retributivism with the command to love?

JOHN RAWLS

TWO CONCEPTS OF PUNISHMENT

John Rawls (1921–2002) was a professor of philosophy at Harvard University and the author of several important works in moral and political philosophy, including *A Theory of Justice*. In this essay, Rawls presents a compromise between rule utilitarianism and retributivism. He makes a sharp distinction between social practices and the actions that fall under various practices; then he points out that utilitarianism justifies social practices, but that something like retributivist considerations are needed to justify the specific actions that fall under those practices. The practice of punishment is justified by utilitarian considerations. However, when we come to a specific instance of punishment, we do not employ the utilitarian justification even if it will result in greater utility. For example, even if framing an innocent man and punishing him would serve as a needed deterrent, we refrain from this act. Instead, in specific applications of the practice of punishment, we resort to retribution-like reasons.

In this paper I want to show the importance of the distinction between justifying a practice [1] and justifying a particular action falling under it, and I want to explain the logical basis of this distinction and how it is possible to miss its significance. While the distinction has frequently been made, and is now becoming commonplace, there remains the task of explaining the tendency either to overlook it altogether, or to fail to appreciate its importance.

To show the importance of the distinction I am going to defend utilitarianism against those objections which have traditionally been made against it in connection with punishment and the obligation to keep promises. I hope to show that if one uses the distinction in question then one can state utilitarianism in a way which makes it a much better explication of our considered moral judgments than these traditional objections would seem to admit. Thus the importance of the distinction is shown by the way it strengthens the utilitarian view regardless of whether that view is completely defensible or not. . . .

The subject of punishment, in the sense of attaching legal penalties to the violation of legal rules, has always been a troubling moral question. The trouble about it has not been that people disagree as to whether or not punishment is justifiable. Most people have held that, freed from certain abuses, it is an acceptable institution. Only a few have rejected punishment entirely, which is rather surprising when one considers all that can be said against it. The difficulty is with the justification of punishment: various arguments for it have been given by moral philosophers, but so far none of them has won any sort of general acceptance; no justification is without those who detest it. I hope to show that the use of the aforementioned distinction enables one to state the utilitarian view in a way which allows for the sound points of its critics.

Reprinted from John Rawls, "Two Concepts of Rules," Part I, *Philosophical Review* 64, 1955, pp. 3–13, by permission of the author and publisher. Most notes have been deleted.

For our purposes we may say that there are two justifications of punishment. What we may call the retributive view is that punishment is justified on the grounds that wrongdoing merits punishment. It is morally fitting that a person who does wrong should suffer in proportion to his wrongdoing. That a criminal should be punished follows from his guilt, and the severity of the appropriate punishment depends on the depravity of his act. The state of affairs where a wrongdoer suffers punishment is morally better than the state of affairs where he does not; and it is better irrespective of any of the consequences of punishing him.

What we may call the utilitarian view holds that on the principle that bygones are bygones and that only future consequences are material to present decisions, punishment is justifiable only by reference to the probable consequences of maintaining it as one of the devices of the social order. Wrongs committed in the past are, as such, not relevant considerations for deciding what to do. If punishment can be shown to promote effectively the interest of society it is justifiable, otherwise it is not.

I have stated these two competing views very roughly to make one feel the conflict between them: one feels the force of *both* arguments and one wonders how they can be reconciled. From my introductory remarks it is obvious that the resolution which I am going to propose is that in this case one must distinguish between justifying a practice as a system of rules to be applied and enforced, and justifying a particular action which falls under these rules; utilitarian arguments are appropriate with regard to questions about practices, while retributive arguments fit the application of particular rules to particular cases.

We might try to get clear about this distinction by imagining how a father might answer the question of his son. Suppose the son asks, "Why was *J* put in jail yesterday?" The father answers, "Because he robbed the bank at *B*. He was duly tried and found guilty. That's why he was put in jail yesterday." But suppose the son had asked a different question, namely, "Why do people put other people in jail?" Then the father might answer, "To protect good people from bad people" or "To stop people from doing things that would make it uneasy for all of us; for otherwise we wouldn't be able to go to bed at night and sleep in peace." There are two very different questions here. One question emphasizes the proper name: it asks why *J* was punished rather than someone else, or it asks what he was punished for. The other question asks why we have the institution of punishment; why do people punish one another rather than, say, always forgiving one another?

Thus the father says in effect that a particular man is punished, rather than some other man, because he is guilty, and he is guilty because he broke the law (past tense). In his case the law looks back, the judge looks back, the jury looks back, and a penalty is visited upon him for something he did. That a man is to be punished, and what his punishment is to be, is settled by its being shown that he broke the law and that the law assigns that penalty for the violation of it.

On the other hand we have the institution of punishment itself, and recommend and accept various changes in it, because it is thought by the (ideal) legislator and by those to whom the law applies that, as a part of a system of law impartially applied from case to case arising under it, it will have the consequence, in the long run, of furthering the interests of society.

One can say, then, that the judge and the legislator stand in different positions and look in different directions: one to the past, the other to the future. The justification of what the judge does, *qua* judge, sounds like the retributive view; the justification of what the (ideal) legislator does, *qua* legislator, sounds like the utilitarian view. Thus both views have a point (this is as it should be since intelligent and sensitive persons have been on both sides of the argument); and one's initial confusion disappears once one sees that these views apply to persons holding different offices with different duties; and situated differently with respect to the system of rules that make up the criminal law.

One might say, however, that the utilitarian view is more fundamental since it applies to a more fundamental office, for the judge carries out the legislator's will so far as he can determine it. Once the legislator decides to have laws and to assign penalties for their violation (as things are there must be both the law and the penalty) an institution is set up which involves a retributive conception of particular cases. It is part of the concept of the criminal law as a system of rules that the application and enforcement of these rules in particular cases should be justifiable by arguments of a retributive character. The decision whether or not to use law rather than some other mechanism of social control, and the decision as to what laws to have and what penalties to assign, may be settled by utilitarian arguments; but if one decides to have laws then one has decided on something whose working in particular cases is retributive in form.

The answer, then, to the confusion engendered by the two views of punishment is quite simple: one distinguishes two offices, that of the judge and that of the legislator, and one distinguishes their different stations with respect to the system of rules which make up the law; and then one notes that the different sorts of considerations which would usually be offered as reasons for what is done under the cover of these offices can be paired off with the competing justifications of punishment. One reconciles the two views by the time-honored device of making them apply to different situations.

But can it really be this simple? Well, this answer allows for the apparent intent of each side. Does a person who advocates the retributive view necessarily advocate, as an *institution,* legal machinery whose essential purpose is to set up and preserve a correspondence between moral turpitude and suffering? Surely not. What retributionists have rightly insisted upon is that no man can be punished unless he is guilty, that is, unless he has broken the law. Their fundamental criticism of the utilitarian account is that, as they interpret it, it sanctions an innocent person's being punished (if one may call it that) for the benefit of society.

On the other hand, utilitarians agree that punishment is to be inflicted only for the violation of law. They regard this much as understood from the concept of punishment itself. The point of the utilitarian account concerns the institution as a system of rules: utilitarianism seeks to limit its use by declaring it justifiable only if it can be shown to foster effectively the good of society. Historically it is a protest against the indiscriminate and ineffective use of the criminal law. It seeks to dissuade us from assigning to penal institutions the improper, if not sacrilegious, task of

matching suffering with moral turpitude. Like others, utilitarians want penal institutions designed so that, as far as humanly possible, only those who break the law run afoul of it. They hold that no official should have discretionary power to inflict penalties whenever he thinks it for the benefit of society; for on utilitarian grounds an institution granting such power could not be justified.

The suggested way of reconciling the retributive and the utilitarian justifications of punishment seems to account for what both sides have wanted to say. There are, however, two further questions which arise, and I shall devote the remainder of this section to them.

First, will not a difference of opinion as to the proper criterion of just law make the proposed reconciliation unacceptable to retributionists? Will they not question whether, if the utilitarian principle is used as the criterion, it follows that those who have broken the law are guilty in a way which satisfies their demand that those punished deserve to be punished? To answer this difficulty, suppose that the rules of the criminal law are justified on utilitarian grounds (it is only for laws that meet his criterion that the utilitarian can be held responsible). Then it follows that the actions which the criminal law specifies as offenses are such that, if they were tolerated, terror and alarm would spread in society. Consequently, retributionists can only deny that those who are punished deserve to be punished if they deny that such actions are wrong. This they will not want to do.

The second question is whether utilitarianism doesn't justify too much. One pictures it as an engine of justification which, if consistently adopted, could be used to justify cruel and arbitrary institutions. Retributionists may be supposed to concede that utilitarians *intend* to reform the law and to make it more humane; that utilitarians do not *wish* to justify any such thing as punishment of the innocent; and that utilitarians may appeal to the fact that punishment presupposes guilt in the sense that by punishment one understands an institution attaching penalties to the infraction of legal rules, and therefore that it is logically absurd to suppose that utilitarians in justifying *punishment* might also have justified punishment (if we may call it that) of the innocent. The real question, however, is whether the utilitarian, in justifying punishment, hasn't used arguments which commit him to accepting the infliction of suffering on innocent persons if it is for the good of society (whether or not one calls this punishment). More generally, isn't the utilitarian committed in principle to accepting many practices which he, as a morally sensitive person, wouldn't want to accept? Retributionists are inclined to hold that there is no way to stop the utilitarian principle from justifying too much except by adding to it a principle which distributes certain rights to individuals. Then the amended criterion is not the greatest benefit of society *simpliciter,* but the greatest benefit of society subject to the constraint that no one's rights may be violated. Now while I think that the classical utilitarians proposed a criterion of this more complicated sort, I do not want to argue that point here.[2] What I want to show is that there is *another* way of preventing the utilitarian principle from justifying too much, or at least of making it much less likely to do so: namely, by stating utilitarianism in a way which accounts for the distinction between the justification of an institution and the justification of a particular action falling under it.

I begin by defining the institution of punishment as follows: a person is said to suffer punishment whenever he is legally deprived of some of the normal rights of a citizen on the ground that he has violated a rule of law, the violating having been established by trial according to the due process of law, provided that the deprivation is carried out by the recognized legal authorities of the state, that the rule of law clearly specifies both the offense and the attached penalty, that the courts construe statutes strictly, and that the statute was on the books prior to the time of the offense. This definition specifies what I shall understand by punishment. The question is whether utilitarian arguments may be found to justify institutions widely different from this and such as one would find cruel and arbitrary.

This question is best answered, I think, by taking up a particular accusation. Consider the following from Carritt:

> . . . the utilitarian must hold that we are justified in inflicting pain always and only to prevent worse pain or bring about greater happiness. This, then, is all we

need to consider in so-called punishment, which must be purely preventive. But if some kind of very cruel crime becomes common, and none of the criminals can be caught, it might be highly expedient, as an example, to hang an innocent man, if a charge against him could be so framed that he were universally thought guilty; indeed this would only fail to be an ideal instance of utilitarian 'punishment' because the victim himself would not have been so likely as a real felon to commit such a crime in the future; in all other respects it would be perfectly deterrent and therefore felicific.[3]

Carritt is trying to show that there are occasions when a utilitarian argument would justify taking an action which would be generally condemned; and thus that utilitarianism justifies too much. But the failure of Carritt's argument lies in the fact that he makes no distinction between the justification of the general system of rules which constitutes penal institutions and the justification of particular applications of these rules to particular cases by the various officials whose job it is to administer them. This becomes perfectly clear when one asks who the "we" are of whom Carritt speaks. Who is this who has a sort of absolute authority on particular occasions to decide that an innocent man shall be "punished" if everyone can be convinced that he is guilty? Is this person the legislator, or the judge, or the body of private citizens, or what? It is utterly crucial to know who is to decide such matters, and by what authority, for all of this must be written into the rules of the institution. Until one knows these things one doesn't know what the institution is whose justification is being challenged; and as the utilitarian principle applies to the institution one doesn't know whether it is justifiable on utilitarian grounds or not.

Once this is understood it is clear what the countermove to Carritt's argument is. One must describe more carefully what the *institution* is which his example suggests, and then ask oneself whether or not it is likely that having this institution would be for the benefit of society in the long run. One must not content oneself with the vague thought that, when it's a question of *this* case, it would be a good thing if *somebody* did something even if an innocent person were to suffer.

Try to imagine, then, an institution (which we may call "telishment") which is such that the officials set up by it have authority to arrange a trial for the condemnation of an innocent man whenever they are of the opinion that doing so would be in the best interests of society. The discretion of officials is limited, however, by the rule that they may not condemn an innocent man to undergo such an ordeal unless there is, at the time, a wave of offenses similar to that with which they charge him and telish him for. We may imagine that the officials having the discretionary authority are the judges of the higher courts in consultation with the chief of police, the minister of justice, and a committee of the legislature.

Once one realizes that one is involved in setting up an *institution,* one sees that the hazards are very great. For example, what check is there on the officials? How is one to tell whether or not their actions are authorized? How is one to limit the risks involved in allowing such systematic deception? How is one to avoid giving anything short of complete discretion to the authorities to telish anyone they like? In addition to these considerations, it is obvious that people will come to have a very different attitude towards their penal system when telishment is adjoined to it. They will be uncertain as to whether a convicted man has been punished or telished. They will wonder whether or not they should feel sorry for him. They will wonder whether the same fate won't at any time fall on them. If one pictures how such an institution would actually work, and the enormous risks involved in it, it seems clear that it would serve no useful purpose. A utilitarian justification for this institution is most unlikely.

It happens in general that as one drops off the defining features of punishment one ends up with an institution whose utilitarian justification is highly doubtful. One reason for this is that punishment works like a kind of price system: by altering the prices one has to pay for the performance of actions it supplies a motive for avoiding some actions and doing others. The defining features are essential if punishment is to work in this way; so that an institution which lacks these features, e.g., an institution which is set up to "punish" the innocent, is likely to have about as much point as a price system (if one may call it that) where the prices of things change at random from day to day and one learns the price of something after one has agreed to buy it.

If one is careful to apply the utilitarian principle to the institution which is to authorize particular actions, then there is *less* danger of its justifying too much. Carritt's example gains plausibility by its indefiniteness and by its concentration on the particular case. His argument will only hold if it can be shown that there are utilitarian arguments which justify an institution whose publicly ascertainable offices and powers are such as to permit officials to exercise that kind of discretion in particular cases. But the requirement of having to build the arbitrary features of the particular decision into the institutional practice makes the justification much less likely to go through.

NOTES

1. I use the word "practice" throughout as a sort of technical term meaning any form of activity specified by a system of rules which defines offices, roles, moves, penalties, defenses, and so on, and which gives the activity its structure. As examples one may think of games and rituals, trials and parliaments.
2. By the classical utilitarians I understand Hobbes, Hume, Bentham, J. S. Mill, and Sidgwick.
3. *Ethical and Political Thinking* (Oxford, 1947), p. 65.

FOR FURTHER REFLECTION

1. Describe Rawls's distinction between justifying an action and a practice. Does it result in an adequate compromise between the retributivist and the utilitarian? Does it neglect valid insights of rehabilitation theories?
2. Now that you have read a number of essays espousing different views on punishment, which theory seems the most defensible? Relate your answer to the discussion of free will and determinism: how will the position you take on the problem of free will influence the position you take on punishment?

PART VI

❧

Moral Philosophy

In all the world and in all of life there is nothing more important to determine than what is right. Whatever the matter which lies before us calling for consideration, whatever the question asked us or the problem to be solved, there is some settlement of it which will meet the situation and is to be sought. . . . Wherever there is a decision to be made or any deliberation is in point, there is a right determination of the matter in hand which is to be found and adhered to, and other possible commitments which would be wrong are to be avoided.

C. I. Lewis, The Ground and Nature of Right

What is it to be a moral person and live a morally good life? Why is morality important? Are moral principles valid only as they depend on cultural approval, or are there universal moral truths? How should I live my life? Are there intrinsic values? Why should I be moral? Is there a right answer to every problem in Life? What is the relationship of morality to religion? What is the correct or best moral theory? These are some of the questions considered in this part of the book. We want to understand the nature of morality. We want to know how we should live.

The terms *morals* and *ethics* come from Latin and Greek, respectively (*mores* and *ethos*), deriving their meaning from the idea of custom. Although people sometimes use these terms interchangeably, two separate ideas may be distinguished: one closer to the idea of custom or actual practice and the other referring to a systematic examination of those practices. I follow the custom of using the term *morality* to refer to the principles or rules of conduct that govern a society or that *ought* to govern a society. That is, "morality" refers to the principles of conduct of both actual moralities (such as the moral code of Victorian England, a primitive tribe, or a twenty-first-century corporate business) and of ideal morality (the best justified or true moral system).

I use the term *moral philosophy*, or *ethics* as it is sometimes called, to designate the systematic endeavor to understand moral concepts and justify moral principles and theories. This endeavor undertakes to analyze such concepts as *right, wrong, permissible, ought, good,* and *evil* in their moral contexts. Ethics seeks to establish principles of right behavior that may serve as action guides for individuals and groups. It investigates which values and virtues are paramount to the worthwhile life or society. It builds and scrutinizes arguments in ethical theories, and seeks to discover valid principles (for example, "Never kill innocent human beings") and the relationship between those principles (for example, may saving a life ever constitute a valid reason for breaking a promise?).

Actually, there are not just two designations of actions, *right* and *wrong*, but three: *right* (that is, the correct or obligatory act), *wrong*, and *permissible*. The notion of a right act is ambiguous, sometimes including the obligatory as well as the permissible, and sometimes meaning only the obligatory, as in "*the* right act." I use the designation *right* in the obligatory sense.

The notion of a *permissible* act needs to be broken up into types: morally neutral acts and acts beyond the call of duty (sometimes referred to as *supererogatory*). A woman's choice of whether to wear jeans or a dress is usually morally neutral, as is a man's choice of whether or not to wear a hat. The choice of which brand of toothpaste to buy is normally morally neutral; but if we find that the company that produces brand X is using its profits to support immoral practices, then it becomes wrong to purchase that brand of toothpaste. Other acts are permissible but not morally neutral, for they have positive merit and deserve praise. These include risking one's life for a stranger and giving all of one's assets to the poor. In biblical times, hosts were obligated to carry their guests' baggage one mile. Jesus called on his disciples to extend the rule to two miles, not out of duty but out of a spirit of altruism. Such is the spirit of supererogation.

Ethics then, in the sense of moral philosophy, is the philosophical study of morality. The morality of a given society is the set of principles that are recognized by that society as guides to proper action. The set recognized in the Unites States at the beginning of twenty-first century includes the following principles:

1. Keep your promises.
2. Don't lie.
3. Don't steal.
4. In a war, don't kill noncombatants, especially women and children.
5. Don't kill innocent people.
6. Don't commit infanticide.
7. Don't take pleasure in seeing others harmed.

The set of moral norms in the ancient Greek state of Sparta lacked principles 2, 4, and 6; stealing and infanticide were considered permissible. The set of principles in the Ik culture in the southern Sudan includes none of the U.S. principles.[1] Iks consider lying, stealing, and the breaking of promises to be virtues, permit infanticide, regularly take pleasure in the misfortune of others, and reveal no guilt feelings. The morality of ancient Israel, as recorded in the first five books of the Old Testament or Hebrew Bible, lacks principles 3 and 4 (although there is an injunction against bearing false witness). They also contain many additional rules that are not part of the mainstream of our culture:

8. Do not eat pork or shellfish or anything with the blood in it.
9. Do not do any work on the Sabbath (Saturday) on pain of death.
10. Women may not own property or have leadership positions.

Some Inuit tribes traditionally leave their parents to die, and the Callatians described by Herodotus (see first reading in section A) believed that it was mandatory to eat one's dead parents to show respect for them. All these observations of cultural norms are descriptive or anthropological in nature, not philosophical.

The philosophical question is whether we have any right to judge other cultures, whether we can say that some principles are good or moral, whereas others are bad or immoral. We examine this question in section A of this book.

ETHICS AS COMPARED WITH OTHER NORMATIVE SUBJECTS

Ethics is concerned with values—not what is, but what ought to be. How should I live my life? What is the right thing to do in this situation? Should one always tell the truth? Do I have a duty to report a student whom I have seen cheating on an exam? Should I tell my friend that his spouse is having an affair? Is premarital sex morally permissible? Ought a woman ever to have an abortion? Ethics has a distinct action-guiding or *normative* aspect and, as such, belongs to the group of practical institutions that include religion, law, and etiquette.

Ethics may be closely allied to religion, but it need not be. There are both religions and secular ethical systems. Secular or purely philosophical ethics is grounded in reason and common human experience. To use a spatial metaphor, secular ethics is horizontal, lacking a vertical or transcendental dimension. Religious ethics has a vertical dimension, being grounded in reelation or divine authority. These two differing orientations often generate different moral principles and standards of evaluation, but they need not. Some versions of relitious ethics, which posit God's revelation of the moral law in nature or conscience, hold that reason can discover what is right or wrong even apart from divine revelation. We discuss this subject in section C.

Ethics is also closely related to law. Many laws are instituted in order to promote well-being and resolve conflicts of interest and/or social harmony, just as morality does, but ethics may judge that some laws are immoral without denying that they are valid laws (for example, laws permitting slavery or unjust discrimination based on race or sex). Furthermore, some aspects of morality are not covered by law (for example, although it is generally agreed that lying is immoral, there is no law against it). Finally, law differs from morality in that physical sanctions enforce the law, but essentially it is the sanctions of conscience and reputation that enforce morality.

Etiquette also differs from morality, although, like ethics and unlike law, it appeals primarily to conscience, social censure, and reputation. People sometimes confuse etiquette with morality, as is the case when students condemn someone for not dressing appropriately for a social event. The two institutions have points in common but are actually quite different.

Law, etiquette, and religion are all important institutions, but each has limitations. The limitation of the law is that you can't have a law against every social malady, nor can you enforce every desirable rule. The limitation of etiquette is that it does not point to what is vitally important for personal and social existence: whether one eats with one's fingers or a knife and fork pales in significance compared with the importance of being honest or trustworthy or just. The limitation of the religious injunction is that it rests on authority: we are not always sure of, nor do we agree about, the authority's credentials or how the authority would rule in ambiguous or new cases. Because religion is founded on revelation, not reason, you have no way to convince someone who does not share your religious views that your view is right.

The following chart characterizes the relationship between these four ways of evaluating behavior.

SUBJECT	EVALUATIVE DISJUNCTS	SANCTIONS
Ethics	Right/wrong/permissible, as defined by conscience or reason	Conscience/praise and blame
Religion	Right/wrong (sin)/permissible as defined by religious authority	Conscience/hope of eternal reward and fear of punishment
Law	Legal/illegal as defined by a legislative body	Punishments executed by the judicial body
Etiquette	Proper/improper as defined by culture	Social disapprobation and approbation

Ethics, as the analysis of morality, distinguishes itself from law and etiquette by going deeper into the essence of rational existence. It distinguishes itself from religion by seeking reason, rather than authority, to justify principles. Its central purpose is to secure valid principles of conduct and values that can be instrumental in guiding human actions and producing good character. As such, it is the most important activity known to humans: it concerns how we are to live.

A central feature of morality is the moral principle. There is no universal agreement concerning the traits a moral principle must contain, but five have commanded widespread consensus. They are (1) prescriptivity, (2) universalizability, (3) overridingness, (4) publicity, and (5) practicability.

1. *Prescriptivity*. Morality has a practical or action-guiding nature. Moral principles are generally phrased as injunctions or imperatives; for example, "Do not kill," "Do no unnecessary harm," "Love your neighbor." They are intended for use, to advise and influence to action. Morality shares this trait with all normative discourse. This feature is used retroactively to appraise behavior, assign praise and blame, and justify feelings of satisfaction or guilt.
2. *Universalizability*. Moral principles must apply to all who are in the relevantly similar situation. If one judges that act X is right for a certain person P, then it is right for anyone relevantly similar to P. This trait is exemplified in (1) the Golden Rule, "Do unto others what you would have them do unto you (if you were in their shoes)," and in (2) the formal principle of justice: "It cannot be right for A to treat B in a manner in which it would be wrong for B to treat A, merely on the ground that they are two different individuals, and without there being any difference between the natures or circumstances of the two that can be stated as a reasonable ground for difference of treatment."[2] The criterion of universalizability applies to all evaluative judgments. If I say that X is a good Y, then I am logically committed to judge that anything relevantly similar to X is a good type of Y. This feature is an extension of the principle of consistency: one ought to be consistent about one's value judgments, including one's moral judgments.

3. *Overridingness.* Moral principles have paramount authority. They are not the only principles, but they take precedence over other considerations, including esthetic, prudential, and legal ones. For example, the artist Paul Gauguin may have been esthetically justified in abandoning his family in 1891 in order to devote his life to painting beautiful Pacific Island pictures, but morally, or all things considered, he probably was not justified. I may find it prudent to lie to save my reputation, but it probably is morally wrong to do so, so I should tell the truth. And when the law becomes immoral, it may be my moral duty to exercise civil disobedience. There is a general moral duty to obey the law, because the law serves an overall moral purpose, and this overall purpose may give us moral reasons to obey laws that may not be moral or ideal, but there may come a time when the injustice of a bad law is intolerable and hence calls for illegal but moral defiance (such as the antebellum laws in the South requiring citizens to return slaves to their owners and the Jim Crow laws that followed in the twentieth century). Religion is a special case, and the religious person may be morally justified in breaking a normal moral rule when following a perceived command from God. For example, John's pacifist religious beliefs may cause him to deny an obligation to fight for his country. Religious morality is still morality, and ethics recognizes its legitimacy. We say more about this in section C of this part of our book.

4. *Publicity.* Moral principles must be made public in order to guide our actions. Because we use principles to prescribe behavior, give advice, and assign praise and blame, it would be self-defeating to keep them a secret. Occasionally, a utilitarian argues that it would be better if some people didn't know or didn't try to follow the correct principles, but even those people would have a higher-order principle—or some reason for this exception—that subsumes such special cases.

5. *Practicability.* A moral system must be workable; its rules must not lay too heavy a burden on agents. John Rawls speaks of the "strains of commitment" that overly idealistic principles may cause in average moral agents. It might be desirable to have a morality enjoining more altruism, but the result of such principles could be moral despair, too much guilt, and ineffective action. Practicability may cause the differences among ethical standards over time and place. For instance, there is a discrepancy in the Bible between the ethics of the Old Testament, or Hebrew Bible, and the New Testament on such topics as divorce and treatment of one's enemy. Jesus explained the difference in the first case by saying that it was because of society's moral immaturity or "hardness of heart" that God permitted divorce in pre-Christian times. In the second case, he pointed toward a time when it would be a valid principle that people would love their enemies and would pray for people who abused them, and he enjoined his disciples to begin living by this ideal morality. Demanding that ordinary people live up to high ideals may impose an impossible burden on them. Most ethical systems take human limitations into consideration and make a distinction between what is obligatory for all and what is ideal or *supererogatory*—beyond the strict call of duty.

These, then, are the traits that moral philosophers generally hold to be necessary for valid moral principles, but there is disagreement over them, and a full discussion would lead to a great deal of qualification. However, they should give you an idea of the general features of moral principles.

DOMAINS OF ETHICAL ASSESSMENT

It might seem at this point that ethics concerns itself entirely with rules of conduct, rules based solely on evaluations of acts. But the situation is more complicated. There are four domains of ethical assessment:

DOMAIN	**EVALUATIVE TERMS**
1. Actions, the act	Right, wrong, permissable
2. Consequences	Good, bad, indifferent
3. Character	Virtuous, vicious
4. Motive	Goodwill, evil will

Let me illustrate these concepts. In Domain 1, the most common distinction may be the classification of right and wrong kinds of actions. For example, lying is generally seen as a wrong type of act (prohibited), whereas telling the truth is generally seen as a right kind of act (obligatory). Whether you wrote your friend a letter via E-mail or the traditional way seems to be morally neutral; either is permissable. Whether you listen to pop or classical music is not morally significant; both are allowed. Whether you decide to marry or remain single is up to you; you are under no obligation to do either, unless you have put yourself under an obligation. Some things, such as deciding whether to marry or not, are very important but still within the domain of permissibility, not obligation.

Within the structure of moral obligation, we may define these terms as follows:

1. The *right* act is the act that is obligatory for you to do. You *ought* to do that act. It is not permissible to refrain from doing it.
2. The *wrong* act is that act which you are forbidden to do. You ought not to do that act. It is not permissible to do the act.
3. A *permissible* act is an act that is neither right nor wrong to do. It is neither obligatory nor forbidden.

Within the range of permissible acts is the notion of *supererogatory* or highly altruistic acts. These acts are not required, but are challenges to go beyond what morality requires, going "beyond the call of duty." You may have an obligation to give to people in dire need, but you are probably not obliged to sell your car, let alone become destitute, in order to help them.

Theories that emphasize the nature of the act are called *deontological*, from the Greek word for duty. The most famous of these systems is Kant's moral theory, which we study in section D.

We turn next to Domain 2, the notion of consequences. As noted earlier, lying is generally wrong and telling the truth generally right. But consider this situation. You are hiding in your home an innocent woman named Laura, who is fleeing gangsters. Gangland Gus knocks on your door. When you open it, he asks if Laura is in your house. What should you do? Should you tell the truth or lie? Those who say that morality has something to do with consequences of action would prescribe lying as the morally right thing to do. Those who deny that we should look at the consequences when considering what to do when there is a clear and absolute rule of action ("Thou shalt not lie") will say that you should either keep silent or tell the truth. When no other rule is at stake, of course, the rule-oriented ethicist allows the foreseeable consequences to determine a course of action. Theories that focus primarily on consequences in determining moral rightness and wrongness are called *teleological* theories, from the Greek word *telos*, meaning "goal directed." The most famous of these theories is utilitarianism, which we shall study in section D.

Some ethical theories emphasize principles of action in themselves, and some emphasize principles involving the consequences of action. Other theories, such as Aristotle's ethics, emphasize character, Domain 3. According to Aristotle, it is most important to develop virtuous characters, for if and only if we have good people can we ensure habitual right action. Although the virtues are not central to other types of moral theories, most include the virtues as important. For example, the majority of us, whatever our moral theory, would judge that the people who passively watched from their Queens, New York, windows as Kitty Genovese was assaulted and killed lacked good character. Different moral systems emphasize different virtues and emphasize them to different degrees. We will study *virtue ethics*, sometimes called *aretaic ethics*, from the Greek word *arete*, meaning "virtue," in section D.

Finally, virtually all ethical systems, especially that of Kant, accept the relevance of motive, Domain 4. It is important to the full assessment of any action that the agent's intention be taken into account. Two acts may be identical, but one may be judged morally culpable and the other excusable. Consider John's pushing Joan off a ledge, causing her to break her leg. In situation A he is angry and intends to harm her, but in situation B he sees a knife flying in her direction and intends to save her life. In A, what he did was clearly wrong, whereas in B he did the right thing. On the other hand, two acts may have opposite results, but the action may be equally good when judged on the basis of intention. For example, two soldiers may try to cross enemy lines to communicate with an allied force, but one gets captured through no fault of his own while the other succeeds. In a full moral description of any act, the motive will be taken into consideration as a relevant factor.

Our first reading, Plato's dialogue called the *Crito*, is a classic example of ethical thinking. Written in the fourth century B.C.E., it is one of the earliest surviving treatises on philosophical ethics. It represents an acutely self-conscious attempt to use reasoning to decide what is the right course of action in a particular situation.

The year is 399 B.C.E., the place, an Athenian jail. Socrates, a seventy-year-old philosopher, has been condemned to death by an Athenian court for not believing in the Greek gods and for corrupting the youth. In fact, he has been unjustly condemned, but his refusal to compromise with the powers that be has provoked extreme behavior. Now his friends, led by Crito, have planned his escape and have arranged passage to Thessaly, where Socrates has been assured of a tranquil retirement among admirers. The moral issue is: Should Socrates escape? Should he avail himself of Crito's help, attempt to free himself from prison, and flee Athens? In other words, should he engage in civil disobedience?

Crito and Socrates engage in a moral argument. As you read this dialogue, identify Crito's arguments and Socrates' counterarguments. Try to identify the major principles that each holds and decide how valid the arguments are. Note especially the relationship between law and morality. In another treatise, the *Apology*, Socrates seems to put one principle above the law. He says that if the law commands him to refrain from teaching, he will not obey it. In fact, some years before the events in the *Crito*, he refused to obey the leaders of Athens when they commanded him to arrest an admiral whom he considered innocent of any crime. Do these actions affect his argument in the *Crito?* Was Socrates correct in his arguments? Did he do the right thing? What would you have done in his position, and why?

NOTES

1. In *The Mountain People* (New York: Simon & Schuster, 1972), Colin Turnbull has written a penetrating analysis of Ik culture.
2. Henry Sidgwick, *The Methods of Ethics*, 7th ed. (New York: Macmillan, 1907), 380. More recently, some moral philosophers have denied that universalilizability is a necessary conditon for moral action. See, for example, Lawrence Blum, *Friendship, Altruism, and Morality* (London: Routledge & Kegan Paul, 1980).

PLATO

SOCRATIC MORALITY

Plato (427–347 B.C.E.) was born in Athens and studied under Socrates. In this dialogue he describes the death of Socrates and the moral arguments given by Socrates against escaping from prison.

Crito: I come to bring you a message which is sad and painful; not, as I believe, to yourself, but to all of us who are your friends, and saddest of all to me.

Socrates: What? Has the ship come from Delos, on the arrival of which I am to die?

Crito: No, the ship has not actually arrived, but she will probably be here to-day, as persons who have come from Sunium tell me that they left her there; and therefore to-morrow, Socrates, will be the last day of your life.

Socrates: Very well, Crito; if such is the will of God, I am willing; but my belief is that there will be a delay of a day.

Crito: Why do you think so?

Socrates: I will tell you. I am to die on the day after the arrival of the ship.

Crito: Yes; that is what the authorities say.

Socrates: But I do not think that the ship will be here until to-morrow; this I infer from a vision which I had last night, or rather only just now, when you fortunately allowed me to sleep.

Crito: And what was the nature of the vision?

Socrates: There appeared to me the likeness of a woman, fair and comely, clothed in bright raiment, who called to me and said: O Socrates, 'The third day hence to fertile Phthia shalt thou go.'

Crito: What a singular dream, Socrates!

Socrates: There can be no doubt about the meaning, Crito, I think.

Crito: Yes; the meaning is only too clear. But, oh! my beloved Socrates, let me entreat you once more to take my advice and escape. For if you die I shall not only lose a friend who can never be replaced, but there is another evil: people who do not know you and me will believe that I might have saved you if I had been willing to give money, but that I did not care. Now, can there be a worse disgrace than this—that I should be thought to value money more than the life

From Plato, "Crito," in the *Dialogues of Plato*, trans. Benjamin Jowett, (Oxford, 1896).

of a friend? For the many will not be persuaded that I wanted you to escape, and that you refused.

Socrates: But why, my dear Crito, should we care about the opinion of the many? Good men, and they are the only persons who are worth considering, will think of these things truly as they occurred.

Crito: But you see, Socrates, that the opinion of the many must be regarded, for what is now happening shows that they can do the greatest evil to any one who has lost their good opinion.

Socrates: I only wish it were so, Crito; and that the many could do the greatest evil; for then they would also be able to do the greatest good—and what a fine thing this would be! But in reality they can do neither; for they cannot make a man either wise or foolish; and whatever they do is the result of chance.

Crito: Well, I will not dispute with you; but please to tell me, Socrates, whether you are not acting out of regard to me and your other friends: are you not afraid that if you escape from prison we may get into trouble with the informers for having stolen you away, and lose either the whole or a great part of our property; or that even a worse evil may happen to us? Now, if you fear on our account, be at ease; for in order to save you, we ought surely to run this, or even a greater risk; be persuaded, then, and do as I say.

Socrates: Yes, Crito, that is one fear which you mention, but by no means the only one.

Crito: Fear not—there are persons who are willing to get you out of prison at no great cost; and as for the informers, they are far from being exorbitant in their demands—a little money will satisfy them. My means, which are certainly ample, are at your service, and if you have a scruple about spending all mine, here are strangers who will give you the use of theirs; and one of them, Simmias the Theban, has brought a large sum of money for this very purpose; and Cebes and many others are prepared to spend their money in helping you to escape. I say, therefore, do not hesitate on our account, and do not say, as you did in the court, that you will have a difficulty in knowing what to do with yourself anywhere else. For men will love you in other places to which you may go, and not in Athens only; there are friends of mine in Thessaly, if you like to go to them, who will value and protect you, and no Thessalian will give you any

trouble. Nor can I think that you are at all justified, Socrates, in betraying your own life when you might be saved; in acting thus you are playing into the hands of your enemies, who are hurrying on your destruction. And further I should say that you are deserting your own children; for you might bring them up and educate them; instead of which you go away and leave them, and they will have to take their chance; and if they do not meet with the usual fate of orphans, there will be small thanks to you. No man should bring children into the world who is unwilling to persevere to the end in their nurture and education. But you appear to be choosing the easier part, not the better and manlier, which would have been more becoming in one who professes to care for virtue in all his actions, like yourself. And indeed, I am ashamed not only of you, but of us who are your friends, when I reflect that the whole business will be attributed entirely to our want of courage. The trial need never have come on, or might have been managed differently; and this last act, or crowning folly, will seem to have occurred through our negligence and cowardice, who might have saved you, if we had been good for anything; and you might have saved yourself, for there was no difficulty at all. See now, Socrates, how sad and discreditable are the consequences, both to us and you. Make up your mind then, or rather have your mind already made up, for the time of deliberation is over, and there is only one thing to be done, which must be done this very night, and if we delay at all will be no longer practicable or possible; I beseech you therefore, Socrates, be persuaded by me, and do as I say.

Socrates: Dear Crito, your zeal is invaluable, if a right one; but if wrong, the greater the zeal the greater the danger; and therefore we ought to consider whether I shall or shall not do as you say. For I am and always have been one of those natures who must be guided by reason, whatever the reason may be which upon reflection appears to me to be the best; and now that this chance has befallen me, I cannot repudiate my own words: the principles which I have hitherto honoured and revered I still honour, and unless we can at once find other and better principles, I am certain not to agree with you; no, not even if the power of the multitude could inflict many more imprisonments, confiscations, deaths, frightening us like children with hobgoblin terrors. What will be the fairest way of considering the question? Shall I return to your old argument about the opinions of men?—we were saying that some of them are to be regarded, and others not. Now were we right in maintaining this before I was condemned? And has the argument which was once good now proved to be talk for the sake of talking—mere childish nonsense? That is what I want to consider with your help, Crito:—whether, under my present circumstances, the argument appears to be in any way different or not; and is to be allowed by me or disallowed. That argument, which, as I believe, is maintained by many persons of authority, was to the effect, as I was saying, that the opinions of some men are to be regarded, and of other men not to be regarded. Now you, Crito, are not going to die tomorrow—at least, there is no human probability of this—and therefore you are disinterested and not liable to be deceived by the circumstances in which you are placed. Tell me then, whether I am right in saying that some opinions, and the opinions of some men only, are to be valued, and that other opinions, and the opinions of other men, are not to be valued. I ask you whether I was right in maintaining this?

Crito: Certainly.

Socrates: The good are to be regarded, and not the bad?

Crito: Yes.

Socrates: And the opinions of the wise are good, and the opinions of the unwise are evil?

Crito: Certainly.

Socrates: And what was said about another matter? Is the pupil who devotes himself to the practice of gymnastics supposed to attend to the praise and blame and opinion of every man, or of one man only—his physician or trainer, whoever he may be?

Crito: Of one man only.

Socrates: And he ought to fear the censure and welcome the praise of that one only, and not of the many?

Crito: Clearly so.

Socrates: And he ought to act and train, and eat and drink in the way which seems good to his single master who has understanding, rather than according to the opinion of all other men put together?

Crito: True.

Socrates: And if he disobeys and disregards the opinion and approval of the one, and regards the opinion of the many who have no understanding, will he not suffer evil?

Crito: Certainly he will.

Socrates: And what will the evil be, whither tending and what affecting, in the disobedient person?

Crito: Clearly, affecting the body; that is what is destroyed by the evil.

Socrates: Very good; and is not this true, Crito, of other things which we need not separately enumerate? In questions of just and unjust, fair and foul, good and evil, which are the subjects of our present consultation, ought we to follow the opinion of the many and to fear them; or the opinion of the one man who has understanding? Ought we not to fear and reverence him more than all the rest of the world: and if we desert him shall we not destroy and injure that principle in us which may be assumed to be improved by justice and deteriorated by injustice;—there is such a principle?

Crito: Certainly there is, Socrates.

Socrates: Take a parallel instance:—if, acting under the advice of those who have no understanding, we destroy that which is improved by health and is deteriorated by disease, would life be worth having? And that which has been destroyed is—the body?

Crito: Yes.

Socrates: Could we live, having an evil and corrupted body?

Crito: Certainly not.

Socrates: And will life be worth having, if that higher part of man be destroyed, which is improved by justice and depraved by injustice? Do we suppose that principle, whatever it may be in man, which has to do with justice and injustice, to be inferior to the body?

Crito: Certainly not.

Socrates: More honourable than the body?

Crito: Far more.

Socrates: Then, my friend, we must not regard what the many say of us: but what he, the one man who has understanding of just and unjust, will say, and what the truth will say. And therefore you begin in error when you advise that we should regard the opinion of the many about just and unjust, good and evil, honourable and dishonourable.—"Well," some one will say, "but the many can kill us."

Crito: Yes, Socrates; that will clearly be the answer.

Socrates: And it is true: but still I find with surprise that the old argument is unshaken as ever. And I should like to know whether I may say the same of another proposition—that not life, but a good life, is to be chiefly valued?

Crito: Yes, that also remains unshaken.

Socrates: And a good life is equivalent to a just and honourable one—that holds also?

Crito: Yes, it does.

Socrates: From these premises I proceed to argue the question whether I ought or ought not to try and escape without the consent of the Athenians: and if I am clearly right in escaping, then I will make the attempt; but if not, I will abstain. The other considerations which you mention, of money and loss of character and the duty of educating one's children, are, I fear, only the doctrines of the multitude, who would be as ready to restore people to life, if they were able, as they are to put them to death—and with as little reason. But now, since the argument has thus far prevailed, the only question which remains to be considered is, whether we shall do rightly either in escaping or in suffering others to aid in our escape and paying them in money and thanks, or whether in reality we shall not do rightly; and if the latter, then death or any other calamity which may ensue on my remaining here must not be allowed to enter into the calculation.

Crito: I think that you are right, Socrates; how then shall we proceed?

Socrates: Let us consider the matter together, and do you either refute me if you can, and I will be convinced; or else cease, my dear friend, from repeating to me that I ought to escape against the wishes of the Athenians: for I highly value your attempts to persuade me to do so, but I may not be persuaded against my own better judgment. And now please to consider my first position, and try how you can best answer me.

Crito: I will.

Socrates: Are we to say that we are never intentionally to do wrong, or that in one way we ought and in another we ought not to do wrong, or is doing wrong always evil and dishonourable, as I was just now saying, and as has been already acknowledged by us? Are all our former admissions which were made within a few days to be thrown away? And have we, at our age, been earnestly discoursing with one another all our life long only to discover that we are no better than children? Or, in spite of the opinion of the many, and in spite of consequences whether better or worse, shall we insist on the truth of what was then said, that injustice is always an evil and dishonour to him who acts unjustly? Shall we say so or not?

Crito: Yes.

Socrates: Then we must do no wrong?

Crito: Certainly not.

Socrates: Nor when injured injure in return, as the many imagine; for we must injure no one at all?

Crito: Clearly not.

Socrates: Again, Crito, may we do evil?

Crito: Surely not, Socrates.

Socrates: And what of doing evil in return for evil, which is the morality of the many—is that just or not?

Crito: Not just.

Socrates: For doing evil to another is the same as injuring him?

Crito: Very true.

Socrates: Then we ought not to retaliate or render evil for evil to any one, whatever evil we may have suffered from him. But I would have you consider, Crito, whether you really mean what you are saying. For this opinion has never been held, and never will be held, by any considerable number of persons; and those who are agreed and those who are not agreed upon this point have no common ground, and can only despise one another when they see how widely they differ. Tell me, then, whether you agree with and assent to my first principle, that neither injury nor retaliation nor warding off evil by evil is ever right. And shall that be the premise of our argument? Or do you decline and dissent from this? For so I have ever thought, and continue to think; but, if you are of another opinion, let me hear what you have to say. If, however, you remain of the same mind as formerly, I will proceed to the next step.

Crito: You may proceed, for I have not changed my mind.

Socrates: Then I will go on to the next point, which may be put in the form of a question:—Ought a man to do what he admits to be right, or ought he to betray the right?

Crito: He ought to do what he thinks right.

Socrates: But if this is true, what is the application? In leaving the prison against the will of the Athenians, do I wrong any? Or rather do I not wrong those whom I ought least to wrong? Do I not desert the principles which were acknowledged by us to be just—what do you say?

Crito: I cannot tell, Socrates; for I do not know.

Socrates: Then consider the matter in this way:—Imagine that I am about to play truant (you may call the proceeding by any name which you like), and the laws and the government come and interrogate me: Tell us, Socrates, they say; what are you about? Are you not going by an act of yours to overturn us—the laws, and the whole state, as far as in you lies? Do you imagine that a state can subsist and not be overthrown, in which the decisions of law have no power, but are set aside and trampled upon by individuals? What will be your answer, Crito, to these and the like words? Any one, and especially a rhetorician, will have a good deal to say on behalf of the law which requires a sentence to be carried out. He will argue that this law should not be set aside; and shall we reply; yes; but the state has injured us and given an unjust sentence. Suppose I say that?

Crito: Very good, Socrates.

Socrates: "And was that our agreement with you?" the law would answer; "or were you to abide by the sentence of the state?" And if I were to express my astonishment at their words, the law would probably add: "Answer, Socrates, instead of opening your eyes—you are in the habit of asking and answering questions. Tell us,—What complaint have you to make against us which justifies you in attempting to destroy us and the state? In the first place did we not bring you into existence? Your father married your mother by our aid and begat you. Say whether you have any objection to urge against those of us who regulate marriage?" None, I should reply. "Or against those of us who after birth regulate the nurture and education of children, in which you also were trained? Were not the laws, which have the charge of educa-tion, right in commanding your father to train you in music and gymnastic?" Right, I should reply. "Well then, since you were brought into the world and nurtured and educated by us, can you deny in the first place that you are our child and slave, as your fathers were before you? And if this is true you are not on equal terms with us; nor can you think that you have a right to do to us what we are doing to you. Would you have any right to strike or revile or do any other evil to your father or your master, if you had one, because you have been struck or reviled by him, or received some other evil at his hands?—you would not say this? And because we think right to destroy you, do you think that you have any right to destroy us in return, and your country as far as in you lies? Will you, O professor of true virtue, pretend that you are justified in this? Has a philosopher like you failed to discover that our country is more to be valued and higher and holier far than mother or father or any ancestor, and more to be regarded in the eyes of the gods and of men of understanding? Also to be soothed, and gently and reverently entreated when angry, even more than a father, and either to be per-suaded, or if not persuaded, to be obeyed? And when we are punished by her, whether with imprisonment or stripes, the punishment is to be endured in silence; and if she leads us to wounds or death in battle, thither we follow as is right; neither may any one yield or retreat or leave his rank, but whether in battle or in a court of law, or in any other place, he must do what his city and his country order him; or he must change their view of what is just: and if he may do no vio-lence to his father or mother, much less may he do violence to his country." What answer shall we make to this, Crito? Do the laws speak truly, or do they not?

Crito: I think that they do.

Socrates: Then the laws will say, "Consider, Socrates, if we are speaking truly that in your present attempt you are going to do us an injury. For, having brought you into the world, and nurtured and educated you, and given you and every other citizen a share in every good which we had to give, we further pro-claim to any Athenian by the liberty which we allow him, that if he does not like us when he has become of age and has seen the ways of the city, and made our acquaintance, he may go where he pleases and take his goods with him. None of our laws will forbid him or interfere with him. Any one who does not like us and the city, and who wants to emigrate to a colony or to any other city, may go where he likes retaining his property. But he who has experience of the manner in which we order justice and administer the state, and still remains, has entered into an implied contract that he will do as we command him. And he who disobeys us is, as we maintain, thrice wrong; first, because in disobeying us he is disobeying his parents; secondly, because we are the authors of his education; thirdly, because he has made an agreement with us that he will duly obey our commands; and he neither obeys them nor convinces us that our commands are unjust; and we do not rudely impose them, but give him the alternative of obeying or convincing us;—that is what we offer, and he does neither.

"These are the sort of accusations to which, as we were saying, you, Socrates, will be exposed if you accomplish your intentions; you, above all other Athenians." Suppose now I ask, why I rather than anybody else? they will justly retort upon me that I above all other men have acknowledged the agreement. "There is clear proof," they will say, "Socrates, that we and the city were not displeasing to you. Of all Athenians you have been the most constant resident in the city, which, as you never leave, you may be supposed to love. For you never went out of the city either to see the games, except once when you went to the Isthmus, or to any other place unless when you were on military service; nor did you travel as other men do. Nor had you any curiosity to know other states or their laws: your affections did not go beyond us and our state; we were your special favourites, and you acquiesced in our government of you; and here in this city you begat your children, which is a proof of your satisfaction. Moreover, you might in the course of the trial, if you had liked, have fixed the penalty at banishment; the state which refuses to let you go now would have let you go then. But you pretended that you preferred death to exile, and that you were not unwilling to die. And now you have forgotten these fine sentiments, and pay no respect to us the laws, of whom you are the destroyer; and are doing what only a miserable slave would do, running away and turning your back upon the compacts and agreements

which you made as a citizen. And first of all answer this question: Are we right in saying that you agreed to be governed according to us in deed, and not in word only? Is that true or not?" How shall we answer, Crito? Must we not assent?

Crito: We cannot help it, Socrates.

Socrates: Then will they not say: "You, Socrates, are breaking the covenants and agreements which you made with us at your leisure, not in any haste or under any compulsion or deception, but after you have had seventy years to think of them, during which time you were at liberty to leave the city, if we were not to your mind, or if our covenants appeared to you to be unfair. You had your choice, and might have gone either to Lacedaemon or Crete, both which states are often praised by you for their good government, or to some other hellenic or foreign state. Whereas you, above all other Athenians, seemed to be so fond of the state, or, in other words, of us her laws (and who would care about a state which has no laws?), that you never stirred out of her; the halt, the blind, the maimed were not more stationary in her than you were. And now you run away and forsake your agreements. Not so, Socrates, if you will take our advice; do not make yourself ridiculous by escaping out of the city.

"For just consider, if you transgress and err in this sort of way, what good will you do either to yourself or to your friends? That your friends will be driven into exile and deprived of citizenship, or will lose their property, is tolerably certain; and you yourself, if you fly to one of the neighbouring cities, as, for example, Thebes or Megara, both of which are well governed, will come to them as an enemy, Socrates, and their government will be against you, and all patriotic citizens will cast an evil eye upon you as a subverter of the laws, and you will confirm in the minds of the judges the justice of their own condemnation of you. For he who is a corrupter of the laws is more than likely to be a corrupter of the young and foolish portion of mankind. Will you then flee from well-ordered cities and virtuous men? And is existence worth having on these terms? Or will you go to them without shame, and talk to them, Socrates? And what will you say to them? What you say here about virtue and justice and institutions and laws being the best things among men? Would that be decent of you?

Surely not. But if you go away from well-governed states to Crito's friends in Thessaly, where there is great disorder and licence, they will be charmed to hear the tale of your escape from prison, set off with ludicrous particulars of the manner in which you were wrapped in a goatskin or some other disguise, and metamorphosed as the manner is of runaways; but will there be no one to remind you that in your old age you were not ashamed to violate the most sacred laws from a miserable desire of a little more life? Perhaps not, if you keep them in a good temper; but if they are out of temper you will hear many degrading things; you will live, but how?—as the flatterer of all men, and the servant of all men; and doing what?—eating and drinking in Thessaly, having gone abroad in order that you may get a dinner. And where will be your fine sentiments about justice and virtue? Say that you wish to live for the sake of your children—you want to bring them up and educate them—will you take them into Thessaly and deprive them of Athenian citizenship? Is this the benefit which you will confer upon them? Or are you under the impression that they will be better cared for and educated here if you are still alive, although absent from them; for your friends will take care of them? Do you fancy that if you are an inhabitant of Thessaly they will take care of them, and if you are an inhabitant of the other world that they will not take care of them? Nay; but if they who call themselves friends are good for anything, they will—to be sure they will.

"Listen, then, Socrates, to us who have brought you up. Think not of life and children first, and of justice afterwards, but of justice first, that you may be justified before the princes of the world below. For neither will you nor any that belong to you be happier or holier or juster in this life, or happier in another, if you do as Crito bids. Now you depart in innocence, a sufferer and not a doer of evil; a victim, not of the laws but of men. But if you go forth, returning evil for evil, and injury for injury, breaking the covenants and agreements which you have made with us, and wronging those whom you ought least of all to wrong, that is to say, yourself, your friends, your country, and us, we shall be angry with you while you live, and our brethren, the laws in the world below, will receive you as an enemy; for they will know that you have done your best to destroy us. Listen, then, to us and not to Crito."

This, dear Crito, is the voice which I seem to hear murmuring in my ears, like the sound of the flute in the ears of the mystic; that voice, I say, is humming in my ears, and prevents me from hearing any other. And I know that nothing more which you may say will be vain. Yet speak, if you have anything to say.

Crito: I have nothing to say, Socrates.

Socrates: Leave me then, Crito, to fulfill the will of God, and to follow whither he leads.

FOR FURTHER REFLECTION

1. Discuss Socrates' reasoning in the *Crito*. Should he have tried to escape? Why or why not? What would you have done?
2. Go over Crito's reasoning and compare it with Socrates' reasoning. Evaluate their arguments.
3. This dialogue is the first recorded essay on the rationale for civil disobedience. Is it sometimes morally correct to engage in civil disobedience? Explain your answer.

A. Moral Relativism

Are there any moral absolutes, or is morality completely relative? *Moral relativism* is the notion that there are no universally valid moral principles, but that all moral principles are valid relative to cultural or individual choice. It should be distinguished from the anthropological notion of *cultural relativism*, the descriptive thesis that cultures differ in their moral norms. It is also to be distinguished from *moral skepticism*, the view that there are no valid moral principles at all (or at least none about which we can be confident). There are two forms of ethical relativism: (1) *subjectivism*, which views morality as a personal decision ("Morality is in the eyes of the beholder"), and (2) *conventionalism*, which views moral validity in terms of social acceptance. Opposed to ethical relativism are various theories of *ethical objectivism*. All forms of objectivism affirm the universal validity of some moral principles. The strongest form, *moral absolutism*, holds that there is exactly one right answer to "What should I do in situation X?" (whatever that situation may be) and that a moral principle can never be overridden—even by another moral principle. A weaker form of objectivism sees moral principles as universally valid but not always applicable. That is, moral principle A could be overridden by moral principle B in a given situation, while in other situations there might not be a right answer. After the ancient Herodotus's illustration of cultural relativism and Ruth Benedict's defense of moral relativism, we go on to my own critique of that theory. Then we study J. L. Mackie's more sophisticated theory about the subjectivity of values, which I answer with a defense of modest objectivism.

Herodotus
‿

CUSTOM IS KING

In this brief passage from his histories, Herodotus (485–430 B.C.E.), a Greek and the first Western historian, illustrates cultural relativism and may suggest that ethical relativism is the better view.

Thus it appears certain to me, by a great variety of proofs, that Cambyses was raving mad; he would not else have set himself to make a mock of holy rites and long-established usages. For if one were to offer men to choose out of all the customs in the world such as seemed to them the best, they would examine the

From Herodotus, in *History of Herodotus*, trans. Geroge Rawlinson (New York: Appleton, 1859), Book 3, Chapter 38.

whole number, and end by preferring their own; so convinced are they that their own usages far surpass those of all others. Unless, therefore, a man was mad, it is not likely that he would make sport of such matters. That people have this feeling about their laws may be seen by very many proofs: among others, by the following. Darius, after he had got the kingdom, called into his presence certain Greeks who were at hand, and asked—"What he should pay them to eat the bodies of their fathers when they died?" To which they answered, that there was no sum that would tempt them to do such a thing. He then sent for certain Indians, of the race called Callatians, men who eat their fathers, and asked them, while the Greeks stood by, and knew by the help of an interpreter all that was said—"What he should give them to burn the bodies of their fathers at their decease?" The Indians exclaimed aloud, and bade him forbear such language. Such is men's wont herein; and Pindar was right, in my judgment, when he said "Custom is the king o'er all."

RUTH BENEDICT

IN DEFENSE OF MORAL RELATIVISM

Ruth Benedict (1887–1948) was a leading U.S. anthropologist who taught at Columbia University and is best known for her book *Patterns of Culture* (1935). Benedict views social systems as communities with common beliefs and practices, which have become more or less well-integrated patterns of ideas and practices. Like a work of art, a social system chooses which theme of its repertoire of basic tendencies to emphasize, and then goes about to produce a holistic, grand design favoring those tendencies. The final systems differ from one another in striking ways, but there is no reason to say that one system is better than another. What is considered normal or abnormal behavior will depend on the choices of these social systems or what Benedict calls the "idea-practice pattern of the culture."

Benedict views morality as dependent on the varying histories and environments of different cultures. In this essay, she assembles an impressive amount of data from her anthropological research of tribal behavior on an island in northwest Melanesia, from which she draws her conclusion that moral relativism is the correct view of moral principles.

Modern social anthropology has become more and more a study of the varieties and common elements of cultural environment and the consequences of these in human behavior. For such a study of diverse social orders primitive peoples fortunately provide a laboratory not yet entirely vitiated by the spread of a standardized worldwide civilization. Dyaks and Hopis, Fijians and Yakuts are significant for psychological

From Ruth Benedict, "Anthropology and the Abnormal," *Journal of General Psychology 10,* 1934, 59–82. Reprinted by permission of the Helen Dwight Reid Educational Foundation.

and sociological study because only among these simpler peoples has there been sufficient isolation to give opportunity for the development of localized social forms. In the higher cultures the standardization of custom and belief over a couple of continents has given a false sense of the inevitability of the particular forms that have gained currency, and we need to turn to a wider survey in order to check the conclusions we hastily base upon this near-universality of familiar customs. Most of the simpler cultures did not gain the wide currency of the one which, out of our experience, we identify with human nature, but this was for various historical reasons, and certainly not for any that gives us as its carriers a monopoly of social good or of social sanity. Modern civilization, from this point of view, becomes not a necessary pinnacle of human achievement but one entry in a long series of possible adjustments.

These adjustments, whether they are in mannerisms like the ways of showing anger, or joy, or grief in any society, or in major human drives like those of sex, prove to be far more variable than experience in any one culture would suggest. In certain fields, such as that of religion or of formal marriage arrangements, these wide limits of variability are well known and can be fairly described. In others it is not yet possible to give a generalized account, but that does not absolve us of the task of indicating the significance of the work that has been done and of the problems that have arisen.

One of these problems relates to the customary modern normal-abnormal categories and our conclusions regarding them. In how far are such categories culturally determined, or in how far can we with assurance regard them as absolute? In how far can we regard inability to function socially as diagnostic of abnormality, or in how far is it necessary to regard this as a function of the culture?

As a matter of fact, one of the most striking facts that emerge from a study of widely varying cultures is the ease with which our abnormals function in other cultures. It does not matter what kind of "abnormality" we choose for illustration, those which indicate extreme instability, or those which are more in the nature of character traits like sadism or delusions of grandeur or of persecution, there are well-described cultures in which these abnormals function at ease and with honor, and apparently without danger or difficulty to the society.

The most notorious of these is trance and catalepsy. Even a very mild mystic is aberrant in our culture. But most peoples have regarded even extreme psychic manifestations not only as normal and desirable, but even as characteristic of highly valued and gifted individuals. This was true even in our own cultural background in that period when Catholicism made the ecstatic experience the mark of sainthood. It is hard for us, born and brought up in a culture that makes no use of the experience, to realize how important a role it may play and how many individuals are capable of it, once it has been given an honorable place in any society. . . .

Cataleptic and trance phenomena are, of course, only one illustration of the fact that those whom we regard as abnormals may function adequately in other cultures. Many of our culturally discarded traits are selected for elaboration in different societies. Homosexuality is an excellent example, for in this case our attention is not constantly diverted, as in the consideration of trance, to the interruption of routine activity which it implies. Homosexuality poses the problem very simply. A tendency toward this trait in our culture exposes an individual to all the conflicts to which all aberrants are always exposed, and we tend to identify the consequences of this conflict with homosexuality. But these consequences are obviously local and cultural. Homosexuals in many societies are not incompetent, but they may be such if the culture asks adjustments of them that would strain any man's vitality. Wherever homosexuality has been given an honorable place in any society, those to whom it is congenial have filled adequately the honorable roles society assigns to them. Plato's *Republic* is, of course, the most convincing statement of such a reading of homosexuality. It is presented as one of the major means to the good life, and it was generally so regarded in Greece at that time.

The cultural attitude toward homosexuals has not always been on such a high ethical plane, but it has been very varied. Among many American Indian tribes there exists the institution of the *berdache,* as the French called them. These men-women were men who at puberty or thereafter took the dress and the occupations of women. Sometimes they married other men and lived with them. Sometimes they were men with no inversion, persons of weak sexual endowment who chose this role to avoid the jeers of the women. The *berdaches* were never regarded as of first-rate supernatural power, as similar men-women were in Siberia, but rather as leaders in women's occupations, good healers in certain diseases, or, among certain tribes, as the genial organizers of social affairs. In any case, they were socially placed. They were not left exposed to the conflicts that visit the deviant who is excluded from participation in the recognized patterns of his society.

The most spectacular illustrations of the extent to which normality may be culturally defined are those cultures where an abnormality of our culture is the cornerstone of their social structure. It is not possible to do justice to these possibilities in a short discussion. A recent study of an island of northwest Melanesia by Fortune describes a society built upon traits which we regard as beyond the border of paranoia. In this tribe the exogamic groups look upon each other as prime manipulators of black magic, so that one marries always into an enemy group which remains for life one's deadly and unappeasable foes. They look upon a good garden crop as a confession of theft, for everyone is engaged in making magic to induce into his garden the productiveness of his neighbors'; therefore no secrecy in the island is so rigidly insisted upon as the secrecy of a man's harvesting of his yams. Their polite phrase at the acceptance of a gift is, "And if you now poison me, how shall I repay you this present?" Their preoccupation with poisoning is constant; no woman ever leaves her cooking pot for a moment untended. Even the great affinal economic exchanges that are characteristic of this Melanesian culture area are quite altered in Dobu since they are incompatible with this fear and distrust that pervades the culture. They go farther and people the whole world outside their own quarters with such malignant spirits that all-night feasts and ceremonials simply do not occur here. They have even rigorous religiously enforced customs that forbid the sharing of seed even in one family group. Anyone else's food is deadly poison to you, so that communality of stores is out of the ques-

tion. For some months before harvest the whole society is on the verge of starvation, but if one falls to the temptation and eats up one's seed yams, one is an outcast and a beachcomber for life. There is no coming back. It involves, as a matter of course, divorce and the breaking of all social ties.

Now in this society where no one may work with another and no one may share with another, Fortune describes the individual who was regarded by all his fellows as crazy. He was not one of those who periodically ran amok and, beside himself and frothing at the mouth, fell with a knife upon anyone he could reach. Such behavior they did not regard as putting anyone outside the pale. They did not even put the individuals who were known to be liable to these attacks under any kind of control. They merely fled when they saw the attack coming on and kept out of the way. "He would be all right tomorrow." But there was one man of sunny, kindly disposition who liked work and liked to be helpful. The compulsion was too strong for him to repress it in favor of the opposite tendencies of his culture. Men and women never spoke of him without laughing; he was silly and simple and definitely crazy. Nevertheless, to the ethnologist used to a culture that has, in Christianity, made his type the model of all virtue, he seemed a pleasant fellow. . . .

. . . Among the Kwakiutl it did not matter whether a relative had died in bed of disease, or by the hand of an enemy, in either case death was an affront to be wiped out by the death of another person. The fact that one had been caused to mourn was proof that one had been put upon. A chief's sister and her daughter had gone up to Victoria, and either because they drank bad whiskey or because their boat capsized they never came back. The chief called together his warriors, "Now I ask you, tribes, who shall wail? Shall I do it or shall another?" The spokesman answered, of course, "Not you, Chief. Let some other of the tribes." Immediately they set up the war pole to announce their intention of wiping out the injury, and gathered a war party. They set out, and found seven men and two children asleep and killed them. "Then they felt good when they arrived at Sebaa in the evening."

The point which is of interest to us is that in our society those who on that occasion would feel good when they arrived at Sebaa that evening would be the definitely abnormal. There would be some, even in our society, but it is not a recognized and approved mood under the circumstances. On the Northwest Coast those are favored and fortunate to whom that mood under those circumstances is congenial, and those to whom it is repugnant are unlucky. This latter minority can register in their own culture only by doing violence to their congenial responses and acquiring others that are difficult for them. The person, for instance, who, like a Plains Indian whose wife has been taken from him, is too proud to fight, can deal with the Northwest Coast civilization only by ignoring its strongest bents. If he cannot achieve it, he is the deviant in that culture, their instance of abnormality.

This head-hunting that takes place on the Northwest Coast after a death is no matter of blood revenge or of organized vengeance. There is no effort to tie up the subsequent killing with any responsibility on the part of the victim for the death of the person who is being mourned. A chief whose son has died goes visiting wherever his fancy dictates, and he says to his host, "My prince has died today, and you go with him." Then he kills him. In this, according to their interpretation, he acts nobly because he has not been downed. He has thrust back in return. The whole procedure is meaningless without the fundamental paranoid reading of bereavement. Death, like all the other untoward accidents of existence, confounds man's pride and can only be handled in the category of insults.

The behavior honored upon the Northwest Coast is one which is recognized as abnormal in our civilization, and yet it is sufficiently close to the attitudes of our own culture to be intelligible to us and to have a definite vocabulary with which we may discuss it. The megalomaniac paranoid trend is a definite danger in our society. It is encouraged by some of our major preoccupations, and it confronts us with a choice of two possible attitudes. One is to brand it as abnormal and reprehensible, and is the attitude we have chosen in our civilization. The other is to make it an essential attribute of ideal man, and this is the solution in the culture of the Northwest Coast.

These illustrations, which it has been possible to indicate only in the briefest manner, force upon us the fact that normality is culturally defined. An adult shaped to the drives and standards of either of these cultures, if he were transported into our civilization, would fall into our categories of abnormality. He would be faced with the psychic dilemmas of the socially unavailable. In his own culture, however, he is the pillar of society, the end result of socially inculcated mores, and the problem of personal instability in his case simply does not arise.

No one civilization can possibly utilize in its mores the whole potential range of human behavior. Just as there are great numbers of possible phonetic articulations, and the possibility of language depends on a selection and standardization of a few of these in order that speech communication may be possible at all, so the possibility of organized behavior of every sort, from the fashions of local dress and houses to the dicta of a people's ethics and religion, depends upon a similar selection among the possible behavior traits. In the field of recognized economic obligations or sex tabus this selection is as nonrational and subconscious a process as it is in the field of phonetics. It is a process which goes on in the group for long periods of time and is historically conditioned by innumerable accidents of isolation or of contact of peoples. In any comprehensive study of psychology, the selection that different cultures have made in the course of history within the great circumference of potential behavior is of great significance.

Every society, beginning with some slight inclination in one direction or another, carries its preference farther and farther, integrating itself more and more completely upon its chosen basis, and discarding those types of behavior that are uncongenial. Most of those organizations of personality that seem to us most uncontrovertibly abnormal have been used by different civilizations in the very foundations of their institutional life. Conversely the most valued traits of our normal individuals have been looked on in differently organized cultures as aberrant. Normality, in short, within a very wide range, is culturally defined. It is primarily a term for the socially elaborated segment of human behavior in any culture; and abnormality, a term for the segment that that particular civilization does not use. The very eyes with which we see the problem are conditioned by the long traditional habits of our own society.

It is a point that has been made more often in relation to ethics than in relation to psychiatry. We do not any longer make the mistake of deriving the morality of our locality and decade directly from the inevitable constitution of human nature. We do not elevate it to the dignity of a first principle. We recognize that morality differs in every society, and is a convenient term for socially approved habits. Mankind has always preferred to say, "It is a moral good," rather than "It is habitual," and the fact of this preference is matter enough for a critical science of ethics. But historically the two phrases are synonymous.

The concept of the normal is properly a variant of the concept of the good. It is that which society has approved. A normal action is one which falls well within the limits of expected behavior for a particular society. Its variability among different peoples is essentially a function of the variability of the behavior patterns that different societies have created for themselves, and can never be wholly divorced from a consideration of culturally institutionalized types of behavior.

Each culture is a more or less elaborate working-out of the potentialities of the segment it has chosen. In so far as a civilization is well integrated and consistent within itself, it will tend to carry farther and farther, according to its nature, its initial impulse toward a particular type of action, and from the point of view of any other culture those elaborations will include more and more extreme and aberrant traits.

Each of these traits, in proportion as it reinforces the chosen behavior patterns of that culture, is for that culture normal. Those individuals to whom it is congenial either congenitally, or as the result of childhood sets, are accorded prestige in that culture, and are not visited with the social contempt or disapproval which their traits would call down upon them in a society that was differently organized. On the other hand, those individuals whose characteristics are not congenial to the selected type of human behavior in that community are the deviants, no matter how valued their personality traits may be in a contrasted civilization.

The Dobuan who is not easily susceptible to fear of treachery, who enjoys work and likes to be helpful, is their neurotic and regarded as silly. On the North-west Coast the person who finds it difficult to read life in terms of an insult contest will be the person upon whom fall all the difficulties of the culturally unprovided for. The person who does not find it easy to humiliate a neighbor, nor to see humiliation in his own experience, who is genial and loving, may, of course, find some unstandardized way of achieving satisfactions in his society, but not in the major patterned responses that his culture requires of him. If he is born to play an important role in a family with many hereditary privileges, he can succeed only by doing violence to his whole personality. If he does not succeed, he has betrayed his culture; that is, he is abnormal.

I have spoken of individuals as having sets toward certain types of behavior, and of these sets as running sometimes counter to the types of behavior which are institutionalized in the culture to which they belong. From all that we know of contrasting cultures it seems clear that differences of temperament occur in every society. The matter has never been made the subject of investigation, but from the available material it would appear that these temperament types are very likely of universal recurrence. That is, there is an ascertainable range of human behavior that is found wherever a sufficiently large series of individuals is observed. But the proportion in which behavior types stand to one another in different societies is not universal. The vast majority of individuals in any group are shaped to the fashion of that culture. In other words, most individuals are plastic to the moulding force of the society into which they are born. In a society that values trance, as in India, they will have supernormal experience. In a society that institutionalizes homosexuality, they will be homosexual. In a society that sets the gathering of possessions as the chief human objective, they will amass property. The deviants, whatever the type of behavior the culture has institutionalized, will remain few in number, and there seems no more difficulty in moulding the vast malleable majority to the "normality" of what we consider an aberrant trait, such as delusions of reference, than to the normality of such accepted behavior patterns as acquisitiveness. The small proportion of the number of the deviants in any culture is not a function of the sure instinct with which that society has built itself upon the fundamental sanities, but of the universal fact that, happily, the majority of mankind quite readily take any shape that is presented to them.

FOR FURTHER REFLECTION

1. Is Benedict correct in saying that our culture is "but one entry in a long series of possible adjustments"? What are the implications of this statement?

2. Can we separate the descriptive aspect of anthropological study from the prescriptive aspect of evaluating cultures? Are there some independent criteria by which we can say that some cultures are better than others? How might this project be begun?

3. What are the implications of Benedict's claim that morality is simply whatever a culture deems as normal behavior? Is this a satisfactory equation? Can you apply it to the institution of slavery or to the Nazi policy of anti-Semitism? Explain.

4. What is the significance of Benedict's statement "The very eyes with which we see the problem are conditioned by the long traditional habits of our own society"? Can you apply the conceptual relativism embodied in this statement to her own position?

LOUIS P. POJMAN

ETHICAL RELATIVISM VERSUS ETHICAL OBJECTIVISM

Louis P. Pojman was a professor of philosophy at the United States Military Academy. He wrote books and articles in the areas of philosophy of religion and ethics, including *Ethics: Discovering Right and Wrong*, 3d ed. (1999), from which this essay is taken. He was the editor of this book.

In this essay Pojman first analyzes the structure of ethical relativism as constituted by two theses, the diversity thesis and dependency thesis, and then goes on to examine two types of ethical relativism: subjectivism and conventionalism. He argues that both types have serious problems. He indicates a way of taking into account the insights of relativism while maintaining an objectivist position, and ends by offering suggestions as to why people have been misled by relativist arguments.

There is one thing a professor can be absolutely certain of: almost every student entering the university believes, or says he believes, that truth is relative. If this belief is put to the test, one can count on the students' reaction: they will be uncomprehending. That anyone should regard the proposition as not self-evident astonishes them, as though he were calling into question 2 + 2 = 4. . . . The danger they have been taught to fear from absolutism is not error but intolerance. Relativism is necessary to openness; and this is the virtue, the only virtue, which all primary education for more than fifty years has dedicated itself to inculcating.

Alan Bloom, The Closing of the American Mind

In the nineteenth century, Christian missionaries sometimes used coercion to change the customs of pagan tribal people in parts of Africa and the Pacific Islands. Appalled by the customs of public nakedness, polygamy, working on the Sabbath, and infanticide, they paternalistically went about reforming the "poor pagans." They clothed the people, separated secondary wives from their polygamous husbands in order to create monogamous households, made the Sabbath a day of rest, and put an end to infanticide. In the process, they sometimes created social malaise, causing the estranged women to despair and their children to be orphaned. The natives often did not understand the new religion, but accepted it in deference to white power. The white people had guns and medicine.

Since the nineteenth century, we've made progress in understanding cultural diversity and realize that the social dissonance caused by do-gooders was a bad thing. In the last century or so, anthropology has exposed our penchant for ethnocentrism—the prejudicial view that interprets all reality through the eyes of our cultural beliefs and values. We have come to see enormous variety in social practices throughout the world.

Some Eskimo tribes allow their elderly to die by starvation, while we believe that this is morally wrong. The Spartans of ancient Greece and Dobu of New Guinea believe that stealing is morally right, but we believe it is wrong. Many cultures, past and present, have practiced or still practice infanticide. A tribe in East Africa once threw deformed infants to the hippopotamus, but our society condemns such acts. Sexual practices vary over time and clime. Some cultures permit, while others condemn, homosexual behavior. Some cultures, including Moslem societies, practice polygamy, while Christian cultures view it as immoral. Ruth Benedict describes a tribe in Melane-

sia that views cooperation and kindness as vices, and Colin Turnbull has documented that the Ik in northern Uganda have no sense of duty toward their children or parents. There are societies that make it a duty for children to kill (sometimes by strangling) their aging parents.

The ancient Greek historian, Herodotus (485–430 B.C.E.) tells the story of how Darius, the king of Persia, once brought together some Callatians (Asian tribal people) and some Greeks. He asked the Callatians how they disposed of their deceased parents. They said they ate their dead parents. The Greeks, who cremated their parents, were horrified at such barbarous behavior. No amount of money could tempt them to do such an irreverent thing. Then Darius asked the Callatians what he could give them to persuade them to burn their dead parents instead. The Callatians were utterly horrified at such barbarous behavior and begged Darius to stop talking so irreverently. Herodotus concludes that "Custom is the king o'er all." [1]

Today we condemn ethnocentrism—the uncritical belief in the inherent superiority of one's own culture—as a variety of prejudice tantamount to racism and sexism. What is right in one culture may be wrong in another, what is good east of the river may be bad west of the same river, what is a virtue in one nation may be seen as a vice in another, so it behooves us not to judge others but to be tolerant of diversity.

This rejection of Western ethnocentrism has helped shift public opinion about morality, so that for a growing number of Westerners, consciousness raising about the validity of other ways of life has gradually eroded belief in moral *objectivism,* the view that there are universal moral principles, valid for all people at all times and climes. For example, in polls taken in my ethics and introduction to philosophy classes (in three different universities, in three areas of the country) over the past several years students by a 2-to-1 ratio affirmed a version of *moral relativism* over *moral absolutism.* Barely 3 percent considered a stance in between these two polar opposites. Of course, I'm not suggesting that all these students clearly understand what relativism entails. Many who

Adapted from Louis Pojman, *Ethics: Discovering Right and Wrong,* 3d ed. (Belmont, CA: Wadsworth, 1999), Chapter 2. Copyright © Louis P. Pojman, 1988.

say they are ethical relativists also may state (on the same questionnaire) that "Abortion except to save the mother's life is always wrong," that "Capital punishment is always morally wrong," or that "Suicide is never morally permissible." The apparent contradictions signal an apparent confusion on the matter.

I want to argue that ethical relativism is a mistaken theory and that the cultural differences do not demonstrate that all ways of life are equally valid from a moral perspective. Indeed, ethical relativism, were it true, would spell the death of ethics. In spite of cultural divergences, there is a universally valid core morality. I call this core morality "moral objectivism" to distinguish it from both moral absolutism and moral relativism.

AN ANALYSIS OF RELATIVISM

Ethical relativism is the theory that there are no universally valid moral principles; that all moral principles are valid relative to *culture* or *individual choice.* There are two types of relativism: *conventionalism* holds that moral principles are relative to the culture or society, and *subjectivism* holds that individual choice determines the validity of a moral principle. We'll start with conventionalism. Philosopher John Ladd, of Brown University, defines *conventional ethical relativism* this way:

> Ethical relativism is the doctrine that the moral rightness and wrongness of actions varies from society to society and that there are no absolute universal moral standards binding on all men at all times. Accordingly, it holds that whether or not it is right for an individual to act in a certain way depends on or is relative to the society to which he belongs.[2]

According to Ladd, ethical relativism consists of two theses: (1) a *diversity thesis,* which specifies that what is considered morally right and wrong varies from society to society, so that there are no moral principles accepted by all societies, and (2) a *dependency thesis,* which specifies that all moral principles derive their validity from cultural acceptance. From these two ideas he concludes that there are no universally valid moral principles, objective standards that apply to all people everywhere and at all times.

The first thesis, the *diversity thesis,* or what may simply be called *cultural relativism,* is an anthropological thesis, registering the fact that moral rules differ from society to society. As noted at the beginning of this essay, there is enormous variety in what may count as a moral principle in a given society. The human condition is extremely malleable, allowing any number of folkways or moral codes. As Ruth Benedict has written,

> The cultural pattern of any civilization makes use of a certain segment of the great arc of potential human purposes and motivations . . . that any culture makes use of certain selected material techniques or cultural traits. The great arc along which all the possible human behaviors are distributed is far too immense and too full of contradictions for any one culture to utilize even any considerable portion of it. Selection is the first requirement.[3]

The second thesis, the *dependency thesis,* asserts that individual acts are right or wrong depending on the nature of the society from which they emanate. What is considered morally right or wrong must be seen in a context, depending on the goals, wants, beliefs, history, and environment of the society in question. As William Graham Sumner says, "We learn the [morals] as unconsciously as we learn to walk and hear and breathe, and they never know any reason why the [morals] are what they are. The justification of them is that when we wake to consciousness of life we find them facts which already hold us in the bonds of tradition, custom, and habit."[4] Trying to see things from an independent, noncultural point of view would be like taking out our eyes in order to examine their contours and qualities. We are simply culturally determined beings.

In a sense, we all live in radically different worlds. Each person has a different set of beliefs and experiences, a particular perspective that colors all of his or her perceptions. Do the farmer, the real estate dealer, and the artist, looking at the same spatiotemporal field, see the *same* field? Not likely. Their different orientations, values, and expectations govern their perceptions, so that different aspects of the field are highlighted and some features are missed. Even as our individual values arise from personal experience, so social values are grounded in the peculiar history of the community. Morality, then, is just the set of common rules, habits, and customs that have won social approval over time, so that they seem part of the nature of things, as facts. There is nothing mysterious or transcendent about these codes of behavior. They are the outcomes of our social history.

The conclusion that there are no absolute or objective moral standards binding on all people follows from the first two propositions. Cultural relativism (the diversity thesis) plus the dependency thesis yield ethical relativism in its classic form. If there are different moral principles from culture to culture and if all morality is rooted in culture, then it follows that there are no universal moral principles, valid for all cultures and people at all times.

SUBJECTIVE ETHICAL RELATIVISM (SUBJECTIVISM)

Some people think that even this conclusion is too tame, and maintain that morality does not depend on the society but on the individual him- or herself. As students sometimes maintain, "Morality is in the eye of the beholder." Ernest Hemingway wrote, "So far, about morals, I know only that what is moral is what you feel good after and what is immoral is what you feel bad after and judged by these moral standards, which I do not defend, the bullfight is very moral to me because I feel very fine while it is going on and have a feeling of life and death and mortality and immortality, and after it is over I feel very sad but very fine."[5]

This form of moral subjectivism has the sorry consequence that it makes morality a useless concept, for on its premises little or no interpersonal criticism or judgment is logically possible. Hemingway may feel good about killing bulls in a bullfight, while Albert Schweitzer or Mother Teresa may feel the opposite. No argument about the matter is possible. The only basis for judging Hemingway or anyone else wrong would be if he failed to live up to his own principles, but, of course, one of Hemingway's principles could be that hypocrisy is morally permissible (he feels good about it), so that it would be impossible for him to do wrong. For Hemingway, both hypocrisy and nonhypocrisy are morally permissible. On the basis of subjectivism, Adolf Hitler is as moral as Gandhi, so long as each believes he is living by his chosen principles. Notions of moral good and bad, right or wrong, cease to have interpersonal evaluative meaning.

Columbia University professor Sidney Morgenbesser once taught a class of philosophy students who argued vehemently for subjectivism. When a test was taken, Morgenbesser returned all the tests marked "F"—even though his comments showed that most of the tests were of a very high quality. When the students expressed outrage at this injustice, Morgenbesser answered that he had accepted the notion of subjectivism for purposes of marking the exams, in which case the principle of justice had no objective validity.

Absurd consequences follow from subjective ethical relativism. If it is correct, then morality reduces to esthetic tastes over which there can be no argument nor interpersonal judgment. Although many people say that they hold this position, it seems to conflict with other of their moral views (for example, that Hitler is really morally bad, or capital punishment is always wrong). There seems to be a contradiction between subjectivism and the very concept of morality it is supposed to characterize, for morality concerns "proper" resolution of interpersonal conflict and the amelioration of the human predicament. Whatever else it does, morality has a minimal aim of preventing a state of chaos where life is "solitary, poor, nasty, brutish, and short." But subjectivism is no help at all in doing this, for it doesn't rest on social *agreement* of principle (as the conventionalist maintains) or on an objectively independent set of norms that bind all people for the common good.

Subjectivism treats individuals as billiard balls on a societal pool table where they meet only in radical collisions, each aiming for its own goal and striving to do in the other fellow first. This atomistic view of personality contrasts with the fact that we develop in families and mutually dependent communities, in which we share a common language, common institutions, and habits, and that we often share each other's joys and sorrows. As John Donne said, "No man is an island, entire of itself; every man is a piece of the continent."

Radical individualistic relativism seems incoherent. So the only plausible form of ethical relativism must be one that grounds morality in the group or culture. This form of relativism is called "conventionalism," at which we looked earlier and to which we now return.

CONVENTIONAL ETHICAL RELATIVISM (CONVENTIONALISM)

Conventional ethical relativism—the view that there are no objective moral principles but that all valid moral principles are justified by virtue of their cultural acceptance—recognizes the social nature of morality. That is precisely its power and virtue. It does not have the same absurd consequences that plague subjectivism. Recognizing the importance of our social environment in generating customs and beliefs, many people suppose that ethical relativism is the correct ethical theory. Furthermore, they are drawn to it for its liberal philosophical stance. It seems an enlightened response to the "sin of ethnocentricity," and seems to entail or strongly imply an attitude of tolerance toward other cultures. As Benedict says, in recognizing ethical relativity "we shall arrive at a more realistic social faith, accepting as grounds of hope and as new bases for tolerance the coexisting and equally valid patterns of life which mankind has created for itself from the raw materials of existence."[6] The most famous person holding this position is anthropologist Melville Herskovits, who argues even more explicitly than Benedict that ethical relativism entails intercultural tolerance.[7]

The view contains a contradiction. If no moral principles are universally valid, how can tolerance be universally valid? Whence comes its validity? If morality is simply relative to each culture and if the culture does not have a principle of tolerance, then its members have no obligation to be tolerant. Herskovits seems to be treating the *principle of tolerance* as the one exception to his relativism—as an absolute moral principle. But from a relativistic point of view there is no more reason to be tolerant than to be intolerant, and neither stance is objectively morally better than the other.

Not only do relativists fail to offer a basis for criticizing those who are intolerant, but they cannot rationally *criticize* anyone who espouses what they might regard as an evil principle. If (as seems to be the case) valid criticism supposes an objective or impartial standard, then relativists cannot morally criticize anyone outside their own culture. Adolf Hitler's genocidal actions, as long as they are culturally accepted, are thus as morally legitimate as Mother Teresa's works of mercy. If conventional relativism is accepted, then racism, genocide of unpopular minorities, oppression of the poor, slavery, and even the advocacy of war for its own sake are as equally moral as their opposites. And if a subculture decided that starting a nuclear war was somehow morally acceptable, we could not morally criticize these people. Any actual morality, whatever its content, is as valid as every other, and more valid than ideal moralities—because the latter aren't adhered to by any culture.

There are other disturbing consequences of ethical relativism. It seems to entail that reformers are always (morally) wrong, because they go against the cultural tide. Thus William Wilberforce was wrong in the eighteenth century to oppose slavery, the British were immoral in opposing suttee in India (the burning of widows, now illegal in India). The early Christians were wrong in refusing to serve in the Roman army or bow down to Caesar because most people in the Roman Empire believed these two acts were moral duties. In fact, Jesus himself was immoral: he broke the law by healing on the Sabbath day and by advocating the principles expressed in the Sermon on the Mount, because few people in his time (or in ours) accepted these principles.

Yet we normally feel just the opposite: that the reformer is the courageous innovator who is right, who has the truth, against the mindless majority. Sometimes the individual must stand alone with the truth, risking social censure and persecution. Dr. Stockman says in Ibsen's *Enemy of the People,* after he loses the battle to declare his town's profitable polluted tourist spa unsanitary, "The most dangerous enemy of the truth and freedom among us—is the compact majority. Yes, the damned, compact and liberal majority. The majority has *might*—unfortunately—but *right* it is not. Right—are I and a few others." Yet if relativism is correct, the opposite is necessarily the case. Truth is with the crowd, and error with the individual.

There is an even more basic problem with the idea that morality depends on cultural acceptance for validity. The problem is that "culture" or "society" is notoriously difficult to define. This is especially so in a pluralistic society like our own, which seems to be vague, with unclear boundary lines. One person may belong to several societies (subcultures) with different value emphases and arrangements of principles. A person may belong to the nation as a single society with certain values of patriotism, honor, courage, and laws (including some that are controversial but have majority acceptance, such as the law on abortion). But a person may also belong to a church that opposes some of the laws of the state. He or she may also be an integral member of a socially mixed community where different principles hold sway, and may belong to clubs and a family where still other rules are adhered to. Relativism would seem to tell us that where people are members of societies with conflicting moralities they must be judged both wrong and not wrong, whatever they do. For example, if Mary is a U.S. citizen and a member of the Roman Catholic Church, she is wrong (as a Catholic) if she chooses to have an abortion and not wrong (as a U.S. citizen) if she acts against the teaching of the Church on abortion. As a member of a racist organization, the Ku Klux Klan or KKK, John has no obligation to treat his fellow black citizen as an equal, but as a member of the university community itself (where the principle of equal rights is accepted) he does have that obligation; but as a member of the surrounding community (which may reject the principle of equal rights) he again has no such obligation; and again, as a member of the nation at large (which accepts the principle), he is obligated to treat his fellow with respect. What is the morally right thing for John to do? The question no longer makes much sense in this moral Babel. It has lost its action-guiding function.

Perhaps the relativist would adhere to a principle that says that in such cases the individual may choose which group to belong to as primary. If Mary chooses to have an abortion, she is choosing to belong to the general society, relative to that principle. And John must likewise choose between groups. The trouble with this option is that it seems to lead back to counterintuitive results. If Gangland Gus of Murder, Incorporated, feels like killing Bank President Ortcutt and wants to feel good about it, he identifies with the Murder, Incorporated, society rather than the general public morality. Does this justify the killing? In fact, couldn't one justify anything simply by forming a small subculture that approved of it? Charles Manson would be morally pure in killing innocents simply by virtue of forming a little coterie. How large must the group be in order to be a legitimate subculture or society? Does it need ten or fifteen people? How about just three? Come to think about it, why can't my burglary partner and I found our own society with a morality of its own? Of course, if my partner died, I could still claim that I was acting from an originally social set of norms. But why can't I dispense with the interpersonal agreements altogether and invent my own morality—since morality, on this view, is only an invention anyway? Conventionalist relativism seems to reduce to subjectivism. And subjectivism leads, as we have seen, to the demise of morality altogether.

Where does the relativist go wrong? I think the relativist makes an unwarranted slide from (1) the observation that different cultures have different rules, to (2) the conclusion that no culture's set of rules are better than any other culture's set of rules or even any ideal set of rules. But some sets of rules *are* better than other sets relative to the purposes of morality. If we suppose that morality answers to a set of social purposes, and that the purposes of morality are the survival of society, alleviation of suffering, encouragement of human flourishing, and the just resolution of conflicts of interest, these purposes will yield a set of common principles that may actually underlie some of the cultural differences reported by anthropologists. E. O. Wilson has identified over a score of common features, and before him Clyde Kluckhohn has noted some significant common ground:

> Every culture has a concept of murder, distinguishing this from execution, killing in war, and other "justifiable homicides." The notions of incest and other regulations upon sexual behavior, the prohibitions upon untruth under defined circumstances, of restitution and reciprocity, of mutual obligations

between parents and children—these and many other moral concepts are altogether universal.[8]

And Colin Turnbull, whose description of the sadistic, semidisplaced Ik in northern Uganda was seen as evidence of a people without principles of kindness and cooperation, has produced evidence that underneath the surface of this dying society, there is a deeper moral code from a time when the tribe flourished. Occasionally this deeper code surfaces and shows its nobler face.

The nonrelativist can accept a certain relativity in the way moral principles are *applied* in various cultures, depending on beliefs, history, and environment. For example, a raw environment with scarce natural resources may justify the Eskimos' brand of euthanasia to the objectivist, who in another environment would consistently reject that practice. The Greeks and Callatians disposed of their parents differently, but that does not prove that conventionalism is correct. Actually, both groups seem to adhere to a common principle of showing respect to one's elders. There can be latitude in how that respect is shown.

The members of a tribe in the Sudan throw their deformed children into the river because of their belief that such infants *belong* to the hippopotamus, the god of the river. We believe that they have a false belief about this, but the point is that the same principles of respect for property and respect for human life are operative in these contrary practices. They differ with us only in belief, not in substantive moral principle. This is an illustration of how nonmoral beliefs (for example, deformed children belong to the hippopotamus) when applied to common moral principles (such as give to each his or her due) generate different actions in different cultures.

In our own culture, differences in nonmoral belief about the status of a fetus generate opposite moral prescriptions. Both the prochoice movement and the antiabortionists agree that it is wrong to kill innocent people, but they disagree as to a fact (not the principle) of whether a fetus is a *person* (someone having a right to life). Roman Catholics believe that the fetus is a person because it has a soul, whereas most liberal Protestants and secularists deny this. Abortion is a serious moral issue, but what divides many of us is not a moral principle but how that principle should be applied. Antiabortionists believe the principle of not killing innocent people applies to fetuses, whereas pro-choicers do not—but they do not disagree on the fundamental principle.

The relativist may respond to this point and argue that even if we do often share deep principles, we don't always share them. Some people may not value life at all. How can we prove them wrong? Who's to say which culture is right and which is wrong? This response seems dubious. We can reason and perform thought experiments in order to make a case for one system over another. We may not be able to *know* with certainty that our moral beliefs are closer to the truth than those of another culture or those of others within our own culture, but we may be *justified* in believing that they are. If we can be closer to the truth regarding factual or scientific matters, why can't we be closer to the truth on moral matters? Why can't a culture simply be confused or wrong about its moral perceptions? Why can't we say that the society like the Ik, which sees nothing wrong with enjoying watching its own children fall into fires, is less moral in that regard than the culture that cherishes children and grants them protection and equal rights? To take such a stand is not to commit the fallacy of ethnocentrism, for we are seeking to derive principles through critical reason, not simply uncritical acceptance of one's own mores.

THE CASE FOR MORAL OBJECTIVISM

The discussion heretofore has been largely negative, against relativism. Now I want to make a positive case for a core set of moral principles that are necessary to the good society and the good life.

First, I must make it clear that I am distinguishing moral *absolutism* from moral *objectivism*. The absolutist believes that there are nonoverridable moral principles that ought never to be violated. Kant's system is a good example: one ought *never* break a promise or tell a lie, no matter what. An objectivist, however, need not posit any nonoverridable principles, at least not in unqualified general form, and so need not be an absolutist. As Renford Bambrough put it,

> To suggest that there is a *right* answer to a moral problem is at once to be accused of or credited with a belief in moral absolutes. But it is no more necessary to believe in moral absolutes in order to believe in moral objectivity than it is to believe in the existence of absolute space or absolute time in order to believe in the objectivity of temporal and spatial relations and of judgments about them.[9]

In the objectivist's account, moral principles are what Oxford University philosopher William Ross (1877–1971) refers to as prima facie principles, valid rules of action that should generally be adhered to, but that may be overridden by another moral principle in cases of moral conflict.[10] For example, while a principle of justice generally outweighs a principle of benevolence, at times enormous good could be done by sacrificing a small amount of justice, so that an objectivist would be inclined to act according to the principle of benevolence. There may be some absolute or nonoverridable principles (indeed, the next principle I mention is probably one), but there need not be any or many for objectivism to be true.

If I can establish or show that it is reasonable to believe that at least one objective moral principle is binding on all people everywhere in some ideal sense, I shall have shown that relativism is probably false and that a limited objectivism is true. Actually, I believe that many qualified general ethical principles are binding on all rational beings, but one will suffice to refute relativism. The principle I've chosen is the following:

1. It is morally wrong to torture people for the fun of it.

I claim that this principle is binding on all rational agents. If some agent, S, rejects Principle 1, we should not let that affect our intuition that Principle 1 is a true principle but rather try to explain S's behavior as perverse, ignorant, or irrational instead. For example, suppose Adolf Hitler doesn't accept Principle 1. Should that affect our confidence in its truth? Isn't it more reasonable to infer that Hitler is morally deficient, morally blind, ignorant, or irrational than to

suppose that his noncompliance is evidence against the truth of Principle 1?

Suppose, further, that a tribe of Hitlerites enjoys torturing people. The whole culture accepts torturing others for the fun of it. Suppose that Mother Teresa and Gandhi try unsuccessfully to convince them that they should stop torturing people altogether, and they respond by torturing Teresa and Gandhi. Should this affect our confidence in 1? Would it not be more reasonable to look for some explanation of Hitlerite behavior? For example, we might hypothesize that this tribe lacked a developed sense of sympathetic imagination that is necessary for the moral life. Or we might theorize that this tribe was on a lower evolutionary level than most *Homo sapiens.* Or we might simply conclude that the tribe was closer to a Hobbesian state of nature than most societies, and as such probably would not survive. But we need not know the correct answer as to why the tribe was in such bad shape, in order to maintain our confidence in Principle 1 as a moral principle. If Principle 1 is a basic or core belief for us, we will be more likely to doubt the Hitlerites' sanity or ability to think morally than to doubt the validity of Principle 1.

We can perhaps produce other candidates for membership in our minimally basic objective moral set. For example,

2. Do not kill innocent people.
3. Do not cause pain or suffering except when a higher duty prescribes it.
4. Do not commit rape.
5. Keep your promises and contracts.
6. Do not deprive another person of his or her freedom.
7. Do justice, treating equals equally and unequals unequally.
8. Tell the truth.
9. Help other people.
10. Obey just laws.

Principles 1 through 10 are examples of the core morality, principles necessary for the good life. Fortunately, it isn't as though 1 to 10 were arbitrary principles, for we can give reasons why we believe that these rules will be necessary to any satisfactory social order. Principles such as the Golden Rule, not killing innocent people, treating equals equally, truth telling, promise keeping, and the like are central to the fluid progression of social interaction and the resolution of conflicts of which ethics are about (at least minimal morality is, even though there may be more to morality than simply these kinds of concerns). For example, language itself depends on a general and implicit commitment to the principle of truth telling. Accuracy of expression is a primitive form of truthfulness. Hence, every time we use words correctly we are telling the truth. Without this behavior, language wouldn't be possible. Likewise, without the recognition of a rule of promise keeping, contracts are of no avail and cooperation is less likely to occur. And without the protection of life and liberty, we could not secure our other goals.

A morality would be adequate if it contained the principles of the core morality, but there could be more than one adequate morality that *applied* these principles differently. That is, there may be a certain relativity to secondary principles (whether to opt for monogamy rather than polygamy, whether to include high altruism in the set of moral duties, whether to allocate more resources to medical care than to environmental concerns, whether to require driving on the left side of the road or on the right side, and so forth). But in every morality a certain core will remain, applied somewhat differently because of differences in environment, belief, tradition, and the like.

The core moral rules are analogous to the core vitamins necessary for a healthy diet. We need an adequate amount of each vitamin—some humans need more of one than another—but in prescribing a nutritious diet we don't have to set forth recipes, specific foods, place settings, or culinary habits. Gourmets, ascetics, and vegetarians may meet the requirements differently, but the basic nutrients may be had by all without rigid regimentation or an absolute set of recipes.

Imagine that you have been miraculously transported to the dark kingdom of hell, and there you get a glimpse of the sufferings of the damned. What is their punishment? Well, they have eternal back itches that ebb and flow constantly. But they cannot scratch their backs, for their arms are paralyzed in a frontal position. And so they writhe with itchiness through eternity. But just as you are beginning to feel the itch in your own back, you are suddenly transported to heaven. What do you see in the kingdom of the blessed? Well, you see people with eternal back itches, who cannot scratch their own backs. But they are all smiling instead of writhing. Why? Because everyone has his or her arms stretched out to scratch someone else's back, and, so arranged in one big circle, a hell is turned into a heaven of ecstasy.

If we can imagine some states of affairs or cultures that are better than others in a way that depends on human action, we can ask what character traits make them so. In our story, people in heaven, but not those in hell, cooperate to ameliorate suffering and produce pleasure. These goods are very primitive, not sufficient for a full-blown morality, but they give us a hint as to the objectivity of morality. Moral goodness has something to do with the amelioration of suffering, the resolution of conflict, and the promotion of human flourishing. If our heaven is really better than the eternal itchiness of hell, then whatever makes it so is constitutively related to moral rightness.

AN EXPLANATION OF THE ATTRACTION OF ETHICAL RELATIVISM

Why, then, is there such a strong inclination toward ethical relativism? I think that there are three reasons, which haven't been emphasized. One is the fact that the options are usually presented as though absolutism and relativism were the only alternatives, so conventionalism wins out against an implausible competitor. The questionnaire I give my students reads as follows: "Are there any ethical absolutes, moral duties binding on all persons at all times, or are moral duties relative to culture? Is there any alternative to these two positions?" Only 3 percent of students suggest a third position, and very few of them identify objectivism. Granted, it takes a little philosophical sophistication to make the crucial distinctions (and it is precisely for lack of this sophistication or reflection that relativism has procured its enormous prestige). But, as Ross and others have shown, and as I have argued in this chapter, one can have an objective morality without being absolutist.

The second reason is that our recent sensitivity to cultural relativism and the evils of ethnocentrism, which have plagued European and American relations with other cultures, has made us conscious of how frail many aspects of our moral repertoire are, so that we tend to wonder "Who's to judge what's really right or wrong?" However, the move from a reasonable cultural relativism, which rightly causes us to rethink our moral systems, to an ethical relativism, which causes us to give up the heart of morality altogether, is an instance of the fallacy of confusing factual or descriptive statements with normative ones. Cultural relativism doesn't entail ethical relativism. The very reason why we are against ethnocentrism is the same reason why we are for an objective moral system: impartial reason draws us to it.

We may well agree that cultures differ and that we ought to be cautious in condemning what we don't understand. But this agreement in no way needs to imply that there are not better and worse ways of living. We can understand and excuse, to some degree at least, people who differ from our best notions of morality, without abdicating the notion that cultures without principles of justice, promise keeping, or protection of the innocent are morally poorer for these omissions.

A third factor, which has driven some to moral nihilism and others to relativism, is the decline of religion in Western society. As one of Dostoyevsky's characters said, "If God is dead, all things are permitted." The person who has lost religious faith feels a deep vacuum and understandably confuses it with a moral vacuum, or may finally resign him- or herself to a form of secular conventionalism. Such people reason that if there is no God to guarantee the validity of the moral order, there must not be a universal moral order. There is just radical cultural diversity and death at the end.

But even if there turns out to be no God and no immortality, we still will want to live happy, meaningful lives during our four-score years on earth. If this is true, then it matters by which principles we live, and those which win out in the test of time will be objectively valid principles.

To sum up: there are moral truths, principles belonging to the core morality, without which society will not long survive and individuals will not flourish. Reason can discover these principles, and it is in our interest to promote them.

So "Who's to judge what's right or wrong?" We are. We are to do so on the basis of the best reasoning we can bring forth, and with sympathy and understanding.

NOTES

1. *History of Herodotus,* trans. George Rawlinson (New York: Appleton, 1859), Book 3, Chapter 38.
2. *Ethical Relativism* (Belmont, CA: Wadsworth, 1973), p. 1.
3. *Patterns of Culture* (New York: Houghton Mifflin, 1934), p. 219.
4. *Folkways* (New York: 1906), Section 80. Ruth Benedict indicates the depth of our cultural conditioning this way: "The very eyes with which we see the problem are conditioned by the long traditional habits of our own society" ("Anthropology and the Abnormal," *Journal of General Psychology,* 1934), pp. 59–82.
5. *Death in the Afternoon* (New York: Scribner's, 1932), p. 4.
6. *Patterns of Culture,* p. 257.
7. *Cultural Relativism* (New York: Random House, 1972).
8. "Ethical Relativity: Sic et Non," *Journal of Philosophy 52,* 1955.
9. *Moral Skepticism and Moral Knowledge* (London: Routledge & Kegan Paul, 1979), p. 33.
10. *The Right and the Good* (Oxford: Oxford University Press, 1931).

FOR FURTHER REFLECTION

1. How do cultural relativism and ethical relativism differ?
2. Are there moral absolutes or is morality completely relative? Are there independent criteria by which we can say that some cultures are better than others?
3. Is Pojman's attempt to ground morality in a common human nature a form of ethical relativism? Might there be different human natures?

J. L. MACKIE

THE SUBJECTIVITY OF VALUES

J. L. Mackie (1917–1982) was a fellow in philosophy at University College, Oxford University. His work covers virtually every major area in philosophy. His book *Ethics: Inventing Right and Wrong*, from which this selection is taken, represents a classical skeptical position on moral values. Mackie disagrees with the noncognitivists who say that ethical language is meaningless. Moral statements make claims about the nature of reality—claims that there are moral facts. Unfortunately, these statements are all false; there are no objective values. Because we naturally believe that our claims are true but are invariably mistaken, Mackie calls his theory an "error theory." We are in error about our moral judgments. He presents two arguments that show why this is the conclusion to which rational people should come.

The first is the argument from relativity or disagreement, which says that since morals seem to be culturally dependent and vary over time and place, the burden of proof is on the person who contends that we should not take this diversity at face value. This argument indicates that there is no separate or supervenient reality. The second argument is the argument from queerness, which contends that if there were objective values, they would have to be very strange things indeed, but that there is no good reason to suppose that there are these queer objects. Thus, by the principle of parsimony (that is, do not multiply objects beyond necessity), we should conclude that there are no such objects.

MORAL SCEPTICISM

There are no objective values. This is a bald statement of the thesis of this chapter, but before arguing for it I shall try to clarify and restrict it in ways that may meet some objections and prevent some misunderstanding.

The statement of this thesis is liable to provoke one of three very different reactions. Some will think it not merely false but pernicious; they will see it as a threat to morality and to everything else that is worthwhile, and they will find the presenting of such a thesis in which purports to be a book on ethics paradoxical or even outrageous. Others will regard it as a trivial truth, almost too obvious to be worth mentioning, and certainly too plain to be worth much argument. Others again will say that it is meaningless or empty, that no real issue is raised by the question whether values are or are not part of the fabric of the world. But, precisely because there can be these three different reactions, much more needs to be said.

The claim that values are not objective, are not part of the fabric of the world, is meant to include not only moral goodness, which might be most naturally

From J. L. Mackie, *Ethics: Inventing Right and Wrong* (Penguin, 1977), by permission of Penguin Books, Ltd.

equated with moral value, but also other things that could be more loosely called moral values or disvalues—rightness and wrongness, duty, obligation, an action's being rotten and contemptible, and so on. It also includes non-moral values, notably aesthetic ones, beauty and various kinds of artistic merit. I shall not discuss these explicitly, but clearly much the same considerations apply to aesthetic and to moral values, and there would be at least some initial implausibility in a view that gave the one a different status from the other.

Since it is with moral values that I am primarily concerned, the view I am adopting may be called moral scepticism. But this name is likely to be misunderstood: "moral scepticism" might also be used as a name for either of two first order views, or perhaps for an incoherent mixture of the two. A moral sceptic might be the sort of person who says "All this talk of morality is tripe," who rejects morality and will take no notice of it. Such a person may be literally rejecting all moral judgements; he is more likely to be making moral judgements of his own, expressing a positive moral condemnation of all that conventionally passes for morality; or he may be confusing these two logically incompatible views, and saying that he rejects all morality, while he is in fact rejecting only a particular morality that is current in the society in which he has grown up. But I am not at present concerned with the merits or faults of such a position. These are first order moral views, positive or negative: the person who adopts either of them is taking a certain practical, normative, stand. By contrast, what I am discussing is a second order view, a view about the status of moral values and the nature of moral valuing, about where and how they fit into the world. These first and second order views are not merely distinct but completely independent: one could be a second order moral sceptic without being a first order one, or again the other way round. A man could hold strong moral views, and indeed ones whose content was thoroughly conventional, while believing that they were simply attitudes and policies with regard to conduct that he and other people held. Conversely, a man could reject all established morality while believing it to be an objective truth that it was evil or corrupt.

With another sort of misunderstanding moral scepticism would seem not so much pernicious as absurd. How could anyone deny that there is a difference between a kind action and a cruel one, or that a coward and a brave man behave differently in the face of danger? Of course, this is undeniable; but it is not to the point. The kinds of behaviour to which moral values and disvalues are ascribed are indeed part of the furniture of the world, and so are the natural, descriptive, differences between them; but not, perhaps, their differences in value. It is a hard fact that cruel actions differ from kind ones, and hence that we can learn, as in fact we all do, to distinguish them fairly well in practice, and to use the words 'cruel' and 'kind' with fairly clear descriptive meanings; but is it an equally hard fact that actions which are cruel in such a descriptive sense are to be condemned? The present issue is with regard to the objectivity specifically of value, not with regard to the objectivity of those natural, factual differences on the basis of which differing values are assigned.

SUBJECTIVISM

Another name often used, as an alternative to "moral scepticism," for the view I am discussing is "subjectivism." But this too has more than one meaning. Moral subjectivism too could be a first order, normative, view, namely that everyone really ought to do whatever he thinks he should. This plainly is a (systematic) first order view; on examination it soon ceases to be plausible, but that is beside the point, for it is quite independent of the second order thesis at present under consideration. What is more confusing is that different second order views compete for the name "subjectivism." Several of these are doctrines about the meaning of moral terms and moral statements. What is often called moral subjectivism is the doctrine that, for example, "This action is right" means "I approve of this action," or more generally that moral judgements are equivalent to reports of the speaker's own feelings or attitudes. But the view I am now discussing is to be distinguished in two vital respects from any such doctrine as this. First, what I have called moral scepticism is a negative doctrine, not a positive one: it says what there isn't, not what there is. It says that there do not exist entities or relations of a certain kind, objective values or requirements, which many people have believed to exist. Of course, the moral sceptic cannot leave it at that. If his position is to be at all plausible, he must give some account of how other people have fallen into what he regards as an error, and this account will have to include some positive suggestions about how values fail to be objective, about what has been mistaken for, or has led to false beliefs about, objective values. But this will be a development of his theory, not its core: its core is the negation. Secondly, what I have called moral scepticism is an ontological thesis, not a linguistic or conceptual one. It is not, like the other doctrine often called moral subjectivism, a view about the meanings of moral statements. Again, no doubt, if it is to be at all plausible, it will have to give some account of their meanings, and I shall say something about this [later]. But this too will be a development of the theory, not its core.

It is true that those who have accepted the moral subjectivism which is the doctrine that moral judgements are equivalent to reports of the speaker's own feelings or attitudes have usually presupposed what I am calling moral scepticism. It is because they have assumed that there are no objective values that they have looked elsewhere for an analysis of what moral statements might mean, and have settled upon subjective reports. Indeed, if all our moral statements were such subjective reports, it would follow that, at least so far as we are aware, there are no objective moral values. If we were aware of them, we would say something about them. In this sense this sort of subjectivism entails moral scepticism. But the converse entailment does not hold. The denial that there are objective values does not commit one to any particular view about what moral statements mean, and certainly not to the view that they are equivalent to subjective reports. No doubt if moral values are not objective they are in some very broad sense subjective, and for this reason I would accept "moral subjectivism" as an alternative name to "moral scepticism." But subjectivism in this broad sense must be distinguished from the specific doctrine about meaning referred to above. Neither name is altogether

satisfactory: we simply have to guard against the (different) misinterpretations which each may suggest.

THE MULTIPLICITY OF SECOND ORDER QUESTIONS

The distinctions drawn in the last two sections rest not only on the well-known and generally recognized difference between first and second order questions, but also on the more controversial claim that there are several kinds of second order moral question. Those most often mentioned are questions about the meaning and use of ethical terms, or the analysis of ethical concepts. With these go questions about the logic of moral statements: there may be special patterns of moral argument, licensed, perhaps, by aspects of the meanings of moral terms—for example, it may be part of the meaning of moral statements that they are universalizable. But there are also ontological, as contrasted with linguistic or conceptual, questions about the nature and status of goodness or rightness or whatever it is that first order moral statements are distinctively about. These are questions of factual rather than conceptual analysis: the problem of what goodness is cannot be settled conclusively or exhaustively by finding out what the word "good" means, or what it is conventionally used to say or to do.

Recent philosophy, biased as it has been towards various kinds of linguistic inquiry, has tended to doubt this, but the distinction between conceptual and factual analysis in ethics can be supported by analogies with other areas. The question of what perception is, what goes on when someone perceives something, is not adequately answered by finding out what words like "see" and "hear" mean, or what someone is doing in saying "I perceive . . . ," by analysing, however fully and accurately, any established concept of perception. There is a still closer analogy with colours. Robert Boyle and John Locke called colours "secondary qualities," meaning that colours as they occur in material things consist simply in patterns of arrangement and movement of minute particles on the surfaces of objects, which make them, as we would now say, reflect light of some frequencies better than others, and so enable these objects to produce colour sensations in us, but that colours as we see them do not literally belong to the surfaces of material things. Whether Boyle and Locke were right about this cannot be settled by finding out how we use colour words and what we mean in using them. Naive realism about colours might be a correct analysis not only of our prescientific colour concepts but also of the conventional meanings of colour words, and even of the meanings with which scientifically sophisticated people use them when they are off their guard, and yet it might not be a correct account of the status of colours.

Error could well result, then, from a failure to distinguish factual from conceptual analysis with regard to colours, from taking an account of the meanings of statements as a full account of what there is. There is a similar and in practice even greater risk of error in moral philosophy. There is another reason, too, why it would be a mistake to concentrate second order ethical discussions on questions of meaning. The more work philosophers have done on meaning, both in ethics and elsewhere, the more complications have come to light. It is by now pretty plain that no simple account of the meanings of first order moral statements will be correct, will cover adequately even the standard, conventional, sense of the main moral terms; I think, none the less, that there is a relatively clear-cut issue about the objectivity of moral values which is in danger of being lost among the complications of meaning.

THE CLAIM TO OBJECTIVITY

If I have succeeded in specifying precisely enough the moral values whose objectivity I am denying, my thesis may now seem to be trivially true. Of course, some will say, valuing, preferring, choosing, recommending, rejecting, condemning, and so on, are human activities, and there is no need to look for values that are prior to and logically independent of all such activities. There may be widespread agreement in valuing, and particular value-judgements are not in general arbitrary or isolated: they typically cohere with others, or can be criticized if they do not, reasons can be given for them, and so on: but if all that

the subjectivist is maintaining is that desires, ends, purposes, and the like figure somewhere in the system of reasons, and that no ends or purposes are objective as opposed to being merely intersubjective, then this may be conceded without much fuss.

But I do not think that this should be conceded so easily. As I have said, the main tradition of European moral philosophy includes the contrary claim, that there are objective values of just the sort I have denied. I have referred already to Plato, Kant, and Sidgwick. Kant in particular holds that the categorical imperative is not only categorical and imperative but objectively so: though a rational being gives the moral law to himself, the law that he thus makes is determinate and necessary. Aristotle begins the Nicomachean Ethics by saying that the good is that at which all things aim, and that ethics is part of a science which he calls "politics," whose goal is not knowledge but practice; yet he does not doubt that there can be knowledge of what is the good for man, nor, once he has identified this as well-being or happiness, eudaimonia, that it can be known, rationally determined, in what happiness consists; and it is plain that he thinks that this happiness is intrinsically desirable, not good simply because it is desired. The rationalist Samuel Clarke holds that

> these eternal and necessary differences of things make it fit and reasonable for creatures so to act . . . even separate from the consideration of these rules being the positive will or command of God; and also antecedent to any respect or regard, expectation or apprehension, of any particular private and personal advantage or disadvantage, reward or punishment, either present or future. . . .

Even the sentimentalist Hutcheson defines moral goodness as "some quality apprehended in actions, which procures approbation . . . ," while saying that the moral sense by which we perceive virtue and vice has been given to us (by the Author of nature) to direct our actions. Hume indeed was on the other side, but he is still a witness to the dominance of the objectivist tradition, since he claims that when we "see that the distinction of vice and virtue is not founded merely on the relations of objects, nor is perceiv'd by reason," this "wou'd subvert all the vulgar systems of morality." And Richard Price insists that right and wrong are "real characters of actions," not "qualities of our minds," and are perceived by the understanding; he criticizes the notion of moral sense on the ground that it would make virtue an affair of taste, and moral right and wrong "nothing in the objects themselves"; he rejects Hutcheson's view because (perhaps mistakenly) he sees it as collapsing into Hume's.

But this objectivism about values is not only a feature of the philosophical tradition. It has also a firm basis in ordinary thought, and even in the meanings of moral terms. No doubt it was an extravagance for Moore to say that "good" is the name of a non-natural quality, but it would not be so far wrong to say that in moral contexts it is used as if it were the name of a supposed non-natural quality, where the description "non-natural" leaves room for the peculiar evaluative, prescriptive, intrinsically action-guiding aspects of this supposed quality. This point can be illustrated by reflection on the conflicts and swings of opinion in recent years between noncognitivist and naturalist views about the central, basic, meanings of ethical terms. If we reject the view that it is the function of such terms to introduce objective values into discourse about conduct and choices of action, there seem to be two main alternative types of account. One (which has importantly different subdivisions) is that they conventionally express either attitudes which the speaker purports to adopt towards whatever it is that he characterizes morally, or prescriptions or recommendations, subject perhaps to the logical constraint of universalizability. Different views of this type share the central thesis that ethical terms have, at least partly and primarily, some sort of noncognitive, non-descriptive, meaning. Views of the other type hold that they are descriptive in meaning, but descriptive of natural features, partly of such features as everyone, even the non-cognitivist, would recognize as distinguishing kind actions from cruel ones, courage from cowardice, politeness from rudeness, and so on, and partly (though these two overlap) of relations between the actions and some human wants, satisfactions, and the like. I believe that views of both these types capture part of the truth. Each approach can account for the fact that moral judgements are action-guiding or practical. Yet each gains much of its plausibility from the felt inadequacy of the other. It is

a very natural reaction to any non-cognitive analysis of ethical terms to protest that there is more to ethics than this, something more external to the maker of moral judgements, more authoritative over both him and those of or to whom he speaks, and this reaction is likely to persist even when full allowance has been made for the logical, formal, constraints of full-blooded prescriptivity and universalizability. Ethics, we are inclined to believe, is more a matter of knowledge and less a matter of decision than any non-cognitive analysis allows. And of course naturalism satisfies this demand. It will not be a matter of choice or decision whether an action is cruel or unjust or imprudent or whether it is likely to produce more distress than pleasure. But in satisfying this demand, it introduces a converse deficiency. On a naturalist analysis, moral judgements can be practical, but their practicality is wholly relative to desires or possible satisfactions of the person or persons whose actions are to be guided; but moral judgements seem to say more than this. This view leaves out the categorical quality of moral requirements. In fact both naturalist and non-cognitive analyses leave out the apparent authority of ethics, the one by excluding the categorically imperative aspect, the other the claim to objective validity or truth. The ordinary user of moral language means to say something about whatever it is that he characterizes morally, for example a possible action, as it is in itself, or would be if it were realized, and not about, or even simply expressive of, his, or anyone else's, attitude or relation to it. But the something he wants to say is not purely descriptive, certainly not inert, but something that involves a call for action or for the refraining from action, and one that is absolute, not contingent upon any desire or preference or policy or choice, his own or anyone else's. Someone in a state of moral perplexity, wondering whether it would be wrong for him to engage, say, in research related to bacteriological warfare, wants to arrive at some judgement about this concrete case, his doing this work at this time in these actual circumstances; his relevant characteristics will be part of the subject of the judgement, but no relation between him and the proposed action will be part of the predicate. The question is not, for example, whether he really wants to do this work, whether it will satisfy or dissatisfy him, whether he will in the long run have a pro-attitude towards it, or even whether this is an action of a sort that he can happily and sincerely recommend in all relevantly similar cases. Nor is he even wondering just whether to recommend such action in all relevantly similar cases. He wants to know whether this course of action would be wrong in itself. Something like this is the everyday objectivist concept of which talk about non-natural qualities is a philosopher's reconstruction.

The prevalence of this tendency to objectify values—and not only moral ones—is confirmed by a pattern of thinking that we find in existentialists and those influenced by them. The denial of objective values can carry with it an extreme emotional reaction, a feeling that nothing matters at all, that life has lost its purpose. Of course this does not follow; the lack of objective values is not a good reason for abandoning subjective concern or for ceasing to want anything. But the abandonment of a belief in objective values can cause, at least temporarily, a decay of subjective concern and sense of purpose. That it does so is evidence that the people in whom this reaction occurs have been tending to objectify their concerns and purposes, have been giving them a fictitious external authority. A claim to objectivity has been so strongly associated with their subjective concerns and purposes that the collapse of the former seems to undermine the latter as well.

This view, that conceptual analysis would reveal a claim to objectivity, is sometimes dramatically confirmed by philosophers who are officially on the other side. Bertrand Russell, for example, says that "ethical propositions should be expressed in the optative mood, not in the indicative"; he defends himself effectively against the charge of inconsistency in both holding ultimate ethical valuations to be subjective and expressing emphatic opinions on ethical questions. Yet at the end he admits

> Certainly there seems to be something more. Suppose, for example, that some one were to advocate the introduction of bullfighting in this country. In opposing the proposal, I should feel, not only that I was expressing my desires, but that my desires in the matter are right, whatever that may mean. As a matter of argument, I can, I think, show that I am not guilty

of any logical inconsistency in holding to the above interpretation of ethics and at the same time expressing strong ethical preferences. But in feeling I am not satisfied.

But he concludes, reasonably enough, with the remark: "I can only say that, while my own opinions as to ethics do not satisfy me, other people's satisfy me still less."

I conclude, then, that ordinary moral judgements include a claim to objectivity, an assumption that there are objective values in just the sense in which I am concerned to deny this. And I do not think it is going too far to say that this assumption has been incorporated in the basic, conventional, meanings of moral terms. Any analysis of the meanings of moral terms which omits this claim to objective, intrinsic, prescriptivity is to that extent incomplete; and this is true of any non-cognitive analysis, any naturalist one, and any combination of the two.

If second order ethics were confined, then, to linguistic and conceptual analysis, it ought to conclude that moral values at least are objective: that they are so is part of what our ordinary moral statements mean: the traditional moral concepts of the ordinary man as well as of the main line of western philosophers are concepts of objective value. But it is precisely for this reason that linguistic and conceptual analysis is not enough. The claim to objectivity, however ingrained in our language and thought, is not self-validating. It can and should be questioned. But the denial of objective values will have to be put forward not as the result of an analytic approach, but as an "error theory," a theory that although most people in making moral judgements implicitly claim, among other things, to be pointing to something objectively prescriptive, these claims are all false. It is this that makes the name "moral scepticism" appropriate.

But since this is an error theory, since it goes against assumptions ingrained in our thought and built into some of the ways in which language is used, since it conflicts with what is sometimes called common sense, it needs very solid support. It is not something we can accept lightly or casually and then quietly pass on. If we are to adopt this view, we must argue explicitly for it. Traditionally it has been supported by arguments of two main kinds, which I shall call the argument from relativity and the argument from queerness, but these can, as I shall show, be supplemented in several ways.

THE ARGUMENT FROM RELATIVITY

The argument from relativity has as its premise the well-known variation in moral codes from one society to another and from one period to another, and also the differences in moral beliefs between different groups and classes within a complex community. Such variation is in itself merely a truth of descriptive morality, a fact of anthropology which entails neither first order nor second order ethical views. Yet it may indirectly support second order subjectivism: radical differences between first order moral judgements make it difficult to treat those judgements as apprehensions of objective truths. But it is not the mere occurrence of disagreements that tells against the objectivity of values. Disagreement on questions in history or biology or cosmology does not show that there are no objective issues in these fields for investigators to disagree about. But such scientific disagreement results from speculative inferences or explanatory hypotheses based on inadequate evidence, and it is hardly plausible to interpret moral disagreement in the same way. Disagreement about moral codes seems to reflect people's adherence to and participation in different ways of life. The causal connection seems to be mainly that way round: it is that people approve of monogamy because they participate in a monogamous way of life rather than that they participate in a monogamous way of life because they approve of monogamy. Of course, the standards may be an idealization of the way of life from which they arise: the monogamy in which people participate may be less complete, less rigid, than that of which it leads them to approve. This is not to say that moral judgements are purely conventional. Of course there have been and are moral heretics and moral reformers, people who have turned against the established rules and practices of their own communities for moral reasons, and often for moral reasons that we would endorse. But this can usually be understood as the extension, in ways which, though new and unconventional, seemed to them to be required for consistency, of rules to which they already adhered as arising out of an existing way of life. In short, the argument from relativity has some force simply because the actual variations in the moral codes are more readily explained by the hypothesis that they reflect ways of life than by the hypothesis that they express perceptions, most of them seriously inadequate and badly distorted, of objective values.

But there is a well-known counter to this argument from relativity, namely to say that the items for which objective validity is in the first place to be claimed are not specific moral rules or codes but very general basic principles which are recognized at least implicitly to some extent in all society—such principles as provide the foundations of what Sidgwick has called different methods of ethics: the principle of universalizability, perhaps, or the rule that one ought to conform to the specific rules of any way of life in which one takes part, from which one profits, and on which one relies, or some utilitarian principle of doing what tends, or seems likely, to promote the general happiness. It is easy to show that such general principles, married with differing concrete circumstances, different existing social patterns or different preferences, will beget different specific moral rules; and there is some plausibility in the claim that the specific rules thus generated will vary from community to community or from group to group in close agreement with the actual variations in accepted codes.

The argument from relativity can be only partly countered in this way. To take this line the moral objectivist has to say that it is only in these principles that the objective moral character attaches immediately to its descriptively specified ground or subject: other moral judgements are objectively valid or true, but only derivatively and contingently—if things had been otherwise, quite different sorts of actions would have been right. And despite the prominence in recent philosophical ethics of universalization, utilitarian principles, and the like, these are very far from constituting the whole of what is actually affirmed as basic in ordinary moral thought. Much of this is concerned rather with what Hare calls "ideals" or, less kindly, "fanaticism." That is, people judge that some things are good or right, and others are bad or wrong, not because—or at any rate not only because—they exemplify some general principle for which widespread implicit acceptance could be claimed, but because something about those things arouses certain responses immediately in them, though they would arouse radically and irresolvably different responses in others. "Moral sense" or "intuition" is an initially more plausible description of what supplies many of our basic moral judgements than "reason." With regard to all these starting points of moral thinking the argument from relativity remains in full force.

THE ARGUMENT FROM QUEERNESS

Even more important, however, and certainly more generally applicable, is the argument from queerness. This has two parts, one metaphysical, the other epistemological. If there were objective values, then they would be entities or qualities or relations of a very strange sort, utterly different from anything else in the universe. Correspondingly, if we were aware of them, it would have to be by some special faculty of moral perception or intuition, utterly different from our ordinary ways of knowing everything else. These points were recognized by Moore when he spoke of non-natural qualities, and by the intuitionists in their talk about a "faculty of moral intuition." Intuitionism has long been out of favour, and it is indeed easy to point out its implausibilities. What is not so often stressed, but is more important, is that the central thesis of intuitionism is one to which any objectivist view of values is in the end committed: intuitionism merely makes unpalatably plain what other forms of objectivism wrap up. Of course the suggestion that moral judgements are made or moral problems solved by just sitting down and having an ethical intuition is a travesty of actual moral thinking. But, however complex the real process, it will require (if it is to yield authoritatively prescriptive conclusions) some input of this distinctive sort, either premises or forms of argument or both. When we ask the awkward question, how we can be aware of this authoritative prescriptivity, of

the truth of these distinctively ethical premises or of the cogency of this distinctively ethical pattern of reasoning, none of our ordinary accounts of sensory perception or introspection or the framing and confirming of explanatory hypotheses or inference or logical construction or conceptual analysis, or any combination of these, will provide a satisfactory answer; "a special sort of intuition" is a lame answer, but it is the one to which the clearheaded objectivist is compelled to resort.

Indeed, the best move for the moral objectivist is not to evade this issue, but to look for companions in guilt. For example, Richard Price argues that it is not moral knowledge alone that such an empiricism as those of Locke and Hume is unable to account for, but also our knowledge and even our ideas of essence, number, identity, diversity, solidity, inertia, substance, the necessary existence and infinite extension of time and space, necessity and possibility in general, power, and causation. If the understanding, which Price defines as the faculty within us that discerns truth, is also a source of new simple ideas of so many other sorts, may it not also be a power of immediately perceiving right and wrong, which yet are real characters of actions?

This is an important counter to the argument from queerness. The only adequate reply to it would be to show how, on empiricist foundations, we can construct an account of the ideas and beliefs and knowledge that we have of all these matters. I cannot even begin to do that here, though I have undertaken some parts of the task elsewhere. I can only state my belief that satisfactory accounts of most of these can be given in empirical terms. If some supposed metaphysical necessities or essences resist such treatment, then they too should be included, along with objective values, among the targets of the argument from queerness.

This queerness does not consist simply in the fact that ethical statements are "unverifiable." Although logical positivism with its verifiability theory of descriptive meaning gave an impetus to non-cognitive accounts of ethics, it is not only logical positivists but also empiricists of a much more liberal sort who should find objective values hard to accommodate. Indeed, I would not only reject the verifiability principle but also deny the conclusion commonly drawn from it, that moral judgements lack descriptive meaning. The assertion that there are objective values or intrinsically prescriptive entities or features of some kind, which ordinary moral judgements presuppose, is, I hold, not meaningless but false.

Plato's Forms give a dramatic picture of what objective values would have to be. The Form of the Good is such that knowledge of it provides the knower with both a direction and an overriding motive; something's being good both tells the person who knows this to pursue it and makes him pursue it. An objective good would be sought by anyone who was acquainted with it, not because of any contingent fact that this person, or every person, is so constituted that he desires this end, but just because the end has to-be-pursuedness somehow built into it. Similarly, if there were objective principles of right and wrong, any wrong (possible) course of action would have not-to-be-doneness somehow built into it. Or we should have something like Clarke's necessary relations of fitness between situations and actions, so that a situation would have a demand for such-and-such an action somehow built into it.

The need for an argument of this sort can be brought out by reflection on Hume's argument that "reason"—in which at this stage he includes all sorts of knowing as well as reasoning—can never be an "influencing motive of the will." Someone might object that Hume has argued unfairly from the lack of influencing power (not contingent upon desires) in ordinary objects of knowledge and ordinary reasoning, and might maintain that values differ from natural objects precisely in their power, when known, automatically to influence the will. To this Hume could, and would need to, reply that this objection involves the postulating of value-entities or value-features of quite a different order from anything else with which we are acquainted, and of a corresponding faculty with which to detect them. That is, he would have to supplement his explicit argument with what I have called the argument from queerness.

Another way of bringing out this queerness is to ask, about anything that is supposed to have some objective moral quality, how this is linked with its nat-

ural features. What is the connection between the natural fact that an action is a piece of deliberate cruelty—say, causing pain just for fun—and the moral fact that it is wrong? It cannot be an entailment, a logical or semantic necessity. Yet it is not merely that the two features occur together. The wrongness must somehow be "consequential" or "supervenient"; it is wrong because it is a piece of deliberate cruelty. But just what in the world is signified by this "because"? And how do we know the relation that it signifies, if this is something more than such actions being socially condemned, and condemned by us too, perhaps through our having absorbed attitudes from our social environment? It is not even sufficient to postulate a faculty which "sees" the wrongness: something must be postulated which can see at once the natural features that constitute the cruelty, and the wrongness, and the mysterious consequential link between the two. Alternatively, the intuition required might be the perception that wrongness is a higher order property belonging to certain natural properties; but what is this belonging of properties to other properties, and how can we discern it? How much simpler and more comprehensible the situation would be if we could replace the moral quality with some sort of subjective response which could be causally related to the detection of the natural features on which the supposed quality is said to be consequential.

It may be thought that the argument from queerness is given an unfair start if we thus relate it to what are admittedly among the wilder products of philosophical fancy—Platonic Forms, nonnatural qualities, self-evident relations of fitness, faculties of intuition, and the like. Is it equally forceful if applied to the terms in which everyday moral judgements are more likely to be expressed—though still . . . with a claim to objectivity—"you must do this," "you can't do that," "obligation," "unjust," "rotten," "disgraceful," "mean," or talk about good reasons for or against possible actions? Admittedly not; but that is because the objective prescriptivity, the element a claim for whose authoritativeness is embedded in ordinary moral thought and language, is not yet isolated in these forms of speech, but is presented along with relations to desires and feelings, reasoning about the means to desired ends, interpersonal demands, the injustice which consists in the violation of what are in the context the accepted standards of merit, the psychological constituents of meanness, and so on. There is nothing queer about any of these, and under cover of them the claim for moral authority may pass unnoticed. But if I am right in arguing that it is ordinarily there, and is therefore very likely to be incorporated almost automatically in philosophical accounts of ethics which systematize our ordinary thought even in such apparently innocent terms as these, it needs to be examined, and for this purpose it needs to be isolated and exposed as it is by the less cautious philosophical reconstructions.

PATTERNS OF OBJECTIFICATION

Considerations of these kinds suggest that it is in the end less paradoxical to reject than to retain the common-sense belief in the objectivity of moral values, provided that we can explain how this belief, if it is false, has become established and is so resistant to criticisms. This proviso is not difficult to satisfy.

On a subjectivist view, the supposedly objective values will be based in fact upon attitudes which the person has who takes himself to be recognizing and responding to those values. If we admit what Hume calls the mind's "propensity to spread itself on external objects," we can understand the supposed objectivity of moral qualities as arising from what we can call the projection or objectification of moral attitudes. This would be analogous to what is called the "pathetic fallacy," the tendency to read our feelings into their objects. If a fungus, say, fills us with disgust, we may be inclined to ascribe to the fungus itself a non-natural quality of foulness. But in moral contexts there is more than this propensity at work. Moral attitudes themselves are at least partly social in origin: socially established—and socially necessary—patterns of behaviour put pressure on individuals, and each individual tends to internalize these pressures and to join in requiring these patterns of behaviour of himself and of others. The attitudes that are objecti-

fied into moral values have indeed an external source, though not the one assigned to them by the belief in their absolute authority. Moreover, there are motives that would support objectification. We need morality to regulate interpersonal relations, to control some of the ways in which people behave towards one another, often in opposition to contrary inclinations. We therefore want our moral judgements to be authoritative for other agents as well as for ourselves: objective validity would give them the authority required. Aesthetic values are logically in the same position as moral ones; much the same metaphysical and epistemological considerations apply to them. But aesthetic values are less strongly objectified than moral ones; their subjective status, and an "error theory" with regard to such claims to objectivity as are incorporated in aesthetic judgements, will be more readily accepted, just because the motives for their objectification are less compelling.

But it would be misleading to think of the objectification of moral values as primarily the projection of feelings, as in the pathetic fallacy. More important are wants and demands. As Hobbes says, "whatsoever is the object of any man's Appetite or Desire, that is it, which he for his part calleth Good"; and certainly both the adjective "good" and the noun "goods" are used in non-moral contexts of things because they are such as to satisfy desires. We get the notion of something's being objectively good, or having intrinsic value, by reversing the direction of dependence here, by making the desire depend upon the goodness, instead of the goodness on the desire. And this is aided by the fact that the desired thing will indeed have features that make it desired, that enable it to arouse a desire or that make it such as to satisfy some desire that is already there. It is fairly easy to confuse the way in which a thing's desirability is indeed objective with its having in our sense objective value. The fact that the word "good" serves as one of our main moral terms is a trace of this pattern of objectification.

Similarly related uses of words are covered by the distinction between hypothetical and categorical imperatives. The statement that someone "ought to" or, more strongly, "must" do such-and-such may be backed up explicitly or implicitly by reference to what he wants or to what his purposes and objects are. Again, there may be a reference to the purposes of someone else, perhaps the speaker: "You must do this"—"Why?"—"Because I want such-and-such." The moral categorical imperative which could be expressed in the same words can be seen as resulting from the suppression of the conditional clause in a hypothetical imperative without its being replaced by any such reference to the speaker's wants. The action in question is still required in something like the way in which it would be if it were appropriately related to a want, but it is no longer admitted that there is any contingent want upon which its being required depends. Again this move can be understood when we remember that at least our central and basic moral judgements represent social demands, where the source of the demand is indeterminate and diffuse. Whose demands or wants are in question, the agent's, or the speaker's, or those of an indefinite multitude of other people? All of these in a way, but there are advantages in not specifying them precisely. The speaker is expressing demands which he makes as a member of a community, which he has developed in and by participation in a joint way of life; also, what is required of this particular agent would be required of any other in a relevantly similar situation; but the agent too is expected to have internalized the relevant demands, to act as if the ends for which the action is required were his own. By suppressing any explicit reference to demands and making the imperatives categorical we facilitate conceptual moves from one such demand relation to another. The moral uses of such words as "must" and "ought" and "should," all of which are used also to express hypothetical imperatives, are traces of this pattern of objectification.

It may be objected that this explanation links normative ethics too closely with descriptive morality, with the mores or socially enforced patterns of behaviour that anthropologists record. But it can hardly be denied that moral thinking starts from the enforcement of social codes. Of course it is not confined to that. But even when moral judgements are detached from the mores of any actual society they are liable to be framed with reference to an ideal community of moral agents, such as Kant's kingdom of ends, which

but for the need to give God a special place in it would have been better called a commonwealth of ends.

Another way of explaining the objectification of moral values is to say that ethics is a system of law from which the legislator has been removed. This might have been derived either from the positive law of a state or from a supposed system of divine law. There can be no doubt that some features of modern European moral concepts are traceable to the theological ethics of Christianity. The stress on quasi-imperative notions, on what ought to be done or on what is wrong in a sense that is close to that of "forbidden," are surely relics of divine commands. Admittedly, the central ethical concepts for Plato and Aristotle also are in a broad sense prescriptive or intrinsically action-guiding, but in concentrating rather on "good" than on "ought" they show that their moral thought is an objectification of the desired and the satisfying rather than of the commanded. Elizabeth Anscombe has argued that modern, non-Aristotelian, concepts of moral obligation, moral duty, of what is morally right and wrong, and of the moral sense of "ought" are survivals outside the framework of thought that made them really intelligible, namely the belief in divine law. She infers that "ought" has "become a word of mere mesmeric force," with only a "delusive appearance of content," and that we would do better to discard such terms and concepts altogether, and go back to Aristotelian ones.

There is much to be said for this view. But while we can explain some distinctive features of modern moral philosophy in this way, it would be a mistake to see the whole problem of the claim to objective prescriptivity as merely local and unnecessary, as a postoperative complication of a society from which a dominant system of theistic belief has recently been rather hastily excised. As Cudworth and Clarke and Price, for example, show, even those who still admit divine commands, or the positive law of God, may believe moral values to have an independent objective but still action-guiding authority. Responding to Plato's Euthyphro dilemma, they believe that God commands what he commands because it is in itself good or right, not that it is good or right merely because and in that he commands it. Otherwise God himself could not be called good. Price asks, "What can be more preposterous, than to make the Deity nothing but will; and to exalt this on the ruins of all his attributes?" The apparent objectivity of moral value is a widespread phenomenon which has more than one source: the persistence of a belief in something like divine law when the belief in the divine legislator has faded out is only one factor among others. There are several different patterns of objectification, all of which have left characteristic traces in our actual moral concepts and moral language.

FOR FURTHER REFLECTION

1. Examine and evaluate Mackie's error theory. Identify Mackie's arguments against the objectivity of moral values. How strong are they?
2. What is the strongest point of Mackie's argument? What is the weakest point?
3. How would a moral realist, one who believes in objective moral principles, respond to Mackie?

LOUIS P. POJMAN

A CRITIQUE OF MACKIE'S THEORY OF MORAL SUBJECTIVISM

A biosketch of Louis P. Pojman appears earlier in this part. In this essay Pojman, who was one of Mackie's students, briefly examines and critiques Mackie's arguments against moral objectivity. The dispute takes place against the background of the debate over moral realism, the thesis that there are moral facts that exist independently of human acceptance. For example, promise breaking would be prima facie wrong whether or not anyone labeled it so.

In 1977, the Oxford philosopher J. L. Mackie in his *Ethics: Inventing Right and Wrong* set forth a Spinozist interpretation of morality. Mackie accepts the cognitivist's analysis of morality as presupposing moral facts, but he denies that there are any. "The denial of objective values will have to be put forward . . . as an 'error theory,' a theory that although most people in making moral judgments implicitly claim, among other things, to be pointing to something objectively prescriptive, these claims are all false."

Moral skeptics, then, doubt or deny that any of our moral theories or judgments are true.

Mackie acknowledges the importance of the realist's claims in holding to objective values but offers two arguments against such views: the *argument from relativity* (or disagreement) and the *argument from queerness*. The argument from relativity points out that there is no universal moral code that all people everywhere adhere to, which seems to indicate that morality is culturally dependent. The argument from

Adapted from Louis P. Pojman, *Ethics: Discovering Right and Wrong*, 3d ed. (Wadsworth, 1999).

queerness aims at showing the implausibility of supposing that such things as values have an independent existence. Hence, according to the *principle of simplicity* (do not multiply kinds of objects beyond necessity), we should conclude that moral facts do not exist.

MACKIE'S ERROR THEORY OF MORALITY

Mackie opens his book with the sentence, "There are no objective values." He elaborates by saying:

> The claim that values are not objective, are not part of the fabric of the world, is meant to include not only moral goodness, which might be most naturally equated with moral value, but also other things that could be more loosely called moral values or disvalues—rightness and wrongness, duty, obligation, an action's being rotten and contemptible, and so on. It also includes non-moral values, notably aesthetic ones, beauty and various kinds of artistic merit. (p. 15)

He distinguishes his view from a moral subjectivism in which the statement "This action is right" *means* "I approve of this action." His view is not about *meaning* but about *facts*, about whether there are any right or good actions. His answer is a skeptical one—we have no good reason to believe that moral facts exist. An example of a theory holding to moral facts is Plato's theory of the forms, and in particular the form of the good, which are eternal realities, "a very central part of the universe." If God exists, then there likewise might be moral truths in God or truths that God created. But Mackie, as an atheist, rejects this possibility. Other notions of objectivity might be the intuitionist notions of moral principles being discoverable by an inner sense or the naturalist notions of objective qualities, such as happiness, being "intrinsically desirable." Certainly, we feel as though certain actions are objectively right or wrong and that happiness is better than misery, but these are just our subjective preferences—even if others agree, intersubjective agreement is still subjective. When we apply a philosophical microscope to our judgments, we are forced to conclude that commonsense morality-qua-objectivity is simply false. However nice it would be to have an infallible or imposing moral authority, there is no reason to believe it exists. There are no moral truths. Nothing is morally wrong.

In explaining the tendency to objectify morality, Mackie refers to Hume, who pointed out in *Treatise of Human Nature* (1739) that when we perceive a murder we do not perceive the *vice* in it, nor can we infer it from what we do perceive by any valid principles of inference.[1] Hume speaks of our mind's "propensity to spread itself on external objects." Mackie calls this the *pathetic fallacy*, "our tendency to read our feelings into their objects. If a fungus, say, fills us with disgust, we may be inclined to ascribe to the fungus itself a non-natural quality of foulness." The difference between this and morality is that, with regard to morality, society influences what we find repulsive or good.

Let us further examine Mackie's two arguments for his error theory. First is his *argument from relativity*. It is an anthropological truism that the content of moral codes varies enormously from culture to culture. Some cultures promote monogamy, whereas others promote polygamy. Some cultures practice euthanasia, and others proscribe it. Our moral beliefs seem largely a product of our cultural upbringing. We tend to internalize the mores of our group. The argument from relativity holds that the best explanation for actual moral diversity is the absence of universal moral truths, rather than the distorted perceptions of objective principles.

We can neutralize this argument from relativity by considering whether the description of the moral life and its constitutive principles can find an independent justification. The fact of cultural diversity doesn't constitute a very strong argument against an objective core morality any more than disagreement about economics is good evidence against the thesis that some theories are better than others. Disagreement about morals could be due to ignorance, immaturity, moral insensitivity, superstition, or irrational authority. A criminal I once knew, whom I will call Sam, was accused of attempted rape. Asked to compare the significance of rape with other actions, he replied, "It's like choosing between chocolate and vanilla ice cream." Why should I allow Sam's perception to undermine my confidence in the principle, "Rape is immoral"? Just as there can be physical blindness or partial blindness, can't there be gross moral blindness? Can't I conclude that something is wrong with Sam—rather than concluding "Oh, well, different strokes for different folks" or "Different morals for different cultures"? I have already dealt with this issue in my previous article in this section of our book. In any case, Mackie acknowledges that his argument from relativity is indecisive, although, if we allow it, it adds weight to his crucial second argument.

The second argument is his *argument from queerness*. If there were objective values, then they would have to be "of a very strange sort, utterly different from anything else in the universe." Mackie thinks that all forms of moral realism boil down to intuitionism and that moral intuitionism requires "a special sort of intuition." The burden of proof seems to rest with the intuitionist to explain why we should espouse this unexplained, extra mechanism—this strange "moral sense." The principle of simplicity favors the simpler explanation that moral principles are merely subjective judgments.

The argument from queerness holds that moral facts, if they existed, would be strange objects, which would require a strange faculty to perceive. What evidence there is suggests that no such strange faculty exists. Rather, there are simpler explanations for our moral beliefs. Hence, we should reject the thesis that moral facts exist. Hence, there is nothing wrong (or right).

We could reject Mackie's characterization, as some have done, by pointing out that moral facts are not independent objects as such, but rather they *supervene* on natural properties or social practices. The concept of *supervenience* is important here. For example, our perception of the color red is a supervenient effect of the reflection of certain light waves off surfaces as communicated to our retinas. The color red supervenes on the noncolored properties of these surfaces. The color is not in the objects themselves, but there is a causal relationship between the light rays and our perceptions. Likewise, moral expressions, such as right and wrong or good and bad, may be supervenient on natural properties, such as happiness or suffering. It may well be that moral properties should be viewed as *functional*, standing for practices that tend to fulfill the purpose of morality (the *right*) or tend to

thwart it (the *wrong*). Morality's purpose is to promote human flourishing and ameliorate suffering and so forth, so *moral truths* are practices that satisfy the conditions for fulfilling that purpose.

We must note one further problem with Mackie's error theory: It seems to dissolve moral discourse altogether. Mackie actually wants to assert that some things really are wrong. He says, for instance, "As the world is, wars and revolutions cannot be ruled to be morally completely out of the question. The death penalty, I believe, can."[2] I confess to being dumbfounded. If nothing is wrong, then how can the death penalty be wrong? This seems a contradiction. Perhaps all Mackie means is "Death penalty—boo!" as an emotivist might exclaim. In that case, his opponents' "Death penalty—hurrah!" is no less valid.

If nothing is morally wrong, then isn't everything morally permissible (morally right)? If rape is not morally wrong, then doesn't that make it morally permissible? Mackie seems to want to say that both wrongness and permissibility are category mistakes. Neither exists. But if this really were so, then does it really matter what we do? Morality doesn't exist at all. We have not merely moral skepticism, but moral *nihilism*. But if this is so, don't we need something else to guide our behavior—practical reason to prohibit certain practices (e.g., rape and killing innocent people) and promote others (e.g., cooperation and promise-keeping)? It seems so. But if we use practical reason to coordinate our practices, then aren't some of these practices *better* than others from the standpoint of optimizing our wants and interests? Cooperation and promise-keeping and respecting others will promote the interests of members of a society more than rape and the killing of innocents. But if the former are more optimific, then aren't they the ones we will advise other societies to follow? Hence, we can judge Hindu Indian society immoral for practicing suttee—the burning of widows—and we can condemn Nazi society for exterminating Jews, and we can judge certain West African societies as wrong for performing clitorectomies on young girls. But given these considerations, it would seem that we can use objective moral language, just so long as we recognize the point of moral discourse.

Mackie holds that morality is an invention, not a discovery. What could this mean? The Greek philosopher Xenophon (570–478 B.C.E.) said that religion is an invention, the making of God in the image of one's own group:

> The Ethiopian make their gods black and snub-nosed; the Thracians say theirs have blue eyes and red hair. Yes, and if oxen and horses or lions had hands, and could paint with their hands, and produce works of art as men do, horses would paint the forms of the gods like horses, and oxen like oxen, and make their bodies in the image of their several kinds.[3]

Is this how we create morality—in our own images and according to our own desires, giving it authority in the process? Does Mackie mean that we consciously invent morality, principles, and sanctions to achieve social control? It seems so, for he writes,

> We need morality to regulate interpersonal relations, to control some of the ways in which people behave towards one another, often in opposition to contrary inclinations. We therefore want our moral judgements to be authoritative for other agents as well as for ourselves: objective validity would give them the authority required. (p. 43)

Suppose that Mackie is correct, and we do invent these practices and institutions. We find ourselves cooperating, then we notice the wonderful benefits it brings, and thus reinforced, the behavior tends to be repeated and promoted. We notice that truth-telling is indispensable for achieving our goals, so we invent sanctions to encourage it. But even if we did create all our moral practices ab initio in the way Mackie seems to suppose, still it would be an objective matter—a matter of *discovery*—to determine whether they really work! Suppose we decide to invent the practice of respecting property. We then discover that it really enhances the freedom and meaning of our lives. Just as the Ethiopian invention of black gods doesn't make it true that gods are black, our invention of moral practices doesn't make these practices true or valid or successful in meeting the relevant conditions. We don't *invent* the fact that respect for property brings us freedom and meaning. It either does or it doesn't. There is a fact of the matter.

CONCLUSION

Are there moral facts? The main arguments against this thesis are (1) the principle of simplicity—that we should not multiply properties or things beyond necessity—and (2) the word-to-world fit—that moral principles are more like prescriptions or imperatives, not descriptions of the world. We have countered the first argument in terms of the explanatory power of moral properties. Our response to the second argument is as follows. Just as we can say of a medical prescription, "Taking an aspirin a day is the correct prescription if you want to prevent a heart attack," we can also correctly say, "Doing benevolent and just deeds is the way to promote human happiness and improve the welfare of society." Both statements are true—or, if they're not, then their opposites are. So moral principles do entail truth claims in this broad conditional sense.

But the moral realist often wants to say more than this. He is making a metaphysical claim about the fabric of the universe. Philosophers like Gilbert Harman and R. M. Hare are correct in pointing out that moral principles cannot be tested by observation in the same way that empirical theories can. But they may be tested, nevertheless. Cultures that fail to instantiate moral principles such as truth telling, promise keeping, and prohibiting stealing, murder, and rape, are not likely to prosper or even survive. Thought experiments, such as William Golding's *Lord of the Flies*, as well as considerable anthropological data, such as Colin Turnbull's *Mountain People* confirm the Hobbesian thesis that without a moderate amount of standard morality we would exist in a state of nature where life is "solitary, poor, nasty, brutish and short, a war of all against all." But even as our scientific theories are always open to revision, so our moral theories should be open to revision in the light of better evidence and deeper reflection.

One other consideration accommodates the view that moral principles have truth value and that they do make up the fabric of the universe. This is the thesis that not all truths about the universe are empirical ones. *Not all facts are empirical.* The laws of logic are not empirical, yet they are true in all possible worlds. Universals exist: the universal property *red* is possessed by all red objects; all horses have the property of horsehood, and the property of being a belief applies to all beliefs. There are two-placed relations such as *being to the left of* something (e.g., aRb, where "R" stands for the relation and "a" and "b" stand for the objects in relation) that characterize objects in space and relations in time (e.g., "a occurred before b"). If universals are admitted as part of the fabric of the universe, then there is no reason to withhold moral properties from the class of these entities, and so moral truths exist as part of the furniture of the world.

Although I have supported the naturalist account of morality, holding that moral properties supervene on natural ones, I have not ruled out intuitionism, the thesis that moral properties are nonnatural, that they are self-evident truths discoverable upon reflection. It could also be the case that moral truths are rooted in a transcendent reality. The naturalism that I have defended is a functional naturalism, not a metaphysical one. The common thesis of these theories is that universal moral truths exist. If so, we have objective guidelines for our actions, ones by which we ought to live and structure our societies.

NOTES

1. "Take any action allowed to be vicious; willful murder, for instance. Examine it in all lights and see if you can find that matter of fact . . . which you call vice. In whichever way you take it, you only find certain passions, motives, volitions and thoughts . . . The vice entirely escapes you, as long as you consider the object. You can never find it till you turn your reflection into your own breast, and find a sentiment of disapprobation, which arises in you, towards that action." (David Hume, A *Treatise of Human Nature*)

2. Jonathan Harrison in his "Mackie's Moral Skepticism" (*Philosophy* 57, 1982) notes this point.

3. Quoted in Wallace Matson's *A New History of Philosophy* (Wadsworth, 1987), vol. 1.

FOR FURTHER REFLECTION

1. Examine and evaluate Pojman's critique of Mackie's Error Theory. How might Mackie respond to it.

2. Explain the concept of *supervenience*. How does it help the moral realist make his case?

3. How plausible is moral realism. Can one be a nonrealist and still be a moral objectivist? Explain.

4. We have asked, "What is the purpose of morality? What function does it serve?" Some philosophers deny that this is a good way to describe morality because they hold that morality has intrinsic value apart from specific functions. Reflect on this controversy and develop your own position.

B. MORALITY AND SELF-INTEREST

Why should you be moral? That is, why should you do what morality requires even when it may not seem to be in your best interest? Is it really in your best interest after all, even if you don't realize it? Or is morality only generally in your best interest, so that you should contemplate breaking its rules whenever they become too burdensome? Or is the question itself confused?

In this section and the next, we look at various responses to that question. In this section, we begin with Glaucon's question to Socrates: whether justice (what we would call morality) was really only a compromise relationship between the better but unattainable state of exploiting others with impunity and the worst situation of being exploited by others. Socrates rejects this way of looking at the problem and argues that justice or morality is intrinsically valuable and brings about a healthy soul. Next, turning to contemporary discussions of the problem, we look at James Rachels's succinct examination of ethical egoism. Finally, we look at J. L. Mackie's attempt to relate the problem of self-interest to evolutionary theory, showing the natural wisdom of reciprocal altruism.

In section C, the same problem is raised in the selections by Mavrodes and Nielsen with regard to the relationship of morality to religion.

PLATO

GYGES' RING, OR IS THE GOOD GOOD FOR YOU?

Plato (427–347 B.C.E.) lived in Athens and is the earliest philosopher for whom extensive works have survived. He immortalized his teacher, Socrates, in a series of dialogues. Perhaps his greatest dialogue is the *Republic*, from which this present reading is taken. The *Republic* is a classic treatise on political philosophy, centering on the concept of justice or moral rightness. In this work, Plato—through his idealization of Socrates—argues there will be justice only when reason rules and the people obey its commands. This utopia is only possible in an aristocracy in which the rulers are philosophers—in fact, philosopher-kings. In our selection, Plato's older brother Glaucon asks Socrates whether justice is good in itself or only a necessary evil. Playing devil's advocate, Glaucon hypothesizes that egotistic power seeking, in which we have complete freedom to indulge ourselves, might be the ideal state of existence. However, the hypothesis continues, reason quickly shows us that others might seek the same power, which would interfere with our freedom and cause a state of chaos in which no one was likely to have any desire fulfilled. So we compromise and limit our acquisitive instincts. Justice or a system of morality is simply the result of that compromise. It has no intrinsic value; it is better than chaos but worse than undisturbed power. It is better to compromise and limit our acquisitive instincts.

To illustrate his point, Glaucon tells the story of a shepherd named Gyges, who finds a ring that at his command makes him invisible. He uses it to escape the external sanctions of society—its laws and censure—and to serve his greed to the fullest. Glaucon asks whether it is not plausible to suppose that we all would do likewise. Then he offers a thought experiment that compares the life of the seemingly just (but really unjust) man who is incredibly successful with the life of the seemingly unjust (but really just) man who is incredibly unsuccessful. Which would we choose?

We enter the dialogue in the second book of the *Republic*. Socrates has just shown that the type of egoism advocated by Thrasymachus is contradictory. Socrates is speaking.

With these words I was thinking that I had made an end of the discussion; but the end, in truth, proved to be only a beginning. For Glaucon, who is always the most pugnacious of men, was dissatisfied at Thrasymachus' retirement; he wanted to have the battle out. So he said to me: Socrates, do you wish really to persuade us, or only to seem to have persuaded us, that to be just is always better than to be unjust?

I should wish really to persuade you, I replied, if I could.

Then you certainly have not succeeded. Let me ask you now:—How would you arrange goods—are there not some which we welcome for their own sakes, and independently of their consequences, as, for example, harmless pleasures and enjoyments, which delight us at the time, although nothing follows from them?

I agree in thinking that there is such a class, I replied.

Is there not also a second class of goods, such as knowledge, sight, health, which are desirable not only in themselves, but also for their results?

Certainly, I said.

And would you not recognize a third class, such as gymnastic, and the care of the sick, and the physician's art; also the various ways of money-making— these do us good but we regard them as disagreeable; and no one would choose them for their own sakes, but only for the sake of some reward or result which flows from them?

There is, I said, this third class also. But why do you ask?

Because I want to know in which of the three classes you would place justice?

In the highest class, I replied, among those goods which he who would be happy desires both for their own sake and for the sake of their results.

Then the many are of another mind; they think that justice is to be reckoned in the troublesome class, among goods which are to be pursued for the sake of rewards and of reputation, but in themselves are disagreeable and rather to be avoided.

I know, I said, that this is their manner of thinking, and that this was the thesis which Thrasymachus was maintaining just now, when he censured justice and praised injustice. But I am too stupid to be convinced by him. . . .

I wish, he said, that you would hear me as well as him, and then I shall see whether you and I agree. For Thrasymachus seems to me, like a snake, to have been charmed by your voice sooner than he ought to have been; but to my mind the nature of justice and injustice have not yet been made clear. Setting aside their rewards and results, I want to know what they are in themselves, and how they inwardly work in the soul. If you please, then, I will revive the argument of Thrasymachus. And first I will speak of the nature and origin of justice according to the common view of them. Secondly, I will show that all men who practice justice do so against their will, of necessity, but not as a good. And thirdly, I will argue that there is reason in this view, for the life of the unjust is after all better far than the life of the just—if what they say is true, Socrates, since I myself am not of their opinion. But still I acknowledge that I am perplexed when I hear the voices of Thrasymachus and myriads of others dinning in my ears; and, on the other hand, I have never yet heard the superiority of justice to injustice maintained by any one in a satisfactory way. I want to hear justice praised in respect of itself; then I shall be satisfied, and you are the person from whom I think that I am most likely to hear this; and therefore I will praise the unjust life to the utmost of my power, and my manner of speaking will indicate the manner in which I desire to hear you too praising justice and censuring injustice. Will you say whether you approve of my proposal?

Indeed I do; nor can I imagine any theme about which a man of sense would oftener wish to converse.

I am delighted, he replied, to hear you say so, and shall begin by speaking, as I proposed, of the nature and origin of justice.

They say that to do injustice is, by nature, good; to suffer injustice, evil; but that the evil is greater than the good. And so when men have both done and suffered injustice and have had experience of both, not being able to avoid the one and obtain the other, they think that they had better agree among themselves to

From Plato, *The Republic,* in *The Dialogues of Plato,* trans. Benjamin Jowett (New York: Scribner's, 1889).

have neither; hence there arise laws and mutual covenants; and that which is ordained by law is termed by them lawful and just. This they affirm to be the origin and nature of justice:—it is a mean or compromise, between the best of all, which is to do injustice and not be punished, and the worst of all, which is to suffer injustice without the power of retaliation; and justice, being at a middle point between the two, is tolerated not as a good, but as the lesser evil, and honoured by reason of the inability of men to do injustice. For no man who is worthy to be called a man would ever submit to such an agreement if he were able to resist; he would be mad if he did. Such is the received account, Socrates, of the nature and origin of justice.

Now that those who practice justice do so involuntarily and because they have not the power to be unjust will best appear if we imagine something of this kind: having given both to the just and the unjust power to do what they will, let us watch and see whither desire will lead them; then we shall discover in the very act the just and unjust man to be proceeding along the same road, following their interest, which all natures deem to be their good, and are only diverted into the path of justice by the force of law. The liberty which we are supposing may be most completely given to them in the form of such a power as is said to have been possessed by Gyges the ancestor of Croesus the Lydian. According to the tradition, Gyges was a shepherd in the service of the king of Lydia; there was a great storm, and an earthquake made an opening in the earth at the place where he was feeding his flock. Amazed at the sight, he descended into the opening, where, among other marvels, he beheld a hollow brazen horse, having doors, at which he stooping and looking in saw a dead body of stature, as appeared to him, more than human, and having nothing on but a gold ring; this he took from the finger of the dead and reascended. Now the shepherds met together, according to custom, that they might send their monthly report about the flocks to the king; into their assembly he came having the ring on his finger, and as he was sitting among them he chanced to turn the collet of the ring inside his hand, when instantly he became invisible to the rest of the company and they began to speak of him as if he were no longer

present. He was astonished at this, and again touching the ring he turned the collet outwards and reappeared; he made several trials of the ring, and always with the same result—when he turned the collet inwards he became invisible, when outwards he reappeared. Whereupon he contrived to be chosen one of the messengers who were sent to the court; where as soon as he arrived he seduced the queen, and with her help conspired against the king and slew him, and took the kingdom. Suppose now that there were two such magic rings, and the just put on one of them and the unjust the other; no man can be imagined to be of such an iron nature that he would stand fast in justice. No man would keep his hands off what was not his own when he could safely take what he liked out of the market, or go into houses and lie with any one at his pleasure, or kill or release from prison whom he would, and in all respects be like a God among men. Then the actions of the just would be as the actions of the unjust; they would both come at last to the same point. And this we may truly affirm to be a great proof that a man is just, not willingly or because he thinks that justice is any good to him individually, but of necessity, for wherever any one thinks that he can safely be unjust, there he is unjust. For all men believe in their hearts that injustice is far more profitable to the individual than justice, and he who argues as I have been supposing, will say that they are right. If you could imagine any one obtaining this power of becoming invisible, and never doing any wrong or touching what was another's, he would be thought by the lookers-on to be a most wretched idiot, although they would praise him to one another's faces, and keep up appearances with one another from a fear that they too might suffer injustice. Enough of this.

Now, if we are to form a real judgment of the life of the just and unjust, we must isolate them; there is no other way; and how is the isolation to be effected? I answer: Let the unjust man be entirely unjust, and the just man entirely just; nothing is to be taken away from either of them, and both are to be perfectly furnished for the work of their respective lives. First, let the unjust be like other distinguished masters of craft; like the skillful pilot or physician, who knows intuitively his own powers and keeps within their limits, and who, if he fails at any point, is able to recover himself. So let the unjust make his unjust attempts in the right way, and lie hidden if he means to be great in his injustice (he who is found out is nobody): for the highest reach of injustice is: to be deemed just when you are not. Therefore I say that in the perfectly unjust man we must assume the most perfect injustice; there is to be no deduction, but we must allow him, while doing the most unjust acts, to have acquired the greatest reputation for justice. If he have taken a false step he must be able to recover himself; he must be one who can speak with effect, if any of his deeds come to light, and who can force his way where force is required by his courage and strength, and command of money and friends. And at his side let us place the just man in his nobleness and simplicity, wishing, as Aeschylus says, to be and not to seem good. There must be no seeming, for if he seem to be just he will be honoured and rewarded, and then we shall now know whether he is just for the sake of justice or for the sake of honours and rewards; therefore, let him be clothed in justice only, and have no other covering; and he must be imagined in a state of life the opposite of the former. Let him be the best of men, and let him be thought the worst; then he will have been put to the proof; and we shall see whether he will be affected by the fear of infamy and its consequences. And let him continue thus to the hour of death; being just and seeming to be unjust. When both have reached the uttermost extreme, the one of justice and the other of injustice, let judgment be given which of them is the happier of the two.

Heavens! my dear Glaucon, I said, how energetically you polish them up for the decision, first one and then the other, as if they were two statues.

I do my best, he said. And now that we know what they are like there is no difficulty in tracing out the sort of life which awaits either of them. This I will proceed to describe; but as you may think the description a little too coarse, I ask you to suppose, Socrates, that the words which follow are not mine.—Let me put them into the mouths of the eulogists of injustice: they will tell you that the just man who is thought unjust will be scourged, racked, bound—will have his eyes burnt out; and, at last, after suffering every kind of evil, he will be impaled: Then he will understand that he ought to seem only, and not to be, just;

the words of Aeschylus may be more truly spoken of the unjust than of the just. For the unjust is pursuing a reality; he does not live with a view to appearances—he wants to be really unjust and not to seem only:—

His mind has a soil deep and fertile.
Out of which spring his prudent counsels.

In the first place, he is thought just, and therefore bears rule in the city; he can marry whom he will, and give in marriage to whom he will; also he can trade and deal where he likes, and always to his own advantage, because he has no misgivings about injustice; and at every contest, whether in public, or private, he gets the better of his antagonists, and gains at their expense, and is rich, and out of his gains he can benefit his friends, and harm his enemies; moreover, he can offer sacrifices, and dedicate gifts to the gods abundantly and magnificently, and can honour the gods or any man whom he wants to honour in a far better style than the just, and therefore he is likely to be dearer than they are to the gods. And thus, Socrates, gods and men are said to unite in making the life of the unjust better than the life of the just. . . .

BOOK 9

"Now that we've gotten this far," I said, "let's go back to that statement made at the beginning, which brought us here: that it pays for a man to be perfectly unjust if he appears to be just. Isn't that what someone said?"

"Yes."

"Then since we've agreed what power justice and injustice each have, let's have a discussion with him."

"How?"

"By molding in words an image of the soul, so that the one who said that will realize what he was saying."

"What kind of image?"

"Oh, something like those natures the myths tell us were born in ancient times—the Chimaera, Scylla, Cerberus, and others in which many different shapes were supposed to have grown into one."

"So they tell us," he said.

"Then mold one figure of a colorful, many-headed beast with heads of wild and tame animals growing in a circle all around it; one that can change and grow all of them out of itself."

"That's a job for a skilled artist. Still, words mold easier than wax or clay, so consider it done."

"And another of a lion, and one of a man. Make the first by far the biggest, the second second largest."

"That's easier, and already done."

"Now join the three together so that they somehow grow."

"All right."

"Next mold the image of one, the man, around them all, so that to someone who can't see what's inside but looks only at the container it appears to be a single animal, man."

"I have."

"Then shall we inform the gentleman that when he says it pays for this man to be unjust, he's saying that it profits him to feast his multifarious beast and his lion and make them grow strong, but to starve and enfeeble the man in him so that he gets dragged wherever the animals lead him, and instead of making them friends and used to each other, to let them bite and fight and eat each other?"

"That's just what he's saying by praising injustice."

"The one who says justice pays, however, would be saying that he should practice and say whatever will give the most mastery to his inner man, who should care for the many-headed beast like a farmer, raising and domesticating its tame heads and preventing the wild ones from growing, making the lion's nature his partner and ally, and so raise them both to be friends to each other and to him."

"That's exactly what he means by praising justice."

"So in every way the commender of justice is telling the truth, the other a lie. Whether we examine pleasure, reputation, or profit, we find that the man who praises justice speaks truly, the one who disparages it disparages sickly and knows nothing of what he disparages."

"I don't think he does at all."

"Then let's gently persuade him—his error wasn't intended—by asking him a question: 'Shouldn't we say that the traditions of the beautiful and the ugly have come about like this: Beautiful things are those that make our bestial parts subservient to the human—or rather, perhaps, to the divine—part of our nature, while ugly ones are those that enslave the tame to the wild?' Won't he agree?"

"If he takes my advice."

"On this argument then, can it pay for a man to take money unjustly if that means making his best part a slave to the worst? If it wouldn't profit a man to sell his son or his daughter into slavery—to wild and evil men at that—even if he got a fortune for it, then if he has no pity on himself and enslaves the most godlike thing in him to the most godless and polluted, isn't he a wretch who gets bribed for gold into a destruction more horrible than Euriphyle's, who sold her husband's life for a necklace?"

"Much more horrible," said Glaucon.

". . . everyone is better off being ruled by the godlike and intelligent; preferably if he has it inside, but if not, it should be imposed on him from without so that we may all be friends and as nearly alike as possible, all steered by the same thing."

"Yes, and we're right," he said.

"Law, the ally of everyone in the city, clearly intends the same thing, as does the rule of children, which forbids us to let them be free until we've instituted a regime in them as in a city. We serve their best part with a similar part in us, install a like guardian and ruler in them, and only then set them free."

"Clearly."

"Then how, by what argument, Glaucon, can we say that it pays for a man to be unjust or self-indulgent or to do something shameful to get more money or power if by doing so he makes himself worse?"

"We can't," he said.

"And how can it pay to commit injustice without getting caught and being punished? Doesn't getting away with it make a man even worse? Whereas if a man gets caught and punished, his beastlike part is taken in and tamed, his tame part is set free, and his whole soul acquires justice and temperance and knowledge. Therefore his soul recovers its best nature and attains a state more honorable than the state the body attains when it acquires health and strength and beauty, by as much as the soul is more honorable than the body."

"Absolutely."

"Then won't a sensible man spend his life directing all his efforts to this end?"

FOR FURTHER REFLECTION

1. Which would you choose to be, Glaucon's good but suffering person or his bad but successful person? Is there a third alternative? Explain.

2. Socrates' answer to Glaucon is that, in spite of appearances, we should choose the life of the "unsuccessful" just person because it's to our advantage to be moral. Socrates' answer depends on a notion of mental health. He contends that immorality corrupts the inner person, so that one is happy or unhappy in exact proportion to one's moral integrity. Is this a plausible reply?

3. Is the good always good for you?

JAMES RACHELS

ETHICAL EGOISM

James Rachels (1941–2003) was professor of philosophy at the University of Alabama at Birmingham and is the author of several articles in moral philosophy. He is the author of *The End of Life: Euthanasia and Morality* (Oxford: Oxford University Press, 1986) and *The Elements of Moral Philosophy* (New York: Random House, 1986), from which latter book this reading is taken. In this succinct essay, Rachels first separates ethical egoism from psychological egoism, the doctrine that people always act out of their own perceived self-interest. Ethical egoism is the doctrine that it is always our duty to act exclusively in our self-interest. He examines three arguments in favor of ethical egoism, showing that they each fail to support their conclusion, and then examines three arguments against the doctrine. He argues that only one of these is sound, but it is enough to invalidate ethical egoism.

IS THERE A DUTY TO CONTRIBUTE FOR FAMINE RELIEF?

Each year millions of people die of malnutrition and related health problems. A common pattern among children in poor countries is death from dehydration caused by diarrhea brought on by malnutrition. James Grant, executive director of the United Nations Children's Fund (UNICEF), estimates that about 15,000 children die in this way *every day*. That comes to 5,475,000 children annually. Even if his estimate is too high, the number that die is staggering.

For those of us in the affluent countries, this poses an acute moral problem. We spend money on ourselves, not only for the necessities of life but for innu-

From James Rachels, *The Elements of Moral Philosophy* (New York: Random House, 1986). Reprinted by permission of McGraw-Hill Publishers.

merable luxuries—for fine automobiles, fancy clothes, stereos, sports, movies, and so on. In our country, even people with modest incomes enjoy such things. The problem is that we *could* forgo our luxuries and give the money for famine relief instead. The fact that we don't suggests that we regard our luxuries as more important than feeding the hungry.

Why do we allow people to starve to death when we could save them? Very few of us actually believe our luxuries are that important. Most of us, if asked the question directly, would probably be a bit embarrassed, and we would say that we probably should do more for famine relief. The explanation of why we do not is, at least in part, that we hardly ever think of the problem. Living our own comfortable lives, we are effectively insulated from it. The starving people are dying at some distance from us; we do not see them, and we can avoid even thinking of them. When we do think of them, it is only abstractly, as bloodless statistics. Unfortunately for the starving, statistics do not have much power to motivate action.

But leaving aside the question of *why* we behave as we do, what is our *duty?* What *should* we do? We might think of this as the "common-sense" view of the matter: morality requires that we balance our own interests against the interests of others. It is understandable, of course, that we look out for our own interests, and no one can be faulted for attending to his own basic needs. But at the same time the needs of others are also important, and when we can help others—especially at little cost to ourselves—we should do so. Suppose you are thinking of spending ten dollars on a trip to the movies, when you are reminded that ten dollars could buy food for a starving child. Thus you could do a great service for the child at little cost to yourself. Common-sense morality would say, then, that you should give the money for famine relief rather than spending it on the movies.

This way of thinking involves a general assumption about our moral duties: it is assumed that we have moral duties *to other people*—and not merely duties that we create, such as by making a promise or incurring a debt. We have "natural" duties to others *simply because they are people who could be helped or harmed by our actions.* If a certain action would benefit (or harm) other people, then that is a reason

why we should (or should not) do that action. The common-sense assumption is that other people's interests *count,* for their own sakes, from a moral point of view.

But one person's common sense is another person's naive platitude. Some thinkers have maintained that, in fact, we have no "natural" duties to other people. *Ethical Egoism* is the idea that each person ought to pursue his or her own self-interest exclusively. It is different from Psychological Egoism, which is a theory of human nature concerned with how people *do* behave—Psychological Egoism says that people do in fact always pursue their own interests. Ethical Egoism, by contrast, is a normative theory—that is, a theory about how we *ought* to behave. Regardless of how we do behave, Ethical Egoism says we have no moral duty except to do what is best for ourselves.

It is a challenging theory. It contradicts some of our deepest moral beliefs—beliefs held by most of us, at any rate—but it is not easy to refute. We will examine the most important arguments for and against it. If it turns out to be true, then of course that is immensely important. But even if it turns out to be false, there is still much to be learned from examining it—we may, for example, gain some insight into the reasons why we *do* have obligations to other people.

But before looking at the arguments, we should be a little clearer about exactly what this theory says and what it does not say. In the first place, Ethical Egoism does not say that one should promote one's own interests *as well as* the interests of others. That would be an ordinary, unexceptional view. Ethical Egoism is the radical view that one's *only* duty is to promote one's own interests. According to Ethical Egoism, there is only one ultimate principle of conduct, the principle of self-interest, and this principle sums up *all* of one's natural duties and obligations.

However, Ethical Egoism does not say that you should *avoid* actions that help others, either. It may very well be that in many instances your interests coincide with the interests of others, so that in helping yourself you will be aiding others willy-nilly. Or it may happen that aiding others is an effective *means* for creating some benefit for yourself. Ethical Egoism does not forbid such actions; in fact, it may demand them. The theory insists only that in such cases the benefit to others is not what makes the act right. What makes the act right is, rather, the fact that it is to one's own advantage.

Finally, Ethical Egoism does not imply that in pursuing one's interests one ought always to do what one wants to do, or what gives one the most pleasure in the short run. Someone may want to do something that is not good for himself or that will eventually cause himself more grief than pleasure—he may want to drink a lot or smoke cigarettes or take drugs or waste his best years at the race track. Ethical Egoism would frown on all this, regardless of the momentary pleasure it affords. It says that a person ought to do what *really is* to his or her own best advantage, *over the long run.* It endorses selfishness, but it doesn't endorse foolishness.

THREE ARGUMENTS IN FAVOR OF ETHICAL EGOISM

What reasons can be advanced to support this doctrine? Why should anyone think it is true? Unfortunately, the theory is asserted more often than it is argued for. Many of its supporters apparently think its truth is self-evident, so that arguments are not needed. When it *is* argued for, three lines of reasoning are most commonly used.

1. The first argument has several variations, each suggesting the same general point:

a. Each of us is intimately familiar with our own individual wants and needs. Moreover, each of us is uniquely placed to pursue those wants and needs effectively. At the same time, we know the desires and needs of other people only imperfectly, and we are not well situated to pursue them. Therefore, it is reasonable to believe that if we set out to be "our brother's keeper," we would often bungle the job and end up doing more mischief than good.

b. At the same time, the policy of "looking out for others" is an offensive intrusion into other people's privacy; it is essentially a policy of minding other people's business.

c. Making other people the object of one's "charity" is degrading to them; it robs them of their individual dignity and self-respect. The offer of charity says, in effect, that they are not competent to care for

themselves; and the statement is self-fulfilling—they cease to be self-reliant and become passively dependent on others. That is why the recipients of "charity" are so often resentful rather than appreciative.

What this adds up to is that the policy of "looking out for others" is self-defeating. If we want to promote the best interests of everyone alike, we should *not* adopt so-called altruistic policies of behavior. On the contrary, if each person looks after his or her *own* interests, it is more likely that everyone will be better off, in terms of both physical and emotional well-being. Thus Robert G. Olson says in his book *The Morality of Self-Interest* (1965), "The individual is most likely to contribute to social betterment by rationally pursuing his own best long-range interests." Or as Alexander Pope said more poetically,

> Thus God and nature formed the general frame
> And bade self-love and social be the same.

It is possible to quarrel with this argument on a number of grounds. Of course no one favors bungling, butting in, or depriving people of their self-respect. But is this really what we are doing when we feed hungry children? Is the starving child in Ethiopia really harmed when we "intrude" into "her business" by supplying food? It hardly seems likely. Yet we can set this point aside, for considered as an argument for Ethical Egoism, this way of thinking has an even more serious defect.

The trouble is that it isn't really an argument *for Ethical Egoism* at all. The argument concludes that we should adopt certain policies of action; and on the surface they appear to be egoistic policies. However, the *reason* it is said we should adopt those policies is decidedly *un*egoistic. The reason is one that to an egoist shouldn't matter. It is said that we should adopt those policies because doing so will promote the "betterment of society"—but according to Ethical Egoism, that is something we should not be concerned about. Spelled out fully, with everything laid on the table, the argument says:

(1) We ought to do whatever will promote the best interests of everyone alike.

(2) The interests of everyone will best be promoted if each of us adopts the policy of pursuing our own interests exclusively.

(3) Therefore, each of us should adopt the policy of pursuing our own interests exclusively.

If we accept this reasoning, then we are not ethical egoists at all. Even though we might end up *behaving* like egoists, our ultimate principle is one of beneficence—we are doing what we think will help everyone, not merely what we think will benefit ourselves. Rather than being egoists, we turn out to be altruists with a peculiar view of what in fact promotes the general welfare.

2. The second argument was put forward with some force by Ayn Rand, a writer little heeded by professional philosophers but who nevertheless was enormously popular on college campuses during the 1960s and 1970s. Ethical Egoism, in her view, is the only ethical philosophy that respects the integrity of the individual human life. She regarded the ethics of "altruism" as a totally destructive idea, both in society as a whole and in the lives of individuals taken in by it. Altruism, to her way of thinking, leads to a denial of the value of the individual. It says to a person: *your* life is merely something that may be sacrificed. "If a man accepts the ethics of altruism," she writes, "his first concern is not how to live his life, but how to sacrifice it." Moreover, those who would *promote* this idea are beneath contempt—they are parasites who, rather than working to build and sustain their own lives, leech off those who do. Again, she writes:

> Parasites, moochers, looters, brutes and thugs can be of no value to a human being—nor can he gain any benefit from living in a society geared to *their* needs, demands and protections, a society that treats him as a sacrificial animal and penalizes him for his virtues in order to reward *them* for their vices, which means: a society based on the ethics of altruism.

By "sacrificing one's life" Rand does not necessarily mean anything so dramatic as dying. A person's life consists (in part) of projects undertaken and goods earned and created. To demand that a person abandon his projects or give up his goods is also a clear effort to "sacrifice his life." Furthermore, throughout her writings Rand also suggests that there is a *metaphysical* basis for egoistic ethics. Somehow, it is the only ethics that takes seriously the *reality* of the

individual person. She bemoans "the enormity of the extent to which altruism erodes men's capacity to grasp . . . the value of an individual life; it reveals a mind from which the reality of a human being has been wiped out."

What, then, of the starving people? It might be argued, in response, that Ethical Egoism "reveals a mind from which the reality of a human being has been wiped out"—namely, the human being who is starving. Rand quotes with approval the evasive answer given by one of her followers: "Once, when Barbara Brandon was asked by a student: 'What will happen to the poor . . . ?'—she answered: 'If *you* want to help them, you will not be stopped.'"

All these remarks are, I think, part of one continuous argument that can be summarized like this:

(1) A person has only one life to live. If we place any value on the individual—that is, if the individual has any moral worth—then we must agree that this life is of supreme importance. After all, it is all one has, and all one is.

(2) The ethics of altruism regards the life of the individual as something one must be ready to sacrifice for the good of others.

(3) Therefore, the ethics of altruism does not take seriously the value of the human individual.

(4) Ethical Egoism, which allows each person to view his or her own life as being of ultimate value, *does* take the human individual seriously—in fact, it is the only philosophy that does so.

(5) Thus, Ethical Egoism is the philosophy that ought to be accepted.

The problem with this argument, as you may already have noticed, is that it relies on picturing the alternatives in such an extreme way. "The ethics of altruism" is taken to be such an extreme philosophy that *nobody,* with the possible exception of certain monks, would find it congenial. As Ayn Rand presents it, altruism implies that one's own interests have *no* value, and that *any* demand by others calls for sacrificing them. If that is the alternative, then any other view, including Ethical Egoism, will look good by comparison. But this is hardly a fair picture of the choices. What we called the common-sense view stands somewhere between the two extremes. It says that one's own interests and the interests of others are both important and must be balanced against one another. Sometimes, when the balancing is done, it will turn out that one should act in the interests of others; other times, it will turn out that one should take care of oneself. So even if the Randian argument refutes the extreme "ethics of altruism," it does not follow that one must accept the other extreme of Ethical Egoism.

3. The third line of reasoning takes a somewhat different approach. Ethical Egoism is usually presented as a *revisionist* moral philosophy, that is, as a philosophy that says our common-sense moral views are mistaken and need to be changed. It is possible, however, to interpret Ethical Egoism in a much less radical way, as a theory that *accepts* common-sense morality and offers a surprising account of its basis.

The less radical interpretation goes as follows. In everyday life, we assume that we are obliged to obey certain rules. We must avoid doing harm to others, speak the truth, keep our promises, and so on. At first glance, these duties appear to be very different from one another. They appear to have little in common. Yet from a theoretical point of view, we may wonder whether there is not some hidden *unity* underlying the hodgepodge of separate duties. Perhaps there is some small number of fundamental principles that explain all the rest, just as in physics there are basic principles that bring together and explain diverse phenomena. From a theoretical point of view, the smaller the number of basic principles, the better. Best of all would be *one* fundamental principle, from which all the rest could be derived. Ethical Egoism, then, would be the theory that all our duties are ultimately derived from the one fundamental principle of self-interest.

Taken in this way, Ethical Egoism is not such a radical doctrine. It does not challenge common-sense morality; it only tries to explain and systematize it. And it does a surprisingly successful job. It can provide plausible explanations of the duties mentioned above, and more:

a. If we make a habit of doing things that are harmful to other people, people will not be reluctant to do things that will harm *us*. We will be shunned and despised; others will not have us as friends and will

not do us favors when we need them. If our offenses against others are serious enough, we may even end up in jail. Thus it is to our own advantage to avoid harming others.

b. If we lie to other people, we will suffer all the ill effects of a bad reputation. People will distrust us and avoid doing business with us. We will often need for people to be honest with us, but we can hardly expect them to feel much of an obligation to be honest with us if they know we have not been honest with them. Thus it is to our own advantage to be truthful.

c. It is to our own advantage to be able to enter into mutually beneficial arrangements with other people. To benefit from those arrangements, we need to be able to rely on others to keep their parts of the bargains we make with them—we need to be able to rely on them to keep their promises to us. But we can hardly expect others to keep their promises to us if we are not willing to keep our promises to them. Therefore, from the point of view of self-interest, we should keep our promises.

Pursuing this line of reasoning, Thomas Hobbes suggested that the principle of Ethical Egoism leads to nothing less than the Golden Rule: we should "do unto others" *because* if we do, others will be more likely to "do unto us."

Does this argument succeed in establishing Ethical Egoism as a viable theory of morality? It is, in my opinion at least, the best try. But there are two serious objections to it. In the first place, the argument does not prove quite as much as it needs to prove. At best, it shows only that *as a general rule* it is to one's own advantage to avoid harming others. It does not show that this is *always* so. And it could not show that, for even though it may usually be to one's advantage to avoid harming others, sometimes it is not. Sometimes one might even *gain* from treating another person badly. In that case, the obligation not to harm the other person could *not* be derived from the principle of Ethical Egoism. Thus it appears that not all our moral obligations can be explained as derivable from self-interest.

But set that point aside. There is still a more fundamental question to be asked about the proposed theory. Suppose it is true that, say, contributing money for famine relief is somehow to one's own advantage.

It does not follow that this is the only reason, or even the most basic reason, why doing so is a morally good thing. (For example, the most basic reason might be *in order to help the starving people.* The fact that doing so is also to one's own advantage might be only a secondary, less important, consideration.) A demonstration that one could *derive* this duty from self-interest does not prove that self-interest is the *only reason* one has this duty. Only if you accept an additional proposition—namely, the proposition that there is no reason for giving *other than* self-interest—will you find Ethical Egoism a plausible theory.

THREE ARGUMENTS AGAINST ETHICAL EGOISM

Ethical Egoism has haunted twentieth-century moral philosophy. It has not been a popular doctrine; the most important philosophers have rejected it outright. But it has never been very far from their minds. Although no thinker of consequence has defended it, almost everyone has felt it necessary to explain why he was rejecting it—as though the very possibility that it might be correct was hanging in the air, threatening to smother their other ideas. As the merits of the various "refutations" have been debated, philosophers have returned to it again and again.

The following three arguments are typical of the refutations proposed by contemporary philosophers.

1. In his book *The Moral Point of View* (1958), Kurt Baier argues that Ethical Egoism cannot be correct because it cannot provide solutions for conflicts of interest. We need moral rules, he says, only because our interests sometimes come into conflict. (If they never conflicted, then there would be no problems to solve and hence no need for the kind of guidance that morality provides.) But Ethical Egoism does not help to resolve conflicts of interest; it only exacerbates them. Baier argues for this by introducing a fanciful example:

> Let B and K be candidates for the presidency of a certain country and let it be granted that it is in the interest of either to be elected, but that only one can succeed. It would then be in the interest of B but against the interest of K if B were elected, and vice

versa, and therefore in the interest of B but against the interest of K if K were liquidated, and vice versa. But from this it would follow that B ought to liquidate K, that it is wrong for B not to do so, that B has not "done his duty" until he has liquidated K; and vice versa. Similarly K, knowing that his own liquidation is in the interest of B and therefore, anticipating B's attempts to secure it, ought to take steps to foil B's endeavors. It would be wrong for him not to do so. He would "not have done his duty" until he had made sure of stopping B. . . .

This is obviously absurd. For morality is designed to apply in just such cases, namely, those where interests conflict. But if the point of view of morality were that of self-interest, then there could never be moral solutions of conflicts of interest.

Does this argument prove that Ethical Egoism is unacceptable? It does, *if* the conception of morality to which it appeals is accepted. The argument assumes that an adequate morality must provide solutions for conflicts of interest in such a way that everyone concerned can live together harmoniously. The conflict between B and K, for example, should be resolved so that they would no longer be at odds with one another. (One would not then have a duty to do something that the other has a duty to prevent.) Ethical Egoism does not do that, and if you think an ethical theory should, then you will not find Ethical Egoism acceptable.

But a defender of Ethical Egoism might reply that *he* does not accept this conception of morality. For him, life is essentially a long series of conflicts in which each person is struggling to come out on top; and the principle he accepts—the principle of Ethical Egoism—simply urges each one to do his or her best to win. On his view, the moralist is not like a courtroom judge, who resolves disputes. Instead, he is like the Commissioner of Boxing, who urges each fighter to do his best. So the conflict between B and K will be "resolved" not by the application of an ethical theory but by one or the other of them winning the struggle. The egoist will not be embarrassed by this—on the contrary, he will think it no more than a realistic view of the nature of things.

2. Some philosophers, including Baier, have leveled an even more serious charge against Ethical Egoism. They have argued that it is a *logically*

inconsistent doctrine—that is, they say it leads to logical contradictions. If this is true, then Ethical Egoism is indeed a mistaken theory, for no theory can be true if it is self-contradictory.

Consider B and K again. As Baier explains their predicament, it is in B's interest to kill K, and obviously it is in K's interest to prevent it. But, Baier says,

> if K prevents B from liquidating him, his act must be said to be both wrong and not wrong—wrong because it is the prevention of what B ought to do, his duty, and wrong for B not to do it; not wrong because it is what K ought to do, his duty, and wrong for K not to do it. But one and the same act (logically) cannot be both morally wrong and not morally wrong.

Now, does *this* argument prove that Ethical Egoism is unacceptable? At first glance it seems persuasive. However, it is a complicated argument, so we need to set it out with each step individually identified. Then we will be in a better position to evaluate it. Spelled out fully, it looks like this:

(1) Suppose it is each person's duty to do what is in his own best interests.

(2) It is in B's best interest to liquidate K.

(3) It is in K's best interest to prevent B from liquidating him.

(4) Therefore B's duty is to liquidate K, and K's duty is to prevent B from doing it.

(5) But it is wrong to prevent someone from doing his duty.

(6) Therefore it is wrong for K to prevent B from liquidating him.

(7) Therefore it is both wrong and not wrong for K to prevent B from liquidating him.

(8) But no act can be both wrong and not wrong—that is a self-contradiction.

(9) Therefore the assumption with which we started—that it is each person's duty to do what is in his own best interests—cannot be true.

When the argument is set out in this way, we can see its hidden flaw. The logical contradiction—that it is both wrong and not wrong for K to prevent B from liquidating him—does *not* follow simply from the principle of Ethical Egoism. It follows from that principle, *and* the additional premise expressed in step (5)—namely, that "it is wrong to prevent someone

from doing his duty." Thus we are not compelled by the logic of the argument to reject Ethical Egoism. Instead, we could simply reject this additional premise, and the contradiction would be avoided. That is surely what the ethical egoist would want to do, for the ethical egoist would never say, without qualification, that it is always wrong to prevent someone from doing his duty. He would say, instead, that *whether one ought to prevent someone from doing his duty depends entirely on whether it would be to one's own advantage to do so.* Regardless of whether we think this is a correct view, it is, at the very least, a *consistent* view, and so this attempt to convict the egoist of self-contradiction fails.

3. Finally, we come to the argument that I think comes closest to an outright refutation of Ethical Egoism. It is also the most interesting of the arguments, because at the same time it provides the most insight into why the interests of other people *should* matter to a moral agent.

Before this argument is presented, we need to look briefly at a general point about moral values. So let us set Ethical Egoism aside for a moment and consider this related matter.

There is a whole family of moral views that have this in common: they all involve dividing people into groups and saying that the interests of some groups count for more than the interests of other groups. Racism is the most conspicuous example; it involves dividing people into groups according to race and assigning greater importance to the interests of one race than to others. The practical result is that members of the preferred race are to be *treated better* than the others. Anti-Semitism works the same way, and so can nationalism. People in the grip of such views will think, in effect: "*My* race counts for more," or "Those who believe in *my* religion count for more," or "*My* country counts for more," and so on.

Can such views be defended? Those who accept them are usually not much interested in argument—racists, for example, rarely try to offer rational grounds for their position. But suppose they did. What could they say?

There is a general principle that stands in the way of any such defense, namely: *We can justify treating people differently only if we can show that there is some factual difference between them that is relevant to justifying the difference in treatment.* For example, if one person is admitted to law school while another is rejected, this can be justified by pointing out that the first graduated from college with honors and scored well on the admissions test, while the second dropped out of college and never took the test. However, if *both* graduated with honors and did well on the entrance examination—in other words, if they are in all relevant respects equally well qualified—then it is merely arbitrary to admit one but not the other.

Can a racist point to any differences between, say, white people and black people that would justify treating them differently? In the past, racists have sometimes attempted to do this by picturing blacks as stupid, lacking in ambition, and the like. *If* this were true, then it might justify treating them differently, in at least some circumstances. (This is the deep purpose of racist stereotypes—to provide the "relevant differences" needed to justify differences in treatment.) But of course it is not true, and in fact there are no such general differences between the races. Thus racism is an *arbitrary* doctrine, in that it advocates treating some people differently even though there are no differences between them to justify it.

Ethical Egoism is a moral theory of the same type. It advocates that each of us divide the world into two categories of people—ourselves and all the rest—and that we regard the interests of those in the first group as more important than the interests of those in the second group. But each of us can ask, what is the difference between myself and others that justifies placing myself in this special category? Am I more intelligent? Do I enjoy my life more? Are my accomplishments greater? Do I have needs or abilities that are so different from the needs or abilities of others? *What is it that makes me so special?* Failing an answer, it turns out that Ethical Egoism is an arbitrary doctrine, in the same way that racism is arbitrary.

The argument, then, is this:

(1) Any moral doctrine that assigns greater importance to the interests of one group than to those of another is unacceptably arbitrary unless there is some difference between the members of the groups that justifies treating them differently.

(2) Ethical Egoism would have each person assign greater importance to his or her own interests than to the interests of others. *But there is no general difference between oneself and others, to which each person can appeal, that justifies this difference in treatment.*

(3) Therefore, Ethical Egoism is unacceptably arbitrary.

And this, in addition to arguing against Ethical Egoism, also sheds some light on the question of why we should care about others.

We should care about the interests of other people *for the very same reason we care about our own interests;* for their needs and desires are comparable to our own. Consider, one last time, the starving people we could feed by giving up some of our luxuries. Why should we care about them? We care about ourselves, of course—if *we* were starving, we would go to almost any lengths to get food. But what is the difference between us and them? Does hunger affect them any less? Are they somehow less deserving than we? If we can find no relevant difference between us and them, then we must admit that if *our* needs should be met, so should *theirs*. It is this realization, that we are on a par with one another, that is the deepest reason why our morality must include some recognition of the needs of others, and why, then, Ethical Egoism fails as a moral theory.

FOR FURTHER REFLECTION

1. Go over the three arguments for ethical egoism. Do you agree with Rachels's assessment that they all fail to establish the theory? Could a slight modification in any of them save the theory from Rachels's attack? Explain.

2. Examine the three arguments against ethical egoism. Do you agree with Rachels that only the third one "comes closest" to refuting ethical egoism? Why doesn't Rachels think that this argument actually does refute the doctrine? Does he give us a reason for thinking ethical egoism is still possibly true? Explain.

3. What sort of response might the ethical egoist make to Rachels's final critique? What if the

egoist responded thus: "It is not arbitrary to love oneself more than others. It is natural, for I have never experienced any other consciousness but my own, never felt the pain of any one else's toothache but my own, never dreamed or longed for any goal but my own. I am ultimately responsible for myself—and no one else is. Sure we need others to accomplish our goals, so we must cooperate with them. My duty to myself often includes helping or not harming them, but I have no direct duties to them. But we really don't know them. It's simply absurd to call on humanity "to love your neighbor as yourself." There is simply no way that I can be preoccupied with whether my neighbor will fulfill his dreams or is suffering or will come to terms with his death in the way I am preoccupied with my dreams and my suffering and my death." How would one criticize this argument?

4. Some philosophers, beginning with Plato, have argued that Ethical Egoism is irrational, since it precludes psychological health. In an article entitled "Ethical Egoism and Psychological Dispositions" (*American Philosophical Quarterly 17,* 1980), Laurence Thomas sets forth the following argument:

> P1. A true friend could never, as a matter of course, be disposed to harm or to exploit anyone with whom he is a friend (definition of a friend).
>
> P2. An egoist could never be a true friend to anyone (for the egoist must be ready to exploit others whenever it is in his or her interest).
>
> P3. Only someone with an unhealthy personality could never be a true friend to anyone. [definition of a healthy personality]
>
> P4. Ethical egoism requires that we have a kind of disposition which is incompatible with our having a healthy personality. [from P1–P3]
>
> Conclusion: Therefore, from the standpoint of our psychological makeup, ethical egoism is unacceptable as a moral theory.

Do you agree with Thomas? Why or why not? How might the ethical egoist respond?

J. L. MACKIE

THE LAW OF THE JUNGLE
Moral Alternatives and Principles of Evolution

J. L. Mackie (1917–1982) was born in Australia but spent most of his academic career teaching philosophy at University College, Oxford University. He made important contributions in the areas of metaphysics, philosophy of religion, epistemology, and ethics. Among his books are *The Cement of the Universe* (1974), *Ethics: Inventing Right and Wrong* (1977), and *The Miracle of Theism* (1982).

In this essay, Mackie examines the relevance of evolutionary theory to ethics. He begins with the work of Richard Dawkins, who invented the powerful metaphor "the selfish gene" and who argues that all adaptive benefits in the evolutionary process occur for the benefit of the individual. Counter to ethologists (that is, those who study animal behavior) like Robert Ardrey and Konrad Lorenz, there is no selection for traits favorable to the group. Mackie challenges Dawkins's position from within the framework of Dawkins's own theory, showing that in certain situations cooperative behavior can actually select for reciprocators (what Dawkins calls "grudgers").

The significance of work by Dawkins and others in relating evolutionary biology to ethical theory is that it shows the reasonableness of limited or reciprocal altruism in contrast to both the egoism of the "cheats" and the complete altruism of the "sucker."

When people speak of "the law of the jungle," they usually mean unrestrained and ruthless competition, with everyone out solely for his own advantage. But the phrase was coined by Rudyard Kipling, in *The Second Jungle Book,* and he meant something very different. His law of the jungle is a law that wolves in a pack are supposed to obey. His poem says that "the strength of the Pack is the Wolf, and the strength of the Wolf is the Pack," and it states the basic principles of social co-operation. Its provisions are a judicious mixture of individualism and collectivism, prescribing graduated and qualified rights for fathers of families, mothers with cubs, and young wolves, which constitute an elementary system of welfare services. Of course, Kipling meant his poem to give moral instruction to human children, but he probably thought it was at least roughly correct as a description of the social behaviour of wolves and other wild animals. Was he right, or is the natural world the scene of unrestrained competition, of an individualistic struggle for existence?

Views not unlike those of Kipling have been presented by some recent writers on ethology, notably Robert Ardrey and Konrad Lorenz. These writers con-

From J. L. Mackie, *Philosophy 53* (1978), 455–64. Reprinted with the permission of Cambridge University Press.

nect their accounts with a view about the process of evolution that has brought this behaviour, as well as the animals themselves, into existence. They hold that the important thing in evolution is the good of the species, or the group, rather than the good of the individual. Natural selection favours those groups and species whose members tend, no doubt through some instinctive programming, to co-operate for a common good; this would, of course, explain why wolves, for example, behave co-operatively and generously towards members of their own pack, if indeed they do.

However, this recently popular view has been keenly attacked by Richard Dawkins in his admirable and fascinating book, *The Selfish Gene*.[1] He defends an up-to-date version of the orthodox Darwinian theory of evolution, with special reference to "the biology of selfishness and altruism." One of his main theses is that there is no such thing as group selection, and that Lorenz and others who have used this as an explanation are simply wrong. This is a question of some interest to moral philosophers, particularly those who have been inclined to see human morality itself as the product of some kind of natural evolution.[2]

It is well, however, to be clear about the issue. It is not whether animals ever behave for the good of the group in the sense that this is their conscious subjective goal, that they *aim* at the well-being or survival of the whole tribe or pack: the question of motives in this conscious sense does not arise. Nor is the issue whether animals ever behave in ways which do in fact promote the well-being of the group to which they belong, or which help the species of which they are members to survive: of course they do. The controversial issue is different from both of these: it is whether the good of the group or the species would ever figure in a correct evolutionary account. That is, would any correct evolutionary account take either of the following forms?

1. The members of this species tend to do these things which assist the survival of this species because their ancestors were members of a sub-species whose members had an inheritable tendency to do these things, and as a result that sub-species survived, whereas other sub-species of the ancestral species at that time had mem-

bers who tended not to do these things and as a result their sub-species did not survive.

2. The members of this species tend to do these things which help the group of which they are members to flourish because some ancestral groups happened to have members who tended to do these things and these groups, as a result, survived better than related groups of the ancestral species whose members tended not to do these things.

In other words, the issue is this: is there natural selection by and for group survival or species survival as opposed to selection by and for individual survival (or, as we shall see, gene survival)? Is behaviour that helps the group or the species, rather than the individual animal, rewarded by the natural selection which determines the course of evolution?

However, when Dawkins denies that there is selection by and for group or species survival, it is not selection by and for individual survival that he puts in its place. Rather it is selection by and for the survival of each single gene—the genes being the unit factors of inheritance, the portions of chromosomes which replicate themselves, copy themselves as cells divide and multiply. Genes, he argues, came into existence right back at the beginning of life on earth, and all more complex organisms are to be seen as their products. We are, as he picturesquely puts it, gene-machines: our biological function is just to protect our genes, carry them around, and enable them to reproduce themselves. Hence the title of his book, *The Selfish Gene*. Of course what survives is not a token gene: each of these perishes with the cell of which it is a part. What survives is a gene-type, or rather what we might call a gene-clone, the members of a family of token genes related to one another by simple direct descent, by replication. The popularity of the notions of species selection and group selection may be due partly to confusion on this point. Since clearly it is only types united by descent, not individual organisms, that survive long enough to be of biological interest, it is easy to think that selection must be by and for species survival. But this is a mistake: genes, not species, are the types which primarily replicate themselves and are selected. Since Dawkins roughly defines the gene as "a genetic unit which is small enough to last for a number of generations and to be distributed around in the form of many copies," it is (as he admits) practically a tautology that the gene is the basic unit of natural selection and therefore, as he puts it, "the fundamental unit of self-interest," or, as we might put it less picturesquely, the primary beneficiary of natural selection. But behind this near-tautology is a synthetic truth, that this basic unit, this primary beneficiary, is a small bit of a chromosome. The reason why this is so, why what is differentially effective and therefore subject to selection is a small bit of chromosome, lies in the mechanism of sexual reproduction by way of meiosis, with crossing over between chromosomes. When male and female cells each divide before uniting at fertilization, it is not chromosomes as a whole that are randomly distributed between the parts, but sections of chromosomes. So sections of chromosomes can be separately inherited, and therefore can be differentially selected by natural selection.

The issue between gene selection, individual selection, group selection, and species selection might seem to raise some stock questions in the philosophy of science. Many thinkers have favoured reductionism of several sorts, including methodological individualism. Wholes are made up of parts, and therefore in principle whatever happens in any larger thing depends upon and is explainable in terms of what happens in and between its smaller components. But though this metaphysical individualism is correct, methodological individualism does not follow from it. It does not follow that we must always conduct our investigations and construct our explanations in terms of component parts, such as the individual members of a group or society. Scientific accounts need not be indefinitely reductive. Some wholes are obviously more accessible to us than their components. We can understand what a human being does without analysing this in terms of how each single cell in his body or his brain behaves. Equally we can often understand what a human society does without analysing this in terms of the behaviour of each of its individual members. And the same holds quite generally: we can often understand complex wholes as units, without analysing them into their parts. So if, in the account of evolution, Dawkins's concentration

upon genes were just a piece of methodological individualism or reductionism, it would be inadequately motivated. But it is not: there is a special reason for it. Dawkins's key argument is that species, populations, and groups, and individual organisms too, are as genetic units too temporary to qualify for natural selection. "They are not stable through evolutionary time. Populations are constantly blending with other populations and so losing their identity," and, what is vitally important, "are also subject to evolutionary change from within" (p. 36).

This abstract general proposition may seem obscure. But it is illustrated by a simple example which Dawkins gives (pp. 197–201).

A species of birds is parasitized by dangerous ticks. A bird can remove the ticks from most parts of its own body, but, having only a beak and no hands, it cannot get them out of the top of its own head. But one bird can remove ticks from another bird's head: there can be mutual grooming. Clearly if there were an inherited tendency for each bird to take the ticks out of any other bird's head, this would help the survival of any group in which that tendency happened to arise—for the ticks are dangerous: they can cause death. Someone who believed in group selection would, therefore, expect this tendency to be favoured and to evolve and spread for this reason. But Dawkins shows that it would not. He gives appropriate names to the different "strategies," that is, the different inheritable behavioural tendencies. The strategy of grooming anyone who needs it he labels "Sucker." The strategy of accepting grooming from anyone, but never grooming anyone else, even someone who has previously groomed you, is called "Cheat." Now if in some population both these tendencies or strategies, and only these two, happen to arise, it is easy to see that the cheats will always do better than the suckers. They will be groomed when they need it, and since they will not waste their time pecking out other birds' ticks, they will have more time and energy to spare for finding food, attracting mates, building nests, and so on. Consequently the gene for the Sucker strategy will gradually die out. So the population will come to consist wholly of cheats, despite the fact that this is likely to lead to the population itself becoming extinct, if the parasites are common enough and dangerous enough, whereas a population consisting wholly of suckers would have survived. The fact that the group is open to evolutionary change from within, because of the way the internal competition between Cheat and Sucker genes works out, prevents the group from developing or even retaining a feature which would have helped the group as a whole.

This is just one illustration among many, and Dawkins's arguments on this point seem pretty conclusive. We need, as he shows, the concept of an *evolutionarily stable strategy* or ESS (p. 74 *et passim*). A strategy is evolutionarily stable, in relation to some alternative strategy or strategies, if it will survive indefinitely in a group in competition with those alternatives. We have just seen that where Cheat and Sucker alone are in competition, Cheat is an ESS but Sucker is not. We have also seen, from this example, that an ESS may not help a group, or the whole species, to survive and multiply. Of course we must not leap to the conclusion that an ESS never helps a group or a species: if that were so we could not explain much of the behaviour that actually occurs. Parents sacrifice themselves for their children, occasionally siblings for their siblings, and with the social insects, bees and ants and termites, their whole life is a system of communal service. But the point is that these results are not to be explained in terms of group selection. They can and must be explained as consequences of the selfishness of genes, that is, of the fact that gene-clones are selected for whatever helps each gene-clone itself to survive and multiply.

But now we come to another remarkable fact. Although the gene is the hero of Dawkins's book, it is not unique either in principle or in fact. It is not the only possible subject of evolutionary natural selection, nor is it the only actual one. What is important about the gene is just that it has a certain combination of logical features. It is a replicator: in the right environment it is capable of producing multiple copies of itself; but in this process of copying some mistakes occur; and these mistaken copies—mutations—will also produce copies of themselves; and, finally, the copies produced may either survive or fail to survive. Anything that has these formal, logical, features is a possible subject of evolution by natural selection. As we have seen, individual organisms, groups, and species do not have the required formal features, though many thinkers have supposed that they do. They cannot reproduce themselves with sufficient constancy of characteristics. But Dawkins, in his last chapter, introduces another sort of replicators. These are what are often called cultural items or traits; Dawkins christens them *memes*—to make a term a bit like "genes"—because they replicate by memory and imitation (mimesis). Memes include tunes, ideas, fashions, and techniques. They require, as the environment in which they can replicate, a collection of minds, that is, brains that have the powers of imitation and memory. These brains (particularly though not exclusively human ones) are themselves the products of evolution by gene selection. But once the brains are there gene selection has done its work: given that environment, memes can themselves evolve and multiply in much the same way as genes do, in accordance with logically similar laws. But they can do so more quickly. Cultural evolution may be much faster than biological evolution. But the basic laws are the same. Memes are selfish in the same sense as genes. The explanation of the widespread flourishing of a certain meme, such as the idea of a god or the belief in hell fire, may be simply that it is an efficiently selfish meme. Something about it makes it well able to infect human minds, to take root and spread in and among them, in the same way that something about the smallpox virus makes it well able to take root and spread in human bodies. There is no need to explain the success of a meme in terms of any benefit it confers on individuals or groups; it is a replicator in its own right. Contrary to the optimistic view often taken of cultural evolution, this analogy shows that a cultural trait can evolve, not because it is advantageous to society, but simply because it is advantageous to itself. It is ironical that Kipling's phrase "the law of the jungle" has proved itself a more efficient meme than the doctrine he tried to use it to propagate.

So far I have been merely summarizing Dawkins's argument. We can now use it to answer the question from which I started. Who is right about the law of the jungle? Kipling, or those who have twisted his phrase to mean almost the opposite of what he intended? The answer is that neither party is right. The law by which nature works is not unrestrained and ruthless competition between individual organisms. But neither does it turn upon the advantages to a group, and its members, of group solidarity, mutual care and respect, and co-operation. It turns upon the self-preservation of gene-clones. This has a strong tendency to express itself in individually selfish behaviour, simply because each agent's genes are more certainly located in him than in anyone else. But it can and does express itself also in certain forms of what Broad called self-referential altruism, including special care for one's own children and perhaps one's siblings, and, as we shall see, reciprocal altruism, helping those (and only those) who help you.

But now I come to what seems to be an exception to Dawkins's main thesis, though it is generated by his own argument and illustrated by one of his own examples. We saw how, in the example of mutual grooming, if there are only suckers and cheats around, the strategy Cheat is evolutionarily stable, while the strategy Sucker is not. But Dawkins introduces a third strategy, Grudger. A grudger is rather like you and me. A grudger grooms anyone who has previously groomed him, and any stranger, but he remembers and bears a grudge against anyone who cheats him—who refuses to groom him in return for having been groomed—and the grudger refuses to groom the cheat ever again. Now when all three strategies are in play, both Cheat and Grudger are evolutionarily stable. In a population consisting largely of cheats, the cheats will do better than the others, and both suckers and grudgers will die out. But in a population that starts off with more than a certain critical proportion of grudgers, the cheats will first wipe out the suckers, but will then themselves become rare and eventually extinct: cheats can flourish only while they have suckers to take advantage of, and yet by doing so they tend to eliminate those suckers.

It is obvious, by the way, that a population containing only suckers and grudgers, in any proportions, but no cheats, would simply continue as it was. Suckers and grudgers behave exactly like one another as long as there are no cheats around, so there would be no tendency for either the Sucker or the Grudger gene to do better than the other. But if there is any risk of an invasion of Cheat genes, either through mutation or through immigration, such a pattern is not

evolutionarily stable, and the higher the proportion of suckers, the more rapidly the cheats would multiply.

So we have two ESSs, Cheat and Grudger. But there is a difference between these two stable strategies. If the parasites are common enough and dangerous enough, the population of cheats will itself die out, having no defence against ticks in their heads, whereas a separate population of grudgers will flourish indefinitely. Dawkins says, "If a population arrives at an ESS which drives it extinct, then it goes extinct, and that is just too bad" (p. 200). True: *but is this not group selection after all?* Of course, this will operate only if the populations are somehow isolated. But if the birds in question were distributed in geographically isolated regions, and Sucker, Cheat and Grudger tendencies appeared (after the parasites became plentiful) in randomly different proportions in these different regions, then some populations would become pure grudger populations, and others would become pure cheat populations, but then the pure cheat populations would die out, so that eventually all surviving birds would be grudgers. And they would be able to re-colonize the areas where cheat populations had perished.

Another name for grudgers is "reciprocal altruists." They act as if on the maxim "Be done by as you did." One implication of this story is that this strategy is not only evolutionarily stable within a population, it is also viable for a population as a whole. The explanation of the final situation, where all birds of this species are grudgers, lies partly in the non-viability of a population of pure cheats. So this is, as I said, a bit of group selection after all.

It is worth noting how and why this case escapes Dawkins's key argument that a population is "not a discrete enough entity to be a unit of natural selection, not stable and unitary enough to be "selected" in preference to another population" (p. 36). Populations can be made discrete by geographical (or other) isolation, and can be made stable and unitary precisely by the emergence of an ESS in each, but perhaps different ESSs in the different regional populations of the same species. This case of group selection is necessarily a second order phenomenon: it arises where gene selection has produced the ESSs which are then persisting selectable features of groups. In other words, an ESS may be a third variety of replicator, along with genes and memes; it is a self-reproducing feature *of groups*.

Someone might reply that this is not really group selection because it all rests ultimately on gene selection, and a full explanation can be given in terms of the long-run self-extinction of the Cheat gene, despite the fact that within a population it is evolutionarily stable in competition with the two rival genes. But this would be a weak reply. The monopoly of cheating *over a population* is an essential part of the causal story that explains the extinction. Also, an account at the group level, though admittedly incomplete, is here correct as far as it goes. The reason why all ultimately surviving birds of this species are grudgers is partly that *populations* of grudgers can survive whereas *populations* of cheats cannot, though it is also partly that although a population of suckers could survive—it would be favoured by group selection, if this possibility arose, just as much as a population of grudgers—internal changes due to gene selection after an invasion of Cheat genes would prevent there being a population of suckers. In special circumstances group selection (or population selection) can occur and could be observed and explained as such, without going down to the gene selection level. It would be unwarranted methodological individualism or reductionism to insist that we not merely can but must go down to the gene selection level here. We must not fall back on this weak general argument when Dawkins's key argument against group selection fails.

I conclude, then, that there can be genuine cases of group selection. But I admit that they are exceptional. They require rather special conditions, in particular geographical isolation, or some other kind of isolation, to keep the populations that are being differentially selected apart. For if genes from one could infiltrate another, the selection of populations might be interfered with. (Though in fact in our example *complete* isolation is not required: since what matters is whether there is more or less than a certain critical proportion of grudgers, small-scale infiltrations would only delay, not prevent, the establishing of pure populations.) And since special conditions are required, there is no valid general principle that features which would enable a group to flourish will be selected. And

even these exceptional cases conform thoroughly to the general logic of Dawkins's doctrine. Sometimes, but only sometimes, group characteristics have the formal features of replicators that are open to natural selection.

Commenting on an earlier version of this paper, Dawkins agreed that there could be group selection in the sort of case I suggested, but stressed the importance of the condition of geographical (or other) isolation. He also mentioned a possible example, that the prevalence of sexual reproduction itself may be a result of group selection. For if there were a mutation by which asexual females, producing offspring by parthenogenesis, occurred in a species, this clone of asexual females would be at once genetically isolated from the rest of the species, though still geographically mixed with them. Also, in most species males contribute little to the nourishment or care of their offspring; so from a genetic point of view males are wasters: resources would be more economically used if devoted only to females. So the genetically isolated population of asexual females would outcompete the normal sexually reproducing population with roughly equal numbers of males and females. So the species would in time consist only of asexual females. But then, precisely because all its members were genetically identical, it would not have the capacity for rapid adaptation by selection to changing conditions that an ordinary sexual population has. So when conditions changed, it would be unable to adapt, and would die out. Thus there would in time be species selection against any species that produced an asexual female mutation. Which would explain why nearly all existing species go in for what, in the short run, is the economically wasteful business of sexual reproduction.

What implications for human morality have such biological facts about selfishness and altruism? One is that the possibility that morality is itself a product of natural selection is not ruled out, but care would be needed in formulating a plausible speculative account of how it might have been favoured. Another is that the notion of an ESS may be a useful one for discussing questions of practical morality. Moral philosophers have already found illumination in such simple items of game theory as the Prisoners' Dilemma; perhaps these rather more complicated evolutionary "games" will prove equally instructive. Of course there is no simple transition from "is" to "ought," no direct argument from what goes on in the natural world and among non-human animals to what human beings ought to do. Dawkins himself explicitly warns against any simple transfer of conclusions. At the very end of the book he suggests that conscious foresight may enable us to develop radically new kinds of behaviour. "We are built as gene machines and cultured as meme machines, but we have the power to turn against our creators. We, alone on earth, can rebel against the tyranny of the selfish replicators" (p. 215). This optimistic suggestion needs fuller investigation. It must be remembered that the human race as a whole cannot act as a unit with conscious foresight. Arrow's Theorem shows that even quite small groups of rational individuals may be unable to form coherently rational preferences, let alone to act rationally. Internal competition, which in general prevents a group from being a possible subject of natural selection, is even more of an obstacle to its being a rational agent. And while we can turn against some memes, it will be only with the help and under the guidance of other memes.

This is an enormous problematic area. For the moment I turn to a smaller point. In the mutual grooming model, we saw that the Grudger strategy was, of the three strategies considered, the only one that was healthy in the long run. Now something closely resembling this strategy, reciprocal altruism, is a well known and long established tendency in human life. It is expressed in such formulae as that justice consists in giving everyone his due, interpreted, as Polemarchus interprets it in the first book of Plato's *Republic,* as doing good to one's friends and harm to one's enemies, or repaying good with good and evil with evil. Morality itself has been seen, for example by Edward Westermarck, as an outgrowth from the retributive emotions. But some moralists, including Socrates and Jesus, have recommended something very different from this, turning the other cheek and repaying evil with good. They have tried to substitute "Do as you would be done by" for "Be done by as you did." Now this, which in human life we characterize as a Christian spirit or perhaps as saintliness, is roughly equivalent to the strategy

Dawkins has unkindly labelled "Sucker." Suckers are saints, just as grudgers are reciprocal altruists, while cheats are a hundred per cent selfish. And as Dawkins points out, the presence of suckers endangers the healthy Grudger strategy. It allows cheats to prosper, and could make them multiply to the point where they would wipe out the grudgers, and ultimately bring about the extinction of the whole population. This seems to provide fresh support for Nietzsche's view of the deplorable influence of moralities of the Christian type. But in practice there may be little danger. After two thousand years of contrary moral teaching, reciprocal altruism is still dominant in all human societies; thoroughgoing cheats and thoroughgoing saints (or suckers) are distinctly rare. The sucker slogan is an efficient meme, but the sucker behaviour pattern far less so. Saintliness is an attractive topic for preaching, but with little practical persuasive force. Whether in the long run this is to be deplored or welcomed, and whether it is alterable or not, is a larger question. To answer it we should have carefully to examine our specifically human capacities and the structure of human societies, and also many further alternative strategies. We cannot simply apply to the human situation conclusions drawn from biological models. Nevertheless they are significant and challenging as models; it will need to be shown how and where human life diverges from them.

NOTES

1. R. Dawkins, *The Selfish Gene* (Oxford, 1976).
2. I am among these: see p. 113 of my *Ethics: Inventing Right and Wrong* (Penguin, Harmondsworth, 1977).

FOR FURTHER REFLECTION

1. An important question that arises with this sort of article is how relevant evolutionary theory is for ethical theory. Many philosophers argue that such work is irrelevant because evolution focuses on the gene as the focal point, while ethics focuses on people who cannot be reduced to genetic endowments. Discuss the pros and cons of this issue.

2. Mackie claims that reciprocal altruism is radically different from Socratic or Christian morality, which advocates complete altruism (what Dawkins calls being a "sucker"). Do you agree with his charge? Has he misunderstood the relationship between morality and religion?

C. Religion and Ethics

Does God love goodness because it is good, or is it good because God loves it? Does morality depend on religion? And are religious ethics essentially different from secular ethics? These questions are related, but not the same. Unlike many religions found in the ancient world, Judaism, Islam, and Christianity are ethical monotheisms. They not only promise salvation to the faithful but also tie ethical responsibility into the matrix of salvation in a very close way, by making the moral life either a necessary condition for God's favor or a consequence of it.

The first question is whether moral standards themselves depend on God for their validity or whether there is an autonomy of ethics, so that even God is subject to the moral order. As Socrates asks in our first reading from Plato's *Euthphro*, "Do the gods love holiness because it is holy, or is it holy because the gods love it?" According to one theory, called the *divine command theory* (DCT), ethical principles are simply the commands of God. The derive their validity from God's commanding them, and they *mean* "commanded by God." Without god, there would be no universally valid morality. As Dostoevsky wrote in *The Brothers Karamazov*, "If God doesn't exist, everything is permissible." Without God, we have moral nihilism.

We can analyze the DVT into three separate theses: (1) Morality (that is, rightness or wrongness) originates with God; (2) Moral rightness simply means willed by God, and moral wrongness means against the will of God; (3) No further reasons for action are necessary. Essentially, morality is based in divine will, not on independently existing reasons for action.

Now, there are many modified versions of the DCT that drop or qualify one or more of the three theses, but the strongest form includes all three of them.

The opposing viewpoint—call it the *autonomy of ethics position*—denies all three theses: morality does not originate with God (although the way God created us may affect the specific nature of morality); rightness and wrongness are based on something other than simply God's will (such as the flourishing of the creation or the perfection of rational beings). Essentially, there are reasons for acting one way or the other which may be known independently of God's will. In sum, ethics is autonomous, and even God must keep the moral law, which exists independently of him- or herself—as do the laws of mathematics and logic.

God, of course, *knows* what is right—better than we do, but in principle we act morally for the same reasons that God does. We both follow moral reasons that are independent of god. If there is no God, in this account, nothing is changed. Morality is left intact, and if we choose to be moral we have the very same duties as we would have as theists.

The motivation for the DCT is to preserve or do justice to the omnipotence or sovereignty of God. God is somehow thought to be less sovereign or necessary to our lives if he or she is not the source of morality. When the believer asks what God's will is, that is a direct appeal to a personal will, not to an independently existing rule.

One problem with the DCT is that it would seem to make the attribution of *goodness* to God redundant. When we say "God is good," we think we are ascribing a property to God, but if *good* simply meant "what God commands or wills," then we are not attributing any property to God. Our statement would merely mean "God wills what God wills," which is a tautology. a second problem is that if God's arbitrary fiat (in the sense of not being based on reasons) is the sole arbiter of right and wrong, it would seem to be logically possible for such "heinous" acts as rape, killing of the innocent for the fun of it, and gratuitous cruelty to become morally good actions—if God suddenly decided to command us to do these things. But then, wouldn't morality be reduced to the right of the powerful? To Nietzsche's "Might makes right"?

The second problem related to the matter of religion and morality is the degree to which religious morality and nonreligious morality are similar to each other. There is a question of adequate motivation. According to some, secularity offers insufficient incentive to live a moral life, or at least an altruistic life. They conclude that the content of secular ethics is less altruistic than that of religious ethics.

According to Immanuel Kant (see the reading "Duty and the Categorical Imperative" in section D), who held to the autonomy of ethics, there could be no difference between valid religious ethics and valid philosophical ethics. God and humanity both must obey the same rational principles, and reason is sufficient to guide us to these principles.

But while Kant exalts ethics as an intrinsic good discoverable by reason alone, he believes that God and immortality are necessary postulates for ethics; immortality is necessary to make sense of the command to become morally perfect. Since "ought" implies "can," we must be *able* to reach moral perfection. But we can't attain perfection in this life because the task is infinite, so there must be an afterlife in which we continue to make progress toward our ideal.

God is a necessary idea for morality, according to Kant, because there must be someone to keep a moral scorecard and enforce the moral law, rewarding each according to his or her desert. The harmonious correlation of virtue with happiness (or vice with unhappiness) does not happen in this life, where the evil often prosper and the good suffer, so it must happen in the next life. So, there must be a God, acting as judge and enforcer of the moral law, without which the moral law would somehow be lacking completion.

The second reading in this section, Bertrand Russell's "A Free Man's Worship," sets forth an opposing viewpoint. Morality does not need a God or an afterlife, and because these notions are irrational, we had better learn to live without their support—the sooner the better. For most educated people, science removed the possibility of religious faith, so the only path left is stoic resignation. As Russell says, "Nature, omnipotent but blind, in the revolutions of her secular hurryings through the abysses of space, has brought forth at last a child, subject still to her power, but gifted with sight, with knowledge of good and evil, with the capacity of judging all the works of his unthinking mother." This conscious power of moral evaluation makes the child superior to the omnipotent mother. People are free to think, to evaluate, to create, and to live committed to inspiring ideals:

in spite of suffering, despair, and death, human beings are free. Life has the meaning we give it.

George Mavrodes, in the third reading, "Religion and the Queerness of Morality," represents the Kantian view that morality without religion lacks justification. He criticizes Russell's view as "queer," as it has no satisfactory answer to the question "Why should I be moral?" In Russell's account, the common goods at which morality in general aims are often just those we sacrifice in carrying out our moral obligations. Why should we sacrifice our own welfare for our moral duty?

The second oddity about secular ethics is that it is superficial, not deeply rooted. It seems to lack that metaphysical basis that a Platonic or Judeo-Christian worldview affords. Mavrodes says,

> Values and obligations cannot be deep in such a [secular] world. What is deep in a Russellian world must be such things as matter and energy, or perhaps natural law, chance, or chaos. If it really were a fact that one had obligations in a Russellian world, then something would be laid upon man that cost a man everything but that went no further than man. And that difference from a Platonic world seems to make all the difference.

Mavrodes outlines how a religious morality can meet these desiderata and (if we are inclined to believe that morality is not queer) can provide some evidence for the religious worldview.

Kai Nielsen's essay "Ethics Without Religion" was written twenty years before Mavrodes's essay on the queerness of morality, but anticipates some of Mavrodes's arguments. Nielsen's thesis is that even if "God is dead," that really doesn't matter—as far as our morality is concerned. There are intrinsically good things in life, which are worth living for and which provide happiness. Furthermore, both the secular basis of ethics and the religious basis involve an objective rationale involving central principles such as respect for people and justice, and benevolence. Our common nature and quest for the good life is all the grounding ethics needs. It is true that morality sometimes calls for sacrifice of nonmoral goods. It would be nice if this were not the case, but life is sometimes hard. We should face the injustices in life without accepting the unaccountable mystery or absurdity of religion.

PLATO

THE DIVINE COMMAND THEORY OF ETHICS

We have already encountered the writings of Plato (427–347 B.C.E.). Here we find his mentor, Socrates, engaged in a dialogue with the self-righteously religious Euthyphro, who is going to court to report his father for having killed a slave. In the course of the discussion Socrates raises the question that has come to be known as the question of the divine command theory of ethics: Is the good, good because God loves it, or does God love the good because it is good?

Socrates: But shall we . . . say that whatever all the gods hate is unholy, and whatever they all love is holy: while whatever some of them love, and others hate, is either both or neither? Do you wish us now to define holiness and unholiness in this manner?

Euthyphro: Why not, Socrates?

Socrates: There is no reason why I should not, Euthyphro. It is for you to consider whether that definition will help you to instruct me as you promised.

Euthyphro: Well, I should say that holiness is what all the gods love, and that unholiness is what they all hate.

Socrates: Are we to examine this definition, Euthyphro, and see if it is a good one? Or are we to be content to accept the bare assertions of other men, or of ourselves, without asking any questions? Or must we examine the assertions?

Euthyphro: We must examine them. But for my part I think that the definition is right this time.

Socrates: We shall know that better in a little while, my good friend. Now consider this question. Do the gods love holiness because it is holy, or is it holy because they love it?

Euthyphro: I do not understand you, Socrates.

Socrates: I will try to explain myself: we speak of a thing being carried and carrying, and being led and leading, and being seen and seeing; and you understand that all such expressions mean different things, and what the difference is.

Euthyphro: Yes, I think I understand.

Socrates: And we talk of a thing being loved, and, which is different, of a thing loving?

Euthyphro: Of course.

Socrates: Now tell me: is a thing which is being carried in a state of being carried, because it is carried, or for some other reason?

Euthyphro: No, because it is carried.

Socrates: And a thing is in a state of being led, because it is led, and of being seen, because it is seen?

Euthyphro: Certainly.

Socrates: Then a thing is not seen because it is in a state of being seen; it is in a state of being seen because it is seen: and a thing is not led because it is in a state of being led; it is in a state of being led because it is led: and a thing is not carried because it is in a state of being carried; it is in a state of being

From Plato, the *Euthyphro,* in *Dialogues of Plato,* trans. Benjamin Jowett (New York: Scribner's, 1889).

carried because it is carried. Is my meaning clear now, Euthyphro? I mean this: if anything becomes or is affected, it does not become because it is in a state of becoming; it is in a state of becoming because it becomes; and it is not affected because it is in a state of being affected: it is in a state of being affected because it is affected. Do you not agree?

Euthyphro: I do.

Socrates: Is not that which is being loved in a state, either of becoming, or of being affected in some way by something?

Euthyphro: Certainly.

Socrates: Then the same is true here as in the former cases. A thing is not loved by those who love it because it is in a state of being loved. It is in a state of being loved because they love it.

Euthyphro: Necessarily.

Socrates: Well, then, Euthyphro, what do we say about holiness? Is it not loved by all the gods, according to your definition?

Euthyphro: Yes.

Socrates: Because it is holy, or for some other reason?

Euthyphro: No, because it is holy.

Socrates: Then it is loved by the gods because it is holy: it is not holy because it is loved by them?

Euthyphro: It seems so.

Socrates: But then what is pleasing to the gods is pleasing to them, and is in a state of being loved by them, because they love it?

Euthyphro: Of course.

Socrates: Then holiness is not what is pleasing to the gods, and what is pleasing to the gods is not holy, as you say, Euthyphro. They are different things.

Euthyphro: And why, Socrates?

Socrates: Because we are agreed that the gods love holiness because it is holy: and that it is not holy because they love it. Is not this so?

Euthyphro: Yes.

Socrates: And that what is pleasing to the gods because they love it, is pleasing to them by reason of

this same love: and that they do not love it because it is pleasing to them.

Euthyphro: True.

Socrates: Then, my dear Euthyphro, holiness, and what is pleasing to the gods, are different things. If the gods had loved holiness because it is holy, they would also have loved what is pleasing to them because it is pleasing to them; but if what is pleasing to them had been pleasing to them because they loved it, then holiness too would have been holiness, because they loved it. But now you see that they are opposite things, and wholly different from each other. For the one is of a sort to be loved because it is loved: while the other is loved, because it is of a sort to be loved. My question, Euthyphro, was, What is holiness? But it turns out that you have not explained to me the essence of holiness; you have been content to mention an attribute which belongs to it, namely, that all the gods love it. You have not yet told me what is its essence. Do not, if you please, keep from me what holiness is; begin again and tell me that. Never mind whether the gods love it, or whether it has other attributes: we shall not differ on that point. Do your best to make it clear to me what is holiness and what is unholiness.

FOR FURTHER REFLECTION

1. This selection records the first known instance of asking whether goodness is something intrinsically good or whether it derives its worth from God's choice. Does God love the good because it really is good in its own right, or is it good only because God values it? If the former is true, then it would appear that even God is limited in what he can do by the nature of goodness, but if the latter is true, it would seem that God could make good, simply by fiat, what is now considered evil. He could make rape or torturing people good. Discuss this dilemma.

BERTRAND RUSSELL

A FREE MAN'S WORSHIP

This essay was written in 1903, during one of Russell's deepest personal crises. It shows his attempt to find meaning and morality in life and is a classic essay on humanist ethics.

    The world, says Russell, is an absurd, godless tragedy in which nature, omnipotent but blind, has brought forth rational children who are superior to their mother and, as such, can discover moral ideals with which to sustain themselves in this ultimately meaningless existence. Morality doesn't need religion for legitimation.

To Dr. Faustus in his study Mephistopheles told the history of the Creation, saying,

> The endless praises of the choirs of angels had begun to grow wearisome; for, after all, did he not deserve their praise? Had he not given them endless joy? Would it not be more amusing to obtain undeserved praise, to be worshiped by beings whom he tortured? He smiled inwardly, and resolved that the great drama should be performed.
>
> For countless ages the hot nebula whirled aimlessly through space. At length it began to take shape, the central mass threw off planets, the planets cooled, boiling seas and burning mountains heaved and tossed, from black masses of cloud hot sheets of rain deluged the barely solid crust. And now the first germ of life grew in the depths of the ocean and developed rapidly in the fructifying warmth into vast forest trees, huge ferns springing from the damp mold, sea monsters breeding, fighting, devouring, and passing away. And from the monsters, as the play unfolded itself, Man was born, with the power of thought, the knowledge of good and evil, and the cruel thirst for worship. And Man saw that all is passing in this mad, monstrous world, that all is struggling to snatch, at any cost, a few brief moments of life before Death's inexorable decree. And Man said, "There is a hidden purpose, could we but fathom it, and the purpose is good; for we must reverence something, and in the visible world there is nothing worthy of reverence." And Man stood aside from the struggle, resolving that God intended harmony to come out of chaos by human efforts. And when he followed the instincts which God had transmitted to him from his ancestry of beasts of prey, he called it Sin, and asked God to forgive him. But he doubted whether he could be justly forgiven, until he invented a divine Plan by which God's wrath was to have been appeased. And seeing the present was bad, he made it yet worse, that thereby the future might be better. And he gave God thanks for the strength that enabled him to forgo even the joys that were possible. And God smiled; and when he saw that Man had become perfect in renunciation and worship, he sent another sun through the sky, which crashed into Man's sun; and all returned again to nebula.

"Yes," he murmured, "it was a good play; I will have it performed again."

Such, in outline, but even more purposeless, more void of meaning, is the world which science presents for our belief. Amid such a world, if anywhere, our ideals henceforward must find a home. That man is

From Bertrand Russell, "A Free Man's Worship."

the product of causes which had no prevision of the end they were achieving; that his origin, his growth, his hopes and fears, his loves and his beliefs, are but the outcome of accidental collocations of atoms; that no fire, no heroism, no intensity of thought and feeling, can preserve an individual life beyond the grave; that all the labors of the ages, all the devotion, all the inspiration, all the noonday brightness of human genius, are destined to extinction in the vast death of the solar system, and that the whole temple of man's achievement must inevitably be buried beneath the debris of a universe in ruins—all these things, if not quite beyond dispute, are yet so nearly certain that no philosophy which rejects them can hope to stand. Only within the scaffolding of these truths, only on the firm foundation of unyielding despair, can the soul's habitation henceforth be safely built.

How, in such an alien and inhuman world, can so powerless a creature as man preserve his aspirations untarnished? A strange mystery it is that nature, omnipotent but blind, in the revolutions of her secular hurryings through the abysses of space, has brought forth at last a child, subject still to her power, but gifted with sight, with knowledge of good and evil, with the capacity of judging all the works of his unthinking mother. In spite of death, the mark and seal of the parental control, man is yet free, during his brief years, to examine, to criticize, to know, and in imagination to create. To him alone, in the world with which he is acquainted, this freedom belongs; and in this lies his superiority to the resistless forces that control his outward life.

The savage, like ourselves, feels the oppression of his impotence before the powers of nature; but having in himself nothing that he respects more than power, he is willing to prostrate himself before his gods, without inquiring whether they are worthy of his worship. Pathetic and very terrible is the long history of cruelty and torture, of degradation and human sacrifice, endured in the hope of placating the jealous gods: surely, the trembling believer thinks, when what is most precious has been freely given, their lust for blood must be appeased, and more will not be required. The religion of Moloch—as such creeds may be generally called—is in essence the cringing submission of the slave, who dare not, even in his heart,

allow the thought that his master deserves no adulation. Since the independence of ideals is not yet acknowledged, power may be freely worshiped and receive an unlimited respect, despite its wanton infliction of pain.

But gradually, as morality grows bolder, the claim of the ideal world begins to be felt; and worship, if it is not to cease, must be given to gods of another kind than those created by the savage. Some, though they feel the demands of the ideal, will still consciously reject them, still urging that naked power is worthy of worship. Such is the attitude inculcated in God's answer to Job out of the whirlwind: the divine power and knowledge are paraded, but of the divine goodness there is no hint. Such also is the attitude of those who, in our own day, base their morality upon the struggle for survival, maintaining that the survivors are necessarily the fittest. But others, not content with an answer so repugnant to the moral sense, will adopt the position which we have become accustomed to regard as specially religious, maintaining that, in some hidden manner, the world of fact is really harmonious with the world of ideals. Thus man created God, all-powerful and all-good, the mystic unity of what is and what should be.

But the world of fact, after all, is not good; and, in submitting our judgment to it, there is an element of slavishness from which our thoughts must be purged. For in all things it is well to exalt the dignity of man, by freeing him as far as possible from the tyranny of nonhuman power. When we have realized that power is largely bad, that man, with his knowledge of good and evil, is but a helpless atom in a world which has no such knowledge, the choice is again presented to us: Shall we worship force, or shall we worship goodness? Shall our God exist and be evil, or shall he be recognized as the creation of our own conscience?

The answer to this question is very momentous and affects profoundly our whole morality. The worship of force, to which Carlyle and Nietzsche and the creed of militarism have accustomed us, is the result of failure to maintain our own ideals against a hostile universe: it is itself a prostrate submission to evil, a sacrifice of our best to Moloch. If strength indeed is to be respected, let us respect rather the strength of those who refuse that false "recognition of facts" which fails to recognize that facts are often bad. Let us admit that, in the world we know, there are many things that would be better otherwise, and that the ideals to which we do and must adhere are not realized in the realm of matter. Let us preserve our respect for truth, for beauty, for the ideal of perfection which life does not permit us to attain, though none of these things meet with the approval of the unconscious universe. If power is bad, as it seems to be, let us reject it from our hearts. In this lies man's true freedom: in determination to worship only the God created by our own love of the good, to respect only the heaven which inspires the insight of our best moments. In action, in desire, we must submit perpetually to the tyranny of outside forces; but in thought, in aspiration, we are free, free from our fellow men, free from the petty planet on which our bodies impotently crawl, free even, while we live, from the tyranny of death. Let us learn, then, that energy of faith which enables us to live constantly in the vision of the good; and let us descend, in action, into the world of fact, with that vision always before us.

When first the opposition of fact and ideal grows fully visible, a spirit of fiery revolt, of fierce hatred of the gods, seems necessary to the assertion of freedom. To defy with Promethean constancy a hostile universe, to keep its evil always in view, always actively hated, to refuse no pain that the malice of power can invent, appears to be the duty of all who will not bow before the inevitable. But indignation is still a bondage, for it compels our thoughts to be occupied with an evil world; and in the fierceness of desire from which rebellion springs there is a kind of self-assertion which it is necessary for the wise to overcome. Indignation is a submission of our thoughts but not of our desires; the Stoic freedom in which wisdom consists is found in the submission of our desires but not of our thoughts. From the submission of our desires springs the virtue of resignation; from the freedom of our thoughts springs the whole world of art and philosophy, and the vision of beauty by which, at last, we half reconquer the reluctant world. But the vision of beauty is possible only to unfettered contemplation, to thoughts not weighted by the load of eager wishes; and thus freedom comes only to those who no longer ask of life that it shall yield them any

of those personal goods that are subject to the mutations of time.

Although the necessity of renunciation is evidence of the existence of evil, yet Christianity, in preaching it, has shown a wisdom exceeding that of the Promethean philosophy of rebellion. It must be admitted that, of the things we desire, some, though they prove impossible, are yet real goods; others, however, as ardently longed for, do not form part of a fully purified ideal. The belief that what must be renounced is bad, though sometimes false, is far less often false than untamed passion supposes; and the creed of religion, by providing a reason for proving that it is never false, has been the means of purifying our hopes by the discovery of many austere truths.

But there is in resignation a further good element: even real goods, when they are unattainable, ought not to be fretfully desired. To every man comes, sooner or later, the great renunciation. For the young, there is nothing unattainable; a good thing desired with the whole force of a passionate will, and yet impossible, is to them not credible. Yet, by death, by illness, by poverty, or by the voice of duty, we must learn, each one of us, that the world was not made for us, and that, however beautiful may be the things we crave, Fate may nevertheless forbid them. It is the part of courage, when misfortune comes, to bear without repining the ruin of our hopes, to turn away our thoughts from vain regrets. This degree of submission to power is not only just and right: it is the very gate of wisdom.

But passive renunciation is not the whole of wisdom; for not by renunciation alone can we build a temple for the worship of our own ideals. Haunting foreshadowings of the temple appear in the realm of imagination, in music, in architecture, in the untroubled kingdom of reason, and in the golden sunset magic of lyrics, where beauty shines and glows, remote from the touch of sorrow, remote from the fear of change, remote from the failures and disenchantments of the world of fact. In the contemplation of these things the vision of heaven will shape itself in our hearts, giving at once a touchstone to judge the world about us and an inspiration by which to fashion to our needs whatever is not incapable of serving as a stone in the sacred temple.

Except for those rare spirits that are born without sin, there is a cavern of darkness to be traversed before that temple can be entered. The gate of the cavern is despair, and its floor is paved with the gravestones of abandoned hopes. There self must die; there the eagerness, the greed of untamed desire, must be slain, for only so can the soul be freed from the empire of Fate. But out of the cavern, the Gate of Renunciation leads again to the daylight of wisdom, by whose radiance a new insight, a new joy, a new tenderness, shine forth to gladden the pilgrim's heart.

When, without the bitterness of impotent rebellion, we have learned both to resign ourselves to the outward rule of Fate and to recognize that the non-human world is unworthy of our worship, it becomes possible at last so to transform and refashion the unconscious universe, so to transmute it in the crucible of imagination, that a new image of shining gold replaces the old idol of clay. In all the multiform facts of the world—in the visual shapes of trees and mountains and clouds, in the events of the life of man, even in the very omnipotence of death—the insight of creative idealism can find the reflection of a beauty which its own thoughts first made. In this way mind asserts its subtle mastery over the thoughtless forces of nature. The more evil the material with which it deals, the more thwarting to untrained desire, the greater is its achievement in inducing the reluctant rock to yield up its hidden treasures, the prouder its victory in compelling the opposing forces to swell the pageant of its triumph. Of all the arts, tragedy is the proudest, the most triumphant; for it builds its shining citadel in the very center of the enemy's country, on the very summit of his highest mountain; from its impregnable watchtowers, his camps and arsenals, his columns and forts, are all revealed; within its walls the free life continues, while the legions of death and pain and despair, and all the servile captains of tyrant Fate, afford the burghers of that dauntless city new spectacles of beauty. Happy those sacred ramparts, thrice happy the dwellers on that all-seeing eminence. Honor to those brave warriors who, through countless ages of warfare, have preserved for us the priceless heritage of liberty and have kept undefiled by sacrilegious invaders the home of the unsubdued.

But the beauty of tragedy does but make visible a quality which, in more or less obvious shapes, is present always and everywhere in life. In the spectacle of death, in the endurance of intolerable pain, and in the irrevocableness of a vanished past, there is a sacredness, an overpowering awe, a feeling of the vastness, the depth, the inexhaustible mystery of existence, in which, as by some strange marriage of pain, the sufferer is bound to the world by bonds of sorrow. In these moments of insight, we lose all eagerness of temporary desire, all struggling and striving for petty ends, all care for the little trivial things that, to a superficial view, make up the common life of day by day; we see, surrounding the narrow raft illumined by the flickering light of human comradeship, the dark ocean on whose rolling waves we toss for a brief hour; from the great night without, a chill blast breaks in upon our refuge; all the loneliness of humanity amid hostile forces is concentrated upon the individual soul, which must struggle alone, with what of courage it can command, against the whole weight of a universe that cares nothing for its hopes and fears. Victory, in this struggle with the powers of darkness, is the true baptism into the glorious company of heroes, the true initiation into the overmastering beauty of human existence. From that awful encounter of the soul with the outer world, renunciation, wisdom, and charity are born; and with their birth a new life begins. To take into the inmost shrine of the soul the irresistible forces whose puppets we seem to be—death and change, the irrevocableness of the past, and the powerlessness of man before the blind hurry of the universe from vanity to vanity—to feel these things and know them is to conquer them.

This is the reason why the past has such magical power. The beauty of its motionless and silent pictures is like the enchanted purity of late autumn, when the leaves, though one breath would make them fall, still glow against the sky in golden glory. The past does not change or strive; like Duncan, after life's fitful fever it sleeps well; what was eager and grasping, what was petty and transitory, has faded away; the things that were beautiful and eternal shine out of it like stars in the night. Its beauty, to a soul not worthy of it, is unendurable; but to a soul which has conquered Fate it is the key of religion.

The life of man, viewed outwardly, is but a small thing in comparison with the forces of nature. The slave is doomed to worship Time and Fate and Death, because they are greater than anything he finds in himself, and because all his thoughts are of things which they devour. But, great as they are, to think of them greatly, to feel their passionless splendor, is greater still. And such thought makes us free men; we no longer bow before the inevitable in Oriental subjection, but we absorb it and make it a part of ourselves. To abandon the struggle for private happiness, to expel all eagerness of temporary desire, to burn with passion for eternal things—this is emancipation, and this is the free man's worship. And this liberation is effected by contemplation of Fate; for Fate itself is subdued by the mind which leaves nothing to be purged by the purifying fire of time.

United with his fellow men by the strongest of all ties, the tie of a common doom, the free man finds that a new vision is with him always, shedding over every daily task the light of love. The life of man is a long march through the night, surrounded by invisible foes, tortured by weariness and pain, toward a goal that few can hope to reach, and where none may tarry long. One by one, as they march, our comrades vanish from our sight, seized by the silent orders of omnipotent death. Very brief is the time in which we can help them, in which their happiness or misery is decided. Be it ours to shed sunshine on their path, to lighten their sorrows by the balm of sympathy, to give them the pure joy of a never- tiring affection, to strengthen failing courage, to instill faith in hours of despair. Let us not weigh in grudging scales their merits and demerits, but let us think only of their need—of the sorrows, the difficulties, perhaps the blindnesses, that make the misery of their lives; let us remember that they are fellow sufferers in the same darkness, actors in the same tragedy with ourselves. And so, when their day is over, when their good and their evil have become eternal by the immortality of the past, be it ours to feel that, where they suffered, where they failed, no deed of ours was the cause; but

wherever a spark of the divine fire kindled in their hearts, we were ready with encouragement, with sympathy, with brave words in which high courage glowed.

Brief and powerless is man's life; on him and all his race the slow, sure doom falls pitiless and dark. Blind to good and evil, reckless of destruction, omnipotent matter rolls on its relentless way; for man, condemned today to lose his dearest, tomorrow himself to pass through the gate of darkness, it remains only to cherish, ere yet the blow fall, the lofty thoughts that ennoble his little day; disdaining the coward terrors of the slave of Fate, to worship at the shrine that his own hands have built; undismayed by the empire of chance, to preserve a mind free from the wanton tyranny that rules his outward life; proudly defiant of the irresistible forces that tolerate, for a moment, his knowledge and his condemnation, to sustain alone, a weary but unyielding Atlas, the world that his own ideals have fashioned despite the trampling march of unconscious power.

FOR FURTHER REFLECTION

1. Russell prescribes stoic freedom. What does he mean by this, and why does he recommend it? Do you agree? Explain.
2. Compare Russell's views on ethics without religion with those of Tolstoy:

> The attempts to found a morality apart from religion are like the attempts of children who, wishing to transplant a flower that pleases them, pluck it from the roots that seem to them unpleasing and superfluous, and stick it rootless into the ground. Without religion there can be no real sincere morality, just as without roots there can be no real flower. (Leo Tolstoy, "Religion and Morality," in *Leo Tolstoy: Selected Essays*)

Who is closer to the truth here? Why?

GEORGE MAVRODES

RELIGION AND THE QUEERNESS
OF MORALITY

George Mavrodes is professor of philosophy at the University of Michigan. He has written widely on philosophy of religion. In this reading, he argues that to completely justify ethics, a benevolent God must make sense of the moral life. Mavrodes refers to Bertrand Russell's views (which are much like Kai Nielsen's in the following selection) and argues that Russell's world of secular morality is odd since it can't satisfactorily answer the question "Why should I be moral?" In Russell's account, the common goods—at which morality in general aims—are often exactly the ones we sacrifice in carrying out our moral obligations. Why should we sacrifice our welfare for our moral duty?

The second oddity about secular ethics is that it is superficial and not deeply rooted. It seems to lack the metaphysical basis offered by a Platonic or Judeo-Christian worldview. Values and obligations are not as deep in a secular world. Mavrodes outlines how a religious morality can meet the desiderata of deepness and values, and—if we are inclined to believe that morality is not queer—can provide some evidence for the religious worldview.

Many arguments for the existence of God may be construed as claiming that there is some feature of the world that would somehow make no sense unless there was something else that had a stronger version of that feature or some analogue of it. So, for example, the cosmological line of argument may be thought of as centering upon the claim that the way in which the world exists (called "contingent" existence) would be incomprehensible unless there were something else—that is, God—that had a stronger grip upon existence (that is, "necessary" existence).

Now, a number of thinkers have held a view something like this with respect to morality. They have claimed that in some important way morality is dependent upon religion—dependent, that is, in such a way that if religion were to fail, morality would fail also. And they have held that the dependence was more than psychological, that is, if religion were to fail, it would somehow be *proper* (perhaps logically or perhaps in some other way) for morality to fail also. One way of expressing this theme is by Dostoevsky's "If there is no God, then everything is permitted," a sentiment that in this century has been prominently echoed by Sartre. But perhaps the most substantial philosophical thinker of the modern period to espouse this view, though in a rather idiosyncratic way, was Immanuel Kant, who held that the existence of God was a necessary postulate of 'practical' (that is, moral) reason.

From *Rationality*, George Mavrodes, in *Religious Belief and Moral Commitment: New Essays in the Philosophy of Religion,* eds. R. Audi and W. Wainwright (Ithaca, NY: Cornell University Press, 1986). Copyright © 1986 by Cornell University. Reprinted by permission of George Mavrodes and Cornell University Press.

On the other hand, it has recently been popular for moral philosophers to deny this theme and to maintain that the dependence of morality on religion is, at best, merely psychological. Were religion to fail, so they apparently hold, this would grant no sanction for the failure of morality. For morality stands on its own feet, whatever those feet may turn out to be.

Now, the suggestion that morality somehow depends on religion is rather attractive to me. It is this suggestion that I wish to explore in this paper, even though it seems unusually difficult to formulate clearly the features of this suggestion that make it attractive. I will begin by mentioning briefly some aspects that I will not discuss.

First, beyond this paragraph I will not discuss the claim that morality cannot survive psychologically without the support of religious belief. At least in the short run, this proposal seems to me false. For there certainly seems to be people who reject religious belief, at least in the ordinary sense, but who apparently have a concern with morality and who try to live a moral life. Whether the proposal may have more force if it is understood in a broader way, as applying to whole cultures, epochs, and so forth, I do not know.

Second, I will not discuss the attempt to define some or all moral terms by the use of religious terms, or vice versa. But this should not be taken as implying any judgment about this project.

Third, beyond this paragraph I shall not discuss the suggestion that moral statements may be entailed by religious statements and so may be "justified" by religious doctrines or beliefs. It is popular now to hold that no such alleged entailment can be valid. But the reason usually cited for this view is the more general doctrine that moral statements cannot be validly deduced from nonmoral statements, a doctrine usually traced to Hume. Now, to my mind the most important problem raised by this general doctrine is that of finding some interpretation of it that is both significant and not plainly false. If it is taken to mean merely that there is *some* set of statements that entails no moral statement, then it strikes me as probably true, but trivial. At any rate, we should then need another reason to suppose that religious statements fall in this category. If, on the other hand, it is taken to mean that one can divide the domain of statements into two classes, the moral and the nonmoral, and that none of the latter entail any of the former, then it is false. I, at any rate, do not know a version of this doctrine that seems relevant to the religious case and that has any reasonable likelihood of being true. But I am not concerned on this occasion with the possibly useful project of deducing morality from religion, and so I will not pursue it further. My interest is closer to a move in the other direction, that of deducing religion from morality. (I am not quite satisfied with this way of putting it and will try to explain this dissatisfaction later on.)

For the remainder of this discussion, then, my project is as follows. I will outline one rather common nonreligious view of the world, calling attention to what I take to be its most relevant features. Then I shall try to portray some sense of the odd status that morality would have in a world of that sort. I shall be hoping, of course, that you will notice that this odd status is not the one that you recognize morality to have in the actual world. But it will perhaps be obvious that the "world-view" amendments required would move substantially toward a religious position.

First, then, the nonreligious view. I take a short and powerful statement of it from a 1903 essay by Bertrand Russell, "A Free Man's Worship."

> That man is the product of causes which had no prevision of the end they were achieving; that his origin, his growth, his hopes and fears, his loves and his beliefs are but the outcome of accidental collocations of atoms; that no fire, no heroism, no intensity of thought and feeling, can preserve an individual life beyond the grave; that all the labors of the ages, all the devotion, all the inspiration, all the noonday brightness of human genius, are destined to extinction in the vast death of the solar system, and that the whole temple of man's achievement must inevitably be buried beneath the debris of a universe in ruins—all these things, if not quite beyond dispute, are yet so nearly certain that no philosophy which rejects them can hope to stand. Only within the scaffolding of these truths, only on the firm foundation of *unyielding despair,* can the soul's habitation henceforth be safely built.[1]

For convenience, I will call a world that satisfies the description given here a "Russellian world." But we are primarily interested in what the status of morality would be in the actual world if that world should turn out to be Russellian. I shall therefore sometimes augment the description of a Russellian world with obvious features of the actual world.

What are the most relevant features of a Russellian world? The following strike me as especially important: (1) Such phenomena as minds, mental activities, consciousness, and so forth are the products of entities and causes that give no indication of being mental themselves. In Russell's words, the causes are "accidental collocations of atoms" with "no prevision of the end they were achieving." Though not stated explicitly by Russell, we might add the doctrine, a commonplace in modern science, that mental phenomena—and indeed life itself—are comparative latecomers in the long history of the earth. (2) Human life is bounded by physical death and each individual comes to a permanent end at his physical death. We might add to this the observation that the span of human life is comparatively short, enough so that in some cases we can, with fair confidence, predict the major consequences of certain actions insofar as they will affect a given individual throughout his whole remaining life. (3) Not only each individual but also the human race as a species is doomed to extinction "beneath the debris of a universe in ruins."

So much, then, for the main features of a Russellian world. Because the notion of benefits and goods plays an important part in the remainder of my discussion, I want to introduce one further technical expression—"Russellian benefit." A Russellian benefit is one that could accrue to a person in a Russellian world. A contented old age would be, I suppose, a Russellian benefit, as would a thrill of sexual pleasure or a good reputation. Going to heaven when one dies, though a benefit, is not a Russellian benefit. Russellian benefits are only the benefits possible in a Russellian world. But one can have Russellian benefits even if the world is not Russellian. In such a case there might, however, also be other benefits, such as going to heaven.

Could the actual world be Russellian? Well, I take it to be an important feature of the actual world that human beings exist in it and that in it their actions fall, at least sometimes, within the sphere of morality—that is, they have moral obligations to act (or to

refrain from acting) in certain ways. And if they do not act in those ways, then they are properly subject to a special and peculiar sort of adverse judgment (unless it happens that there are special circumstances that serve to excuse their failure to fulfill the obligations). People who do not fulfill their obligations are not merely stupid or weak or unlucky; they are morally reprehensible.

Now, I do not have much to say in an illuminating manner about the notion of moral obligation, but I could perhaps make a few preliminary observations about how I understand this notion. First, I take it that morality includes, or results in, judgments of the form "N ought to do (or to avoid doing) ————" or "It is N's duty to do (or to avoid doing) ————." That is, morality ascribes to particular people an obligation to do a certain thing on a certain occasion. No doubt morality includes other things as well—general moral rules, for example. I shall, however, focus on judgments of the sort just mentioned, and when I speak without further qualification of someone's having an obligation I intend it to be understood in terms of such a judgment.

Second, many authors distinguish prima facie obligations from obligations "all things considered." Probably this is a useful distinction. For the most part, however, I intend to ignore prima facie obligations and to focus upon our obligations all things considered, what we might call our "final obligations." These are the obligations that a particular person has in some concrete circumstance at a particular place and time, when all the aspects of the situation have been taken into account. It identifies the action that, if not done, will properly subject the person to the special adverse judgment.

Finally, it is, I think, a striking feature of moral obligations that a person's being unwilling to fulfill the obligation is irrelevant to having the obligation and is also irrelevant to the adverse judgment in case the obligation is not fulfilled. Perhaps even more important is the fact that, at least for some obligations, it is also irrelevant in both these ways for one to point out that he does not see how fulfilling the obligations can do him any good. In fact, unless we are greatly mistaken about our obligations, it seems clear that in a Russellian world there are an appreciable number of cases in which fulfilling an obligation would result in a loss of good to ourselves. On the most prosaic level, this must be true of some cases of repaying a debt, keeping a promise, refraining from stealing, and so on. And it must also be true of those rarer but more striking cases of obligation to risk death or serious injury in the performance of a duty. People have, of course, differed as to what is good for humans. But so far as I can see, the point I have been making will hold for any candidate that is plausible in a Russellian world. Pleasure, happiness, esteem, contentment, self-realization, knowledge—all of these can suffer from the fulfillment of a moral obligation.

It is not, however, a *necessary* truth that some of our obligations are such that their fulfillment will yield no net benefit, within Russellian limits, to their fulfiller. It is not contradictory to maintain that, for every obligation that I have, a corresponding benefit awaits me within the confines of this world and this life. While such a contention would not be contradictory, however, it would nevertheless be false. I discuss below one version of this contention. At present it must suffice to say that a person who accepts this claim will probably find the remainder of what I have to say correspondingly less plausible.

Well, where are we now? I claim that in the actual world we have some obligations that, when we fulfill them, will confer on us no net Russellian benefit—in fact, they will result in a Russellian loss. If the world is Russellian, then Russellian benefits and losses are the only benefits and losses, and also then we have moral obligations whose fulfillment will result in a net loss of good to the one who fulfills them. I suggest, however, that it would be very strange to have such obligations—strange not simply in the sense of being unexpected or surprising but in some deeper way. I do not suggest that it is strange in the sense of having a straightforward logical defect, of being self-contradictory to claim that we have such obligations. Perhaps the best thing to say is that were it a fact that we had such obligations, then the world that included such a fact would be absurd—we would be living in a crazy world.

Now, whatever success I may have in this paper will in large part be a function of my success (or lack thereof) in getting across a sense of that absurdity, that

queerness. On some accounts of morality, in a Russellian world there would not be the strangeness that I allege. Perhaps, then, I can convey some of that strangeness by mentioning those views of morality that would eliminate it. In fact, I believe that a good bit of their appeal is just the fact that they do get rid of this queerness.

First, I suspect that morality will not be queer in the way I suggest, even in a Russellian world, if judgments about obligations are properly to be analyzed in terms of the speaker rather than in terms of the subject of the judgment. And I more than suspect that this will be the case if such judgments are analyzed in terms of the speaker's attitude or feeling toward some action, and/or his attempt or inclination to incite a similar attitude in someone else. It may be, of course, that there is something odd about the supposition that human beings, consciousness, and so forth, could arise at all in a Russellian world. A person who was impressed by that oddity might be attracted toward some "teleological" line of reasoning in the direction of a more religious view. But I think that this oddity is not the one I am touching on here. Once given the existence of human beings with capacities for feelings and attitudes, there does not seem to be anything further that is queer in the supposition that a speaker might have an attitude toward some action, might express that attitude, and might attempt (or succeed) in inciting someone else to have a similar attitude. Anyone, therefore, who can be satisfied with such an analysis will probably not be troubled by the queerness that I allege.

Second, for similar reasons, this queerness will also be dissipated by any account that understands judgments about obligations purely in terms of the feelings, attitudes, and so forth of the subject of the judgment. For, given again that there are human beings with consciousness, it does not seem to be any additional oddity that the subject of a moral judgment might have feelings or attitudes about an actual or prospective action of his own. The assumption that morality is to be understood in this way takes many forms. In a closely related area, for example, it appears as the assumption—so common now that it can pass almost unnoticed—that guilt could not be anything other than guilt *feelings,* and that the "problem" of guilt is just the problem generated by such feelings.

In connection with our topic here, however, we might look at the way in which this sort of analysis enters into one plausible-sounding explanation of morality in a Russellian world, an explanation that has a scientific flavor. The existence of morality in a Russellian world, it may be said, is not at all absurd because its existence there can be given a perfectly straightforward explanation: morality has a survival value for a species such as ours because it makes possible continued cooperation and things of that sort. So it is no more absurd that people have moral obligations than it is absurd that they have opposable thumbs.

I think that this line of explanation will work only if one analyzes obligations into feelings, or beliefs. I think it is plausible (though I am not sure it is correct) to suppose that everyone's having feelings of moral obligation might have survival value for a species such as Man, given of course that these feelings were attached to patterns of action that contributed to such survival. And if that is so, then it is not implausible to suppose that there may be a survival value for the species even in a moral feeling that leads to the death of the individual who has it. So far so good. But this observation, even if true, is not relevant to the queerness with which I am here concerned. For I have not suggested that the existence of moral feelings would be absurd in a Russellian world; it is rather the existence of moral *obligations* that is absurd, and I think it important to make the distinction. It is quite possible, it seems to me, for one to feel (or to believe) that he has a certain obligation without actually having it, and also vice versa. Now, beliefs and feelings will presumably have some effect upon actions, and this effect may possibly contribute to the survival of the species. But, so far as I can see, the addition of actual moral obligations to these moral beliefs and feelings will make no further contribution to action nor will the actual obligations have an effect upon action in the absence of the corresponding feelings and beliefs. So it seems that neither with nor without the appropriate feelings will moral obligations contribute to the survival of the species. Consequently, an "evolutionary" approach such as this cannot serve to explain the existence of moral obligations, unless one rejects my distinction and equates the obligations with the feelings.

And finally, I think that morality will not be queer in the way I allege, or at least it will not be as queer as I think, if it should be the case that every obligation yields a Russellian benefit to the one who fulfills it. Given the caveat expressed earlier, one can perhaps make some sense out of the notion of a Russellian good or benefit for a sentient organism in a Russellian world. And one could, I suppose, without further queerness imagine that such an organism might aim toward achieving such goods. And we could further suppose that there were certain actions—those that were "obligations"—that would, in contrast with other actions, actually yield such benefits to the organism that performed them. And finally, it might not be too implausible to claim that an organism that failed to perform such an action was defective in some way and that some adverse judgment was appropriate.

Morality, however, seems to require us to hold that certain organisms (namely, human beings) have in addition to their ordinary properties and relations another special relation to certain actions. This relation is that of being "obligated" to perform those actions. And some of those actions are pretty clearly such that they will yield only Russellian losses to the one who performs them. Nevertheless, we are supposed to hold that a person who does not perform an action to which he is thus related is defective in some serious and important way and an adverse judgment is appropriate against him. And that certainly does seem odd.

The recognition of this oddity—or perhaps better, this absurdity—is not simply a resolution to concern ourselves only with what "pays." Here the position of Kant is especially suggestive. He held that a truly moral action is undertaken purely out of respect for the moral law and with no concern at all for reward. There seems to be no room at all here for any worry about what will "pay." But he also held that the moral enterprise needs, in a deep and radical way, the postulate of a God who can, and will, make happiness correspond to virtue. This postulate is "necessary" for a practical reason. Perhaps we could put this Kantian demand in the language I have been using here, saying that the moral enterprise would make no sense in a world in which that correspondence ultimately failed.

I suspect that what we have in Kant is the recognition that there cannot be, in any "reasonable" way, a moral demand upon me, unless reality itself is committed to morality in some deep way. It makes sense only if there is a moral demand on the world too and only if reality will in the end satisfy that demand. This theme of the deep grounding of morality is one to which I return briefly near the end of this paper.

The oddity we have been considering is, I suspect, the most important root of the celebrated and somewhat confused question, "Why should I be moral?" Characteristically, I think, the person who asks that question is asking to have the queerness of that situation illuminated. From time to time there are philosophers who make an attempt to argue—perhaps only a halfhearted attempt—that being moral really is in one's interest after all. Kurt Baier, it seems to me, proposes a reply of this sort. He says:

> Moralities are systems of principles whose acceptance by everyone as overruling the dictates of self-interest is in the interest of everyone alike though following the rules of a morality is not of course identical with following self-interest. . . .
>
> The answer to our question 'Why should we be moral?' is therefore as follows. We should be moral because being moral is following rules designed to overrule self-interest whenever it is in the interest of everyone alike that everyone should set aside his interest.[2]

As I say, this seems to be an argument to the effect that it really is in everyone's interest to be moral. I suppose that Baier is here probably talking about Russellian interests. At least, we must interpret him in that way if his argument is to be applicable in this context, and I will proceed on that assumption. But how exactly is the argument to be made out?

It appears here to begin with a premise something like

(A) It is in everyone's best interest (including mine, presumably) for everyone (including me) to be moral.

This premise itself appears to be supported earlier by reference to Hobbes. As I understand it, the idea is

that without morality people will live in a "state of nature," and life will be nasty, brutish, and short. Well, perhaps so. At any rate, let us accept (A) for the moment. From (A) we can derive

(B) It is in my best interest for everyone (including me) to be moral.

And from (B) perhaps one derives

(C) It is in my best interest for me to be moral.

And (C) may be taken to answer the question, "Why should I be moral?" Furthermore, if (C) is true, then moral obligation will at least not have the sort of queerness that I have been alleging.

Unfortunately, however, the argument outlined above is invalid. The derivation of (B) from (A) *may* be all right, but the derivation of (C) from (B) is invalid. What does follow from (B) is

(C′) It is in my best interest for me to be moral *if everyone else is moral.*

The argument thus serves to show that it is in a given person's interest to be moral only on the assumption that everyone else in the world is moral. It might, of course, be difficult to find someone ready to make that assumption.

There is, however, something more of interest in this argument. I said that the derivation of (B) from (A) may be all right. But in fact is it? If it is not all right, then this argument would fail even if everyone else in the world were moral. Now (A) can be interpreted as referring to "everyone's best interest" ("the interest of everyone alike," in Baier's own words) either collectively or distributively; that is, it may be taken as referring to the best interest of the whole group considered as a single unit, or as referring to the best interest of each individual in the group. But if (A) is interpreted in the collective sense, then (B) does not follow from it. It may not be in *my* best interest for everyone to act morally, even if it is in the best interest of the group as a whole, for the interest of the group as a whole may be advanced by the sacrificing of my interest. On this interpretation of (A), then, the argument will not answer the question "Why should I be moral?" even on the supposition that everyone else is moral.

If (A) is interpreted in the distributive sense, on the other hand, then (B) does follow from it, and the foregoing objection is not applicable. But another objection arises. Though (A) in the collective sense has some plausibility, it is hard to imagine that it is true in the distributive sense. Hobbes may have been right in supposing that life in the state of nature would be short, etc. But some lives are short anyway. In fact, some lives are short just because the demands of morality are observed. Such a life is not bound to have been shorter in the state of nature. Nor is it bound to have been less happy, less pleasurable, and so forth. In fact, does it not seem obvious that *my* best Russellian interest will be further advanced in a situation in which everyone else acts morally but I act immorally (in selected cases) than it will be in case everyone, including me, acts morally? It certainly seems so. It can, of course, be observed that if I act immorally then so will other people, perhaps reducing my benefits. In the present state of the world that is certainly true. But in the present state of the world it is also true, as I observed earlier, that many other people will act immorally *anyway,* regardless of what I do.

A more realistic approach is taken by Richard Brandt.[3] He asks, "Is it *reasonable* for me to do my duty if it conflicts seriously with my personal welfare?" After distinguishing several possible senses of this question, he chooses a single one to discuss further, presumably a sense that he thinks important. As reformulated, the question is now: "Given that doing *x* is my duty and that doing some conflicting act *y* will maximize my personal welfare, will the performance of *x* instead of *y* satisfy my reflective preferences better?" And the conclusion to which he comes is that "the correct answer may vary from one person to another. It depends on what kind of person one is, what one cares about." And within Russellian limits Brandt must surely be right in this. But he goes on to say, "It is, of course, no defense of one's failure to do one's duty, before others or society, to say that doing so is not 'reasonable' for one in this sense." And this is just to bring the queer element back in. It is to suppose that besides "the kind of person" I am and my particular pattern of "cares" and interests there is something else, my duty, which may go against these

and in any case properly overrides them. And one feels that there must be some sense of "reasonable" in which one can ask whether a world in which that is true is a reasonable world, whether such a world makes any sense.

This completes my survey of some ethical or meta-ethical views that would eliminate or minimize this sort of queerness of morality. I turn now to another sort of view, stronger I think than any of these others, which accepts that queerness but goes no further. And one who holds this view will also hold, I think, that the question "Why should I be moral?" must be rejected in one way or another. A person who holds this view will say that it is simply a fact that we have the moral obligations that we do have, and that is all there is to it. If they sometimes result in a loss of good, then that too is just a fact. These may be puzzling and surprising facts, but there are lots of puzzling and surprising things about the world. In a Russellian world, morality will be, I suppose, an "emergent" phenomenon; it will be a feature of certain effects though it is not a feature of their causes. But the wetness of water is an emergent feature, too. It is not a property of either hydrogen or oxygen. And there is really nothing more to be said; somewhere we must come to an end of reasons and explanations. We have our duties. We can fulfill them and be moral, or we can ignore them and be immoral. If all that is crazy and absurd—well, so be it. Who are we to say that the world is not crazy and absurd?

Such a view was once suggested by William Alston in a criticism of Hasting Rashdall's moral argument for God's existence. Alston attributed to Rashdall the view that "God is required as a locus for the moral law." But Alston then went on to ask, "Why could it not just be an ultimate fact about the universe that kindness is good and cruelty bad? This seems to have been Plato's view." And if we rephrase Alston's query slightly to refer to obligations, we might be tempted to say, "Why not indeed?"

I say that this is perhaps the strongest reply against me. Since it involves no argument, there is no argument to be refuted. And I have already said that, so far as I can see, its central contention is not self-contradictory. Nor do I think of any other useful argument to the effect that the world is not absurd and crazy in this way. The reference to Plato, however, might be worth following for a moment. Perhaps Plato did think that goodness, or some such thing related to morality, was an ultimate fact about the world. But a Platonic world is not very close to a Russellian world. Plato was not a Christian, of course, but his world view has very often been taken to be congenial (especially congenial compared to some other philosophical views) to a religious understanding of the world. He would not have been satisfied, I think, with Russell's "accidental collocations of atoms," nor would he have taken the force of the grave to be "so nearly certain." The idea of the Good seems to play a metaphysical role in his thought. It is somehow fundamental to what *is* as well as to what ought to be, much more fundamental to reality than are the atoms. A Platonic man, therefore, who sets himself to live in accordance with the Good aligns himself with what is deepest and most basic in existence. Or to put it another way, we might say that whatever values a Platonic world imposes on a man are values to which the Platonic world itself is committed, through and through.

Not so, of course, for a Russellian world. Values and obligations cannot be deep in such a world. They have a grip only upon surface phenomena, probably only upon man. What is deep in a Russellian world must be such things as matter and energy, or perhaps natural law, chance, or chaos. If it really were a fact that one had obligations in a Russellian world, then something would be laid upon man that might cost a man everything but that went no further than man. And that difference from a Platonic world seems to make all the difference.

This discussion suggests, I think, that there are two related ways in which morality is queer in a Russellian world. Or maybe they are better construed as two aspects of the queerness we have been exploring. In most of the preceding discussion I have been focusing on the strangeness of an overriding demand that does not seem to conduce to the *good* of the person on whom it is laid. (In fact, it does not even promise his good.) Here, however, we focus on the fact that this demand—radical enough in the human life on which it is laid—is *superficial* in a Russellian world. Some-

thing that reaches close to the heart of my own life, perhaps even demanding the sacrifice of that life, is not deep at all in the world in which (on a Russellian view) that life is lived. And that, too, seems absurd.

This brings to an end the major part of my discussion. If I have been successful at all you will have shared with me to some extent in the sense of the queerness of morality, its absurdity in a Russellian world. If you also share the conviction that it cannot in the end be absurd in that way, then perhaps you will also be attracted to some religious view of the world. Perhaps you also will say that morality must have some deeper grip upon the world than a Russellian view allows. And, consequently, things like mind and purpose must also be deeper in the real world than they would be in a Russellian world. They must be more original, more controlling. The accidental collocation of atoms cannot be either primeval or final, nor can the grave be an end. But of course that would be only a beginning, a sketch waiting to be filled in.

We cannot here do much to fill it in further. But I should like to close with a final, and rather tentative suggestion, as to a direction in which one might move in thinking about the place of morality in the world. It is suggested to me by certain elements in my own religion, Christianity.

I come more and more to think that morality, while a fact, is a twisted and distorted fact. Or perhaps better, that it is a barely recognizable version of another fact, a version adapted to a twisted and distorted world. It is something like, I suppose, the way in which the pine that grows at timberline, wind blasted and twisted low against the rock, is a version of the tall and symmetrical tree that grows lower on the slopes. I think it may be that the related notions of sacrifice and gift represent (or come close to representing) the fact, that is, the pattern of life, whose distorted version we know here as morality. Imagine a situation, an "economy" if you will, in which no one ever buys or trades for or seizes any good thing. But whatever good he enjoys it is either one which he himself has created or else one which he receives as a free and unconditional gift. And as soon as he has tasted it and seen that it is good he stands ready to give it away in his turn as soon as the opportunity arises. In such a place, if one were to speak either of his rights or his duties, his remark might be met with puzzled laughter as his hearers struggled to recall an ancient world in which those terms referred to something important.

We have, of course, even now some occasions that tend in this direction. Within some families perhaps, or even in a regiment in desperate battle, people may for a time pass largely beyond morality and live lives of gift and sacrifice. On those occasions nothing would be lost if the moral concepts and the moral language were to disappear. But it is probably not possible that such situations and occasions should be more than rare exceptions in the daily life of the present world. Christianity, however, which tells us that the present world is "fallen" and hence leads us to expect a distortion in its important features, also tells us that one day the redemption of the world will be complete and that then all things shall be made new. And it seems to me to suggest an "economy" more akin to that of gift and sacrifice than to that of rights and duties. If something like that should be true, then perhaps morality, like the Marxist state, is destined to wither away (unless perchance it should happen to survive in hell).

Christianity, then, I think is related to the queerness or morality in one way and perhaps in two. In the first instance, it provides a view of the world in which morality is not an absurdity. It gives morality a deeper place in the world than does a Russellian view and thus permits it to "make sense." But in the second instance, it perhaps suggests that morality is not the deepest thing, that it is provisional and transitory, that it is due to serve its use and then to pass away in favor of something richer and deeper. Perhaps we can say that it begins by inverting the quotation with which I began and by telling us that, since God exists, not everything is permitted; but it may also go on to tell us that, since God exists, in the end there shall be no occasion for any prohibition.

NOTES

1. Bertrand Russell, *Mysticism and Logic* (New York: Barnes & Noble, 1917), pp. 47–48. Italics added.
2. Kurt Baier, *The Moral Point of View* (Ithaca: Cornell University Press, 1958), p. 314.
3. Richard Brandt, *Ethical Theory* (Englewood Cliffs, N.J.: Prentice-Hall, 1959), pp. 375–78.

FOR FURTHER REFLECTION

1. Go over Mavrodes's arguments for the inadequacy of secular morality. Do you agree with him that secularists have no satisfactory answer to the question "Why should I be moral?" Why or why not?
2. Do you agree with Mavrodes that by comparison with Platonic and Christian ethics secular ethics are superficial, lacking an adequate metaphysical basis? Explain your answer.

KAI NIELSEN

ETHICS WITHOUT RELIGION

Kai Nielsen is professor of philosophy at Calgary University in Canada. This essay was written twenty years before Mavrodes's paper on the queerness of morality, and it anticipates some of Mavrodes's arguments. Nielsen's thesis is that even if "God is dead," it really doesn't matter—as far as our morality is concerned. First of all, with the loss of faith all our essential moral values are left intact. We still can be happy, find security and emotional peace, experience love and friendship, enjoy creative work and a rich variety of experiences. Second, both the secular basis of ethics and the religious basis involve an objective rationale involving central principles such as respect for people and justice, and benevolence. Our common nature and quest for the good life is all the grounding that ethics needs. It is true that morality sometimes calls for sacrifice of nonmoral goods. It would be nice if this were not the case, but life is sometimes hard.

There certainly are fundamental difficulties and perhaps even elements of incoherence in Christian ethics, but what can a secular moralist offer in its stead? Religious morality—and Christian morality in particular—may have its difficulties, but secular morality, religious apologists argue, has still greater difficulties. It leads they claim, to ethical scepticism, nihilism, or, at best, to a pure conventionalism. Such apologists could point out that if we look at morality with the cold eye of an anthropologist we will—assuming we are clear-headed—find morality to be nothing more than the often conflicting *mores* of the various tribes spread around the globe. If we eschew the kind of insight that religion can give us, we will have no Archimedean point in accordance with which we can decide how it is that we ought to live and die. If we look at ethics from such a purely secular point of view, we will discover that it is constituted by tribal conventions, conventions which we are free to reject

if we are sufficiently free from ethnocentrism. We can continue to act in accordance with them or we can reject them and adopt a different set of conventions; but whether we act in accordance with the old conventions or forge "new tablets," we are still acting in accordance with certain conventions. Relative to them certain acts are right or wrong, reasonable or unreasonable, but we cannot justify these fundamental moral conventions themselves or the ways of life which they partially codify.

When these points are conceded, theologians are in a position to press home a powerful apologetic point. When we become keenly aware, they argue, of the true nature of such conventionalism and when we become aware that there is no overarching purpose that men were destined to fulfill, the myriad purposes, the aims and goals humans create for themselves, will be seen not to be enough. When we realize that life does not have a meaning—that is, a significance—

From Kai Nielsen, "Ethics without Religion," *Ohio University Review 6,* 1964, 48–51, 57–62, by permission of the publisher and author.

which is there to be found, but that we human beings must by our deliberate decisions give it whatever meaning it has, we will (as Sartre so well understood) undergo estrangement and despair. We will drain our cup to its last bitter drop and feel our alienation to the full. Perhaps there are human purposes, purposes to be found *in* life, and we can and do have them even in a Godless world, but without God there can be no one overarching purpose, no one basic scheme of human existence, in virtue of which we could find a meaning for our grubby lives. It is this overall sense of meaning that man so ardently strives for, but it is not to be found in a purely secular worldview. You secularists, a new Pascal might argue, must realize, if you really want to be clear-headed, that no purely human purposes are ultimately worth striving for. What you humanists can give us by way of a scheme of human existence will always be a poor second-best and not what the human heart most ardently longs for.

The considerations for and against an ethics not rooted in a religion are complex and involuted; a fruitful discussion of them is difficult, for in considering the matter our passions, our anxieties, our (if you will) ultimate concerns are involved, and they tend to blur our vision, enfeeble our understanding, of what exactly is at stake. But we must not forget that what is at stake here is just what kind of ultimate commitments or obligations a man could have without evading any issue, without self-deception or without delusion. I shall be concerned to display and assess, to make plain but also to weigh, some of the most crucial considerations for and against a purely secular ethic. While I shall in an objective fashion try to make clear what the central issues are, I shall also give voice to my reflective convictions on this matter. I shall try to make evident my reasons for believing that we do not need God or any religious conception to support our moral convictions. I shall do this, as I think one should in philosophy, by making apparent the dialectic of the problem (by bringing to the fore the conflicting and evolving considerations for and against) and by arguing for what I take to be their proper resolution.

I am aware that Crisis Theologians would claim that I am being naive, but I do not see why purposes of purely human devising are not ultimately worth striving for. There is much that we humans prize and would continue to prize even in a Godless world. Many things would remain to give our lives meaning and point even after "the death of God."

Take a simple example. All of us *want* to be happy. But in certain bitter or sceptical moods we question what happiness is or we despairingly ask ourselves whether anyone can really be happy. Is this, however, a sober, sane view of the situation? I do not think that it is. Indeed we cannot adequately define "happiness" in the way that we can "bachelor," but neither can we in that way define "chair," "wind," "pain," and the vast majority of words in everyday discourse. For words like "bachelor," "triangle," or "father" we can specify a consistent set of properties that all the things and only the things denoted by these words have, but we cannot do this for "happiness," "chair," "pain," and the like. In fact, we cannot do it for the great majority of our words. Yet there is no greater loss here. Modern philosophical analysis has taught us that such an essentially Platonic conception of definition is unrealistic and unnecessary.[1] I may not be able to define "chair" in the way that I can define "bachelor," but I understand the meaning of "chair" perfectly well. In normal circumstances, at least, I know what to sit on when someone tells me to take a chair. I may not be able to define "pain," but I know what it is like to be in pain, and sometimes I can know when others are in pain. Similarly, though I cannot define "happiness" in the same way that I can define "bachelor," I know what it is like to be happy, and I sometimes can judge with considerable reliability whether others are happy or sad. "Happiness" is a slippery word, but it is not so slippery that we are justified in saying that nobody knows what happiness is.

A man could be said to have lived a happy life if he had found lasting sources of satisfaction in his life and if he had been able to find certain goals worthwhile and to achieve at least some of them. He could indeed have suffered some pain and anxiety, but his life must, for the most part, have been free from pain, estrangement, and despair, and must, on balance, have been a life which he has liked and found worthwhile. But surely we have no good grounds for saying that no one achieves such a balance or that no one is ever happy even for a time. We all have some idea of what would make us happy and of what would make us unhappy; many people, at least, can remain happy even after "the death of God." At any rate, we need not strike Pascalian attitudes, for even in a purely secular world there are permanent sources of human happiness for anyone to avail himself of.

What are they? What are these relatively permanent sources of human happiness that we all want or need? What is it which, if we have it, will give us the basis for a life that could properly be said to be happy? We all desire to be free from pain and want. Even masochists do not seek pain for its own sake; they endure pain because this is the only psychologically acceptable way of achieving something else (usually sexual satisfaction) that is so gratifying to them that they will put up with the pain to achieve it. We all want a life in which sometimes we can enjoy ourselves, in which we can attain our fair share of some of the simple pleasures that we all desire. They are not everything in life, but they are important, and our lives would be impoverished without them.

We also need security and emotional peace. We need and want a life in which we will not be constantly threatened with physical or emotional harassment. Again this is not the only thing worth seeking, but it is an essential ingredient in any adequate picture of the good life.

Human love and companionship are also central to a significant or happy life. We prize them, and a life which is without them is most surely an impoverished life, a life that no man, if he would take the matter to heart, would desire. But I would most emphatically assert that human love and companionship are quite possible in a Godless world, and the fact that life will some day inexorably come to an end and cut off love and companionship altogether enhances rather than diminishes their present value.

Furthermore, we all need some sort of creative employment or meaningful work to give our lives point, to save them from boredom, drudgery, and futility. A man who can find no way to use the talents he has or a man who can find no work which is meaningful to him will indeed be a miserable man. But again there is work—whether it be as a surgeon, a farmer, or a fisherman—that has a rationale even in a world without God. And poetry, music, and art retain their beauty and enrich our lives even in the complete absence of God or the gods.

We want and need art, music, and the dance. We find pleasure in travel and conversation and in a rich variety of experiences. The sources of human enjoyment are obviously too numerous to detail. But all of them are achievable in a Godless universe. If some can be ours, we can attain a reasonable measure of happiness. Only a Steppenwolfish personality beguiled by impossible expectations and warped by irrational guilts and fears can fail to find happiness in the realization of such ends. But to be free of impossible expectations people must clearly recognize that there is no "one big thing" or, for that matter, "small thing" which would make them permanently happy; almost anything permanently and exclusively pursued will lead to that nausea that Sartre has so forcefully brought to our attention. But we can, if we are not too sick and if our situation is not too precarious, finding lasting sources of human happiness in a purely secular world.

It is not only happiness for ourselves that can give us something of value, but there is the need to do what we can to diminish the awful sum of human misery in the world. I have never understood those who say that they find contemporary life meaningless because they find nothing worthy of devoting their energies to. Throughout the world there is an immense amount of human suffering, suffering that can, through a variety of human efforts, be partially alleviated. Why can we not find a meaningful life in devoting ourselves, as did Doctor Rieux in Albert Camus's *The Plague,* to relieving somewhat the sum total of human suffering? Why cannot this give our lives point, and for that matter an over-all rationale? It is childish to think that by human effort we will someday totally rid the world of suffering and hate, of deprivation and sadness. This is a permanent part of the human condition. But specific bits of human suffering can be alleviated. The plague is always potentially with us, but we can destroy the Nazis and we can fight for racial and social equality throughout the world. And as isolated people, as individuals in a mass society, we find people turning to us in dire need, in suffering and in emotional deprivation, and we can as individuals respond to those people and alleviate or at least acknowledge that suffering and deprivation. A man who says, "If God is dead, nothing matters," is a spoilt child who has never looked at his fellow men with compassion.

Yet, it might be objected, if we abandon a Judaeo-Christian *Weltanschauung,* there can, in a secular world, be no "one big thing" to give our lives an overall rationale. We will not be able to see written in the stars the final significance of human effort. There will be no architectonic purpose to give our lives such a rationale. Like Tolstoy's Pierre in *War and Peace,* we desire *somehow* to gather the sorry scheme of things entire into one intelligible explanation so that we can finally crack the riddle of human destiny. We long to understand why it is that men suffer and die. If it is a factual answer that is wanted when such a question is asked, it is plain enough. Ask any physician. But clearly this is not what people who seek such answers are after. They want some *justification* for suffering; they want some way of showing that suffering is after all for a good purpose. It can, of course, be argued that suffering sometimes is a good thing, for it occasionally gives us insight and at times even brings about in the man who suffers a capacity to love and to be kind. But there is plainly an excessive amount of human suffering—the suffering of children in children's hospitals, the suffering of people devoured by cancer, and the sufferings of millions of Jews under the Nazis—for which there simply is no justification. Neither the religious man nor the secularist can explain, that is justify, such suffering and find some overall "scheme of life" in which it has some place, but only the religious man needs to do so. The secularist understands that suffering is not something to be justified but simply to be struggled against with courage and dignity. And in this fight, even the man who has been deprived of that which could give him some measure of happiness can still find or make for himself a meaningful human existence. . . .

The dialectic of our problem has not ended. The religious moralist might acknowledge that human happiness is indeed plainly a good thing while contending that secular morality, where it is consistent and reflective, will inevitably lead to some variety of egoism. An individual who recognized the value of happiness and self-consciousness might, if he were free of religious restraints, ask himself why he should be concerned with the happiness and self-awareness of *others,* except where their happiness and self-awareness would contribute to his own good. We must face the fact that sometimes, as the world goes, people's interests clash. Sometimes the common good is served only at the expense of some individual's interests. An individual must therefore, in such a circumstance, sacrifice what will make him happy for the common good. Morality requires this sacrifice of us, *when it is necessary* for the common good; morality, any morality, exists in part at least to adjudicate between the conflicting interests and demands of people. It is plainly evident that everyone cannot be happy all the time and that sometimes one person's happiness or the happiness of a group is at the expense of another person's happiness. Morality requires that we attempt to distribute happiness as evenly as possible. We must be fair: each person is to count for one and none is to count for more than one. Whether we like a person or not, whether he is useful to his society or not, his interests, and what will make him happy, must also be considered in any final decision as to what ought to be done. The requirements of justice make it necessary that each person be given equal consideration. I cannot justify my neglect of another person in some matter of morality simply on the grounds that I do not like him, that he is *not* a member of my set, or that he is *not* a productive member of society. The religious apologist will argue that behind these requirements of justice as fairness there lurks the ancient religious principle that men are creatures of God, each with an infinite worth, and thus men are never to be treated only as means but as persons deserving of respect in their own right. They have an infinite worth simply as persons.

My religious critic, following out the dialectic of the problem, should query: why should you respect someone, why should you treat all people equally, if doing this is not in your interest or not in the interests of your group? No purely secular justification can be given for so behaving. My critic now serves his *coup de grâce:* the secularist, as well as the "knight of faith," acknowledges that the principle of respect for persons is a precious one—a principle that he is unequivocally committed to, but the religious man alone can *justify* adherence to this principle. The secularist is surreptitiously drawing on Christian inspiration when he insists that all men should be considered equal and that people's rights must be respected. For a secular morality to say all it wants and needs to say, it must, at this crucial point, be parasitical upon a God-centered morality. Without such a dependence on religion, secular morality collapses into egoism.

It may well be the case that, as a historical fact, our moral concern for persons came from our religious conceptions, but it is a well known principle of logic that the validity of a belief is independent of its origin. What the religious moralist must do is to show that only on religious grounds could such a principle of respect for persons be justifiably asserted. But he has not shown that this is so; and there are good reasons for thinking that it is not so. Even if the secularist must simply subscribe to the Kantian principle, "Treat every man as an end and never as a means only," as he must subscribe to the claim, "Happiness is good," it does not follow that he is on worse ground than the religious moralist, for the religious moralist too, as we have seen, must simply subscribe to his ultimate moral principle, "Always do what God wills." *In a way,* the religious moralist's position here is simpler than the secularist's, for he needs only the fundamental moral principle that he ought to do what God wills. The secularist appears to need at least two fundamental principles. But in another and more important way the religious moralist's position is more complex, for he must subscribe to the extraordinarily obscure notion that man is a creature of God and as such has infinite worth. The Kantian principle may in the last analysis simply require subscription, but it is not inherently mysterious. To accept it does not require a crucifixion of the intellect. And if we are prepared simply to commit ourselves to one principle, why not to two principles, neither of which involves any appeal to conceptions whose very intelligibility is seriously in question?

The above argument is enough to destroy the believer's case here. But need we even make those

concessions? I do not think so. There is a purely secular rationale for treating people fairly, for regarding them as persons. Let me show how this is so. We have no evidence that men ever lived in a pre-social state of nature. Man, as we know him, is an animal with a culture; he is part of a community, and the very *concept* of community implies binding principles and regulations—duties, obligations and rights. Yet, by an exercise in imagination, we could conceive, in broad outline at any rate, what it would be like to live in such a pre-social state. In such a state no one would have any laws or principles to direct his behaviour. In that sense man would be completely free. But such a life, as Hobbes graphically depicted, would be a clash of rival egoisms. Life in that state of nature would, in his celebrated phrase, "be nasty, brutish and short." Now if men were in such a state and if they were perfectly rational egoists, what kind of community life would they choose, given the fact that they were, very roughly speaking, nearly equal in strength and ability? (That in communities as we find them men are not so nearly equal in power is beside the point, for our *hypothetical* situation.) Given that they all start from scratch and have roughly equal abilities, it seems to me that it would be most reasonable, even for rational egoists, to band together into a community where each man's interests were given equal consideration, where each person was treated as deserving of respect. Each rational egoist would want others to treat him with respect, for his very happiness is contingent upon that; and he would recognize, if he were rational, that he could attain the fullest cooperation of others only if other rational egoists knew or had good grounds for believing that their interests and their persons would also be respected. Such cooperation is essential for each egoist if all are to have the type of community life which would give them the best chance of satisfying their own interests to the fullest degree. Thus, even if men were thorough egoists, we would still have rational grounds for subscribing to a principle of respect for persons. That men are not thoroughly rational, do not live in a state of nature, and are not thorough egoists, does not gainsay the fact that we have rational grounds for regarding social life, organized in accordance with such a principle, as being objectively better than a social life which ignored this principle. The point here is that even rational egoists could see that this is the best possible social organization where men are nearly equal in ability.

Yet what about the world we live in—a world in which, given certain extant social relationships, men are not equal or even nearly equal in power and opportunity? What reason is there for an egoist who is powerfully placed to respect the rights of others, when they cannot hurt him? We can say that his position, no matter how strong, might change and he might be in a position where he would need his rights protected, but this is surely not a strong enough reason for respecting those rights. To be moral involves respecting those rights, but our rational egoist may not propose to be moral. In considering such questions we reach a point in reasoning at which we must simply *decide* what sort of person we shall strive to become. But, as I have said, the religious moralist reaches the same point. He too must make a decision of principle, but the principle he adopts is a fundamentally incoherent one. He not only must decide, but his decision must involve the acceptance of an absurdity.

It is sometimes argued by religious apologists that only if there is a God who can punish men will we be assured that naturally selfish men will be fair and considerate of others. Without this punitive sanction or threat men would go wild. Men will respect the rights of others only if they fear a wrathful and angry God. Yet it hardly seems to be the case that Christians, with their fear of hell, have been any better at respecting the rights of others than non-Christians. A study of the Middle Ages or the conquest of the non-Christian world makes this plain enough. And even if it were true (as it is not) that Christians were better in this respect than non-Christians, it would not show that they had a superior moral reason for their behavior, for in so acting and in so reasoning, they are not giving a morally relevant reason at all but are simply acting out of fear for their own hides. Yet Christian morality supposedly takes us beyond the clash of the rival egoisms of secular life.

In short, Christian ethics has not been able to give us a sounder ground for respecting persons than we have with a purely secular morality. The Kantian principle of respect for persons is actually bound up in the very idea of morality, either secular or religious, and there are good reasons, of a perfectly mundane sort, why we should have the institution of morality as we now have it, namely, that our individual welfare is dependent on having a device which equitably resolves social and individual conflicts. Morality has an objective rationale in complete independence of religion. Even if God is dead, it doesn't really matter.

It is in just this last thrust, it might be objected, that you reveal your true colors and show your own inability to face a patent social reality. At this point the heart of your rationalism is very irrational. For millions of people "the death of God" means very much. It really does matter. In your somewhat technical sense, the concept of God may be chaotic or unintelligible, but this concept, embedded in our languages—embedded in "the stream of life"—has an enormous social significance for many people. Jews and Christians, if they take their religion to heart, could not but feel a great rift in their lives with the loss of God, for they have indeed organized a good bit of their lives around their religion. Their very life-ideals have grown out of these, if you will, myth-eaten concepts. What should have been said is that if "God is dead" it matters a lot, but we should stand up like men and face this loss and learn to live in the Post-Christian era. As Nietzsche so well knew, to do this involves a basic reorientation of one's life and not just an intellectual dissent to a few statements of doctrine.

There is truth in this and a kind of "empiricism about man" that philosophers are prone to neglect. Of course it does matter when one recognizes that one's religion is illusory. For a devout Jew or Christian to give up his God most certainly is important and does take him into the abyss of a spiritual crisis. But in saying that it doesn't *really* matter I was implying what I have argued for in this essay, namely, that if a believer loses his God but can keep his nerve, think the matter over, and thoroughly take it to heart, life can still be meaningful and morality yet have an objective rationale. Surely, for good psychological reasons, the believer is prone to doubt this argument, but if he will only "hold on to his brains" and keep his courage, he will come to see that it is so. In this crucial sense it remains true that if "God is dead" it doesn't really matter.

NOTE

1. This is convincingly argued in Michael Scriven's essay "Definitions, Explanations, and Theories," in Herbert Feigl, Michael Scriven, and Grover Maxwell, eds., *Minnesota Studies in the Philosophy of Science,* III (Minneapolis, 1958), pp. 99–195.

FOR FURTHER REFLECTION

1. Do you agree with Nielsen that even if "God is dead," that the finality of death really doesn't matter for the moral life? How would a Christian like Mavrodes respond to Nielsen?
2. Has Nielsen shown why we should sacrifice our own good for the common good? Explain.
3. Nielsen claims that morality requires that happiness be distributed as evenly as possible. Does he give an argument for this position? What does he mean, and is he correct? Why or why not?

D. Standards of Moral Evaluation

Western philosophy has produced three major types of theories regarding the ultimate standard of moral evaluation. First, virtue ethics state that the emphasis in ethics should be put not on rules, but on character, on the virtues and vices people demonstrate in their lives: ethical goodness is primarily a state of being, and only secondarily a doing.

Second, teleological ethics assert that the rightness of an act is determined by the goodness of its consequences. Utilitarianism is the most important of the teleological theories. Classical utilitarianism advocates the greatest happiness to the greatest number: always do that act that is likely to maximize utility.

Third, deontological ethics affirm that ethics is primarily a following of rules or principles of action, for these principles of action have inherent value: in every moral act, we are acting in accordance with an appropriate principle.

The first three readings in this section represent each of these three types of theories. We begin with Aristotle's virtue theory, one of the oldest accounts of ethics in the history of philosophy. Next Thomas Hobbes offers a contractual defense of ethics. Then we examine the most famous utilitarian document, John Stuart Mill's classic *Utilitarianism.* Finally, we read a section from the most important representative of deontological ethics, Immanuel Kant's *The Foundations of a Metaphysics of Morals.*

ARISTOTLE

VIRTUES

Aristotle (384–322 B.C.E.) was one of the most important philosophers who ever lived. (See biosketch in Part V.) Although deeply indebted to him, Aristotle broke with Plato over the idea of Forms (Plato thought that the Forms had independent existence, whereas Aristotle thought that they were in things). Aristotle tended to be more empirical than Plato. His break with his master led to the formation of the second major school of philosophy in Athens, Aristotle's Lyceum.

In this selection from the *Nicomachean Ethics*, Aristotle discusses the nature of ethics and its relationship to human existence. He next turns to the nature of virtue, which he characterizes as traits that enable individuals to live well in communities. In order to achieve well-being (*eudaimonia*, happiness), proper social institutions are necessary. Thus the moral person cannot really exist apart from a flourishing political setting that enables the individual to develop the requisite virtues for the good life. For this reason, Aristotle considers ethics to be a branch of politics.

After locating ethics as a part of politics, Aristotle explains that moral virtues differ from intellectual ones. Although intellectual virtues may be taught directly, moral ones must be lived in order to be learned. By living well, we acquire the right habits. These habits are in fact the virtues, which are to be sought as the best guarantee to the happy life. But again, happiness requires that one be lucky enough to live in a flourishing state. The morally virtuous life consists in living in moderation, according to the Golden Mean.

BOOK I
[ALL HUMAN ACTIVITIES AIM AT SOME GOOD]

Chapter 1

Every art and every scientific inquiry, and similarly every action and purpose, may be said to aim at some good. Hence the good has been well defined as that at which all things aim. But it is clear that there is a difference in ends; for the ends are sometimes activities, and sometimes results beyond the mere activities. Where there are ends beyond the action, the results are naturally superior to the action.

As there are various actions, arts, and sciences, it follows that the ends are also various. Thus health is the end of the medical art, a ship of shipbuilding, victory of strategy, and wealth of economics. It often happens that a number of such arts or sciences combine for a single enterprise, as the art of making bri-

From Aristotle, *Nicomachean Ethics,* trans. James Weldon (New York: Macmillan, 1897).

dles and all such other arts as furnish the implements of horsemanship combine for horsemanship, and horsemanship and every military action for strategy; and in the same way, other arts or sciences combine for others. In all these cases, the ends of the master arts or sciences, whatever they may be, are more desirable than those of the subordinate arts or sciences, as it is for the sake of the former that the latter are pursued. It makes no difference to the argument whether the activities themselves are the ends of the action, or something beyond the activities, as in the above-mentioned sciences.

If it is true that in the sphere of action there is some end which we wish for its own sake, and for the sake of which we wish everything else, and if we do not desire everything for the sake of something else (for, if that is so, the process will go on *ad infinitum,* and our desire will be idle and futile), clearly this end will be good and the supreme good. Does it not follow then that the knowledge of this good is of great importance for the conduct of life? Like archers who have a mark at which to aim, shall we not have a better chance of attaining what we want? If this is so, we must endeavor to comprehend, at least in outline, what this good is, and what science or faculty makes it its object.

It would seem that this is the most authoritative science. Such a kind is evidently the political, for it is that which determines what sciences are necessary in states, and what kinds should be studied, and how far they should be studied by each class of inhabitant. We see too that even the faculties held in highest esteem, such as strategy, economics, and rhetoric, are subordinate to it. Then since politics makes use of the other sciences and also rules what people may do and what they may not do, it follows that its end will comprehend the ends of the other sciences, and will therefore be the good of mankind. For even if the good of an individual is identical with the good of a state, yet the good of the state is evidently greater and more perfect to attain or to preserve. For though the good of an individual by himself is something worth working for, to ensure the good of a nation or a state is nobler and more divine.

These then are the objects at which the present inquiry aims, and it is in a sense a political inquiry. . . .

THE SCIENCE OF THE GOOD FOR MAN IS POLITICS

Chapter 2

As every science and undertaking aims at some good, what is in our view the good at which political science aims, and what is the highest of all practical goods? As to its name there is, I may say, a general agreement. The masses and the cultured classes agree in calling it happiness, and conceive that "to live well" or "to do well" is the same thing as "to be happy." But as to what happiness is they do not agree, nor do the masses give the same account of it as the philosophers. The former take it to be something visible and palpable, such as pleasure, wealth, or honor; different people, however, give different definitions of it, and often even the same man gives different definitions at different times. When he is ill, it is health, when he is poor, it is wealth; if he is conscious of his own ignorance, he envies people who use grand language above his own comprehension. Some philosophers, on the other hand, have held that, besides these various goods, there is an absolute good which is the cause of goodness in them all.[1] It would perhaps be a waste of time to examine all these opinions; it will be enough to examine such as are most popular or as seem to be more or less reasonable.

Chapter 3

Men's conception of the good or of happiness may be read in the lives they lead. Ordinary or vulgar people conceive it to be a pleasure, and accordingly choose a life of enjoyment. For there are, we may say, three conspicuous types of life, the sensual, the political, and, thirdly, the life of thought. Now the mass of men present an absolutely slavish appearance, choosing the life of brute beasts, but they have ground for so doing because so many persons in authority share the tastes of Sardanapalus.[2] Cultivated and energetic people, on the other hand, identify happiness with honor, as honor is the general end of political life. But this seems too superficial an idea for our present purpose; for honor depends more upon the people who pay it than upon the person to whom it is paid, and the good we feel is something which is proper to a man himself and cannot be easily taken away from him. Men too appear to seek honor in order to be assured of their own goodness. Accordingly, they seek it at the hands of the sage and of those who know them well, and they seek it on the ground of their virtue; clearly then, in their judgment at any rate, virtue is better than honor. Perhaps then we might look on virtue rather than honor as the end of political life. Yet even this idea appears not quite complete; for a man may possess virtue and yet be asleep or inactive throughout life, and not only so, but he may experience the greatest calamities and misfortunes. Yet no one would call such a life a life of happiness, unless he were maintaining a paradox. But we need not dwell further on this subject, since it is sufficiently discussed in popular philosophical treatises. The third life is the life of thought, which we will discuss later.

The life of money making is a life of constraint; and wealth is obviously not the good of which we are in quest; for it is useful merely as a means to something else. It would be more reasonable to take the things mentioned before—sensual pleasure, honor, and virtue— as ends than wealth, since they are things desired on their own account. Yet these too are evidently not ends, although much argument has been employed to show that they are. . . .

CHARACTERISTICS OF THE GOOD

Chapter 5

But leaving this subject for the present, let us revert to the good of which we are in quest and consider what it may be. For it seems different in different activities or arts; it is one thing in medicine, another in strategy, and so on. What is the good in each of these instances? It is presumably that for the sake of which all else is done. In medicine this is health, in strategy victory, in architecture a house, and so on. In every activity and undertaking it is the end, since it is for the sake of the end that all people do whatever else they do. If then there is an end for all our activity, this will be the good to be accomplished; and if there are several such ends, it will be these.

Our argument is arrived by a different path at the same point as before; but we must endeavor to make it still plainer. Since there are more ends than one, and some of these ends—for example, wealth, flutes, and instruments generally—we desire as means to something else, it is evident that not all are final ends. But the highest good is clearly something final. Hence if there is only one final end, this will be the object of which we are in search; and if there are more than one, it will be the most final. We call that which is sought after for its own sake more final than that which is sought after as a means to something else; we call that which is never desired as a means to something else more final than things that are desired both for themselves and as means to something else. Therefore, we call absolutely final that which is always desired for itself and never as a means to something else. Now happiness more than anything else answers to this description. For happiness we always desire for its own sake and never as a means to something else, whereas honor, pleasure, intelligence, and every virtue we desire partly for their own sakes (for we should desire them independently of what might result from them), but partly also as means to happiness, because we suppose they will prove instruments of happiness. Happiness, on the other hand, nobody desires for the sake of these things, nor indeed as a means to anything else at all.

If we start from the point of view of self-sufficiency, we reach the same conclusion; for we assume that the final good is self-sufficient. By self-sufficiency we do not mean that a person leads a solitary life all by himself, but that he has parents, children, wife and friends and fellow citizens in general, as man is naturally a social being. Yet here it is necessary to set some limit; for if the circle must be extended to include ancestors, descendants, and friends' friends, it will go on indefinitely. Leaving this point, however, for future investigation, we call the self-sufficient that which, taken even by itself, makes life desirable and wanting nothing at all; and this is what we mean by happiness.

Again, we think happiness the most desirable of all things, and that not merely as one good thing among others. If it were only that, the addition of the smallest more good would increase its desirableness; for the addition would make an increase of goods, and the greater of two goods is always the more desirable. Happiness is something final and self-sufficient and the end of all action.

Chapter 6

Perhaps, however, it seems a commonplace to say that happiness is the supreme good; what is wanted is to define its nature a little more clearly. The best way of arriving at such a definition will probably be to ascertain the function of man. For, as with a flute player, a sculptor, or any artist, or in fact anybody who has a special function or activity, his goodness and excellence seem to lie in his function, so it would seem to be with man, if indeed he has a special function. Can it be said that, while a carpenter and a cobbler have special functions and activities, man, unlike them, is naturally functionless? Or, as the eye, the hand, the foot, and similarly each part of the body has a special function, so may man be regarded as having a special function apart from all these? What, then, can this function be? It is not life; for life is apparently something that man shares with plants; and we are looking for something peculiar to him. We must exclude therefore the life of nutrition and growth. There is next what may be called the life of sensation. But this too, apparently, is shared by man with horses, cattle, and all other animals. There remains what I may call the active life of the rational part of man's being. Now this rational part is twofold; one part is rational in the sense of being obedient to reason, and the other in the sense of possessing and exercising reason and intelligence. The active life too may be conceived of in two ways, either as a state of character, or as an activity; but we mean by it the life of activity, as this seems to be the truer form of the conception.

The function of man then is activity of soul in accordance with reason, or not apart from reason. Now, the function of a man of a certain kind, and of a man who is good of that kind—for example, of a harpist and a good harpist—are in our view the same in kind. This is true of all people of all kinds without exception, the superior excellence being only an addition to the function; for it is the function of a harpist to play the harp, and of a good harpist to play the harp well. This being so, if we define the function of man as a kind of life, and this life as an activity of the soul or a course of action in accordance with reason, and if the function of a good man is such activity of a good and noble kind, and if everything is well done when it is done in accordance with its proper excellence, it follows that the good of man is activity of soul in accordance with virtue, or, if there are more virtues than one, in accordance with the best and most complete virtue. But we must add the words "in a complete life." For as one swallow or one day does not make a spring, so one day or a short time does not make a man blessed or happy. . . .

Inasmuch as happiness is an activity of soul in accordance with perfect virtue, we must now consider virtue, as this will perhaps be the best way of studying happiness. . . . Clearly it is human virtue we have to consider; for the good of which we are in search is, as we said, human good, and the happiness, human happiness. By human virtue or excellence we mean not that of the body, but that of the soul, and by happiness we mean an activity of the soul. . . .

BOOK II

Moral virtues can best be acquired by practice and habit. They imply a right attitude toward pleasures and pains. A good man deliberately chooses to do what is noble and right for its own sake. What is right in matters of moral conduct is usually a mean between two extremes.

Chapter 1

Virtue then is twofold, partly intellectual and partly moral, and intellectual virtue is originated and fostered mainly by teaching; it demands therefore experience and time. Moral virtue on the other hand is the outcome of habit, and accordingly its name, *ethike,* is derived by a slight variation from *ethos,* habit. From this fact it is clear that moral virtue is not implanted in us by nature; for nothing that exists by nature can be transformed by habit. Thus a stone, that naturally tends to fall downwards, cannot be habituated or trained to rise upwards, even if we tried to train it by throwing it up ten thousand times. Nor again can fire be trained to sink downwards, nor anything else that follows one natural law be habituated or trained to follow another. It is neither by nature then nor in defiance of nature that virtues grow in us. Nature gives us the capacity to receive them, and that capacity is perfected by habit.

Again, if we take the various natural powers which belong to us, we first possess the proper faculties and afterwards display the activities. It is obviously so with the senses. Not by seeing frequently or hearing frequently do we acquire the sense of seeing or hearing; on the contrary, because we have the senses we make use of them; we do not get them by making use of them. But the virtues we get by first practicing them, as we do in the arts. For it is by doing what we ought to do when we study the arts that we learn the arts themselves; we become builders by building and harpists by playing the harp. Similarly, it is by doing just acts that we become just, by doing temperate acts that we become temperate, by doing brave acts that we become brave. The experience of states confirms this statement, for it is by training in good habits that lawmakers make the citizens good. This is the object all lawmakers have at heart; if they do not succeed in it, they fail of their purpose; and it makes the distinction between a good constitution and a bad one.

Again, the causes and means by which any virtue is produced and destroyed are the same; and equally so in any part. For it is by playing the harp that both good and bad harpists are produced; and the case of builders and others is similar, for it is by building well that they become good builders and by building badly that they become bad builders. If it were not so, there would be no need of anybody to teach them; they would all be born good or bad in their several crafts. The case of the virtues is the same. It is by our actions in dealings between man and man that we become either just or unjust. It is by our actions in the face of danger and by our training ourselves to fear or to courage that we become either cowardly or courageous. It is much the same with our appetites and angry passions. People become temperate and gentle, others licentious and passionate, by behaving in one

or the other way in particular circumstances. In a word, moral states are the results of activities like the states themselves. It is our duty therefore to keep a certain character in our activities, since our moral states depend on the differences in our activities. So the difference between one and another training in habits in our childhood is not a light matter, but important, or rather, all-important.

Chapter 2

Our present study is not, like other studies, purely theoretical in intention; for the object of our inquiry is not to know what virtue is but how to become good, and that is the sole benefit of it. We must, therefore, consider the right way of performing actions, for it is acts, as we have said, that determine the character of the resulting moral states.

That we should act in accordance with right reason is a common general principle, which may here be taken for granted. The nature of right reason, and its relation to the virtues generally, will be discussed later. But first of all it must be admitted that all reasoning on matters of conduct must be like a sketch in outline; it cannot be scientifically exact. We began by laying down the principle that the kind of reasoning demanded in any subject must be such as the subject matter itself allows; and questions of conduct and expediency no more admit of hard and fast rules than questions of health.

If this is true of general reasoning on ethics, still more true is it that scientific exactitude is impossible in treating of particular ethical cases. They do not fall under any art or law, but the actors themselves have always to take account of circumstances, as much as in medicine or navigation. Still, although such is the nature of our present argument, we must try to make the best of it.

The first point to be observed is that in the matters we are now considering deficiency and excess are both fatal. It is so, we see, in questions of health and strength. (We must judge of what we cannot see by the evidence of what we do see.) Too much or too little gymnastic exercise is fatal to strength. Similarly, too much or too little meat and drink is fatal to health, whereas a suitable amount produces, increases, and sustains it. It is the same with temperance, courage, and other moral virtues. A person who avoids and is afraid of everything and faces nothing becomes a coward; a person who is not afraid of anything but is ready to face everything becomes foolhardy. Similarly, he who enjoys every pleasure and abstains from none is licentious; he who refuses all pleasures, like a boor, is an insensible sort of person. For temperance and courage are destroyed by excess and deficiency but preserved by the mean.

Again, not only are the causes and agencies of production, increase, and destruction in moral states the same, but the field of their activity is the same also. It is so in other more obvious instances, as, for example, strength; for strength is produced by taking a great deal of food and undergoing a great deal of exertion, and it is the strong man who is able to take most food and undergo most exertion. So too with the virtues. By abstaining from pleasures we become temperate, and, when we have become temperate, we are best able to abstain from them. So again with courage; it is by training ourselves to despise and face terrifying things that we become brave, and when we have become brave, we shall be best able to face them.

The pleasure or pain which accompanies actions may be regarded as a test of a person's moral state. He who abstains from physical pleasures and feels pleasure in so doing is temperate; but he who feels pain at so doing is licentious. He who faces dangers with pleasure, or at least without pain, is brave; but he who feels pain at facing them is a coward. For moral virtue is concerned with pleasures and pains. It is pleasure which makes us do what is base, and pain which makes us abstain from doing what is noble. Hence the importance of having a certain training from very early days, as Plato says, so that we may feel pleasure and pain at the right objects; for this is true education. . . .

Chapter 3

But we may be asked what we mean by saying that people must become just by doing what is just and temperate by doing what is temperate. For, it will be said, if they do what is just and temperate they are already just and temperate themselves, in the same way as, if they practice grammar and music, they are grammarians and musicians.

But is this true even in the case of the arts? For a person may speak grammatically either by chance or at the suggestion of somebody else; hence he will not be a grammarian unless he not only speaks grammatically but does so in a grammatical manner, that is, because of the grammatical knowledge which he possesses.

There is a point of difference too between the arts and the virtues. The productions of art have their excellence in themselves. It is enough then that, when they are produced, they themselves should possess a certain character. But acts in accordance with virtue are not justly or temperately performed simply because they are in themselves just or temperate. The doer at the time of performing them must satisfy certain conditions; in the first place, he must know what he is doing; secondly, he must deliberately choose to do it and do it for his own sake; and thirdly, he must do it as part of his own firm and immutable character. If it be a question of art, these conditions, except only the condition of knowledge, are not raised; but if it be a question of virtue, mere knowledge is of little or no avail; it is the other conditions, which are the results of frequently performing just and temperate acts, that are not slightly but all-important. Accordingly, deeds are called just and temperate when they are such as a just and temperate person would do; and a just and temperate person is not merely one who does these deeds but one who does them in the spirit of the just and the temperate.

It may fairly be said that a just man becomes just by doing what is just, and a temperate man becomes temperate by doing what is temperate, and if a man did not so act, he would not have much chance of becoming good. But most people, instead of acting, take refuge in theorizing; they imagine that they are philosophers and that philosophy will make them virtuous; in fact, they behave like people who listen attentively to their doctors but never do anything that their doctors tell them. But a healthy state of the soul will no more be produced by this kind of philosophizing than a healthy state of the body by this kind of medical treatment.

Chapter 4

We have next to consider the nature of virtue. Now, as the properties of the soul are three, namely, emotions, faculties, and moral states, it follows that virtue must be one of the three. By emotions I mean desire, anger, fear, pride, envy, joy, love, hatred, regret, ambition, pity—in a word, whatever feeling is attended by pleasure or pain. I call those faculties through which we are said to be capable of experiencing these emotions, for instance, capable of getting angry or being pained or feeling pity. And I call those moral states through which we are well or ill disposed in our emotions, ill disposed, for instance, in anger, if our anger be too violent or too feeble, and well disposed, if it be rightly moderate; and similarly in our other emotions.

Now neither the virtues nor the vices are emotions; for we are not called good or bad for our emotions but for our virtues or vices. We are not praised or blamed simply for being angry, but only for being angry in a certain way; but we are praised or blamed for our virtues or vices. Again, whereas we are angry or afraid without deliberate purpose, the virtues are matters of deliberate purpose, or require deliberate purpose. Moreover, we are said to be moved by our emotions, but by our virtues or vices we are not said to be moved but to have a certain disposition.

For these reasons the virtues are not faculties. For we are not called either good or bad, nor are we praised or blamed for having simple capacity for emotion. Also while Nature gives us our faculties, it is not Nature that makes us good or bad; but this point we have already discussed. If then the virtues are neither emotions nor faculties, all that remains is that they must be moral states.

Chapter 5

The nature of virtue has been now described in kind. But it is not enough to say merely that virtue is a moral state; we must also describe the character of that moral state.

We may assert then that every virtue or excellence puts into good condition that of which it is a virtue or excellence, and enables it to perform its work well. Thus excellence in the eye makes the eye good and its function good, for by excellence in the eye we see well. Similarly, excellence of the horse makes a horse excellent himself and good at racing, at carrying its rider and at facing the enemy. If then this rule is universally true, the virtue or excellence of a man will be such a moral state as makes a man good and able to perform his proper function well. How this will be the case we have already explained, but another way of making it clear will be to study the nature or character of virtue.

Now of everything, whether it be continuous or divisible, it is possible to take a greater, a smaller, or an equal amount, and this either in terms of the thing itself or in relation to ourselves, the equal being a mean between too much and too little. By the mean in terms of the thing itself, I understand that which is equally distinct from both its extremes, which is one and the same for every man. By the mean relatively to ourselves, I understand that which is neither too much nor too little for us; but this is not one nor the same for everybody. Thus if 10 be too much and 2 too little, we take 6 as a mean in terms of the thing itself; for 6 is as much greater than 2 as it is less than 10, and this is a mean in arithmetical proportion. But the mean considered relatively to ourselves may not be ascertained in that way. It does not follow that if 10 pounds of meat is too much and 2 too little for a man to eat, the trainer will order him 6 pounds, since this also may be too much or too little for him who is to take it; it will be too little, for example, for Milo but too much for a beginner in gymnastics. The same with running and wrestling; the right amount will vary with the individual. This being so, the skillful in any art avoids alike excess and deficiency; he seeks and chooses the mean, not the absolute mean, but the mean considered relatively to himself.

Every art then does its work well, if it regards the mean and judges the works it produces by the mean. For this reason we often say of successful works of art that it is impossible to take anything from them or to add anything to them, which implies that excess or deficiency is fatal to excellence but that the mean state ensures it. Good artists too, as we say, have an eye to the mean in their works. Now virtue, like Nature herself, is more accurate and better than any art; virtue, therefore, will aim at the mean. I speak of moral virtue, since it is moral virtue which is concerned with emotions and actions, and it is in these we have excess and deficiency and the mean. Thus it is possible to go too far, or not far enough in fear, pride, desire, anger, pity, and pleasure and pain generally, and the excess and the deficiency are alike wrong; but to feel these emotions at the right times, for the right objects, towards the right persons, for the right motives, and in the right manner, is the mean or the best good, which signifies virtue. Similarly, there may be excess, deficiency, or the mean, in acts. Virtue is concerned with both emotions and actions, wherein excess is an error and deficiency a fault, while the mean is successful and praised, and success and praise are both characteristics of virtue.

It appears then that virtue is a kind of mean because it aims at the mean.

On the other hand, there are many different ways of going wrong; for evil is in its nature infinite, to use the Pythagorean phrase, but good is finite and there is only one possible way of going right. So the former is easy and the latter is difficult; it is easy to miss the mark but difficult to hit it. And so by our reasoning excess and deficiency are characteristics of vice and the mean is a characteristic of virtue.

For good is simple, evil manifold.

Chapter 6

Virtue then is a state of deliberate moral purpose, consisting in a mean relative to ourselves, the mean being determined by reason, or as a prudent man would determine it. It is a mean, firstly, as lying between two vices, the vice of excess on the one hand, the vice of deficiency on the other, and, secondly, because, whereas the vices either fall short of or go beyond what is right in emotion and action, virtue discovers and chooses the mean. Accordingly, virtue, if regarded in its essence or theoretical definition, is a mean, though, if regarded from the point of view of what is best and most excellent, it is an extreme.

But not every action or every emotion admits of a mean. There are some whose very name implies wickedness, as, for example, malice, shamelessness,

and envy among the emotions, and adultery, theft, and murder among the actions. All these and others like them are marked as intrinsically wicked, not merely the excesses or deficiencies of them. It is never possible then to be right in them; they are always sinful. Right or wrong in such acts as adultery does not depend on our committing it with the right woman, at the right time, or in the right manner; on the contrary, it is wrong to do it at all. It would be equally false to suppose that there can be a mean or an excess or deficiency in unjust, cowardly or licentious conduct; for, if that were so, it would be a mean of excess and deficiency, an excess of excess and a deficiency of deficiency. But as in temperance and courage there can be no excess or deficiency, because the mean there is in a sense an extreme, so too in these other cases there cannot be a mean or an excess or a deficiency, but however the acts are done, they are wrong. For in general an excess or deficiency does not have a mean, nor a mean an excess or deficiency. . . .

Chapter 8

There are then three dispositions, two being vices, namely, excess and deficiency, and one virtue, which is the mean between them; and they are all in a sense mutually opposed. The extremes are opposed both to the mean and to each other, and the mean is opposed to the extremes. For as the equal if compared with the less is greater, but if compared with the greater is less, so the mean state, whether in emotion or action, if compared with deficiency is excessive, but if compared with excess is deficient. Thus the brave man appears foolhardy compared with the coward, but cowardly compared with the foolhardy. Similarly, the temperate man appears licentious compared with the insensible man but insensible compared with the licentious; and the liberal man appears extravagant compared with the stingy man but stingy compared with the spendthrift. The result is that the extremes each denounce the mean as belonging to the other extreme; the coward calls the brave man foolhardy, and the foolhardy man calls him cowardly; and so on in other cases.

But while there is mutual opposition between the extremes and the mean, there is greater opposition between the two extremes than between extreme and the mean; for they are further removed from each other than from the mean, as the great is further from the small and the small from the great than either from the equal. Again, while some extremes show some likeness to the mean, as foolhardiness to courage and extravagance to liberality, there is the greatest possible dissimilarity between extremes. But things furthest removed from each other are called opposites; hence the further things are removed, the greater is the opposition between them.

In some cases it is deficiency and in others excess which is more opposed to the mean. Thus it is not foolhardiness, an excess, but cowardice, a deficiency, which is more opposed to courage, nor is it insensibility, a deficiency, but licentiousness, an excess, which is more opposed to temperance. There are two reasons why this should be so. One lies in the nature of the matter itself; for when one of two extremes is nearer and more like the mean, it is not this extreme but its opposite that we chiefly contrast with the mean. For instance, as foolhardiness seems more like and nearer to courage than cowardice, it is cowardice that we chiefly contrast with courage; for things further removed from the mean seem to be more opposite to it. This reason lies in the nature of the matter itself; there is a second which lies in our own nature. The things to which we ourselves are naturally more inclined we think more opposed to the mean. Thus we are ourselves naturally more inclined to pleasures than to their opposites, and are more prone therefore to self-indulgence than to moderation. Accordingly we speak of those things in which we are more likely to run to great lengths as more opposed to the mean. Hence licentiousness, which is an excess, seems more opposed to temperance than insensibility.

Chapter 9

We have now sufficiently shown that moral virtue is a mean, and in what sense it is so; that it is a mean as lying between two vices, a vice of excess on the one side and a vice of deficiency on the other, and as aiming at the mean in emotion and action.

That is why it is so hard to be good; for it is always hard to find the mean in anything; it is not everyone but only a man of science who can find the mean or center of a circle. So too anybody can get angry—that is easy—and anybody can give or spend money, but to give it to the right person, to give the right amount of it, at the right time, for the right cause and in the right way, this is not what anybody can do, nor is it easy. That is why goodness is rare and praise worthy and noble. One then who aims at a mean must begin by departing from the extreme that is more contrary to the mean; he must act in the spirit of Calypso's advice,

Far from this spray and swell hold thou thy ship,

for of the two extremes one is more wrong than the other. As it is difficult to hit the mean exactly, we should take the second best course, as the saying is, and choose the lesser of two evils. This we shall best do in the way described, that is, steering clear of the evil which is further from the mean. We must also note the weaknesses to which we are ourselves particularly prone, since different natures tend in different ways; and we may ascertain what our tendency is by observing our feelings of pleasure and pain. Then we must drag ourselves away towards the opposite extreme; for by pulling ourselves as far as possible from what is wrong we shall arrive at the mean, as we do when we pull a crooked stick straight.

In all cases we must especially be on our guard against the pleasant, or pleasure, for we are not impartial judges of pleasure. Hence our attitude towards pleasure must be like that of the elders of the people in the *Iliad* towards Helen, and we must constantly apply the words they use; for if we dismiss pleasure as they dismissed Helen, we shall be less likely to go wrong. By action of this kind, to put it summarily, we shall best succeed in hitting the mean.

Undoubtedly this is a difficult task, especially in individual cases. It is not easy to determine the right manner, objects, occasion and duration of anger. Sometimes we praise people who are deficient in anger, and call them gentle, and at other times we praise people who exhibit a fierce temper as high spirited. It is not however a man who deviates a little from goodness, but one who deviates a great deal, whether on the side of excess or of deficiency, that is blamed; for he is sure to call attention to himself. It is not easy to decide in theory how far and to what extent a man may go before he becomes blameworthy, but neither is it easy to define in theory anything else in the region of the senses; such things depend on circumstances, and our judgment of them depends on our perception.

So much then is plain, that the mean is everywhere praiseworthy, but that we ought to aim at one time towards an excess and at another towards a deficiency; for thus we shall most easily hit the mean, or in other words reach excellence.

NOTES

1. Plato.
2. A half-legendary ruler whose name to the Greeks stood for extreme mental luxury and extravagance.

FOR FURTHER REFLECTION

1. Is Aristotle's concept of happiness clear? Is it a subjective or an objective notion? That is, is it subjective, in the mind of the beholder, so you are just as happy as you feel yourself to be; or is it objective, defined by a state of being, and having certain characteristics regardless of how you feel? According to Aristotle, could a criminal be happy?

2. Is Aristotle's ethics sufficiently action guiding? Does it help you make decisions? If you ask what you should do in Situation X, Aristotle would seem to say, "Do what the virtuous person would do." But if you ask how you are to recognize such a person, he would seem to say, "The virtuous person is one who acts justly." Is there something circular about this reasoning? Does virtue ethics need supplementation from other ethical systems, or can it solve this problem? Explain.

THOMAS HOBBES

THE SOCIAL CONTRACT

Thomas Hobbes (1588–1679), one of the greatest English political philosophers, gave classic expression to the idea that morality and politics arise out of a social contract. He was born in the year of the Spanish Armada, was educated at Oxford University, and lived through an era of political revolutions as a scholar and tutor (he was tutor to Prince Charles, later King Charles II, of England). He was widely traveled and was in communication with most of the intellectual luminaries of his day, both on the continent (Galileo, Gassendi, and Descartes) and in England (Francis Bacon, Ben Jonson, and William Harvey), and was regarded as a brilliant, if somewhat unorthodox and controversial, intellectual.

Hobbes is known today primarily for his masterpiece in political theory, *Leviathan* (1651), a book that was suppressed in his own day for its controversial ideas. In this book, from which our selection is taken, he develops a moral and political theory based on psychological egoism. Hobbes argues that people are all egoists who always act in their own self-interest, to obtain gratification and avoid harm. However, we cannot obtain any of the basic goods because of the inherent fear and insecurity in an unregulated "state of nature," in which life is "solitary, poor, nasty, brutish, and short." We cannot relax our guard, for everyone is constantly in fear of everyone else. In this state of anarchy the prudent person concludes that it really is in everyone's self-interest to make a contract to keep to a minimal morality of respecting human life, keeping covenants made, and obeying the society's laws. This minimal morality, which Hobbes refers to as "the laws of nature," is nothing more than a set of maxims of prudence. To ensure that we all obey this covenant Hobbes proposes a strong sovereign or "Leviathan" to impose severe penalties on those who disobey the laws, for "covenants without the sword are but words."

OF THE NATURAL CONDITION OF MANKIND AS CONCERNING THEIR FELICITY, AND MISERY

Nature hath made men so equal, in the faculties of the body, and mind; as that though there be found one man sometimes manifestly stronger in body, or of quicker mind than another; yet when all is reckoned together, the difference between man, and man, is not so considerable, as that one man can thereupon claim to himself any benefit, to which another may not pretend, as well as he. For as to the strength of body, the weakest has strength enough to kill the strongest, either by secret machination, or by confederacy with others, that are in the same danger with himself.

And as to the faculties of the mind, setting aside the arts grounded upon words, and especially that

From Thomas Hobbes, *Leviathan* (1651).

skill of proceeding upon general, and infallible rules, called science; which very few have, and but in few things; as being not a native faculty, born with us; nor attained, as prudence, while we look after somewhat else, I find yet a greater equality amongst men, than that of strength. For prudence, is but experience; which equal time, equally bestows on all men, in those things they equally apply themselves unto. That which may perhaps make such equality incredible, is but a vain conceit of one's own wisdom, which almost all men think they have in a greater degree, than the vulgar; that is, than all men but themselves, and a few others, whom by fame, or for concurring with themselves, they approve. For such is the nature of men, that howsoever they may acknowledge many others to be more witty, or more eloquent, or more learned; yet they will hardly believe there be many so wise as themselves; for they see their own wit at hand, and other men's at a distance. But this proveth rather that men are in that point equal, than unequal. For there is not ordinarily a greater sign of the equal distribution of any thing, than that every man is contented with his share.

From this equality of ability, ariseth equality of hope in the attaining of our ends. And therefore if any two men desire the same thing, which nevertheless they cannot both enjoy, they become enemies; and in the way to their end, which is principally their own conservation, and sometimes their delectation only, endeavour to destroy, or subdue one another. And from hence it comes to pass, that where an invader hath no more to fear, than another man's single power; if one plant, sow, build, or possess a convenient seat, others may probably be expected to come prepared with forces united, to dispossess, and deprive him, not only of the fruit of his labour, but also of his life, or liberty. And the invader again is in the like danger of another.

And from this diffidence of one another, there is no way for any man to secure himself, so reasonable, as anticipation; that is, by force, or wiles, to master the persons of all men he can, so long, till he see no other power great enough to endanger him: and this is no more than his own conservation requireth, and is generally allowed. Also because there be some, that taking pleasure in contemplating their own power in the acts of conquest, which they pursue farther than their security requires; if others, that otherwise would be glad to be at ease within modest bounds, should not by invasion increase their power, they would not be able, long time, by standing only on their defence, to subsist. And by consequence, such augmentation of dominion over men being necessary to a man's conservation, it ought to be allowed him.

Again, men have no pleasure, but on the contrary a great deal of grief, in keeping company, where there is no power able to over-awe them all. For every man looketh that his companion should value him, at the same rate he sets upon himself: and upon all signs of contempt, or undervaluing, naturally endeavours, as far as he dares, (which amongst them that have no common power to keep them in quiet, is far enough to make them destroy each other), to extort a greater value from his contemners, by damage; and from others, by the example.

So that in the nature of man, we find three principle causes of quarrel. First, competition; secondly, diffidence; thirdly, glory.

The first, maketh men invade for gain; the second, for safety; and the third, for reputation. The first use violence, to make themselves masters of other men's persons, wives, children, and cattle; the second, defend them; the third, for trifles, as a word, a smile, a different option, and any other sign of undervalue, either direct in their persons, or by reflection in their kindred, their friends, their nation, their profession, or their name.

Hereby it is manifest, that during the time men live without a common power to keep them all in awe, they are in that condition which is called war; and such a war, as is of every man, against every man. For war, consisteth not in battle only, or the act of fighting; but in a tract of time, wherein the will to contend by battle is sufficiently known: and therefore the notion of *time,* is to be considered in the nature of war; as it is in the nature of weather. For as the nature of foul weather, lieth not in the shower or two of rain; but in an inclination thereto of many days together: so the nature of war, consisteth not in actual fighting; but in the known disposition thereto, during all the time there is no assurance to the contrary. All other time is PEACE.

Whatsoever therefore is consequent to a time of war, where every man is enemy to every man; the same is consequent to the time, wherein men live without other security, than what their own strength, and their own invention shall furnish them withal. In such condition, there is no place for industry; because the fruit thereof is uncertain: and consequently no culture of the earth; no navigation, nor use of the commodities that may be imported by sea; no commodious building; no instruments of moving, and removing, such things as require much force; no knowledge of the face of the earth; no account of time; no arts; no letters; no society; and which is worst of all, continual fear, and danger of violent death; and the life of man, solitary, poor, nasty, brutish, and short.

It may seem strange to some man, that has not well weighed these things; that nature should thus dissociate, and render men apt to invade, and destroy one another: and he may therefore, not trusting to this inference, made from the passions, desire perhaps to have the same confirmed by experience. Let him therefore consider with himself, when taking a journey, he arms himself, and seeks to go well accompanied; when going to sleep, he locks his doors; when even in his house he locks his chests; and this when he knows there be laws, and public officers, armed, to revenge all injuries shall be done him; what opinion he has of his fellow-subjects, when he rides armed; of his fellow citizens, when he locks his doors; and of his children, and servants, when he locks his chests. Does he not there as much accuse mankind by his actions, as I do by my words? But neither of us accuse man's nature in it. The desires, and other passions of man, are in themselves no sin. No more are the actions, that proceed from those passions, till they know a law that forbids them: which till laws be made they cannot know: nor can any law be made, till they have agreed upon the person that shall make it.

It may peradventure be thought, there was never such a time, nor condition of war as this; and I believe it was never generally so, over all the world: but there are many places, where they live so now. For the savage people in many places of America, except the government of small families, the concord whereof dependeth on natural lust, have no government at all;

and live at this day in that brutish manner, as I said before. Howsoever, it may be perceived what manner of life there would be, where there were no common power to fear, by the manner of life, which men that have formerly lived under a peaceful government, use to degenerate into, in a civil war.

But though there had never been any time, wherein particular men were in a condition of war one against another; yet in all times, kings, and persons of sovereign authority, because of their independency, are in continual jealousies, and in the state and posture of gladiators; having their weapons pointing, and their eyes fixed on one another; that is, their forts, garrisons, and guns upon the frontiers of their kingdoms; and continual spies upon their neighbours; which is a posture of war. But because they uphold thereby, the industry of their subjects; there does not follow from it, that misery, which accompanies the liberty of particular men.

To this war of every man, against every man, this also is consequent; that nothing can be unjust. The notions of right and wrong, justice and injustice have there no place. Where there is no common power, there is no law: where no law, no injustice. Force, and fraud, are in war the two cardinal virtues. Justice, and injustice are none of the faculties neither of the body, nor mind. If they were, they might be in a man that were alone in the world, as well as his senses, and passions. They are qualities, that relate to men in society, not in solitude. It is consequent also to the same condition, that there be no propriety, no dominion, no *mine* and *thine* distinct; but only that to be every man's, that he can get; and for so long, as he can keep it. And thus much for the ill condition, which man by mere nature is actually placed in; though with a possibility to come out of it, consisting partly in the passions, partly in his reason.

The passions that incline men to peace, are fear of death; desire of such things as are necessary to commodious living; and a hope by their industry to obtain them. And reason suggesteth convenient articles of peace, upon which men may be drawn to agreement. These articles, are they, which otherwise are called the Laws of Nature: whereof I shall speak more particularly, in the two following chapters.

OF THE FIRST AND SECOND NATURAL LAWS, AND OF CONTRACTS

The right of nature, which writers commonly call *jus naturale,* is the liberty each man hath, to use his own power, as he will himself, for the preservation of his own nature; that is to say, of his own life; and consequently, of doing any thing, which in his own judgment, and reason, he shall conceive to be the aptest means thereunto.

By LIBERTY, is understood, according to the proper signification of the word, the absence of external impediments: which impediments, may oft take away part of a man's power to do what he would; but cannot hinder him from using the power left him, according as his judgment, and reason shall dictate to him.

A LAW OF NATURE, *lex naturalis,* is a precept or general rule, found out by reason, by which a man is forbidden to do that, which is destructive of his life, or taketh away the means of preserving the same; and to omit that, by which he thinketh it may be best preserved. For though they that speak of this subject, use to confound *jus,* and *lex, right* and *law:* yet they ought to be distinguished; because RIGHT, consisteth in liberty to do, or to forbear; whereas LAW, determineth, and bindeth to one of them: so that law, and right, differ as much, as obligation, and liberty; which in one and the same matter are inconsistent.

And because the condition of man, as hath been declared in the precedent chapter, is a condition of war of every one against every one; in which case every one is governed by his own reason; and there is nothing he can make use of, that may not be a help unto him, in preserving his life against his enemies; it followeth, that in such a condition, every man has a right to every thing; even to one another's body. And therefore, as long as this natural right of every man to every thing endureth, there can be no security to any man, how strong or wise soever he be, of living out the time, which nature ordinarily alloweth men to live. And consequently it is a precept, or general rule of reason, *that every man, ought to endeavour peace, as far as he has hope of obtaining it; and when be cannot obtain it, that he may seek, and use, all helps, and advantages of war.* The first branch of which rule, containeth the first, and fundamental law of nature; which is, *to seek peace, and follow it.* The second, the sum of the right of nature; which is, *by all means we can, to defend ourselves.*

From this fundamental law of nature, by which men are commanded to endeavour peace, is derived this second law; *that a man be willing, when others are so too, as far-forth, as for peace, and defence of himself he shall think it necessary, to lay down this right to all things; and be contented with so much liberty against other men, as he would allow other men against himself.* For as long as every man holdeth this right, of doing any thing he liketh; so long are all men in the condition of war. But if other men will not lay down their right, as well as he; then there is no reason for any one, to divest himself of his: for that were to expose himself to prey, which no man is bound to, rather than to dispose himself to peace. This is that law of the Gospel; *whatsoever you require that others should do to you, that do ye to them.* And that law of all men, *quod tibi fieri non vis, alteri ne feceris.* ["What you do not want done to you, do not do to others."—Ed.].

To *lay down* a man's *right* to any thing, *divest* himself of the *liberty,* of hindering another of the benefit of his own right to the same. For he that renounceth, or passeth away his right, giveth not to any other man a right which he had not before; because there is nothing to which every man had not right by nature: but only standeth out of his way, that he may enjoy his own original right, without hindrance from him; not without hindrance from another. So that the effect which redoundeth to one man, by another man's defect of right, is but so much diminution of impediments to the use of his own right original.

Right is laid aside, either by simply renouncing it; or by transferring it to another. By *simply* RENOUNCING; when he cares not to whom the benefit thereof redoundeth. By TRANSFERRING; when he intendeth the benefit thereof to some certain person, or persons. And when a man hath in either manner abandoned, or granted away his right; then is he said to be OBLIGED, or BOUND, not to hinder those, to whom such right is granted, or abandoned, from the benefit of it: and that he *ought,* and it is his DUTY, not to make void that voluntary act of his own: and that such hindrance is INJUSTICE, and INJURY, as being *sine jure* [that is, without right.—Ed.], the right being before renounced, or transferred. So that *injury,* or *injustice,* in the controversies of the world, is somewhat like to that, which in the disputations of scholars is called *absurdity.* For as it is there called an absurdity, to contradict what one maintained in the beginning: so in the world, it is called injustice, and injury, voluntarily to undo that, which from the beginning he had voluntarily done. The way by which a man either simply renounceth, or transferreth his right, is a declaration, or signification, by some voluntary and sufficient sign, or signs, that he doth so renounce, or transfer; or hath so renounced, or transferred the same, to him that accepteth it. And these signs are either words only, or actions only; or, as it happeneth most often, both words, and actions. And the same are the BONDS, by which men are bound, and obliged: bonds, that have their strength, not from their own nature, for nothing is more easily broken than a man's word, but from fear of some evil consequence upon the rupture.

Whensoever a man transferreth his right, or renounceth it; it is either in consideration of some right reciprocally transferred to himself; or for some other good he hopeth for thereby. For it is a voluntary act: and of the voluntary acts of every man, the object is some *good to himself.* And therefore there be some rights, which no man can be understood by any words, or other signs, to have abandoned, or transferred. At first a man cannot lay down the right of resisting them, that assault him by force, to take away his life; because he cannot be understood to aim thereby, at any good to himself. The same may be said of wounds, and chains, and imprisonment; both because there is no benefit consequent to such patience; as there is to the patience of suffering another to be wounded, or imprisoned: as also because a man cannot tell, when he seeth men proceed against him by violence, whether they intend his death or not. And lastly the motive, and end for which this renouncing, and transferring of right is introduced, is nothing else but the security of a man's person, in his life, and in the means of so preserving life, as not to be weary of it. And therefore if a man by words, or other signs, seem

to despoil himself of the end, for which those signs were intended; he is not to be understood as if he meant it, or that it was his will; but that he was ignorant of how such words and actions were to be interpreted.

The mutual transferring of right, is that which men call CONTRACT.

There is a difference between transferring of right to the thing; and transferring, or tradition, that is delivery of the thing itself. For the thing may be delivered together with the translation of the right; as in buying and selling with ready-money; or exchange of goods, or lands: and it may be delivered some time after.

Again, one of the contractors, may deliver the thing contracted for on his part, and leave the other to perform his part at some determinate time after, and in the mean time be trusted; and then the contract on his part, is called PACT, or COVENANT: or both parts may contract now, to perform hereafter: in which cases, he that is to perform in time to come, being trusted, his performance is called *keeping of promise,* or faith; and the failing of performance, if it be voluntary, *violation of faith.*

When the transferring of right, is not mutual: but one of the parties transferreth, in hope to gain thereby friendship, or service from another, or from his friends; or in hope to gain the reputation of charity, or magnanimity; or to deliver his mind from the pain of compassion; or in hope of reward in heaven, this is not contract, but GIFT, FREE-GIFT, GRACE: which words signify one and the same thing.

Signs of contract, are either *express,* or *by inference.* Express, are words spoken with understanding of what they signify: and such words are either of the time *present,* or *past;* as, *I give, I grant, I have given, I have granted, I will that this be yours:* or of the future; as, *I will give, I will grant:* which words of the future are called PROMISE.

If a covenant be made, wherein neither of the parties perform presently, but trust one another; in the condition of mere nature, which is a condition of war of every man against every man, upon any reasonable suspicion, it is void: but if there be a common power set over them both, with right and force sufficient to compel performance, it is not void. For he that performeth first, has no assurance the other will perform after; because the bonds of words are too weak to bridle men's ambition, avarice, anger, and other passions, without the fear of some coercive power; which in the condition of mere nature, where all men are equal, and judges of the justness of their own fears, cannot possibly be supposed. And therefore he which performeth first, does but betray himself to his enemy; contrary to the right, he can never abandon, of defending his life, and means of living.

But in a civil estate, where there is a power set up to constrain those that would otherwise violate their faith, that fear is no more reasonable: and for that cause, he which by the covenant is to perform first, is obliged so to do.

The cause of fear, which maketh such a covenant invalid, must be always something arising after the covenant made; as some new fact, or other sign of the will not to perform: else it cannot make the covenant void. For that which could not hinder a man from promising, ought not to be admitted as a hindrance of performing.

OF OTHER LAWS OF NATURE

From that law of nature, by which we are obliged to transfer to another, such rights, as being retained, hinder the peace of mankind, there followeth a third; which is this, *that men perform their covenants made:* without which, covenants are in vain, and but empty words; and the right of all men to all things remaining, we are still in the condition of war.

And in this law of nature, consisteth the fountain and origin of JUSTICE. For where no covenant hath preceded, there hath no right been transferred, and every man has right to every thing; and consequently, no action can be unjust. But when a covenant is made, then to break it is *unjust:* and the definition of INJUSTICE, is no other than *the not performance of covenant.* And whatsoever is not unjust, is *just.*

But because covenants of mutual trust, where there is a fear of no performance on either part, as hath been said in the former chapter, are invalid; though the origin of justice be the making of covenants; yet injustice actually there can be none, till the cause of such fear be taken away; which while men are in the nat-ural condition of war, cannot be done. Therefore before the names of just, and unjust can have place, there must be some coercive power, to compel men equally to the performance of their covenants, by the terror of some punishment, greater than the benefit they expect by the breach of their covenant; and to make good that propriety, which by mutual contract men acquire, in recompense of the universal right they abandon: and such power there is none before the erection of a commonwealth. And this is also to be gathered out of the ordinary definition of justice in the Schools: for they say, that *justice is the constant will of giving to every man his own,* and therefore where there is no *own,* that is, no propriety, there is no injustice; and where there is no coercive power erected, that is, where there is no commonwealth, there is no propriety; all men having right to all things: therefore where there is no commonwealth, there nothing is unjust. So that the nature of justice, consisteth in keeping of valid covenants: but the validity of covenants begins not but with the constitution of a civil power, sufficient to compel men to keep them: and then it is also that propriety begins. . . .

And because, though men be never so willing to observe these laws, there may nevertheless arise questions concerning a man's action; first, whether it were done, or not done; secondly, if done, whether against the law, or not against the law; the former whereof, is called a question *of fact;* the latter a question *of right,* therefore unless the parties to the question, covenant mutually to stand to the sentence of another, they are as far from peace as ever. This other to whose sentence they submit is called an ARBITRATOR. And therefore it is of the law of nature, *that they that are at controversy, submit their right to the judgment of an arbitrator.*

And seeing every man is presumed to do all things in order to his own benefit, no man is a fit arbitrator in his own cause; and if he were never so fit; yet equity allowing to each party equal benefit, if one be admitted to the judge, the other is to be admitted also; and so the controversy, that is, the cause of war, remains, against the law of nature.

For the same reason no man in any cause ought to be received for arbitrator, to whom greater profit, or honour, or pleasure apparently ariseth out of the victory of one party, than of the other: for he hath taken, though an unavoidable bribe, yet a bribe; and no man can be obliged to trust him. And thus also the controversy, and the condition of war remaineth, contrary to the law of nature.

And in a controversy of *fact,* the judge being to give no more credit to one, than to the other, if there be no other arguments, must give credit to a third; or to a third and fourth; or more: for else the question is undecided, and left to force, contrary to the law of nature.

These are the laws of nature, dictating peace, for a means of the conservation of men in multitudes; and which only concern the doctrine of civil society. There be other things tending to the destruction of particular men; as drunkenness, and all other parts of intemperance; which may therefore also be reckoned amongst those things which the law of nature hath forbidden; but are not necessary to be mentioned, nor are pertinent enough to this place.

And though this may seem too subtle a deduction of the laws of nature, to be taken notice of by all men; whereof the most part are too busy in getting food, and the rest too negligent to understand; yet to leave all men inexcusable, they have been contracted into one easy sum, intelligible even to the meanest capacity, and that is, *Do not that to another, which thou wouldest not have done to thyself;* which sheweth him, that he has no more to do in learning the laws of nature, but, when weighing the actions of other men with his own, they seem too heavy, to put them into the other part of the balance, and his own into their place, that his own passions, and self-love, may add nothing to the weight; and then there is none of these laws of nature that will not appear unto him very reasonable.

The laws of nature oblige *in foro interno* [Literally, "in the internal forum"—that is, in a person's mind or conscience.—Ed.], that is to say, they bind to a desire they should take place: but *in foro extern* [Literally, "in the external forum"—that is, in the public world of action.—Ed.], that is, to the putting them in act, not always. For he that should be modest, and tractable, and perform all he promises, in such time, and place, where no man else should do so, should but make himself a prey to others, and procure his own certain ruin, contrary to the ground of all laws of nature,

which tend to nature's preservation. And again, he that having sufficient security, that others shall observe the same laws towards him, observes them not himself, seeketh not peace, but war; and consequently the destruction of his nature by violence.

And whatsoever laws bind *in foro interno,* may be broken, not only by a fact contrary to the law, but also by a fact according to it, in case a man think it contrary. For though his action in this case, be according to the law; yet his purpose was against the law; which, where the obligation is *in foro interno,* is a breach.

The laws of nature are immutable and eternal; for injustice, ingratitude, arrogance, pride, iniquity, acception of persons, and the rest, can never be made lawful. For it can never be that war shall preserve life, and peace destroy it.

The same laws, because they oblige only to a desire, and endeavour, I mean an unfeigned and constant endeavour, are easy to be observed. For in that they require nothing but endeavour, he that endeavoureth their performance, fulfilleth them; and he that fulfilleth the law, is just.

And the science of them, is the true and only moral philosophy. For moral philosophy is nothing else but the science of what is *good,* and *evil,* in the conversation, and society of mankind. *Good,* and *evil,* are names that signify our appetites, and aversions; which in different tempers, customs, and doctrines of men, are different: and divers men, differ not only in their judgment, on the sense of what is pleasant, and unpleasant to the taste, smell, hearing, touch, and sight; but also of what is conformable, or disagreeable to reason, in the actions of common life. Nay, the same man, in divers times, differs from himself; and one time praiseth, that is, calleth good, what another time he dispraiseth, and called evil: from whence arise disputes, controversies, and at last war. And therefore so long as a man is in the condition of mere nature, which is a condition of war, as private appetite is the measure of good, and evil: and consequently all men agree on this, that peace is good, and therefore also the way, or means of peace, which, as I have shewed before, are *justice, gratitude, modesty, equity, mercy,* and the rest of the laws of nature, are good; that is to say; *moral virtues;* and their contrary *vices,* evil. Now the science of virtue and vice, is moral philosophy;

and therefore the true doctrine of the laws of nature, is the true moral philosophy. But the writers of moral philosophy, though they acknowledge the same virtues and vices; yet not seeing wherein consisted their goodness; nor that they come to be praised, as the means of peaceable, sociable, and comfortable living, place them in a mediocrity of passions: as if not the cause, but the degree of daring, made fortitude; or not the cause, but the quantity of a gift, made liberality.

These dictates of reason, men used to call by the name of laws, but improperly: for they are but conclusions, of theorems concerning what conduceth to the conservation and defence of themselves; whereas law, properly, is the word of him, that by right hath command over others. But yet if we consider the same theorems, as delivered in the word of God, that by right commandeth all things; then are they properly called laws.

OF THE CAUSES, GENERATION, AND DEFINITION OF A COMMONWEALTH

The final cause, end, or design of men, who naturally love liberty, and dominion over others, in the introduction of that restraint upon themselves, in which we see them live in commonwealths, is the foresight of their own preservation, and of a more contented life thereby; that is to say, of getting themselves out from that miserable condition of war, which is necessarily consequent, as hath been shown in chapter XIII, to the natural passions of men, when there is no visible power to keep them in awe, and tie them by fear of punishment to the performance of their covenants, and observation of those laws of nature set down in the fourteenth and fifteenth chapters.

For the laws of nature, as *justice, equity, modesty, mercy,* and, in sum, *doing to others, as we would be done to,* of themselves, without the terror of some power, to cause them to be observed, are contrary to our natural passions, that carry us to partiality, pride, revenge, and the like. And covenants, without the sword, are but words, and of no strength to secure a man at all. Therefore notwithstanding the laws of nature, which every one hath then kept, when he has the will to keep them, when he can do it safely, if there be no power erected, or not great enough for our security; every man will, and may lawfully rely on his own strength and art, for caution against all other men. And in all places, where men have lived by small families, to rob and spoil one another, has been a trade, and so far from being reputed against the law of nature, that the greater spoils they gained, the greater was their honour; and men observed no other laws therein, but the laws of honour; that is, to abstain from cruelty, leaving to men their lives, and instruments of husbandry. And as small families did then; so now do cities and kingdoms which are but greater families, for their own security, enlarge their dominions, upon all pretences of danger, and fear of invasion, or assistance that may be given to invaders, and endeavour as much as they can, to subdue, or weaken their neighbours, by open force, and secret arts, for want of other caution, justly; and are remembered for it in after ages with honour.

It is true, that certain living creatures, as bees, and ants, live sociably one with another, which are therefore by Aristotle numbered amongst political creatures; and yet have no other direction, than their particular judgments and appetites; nor speech, whereby one of them can signify to another, what he thinks expedient for the common benefit: and therefore some man may perhaps desire to know, why mankind cannot do the same. To which I answer,

First, that men are continually in competition for honour and dignity, which these creatures are not; and consequently amongst men there ariseth on that ground, envy and hatred, and finally war; but amongst these not so.

Secondly, that amongst these creatures, the common good differeth not from the private; and being by nature inclined to their private, they procure thereby the common benefit. But man, whose joy consisteth in comparing himself with other men, can relish nothing but what is eminent.

Thirdly, that these creatures, having not, as man, the use of reason, do not see, nor think they see any fault, in the administration of their common business; whereas amongst men, there are very many, that think themselves wiser, and abler to govern the public, better than the rest; and these strive to reform and innovate, one this way, another that way; and thereby bring it into distraction and civil war.

Fourthly, that these creatures, though they have some use of voice, in making known to one another their desires, and other affections; yet they want that art of words, by which some men can represent to others, that which is good, in the likeness of evil; and evil, in the likeness of good; and augment, or diminish the apparent greatness of good and evil; discontenting men, and troubling their peace at their pleasure.

Fifthly, irrational creatures cannot distinguish between *injury,* and *damage;* and therefore as long as they be at ease, they are not offended with their fellows: whereas man is then most troublesome, when he is most at ease: for then it is that he loves to shew his wisdom, and control the actions of them that govern the commonwealth.

Lastly, the agreement of these creatures is natural; that of men, is by covenant only, which is artificial: and therefore it is no wonder if there be somewhat else required, besides covenant, to make their agreement constant and lasting; which is a common power, to keep them in awe, and to direct their actions to the common benefit.

The only way to erect such a common power, as may be able to defend them from the invasion of foreigners, and the injuries of one another, and thereby to secure them in such sort, as that by their own industry, and by the fruits of the earth, they may nourish themselves and live contentedly; is, to confer all their power and strength upon one man, or upon one assembly of men, that may reduce all their wills, by plurality of voices, unto one will: which is as much as to say, to appoint one man, or assembly of men, to bear their person; and every one to own, and acknowledge himself to be author of whatsoever he that so beareth their person, shall act, or cause to be acted, in those things which concern the common peace and safety; and therein to submit their wills, every one to his will, and their judgments, to his judgment. This is more than consent, or concord; it is a real unity of them all, in one and the same person, made by covenant of every man with every man, in such manner, as if every man should say to every man, *I authorize and give up my right of governing myself, to this man, or to this*

assembly of men, on this condition, that thou give up thy right to him, and authorize all his actions in like manner. This done, the multitude so united in one person, is called a COMMONWEALTH, in Latin *civitas.* This is the generation of that great LEVIATHAN, or rather, to speak more reverently, of that *mortal god,* to which we owe under the *immortal God,* our peace and defence. For by this authority, given him by every particular man in the commonwealth, he hath the use of so much power and strength conferred on him, that by terror thereof, he is enabled to perform the wills of them all, to peace at home, and mutual aid against their enemies abroad. And in him consisteth the essence of the commonwealth; which, to define it, is *one person, of whose acts a great multitude, by mutual covenants one with another, have made themselves every one the author, to the end he may use the strength and means of them all, as he shall think expedient, for their peace and common defence.*

And he that carrieth this person, is called SOVEREIGN, and said to have *sovereign* power; and every one besides, his SUBJECT.

FOR FURTHER REFLECTION

1. Hobbes wrote, "The utility of morality and civil philosophy is to be estimated, not so much by the commodities we have by knowing these sciences, as by the calamities we receive from not knowing them." What does he mean by this, and does the selection illustrate it?

2. Is Hobbes's view of human nature accurate? Do we always act out of the motivations of fear and distrust? Are people entirely self-interested egoists? Is psychological egoism, the view that we always do what we perceive to be in our best interest, too bleak and one sided?

3. Hobbes thought that only an absolute sovereign could establish or ensure peace and civil society. Is he correct? What would his estimation of democracy be? Could democratic society make use of his analysis? How would democrats modify Hobbes's theory?

4. David Hume criticized the idea that contract theories provide a justification for political

authority. First, there is no evidence of an original contract ever being made, and second, even if our ancestors did sign an original contract, why should that give us any reason for obeying the laws of the state? Even as we are not bound by the marriage or business contracts of our ancestors, why should we be obliged by their political contracts?

JOHN STUART MILL

UTILITARIANISM AND PLEASURE

John Stuart Mill (1806–1873), one of the most important British philosophers of the nineteenth century, was born in London and educated by his father, learning Greek at age three and Latin at age eight. By the time he was fourteen, he had received a thorough classic education at home. He began work as a clerk for the East India Company at age seventeen and eventually became director of the company. He was elected to Parliament in 1865. A man of liberal ideas and a penetrating mind, he made significant contributions to logic, philosophy of science, philosophy of religion, political theory, and ethics. His principal works are *A System of Logic* (1843), *Utilitarianism* (1863), *On Liberty* (1859), and *The Subjection of Women* (1869).

Mill defends utilitarianism, a form of teleological ethics, against more rule-bound "deontological" systems, the sort of system we consider in the next selection on Kant's categorical imperative. Traditionally, two major types of ethical systems have dominated the field: one in which the locus of value is the act or kind of act, the other in which the locus of value is the outcome or consequences of the act. The former type of theory is called *deontological* (from the Greek *deon*, which means "duty") and the latter is called *teleological* (from the Greek *telos*, which means "end" or "goal").

That is, the standard of right or wrong action for the teleologists is the comparative consequences of the available actions. The right act is the one that produces the best consequences. Whereas the deontologist is concerned only with the rightness of the act itself, the teleologist asserts there is no such thing as an act's having intrinsic worth. Although for the deontologist there is something intrinsically bad about lying, for the teleologist the only thing wrong with lying is its bad consequences. If you can reasonably calculate that a lie will do even slightly more good than telling the truth, in fact, you have an obligation to lie.

The present selection was written against the background of a debate over Jeremy Bentham's hedonistic version of utilitarianism, which failed to differentiate between kinds and quality of pleasure, and so received the name of "pig philosophy." Mill meets this charge by substituting a more complex theory of happiness for Bentham's undifferentiated pleasure.

WHAT UTILITARIANISM IS

... The creed which accepts as the foundation of morals, Utility, or the Greatest Happiness Principle, holds that actions are right in proportion as they tend to promote happiness, wrong as they tend to produce the reverse of happiness. By happiness is intended pleasure, and the absence of pain; by unhappiness, pain, and the privation of pleasure. To give a clear view of the moral standard set up by the theory, much more requires to be said; in particular, what things it includes in the ideas of pain and pleasure; and to what extent this is left an open question. But these supplementary explanations do not affect the theory of life on which this theory of morality is grounded—namely, that pleasure, and freedom from pain, are the only things desirable as ends; and that all desirable things (which are as numerous in the utilitarian as in any other scheme) are desirable either for the pleasure inherent in themselves, or as a means to the promotion of pleasure and the prevention of pain.

Now, such a theory of life excites in many minds, and among them in some of the most estimable in feeling and purpose, inveterate dislike. To suppose that life has (as they express it) no higher end than pleasure—no better and nobler object of desire and pursuit—they designate as utterly mean and grovelling; as a doctrine worthy only of swine, to whom the followers of Epicurus were, at a very early period, contemptuously likened; and modern holders of the doctrine are occasionally made the subject of equally polite comparisons by its German, French, and English assailants.

When thus attacked, the Epicureans have always answered, that it is not they, but their accusers, who represent human nature in a degrading light; since the accusation supposes human beings to be capable of no pleasures except those of which swine are capable. If this supposition were true, the charge could not be gainsaid, but would then be no longer an imputation; for if the sources of pleasure were precisely the same to human beings and to swine, the rule of life which is good enough for the one would be good enough for the other. The comparison of the Epicurean life to

that of beasts is felt as degrading, precisely because a beast's pleasures do not satisfy a human being's conception of happiness. Human beings have faculties more elevated than the animal appetites, and when once made conscious of them, do not regard anything as happiness which does not include their gratification. I do not, indeed, consider the Epicureans to have been by any means faultless in drawing out their scheme of consequences from the utilitarian principle. To do this in any sufficient manner, many Stoic, as well as Christian elements require to be included. But there is no known Epicurean theory of life which does not assign to the pleasures of the intellect, of the feelings and imagination, and of the moral sentiments, a much higher value as pleasures than to those of mere sensation. It must be admitted, however, that utilitarian writers in general have placed the superiority of mental over bodily pleasures chiefly in the greater permanency, safety, uncostliness, etc., of the former—that is, in their circumstantial advantages rather than in their intrinsic nature. And on all these points utilitarians have fully proved their case; but they might have taken the other, and, as it may be called, higher ground, with entire consistency. It is quite compatible with the principle of utility to recognise the fact, that some *kinds* of pleasure are more desirable and more valuable than others. It would be absurd that while, in estimating all other things, quality is considered as well as quantity, the estimation of pleasures should be supposed to depend on quantity alone.

If I am asked, what I mean by difference of quality in pleasures, or what makes one pleasure more valuable than another, merely as a pleasure, except its being greater in amount, there is but one possible answer. Of two pleasures, if there be one which all or almost all who have experience of both give a decided preference, irrespective of any feeling of moral obligation to prefer it, that is the more desirable pleasure. If one of the two is, by those who are competently acquainted with both, placed so far above the other that they prefer it, even though knowing it to be attended with a great amount of discontent, and would not resign it for any quantity of the other pleasure which their nature is capable of, we are justified in

From John Stuart Mill, *Utilitarianism* (1861), Chapters 2 and 4.

ascribing to the preferred enjoyment a superiority in quality, so far outweighing quantity as to render it, in comparison, of small account.

Now it is an unquestionable fact that those who are equally acquainted with, and equally capable of appreciating and enjoying, both, do give a most marked preference to the manner of existence which employs their higher faculties. Few human creatures would consent to be changed into any of the lower animals, for a promise of the fullest allowance of a beast's pleasures; no intelligent human being would consent to be a fool, no instructed person would be an ignoramus, no person of feeling and conscience would be selfish and base, even though they should be persuaded that the fool, the dunce, or the rascal is better satisfied with his lot than they are with theirs. They would not resign what they possess more than he for the most complete satisfaction of all the desires which they have in common with him. If they ever fancy they would, it is only in cases of unhappiness so extreme, that to escape from it they would exchange their lot for almost any other, however undesirable in their own eyes. A being of higher faculties requires more to make him happy, is capable probably of more acute suffering, and certainly accessible to it at more points, than one of an inferior type; but in spite of these liabilities, he can never really wish to sink into what he feels to be a lower grade of existence. We may give what explanation we please of this unwillingness; we may attribute it to pride, a name which is given indiscriminately to some of the most and to some of the least estimable feelings of which mankind are capable; we may refer it to the love of liberty and personal independence, an appeal to which was with the Stoics one of the most effective means for the inculcation of it; to the love of power, or to the love of excitement, both of which do really enter into and contribute to it: but its most appropriate appellation is a sense of dignity, which all human beings possess in one form or another, and in some, though by no means in exact, proportion to their higher faculties, and which is so essential a part of the happiness of those in whom it is strong, that nothing which conflicts with it could be, otherwise than momentarily, an object of desire to them. Whoever supposes that this preference takes place at a sacrifice of happiness—

that the superior being, in anything like equal circumstances, is not happier than the inferior—confounds the two very different ideas, of happiness, and content. It is indisputable that the being whose capacities of enjoyment are low, has the greatest chance of having them fully satisfied; and a highly endowed being will always feel that any happiness which he can look for, as the world is constituted, is imperfect. But he can learn to bear its imperfections, if they are at all bearable; and they will not make him envy the being who is indeed unconscious of the imperfections, but only because he feels not at all the good which those imperfections qualify. It is better to be a human being dissatisfied than a pig satisfied; better to be Socrates dissatisfied than a fool satisfied. And if the fool, or the pig, are of a different opinion, it is because they only know their own side of the question. The other party to the comparison knows both sides.

It may be objected, that many who are capable of the higher pleasures, occasionally, under the influence of temptation, postpone them to the lower. But this is quite compatible with a full appreciation of the intrinsic superiority of the higher. Men often, from infirmity of character, make their election for the nearer good, though they know it to be the less valuable; and this is no less when the choice is between two bodily pleasures, than when it is between bodily and mental. They pursue sensual indulgences to the injury of health, though perfectly aware that health is the greater good. It may be further objected, that many who begin with youthful enthusiasm for everything noble, as they advance in years sink into indolence and selfishness. But I do not believe that those who undergo this very common change, voluntarily choose the lower description of pleasures in preference to the higher. I believe that before they devote themselves exclusively to the one, they have already become incapable of the other. Capacity for the nobler feelings is in most natures a very tender plant, easily killed, not only by hostile influences, but by mere want of sustenance; and in the majority of young persons it speedily dies away if the occupations to which their position in life has devoted them, and the society into which it has thrown them, are not favourable to keeping that higher capacity in exercise. Men lose their high aspirations as they lose their intellectual tastes, because they have not time or opportunity for indulging them; and they addict themselves to inferior pleasures, not because they deliberately prefer them, but because they are either the only ones to which they have access, or the only ones which they are any longer capable of enjoying. It may be questioned whether any one who has remained equally susceptible to both classes of pleasures, ever knowingly and calmly preferred the lower; though many, in all ages, have broken down in an ineffectual attempt to combine both.

From this verdict of the only competent judges, I apprehend there can be no appeal. On a question which is the best worth having of two pleasures, or which of two modes of existence is the most grateful to the feelings, apart from its moral attributes and from its consequences, the judgment of those who are qualified by knowledge of both, or, if they differ, that of the majority among them, must be admitted as final. And there needs to be the less hesitation to accept this judgment respecting the quality of pleasures, since there is no other tribunal to be referred to even on the question of quantity. What means are there of determining which is the acutest of two pains, or the intensest of two pleasurable sensations, except the general suffrage of those who are familiar with both? Neither pains nor pleasures are homogeneous, and pain is always heterogeneous with pleasure. What is there to decide whether a particular pleasure is worth purchasing at the cost of a particular pain, except the feelings and judgment of the experienced? When, therefore, those feelings and judgment declare the pleasures derived from the higher faculties to be preferable *in kind,* apart from the question of intensity, to those of which the animal nature, disjoined from the higher faculties, is susceptible, they are entitled on this subject to the same regard.

I have dwelt on this point, as being a necessary part of a perfectly just conception of Utility or Happiness, considered as the directive rule of human conduct. But it is by no means an indispensable condition to the acceptance of the utilitarian standard; for that standard is not the agent's own greatest happiness, but the greatest amount of happiness altogether; and if it may possibly be doubted whether a noble character is always the happier for its nobleness, there can be no

doubt that it makes other people happier, and that the world in general is immensely a gainer by it. Utilitarianism, therefore, could only attain its end by the general cultivation of nobleness of character, even if each individual were only benefited by the nobleness of others, and his own, so far as happiness is concerned, were a sheer deduction from the benefit. But the bare enunciation of such an absurdity as this last, renders refutation superfluous.

According to the Greatest Happiness Principle, as above explained, the ultimate end, with reference to and for the sake of which all other things are desirable (whether we are considering our own good or that of other people), is an existence exempt as far as possible from pain, and as rich as possible in enjoyments, both in point of quantity and quality; the test of quality, and the rule for measuring it against quantity, being the preference felt by those who in their opportunities of experience, to which must be added their habits of self-consciousness and self-observation, are best furnished with the means of comparison. This, being, according to the utilitarian opinion, the end of human action, is necessarily also the standard of morality; which may accordingly be defined, the rules and precepts for human conduct, by the observance of which an existence such as has been described might be, to the greatest extent possible, secured to all mankind; and not to them only, but, so far as the nature of things admits, to the whole sentient creation. . . .

The objectors to utilitarianism cannot always be charged with representing it in a discreditable light. On the contrary, those among them who entertain anything like a just idea of its disinterested character, sometimes find fault with its standard as being too high for humanity. They say it is exacting too much to require that people shall always act from the inducement of promoting the general interests of society. But this is to mistake the very meaning of a standard of morals, and confound the rule of action with the motive of it. It is the business of ethics to tell us what are our duties, or by what test we may know them; but no system of ethics requires that the sole motive of all we do shall be a feeling of duty; on the contrary, ninety-nine hundredths of all our actions are done from other motives, and rightly so done, if the rule of duty does not condemn them. It is the more unjust to utilitarianism that this particular misapprehension should be made a ground of objection to it, inasmuch as utilitarian moralists have gone beyond almost all others in affirming that the motive has nothing to do with the morality of the action, though much with the worth of the agent. He who saves a fellow-creature from drowning does what is morally right, whether his motive be duty, or the hope of being paid for his trouble; he who betrays the friend that trusts him, is guilty of a crime, even if his object be to serve another friend to whom he is under greater obligation. But to speak only of actions done from the motive of duty, and in direct obedience to principle: it is a misapprehension of the utilitarian mode of thought, to conceive it as implying that people should fix their minds upon so wide a generality as the world, or society at large. The great majority of good actions are intended not for the benefit of the world, but for that of individuals, of which the good of the world is made up; and the thoughts of the most virtuous man need not on these occasions travel beyond the particular persons concerned, except so far as is necessary to assure himself that in benefiting them he is not violating the rights, that is, the legitimate and authorised expectations, of any one else. The multiplication of happiness is, according to the utilitarian ethics, the object of virtue: the occasions on which any person (except one in a thousand) has it in his power to do this on an extended scale, in other words to be a public benefactor, are but exceptional; and on these occasions alone is he called on to consider public utility; in every other case, private utility, the interest or happiness of some few persons, is all he has to attend to. Those alone the influence of whose actions extends to society in general, need concern themselves habitually about so large an object. In the case of abstinences indeed—of things which people forbear to do from moral considerations, though the consequences in the particular case might be beneficial—it would be unworthy of an intelligent agent not to be consciously aware that the action is of a class which, if practised generally, would be generally injurious, and that this is the ground of the obligation to abstain from it. The amount of regard for the public interest implied in this recognition, is no greater than is demanded by every system of morals, for they all enjoin to abstain from whatever is manifestly pernicious to society. . . .

CHAPTER IV
OF WHAT SORT OF PROOF THE PRINCIPLE OF UTILITY IS SUSCEPTIBLE

It has already been remarked, that questions of ultimate ends do not admit of proof, in the ordinary acceptation of the term. To be incapable of proof by reasoning is common to all first principles; to the first premises of our knowledge, as well as to those of our conduct. But the former, being matters of fact, may be the subject of a direct appeal to the faculties which judge of fact—namely, our senses, and our internal consciousness. Can an appeal be made to the same faculties on questions of practical ends? Or by what other faculty is cognisance taken of them?

Questions about ends are, in other words, questions about what things are desirable. The utilitarian doctrine is, that happiness is desirable, and the only thing desirable, as an end; all other things being desirable as means to that end. What ought to be required of this doctrine—what conditions is it requisite that the doctrine should fulfil—to make good its claim to be believed?

The only proof capable of being given that an object is visible, is that people actually see it. The only proof that a sound is audible, is that people hear it: and so of the other sources of our experience. In like manner, I apprehend, the sole evidence it is possible to produce that anything is desirable, is that people do actually desire it. If the end which the utilitarian doctrine proposes to itself were not, in theory and in practice, acknowledged to be an end, nothing could ever convince any person that it was so. No reason can be given why the general happiness is desirable, except that each person, so far as he believes it to be attainable, desires his own happiness. This, however, being a fact, we have not only all the proof which the case admits of, but all which it is possible to require, that happiness is a good: that each person's happiness is a good to that person, and the general happiness, therefore, a good to the aggregate of all persons. Happiness has made out its title as *one* of the ends of conduct, and consequently one of the criteria of morality.

But it has not, by this alone, proved itself to be the sole criterion. To do that, it would seem, by the same rule, necessary to show, not only that people desire happiness, but that they never desire anything else. . . .

We have now, then, an answer to the question, of what sort of proof the principle of utility is susceptible. If the opinion which I have now stated is psychologically true—if human nature is so constituted as to desire nothing which is not either a part of happiness or a means of happiness, we can have no other proof, and we require no other, that these are the only things desirable. If so, happiness is the sole end of human action, and the promotion of it the test by which to judge of all human conduct; from whence it necessarily follows that it must be the criterion of morality, since a part is included in the whole.

And now to decide whether this is really so; whether mankind do desire nothing for itself but that which is a pleasure to them, or of which the absence is a pain; we have evidently arrived at a question of fact and experience, dependent, like all similar questions, upon evidence. It can only be determined by practised self-consciousness and self-observation, assisted by observation of others. I believe that these sources of evidence, impartially consulted, will declare that desiring a thing and finding it pleasant, aversion to it and thinking of it as painful, are phenomena entirely inseparable, or rather two parts of the same phenomenon; in strictness of language, two different modes of naming the same psychological fact: that to think of an object as desirable (unless for the sake of its consequences), and to think of it as pleasant, are one and the same thing; and that to desire anything, except in proportion as the idea of it is pleasant, is a physical and metaphysical impossibility.

FOR FURTHER REFLECTION

1. How does Mill reply to the charge that utilitarianism is a "pig philosophy"? What is meant by "Better to be Socrates dissatisfied than a pig satisfied"?
2. In order to get a better grasp on the difference between utilitarianism and deontological ethics,

consider this example: Suppose there is a raft floating in the Pacific Ocean. On the raft are two men who are starving to death. One day they discover some food in an inner compartment of a box on the raft. They have reason to believe that the food is enough to keep one of them alive until the raft reaches a certain island where help is available, but that if they share the food most likely both will die. Now, one of these men is a brilliant scientist who has in his mind the cure for cancer. The other man is undistinguished. Otherwise there is no relevant difference between the two men. What is the morally right thing to do? Share the food and hope against the odds for a miracle? Flip a coin in order to see which man gets the food? Give the food to the scientist?

If you voted to flip a coin or share the food, you sided with the deontologist, but if you voted to give the food to the scientist, then you sided with the teleologist, the utilitarian, who would calculate that greater good would be accomplished as a result of the scientist getting the food and living than in any of the other likely outcomes.

It has often been admitted that utilitarianism could easily be misused. If people tried to "play God" and decide each case on the basis of what they thought would be the "best" consequences, chaos might result, so that some utilitarians have advocated keeping their doctrine a secret. What do you think of both the prediction of the antiutilitarian consequences of widespread utilitarianism and the prescription of keeping the doctrine a secret?

3. John Rawls has argued that utilitarianism makes a false inference from (a) what one is allowed to do with one's own life to (b) what one is allowed to do with other people's lives. We often have a right to forgo some present enjoyment for the sake of a future personal higher goal, but, he argues, we don't have the same right to restrict some other person from a present enjoyment for one that we deem to be his or her higher future goal. That is, utilitarianism paternalistically violates human rights. It treats

rights as expendable. Do you agree with this criticism?

4. What do you see as the overall merits and liabilities of deontological and utilitarian systems? Where do you stand at this juncture?

5. Friedrich Nietzsche wrote, "If we possess our *why* of life we can put up with almost any *how*—Man does not strive after happiness; only the Englishman does that" (*Twilight of the Idols*). Do you agree or disagree with Nietzsche on the unimportance of the search for happiness?

IMMANUEL KANT

DUTY AND THE CATEGORICAL IMPERATIVE

This reading is from Kant's classic work, *The Foundations of the Metaphysic of Morals*, written in 1785, in which he outlines his ethical system. Kant is concerned to reject those ethical theories, such as the theory of moral sentiments set forth by the Scottish moralists Francis Hutcheson (1694) and David Hume (1711–1776), in which morality is contingent and hypothetical. The moral sentiment view is contingent in that it is based on human nature and, in particular, on our feelings or sentiments. Had we been created differently, we would have a different nature and hence a different morality with different moral duties. According to the moral sentiment theory, all duties are hypothetical in that they depend on our desires for their realization. For example, we should obey the law because we want a peaceful, orderly society.

Kant rejects this naturalistic account of ethics. Ethics are not contingent but absolute, and its duties or imperatives are not hypothetical but categorical (unconditional). Ethics are based not on feeling but on reason. It is because we are rational beings that we are valuable and capable of discovering moral laws binding on all people at all times. As such, our moral duties depend not on feelings but on reason. They are unconditional, universally valid, and necessary, regardless of the possible consequences or opposition to our inclinations.

Kant's first formulation of his *categorical imperative* is "Act only on that maxim whereby thou canst at the same time will that it would become a universal law." This imperative is given as the criterion (or second-order principle) by which to judge all other principles. If we could consistently will that everyone would do some type of action, then there is an application of the categorical imperative enjoining that type of action. If we cannot consistently will that everyone would do some type of action, then that type of action is morally wrong. Kant argues, for example, that we cannot consistently will that everyone make lying promises, for the very institution of promising entails or depends on general adherence to keeping the promise or an intention to do so.

Kant offers a second formulation of the categorical imperative: "So act as to treat humanity, whether in your own person or in that of any other, in every case as an end and never as merely a means only." Each person, by virtue of his or her reason, has dignity and profound worth, which entails that he or she must never be exploited or manipulated or merely used as a means to our idea of what is for the general good. Kant thought that this formulation was substantively identical with the first, but the view is controversial.

The first formulation seems to be purely formal, suggesting that only universalizable principles are moral principles. The second formulation seems to suggest a substantive directive of treating all rational creatures as equally intrinsically valuable. Someone like Aristotle, Hobbes, or Nietzsche could accept Kant's first form, but reject the second one on the basis of inegalitarianism (the view that states that not all rational beings are equally valuable). (See Part II for a biographical sketch of Kant.)

PREFACE

As my concern here is with moral philosophy, I limit the question suggested to this: Whether it is not of the utmost necessity to construct a pure moral philosophy, perfectly cleared of everything which is only empirical, and which belongs to anthropology? for that such a philosophy must be possible is evident from the common idea of duty and of the moral laws. Everyone must admit that if a law is to have moral force, *i.e.* to be the basis of an obligation, it must carry with it absolute necessity; that, for example, the precept, "Thou shall not lie," is not valid for men alone, as if other rational beings had no need to observe it; and so with all the other moral laws properly so called; that, therefore, the basis of obligation must not be sought in the nature of man, or in the circumstances in the world in which he is placed, but a priori simply in the conception of pure reason; and although any other precept which is founded on principles of mere experience may be in certain respects universal, yet in as far as it rests even in the least degree on an empirical basis, perhaps only as to a motive, such a precept, while it may be a practical rule, can never be called a moral law. . . .

THE GOOD WILL

Nothing can possibly be conceived in the world, or even out of it, which can be called good, without qualification, except a Good Will. Intelligence, wit, judgment, and the other *talents* of the mind, however they may be named, or courage, resolution, perseverance, as qualities of temperament, are undoubtedly good and desirable in many respects; but these gifts of nature may also become extremely bad and mischievous if the will which is to make use of them, and which, therefore, constitutes what is called *character,* is not good. It is the same with the *gifts of fortune.* Power, riches, honour, even health, and the general well-being and contentment with one's conditions which is called *happiness,* inspire pride, and often presumption, if there is not a good will to correct the influence of these on the mind, and with this also to rectify the whole principle of acting, and adapt it to its end. The sight of a being who is not adorned with a single feature of a pure and good will, enjoying unbroken prosperity, can never give pleasure to an impartial rational spectator. Thus a good will appears to constitute the indispensable condition even of being worthy of happiness.

There are even some qualities which are of service to this good will itself, and may facilitate its action, yet which have no intrinsic unconditional value, but always presuppose a good will, and this qualifies the esteem that we justly have for them, and does not permit us to regard them as absolutely good. Moderation in the affections and passions, self-control, and calm deliberation are not only good in many respects, but even seem to constitute part of the intrinsic worth

From Immanuel Kant, *The Foundations of the Metaphysic of Morals,* trans. T. K. Abbott (1873).

of the person; but they are far from deserving to be called good without qualification, although they have been so unconditionally praised by the ancients. For without the principles of a good will, they may become extremely bad; and the coolness of a villain not only makes him far more dangerous, but also directly makes him more abominable in our eyes than he would have been without it.

A good will is good not because of what it performs or effects, not by its aptness for the attainment of some proposed end, but simply by virtue of the volition, that is, it is good in itself, and considered by itself to be esteemed much higher than all that can be brought about by it in favour of any inclination, nay, even of the sum-total of all inclinations. Even if it should happen that, owing to special disfavour of fortune, or the niggardly provision of a step-motherly nature, this will should wholly lack power to accomplish its purpose, if with its greatest efforts it should yet achieve nothing, and there should remain only the good will (not, to be sure, a mere wish, but the summoning of all means in our power), then, like a jewel, it would still shine by its own light, as a thing which has its whole value in itself. Its usefulness or fruitlessness can neither add to nor take away anything from this value. It would be, as it were, only the setting to enable us to handle it the more conveniently in common commerce, or to attract to it the attention of those who are not yet connoisseurs, but not to recommend it to true connoisseurs, or to determine its value.

WHY REASON WAS MADE TO GUIDE THE WILL

There is, however, something so strange in this idea of the absolute value of the mere will, in which no account is taken of its utility, that notwithstanding the thorough assent of even common reason to the idea, yet a suspicion must arise that it may perhaps really be the product of mere high-blown fancy, and that we may have misunderstood the purpose of nature in assigning reason as the governor of the will. Therefore we will examine this idea from this point of view.

In the physical constitution of an organized being, that is, a being adapted suitably to the purposes of life, we assume it as a fundamental principle that no organ for any purpose will be found but what is also the fittest and best adapted for that purpose. Now in a being which has reason and a will, if the proper object of nature were its *conservatism,* its *welfare,* in a word, its *happiness,* then nature would have hit upon a very bad arrangement in selecting the reason of the creature to carry out this purpose. For all the actions which the creature has to perform with a view to this purpose, and the whole rule of its conduct, would be far more surely prescribed to it by instinct, and that end would have been attained thereby much more certainly than it ever can be by reason. Should reason have been communicated to this favoured creature over and above, it must only have served it to contemplate the happy constitution of its nature, to admire it, to congratulate itself thereon, and to feel thankful for it to the beneficent cause, but not that it should subject its desires to that weak and delusive guidance, and meddle bunglingly with the purpose of nature. In a word, nature would have taken care that reason should not break forth into *practical exercise,* nor have the presumption, with its weak insight, to think out for itself the plan of happiness, and of the means of attaining it. Nature would not only have taken on herself the choice of the ends, but also of the means, and with wise foresight would have entrusted both to instinct.

And, in fact, we find that the more a cultivated reason applies itself with deliberate purpose to the enjoyment of life and happiness, so much the more does the man fail of true satisfaction. And from this circumstance there arises in many, if they are candid enough to confess it, a certain degree of *misology,* that is, hatred of reason, especially in the case of those who are most experienced in the use of it, because after calculating all the advantages they derive, I do not say from the invention of all the arts of common luxury, but even from the sciences (which seem to them to be after all only a luxury of the understanding), they find that they have, in fact, only brought more trouble on their shoulders, rather than gained in happiness; and they end by envying, rather than despising, the more common stamp of men who keep closer to the guidance of mere instinct, and do not allow their reason much influence on their conduct. And this we must admit, that the judgment of those who would very much lower the lofty eulogies of the advantages which reason gives us in regard to the happiness and satisfaction of life, or who would even reduce them below zero, is by no means morose or ungrateful to the goodness with which the world is governed, but that there lies at the root of these judgments the idea that our existence has a different and far nobler end, for which, and not for happiness, reason is properly intended, and which must, therefore, be regarded as the supreme condition to which the private ends of man must, for the most part, be postponed.

For as reason is not competent to guide the will with certainty in regard to its objects and the satisfaction of all our wants (which it to some extent even multiplies), this being an end to which an implanted instinct would have led with much greater certainty; and since, nevertheless, reason is imparted to us as a practical faculty, *i.e.* as one which is to have influence on the *will,* therefore, admitting that nature generally in the distribution of her capacities has adapted the means to the end, its true destination must be to produce a *will,* not merely good as a *means* to something else, but *good in itself,* for which reason was absolutely necessary. This will then, though not indeed the sole and complete good, must be the supreme good and the condition of every other, even of the desire of happiness. Under these circumstances, there is nothing inconsistent with the wisdom of nature in the fact that the cultivation of the reason, which is requisite for the first and unconditional purpose, does in many ways interfere, at least in this life, with the attainment of the second, which is always conditional, namely, happiness. Nay, it may even reduce it to nothing, without nature thereby failing in her purpose. For reason recognizes the establishment of a good will as its highest practical destination, and in attaining this purpose is capable only of a satisfaction of its own proper kind, namely, that from the attainment of an end, which end again is determined by reason only, notwithstanding that this may involve many a disappointment to the ends of inclination.

THE FIRST PROPOSITION OF MORALITY

[An action must be done from a sense of duty, if it is to have moral worth]

We have then to develop the notion of a will which deserves to be highly esteemed for itself, and is good without a view to anything further, a notion which exists already in the sound natural understanding, requiring rather to be cleared up than to be taught, and which in estimating the value of our actions always takes the first place, and constitutes the condition of all the rest. In order to do this, we will take the notion of duty, which includes that of a good will, although implying certain subjective restrictions and hindrances. These, however, far from concealing it, or rendering it unrecognizable, rather bring it out by contrast, and make it shine forth so much the brighter.

I omit here all actions which are already recognized as inconsistent with duty although they may be useful for this or that purpose, for with these the question whether they are done *from duty* cannot arise at all, since they even conflict with it. I also set aside those actions which really conform to duty, but to which men have *no* direct *inclination,* performing them because they are impelled thereto by some other inclination. For in this case we can readily distinguish whether the action which agrees with duty is done *from duty,* or from a selfish view. It is much harder to make this distinction when the action accords with duty, and the subject has besides a *direct* inclination to it. For example, it is always a matter of duty that a dealer should not overcharge an inexperienced purchaser; and wherever there is much commerce the prudent tradesman does not overcharge, but keeps a fixed price for everyone, so that a child buys of him as well as any other. Men are thus *honestly* served; but this is not enough to make us believe that the tradesman has so acted from duty and from principles of honesty: his own advantage required it; it is out of the question in this case to suppose that he might besides have a direct inclination in favour of the buyers, so that, as it were, from love he should give no advantage to one over another. Accordingly the action was done neither from duty nor from direct inclination, but merely with a selfish view.

On the other hand, it is a duty to maintain one's life; and, in addition, everyone has also a direct inclination to do so. But on this account the often anxious care which most men take for it has no intrinsic worth, and their maxim has no moral import. They preserve their life *as duty requires,* no doubt, but not *because duty requires.* On the other hand, if adversity and hopeless sorrow have completely taken away the relish for life; if the unfortunate one, strong in mind, indignant at his fate rather than desponding or dejected, wishes for death, and yet preserves his life without loving it—not from inclination or fear, but from duty—then his maxim has a moral worth.

To be beneficent when we can is a duty; and besides this, there are many minds so sympathetically constituted that, without any other motive of vanity or self-interest, they find a pleasure in spreading joy around them, and can take delight in the satisfaction of others so far as it is their own work. But I maintain that in such a case an action of this kind, however proper, however amiable it may be, has nevertheless no true moral worth, but is on a level with other inclinations, *e.g.* the inclination to honour, which, if it is happily directed to that which is in fact of public utility and accordant with duty, and consequently honourable, deserves praise and encouragement, but not esteem. For the maxim lacks the moral import, namely, that such actions be done *from duty,* not from inclination. Put the case that the mind of that philanthropist was clouded by sorrow of his own, extinguishing all sympathy with the lot of others, and that while he still has the power to benefit others in distress, he is not touched by their trouble because he is absorbed with his own; and now suppose that he tears himself out of this dead insensibility, and performs the action without any inclination to it, but simply from duty, then first has his action its genuine moral worth. Further still; if nature has put little sympathy in the heart of this or that man; if he, supposed to be an upright man, is by temperament cold and indifferent to the sufferings of others, perhaps because in respect of his own he is provided with the special gift of patience and fortitude, and supposes, or even requires,

that others should have the same—and such a man would certainly not be the meanest product of nature—but if nature had not specially framed him for a philanthropist, would he not still find in himself a source from whence to give himself a far higher worth than that of a good-natured temperament could be? Unquestionably. It is just in this that the moral worth of the character is brought out which is incomparably the highest of all, namely, that he is beneficent, not from inclination, but from duty.

To secure one's own happiness is a duty, at least indirectly; for discontent with one's condition, under a pressure of many anxieties and amidst unsatisfied wants, might easily become a great *temptation to transgression of duty.* But here again, without looking to duty, all men have already the strongest and most intimate inclination to happiness, because it is just in this idea that all inclinations are combined in one total. But the precept of happiness is often of such a sort that it greatly interferes with some inclinations, and yet a man cannot form any definite and certain conception of the sum of satisfaction of all of them which is called happiness. It is not then to be wondered at that a single inclination, definite both as to what it promises and as to the time within which it can be gratified, is often able to overcome such a fluctuating idea, and that a gouty patient, for instance, can choose to enjoy what he likes, and to suffer what he may, since, according to his calculation, on this occasion at least, he has [only] not sacrificed the enjoyment of the present moment to a possibly mistaken expectation of a happiness which is supposed to be found in health. But even in this case, if the general desire for happiness did not influence his will, and supposing that in his particular case health was not a necessary element in this calculation, there yet remains in this, as in all other cases, this law, namely, that he should promote his happiness not from inclination but from duty, and by this would his conduct first acquire true moral worth.

It is in this manner, undoubtedly, that we are to understand those passages of Scripture also in which we are commanded to love our neighbour, even our enemy. For love, as an affection, cannot be commanded, but beneficence for duty's sake may; even though we are not impelled to it by any inclination—nay, are even repelled by a natural and unconquerable aversion. This is *practical* love, and not *pathological* [passional or emotional–Ed.]—a love which is seated in the will, and not in the propensions of sense—in principles of action and not of tender sympathy; and it is this love alone which can be commanded.

THE SECOND PROPOSITION OF MORALITY

The second proposition is: That an action done from duty derives its moral worth, *not from the purpose* which is to be attained by it, but from the maxim by which it is determined, and therefore does not depend on the realization of the object of the action, but merely on the *principle of volition* by which the action has taken place, without regard to any object of desire. It is clear from what precedes that the purposes which we may have in view in our actions, or their effects regarded as ends and springs of the will, cannot give to actions any unconditional or moral worth. In what, then, can their worth lie, if it is not to consist in the will and in reference to its expected effect? It cannot lie anywhere but in the *principle of the will* without regard to the ends which can be attained by the action. For the will stands between its *a priori principle,* which is formal, and its *a posteriori* spring, which is material, as between two roads, and as it must be determined by something, it follows that it must be determined by the formal principle of volition when an action is done from duty, in which case every material principle has been withdrawn from it.

THE THIRD PROPOSITION OF MORALITY

The third proposition, which is a consequence of the two preceding, I would express thus: *Duty is the necessity of acting from respect for the law.* I may have *inclination* for an object as the effect of my proposed action, but I cannot have *respect* for it, just for this reason, that it is an effect and not an energy of will. Similarly, I cannot have respect for inclination, whether my own or another's; I can at most, if my

own, approve it; if another's, sometimes even love it; *i.e.* look on it as favourable to my own interest. It is only what is connected with my will as a principle, by no means as an effect—what does not subserve my inclination, but overpowers it, or at least in case of choice excludes it from its calculation—in other words, simply the law of itself, which can be an object of respect, and hence a command. Now an action done from duty must wholly exclude the influence of inclination, and with it every object of the will, so that nothing remains which can determine the will except objectively the *law,* and subjectively *pure respect* for this practical law, and consequently the maxim that I should follow this law even to the thwarting of all my inclinations.

Thus the moral worth of an action does not lie in the effect expected from it, nor in any principle of action which requires to borrow its motive from this expected effect. For all these effects—agreeableness of one's condition, and even the promotion of the happiness of others—could have been also brought about by other causes, so that for this there would have been no need of the will of a rational being; whereas it is in this alone that the supreme and unconditional good can be found. The pre-eminent good which we call moral can therefore consist in nothing else than *the conception of law* in itself, *which certainly is only possible in a rational being,* in so far as this conception, and not the expected effect, determines the will. This is a good which is already present in the person who acts accordingly, and we have not to wait for it to appear first in the result.

THE SUPREME PRINCIPLE OF MORALITY: THE CATEGORICAL IMPERATIVE

But what sort of law can that be, the conception of which must determine the will, even without paying any regard to the effect expected from it, in order that this will may be called good absolutely and without qualification? As I have deprived the will of every impulse which could arise to it from obedience to any law, there remains nothing but the universal conformity of its actions to law in general, which alone is to serve the will as a principle, i.e., I am never to act otherwise than so *that I could also will that my maxim should become a universal law.* Here, now, it is the simple conformity to law in general, without assuming any particular law applicable to certain actions, that serves the will as its principle, and must so serve it, if duty is not to be a vain delusion and a chimerical notion. The common reason of men in its practical judgments perfectly coincides with this, and always has in view the principle here suggested. Let the question be, for example: May I when in distress make a promise with the intention not to keep it? I readily distinguish here between the two significations which the question may have: Whether it is prudent, or whether it is right, to make a false promise? The former may undoubtedly often be the case. I see clearly indeed that it is not enough to extricate myself from a present difficulty by means of this subterfuge, but it must be well considered whether there may not hereafter spring from this lie much greater inconvenience than that from which I now free myself, and as, with all my supposed *cunning,* the consequences cannot be so easily foreseen but that credit once lost may be much more injurious to me than any mischief which I seek to avoid at present, it should be considered whether it would not be more *prudent* to act herein according to a universal maxim, and to make it a habit to promise nothing except with the intention of keeping it. But it is soon clear to me that such a maxim will still only be based on the fear of consequences. Now it is a wholly different thing to be truthful from duty, and to be so from apprehension of injurious consequences. In the first case, the very notion of the action already implies a law for me; in the second case, I must first look about elsewhere to see what results may be combined with it which would affect myself. For to deviate from the principle of duty is beyond all doubt wicked; but to be unfaithful to my maxim of prudence may often be very advantageous to me, although to abide by it is certainly safer. The shortest way, however, and an unerring one, to discover the answer to this question whether a lying promise is consistent with duty, is to ask myself, Should I be content that my maxim (to extricate myself from difficulty by a false promise) should hold good as a universal law, for myself as well as for others? and should I be able to say to myself, "Every one may make a deceitful promise when he finds himself in a difficulty from which he cannot otherwise extricate himself"? Then I presently become aware that while I can will the lie, I can by no means will that lying should be a universal law. For with such a law there would be no promises at all, since it would be in vain to allege my intention in regard to my future actions to those who would not believe this allegation, or if they over-hastily did so, would pay me back in my own coin. Hence my maxim, as soon as it should be made a universal law, would necessarily destroy itself.

I do not, therefore, need any far-reaching penetration to discern what I have to do in order that my will may be morally good. Inexperienced in the course of the world, incapable of being prepared for all its contingencies, I only ask myself: Canst thou also will that thy maxim should be a universal law? If not, then it must be rejected, and that not because of a disadvantage accruing from myself or even to others, but because it cannot enter as a principle into a possible universal legislation, and reason extorts from me immediate respect for such legislation. I do not indeed as yet *discern* on what this respect is based (this the philosopher may inquire), but at least I understand this, that it is an estimation of the worth which far outweighs all worth of what is recommended by inclination, and that the necessity of acting from *pure* respect for the practical law is what constitutes duty, to which every other motive must give place, because it is the condition of a will being good *in itself,* and the worth of such a will is above everything.

Thus, then, without quitting the moral knowledge of common human reason, we have arrived at its principle. And although, no doubt, common men do not conceive it in such an abstract and universal form, yet they always have it really before their eyes, and use it as the standard of their decision. . . .

Nor could anything be more fatal to morality than that we should wish to derive it from examples. For every example of it that is set before me must be first itself tested by principles of morality, whether it is worthy to serve as an original example, *i.e.* as a pattern, but by no means can it authoritatively furnish the conception of morality. Even the Holy One of the

Gospels must first be compared with our ideal of moral perfection before we can recognize Him as such; and so He says of Himself, "Why call ye Me [whom you see] good; none is good [the model of good] but God only [whom ye do not see]." But whence have we the conception of God as the supreme good? Simply from the *idea* of moral perfection, which reason frames a priori, and connects inseparably with the notion of a free will. Imitation finds no place at all in morality, and examples serve only for encouragement, i.e., they put beyond doubt the feasibility of what the law commands, they make visible that which the practical rule expresses more generally, but they can never authorize us to set aside the true original which lies in reason, and to guide ourselves by examples.

From what has been said, it is clear that all moral conceptions have their seat and origin completely *a priori* in the reason, and that, moreover, in the commonest reason just as truly as in that which is in the highest degree speculative; that they cannot be obtained by abstraction from any empirical, and therefore merely contingent knowledge; that it is just this purity of their origin that makes them worthy to serve as our supreme practical principle, and that just in proportion as we add anything empirical, we detract from their genuine influence, and from the absolute value of actions; that it is not only of the greatest necessity, in a purely speculative point of view, but is also of the greatest practical importance, to derive these notions and laws from pure reason, to present them pure and unmixed, and even to determine the compass of this practical or pure rational knowledge, *i.e.* to determine the whole faculty of pure practical reason; and, in doing so, we must not make its principles dependent on the particular nature of human reason, though in speculative philosophy this may be permitted, or may even at times be necessary; but since moral laws ought to hold good for every rational creature, we must derive them from the general concept of a rational being. In this way, although for its *application* to man morality has need of anthropology, yet, in the first instance, we must treat it independently as pure philosophy, i.e., as metaphysic, complete in itself (a thing which in such distinct branches of science is easily done); knowing well that

unless we are in possession of this, it would not only be vain to determine the moral element of duty in right actions for purposes of speculative criticism, but it would be impossible to base morals on their genuine principles, even for common practical purposes, especially of moral instruction, so as to produce pure moral dispositions, and to engraft them on men's minds to the promotion of the greatest possible good in the world. . . .

THE RATIONAL GROUND OF THE CATEGORICAL IMPERATIVE

. . . the question, how the imperative of *morality* is possible, is undoubtedly one, the only one, demanding a solution, as this is not at all hypothetical, and the objective necessity which it presents cannot rest on any hypothesis, as is the case with the hypothetical imperatives. Only here we must never leave out of consideration that we *cannot* make out *by any example,* in other words empirically, whether there is such an imperative at all; but it is rather to be feared that all those which seem to be categorical may yet be at bottom hypothetical. For instance, when the precept is: Thou shalt not promise deceitfully; and it is assumed that the necessity of this is not a mere counsel to avoid some other evil, so that it should mean: Thou shalt not make a lying promise, lest if it become known thou shouldst destroy thy credit, but that an action of this kind must be regarded as evil in itself, so that the imperative of the prohibition is categorical; then we cannot show with certainty in any example that the will was determined merely by the law, without any other spring of action, although it may appear to be so. For it is always possible that fear of disgrace, perhaps also obscure dread of other dangers, may have a secret influence on the will. Who can prove by experience the nonexistence of a cause when all that experience tells us is that we do not perceive it? But in such a case the so-called moral imperative, which as such appears to be categorical and unconditional, would in reality be only a pragmatic precept, drawing our attention to our own interests, and merely teaching us to take these into consideration.

We shall therefore have to investigate *a priori* the possibility of a categorical imperative, as we have not in this case the advantage of its reality being given in experience, so that [the elucidation of] its possibility should be requisite only for its explanation, not for its establishment. In the meantime it may be discerned beforehand that the categorical imperative alone has the purport of a practical law: all the rest may indeed be called *principles* of the will but not laws, since whatever is only necessary for the attainment of some arbitrary purpose may be considered as in itself contingent, and we can at any time be free from the precept if we give up the purpose: on the contrary, the unconditional command leaves the will no liberty to choose the opposite; consequently it alone carries with it that necessity which we require in a law.

Secondly, in the case of this categorical imperative or law of morality, the difficulty (of discerning its possibility) is a very profound one. It is an a priori synthetical practical proposition; and as there is so much difficulty in discerning the possibility of speculative propositions of this kind, it may readily be supposed that the difficulty will be no less with the practical.

FIRST FORMULATION OF THE CATEGORICAL IMPERATIVE: UNIVERSAL LAW

In this problem we will first inquire whether the mere conception of a categorical imperative may not perhaps supply us also with the formula of it, containing the proposition which alone can be a categorical imperative; for even if we know the tenor of such an absolute command, yet how it is possible will require further special and laborious study, which we postpone to the last section.

When I conceive a hypothetical imperative, in general I do not know beforehand what it will contain until I am given the condition. But when I conceive a categorical imperative, I know at once what it contains. For as the imperative contains besides the law only the necessity that the maxims shall conform to this law, while the law contain no conditions restricting it, there remains nothing but the general state-

ment that the maxim of the action should conform to a universal law, and it is this conformity alone that the imperative properly represents as necessary.

There is therefore but one categorical imperative, namely, this: *Act only on that maxim whereby thou canst at the same time will that it should become a universal law.*

Now if all imperatives of duty can be deduced from this one imperative as from their principle, then, although it should remain undecided whether what is called duty is not merely a vain notion, yet at least we shall be able to show what we understand by it and what this notion means.

Since the universality of the law according to which effects are produced constitutes what is properly called *nature* in the most general sense (as to form), that is the existence of things so far as it is determined by general laws, the imperative of duty may be expressed thus: *Act as if the maxim of thy action were to become by thy will a universal law of nature.*

FOUR ILLUSTRATIONS

We will now enumerate a few duties, adopting the usual division of them into duties to ourselves and to others, and into perfect and imperfect duties.

1. A man reduced to despair by a series of misfortunes feels wearied of life, but is still so far in possession of his reason that he can ask himself whether it would not be contrary to his duty to himself to take his own life. Now he inquires whether the maxim of his action could become a universal law of nature. His maxim is: From self-love I adopt it as a principle to shorten my life when its longer duration is likely to bring more evil than satisfaction. It is asked then simply whether this principle founded on self-love can become a universal law of nature. Now we see at once that a system of nature of which it should be a law to destroy life by means of the very feeling whose special nature it is to impel to the improvement of life would contradict itself, and therefore could not exist as a system of nature; hence the maxim cannot possibly exist as a universal law of nature, and consequently would be wholly inconsistent with the supreme principle of all duty.

2. Another finds himself forced by necessity to borrow money. He knows that he will not be able to repay it, but sees also that nothing will be lent to him, unless he promises stoutly to repay it in a definite time. He desires to make this promise, but he has still so much conscience as to ask himself: Is it not unlawful and inconsistent with duty to get out of a difficulty in this way? Suppose, however, that he resolves to do so, then the maxim of his action would be expressed thus: When I think myself in want of money, I will borrow money and promise to repay it, although I know that I never can do so. Now this principle of self-love or of one's own advantage may perhaps be consistent with my whole future welfare; but the question is, Is it right? I change then the suggestion of self-love into a universal law, and state the question thus: How would it be if my maxim were a universal law? Then I see at once that it could never hold as a universal law of nature, but would necessarily contradict itself. For supposing it to be a universal law that everyone when he thinks himself in a difficulty should be able to promise whatever he pleases, with the purpose of not keeping his promise, the promise itself would become impossible, as well as the end that one might have in view in it, since no one would consider that anything was promised to him, but would ridicule all such statements as vain pretenses.

3. A third finds in himself a talent which with the help of some culture might make him a useful man in many respects. But he finds himself in comfortable circumstances, and prefers to indulge in pleasure rather than to take pains in enlarging and improving his happy natural capacities. He asks, however, whether his maxim of neglect of his natural gifts, besides agreeing with his inclination to indulgence, agrees also with what is called duty. He sees then that a system of nature could indeed subsist with such a universal law although men (like the South Sea islanders) should let their talents rest, and resolve to devote their lives merely to idleness, amusement, and propagation of their species—in a word, to enjoyment; but he cannot possibly *will* that this should be a universal law of nature, or be implanted in us as such by a natural instinct. For, as a rational being, he necessarily wills that his faculties be developed, since they serve him, and have been given him, for all sorts of possible purposes.

4. A fourth, who is in prosperity, while he sees that others have to contend with great wretchedness and that he could help them, thinks: What concern is it of mine? Let everyone be as happy as Heaven pleases, or as he can make himself; I will take nothing from him nor even envy him, only I do not wish to contribute anything to his welfare or to his assistance in distress! Now no doubt if such a mode of thinking were a universal law, the human race might very well subsist, and doubtless even better than in a state in which everyone talks of sympathy and good-will, or even takes care occasionally to put it into practice, but, on the other side, also cheats when he can, betrays the rights of men, or otherwise violates them. But although it is possible that a universal law of nature might exist in accordance with that maxim, it is impossible to *will* that such a principle should have the universal validity of a law of nature. For a will which resolved this would contradict itself, inasmuch as many cases might occur in which one would have need of the love and sympathy of others, and in which, by such a law of nature, sprung from his own will, he would deprive himself of all hope of the aid he desires.

These are a few of the many actual duties, or at least what we regard as such, which obviously fall into two classes on the one principle that we have laid down. We must be *able to will* that a maxim of our action should be a universal law. This is the canon of the moral appreciation of the action generally. Some actions are of such a character that their maxim cannot without contradiction be even *conceived* as a universal law of nature, far from it being possible that we should *will* that it *should* be so. In others this intrinsic impossibility is not found, but still it is impossible to *will* that their maxim should be raised to the universality of a law of nature, since such a will would contradict itself. It is easily seen that the former violate strict or rigorous (inflexible) duty; the latter only laxer (meritorious) duty. Thus it has been completely shown by these examples how all duties depend as regards the nature of the obligation (not the object of the action) on the same principle. . . .

SECOND FORMULATION OF THE CATEGORICAL IMPERATIVE: HUMANITY AS AN END IN ITSELF

Now I say: man and generally any rational being *exists* as an end in himself, *not merely as a means* to be arbitrarily used by this or that will, but in all his actions, whether they concern himself or other rational beings, must be always regarded at the same time as an end. All objects of the inclinations have only a conditional worth; for if the inclinations and the wants founded on them did not exist, then their object would be without value. But the inclinations themselves being sources of want are so far from having an absolute worth for which they should be desired, that, on the contrary, it must be the universal wish of every rational being to be wholly free from them. Thus the worth of any object which is *to be acquired* by our action is always conditional. Beings whose existence depends not on our will but on nature's, have nevertheless, if they are nonrational beings, only a relative value as means, and are therefore called *things;* rational beings, on the contrary, are called *persons,* because their very nature points them out as ends in themselves, that is as something which must not be used merely as means, and so far therefore restricts freedom of action (and is an object of respect). These, therefore, are not merely subjective ends whose existence has a worth *for us* as an effect of our action, but *objective ends,* that is things whose existence is an end in itself: an end moreover for which no other can be substituted, which they should subserve *merely* as means, for otherwise nothing whatever would possess *absolute worth;* but if all worth were conditioned and therefore contingent, then there would be no supreme practical principle of reason whatever.

If then there is a supreme practical principle or, in respect of the human will, a categorical imperative, it must be one which, being drawn from the conception of that which is necessarily an end for everyone because it is *an end in itself,* constitutes an *objective* principle of will, and can therefore serve as a universal practical law. The foundation of this principle is: *rational nature exists as an end in itself.* Man neces-

sarily conceives his own existence as being so: so far then this is a *subjective* principle of human actions. But every other rational being regards its existence similarly, just on the same rational principle that holds for me: so that it is at the same time an objective principle, from which as a supreme practical law all laws of the will must be capable of being deduced. Accordingly the practical imperative will be as follows: *So act as to treat humanity, whether in thine own person or in that of any other, in every case as an end withal, never as means only. . . .*

. . . Looking back now on all previous attempts to discover the principle of morality, we need not wonder why they all failed. It was seen that man was bound to laws by duty, but it was not observed that the laws to which he is subject are *only those of his own giving,* though at the same time they are *universal,* andthat he is only bound to act in conformity with his own will; a will, however, which is designed by nature to give universal laws. For when one has conceived man only as subject to a law (no matter what), then this law required some interest, either by way of attraction or constraint, since it did not originate as a law from *his own* will, but this will was according to a law obliged by *something else* to act in a certain manner. Now by this necessary consequence all the labour spent in finding a supreme principle of *duty* was irrevocably lost. For men never elicited duty, but only a necessity of acting from a certain interest. Whether this interest was private or otherwise, in any case the imperative must be conditional, and could not by any means be capable of being a moral command. I will therefore call this the principle of *Autonomy* of the will, in contrast with every other which I accordingly reckon as *Heteronomy.*

THE KINGDOM OF ENDS

The conception of every rational being as one which must consider itself as giving in all the maxims of its will universal laws, so as to judge itself and its actions from this point of view—this conception leads to another which depends on it and is very fruitful, namely, that of a *kingdom of ends.*

By a *kingdom* I understand the union of different rational beings in a system by common laws. Now since it is by laws that ends are determined as regards their universal validity, hence, if we abstract from the personal differences of rational beings, and likewise from all the content of their private ends, we shall be able to conceive all ends combined in a systematic whole (including both rational beings as ends in themselves, and also the special ends which each may propose to himself), that is to say, we can conceive a kingdom of ends, which on the preceding principles is possible.

For all rational beings come under the *law* that each of them must treat itself and all others *never merely as means,* but in every case *at the same time as ends in themselves.* Hence results a systematic union of rational beings by common objective laws, *i.e.,* a kingdom which may be called a kingdom of ends, since what these laws have in view is just the relation of these beings to one another as ends and means. . . .

FOR FURTHER REFLECTION

1. What is the aim of Kant's work? Why does he want to reject empirical (that is, sociological and anthropological) data in constructing a "pure moral philosophy"?

2. What is the only quality that is good without qualification? Analyze Kant's reasoning here. Is it cogent? Why or why not?

3. Is Kant's philosophy merely a development of the Golden Rule: "Do unto others what you would have them do unto you"? If it is equivalent, does that make Kant's system more intuitively plausible? Does it lead to problems with what Kant thought were the implications of his system? (For example, on the basis of the Golden Rule one might endorse certain instances of euthanasia, but Kant's discussion of suicide seems to rule this endorsement out.) Explain.

4. Kant's ethics are called *deontological* (from the Greek word "duty") because he believes that the value of an act is in the act itself, rather than in its consequences (as teleologists hold). Deontological ethics have been criticized as being too rigid. Do you agree? Should the notion of consequences be taken into consideration? Explain your answer.

5. How would Kant deal with moral conflicts? When two universal principles conflict, how would Kant resolve the dilemma?

6. Kant's categorical imperative has also been criticized for being more wide open than he realized because it doesn't limit what could be universalized. How would Kant respond to the following counterexamples? (a) "Everyone should tie his or her right shoe before the left shoe." (b) "All retarded or senile people should be executed by the government" (also, "If I should become retarded or senile, I should also undergo this fate").

E. Challenges to Traditional Moral Theories

We have examined several types of traditional moral theories, but not every philosopher accepts a form of these theories. Ethical relativism, which denies the objectivity and universal validity of morality, is not the only challenge to traditional moral theories. Four others may be examined.

The first challenge comes from David Hume, who questions the traditional conception of moral reasoning that maintained that moral assessments are the result of a rational exercise of human reason. Hume argues instead that moral assessments are special feelings of pleasure and pain that we experience when we see someone perform a good or bad action. Hume's view is captured in the expression, "Ought cannot be Derived from Is," that is, moral assessments cannot be rationally deduced from a mere collection of factual statements. In more recent years A. J. Ayer continued Hume's line of attack by arguing that moral utterances are not factual at all, but merely express our feelings, such as the statement "Hoorary for Charity!" or "Boo for stealing!"

The second challenge is Friedrich Nietzsche's interpretation of morality as the will to power. Each of us seeks to affirm him- or herself, to dominate. Unlike utilitarianism, Nietzsche's ethic is not about maximizing happiness: "Man does not want happiness, only the Englishman wants happiness. Man wants power," he wrote. There are two ways to attempt to achieve this end, which Nietzsche designates *slave morality* and *master morality*. Master morality is the natural mode of the natural aristocracy (*Übermenchen*) who spontaneously live out of their own instincts and drives, seeking to fulfill themselves. Sometimes this seems to be an aesthetic way of life, in which the noble person seeks to realize himself as a magnificent work of art. Slave morality is a reaction, a resentment against noble souls. It asserts itself by trying to pull down the edifice of nobility. It advocates peace, humility, mercy, pity, endurance, equality—in short, the "Christian virtues," which are really indirect ways of maintaining the power of the mediocre masses over the elite.

The third challenge to traditional moral theories consists of criticism of the abstract nature of traditional morality. The philosopher-novelist William Gass argues that the abstract nature of traditional morality fails to do justice to the concreteness of our everyday moral decisions, which are ineluctably particular. He imagines an obliging stranger who agrees to be part of an experiment, whereupon Gass knocks him out and puts him into an oven, at which point the question becomes: Why is this act wrong? The classical theories fail because they try to give reasons where none are needed. Gass's alternative might be called *particularist intuitionism.* In Part III of his reading, Gass satirizes traditional moral theories as giving reasons to refrain from actions that are obviously wrong: "The moralist can say, with conviction, what is wrong, but he can't say why."

The fourth challenge comes from Thomas Nagel, who questions the typical conception of moral responsibility. Most moral theories, particularly those that follow Kant, emphasize our free-will choices to make moral decisions and the responsibility that we bear when we choose the wrong course of action. But what if many of our moral decisions rest on factors that are completely beyond our control? Consider, for example, how a Nazi concentration camp officer might have lived his life if the Nazis never came to power; he might have lived an otherwise virtuous life. Thus, being good seems to involve some moral luck as much as it does moral choice.

DAVID HUME

〜

MORALITY NOT DERIVED FROM REASON

Born in Edinburgh, Scotland, David Hume (1711–1776) is one of the great philosophers of the English-speaking world and is famous for his skeptical views in epistemology, the philosophy of religion, and ethics. In two of his works, *A Treatise of Human Nature* (1739–1740) and *An Enquiry Concerning the Principles of Morals* (1751), he challenges traditional assumptions about the role of reason in morality; selections from both of these appear here.

Since ancient times, philosophers have typically believed that morality is a rational phenomenon; first, we discover moral principles through reason, and, second, reason motivates us to follow these principles. Hume attacks both of these positions and argues instead that morality is a function of human emotion, not reason. He recognizes that there are arguments supporting the roles of both reason and emotion in moral matters; ultimately, though, he concludes that moral approval is only a pleasing feeling or sentiment, not a rational judgment. For example, when I assess that Jill's act of charity is morally good, I am feeling only a special kind of pleasure about her action; I am not rationally discovering any moral truth. Furthermore, Hume argues, reason can never motivate us to act: reason only presents us with facts, and facts alone cannot prompt action. No matter how many starving people I see, I will never be motivated to help feed these people unless I am driven by emotion, not by reason. Hume closes with his famous position that *ought cannot be derived from is*. That is, it is impossible to rationally deduce statements of obligation from statements of fact in the manner that traditional moral philosophers have attempted to do.

REASON VERSUS SENTIMENT

There has been a controversy started of late . . . concerning the general foundation of morals: whether they be derived from reason or from sentiment; whether we attain the knowledge of them by a chain of argument and induction or by an immediate feeling and finer internal sense; whether, like all sound judgment of truth and falsehood, they should be the same to every rational intelligent being or whether, like the perception of beauty and deformity, they be founded entirely on the particular fabric and constitution of the human species.

The ancient philosophers, though they often affirm that virtue is nothing but conformity to reason, yet, in general, seem to consider morals as deriving their existence from taste and sentiment. On the other hand, our modern inquirers (though they also talk much of the beauty of virtue and deformity of vice, yet) have commonly endeavored to account for these distinctions by

From David Hume, *An Enquiry Concerning the Principles of Morals* (1751), Section 1 and Appendix 1. Two additional paragraphs are from Hume's *A Treaise of Human Nature* (1739–1740), as indicated in the footnotes. Section headings have been added, and spelling and punctuation have been modernized by the editor.

metaphysical reasonings, and by deductions from the most abstract principles of the understanding. Such confusion reigned in these subjects, that an opposition of the greatest consequence could prevail between one system and another, and even in the parts of almost each individual system. And yet nobody, till very lately, was ever sensible of it.

The Case for Reason

It must be acknowledged that both sides of the question are susceptible of specious arguments. Moral distinctions, it may be said, are discernible by pure reason. Else, whence the many disputes that reign in common life as well as in philosophy with regard to this subject: the long chain of proofs often produced on both sides, the examples cited, the authorities appealed to, the analogies employed, the fallacies detected, the inferences drawn, and the several conclusions adjusted to their proper principles. Truth is disputable, not taste. What exists in the nature of things is the standard of our judgment, [but] what each man feels within himself is the standard of sentiment. Propositions in geometry may be proved, systems in physics may be controverted. But the harmony of verse, the tenderness of passion, the brilliance of wit must give immediate pleasure. No man reasons concerning another's beauty, but frequently concerning the justice or injustice of his actions. In every criminal trial the first object of the prisoner is to disprove the facts alleged, and deny the actions imputed to him. The second [is] to prove that, even if these actions were real, they might be justified as innocent and lawful. It is confessedly by deductions of the understanding that the first point [of alleged facts] is ascertained. How can we suppose that a different faculty of the mind is employed in fixing the other [point regarding moral justification]?

The Case for Sentiment

On the other hand, those who would resolve all moral determinations into *sentiment* may endeavor to show that it is impossible for reason ever to draw conclusions of this nature. To virtue, say they, it belongs to be *amiable*, and [to] vice *odious*. This

forms their very nature or essence. But can reason or argumentation distribute these different epithets to any subjects, and pronounce beforehand that this must produce love, and that hatred? Or what other reason can we ever assign for these affections but the original fabric and formation of the human mind, which is naturally adapted to receive them?

The end of all moral speculations is to teach us our duty and (by proper representations of the deformity of vice and beauty of virtue) beget correspondent habits and engage us to avoid the one and embrace the other. But is this ever to be expected from the inferences and conclusions of the understanding, which, of themselves, have no hold of the affections nor set in motion the active powers of men? They discover truths. But where the truths which they discover are indifferent and beget no desire or aversion, they can have no influence on conduct and behavior. What is honorable, what is fair, what is becoming, what is noble, what is generous, takes possession of the heart and animates us to embrace and maintain it. What is intelligible, what is evident, what is probable, what is true, procures only the cool assent of the understanding, and gratifying a speculative curiosity, puts an end to our researches.

It is not contrary to reason to prefer the destruction of the whole world to the scratching of my finger. It is not contrary to reason for me to choose my total ruin, to prevent the least uneasiness of an *Indian* or person wholly unknown to me. It is as little contrary to reason to prefer even my own acknowledged lesser good to my greater, and have a more ardent affection for the former than the latter. A trivial good may, from certain circumstances, produce a desire superior to what arises from the greatest and most valuable enjoyment. Nor is there anything more extraordinary in this than in [the field of] mechanics to see [a] one pound weight raise up a hundred by the advantage of its situation [such as by a lever]. In short, a passion must be accompanied with some false judgment in order to its being unreasonable.[1]

Extinguish all the warm feelings and prepossessions in favor of virtue and all disgust or aversion to vice; render men totally indifferent towards these distinctions, and morality is no longer a practical study, nor has any tendency to regulate our lives and actions.

The Limited Role of Reason

These arguments on each side (and many more might be produced) are so plausible that I am apt to suspect they may, the one as well as the other, be solid and satisfactory, and that *reason* and *sentiment* concur in almost all moral determinations and conclusions. The final sentence, it is probable, which pronounces characters and actions amiable or odious, praise-worthy or blamable; that which stamps on them the mark of honor or infamy, approbation or censure; that which renders morality an active principle and constitutes virtue our happiness, and vice our misery; it is probable, I say, that this final sentence depends on some internal sense or feeling which nature has made universal in the whole species. For what else can have an influence of this nature? But in order to pave the way for such a *sentiment*, and give a proper discernment of its object, it is often necessary, we find, that much *reasoning* should precede, [so] that nice distinctions be made, just conclusions drawn, distant comparisons formed, complicated relations examined, and general facts fixed and ascertained.

Some species of beauty, especially the natural kinds, on their first appearance, command our affection and approbation. And where they fail of this effect, it is impossible for any reasoning to redress their influence, or adapt them better to our taste and sentiment. But in many orders of beauty, particularly those of the finer arts, it is requisite to employ much reasoning in order to feel the proper sentiment. And a false relish may frequently be corrected by argument and reflection. There are just grounds to conclude that moral beauty partakes much of this latter species, and demands the assistance of our intellectual faculties, in order to give it a suitable influence on the human mind....

ARGUMENTS AGAINST OTHER ROLES OF REASON IN MORALITY

This partition between the faculties of understanding and sentiment, in all moral decisions, seems clear from the preceding hypothesis. But I shall suppose that hypothesis false: it will then be requisite to look out for some other theory that may be satisfactory. And I dare venture to affirm that none such will ever be found, so long as we suppose reason to be the sole source of morals. To prove this, it will be proper to weigh the five following considerations.

Approval as Not a Judgment About Fact or Relations

It is easy for a false hypothesis to maintain some appearance of truth, while it keeps wholly in generals, makes use of undefined terms, and employs comparisons, instead of [citing] instances. This is particularly remarkable in that philosophy which ascribes the discernment of all moral distinctions to reason alone, without the concurrence of sentiment. It is impossible that, in any particular instance, this hypothesis can so much as be rendered intelligible, whatever specious figure it may make in general declamations and discourses. Examine the crime of *ingratitude*, for instance (which has place, wherever we observe good will, expressed and known, together with good offices performed, on the one side, and a return of ill-will or indifference, with ill-offices or neglect on the other). Anatomize all these circumstances and examine by your reason alone in what consists the demerit or blame. You never will come to any issue or conclusion.

Reason Judges Either of Matter of Fact or of Relations[2]

Inquire then, *first*, where is that matter of fact which we here call *crime*. Point it out. Determine the time of its existence. Describe its essence or nature. Explain the sense or faculty to which it discovers itself. [You may say that] it resides in the mind of the person who is ungrateful, [and that] he must, therefore, feel it and be conscious of it. But [in reply] nothing is there except the passion of ill-will or absolute indifference. You cannot say that these, of themselves, always and in all circumstances are crimes. No: they are only crimes when directed towards persons who have before expressed and displayed good will towards us. Consequently, we may infer that the crime of ingratitude is not any particular individual *fact*; but arises from a complication of circumstances which, being presented to the spectator, excites the *sentiment* of blame by the particular structure and fabric of his mind. ...

No New Fact Is Discovered

When a man, at any time, deliberates concerning his own conduct (as whether he had better, in a particular emergence, assist a brother or a benefactor), he must consider these separate relations, with all the circumstances and situations of the persons, in order to determine the superior duty and obligation. And in order to determine the proportion of lines in any triangle, it is necessary to examine the nature of that figure, and the relations which its several parts bear to each other. But notwithstanding this appearing similarity in the two cases, there is, at bottom, an extreme difference between them. A speculative reasoner concerning triangles or circles considers the several known and give relations of the parts of these figures, and thence infers some unknown relation which is dependent on the former. But in moral deliberations, we must be acquainted *beforehand* with all the objects, and all their relations to each other. And from a comparison of the whole, [we] fix our choice or approbation. No new fact to be ascertained. No new relation to be discovered. All the circumstances of the case are supposed to be laid before us, ere we can fix any sentence of blame or approbation. If any material circumstance be yet unknown or doubtful, we must first employ our inquiry or intellectual faculties to assure us of it and must suspend for a time all moral decision or sentiment. While we are ignorant whether a man were aggressor or not, how can we determine whether the person who killed him be criminal or innocent? But after every circumstance, every relation is known [and] the understanding has no further room to operate, nor any object on which it could employ itself. The approbation or blame which then ensues cannot be the work of the judgment, but of the heart, and is not a speculative proposition or affirmation, but an active feeling or sentiment. In the disquisitions of the understanding, from known circumstances and relations, we infer some[thing] new and unknown. In moral decisions, all the circumstances and relations must be previously known. And the mind, from the contemplation of the whole, feels some new impression of affection or disgust, esteem or contempt, approbation or blame.

Hence the great difference between a mistake of *fact* and one of *right*. And hence the reason why the one is commonly criminal and not the other. When Oedipus killed Laius, he was ignorant of the relation, and from circumstances, innocent and involuntary, formed erroneous opinions concerning the action which he committed. But when Nero killed Agrippina, all the relations between himself and the person and all the circumstances of the fact were previously known to him. But the motive of revenge, or fear, or interest, prevailed in his savage heart over the sentiments of duty and humanity. And when we express that detestation against him (to which he, himself, in a little time became insensible), it is not that we see any relations of which he was ignorant. But that, from the rectitude of our disposition, we feel sentiments against which he was hardened, from flattery and a long perseverance in the most enormous crimes. In these sentiments, then, [and] not in a discovery of relations of any kind, do all moral determinations consist. Before we can pretend to form any decision of this kind, everything must be known and ascertained on the side of the object or action. Nothing remains but to feel, on our part, some sentiment of blame or approbation; whence we pronounce the action criminal or virtuous.

Similarity Between Moral and Aesthetic Perception

This doctrine will become still more evident if we compare moral beauty with natural, to which, in many particulars, it bears so near a resemblance. It is on the proportion, relation, and position of parts that all natural beauty depends. But it would be absurd to infer that the perception of beauty, like that of truth in geometrical problems, consists wholly in the perception of relations and was performed entirely by the understanding or intellectual faculties. In all the sciences, our mind, from the known relations, investigates the unknown. But in all decisions of taste or external beauty, all the relations are beforehand obvious to the eye. And we thence proceed to feel a sentiment of complacency or disgust, according to the nature of the object and disposition of our organs.

Euclid has fully explained all the qualities of the circle, but has not, in any proposition, said a word of its beauty. The reason is evident. The beauty is not a quality of the circle. It lies not in any part of the line, whose parts are equally distant from a common center. It is only the effect which that figure produces upon the mind, whose peculiar fabric or structure renders it susceptible of such sentiments. In vain would you look for it in the circle, or seek it either by your senses, or by mathematical reasonings in all the properties of that figure.

Attend to Palladio and Perrault, while they explain all the parts and proportions of a pillar. They talk of the cornice and frieze and base and entablature and shaft and architrave, and give the description and position of each of these members. But should you ask the description and position of its beauty, they would readily reply that the beauty is not in any of the parts or members of a pillar, but results from the whole, when that complicated figure is presented to an intelligent mind, susceptible to those finer sensations. Until such a spectator appears, there is nothing but a figure of such particular dimensions and proportions. From his sentiments alone arise its elegance and beauty.

Again, attend to Cicero while he paints the crimes of a Verres or a Catiline. You must acknowledge that the moral turpitude results, in the same manner, from the contemplation of the whole, when presented to a being whose organs have such a particular structure and formation. The orator may paint rage, insolence, barbarity on the one side; meekness, suffering, sorrow, innocence on the other. But if you feel no indignation or compassion arise in you from this complication of circumstances, you would in vain ask him, in what consists the crime or villainy which he so vehemently exclaims against; at what time or on what subject it first began to exist; and what has a few months afterwards become of it, when every disposition and thought of all the actors is totally altered or annihilated. No satisfactory answer can be given to any of these questions, upon the abstract hypothesis of morals. And we must at last acknowledge that the crime or immorality is no particular fact or relation, which can be the object of the understanding. But, [it] arises entirely from the sentiment of disapprobation which, by the structure of human nature, we unavoidably feel on the apprehension of barbarity or treachery.

No Distinctly Moral Relation

Inanimate objects may bear to each other all the same relations which we observe in moral agents, though the former can never be the object of love or hatred, nor are consequently susceptible of merit or iniquity. A young tree which over-tops and destroys its parent, stands in all the same relations with Nero when he murdered [his mother] Agrippina. And if morality consisted merely in relations, [this] would, no doubt, be equally criminal. ...

CONCLUSION

Thus, the distinct boundaries and offices of *reason* and of *taste* are easily ascertained. The former conveys the knowledge of truth and falsehood. The latter gives the sentiment of beauty and deformity, vice and virtue. The one discovers objects as they really stand in nature, without addition or diminution. The other has a productive faculty and (gilding or staining all natural objects with the colors borrowed from internal sentiment) raises in a manner a new creation. Reason, being cool and disengaged, is no motive to action and directs only the impulse received from appetite or inclination, by showing us the means of attaining happiness or avoiding misery. Taste, as it gives pleasure or pain (and thereby constitutes happiness or misery), becomes a motive to action and is the first spring or impulse to desire and volition. From circumstances and relations known or supposed, the former leads us to the discovery of the concealed and unknown. After all circumstances and relations are laid before us, the latter makes us feel from the whole a new sentiment of blame or approbation. The standard of the one, being founded on the nature of things, is eternal and inflexible, even by the will of the Supreme Being. The standard of the other, arising from the internal frame and constitution of animals, is ultimately derived from that Supreme will, which bestowed on each being its peculiar nature and arranged the several classes and orders of existence.

Deriving Ought from Is

I cannot forbear adding to these reasonings an observation, which may, perhaps, be found of some importance. In every system of morality which I have hitherto met with, I have always remarked that the author proceeds for some time in the ordinary way of reasoning and establishes the being of a God or makes observations concerning human affairs. When of a sudden, I am surprised to find that, instead of the usual copulations of propositions, *is* and *is not*, I meet with no proposition that is not connected with an *ought* or an *ought not*. The change is imperceptible, but is, however, of the last [and greatest] consequence. For as this *ought* or *ought not* expresses some new relation or affirmation, it is necessary that it should be observed and explained. And at the same time, [it is necessary] that a reason should be given for (what seems altogether inconceivable) how this new relation can be a deduction from others, which are entirely different from it. But as authors do not commonly use this precaution, I shall presume to recommend it to the readers. And [I] am persuaded that this small attention would subvert all the vulgar systems of morality, and let us see that the distinction of vice and virtue is not founded merely on the relations of objects nor is perceived by reason.³

NOTES

1. [The preceding paragraph is from *A Treatise of Human Nature*, Book 2, Part 3, Section 3.]

2. [A matter of fact is a fact about the world that we know through our experience, such as the sun will rise tomorrow. A relation is an abstract mathematical or logical truth that we know through reflection, such as three times five equals half of thirty. Hume's point is that the sole function of reason is to assess matters of fact or relations. Since moral approval is not a judgment about matters of fact or relations, then moral approval is not an act of reason.]
3. [The preceding paragraph is from *A Treatise of Human Nature*, Book 3, Part 1, Section 1.]

FOR FURTHER REFLECTION

1. Hume comments that "it is not contrary to reason to prefer the destruction of the whole world to the scratching of my finger." How does this example show the need for sentiment or feeling in morality, and is he correct in his point?
2. The faculty of reason, according to Hume, is restricted to judgments concerning relations of ideas and matters of fact. Is there another area of human reasoning that doesn't fall into these two categories?
3. According to Hume, morality is not a judgment about matters of fact. Is there anything factual about moral judgments beyond what Hume claims?
4. Hume argues that we cannot derive statements of obligation from statements of fact (i.e., *ought* statements from *is* statements). Give an example of what he is talking about.

ALFRED JULES AYER

EMOTIVISM AND PRESCRIPTIVISM

Alfred Jules Ayer (1910–1989) was a philosophy professor at University College, London, and New College, Oxford. Among his many publications, his first work *Language, Truth and Logic* (1936) is his most famous, in which he defends the radically empiricist theory of logical positivism. In that work, Ayer challenges the traditional rationalist view of morality with the following argument:

(1) A statement is a factual judgment if only if it is either (a) capable of empirical verification or (b) true by definition.
(2) Moral evaluations are neither (a) capable of empirical verification nor (b) true by definition.
(3) Therefore, moral evaluations are not factual judgments.

Rejecting the view that moral evaluations are factual judgments, Ayer concludes that moral utterances merely (1) express our feelings and (2) make commands to other people. For example, when I say "it is good for Jill to donate to charity," I am (1) expressing my favorable emotions about Jill and (2) commanding you to approve of Jill's conduct. Philosophers today refer to the first of these components as *emotive* and the second as *prescriptive*. For Ayer, insofar as moral evaluations are only emotive and prescriptive, "They are unverifiable for the same reason as a cry of pain or a word of command is unverifiable—because they do not express genuine propositions." Ayer emphasizes the difference between (1) expressing an emotion and (2) asserting or reporting an emotion. Although some philosophers hold that moral judgments involve assertions or reports about our emotions, Ayer disagrees: moral judgments are simply expressions of feelings without any factual assertion or report of our feelings.

THE NATURE AND LIMITS OF ETHICAL PHILOSOPHY

The ordinary system of ethics, as elaborated in the works of ethical philosophers, is very far from being a homogeneous whole. Not only is it apt to contain pieces of metaphysics, and analyses of non-ethical concepts: its actual ethical contents are themselves of very different kinds. We may divide them, indeed, into four main classes. There are, first of all, propositions which express definitions of ethical terms, or judgements about the legitimacy or possibility of certain definitions. Secondly, there are propositions describing the phenomena of moral experience, and their causes. Thirdly, there are exhortations to moral virtue. And, lastly, there are actual ethical judgements. It is unfortunately the case that the distinction between these four classes, plain as it is, is commonly

From A. J. Ayer, *Language Truth and Logic* (New York, Dover, 1952), Chapter 6. Section titles have been added by the editor.

ignored by ethical philosophers; with the result that it is often very difficult to tell from their works what it is that they are seeking to discover or prove.

In fact, it is easy to see that only the first of our four classes, namely that which comprises the propositions relating to the definitions of ethical terms, can be said to constitute ethical philosophy. The propositions which describe the phenomena of moral experience, and their causes, must be assigned to the science of psychology, or sociology. The exhortations to moral virtue are not propositions at all, but ejaculations or commands which are designed to provoke the reader to action of a certain sort. Accordingly, they do not belong to any branch of philosophy or science. As for the expressions of ethical judgements, we have not yet determined how they should be classified. But inasmuch as they are certainly neither definitions nor comments upon definitions, nor quotations, we may say decisively that they do not belong to ethical philosophy. A strictly philosophical treatise on ethics should therefore make no ethical pronouncements. But it should, by giving an analysis of ethical terms, show what is the category to which all such pronouncements belong. And this is what we are now about to do.

A question which is often discussed by ethical philosophers is whether it is possible to find definitions which would reduce all ethical terms to one or two fundamental terms. But this question, though it undeniably belongs to ethical philosophy, is not relevant to our present inquiry. We are not now concerned to discover which term, within the sphere of ethical terms, is to be taken as fundamental; whether, for example, "good" can be defined in terms of "right" or "right" in terms of "good," or both in terms of "value." What we are interested in is the possibility of reducing the whole sphere of ethical terms to non-ethical terms. We are inquiring whether statements of ethical value can be translated into statements of empirical fact. . . .

MEANINGLESSNESS OF ETHICAL STATEMENTS

We begin by admitting that the fundamental ethical concepts are unanalysable, inasmuch as there is no criterion by which one can test the validity of the judgements in which they occur. So far we are in agreement with the absolutists [who hold that statements of value are not controlled by observation, but by a mysterious intellectual intuition]. But, unlike the absolutists, we are able to give an explanation of this fact about ethical concepts. We say that the reason why they are unanalysable is that they are mere pseudo-concepts. The presence of an ethical symbol in a proposition adds nothing to its factual content. Thus if I say to someone, "You acted wrongly in stealing that money," I am not stating anything more than if I had simply said, "You stole that money." In adding that this action is wrong I am not making any further statement about it. I am simply evincing my moral disapproval of it. It is as if I had said, "You stole that money," in a peculiar tone of horror, or written it with the addition of some special exclamation marks. The tone, or the exclamation marks, adds nothing to the literal meaning of the sentence. It merely serves to show that the expression of it is attended by certain feelings in the speaker.

If now I generalize my previous statement and say, "Stealing money is wrong," I produce a sentence which has no factual meaning—that is, expresses no proposition which can be either true or false. It is as if I had written "Stealing money!!"—where the shape and thickness of the exclamation marks show, by a suitable convention, that a special sort of moral disapproval is the feeling which is being expressed. It is clear that there is nothing said here which can be true or false. Another man may disagree with me about the wrongness of stealing, in the sense that he may not have the same feelings about stealing as I have, and he may quarrel with me on account of my moral sentiments. But he cannot, strictly speaking, contradict me. For in saying that a certain type of action is right or wrong, I am not making any factual statement, not even a statement about my own state of mind. I am merely expressing certain moral sentiments. And the man who is ostensibly contradicting me is merely expressing his moral sentiments. So that there is plainly no sense in asking which of us is in the right. For neither of us is asserting a genuine proposition.

What we have just been saying about the symbol "wrong" applies to all normative ethical symbols. Sometimes they occur in sentences which record ordinary empirical facts besides expressing ethical feeling about those facts: sometimes they occur in sentences which simply express ethical feeling about a certain type of action, or situation, without making any statement of fact. But in every case in which one would commonly be said to be making an ethical judgement, the function of the relevant ethical word is purely "emotive." It is used to express feeling about certain objects, but not to make any assertion about them.

EXPRESSING FEELINGS AND COMMANDS

It is worth mentioning that ethical terms do not serve only to express feeling. They are calculated also to arouse feeling, and so to stimulate action. Indeed some of them are used in such a way as to give the sentences in which they occur the effect of commands. Thus the sentence "It is your duty to tell the truth" may be regarded both as the expression of a certain sort of ethical feeling about truthfulness and as the expression of the command "Tell the truth." The sentence "You ought to tell the truth" also involves the command "Tell the truth," but here the tone of the command is less emphatic. In the sentence "It is good to tell the truth" the command has become little more than a suggestion. And thus the "meaning" of the word "good," in its ethical usage, is differentiated from that of the word "duty" or the word "ought." In fact we may define the meaning of the various ethical words in terms both of the different feelings they are ordinarily taken to express, and also the different responses which they are calculated to provoke.

We can now see why it is impossible to find a criterion for determining the validity of ethical judgements. It is not because they have an "absolute" validity which is mysteriously independent of ordinary sense-experience, but because they have no objective validity whatsoever. If a sentence makes no statement at all, there is obviously no sense in asking whether what it says is true or false. And we have seen that sentences which simply express moral judgements do not say anything. They are pure expressions of feeling and as such do not come under the category of truth and falsehood. They are unverifiable for the same reason as a cry of pain or a word of command is unverifiable—because they do not express genuine propositions.

EXPRESSING FEELINGS VS. ASSERTING FEELINGS

Thus, although our theory of ethics might fairly be said to be radically subjectivist, it differs in a very important respect from the orthodox subjectivist theory. For the orthodox subjectivist does not deny, as we do, that the sentences of a moralizer express genuine propositions. All he denies is that they express propositions of a unique non-empirical character. His own view is that they express propositions about the speaker's feelings. If this were so, ethical judgements clearly would be capable of being true or false. They would be true if the speaker had the relevant feelings, and false if he had not. And this is a matter which is, in principle, empirically verifiable. Furthermore they could be significantly contradicted. For if I say, "Tolerance is a virtue," and someone answers, "You don't approve of it," he would, on the ordinary subjectivist theory, be contradicting me. On our theory, he would not be contradicting me, because, in saying that tolerance was a virtue, I should not be making any statement about my own feelings or about anything else. I should simply be evincing my feelings, which is not at all the same thing as saying that I have them.

The distinction between the expression of feeling and the assertion of feeling is complicated by the fact that the assertion that one has a certain feeling often accompanies the expression of that feeling, and is then, indeed, a factor in the expression of that feeling. Thus I may simultaneously express boredom and say that I am bored, and in that case my utterance of the words, "I am bored," is one of the circumstances which make it true to say that I am expressing or evincing boredom. But I can express boredom without actually saying that I am bored. I can express it by my tone and gestures, while making a statement about something wholly unconnected with it, or by an ejaculation, or without uttering any words at all. So that even if the assertion that one has a certain feeling always involves the expression of that feeling, the expression of a feeling assuredly does not always involve the assertion that one has it. And this is the important point to grasp in considering the distinction between our theory and the ordinary subjectivist theory. For whereas the subjectivist holds that ethical statements actually assert the existence of certain feelings, we hold that ethical statements are expressions and excitants of feeling which do not necessarily involve any assertions.

We have already remarked that the main objection to the ordinary subjectivist theory is that the validity of ethical judgements is not determined by the nature of their author's feelings. And this is an objection which our theory escapes. For it does not imply that the existence of any feelings is a necessary and sufficient condition of the validity of an ethical judgement. It implies, on the contrary, that ethical judgements have no validity.

IMPOSSIBILITY OF TRUE MORAL DISPUTES

There is, however, a celebrated argument against subjectivist theories which our theory does not escape. It has been pointed out by Moore that if ethical statements were simply statements about the speaker's feelings, it would be impossible to argue about questions of value.[1] To take a typical example: if a man said that thrift was a virtue, and another replied that it was a vice, they would not, on this theory, be disputing with one another. One would be saying that he approved of thrift and the other that *he* didn't; and there is no reason why both these statements should not be true. Now Moore held it to be obvious that we do dispute about questions of value, and accordingly concluded that the particular for-in of subjectivism which he was discussing was false.

It is plain that the conclusion that it is impossible to dispute about questions of value follows from our theory also. For as we hold that such sentences as "Thrift is a virtue" and "Thrift is a vice" do not express propositions at all, we clearly cannot hold that they express incompatible propositions. We must therefore admit that if Moore's argument really refutes the ordinary subjectivist theory, it also refutes ours. But, in fact, we deny that it does refute even the ordinary subjectivist theory. For we hold that one really never does dispute about questions of value.

This may seem, at first sight, to be a very paradoxical assertion. For we certainly do engage in disputes which are ordinarily regarded as disputes about questions of value. But, in all such cases, we find, if we consider the matter closely, that the dispute is not really about a question of value, but about a question of fact. When someone disagrees with us about the moral value of a certain action or type of action, we do admittedly resort to argument in order to win him over to our way of thinking. But we do not attempt to show by our arguments that he has the "wrong" ethical feeling towards a situation whose nature he has correctly apprehended. What we attempt to show is that he is mistaken about the facts of the case. We argue that he has misconceived the agent's motive: or that he has misjudged the effects of the action, or its probable effects in view of the agent's knowledge; or that he has failed to take into account the special circumstances in which the agent was placed. Or else we employ more general arguments about the effects which actions of a certain type tend to produce, or the qualities which are usually manifested in their performance. We do this in the hope that we have only to get our opponent to agree with us about the nature of the empirical facts for him to adopt the same moral attitude towards them as we do. And as the people with whom we argue have generally received the same moral education as ourselves, and live in the same social order, our expectation is usually justified. But if our opponent happens to have undergone a different process of moral "conditioning" from ourselves, so that, even when he acknowledges all the facts, he still disagrees with us about the moral value of the actions under discussion, then we abandon the attempt to convince him by argument. We say that it is impossible to argue with him because he has a distorted or undeveloped moral sense; which signifies merely that he employs a different set of values from our own. We feel that our own system of values is superior, and therefore speak in such derogatory terms of his. But we cannot bring forward any arguments to show that our system is superior. For our judgement that it is so is itself a judgement of value, and accordingly outside the scope of argument. It is because argument fails us when we come to deal with pure questions of value, as distinct from questions of fact, that we finally resort to mere abuse.

In short, we find that argument is possible on moral questions only if some system of values is presupposed. If our opponent concurs with us in expressing moral disapproval of all actions of a given type t, then we may get him to condemn a particular action A, by bringing forward arguments to show that A is of type t. For the question whether A does or does not belong to that type is a plain question of fact. Given that a man has certain moral principles, we argue that he must, in order to be consistent, react morally to certain things in a certain way. What we do not and cannot argue about is the validity of these moral principles. We merely praise or condemn them in the light of our own feelings.

If anyone doubts the accuracy of this account of moral disputes, let him try to construct even an imaginary argument on a question of value which does not reduce itself to an argument about a question of logic or about an empirical matter of fact. I am confident that he will not succeed in producing a single example. And if that is the case, he must allow that its involving the impossibility of purely ethical arguments is not, as Moore thought, a ground of objection to our theory, but rather a point in favor of it.

ETHICS AS A BRANCH OF PSYCHOLOGY

Having upheld our theory against the only criticism which appeared to threaten it, we may now use it to define the nature of all ethical inquires. We find that ethical philosophy consists simply in saying that ethical concepts are pseudo-concepts and therefore unanalysable. The further task of describing the different feelings that the different ethical terms are used to express, and the different reactions that they customarily provoke, is a task for the psychologist. There cannot be such a thing as ethical science, if by ethical science one means the elaboration of a "true" system of morals. For we have seen that, as ethical judgements are mere expressions of feeling, there can be no

way of determining the validity of any ethical system, and, indeed, no sense in asking whether any such system is true. All that one may legitimately inquire in this connection is, What are the moral habits of a given person or group of people, and what causes them to have precisely those habits and feelings? And this inquiry falls wholly within the scope of the existing social sciences.

It appears, then, that ethics, as a branch of knowledge, is nothing more than a department of psychology and sociology. And in case anyone thinks that we are overlooking the existence of casuistry, we may remark that casuistry is not a science, but is a purely analytical investigation of the structure of a given moral system. In other words, it is an exercise in formal logic.

When one comes to pursue the psychological inquiries which constitute ethical science, one is immediately enabled to account for the Kantian and hedonistic theories of morals. For one finds that one of the chief causes of moral behavior is fear, both conscious and unconscious, of a god's displeasure, and fear of the enmity of society. And this, indeed, is the reason why moral precepts present themselves to some people as "categorical" commands. And one finds, also, that the moral code of a society is partly determined by the beliefs of that society concerning the conditions of its own happiness-or, in other words, that a society tends to encourage or discourage a given type of conduct by the use of moral sanctions according as it appears to promote or detract from the contentment of the society as a whole. And this is the reason why altruism is recommended in most moral codes and egotism condemned. It is from the observation of this connection between morality and happiness that hedonistic or eudæmonistic theories of morals ultimately spring, just as the moral theory of Kant is based on the fact, previously explained, that moral precepts have for some people the force of inexorable commands. As each of these theories ignores the fact which lies at the root of the other, both may be criticized as being onesided; but this is not the main objection to either of them. Their essential defect is that they treat propositions which refer to the causes and attributes of our ethical feelings as if they were definitions of ethical concepts. And thus they fail to recognize that ethical concepts are pseudo-concepts and consequently indefinable.

NOTES

1. [G.E. Moore] cf. *Philosophical Studies*, "The Nature of Moral Philosophy."

FOR FURTHER REFLECTION

1. Ayer writes that "The presence of an ethical symbol in a proposition adds nothing to its factual content." What does he mean, and is he correct?

2. Ayer writes that "We can now see why it is impossible to find a criterion for determining the validity of ethical judgements." Why, according to him, is it impossible, and is he correct?

3. Ayer maintains that his emotivist theory differs significantly from the "orthodox subjectivist theory," as he calls it. What is the main point of difference, and is that difference really as big as he claims?

4. Ayer maintains that we "finally resort to mere abuse" when we have moral disagreements. Are moral disagreements really battles of emotions as Ayer suggests?

FRIEDRICH NIETZSCHE

BEYOND GOOD AND EVIL

Friedrich Nietzsche (1844–1900) was a German existentialist who has played a major role in contemporary intellectual development. Descended through both his parents from Christian ministers, Nietzsche was brought up in a pious German Lutheran home and was known as "the little Jesus" by his schoolmates. He studied theology at the University of Bonn and philology at Leipzig, becoming an atheist in the process. At age twenty-four, he was appointed professor of classical philology at the University of Basel in Switzerland, where he taught for ten years until ill health forced him to retire. Eventually he also became mentally ill. He died on August 25, 1900.

Nietzsche believes that the fundamental force that motivates all creation is the will to power. We all seek to affirm ourselves, to flourish and dominate. Because people are essentially unequal in ability, it follows that the fittest will survive and be victorious in the contest with the weaker and baser. There is great esthetic beauty in the noble spirit coming to fruition, but this process is hampered by Judeo-Christian morality, which Nietzsche labels "slave morality." Slave morality, which is the invention of jealous priests envious and resentful of the power of the noble, prescribes that we give up the will to power and excellence and become meek and mild, that we believe the Judeo-Christian lie that all humans are of equal worth. In our reading, Nietzsche also refers to this morality as the "ethics of resentment."

Nietzsche's ideas of inegalitarian ethics are based on his notion of God's death. God plays no vital role in our culture—except as protector of the slave morality, including egalitarianism. If we recognize that there is no rational basis for believing in God, we see that the whole structure of slave morality must crumble, and with it the notion of equal worth. In its place arises the morality of the noble person, based on the virtues of high courage, discipline, and intelligence in the pursuit of self-affirmation and excellence.

We begin this section with Nietzsche's famous description of the madman who announces the death of God, and then we turn to selections from *Beyond Good and Evil, The Genealogy of Morals,* and *The Twilight of the Idols.*

THE MADMAN AND THE DEATH OF GOD

Have you ever heard of the madman who on a bright morning lighted a lantern and ran to the market-place calling out unceasingly: "I seek God! I seek God!"— As there were many people standing about who did not believe in God, he caused a great deal of amusement. Why! is he lost? said one. Has he strayed away like a child? said another. Or does he keep himself hidden? Is he afraid of us? Has he taken a sea-voyage? Has he emigrated?—the people cried out laughingly, all in a hubbub. The insane man jumped into their midst and transfixed them with his glances. "Where is God gone?" he called out. "I mean to tell you! *We have killed him,*—you and I! We are all his murderers! But how have we done it? How were we able to drink up the sea? Who gave us the sponge to wipe away the whole horizon? What did we do when we loosened this earth from its sun? Whither does it now move? Whither do we move? Away from all suns? Do we not dash on unceasingly? Backwards, sideways, forewards, in all directions? Is there still an above and below? Do we not stray, as through infinite nothingness? Does not empty space breathe upon us? Has it not become colder? Does not night come on continually, darker and darker? Shall we not have to light lanterns in the morning? Do we not hear the noise of the grave-diggers who are burying God? Do we not smell the divine putrefaction?—for even Gods putrefy! God is dead! God remains dead! And we have killed him! How shall we console ourselves, the most murderous of all murderers? The holiest and the mightiest that the world has hitherto possessed, has bled to death under our knife,—who will wipe the blood from us? With what water could we cleanse ourselves? What lustrums, what sacred games shall we have to devise? Is not the magnitude of this deed too great for us? Shall we not ourselves have to become Gods, merely to seem worthy of it? There never was a greater event,—and on account of it, all who are born after us belong to a higher history than any history hitherto!"—Here the madman was silent and looked again at his hearers; they also were silent and looked at him in surprise. At last he threw his lantern on the ground, so that it broke in pieces and was extinguished. "I come too early," he then said, "I am not yet at the right time. This prodigious event is still on its way, and is travelling,—it has not yet reached men's ears. Lightning and thunder need time, the light of the stars needs time, deeds need time, even after they are done, to be seen and heard. This deed is as yet further from them than the furthest star,—*and yet they have done it!*"—It is further stated that the madman made his way into different churches on the same day, and there intoned his *Requiem aeternam deo.* When led out and called to account, he always gave the reply: "What are these churches now, if they are not the tombs and monuments of God?"—. . . .

WHAT IS NOBLE?

Every elevation of the type "man," has hitherto been the work of an aristocratic society and so it will always be—a society believing in a long scale of gradations of rank and differences of worth among

From Friedrich Nietzsche, in *The Complete Works of Nietzsche,* ed. and trans. Oscar Levy, vols. 10 and 11 (T. N. Foulis, 1910). Some passages have been adapted by the editor for clarity.

human beings, and requiring slavery in some form or other. Without the *pathos of distance,* such as grows out of the incarnated difference of classes, out of the constant outlooking and downlooking of the ruling caste on subordinates and instruments, and out of their equally constant practice of obeying and commanding, of keeping down and keeping at a distance—that other more mysterious pathos could never have arisen, the longing for an ever new widening of distance within the soul itself, the formation of ever higher, rarer, further, more extended, more comprehensive states, in short, just the elevation of the type "man," the continued "self-surmounting of man," to use a moral formula in a supermoral sense. To be sure, one must not resign oneself to any humanitarian illusions about the history of the origin of an aristocratic society (that is to say, of the preliminary condition for the elevation of the type "man"): the truth is hard. Let us acknowledge unprejudicedly how ever higher civilisation hitherto has *originated!* Men with a still natural nature, barbarians in every terrible sense of the word, men of prey, still in possession of unbroken strength of will and desire for power, threw themselves upon weaker, more moral, more peaceful races (perhaps trading or cattle-rearing communities), or upon old mellow civilisations in which the final vital force was flickering out in brilliant fireworks of wit and depravity. At the commencement, the noble caste was always the barbarian caste: their superiority did not consist first of all in their physical, but in their psychical power—they were more *complete* men (which at every point also implies the same as "more complete beasts").

Corruption—as the indication that anarchy threatens to break out among the instincts, and that the foundation of the emotions, called "life," is convulsed—is something radically different according to the organisation in which it manifests itself. When, for instance, an aristocracy like that of France at the beginning of the Revolution, flung away its privileges with sublime disgust and sacrificed itself to an excess of its moral sentiments, it was corruption:—it was really only the closing act of the corruption which had existed for centuries, by virtue of which that aristocracy had abdicated step by step its lordly prerogatives and lowered itself to a *function* of royalty (in the end even to its decoration and parade-dress). The essential thing, however, in a good and healthy aristocracy is that it should *not* regard itself as a function either of the kingship or the commonwealth, but as the *significance* and highest justification thereof—that it should therefore accept with a good conscience the sacrifice of a legion of individuals, who, *for its sake,* must be suppressed and reduced to imperfect men, to slaves and instruments. Its fundamental belief must be precisely that society is *not* allowed to exist for its own sake, but only as a foundation and scaffolding, by means of which a select class of beings may be able to elevate themselves to their higher duties, and in general to a higher *existence:* like those sun-seeking climbing plants in Java—they are called *Sipo Matador,*—which encircle an oak so long and so often with their arms, until at last, high above it, but supported by it, they can unfold their tops in the open light, and exhibit their happiness.

To refrain mutually from injury, from violence, from exploitation, and put one's will on a par with that of others: this may result in a certain rough sense in good conduct among individuals when the necessary conditions are given (namely, the actual similarity of the individuals in amount of force and degree of worth, and their co-relation within one organisation). As soon, however, as one wished to take this principle more generally, and if possible even as *the fundamental principle of society,* it would immediately disclose what it really is—namely, a Will to the *denial* of life, a principle of dissolution and decay. Here one must think profoundly to the very basis and resist all sentimental weakness: life itself is *essentially* appropriation, injury, conquest of the strange and weak, suppression, severity, obtrusion of peculiar forms, incorporation, and at the least, putting it mildest, exploitation;—but why should one for ever use precisely these words on which for ages a disparaging purpose has been stamped? Even the organisation within which, as was previously supposed, the individuals treat each other as equal—it takes place in every healthy aristocracy—must itself, if it be a living and not a dying organisation, do all that towards other bodies, which the individuals within it refrain from doing to each other: it will have to be the incarnated Will to Power, it will endeavour to grow, to gain ground, attract to itself and acquire ascendency—not owing to any morality or immorality, but because it *lives,* and because life *is* precisely Will to Power. On no point, however, is the ordinary consciousness of Europeans more unwilling to be corrected than on this matter; people now rave everywhere, even under the guise of science, about coming conditions of society in which "the exploiting character" is to be absent:—that sounds to my ears as if they promised to invent a mode of life which should refrain from all organic functions. "Exploitation" does not belong to a depraved, or imperfect and primitive society: it belongs to the *nature* of the living being as a primary organic function; it is a consequence of the intrinsic Will to Power, which is precisely the Will to Life.— Granting that as a theory this is a novelty—as a reality it is the *fundamental fact* of all history: let us be so far honest towards ourselves!

MASTER AND SLAVE MORALITY

In a tour through the many finer and coarser moralities which have hitherto prevailed or still prevail on the earth, I found certain traits recurring regularly together, and connected with one another, until finally two primary types revealed themselves to me, and a radical distinction was brought to light. There is *master-morality* and *slave-morality;*—I would at once add, however, that in all higher and mixed civilisations, there are also attempts at the reconciliation of the two moralities; but one finds still oftener the confusion and mutual misunderstanding of them, indeed, sometimes their close juxtaposition—even in the same man, within one soul. The distinctions of moral values have either originated in a ruling caste, pleasantly conscious of being different from the ruled—or among the ruled class, the slaves and dependents of all sorts. In the first case, when it is the rulers who determine the conception "good," it is the exalted, proud disposition which is regarded as the distinguishing feature, and that which determines the order of rank. The noble type of man separates from himself the beings in whom the opposite of this exalted, proud disposition displays itself: he despises them. Let it at once be noted that in this first kind of moral-

ity the antithesis "good" and "bad" means practically the same as "noble" and "despicable";—the antithesis "good" and "*evil*" is of a different origin. The cowardly, the timid, the insignificant, and those thinking merely of narrow utility are despised; moreover, also, the distrustful, with their constrained glances, the self-abasing, the dog-like kind of men who let themselves be abused, the mendicant flatterers, and above all the liars:—it is a fundamental belief of all aristocrats that the common people are untruthful. "We truthful ones"—the nobility in ancient Greece called themselves. It is obvious that everywhere the designations of moral value were at first applied to *men,* and were only derivatively and at a later period applied to *actions;* it is a gross mistake, therefore, when historians of morals start with questions like, "Why have sympathetic actions been praised?" The noble type of man regards *himself* as a determiner of values; he does not require to be approved of; he passes the judgment: "What is injurious to me is injurious in itself"; he knows that it is he himself only who confers honour on things; he is a *creator of values.* He honours whatever he recognises in himself: such morality is self-glorification. In the foreground there is the feeling of plenitude, of power, which seeks to overflow, the happiness of high tension, the consciousness of a wealth which would fain give and bestow:—the noble man also helps the unfortunate, but not—or scarcely—out of pity, but rather from an impulse generated by the super-abundance of power. The noble man honours in himself the powerful one, him also who has power over himself, who knows how to speak and how to keep silence, who takes pleasure in subjecting himself to severity and hardness, and has reverence for all that is severe and hard. "Wotan placed a hard heart in my breast," says an old Scandinavian Saga: it is thus rightly expressed from the soul of a proud Viking. Such a type of man is even proud of *not* being made for sympathy; the hero of the Saga therefore adds warningly: "He who has not a hard heart when young, will never have one." The noble and brave who think thus are the furthest removed from the morality which sees precisely in sympathy, or in acting for the good of others, or in *désintéressement,* the characteristic of the moral; faith in oneself, pride in oneself, a radical enmity and irony towards "selflessness," belong as definitely to noble morality, as do a careless scorn and precaution in presence of sympathy and the "warm heart."—It is the powerful who *know* how to honour, it is their art, their domain for invention. The profound reverence for age and for tradition—all law rests on this double reverence,—the belief and prejudice in favour of ancestors and unfavourable to newcomers, is typical in the morality of the powerful; and if, reversely, men of "modern ideas" believe almost instinctively in "progress" and the "future," and are more and more lacking in respect for old age, the ignoble origin of these "ideas" has complacently betrayed itself thereby. A morality of the ruling class, however, is more especially foreign and irritating to present-day taste in the sternness of its principle that one has duties only to one's equals; that one may act towards beings of a lower rank, towards all that is foreign, just as seems good to one, or "as the heart desires," and in any case "beyond good and evil": it is here that sympathy and similar sentiments can have a place. The ability and obligation to exercise prolonged gratitude and prolonged revenge—both only within the circle of equals,—artfulness in retaliation, *raffinement* of the idea in friendship, a certain necessity to have enemies (as outlets for the emotions of envy, quarrelsomeness, arrogance—in fact, in order to be a good *friend*): all these are typical characteristics of the noble morality, which, as has been pointed out, is not the morality of "modern ideas," and is therefore at present difficult to realise and also to unearth and disclose.—It is otherwise with the second type of morality, *slave-morality*. Supposing that the abused, the oppressed, the suffering, the unemancipated, the weary, and those uncertain of themselves, should moralise, what will be the common element in their moral estimates? Probably a pessimistic suspicion with regard to the entire situation of man will find expression, perhaps a condemnation of man, together with his situation. The slave has an unfavourable eye for the virtues of the powerful; he has a scepticism and distrust, a *refinement* of distrust of everything "good" that is there honoured—he would fain persuade himself that the very happiness there is not genuine. On the other hand, *those* qualities which serve to alleviate the existence of sufferers are brought into promi-

nence and flooded with light; it is here that sympathy, the kind, helping hand, the warm heart, patience, diligence, humility, and friendliness attain to honour; for here these are the most useful qualities, and almost the only means of supporting the burden of existence. Slave-morality is essentially the morality of utility. Here is the seat of the origin of the famous antithesis "good" and "evil":—power and dangerousness are assumed to reside in the evil, a certain dreadfulness, subtlety, and strength, which do not admit of being despised. According to slave-morality, therefore, the "evil" man arouses fear; according to master-morality, it is precisely the "good" man who arouses fear and seeks to arouse it, while the bad man is regarded as the despicable being. The contrast attains its maximum when, in accordance with the logical consequences of slave-morality, a shade of depreciation—it may be slight and well-intentioned—at last attaches itself to the "good" man of this morality; because, according to the servile mode of thought, the good man must in any case be the *safe* man: he is good-natured, easily deceived, perhaps a little stupid, *un bonhomme*. Everywhere that slave-morality gains the ascendency, language shows a tendency to approximate the significations of the words "good" and "stupid."—A last fundamental difference: the desire for *freedom,* the instinct for happiness and the refinements of the feeling of liberty belong as necessarily to slave-morals and morality, as artifice and enthusiasm in reverence and devotion are the regular symptoms of an aristocratic mode of thinking and estimating.—Hence we can understand without further detail why love *as a passion*—it is our European specialty—must absolutely be of noble origin; as is well known, its invention is due to the Provençal poet-cavaliers, those brilliant, ingenious men of the "*gai saber,*" to whom Europe owes so much, and almost owes itself. . . .

There is an *instinct for rank,* which more than anything else is already the sign of a *high* rank; there is a *delight* in the *nuances* of reverence which leads one to infer noble origin and habits. The refinement, goodness, and loftiness of a soul are put to a perilous test when something passes by that is of the highest rank, but is not yet protected by the awe of authority from obtrusive touches and incivilities: something that goes its way like a living touchstone, undistinguished, undiscovered, and tentative, perhaps voluntarily veiled and disguised. He whose task and practice it is to investigate souls, will avail himself of many varieties of this very art to determine the ultimate value of a soul, the unalterable, innate order of rank to which it belongs: he will test it by its *instinct for reverence. Différence engendre haine* [Difference engenders hate.—Ed.]: the vulgarity of many a nature spurts up suddenly like dirty water, when any holy vessel, any jewel from closed shrines, any book bearing the marks of great destiny, is brought before it; while on the other hand, there is an involuntary silence, a hesitation of the eye, a cessation of all gestures, by which it is indicated that a soul *feels* the nearness of what is worthiest of respect. . . .

The revolt of the slaves in morals begins in the very principle of *resentment* becoming creative and giving birth to values—a resentment experienced by creatures who, deprived as they are of the proper outlet of action, are forced to find their compensation in an imaginary revenge. While every aristocratic morality springs from a triumphant affirmation of its own demands, the slave-morality says "no" from the very outset to what is "outside itself," "different from itself," and "not itself": and this "no" is its creative deed. This reversal of the valuing standpoint—this *inevitable* gravitation to the objective instead of back to the subjective—is typical of "resentment": the slave-morality requires as the condition of its existence an external and objective world, to employ physiological terminology, it requires objective stimuli to be capable of action at all—its action is fundamentally a reaction. The contrary is the case when we come to the aristocrat's system of values: it acts and grows spontaneously, it merely seeks its antithesis in order to pronounce a more grateful and exultant "yes" to its own self;—its negative conception, "low," "vulgar," "bad," is merely a pale late-born foil in comparison with its positive and fundamental conception (saturated as it is with life and passion), of "we aristocrats, we good ones, we beautiful ones, we happy ones."

When the aristocratic morality goes astray and commits sacrilege on reality, this is limited to that particular sphere with which it is *not* sufficiently acquainted—a sphere, in fact, from the real knowledge of which it disdainfully defends itself. It misjudges, in some cases, the sphere which it despises, the sphere of the common vulgar man and the low people: on the other hand, due weight should be given to the consideration that in any case the mood of contempt, of disdain, of superciliousness, even on the supposition that it *falsely* portrays the object of its contempt, will always be far removed from that degree of falsity which will always characterise the attacks—in effigy, of course—of the vindictive hatred and revengefulness of the weak in onslaughts on their enemies. In point of fact, there is in contempt too strong an admixture of nonchalance, of casualness, of boredom, of impatience, even of personal exultation, for it to be capable of distorting its victim into a real caricature or a real monstrosity. Attention again should be paid to the almost benevolent *nuances* which, for instance, the Greek nobility imports into all the words by which it distinguishes the common people from itself; note how continuously a kind of pity, care, and consideration imparts its honeyed fl*avour,* until at last almost all the words which are applied to the vulgar man survive finally as expressions for "unhappy," "worthy of pity" . . . —and how, conversely, "bad," "low," "unhappy" have never ceased to ring in the Greek ear with a tone in which "unhappy" is the predominant note: this is a heritage of the old noble aristocratic morality, which remains true to itself even in contempt. . . . The "well-born" simply *felt* themselves the "happy"; they did not have to manufacture their happiness artificially through looking at their enemies, or in cases to talk and lie themselves into happiness (as is the custom with all resentful men); and similarly, complete men as they were, exuberant with strength, and consequently *necessarily* energetic, they were too wise to dissociate happiness from action—activity becomes in their minds necessarily counted as happiness (that is the etymology of ευ∴ πραστειν)—all in sharp contrast to the "happiness" of the weak and the oppressed, with their festering venom and malignity, among whom happiness appears essentially as a narcotic, a deadening, a quietude, a peace, a "Sabbath," an enervation of the mind and relaxation of the limbs,—in short, a purely *passive* phenomenon. While the aristocratic man lived in confidence and openness with himself (γεν–ναῖος, "noble-born," emphasises the nuance "sincere," and perhaps also "naïf"), the resentful man, on the other hand, is neither sincere nor naïf, nor honest and candid with himself. His soul *squints;* his mind loves hidden crannies, tortuous paths and backdoors, everything secret appeals to him as *his* world, *his* safety, *his* balm; he is past master in silence, in not forgetting, in waiting, in provisional self-depreciation and self-abasement. A race of such *resentful* men will of necessity eventually prove more *prudent* than any aristocratic race, it will honour prudence on quite a distinct scale, as, in fact, a paramount condition of existence, while prudence among aristocratic men is apt to be tinged with a delicate flavour of luxury and refinement; so among them it plays nothing like so integral a part as that complete certainty of function of the governing *unconscious* instincts, or as indeed a certain lack of prudence, such as a vehement and valiant charge, whether against danger or the enemy, or as those ecstatic bursts of rage, love, reverence, gratitude, by which at all times noble souls have recognised each other. When the resentment of the aristocratic man manifests itself, it fulfils and exhausts itself in an immediate reaction, and consequently instills no *venom:* on the other hand, it never manifests itself at all in countless instances, when in the case of the feeble and weak it would be inevitable. An inability to take seriously for any length of time their enemies, their disasters, their *misdeeds*—that is the sign of the full strong natures who possess a superfluity of moulding plastic force, that heals completely and produces forgetfulness: a good example of this in the modern world is Mirabeau, who had no memory for any insults and meannesses which were practised on him, and who was only incapable of forgiving because he forgot. Such a man indeed shakes off with a shrug many a worm which would have buried itself in another; it is only in characters like these that we see the possibility (supposing, of course, that there is such a possibility in the world) of the real "*love* of one's enemies." What respect for his enemies is found, forsooth, in an aristocratic man—and such a

reverence is already a bridge to love! He insists on having his enemy to himself as his distinction. He tolerates no other enemy but a man in whose character there is nothing to despise and *much* to honour! On the other hand, imagine the "enemy" as the resentful man conceives him—and it is here exactly that we see his work, his creativeness; he has conceived "the evil enemy," the "evil one," and indeed that is the root idea from which he now evolves as a contrasting and corresponding figure a "good one," himself—his very self!

The method of this man is quite contrary to that of the aristocratic man, who conceives the root idea "good" spontaneously and straight away, that is to say, out of himself, and from that material then creates for himself a concept of "bad"! This "bad" of aristocratic origin and that "evil" out of the cauldron of unsatisfied hatred—the former an imitation, an "extra," an additional nuance; the latter, on the other hand, the original, the beginning, the essential act in the conception of a slave-morality—these two words "bad" and "evil," how great a difference do they mark, in spite of the fact that they have an identical contrary in the idea "good." But the idea "good" is *not* the same: much rather let the question be asked, "Who is really evil according to the meaning of the morality of resentment?" In all sternness let it be answered thus:— *just* the good man of the other morality, just the aristocrat, the powerful one, the one who rules, but who is distorted by the venomous eye of resentfulness, into a new colour, a new signification, a new appearance. This particular point we would be the last to deny: the man who learnt to know those "good" ones only as enemies, learnt at the same time not to know them only as "*evil enemies,*" and the same men who . . . were kept so rigorously in bounds through convention, respect, custom, and gratitude, though much more through mutual vigilance and jealousy, . . . these men who in their relations with each other find so many new ways of manifesting consideration, self-control, delicacy, loyalty, pride, and friendship, these men are in reference to what is outside their circle (where the foreign element, a *foreign* country, begins), not much better than beasts of prey, which have been let loose. They enjoy there freedom from all social control, they feel that in the wilderness they can give vent with impunity to that tension which is produced by enclosure and imprisonment in the peace of society, they *revert* to the innocence of the beast-of-prey conscience, like jubilant monsters, who perhaps come from a ghostly bout of murder, arson, rape, and torture, with bravado and a moral equanimity, as though merely some wild student's prank had been played, perfectly convinced that the poets have now an ample theme to sing and celebrate. It is impossible not to recognise at the core of all these aristocratic races the beast of prey; the magnificent *blonde brute,* avidly rampant for spoil and victory; this hidden core needed an outlet from time to time, the beast must get loose again, must return into the wilderness—the Roman, Arabic, German, and Japanese nobility, the Homeric heroes, the Scandinavian Vikings, are all alike in this need. It is the aristocratic races who have left the idea "Barbarian" on all the tracks in which they have marched; nay, a consciousness of this very barbarianism, and even a pride in it, manifests itself even in their highest civilisation (for example, when Pericles says to his Athenians in that celebrated funeral oration, "Our audacity has forced a way over every land and sea, rearing everywhere imperishable memorials of itself for *good* and for *evil*"). This audacity of aristocratic races, mad, absurd, and spasmodic as may be its expression; the incalculable and fantastic nature of their enterprises, . . . their nonchalance and contempt for safety, body, life, and comfort, their awful joy and intense delight in all destruction, in all the ecstasies of victory and cruelty,— all these features become crystallised, for those who suffered thereby in the picture of the "barbarian," of the "evil enemy," perhaps of the "Goth" and of the "Vandal." The profound, icy mistrust which the German provokes, as soon as he arrives at power,—even at the present time,—is always still an aftermath of that inextinguishable horror with which for whole centuries Europe has regarded the wrath of the blonde Teuton beast. . . .

. . . One may be perfectly justified in being always afraid of the blonde beast that lies at the core of all aristocratic races, and in being on one's guard: but who would not a hundred times prefer to be afraid, when one at the same time admires, than to be immune from fear, at the cost of being perpetually obsessed with the loathsome spectacle of the distorted, the dwarfed, the stunted, the envenomed? And is that not our fate? What produces to-day our repulsion towards "man"?—for we *suffer* from "man," there is no doubt about it. It is not fear; it is rather that we have nothing more to fear from men; it is that the worm "man" is in the foreground and pullulates; it is that the "tame man," the wretched mediocre and unedifying creature, has learnt to consider himself a goal and a pinnacle, an inner meaning, an historic principle, a "higher man"; yes, it is that he has a certain right so to consider himself, in so far as he feels that in contrast to that excess of deformity, disease, exhaustion, and effeteness whose odour is beginning to pollute present-day Europe, he at any rate has achieved a relative success, he at any rate still says "yes" to life.

GOODNESS AND THE WILL TO POWER

What is good?—All that enhances the feeling of power, the Will to Power, and the power itself in man. What is bad?—All that proceeds from weakness. What is happiness?—The feeling that power is increasing—that resistance has been overcome.

Not contentment, but more power; not peace at any price but war; not virtue, but competence (virtue in the Renaissance sense, *virtu,* free from all moralistic acid). The first principle of our humanism: The weak and the failures shall perish. They ought even to be helped to perish.

What is more harmful than any vice?—Practical sympathy and pity for all the failures and all the weak: Christianity.

Christianity is the religion of pity. Pity opposes the noble passions which heighten our vitality. It has a depressing effect, depriving us of strength. As we multiply the instances of pity we gradually lose our strength of nobility. Pity makes suffering contagious and under certain conditions it may cause a total loss of life and vitality out of all proportion to the magnitude of the cause. . . . Pity is the practice of nihilism.

FOR FURTHER REFLECTION

1. What do you make of the parable of God's death? What is its significance for ethics?
2. A good exercise for getting a grip on the radicality of Nietzsche's ethics is to read Jesus' Sermon on the Mount (Matthew 5–7) after reading Nietzsche. Discuss the contrast.
3. Compare Nietzsche's ethics with Aristotle's ethics of virtue. What are the similarities and differences? How might Aristotle respond to the charge that his ethics are really a "gentleman's" version of Nietzsche's more shocking ideas?

WILLIAM GASS

THE CASE OF THE OBLIGING STRANGER

William Gass (b. 1924), long a professor at Washington University in St. Louis, is the author of many short stories and novels, including *Omensetter's Luck* (1966). In this essay, Gass challenges the standard moral theories with their emphasis on reasoning from abstract principles. He argues that in ordinary life moral decisions are made quite differently from the way the theoreticians suppose.

I

Imagine I approach a stranger on the street and say to him, "If you please sir, I desire to perform an experiment with your aid." The stranger is obliging, and I lead him away. In a dark place conveniently by, I strike his head with the broad of an axe and cart him home. I place him, buttered and trussed, in an ample electric oven. The thermostat reads 450°F. Thereupon I go off to play poker with friends and forget all about the obliging stranger in the stove. When I return, I realize I have overbaked my specimen, and the experiment, alas, is ruined.

Something has been done wrong. Or something wrong has been done.

Any ethic that does not roundly condemn my action is vicious. It is interesting that none is vicious for this reason. It is also interesting that no more convincing refutation of any ethic could be given than by showing that it approved of my baking the obliging stranger.

This is really all I have to say, but I shall not stop on that account. Indeed, I shall begin again.

II

The geometer cannot demonstrate that a line is beautiful. The beauty of lines is not his concern. We do not chide him when he fails to observe uprightness in his

From William Gass, "The Case of the Obliging Stranger," *The Philosophy Review* 66 (1957), by permission of the author and the publisher.

verticals, when he discovers no passions between sinuosities. We would not judge it otherwise than foolish to berate him for neglecting to employ the methods successful in biology or botany merely because those methods dealt fairly with lichens and fishes. Nor do we despair of him because he cannot give us reasons for doing geometry which will equally well justify our drilling holes in teeth. There is a limit, as Aristotle said, to the questions which we may sensibly put to each man of science; and however much we may desire to find unity in the purposes, methods, and results of every fruitful sort of inquiry, we must not allow that desire to make much of their necessary differences.

Historically, with respect to the fundamental problems of ethics, the limit has not been observed. Moreover, the analogy between mathematics and morals, or between the methods of empirical science and the good life, has always been unfairly one-sided. Geometers never counsel their lines to be moral, but moralists advise men to be like lines and go straight. There are triangles of lovers, but no triangles in love. And who says the organism is a state?

For it is true that the customary methods for solving moral problems are the methods which have won honors by leaping mathematical hurdles on the one hand or scientific and physical ones on the other: the intuitive and deductive method and the empirical and inductive one. Nobody seems to have minded very much that the moral hurdle has dunked them both in the pool beyond the wall, for they can privately laugh at each other for fools, and together they can exclaim how frightfully hard is the course.

The difficulty for the mathematical method is the discovery of indubitable moral first premises which do not themselves rest on any inductive foundation and which are still applicable to the complicated tissue of factors that make up moral behavior. The result is that the premises are usually drawn from metaphysical speculations having no intimate relation to moral issues or from rational or mystical revelations which only the intuiter and his followers are willing to credit. For the purposes of deduction, the premises have to be so broad and, to satisfy intuition, so categorically certain, that they become too thin for touch and too heavy for bearing. All negative instances are pruned as unreal or parasitic. Conse-

quently, the truth of the ultimate premises is constantly called into question by those who have intuited differently or have men and actions in mind that they want to call good and right but cannot.

Empirical solutions, so runs the common complaint, lop off the normative branch altogether and make ethics a matter of expediency, taste, or conformity to the moral etiquette of the time. One is told what people do, not what they ought to do; and those philosophers who still wish to know what people ought to do are told, by some of the more uncompromising, that they can have no help from empiricism and are asking a silly question. Philosophers, otherwise empiricists, who admit that moral ends lie beyond the reach of factual debate turn to moral sentiment or some other *bonum ex machina* [literally, good from a machine; contrived appeal to a theory of the good.—Ed.], thus generously embracing the perplexities of both methods.

III

Questions to which investigators return again and again without success are very likely improperly framed. It is important to observe that the ethical question put so directly as "What is good?" or "What is right?"[1] aims in its answer not, as one might immediately suppose, at a catalogue of the world's good, right things. The moralist is not asking for a list of sheep and goats. The case of the obliging stranger is a case of immoral action, but this admission is not an answer, even partially, to the question, "What is wrong?"

Furthermore, the ethical question is distressingly short. "Big" questions, it would seem, ought to be themselves big, but they almost never are; and they tend to grow big simply by becoming short—too short, in fact, ever to receive an answer. I might address, to any ear that should hear me, the rather less profound-sounding, but none the less similar question, "Who won?" or perhaps the snappier, "What's a winner?" I should have to ask this question often because, if I were critical, I should never find an answer that would suit me; while at the same time there would be a remarkable lot of answers that suited a remarkable lot of people. The more answers I had— the more occasions on which I asked the question—

the more difficult, the more important, the more "big" the question would become.

If the moralist does not want to hear such words as "Samson," "money," or "brains" when he asks his question, "What is good?," what does he want to hear? He wants to hear a word like "power." He wants to know what is good in the things that are good that makes them good. It should be perfectly clear it is not the things themselves that he thinks good or bad but the qualities they possess, the relations they enter into, or the consequences they produce. Even an intuitionist, who claims to perceive goodness directly, perceives a property of things when he perceives goodness, and not any *thing,* except incidentally. The wrong done the obliging stranger was not the act of cooking him but was something belonging to the act in some one of many possible ways. It is not I who am evil (if I am not mad) but something which I *have* that is; and while, of course, I may be adjudged wicked for having whatever it is I have that is bad, it is only because I have it that I am wicked—as if I owned a vicious and unruly dog.

I think that so long as I look on my act in this way, I wrong the obliging stranger a second time.

The moralist, then, is looking for the ingredient that perfects or spoils the stew. He wants to hear the world "power." He wants to know what is good in what is good that makes it good; and the whole wretched difficulty is that one is forced to reply either that what is good in what is good makes the good in what is good good, or that it is, in fact, made good by things which are not in the least good at all. So the next question, which is always, "And why is power good?," is answered by saying that it is good because it is power and power is good; or it is put off by the promise that power leads to things worth much; or it is shrugged aside with the exclamation, "Well, that's life!" This last is usually accompanied by an exhortation not to oppose the inevitable course of nature.

You cannot ask questions forever. Sooner or later the questioning process is brought up short by statements of an apparently dogmatic sort. Pleasure is sought for pleasure's sake. The principle of utility is susceptible of no demonstration. Every act and every inquiry aims at well-being. The nonnatural property of goodness fastens itself to its object and will remain there whatever world the present world may madly

become. Frustrated desires give rise to problems, and problems are bad. We confer the title of The Good upon our natural necessities.

I fail to see why, if one is going to call a halt in this way, the halt cannot be called early, and the evident, the obvious, the axiomatic, the indemonstrable, the intrinsic, or whatever one wants to name it be deemed those clear cases of moral goodness, badness, obligation, or wrong which no theory can cloud, and for which men are prepared to fight to the last ditch. For if someone asks me, now I am repentant, why I regard my act of baking the obliging stranger as wrong, what can I do but point again to the circumstances comprising the act? "Well, I put this fellow in an oven, you see. The oven was on, don't you know." And if my questioner persists in saying, "Of course, I know all about *that;* but what I want to know is, why is *that* wrong?," I should recognize there is no use in replying that it is wrong because of the kind of act it is, a wrong one, for my questioner is clearly suffering from a sort of *folie de doute morale* [the madness of doubting morality.—Eds.], which forbids him to accept any final answer this early in the game, although he will have to accept precisely the same kind of answer at some time or other.

Presumably there is some advantage in postponing the stop, and this advantage lies in the explanatory power of the higher-level answer. It cannot be that my baking the stranger is wrong for no reason at all. It would then be inexplicable. I do not think this is so, however. It is not inexplicable; it is transparent. Furthermore, the feeling of elucidation, of greater insight or knowledge, is a feeling only. It results, I suspect, from the satisfaction one takes in having an open mind. The explanatory factor is always more inscrutable than the event it explains. The same questions can be asked of it as were asked of the original occasion. It is either found in the situation and brought forward to account for all, as one might advance pain, in this case, out of the roaster; or it resides there mysteriously, like an essence, the witch in the oven; or it hovers, like a coil of smoke, as hovers the greatest unhappiness of the greatest number.

But how ludicrous are the moralist's "reasons" for condemning my baking the obliging stranger. They sound queerly unfamiliar and out of place. This is partly because they intrude where one expects to find denunciation only and because it is true they are seldom if ever *used*. But their strangeness is largely due to the humor in them.

Consider:

1. My act produced more pain than pleasure.
2. Baking this fellow did not serve the greatest good to the greatest number.
3. I acted wrongly because I could not consistently will that the maxim of my action become a universal law.
4. God forbade me, but I paid no heed.
5. Anyone can apprehend the property of wrongness sticking plainly to the whole affair.
6. Decent men remark it and are moved to tears.

But I should say that my act was wrong even if my stranger were tickled into laughter while he cooked; or even if his baking did the utmost good it could; or if, in spite of all, I could consistently will that whatever maxim I might have had might become a universal law; or even if God had spoken from a bush to me, "Thou shalt!" How redundant the property of wrongness, as if one needed *that,* in such a case! And would the act be right if the whole world howled its glee? Moralists can say, with conviction, that the act is wrong; but none can *show* it.

Such cases, like that of the obliging stranger, are cases I call clear. They have the characteristic of moral transparency, and they comprise the core of our moral experience. When we try to explain why they are instances of good or bad, of right or wrong, we sound comic, as anyone does who gives elaborate reasons for the obvious, especially when these reasons are so shamefaced before reality, so miserably beside the point. What we must explain is not why these cases have the moral nature they have, for that needs no explaining, but *why they are so clear.* It is an interesting situation: Any moralist will throw over his theory if it reverses the decision on cases like the obliging stranger's. The most persuasive criticism of any ethical system has always been the demonstration, on the critic's part, that the system countenances moral absurdities, despite the fact that, in the light of the whole theoretical enterprise, such criticisms beg the question. Although the philosopher who is caught by a criticism of this sort may protest his circularity or even manfully swallow the dreadful conclusion, his system has been scotched, if it has not been killed.

Not all cases are clear. But the moralist will furrow his brow before even this one. He will pursue principles which do not apply. He does not believe in clear cases. He refuses to believe in clear cases. Why?

I V

His disbelief is an absolute presupposition with him. It is a part of his methodological commitments and a part of his notion of profundity and of the nature of philosophy. It is a part of his reverence for intellectual humility. It is a part of his fear of being arbitrary. So he will put the question bravely to the clear cases, even though no state of fact but only his state of mind brings the question up, and even though putting the question, revealing the doubt, destroys immediately the validity of any answer he has posed the question to announce.

Three children are killed by a drunken driver. A family perishes in a sudden fire. Crowded bleachers collapse. Who is puzzled, asking why these things are terrible, why these things are wrong? When is such a question asked? It is asked when the case is not clear, when one is in doubt about it. "Those impious creatures! . . . At the movies . . . today, . . . which is the Lord's!" Is that so bad? Is being impious, even, so bad? I do not know. It is unclear, so I ask why. Or I disagree to pick a quarrel. Or I am a philosopher whose business it is to be puzzled. But do I imagine there is nothing the matter when three children are run over by drunkenness, or when a family goes up in smoke, or when there is a crush of people under timbers? There is no lack of clarity here, there is only the philosopher: patient, persistent as the dung beetle, pushing his "whys" up his hillocks with his nose. His doubts are never of the present case. They are always general. They are doubts in legion, regiment, and principle.

The obliging stranger is overbaked. I wonder whether this is bad or not. I ask about it. Presumably there is a reason for my wonderment. What is it? Well, of course there is not any reason that is a reason about the obliging stranger. There is only a reason because I am a fallibilist, or because one must not be arbitrary, or because all certainties in particular cases are certain only when deduced from greater, grander certainties. The reason I advance may be advanced upon itself. The entire moral structure tumbles at once. It is a test of the clarity of cases that objections to them are objections in principle; that the principle applies as well to all cases as to any one; and that these reasons for doubt devour themselves with equal right and the same appetite. That is why the moralist is really prepared to fight for the clear cases to the last ditch; why, when he questions them, he does so to display his philosophical breeding, because it is good form: He knows that if these cases are not clear, none are, and if none are, the game is up.

If there are clear cases, and if every moralist, at bottom, behaves as if there were, why does he still, at the top, behave as if there were none?

V

He may do so because he is an empiricist practicing induction. He believes, with Peirce, that "the inductive method springs directly out of dissatisfaction with existing knowledge." To get more knowledge he must become dissatisfied with what he has, all of it, by and large, often for no reason whatever. Our knowledge is limited, and what we do know, we know inexactly. In the sphere of morals the moralist has discovered how difficult it is to proceed from facts to values, and although he has not given up, his difficulties persuade him not that no one knows but that no one can be sure.

Above all, the empiricist has a hatred of certainty. His reasons are not entirely methodological. Most are political: Certainty is evil; it is dictatorial; it is undemocratic; all cases should be scrutinized equally; there should be no favoritism; the philosopher is fearless. "Thought looks into the pit of hell and is not afraid."

The moralist may behave as if there were no clear cases because he is a rationalist practicing deduction. He knows all about the infinite regress. He is familiar with the unquestioned status of first principles. He is beguiled by the precision, rigor, and unarguable moves of logical demonstration. Moreover, he is such an accomplished doubter of the significance of sen-

sation that he has persuaded the empiricist also to doubt that significance. He regards the empiricist as a crass, anti-intellectual booby, a smuggler where he is not an honest skeptic, since no fact, or set of facts, will account for the value we place on the obliging stranger unless we are satisfied to recount again the precise nature of the case.

Suppose our case concerned toads. And suppose we were asking of the toads, "Why? Why are you toads?" They would be unable to reply, being toads. How far should we get in answering our own question if we were never sure of any particular toad that he was one? How far should we get with our deductions if we were going to deduce one from self-evident toadyisms? What is self-evident about toads except that some are toads? And if we had a toad before us, and we were about to investigate him, and someone doubted that we had a toad before us, we could only say our creature was tailless and clumsy and yellow-green and made warts. So if someone still wanted to doubt our toad, he would have to change the definition of "toad," and someone might want to do that; but who wants to change our understanding of the word "immoral" so that the baking of the obliging stranger is not to be called immoral?

The empiricist is right: The deductive ethic rests upon arbitrary postulation. The rationalist is right: The inductive ethic does not exist; or worse, it consists of arbitrary values disguised as facts. Both are guilty of the most elaborate and flagrant rationalizations. Both know precisely what it is they wish to save. Neither is going to be surprised in the least by what turns out to be good or bad. They are asking of their methods answers that their methods cannot give.

VI

It is confusion which gives rise to doubt. What about the unclear cases? I shall be satisfied to show that there are clear ones, but the unclear ones are more interesting, and there are more of them. How do we decide about blue laws, supposing that there is nothing to decide about the obliging stranger except how to prevent the occurrence from happening again? How do we arbitrate conflicts of duty where each duty, even, may be clear? What of principles, after all? Are there none? Are they not used by people? Well, they talk about them more than they use them, but they use them a little.

I should like to try to answer these questions another time. I can only indicate, quite briefly, the form these answers will take.

I think we decide cases where there is some doubt by stating what it is about them that puzzles us. We hunt for more facts, hoping that the case will clear:

"She left her husband with a broken hand and took the children."

"She did!"

"He broke his hand on her head."

"Dear me; but even so!"

"He beat her every Thursday after tea and she finally couldn't stand it any longer."

"Ah, of course, but the poor children?"

"He beat them, too."

"My, my, and was there no other way?"

"The court would grant her no injunction."

"Why not?"

"Judge Bridlegoose is a fool."

"Ah, of course, she did right, no doubt about it."

If more facts do not clear the case, we redescribe it, emphasizing first this fact and then that until it is clear, or until we have several clear versions of the original muddle. Many ethical disputes are due to the possession, by the contending parties, of different accounts of the same occasion, all satisfactorily clear, and this circumstance gives the disputants a deep feeling for the undoubted rightness of each of their versions. Such disputes are particularly acrimonious, and they cannot be settled until an agreement is reached about the true description of the case.

There are, of course, conflicts of duty which are perfectly clear. I have promised to meet you at four to bowl, but when four arrives I am busy rescuing a baby from the jaws of a Bengal tiger and cannot come. Unclear conflicts we try to clarify. And it sometimes happens that the tug of obligations is so equal as to provide no reasonable solution. If some cases are clear, others are undecidable.

It is perfectly true that principles are employed in moral decisions—popular principles, I mean, like the golden rule and the laws of God. Principles really obscure matters as often as they clear them. They are generally flags and slogans to which the individual is greatly attached. Attack the principle and you attack the owner: his good name, his reputation, his sense of righteousness. Love me, love my maxims. People have been wrongly persuaded that principles decide cases and that a principle which fails in one case fails in all. So principles are usually vehicles for especially powerful feelings and frequently get in the way of good sense. We have all observed the angry arguer who grasps the nettle of absurdity to justify his bragging about the toughness of his skin.

I should regard useful principles as summaries of what may be present generally in clear cases, as for instance: Cases where pain is present are more often adjudged bad than not. We might, if the reverse were true for pleasure, express our principle briefly in hedonistic terms: Pleasure is the good. But there may be lots of principles of this sort, as there may be lots of rather common factors in clear cases. Principles state more or less prevalent identifying marks, as cardinals usually nest in low trees, although there is nothing to prevent them from nesting elsewhere, and the location of the nest is not the essence of the bird. When I appeal to a principle, then, the meaning of my appeal consists of the fact that before me is a case about which I can reach no direct decision; of the fact that the principle I invoke is relevant, since not every principle is (the laws of God do not cover everything, for instance). In this way I affirm my loyalty to those clear cases the principle so roughly summarizes and express my desire to remain consistent with them.

VII

Insofar as present moral theories have any relevance to our experience, they are elaborate systems designed to protect the certainty of the moralist's last-ditch data. Although he may imagine he is gathering his principles from the purest vapors of the mind, the moralist will in fact be prepared to announce as such serenities only those which support his most cherished goods. And if he is not careful to do just this, he will risk being charged with irrelevancy by those who will employ the emptiness and generality of his principles to demonstrate the value of trivialities: as for example, the criticism of the categorical imperative that claims one can universally will all teeth be brushed with powder in the morning, and so on in like manner.

Ethics, I wish to say, is about something, and in the rush to establish principles, to elicit distinctions from a recalcitrant language, and to discover "laws," those lovely things and honored people, those vile seducers and ruddy villains our principles and laws are supposed to be based upon and our ethical theories to be about are overlooked and forgotten.

NOTE

1. The order in which these questions are asked depends on one's view of the logical primacy of

moral predicates. I shall not discriminate among them since I intend my remarks to be indiscriminate.

FOR FURTHER REFLECTION

1. Consider Gass's claim that none of the standard moral principles could justify refraining from baking the obliging stranger. Is Gass correct? Explain.
2. What is Gass's account of moral reasoning? What is the role of reason in the moral life? Do you agree with his assessment of moral reasoning?

Thomas Nagel

MORAL LUCK

Thomas Nagel is professor of philosophy at New York University and the author of several important works in philosophy of the mind and moral theory. In this essay Nagel questions the whole Kantian way of looking at morality, which presumes that we are all, qua rational, equal participants in the moral enterprise who have equal opportunity to be moral. The locus of the moral enterprise is the good will, the will to do our duty according to reason's dictates, the only purely good thing in the world. Although we all have different nonmoral abilities, even different characters inclining us to virtue, only the resolved intention to do one's duty matters.

Nagel argues that this view is too simple and doesn't take into account the way external factors impinge upon us. External factors introduce the notion of moral luck, which Nagel defines thusly: "Where a significant aspect of what someone does depends on factors beyond his control, yet we continue to treat him in that respect as an object of moral judgment, it can be called moral luck."

Nagel discusses four types of moral luck: constitutional luck, circumstantial luck, consequential luck in which consequences retrospectively justify an otherwise immoral act (or fail to justify an otherwise moral act), and consequential luck in which the consequences affect the type or quality of blame or remorse (or moral praise). Nagel's article challenges our traditional way of viewing ethics as being beyond accident and luck.

From Thomas Nagel, *Mortal Questions* (1979), 24–38, by permission of Cambridge University Press.

Kant believed that good or bad luck should influence neither our moral judgment of a person and his actions, nor his moral assessment of himself.

> The good will is not good because of what it effects or accomplishes or because of its adequacy to achieve some proposed end; it is good only because of its willing, i.e., it is good of itself. And, regarded for itself, it is to be esteemed incomparably higher than anything which could be brought about by it in favor of any inclination or even of the sum total of all inclinations. Even if it should happen that, by a particular unfortunate fate or by the niggardly provision of a stepmotherly nature, this will should be wholly lacking in power to accomplish its purpose, and if even the greatest effort should not avail it to achieve anything of its end, and if there remained only the good will (not as a mere wish but as the summoning of all the means in our power), it would sparkle like a jewel in its own right, as something that had its full worth in itself. Usefulness or fruitlessness can neither diminish nor augment this worth.[1]

He would presumably have said the same thing about a bad will: whether it accomplishes its evil purposes is morally irrelevant. And a course of action that would be condemned if it had a bad outcome cannot be vindicated if by luck it turns out well. There cannot be moral risk. This view seems to be wrong, but it arises in response to a fundamental problem about moral responsibility to which we possess no satisfactory solution.

The problem develops out of the ordinary conditions of moral judgment. Prior to reflection it is intuitively plausible that people cannot be morally assessed for what is not their fault, or for what is due to factors beyond their control. Such judgment is different from the evaluation of something as a good or bad thing, or state of affairs. The latter may be present in addition to moral judgment, but when we blame someone for his actions we are not merely saying it is bad that they happened, or bad that he exists: we are judging him, saying he is bad, which is different from his being a bad thing. This kind of judgment takes only a certain kind of object. Without being able to explain exactly why, we feel that the appropriateness of moral assessment is easily undermined by the dis-

covery that the act or attribute, no matter how good or bad, is not under the person's control. While other evaluations remain, this one seems to lose its footing. So a clear absence of control, produced by involuntary movement, physical force, or ignorance of the circumstances, excuses what is done from moral judgment. But what we do depends in many more ways than these on what is not under our control—what is not produced by a good or a bad will in Kant's phrase. And external influences in this broader range are not usually thought to excuse what is done from moral judgment, positive or negative.

Let me give a few examples, beginning with the type of case Kant has in mind. Whether we succeed or fail in what we try to do nearly always depends to some extent on factors beyond our control. This is true of murder, altruism, revolution, the sacrifice of certain interests for the sake of others—almost any morally important act. What has been done, and what is morally judged, is partly determined by external factors. However jewel-like the good will may be in its own right, there is a morally significant difference between rescuing someone from a burning building and dropping him from a twelfth-story window while trying to rescue him. Similarly, there is a morally significant difference between reckless driving and manslaughter. But whether a reckless driver hits a pedestrian depends on the presence of the pedestrian at the point where he recklessly passes a red light. What we do is also limited by the opportunities and choices with which we are faced, and these are largely determined by factors beyond our control. Someone who was an officer in a concentration camp might have led a quiet and harmless life if the Nazis had never come to power in Germany. And someone who led a quiet and harmless life in Argentina might have become an officer in a concentration camp if he had not left Germany for business reasons in 1930.

I shall say more later about these and other examples. I introduce them here to illustrate a general point. Where a significant aspect of what someone does depends on factors beyond his control, yet we continue to treat him in that respect as an object of moral judgment, it can be called moral luck. Such luck can be good or bad. And the problem posed by this phenomenon, which led Kant to deny its possibility, is that the broad range of external influences here identified seems on close examination to undermine moral assessment as surely as does the narrower range of familiar excusing conditions. If the condition of control is consistently applied, it threatens to erode most of the moral assessments we find it natural to make. The things for which people are morally judged are determined in more ways than we at first realize by what is beyond their control. And when the seemingly natural requirement of fault or responsibility is applied in light of these facts, it leaves few pre-reflective moral judgments intact. Ultimately, nothing or almost nothing about what a person does seems to be under his control.

Why not conclude, then, that the condition of control is false—that it is an initially plausible hypothesis refuted by clear counter-examples? One could in that case look instead for a more refined condition which picked out the kinds of lack of control that really undermine certain moral judgments, without yielding the unacceptable conclusion derived from the broader condition, that most or all ordinary moral judgments are illegitimate.

What rules out this escape is that we are dealing not with a theoretical conjecture but with a philosophical problem. The condition of control does not suggest itself merely as a generalization from certain clear cases. It seems correct in the further cases to which it is extended beyond the original set. When we undermine moral assessment by considering new ways in which control is absent, we are not just discovering what would follow given the general hypothesis, but are actually being persuaded that in itself the absence of control is relevant in these cases too. The erosion of moral judgment emerges not as the absurd consequence of an over-simple theory, but as a natural consequence of the ordinary idea of moral assessment, when it is applied in view of a more complete and precise account of the facts. It would therefore be a mistake to argue from the unacceptability of the conclusions to the need for a different account of the conditions of moral responsibility. The view that moral luck is paradoxical is not a mistake, ethical or logical, but a perception of one of the ways in which

the intuitively acceptable conditions of moral judgment threaten to undermine it all.

It resembles the situation in another area of philosophy, the theory of knowledge. There too conditions which seem perfectly natural, and which grow out of the ordinary procedures for challenging and defending claims to knowledge, threaten to undermine all such claims if consistently applied. Most skeptical arguments have this quality: they do not depend on the imposition of arbitrarily stringent standards of knowledge, arrived at by misunderstanding, but appear to grow inevitably from the consistent application of ordinary standards.[2] There is a substantive parallel as well, for epistemological skepticism arises from consideration of the respects in which our beliefs and their relation to reality depend on factors beyond our control. External and internal causes produce our beliefs. We may subject these processes to scrutiny in an effort to avoid error, but our conclusions at this next level also result, in part, from influences which we do not control directly. The same will be true no matter how far we carry the investigation. Our beliefs are always, ultimately, due to factors outside our control, and the impossibility of encompassing those factors without being at the mercy of others leads us to doubt whether we know anything. It looks as though, if any of our beliefs are true, it is pure biological luck rather than knowledge.

Moral luck is like this because while there are various respects in which the natural objects of moral assessment are out of our control or influenced by what is out of our control, we cannot reflect on these facts without losing our grip on the judgments.

There are roughly four ways in which the natural objects of moral assessment are disturbingly subject to luck. One is the phenomenon of constitutive luck—the kind of person you are, where this is not just a question of what you deliberately do, but of your inclinations, capacities, and temperament. Another category is luck in one's circumstances—the kind of problems and situations one faces. The other two have to do with the causes and effects of action: luck in how one is determined by antecedent circumstances, and luck in the way one's actions and projects turn out. All of them present a common problem. They are all opposed by the idea that one cannot be more culpable or estimable for anything than one is for that fraction of it which is under one's control. It seems irrational to take or dispense credit or blame for matters over which a person has no control, or for their influence on results over which he has partial control. Such things may create the conditions for action, but action can be judged only to the extent that it goes beyond these conditions and does not just result from them.

Let us first consider luck, good and bad, in the way things turn out. Kant, in the above-quoted passage, has one example of this in mind, but the category covers a wide range. It includes the truck driver who accidentally runs over a child, the artist who abandons his wife and five children to devote himself to painting,[3] and other cases in which the possibilities of success and failure are even greater. The driver, if he is entirely without fault, will feel terrible about his role in the event, but will not have to reproach himself. Therefore this example of agent-regret[4] is not yet a case of moral bad luck. However, if the driver was guilty of even a minor degree of negligence—failing to have his brakes checked recently, for example— then if that negligence contributes to the death of the child, he will not merely feel terrible. He will blame himself for the death. And what makes this an example of moral luck is that he would have to blame himself only slightly for the negligence itself if no situation arose which required him to brake suddenly and violently to avoid hitting a child. Yet the negligence is the same in both cases, and the driver has no control over whether a child will run into his path.

The same is true at higher levels of negligence. If someone has had too much to drink and his car swerves onto the sidewalk, he can count himself morally lucky if there are no pedestrians in his path. If there were, he would be to blame for their deaths, and would probably be prosecuted for manslaughter. But if he hurts no one, although his recklessness is exactly the same, he is guilty of a far less serious legal offense and will certainly reproach himself and be reproached by others much less severely. To take another legal example, the penalty for attempted murder is less than that for successful murder—however similar the intentions and motives of the assailant

may be in the two cases. His degree of culpability can depend, it would seem, on whether the victim happened to be wearing a bullet-proof vest, or whether a bird flew into the path of the bullet—matters beyond his control.

Finally, there are cases of decision under uncertainty—common in public and in private life. Anna Karenina goes off with Vronsky, Gauguin leaves his family, Chamberlain signs the Munich Agreement, the Decembrists persuade the troops under their command to revolt against the czar, the American colonies declare their independence from Britain, you introduce two people in an attempt at match-making. It is tempting in all such cases to feel that some decision must be possible, in the light of what is known at the time, which will make reproach unsuitable no matter how things turn out. But this is not true; when someone acts in such ways he takes his life, or his moral position, into his hands, because how things turn out determines what he has done. It is possible also to assess the decision from the point of view of what could be known at the time, but this is not the end of the story. If the Decembrists had succeeded in overthrowing Nicholas I in 1825 and establishing a constitutional regime, they would be heroes. As it is, not only did they fail and pay for it, but they bore some responsibility for the terrible punishments meted out to the troops who had been persuaded to follow them. If the American Revolution had been a bloody failure resulting in greater repression, then Jefferson, Franklin, and Washington would still have made a noble attempt, and might not even have regretted it on their way to the scaffold, but they would also have had to blame themselves for what they had helped to bring on their compatriots. (Perhaps peaceful efforts at reform would eventually have succeeded.) If Hitler had not overrun Europe and exterminated millions, but instead had died of a heart attack after occupying the Sudetenland, Chamberlain's action at Munich would still have utterly betrayed the Czechs, but it would not be the great moral disaster that has made his name a household word.[5]

In many cases of difficult choice the outcome cannot be foreseen with certainty. One kind of assessment of the choice is possible in advance, but another kind must await the outcome, because the outcome determines what has been done. The same degree of culpability or estimability in intention, motive, or concern is compatible with a wide range of judgments, positive or negative, depending on what happened beyond the point of decision. The mens rea which could have existed in the absence of any consequences does not exhaust the grounds of moral judgment. Actual results influence culpability or esteem in a large class of unquestionably ethical cases ranging from negligence through political choice.

That these are genuine moral judgments rather than expressions of temporary attitude is evident from the fact that one can say in advance how the moral verdict will depend on the results. If one negligently leaves the bath running with the baby in it, one will realize, as one bounds up the stairs toward the bathroom, that if the baby has drowned one has done something awful, whereas if it has not one has merely been careless. Someone who launches a violent revolution against an authoritarian regime knows that if he fails he will be responsible for much suffering that is in vain, but if he succeeds he will be justified by the outcome. I do not mean that any action can be retroactively justified by history. Certain things are so bad in themselves, or so risky, that no results can make them all right. Nevertheless, when moral judgment does depend on the outcome, it is objective and timeless and not dependent on a change of standpoint produced by success or failure. The judgment after the fact follows from an hypothetical judgment that can be made beforehand, and it can be made as easily by someone else as by the agent.

From the point of view which makes responsibility dependent on control, all this seems absurd. How is it possible to be more or less culpable depending on whether a child gets into the path of one's car, or a bird into the path of one's bullet? Perhaps it is true that what is done depends on more than the agent's state of mind or intention. The problem then is, why is it not irrational to base moral assessment on what people do, in this broad sense? It amounts to holding them responsible for the contributions of fate as well as for their own—provided they have made some contribution to begin with. If we look at cases of negligence or attempt, the pattern seems to be that overall culpability corresponds to the product of mental or intentional fault and the seriousness of the outcome. Cases of decision under uncertainty are less easily explained in this way, for it seems that the overall judgment can even shift from positive to negative depending on the outcome. But here too it seems rational to subtract the effects of occurrences subsequent to the choice, that were merely possible at the time, and concentrate moral assessment on the actual decision in light of the probabilities. If the object of moral judgment is the person, then to hold him accountable for what he has done in the broader sense is akin to strict liability, which may have its legal uses but seems irrational as a moral position.

The result of such a line of thought is to pare down each act to its morally essential core, an inner act of pure will assessed by motive and intention. Adam Smith advocates such a position in *The Theory of Moral Sentiments*, but notes that it runs contrary to our actual judgments.

> But how well soever we may seem to be persuaded of the truth of this equitable maxim, when we consider it after this manner, in abstract, yet when we come to particular cases, the actual consequences which happen to proceed from any action, have a very great effect upon our sentiments concerning its merit or demerit, and almost always either enhance or diminish our sense of both. Scarce, in any one instance, perhaps, will our sentiments be found, after examination, to be entirely regulated by this rule, which we all acknowledge ought entirely to regulate them.[6]

Joel Feinberg points out further that restricting the domain of moral responsibility to the inner world will not immunize it to luck. Factors beyond the agent's control, like a coughing fit, can interfere with his decisions as surely as they can with the path of a bullet from his gun.[7] Nevertheless the tendency to cut down the scope of moral assessment is pervasive, and does not limit itself to the influence of effects. It attempts to isolate the will from the other direction, so to speak, by separating out constitutive luck. Let us consider that next.

Kant was particularly insistent on the moral irrelevance of qualities of temperament and personality that are not under the control of the will. Such qualities as sympathy or coldness might provide the background against which obedience to moral requirements is more or less difficult, but they could not be objects of moral assessment themselves, and might well interfere with confident assessment of its proper object—the determination of the will by the motive of duty. This rules out moral judgment of many of the virtues and vices, which are states of character that influence choice but are certainly not exhausted by dispositions to act deliberately in certain ways. A person may be greedy, envious, cowardly, cold, ungenerous, unkind, vain, or conceited, but behave perfectly by a monumental effort of will. To possess these vices is to be unable to help having certain feelings under certain circumstances, and to have strong spontaneous impulses to act badly. Even if one controls the impulses, one still has the vice. An envious person hates the greater success of others. He can be morally condemned as envious even if he congratulates them cordially and does nothing to denigrate or spoil their success. Conceit, likewise, need not be displayed. It is fully present in someone who cannot help dwelling with secret satisfaction on the superiority of his own achievements, talents, beauty, intelligence, or virtue. To some extent such a quality may be the product of earlier choices; to some extent it may be amenable to change by current actions. But it is largely a matter of constitutive bad fortune. Yet people are morally condemned for such qualities, and esteemed for others equally beyond control of the will: they are assessed for what they are like.

To Kant this seems incoherent because virtue is enjoined on everyone and therefore must in principle be possible for everyone. It may be easier for some than for others, but it must be possible to achieve it by making the right choices, against whatever temperamental background.[8] One may want to have a generous spirit, or regret not having one, but it makes no sense to condemn oneself or anyone else for a quality which is not within the control of the will. Condemnation implies that you should not be like that, not that it is unfortunate that you are.

Nevertheless, Kant's conclusion remains intuitively unacceptable. We may be persuaded that these moral judgments are irrational, but they reappear involuntarily as soon as the argument is over. This is the pattern throughout the subject.

The third category to consider is luck in one's circumstances, and I shall mention it briefly. The things we are called upon to do, the moral tests we face, are importantly determined by factors beyond our control. It may be true of someone that in a dangerous situation he would behave in a cowardly or heroic fashion, but if the situation never arises, he will never have the chance to distinguish or disgrace himself in this way, and his moral record will be different.[9]

A conspicuous example of this is political. Ordinary citizens of Nazi Germany had an opportunity to behave heroically by opposing the regime. They also had an opportunity to behave badly, and most of them are culpable for having failed this test. But it is a test to which the citizens of other countries were not subjected, with the result that even if they, or some of them, would have behaved as badly as the Germans in like circumstances, they simply did not and therefore are not similarly culpable. Here again one is morally at the mercy of fate, and it may seem irrational upon reflection, but our ordinary moral attitudes would be unrecognizable without it. We judge people for what they actually do or fail to do, not just for what they would have done if circumstances had been different.

This form of moral determination by the actual is also paradoxical, but we can begin to see how deep in the concept of responsibility the paradox is embedded. A person can be morally responsible only for what he does; but what he does results from a great deal that he does not do; therefore he is not morally responsible for what he is and is not responsible for. (This is not a contradiction, but it is a paradox.)

It should be obvious that there is a connection between these problems about responsibility and control and an even more familiar problem, that of freedom of the will. That is the last type of moral luck I want to take up, though I can do no more within the scope of this essay than indicate its connection with the other types.

If one cannot be responsible for consequences of one's acts due to factors beyond one's control, or for antecedents of one's acts that are properties of temperament not subject to one's will, or for the circumstances that pose one's moral choices, then how can one be responsible even for the stripped-down acts of the will itself, if they are the product of antecedent circumstances outside of the will's control?

The area of genuine agency, and therefore of legitimate moral judgment, seems to shrink under this scrutiny to an extensionless point. Everything seems to result from the combined influence of factors, antecedent and posterior to action, that are not within the agent's control. Since he cannot be responsible for them, he cannot be responsible for their results—though it may remain possible to take up the aesthetic or other evaluative analogues of the moral attitudes that are thus displaced.

It is also possible, of course, to brazen it out and refuse to accept the results, which indeed seem unacceptable as soon as we stop thinking about the arguments. Admittedly, if certain surrounding circumstances had been different, then no unfortunate consequences would have followed from a wicked intention, and no seriously culpable act would have been performed; but since the circumstances were not different, and the agent in fact succeeded in perpetrating a particularly cruel murder, that is what he did, and that is what he is responsible for. Similarly, we may admit that if certain antecedent circumstances had been different, the agent would never have developed into the sort of person who would do such a thing; but since he did develop (as the inevitable result of those antecedent circumstances) into the sort of swine he is, and into the person who committed such a murder, that is what he is blamable for. In both cases one is responsible for what one actually does—even if what one actually does depends in important ways on what is not within one's control. This [compatibilist] account of our moral judgments would leave room for the ordinary conditions of responsibility—the absence of coercion, ignorance, or involuntary movement—as part of the determination of what someone has done—but it is understood not to exclude the influence of a great deal that he has not done.

The only thing wrong with this solution is its failure to explain how skeptical problems arise. For they arise not from the imposition of an arbitrary external requirement, but from the nature of moral judgment itself. Something in the ordinary idea of what someone does must explain how it can seem necessary to subtract from it anything that merely happens—even though the ultimate consequence of such subtraction is that nothing remains. And something in the ordinary idea of knowledge must explain why it seems to be undermined by any influences on belief not within the control of the subject—so that knowledge seems impossible without an impossible foundation in autonomous reason. But let us leave epistemology aside and concentrate on action, character, and moral assessment.

The problem arises, I believe, because the self which acts and is the object of moral judgment is threatened with dissolution by the absorption of its acts and impulses into the class of events. Moral judgment of a person is judgment not of what happens to him, but of him. It does not say merely that a certain event or state of affairs is fortunate or unfortunate or even terrible. It is not an evaluation of a state of the world, or of an individual as part of the world. We are not thinking just that it would be better if he were different, or did not exist, or had not done some of the things he has done. We are judging him, rather than his existence or characteristics. The effect of concentrating on the influence of what is not under his control is to make this responsible self seem to disappear, swallowed up by the order of mere events.

What, however, do we have in mind that a person must be to be the object of these moral attitudes? While the concept of agency is easily undermined, it is very difficult to give it a positive characterization. That is familiar from the literature on Free Will.

I believe that in a sense the problem has no solution, because something in the idea of agency is incompatible with actions being events, or people being things. But as the external determinants of what someone has done are gradually exposed, in their effect on consequences, character, and choice itself, it becomes gradually clear that actions are events and people things. Eventually nothing remains which can be ascribed to the responsible self, and we are left with nothing but a portion of the larger sequences of events, which can be deplored or celebrated, but not blamed or praised.

Though I cannot define the idea of the active self that is thus undermined, it is possible to say something about its sources. There is a close connection between our feelings about ourselves and our feelings about others. Guilt and indignation, shame and contempt, pride and admiration are internal and external sides of the same moral attitudes. We are unable to view ourselves simply as portions of the world, and from inside we have a rough idea of the boundary between what is us and what is not, what we do and what happens to us, what is our personality and what is an accidental handicap. We apply the same essentially internal conception of the self to others. About ourselves we feel pride, shame, guilt, remorse—and agent-regret. We do not regard our actions and our characters merely as fortunate or unfortunate episodes—though they may also be that. We cannot simply take an external evaluative view of ourselves—of what we most essentially are and what we do. And this remains true even when we have seen that we are not responsible for our own existence, or our nature, or the choices we have to make, or the circumstances that give our acts the consequences they have. Those acts remain ours and we remain ourselves, despite the persuasiveness of the reasons that seem to argue us out of existence.

It is this internal view that we extend to others in moral judgment—when we judge them rather than their desirability or utility. We extend to others the refusal to limit ourselves to external evaluation, and we accord to them selves like our own. But in both cases this comes up against the brutal inclusion of humans and everything about them in a world from which they cannot be separated and of which they are nothing but contents. The external view forces itself on us at the same time that we resist it. One way this occurs is through the gradual erosion of what we do by the subtraction of what happens.

The inclusion of consequences in the conception of what we have done is an acknowledgment that we are parts of the world, but the paradoxical character of moral luck which emerges from this acknowledgment shows that we are unable to operate with such a view, for it leaves us with no one to be. The same thing is revealed in the appearance that determinism obliterates responsibility. Once we see an aspect of what we or someone else does as something that happens, we lose our grip on the idea that it has been done and that we can judge the doer and not just the happening. This explains why the absence of determinism is no

more hospitable to the concept of agency than is its presence—a point that has been noticed often. Either way the act is viewed externally, as part of the course of events.

The problem of moral luck cannot be understood without an account of the internal conception of agency and its special connection with the moral attitudes as opposed to other types of value. I do not have such an account. The degree to which the problem has a solution can be determined only by seeing whether in some degree the incompatibility between this conception and the various ways in which we do not control what we do is only apparent. I have nothing to offer on that topic either. But it is not enough to say merely that our basic moral attitudes toward ourselves and others are determined by what is actual; for they are also threatened by the sources of that actuality, and by the external view of action which forces itself on us when we see how everything we do belongs to a world that we have not created.

NOTES

1. Immanuel Kant, *Foundations of the Metaphysics of Morals*, L. W. Beck, trans. (Bobbs-Merrill, 1959), sec. I, paragraph 3.
2. See Thompson Clark, "The Legacy of Skepticism," *Journal of Philosophy*, LXIX, no. 20 (November 9, 1972): 754–69.
3. Such a case, modelled on the life of Gauguin, is discussed by Bernard Williams in "Moral Luck," *Proceedings of the Aristotelian Society*, supplementary vol. L (1976): 115–35 (to which the original version of this essay was a reply). He points out that though success or failure cannot be predicted in advance, Gauguin's most basic retrospective feelings about the decision will be determined by the development of his talent. My disagreement with Williams is that his account fails to explain why such retrospective attitudes can be called moral. If success does not permit Gauguin to justify himself to others, but still determines his most basic feelings, that shows only that his most basic feelings need not be moral. It does not show that morality is subject to luck. If the retrospective judgment were moral, it would imply the truth of a hypothetical judgment made in advance, of the form 'If I leave my family and become a great painter, I will

be justified by success; if I don't become a great painter, the act will be unforgivable.'

4. Williams's term (ibid.).

5. For a fascinating but morally repellent discussion of the topic of justification by history, see Maurice Merleau-Ponty, *Humanisme et Terreur* (Paris: Gallimard, 1947), translated as *Humanism and Terror* (Boston: Beacon Press, 1969).

6. Adam Smith, *The Theory of Moral Sentiments*, 1759, Pt. II, sec. 3, Introduction, para. 5.

7. "Problematic Responsibility in Law and Morals," in Joel Feinberg, *Doing and Deserving* (Princeton: Princeton University Press, 1970).

8. 'If nature has put little sympathy in the heart of a man, and if he, though an honest man, is by temperament cold and indifferent to the sufferings of others, perhaps because he is provided with special gifts of patience and fortitude and expects or even requires that others should have the same—and such a man would certainly not be the meanest product of nature—would not he find in himself a source from which to give himself a far higher worth than he could have got by having a good-natured temperament?' (Kant, Foundations of the *Metaphysics of Morals*, first section, eleventh paragraph).

9. Cf. Thomas Gray, 'Elegy Written in a Country Churchyard':

Some mute inglorious Milton here may rest,
Some Cromwell, guiltless of his country's blood.

An unusual example of circumstantial moral luck is provided by the kind of moral dilemma with which someone can be faced through no fault of his own, but which leaves him with nothing to do which is not wrong.

FOR FURTHER REFLECTION

1. Is there moral luck? Who is right, Kant or Nagel? Review Kant's ethical theory and compare it with Nagel's considerations of external force on moral agents.

2. Describe the four kinds of moral luck discussed by Nagel. Evaluate their strengths and weaknesses.

3. How does Nagel's essay bear on the problem of free will and determinism? (covered in Part V of this book). What difference would it make if we discovered that all of our actions were affected by moral luck?

‿

How to Read and Write
a Philosophy Paper

Nothing worthwhile was ever accomplished without great difficulty.
Plato, The Republic

Just about everyone who comes to philosophy—usually in college—feels a sinking sensation in his or her stomach when first encountering this very strange material, involving a different sort of style and method from anything else they have ever dealt with. It was certainly my first reaction as a student. Lured by questions such as "Is there a God? What can I truly know? What is the meaning of life? How shall I live my life?" I began to read philosophy on my own. My first book was Bertrand Russell's *History of Western Philosophy,* which is much more than a history of the subject, being also Russell's own analysis and evaluation of major themes in the history of Western philosophy. Although it is not a terribly difficult text, most of the ideas and arguments were new to me. Since he opposed many of the beliefs that I had been brought up with, I felt angry with him. But since he seemed to argue so persuasively, my anger gave way to confusion and then to a sense of defeat and despair. Yet I felt compelled to go on with this "forbidden fruit," finishing Russell's long work and going on to read Plato's *Republic,* René Descartes's *Meditations,* David Hume's *Dialogues on Natural Religion,* selected writings of Immanuel Kant, William James's *Will to Believe,* and finally contemporary readings by Antony Flew, R. M. Hare, John Hick, and Ludwig Wittgenstein. Gradually, I became aware that on every issue on which I disagreed with Hume or Russell, Kant or Hick, someone else had a plausible counterargument. Eventually, I struggled to the place where I could see weaknesses in arguments (sometimes in the arguments of those figures with whom I had agreed) and finally I came to the point where I could write out arguments of my own. The pain of the process slowly gave way to joy—almost addictive joy, let me warn you—so that I decided to go to graduate school to get an advanced degree in philosophy.

It was a gnawing worry about fundamental questions of existence that drew me to philosophy. Is there a God? What can I know for sure? Do I have a soul that will live forever?

Am I truly free, or simply determined by my heredity and environment? What is it to live a moral life? If you have asked these questions and pondered alternative responses, most of the essays in this book will make sense to you. But if you have not spent a lot of time thinking about this sort of subject matter, you might ask yourself whether or not these questions are important and you might outline your own present responses to them. For unless you've asked the question, the proposed answers may sound like only one end of a telephone conversation.

This textbook is meant to suggest responses in order to stimulate you to work out your own position on the questions addressed herein. This text, offering readings on alternative sides of each issue, along with a teacher to serve as a guide—and, I hope, some fellow students with whom to discuss the material—should challenge you to begin to work out your own philosophy of life.

However, neither the textbook nor the teacher will be sufficient to save you from a sense of disorientation and uncertainty in reading and writing about philosophy, so let me offer a few tips from my experience as a student and as a teacher of philosophy.

SUGGESTIONS ON READING A PHILOSOPHY TEXT

The styles and methods of philosophy are different from other subjects with which you have been acquainted since grammar school, e.g., English, history, mathematics, and science. Of course, there are many methods, and some writings—for example, the existentialists, Søren Kierkegaard, Friedrich Nietzsche, Albert Camus, and Jean Paul Sartre—do resemble what we encounter in literature more than more typical essays in philosophical analysis. In some ways philosophy resembles mathematics, since it usually strives to develop a deductive argument much like a mathematical proof, only the premises of the argument are usually in need of a lot of discussion and objections need to be considered. Sometimes I think of arguing about a philosophical problem as a kind of legal reasoning before a civil court. Each side presents its evidence and gives reasons for accepting its conclusion rather than the opponent's. For example, suppose you believe in freedom of the will and I believe in determinism. We each set forth the best reasons we have for accepting our respective conclusions. The difference between philosophical argument and the court case is that we are also the jury. We can change our minds on hearing the evidence and even change sides by hearing our opponent make a persuasive case.

SUGGESTIONS ON WRITING A PHILOSOPHY PAPER

Talking about philosophy and writing philosophy is an excellent way to improve your understanding of the content and process of the subject as well as to improve your philosophical reasoning skill. Writing an essay on a philosophical issue focuses your mind and forces you to concentrate on the essential arguments connected with the issue. Though the process is hard, it's amazing how much progress one can make—some faster than others, but in my experience some of those who have the hardest time at first end up doing the deepest, most thorough work.

First of all, identify a *problem* you want to shed light on or solve or a *thesis* you want to defend. Be sure that you have read at least a few good articles on different sides of the issue and can put the arguments in your own words.

Now you are ready to begin to write. Here are some suggestions that may help you.

1. Identify the problem you want to analyze. For example, you might want to show that W. T. Stace (in Part V) has put forth an unsound argument for the thesis that free will and determinism are compatible.
2. As clearly as possible, state the problem and what you intend to show (for example, "I intend to analyze Stace's argument for compatibilism and show that he has misconstrued the issue. His argument for compatibilism is unsound").
3. Set forth your argument in logical order, supporting your own premises with reasons. It may help to illustrate your points with examples or to point out counterexamples to the opposing points of view.
4. Consider points of view that differ from your own as well as objections to your position. Try to meet these charges and to show why your position is more plausible.
5. End your paper with a summary and a conclusion: review your argument and show its implications for other issues.
6. You will probably need to write at least two drafts before you have a working copy. It helps to have another philosophy student go over the preliminary draft before you write a final draft. Make sure that your argument is well constructed and that your paper as a whole is coherent.
7. Regarding style, write *clearly,* in an active voice, put other people's ideas in your own words as much as possible, and give credit in the text and in bibliographic notes wherever you have used someone else's idea or quoted someone.
8. Include a bibliography at the end of your paper, listing all the sources you used for your paper.

When you have a serious problem, do not hesitate to contact your teacher. That is what he or she is there for: to help you make progress in doing philosophical reasoning.

Good luck, and I hope you come to enjoy the philosophical quest for truth and wisdom as much as I have.

APPENDIX II

❧

A Little Bit of Logic

Philosophy is centered in the analysis and construction of *arguments*. We call the study of arguments *logic*. Let us devote a little time to the rudiments of logic. By argument we do not mean a verbal fight but a process of supporting a thesis (called the *conclusion*) with reasons (called *premises*). An argument consists of at least two declarative sentences (sometimes called *propositions*), one of which (the conclusion) logically follows from the others (the premises). The connection by which the conclusion follows from the premises is called an *inference:*

The Structure of An Argument

Premise 1

Premise 2 —⟩——— **Inference**

Conclusion

DEDUCTIVE AND INDUCTIVE REASONING

Deductive Arguments

A *valid deductive argument* is one that follows a correct logical form, so that if the premises are true, the conclusion must also be true. If the form is not a good one, the argument is invalid. We say that a valid deductive argument *preserves truth*. It does so in much the same way as a good refrigerator preserves food. If the food is good, a good refrigerator will preserve it; but if the food is already spoiled, the refrigerator will not make it good. Similarly, the same is true with premises of a valid argument. If the statements are true and the form is correct, the conclusion will be true; but if the premises are not true, a valid argument will not guarantee a true conclusion.

A classic example of a valid argument is the following:

1. Socrates is a man.
2. All men are mortal.
3. ∴ Socrates is mortal.

To identify the form, let us look at the conclusion, 3, and identify the two major components: a subject (*S*) and a predicate (*P*). *Socrates* is the subject term, and *mortal* is the predicate term. Now return to the two premises and identify these two terms in them. We discover that the two terms are connected by a third term, *man* (or the plural *men*). We call this the *middle term* (*M*).

The form of the argument is as follows:

1. *S* is *M*.
2. All *M* are *P*.
3. Therefore *S* is *P*.

This is an example of a valid deductive form. If premises 1 and 2 are true, we will always get a true conclusion by using this form. But note how easy it would be to get an invalid form. Change the order of the second premise to read "All *P* are *M*." Let the first premise read, "My roommate is a mammal" and the second premise read, "All dogs are mammals." What do you get? The following:

1. My roommate, Sam Smith, is a mammal. (Premise)
2. Dogs are mammals. (Premise)
3. ∴ My roommate is a dog. (Conclusion)

Regardless of how badly you might treat your roommate, the argument has improper form and cannot yield a valid conclusion. It is *invalid*. Every argument is either valid or invalid. Like a woman who cannot be a little pregnant, an argument cannot be partly valid or invalid but must be completely one or the other. By seeking to find counterexamples for argument forms, we can discover which are correct forms. (A full study of this would have to wait for a course in logic.)

Validity is not the only concept we need to examine. *Soundness* is also important. An argument can be valid but still unsound. An argument is sound if it has a valid form and all its premises are true. If at least one premise is false, the argument is *unsound*. Here is an example of a sound argument:

1. If Mary is a mother, she must be a woman.
2. Mary is a mother (for she has just given birth to a baby).
3. ∴ Mary is a woman.

If Mary hasn't given birth, then premise 2 is false, and the argument is unsound.

There are four deductive argument forms of which you should be aware: *modus ponens, modus tollens, disjunctive syllogism,* and *reductio ad absurdum.* Here are their forms:

Modus Ponens (MP)	*Modus Tollens (MT)*
(Affirming the Antecedent)	*(Denying the Consequent)*
1. If *P,* then *Q.*	1. If *P,* then *Q.*
2. *P.*	2. Not *Q.*
3. ∴ *Q.*	3. ∴ Not *P.*

Note that in a hypothetical proposition (if *P,* then *Q*) the first term (the proposition *P*) is called the antecedent and the second term (*Q*) the consequent. Both affirming the antecedent and denying the consequent yield valid forms:

Disjunctive Syllogism (DS) (or Denying the Disjunct)

1. Either *P* or *Q.*
2. Not *Q.*
3. ∴ *P.*

Reductio ad Absurdum (RAA)
(*Reduce to a Contradiction*)

1. Assume *A* (*A* is the logical opposite of the conclusion you seek to prove).
2. Logically deduce a contradiction from *A* (This shows that *A* implies a contradiction).
3. This proves *A* is false, since a contradiction cannot be true. So not-*A* must be true.

We have already given an example of modus ponens:

1. If Mary is a mother, she must be a woman.
2. Mary is a mother.
3. ∴ Mary is a woman.

Here is an example of modus tollens:

1. If Leslie is a mother, she is a woman.
2. Leslie is not a woman (but a man).
3. ∴ Leslie is not a mother.

Here is an example of a disjunctive syllogism (sometimes called "denying the disjunct"— a *disjunct* refers to a proposition with an "or" statement in it, such as "*P* or *Q*").

1. John is either a bachelor or a married man.
2. We know for certain that John is not married.
3. ∴ John is a bachelor.

We turn to *reductio ad absurdum* (RAA). This is an indirect method of proving or establishing a thesis. You assume the opposite of what you want to prove and show that it produces an absurd conclusion. Therefore, your thesis must be true. Here is an example of a *reductio ad absurdum*. It is a little more complicated than the other forms, but it is important especially in reference to the ontological argument (see Anselm in Part III A). Suppose that someone denies that there is such a thing as a self, and you want to refute the assertion. You might argue in the following manner:

1. Suppose that you're correct, and there is no such thing as a self (not *A*).
2. But if there is no such thing as a self, then no one ever acts (if not *A,* then not *B*).

3. But if no one ever acts, then no one can utter meaningful statements (if not *B,* then not *C*).

4. But you have purported to utter a meaningful statement in saying that there is no such thing as a self, so there is at least one meaningful statement (*C*).

5. According to your argument, there is and there is not at least one meaningful statement (*C* and not *C*).

6. ∴ It must be false that there is no such thing as a self (not, not *A*—which by double negation yields *A*). Thus, we have proved by reductio ad absurdum that there is such a thing as a self.

Before we leave the realm of deductive argument, we must point out two invalid forms that often give students trouble. To understand them, look back at forms MP and MT (page 670), which respectively argue by affirming the antecedent and denying the consequent. But notice that there are two other possible forms. You can also deny the antecedent and affirm the consequent in the following manner:

Denying the Antecedent (DA)   *Affirming the Consequent (AC)*

1. If *P,* then *Q.*   1. If *P,* then *Q.*

2. Not *P.*   2. *Q.*

3. ∴ Not *Q.*   3. ∴ *P.*

Are these valid forms? Remember a valid form must always yield true conclusions if the premises are true. Try to find a counterexample that will show that these two forms are invalid. You might let proposition 1 (if *P,* then *Q*) be represented by the previous proposition, "If Mary is a mother, then she is a woman." First, deny the antecedent. Does it necessarily yield a true conclusion? Not necessarily. The conclusion says that Mary is not a woman, but there are many women who are not mothers. So DA is an invalid form:

1. If Mary is a mother, she is a woman.

2. Mary is not a mother.

3. ∴ Mary is not a woman.

Take the same initial proposition and affirm the consequent "Mary is a woman." Does this in itself yield the conclusion that she is a mother? Of course not. She could be a woman without being a mother:

1. If Mary is a mother, she is a woman.

2. She is a woman.

3. ∴ Mary is a mother.

Thus, whereas MP and MT are valid forms, DA and AC are not. Be careful here. Many students slur over these distinctions. Work out your own examples of each form of argument.

These are just simple examples of deductive argument forms. Often, alas, it is difficult to state exactly what the author's premises are.

Inductive Arguments

Let us turn our attention to inductive arguments. Unlike their counterparts, valid deductive arguments, *inductive arguments* are not truth preserving. That is, they do not guarantee that if we have true premises, we will obtain a true conclusion. They bring only *probability*, but in most of life, that is the best we can hope for. Thus, David Hume (1711–1776) said that "probability is the guide of life." The wise person guides his or her life by the best evidence available, always realizing that one could be mistaken. We usually do not speak of inductive arguments as valid/ invalid or sound/unsound but as strong or weak—or as cogent or implausible. In inductive arguments, the premises are *evidence* for the conclusion or hypothesis. If the evidence for the conclusion is substantial, we call the argument a strong inductive argument; but if the evidence is weak, so is the argument as a whole. An inductive argument has the following form:

1. A_1 is a B.
2. A_2 is a B.
3. A_3 is a B.
4. So probably the next A we encounter (A_4) will also be a B.

For example, suppose that you are surrounded by four islands somewhere in the Pacific Ocean. You examine all the trees on three of the islands, but you cannot get to the fourth. Nevertheless, you might make some predictions on the basis of your experience on the first three islands. For example, you note that all the trees on islands A, B, and C are coconut trees. From this you predict that there will be coconut trees on island D and that probably only coconut trees will be found there.

We learn from experience, that is, by induction. We observe resemblances and regularities in life and generalize from them. After a few experiences of getting burned by fire (or after a few experiences with people of a certain type), we learn to avoid fire (or people of a certain type). The human race has learned by inductive experience that cooperation generally produces more benefits than noncooperation, so we advocate cooperative ventures.

Naturally, the greater the sample size of our observation, the greater the probability of our generalization. Asking 1,000 representative Americans whom they will vote for is likely to yield a more accurate prediction of who will be elected than asking only 100 Americans. Sometimes we generalize or make predictions from an inadequate sample. When we should know better, we call this type of malformed induction *prejudice*. If a child infers from his only six bad experiences with people from Podunkville that all people in Podunkville are bad, that might be acceptable. However, if an adult, who could easily have evidence that many good people live in Podunkville, still generalizes about the people of Podunkville and acts accordingly, we label this an irrational bias, a prejudice.

Inductive reasoning can lead us astray—it can be dangerous. The chicken who innately reasons that the farmer will feed her again today because he has done so twice a day for a long time, is in for a cruel shock when he wrings her neck in preparation for his meal.

A special kind of induction reasoning is called *reasoning by analogy* (see the teleological arguments by Paley and Hume in Part III). Reasoning by analogy allows us to reason from the similarity of two things in some relevant respects to their similarity in an unexpected respect. For example, suppose I am lost in the forest and I want to determine whether to eat a certain mushroom, which my hungry stomach craves. I note that it is similar in shape, color, and constituency with other mushrooms that turned out to be edible. Thus, I infer that this mushroom will probably be edible, too.

ABDUCTIVE REASONING

We said earlier that there were two main types of argument, deductive and inductive. There is a lesser known type of reasoning, first formulated by the American philosopher Charles S. Peirce (1839–1914), called *abductive reasoning* or *reasoning to the best explanation.* Like inductive reasoning, abduction yields only probable truth. Whereas induction establishes general premises or probabilities about future occurrences, abduction provides explanatory hypotheses. It answers the question, Why is such and such the case? We can illustrate abductive reasoning with the following example of Sherlock Holmes's reasoning:

The portly client puffed out his chest with an appearance of some little pride and pulled a dirty and wrinkled newspaper from the inside pocket of his greatcoat. As he glanced down the advertisement column with his head thrust forward and the paper flattened out upon his knee, I took a good look at the man and endeavored, after the fashion of my companion, to read the indications which might be presented by his dress or appearance.

I did not gain very much, however, by my inspection. Our visitor bore every mark of being an average commonplace British tradesman, obese, pompous, and slow. He wore rather baggy gray shepherd's check trousers, a not over-clean black frock-coat, unbuttoned in the front, and a drab waistcoat with a heavy brassy Albert chain, and a square pierced bit of metal dangling down as an ornament. A frayed top-hat and a faded brown overcoat with a wrinkled velvet collar lay upon a chair beside him. Altogether, look as I would, there was nothing remarkable about the man save his blazing red head and the expression of extreme chagrin and discontent upon his features.

Sherlock Holmes's quick eye took in my occupation, and he shook his head with a smile as he noticed my questioning glances. "Beyond the obvious facts that he has at some time done manual labour, that he takes snuff, that he is a Freemason, that he has been in China, and that he has done a considerable amount of writing lately, I can *deduce* nothing else." Mr. Jabez Wilson started up in his chair, with his forefinger upon the paper, but his eyes upon my companion.

"How, in the name of good-fortune did you know all that, Mr. Holmes?" he asked. "How did you know, for example, that I did manual labour? It's as true as gospel, for I began as a ship's carpenter."

"Your hands, my dear sir. Your right hand is quite a size larger than your left. You have worked with it, and the muscles are more developed."

"Well, the snuff, then, and the Freemasonry?"

"I won't insult your intelligence by telling you how I read that, especially as, rather against the strict rules of your order, you use an arc-and-compass breastpin."

"Ah, of course, I forgot that. But the writing?"

"What else can be indicated by that right cuff so very shiny for five inches, and the left one with the smooth patch near the elbow where you rest it upon the desk?"

"Well, but China?"

"The fish which you have tattooed immediately above your right wrist could only have been done in China. I have made a small study of tattoo marks and have even contributed to the literature of the subject. That trick of staining the fishes' scales of a delicate pink is quite peculiar to China. When, in addition, I see a Chinese coin hanging from your watchchain, the matter becomes even more simple."

Mr. Jabez Wilson laughed heavily. "Well, I never!" said he. "I thought at first that you had done something clever, but I see that there was nothing in it, after all."[1]

Philosophers appreciate Mr. Wilson's final remark, that Holmes's explanation makes so much sense that one wonders why one didn't think of it oneself. Holmes often chided Watson: "You see, but you do not observe." A good philosopher, like a good detective or scientist, observes while he or she sees.

There is, however, a significant inaccuracy in Holmes's description of what he does. He claims to be deducing the conclusions about Mr. Wilson from the telltale signs. Strictly speaking, he is doing no such thing. In deductive reasoning, if the form is correct and the premises are true, one cannot help but obtain a true conclusion, but such is not the case with Mr. Holmes's reasoning. For example, consider Wilson's arc-and-compass breastpin, which leads Holmes to conclude that Wilson is a Freemason. If the reasoning were deductive, the argument would go something like this:

1. Everyone wearing an arc-and-compass breastpin is a Freemason.
2. Mr. Wilson is wearing an arc-and-compass breastpin.
3. ∴ Mr. Wilson is a Freemason.

Is this a sound argument? Of course not. Imagine that Mr. Wilson, who is not a Freemason, bought a similar arc-and-compass breastpin at a pawnshop and wore it, thinking it was a beautiful bit of Moslem design. In that case, premise 1 would be false. Not everyone wearing an arc-and-compass breastpin is a Freemason. Because it is possible that non-Freemasons wear that pin, the above deductive argument is not sound.

What Holmes has really done is reason abductively, that is, reason to the best explanation of the facts. Like inductive reasoning, abduction does not guarantee the truth of the conclusions. Unlike induction, it is not simply about the probability of such and such being the case based on the evidence. Abductive reasoning attempts to offer explanations of the facts, why things are the way they are. The best explanation of Mr. Wilson's wearing the arc-and-compass breastpin is his belonging to the Freemasons. The best explanation of a child's having a fever and red spots is that she has the measles. The best explanation of the puddles outside is that it has recently rained.

The notion of the best explanation is fascinating in its own right. How do we discover the best explanation? What characteristics does it have? How do we rank the various virtues of a good explanation? There are no definite answers to these questions, but it is generally agreed that such traits as predictability, coherence, simplicity, and fruitfulness are among the main characteristics. If a theory helps us predict future events, that is a powerful weapon. If it coheres well with everything or nearly everything else that we hold true in the field, that lends support to it. If it is simpler than its rivals, if it demands fewer *ad hoc,* or auxiliary, hypotheses, that is a virtue. If it leads to new insight and discoveries, that is also a point in its favor. But what if explanatory theory A has more of one of these features and theory B more of another? Which should we prefer? There is no decision-making procedure to decide the matter with any finality. In a sense, abduction is educated guesswork or intuition. Counterevidence counts strongly against a hypothesis, so that if we can falsify our thesis, we have good reason to drop it; however, sometimes we can make adjustments in our hypothesis to accommodate the counterevidence.

Abduction has been neglected in philosophy, but it really is of the utmost importance. Consider the following questions: Why do you believe in God? Why do you believe in evolutionary theory? Why do you believe that there are universal moral principles? Why do you believe that all events are caused? In one way or another, the answer will probably be abductive: What you believe seems to you to be the best explanation among all the competitors of certain phenomena. We will have opportunity to use abductive reasoning at several points during our course of study.

SOME APPLICATIONS

Let us apply these brief lessons of logic to reading philosophy. Because the key to philosophy is the argument, you will want to concentrate and even outline the author's reasoning. Find his or her thesis or conclusion. Usually, it is stated quite early on. After this, identify the premises that support or lead to the conclusion. For example, Thomas Aquinas (1225–1274) holds the conclusion that God exists. He argues for this conclusion in five different ways. In the second argument, he uses the following premises to reach his conclusion: There is motion, and there cannot be motion without something initiating the motion.

It helps to outline the premises of the argument. For example, here's how we might set forth Aquinas's second argument:

1. Some things are in motion. (Premise)
2. Nothing in the world can move itself but must be moved by another. (Premise)
3. There cannot be an infinite regress of motions. (Premise)
4. There must be a First Mover who is responsible for all other motion. (Conclusion of premises 1–3, which in turn becomes a premise for the rest of the argument)
5. This First Mover is what we call God (Explanation of the meaning of God). (Premise)
6. ∴ God exists. (Conclusion of second part of the argument, premises 4 and 5)

After you have identified the premises and conclusion, analyze them, looking for mistakes in the reasoning process. Sometimes arguments are weak or unsound, but not obviously so. Then stretch your imagination and think of possible counterexamples to the claims of the author. I found this process almost impossible at first, but gradually it became second nature.

Because philosophical arguments are often complex and subtle (and because philosophers do not always write as clearly as they should), a full understanding of an essay is not readily available after a single reading. So read it two or even three times. The first time I read a philosophy essay, I read it for understanding. I want to know where the author is coming from and what he or she is trying to establish. After the first reading, I leave the essay for some time, ruminating on it. Sometimes objections to the arguments awaken me at night or while I am working at something else. Then I go back a day or so later and read the essay a second time, this time, trying to determine its soundness.

A few pointers should be mentioned along the way. Some students find it helpful to keep a notebook on their reflections on the readings. If you own this book, I suggest that you make notes in the margins—initially in pencil because you may want to revise your impressions after a second reading.

Finally, practice charity. Give the author the best possible interpretation in order to see if the argument has merit. Always try to deal with the most generous version of the argument, especially if you don't agree with its conclusion. A position has not been seriously challenged unless the best arguments for it have been refuted. That's why it is necessary to construe all arguments, including those of your opponents, as charitably as possible. The exercise will broaden your horizons and help you develop sharper reasoning skills.

FALLACIES OF REASONING

Before we sum up this chapter, I would like to identify a number of common fallacies of reasoning. Good reasoning depends on justified beliefs (acceptable premises) and valid logic form. But many arguments fail to satisfy these conditions. I have listed some of the main fallacies of reasoning. See if you can illustrate them with examples of your own.

Ad Hominem Argument (or an argument against the man)

This argument attacks the person instead of the position—for example, if I say to you, "You can't trust what Joan says about abortion, she is an immoral person." But, of course, her argument for or against abortion might be sound on independent grounds. Even the devil has true beliefs. The character of the person is irrelevant to the soundness of the argument.

Argument from Authority

Suppose we are arguing about the death penalty, and I tell you that we should believe in the death penalty because Plato believed in it. Since you don't know Plato's reasons (I might not either), it is not sufficient grounds for either of us to believe in the death penalty. We need positive arguments, not simply authority. Advertisements are notorious for subtly and sometimes not so subtly using this device. In a beer commercial, a famous athlete (nicely remunerated for the exercise) can be seen gratifying his thirst, proclaiming the ecstasy of the beverage, as if that were proof of its quality.

Of course, authority might sometimes be the best we can get and sufficient for justified belief, as when a physicist tells us the conclusions of a complicated physics research or a friend from Australia gives you pertinent information for your upcoming visit to that country. We sometimes do need to trust authority, but often it is an improper substitute for good reasoning.

Arguing in a Circle (sometimes referred to as "begging the question")

Suppose that I argue that you should believe that God exists. You ask why. I say, "Because the Bible says so." You ask, "Why should I believe what the Bible says?" I reply, "Because it's the Word of God." That is, I argue in a circle, using my conclusion as a premise to prove the conclusion. Note that all valid deductive argument can appear as arguing in a circle, since the conclusion of such an argument is contained in the premises. The difference is that in a valid argument the conclusion brings out a nontrivial feature of the premises. Essentially, arguing in a circle is not invalid, just trivial and unconvincing, having no power to convince an opponent.

Argument from Ignorance

This kind of argument occurs when I claim that because you cannot prove a proposition is false, I am justified in believing it to be true. For example, because you can't prove God doesn't exist, I am free to believe that He does exist. Or because you can't prove that we do not have a soul, I am free to believe that we do.

False Dilemma

This happens when we reduce several possibilities to two alternatives. I once read of two travelers facing a swamp in which traveler A said to traveler B: "Since you admit you don't know the way through the swamp and there must be a way, follow me. I must know the way." Of course, neither might know the way. Likewise, someone can argue that since your answer to a problem isn't correct, his or hers must be. But, of course, both can be wrong.

Slippery Slope Fallacy

This is sometimes called the Edge of the Wedge Argument. Once you let the camel nose under the wedge of the tent, it will collapse the entire tent. Likewise, it will be argued, once we allow act *A* to occur, event *B,* which is evil, will occur. Robert Wright has argued that "once you buy the premise that animals can experience pain and pleasure, and that their welfare therefore deserves *some* consideration, you're on the road to comparing yourself with a lobster. There may be some exit ramps along the way—plausible places to separate welfare from rights—but I can't find any." Others have argued that if we allow voluntary euthanasia, we are on the slippery slope to involuntary euthanasia, even eventually to a holocaust. Still others have argued that if we pass a National Health Care bill, it will inevitably lead to socialism and communism. The slippery slope fallacy ignores the truth that very often wise policy is a moderate stance between two extremes and that rational people can hold to a rational position without going to an extreme.

Straw Man Argument

This is an instance of misrepresenting an opponent's position. It occurs when someone ignores the evidence for a position and instead attacks an inferior version of the position. In the heat of debate on whether our nation should reduce its military spending, a militarist might argue that his opponent wants to leave our nation defenseless or a willing prey to communism. I once heard of a Russian tourist guide who claimed that she knew that God didn't exist, because if He did, He would announce His presence from heaven. The straw man argument is often a distortion of the other person's position. There is a tendency in all of us to attack a weaker, less plausible version of our opponent's position. The *principle of charity* is the opposite of the straw man argument. It instructs us to give our opponent's position the very best form we can find—and then try to show it is unsound.

Genetic Fallacy

Arguing against a position or argument because its origins are suspect. Suppose I tell you not to believe in the principles of chemistry because they originated in superstitious alchemy or that I tell you not to believe in an astronomical theory because it arose from astrological sources. The fact that a theory or position originated in discredited circumstances is irrelevant if the theory is supported by the evidence. Chemistry and astronomy can produce impressive evidence for their theories that is independent of the authority of alchemy and astrology. It doesn't matter where the truth comes from, as long as it is true.

Fallacy of Composition

When the conclusion of an argument depends on an erroneous inference from the part to the whole. That is, because each part has an attribute, the whole is said to have the same attribute. For example sodium and chlorine are each deadly poisons, so that sodium chloride must be a deadly poison. But it's not. It's ordinary table salt. The whole can have different properties from its parts. Here is another example: Each member of the football team is an excellent player, therefore the team must be excellent. But it might not be, for their individual excellences might not transfer into the right combination. For example, they might all be excellent half-backs and quarterbacks, but none be good at blocking. Is the following an example of this fallacy: *Because every part of the world exhibits design, the whole must exhibit design?*

Inconsistency

When we argue inconsistently, we argue from contradictory premises. In trying to win votes from one constituency, politicians sometimes contradict what they have said to other constituencies. For an illustration, consider some statements made by former President Ronald Reagan at different periods of his political career:

On Civil Rights
1. I favor the Civil Rights Act of 1964 and it must be enforced at the point of a bayonet, if necessary. (October 19, 1965)
2. I would have voted against the Civil Rights Act of 1964." (June 16, 1966)

On Redwood National Park
1. I believe our country can and should have a Redwood National Park in California. (April 17, 1967)
2. There can be no proof given that a national park is necessary to preserve the redwoods. The state of California has already maintained a great conservation program. (April 18, 1967—the next day)

On the Soft Grain Embargo
1. I just don't believe the farmers should be made to pay a special price for our diplomacy, and I'm opposed to [the Soviet grain embargo]. (January 7, 1980)
2. If we are going to do such a thing to the Soviet Union as a full grain embargo, which I support, first we have to be sure our own allies would join us on this." (January 8, 1980, the next day)[2]

Of course, people change their minds and come to believe the opposite of what they formerly believed. That might show progress. But many of us are not aware of the inconsistencies in our own belief systems. For example, Fred might believe that morality entails universalizing principles (what's good for the goose is good for the gander), but fail to note that his view that premarital sex is morally permissible for men but not for women is inconsistent with that principle.

SUMMARY

In a valid deductive argument, if the premises are true, the conclusion must be true by virtue of a logically necessary form.

In a strong inductive argument, the premises, if true, make the conclusion probable but do not guarantee the truth of the conclusion.

In a good abductive argument, the conclusion or hypothesis offers the best explanation of the data.

LOGIC EXERCISES

Show the form of the following arguments and tell whether they are valid:

1) 1. If Mary gets the job, then she will be happy.
   2. Mary will get the job.
   3. Therefore, Mary will be happy.

2) 1. If Napoleon was born in Chicago, he was Emperor of France.
   2. Napoleon was not born in Chicago.
   3. Therefore Napoleon was not Emperor of France.

3) An Environmental Argument:
   1. If I wash, I'll pollute the water.
   2. If I don't wash, I'll pollute the air.
   3. Therefore whatever I do I will be a polluter.

4) 1. All cadets at military institutions are drug free.
   2. Timothy Leary was once a West Point cadet (a true statement).
   3. Therefore Timothy was drug free.

5) 1. If John is a bachelor, he is unmarried.
   2. John is married.
   3. Therefore [fill in blank].

6) 1. If Mary gets the job, she will be happy.
   2. If she is happy, then her husband will be happy.
   3. If her husband is happy, her mother-in-law will be happy.
   4. If her mother-in-law is happy, her mother-in-law's boss, Bob, will be happy.
   5. If Bob will be happy, his dog will be happy.
   6. Therefore [fill in the blank].

7) 1. All dogs are animals.
   2. All cats are animals.
   3. Therefore all dogs are cats.

8) 1. If the fetus is a person, abortion is immoral.
   2. Abortion is not immoral.
   3. Therefore, the fetus is not a person.

FOR FURTHER REFLECTION

1. What is an argument? Using the argument forms discussed in this chapter, construct an argument of your own for each form shown.

2. Explain the differences between deductive, inductive, and abductive reasoning.
3. Explain the difference between validity and soundness.
4. Get a copy of your student newspaper or your local newspaper and analyze two arguments therein. Begin to look at the claims of others in argument form.
5. Philosophy can be seen as an attempt to solve life's perennial puzzles. Taking the material at hand, it tries to unravel enigmas by thought alone. See what you can do with the puzzles and paradoxes included here.
   a. There is a barber in Barberville who shaves all and only those barbers who do not shave themselves. Does this barber shave himself?

   (Who does shave him?)

   b. You are the sole survivor of a shipwreck and are drifting in a small raft parallel to the coast of an island. You know that on this island there are only two tribes of natives: Nobles, kind folk who *always* tell the truth, and Savages, cannibals who *always* lie. Naturally, you want to find refuge with the Nobles. You see a man standing on the shore and call out, "Are you a Noble or a Savage?" The man answers the question, but a wave breaks on the beach at that very moment, so you don't hear the reply. The boat drifts farther down along the shore when you see another man. You ask him the same question, and he replies, pointing to the first man, "He said he was a Noble." Then he continues, "I am a Noble." Your boat drifts farther down the shore where you see a third man. You ask him the same question. The man seems very friendly as he calls out, "They are both liars. I am a Noble. They are Savages."

   The puzzle: Are the data given sufficient to tell you any man's tribe? Are they sufficient to tell you each man's tribe?

   c. Mrs. Smith, a schoolteacher, announces to her class on Friday that there will be a surprise test during the following week. She defines "surprise test" as one that no one could reasonably predict on the day of the test. Johnny, one of her students, responds that she may not give the test on pain of contradicting herself. Mrs. Smith asks, "Why not?" Johnny replies, "You cannot give the test on Friday because on Friday everyone would know that the test would take place on that day, and so it would not be a surprise. So the test must take place on a day between Monday and Thursday. But it cannot take place on Thursday, for if it hasn't taken place by then, it would not be a surprise on Thursday. So the test must take place between Monday and Wednesday. But it cannot take place on Wednesday for the same reason that we rejected Friday and Thursday. Similarly, we can use the same reason to exclude Tuesday and Monday. On no day of the week can a surprise test be given. So the test cannot be given next week."

   Mrs. Smith heard Johnny's argument and wondered what the solution was. She gave the test on Tuesday, and everyone was surprised, including Johnny. How was this possible?

   d. What follows from this puzzle?

   It is sometimes said that space is empty, which means presumably that there is nothing between two stars. But if there is nothing between stars, then they are not separated by anything, and, thus, they must be right up against one another, perhaps forming some peculiar sort of double star. We know this not to be the case, of course.[3]

6. A good reason to be a critical thinker is to avoid getting cheated. Occasionally, you may be in danger of being duped by an unscrupulous salesperson. Thinking clearly may save you. Here is an example of such a situation that occurred after the Loma Prieta earthquake in the California Bay area in 1989.

Last week the 55 year old [Eva] Davis was evicted from her . . . home of 22 years by San Francisco sheriff's deputies. Her troubles began in 1990 when a contractor offered to repair front steps damaged in the Loma Prieta earthquake. Two hours later came a disaster worse than an earthquake, a disaster with a smile, a representative of Congress Mortgage Co. of San Jose. Convinced that she was getting a federal loan that didn't have to be repaid until the house was sold, Davis signed a 15 percent loan with a 15 percent origination fee. The 15 points meant a $23,000 fee, instead of a usual $4,000 or so. Suddenly, Davis had an $1,800 monthly payment instead of $459. It was only a matter of time before the house belonged to Congress Mortgage.

Congress Mortgage sold the home, valued at $225,000. The company makes some 400 loans a year and has scheduled 51 foreclosure sales in the next month alone. The bust business is booming. (Rob Morse, *San Francisco Chronicle,* Feb. 20, 1994)

Think of other examples of how critical thinking can save people from evil.

NOTES

1. Arthur Conan Doyle, *The Red-Headed League* (New York: Harper & Bros., 1892).
2. Marc Green and Gail MacCall, *There He Goes Again: Ronald Reagan's Reign of Error* (New York: Pantheon, 1983).
3. Jay Rosenberg, *The Practice of Philosophy* (Englewood Cliffs, NJ: Prentice-Hall, 1978), 99.

GLOSSARY

ぐ

ABSOLUTE   A moral absolute is a principle that is universally binding. It can never be overridden by another principle. Utilitarianism is a type of system that has only one ethical absolute principle: "Do that action that maximizes utility." Kant's system has several absolutes, whereas other deontological systems may have only a few broad absolutes, such as "Never cause unnecessary harm." Sometimes *ethical absolutism* refers to the notion that there is only one correct answer to every moral problem. Diametrically opposed to ethical absolutism is ethical relativism (see the definition of *relativism,* later), which says that the validity of ethical principles depends on social acceptance. In between these polar opposites is ethical objectivism (see the definition of *objectivism,* later).

AD HOC   A proposition added to a theory in order to save it from being considered logically impossible or implausible. As ad hoc, the proposition may have little or no support itself but may simply serve to stave off rejection of the original theory.

AGNOSTICISM   The view that we do not know whether God exists. It is contrasted with *theism,* belief in God, and with *atheism,* the belief that there is no such being.

AKRASIA   From the Greek, meaning "weakness of will." A moral defect, signifying the inability to carry out one's intentions. For example, a drug addict may want to refrain from taking cocaine or heroine but be unable because of his addiction. (See Michael Levin's essay, "A Compatibilist Defense of Moral Responsibility," Part V B reading 3.)

A POSTERIORI   From the Latin for "the following," a posteriori describes knowledge that is obtained only from experience, such as sense perceptions or pain sensations.

A PRIORI   From the Latin for "preceding," a priori describes knowledge that is not based on sense experience but is innate or known simply by the meaning of words or definitions. Hume limited the term to "relations of ideas," referring to analytic truths and mathematics.

ARETAIC ETHICS   The word *aretaic* is derived from the Greek *arete,* "virtue." The theory, first presented by Aristotle, says that the basis of ethical assessment is character. Rather than considering the heart of ethics to lie in actions or duties, it focuses on the character and dispositions of the agent. Whereas *deontological* and *teleological* ethical systems emphasize *doing,* aretaic or virtue ethics emphasize *being,* being a certain type of person who will no doubt manifest his or her being in appropriate actions. (See Part VI D.)

ARGUMENT A process of reasoning from a set of statements or premises to a conclusion. Arguments are either valid or invalid. They are valid if they have proper logical form and invalid if they do not. (See *deductive argument* and *inductive argument.*)

ASSUMPTION A principle or proposition that is taken for granted in an argument.

ATHEISM The view that there is no such being as God. (See *agnosticism* and *theism.*)

CATEGORICAL IMPERATIVE The categorical imperative commands actions that are necessary of themselves without reference to other ends. This is contrasted with *hypothetical imperatives* (see below) that command actions not for their own sakes but for some other good. For Kant, moral duties command categorically. They represent the injunctions of reason, which endows them with universal validity and objective necessity. (See Part VI D.)

COMPATIBILISM The view that an act may be entirely determined and yet be free in the sense that it was done voluntarily and not under external coercion. Stace represents this position in Part V A. It is sometimes referred to as *soft determinism.* However, whereas the soft determinist positively holds to determinism, the compatibilist may be agnostic on the truth of determinism, holding only that *if* we are determined, we could still be said to act freely under some conditions.

CONTINGENT A proposition is contingent if its denial is logically possible; its denial is not contradictory. A being is contingent if it is not logically necessary.

CONTRADICTION When one statement denies another, both of which cannot be true: for example, "God exists" and "God does not exist."

DEDUCTIVE ARGUMENT An argument is a sound deductive argument if it follows a valid form and has true premises. In that case, the truth of its conclusion is guaranteed. A deductive argument is valid (but not necessarily sound) if it follows an approved form that would guarantee the truth of the conclusion if the premises were true.

DEISM The view that God exists but takes no interest in human affairs. He wound up the world like a clock, and then left it to run itself.

DEONTOLOGICAL ETHICS Deontological (from the Greek *deon,* which means "duty") ethical systems see certain features in the moral act itself as having intrinsic value. These are contrasted with *teleological systems,* which see the ultimate criterion of morality in some nonmoral value that results from actions. For example, for the deontologist there is something right about truth telling even when it may cause pain or harm, and there is something wrong about lying even when it may produce good consequences. (See Part VI D.)

DETERMINISM The theory that all events and states of affairs in the world, including human actions, are caused. There are two versions of determinism: (1) *hard determinism,* which states that because every event is caused, no one is responsible for his or her actions; and (2) *soft determinism* or *compatibilism,* which states that rational creatures can still be held accountable for their actions in so far as they acted voluntarily. (See Part V A.)

EUDAIMONIA Aristotle's word for "happiness."

EXISTENTIALISM The philosophical method that studies human existence from inside the subject's experience rather than from outside. It takes a first-person or subjective approach to the ultimate questions rather than a third-person or objective approach. Examples of this view are the nineteenth-century Danish philosopher Søren Kierkegaard (1813–1855) and the French philosophers Jean Paul Sartre (1905–1980) and Albert Camus (1913–1960).

FOLK PSYCHOLOGY Our commonsense view about mental events (for example, pains, beliefs, desires, emotions, and intentions) that sees them as being of a different nature from physical events and substance. (See Part IV A.)

FUNCTIONALISM This theory denies that there need be a type-type relationship between mental events and mental states. Although mental events may be identical to certain processes in one brain, they may be identical to a different process in a different brain, and they may be eventually produced in robots without brains like ours. (See Part IV A.)

HEDONIC From the Greek *hedone,* "pleasure." Possessing pleasurable or painful quality. Sometimes *hedon* is used to stand for a quantity of pleasure.

HEDONISM Psychological hedonism is the theory that motivation is explained exclusively in terms of desire for pleasure and aversion from pain. Ethical hedonism is the theory that pleasure is the only intrinsic positive value and pain or "unpleasant consciousness" is the only thing that has negative intrinsic value or intrinsic *dis*value. All other values are derived from these two.

HEDONISTIC PARADOX This is the apparent contradiction arising from the doctrine that pleasure is the only thing worth seeking and the fact that whenever one seeks pleasure, it is not found. Pleasure normally arises as an accompaniment of satisfaction of desire whenever one reaches one's goal.

HETERONOMY OF THE WILL This is Kant's term for the determination of the will on nonrational grounds. It is contrasted with *autonomy of the will,* in which the will is guided by reason. (See Part VI.)

HYPOTHETICAL IMPERATIVE Hypothetical imperatives command actions because they are useful for attaining some end that one may or may not desire to obtain. Ethicists who view moral duties to be dependent on consequences would view moral principles as hypothetical imperatives. They have the form: if you want *X,* do action *A* (for example, if you want to live in peace, do all in your power to prevent violence). This is contrasted with the *categorical imperative.*

IDENTITY OF INDISCERNIBLES Known as *Leibniz's law,* which states that two things are numerically identical if and only if they have all the same properties in common. It can be stated formally as: If (x) (y) $[(x=y)$, then (P) $(Px$, if and only if $Py)]$. (See Part IV.)

INDETERMINISM The view that some events are uncaused. Some versions state that some events are uncaused because they happen by chance. Others hold the minimal thesis that some events or states of being (such as the self) are uncaused, so that free will is consistent with the position. This view is contrasted with *determinism.*

INDUCTIVE ARGUMENT An argument in which the premises support the truth of the conclusion but do not guarantee it (as would a valid deductive argument).

INNATE IDEAS The theory that we first read in Plato's *Meno* (Part II) and later in Descartes (also Part II) that says all humans are born with certain knowledge.

INTENTIONALITY (from Latin *intendo*, "to aim at"). Refers to the directedness (*aboutness*) of mental states. Consciousness is often directed at an object, its content— objects of desire, fear, belief, and appearances. Intentions are bidirectional: (1) from Mind to World and (2) from World to Mind. An example of (1) from Mind to World is our desire to change the world, such as when I kick a ball, aiming to score a goal, or invest money in stocks, aiming to increase my wealth. An example of (2) from World to Mind is acquiring a belief through perceiving the environment. (See Part IV.)

INTUITIONISM This is the ethical theory that the good or the right thing to do can be known directly via the intuition. G. E. Moore is an intuitionist about the good, defining it as a simple, unanalyzable property.

LIBERTARIANISM The theory that humans have free will in the sense that given the same antecedent conditions, one can do otherwise. That is, the self is underdetermined by causes and is itself the determining cause of action. This view, represented by Richard Taylor and Lois Hope Walker in Part V, is contrasted with *compatibilism* and *determinism.*

MATERIALISM The metaphysical view that only physical matter and its properties exist. What appears to be nonmaterial (such as consciousness) is really either physical or a property of what is physical. (See Part IV A.)

MEME A cultural artifact that tends to replicate in the social world as genes tend to replicate in the biological world. Language, technology, and morality itself are characterized as *memes*. See Dennett's essay in Part II.

METAPHYSICS "Beyond physics." The study of ultimate reality, that which is not readily accessible through ordinary empirical experience. Metaphysics includes within its domain such topics as free will, causality, the nature of matter, immortality, and the existence of God. Ontology is a further branch of metaphysics (see *ontology*).

MONISM The theory that reality is all of one substance, rather than two or more. Examples are materialist monism, which holds that matter is the single substance that makes up all there is, and idealism, which holds that all reality is spiritual or made up of ideas. The ancient philosophers Lucretius and Democritus, as well as twentieth-century philosophers Bertrand Russell, Paul Churchland, and John Bickle, all hold to materialistic monism. Spinoza and Berkeley, as well as Hinduism, are examples of proponents or systems of idealism.

NATURALISM The theory that ethical terms are defined through factual terms in that ethical terms refer to natural properties. Ethical hedonism is one version of ethical naturalism, for it states that the good at the basis of all ethical judgment refers to the experience of pleasure. Other naturalists, like Geoffrey Warnock, speak of the content of morality in terms of promoting human flourishing or ameliorating the human predicament.

NATURAL THEOLOGY The view that knowledge of God can be obtained through the use of reason. Strong versions hold that we can prove the existence of God.

It is contrasted with *revealed theology,* which holds that all knowledge of God must come from a revelation of God. (See Part III A.)

NECESSARY TRUTH A proposition that cannot be false, such as analytic propositions (for example, "All bachelors are male"). They are true in all possible worlds.

NONCOGNITIVISM The theory that ethical judgments have no truth value but express attitudes or prescriptions.

OBJECTIVISM The view that moral principles have objective validity whether or not people recognize them as such; that is, moral rightness or wrongness does not depend on social approval but on independent considerations. Objectivism differs from absolutism in that it allows that all or many of its principles are overridable in given situations. (See Part VI A.)

OCCAM'S RAZOR named after William of Occam (1290–1349). Sometimes called the *principle of parsimony*, it states that "entities are not to be multiplied beyond necessity." The razor metaphor connotes that useless or unnecessary information should be cut away from any explanation, so that, all things being equal, the simpler the hypothesis, the better.

ONTOLOGY The study of the essence of things and of what there is. What kinds of things are there in the universe? For example, the mind-body problem is in part a debate over whether mental events are of a separate substance or property from physical events or things. Descartes thought there were three different kinds of things: God, created souls, and created material things (see *metaphysics*).

PANTHEISM The view that God is everything and everything is God.

PRAGMATISM The theory, set forth by C. S. Peirce and William James, that interprets the meaning of a statement in terms of its practical consequences. They sometimes go on, as James does, to say that a proposition is true or false according to its results.

PRIMA FACIE The Latin term that means "at first glance." It signifies an initial status of an idea or principle. In ethics, beginning with W. D. Ross, it stands for a duty that has a presumption in its favor but that may be overridden by another duty. Prima facie duties are contrasted with *actual duties* or *all things considered duties.*

PRINCIPLE OF SUFFICIENT REASON The theory set forth by G. W. Leibniz (1646–1716) and used by Samuel Clarke and Frederick Copleston (see readings in Part III) stating that every being or event must have an adequate explanation for its existence. Put another way, every being (that exists or has ever existed) is either a dependent being or a self-existent being. Since not every being can be dependent, there must exist a self-existent being. Leibniz and Clarke and other theists use this principle as the basis for a version of the cosmological argument known as the argument from contingency. David Hume and Bertrand Russell have argued against the principle.

PROPOSITION A sentence or statement that must either be true or false. Every statement that "states" how the world is is a proposition. Questions and imperatives are not propositions. "Would you open the door?" and "Please, open the door" are not propositions, but "The door is open" is, because it claims to describe a situation.

RATIONALISM The school of philosophy that holds that there are important truths that can be known by the mind even though we have never experienced them. The rationalist generally believes in innate knowledge (or ideas), so that we can have certainty about metaphysical truth. Plato and Descartes are two classic examples of rationalists.

REDUCTIONIST MATERIALISM The view that all mental states can be identified with states in the brain. (See Part IV.)

RELATIVISM There are two main types of relativism: cultural and ethical. *Cultural relativism* is a descriptive thesis, stating that there is enormous variety of moral beliefs across cultures. It is neutral as to whether this is the way things ought to be. *Ethical relativism* is an evaluative thesis that holds that the truth of a moral judgment depends on whether a culture recognizes the principle in question. (See Part VI A.)

RETRIBUTIVISM The view on punishment that the criminal (or moral offender) deserves to be punished in exact proportion to the seriousness of the offense. (See Part V C.)

SKEPTICISM The view that we can have no knowledge. Universal skepticism holds that we cannot know anything at all, whereas local or particular skepticism holds that there are important realms in which we are ignorant (for example, read Hume on metaphysics in Part II).

SOFT DETERMINISM A version of determinism that holds that although we are determined by antecedent causal conditions, we act freely just so long as we voluntarily do what we have been caused to do. (See *compatibilism.*)

STOIC, STOICISM An ancient Greek school of philosophy that taught we should control our passions and endure what fate brings our way. Bertrand Russell's essay "A Free Man's Worship" (Part VI C) is a modern expression of this view.

SUPEREROGATORY From the Latin *supererogatus*—"beyond the call of duty." A supererogatory act is one that is not required by moral principles but contains enormous value. Supererogatory acts are those beyond the call of duty, such as risking one's life to save a stranger. Although most moral systems allow for the possibility of supererogatory acts, some theories (most versions of classical utilitarianism) deny that there can be such acts.

TELEOLOGICAL ETHICS Teleological ethical theories place the ultimate criterion of morality in some nonmoral value (for example, happiness or welfare) that results from acts. Whereas *deontological* ethical theories (see earlier) ascribe intrinsic value to features of the acts themselves, teleological theories see only instrumental value in the acts but intrinsic value in the consequences of those acts. Both *ethical egoism* and *utilitarianism* are teleological theories. (See Part VI D.)

THEISM The belief that a personal God exists and is providentially involved in human affairs. It is to be contrasted with *atheism,* which believes that no such being exists, and with *deism,* which holds that God exists but is not providentially concerned with human affairs.

THEODICY The view that evil can be explained in the light of an overall plan of God and that, rightly understood, this world is the best of all possible worlds. (See Part III B.)

TRUTH   The standard definition, going back to Plato and Aristotle, is that a proposition or statement is true if it corresponds to the facts. Aristotle said, "To say of what is that it is not or of what is not that it is, is false, while to say of what is that it is, or of what is not that it is not, is true." Other theories of truth include the coherence theory, which states that a statement is true only if it coheres within a system of propositions that mutually entail or support each other. According to John Locke, philosophy can be characterized as the pursuit of truth. (See Part I, reading 2.)

UNIVERSALIZABILITY   This principle, which is found explicitly in Kant's and R. M. Hare's philosophy and implicitly in most ethicists' work, states that if some act is right (or wrong) for one person in a situation, it is right (or wrong) for any relevantly similar person in that kind of a situation. It is a principle of consistency, which aims to eliminate irrelevant considerations from ethical assessment.

UTILITARIANISM   The theory that the right action is that which maximizes utility. Sometimes utility is defined in terms of *pleasure* (Jeremy Bentham), *happiness* (J. S. Mill), *ideals* (G. E. Moore and H. Rashdall), or *interests* (R. B. Perry). Its motto, which characterizes one version of utilitarianism, is "The Greatest Happiness for the Greatest Number." Utilitarians further divide into act and rule utilitarians. *Act utilitarians* hold that the right act in a situation is that which results (or is most likely to result) in the best consequences, whereas *rule utilitarians* hold that the right act is that which conforms to the set of rules which in turn will result in the best consequences (relative to other sets of rules). (See Part VI.)

VIRTUE ETHICS   See *aretaic ethics.*

Suggestions for Further Reading

PART I   WHAT IS PHILOSOPY?

Audi, Robert, ed. *The Cambridge Dictionary of Philosophy*. Cambridge, England: Cambridge University Press, 1999. The best dictionary of philosophy available.

Craig, Edward, ed. *Routledge Encyclopedia of Philosophy*. 10 vols. London: Routledge, 1998. Contains a rich and comprehensive set of essays on virtually every problem in philosophy.

Copleston, F. C. *History of Philosophy*. Westminster, MD: Newman Press, 1966. This nine-volume set is the most comprehensive contemporary work in the history of philosophy.

Cornman, James, and Keith Lehrer. *Philosophical Problems and Arguments*. New York: Macmillan, 1984. A contemporary paradigm of the analytic method.

Borchert, Donald M., ed. *Encyclopedia of Philosophy*. 10 vols. New York: Macmillan, 1967. A second and thoroughly revised version of the eight-volume 1967 work originally edited by Paul Edwards.

Guthrie, W. K. C. *Socrates*. Cambridge, England: Cambridge University Press, 1971. A clear, accessible, scholarly work of the first order.

Jones, W. T. *A History of Western Philosophy*. 5 vols. New York: Harper & Row, 1976. A lucid, accessible work.

Lawhead, William. *A Voyage of Discovery: A History of Western Philosophy*. Belmont, CA: Wadsworth, 2002. A reliable, user-friendly introduction to the subject.

Matson, Wallace. *A New History of Philosophy*. 2 vols. New York: Harcourt Brace Jovanovich, 1999. An insightful, acute, short introduction to the history of philosophy.

Miller, Ed. *Questions that Matter*. New York: McGraw-Hill, 2003. A clear introduction.

Nagel, Thomas. *What Does It All Mean?* Oxford: Oxford University Press, 2004. A succinct, thoughtful invitation to philosophical reflection.

Olen, Jeffrey. *Persons and Their World*. New York: Random House, 1983. One of the best single-author introductions to philosophy.

Rosenberg, Jay. *The Practice of Philosophy*. Englewood Cliffs, NJ: Prentice-Hall, 1995. An excellent handbook of philosophy for beginners: concise, witty, and philosophically rich.

Russell, Bertrand. *The Problems of Philosophy*. Oxford: Oxford University Press, 1912. Although a little dated, this marvelously lucid book, reputedly written in ten days, is a gold mine of ideas and pressing arguments.

Woodhouse, Mark. *A Preface for Philosophy*. Belmont, CA: Wadsworth, 2006. This little gem is useful in discussing the purposes and methods of philosophical inquiry. It contains lively discussions on informal logic, reading philosophy, and writing philosophical papers.

Stumpf, Samuel, and James Fieser, *Socrates to Sartre and Beyond*. New York: McGraw-Hill, 2008. Historical overview of the key figures in the history of Western philosophy

PART II: THEORY OF KNOWLEDGE

Audi, Robert. *Belief, Justification, and Knowledge.* Belmont, CA: Wadsworth, 2007. An excellent short introduction to the subject.

Chisholm, Roderick. *Theory of Knowledge.* Englewood Cliffs, NJ: Prentice-Hall, 1988. A rich exposition of the major problems.

Dancy, Jonathan. *Contemporary Epistemology.* New York: Basil Blackwell, 1985. This book defends a coherentist position against foundationalism.

Dancy, Jonathan, and Ernest Sosa, eds. *A Companion to Epistemology.* London: Basil Blackwell, 1992. An excellent comprehensive encyclopedia of epistemology.

Descartes, Rene. *The Philosophical Writings of Descartes.* Trans. John Cottingham et al. Cambridge, England: Cambridge University Press, 1985. See especially Descartes's classic *Meditations.*

Klein, Peter. *Certainty: A Refutation of Skepticism.* Minneapolis: University of Minnesota Press, 1981. A clear and cogent argument against skepticism.

Koertge, Noretta, ed. *A House Built on Sand: Exposing Postmodernist Myths and Science.* New York: Oxford University Press, 2000.

Landesman, J. Charles. *Skepticism.* Oxford: Blackwell, 2002. An excellent survey and analysis of philosophical skepticism from the ancient Greeks to contemporary philosophy.

Lehrer, Keith. *Theory of Knowledge.* Boulder, CO: Westview Press, 2000. A thorough and thoughtful survey of the subject.

Moser, Paul K. *The Oxford Handbook of Epistemology.* New York: Oxford University Press, 2005. Essays by established scholars on various aspects of the debate.

Plantinga, Alvin. *Warrant and Proper Function.* Oxford: Oxford University Press, 1993. A penetrating and comprehensive work in contemporary epistemology.

———. Warrant: *The Current Debate.* Oxford: Oxford University Press, 1993. A thorough critique of contemporary epistemology. A clearly written text, advanced, but accessible to a beginning philosopher.

Pojman, Louis. *The Theory of Knowledge: Classical and Contemporary Readings.* Belmont, CA: Wadsworth, 2007. A comprehensive anthology containing many of the authors referred to and works used in this part of our book.

———. *What Can We Know?* Belmont, CA: Wadsworth, 2001. A comprehensive overview of epistemological theory.

Pollock, John. *Contemporary Theories of Knowledge.* Totowa, NJ: Rowman & Littlefield, 1999. A lively, challenging study that focuses primarily on epistemic justification.

Rorty, Richard. *Philosophy and the Mirror of Nature.* Princeton, NJ: Princeton University Press, 1979. A critique of the whole enterprise of epistemology, aiming to replace it with "social knowledge" and intellectual conversation.

Russell, Bertrand. *The Problems of Philosophy.* Oxford: Oxford University Press, 1912. A classic—pithy, succinct, and engaging. Contains a classic treatment of the correspondence theory of truth.

Stroud, Barry. *The Significance of Philosophical Skepticism.* Oxford: Oxford University Press, 1984. A sympathetic exposition of the major skeptical arguments.

Unger, Peter. *Ignorance*: *A Case for Skepticism.* Oxford: Clarendon Press, 1975. A radical, superglobal skeptical view.

PART III: PHILOSOPHY OF RELIGION

Adams, Marilyn McCord. *Horrendous Evils and the Goodness of God.* Ithaca, NY: Cornell University Press, 1999. A comprehensive and illuminating contemporary treatment of the problem of horrendous evil.

Anders, Timothy. *The Evolution of Evil.* Chicago: Open Court Books, 1994. A good account of the thesis set forth at the end of this chapter, defending an evolutionary explanation of evil.